HORNGREN'S ACCOUNTING

HORNGREN'S ACCOUNTING

TRACIE L. MILLER-NOBLES
Austin Community College

BRENDA MATTISON
Tri-County Technical College

ELLA MAE MATSUMURA
University of Wisconsin—Madison

CAROL A. MEISSNER
Georgian College

JO-ANN L. JOHNSTON
British Columbia Institute of Technology

PETER R. NORWOOD
Langara College

VOLUME ONE

11TH CANADIAN EDITION

Pearson Canada Inc., 26 Prince Andrew Place, North York, Ontario M3C 2H4.

ISBN 9780134735337

1 20

Library and Archives Canada Cataloguing in Publication

Miller-Nobles, Tracie L., author
Horngren's accounting / Tracie Miller-Nobles, Texas State University-San Marcos [and five others]. — 11th Canadian edition.

Includes indexes.
ISBN 978-0-13-473533-7 (v. 1 : softcover)

1. Accounting--Textbooks. 2. Textbooks.
I. Title. II. Title: Accounting.

HF5636.M54 2019 657 C2018-906037-9

In memory of *Charles T. Horngren* 1926–2011

Whose vast contributions to the teaching and learning of accounting impacted and will continue to impact generations of accounting students and professionals.

I would like to thank my students for keeping me on my toes. Hearing their new ideas and how they think about accounting makes teaching such a wonderful job.

Carol A. Meissner

I would like to thank my husband, Bill, and my family for their encouragement and support.

Jo-Ann L. Johnston

I would like to thank my wife, Helen, and my family very much for their support and encouragement.

Peter R. Norwood

Pearson

Brief Contents

VOLUME 1

VOLUME 2

Contents

Part 1 The Basic Structure of Accounting

About the Authors

TRACIE L. MILLER-NOBLES, CPA, received her bachelor's and master's degrees in accounting from Texas A&M University and is currently pursuing her Ph.D. in adult education also at Texas A&M University. She is an associate professor at Austin Community College, Austin, Texas. Previously she served as a senior lecturer at Texas State University, San Marcos, Texas, and she has taught as an adjunct at University of Texas-Austin. Tracie has public accounting experience with Deloitte Tax LLP and Sample & Bailey, CPAs.

Tracie is a recipient of the following awards: American Accounting Association J. Michael and Mary Anne Cook prize, Texas Society of CPAs Rising Star TSCPA Austin Chapter CPA of the Year, TSCPA Outstanding Accounting Educator, NISOD Teaching Excellence and Aims Community College Excellence in Teaching. She is a member of the Teachers of Accounting at Two Year Colleges, the American Accounting Association, the American Institute of Certified Public Accountants, and the Texas State Society of Certified Public Accountants. She is currently serving on the board of directors as secretary/webmaster of Teachers of Accounting at Two Year Colleges and as a member of the American Institute of Certified Public Accountants financial literacy committee. In addition, Tracie served on the Commission on Accounting Higher Education: Pathways to a Profession.

Tracie has spoken on such topics as using technology in the classroom, motivating non-business majors to learn accounting, and incorporating active learning in the classroom at numerous conferences. In her spare time she enjoys camping and hiking and spending time with friends and family.

BRENDA L. MATTISON, CMA, has a bachelor's degree in education and a master's degree in accounting, both from Clemson University. She is currently an accounting instructor at Tri-County Technical College in Pendleton, South Carolina. Brenda previously served as accounting program coordinator at TCTC and has prior experience teaching accounting at Robeson Community College, Lumberton, North Carolina; University of South Carolina Upstate, Spartanburg, South Carolina; and Rasmussen Business College, Eagan, Minnesota. She also has accounting work experience in retail and manufacturing businesses and is a Certified Management Accountant.

Brenda is a member of the American Accounting Association, Institute of Management Accountants, South Carolina Technical Education Association, and Teachers of Accounting at Two Year Colleges. She is currently serving on the board of directors as vice-president of Conference Administration of Teachers of Accounting at Two Year Colleges.

Brenda previously served as Faculty Fellow at Tri-County Technical College. She has presented at state, regional, and national conferences on topics including active learning, course development, and student engagement.

In her spare time, Brenda enjoys reading and spending time with her family. She is also an active volunteer in the community, serving her church and other organizations.

ELLA MAE MATSUMURA, PH.D., is a professor in the Department of Accounting and Information Systems in the School of Business at the University of Wisconsin–Madison, and is affiliated with the university's Center for Quick Response Manufacturing. She received an A.B. in mathematics from the University of California, Berkeley, and M.Sc. and Ph.D. degrees from the University of British Columbia. Ella Mae has won two teaching excellence awards at the University of Wisconsin–Madison and was elected as a lifetime fellow of the university's Teaching Academy, formed to promote effective teaching. She is a member of the university team awarded an IBM Total Quality Management Partnership grant to develop curriculum for total quality management education.

Ella Mae was a co-winner of the 2010 Notable Contributions to Management Accounting Literature Award. She has served in numerous leadership positions in the American Accounting Association (AAA). She was coeditor of *Accounting Horizons* and has chaired and served on numerous AAA committees. She has been secretary-treasurer and president of the AAA's Management Accounting Section. Her past and current research articles focus on decision making, performance evaluation, compensation, supply chain relationships, and sustainability. She coauthored a monograph on customer profitability analysis in credit unions.

About the Canadian Authors

CAROL A. MEISSNER is a professor in both Business and Management Studies and the Automotive Business School of Canada at Georgian College in Barrie, Ontario. She teaches in the Accounting Diploma, Automotive Business Diploma, and business degree programs.

Carol has always been a teacher. She started as a part-time college instructor when she completed her first degree and has taught full time since 2005. In 2014, Carol was awarded the Georgian College Board of Governors' Award of Excellence Academic for outstanding contributions to the college and an ongoing commitment to excellence.

Her "real world" experience includes car dealership controllership and self-employment as a part-time controller and consultant for a wide variety of businesses.

Carol has broad experience in curriculum development. She has been a curriculum chair, program coordinator, member of several curriculum committees, and has been involved in writing and renewing degree, diploma, and graduate certificate programs.

A self-professed "learning junkie," Carol holds a Bachelor of Commerce degree, a Master of Business Administration degree, a Master of Arts degree in Education (Community College concentration), and a CPA designation. She has also earned Georgian College's Professional Development Teaching Practice Credential and is a graduate of Georgian's Aspiring Leaders program. She is a regular attendee and occasional presenter at conferences related to teaching, accounting, and the automotive industry. Outside of work she is an esports mom who spends many hours watching tournaments online.

JO-ANN JOHNSTON is an instructor in the Accounting, Finance and Insurance Department at the British Columbia Institute of Technology (BCIT). She obtained her Diploma of Technology in Financial Management from BCIT, her Bachelor in Administrative Studies degree from British Columbia Open University, and her Master of Business Administration degree from Simon Fraser University. She is also a certified general accountant, has CPA designation, and completed the Canadian securities course.

Prior to entering the field of education, Jo-Ann worked in public practice and industry for over 10 years. She is a past member of the board of governors of the Certified General Accountants Association of British Columbia and has served on various committees for the association. She was also a member of the board of directors for the BCIT Faculty and Staff Association and served as treasurer during that tenure.

In addition to teaching duties and committee work for BCIT, Jo-Ann is the financial officer for a family-owned business.

PETER R. NORWOOD is an instructor in accounting and coordinator of the Accounting program at Langara College in Vancouver. A graduate of the University of Alberta, he received his Master of Business Administration from the University of Western Ontario. He is a CPA, a fellow of the Institute of Chartered Accountants of British Columbia, a certified management accountant, and a fellow of the Society of Management Accountants of Canada.

Before entering the academic community, Peter worked in public practice and industry for over 15 years. He is a past president of the Institute of Chartered Accountants of British Columbia and chair of the Chartered Accountants School of Business (CASB). He is also the chair of the Chartered Accountants Education Foundation for the British Columbia Institute of Chartered Accountants and has been active on many provincial and national committees, including the Board of Evaluators of the Canadian Institute of Chartered Accountants. Peter is also a sessional lecturer in the Sauder School of Business at the University of British Columbia.

Changes to This Edition

General

Revised end-of-chapter starters, exercises, practice sets, challenge exercises, ethical issues, problems, challenge problems, decision problems, and financial statement cases.

Moved IFRS Mini-Cases and Comprehensive Problems for each Part) to MyLab Accounting.

Learning Objectives in all chapters have been reviewed against current CPA competencies and correlation provided at the beginning of each chapter. Many of the problems in the text (Beyond the Numbers, Ethical issues, Decision Problems, Financial Statements Cases) give opportunities to develop CPA competencies, in particular Enabling Competencies, such as Communication, Problem Solving, and Professional and Ethical Behaviour.

- **NEW! Using Excel.** This end-of-chapter exercise in select chapters introduces students to Excel to solve common accounting problems as they would in the business environment.
- **NEW! Practice Set.** Practice Set questions for Chapters 2 through 9 provide another opportunity for students to practise the entire accounting cycle. The practice set uses the same company in each chapter but is often not as extensive as the serial exercises.
- **NEW! Serial Exercises.** Serial exercises in all chapters expose students to recording entries for a service company which grows to become a merchandiser later in the text.
- **NEW! Ethics box.** This feature provides common questions and potential solutions business owners face. Students are asked to determine the course of action they would take based on concepts covered in the chapter and are then given potential solutions. Available in most chapters.
- **NEW!** List of acronyms has been expanded and added to inside back cover for easier student reference.

Chapter 1

- Updated Try It! questions.
- Additional starters and exercises.
- Updated format for transaction analysis.

Chapter 2

NEW! chapter-opening vignette.

- Rules of debit and credit are colour-coded.
- Refreshed the journal entries example.
- Added dates to journal entries and T-accounts to match with how work is done in the end-of-chapter questions.
- Updated posting to ledger.
- Updated Try It! questions.
- Additional exercises, problems for journal entries.

Chapter 3

NEW! chapter-opening vignette.

- Streamlined recognition criteria explanation.

Chapter 4

NEW! annotated worksheet exhibit, and reduced repetition in this section.

- Streamlined closing entries.
- Reordered Learning Objective 2.
- New example in appendix.

Chapter 5

NEW! chapter-opening vignette.

- Simplified introduction to periodic inventory systems and moved most periodic information to the Appendix.
- Included debit and credit memos where topics introduced (moved from Chapter 7). Added images of source documents.
- Purchase and sales transactions now all from the perspective of Slopes (rather than switching companies for the sales section).
- Additional starters and exercises.

Chapter 6

NEW! chapter-opening vignette.

- New example for whole chapter tied to the vignette.
- Added additional starters and exercises.

Chapter 7

NEW! chapter opening vignette.

- Simplified general ledger discussion (moving debit/credit memos to Chapter 5).
- Moved PST/GST for special journals to MyLab.

Chapter 8

NEW! chapter-opening vignette.

- Greater use of bank statements (authentic-looking source documents).
- More bank reconciliations to practise.
- Added additional starters.

Chapter 9

- Updated several exhibits for clarity and currency.
- Added internal control for receivables.
- Added cryptocurrencies to types of payments.
- Added Accounts Receivable Turnover.
- Additional starters and exercises.

Chapter 10

NEW! additional starters and exercises.

Chapter 11

NEW! exhibit to explain current portion of long-term debt.

- Removed duplication of journal entries in the payroll section.
- Updated taxes and payroll to 2018 rates.
- Additional starters and exercises.
- Updated examples/questions to current wage rates.

Horngren's Accounting ...
Expanding on Proven Success

Accounting Cycle Tutorial

This interactive tutorial in MyLab Accounting helps students master the Accounting Cycle for early and continued success in introduction to accounting courses. The tutorial, accessed by computer, smartphone, or tablet, provides students with brief explanations of each concept of the Accounting Cycle through engaging, interactive activities. Students are immediately assessed on their understanding, and their performance is recorded in the MyLab gradebook. Whether the Accounting Cycle Tutorial is used as a remediation self-study tool or course assignment, students have yet another resource within MyLab to help them be successful with the accounting cycle.

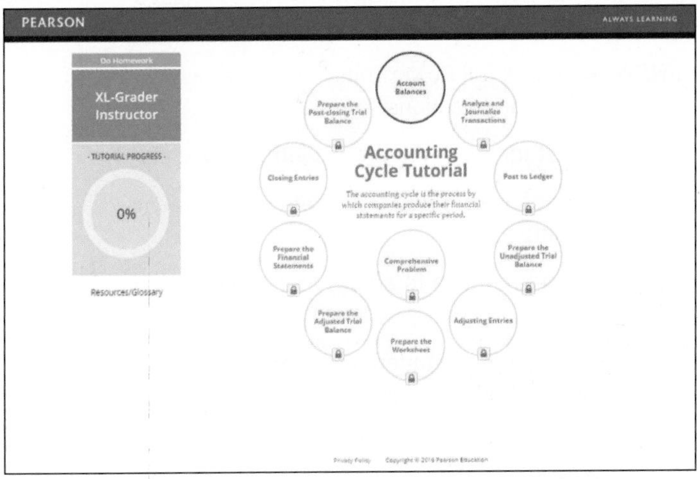

NEW! ACT Comprehensive Problem

The Accounting Cycle Tutorial now includes a comprehensive problem that allows students to work with the same set of transactions throughout the accounting cycle. The comprehensive problem, which can be assigned at the beginning or the end of the full cycle, reinforces the lessons learned in the Accounting Cycle Tutorial activities by emphasizing the connections between the accounting cycle concepts.

Study Plan

The Study Plan acts as a tutor, providing personalized recommendations for each of your students based on his or her ability to master the learning objectives in your course. This allows students to focus their study time by pinpointing the precise areas they need to review and allowing them to use customized practice and learning aids–such as videos, eText, tutorials, and more–to get them back on track. Using the report available in the gradebook, you can then tailor course lectures to prioritize the content where students need the most support–offering you better insight into classroom and individual performance.

Dynamic Study Modules

New! Chapter-specific Dynamic Study Modules help students study effectively on their own by continuously assessing their activity and performance in real time. Here's how it works: students complete a set of questions with a unique answer format that also asks them to indicate their confidence level. Questions repeat until the student can answer them all correctly and confidently. Dynamic Study Modules explain the concept using materials from the text. These are available as graded assignments and are accessible on smartphones, tablets, and computers.

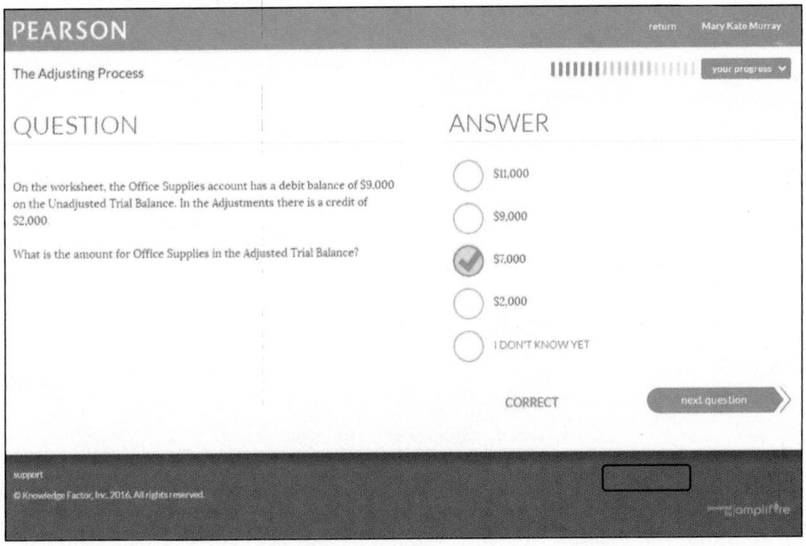

Learning Catalytics

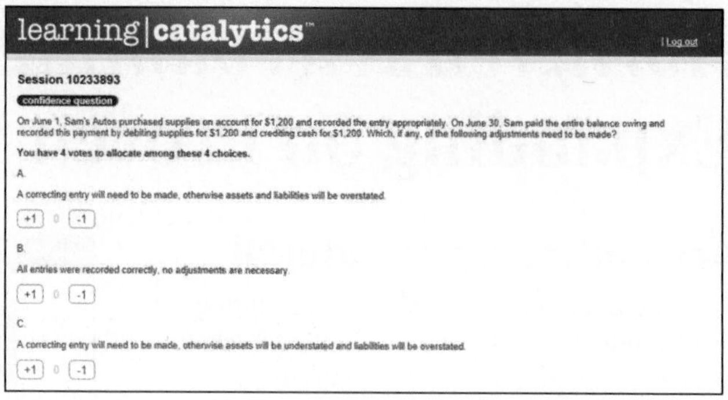

Text-specific Learning Catalytics helps you generate class discussion, customize your lecture, and promote peer-to-peer learning with real-time analytics. As a student response tool, Learning Catalytics uses students' smartphones, tablets, or laptops to engage them in more interactive tasks and thinking.

- **NEW!** Upload a full PowerPoint® deck for easy creation of slide questions.
- Help your students develop critical thinking skills.
- Monitor responses to find out where your students are struggling.
- Rely on real-time data to adjust your teaching strategy.
- Automatically group students for discussion, teamwork, and peer-to-peer learning.

Pearson Etext

Pearson eText gives students access to their textbook anytime, anywhere. In addition to note-taking, highlighting, and bookmarking, the Pearson eText offers interactive and sharing features. Instructors can share their comments or highlights, and students can add their own, creating a tight community of learners within the class.

Textbook Features

Making Connections

CONNECTING CHAPTER boxes appear at the beginning of each chapter. This feature combines the chapter outline with the learning objectives, key questions, and page references.

4 Completing the Accounting Cycle

CONNECTING CHAPTER 4

LEARNING OBJECTIVES

The **Summary** for Chapter 4 appears on pages 204–205.
Key Terms with definitions for this chapter's material appears on page 205.

LEARNING OBJECTIVES provide a roadmap showing what will be covered and what is especially important in each chapter.

KEY QUESTIONS are questions about the important concepts in the chapter, expressed in everyday language.

PAGE REFERENCES give students the ability to quickly connect to the topic they are seeking within the chapter.

CPA competencies

This text covers material outlined in **Section 1: Financial Reporting of the CPA Competency Map**. The Learning Objectives for each chapter have been aligned with the CPA Competency Map to ensure the best coverage possible.

1.1.2 Evaluates the appropriateness of the basis of financial reporting

1.3.1 Prepares financial statements

1.4.2 Evaluates financial statements including note disclosure

CPA COMPETENCY MAP Each chapter's Learning Objectives have been aligned with the latest CPA competencies, which are provided here.

CHAPTER OPENERS

Chapter openers set up the concepts to be covered in the chapter using stories students can relate to. The implications of those concepts on a company's reporting and decision-making processes are then discussed.

Susan Schmitz/Shutterstock

When Danielle Rodriguez started her business in January 2015, she wasn't thinking about accounting. As an IT professional, she was looking to combine her business skills with her love of dogs. Her "fur babies," Zoey and Maggie Mae, are an important part of her #Barknfun Team.

Her business, The Bark'N Fun Company, is a monthly subscription box service that offers premium toys, treats, and accessories for dogs and puppies. The business is online, but her office is located in the small town of Courtice, Ontario.

The majority of small businesses fail within the first three years. So how has The Bark'N Fun Company stayed in business in a competitive online market for luxury items? Danielle, The Bark'N Fun Company's owner, uses accounting information to make her business decisions. Is she an accountant? No! She is a smart businessperson who knows that she needs to understand the business's monthly revenues and expenses so that her business can survive in the short-term and thrive in the long-term. The Bark'N Fun Company needs to know if the prices of their toys and treats are high enough to cover operating expenses, or if they can afford to offer free shipping. Is it working? Yes. The Bark'N Fun Company has not only been able to stay in business but also supports charities that are important to dogs, such as canine rescue organizations and humane society shelters.

This chapter shows how The Bark'N Fun Company and other businesses record their transactions and update their financial records. The procedures outlined in this chapter are followed by businesses ranging in size from giant multinational corporations like PetSmart Inc. to micro-enterprises like The Bark'N Fun Company and Hunter Environmental Consulting, who we will continue to follow through this chapter.

57

SPREADSHEET FORMATS USED IN EXHIBITS

NEW! Excel-based financial documents are used so students will familiarize themselves with the accounting information used in the business world.

EXHIBIT 10–6 | Units-of-Production Amortization for a Truck

	A	B	C	D	E	F	G	H	I
1			Amortization for the Year						
2		Asset	Amortization		Number of		Amortization	Accumulated	Asset
3	Date	Cost	Per Kilometre		Kilometres		Expense	Amortization	Book Value
4	Jan. 1, 2020	$65,000	❶		❷				$65,000
5	Dec. 31, 2020		$0.15	×	90,000	=	$13,500	$13,500	51,500
6	Dec. 31, 2021		0.15	×	120,000	=	18,000	31,500	33,500
7	Dec. 31, 2022		0.15	×	100,000	=	15,000	46,500	18,500
8	Dec. 31, 2023		0.15	×	60,000	=	9,000	55,500	9,500
9	Dec. 31, 2024		0.15	×	30,000	=	4,500	60,000	5,000

Residual value

EXHIBIT 2–8 | The Journal

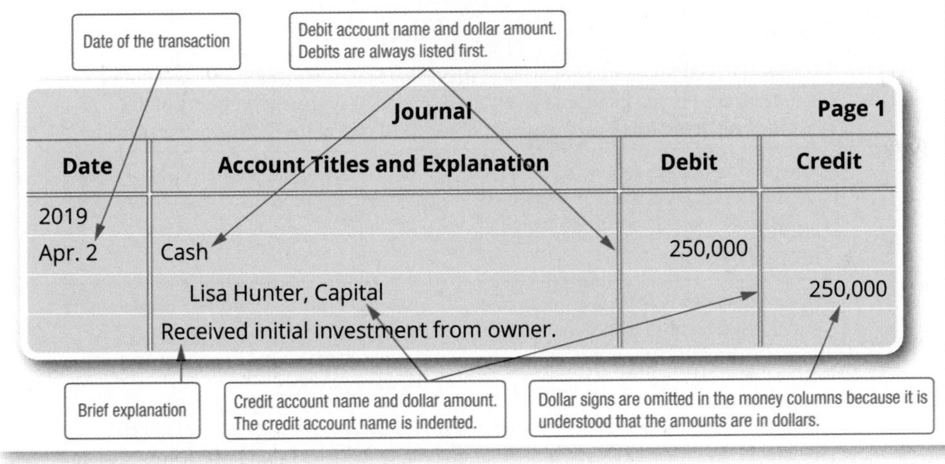

Date of the transaction

Debit account name and dollar amount.
Debits are always listed first.

Journal			Page 1
Date	**Account Titles and Explanation**	**Debit**	**Credit**
2019			
Apr. 2	Cash	250,000	
	Lisa Hunter, Capital		250,000
	Received initial investment from owner.		

Brief explanation

Credit account name and dollar amount.
The credit account name is indented.

Dollar signs are omitted in the money columns because it is
understood that the amounts are in dollars.

INSTRUCTOR TIPS & TRICKS Found throughout the text, these handwritten notes mimic the experience of having an experienced teacher walk a student through concepts on the "board." Many include mnemonic devices or examples to help students remember the rules of accounting.

One way to memorize this is to use an acronym, such as AWE ROL. In this case, the (A)sset, (W)ithdrawal, and (E)xpense accounts all have debit balances, while the (R)evenue, (O)wner's Equity, and (L)iability accounts all have credit balances.
Or memorize which side has the "+" (increase), and then all the "−" (decreases) are the opposite. This way you only have to memorize half of them!
Try DR. AWE—the debits (dr) belong with the (A)sset, (W)ithdrawal, and (E)xpense accounts.

EXHIBIT 2–6 | Expanded Accounting Equation

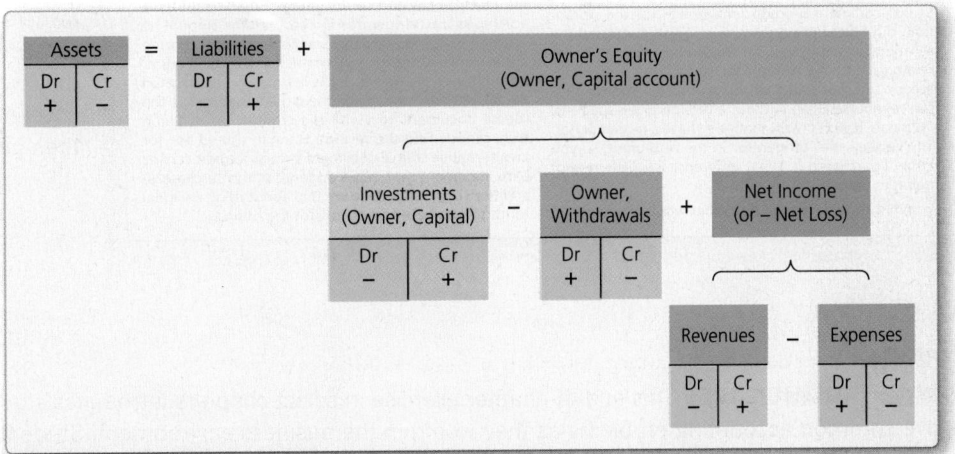

TRY IT! BOXES Found after each learning objective, Try It! boxes give students opportunities to apply the concept they've just learned by completing an accounting problem. Links to these exercises appear throughout the eText, allowing students to practise in MyLab Accounting without interruption.

Try It!

8. Using the following accounts and their balances, prepare the unadjusted trial balance for Cooper Furniture Repair as of December 31, 2018. All accounts have normal balances.

Cash	$7,000	Advertising Expense	$1,200
Unearned Revenue	4,500	Utilities Expense	800
Equipment	10,000	Rent Expense	5,000
Service Revenue	8,000	Accounts Payable	2,300
M. Cooper, Capital	12,200	M. Cooper, Withdrawals	3,000

Solutions appear at the end of this chapter and on **MyLab Accounting**

IFRS/ASPE COMPARISON Provides guidance on how IFRS differs from ASPE.

EXHIBIT 1–16 | How IFRS Differ from What We See in the Chapter

ASPE	IFRS
In Canada, both International Financial Reporting Standards (IFRS) and Accounting Standards for Private Enterprises (ASPE) are prepared under the authority of the **Accounting Standards Board** and are published as part of the CPA *Canada Handbook.*	
Sole proprietorships follow ASPE, which are simpler and less costly to implement. Private corporations can choose to follow ASPE or IFRS.	Publicly accountable enterprises or those planning to become one must follow IFRS.
Financial reports contain less information under ASPE because readers have more access to the details themselves.	Financial reports under IFRS contain more detailed information than under ASPE because users do not have easy access to the information.
Companies reporting under either method must also provide notes to the financial statements, which include significant accounting policies and explanatory information.	

ETHICS Are receipts really important?

Elijah Morris, assistant manager for Red's Big Burger Restaurant, is responsible for purchasing equipment and supplies for the restaurant. Elijah recently purchased a $4,000 commercial-grade refrigerator for the restaurant, but he can't find the receipt. Elijah purchased the refrigerator with personal funds and is asking to be reimbursed by the restaurant. Hannah, the restaurant's accountant, has said that she is unsure if the business can reimburse Elijah without a receipt. Elijah suggests: "Hannah, it won't really matter if I have a receipt or not. You've seen the refrigerator in the restaurant, so you know I purchased it. What difference is a little receipt going to make?"

What should Hannah do? What would you do?

Solution

Hannah should not reimburse Elijah until she receives the receipt—the source document. Elijah could have purchased the refrigerator for less than the amount he is asking in reimbursement. Source documents provide the evidence of the amount of the transaction. If either an auditor or the owner of the restaurant investigated the $4,000 purchase, he or she would need to see the source document to verify the transaction. If Elijah truly cannot find the receipt, Hannah should ask for an alternative source document such as a credit card or bank statement that shows evidence of the purchase. In addition, Elijah should be warned about using personal funds to purchase equipment for the business.

ETHICS BOXES This feature provides common questions and potential solutions business owners face. Students are asked to determine the course of action they would take based on concepts covered in the chapter and are then given potential solutions.

NEW! **USING EXCEL** This end-of-chapter exercise in select chapters introduces students to Excel to solve common accounting problems as they would in the business environment. Students will work from a template that will aid them in solving the problem related to accounting concepts taught in the chapter.

NEW! **SERIAL EXERCISE** starts in Chapter 1 and run through Volume 1, exposing students to recording entries for a service company and then moving into recording transactions for a merchandiser later in the text.

NEW! **PRACTICE SET** The Practice Set for Chapters 2–9 provide another opportunity for students to practise the entire accounting cycle. The practice set uses the same company in each chapter, but is often not as extensive as the serial exercise.

Acknowledgments for *Horngren's Accounting*, Eleventh Canadian Edition

Acknowledgements for *Horngren's Accounting*, Eleventh Canadian Edition

Horngren's Accounting, Eleventh Canadian Edition, is the product of a rigorous research process that included multiple reviews in the various stages of development to ensure the revision meets the needs of Canadian students and instructors. The extensive feedback from the following reviewers helped shape this edition into a clearer, more readable and streamlined textbook in both the chapter content and assignment material:

- Gregory Springate, Red Deer College
- Deirdre Fitzpatrick, George Brown College
- Joan Baines, Red River College
- Robert Cinapri, Humber College
- Arsineh Garabedian, Douglas College
- Darlene Lowe, MacEwan University
- Jerry Aubin, Algonquin College
- Meredith Delaney, Seneca College
- Heather Cornish, Northern Alberta Institute of Technology
- Cheryl Wilson, Durham College

We would also like to thank the late Charles Horngren and Tom Harrison for their support in writing the original material.

We would like to give special thanks to Chris Deresh, CPA, Manager, Curriculum Content, at Chartered Professional Accountants of Canada for his guidance and technical support. His willingness to review and discuss portions of the manuscript was generous and insightful, and it is gratefully acknowledged.

The Chartered Professional Accountants, as the official administrator of generally accepted accounting principles in Canada, and the *CPA Canada Handbook*, are vital to the conduct of business and accounting in Canada. We have made every effort to incorporate the most current *Handbook* recommendations in this new edition of *Accounting*. We would also like to thank Sarah Magdalinski, Northern Alberta Institute of Technology, for her work in assessing and adapting this edition's Serial Exercises.

Thanks are extended to Indigo Books & Music Inc. and TELUS Corporation for permission to use portions of their annual reports in Volumes I and II of this text and on MyLabAccounting. We acknowledge the support provided by the websites of various news organizations and by the annual reports of a large number of public companies.

We would like to acknowledge the people of Pearson Canada, in particular senior portfolio manager Keara Emmett and marketing manager Darcey Pepper. Special thanks to Suzanne Simpson Millar, Queen Bee at Simpson Editorial Services, who was an awesome content developer on this edition. Thanks also to Sarah Gallagher, project manager; Nicole Mellow and Sogut Gulec, content managers, for their diligence in keeping everything on track.

Our task is to provide educational material in the area of accounting to instructors and students to aid in the understanding of this subject area. We welcome your suggestions and comments on how to serve you better.

1 Accounting and the Business Environment

Learning Objectives are a "roadmap" showing what will be covered and what is especially important in each chapter.

Connecting Chapter "X" appears at the beginning of each chapter and gives a guide to the content of the chapter with page references.

CONNECTING CHAPTER 1

LEARNING OBJECTIVES

Key Questions are questions about the important concepts in the chapter expressed in everyday language.

The **Summary** for Chapter 1 appears on page 27.

Key Terms with definitions for this chapter's material appear on page 28.

CPA competencies

This text covers material outlined in **Section 1: Financial Reporting of the CPA Competency Map**. The Learning Objectives for each chapter have been aligned with the CPA Competency Map to ensure the best coverage possible.

1.1.1 Evaluates financial reporting issues

1.1.2 Evaluates the appropriateness of the basis of financial reporting

1.3.1 Prepares financial statements

Pixzzle/E+/Getty Images

Lisa Hunter graduated from university with a degree in environmental studies. She then went to work with an environmental consulting company and gained extensive experience in the area of environmental sustainability. Lisa soon came to realize that many small businesses were looking to optimize the benefits of "going green."

Lisa decided to start her own consulting firm, but she did not have a lot of knowledge about businesses or their record keeping. She had so many questions. What kind of business should she set up? How would she know if the business was making any money? How would she know how much money she could take out of her business? She took some night school courses in accounting and small business management before starting her business to make sure she could answer those questions.

She named her new company Hunter Environmental Consulting. She was now an entrepreneur! She realized she needed to develop a business plan, secure clients, set up an office, and hire staff.

Lisa's first year in business was stressful and successful. Her work in the first year was in the area of energy efficiency and suggesting how her clients could reduce their energy consumption and their energy costs.

"My previous training and experience gave me the confidence to know that I could be successful in this field. However, I did not realize how carefully you have to watch business finances—costs can get out of control in a hurry if you're not careful!"

A **chapter-opening story** shows why the topics in the chapter are important to real companies and businesspeople. We refer to this story throughout the chapter.

What role does accounting play in Lisa Hunter's situation? Lisa had to decide how to organize her company. She set up her business as a proprietorship—a single-owner company—with herself as the owner. As her business grows, she may decide to expand it by taking on a partner. She might also choose to incorporate—that is, to form a corporation. In this chapter, we discuss all three forms of business organization—proprietorships, partnerships, and corporations—in addition to answering other questions Lisa asked.

You may already know various accounting terms and relationships because accounting affects people's lives in many ways. This first accounting course will help you see this by explaining how accounting works. As you progress through this course, you will see how accounting helps people like Lisa Hunter—and you—achieve business goals.

Accounting: The Language of Business

LO 1

Why is accounting important, and who uses the information?

Each new learning objective starts with a question in the margin.

Accounting is the information system that measures **business** financial activities, processes that information into reports, and communicates the results to decision makers. For this reason it is called "the language of business." The better you understand the language, the better your decisions will be, and the better you can manage financial information. And as with any language, there is unique terminology that takes practice to learn. Students must practise using this new language as much as possible. Many business managers believe it is more important for students to learn accounting than any other business subject.

Boldface words are new terms that are explained here and defined in the Key Terms section at the end of this chapter and the Glossary at the end of the book.

Financial statements are a key product of an accounting system and provide information that helps people make informed business decisions. Financial statements report on a business in monetary terms and help you answer questions such as, Is my business making a **profit**? Should I hire assistants? Who owes me money? Am I earning enough money to expand my business?

Students sometimes mistake bookkeeping for accounting. **Bookkeeping** is a procedural element of accounting, just as arithmetic is a step used when solving a mathematical problem (or just as skating is an important part of hockey). There are many accounting software packages that will handle detailed bookkeeping. Recording the information is important, but understanding what it all means and how it helps you make better decisions is even more important. Exhibit 1–1 illustrates the role of accounting in business.

Exhibits summarize key ideas in a visual way.

EXHIBIT 1–1 | The Accounting System: The Flow of Information

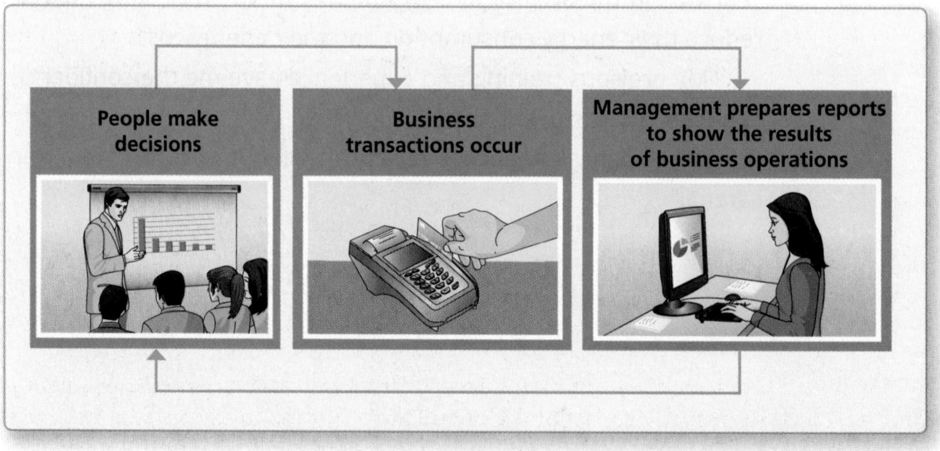

People make decisions
Business transactions occur
Management prepares reports to show the results of business operations

Users of Accounting Information

It seems that almost everyone uses accounting information to make decisions.

Individuals People use accounting information in day-to-day affairs to manage bank accounts, evaluate job prospects, make investments, and decide whether to lease or buy a new car.

Businesses Business owners and managers use accounting information to set goals for their organizations. They evaluate their progress toward those goals, and they make changes when necessary. For example, Lisa Hunter knows the amount of money that will be earned, since she and her client will agree on a fee for the consulting work she will perform. She needs to determine the scope of the work, how many consultants she will require, and how many hours it will take to complete the project. She needs to make sure that her costs do not exceed the fee she will receive from her client if she wants to make sure that she maintains a profitable business.

Investors and Creditors Investors and creditors provide the money to finance business activities. To decide whether to invest, **investors** predict the amount of income that will be earned on their investment. Before lending money, **creditors** such as banks and suppliers evaluate the borrower's ability to pay them back.

Government and Regulatory Bodies Provincial and federal governments levy taxes on individuals and businesses. Income tax is calculated by using accounting information as a starting point. A business's accounting system is required to keep track of provincial sales tax, goods and services tax, and harmonized sales tax that a business collects from its customers and pays to its suppliers. In addition, some companies are regulated by provincial securities commissions, such as the British Columbia Securities Commission or the Ontario Securities Commission, which dictate that businesses selling their shares to and borrowing money from the public disclose certain financial information.

Not-for-Profit Organizations Organizations such as churches, hospitals, government agencies, universities, and colleges, which operate for purposes other than to earn a profit, use accounting information to make decisions related to the organization in much the same way that profit-oriented businesses do.

Other Users Employees and labour unions may make wage demands based on the accounting information that shows their employer's reported income. Consumer groups and the general public are also interested in the amount of income that businesses earn.

Financial Accounting and Management Accounting

Users of accounting information may be grouped as external users or internal users. This distinction allows us to classify accounting into two fields—financial accounting and management accounting.

Financial accounting provides information primarily to people outside the company. Creditors and outside investors, for example, are not part of the day-to-day management of the company. Creditors want to know if the business can pay them back. Investors will want to know if the business is profitable and they should invest in it. Likewise, government agencies and the general public are **external users** of a company's accounting information. This text deals primarily with financial accounting.

Management accounting generates information for internal decision makers, such as company executives, department managers, and hospital administrators. **Internal users** ask questions such as, What price should we set for our product in order to make the most money? How much of a raise can we afford to give our employees?

Exhibit 1–2 shows how financial accounting and management accounting are used by Hunter Environmental Consulting's internal and external decision makers.

EXHIBIT 1–2 | How Financial Accounting and Management Accounting Are Used

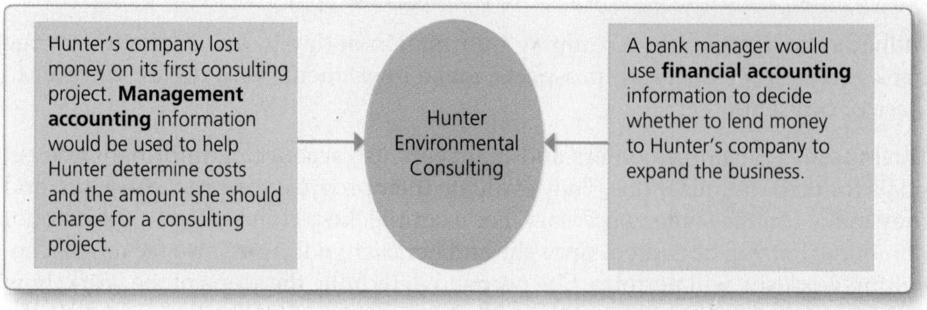

Accountants

Designated accountants in Canada are called **Chartered Professional Accountants (CPAs)**. Until recently, there were three **professional designations** for accountants in Canada—Chartered Accountants (CAs), Certified General Accountants (CGAs), and Certified Management Accountants (CMAs). Those accountants who joined the CPA as a result of the merger of these organizations currently retain their **legacy designation** on their business cards.

Professional Conduct Professional accountants are governed by standards of professional conduct. Many of these standards apply whether the members are **public accountants** who perform work for other businesses or **private accountants** who are employed by a particular business. These rules concern the confidentiality of information the accountant is privy to, maintenance of the profession's reputation, the need to work with integrity and due care, competence, refusal to be associated with false or misleading information, and compliance with professional standards. Other rules are applicable only to those members in public practice and deal with things like the need for **independence** and how to advertise, seek clients, and conduct a practice. This helps the public determine its expectations of members' behaviour. However, the rules of professional conduct should be considered a minimum standard of performance; ideally, the members should continually strive to exceed them.

Audits One type of work done by **designated accountants** is an **audit**. An audit is a financial examination. Audits are conducted by independent accountants who express an opinion on whether or not the financial statements fairly reflect the economic events that occurred during the accounting period. Companies and their auditors must behave in an ethical manner. Exhibit 1–3 illustrates the relationship among accounting and business entities that are **publicly traded companies**.

EXHIBIT 1–3 | Relationship among Accounting and Business Entities

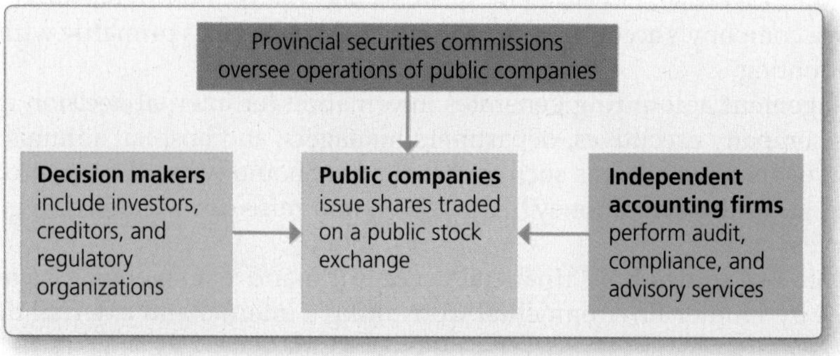

CPA Canada Advanced Certificate in Accounting and Finance (ACAF) The ACAF program prepares people for intermediate-level accounting and finance roles. Courses are delivered through accredited programs at postsecondary institutions as an alternative to pursuing a professional designation.

Ethics in Accounting and Business

We need to consider **ethics** in all areas of accounting and business. Investors, creditors, and regulatory bodies need reliable information about a company. Naturally, companies want to make themselves look as good as possible to attract investors, so there is a potential for conflict. Unfortunately for the accounting profession, accounting scandals involving both public companies and their auditors have made the headlines over the years. At the turn of this century, Enron Corporation, which was the seventh-largest company in the United States, issued misleading financial statements. Enron was forced into bankruptcy, and its auditors' actions were questioned. The impact of the Enron bankruptcy was felt by many different parties, including Enron shareholders, who saw their investments become worthless; employees, who lost their jobs and their pensions; and the accounting profession, which lost some of its integrity and reputation as gatekeepers and stewards for the investing public. This situation shocked the business community and caused investors to question the reliability of financial information.

In an effort to increase the reliability of financial information, a number of changes were made after the Enron scandal. Chapter 8 discusses this in greater detail.

Since the financial health of a company is important to many different groups of users, these users must be confident that they can rely on the financial information they are given when they are making decisions. To increase users' confidence, the accounting profession and other interested stakeholder groups made important changes over the past decade to improve the quality of the financial information provided.

Try It! questions appear at the end of each learning-objective section, allowing you to test your understanding of the concepts before moving on to the next learning objective. The solutions appear at the end of the chapter and on MyLab Accounting. For this chapter, look on page 54.

Try It!

1. Indicate if the following users of accounting information are internal or external users.

	Internal	External
a. Supplier		
b. Owner (who manages the business)		
c. Marketing manager		
d. Lender		
e. Ontario Securities Commission		

Solutions appear at the end of this chapter and on **MyLab Accounting**

Forms of Business Organizations

LO 2
In what form can we set up a company?

A business can be organized as a

- Proprietorship
- Partnership
- Corporation

Exhibit 1–4 summarizes some of the differences between the three forms of business organization.

Proprietorship

A **proprietorship** has a single owner, called the proprietor, who often manages the business. Proprietorships tend to be small retail stores, restaurants, and service businesses, but they can also be very large. From an accounting viewpoint, each

EXHIBIT 1-4 | Comparison of the Forms of Business Organization

	Proprietorship	Partnership	Corporation
Owner(s)	Proprietor—one owner	Partners—two or more owners	Shareholder(s)—one or many owners
Life of organization	Limited by owner's choice or death	Limited by owners' choices or death of one of the partners	Indefinite
Personal liability of owner(s) for business debts	Owner is personally liable	Partners are personally liable*	Shareholders are not personally liable
Legal status	The owner and the business are not legally separate	The partnership is the partners; they are not legally separate	The corporation is separate from the shareholders (owners)
Taxation	The owner pays tax on the proprietorship's earnings; income is added onto the owner's personal tax return	The owners each pay tax on their share of the partnership's earnings; income is added onto each partner's personal tax return	Separate taxable entity; the corporation pays tax on its earnings

* Unless it is a limited liability partnership (LLP)

proprietorship is distinct from its owner. Thus, the accounting records of the proprietorship do not include the proprietor's personal accounting records. However, from a legal perspective, the business *is* the proprietor, so if the business cannot pay its debts, lenders can take the proprietor's personal assets (cash and belongings) to pay the proprietorship's debt.

Partnership

A **partnership** joins two or more individuals together as co-owners. Each owner is a partner. Many retail stores and professional organizations of physicians, lawyers, and accountants are partnerships. Accounting treats the partnership as a separate organization distinct from the personal affairs of each partner. From a legal perspective, though, a partnership *is* the partners in a manner similar to a proprietorship. If the partnership cannot pay its debts, lenders can take each partner's personal assets to pay the partnership's debts.

Limited Liability Partnership (LLP) A **limited liability partnership (LLP)** is a partnership in which one partner cannot create a large liability for the other partners. Each partner is liable only for his or her own actions and those actions under his or her control.

Corporation

A **corporation** is a business owned by **shareholders**. These are the people or other corporations who own shares of ownership in the business. Although proprietorships and partnerships are more numerous, corporations engage in more business and are generally larger in terms of total assets, income, and number of employees. In Canada, corporations generally have *Ltd.* or *Limited, Inc.* or *Incorporated*, or *Corp.* or *Corporation* in their legal name to indicate that they are incorporated. Corporations need not be large; a business with only one owner and only a few assets could be organized as a corporation.

From a legal perspective, a corporation is formed when the federal or provincial government approves its articles of incorporation. Unlike a proprietorship or a partnership, once a corporation is formed it is a legal entity separate and distinct from its owners. The corporation operates as an "artificial person" that exists apart from its owners and that conducts business in its own name. The corporation has

There are a lot of acronyms and abbreviations in accounting. At the end of each chapter there is a list of **Similar Terms**, and they are also summarized on the inside back cover.

many of the rights that a person has. For example, a corporation may buy, own, and sell property; the corporation may enter into contracts and sue and be sued.

Corporations differ significantly from proprietorships and partnerships in another way. If a proprietorship or partnership cannot pay its debts, lenders can take the owners' personal assets to satisfy the business's obligations. But if a corporation goes bankrupt, lenders cannot take the personal assets of the shareholders. This **limited personal liability** of shareholders for corporate debts explains why corporations are so popular compared to proprietorships and partnerships, which have **unlimited personal liability**.

Corporations divide ownership into individual shares. Companies such as WestJet Airlines Ltd. and Canadian Tire Corporation, Limited, have issued millions of shares of stock and have tens of thousands of shareholders. An investor with no personal relationship either to the corporation or to any other shareholder can become an owner by buying 30, 100, 5,000, or any number of shares of its stock. For most corporations, the investor may sell the shares at any time. It is usually harder to sell one's investment in a proprietorship or a partnership than to sell one's investment in a corporation.

Accounting for corporations includes some unique complexities. For this reason, we initially focus on proprietorships. We cover partnerships in Chapter 12 and begin our discussion of corporations in Chapter 13.

Try It!

2. For each of the following scenarios, indicate the applicable form of business in the space provided.

	Proprietorship	Partnership	Corporation
a. The business is not making enough money to pay its bills. The owners do not have to make up the difference with their personal funds.			
b. Anna and Sui have owned their business together for five years. Anna dies. The business must be closed if they chose this form of business.			
c. An unincorporated business with five owners is a . . .			
d. The profits of Chi's business must be reported on her tax return.			
e. There is a lawsuit against a business and there is not enough money to pay the claim. The owners only lose the amount they have invested into the business.			

Solutions appear at the end of this chapter and on **MyLab Accounting**

Accounting Concepts

LO 3

What are some of the guidelines for accounting, and why do we need them?

Earlier in this chapter, we discussed the importance of financial information to various user groups. Users must be confident that they can rely on the financial information they are given when they are making decisions. To increase users' confidence, accounting practices need to follow certain guidelines that govern how accountants measure, process, and communicate financial information. They are known as **generally accepted accounting principles**, or **GAAP**.

Individual countries determine their own GAAP. In the past, the standards used around the world were very different. Over time, as more businesses operated in multiple countries, the preparation of different statements for each country became costly and inefficient. For example, a Canadian company that sold its shares on a

Both IFRS and ASPE are "principles-based." This means that standards cannot possibly be developed for every accounting transaction a company will encounter, so the accountant must use professional judgment in some circumstances. Professional judgment is an acquired skill—you need a good knowledge of accounting standards and many years of experience in order to exercise sound professional judgment. However, it is important to note that the starting point in acquiring professional judgment is a solid understanding of the concepts of accounting.

Margin notes provide additional, useful information which may include real-world examples, learning tips, or key points for review.

stock exchange in Germany had to prepare one set of financial statements under Canadian GAAP and another under German GAAP or, at least, provide a reconciliation from one to the other. To address this issue, the **International Accounting Standards Board (IASB)** developed **International Financial Reporting Standards**, or **IFRS**. In 2016, PwC reported that 89% of countries require or permit IFRS for **listed companies** (those traded on a stock exchange).

IFRS Canadian guidelines are developed by the Accounting Standards Board and published in the *CPA Canada Handbook – Accounting*. There are several parts to this *Handbook* for different types of business entities. Part I covers IFRS for companies that qualify as publicly accountable enterprises. **Publicly accountable enterprises**, generally speaking, are companies that are publicly traded or for which a strong public interest exists. In Canada, they are small in number but contribute heavily to our economy. The Indigo Books & Music Inc. financial statements in Appendix A and the TELUS Corporation annual report posted in MyLab Accounting provide you with examples of IFRS reporting.

ASPE Most Canadian businesses are small to medium in size and are **private enterprises**. The most significant users of their financial information are their creditors (likely their bank) and the government (for computing income taxes and sales taxes). Consequently, a second set of accounting standards, **Accounting Standards for Private Enterprises**, or **ASPE**, was developed for these types of businesses and forms Part II* of the *Handbook*. The primary reason for this second standard is related to users' access to a company's financial information. For smaller, private enterprises, whether they are proprietorships, partnerships, or corporations, the various user groups that interact with the company typically have better access to the owners and managers of the company. Therefore, the users do not need as much information from the financial statements. If a banker has a question about a private company's purchases of equipment, the banker can ask the owner directly. However, many of the user groups who need financial information about larger, publicly traded companies do not have the same access to the managers and, therefore, need more information, which is included in the IFRS-based financial statements.

Because of the large number of businesses in Canada that follow ASPE, and because most later accounting courses focus on IFRS, this text will focus on ASPE, with IFRS material appearing as the final learning objective when appropriate.

Framework for Financial Reporting

Objective

Fundamental accounting concepts form the basis of how accounting should be done and reported to users. The hierarchy of financial statement concepts shown in Exhibit 1–5 is the framework for financial reporting. As the pyramid shape indicates, the financial reports issued by a company are the end product to meet the *objective of financial reporting*, which is to provide *useful* information to investors, creditors, and other users in making investment decisions or assessing the success of a company by looking at the financial statements. They are built on a strong foundation of accounting principles. We refer to these concept throughout the text as they are the reason we do things the way we do.

Qualitative Characteristics

The *qualitative characteristics of accounting information* of relevance, reliability, comparability, and understandability explain what makes information useful to the various users of financial reports. Assume that you have decided that you would like to invest some of your savings in the shares of a company. How would you decide on a company to invest in? Your starting point would likely be the financial statements. You expect that the financial statements include information that is:

- **Relevant**: It provides important information upon which you can base your investment decision.

*The *CPA Canada Handbook* has five parts. The others are: Part III—accounting standards for not-for-profit organizations, Part IV—accounting standards for pension plans, and Part V—pre-changeover accounting standards.

EXHIBIT 1–5 | A Hierarchy of Financial Statement Concepts

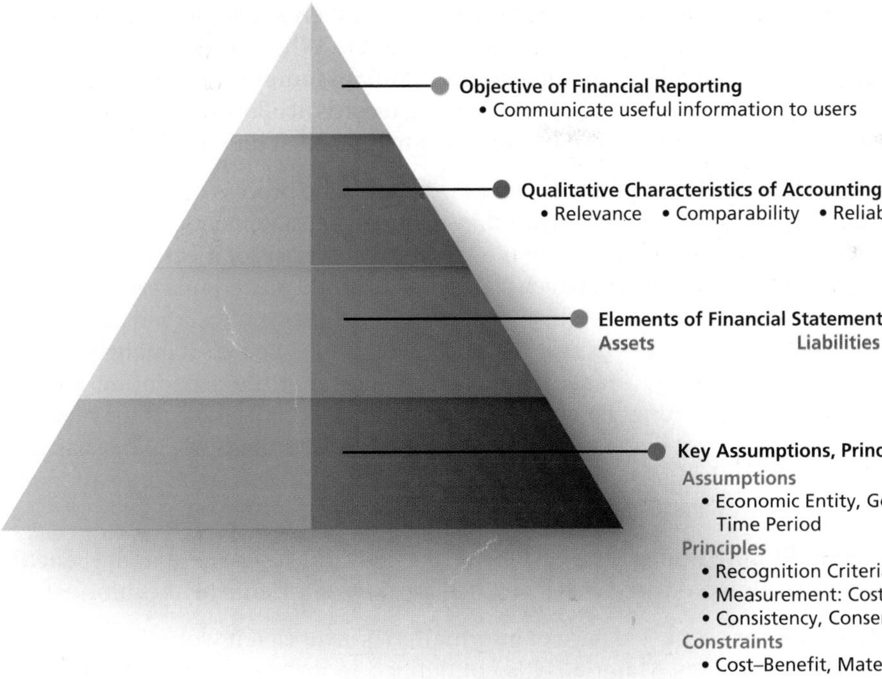

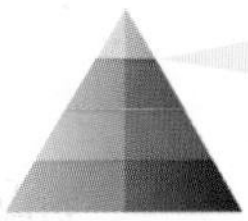

You will refer to this exhibit in later chapters. A triangle icon will remind you to review this exhibit.

- **Reliable**: The information reported accurately reflects the business events that affect the company.
- **Comparable**: You should be able to compare the information against the business's own financial results in previous years or against the results of another company in the same industry.
- **Understandable**: It is clear and concise so that information is not misunderstood.

Certainly there is other information that you may want to study before you make your decision, but the financial statements are a good starting point.

Elements of financial statements are the accounts that are explained in the next learning objective in this chapter.

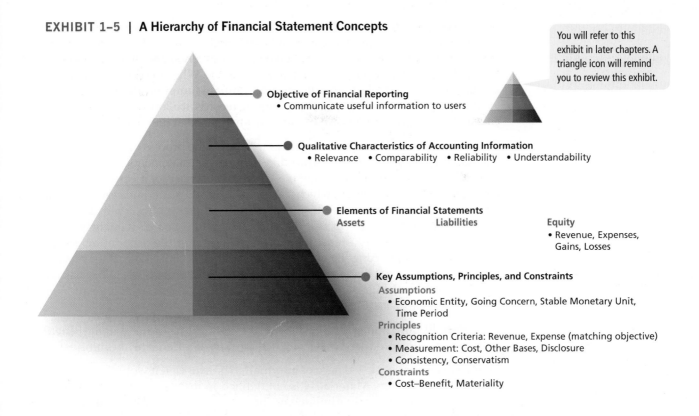

Elements

The bottom level forms the foundation of understanding financial information, through *assumptions, recognition and measurement criteria,* and *constraints,* some of which are discussed below.

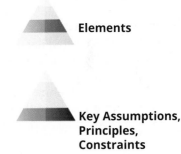

Key Assumptions, Principles, Constraints

Economic Entity Assumption In accounting, an *entity* is an organization or a section of an organization that stands apart from other organizations and individuals as a separate economic unit. This is known as the **economic entity assumption**. Each entity keeps separate accounting records. This means you keep your business's accounting separate from your personal accounting so that you can evaluate the success of your business. It also means companies may keep each department's accounting separate from all the other departments to assess and evaluate the performance of each department.

Going Concern Assumption When accountants record financial information, they assume that the entity is going to be in business for the foreseeable future. Under the **going concern assumption**, accountants *assume* that the business will remain in operation long enough to use its resources rather than being forced to accept whatever price it can get because it is going out of business.

Stable Monetary Unit Assumption In Canada, accountants record transactions in dollars because the dollar is the measure we use when we make purchases and sales. However, unlike other measures like a kilometre or a tonne, the value of a dollar can change over time. A rise in the general level of prices is called **inflation**. During inflation, a dollar will purchase less milk, less toothpaste, and less of other goods over time. In Canada, prices are considered to be relatively stable—there is little inflation—so the purchasing power of money is also stable. When the dollar's purchasing power is relatively stable, the **stable monetary unit assumption** allows accountants to ignore the effect of inflation in the accounting records. It allows accountants to add and subtract dollar amounts for activities that happened at different times.

Cost Principle of Measurement **Measurement** is the process of determining the amount at which an item is recognized in the financial statements. Financial statements are prepared primarily using the historical-cost basis of measurement, commonly called the *cost principle*, which states that acquired assets and services should be recorded at their actual cost (historical cost). Purchases are recorded at the price actually paid and not at the "expected" cost or what someone feels it might be worth.

The **cost principle of measurement** also holds that the accounting records should continue reporting the historical cost of an asset for as long as the business holds the asset. Why? Because historical cost is a *reliable* measure. Other bases of measurement can be used but only in limited circumstances. In later chapters we will look at them when they are appropriate.

Cost–Benefit Constraint The **cost–benefit constraint** stipulates that the benefits of the information produced should exceed the costs of producing the information.

Materiality Constraint A piece of information is *material* if it would affect a decision maker's decision. **Materiality** is not defined in the standards but is a matter of the information preparer's judgment. For example, information about inventory is important to users of Canadian Tire Corporation, Limited's financial statements, since a large change in inventory could change a decision about investing in Canadian Tire. Thus, such information would be provided to decision makers. However, information about the office supplies at Canadian Tire would not likely change an investment decision, so details about office supplies are not provided.

Try It!

3. Suppose you are considering the purchase of a building. The seller is asking $200,000 for a building that cost her $100,000. An appraisal shows the building has a value of $180,000. You first offer $160,000. The seller counteroffers with $190,000. Finally, you and the seller agree on a price of $185,000. What dollar amount for this building is reported on your financial statements? Which accounting assumption or principle guides your answer?
4. Suppose you own a company that delivers newspapers. The company owns two trucks that are used for delivering the papers. You have decided that you need a new car for mainly personal purposes, but you want the company to buy it for you. Is this appropriate? Name the assumption or principle that must be considered.

Solutions appear at the end of this chapter and on **MyLab Accounting**

The Accounting Equation

LO 4

How do business activities affect the accounting records of a company?

Financial statements tell us how a business is performing. They are the final product of the accounting process. But how do we arrive at the items and amounts that make up the financial statements? The most basic tool is the **accounting equation**. It measures the resources of a business and the claims to those resources.

The accounting equation in Exhibit 1–6 shows how assets, liabilities, and owner's equity are related. Assets appear on the left side of the equation. The legal and economic claims against the assets—the liabilities and owner's equity—appear on the right side of the equation. As the exhibit shows, *the two sides must be equal.*

EXHIBIT 1–6 | The Accounting Equation

Assets	=	Liabilities	+	Owner's Equity
Economic Resources		**Claims to Economic Resources**		

The basic summary device of accounting is the **account**, which is the detailed record of the changes that have occurred in a particular asset, liability, or item of owner's equity during a period of time and the total at any point in time. Business activities cause the changes.

Assets

Assets are economic resources controlled by an entity that are expected to benefit the business in the future. Most firms use the asset accounts similar to the ones shown in Exhibit 1–7.

Hint: A receivable is always an asset. A payable is always a liability.

EXHIBIT 1–7 | Asset Accounts

Account Name	Explanation
Cash	A business's money. Includes bank balances, bills, coins, and cheques.
Accounts Receivable	A business may sell its goods or services in exchange for an oral or implied promise of future cash receipts. Such sales are made on credit—*on account*—to customers who buy a business's products or services and recorded in the **Accounts Receivable** account.
Note Receivable	A business may sell its goods or services in exchange for a **promissory note**, which is a written pledge that the customer will pay the business a fixed amount of money by a certain date. A **note receivable** offers more **security** for collection than an account receivable does, and it can require the customer to pay interest on the amount the customer owes.
Prepaid Expenses	A business often pays certain expenses in advance. A **prepaid expense** is an asset because it provides future benefits to the business. The business avoids having to pay cash in the future for the specified expense. Examples include: Prepaid Rent, Prepaid Insurance, and Prepaid Advertising.
Land	The cost of land a business owns and uses in its operations.
Building	The cost of a business's buildings—office, warehouse, garage, or store. These are the buildings used in the operation of the business.
Equipment, Furniture, and Fixtures	A business has a separate asset account for each type of equipment—Computer Equipment, Office Equipment, and Store Equipment, for example.

Liabilities

Liabilities are debts that are payable to creditors. For example, a creditor who has lent money to a business has a claim—a legal right—to a part of the assets until the business pays the debt. Many liabilities have the word *payable* in their title. A business generally has fewer liability accounts than asset accounts because a business's liabilities can be summarized under relatively few categories. Some are shown in Exhibit 1–8, while others will be added in later chapters. A more comprehensive list of typical account names for **service proprietorships** is given in Appendix B at the end of this book.

Account names are not the same for all companies. Once an account name is used, then the same name is used all the time for that company.

EXHIBIT 1–8 | Liability Accounts

Account Name	Explanation
Accounts Payable	The oral or implied promise to pay off debts arising from credit purchases. Such purchases are said to be made *on account*. **Accounts payable** are usually amounts owed to a business's suppliers for goods or services purchased.
Note Payable	A **note payable** account represents an amount that the business must pay because it signed a promissory note to borrow money. Interest must be paid in addition to the amount borrowed.
Unearned Revenue	An **unearned revenue** is a liability created when a business collects cash from customers in advance of doing work for the customer. There is an obligation to provide a product or service in the future.

Owner's Equity

The equity accounts, as shown in Exhibit 1–9, show the owner's claims to the business assets. Keep this perspective in mind when working through transactions. Always remember to record information from the company's perspective.

EXHIBIT 1–9 | Equity Accounts

Account Name	Explanation
Capital	Owner's claims to the business assets are called **owner's equity** or **capital**. In this text, the account to represent this equity is written as Lisa Hunter, Capital or L. Hunter, Capital, although Hunter, Capital is also considered correct.
Withdrawals	Distributions of cash or other assets to the owner. Withdrawals *decrease equity*. The amounts taken out of the business appear in a separate account entitled Lisa Hunter, Withdrawals. **Owner withdrawals** do not represent a business expense because the cash is used for the owner's personal affairs unrelated to the business.
Revenues	The purpose of business is to *increase owner's equity* through **revenues**, which are amounts earned by delivering goods or services to customers. Typical accounts include Service Revenue, Sales Revenue (see Chapter 5 on the sale of goods), Interest Revenue (if a business lends money), and Rent Revenue.
Expenses	**Expenses** result in a *decrease in owner's equity*. They occur when a business uses or consumes assets or increases liabilities in the course of delivering goods and services to customers. Expenses are often thought of as the "costs of doing business." Examples include Salaries Expense, Office Supplies Expense, Rent Expense, Advertising Expense, and Utilities Expense.

Partnerships and corporations have similar terms for their equity: The owner's equity category of accounts is called **partners' equity** in a partnership and **shareholders' equity** in a corporation. Profits paid to owners in a corporation are called **dividends**. We use these accounts in Volume 2 of the text.

	Sole Proprietorship	Partnership	Corporation
Equity terminology	Owner's Equity	Partners' Equity	Shareholders' Equity
Resources removed from the business by the owner	Withdrawals, or Drawings	Withdrawals, or Drawings	Dividends

The accounting equation you first saw in Exhibit 1–6 can be expanded to show details of the Owner's Equity accounts. We will learn shortly that the calculation of revenues less expenses tells us whether the business earns a net income or has incurred a net loss. This means we can further expand the accounting equation as shown in Exhibit 1–10.

EXHIBIT 1–10 | Expanded Accounting Equation

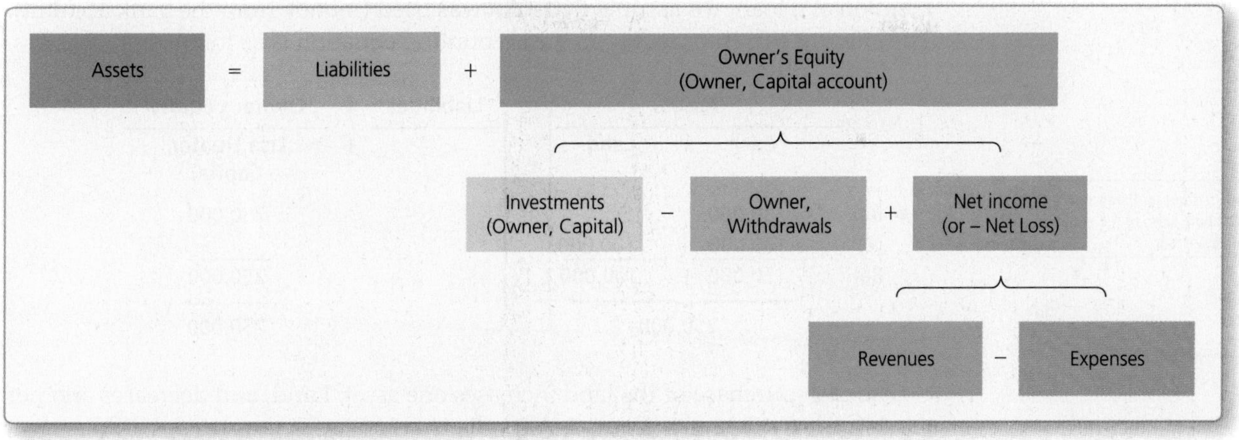

Accounting for Business Transactions

Accounting is based on transactions, not opinions or desires. A **transaction** is any event that affects the financial position of the business entity *and* can be measured reliably. Many events may affect a company, including elections and economic booms, but accountants do not record the effects of these events because they cannot be measured reliably. An accountant records as transactions only events with dollar amounts that can be measured reliably, such as purchases and sales of merchandise inventory, payment of rent, and collection of cash from customers. In Exhibit 1–1 on page 4, transactions are the middle step in the flow of information in an accounting system.

A transaction is an event that must always satisfy these two conditions:
1. It affects the financial position of a business entity.
2. It can be measured reliably.

To illustrate accounting for business transactions, let's go back to our opening story and look at the transactions for Lisa Hunter's company, Hunter Environmental Consulting (HEC), in the first month of her business. We will consider 12 events and analyze each in terms of its effect on the accounting equation of HEC.

Transaction 1: Starting the Business Hunter invests $250,000 of her money to start the business. Specifically, she deposits $250,000 in a bank account set up for Hunter Environmental Consulting.

We do not use an account called Bank. Why not? It is just how we do it in this text. Could a real business call this account Bank? Yes! But throughout this text, we always use an account called Cash.

The effect of this transaction on the accounting equation of the HEC business entity is as follows:

	Assets		Liabilities	+	Owner's Equity
	Cash	=			Lisa Hunter, Capital
(1)	+250,000				+250,000

For every transaction, the amount on the left side of the equation must equal the amount on the right side. The first transaction increases both the assets (in this case, Cash) and the owner's equity of the business (Lisa Hunter, Capital). When we update the owner's equity, what we are saying is that the business has increased the owner's claim on the assets of the business. The transaction involves no liabilities of the business because it creates no obligation for HEC to pay an outside party. The assets and liabilities elements of the accounting equation will be expanded to show the specific accounts affected by a transaction, but owner's equity will not be expanded. Therefore, to the right of the transaction, we write "owner investment" to keep track of the reason for the effect on owner's equity.

Transaction 2: Purchase of Land HEC purchases land for a future office location, paying $100,000. How do you purchase something? In this case, since there is no mention of a loan, we assume that cash was used (money from the bank account). The effect of this transaction on the accounting equation is as follows:

Bal. is short for Balance. We check that both sides of the equation are always equal.

	Assets				Liabilities	+	Owner's Equity
	Cash	+	Land			+	Lisa Hunter, Capital
Bal.	250,000			=			250,000
(2)	−100,000		+100,000				
Bal.	150,000	+	100,000				250,000
	250,000						250,000

The cash purchase of the land increases one asset, Land, and decreases another asset, Cash, by the same amount. After the transaction is completed, HEC has cash of $150,000, land of $100,000, no liabilities, and Lisa Hunter, Capital of $250,000. Note that the sum of the balances on both sides of the equation are equal.

Office Supplies that are held for future use are an asset. When they are used, they become an expense. Because there is a gap in time between buying $7,000 worth of supplies and using them, we record each event separately.

Transaction 3: Purchase of Office Supplies on Account HEC buys stationery and other office supplies, agreeing to pay $7,000 within 30 days. This transaction increases both the assets and the liabilities of the company, as follows:

	Assets						Liabilities	+	Owner's Equity
	Cash	+	Office Supplies	+	Land		Accounts Payable	+	Lisa Hunter, Capital
Bal.	150,000			+	100,000	=		+	250,000
(3)			+7,000				+7,000		
Bal.	150,000	+	7,000	+	100,000		7,000	+	250,000
	257,000						257,000		

The asset increased is Office Supplies, and the liability increased is called Accounts Payable because the office supplies were purchased *on account*. A payable is always a liability. (If a promissory note had been signed, we would have recorded the liability as a note payable.)

Transaction 4: Earning of Service Revenue HEC earns service revenue by providing environmental consulting services for clients. Assume the business earns $30,000 and collects this amount in cash. The effect on the accounting equation is an increase in the asset Cash and an increase in Service Revenue as follows:

	Assets						Liabilities	+	Owner's Equity		
	Cash	+	Office Supplies	+	Land		Accounts Payable	+	Lisa Hunter, Capital	+	Service Revenue
Bal.	150,000	+	7,000	+	100,000	=	7,000	+	250,000		
(4)	+30,000										+30,000
Bal.	180,000	+	7,000	+	100,000		7,000	+	250,000	+	30,000
	287,000						287,000				

A revenue transaction causes the business to grow, as shown by the increase in total assets and owner's equity. A company like RONA or Canadian Tire that sells goods to customers is a **merchandising business**. Its revenue is called **sales revenue**. In contrast, HEC performs services for clients, so HEC's revenue is called **service revenue**.

Transaction 5: Earning of Service Revenue on Account HEC performs consulting services for clients who do not pay immediately. In return for the services, HEC issues an invoice, and the clients will pay the $25,000 amount within one month. This amount owed to HEC is an asset to HEC, an account receivable, because the business expects to collect the cash in the future. Performing the service, not collecting the cash, earns the revenue. HEC records an increase in the asset Accounts Receivable and an increase in Service Revenue, which increases owner's equity as follows:

The term *on account* can be used for payables or receivables. If you will *receive* cash in the future, it is an Accounts *Receivable* transaction. If you will *pay* cash in the future, it is an Accounts *Payable* transaction.

	Assets					Liabilities +	Owner's Equity	
	Cash +	Accounts Receivable +	Office Supplies +	Land		Accounts Payable +	Lisa Hunter, Capital +	Service Revenue
Bal.	180,000		+ 7,000	+ 100,000	=	7,000	+ 250,000	+ 30,000
(5)		+25,000						+25,000
Bal.	180,000 +	25,000	+ 7,000	+ 100,000		7,000	+ 250,000	+ 55,000
		312,000					312,000	

Transactions 6, 7, and 8: Payment of Expenses During the month, HEC pays $12,000 in cash expenses: office rent, $4,000 (HEC purchased land to build an office in the future [Transaction 2], but the company is renting fully furnished office space in the meantime); employee salaries, $6,500 (for a full-time assistant and a junior consultant); and total utilities, $1,500. The effects on the accounting equation are as follows:

	Assets					Liabilities +	Owner's Equity				
	Cash +	Accounts Receivable +	Office Supplies +	Land		Accounts Payable +	Lisa Hunter, Capital +	Service Revenue −	Rent Expense −	Salaries Expense −	Utilities Expense
Bal.	180,000 +	25,000 +	7,000 +	100,000		7,000 +	250,000 +	55,000			
(6)	−4,000				=				−4,000		
(7)	−6,500									−6,500	
(8)	−1,500										−1,500
Bal.	168,000 +	25,000 +	7,000 +	100,000		7,000 +	250,000 +	55,000 −	4,000 −	6,500 −	1,500
		300,000						300,000			

Expenses have the opposite effect of revenues. Expenses cause the business to shrink, as shown by the decreased balances of total assets and owner's equity.

Each expense should be recorded in a separate transaction because they would likely be three separate payments (cheques or online payments) to different people or companies.

Pay attention to the specific words and phrases used. "Paid" means they "paid using Cash." A "payment on account" means that a prior bill (account) is what got paid.

Transaction 9: Payment on Account HEC pays $5,000 to the store from which it purchased $7,000 worth of office supplies in Transaction 3. In accounting, we say that the business *paid the account*. The effect on the accounting equation is a decrease in the asset Cash and a decrease in the liability Accounts Payable as follows:

	Assets					Liabilities +	Owner's Equity				
	Cash +	Accounts Receivable +	Office Supplies +	Land		Accounts Payable +	Lisa Hunter, Capital +	Service Revenue −	Rent Expense −	Salaries Expense −	Utilities Expense
Bal.	168,000 +	25,000 +	7,000 +	100,000	=	7,000 +	250,000 +	55,000 −	4,000 −	6,500 −	1,500
(9)	−5,000					−5,000					
Bal.	163,000 +	25,000 +	7,000 +	100,000		2,000 +	250,000 +	55,000 −	4,000 −	6,500 −	1,500
		295,000						295,000			

HEC now has less cash and it owes less money to a supplier than it did before the payment. The payment of cash on account has no effect on the asset Office Supplies because the payment does not increase or decrease the supplies available to the business. Likewise, the payment on account does not affect expenses. HEC was paying off a liability (the account), not an expense.

Transaction 10: Home Remodel Paid from Personal Funds Lisa Hunter remodels her home at a cost of $30,000, paying cash from personal funds. This event is *not* a transaction of HEC. It has no effect on HEC's business affairs and, therefore, is not recorded by the business. It is a transaction of the Hunter *personal* entity, not the HEC business entity. We are focusing solely on the *business* entity, and this event does not affect it. This transaction illustrates the *economic entity assumption.*

When recording a transaction, always look at what is happening "at the moment" and update only what accounts are affected *at that time.*

Transaction 11: Collection on Account In Transaction 5, HEC performed consulting services for clients on account. We set up our accounting records in Transaction 5 to show that HEC will receive payment "later." Well, now is the time we are receiving that payment. The business collects $15,000 from the client. We say that it collects the cash *on account.* The business will record an increase in the asset Cash and a decrease in the asset Accounts Receivable. Should it also record an increase in service revenue? No, because HEC already recorded the revenue when it performed the service in Transaction 5. The effect on the accounting equation is as follows:

	Assets					Liabilities +	Owner's Equity				
	Cash	+ Accounts Receivable	+ Office Supplies	+ Land		Accounts Payable	+ Lisa Hunter, Capital	+ Service Revenue	− Rent Expense	− Salaries Expense	− Utilities Expense
Bal.	163,000	+ 25,000	+ 7,000	100,000	=	2,000	+ 250,000	+ 55,000	− 4,000	− 6,500	− 1,500
(11)	+15,000	−15,000									
Bal.	178,000	+ 10,000	+ 7,000	+ 100,000		2,000	+ 250,000	+ 55,000	− 4,000	− 6,500	− 1,500
	295,000					295,000					

Total assets are unchanged from the preceding transaction's total. Why? Because HEC merely exchanged one asset for another.

Transaction 12: Withdrawing of Cash Lisa withdraws $6,000 cash for her personal use. The difference between this transaction and Transaction 10 is that this money comes from the business's bank account, so this event *does* affect the business and must be recorded in the business's records. The effect on the accounting equation is as follows:

	Assets					Liabilities +	Owner's Equity					
	Cash	+ Accounts Receivable	+ Office Supplies	+ Land		Accounts Payable	+ Lisa Hunter, Capital	− Lisa Hunter, Withdrawals	+ Service Revenue	− Rent Expense	− Salaries Expense	− Utilities Expense
Bal.	178,000	+ 10,000	+ 7,000	+ 100,000	=	2,000	+ 250,000		+ 55,000	− 4,000	− 6,500	− 1,500
(12)	−6,000							−6,000				
Bal.	172,000	+ 10,000	+ 7,000	+ 100,000		2,000	+ 250,000	− 6,000	+ 55,000	− 4,000	− 6,500	− 1,500
	289,000					289,000						

Owner withdrawals do not represent a business expense because the cash is used for the owner's personal affairs unrelated to the business.

Hunter's withdrawal of $6,000 decreases the asset Cash and also increases the total amount of owner's withdrawals from the business.

The double underlines below each column indicate a final total after the last transaction.

Exhibit 1–11 summarizes the 12 preceding transactions.

EXHIBIT 1–11 | Analysis of Transactions of Hunter Environmental Consulting

Panel A: DETAILS OF TRANSACTIONS

(1) The business recorded the $250,000 cash investment made by Lisa Hunter.
(2) Paid $100,000 cash for land.
(3) Bought $7,000 of office supplies on account.
(4) Received $30,000 cash from clients for service revenue earned.
(5) Performed services for clients on account, $25,000.
(6) Paid cash expense for rent, $4,000.
(7) Paid cash expense for employee salaries, $6,500.
(8) Paid cash expense for utilities, $1,500.
(9) Paid $5,000 on the account payable created in Transaction 3.
(10) Remodelled Hunter's personal residence. This is not a transaction of the business.
(11) Collected $15,000 on the account receivable created in Transaction 5.
(12) The business paid $6,000 cash to Hunter as a withdrawal.

Panel B: ANALYSIS OF TRANSACTIONS

	Assets				=	Liabilities +	Owner's Equity					
	Cash	+ Accounts Receivable	+ Office Supplies	+ Land		Accounts Payable	+ Lisa Hunter, Capital	− Lisa Hunter, Withdrawals	+ Service Revenue	− Rent Expense	− Salaries Expense	− Utilities Expense
(1)	+250,000						+250,000					
Bal.	250,000						+ 250,000					
(2)	−100,000			+100,000								
Bal.	150,000			+ 100,000			+ 250,000					
(3)			+7,000			+7,000			+30,000			
Bal.	150,000		+ 7,000	+ 100,000		7,000	+ 250,000		+ 30,000			
(4)	+30,000								+25,000			
Bal.	180,000		+ 7,000	+ 100,000		7,000	+ 250,000		+ 55,000			
(5)		+25,000								−4,000		
Bal.	180,000	+ 25,000	+ 7,000	+ 100,000	=	7,000	+ 250,000		+ 55,000	− 4,000		
(6)	−4,000										−6,500	
(7)	−6,500								+ 55,000	− 4,000	− 6,500	
(8)	−1,500											−1,500
Bal.	168,000	+ 25,000	+ 7,000	+ 100,000		7,000	+ 250,000		+ 55,000	− 4,000	− 6,500	− 1,500
(9)	−5,000					−5,000						
Bal.	163,000	+ 25,000	+ 7,000	+ 100,000		2,000	+ 250,000		+ 55,000	− 4,000	− 6,500	− 1,500
(10)	Not a transaction of the business											
(11)	+15,000	−15,000							+ 55,000	− 4,000	− 6,500	− 1,500
Bal.	178,000	+ 10,000	+ 7,000	+ 100,000		2,000	+ 250,000					
(12)	−6,000							−6,000				
Bal.	172,000	+ 10,000	+ 7,000	+ 100,000		2,000	+ 250,000	− 6,000	+ 55,000	− 4,000	− 6,500	− 1,500
	289,000					289,000						

Notice that every transaction maintains the equality of the accounting equation:
Assets = Liabilities + Owner's Equity

Try It!

5. a. If the assets of a business are $75,000 and the liabilities total $65,000, how much is the owner's equity?
   b. If the owner's equity in a business is $50,000 and the liabilities are $20,000, how much are the assets?
6. Indicate whether each account listed below is a(n) asset (A), liability (L), owner's equity (OE), revenue (R), or expense (E) account.

Accounts Receivable	________	Salaries Expense	________
Computer Equipment	________	Consulting Service Revenue	________
S. Scott, Capital	________	Cash	________
Rent Expense	________	Note Payable	________
Supplies	________	Supplies Expense	________
S. Scott, Withdrawals	________	Accounts Payable	________

7. Using the information provided, analyze the effects of Lawlor Lawn Service's transactions on the accounting equation.

May	1	Received $1,700 and gave capital to Eric Lawlor.
May	3	Purchased a mower on account, $1,440.
May	5	Performed lawn services for client on account, $200.
May	17	Paid $60 cash for gas used in mower.
May	28	Eric Lawlor withdrew cash of $300.

Create a chart using the following format to record your answers:

	Assets			Liabilities	Owners Equity			
	Cash +	Accounts Receivable +	Equipment =	Accounts Payable +	E. Lawlor, Capital −	Withdrawals +	Service Revenue −	Gas Expense
May 1								

Solutions appear at the end of this chapter and on **MyLab Accounting**

The Financial Statements

LO 5

What financial statements are prepared by a company, and how do we create them?

Once the analysis of the transactions is complete, how does a business present the results of the transactions? We now look at the *financial statements*, which are the formal reports of an entity's financial information.

In order to create these reports, we use the totals from Exhibit 1–11.

Income Statement

Is the business making any profit?

The **income statement**, as shown in Exhibit 1–12, presents a summary of the *revenues* and *expenses* of an entity for a period of time, such as a month or a year. Businesspeople run their businesses with the objective of having more revenues than expenses. An excess of total revenues over total expenses is called **net income**, **net earnings**, or **net profit**. If total expenses exceed total revenues, the result is called a **net loss**.

The income statement, also called the **statement of earnings** or **statement of operations**, is often described as a video of the entity's operations—a moving financial picture of business operations during the period.

EXHIBIT 1–12 | Income Statement

The header includes the name of the business, the title of the statement, and the time period. An income statement always represents a period of time, for example, a month or a year.

HUNTER ENVIRONMENTAL CONSULTING Income Statement For the Month Ended April 30, 2019		
Revenues		
Service revenue		$55,000
Expenses		
Rent expense	$4,000	
Salaries expense	6,500	
Utilities expense	1,500	
Total expenses		12,000
Net income		$43,000

Dollar signs appear at the top of each column and on the total.

The revenue accounts are always listed first and then subtotalled, if necessary.

Net income is calculated as total revenues minus total expenses. If this amount is negative, the label changes to read Net loss.

Each expense account is listed separately. Here we are using the convention of alphabetical order. Other ways of listing accounts are possible. It is popular to list them from the largest amount to the smallest amount.

The double underline signals the reader that this is the total of the report.

Statement of Owner's Equity

The **statement of owner's equity** presents a summary of the changes that occurred in the entity's *owner's equity* during a specific period of time, such as a month or a year. Exhibit 1–13 illustrates how to lay it out and calculate the total.

EXHIBIT 1–13 | Statement of Owner's Equity

The header includes the name of the business, the title of the statement, and the time period. A statement of owner's equity always represents a period of time.

HUNTER ENVIRONMENTAL CONSULTING Statement of Owner's Equity For the Month Ended April 30, 2019	
Lisa Hunter, capital, April 1, 2019	$ 0
Add: Investment by owner	250,000
Net income for the month	43,000
	293,000
Less: Withdrawals by owner	6,000
Lisa Hunter, capital, April 30, 2019	$287,000

The beginning capital is $0 because Hunter Environmental Consulting began this month; therefore, it had no beginning capital. The beginning capital will always be the ending capital from the previous time period.

Net income is transferred from the income statement.

The owner withdrawal is subtracted from capital. If there had been a net loss, this would also be subtracted.

This text uses a convention to write the word *less* and not show the number as a negative. Some businesses will not include the word *less* and show the amounts as either −6,000 or (6,000).

The owner's investment and net income are added to the beginning capital.

Balance Sheet

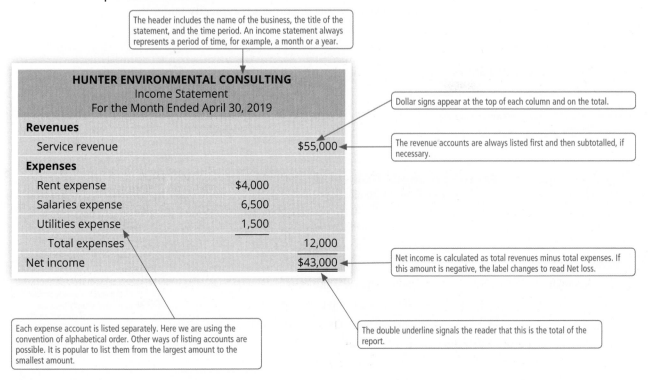

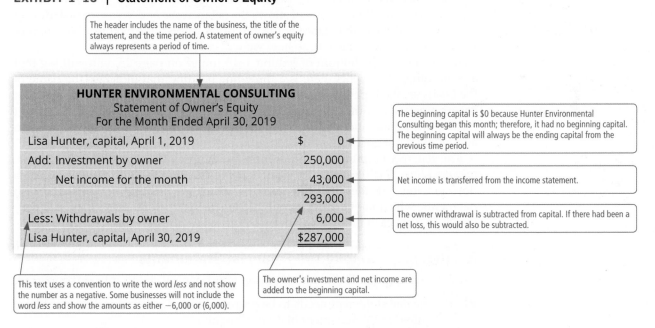

The **balance sheet** (or **statement of financial position**) lists all the assets, liabilities, and owner's equity of an entity as of a specific date, usually the end of a month or a year. The balance sheet is like a snapshot of the entity because it captures values at a moment in time. For HEC, this means the end of the business day on April 30. Exhibit 1–14 shows how this document is typically laid out.

EXHIBIT 1–14 | Balance Sheet

Each asset account is listed separately and then totalled. Cash is always listed first. Pay attention to the order of the other accounts, too.

The heading again shows the name of the business and the title of the financial statement. Notice that the date is different. The balance sheet shows the date as a specific date, not a period of time.

HUNTER ENVIRONMENTAL CONSULTING
Balance Sheet
April 30,2019

Assets		**Liabilities**	
Cash	$172,000	Accounts payable	$ 2,000
Accounts receivable	10,000		
Office supplies	7,000	**Owner's Equity**	
Land	100,000	Lisa Hunter, capital	287,000
Total assets	$289,000	Total liabilities and owner's equity	$289,000

Liabilities are listed separately and then totalled unless there is only one listed. Liabilities that are to be paid first are listed first.

The ending owner's capital is taken directly from the statement of owner's equity.

The balance sheet must always balance. Assets = Liabilities + Owner's Equity. Notice that the layout of this document also shows assets on the left and liabilities and equity on the right. This is no coincidence.

Cash Flow Statement

The **cash flow statement** reports the cash coming in and the cash going out during a period. The cash flow statement shows the net increase or decrease in cash during the period and the cash balance at the end of the period. We devote all of Chapter 17 to the cash flow statement, so here we will only look at it briefly.

If you review the bottom of Exhibit 1–15 found on page 23, you will see that as with other statements there is a three-line heading that indicates the name of the business, the type of financial statement, and the date. A cash flow statement covers a period of time. It explains the change in the balance of the cash account during this period and answers the questions, Where did the money come from and where did it go?

The statement reports cash flows from three types of business activities (*operating*, *investing*, and *financing* activities) during the month. Each category of cash flow activities includes both cash receipts, which are positive amounts, and cash payments, which are negative amounts (denoted by parentheses). Each category results in a net cash inflow or a net cash outflow for the period.

Relationships among the Financial Statements

Exhibit 1–15 on page 23 illustrates how all four financial statements are connected.

1. The income statement needs to be prepared first. The net income (or net loss) is required in the statement of owner's equity.
2. The balance in the capital account is needed for the balance sheet.
3. The balance in the cash account must be the same on both the balance sheet and the cash flow statement.

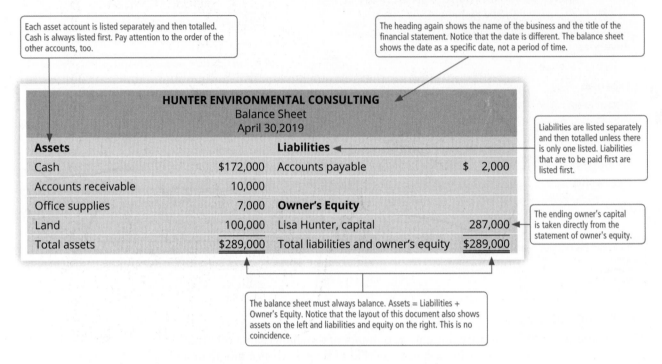

EXHIBIT 1-15 | Financial Statements of Hunter Environmental Consulting

HUNTER ENVIRONMENTAL CONSULTING
Income Statement
For the Month Ended April 30, 2019

Revenue		
Service revenue		$55,000
Expenses		
Rent expense	$4,000	
Salaries expense	6,500	
Utilities expense	1,500	
Total expenses		12,000
Net income		$43,000

HUNTER ENVIRONMENTAL CONSULTING
Statement of Owner's Equity
For the Month Ended April 30, 2019

Lisa Hunter, capital, April 1, 2019	$ 0
Add: Investment by owner	250,000
Net income for the month	43,000
	293,000
Less: Withdrawals by owner	6,000
Lisa Hunter, capital, April 30, 2019	$287,000

1

2

HUNTER ENVIRONMENTAL CONSULTING
Balance Sheet
April 30, 2019

Assets		**Liabilities**	
Cash	$172,000	Accounts payable	$ 2,000
Accounts receivable	10,000		
Office supplies	7,000	**Owner's Equity**	
Land	100,000	Lisa Hunter, capital	287,000
Total assets	$289,000	Total liabilities and owner's equity	$289,000

3

HUNTER ENVIRONMENTAL CONSULTING
Cash Flow Statement*
For the Month Ended April 30, 2019

Cash flows from operating activities		
Cash collections from customers**		$ 45,000
Cash payments to suppliers***	$ (10,500)	
Cash payments to employees	(6,500)	(17,000)
Net cash inflow from operating activities		28,000
Cash flows from investing activities		
Acquisition of land	$(100,000)	
Net cash outflow from investing activities		(100,000)
Cash flows from financing activities		
Investment by owner	$ 250,000	
Withdrawal by owner	(6,000)	
Net cash inflow from financing activities		244,000
Net increase in cash		$172,000
Cash balance, April 1, 2019		0
Cash balance, April 30, 2019		$172,000

*Chapter 17 explains how to prepare this statement.
**$30,000 + $15,000 = $45,000
***$4,000 + $1,500 + $5,000 = $10,500

You will look at the notes to the financial statements in many of the Financial Statement Case questions at the end of each chapter.

Notes to the Financial Statements The four financial statements are accompanied by *notes* that provide more information about what is presented in the statements. The *CPA Canada Handbook* identifies the information that is required, which varies by the type of business or not-for-profit organization. Preparation of the notes is beyond the scope of this text, but reading and understanding them is a useful skill for all users of financial information.

Try It!

8. Using the following information, complete the income statement, statement of owner's equity, and balance sheet for DR Painting for the month of March 2020. The business began operations on March 1, 2020.

Accounts receivable	$1,400
Accounts payable	1,000
Cash	22,300
Owner contribution during March	40,000
Owner withdrawal during March	1,500
D. Richardson, Capital, March 1, 2020	0
Salaries expense	800
Service revenue	7,000
Office supplies	1,800
Land	20,000
Utilities expense	200

Solutions appear at the end of this chapter and on **MyLab Accounting**

This text illustrates accounting for businesses that follow Accounting Standards for Private Enterprises (ASPE). When there are differences from International Financial Reporting Standards (IFRS), this information is noted with a chart as the last learning objective for a chapter. Some chapters won't have a chart, because in many cases the standards are the same! In Volume 2, these charts will become more detailed.

LO 6
What are IFRS and ASPE?

EXHIBIT 1–16 | How IFRS Differ from What We See in the Chapter

ASPE	IFRS
In Canada, both International Financial Reporting Standards (IFRS) and Accounting Standards for Private Enterprises (ASPE) are prepared under the authority of the **Accounting Standards Board** and are published as part of the CPA *Canada Handbook*.	
Sole proprietorships follow ASPE, which are simpler and less costly to implement. Private corporations can choose to follow ASPE or IFRS.	Publicly accountable enterprises or those planning to become one must follow IFRS.
Financial reports contain less information under ASPE because readers have more access to the details themselves.	Financial reports under IFRS contain more detailed information than under ASPE because users do not have easy access to the information.
Companies reporting under either method must also provide notes to the financial statements, which include significant accounting policies and explanatory information.	

Summary Problem for Your Review

Todor Biris opened a website design business in Calgary. He is the sole owner of the proprietorship, which he names Biris Web Design. During the first month of operations, July 2019, the following transactions occurred:

a. Biris invests $50,000 of personal funds to start the business.
b. The business purchases, on account, office supplies costing $2,000.
c. Biris Web Design pays cash of $26,000 to acquire a parcel of land. The business intends to use the land as a future building site for its business office.
d. The business provides services for clients and receives cash of $10,000.
e. The business pays $1,000 on the account payable created in Transaction (b).
f. Biris pays $2,750 of personal funds for a vacation for his family.
g. The business pays cash expenses for office rent, $2,500, and utilities, $500.
h. The business returns to the supplier office supplies that cost $300. The wrong supplies were shipped.
i. Biris withdraws $3,000 cash for personal use.

The **Summary Problem for Your Review** is an extensive, solved review problem that pulls together the chapter concepts.

Required

1. Analyze the preceding transactions in terms of their effects on the accounting equation of Biris Web Design. Use Exhibit 1–11 on page 19 as a guide, but show balances only after the last transaction.
2. Prepare the income statement, statement of owner's equity, and balance sheet of Biris Web Design after recording the transactions. Use Exhibit 1–15 on page 23 as a guide.

As you review the details of each transaction, think of the parts of the accounting equation that will be affected.

SOLUTION

Requirement 1

For each transaction, make sure the accounting equation, Assets = Liabilities + Owner's Equity, balances before going on to the next transaction.

	Assets			=	Liabilities +	Owner's Equity				
	Cash +	Office Supplies +	Land		Accounts Payable +	Todor Biris, Capital −	Todor Biris, Withdrawals −	Service Revenue −	Rent Expense −	Utilities Expense
(a)	+50,000					+50,000				
(b)		+2,000			+2,000					
(c)	−26,000		+26,000							
(d)	+10,000							+10,000		
(e)	−1,000				−1,000					
(f)	Not a business transaction									
(g)	−2,500								−2,500	
	−500									−500
(h)		−300			−300					
(i)	−3,000						−3,000			
Bal.	27,000 +	1,700 +	26,000		700 +	50,000 −	3,000 −	10,000 −	25,000 −	5,000
	54,700				54,700					

Requirement 2

BIRIS WEB DESIGN Income Statement For the Month Ended July 31, 2019		
Revenue		
Service revenue		$10,000
Expenses		
Rent expense	$2,500	
Utilities expense	500	
Total expenses		3,000
Net income		$ 7,000

The header must include the name of the company, "Income Statement," and the specific period of time covered.

Gather all the revenue and expense account names and amounts from Requirement 1. They appear in the owner's equity columns.

- List the revenue account first.
- List the expense accounts next. In this text, expenses are often listed in alphabetical order.

BIRIS WEB DESIGN Statement of Owner's Equity For the Month Ended July 31, 2019	
Todor Biris, capital, July 1, 2019	$ 0
Add: Investment by owner	50,000
Net income for July	7,000
	57,000
Less: Withdrawal by owner	3,000
Todor Biris, capital, July 31, 2019	$54,000

The header must include the name of the company, "Statement of Owner's Equity," and the specific period of time covered.

The net income amount (or net loss amount) is transferred from the income statement.

The withdrawal amount is found in the solution to Requirement 1 in the Todor Biris, Withdrawals column.

The header must include the name of the company, "Balance Sheet," and the date of the balance sheet. It shows the financial position on one specific date.

BIRIS WEB DESIGN Balance Sheet July 31, 2019			
Assets		**Liabilities**	
Cash	$27,000	Accounts payable	$ 700
Office supplies	1,700	**Owner's Equity**	
Land	26,000	Todor Biris, capital	54,000
Total assets	$54,700	Total liabilities and owner's equity	$54,700

Gather all the asset and liability accounts and Bal. amounts from the solution to Requirement 1. List assets on the left. Cash always goes first on the asset side. See Appendix B for more accounts and their typical order.

The capital account amount is transferred from the statement of owner's equity.

Check: Total Assets = Total Liabilities + Owner's Equity

Summary

The **Summary** gives a concise description of the material covered in the chapter along with page references, so you can link back into the chapter if you want to review particular material. It is organized by learning objective.

Learning Objectives

① Define accounting, and describe the users of accounting information **Pg. 4**

Why is accounting important, and who uses the information?

- Accounting is an information system for measuring, processing, and communicating financial information.
- As the "language of business," accounting helps a wide range of users (such as individual investors, businesses, government agencies, and lenders) make business decisions.

② Compare and contrast the forms of business organizations **Pg. 7**

In what form can we set up a company?

- The three basic forms of business organizations are
  - Proprietorship
  - Partnership (a limited liability partnership is a special form of partnership)
  - Corporation
- See Exhibit 1-4 on page 8 for a comparison of the three forms.

③ Describe some concepts and principles of accounting **Pg. 9**

What are some of the guidelines for accounting, and why do we need them?

- Accountants use Generally Accepted Accounting Principles (GAAP) to guide their work. The framework for financial reporting in Exhibit 1-5 on page 11 introduces some key accounting concepts.
  - The primary objective of financial statements is to provide information that is useful for users in their decision making.
  - To be useful, the information must have the qualitative characteristics of understandability, reliability, relevance, and comparability.
  - Key assumptions and principles discussed in this chapter are the economic entity assumption, the going concern assumption, the stable monetary unit assumption, and the cost principle of measurement. They are subject to both the cost–benefit and materiality constraints.

④ Use the accounting equation to analyze business transactions **Pg. 12**

How do business activities affect the accounting records of a company?

- The accounting equation is

Assets = Liabilities + Owner's Equity

- A *transaction* is an event that affects the financial position of an entity *and* can be reliably measured.
- To analyze a transaction's effect on the accounting equation, first select the accounts and then decide if each balance goes up or down. Always check if the equation is in balance.

⑤ Prepare financial statements **Pg. 20**

What financial statements are prepared by a company, and how do we create them?

Financial Statement	Information Provided and Purpose	How is it Prepared
Income statement	Provides information about profitability for a particular period for the company at a point in time.	Revenues − Expenses = Net Income
Statement of owner's equity	Shows the changes in the owner's capital account for a particular period.	Owner, Capital, Beginning + Owner Investment + Net Income or − Net Loss − Owner, Withdrawal = Owner, Capital, Ending
Balance sheet	Provides information to financial statement users about economic resources the company has (assets) as well as debts the company owes (liabilities). Allows decision makers to determine their opinion about the financial position of the company at a point in time.	Assets = Liabilities + Owner's Equity
Statement of cash flows	Reports on a business's cash receipts and cash payments for a period of time.	Cash flows from operating activities Cash flows from investing activities Cash flows from financing activities

- See Exhibit 1-15 on page 23 for model statements.

6 Briefly explain the different accounting standards Pg. 24

What are IFRS and ASPE?

- ASPE = Accounting Standards for Private Enterprises
- IFRS = International Financial Reporting Standards

Key Terms for the chapter are shown next and are in the **Glossary** at the back of the book. **Similar Terms** are shown after **Key Terms**.

Key Terms lists all the new boldface terms that were explained in the chapter with their definitions. They are also defined in the Glossary. Page references help you to review the terms.

KEY TERMS

Like many other subjects, accounting has a special vocabulary. It is important that you understand the following terms:

Account The detailed record of the changes that have occurred in a particular asset, liability, or item of owner's equity during a period *(p. 13)*.

Accounting The system that measures business activities, processes that information into reports and financial statements, and communicates the findings to decision makers *(p. 4)*.

Accounting equation The most basic tool of accounting: Assets = Liabilities + Owner's Equity (proprietorship) or Assets = Liabilities + Shareholders' Equity (corporation) *(p. 12)*.

Account payable The oral or implied promise to pay off debts arising from credit purchases. A liability that is backed by the general reputation and credit standing of the debtor *(p. 14)*.

Account receivable An asset; a promise to receive cash in the future from customers to whom the business has sold goods or services *(p. 13)*.

Accounting Standards Board The Canadian Accounting Standards Board establishes accounting standards for non-publicly accountable enterprises and contributes to the development of International Financial Reporting Standards *(p. 24)*.

Accounting Standards for Private Enterprises (ASPE) Canadian accounting standards that specify the generally accepted accounting principles applicable to private enterprises and those corporations that chose not to apply IFRS *(p. 10)*.

Asset An economic resource a business owns that is expected to be of benefit in the future *(p. 13)*.

Audit The examination of financial statements by outside accountants. The conclusion of an audit is the accountant's professional opinion about the financial statements *(p. 6)*.

Balance sheet A list of an entity's assets, liabilities, and owner's equity (proprietorship) or shareholders' equity (corporation) as of a specific date. Also called the *statement of financial position (p. 21)*.

Bookkeeping A procedural element of accounting; the keeping of the financial records and the recording of financial information *(p. 4)*.

Business One or more individuals selling goods or services with the intent of making a profit *(p. 4)*.

Capital Another name for the owner's equity of a business *(p. 14)*.

Cash flow statement Reports cash receipts and cash payments classified according to the entity's major activities: operating, investing, and financing *(p. 22)*.

Chartered Professional Accountant (CPA) An accountant who has met the examination and experience requirements of CPA Canada *(p. 6)*.

Comparable A qualitative characteristic of accounting information that says financial statements should be able to be measured against results in previous years or other businesses in the same industry *(p. 11)*.

Corporation A business owned by shareholders that begins when the federal or provincial government approves its articles of incorporation. A corporation is a legal entity, an "artificial person," in the eyes of the law *(p. 8)*.

Cost–benefit constraint An accounting constraint that says the benefits of the information produced should exceed the costs of producing the information *(p. 12)*.

Cost principle of measurement States that assets and services are recorded at their purchase cost and that the accounting record of the asset continues to be based on cost rather than current market value *(p. 12)*.

Creditors Businesses or individuals to which payment is owed *(p. 5)*.

Designated accountants Accountants who have met the education, examination, and experience requirements of an accounting body *(p. 6)*

Dividends Distributions by a corporation to its shareholders *(p. 14)*.

Economic entity assumption The accounting assumption that an organization or a section of an organization stands apart from other organizations and individuals as a separate economic unit for accounting purposes *(p. 12)*.

Ethics Rules of behaviour based on what is good or bad *(p. 7)*.

Expenses Costs incurred when running a business (or the using up of assets). Decrease in owner's equity that occurs in the course of delivering goods or services to customers or clients *(p. 14)*.

External users Readers of financial information who do not work for the business *(p. 5)*.

Financial accounting The branch of accounting that provides information to people outside the business *(p. 5)*.

Financial statements Business documents that report financial information about an entity to persons and organizations outside the business *(p. 4)*.

Generally accepted accounting principles (GAAP) Accounting guidelines, formulated by the Accounting Standards Board, that specify the standards for how accountants must record, measure, and report financial information *(p. 9)*.

Going concern assumption An accounting assumption that the business will continue operating in the foreseeable future *(p. 12)*.

Income statement A list of an entity's revenues, expenses, and net income or net loss for a specific period. Also called the *statement of earnings* or *statement of operations* *(p. 20)*.

Independence In accounting, this refers to there being no financial interest outside of the current business relationship. Auditors and other accountants must not be influenced by personal or professional gain from their auditing or accounting decisions *(p. 6)*.

Inflation A rise in the general level of prices *(p. 12)*.

Internal users Readers of financial information who either own the business or are employed by it and who are making decisions on behalf of the business *(p. 5)*.

International Accounting Standards Board (IASB) The body that sets International Financial Reporting Standards *(p. 10)*.

International Financial Reporting Standards (IFRS) The accounting standards that specify the generally accepted accounting principles that must be applied by publicly accountable enterprises in Canada and many other countries *(p. 10)*.

Investors A person or business that provides capital (usually money) to a business with the expectation of receiving financial gain *(p. 5)*.

Legacy designation The accounting designation of CPAs who joined as part of the initial merger of accounting bodies. It is the name of their prior accounting designation that must be used in conjunction with the CPA designation until November 1, 2022 *(p. 6)*.

Liability An economic obligation (a debt) payable to an individual or an organization outside the business *(p. 14)*.

Limited liability partnership (LLP) A form of partnership in which each partner's personal liability for the business's debts is limited to a certain amount *(p. 8)*.

Limited personal liability The owner's legal and financial liability is limited to the amount he or she invested into the business *(p. 9)*.

Listed companies Corporations that have shares traded on a stock exchange *(p. 10)*.

Management accounting The branch of accounting that generates information for internal decision makers of a business *(p. 5)*.

Materiality The accounting constraint that says information should be reported if it is material to the user—that is, if knowing it might affect a decision maker's decision *(p. 12)*.

Measurement The process of determining the amount at which an item is included in the financial statements *(p. 12)*.

Merchandising business A business that resells products previously bought from suppliers *(p. 17)*.

Net earnings Excess of total revenues over total expenses. Also called *net income* or *net profit* *(p. 20)*.

Net income Excess of total revenues over total expenses. Also called *net earnings* or *net profit* *(p. 20)*.

Net loss Excess of total expenses over total revenues *(p. 20)*.

Net profit Excess of total revenues over total expenses. Also called *net earnings* or *net income* *(p. 20)*.

Note payable A liability evidenced by a written promise to make a future payment *(p. 14)*.

Note receivable An asset evidenced by another party's written promise that entitles you to receive cash in the future *(p. 13)*.

Owner's equity In a proprietorship, the claim of an owner of a business to the assets of the business. Also called *capital* *(p. 14)*.

Owner withdrawals Amounts removed from the business by an owner *(p. 14)*.

Partnership An unincorporated business with two or more owners *(p. 8)*.

Partners' equity The name for owner's equity when there is more than one owner. In this case, the owners are called partners *(p. 14)*.

Prepaid expense A category of assets that are paid for first, then expire or get used up in the near future *(p. 13)*.

Private accountants Accountants that only work for one employer that is not a public accounting firm *(p. 6)*.

Private enterprise A corporation that does not offer its shares for sale to the public *(p. 10)*.

Professional designations Acknowledgement of educational achievement from an agency to assure qualification to perform a job *(p. 6)*.

Profit Excess of total revenues over total expenses. Also called *net earnings*, *net income*, or *net profit* *(p. 4)*.

Promissory note A written promise to pay a specified amount of money at a particular future date *(p. 13)*.

Proprietorship An unincorporated business with a single owner *(p. 7)*.

Public accountants Designated accountants that provide services to clients in the practice of public accounting *(p. 6)*.

Publicly accountable enterprise A corporation that has its shares traded on a stock exchange or for which a strong public interest exists *(p. 10)*.

Publicly traded companies Businesses that are incorporated and list/sell their shares on a public stock exchange. *(p. 6)*.

Relevant Information that might influence a decision is considered relevant *(p. 10)*.

Reliable A qualitative characteristic of accounting information that says financial information is only useful if it accurately represents the impact of transactions—that is, it is free of error and bias *(p. 11)*.

Revenue Amounts earned from delivering goods or services to customers. The increase in owner's equity that is earned by delivering goods or services to customers or clients *(p. 14)*.

Sales revenue The amount that a merchandiser earns from selling its inventory before subtracting expenses. Also called *sales (p. 17)*.

Security An asset that will become the property of the lender if the debt that is owed to the lender is not paid *(p. 13)*.

Service proprietorship An unincorporated business with one owner that earns income from selling services *(p. 14)*.

Service revenue The amount of revenue that a business earns from selling services *(p. 17)*.

Shareholder A person or company who owns one or more shares of stock in a corporation *(p. 8)*.

Shareholders' equity The name for owner's equity when the business is a corporation. In this case, the owners are called shareholders *(p. 14)*.

Stable monetary unit assumption Accountants' basis for ignoring the effect of inflation and making no adjustments for the changing value of the dollar *(p. 12)*.

Statement of earnings Another name for the *income statement (p. 20)*.

Statement of financial position Another name for the *balance sheet (p. 21)*.

Statement of operations Another name for the *income statement*. Also called the *statement of earnings (p. 20)*.

Statement of owner's equity A summary of the changes in an entity's owner's equity during a specific period *(p. 21)*.

Transaction An event that has a financial impact on a business and that can be reliably measured *(p. 15)*.

Understandable A qualitative characteristic of accounting information that says users should be able to understand the information in financial statements *(p. 11)*.

Unearned revenue An unearned revenue is a liability created when a business collects cash from customers in advance of doing work for the customer. The obligation to provide a product or service in the future *(p. 14)*.

Unlimited personal liability When the debts of a business are greater than its resources, the owner is (owners are) responsible for their payment *(p. 9)*.

SIMILAR TERMS

Similar Terms are acronyms and other related terms you might have heard outside your accounting class in the media or your day-to-day business dealings.

ACAF	Advanced Certificate in Accounting and Finance
Accounting equation	Assets = Liabilities + Owner's Equity
ASPE	Accounting Standards for Private Enterprises
Balance sheet	Statement of financial position
Business	Company; enterprise; firm
CA	Chartered Accountant
Capital	Owner's equity
CGA	Certified General Accountant
CMA	Certified Management Accountant
Corp.	Corporation
CPA	Chartered Professional Accountant
GAAP	Generally accepted accounting principles
Historical cost	Cost basis; cost principle
IASB	International Accounting Standards Board
IFRS	International Financial Reporting Standards
Inc.	Incorporated
Income statement	Statement of operations; statement of earnings
LLP	Limited liability partnership
Ltd.	Limited
Management accounting	Managerial accounting
Net income	Net earnings; net profit; profit
Profit	Income

Sales	Revenue
Statement of owner's equity	Statement of equity
Withdrawals	Drawings

SELF-STUDY QUESTIONS

Test your understanding with these multiple-choice **Self-Study Questions.** Page references are given if you need review, and the answers are given after Self-Study Question 10.

Test your understanding of the chapter by marking the correct answer for each of the following questions:

1. Which of the following forms of business organization is an "artificial person" and must obtain legal approval from the federal or provincial government to conduct business? *(p. 8)*
   a. Law firm
   b. Proprietorship
   c. Partnership
   d. Corporation
2. You have purchased some T-shirts for $6,000 and can sell them immediately for $8,000. What accounting assumption, criteria, or constraint governs the amount at which to record the goods you purchased? *(p. 12)*
   a. Economic entity assumption
   b. Reliability characteristic
   c. Cost principle
   d. Going concern assumption
3. The economic resources of a business are called *(p. 13)*
   a. Assets
   b. Liabilities
   c. Owner's equity
   d. Accounts payable
4. If the assets of a business are $200,000 and the liabilities are $90,000, how much is the owner's equity? *(p. 13)*
   a. $290,000
   b. $110,000
   c. $200,000
   d. $90,000
5. If the owner's equity in a business is $70,000 and the liabilities are $35,000, how much are the assets? *(p. 13)*
   a. $35,000
   b. $70,000
   c. $105,000
   d. $45,000
6. Purchasing office supplies on account will *(p. 16)*
   a. Increase an asset and increase a liability
   b. Increase an asset and increase owner's equity
   c. Increase one asset and decrease another asset
   d. Increase an asset and decrease a liability
7. Performing a service for a customer or client and receiving the cash immediately will *(p. 16)*
   a. Increase one asset and decrease another asset
   b. Increase an asset and increase owner's equity
   c. Decrease an asset and decrease a liability
   d. Increase an asset and increase a liability
8. Paying an account payable will *(p. 17)*
   a. Increase one asset and decrease another asset
   b. Decrease an asset and decrease owner's equity
   c. Decrease an asset and decrease a liability
   d. Increase an asset and increase a liability
9. The financial statement that summarizes assets, liabilities, and owner's equity is called the *(p. 21)*
   a. Cash flow statement
   b. Balance sheet
   c. Income statement
   d. Statement of owner's equity
10. The financial statements that are dated for a time period (rather than for a specific point in time) are the *(p. 23)*
    a. Balance sheet and income statement
    b. Balance sheet and statement of owner's equity
    c. Income statement, statement of owner's equity, and cash flow statement
    d. All financial statements are dated for a time period

Answers to Self-Study Questions

1. d 2. c 3. a 4. b 5. c 6. a 7. b 8. c 9. b 10. c

Check how well you answered the Self-Study Questions.

Assignment Material

MyLab Accounting Make the grade with MyLab Accounting: The Starters, Exercises, and Problems can be found on MyLab. You can practise them as often as you want, and most feature step-by-step guided instructions to help you find the right answer.

QUESTIONS

1. Distinguish between accounting and bookkeeping.
2. Identify five users of accounting information and explain how they use it.
3. What is the difference between financial accounting and management accounting?
4. What accounting credentials are available for accountants from the CPA, and how do they differ?
5. What organization formulates generally accepted accounting principles in Canada?
6. Explain the differences between proprietorships, partnerships, and corporations based on owners, life of the organization, liability of owners, and legal status.
7. Identify the owner(s) of a proprietorship, a partnership, and a corporation.
8. Identify two advantages of the corporate form of business over a proprietorship.
9. Why is the economic entity assumption so important to accounting?
10. Explain why the going concern assumption is important to know when reading a financial statement.
11. What role does the cost principle of measurement play in accounting?
12. If assets = liabilities + owner's equity, then liabilities = ?
13. Explain the difference between an account receivable and an account payable.
14. A company reported monthly revenues of $92,000 and expenses of $96,400. What is the result of operations for the month?
15. Give a more descriptive title for the balance sheet.
16. What feature of the balance sheet gives this financial statement its name?
17. Give another title for the income statement.
18. Which financial statement is like a snapshot of the entity at a specific time? Which financial statement is like a video of the entity's operation during a period of time?
19. What information does the statement of owner's equity report?
20. What piece of information flows from the income statement to the statement of owner's equity? What information flows from the statement of owner's equity to the balance sheet? What balance sheet item is explained by the cash flow statement?
21. Why does it make sense that Canadian companies whose shares are publicly traded on stock exchanges in Canada follow International Financial Reporting Standards instead of standards developed for private companies in Canada?

A brief description and the learning objectives covered appear beside each Starter, Exercise, and Problem.

STARTERS

(1) Financial and management accounting

S1–1 For each of the following users of accounting, indicate if the user would use financial accounting (FA) or management accounting (MA).

a. Investor
b. Banker
c. Canada Revenue Agency
d. Owner
e. Human resources department manager

(1) Users of financial information

S1–2 Suppose you need a bank loan to purchase lawn equipment for Ralph's Landscaping Service. In evaluating your loan request, the banker asks about the assets and liabilities of your business. In particular, the banker wants to know the amount of the business's owner's equity.

1. Is the banker considered an internal or an external user of financial information?
2. Which financial statement would provide the best information to answer the banker's questions?

S1–3 For each of the users of accounting information, indicate whether they are an external decision maker (E) or an internal decision maker (I).

(1) Internal and external users of financial information

a. Marketing manager ________
b. Canada Revenue Agency ________
c. Investor ________
d. Controller ________
e. Supplier ________

S1–4 Louise Layton plans to open Louise's Floral Designs. She is considering the various types of business organizations and wishes to organize her business with unlimited life and limited liability features. Which type of business organization will meet Louise's needs best?

(2) Forms of business organizations

S1–5 Match the assumption, principle, or constraint description with the appropriate term by placing a, b, c, d, e, and f on the appropriate line.

(3) Describing accounting assumptions, principles, and constraints

a. Cost principle of measurement	________	Benefits of the information produced by an accounting system must be greater than the costs
b. Going concern assumption	________	Amounts may be ignored if the effect on a decision maker's decision is not significant
c. Stable monetary unit assumption	________	Transactions are recorded based on the cash amount received or paid
d. Economic entity assumption	________	Ignore the effects of inflation in the accounting records
e. Cost–benefit constraint	________	Assumes that a business is going to continue operations indefinitely
f. Materiality constraint	________	A business must keep its accounting records separate from its owner's accounting records

S1–6 A potential customer is extremely interested in renting a bicycle from Toronto Island Bike Rentals and emails his intention to rent a bike next month and sets up the date and time for the rental. Would an accountant consider this event a transaction to be recorded in the accounting records? Explain.

(3) Defining transactions

S1–7 Ryan's Wedding Services has been open for one year, and Shu Ryan, the owner, wants to know whether the business earned a net income or a net loss for the year. First, she must identify the revenues earned and the expenses incurred during the year. What are revenues and expenses?

(4) Explaining revenues and expenses

S1–8 Yijie Chan is the proprietor of a property management company near the campus of a local university. The business has cash of $72,000 and furniture that cost $24,000 and has a market value of $30,000. Debts include accounts payable of $20,000. Chan's personal home is valued at $800,000, and her personal bank account contains $22,000.

(3) (4) Applying accounting concepts and principles

1. Consider the accounting assumptions, principles, and constraints discussed in the chapter, and identify the one that best matches each of the following situations:
   a. Chan's personal assets are not recorded on the property management company's balance sheet.
   b. Chan records furniture at its cost of $24,000, not the market value of $30,000.
   c. Chan does not make adjustments for inflation.
   d. Chan missed recording a $2.50 cup of coffee on her financial statements. She does not ask her accountant to redo the financial statements because that would cost her an extra $400.
2. How much is the owner's equity of the property management company?

(4) Identifying accounts

S1–9 Identify each of the following accounts as: Asset (A), Liability (L), or Owner's Equity (OE).

a. Accounts Payable
b. Cash
c. M. Abbas, Capital
d. Accounts Receivable
e. Rent Expense
f. Service Revenue
g. Office Supplies
h. M. Abbas, Withdrawals
i. Land
j. Salaries Expense

(4) Using the accounting equation

S1–10 Suppose Northern Adventures rents stand-up paddleboards to tourists. The company purchased a storage building for the boards for $200,000 and financed the purchase with a loan of $150,000 and an investment by the owner for the remainder. Use the accounting equation to calculate the owner's equity amount.

(5) Identifying accounts in statements

S1–11 Indicate whether each account listed below appears on the balance sheet (B), income statement (I), statement of owner's equity (OE), or cash flow statement (CF). Some items appear on more than one statement.

Accounts Receivable	________	Salaries Expense	________
Computer Equipment	________	Consulting Service Revenue	________
S. Scott, Capital	________	Cash	________
Rent Expense	________	Note Payable	________
Supplies	________	Supplies Expense	________
S. Scott, Withdrawals	________	Accounts Payable	________

(5) Calculating missing information

S1–12 Determine the expenses for September based on the following data:

September net income	$10,000
Beginning owner's equity	$25,000
Owner's withdrawals	$ 5,000
Ending owner's equity	$30,000
September revenue	$42,000

(5) Preparing a balance sheet

S1–13 Picture Perfect Pet Photography specializes in taking pictures of families and their pets. Prepare the balance sheet as at January 31, 2020, using the following accounts and balances, which are currently presented in alphabetical order.

Accounts Payable	$ 6,000
Accounts Receivable	2,000
C. Loranger, Capital	17,200
Camera Equipment	15,000
Cash	5,000
Supplies	1,200

(5) Preparing the income statement

Net income, $78,000

Check figures appear in the margin when applicable to help you make sure you are "on track."

S1–14 Black Canary Sound Studio has just completed operations for the year ended December 31, 2019. This is the third year of operations for the company. As the owner, you want to know how well the company performed during the year. To address this question, you have assembled the data below. Use this data to prepare the income statement of Black Canary Sound Studio for the year ended December 31, 2019.

Insurance Expense	$ 3,000	Salaries Expense	$50,000
Service Revenue	150,000	Accounts Payable	8,000
Supplies Expense	1,000	Supplies	2,500
Rent Expense	18,000	Withdrawals	40,000

S1–15 Jacob's Overhead Doors reports the following financial information:

Assets	$45,800
Liabilities	15,230
Jacob's Investment	28,700
Jacob's Withdrawal	7,000
Service Revenues	10,890
Expenses	?

1. Use the accounting equation to solve for the missing information.
2. Was it a good year or a bad year for the business?

(5) Using the income statement to assess a business

EXERCISES

E1–1 Navneet Kaur is new to Canada. Having studied in a culinary program, she wants to buy a food truck and open her own business. She knows that she needs $40,000 to buy the truck, but she has little knowledge of the lending process. Explain to her what sort of information the lender would review and why.

(1) Users of financial statements

E1–2 Indicate whether each statement below applies to a sole proprietorship, a partnership, or a corporation.

a. The life of the business is limited by the death of the owner.
b. Each owner is personally liable for claims against the business.
c. A business in which there is only one owner and "he or she is the business."
d. Owners are not personally liable for claims against the business.
e. The form of business typically used by accountants and lawyers.
f. Canadian Tire and TELUS are examples of this form of business.

(2) Forms of business organizations

E1–3 Match the situation with the best term to explain why things are done this way.

(3) Describing accounting assumptions, principles, and constraints

1. Every year a business uses the same account names so it can evaluate results between years.	a. Cost principle
2. When we prepare a financial statement, we show all assets at the price we paid for them.	b. Going concern assumption
3. A business should not spend $1,000 on counting and recounting $500 worth of inventory.	c. Relevance characteristic
4. If we assume the business is going to go bankrupt and, as a result, we record a truck on the financial statement at the price we could get for it if we tried to sell it quickly, we are following this accounting assumption.	d. Cost–benefit constraint
5. We try to include information in the accounting records such that financial statements provide enough information for readers to make an investment decision.	e. Economic entity assumption
6. A car dealership will report profits for the parts department separate from the service department so that senior management can see how well each part of their business is doing.	f. Comparability characteristic

E1–4 For each of the following independent transactions, indicate the change in total assets.

a. Purchased $750 of supplies on account.
b. Paid cash to employees for their salaries, $5,000.
c. Purchased furniture for $1,600 on account.
d. Received telephone bill for $200, to be paid in the following period.
e. Work performed; customer will pay $150 next month.
f. Earned $800 of revenue by performing a service for cash.
g. Performed $3,000 of services on account.

(4) Using the accounting equation

4 Using the accounting equation

Marpole Dry Cleaners liabilities, $50,000

E1–5 Compute the missing amount in the accounting equation for each business.

	Assets	Liabilities	Owner's Equity
Economy Cuts	$	$120,000	$40,000
Marpole Dry Cleaners	100,000		50,000
Dauphin Gift and Cards	145,000	115,000	

4 Using the accounting equation

Owner's equity, $21,000

E1–6 Samson Kodua owns Grinds Coffee House, near the campus of Western Community College. The company has cash of $18,000 and furniture that cost $40,000. Debts include accounts payable of $7,000 and a $30,000 note payable.

Required

1. Write the accounting equation of Grinds Coffee House.
2. What is the owner's equity of the company?

4 Transaction analysis

E1–7 Indicate the effects of the following business transactions on the accounting equation of a proprietorship. Transaction *a* is answered as a guide.

a. Received $50,000 cash from the owner.
   Answer: Increase asset (Cash)
   Increase owner's equity (Owner, Capital)
b. Paid the current month's office rent of $4,000.
c. Paid $3,500 cash to purchase office supplies.
d. Performed engineering services for a client on account, $6,000.
e. Purchased office furniture on account at a cost of $5,000.
f. Received cash on account, $3,000.
g. Paid cash on account, $2,500.
h. Sold land for $50,000 cash, which was the business's cost of the land.
i. Performed engineering services for a client and received cash of $6,000.

4 Transaction analysis, accounting equation

Total assets, $266,500

This margin note reminds you that an Excel template is available in MyLab Accounting to help you answer this question.

E1–8 Gayle Hayashi, MD, opens a medical clinic. During her first month of operation, January, the clinic, named Hayashi Medical Clinic, experienced the following events:

Jan.	6	Hayashi invested $250,000 in the clinic by opening a bank account in the name of Hayashi Medical Clinic.
	9	Hayashi Medical Clinic paid cash for land costing $150,000. There are plans to build a clinic on the land. Until then, the business will rent an office.
	12	The clinic purchased medical supplies for $10,000 on account.
	15	On January 15, Hayashi Medical Clinic officially opened for business.
	15–31	During the rest of the month, the clinic earned professional fees of $20,000 and received cash immediately.
	15–31	The clinic paid cash expenses: employee salaries, $5,000; office rent, $4,000; utilities, $500.
	28	The clinic sold supplies to another clinic at cost for $1,000.
	31	The clinic paid $4,000 on the account from January 12.

Required Analyze the effects of these events on the accounting equation of Hayashi Medical Clinic. Use a format similar to that of Exhibit 1–11, Panel B, on page 19 with headings for Cash; Medical Supplies; Land; Accounts Payable; Gayle Hayashi, Capital; Service Revenue; Rent Expense; Salaries Expense; and Utilities Expense.

E1-9 Match each of the following accounting terms with its correct definition:

(4)(5) Using accounting vocabulary

Terms	Definitions
1. Accounting equation	a. An economic resource that is expected to be of benefit in the future
2. Asset	b. An economic obligation (a debt) payable to an individual or an organization outside the business
3. Balance sheet	c. Excess of total expenses over total revenues
4. Expense	d. Excess of total revenues over total expenses
5. Income statement	e. The basic tool of accounting, stated as Assets = Liabilities + Owner's Equity
6. Liability	f. The decrease in equity that occurs from using assets or increasing liabilities in the course of delivering goods or services to customers
7. Net income	g. Amounts earned by delivering goods or services to customers
8. Net loss	h. Report that shows cash receipts and cash payments during a period
9. Revenue	i. Report that shows an entity's assets, liabilities, and owner's equity as of a specific date
10. Cash flow statement	j. Report that shows an entity's revenues, expenses, and net income or net loss for a period of time
11. Statement of owner's equity	k. Report that shows the changes in owner's equity for a period of time

E1-10 The accounting records of Chiang Consulting Services contain the following accounts, which you are to classify. First, indicate whether each account listed is a(n) asset (A), liability (L), owner's equity (OE), revenue (R), or expense (E) account. Then indicate whether each account listed appears on the balance sheet (B), income statement (I), statement of owner's equity (SOE), or cash flow statement (CF). Some accounts can appear on more than one statement.

(4)(5) Classifying accounts, working with financial statements

Account	1. Type of Account	2. Statement(s)
Supplies Expense		
Accounts Receivable		
J. Chiang, Capital		
Computer Equipment		
Consulting Service Revenue		
Accounts Payable		
Rent Expense		
Cash		
J. Chiang, Withdrawals		
Supplies		
Note Payable		

E1-11 The analysis of the transactions that Oakdale Equipment Rental engaged in during its first month of operations follows. The business buys electronic equipment that it rents out to earn rental revenue. The owner of the business, Gary Oake, made only one investment to start the business and made no withdrawals from Oakdale Equipment Rental.

(4)(5) Business organizations, transactions, net income

Net income, $4,500

	Cash	+	Accounts Receivable	+	Rental Equipment	=	Accounts Payable	+	G. Oake, Capital	+	Rental Revenue	−	Gas Expense
a.	+50,000								+50,000				
b.					+80,000		+80,000						
c.	+1,000										+1,000		
d.			+1,000								+1,000		
e.	−2,000												−2,000
f.	+4,500										+4,500		
g.	+500		−500										
h.	−5,000						−5,000						

Required

1. Describe each transaction of Oakdale Equipment Rental.
2. If these transactions fully describe the operations of Oakdale Equipment Rental during the month, what was the amount of net income or net loss?

(2) (5)
Business organization, balance sheet
Total assets, $125,000

E1–12 Presented below are the balances of the assets and liabilities of Bonicalzi Sales Training as of September 30, 2020. Also included are the revenue and expense account balances of the business for September.

Consulting Service Revenue	$ 62,000	Computer Equipment	$ 80,000
Accounts Receivable	25,000	Supplies	5,000
Accounts Payable	26,000	Note Payable	50,000
Salaries Expense	10,000	Rent Expense	4,000
M. Bonicalzi, Capital	?	Cash	15,000

Required

1. What type of business entity or organization is Bonicalzi Sales Training? How can you tell?
2. Prepare the balance sheet of Bonicalzi Sales Training as of September 30, 2020.
3. What does the balance sheet report—financial position or operating results? Which financial statement reports the other information?

(5)
Income statement for a proprietorship
Net income, $57,000

E1–13 The assets, liabilities, owner's equity, revenue, and expenses of Philpott Company, a proprietorship, have the following final balances at December 31, 2020, the end of its first year of business. To start the business, Brian Philpott invested $90,000.

Note Payable	$ 50,000	Office Furniture	$ 50,000
Utilities Expense	18,000	Rent Expense	48,000
Accounts Payable	12,000	Cash	15,000
B. Philpott, Capital	90,000	Office Supplies	14,000
Service Revenue	610,000	Salaries Expense	430,000
Accounts Receivable	35,000	Salaries Payable	5,000
Supplies Expense	30,000	Research Expense	27,000
Equipment	100,000		

Required Prepare the income statement of Philpott Company for the year ended December 31, 2020. What is Philpott Company's net income or net loss for 2020? (Hint: Ignore balance sheet items.)

Use the following information to answer E1–14 through E1–16.

The account balances of Wilson Towing Service at June 30, 2020, follow:

Equipment	$ 25,850	Service Revenue	$ 15,000
Office Supplies	1,000	Accounts Receivable	9,000
Note Payable	6,800	Accounts Payable	8,000
Rent Expense	900	J. Wilson, Capital, June 1, 2020	3,250
Cash	1,400	Salaries Expense	2,400
J. Wilson, Withdrawals	3,500		

(5)
Preparing the income statement
Net Income $11,700

E1–14 *Required*

1. Prepare the income statement for Wilson Towing Service for the month ending June 30, 2020. List expenses from the highest to the lowest dollar amount.
2. What does the income statement report?

(5)
Preparing the statement of owner's equity
Ending Capital $22,450

E1–15 *Required*

1. Prepare the statement of owner's equity for Wilson Towing Service for the month ending June 30, 2020. Assume Wilson invested $11,000 during June.
2. What does the statement of owner's equity report?

E1-16 *Required*

1. Prepare the balance sheet for Wilson Towing Service as of June 30, 2020.
2. What does the balance sheet report?

(5)
Preparing the balance sheet

Total Assets $37,250

USING EXCEL

E1-17 *Download an Excel template for this problem online in MyLab Accounting.*

(5)
Using Excel to prepare transaction analysis and financial statements

Echo Lake started operations on November 1, 2018. Nine transactions occur during November. Financial statements are prepared at the end of the month.

Required

1. Use Excel to prepare a transaction analysis of the nine transactions. Use the blue shaded areas for inputs.
2. Prepare the income statement, statement of owner's equity, and balance sheet. Each financial statement appears on a separate worksheet tab. Fill in the blue shaded areas using a formula that references the account balances at the end of the month in the Transaction Analysis tab.

SERIAL EXERCISE

E1-18 *The Serial Exercise involves a company that will be revisited throughout relevant chapters in Volume 1 and Volume 2. You can complete the Serial Exercises using MyLab Accounting.*

(3)(4)(5)
Using the accounting equation for transaction analysis and preparing financial statements

2. Net income, $1,375

Canyon Canoe Company is a company that rents canoes for use on local lakes and rivers. Amber Wilson graduated from university about 10 years ago. She worked for a large accounting firm and became a CPA. Because she loves the outdoors, she decided to begin a new business that will combine her love of outdoor activities with her business knowledge. Amber decides that she will create a new sole proprietorship, Canyon Canoe Company. The business began operations on November 1, 2020.

Nov.	1	Amber Wilson invested $16,000 cash in the business by opening a bank account in the name of Canyon Canoe Company.
	2	The company leased a building and paid $1,200 for the first month's rent.
	3	The company purchased canoes for $4,800 on account.
	4	The company purchased office supplies on account, $750.
	7	The company earned $1,400 cash for the rental of canoes.
	13	The company paid $1,500 cash for salaries.
	15	Amber Wilson withdrew $50 cash from the business for personal use.
	16	The company received a bill for $150 for utilities, which will be paid later.
	20	The company received a bill for $175 for cellphone expenses. The bill will be paid later.
	22	The company rented canoes to Early Start Daycare on account, $3,000.
	26	Canyon Canoe Company paid $1,000 of the amount owed for the November 3 purchase that was made on account.
	28	The company received $750 from Early Start Daycare as partial payment for the canoe rental on November 22.
	30	Amber Wilson withdrew $100 cash from the business for personal use.

Required

1. Analyze the effects of Canyon Canoe Company's transactions on the accounting equation. Use the format of Exhibit 1–11, Panel B on page 19, and include these headings: Cash; Accounts Receivable; Office Supplies; Canoes; Accounts Payable; Amber Wilson, Capital; Amber Wilson, Withdrawals; Canoe Rental Revenue; Rent Expense; Salaries Expense; Utilities Expense; and Telephone Expense.
2. Prepare the income statement of Canyon Canoe Company for the month ended November 30, 2020. List expenses in this order: Rent Expense; Salaries Expense; Utilities Expense; and Telephone Expense.
3. Prepare the statement of owner's equity for the month ended November 30, 2020.
4. Prepare the balance sheet as of November 30, 2020.

CHALLENGE EXERCISES

(4)(5)
Using the financial statements

Net income:
Fraser Co., $200,000
Delta Co., $170,000
Pine Co., $225,000

E1–19 Compute the missing amounts for each of the following businesses:

	Fraser Co.	Delta Co.	Pine Co.
Beginning			
Assets	$350,000	$300,000	$540,000
Liabilities	200,000	120,000	360,000
Ending			
Assets	$500,000	$360,000	$______
Liabilities	250,000	160,000	480,000
Owner's equity			
Investments by owner	$______	$ 0	$ 50,000
Withdrawals by owner	250,000	150,000	220,000
Income Statement			
Revenues	$660,000	$350,000	$900,000
Expenses	460,000	______	675,000

(4)(5)
Using the accounting equation, preparing the statement of owner's equity

Net income: $10,000

E1–20 Star Esports' balance sheet data are shown below:

	January 1, 2020	December 31, 2020
Total assets	$300,000	$410,000
Total liabilities	260,000	340,000

Required

1. Compute the amount of net income or net loss for the company during the year ended December 31, 2020, if the owner invested $50,000 in the business and withdrew $30,000 during the year. Show all calculations.
2. Prepare the statement of owner's equity for Duncan Shields, the owner of Star Esports, for the year ended December 31, 2020.

BEYOND THE NUMBERS

BN1–1

①⑤ Analyzing a loan request

As an analyst for Royal Bank, it is your job to write recommendations to the bank's loan committee. Vernon Engineering Co., a client of the bank, has submitted these summary data to support the company's request for a $150,000 loan:

Income Statement Data	2020	2019	2018
Total revenues	$550,000	$490,000	$475,000
Total expenses	400,000	345,000	305,000
Net income	$150,000	$145,000	$170,000

Statement of Owner's Equity Data	2020	2019	2018
Beginning capital	$230,000	$205,000	$215,000
Add: Net income	150,000	145,000	170,000
	$380,000	$350,000	$385,000
Less: Withdrawals	175,000	120,000	180,000
Ending capital	$205,000	$230,000	$205,000

Balance Sheet Data	2020	2019	2018
Total assets	$450,000	$425,000	$375,000
Total liabilities	$245,000	$195,000	$170,000
Total owner's equity	205,000	230,000	205,000
Total liabilities and owner's equity	$450,000	$425,000	$375,000

Required Analyze these financial statement data to decide whether the bank should lend $150,000 to Vernon Engineering Co. Consider the trends in net income and owner's equity and the change in total liabilities in making your decision. Write a one-paragraph recommendation to the bank's loan committee.

ETHICAL ISSUE

EI1–1

Transaction analysis, effects on financial statements

The board of directors of Cloutier Inc. is meeting to discuss the past year's results before releasing financial statements to the public. The discussion includes this exchange:

Sue Cloutier, company president: "Well, this has not been a good year! Revenue is down and expenses are up—way up. If we don't do some fancy stepping, we'll report a loss for the third year in a row. I can temporarily transfer some land that I own into the company's name, and that will beef up our balance sheet. Rob, can you shave $500,000 from expenses? Then we can probably get the bank loan that we need."

Rob Samuels, company chief accountant: "Sue, you are asking too much. Generally accepted accounting principles are designed to keep this sort of thing from happening."

Required

1. What is the fundamental ethical issue in this situation?
2. Discuss how Cloutier's proposals violate generally accepted accounting principles. Identify the specific concept(s) or principle(s) involved.

PROBLEMS (GROUP A)

(3)
Accounting concepts/principles

P1–1A Tanner Kerekes operates a law practice in Mississauga under the name Tanner Kerekes, Lawyer. The following business transactions took place during the month of May 2019:

May	1	Kerekes deposited $30,000 cash into the business bank account.
	3	Kerekes completed legal work for a home builder. He charged the builder $5,000, not the $6,000 the work was worth, in order to earn more business from the builder.
	5	The business bought furniture from Ajax Furniture for $8,000, paying $2,000 cash and promising to pay $1,000 per month at the beginning of each month starting June 1, 2019, for six months. Kerekes would like to expense the entire amount to reduce net income for tax reasons.
	10	The business signed a lease to rent additional space at a cost of $2,000 per month. Kerekes will occupy the premises effective June 1, 2019.
	18	Determining that the business would need more cash in June, Kerekes went to the bank and borrowed $20,000 on a personal loan and transferred the money to the company.
	25	Kerekes purchased a painting for his home from one of his clients. He paid for the $3,000 purchase with his personal credit card.
	28	Kerekes withdrew $5,000 from the business. He used $2,000 of the money to repay a portion of the loan arranged on May 18.
	31	The business did legal work with a value of $10,000 for Apex Computers Ltd. Apex paid for the work by giving the company computer equipment with a selling price of $12,000.

Required Identify the accounting characteristic, assumption, or principle that would be applicable to each of the transactions and discuss the effects it would have on the transactions of Tanner Kerekes, Lawyer.

(3)(4)
Entity concept, transaction analysis, accounting equation

Total assets, $61,000

P1–2A Jon Conlin, CPA, was an accountant and partner in a large firm. Recently, he resigned his position to open his own accounting business, which he operates as a proprietorship.

The following events took place during the organizing phase of his new business and its first month of operations:

Jul.	4	Conlin received $100,000 cash from his former partners in the firm from which he resigned.
	5	Conlin invested $50,000 cash in his business.
	5	The business paid office rent expense for the month of July, $3,000.
	6	The business paid $1,000 cash for letterhead stationery for the office.
	7	The business purchased office furniture on account for $7,000, promising to pay within six months.
	10	Conlin sold 2,000 shares of Royal Bank stock, which he had owned for several years, receiving $25,000 cash from his stockbroker.
	11	Conlin deposited the $25,000 cash from sale of the Royal Bank shares in his personal bank account.
	12	A representative of a large construction company telephoned Conlin and told him of the company's intention to transfer its accounting work to Conlin's business.
	29	The business performed an audit for a client and submitted the bill for services, $10,000. The business expected to collect from this client within two weeks.
	31	Conlin withdrew $3,000 cash from the business.

Required

1. Classify each of the preceding events as one of the following (list each date, then choose a, b, or c):
   a. A business transaction to be accounted for by the business.

b. A business-related event but not a transaction to be accounted for by the business at this time.

c. A personal transaction not to be accounted for by the business.

2. Analyze the effects of the above events on the accounting equation of the business. Use a format similar to Exhibit 1–11, Panel B, on page 19.

P1–3A Jamate Company, a sole proprietorship, shows the following changes to its business accounts. The balance of each item in the business's accounting equation is shown below for June 21 and for each of the nine following business days:

(4) Business transactions and analysis

	Cash	Accounts Receivable	Office Supplies	Equipment	Accounts Payable	Owner's Equity
Jun. 21	$19,000	$9,000	$ 3,000	$18,000	$ 9,000	$40,000
22	26,000	9,000	3,000	18,000	9,000	47,000
23	16,000	9,000	3,000	28,000	9,000	47,000
24	16,000	9,000	7,000	28,000	13,000	47,000
25	12,000	9,000	7,000	28,000	9,000	47,000
26	15,000	6,000	7,000	28,000	9,000	47,000
27	22,000	6,000	7,000	28,000	9,000	54,000
28	17,000	6,000	7,000	28,000	4,000	54,000
29	14,000	6,000	10,000	28,000	4,000	54,000
30	4,000	6,000	10,000	28,000	4,000	44,000

Required Assuming that a single transaction took place on each day, briefly describe the transaction that was most likely to have occurred. Begin with June 22 and complete up to June 30. Indicate which accounts were affected, whether the account balances increased or decreased, and by what amount. No revenue or expense transactions occurred on these dates.

P1–4A Shawn Steele is a realtor. He buys and sells properties on his own, and he also earns commission revenue as a real estate agent. He organized his business as a sole proprietorship on November 15, 2019. Consider the following facts as of November 30, 2019:

(2)(3)(5) Balance sheet for a proprietorship, entity concept

Total assets, $113,500

a. The business owed $30,000 on a note payable for some undeveloped land. This land had been acquired by the business for a total price of $70,000.

b. Steele's business had spent $15,000 for a RE/MAX Ltd. real estate franchise, which entitled him to represent himself as a RE/MAX agent. RE/MAX is a national affiliation of independent real estate agents. This franchise is a business asset.

c. Steele owed $250,000 on a personal mortgage on his personal residence, which he acquired in 2001 for a total price of $500,000.

d. Steele had $25,000 in his personal bank account and $19,000 in his business bank account.

e. Steele owed $1,000 on a personal charge account with Hudson's Bay.

f. The business acquired business furniture for $9,000 on November 25. Of this amount, the company owed $3,000 on account at November 30.

g. The real estate office had $500 worth of office supplies on hand on November 30.

Required

1. Steele is concerned about liability exposure. Which proprietorship feature, if any, limits his personal liability?

2. Identify the personal items given in the preceding facts that would not be reported in the financial records of the business.

3. Prepare the balance sheet of the real estate business of Shawn Steele, Realtor, at November 30, 2019.

(4)(5)

Income statement, statement of owner's equity, balance sheet, evaluating business performance

1. Net income, $135,000

P1–5A Presented below are the amounts of the assets and liabilities of Canadian Gardening Consultants as of December 31, 2020, and the revenues and expenses of the company for the year ended December 31, 2020. The items are listed in alphabetical order.

Accounts Payable	$ 57,000	Insurance Expense	$ 4,500
Accounts Receivable	36,000	Interest Expense	15,000
Advertising Expense	48,500	Land	37,500
		J. Wu, Withdrawals	$103,500
Building	300,000	Note Payable	195,000
Cash	15,000	Salaries Expense	240,000
Computer Equipment	165,000	Salaries Payable	22,500
Courier Expense	7,000	Service Revenue	450,000
Furniture	45,000	Supplies	7,500

The opening balance of owner's equity was $300,000. During the year the owner made no investments.

Required

1. Prepare the business's income statement for the year ended December 31, 2020. List expenses in order from highest to lowest amount.
2. Prepare the statement of owner's equity of the business for the year ended December 31, 2020.
3. Prepare the balance sheet of the business at December 31, 2020.
4. Answer these questions about the business:
   a. Was the result of operations for the year a profit or a loss? How much was it?
   b. Did the business's owner's equity increase or decrease during the year? How would this affect the business's ability to borrow money from a bank in the future?
   c. How much in total economic resources does the business have at December 31, 2020, as it moves into the new year? How much does the business owe? What is the dollar amount of the owner's portion of the business at December 31, 2020?

(5)

Correcting a balance sheet

1. Total assets, $330,000

P1–6A The bookkeeper of Oliver Services Co., a proprietorship, prepared the balance sheet of the company while the accountant was ill. The balance sheet is not correct. The bookkeeper knew that the balance sheet should balance, so he "plugged in" the owner's equity amount needed to achieve this balance. The owner's equity amount, however, is not correct. All other amounts are accurate except the "Total assets" amount.

OLIVER SERVICES CO. Balance Sheet For the Month Ended July 31, 2019			
Assets		**Liabilities**	
Cash	$ 70,000	Service revenue	$220,000
Office supplies	5,000	Note payable	55,000
Land	130,000	Accounts payable	45,000
Advertising expense	10,000		
Furniture	50,000		
Accounts receivable	75,000	**Owner's Equity**	
Rent expense	22,000	J. Oliver, capital	42,000
Total assets	$362,000	Total liabilities and owner's equity	$362,000

Required

1. Prepare the corrected balance sheet with the right accounts in the order presented in Appendix B, and date it correctly. Compute total assets, total liabilities, and owner's equity.
2. Consider the original balance sheet as presented and the corrected balance sheet you prepared for Requirement 1. Did the total assets presented in your corrected balance sheet increase, decrease, or stay the same compared to the original balance sheet? Why?

P1–7A Mary Reaney is the proprietor of a career counselling and employee search business, Reaney Personnel Services. The following amounts summarize the financial position of the business on August 31, 2020:

(4) (5)
Transaction analysis, accounting equation, financial statements

2. Net income, $44,000

	Assets				= Liabilities +	Owner's Equity
	Cash +	Accounts Receivable +	Office Supplies +	Furniture =	Accounts Payable +	M. Reaney, Capital
Bal.	40,000	35,000		95,000	55,000	115,000

During September 2020 the following company transactions occurred:

Sep. 3	Reaney deposited $80,000 cash in the business bank account.
4	Performed services for a client and received cash of $5,000.
9	Paid off the August 31 balance of accounts payable.
15	Purchased office supplies on account, $6,000.
18	Collected cash from a customer on account, $7,500.
19	Consulted on a large downsizing by a major corporation and billed the client for services rendered, $48,000.
22	Recorded the following business expenses for the month: (1) Paid co-op students for salaries—$5,000. (2) Paid advertising—$4,000.
24	Purchased office supplies at an auction for $1,000 cash.
29	Reaney withdrew $8,000 cash.

Required

1. Analyze the effects of the above transactions on the accounting equation of Reaney Personnel Services. Adapt the format of Exhibit 1–11, Panel B, on page 19. Add additional columns to the chart as needed.
2. Prepare the income statement of Reaney Personnel Services for the month ended September 30, 2020. List expenses in decreasing order of amount.
3. Prepare the business's statement of owner's equity for the month ended September 30, 2020.
4. Prepare the balance sheet of Reaney Personnel Services at September 30, 2020.

P1–8A Terrace Board Rentals was started on January 1, 2019, by Ryan Terrace with an investment of $50,000 cash. The company rents out snowboards and related gear from a small store. During the first 11 months, Terrace made additional investments of $20,000 and borrowed $40,000 from the bank for the business. He did not withdraw any funds. The balance sheet accounts, excluding Terrace's capital account, at November 30, 2019, are as follows:

(4) (5)
Transaction analysis, accounting equation, financial statements, evaluation

3. Net income, $54,000

Cash	$45,000
Accounts Receivable	15,000
Rental Gear	32,000
Rental Snowboards	48,000
Store Equipment	30,000
Accounts Payable	12,000
Note Payable	40,000

The following transactions took place during the month of December 2019:

Dec.	1	The business paid $5,000 for the month's rent on the store space.
	4	The business signed a one-year lease for the rental of additional store space at a cost of $4,000 per month. The lease is effective January 1. The business will pay the first month's rent in January.
	6	Rental revenues for the week were Gear, $4,000; Boards, $10,000. Three-quarters of the fees were paid in cash and the rest on account.
	10	The business paid the accounts payable from November 30, 2019.
	12	The business purchased gear for $20,000 and boards for $40,000, all on account.
	13	Rental revenues for the week were Gear, $7,000; Boards, $14,000. All the fees were paid in cash.
	15	The company received payment for the accounts receivable owing at November 30, 2019.
	18	The company purchased store equipment for $10,000 by paying $3,000 cash with the balance due in 60 days.
	20	Rental revenues for the week were Gear, $8,000; Boards, $14,000. Half the fees were paid in cash and half on account.
	21	Terrace withdrew $7,000.
	24	The company paid the balance owing for the purchases made on December 12.
	27	Rental revenues for the week were Gear, $6,000; Boards, $10,000. All the fees were paid in cash.
	27	The company received payment for rental fees on account from December 6.
	31	The company paid its employees for the month of December. The total salaries expense was $10,000.
	31	Terrace paid the utility bill for the month of December, which was $4,000.

Required

1. What is the total net income earned by the business over the period of January 1, 2019, to November 30, 2019?
2. Analyze the effects of the December 2019 transactions on the accounting equation of Terrace Board Rentals. Include the account balances from November 30, 2019. Adapt the format of Exhibit 1–11, Panel B, on page 19.
3. Prepare the income statement for Terrace Board Rentals for the month ended December 31, 2019. List expenses in decreasing order of amount.
4. Prepare the statement of owner's equity for Terrace Board Rentals for the month ended December 31, 2019.
5. Prepare the balance sheet for Terrace Board Rentals at December 31, 2019.
6. Terrace has expressed concern that although the business seems to be profitable and growing, he constantly seems to be investing additional money into it. Prepare a reply to his concerns.

PROBLEMS (GROUP B)

3 Accounting concepts/principles

P1–1B John Chang operates a plumbing business as a proprietorship (John Chang Plumbing). The following events took place during the month of June 2019:

Jun.	1	John's brother retired and sold his equipment to John for $30,000. The equipment had cost $50,000 and had a replacement cost of $38,000.
	3	The business did some plumbing repairs for a customer. The business would normally have charged $1,500 for the work but had agreed to do it for $1,000 cash in order to encourage more business from the customer.
	10	The business signed a lease to rent additional shop space for the business at a cost of $3,000 per month. The business will occupy the premises effective July 1, 2019.
	18	Finding he was low on cash, John went to the bank and borrowed $8,000 on a personal loan.
	28	John withdrew $12,000 from the business and used $7,000 to repay the personal bank loan of June 18.
	30	The accountant is preparing the financial statements. The value of John's equipment has increased to $35,000. John does not understand why accountants ignore the effect of inflation in the accounting records.

Required Identify the accounting assumption, principle, or characteristic that would be applicable to each of the events, and discuss the effects it would have on the transactions of John Chang Plumbing.

P1–2B Linda Horowitz is an architect and was a partner with a large firm, a partnership, for 10 years after graduating from university. Recently she resigned her position to open her own architecture office, which she operates as a proprietorship. The name of the new entity is Horowitz Design.

(3) (4) Entity concept, transaction analysis, accounting equation

The following events occurred during the organizing phase of her new business and its first month of operations:

Jul.	1	Horowitz sold 1,000 shares of Canadian Tire stock, which she had owned for several years, receiving $60,000 cash from her stockbroker.
	2	Horowitz deposited the $60,000 cash from the sale of the Canadian Tire shares into her personal bank account.
	3	Horowitz received $100,000 cash from her former partners in the architecture firm from which she resigned.
	5	Horowitz deposited $80,000 into a bank account in the name of Horowitz Design.
	5	Horowitz Design paid office rent for the month of July, $4,000.
	6	A representative of a large real estate company telephoned Linda Horowitz and told her of the company's intention to transfer its design business to Horowitz Design.
	7	Horowitz Design paid $3,000 cash for office supplies, including letterhead and stationery.
	9	Horowitz Design purchased office furniture on account for $10,000, promising to pay in three months.
	23	Horowitz Design finished design work for a client and submitted the bill for design services, $12,000. It expects to collect from this client within one month.
	31	Horowitz withdrew $5,000 for personal use.

Required

1. Classify each of the preceding events as one of the following (list each date and then choose a, b, or c):
   a. A business transaction to be accounted for by the business.
   b. A business-related event but not a transaction to be accounted for by Horowitz Design.
   c. A personal transaction not to be accounted for by the business.
2. Analyze the effects of the above events on the accounting equation of Horowitz Design. Use a format similar to Exhibit 1–11, Panel B, on page 19.

P1–3B Recently, Yu Gan formed a home staging business called Home 4 Yu. The balance of each item in the accounting equation follows for November 16 and for each of the eight following business days:

(4) Business transactions and analysis

	Cash	Accounts Receivable	Office Supplies	Furniture	Accounts Payable	Owner's Equity
Nov. 16	$6,000	$10,000	$1,000	$8,000	$6,000	$19,000
17	7,000	9,000	1,000	8,000	6,000	19,000
18	6,000	9,000	1,000	8,000	5,000	19,000
19	6,000	9,000	1,500	8,000	5,500	19,000
20	8,000	9,000	1,500	8,000	5,500	21,000
23	7,000	9,000	1,500	8,000	4,500	21,000
24	9,000	9,000	1,500	6,000	4,500	21,000
25	8,500	9,000	2,000	6,000	4,500	21,000
26	7,500	9,000	2,000	6,000	4,500	20,000

Required Assuming that a single transaction took place on each day, briefly describe the transaction that was most likely to have occurred. Begin with November 17 and complete up to November 26. Indicate which accounts were affected, whether the account balances increased or decreased, and by what amount. Assume that no revenue or expense transactions occurred on these dates.

③ ⑤
Balance sheet, entity concept

P1–4B Lupita Goodwin is a realtor. She buys and sells properties on her own, and she also earns commission revenue as a real estate agent. She invested $70,000 on March 10, 2020, in her business, Lupita Goodwin Realty. Consider the following facts as of March 31, 2020:

a. Goodwin had $10,000 in her personal bank account and $90,000 in the business bank account.

b. The real estate office had $6,000 of office supplies on hand on March 31, 2020.

c. Lupita Goodwin Realty had spent $25,000 for a Royal LePage franchise, which entitled the company to represent itself as a Royal LePage member firm. This franchise is a business asset.

d. The company owed $160,000 on a note payable for a building that had been acquired by the company for $195,000.

e. Goodwin owed $185,000 on a personal mortgage on her personal residence. She originally paid $320,000 for it.

f. Goodwin owed $2,500 on a personal charge account with Best Buy.

g. The company acquired business furniture for $18,000 on March 26. Of this amount, Lupita Goodwin Realty owed $14,000 on account at March 31, 2020.

Required

1. Goodwin is concerned about liability exposure. Which proprietorship feature, if any, limits her personal liability?
2. Identify the personal items given in the preceding facts that would not be reported on the balance sheet of the business.
3. Prepare the balance sheet of the real estate business of Lupita Goodwin Realty at March 31, 2020.

⑤
Income statement, statement of owner's equity, balance sheet

P1–5B The amounts of the assets and liabilities of Harada Office Cleaning as of December 31, 2020, and the revenues and expenses of the company for the year ended on December 31, 2020, appear below. The items are listed in alphabetical order.

Accounts Payable	$ 40,000	Land	$100,000
Accounts Receivable	50,000	Note Payable	200,000
Building	350,000	Property Tax Expense	10,000
Cash	25,000	Repairs Expense	30,000
Equipment	110,000	Salaries Expense	280,000
Furniture	18,000	Service Revenue	650,000
Interest Expense	14,000	Supplies	10,000
Interest Payable	3,000	Utilities Expense	25,000
		Y, Harada, Withdrawals	$ 71,000

The beginning amount of owner's equity was $200,000. During the year, the owner made no investments.

Required

1. Prepare the income statement of Harada Office Cleaning for the year ended December 31, 2020. List expenses in order from highest to lowest amount.
2. Prepare the statement of owner's equity of the business for the year ended December 31, 2020.
3. Prepare the balance sheet of the business at December 31, 2020.
4. Answer these questions about Harada Office Cleaning:
   a. Was the result of operations for the year a profit or a loss? How much was it?
   b. Did the business's owner's equity increase or decrease during the year? How would this affect the business's ability to borrow money from a bank in the future?
   c. How much in total economic resources does the company have at December 31, 2020, as it moves into the new year? How much does the company owe? What is the dollar amount of the owner's portion of the business at December 31, 2020?

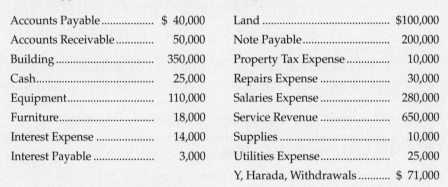

P1–6B The bookkeeper of McBride Insurance Agency prepared the balance sheet of the company while the accountant was ill. The balance sheet contains errors. In particular, the bookkeeper knew that the balance sheet should balance, so she "plugged in" the owner's equity amount needed to achieve this balance. The owner's equity amount, however, is not correct. All other amounts are accurate except the "Total assets" amount.

(5) Correcting a balance sheet

MCBRIDE INSURANCE AGENCY Balance Sheet For the Month Ended October 31, 2019			
Assets		**Liabilities**	
Cash	$ 24,000	Premium revenue	$ 53,000
Insurance expense	2,000	Accounts payable	23,000
Rent expense	6,000	Note payable	40,000
Salaries expense	8,000		
Furniture	20,000		
Accounts receivable	22,000	**Owner's Equity**	
Utilities expense	2,000	C. McBride, capital	(8,000)
Prepaid rent	24,000		
Total assets	$108,000	Total liabilities and owner's equity	$108,000

Required

1. Prepare the corrected balance sheet with the right accounts in the order presented in Appendix B, and date it correctly. Compute total assets, total liabilities, and owner's equity.
2. Identify the accounts listed above that should *not* be presented on the balance sheet and state why you excluded them from the corrected balance sheet you prepared for Requirement 1.

P1–7B Miranda Sykes operates an interior design business called Sykes Design Studio. The following amounts summarize the financial position of the business on April 30, 2020:

(4) (5) Transaction analysis, accounting equation, financial statements

Assets							=	Liabilities	+	Owner's Equity
Cash	+	Accounts Receivable	+	Supplies	+	Land	=	Accounts Payable	+	M. Sykes, Capital
Bal. 27,000		26,000				102,000		33,000		122,000

During May 2020, the company did the following:

May 4 Sykes received $20,000 as a gift and deposited the cash in the business bank account.

6 Paid the beginning balance of accounts payable.

9 Performed services for a client and received cash of $5,000.

10 Collected cash from a customer on account, $4,000.

12 Purchased supplies on account, $3,000.

13 Consulted on the interior design of a major office building and billed the client for services rendered, $16,000.

19 Recorded the following business expenses for the month:
(1) Paid office assistants their salaries for the month, $6,000.
(2) Paid advertising—$4,000.

24 Sold supplies to another interior designer for $1,000 cash, which was the cost of the supplies.

26 Sykes withdrew $7,000 cash for personal use.

Required

1. Analyze the effects of the above transactions on the accounting equation of Sykes Design Studio. Adapt the format of Exhibit 1–11, Panel B, on page 19. Add columns to the chart as needed.
2. Prepare the income statement of Sykes Design Studio for the month ended May 31, 2020. List expenses in decreasing order of amount.
3. Prepare the statement of owner's equity of Sykes Design Studio for the month ended May 31, 2020.
4. Prepare the balance sheet of Sykes Design Studio at May 31, 2020.

(4) (5)
Transaction analysis, accounting equation, financial statements, evaluation

P1–8B Wilson Marketing Consulting, a proprietorship owned by Lin Wilson, was started on January 1, 2019, with an investment of $50,000 cash. The company prepares marketing plans for clients. It has been operating for one year. Business was quite slow in the first year of operations but has steadily increased. Wilson has made additional investments of $30,000 but has not made any withdrawals. The general ledger showed the following balances as of December 31, 2019:

Cash	$ 25,000
Accounts Receivable	30,000
Software	21,000
Office Furniture	15,000
Computer Equipment	32,000
Accounts Payable	18,000
L. Wilson, Capital	105,000

The following transactions took place during the month of January 2020:

Jan.	2	Wilson invested $20,000 in the business.
	2	The business paid $4,000 for the month's rent on the office space.
	4	The business signed a lease for the rental of additional office space at a cost of $3,500 per month. The lease is effective February 1. The business will pay the first month's rent in February.
	6	The business developed a marketing plan for Banting Ltd. and received $10,000 now plus additional $7,000 payments to be received on the 15th of the month for the next three months.
	10	The business paid $1,000 to a courier service.
	12	Wilson signed an agreement to provide a marketing plan to Smith Inc. for $15,000 to be paid upon completion of the work.
	14	The company purchased $5,000 of software that will be required for the Smith assignment. The company paid $3,000 and promised to pay the balance by the end of the month.
	15	The company received $7,000 as the monthly payment from Banting Ltd. from January 6.
	18	The company purchased computer equipment for $10,000 by paying $4,000 cash with the balance due in 60 days.
	23	The company completed a marketing plan for Salem Ltd., which promised to pay $12,000 by the end of the month.
	29	The company paid the balance owing for the software purchased on January 14.
	31	Employees of Wilson Marketing Consulting are paid at the end of each month. The total salaries expense for January was $10,000.
	31	Wilson Marketing Consulting paid the utilities expense for January, $1,000.
	31	Lin Wilson withdrew $5,000 for personal use.

Required

1. What is the total net income earned by the business over the period of January 1, 2019, to December 31, 2019?
2. Analyze the effects of the January 2020 transactions on the accounting equation of Wilson Marketing Consulting. Be sure to include the account balances from December 31, 2019. Adapt the format of Exhibit 1–11, Panel B, on page 19.
3. Prepare the income statement for Wilson Marketing Consulting for the month ended January 31, 2020. List expenses in decreasing order of amount.
4. Prepare the statement of owner's equity for Wilson Marketing Consulting for the month ended January 31, 2020.
5. Prepare the balance sheet for Wilson Marketing Consulting at January 31, 2020.
6. Lin Wilson has expressed concern that although the business seems to be profitable and growing, she constantly seems to be investing additional money into it and has been unable to make many withdrawals for the work she has put into it. Prepare a reply to her concerns.

CHALLENGE PROBLEMS

(3) Understanding the going concern assumption

P1–1C The going concern assumption is becoming an increasing source of concern for users of financial statements. There are instances of companies filing for bankruptcy several months after issuing their annual audited financial statements. The question is, Why didn't the financial statements predict the problem?

A friend has just arrived on your doorstep; you realize she is very angry. After calming her down, you ask what the problem is. She tells you that she had inherited $40,000 from an uncle and invested the money in the common shares of Outdoor Sports Equipment Corp. (OSEC). She had carefully examined OSEC's financial statements for the latest year-end and had concluded that the company was financially sound. This morning, she had read in the local paper that the company had gone bankrupt and her investment was worthless. She asks you why the financial statements valued the assets at values that are in excess of those the trustee in bankruptcy expects to realize from liquidating the assets. Why have the assets suddenly lost so much of the value they had six months ago?

Required Explain to your friend why assets are valued on a going concern basis in the financial statements and why they are usually worth less when the company goes out of business. Use inventory and accounts receivable as examples.

(4) Accounting for business transactions

P1–2C You and three friends have decided to go into the landscape business for the summer to earn money to pay for your schooling in the fall. Your first step was to sign up customers to satisfy yourselves that the business had the potential to be profitable. Next, you planned to go to the bank to borrow money to buy the equipment you would need.

After considerable effort, your group obtained contracts from customers for 200 residences for the summer. One of your partners wants to prepare a balance sheet showing the value of the contracts as an asset. She is sure that you will have no trouble with borrowing the necessary funds from the bank on the basis of the proposed balance sheet.

Required Explain to your friend why the commitments (signed contracts) from customers cannot be recognized as assets. What suggestions do you have that might assist your group in borrowing the necessary funds?

Extending Your Knowledge

DECISION PROBLEMS

1 5

Using financial statements to evaluate a request for a loan

DP1–1

Two businesses, Tyler's Bicycle Centre and Ryan's Catering, have sought business loans from you. To decide whether to make the loans, you have requested their balance sheets.

"Inventory" is the cost of the bicycles and accessories the business has available to sell to customers.

TYLER'S BICYCLE CENTRE Balance Sheet December 31, 2019			
Assets		**Liabilities**	
Cash	$ 27,000	Accounts payable	$ 36,000
Accounts receivable	42,000	Note payable	354,000
Inventory	55,000	Total liabilities	390,000
Store supplies	2,000		
Furniture and fixtures	26,000	**Owner's Equity**	
Building	246,000	T. Jones, capital	230,000
Land	222,000		
Total assets	$620,000	Total liabilities and owner's equity	$620,000

"Inventory" is the cost of the food the business has available to sell to customers.

RYAN'S CATERING Balance Sheet December 31, 2019			
Assets		**Liabilities**	
Cash	$ 30,000	Accounts payable	$ 9,000
Accounts receivable	12,000	Note payable	204,000
Office supplies	6,000	Total liabilities	213,000
Inventory	60,000		
Office furniture	15,000	**Owner's Equity**	
Note receivable, Long-term*	600,000	R. Smith, capital	510,000
Total assets	$723,000	Total liabilities and owner's equity	$723,000

*The investments of $600,000 can be sold today for $750,000.

Required

1. Based solely on these balance sheets, which entity would you be more comfortable lending money to? Explain fully, citing specific items and amounts from the balance sheets.
2. In addition to the balance sheet data, what other financial statement information would you require? Be specific.

FINANCIAL STATEMENT CASES

Indigo Books and Music Inc. (Indigo) is a Canadian retail bookstore chain. It sells books, music, and gifts both online and in stores. It owns Chapters and Coles as well as a number of other smaller bookstores.

Vancouver-based TELUS Corporation (TELUS) is a national telecommunications company that many people recognize as a wireless communications provider from their friendly and colourful advertising campaigns featuring animals and nature. They also operate a broad variety of services for both consumers and businesses, including Internet, data, television, entertainment, and more.

Using these two companies, you will gradually build the confidence to understand and use financial statements of large corporations in addition to the smaller businesses we look at throughout the text.

These and similar cases in later chapters focus on the financial statements of two real Canadian companies—Indigo Books & Music Inc. and TELUS Corporation.

FSC1–1

(4) (5)

Identifying items from a company's financial statements

5. April 1, 2017, net earnings of $20,918,000

Refer to the Indigo financial statements located in Appendix A at the end of this text and on MyLab Accounting. Notice that all amounts are reported in thousands of Canadian dollars. Also, Indigo has a fiscal year-end that changes from year to year. In these statements, the statements are for a 52-week period ended April 1 in 2017 and a 53-week period ended April 2 in 2016.

Required

1. How much accounts receivable did Indigo have at April 1, 2017?
2. What were the total assets at April 1, 2017? At April 2, 2016?
3. Write the company's accounting equation at April 1, 2017, by filling in the dollar amounts:

Assets = Liabilities + Equity

4. Identify total revenue for the fiscal period ended April 1, 2017. Indigo presents this information on a "Consolidated Statements of Earnings" report rather than calling it an income statement. What was the revenue for the period ended April 2, 2016? Did revenue increase or decrease during fiscal 2017?
5. How much net income or net loss did Indigo experience for the 52-week period ended April 1, 2017? Was 2017 a good year or bad year compared to 2016?

Most companies' financial statements are stated at a month end, but many retail and merchandising companies (companies that sell products rather than services) choose to use a 52-week or 53-week period instead.

FSC1–2

(4) (5)

Identifying items from a company's financial statements

5. Dec. 31, 2016, net income, $1,236,000,000

Refer to the TELUS financial statements located on MyLab Accounting. TELUS calls their balance sheet a "Consolidated Statement of Financial Position," and their income statement is called a "Consolidated Statement of Income." The term "consolidated" means the results of many companies owned by TELUS are included in the totals presented.

Required

1. How much accounts receivable did TELUS have at December 31, 2016?
2. What were the total assets at December 31, 2016? At December 31, 2015? Note: There is no title for this amount, but there is a total on the statement.
3. Write the company's accounting equation at December 31, 2016, by filling in the dollar amounts:

Assets = Liabilities + Owners' Equity

4. Identify total operating revenues for the year ended December 31, 2016, and the year ended December 31, 2015. Did revenue increase or decrease during 2016?
5. How much net income or net loss did TELUS experience for the year ended December 31, 2016? Was 2016 a good year or bad year compared to 2015?

IFRS MINI-CASE

The IFRS Mini-Case is now available online, at **MyLab Accounting** in Chapter Resources.

IFRS Mini-Cases are available in MyLab, Chapter Resources, for Chapters 1, 4, 5, 9, 10, and 11, and highlight the similarities and differences between ASPE and IFRS.

Try It! Solutions for Chapter 1

1. internal = b, c; external = a, d, e
2.

	Proprietorship	Partnership	Corporation
a.			X
b.		X	
c.		X	
d.	X		
e.			X

3. The measurement criteria in Exhibit 1–5 tell us that the cost principle of measurement should be used. This transaction would be recognized at the amount of cash paid for the building. You paid $185,000 for the building. Therefore, $185,000 is the cost to report on your financial statements.
4. If the car is not going to be used for business purposes, the car should be the personal responsibility of the owner. The economic entity assumption means that the assets of the business should not be mixed with the assets of the owner to ensure that the results of the business can be identified and analyzed accurately.
5. To answer both questions, use the accounting equation:
   a. **Assets − Liabilities = Owner's Equity**
   $75,000 − $65,000 = $10,000
   b. **Assets = Liabilities + Owner's Equity**
   $70,000 = $20,000 + $50,000
6.

Accounts Receivable	A
Computer Equipment	A
S. Scott, Capital	OE
Rent Expense	E
Supplies	A
S. Scott, Withdrawals	OE
Salaries Expense	E
Consulting Service Revenue	R
Cash	A
Note Payable	L
Supplies Expense	E
Accounts Payable	L

7.

	Assets				Liabilities		Owner's Equity						
	Cash	+ Accounts Receivable	+ Equipment	=	Accounts Payable	+	E. Lawlor, Capital	−	E. Lawlor, Withdrawals	+	Service Revenue	−	Gas Expense
May 1	+ 1,700						+ 1,700						
May 3			+1,440		+1,440								
May 5		+200									+200		
May 17	−60												−60
May 28	−300								−300				
Bal.	1,340	200	1,440		1,440		1,700		300		200		60
		2,980							2,980				

8.

DR PAINTING
Income Statement
For the Month Ended March 31, 2020

Revenue		
Service revenue		$7,000
Expenses		
Salaries expense	$800	
Utilities expense	200	
Total expenses		1,000
Net income		$6,000

DR PAINTING
Statement of Owner's Equity
For the Month Ended March 31, 2020

D. Richardson, capital, March 1, 2020	$ 0
Add: Investment by owner	40,000
Net income for the month	6,000
Less: Withdrawals by owner	1,500
D. Richardson, capital, March 31, 2020	$44,500

DR PAINTING
Balance Sheet
March 31, 2020

Assets		**Liabilities**	
Cash	$22,300	Accounts payable	$ 1,000
Accounts receivable	1,400		
Office supplies	1,800	**Owner's equity**	
Land	20,000	D. Richardson, capital	44,500
Total assets	$45,500	Total liabilities and owner's equity	$45,500

2 Recording Business Transactions

CONNECTING CHAPTER 2

LEARNING OBJECTIVES

The **Summary** for Chapter 2 appears on page 83.
Key Terms with definitions for this chapter's material appear on page 84.

CPA competencies

This text covers material outlined in **Section 1: Financial Reporting of the CPA Competency Map**. The Learning Objectives for each chapter have been aligned with the CPA Competency Map to ensure the best coverage possible.

1.3.1 Prepares financial statements

Susan Schmitz/Shutterstock

When Danielle Rodriguez started her business in January 2015, she wasn't thinking about accounting. As an IT professional, she was looking to combine her business skills with her love of dogs. Her "fur babies," Zoey and Maggie Mae, are an important part of her #Barknfun Team.

Her business, The Bark'N Fun Company, is a monthly subscription box service that offers premium toys, treats, and accessories for dogs and puppies. The business is online, but her office is located in the small town of Courtice, Ontario.

The majority of small businesses fail within the first three years. So how has The Bark'N Fun Company stayed in business in a competitive online market for luxury items? Danielle, The Bark'N Fun Company's owner, uses accounting information to make her business decisions. Is she an accountant? No! She is a smart businessperson who knows that she needs to understand the business's monthly revenues and expenses so that her business can survive in the short-term and thrive in the long-term. The Bark'N Fun Company needs to know if the prices of their toys and treats are high enough to cover operating expenses, or if they can afford to offer free shipping. Is it working? Yes. The Bark'N Fun Company has not only been able to stay in business but also supports charities that are important to dogs, such as canine rescue organizations and humane society shelters.

This chapter shows how The Bark'N Fun Company and other businesses record their transactions and update their financial records. The procedures outlined in this chapter are followed by businesses ranging in size from giant multinational corporations like PetSmart Inc. to micro-enterprises like The Bark'N Fun Company and Hunter Environmental Consulting, who we will continue to follow through this chapter.

Chapter 1 introduced transaction analysis and the financial statements by using a table based on the accounting equation to list all the transactions. This method of tracking account balances was useful to show how accounts and statements connect, but there are too many transactions in a typical business to record information this way. In this chapter we will look at the way bookkeeping is done in the real world. First we look at the entire process and then we will go back and do it step by step.

The Accounting Cycle

LO 1

What are the key terms used when recording transactions?

The **accounting cycle** is the formal process by which companies produce their financial statements and update their financial records for a specific period of time. Exhibit 2–1 outlines the complete accounting cycle. In this chapter, we will look at steps 1 through 4, which represent what is done *during* the **accounting period**. The next two chapters will introduce the last steps in the cycle, which are done *at the end* of the period.

EXHIBIT 2–1 | The Accounting Cycle

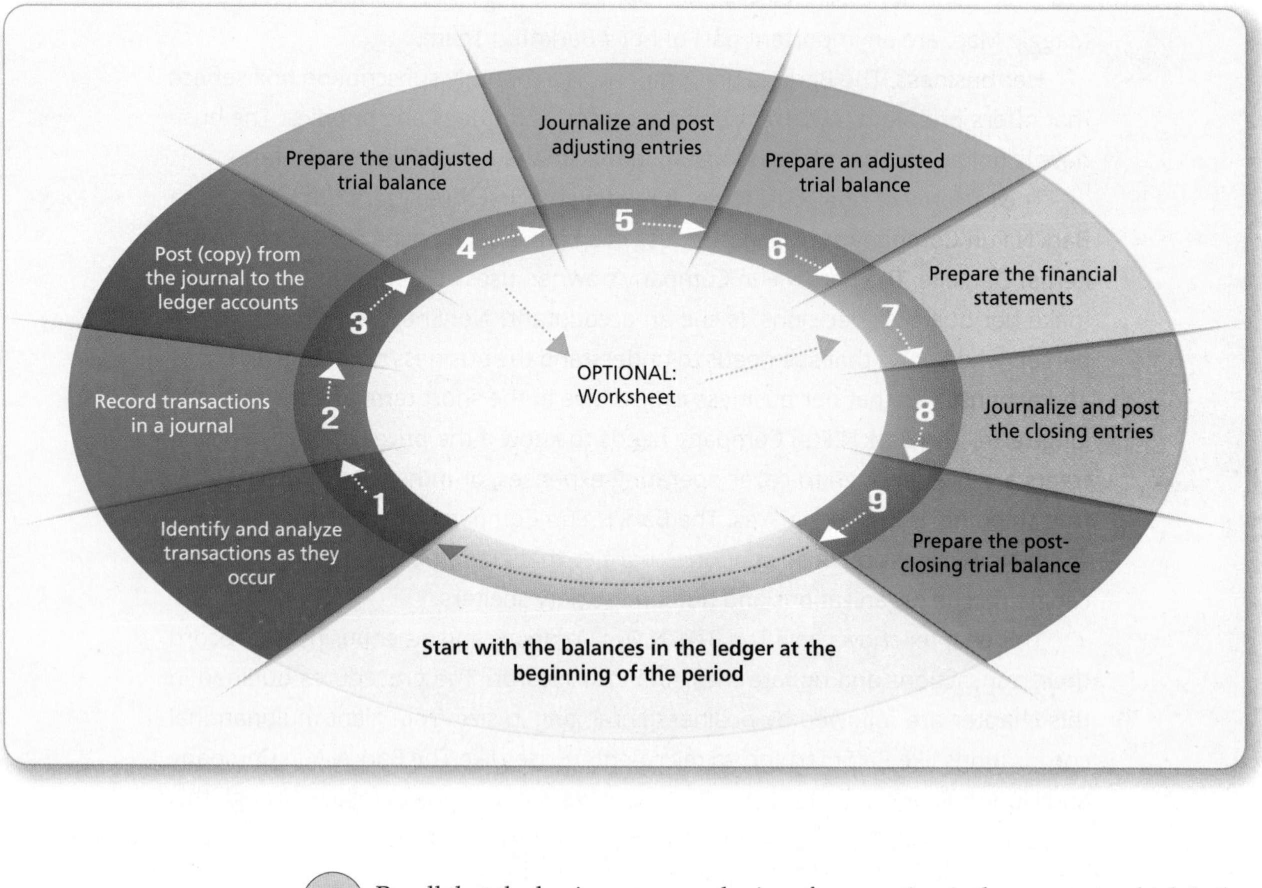

Identify and analyze transactions as they occur
1
Record transactions in a journal
2
Post (copy) from the journal to the ledger accounts
3
Prepare the unadjusted trial balance
4
Journalize and post adjusting entries
5
Prepare an adjusted trial balance
6
Prepare the financial statements
7
Journalize and post the closing entries
8
Prepare the post-closing trial balance
9
OPTIONAL: Worksheet
Start with the balances in the ledger at the beginning of the period

Start Recall that the basic summary device of accounting is the account, which is the detailed record of the changes that have occurred in a particular asset, liability, or item of owner's equity during a period of time. Business transactions cause these changes.

For a new business, the cycle begins with setting up (opening) the ledger accounts. Lisa Hunter started Hunter Environmental Consulting (HEC) on April 2, 2019, so the first step in the cycle was to plan and open the accounts.

Account balances carry over from period to period until the accounting cycle is complete, for example, at the end of one year. Therefore, the accounting cycle usually starts with the account balances at the beginning of the period.

1. Our first step is to analyze the transaction to identify changes in accounts.
2. Accountants record transactions first in a **journal**, which is the chronological record of transactions.
3. Accountants then copy (post) the data to a record of all the accounts called the **ledger**. (One way to think of a ledger is as a binder, with each page in the binder representing one account.) In the phrase "keeping the books," *books* refers to the ledger. Exhibit 2–2 shows how asset, liability, and owner's equity accounts can be grouped into the ledger.

EXHIBIT 2–2 | The Ledger (Asset, Liability, and Owner's Equity Accounts)

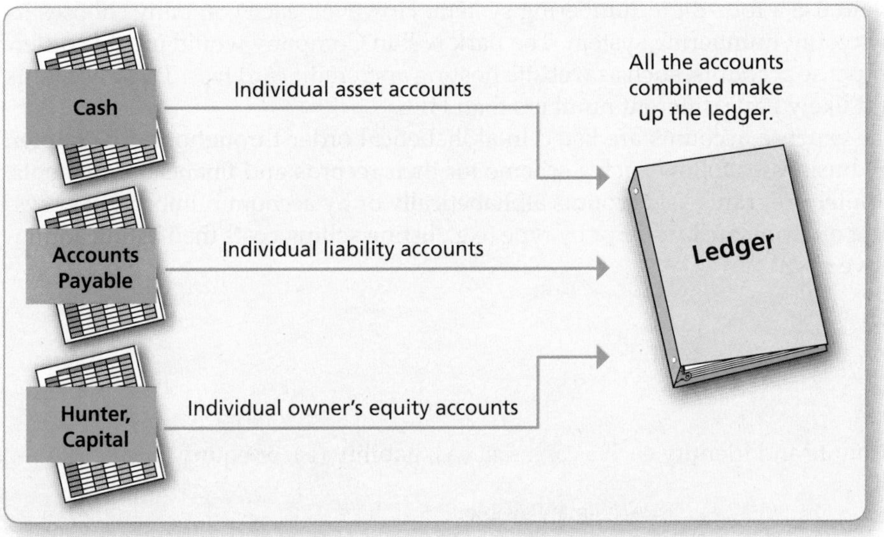

4. Then a list of all the ledger accounts and their balances is prepared. This is called a **trial balance**, or more precisely, an unadjusted trial balance at this stage.

Chart of Accounts

Companies use a **chart of accounts** to list all their accounts. This is just a list and not a financial statement. In many cases, the account names are listed along with the account numbers. Account numbers are just shorthand versions of the account names. One number equals one account name—just like your social insurance number is unique to you. This numbering system makes it easy to locate individual accounts in the ledger and to key in entries in an accounting software program.

Accounts are identified by account numbers with two or more digits. Assets are often numbered beginning with 1, liabilities with 2, owner's equity with 3, revenues with 4, and expenses with 5. The second, third, and higher digits in an account number indicate the position of the individual account within the category.

Hint: It would be helpful to make your own list of accounts as you learn new account names. Appendix B has the start of a list for you to use.

The chart of accounts for Hunter Environmental Consulting appears in Exhibit 2–3. Notice the gap in account numbers between 1200 and 1400. Lisa Hunter realizes that at some later date the business may need to add another category of

EXHIBIT 2-3 | Chart of Accounts—Hunter Environmental Consulting

Balance Sheet Accounts		
Assets	**Liabilities**	**Owner's Equity**
1100 Cash	2100 Accounts Payable	3000 Lisa Hunter, Capital
1200 Accounts Receivable	2300 Note Payable	3100 Lisa Hunter, Withdrawals
1400 Office Supplies	**Income Statement Accounts**	
1500 Furniture	**Revenues**	**Expenses**
1900 Land	4000 Service Revenue	5100 Rent Expense
		5200 Salaries Expense
		5300 Utilities Expense

Companies do not need to use the numbering system illustrated here. They can develop any system that makes sense to them. For example, a Ford dealership uses account 7630 for Parts Department Advertising Expense and a General Motors dealership uses account number 065-07 for the exact same expense.

receivables—for example, Note Receivable—to be numbered 1210. This company chose to use a four-digit numbering system. However, each company chooses its own account numbering system. The Bark'N Fun Company would include different expense accounts, such as website hosting and credit card fees. These accounts would likely have different numbers than HEC.

The expense accounts are listed in alphabetical order throughout this chapter. Many businesses follow such a scheme for their records and financial statements. Computer programs list accounts alphabetically or by account number. Other systems of ordering are by size or by type (e.g., listing selling costs then listing administrative costs).

Try It!

1. Consider the following accounts and identify each as an asset (A), liability (L), or equity (E).

a) Rent Expense	________	f) Accounts Payable	________
b) R. Brock, Capital	________	g) Land	________
c) Furniture	________	h) Notes Receivable	________
d) Service Revenue	________	i) R. Brock, Withdrawals	________
e) Prepaid Insurance	________	j) Insurance Expense	________

2. Create a chart of accounts by matching each of the following account names with an appropriate account number. Assume this company uses a system similar to that described in the chapter, with asset numbers beginning with 1 and expense numbers beginning with 5.

Accounts Payable	30200
Rent Expense	10100
Furniture and Fixtures	50600
Service Revenue	20100
L. Starks, Capital	40100
Accounts Receivable	10400
Cash	30100
Income Taxes Payable	20500
L. Starks, Withdrawals	10200

Solutions appear at the end of this chapter and on **MyLab Accounting**

Double-Entry Accounting

LO (2)

How do we track changes in accounts?

Accounting uses the *double-entry system*, which means that we record the dual, or two, effects of each transaction. As a result, *every transaction affects at least two accounts*.

Consider a cash purchase of supplies. What are the dual effects of this transaction?

1. Increases supplies (the business *received* supplies)
2. Decreases cash (the business *gave* cash)

Similarly, a purchase of a truck (made with a bank loan):

1. Increases vehicles (the business *received* the truck)
2. Increases the bank loan payable (the business *gave* a promise to pay in the future)

The T-Account

The form of account used for most illustrations in this text is called the *T-account* because it takes the form of the capital letter "T." A T-account is a quick way to show the effect of transactions on a particular account—a useful shortcut or tool used in accounting. T-accounts are not part of the formal accounting records.

One way to think about this is to remember the old adage … "you don't get something for nothing." In accounting, money does not just appear and goods are not received without payment.

The vertical line divides the account into its left and right sides, with the account title at the top. For example, the Cash account appears in the following T-account format:

Cash	
(Left side)	**(Right side)**
Debit	*Credit*
Dr.	Cr.

The left side of the account is called the **debit** side, and the right side is called the **credit** side. They are often abbreviated as Dr and Cr.

Even though *left side* and *right side* may be more convenient, *debit* and *credit* are what they are called in a business environment.[1]

Debits are not "good" or "bad." Neither are credits. Debits are not always increases, and credits are not always decreases. Debit simply means left side, and credit means right side.

Increases and Decreases in the Accounts

The type of an account (asset, liability, owner's equity) determines how we record increases and decreases. For any given type of account, all increases are recorded on one side, and all decreases are recorded on the other side. Increases in *assets* are recorded in the left (debit) side of the account. Decreases in assets are recorded in the right (credit) side of the account. Conversely, increases in liabilities and owner's equity are recorded by *credits*. Decreases in liabilities and owner's equity are recorded by *debits*.

This pattern of recording debits and credits is based on the accounting equation:

ASSETS = LIABILITIES + OWNER'S EQUITY
DEBITS = CREDITS

In a computerized accounting system, the software interprets debits and credits as increases or decreases based on the account type that is programmed into it. For example, software reads a debit to Cash as an increase because it is an asset account, and it reads a debit to Accounts Payable as a decrease because it is a liability account.

Assets are on the opposite side of the accounting equation from liabilities and owner's equity. Therefore, increases and decreases in assets are recorded in the opposite manner from increases and decreases in liabilities and owner's equity. Liabilities and owner's equity are on the same side of the equal sign, so they are treated in the same way. Exhibit 2–4 shows the relationship between the accounting equation and the rules of debit and credit.

---

[1]The words *debit* and *credit* abbreviate the Latin terms *debitum* and *creditum*. Luca Pacioli, the Italian monk who wrote about accounting in the 15th century, used these terms.

EXHIBIT 2–4 | The Accounting Equation and the Rules of Debit and Credit

	DEBITS		=	CREDITS				
Accounting Equation:	ASSETS		=	LIABILITIES		+	OWNER'S EQUITY	
Rule of Debit and Credit:	Debit +	Credit −		Debit −	Credit +		Debit −	Credit +

To demonstrate the rules shown in Exhibit 2–4, reconsider Transactions 1 and 2 from Chapter 1. Dates are being added to all transactions.

Transaction 1: Starting the Business On April 2, Lisa Hunter invested $250,000 cash to begin her environmental consulting firm. The company received $250,000 cash from Hunter and gave her the owner's equity. We are accounting for the business entity, Hunter Environmental Consulting (HEC). What accounts of HEC are affected? By what amounts? On what side (debit or credit)? The answer is that both assets and owner's equity would increase by $250,000, as the following T-accounts show:

In each transaction, total debits must equal total credits.

ASSETS = LIABILITIES + OWNER'S EQUITY

Cash	
Apr. 2 250,000	

↑ Debit for increase

Lisa Hunter, Capital	
	Apr. 2 250,000

↑ Credit for increase

Transaction 2: Purchase of Land On April 3, HEC spent $100,000 cash to purchase land. This transaction affects two assets: Cash and Land. It decreases (credits) Cash and increases (debits) Land, as shown in the T-accounts:

ASSETS = LIABILITIES + OWNER'S EQUITY

Cash	
Apr. 2 250,000	**Apr. 3** 100,000
Balance 150,000	

Land	
Apr. 3 100,000	

Lisa Hunter, Capital	
	Apr. 2 250,000

An account with only one transaction does not need the balance shown. It is understood that the amount shown is the balance.

The amount remaining in an account is called its *balance*.

After this transaction, Cash has a $150,000 debit balance ($250,000 debit balance from the previous transaction reduced by the $100,000 credit amount), Land has a debit balance of $100,000, and Lisa Hunter, Capital has a $250,000 credit balance. This is shown in the section of Exhibit 2–5 labelled Transaction 2. Notice that the debits still equal the credits, but there are now two accounts on the left side.

Opening Accounts We create accounts as they are needed. The process of creating a new account in preparation for recording a transaction is called *opening the account*. For Transaction 1, we opened the Cash account and the Lisa Hunter, Capital account. For Transaction 2, we opened the Land account.

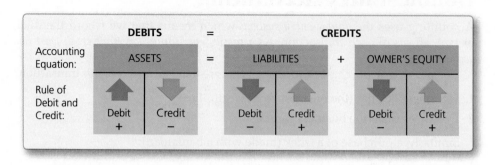

EXHIBIT 2-5 | Debits and Credits for the First Two Transactions of Hunter Environmental Consulting

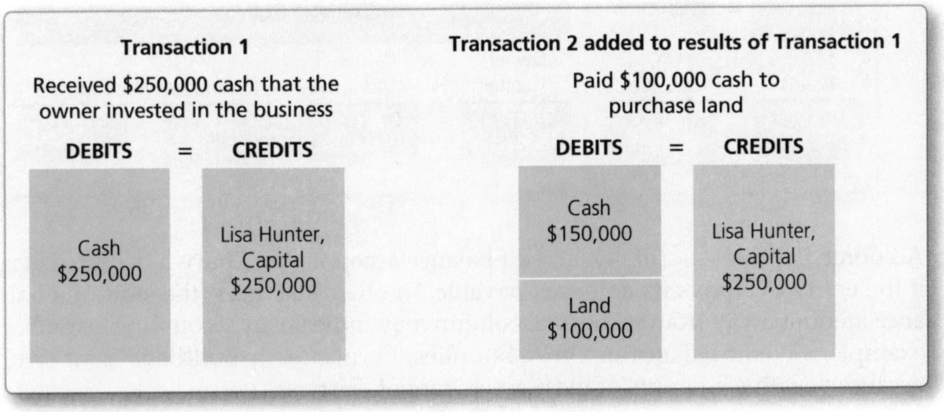

Expanding the Rules of Debit and Credit: Revenues and Expenses

Owner's equity includes revenues and expenses because revenues and expenses make up net income or net loss, which flows into owner's equity. As we discussed in Chapter 1, *revenues* are increases in owner's equity from providing goods and services to customers. *Expenses* are decreases in owner's equity from using assets or increasing liabilities in the course of operating the business. Therefore, we must expand the accounting equation as we did in Exhibit 1–10. Exhibit 2–6 shows revenues and expenses under equity because they directly affect owner's equity.

Think about this for a moment. *Why is an increase to an expense a debit?* Because the overall effect of an increase in an expense is a decrease to equity by reducing net income or creating a net loss. A loss reduces the capital balance. To reduce a capital balance, the account is debited.

EXHIBIT 2-6 | Expanded Accounting Equation

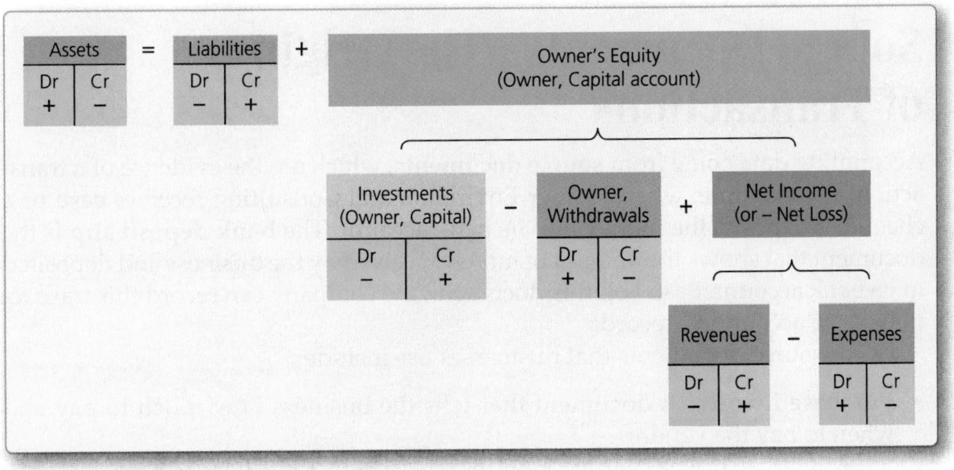

Normal Balance of an Account

An account's **normal balance** appears on the side of the account—debit or credit—where *increases* are recorded. For example, Cash and other assets usually have a debit balance, so the normal balance of assets is on the debit side. Conversely, liabilities and owner's equity usually have a credit balance, so their normal balances are on the credit side. Exhibit 2–7 illustrates the normal balances by highlighting the side where the balance is increased.

An account that normally has a debit balance may occasionally have a credit balance, which indicates a negative amount of the item. For example, Cash will have a credit balance if the entity **overdraws** its bank account. Similarly, the liability

One way to memorize this is to use an acronym, such as AWE ROL. In this case, the (A)sset, (W)ithdrawal, and (E)xpense accounts all have debit balances, while the (R)evenue, (O)wner's Equity, and (L)iability accounts all have credit balances. Or memorize which side has the "+" (increase), and then all the "−" (decreases) are the opposite. This way you only have to memorize half of them! Try DR. AWE–the debits (dr) belong with the (A)sset, (W)ithdrawal, and (E)xpense accounts.

EXHIBIT 2–7 | Final Rules of Debit and Credit

Assets	=	Liabilities	+	Owner's Equity							
Assets	=	Liabilities	+	Owner, Capital	−	Owner, Withdrawals	+	Revenues	−	Expenses	
Dr + / Cr −		Dr − / Cr +		Dr − / Cr +		Dr + / Cr −		Dr − / Cr +		Dr + / Cr −	

Accounts Payable—normally a credit balance account—will have a debit balance if the entity overpays its accounts payable. In other instances, the shift of a balance amount away from its normal column may indicate an accounting error. For example, a credit balance in Office Supplies, Furniture, or Buildings is an error because negative amounts of these assets cannot exist.

Try It!

3. For each account, identify if the change would be recorded as a debit (DR) or credit (CR).

a) Increase to Cash
b) Decrease to Accounts Payable
c) Increase to Owner, Capital
d) Increase to Unearned Revenue
e) Decrease to Accounts Receivable
f) Increase to Interest Revenue
g) Increase to Rent Expense
h) Decrease to Office Supplies
i) Increase to Prepaid Rent
j) Increase to Note Payable

Solutions appear at the end of this chapter and on **MyLab Accounting**

Source Documents—The Origin of Transactions

LO 3

How do we record business transactions?

Accounting data come from **source documents**, which are the evidence of a transaction. For example, when Hunter Environmental Consulting receives cash or a cheque, it deposits the money into its bank account. The **bank deposit slip** is the document that shows the amount of money received by the business and deposited in its bank account. Based on this document, the company can record this transaction in the accounting records.

Other source documents that businesses use include:

- **Purchase invoice**: A document that tells the business how much to pay and when to pay the vendor.
- **Bank cheque**: A document that tells the amount and the date of cash payments.
- **Sales invoice**: A document sent to the customer when a business sells goods or services and tells the business how much revenue to record.

Recording Transactions in the Journal

We could record all transactions directly in the ledger accounts, as we have shown for the first two HEC transactions. However, that way of accounting does not leave a clear record of each transaction. You may have to search through all the accounts to find both sides of a particular transaction. To stay organized and keep all information about a transaction in one place, accountants first keep a record of each transaction in a *journal*, the chronological (listed by date) record of the entity's transactions. They then transfer this information from the journal into the accounts.

The process for thinking through how to write a journal entry is as follows:

Transaction: Identify the transactions from source documents.

Analysis: Identify each account affected by the transaction and its type (asset, liability, owner's equity, revenue, or expense).
Determine whether each account is increased or decreased by the transaction.
Use the rules of debit and credit to determine whether to debit or credit the account to record its increase or decrease.

Accounting Equation: Verify that the increases and decreases result in an accounting equation that is still in balance.

Journal Entry: Record the transaction in the journal, as explained in Exhibit 2–8. Total debits must always equal total credits. This step is also called *making the journal entry* or *journalizing the transaction.*

EXHIBIT 2–8 | The Journal

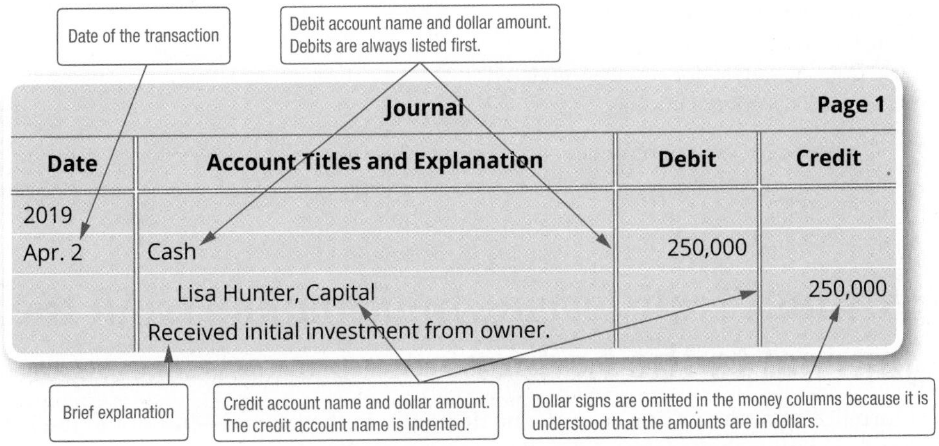

Date of the transaction
Debit account name and dollar amount. Debits are always listed first.
Journal
Page 1
Date
Account Titles and Explanation
Debit
Credit
2019
Apr. 2
Cash
250,000
Lisa Hunter, Capital
250,000
Received initial investment from owner.
Brief explanation
Credit account name and dollar amount. The credit account name is indented.
Dollar signs are omitted in the money columns because it is understood that the amounts are in dollars.

Regardless of the accounting system in use—computerized or manual—an accountant must analyze every business transaction in the manner we are presenting in these opening chapters. Accounting software performs the same actions as accountants do in a manual system. For example, when a sales clerk swipes your VISA card through the credit card reader, the accounting system records both the store's sales revenue and the receivable from VISA. The software automatically records the transaction as a journal entry, but an accountant had to program the computer to do so. A computer's ability to perform routine tasks and mathematical operations quickly and without error frees accountants for decision making.

ETHICS Are receipts really important?

Elijah Morris, assistant manager for Red's Big Burger Restaurant, is responsible for purchasing equipment and supplies for the restaurant. Elijah recently purchased a $4,000 commercial-grade refrigerator for the restaurant, but he can't find the receipt. Elijah purchased the refrigerator with personal funds and is asking to be reimbursed by the restaurant. Hannah, the restaurant's accountant, has said that she is unsure if the business can reimburse Elijah without a receipt. Elijah suggests: "Hannah, it won't really matter if I have a receipt or not. You've seen the refrigerator in the restaurant, so you know I purchased it. What difference is a little receipt going to make?"

What should Hannah do? What would you do?

Solution

Hannah should not reimburse Elijah until she receives the receipt—the source document. Elijah could have purchased the refrigerator for less than the amount he is asking in reimbursement. Source documents provide the evidence of the amount of the transaction. If either an auditor or the owner of the restaurant investigated the $4,000 purchase, he or she would need to see the source document to verify the transaction. If Elijah truly cannot find the receipt, Hannah should ask for an alternative source document such as a credit card or bank statement that shows evidence of the purchase. In addition, Elijah should be warned about using personal funds to purchase equipment for the business.

Try It!

4. For each of the following transactions, select the source document that provides the best evidence of the transaction. Choose from these source documents: bank deposit slip, bank cheque, invoice received from a vendor, or invoice sent to a customer.
   a. A company purchases supplies on account.
   b. A company pays for the supplies it purchased in Transaction a.
   c. A company performs services on account for a college.
   d. The college pays the company for the services performed in Transaction c.
   e. A customer pays the company immediately for services performed.
   f. The company hires a student to provide office support during the summer.

5. EMB Consulting Services had the following transactions for the month of November. Journalize the transactions and include an explanation with each entry.

Nov.	1	The business received $10,000 cash and gave capital to Eloise Martinez, the owner.
	15	Purchased office supplies on account, $400.
	18	Paid advertising bill, $150.
	20	Received $1,000 from customers for services rendered.
	28	Martinez withdrew $500 from the business.

Solutions appear at the end of this chapter and on **MyLab Accounting**

Posting (Transferring Information) from the Journal to the Ledger

LO 4

What is the next step after recording the transaction?

Journalizing a transaction records the data only in the journal—but not in the ledger. Remember, the ledger tracks all transactions related to an account. To appear in the ledger, the data must be copied or transferred there. The process of transferring data from the journal to the ledger is called **posting**.

Posting really just means *copying* a debit in the journal to a debit in the ledger and a credit in the journal to a credit in the ledger. The first transaction of Hunter Environmental Consulting is posted to the ledger as shown in Exhibit 2–9. Here we are using a T-account as a short form for a ledger. In Exhibit 2–11 we illustrate posting the same transaction in a three-column ledger, which is used in formal accounting records. The Post. Ref. column and page number will be explained at that time.

EXHIBIT 2–9 | Making a Journal Entry and Posting to the Ledger

Journal — **Page 1**

Date	Account Titles and Explanation	Post. Ref.	Debit	Credit
2019				
Apr. 2	Cash		250,000	
	Lisa Hunter, Capital			250,000
	Received initial investment from owner.			

Cash

Debit	Credit
Apr. 2 **250,000**	

Lisa Hunter, Capital

Debit	Credit
	Apr. 2 **250,000**

Accounting for Business Transactions

So, to recap, the first steps of the accounting cycle are as follows:

1. Identify and analyze transactions as they occur.
2. Record transactions in a journal.
3. Post (copy) from the journal to the ledger accounts.

In the pages that follow, we record the transactions of Hunter Environmental Consulting (HEC) from Chapter 1. Keep in mind that we are accounting for the business entity and not recording Lisa Hunter's personal transactions.

To simplify the illustrations, we post transactions here to the T-account instead of the ledger. The Summary Problem at the end of the chapter demonstrates the three-column ledger.

Transaction 1: Starting the Business

Transaction:

Lisa Hunter invested $250,000 cash to begin her environmental consulting business, Hunter Environmental Consulting. The money was deposited in the company's bank account on April 2, as shown by the following deposit slip:

CREDIT ACCOUNT OF:
HUNTER ENVIRONMENTAL CONSULTING
10300 004 06000303600

DATE

DAY	MONTH	YEAR
02	04	19

LIST OF CHEQUES

CHEQUE IDENTIFICATION	
1 Lisa Hunter	250,000.00
2	
3	
4	
5	
6	
7	
8	
9	
10	
11	
12	
CHEQUE SUBTOTAL $	250,000.00

BUSINESS ACCOUNT DEPOSIT SLIP

BANK OF THE PEOPLE
SHOPPING CONCOURSE BRANCH
VANCOUVER, BC Y2R 2X1

CREDIT ACCOUNT OF:
HUNTER ENVIRONMENTAL CONSULTING
10300 004 06000303600

DATE			INITIALS	
DAY	MONTH	YEAR	DEPOSITORS	TELLERS
02	04	19	LH	SM

CASH COUNT

× 5		
× 10		
× 20		
× 50		
× 100		
× $2 COIN		
× $1 COIN		
COIN		
CASH SUBTOTAL		
ENTER CREDIT CARD VOUCHER TOTAL		
CASH SUBTOTAL		
CHEQUE SUBTOTAL	250,000	00
DEPOSIT TOTAL $	250,000	00

⑆10300⑈004⑆ 0600⑈ 0303600⑈

Analysis:

Hunter's investment in Hunter Environmental Consulting increased its asset cash; to record this increase, debit Cash. The investment also increased its owner's equity; to record this increase, credit Lisa Hunter, Capital.

Accounting Equation:

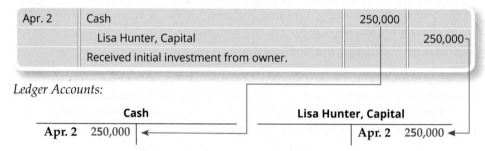

Assets		Liabilities	+	Owner's Equity
Cash	=			Lisa Hunter, Capital
+250,000		0	+	250,000

The journal entry records the same information that you learned by using the accounting equation in Chapter 1. Both accounts—Cash and Lisa Hunter, Capital—increased because the business received $250,000 cash and gave Hunter $250,000 of capital (owner's equity) in the business.

Journal Entry:

Apr. 2	Cash	250,000	
	Lisa Hunter, Capital		250,000
	Received initial investment from owner.		

Ledger Accounts:

Cash

Apr. 2 250,000	

Lisa Hunter, Capital

	Apr. 2 250,000

Don't forget! Use this to help with the analysis:

Assets		=	Liabilities		+	Owner, Capital		−	Owner, Withdrawals		+	Revenues		−	Expenses	
Dr	Cr		Dr	**Cr**		Dr	**Cr**		**Dr**	Cr		Dr	**Cr**		**Dr**	Cr
+	−		−	+		−	+		+	−		−	+		+	−

Transaction 2: Purchase of Land

Transaction:

On April 3, Hunter Environmental Consulting paid $100,000 cash for land as a future office location.

Analysis:

The purchase decreased cash; therefore, credit Cash. The purchase increased the entity's asset, land; to record this increase, debit Land.

Accounting Equation:

Assets				Liabilities	+	Owner's Equity
Cash	+	Land	=			
−100,000	+	100,000		0	+	0

This transaction increased one asset, land, and decreased another asset, cash. The net effect on the business's total assets was zero, and there was no effect on liabilities or owner's equity. We use the term *net* in business to mean an amount after a subtraction.

Journal Entry:

Debits are always shown first in a journal entry.

Apr. 3	Land	100,000	
	Cash		100,000
	Paid cash for land.		

Ledger Accounts:

Cash

Apr. 2 250,000	Apr. 3 100,000

Land

Apr. 3 100,000	

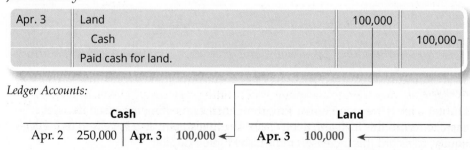

Transaction 3: Purchase of Office Supplies on Account

Transaction:

The business purchased office supplies for $7,000 on account, as shown by the purchase invoice dated April 3 on the next page.

Analysis:

The purchase of office supplies increased this asset, so we debit Office Supplies. The purchase was *on account,* so it also increased a liability; to record this increase, credit Accounts Payable.

Accounting Equation:

Assets		Liabilities	+	Owner's Equity
Office Supplies	=	**Accounts Payable**		
+ 7,000		+ 7,000	+	0

INVOICE (purchase)

WHOLESALE OFFICE SUPPLY
500 HENDERSON ROAD
VANCOUVER, BC

Date: April 3, 2019 — Invoice No: 9623
Terms: 30 days
Sold to: **Hunter Environmental Consulting**
281 Wave Avenue
Vancouver, BC V6R 9C8

Quantity	Item	Price	Total
580	Laser paper	$10	$5,800.00
80	Desk calendars	15	1,200.00
	Total amount due:		**$7,000.00**

Journal Entry:

Apr. 3	Office Supplies	7,000	
	Accounts Payable		7,000
	Purchased office supplies on account.		

Ledger Accounts:

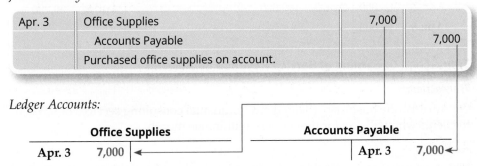

Office Supplies			
Apr. 3	7,000		

Accounts Payable			
		Apr. 3	7,000

Transaction 4: Earning of Service Revenue

Transaction:

The business provided environmental consulting services for clients and received $30,000 cash. The source document is Hunter Environmental Consulting's April 8 sales invoice shown here. There would also be a deposit slip like the one on page 67.

INVOICE (sale)

Hunter Environmental Consulting
281 Wave Avenue
Vancouver, BC V2R 9C8

Date:	April 8, 2019
Sold to:	**Allied Energy Corporation** **325 Brooks Street** **Vancouver, BC**
Invoice No:	**0001**
Service:	1000 DVD0503 service for all locations

PAID

Total amount due: $30,000

All accounts are due and payable within 30 days.

Analysis:

The asset, cash, is increased; therefore, debit Cash. The revenue account, service revenue, is increased; credit Service Revenue.

Accounting Equation:

Assets		Liabilities	+	Owner's Equity
Cash	=			Service Revenue
+30,000		0	+	30,000

Journal Entry:

Apr. 8	Cash	30,000	
	Service Revenue		30,000
	Performed service and received cash.		

Ledger Accounts:

Cash

Apr. 2	250,000	Apr. 3	100,000
Apr. 8	**30,000**		

Service Revenue

		Apr. 8	**30,000**

Transaction 5: Earning of Service Revenue on Account

Transaction:

On April 10, the business provided environmental consulting services of $25,000 to clients who will pay for the services within one month.

Analysis:

The asset, ACCOUNTS RECEIVABLE, is increased; therefore, debit Accounts Receivable. Service revenue is increased; credit Service Revenue.

Accounting Equation:

Assets		Liabilities	+	Owner's Equity
Accounts Receivable	=			Service Revenue
+ 25,000		0	+	25,000

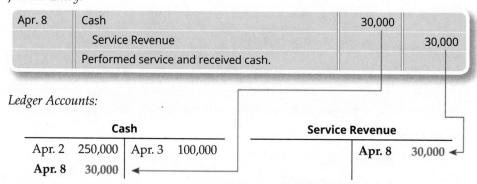

Journal Entry:

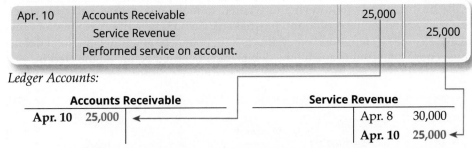

Apr. 10	Accounts Receivable	25,000	
	Service Revenue		25,000
	Performed service on account.		

Ledger Accounts:

Accounts Receivable

Apr. 10 25,000	

Service Revenue

	Apr. 8 30,000
	Apr. 10 25,000

Notice the differences and the similarities between Transactions 4 and 5. In both transactions, Service Revenue was increased because in both cases the company earned revenue. However, in Transaction 4 the company was paid at the time of service. In Transaction 5 the company will receive cash later (Accounts Receivable). The amount of earnings is not determined by when the company receives cash. Earnings (revenue) are recorded when the company does the work, or earns revenue.

Transactions 6, 7, 8: Payment of Expenses

Transactions:

On April 17, the business paid the following expenses: office rent, $4,000; employee salaries, $6,500; and utilities, $1,500. In practice, the business would record these three transactions separately when they are paid with separate cheques.

Analysis:

The asset cash is decreased; therefore, credit Cash for each of the three expense amounts. The following expenses are increased: Rent Expense, Salaries Expense, and Utilities Expense. Each should be debited for the appropriate amount.

Accounting Equation:

	Assets		Liabilities	+	Owner's Equity		
	Cash	=			Rent Expense	Salaries Expense	Utilities Expense
(6)	−4,000		0		−4,000		
(7)	−6,500		0			−6,500	
(8)	−1,500		0				−1,500

Journal Entry:

Apr. 17	Rent Expense	4,000	
	Cash		4,000
	Issued cheque to pay for office rent expense.		
Apr. 17	Salaries Expense	6,500	
	Cash		6,500
	Issued cheque to pay for employees' salaries.		
Apr. 17	Utilities Expense	1,500	
	Cash		1,500
	Issued cheque to pay for utilities.		

Ledger Accounts:

Cash

Apr. 2 250,000	Apr. 3 100,000
Apr. 8 30,000	**Apr. 17** 4,000
	Apr. 17 6,500
	Apr. 17 1,500

Rent Expense

Apr. 17 4,000	

Salaries Expense

Apr. 17 6,500	

Utilities Expense

Apr. 17 1,500	

Alternative journal entry:

If the business truly paid cash and wanted to make one journal entry to reflect this transaction then a **compound journal entry** would be written. No matter how many accounts a compound entry affects—there may be any number—total debits must equal total credits and all the debits must be listed before all the credits.

Apr. 17	Rent Expense	4,000	
	Salaries Expense	6,500	
	Utilities Expense	1,500	
	Cash		12,000
	Paid cash for expenses.		

Transaction 9: Payment on Account

Transaction:

The business paid $5,000 on the account payable created in Transaction 3. The cheque dated April 20 is Hunter Environmental Consulting's source document, or proof, for this transaction.

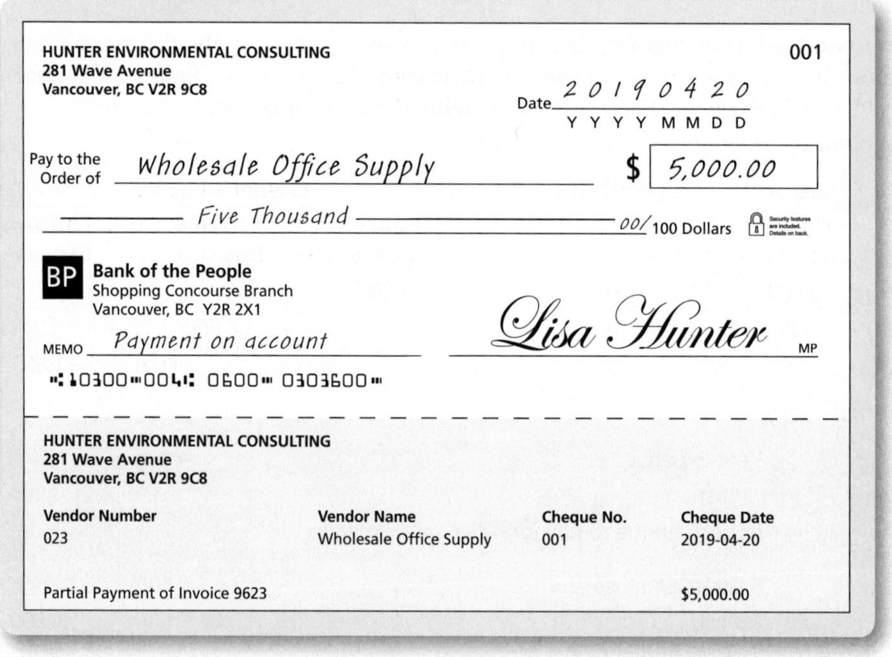
HUNTER ENVIRONMENTAL CONSULTING
281 Wave Avenue
Vancouver, BC V2R 9C8

001

Date 2 0 1 9 0 4 2 0
Y Y Y Y M M D D

Pay to the Order of Wholesale Office Supply $ 5,000.00

Five Thousand 00/100 Dollars

BP Bank of the People
Shopping Concourse Branch
Vancouver, BC Y2R 2X1

MEMO Payment on account

Lisa Hunter MP

HUNTER ENVIRONMENTAL CONSULTING
281 Wave Avenue
Vancouver, BC V2R 9C8

Vendor Number	Vendor Name	Cheque No.	Cheque Date
023	Wholesale Office Supply	001	2019-04-20

Partial Payment of Invoice 9623 $5,000.00

Analysis:

The payment decreased the asset cash; therefore, credit Cash. The payment also decreased the liability accounts payable, so we debit Accounts Payable.

Accounting Equation:

Assets		**Liabilities**	+	**Owner's Equity**
Cash	=	**Accounts Payable**		
−5,000		−5,000	+	0

Journal Entry:

Apr. 20	Accounts Payable	5,000	
	Cash		5,000
	Paid cash on account.		

Ledger Accounts:

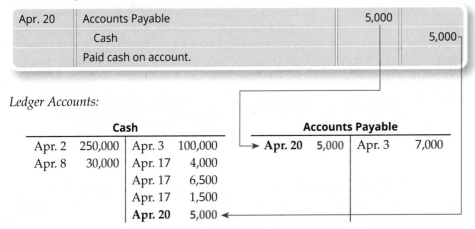

Cash

Apr. 2	250,000	Apr. 3	100,000
Apr. 8	30,000	Apr. 17	4,000
		Apr. 17	6,500
		Apr. 17	1,500
		Apr. 20	**5,000**

Accounts Payable

Apr. 20	**5,000**	Apr. 3	7,000

Transaction 10: Home Remodel Paid from Personal Funds

Transaction:

Lisa Hunter remodelled her personal residence with personal funds on April 25. This is not a business transaction of the environmental consulting business and the *economic entity assumption* tell us to not make a journal entry for it in the business.

Transaction 11: Collection on Account

Transaction:

On April 27, the business received $15,000 cash from one of the clients discussed in Transaction 5.

Analysis:

The asset cash is increased; therefore, debit Cash. The asset accounts receivable is decreased; therefore, credit Accounts Receivable. This transaction has no effect on revenue; the related revenue was accounted for in Transaction 5.

Accounting Equation:

Assets				Liabilities	+	Owner's Equity
Cash	+	**Accounts Receivable**	=			
+ 15,000	+	− 15,000		0	+	0

Journal Entry:

Apr. 27	Cash	15,000	
	Accounts Receivable		15,000
	Received cash on account.		

Ledger Accounts:

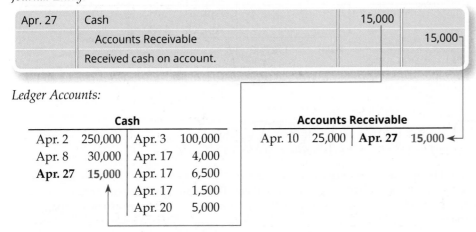

Cash

Apr. 2	250,000	Apr. 3	100,000
Apr. 8	30,000	Apr. 17	4,000
Apr. 27	**15,000**	Apr. 17	6,500
		Apr. 17	1,500
		Apr. 20	5,000

Accounts Receivable

Apr. 10	25,000	**Apr. 27**	**15,000**

Transaction 12: Withdrawing of Cash

Transaction:

Lisa Hunter withdrew $6,000 cash for personal living expenses on April 29.

This is an example of the *economic entity assumption*. The personal expenses of the owner are not reported as expenses for the business. At this point we record only the removal of cash.

Analysis:

The withdrawal decreased the entity's cash; therefore, credit Cash. The transaction also decreased the owner's equity of the entity. Decreases in the owner's equity of a proprietorship that result from owner withdrawals are debited to a separate owner's equity account entitled Withdrawals. Therefore, debit Lisa Hunter, Withdrawals.

Accounting Equation:

Assets		**Liabilities**	+	**Owner's Equity**
Cash	=			**Lisa Hunter, Withdrawals**
−6,000		0		−6,000

Journal Entry:

Apr. 29	Lisa Hunter, Withdrawals	6,000	
	Cash		6,000
	Withdrawal of cash by owner.		

Ledger Accounts:

Cash

Apr. 2	250,000	Apr. 3	100,000
Apr. 8	30,000	Apr. 17	4,000
Apr. 27	15,000	Apr. 17	6,500
		Apr. 17	1,500
		Apr. 20	5,000
		Apr. 29	6,000

Lisa Hunter, Withdrawals

Apr. 29	6,000		

T-Account Balances

Exhibit 2–10 shows the accounts of Hunter Environmental Consulting after posting. Each account has a balance that is the difference between the account's total debits and its total credits. We set a balance apart by a horizontal line. If an account has only one entry, you can total the account and label its balance, but you do not have to since the balance is obvious.

Cash #1100

Notice that the account number is sometimes included with the name.

(= 295,000)	Apr. 2	250,000	Apr. 3	100,000	(= 123,000)
	Apr. 8	30,000	Apr. 17	4,000	
	Apr. 27	15,000	Apr. 17	6,500	
			Apr. 17	1,500	
			Apr. 20	5,000	
			Apr. 29	6,000	
	Bal.	= 172,000			

The balance of the account is labelled Bal. to save space.

(= 295,000 − 123,000)

Why It's Done This Way

Companies record transactions, summarize them, and report them in a format that is recognizable to user groups and *communicates useful information* for them. The financial statements produced by a company are the end result of the accounting cycle. The starting point, as you have seen in this chapter, is to properly record transactions.

The first question that must be asked is whether the transaction represents a financial event that should be recorded in the company's ledger. If the answer to that question is yes, then we say it is *recognized*.

If the transaction is recognized, then we use the *elements* of the financial statements—the accounts—to record information in a way that is *understandable* to everyone.

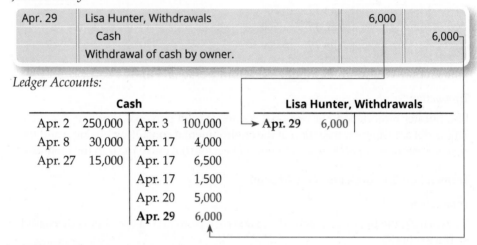

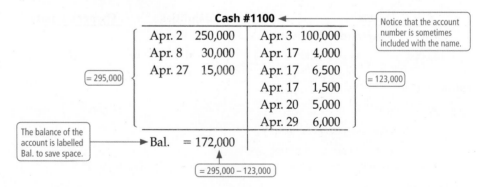

EXHIBIT 2–10 | Hunter Environmental Consulting's Ledger Accounts after Posting

Assets	=	Liabilities	+	Owner's Equity

Cash #1100

Apr. 2	250,000	Apr. 3	100,000
Apr. 8	30,000	Apr. 17	4,000
Apr. 27	15,000	Apr. 17	6,500
		Apr. 17	1,500
		Apr. 20	5,000
		Apr. 29	6,000
Bal.	172,000		

Accounts Receivable #1200

Apr.10	25,000	Apr. 27	15,000
Bal.	10,000		

Office Supplies #1400

Apr. 3	7,000		
Bal.	7,000		

Land #1900

Apr. 3	100,000		
Bal.	100,000		

Accounts Payable #2100

Apr. 20	5,000	Apr. 3	7,000
		Bal.	2,000

Lisa Hunter, Capital #3000

		Apr. 2	250,000
		Bal.	250,000

Lisa Hunter, Withdrawals #3100

Apr. 29	6,000		
Bal.	6,000		

REVENUE

Service Revenue #4000

		Apr. 8	30,000
		Apr. 10	25,000
		Bal.	55,000

EXPENSES

Rent Expense #5100

Apr. 17	4,000		
Bal.	4,000		

Salaries Expense #5200

Apr. 17	6,500		
Bal.	6,500		

Utilities Expense #5300

Apr. 17	1,500		
Bal.	1,500		

Try It!

6. Calculate the account balance for each of the following:

Supplies Expense

110	
290	
544	

Accounts Payable

150	400
800	2,900
475	1,600
	750

Cash

5,000	150
12,600	800
926	475
6,200	290

7. Compute the missing amount represented by *X* in each account:

(1) Cash

Bal.	10,000	13,000
	20,000	
Bal.	X	

(2) Accounts Payable

X	Bal. 12,800
	45,600
	Bal. 23,500

Solutions appear at the end of this chapter and on **MyLab Accounting**

Posting to the Three-Column Ledger

Posting means transferring information from the journal to the ledger accounts. We saw how to do this in Exhibit 2–9 using a T-account as the ledger. Exhibit 2–11, Panel B, presents the ledger in the **three-column format**. Each account has its own record in the ledger. Our example shows Hunter Environmental Consulting's accounts for Cash, Land, and Lisa Hunter, Capital and illustrates the system of cross-referencing used by accountants to find information and follow the "trail" of transactions for future reference.

EXHIBIT 2–11 | Posting to the Three Column Ledger

4 Enter the account number in the posting reference column of the journal once the figure has been posted to the ledger.

Panel A - The Journal — Page 1

Date	Account Titles and Explanations	Post. Ref.	Debit	Credit
2019				
Apr. 2	Cash	1100	250,000	
	Lisa Hunter, Capital	3000		250,000
	Received initial investment from owner.			
Apr. 3	Land	1900	100,000	
	Cash	1100		100,000
	Purchased land.			

1 Transfer the date of the transaction from the journal to the ledger.

Panel B - The Ledger

Account: Cash — **Account No. 1100**

Date	Item	Jrnl. Ref.	Debit	Credit	Balance
2019					
Apr. 2		J.1	250,000		250,000 Dr
Apr. 3		J.1		100,000	150,000 Dr

This is a running balance.

2 Transfer the page number from the journal to the journal reference column of the ledger. "J.1" signifies Journal Page 1.

3 Post the debit figure from the journal as a debit figure in the ledger account.

Account: Land — **Account No. 1900**

Date	Item	Jrnl. Ref.	Debit	Credit	Balance
2019					
Apr. 3		J.1	100,000		100,000 Dr

Account: Lisa Hunter, Capital — **Account No. 3000**

Date	Item	Jrnl. Ref.	Debit	Credit	Balance
2019					
Apr. 2		J.1		250,000	250,000 Cr

Do you see the T-account hiding in here?

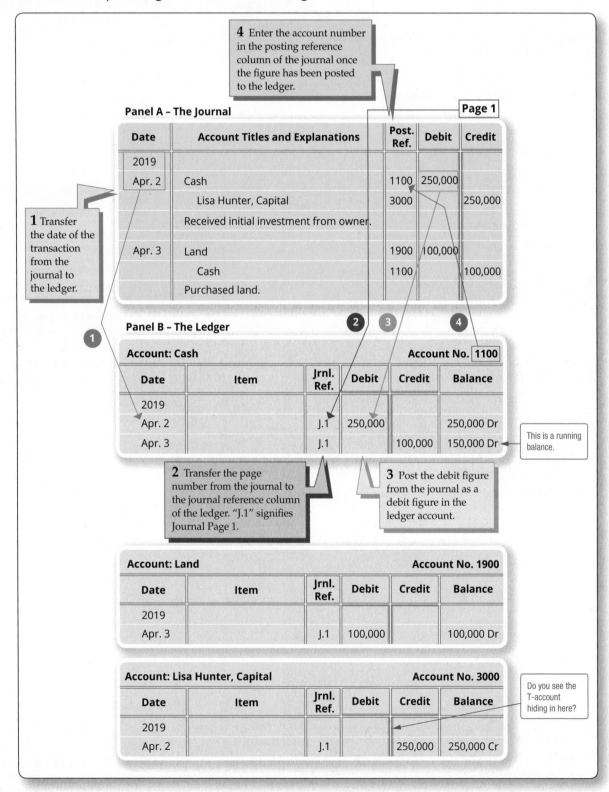

These are the steps to posting Hunter Environmental Consulting's first two transactions into a three-column ledger:

- ① The date is transferred from the journal to the ledger. Notice that the year appears directly under the Date heading at the top of each journal and ledger page or when the year has changed.
- The Item column in the ledger is often left blank because special notations are rarely used other than for an opening balance or a balance brought forward from a previous period.
- ② Each page in a journal is numbered at the top. Panel A shows this is journal page 1. In the ledger in Panel B, the Jrnl. Ref. column means Journal Reference. The short code *J.1* tells the reader that the information in this line comes from page 1 of the journal. In later chapters you will see other journals and cross-reference codes.
- ③ Post (copy) the debit amount in a journal entry to the debit column of the ledger. A credit amount will get copied to the credit column.
- ④ Now go back to the journal in Panel A and update the **posting reference**. The posting reference, abbreviated Post. Ref. (or sometimes PR) tells the reader in which ledger (and in which account in that ledger) the information was posted. The account number 1100 indicates that the $250,000 debit to Cash has been posted to the Cash account in the ledger. These account numbers come from the chart of accounts, which for Hunter, are shown in Exhibit 2–3 on page 60.
- The balance column in the ledger keeps a *running total* of the account balance. The balance can be followed by the letters Dr or Cr (indicating a debit or credit, respectively); however, this is not always required.

The Trial Balance

LO ⑤

How can we check if the records are in balance?

A *trial balance* summarizes the ledger by listing all accounts with their balances—assets first, followed by liabilities, and then owner's equity. Before computers, the trial balance provided an accuracy check by showing whether the total debits equalled the total credits. The trial balance is still useful as a summary of all the accounts and their balances. A trial balance may be created at any time the postings are up to date. The most common time is at the end of the accounting period. Exhibit 2–12 is the trial balance of Hunter Environmental Consulting at April 30, 2019, the end of the first month of operations before any adjustments are made. Therefore it is more accurately called the *unadjusted trial balance* at this stage. (Other trial balances will be introduced in later chapters.) The totals on this report came from the balances in Exhibit 2–10. Most trial balances include the account numbers from the chart of accounts. Accounts with zero balances typically are not listed on the trial balance.

The trial balance is a report and not a formal financial statement. For the purpose of this text we ask that you follow the same layout formatting as other financial statements to encourage neatness and consistency in reporting.

Correcting Trial Balance Errors

Throughout the accounting process, total debits should always equal total credits. If they are not equal, then accounting errors exist. Computerized accounting systems eliminate many errors because most software will not let you make a journal entry that doesn't balance. But computers cannot eliminate *all* errors because humans sometimes input the wrong data or input data to the wrong accounts.

If you are working with a manual system—such as in your course work—you might appreciate some strategies to help you figure out errors:

- Search the trial balance for a missing account. For example, suppose the accountant omitted Lisa Hunter, Withdrawals from the trial balance in Exhibit 2–12. Total debits would then be $301,000 ($307,000 − $6,000) and total credits would be $307,000, a difference of $6,000. Look through the ledger to see if all the accounts are listed in the trial balance and if they are showing the correct amounts.

EXHIBIT 2-12 | Trial Balance

Note:
Do not confuse the trial balance with the balance sheet. A trial balance is an internal document seen only by the company's owners, managers, and accountants. The trial balance is merely a step in the preparation of the financial statements. The balance sheet, on the other hand, is a financial statement used by other internal and external users.

HUNTER ENVIRONMENTAL CONSULTING Unadjusted Trial Balance April 30, 2019			
Account Number	**Account Title**	**Debit**	**Credit**
1100	Cash	$172,000	
1200	Accounts receivable	10,000	
1400	Office supplies	7,000	
1900	Land	100,000	
2100	Accounts payable		$ 2,000
3000	Lisa Hunter, capital		250,000
3100	Lisa Hunter, withdrawals	6,000	
4000	Service revenue		55,000
5100	Rent expense	4,000	
5200	Salaries expense	6,500	
5300	Utilities expense	1,500	
	Total	$307,000	$307,000

- Search the journal for the amount of the difference. For example, suppose the total credits on Hunter Environmental Consulting's trial balance equal $307,000 and total debits equal $306,000. A $1,000 transaction may have been posted incorrectly to the ledger by omitting the debit entry. Search the journal for a $1,000 transaction and check its posting to the ledger.
- Divide the difference between total debits and total credits by 2. A debit treated as a credit, or vice versa, doubles the amount of error. Suppose the accountant paid $1,000 cash for the utilities expenses. This transaction was recorded correctly in the journal but was posted as a debit to Cash and a debit to Utilities Expense. Thus, $2,000 appears on the debit side of the trial balance, and there is nothing on the credit side relating to this transaction. The out-of-balance amount is $2,000, and dividing by 2 reveals that the relevant transaction may have had a value of $1,000. Search the journal for a $1,000 transaction and check the posting to the ledger.
- Divide the out-of-balance amount by 9. If the result is evenly divisible by 9, the error may be a **slide**, which is adding or deleting one or several zeros in a figure (e.g., writing $61 as $610), or a **transposition** (e.g., treating $61 as $16). Suppose the accountant listed the $6,000 balance in Lisa Hunter, Withdrawals as $60,000 on the trial balance—a slide-type error. Total debits would differ from total credits by $54,000 (i.e., $60,000 − $6,000 = $54,000). Dividing $54,000 by 9 yields $6,000, the correct amount of the withdrawals. Trace this amount through the ledger until you reach the Lisa Hunter, Withdrawals account with a balance of $6,000. Dividing by 9 can give the correct transaction amount for a slide but not for a transposition.

Try It!

8. Using the following accounts and their balances, prepare the unadjusted trial balance for Cooper Furniture Repair as of December 31, 2018. All accounts have normal balances.

Cash	$ 7,000	Advertising Expense	$ 1,200
Unearned Revenue	4,500	Utilities Expense	800
Equipment	10,000	Rent Expense	5,000
Service Revenue	8,000	Accounts Payable	2,300
M. Cooper, Capital	12,200	M. Cooper, Withdrawals	3,000

Solutions appear at the end of this chapter and on **MyLab Accounting**

Summary Problem for Your Review

The unadjusted trial balance of Wawa Cottage Management Services on March 1, 2019, lists the company's assets, liabilities, and owner's equity on that date.

WAWA COTTAGE MANAGEMENT SERVICES Unadjusted Trial Balance March 1, 2019			
Account Number	**Account Title**	**Debit**	**Credit**
1100	Cash	$26,000	
1200	Accounts receivable	4,500	
2100	Accounts payable		$ 2,000
3100	Lenni Champlain, capital		28,500
	Total	$30,500	$30,500

During March the business engaged in the following transactions:

Mar.	3	Borrowed $45,000 from the bank and signed a note payable in the name of the business.
	5	Paid cash of $40,000 to a real estate company to acquire land worth $10,000 and a building worth $30,000 just north of the town of Wawa. Use a compound journal entry to record this transaction.
	11	Performed services for a customer and received cash of $5,000.
	12	Purchased supplies on account, $300.
	14	Performed services for a customer and earned revenue on account, $2,600.
	17	Paid $1,200 of the Accounts Payable balance shown on the March 1, 2019, unadjusted trial balance.
	19	Paid the following cash expenses: salaries, $3,000; rent, $1,500; and interest, $400.
	20	Received $3,100 of the Accounts Receivable balance shown on the March 1, 2019, trial balance.
	24	Received a $200 utility bill that will be paid next week.
	28	Lenni Champlain withdrew $1,800 for personal use.

Required

1. Open the accounts and balances shown in the unadjusted trial balance in the ledger of Wawa Cottage Management Services. Use the three-column ledger format. Also set up the following accounts and numbers with no balances:

Supplies, #1400	Service Revenue, #4000
Land, #1900	Interest Expense, #5100
Building, #1905	Rent Expense, #5200
Note Payable, #2300	Salaries Expense, #5300
Lenni Champlain, Withdrawals, #3100	Utilities Expense, #5400

2. Journalize the preceding transactions on page 2 of the journal.
3. Post the transactions to the ledger.
4. Prepare the unadjusted trial balance of Wawa Cottage Management Services at March 31, 2019.

Prepare a ledger account for each account name. Place the opening balance in the ledger account, remembering that the normal balance is a debit for asset and expense accounts and a credit for liability, equity, and revenue accounts.

Refer to the rules of debit and credit shown in Exhibit 2–7 on page 64.

(3) Analyze and record transactions in the journal **Pg. 64**

How do we record business transactions?

- The accountant begins the recording process by analyzing the transaction, deciding if it is a transaction, and then entering the transaction's information in the *journal*, a chronological list of all the entity's transactions.

Date	Account Titles and Explanation	Debit	Credit
Date	Debit account name	Amount	
	Indent the credit account name		Amount
	Explanation of transaction		

(4) Post from the journal to the ledger **Pg. 66**

What is the next step after recording the transaction?

- *Posting* means transferring information from the journal to the *ledger* accounts. We often use T-accounts as a shortcut to represent ledgers in this text. Posting references are used to trace amounts back and forth between the journal and the ledger.

(5) Prepare and use a trial balance **Pg. 77**

How can we check if the records are in balance?

- The *trial balance* is a summary of all the non-zero account balances in the ledger. When *double-entry accounting* has been done correctly, the total debits and the total credits in the trial balance are equal.

Key Terms for the chapter are shown next and are in the **Glossary** at the back of the book. **Similar Terms** are shown after **Key Terms**.

KEY TERMS

Accounting cycle The process by which accountants produce an entity's financial statements and update the financial reports for a period of time *(p. 58).*

Accounting period The time frame, or period of time, covered by financial statements and other reports *(p. 58).*

Bank cheque A document that instructs the bank to pay the designated person or business the specified amount of money *(p. 64).*

Bank deposit slip A document that shows the amount of cash deposited into a person's or business's bank account *(p. 64).*

Chart of accounts A list of all the accounts and their account numbers in the ledger *(p. 59).*

Compound journal entry A journal entry with more than one debit and credit *(p. 72).*

Credit The right side of an account *(p. 61).*

Debit The left side of an account *(p. 61).*

Journal The chronological accounting record of an entity's transactions *(p. 59).*

Ledger The book (or printout) of accounts *(p. 59).*

Normal balance The balance that appears on the side of an account—debit or credit—where we record increases *(p. 63).*

Overdraw To remove more money from a bank account than exists in the bank account. This puts the bank account into a negative balance. This becomes a loan from the bank *(p. 63).*

Posting Transferring of amounts from the journal to the ledger *(p. 66).*

Posting reference A column in the journal that indicates to the reader to which account the journal entry has been posted *(p. 77).*

Purchase invoice A document from a vendor that shows a customer what was purchased, when it was purchased, and how much it cost *(p. 64).*

Sales invoice A seller's request for cash from the purchaser. This document gives the seller the amount of revenue to record *(p. 64).*

Slide A type of error in which one or several zeros are added or deleted in a figure; for example, writing $30 as $300 *(p. 78).*

Source document A document that is evidence of a transaction, such as an invoice *(p. 64).*

Three-column format One common type of ledger format that includes three columns for dollar amounts—one for debit amounts, one for credit amounts, and the other for a running balance *(p. 76).*

Transposition A type of error in which two digits in a number are shown in reverse order *(p. 78).*

Trial balance A list of all the ledger accounts with their balances *(p. 59).*

SIMILAR TERMS

Cr	Credit; right
Dr	Debit; left
Entering the transaction in a journal	Making the journal entry; journalizing the transaction
J.1	page 1 of the journal
Jrnl. Ref.	Journal reference
Open the accounts	Set up the accounts; create the ledger accounts
Post. Ref.	Posting reference
P.R.	Posting reference

SELF-STUDY QUESTIONS

Test your understanding of the chapter by marking the correct answer for each of the following questions:

1. Which sequence correctly summarizes the accounting process? *(p. 58)*
   a. Journalize transactions, post to the accounts, prepare a trial balance
   b. Journalize transactions, prepare a trial balance, post to the accounts
   c. Post to the accounts, journalize transactions, prepare a trial balance
   d. Prepare a trial balance, journalize transactions, post to the accounts
2. The detailed record of the changes in a particular asset, liability, or owner's equity is called *(p. 61)*
   a. An account
   b. A journal
   c. A ledger
   d. A trial balance
3. A T-account has two sides, called the *(p. 61)*
   a. Debit and credit
   b. Asset and liability
   c. Revenue and expense
   d. Journal and ledger
4. Increases in liabilities are recorded by *(p. 61)*
   a. Debits
   b. Credits
5. Why do accountants record transactions in the journal? *(p. 64)*
   a. To ensure that all transactions are posted to the ledger
   b. To ensure that total debits equal total credits
   c. To have a chronological record of all transactions
   d. To help prepare the financial statements
6. Posting is the process of transferring information from the *(p. 66)*
   a. Journal to the trial balance
   b. Ledger to the trial balance
   c. Ledger to the financial statements
   d. Journal to the ledger
7. The purchase of land for cash is recorded by a *(p. 68)*
   a. Debit to Cash and a credit to Land
   b. Debit to Cash and a debit to Land
   c. Debit to Land and a credit to Cash
   d. Credit to Cash and a credit to Land
8. Simpson Transport earned revenue on account. The earning of revenue on account is recorded by a *(p. 70)*
   a. Debit to Cash and a credit to Revenue
   b. Debit to Accounts Receivable and a credit to Revenue
   c. Debit to Accounts Payable and a credit to Revenue
   d. Debit to Revenue and a credit to Accounts Receivable
9. The account credited for a receipt of cash on account is *(p. 73)*
   a. Cash
   b. Accounts Payable
   c. Service Revenue
   d. Accounts Receivable
10. The purpose of the trial balance is to *(p. 77)*
    a. List all accounts with their balances
    b. Ensure that all transactions have been recorded
    c. Speed up the collection of cash receipts from customers
    d. Increase assets and owner's equity

Answers to Self-Study Questions

1. a 2. a 3. a 4. b 5. c 6. d 7. c 8. d 9. a 10. b

Assignment Material

MyLab Accounting Make the grade with MyLab Accounting: The Starters, Exercises, and Problems can be found on MyLab. You can practise them as often as you want, and most feature step-by-step guided instructions to help you find the right answer.

QUESTIONS

1. Is the following statement true or false? Debit means decrease and credit means increase. Explain your answer.
2. Explain the rules of debits and credits for each type of account.
3. What are the three basic types of accounts? Name two additional types of accounts. To which one of the three basic types are these two additional types of accounts most closely related?
4. Suppose you are the accountant for Whistler Marketing Enterprises. Keeping in mind double-entry bookkeeping, identify the *dual effects* of Sasha Chandler's investment of $10,000 cash in her business.
5. Briefly describe the flow of accounting information using the accounting cycle.
6. To what does the *normal balance* of an account refer?
7. Indicate the normal balance of the five types of accounts.

Account Type	**Normal Balance**
Assets	________
Liabilities	________
Owner's equity	________
Revenues	________
Expenses	________

8. What does posting accomplish? Why is it important? Does it come before or after journalizing?
9. Label each of the following transactions as increasing owner's equity (+), decreasing owner's equity (−), or having no effect on owner's equity (0). Write the appropriate symbol in the space provided.
   a. ______ Investment by owner
   b. ______ Invoice customer for services
   c. ______ Purchase of supplies on credit
   d. ______ Pay expenses with cash
   e. ______ Cash payment on account
   f. ______ Withdrawal of cash by owner
   g. ______ Borrowing money on a note payable
   h. ______ Sale of services on account
10. What four steps does the posting process include? Which step is the fundamental purpose of posting?
11. Rearrange the following accounts in their logical sequence in the chart of accounts:

Note Payable	Salaries Expense
Accounts Receivable	Cash
Sales Revenue	Sam Westman, Capital

12. What is the meaning of the statement "Accounts Payable has a credit balance of $2,800"?
13. Spiffy Cleaners launders the shirts of customer Bobby Ng, who has a charge account at the cleaners. When Ng picks up his clothes and is short of cash, he charges it. Later, when he receives his monthly statement from the cleaners, Ng writes a cheque on his bank account and mails the cheque to the cleaners. Identify the two business transactions described here for Spiffy Cleaners. Which transaction increases the business's owner's equity? Which transaction increases Spiffy Cleaners's cash?
14. Explain the difference between the ledger and the chart of accounts.
15. Why do accountants prepare a trial balance?
16. What is a compound journal entry?
17. What is the difference between the trial balance and the balance sheet?
18. The accountant for Wingers Construction mistakenly recorded a $600 purchase of supplies on account as $6,000. He debited Supplies and credited Accounts Payable for $6,000. Does this error cause the trial balance to be out of balance? Explain your answer.
19. What is the effect on total assets of collecting cash on account from customers?
20. If total debits equals total credits on the trial balance, is the trial balance error free? Explain your answer.

STARTERS

S2–1 Put the steps in the accounting cycle in the proper sequence by inserting the numbers 1 to 11.

(1) The accounting cycle

a. Prepare a post-closing trial balance ________
b. Prepare an adjusted trial balance ________
c. Identify and analyze the transaction ________
d. Prepare the unadjusted trial balance ________
e. Post adjusting journal entries to the ledger ________
f. Post from the journal to the ledger accounts ________
g. Journalize adjusting journal entries ________
h. Journalize closing entries ________
i. Prepare financial statements ________
j. Post closing entries to the ledger ________
k. Record transaction in a journal ________

S2–2 Fill in the blanks to review some key definitions.

(1) Using accounting terms

Josh Stone is describing the accounting process to a friend who is a philosophy major. Josh states, "The basic summary device in accounting is the _____. The left side is called the _____ side, and the right side is called the ___ side. We record transactions first in a _____. Then we post (copy the data) to the _____. It is helpful to list all the accounts with their balances on a _____."

S2–3 Accounting has its own vocabulary and basic relationships. Match the accounting terms at left with the corresponding definitions at right.

(1) Using accounting terms

_____	1. Credit	a. Record of transactions
_____	2. Normal balance	b. Always an asset
_____	3. Payable	c. Right side of an account
_____	4. Journal	d. Side of an account where increases are recorded
_____	5. Receivable	e. Copying data from the journal to the ledger
_____	6. Capital	f. Increases in equity from providing goods and services
_____	7. Posting	g. Always a liability
_____	8. Revenue	h. Revenues – Expenses (where expenses exceed revenues)
_____	9. Net loss	i. Grouping of accounts
_____	10. Ledger	j. Owner's equity in the business

S2–4 For each of the following changes, indicate whether a debit or credit entry would be made to the balance sheet account:

(2) Explaining the rules of debit and credit

a. To decrease Accounts Payable
b. To increase Cash
c. To increase Note Payable
d. To increase Office Supplies
e. To increase Equipment
f. To increase Accounts Payable
g. To increase Land
h. To increase Owner, Capital

S2–5 For each of the following accounts, identify whether the normal balance is a debit or a credit:

(2) Normal balances

a. Accounts Payable
b. J. Yuen, Withdrawals
c. Utilities Expense
d. Cash
e. Service Revenue
f. Rent Expense
g. Accounts Receivable

② Identifying accounts

S2-6 State the account to be debited and the account to be credited for the following transactions. Choose from the following list of accounts: Cash, Accounts Receivable, Supplies, Equipment, Land, Accounts Payable, Note Payable, Capital, Withdrawals, Service Revenue, Utilities Expense, and Salaries Expense.

(Hint: Not all accounts will be used.)

	Debit	Credit
a. Owner invests cash into the business.	________	________
b. Purchased supplies for cash.	________	________
c. Performed services for cash.	________	________
d. Purchased equipment by issuing a note payable.	________	________
e. Purchased supplies on account.	________	________
f. Performed services on account.	________	________
g. Received cash on account.	________	________
h. Paid a creditor on account.	________	________

③ Recording transactions

S2-7 Jonathan Wen started a business to offer development of online stores for small businesses. Record the following transactions in the journal of the business. Include an explanation with each journal entry.

Sep.	1	Wen invested $29,000 cash in a business bank account to start his business. The business received the cash and gave Wen owner's equity in the business.
	2	Purchased computer equipment on account, $9,500.
	2	Paid cash for September's office rent of $4,100.
	3	Recorded $6,800 revenue for services rendered to clients on account.

③ Recording transactions

S2-8 After operating for a couple of weeks, Jonathan Wen's business completed the following transactions during the latter part of September:

Sep.	22	Performed service for clients on account, $6,000.
	30	Received cash on account from clients, $4,500.
	30	Received an Internet bill, $150, which will be paid during November.
	30	Paid cash for advertising expense of $900.
	30	Paid cash for monthly salary to his assistant, $3,900.

Journalize the business transactions. Include an explanation with each journal entry.

④ Posting to accounts and calculating balances

S2-9 Your co-worker wanted the afternoon off and you graciously agreed to finish up his work for him. Use the completed journal entries provided and post them to their T-accounts. Assume all accounts start with a zero balance. Compute the balance of each account and mark it as *Bal.*

Journal

Date	Account Titles and Explanations	Post. Ref.	Debit	Credit
Apr. 1	Cash		32,000	
	Jatin Singh, Capital			32,000
	Received investment from owner.			
2	Medical Supplies		9,500	
	Accounts Payable			9,500
	Purchased supplies on account.			
2	Rent Expense		2,900	
	Cash			2,900
	Paid office rent for April.			
3	Cash		6,800	
	Service Revenue			6,800
	Performed service for cash.			
5	Accounts Payable		2,700	
	Cash			2,700
	Partial payment of balance on account.			

S2-10 Nancy Carpenter Optical Dispensary bought supplies on account for $10,000 on September 8. On September 22, the company paid $4,000 on account.

(3)(4) Journalizing transactions; posting to T-accounts

1. Journalize the two transactions for Nancy Carpenter Optical Dispensary. Include an explanation for each transaction.
2. Open the Accounts Payable T-account and post to Accounts Payable. Compute the balance and denote it as *Bal.*

S2-11 On October 5, Tina Serelio performed legal services for a client who could not pay immediately. The business expected to collect the $12,000 the following month. On November 4, the business received $5,500 cash from the client.

(3)(4) Journalizing transactions; posting to T-accounts

3. a. Earned $12,000

1. Record the two transactions for Tina Serelio, Lawyer. Include an explanation for each transaction.
2. Open these T-accounts: Cash; Accounts Receivable; Service Revenue. Post to all three accounts. Compute each account's balance and denote it as *Bal.*
3. Answer these questions based on your analysis:
   a. How much did the business earn? Which account shows this amount?
   b. How much in total assets did the business acquire as a result of the two transactions? Identify each asset and show its amount.

S2-12 Calculate the account balance for each of the following T-accounts:

(4) Calculate T-account balances

Accounts Receivable

2,700	2,700
5,800	1,100
4,900	850
	4,090

Cash

67,500	4,200
16,800	12,300

Accounts Payable

1,100	4,800
	700

S2-13 Compute the missing amount represented by X in each account:

(4) Find missing amounts

R. Glennie, Capital

22,000	Bal.	X
		56,000
		15,000
	Bal.	73,000

Accounts Receivable

Bal.	21,800	X
	55,100	
Bal.	47,000	

S2-14 Use the information shown below to prepare the unadjusted trial balance for Balzy Indoor Tennis Club at November 30, 2020. Include the account number in the trial balance.

(4)(5) Preparing a trial balance from T-accounts

Total, $36,240

Balzy Indoor Tennis Club
General Ledger

Cash 10002

5,000	150
12,600	800
955	475
6,200	290

Furniture 17500

5,500	

Accounts Payable 20001

3,000	9,640
3,000	100

Stan Balzy, Capital 30001

	27,000

Stan Balzy, Withdrawals 30002

1,200	

Sales Revenue 40001

	5,500

Supplies Expense 51200

2,500	

Rent Expense 53200

4,000	

5
Preparing a trial balance
Trial bal. total, $75,000

S2–15 A+ Roofers reported the following summarized data at December 31, 2020. Accounts appear in no particular order.

Revenue	$32,000	Note Payable	$17,000
Equipment	43,000	Cash	6,000
Accounts Payable	1,000	Expenses	26,000
Capital	25,000		

Prepare the unadjusted trial balance of A+ Roofers at December 31, 2020. List the accounts in proper order, as in Exhibit 2–12.

5
Finding errors
Equipment is wrong amount

S2–16 Suppose you are told that the following incorrect trial balance contains a *slide*—where someone accidentally listed one of the account balances wrong. How would you go about finding the error? What should be corrected?

SHINY FLOOR CLEANING
Incorrect Trial Balance
December 31, 2019

Account Title	Debit	Credit
Cash	$13,000	
Accounts receivable	12,500	
Supplies	7,500	
Equipment	200	
Accounts payable		$ 1,000
S. Shaw, capital		15,000
S. Shaw, withdrawals	5,000	
Cleaning revenue		30,000
Supplies expense	6,000	
Total	$44,200	$46,000

5
Correcting a trial balance
Incorrect trial bal. total debits, $557,000

S2–17 Hunter Environmental Consulting prepared its unadjusted trial balance on page 78. Suppose Lisa Hunter made an error: She listed the Capital balance of $250,000 as a debit rather than a credit by mistake.

Compute the incorrect trial balance totals for debits and credits. Then refer to the discussion of correcting errors on pages 77 and 78 and show how to correct this error.

EXERCISES

1
Using accounting vocabulary

E2–1 Your employer, Prairie Tours, has just hired an office manager who does not understand accounting. The Prairie Tours unadjusted trial balance lists Cash of $57,800. Write a short memo to the office manager explaining the accounting process that produced this listing on the trial balance. Mention *debits, credits, journal, ledger, posting,* and *trial balance.*

1
Using accounting vocabulary

E2–2 Review accounting terms by completing the following crossword puzzle.

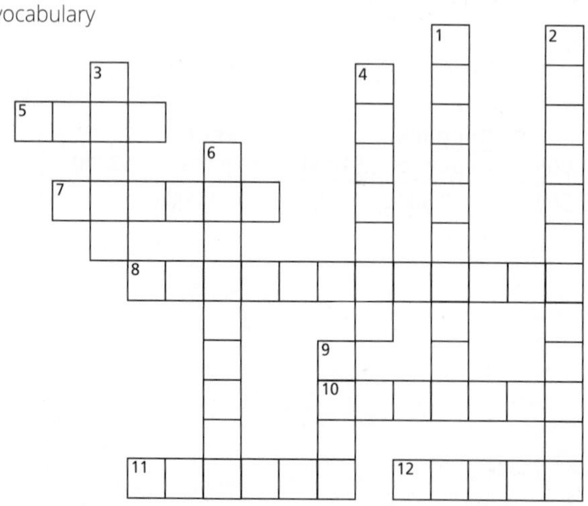

Across:
5. Copy data from the journal to the ledger
7. Book of accounts
8. List of accounts with their balances
10. Revenue – net income
11. Records an increase in a liability
12. Left side of an account

Down:
1. Amount collectible from a customer
2. Statement of financial position
3. An economic resource
4. Record of transactions
6. "Bottom line" of an income statement
9. Another word for liability

E2–3 Indicate whether each account listed below is a(n) asset (A), liability (L), owner's equity (OE), revenue (R), or expense (E) account.

(2) Accounts and normal balances

Salaries Payable	_____	Salaries Expense	_____
Land	_____	Rent Revenue	_____
L. Graham, Capital	_____	Computer Equipment	_____
Rent Expense	_____	Note Payable	_____
Supplies	_____	Prepaid Rent	_____
Accounts Payable	_____	L. Graham, Withdrawals	_____

E2–4 Refer to the Summary Problem for Your Review, specifically the unadjusted trial balance on page 83.

(1)(2) Using debits and credits with the accounting equation

2. Net income, $2,500

Required

1. Write the company's accounting equation and label each element as a debit amount or a credit amount. If you use $28,500 for the owner's equity, why is the accounting equation out of balance?
2. Write the equation to compute Wawa Cottage Management Services's net income or net loss for March 2019. Indicate which element is a debit amount and which element is a credit amount. Does net income represent a net debit or a net credit? Does net loss represent a net debit or a net credit?
3. How much did the owner, Lenni Champlain, withdraw during March 2019? Did the withdrawal represent a debit amount or a credit amount?
4. Considering both the net income (or net loss) and withdrawal for March 2019, by how much did the company's owner's equity increase or decrease? Was the change in owner's equity a debit amount or a credit amount?

E2–5 Indicate whether each account listed below is a(n) asset (A), liability (L), owner's equity (OE), revenue (R), or expense (E) account. Next to each answer, indicate whether the account's normal balance is a debit (Dr) or a credit (Cr).

(2) Accounts and normal balances

Accounts Payable	_____; _____	Cash	_____; _____
Service Revenue	_____; _____	Rent Expense	_____; _____
K. Lockyer, Withdrawals	_____; _____	Vehicles	_____; _____
Rent Revenue	_____; _____	Note Payable	_____; _____
Accounts Receivable	_____; _____	Land	_____; _____
Insurance Expense	_____; _____	K. Lockyer, Capital	_____; _____

E2–6 a. Indicate on which side of these accounts—debit (Dr) or credit (Cr)—you would record an increase.

(2) Normal balances

________	Accounts Receivable	________	Salaries Expense
________	John Ladner, Capital	________	Interest Payable
________	Service Revenue	________	Furniture

b. Indicate on which side of these accounts—debit (Dr) or credit (Cr)—you would record a decrease.

________	Note Payable	________	Land
________	Cash	________	Accounts Payable
________	Income Tax Payable	________	Income Tax Expense

(2)(3) Analyzing and journalizing transactions

E2–7 The following transactions occurred for Anderson Moving Company:

Jul.	2	Received $10,000 contribution from Bill Anderson in exchange for capital.
	4	Paid utilities expense of $400.
	5	Purchased equipment on account for $2,100.
	10	Performed services for a client on account, $2,000.
	12	Borrowed $7,000 cash, signing a note payable.
	19	The owner, Bill Anderson, withdrew $500 cash from the business.
	21	Purchased office supplies for $800 and paid cash.
	27	Paid the liability from July 5.

Required Journalize the transactions of Anderson Moving Company. Include an explanation with each journal entry. Use the following accounts: Cash; Accounts Receivable; Office Supplies; Equipment; Accounts Payable; Note Payable; B. Anderson, Capital; B. Anderson, Withdrawals; Service Revenue; Utilities Expense.

(2)(3) Analyzing and journalizing transactions

E2–8 Analyze the following transactions of Pretty Party Planners in the manner shown for the December 1 transaction. Also, record each transaction in the journal.

Dec. 1 Paid monthly utilities expense of $200.
(Analysis: The expense, utilities expense, is increased; therefore, debit Utilities Expense. The asset, cash, is decreased; therefore, credit Cash.)

Dec. 1	Utilities Expense	200	
	Cash		200

Dec.	4	Borrowed $20,000 cash, signing a note payable.
	8	Purchased equipment on account, $4,000.
	12	Performed service on account for a customer, $6,000.
	19	Sold land for $24,000 cash that had cost this same amount.
	22	Purchased supplies for $1,200 and paid cash.
	27	Paid the liability created on December 8.

(3) Journalizing transactions

E2–9 Yula's Yoga engaged in the following transactions during March 2020, its first month of operations:

Mar.	1	The business received a $15,000 cash investment from Yula Gregore to start Yula's Yoga.
	1	Paid $4,000 cash to rent a yoga studio for the month of March.
	4	Purchased studio supplies for $4,000 on account.
	6	Presented a wellness seminar for a corporate customer and received cash, $3,000.
	9	Paid $1,000 on accounts payable.
	17	Taught yoga classes for customers on account, $800.

Required Record the preceding transactions in the journal of Yula's Yoga. Identify transactions by their date and include an explanation for each entry, as illustrated in the chapter. Use the following accounts: Cash; Accounts Receivable; Studio Supplies; Accounts Payable; Yula Gregore, Capital; Service Revenue; Rent Expense.

(3) Journalize transactions

E2–10 Journalize the following transactions for Deresh DJ Services:

May	3	Owner, Liam Deresh, invested $2,500 cash into the business.
	4	Rented a sound system and paid one month's rent, $1,100.
	6	Performed DJ services on account, $1,700.
	11	Paid $600 cash for equipment.
	14	Owner, Liam Deresh, withdrew $500 cash for personal use.
	18	Purchased $40 of supplies for cash.

E2–11 The first five transactions of Lin's Tai Chi Retreat have been posted to the company's accounts as shown here:

③ Journalizing transactions

Cash

(1)	7,500	(3)	5,250
(4)	1,375	(5)	1,500

Supplies

(2)	275		

Exercise Equipment

(5)	1,500		

Land

(3)	5,250		

Accounts Payable

		(2)	275

Note Payable

		(4)	1,375

S. Lin, Capital

		(1)	7,500

Required Prepare the journal entries that served as the sources for posting the five transactions. Date each entry April 30, 2020, and include an explanation for each entry as illustrated in the chapter.

E2–12 The journal of Anisah's Baking School for July 2019 is shown below:

③④ Describing transactions, posting using T-accounts

3. Accounts Payable total, $564

Journal — **Page 5**

Date	Account Titles and Explanations	Post. Ref.	Debit	Credit
Jul. 2	Cash		5,600	
	Anisah Kaur, Capital			5,600
3	Rent Expense		1,400	
	Cash			1,400
9	Baking Supplies		54	
	Accounts Payable			54
11	Accounts Receivable		1,620	
	Service Revenue			1,620
22	Cash		280	
	Accounts Receivable			280
25	Advertising Expense		590	
	Cash			590
27	Accounts Payable		54	
	Cash			54
31	Utilities Expense		564	
	Accounts Payable			564

Required

1. Describe each transaction.
2. Set up T-accounts using the following account numbers: Cash, #1000; Accounts Receivable, #1200; Baking Supplies, #1400; Accounts Payable, #2000; Anisah Kaur, Capital, #3000; Service Revenue, #4000; Advertising Expense, #5100; Rent Expense, #5600; Utilities Expense, #5800. This is the first month of business so all opening balances are zero.
3. Post to the T-accounts. Identify each transaction by date. You may write the account numbers as posting references directly in the journal in your book unless directed otherwise by your instructor. Compute the balance in each account after posting.

E2–13 On July 2, 2020, Efficient Energy Services performed an energy audit for an industrial client and earned $4,000 of revenue on account. On July 14, 2020, the company received a cheque for the entire amount.

③④ Practise using a three-column ledger

Required

1. Journalize the two transactions on the sixth page of the journal. Include an explanation for each transaction.
2. Create the Accounts Receivable three-column ledger and post the two transactions. The account number for Accounts Receivable is 12001.

③ ④
Journalize and post to two-column ledger
Total debits, $45,000

E2–14 Peterson Engineering engaged in the following September transactions.

Sep.	1	Paid monthly utilities expense of $140.
	4	Borrowed $10,000 cash, signing a note payable.
	8	Performed service on account for a customer, $3,000.
	12	Purchased equipment on account, $2,000.
	24	Purchased supplies for $600 and paid cash.
	27	Paid the liability created on September 12.

Required

1. Prepare journal entries for the transactions in page 18 of the journal. Include an explanation for each transaction.
2. Open T-accounts with the following September 1 balances: Cash #101, debit balance $3,000; Accounts Receivable #103, $0; Supplies #105, $0; Equipment #107, $0; Land #110, debit balance $29,000; Accounts Payable #201, $0; Note Payable #205, $0; R. Peterson, Capital #301, credit balance $32,000; Service Revenue #401, $0; Utilities Expense #501, $0.
3. Post the transactions to T-accounts and compute the account balances.
4. Add the balances to prove that total debits equal total credits.

③ ④
Journalizing and posting transactions to a three-column ledger

E2–15 Open the following three-column ledger accounts for Yarrow Strategic Consulting at May 1, 2020: Cash, #1100; Accounts Receivable, #1300; Office Supplies, #1500; Office Furniture, #1800; Accounts Payable, #2100; Florence Yarrow, Capital, #3100; Florence Yarrow, Withdrawals, #3200; Consulting Revenue, #4100; Rent Expense, #5500; Salaries Expense, #5600.

Journalize the following May 2020 transactions on the ninth page of the journal, then post to the ledger accounts. Use the dates to identify the transactions.

May	2	Florence Yarrow opened a strategic consulting firm by investing $39,200 cash and office furniture valued at $16,200.
	2	Paid cash for May's rent of $2,500.
	2	Purchased office supplies on account, $1,800.
	15	Paid employee salary, $4,000 cash.
	17	Paid $1,200 of the account payable from May 2.
	19	Performed consulting service on account, $69,000.
	30	Withdrew $8,000 cash for personal use.

④ ⑤
Posting transactions using T-accounts, preparing a trial balance
2. Trial bal. total, $21,800

E2–16 Refer to E2-9 for the transactions of Yula's Yoga.

Required

1. After journalizing the transactions of E2-9, post the entries to T-accounts. Identify transactions by their date. Date the ending balance of each account Mar. 31.
2. Prepare the unadjusted trial balance of Yula's Yoga at March 31, 2020.

⑤
Preparing a trial balance
Trial bal. total, $46,000

E2–17 Honey Bee Apiary is a leading consulting business that specializes in teaching farmers how to raise bees. Their accounting records reported the following data on December 31, 2019. Accounts appear in no particular order.

Supplies	$ 7,500	S. Shaw, Withdrawals	$ 5,000
Equipment	2,000	Cash	13,000
Accounts Payable	1,000	Supplies Expense	6,000
S. Shaw, Capital	15,000	Accounts Receivable	12,500
Consulting Revenue	30,000		

Prepare the unadjusted trial balance of Honey Bee Apiary at December 31, 2019. List the accounts in the order shown in Exhibit 2–12.

E2–18 The accounts of Boots Consulting are listed below with their normal balances at October 31, 2020. The accounts are listed in no particular order.

(5) Preparing a trial balance
Trial bal. total, $720,600

Account	Balance
M. Boots, capital	$252,800
Advertising expense	9,900
Accounts payable	33,800
Service revenue	164,000
Land	174,000
Note payable	270,000
Cash	30,000
Salaries expense	36,000
Building	390,000
Computer rental expense	2,000
M. Boots, withdrawals	36,000
Utilities expense	2,400
Accounts receivable	35,000
Supplies expense	3,800
Supplies	1,500

Required Prepare the company's unadjusted trial balance at October 31, 2020, listing accounts in the sequence illustrated in the chapter. (Hints: Supplies are listed before Building and Land. List the expenses alphabetically.)

E2–19 After recording the transactions in E2-15 prepare the unadjusted trial balance of Yarrow Strategic Consulting at May 31, 2020.

(5) Preparing a trial balance
Trial bal. total, $125,000

E2–20 The unadjusted trial balance of Mia's Memories at February 28, 2020, does not balance.

(5) Correcting errors in a trial balance
Trial bal. total, $35,300

Cash	$ 3,100	
Accounts receivable	1,900	
Supplies	700	
Land	26,100	
Accounts payable		$11,400
M. Mia, capital		11,900
Service revenue		9,600
Rent expense	900	
Salaries expense	1,600	
Utilities expense	500	
Total	$34,800	$32,900

Investigation of the accounting records reveals that the bookkeeper made the following errors:

a. Recorded a $400 cash revenue transaction by debiting Accounts Receivable. The credit entry was correct.
b. Posted a $2,000 credit to Accounts Payable as $200.
c. Did not record utilities expense or the related account payable in the amount of $500.
d. Understated M. Mia, Capital by $100.

Required Prepare the corrected unadjusted trial balance at February 28, 2020, complete with a heading. Journal entries are not required.

USING EXCEL

(2)(3)(4)(5) Using Excel to journalize and post transactions and to create financial statements

E2–21 *Download an Excel template for this problem online in MyLab Accounting.*

Redmond Company started operations on April 1, 2020. Seventeen transactions occurred during April which need to be journalized and posted. Prepare the financial statements at the end of the month.

Required

1. Use Excel to record the transactions for April.
2. Post the journal entries to the T-accounts and prepare a trial balance.
3. Prepare the income statement, statement of owner's equity, and balance sheet for the company.

SERIAL EXERCISE

③④⑤
Journalizing transactions, posting to T-accounts, and preparing an unadjusted trial balance

5. Net income, **$6,955**

E2-22 *The Serial Exercise involves a company that will be revisited throughout relevant chapters in Volume 1 and Volume 2. You can complete the Serial Exercises using MyLab Accounting.*

This Exercise continues with the company introduced in Chapter 1, Canyon Canoe Company. Here you will account for Canyon Canoe Company's transactions as it is actually done in practice. Begin by reviewing the transactions from Chapter 1 that are reprinted here:

Nov.	1	Amber Wilson invested $16,000 cash in the business by opening a bank account in the name of Canyon Canoe Company.
	2	The company leased a building and paid $1,200 for the first month's rent.
	3	The company purchased canoes for $4,800 on account.
	4	The company purchased office supplies on account, $750.
	7	The company earned $1,400 cash for the rental of canoes.
	13	The company paid $1,500 cash for salaries.
	15	Amber Wilson withdrew $50 cash from the business for personal use.
	16	The company received a bill for $150 for utilities, which will be paid later.
	20	The company received a bill for $175 for cellphone expenses. The bill will be paid later.
	22	The company rented canoes to Early Start Daycare on account, $3,000.
	26	Canyon Canoe Company paid $1,000 of the amount owed for the November 3 purchase that was made on account.
	28	The company received $750 from Early Start Daycare for canoe rental on November 22.
	30	Amber Wilson withdrew cash of $100 from the business for personal use.

In addition, Canyon Canoe Company completed the following transactions for December.

Dec.	1	Amber Wilson contributed land on the river (worth $85,000) and a small building to use as a rental office (worth $35,000) in exchange for owner's equity.
	1	The company prepaid $3,000 for three months' rent on the warehouse where the company stores the canoes. (Use the Prepaid Rent account.)
	2	The company purchased canoes, signing a note payable for $7,200.
	4	The company purchased office supplies on account for $500.
	9	The company received $4,500 cash for canoe rentals to customers.
	15	Canyon Canoe Company rented canoes to customers for $3,500, but will be paid next month.
	16	Canyon Canoe Company received a $750 rental deposit from a group that will use the canoes next month. (Use the Unearned Revenue account.)
	18	The company paid the utilities and telephone bills from last month.
	19	The company paid other accounts payable in the amount of $2,000.
	20	Canyon Canoe Company received bills for the telephone ($325) and utilities ($295), which will be paid later.
	31	The company paid salaries of $1,800.
	31	Amber Wilson withdrew $300 from the business for personal use.

Required

1. Journalize the transactions for both November and December, using the following accounts: Cash; Accounts Receivable; Office Supplies; Prepaid Rent; Land; Building; Canoes; Accounts Payable; Unearned Revenue; Note Payable; Amber Wilson, Capital; Amber Wilson, Withdrawals; Canoe Rental Revenue; Rent Expense; Salaries Expense; Utilities Expense; and Telephone Expense. Explanations are not required. (Hint: For November transactions, refer to your answer for E1-18 if you completed it.)
2. Open a T-account for each of these accounts in the order presented in requirement 1.
3. Post the journal entries to the T-accounts, and calculate account balances. Formal posting references are not required.

4. Prepare an unadjusted trial balance as of December 31, 2020.
5. Prepare the income statement of Canyon Canoe Company for the two months ended December 31, 2020. List expenses in this order: Rent Expense; Salaries Expense; Utilities Expense; and Telephone Expense.
6. Prepare the statement of owner's equity for the two months ended December 31, 2020.
7. Prepare the balance sheet as of December 31, 2020.

PRACTICE SET

(3) (4) (5)
Journalizing transactions, posting to T-accounts, and preparing a trial balance
Trial balance total, $75,345

E2–23 *This Practice Set appears in Chapters 2 through 9. These questions provide another opportunity to practise the entire accounting cycle. The Practice Set uses the same company in each chapter but is not as extensive as the Serial Exercise.*

Consider the following transactions for the first month of operations of a new small business called Crystal Clear Cleaning.

Nov.	1	Aaron Hideaway invested $15,000 and a truck, with a market value of $3,000, in the business.
	2	The business paid $4,000 to Pleasant Properties for November through February rent. (Hint: Debit Prepaid Rent.)
	3	Paid $4,800 for a business insurance policy for the term November 1, 2019, through October 31, 2020. (Hint: Debit Prepaid Insurance.)
	4	Purchased cleaning supplies on account, $320.
	5	Purchased on account an industrial vacuum cleaner costing $1,500. The invoice is payable November 25.
	7	Paid $3,900 for a computer and printer.
	9	Performed cleaning services on account in the amount of $4,700.
	10	Received $200 for services rendered on November 9.
	15	Paid employees, $400.
	16	Received $15,000 for a 1-year contract beginning November 16 for cleaning services to be provided. Contract begins November 16, 2019, and ends November 15, 2020. (Hint: Credit Unearned Revenue.)
	17	Provided cleaning services and received $400 cash.
	18	Received a utility bill for $175 with a due date of December 4, 2019.
	20	Borrowed $36,000 from bank and signed a note payable with interest rate of 6% per year.
	21	Received $500 on account for services performed on November 9.
	25	Paid $750 on account for vacuum cleaner purchased on November 5.
	29	Paid $200 for advertising.
	30	Aaron Hideaway withdrew cash of $1,400 from the business.

Required

1. Journalize the transactions, using the following accounts: Cash; Accounts Receivable; Cleaning Supplies; Prepaid Rent; Prepaid Insurance; Equipment; Truck; Accounts Payable; Unearned Revenue; Note Payable; A. Hideaway, Capital; A. Hideaway, Withdrawals; Service Revenue; Salaries Expense; Advertising Expense; and Utilities Expense. Explanations are not required.
2. Open a T-account for each account.
3. Post the journal entries to the T-accounts, and calculate account balances.
4. Prepare an unadjusted trial balance as of November 30, 2019.

CHALLENGE EXERCISES

(2) (5)
Computing financial statement amounts
b. Cash paid, $10,880

E2–24 The owner of Fergus Technical Services is an architect with little understanding of accounting. She needs to compute the following summary information from the accounting records:

a. Net income for the month of March
b. Total cash paid during March
c. Cash collections from customers during March
d. Payments on account during March

Analyze the following accounts to compute the desired amounts:

	Balance		Additional Information for the Month of March
Account	Feb. 28	Mar. 31	
a. B. Fergus, Capital	$1,440	$2,400	Withdrawals, $640
b. Cash	1,800	1,640	Cash receipts, $10,720
c. Accounts Receivable	3,840	6,160	Sales on account, $12,160
d. Accounts Payable............	2,080	2,560	Purchases on account, $508

The solution to a (solve for the net income for March) can be computed as follows:

B. Fergus, Capital

March withdrawals	640	Feb. 28 bal.	1,440
		March net income	x = $1,600
		March 31 bal.	2,400

Use a similar approach to compute the other three items.

(2) (3) (5)
Analyzing accounting errors

E2–25 Bridget Battle has trouble keeping her debits and credits equal. During a recent month, Bridget made the following errors:

a. In preparing the trial balance, Bridget omitted a $5,000 note payable.

b. Bridget recorded a $340 purchase of supplies on account by debiting Supplies and crediting Accounts Payable for $430.

c. In recording a $200 payment on account, Bridget debited Supplies instead of Accounts Payable.

d. In journalizing a receipt of cash from service revenue, Bridget debited Cash for $50 instead of the correct amount of $500. The credit was correctly recorded in the amount of $500.

e. Bridget posted a $1,000 utility expense as $100. The credit to Cash was correct.

Required

1. For each of these errors, state whether the total debits equal total credits on the trial balance.
2. Identify each account that has an incorrect balance and indicate the amount and direction of the error (e.g., "Accounts Receivable $500 too high").

BEYOND THE NUMBERS

(1)
Creating a chart of accounts

BN2–1

Victor Yang asks your advice in setting up the accounting records for his new business, Victor's Bike Shop. The business will begin as a bicycle repair shop and will operate in a rented building. Victor's Bike Shop will need office equipment and repair equipment. The business will borrow money using a note payable to buy the needed equipment. Victor's Bike Shop will purchase on account repair supplies and office supplies.

The business will need a store manager. This person will be paid a weekly salary of $1,800. Other expenses will include advertising and insurance. Victor's Bike Shop will want to know which aspects of the business generate the most and the least revenue so that when he starts to sell bikes next year he will know which ones to stock. The business will use separate service revenue accounts for mountain bike, road bike, and tandem bike repairs. Victor's better customers will be allowed to open accounts with the business.

Required List all the accounts Victor's Repair Shop will need, starting with the assets and ending with the expenses. Indicate which accounts will be reported on the balance sheet and which accounts will appear on the income statement.

ETHICAL ISSUE

EI2–1

Associated Charities Trust, a charitable organization in Brandon, Manitoba, has a standing agreement with Prairie Bank. The agreement allows Associated Charities Trust to overdraw its cash balance at the bank when donations are running low. In the past, Associated Charities Trust managed funds wisely and rarely used this privilege. Greg Glowa has recently become the president of Associated Charities Trust. To expand operations, Glowa is acquiring office equipment and spending large amounts for fundraising. During his presidency, Associated Charities Trust has maintained a negative bank balance (a credit Cash balance) of approximately $28,000.

Required What is the ethical issue in this situation? State why you approve or disapprove of Glowa's management of Associated Charities Trust's funds.

PROBLEMS (GROUP A)

P2–1A Baycrest Cinema Company owns movie theatres. Baycrest Cinema engaged in the following transactions in November 2019:

(2) (3) Analyzing and journalizing transactions

Nov.	1	Darrell Palusky invested $350,000 personal cash in the business by depositing that amount in a bank account titled Baycrest Cinema Company. The business gave capital to Palusky.
	1	Paid November's rent on a theatre building with cash, $6,000.
	2	Paid $320,000 cash to purchase land for a theatre site.
	5	Borrowed $220,000 from the bank to finance the first phase of construction of the new theatre. Palusky signed a note payable to the bank in the name of Baycrest Cinema Company.
	10	Purchased theatre supplies on account, $1,000.
	16	Paid employees' salaries of $2,900 cash.
	22	Paid $600 on account.
	28	Palusky withdrew $8,000 cash.
	29	Paid property tax expense on the land for the new theatre, cash of $1,400.
	30	Received $20,000 cash from service revenue and deposited that amount in the bank.

Baycrest uses the following accounts: Cash; Supplies; Land; Accounts Payable; Note Payable; Darrell Palusky, Capital; Darrell Palusky, Withdrawals; Service Revenue; Property Tax Expense; Rent Expense; Salaries Expense.

Required

1. Prepare an analysis of each business transaction of Baycrest Cinema Company as shown for the November 1 transaction:

   Nov. 1 The asset cash is increased. Increases in assets are recorded by debits; therefore, debit Cash. The owner's equity of the entity is increased. Increases in owner's equity are recorded by credits; therefore, credit Darrell Palusky, Capital.

2. Record each transaction in the journal with an explanation, using the account titles given. Identify each transaction by its date.

P2–2A Vince York practises medicine under the business title Vince York, MD. During July, the medical practice completed the following transactions:

(2) (3) Journalizing transactions

Jul.	1	York contributed $63,000 cash to the business in exchange for capital.
	5	Paid monthly rent on medical equipment, $510.
	9	Paid $23,000 cash to purchase land to be used in operations.
	10	Purchased office supplies on account, $1,600.
	19	Borrowed $22,000 from the bank for business use.
	22	Paid $1,100 on account.
	28	The business received a bill for advertising in the daily newspaper to be paid in August, $240.

31	Revenues earned during the month included $6,400 cash and $6,000 on account.
31	Paid employees' salaries $2,200, office rent $1,900, and utilities $560. Record as a compound entry.
31	The business received $1,120 for medical screening services to be performed next month.
31	York withdrew cash of $7,200.

The business uses the following accounts: Cash; Accounts Receivable; Office Supplies; Land; Accounts Payable; Unearned Revenue; Note Payable; V. York, Capital; V. York, Withdrawals; Service Revenue; Salaries Expense; Rent Expense; Utilities Expense; and Advertising Expense.

Required Journalize each transaction. Explanations are not required.

(2) (3)
Journalizing transactions

P2–3A Zeb Slipewicz opened a renovation business called WeReDoIt Construction on September 3, 2020. During the first month of operations, the business completed the following transactions:

Sep.	3	Slipewicz deposited a cheque for $72,000 into the business bank account to start the business.
	4	Purchased supplies, $600, and furniture, $4,400, on account.
	5	Paid September rent expense, $1,500 cash.
	6	Performed design services for a client and received $2,400 cash.
	7	Paid $44,000 cash to acquire land for a future office site.
	10	Designed a bathroom for a client, billed the client, and received her promise to pay the $5,800 within one week.
	14	Paid for the furniture purchased September 4 on account.
	15	Paid assistant's salary, $940 cash.
	17	Received cash on account, $3,400.
	22	Received $5,000 cash from a client for renovation of a cottage.
	25	Prepared a recreation room design for a client on account, $1,600.
	30	Paid assistant's salary, $940 cash.
	30	Slipewicz withdrew $5,600 cash for personal use.

Required Record each transaction in the journal with an explanation. Identify each transaction by date. Use the following accounts: Cash; Accounts Receivable; Supplies; Furniture; Land; Accounts Payable; Z. Slipewicz, Capital; Z. Slipewicz, Withdrawals; Service Revenue; Rent Expense; Salaries Expense.

(2) (3) (4)
Journalizing transactions and posting to ledger accounts

P2–4A The trial balance of Kiki's Jewellery Repair at February 29, 2020, is shown below:

KIKI'S JEWELLERY REPAIR
Unadjusted Trial Balance
February 29, 2020

Account Number	Account Title	Debit	Credit
1100	Cash	$ 4,000	
1200	Accounts receivable	16,000	
1300	Supplies	3,600	
1600	Equipment	37,200	
2000	Accounts payable		$ 8,000
3000	K. Kalani, capital		50,000
3100	K. Kalani, withdrawals	4,400	
5000	Service revenue		16,400
6100	Rent expense	2,000	
6200	Salaries expense	7,200	
	Total	$74,400	$74,400

During March, Kiki's Jewellery Repair completed the following transactions:

Mar.	4	Collected $600 cash from a client on account.
	8	Provided an heirloom jewellery redesign service for a client on account, $580.
	13	Paid for items previously purchased on account, $320.
	18	Purchased supplies on account, $120.
	20	Kalani withdrew $200 cash for personal use.
	21	Received a verbal promise of a $200 commission.
	22	Received cash of $620 for work just completed.
	31	Paid employees' salaries, $1,300 cash.

Required

1. Record the March transactions in page 3 of the journal. Include an explanation for each entry.
2. Open three-column ledger accounts for the accounts listed in the trial balance, together with their balances at February 29. Enter Bal. (for previous balance) in the Item column, and place a check mark (✓) in the journal reference column for the February 29 balance in each account.
3. Post the transactions to the ledger, using dates, account numbers, journal references, and posting references.

P2–5A Sophie Vaillancourt started an investment management business, Vaillancourt Management, on June 1, 2020. During the first month of operations, the business completed the following selected transactions:

(2) (3) (4) (5)
Recording transactions, using three-column ledger accounts, preparing a trial balance

Jun.	1	Vaillancourt began the business with an investment of $20,000 cash, land valued at $60,000, and a building valued at $120,000. The business gave her owner's equity in the business for the value of the cash, land, and building. (Hint: This is a compound journal entry.)
	3	Purchased office supplies on account, $2,600.
	4	Paid $15,000 cash for office furniture.
	12	Paid employee salary, $2,200 cash.
	15	Performed consulting service on account for clients, $12,100.
	22	Paid in cash $800 of the account payable created by purchasing office supplies on June 3.
	24	Received a $2,000 bill for advertising expense that will be paid in the near future.
	25	Performed consulting services for customers and received cash, $5,600.
	26	Received cash on account, $2,400.
	29	Paid the following expenses with two separate cheques: (1) Rent of photocopier, $1,700. (2) Utilities, $400.
	30	Vaillancourt withdrew $6,500 cash for personal use.

Required

1. Record each transaction in the journal.
2. Open the following three-column ledger accounts: Cash, #1100; Accounts Receivable, #1300; Office Supplies, #1400; Office Furniture, #1500; Building, #1700; Land, #1800; Accounts Payable, #2100; Sophie Vaillancourt, Capital, #3100; Sophie Vaillancourt, Withdrawals, #3200; Service Revenue, #4100; Advertising Expense, #5100; Equipment Rental Expense, #5300; Salaries Expense, #5500; Utilities Expense, #5700.
3. Post to the accounts and keep a running balance for each account.
4. Prepare the unadjusted trial balance of Vaillancourt Management at June 30, 2020.

(2) (5)

Correcting errors in a trial balance

Trial bal. total, $70,000

P2–6A The following trial balance does not balance:

A-PLUS TRAVEL PLANNERS Unadjusted Trial Balance June 30, 2020		
Cash	$ 1,600	
Accounts receivable	10,000	
Supplies	900	
Office furniture	3,600	
Land	46,600	
Accounts payable		$ 3,800
Note payable		23,000
R. Minter, capital		31,600
R. Minter, withdrawals	2,000	
Consulting service revenue		7,300
Advertising expense	400	
Rent expense	1,000	
Salaries expense	2,100	
Utilities expense	410	
Total	$68,610	$65,700

The following errors were detected:

a. The cash balance is understated by $1,300.

b. The cost of the land was $44,600, not $46,600.

c. A $400 purchase of supplies on account was neither journalized nor posted.

d. A $3,000 credit to Consulting Service Revenue was not posted.

e. Rent Expense of $200 was posted as a credit rather than a debit.

f. The balance of Advertising Expense is $600, but it was listed as $400 on the trial balance.

g. A $300 debit to Accounts Receivable was posted as $30. The credit to Consulting Service Revenue was correct.

h. The balance of Utilities Expense is overstated by $80.

i. A $900 debit to the R. Minter, Withdrawals account was posted as a debit to R. Minter, Capital.

Required Prepare the corrected unadjusted trial balance at June 30, 2020. Journal entries are not required.

(2) (3) (4) (5)

Journalizing entries, posting to ledger accounts, preparing a trial balance

Total, $442,300

P2–7A Canada-Wide Movers had the following account balances, in random order, on December 15, 2020 (all accounts have their "normal" balances):

Moving fees income	$259,800	Cash	$ 17,200
Accounts receivable	7,400	Storage fees income	57,900
Rent expense	47,100	Note receivable	45,000
H. Martinez, capital	53,000	Utilities expense	2,400
Office supplies expense	2,100	Office supplies	9,600
Mortgage payable	39,000	Accounts payable	33,000
Salaries expense	161,100	Office equipment	12,300
Insurance expense	6,300	Moving equipment	132,200

The following events took place during the final weeks of the year:

Dec. 17 Moved a customer's goods to Canada-Wide's rented warehouse for storage. The moving fees were $4,000. Storage fees are $600 per month. The customer was billed for 1 month's storage and the moving fees.

18 Collected a $15,000 note owed to Canada-Wide Movers and collected interest income of $1,800 cash.

19 Used a company cheque to pay for Martinez's personal hydro bill in the amount of $400.

21 Purchased storage racks for $12,000. Paid $3,600 cash, provided moving services for $1,500, and promised to pay the balance in 60 days.

23 Collected $3,000 cash; $2,600 of this was for moving goods on December 15 (recorded as an account receivable at that time), and the balance was for storage fees for the period of December 16 to 23.

24 Canada-Wide Movers paid cash of $18,000 owing on the mortgage.

27 Martinez withdrew $5,000 cash for personal use.

29 Provided moving services to a lawyer for $2,400. The lawyer paid Canada-Wide Movers $1,500 and provided legal work for the balance.

31 Martinez, the owner of Canada-Wide Movers, sold 2,000 shares he held in Brandon Haulage Inc. for $12,000.

Required

1. Where appropriate, record each transaction from December 17 to 31 in the journal. Include an explanation for each journal entry.
2. Enter December 15 balances in the T-accounts.
3. Post entries in T-accounts and calculate the balance of each one.
4. Prepare the unadjusted trial balance of Canada-Wide Movers at December 31, 2020.

PROBLEMS (GROUP B)

(2) (3) Analyzing and journalizing transactions

P2–1B Gladys Yuan is a research analyst who operates under the business title Yuan Research. During April 2020, the company engaged in the following transactions:

Apr. 1 Yuan deposited $40,000 cash in the business bank account. The business gave Yuan owner's equity in the business.

5 Paid April's rent on a shared office space with cash, $400.

10 Purchased supplies on account, $600.

19 Paid $100 on account for supplies purchased on April 10.

21 Paid $25,000 cash to purchase land for a future office location.

22 Borrowed $15,000 from the bank for business use. Yuan signed a note payable to the bank in the name of the business.

30 Paid cash for employee salaries of $3,500 and utilities of $350.

30 Revenues earned during the month included $1,300 cash and $2,400 on account.

30 Yuan withdrew $1,200 cash from the business for personal use.

Yuan Research uses the following accounts: Cash; Accounts Receivable; Supplies; Land; Accounts Payable; Note Payable; G. Yuan, Capital; G. Yuan, Withdrawals; Service Revenue; Office Rent Expense; Salaries Expense; Utilities Expense.

Required

1. Prepare an analysis of each business transaction of Yuan Research, as shown for the April 1 transaction:

   Apr. 1 The asset cash is increased. Increases in assets are recorded by debits; therefore, debit Cash. The owner's equity is increased. Increases in owner's equity are recorded by credits; therefore, credit G. Yuan, Capital.

2. Record each transaction in the journal with an explanation, using the dates and account titles given.

(2) (3)
Journalizing transactions

P2–2B Victor Yang practices medicine under the business title Victor Yang, M.D. During March, the medical practice completed the following transactions:

Mar.	1	Yang contributed $62,000 cash to the business in exchange for capital.
	5	Paid monthly rent on medical equipment, $570.
	9	Paid $14,000 cash to purchase land to be used in operations.
	10	Purchased office supplies on account, $1,500.
	19	Borrowed $27,000 from the bank for business use by signing a note payable.
	22	Paid $1,400 on account.
	28	The business received a bill for advertising in the daily newspaper to be paid in April, $220.
	31	Revenues earned during the month included $6,700 cash and $5,800 on account.
	31	Paid employees' salaries $2,100, office rent $1,500, and utilities $350. Record as a compound entry.
	31	The business received $1,000 for medical screening services to be performed next month.
	31	Yang withdrew cash of $7,100.

The business uses the following accounts: Cash; Accounts Receivable; Office Supplies; Land; Accounts Payable; Unearned Revenue; Note Payable; V. Yang, Capital; V. Yang, Withdrawals; Service Revenue; Salaries Expense; Rent Expense; Utilities Expense; and Advertising Expense.

Required Journalize each transaction. Explanations are not required.

(2) (3)
Journalizing transactions

P2–3B Scott Jameson opened Jameson Translation Services on January 2, 2020. During the first month of operations, the business completed the following transactions:

Jan.	2	The business received $60,000 cash from Jameson, which was deposited in a business bank account.
	3	Purchased supplies, $750, and furniture, $2,800, on account.
	3	Paid January's rent expense with cash, $1,100.
	4	Performed translation services for a client and received cash, $2,250.
	7	Paid $38,000 cash to acquire land for a future office site.
	11	Translated a brochure for a client and billed the client $1,200.
	15	Paid the office manager his salary, $975 cash.
	16	Paid cash for the furniture purchased January 3 on account.
	18	Received partial payment from a client on account, $600 cash.
	19	Translated legal documents for a client on account, $11,350.
	22	Paid cash for the water and electricity bills, $300.
	29	Received $2,700 cash for translation for a client in an overseas business transaction.
	31	Paid the office manager's salary, $975 cash.
	31	Jameson withdrew $12,000 cash for personal use.

Required Record each transaction in the journal with an explanation, using the account titles given. Use the following accounts: Cash; Accounts Receivable; Supplies; Furniture; Land; Accounts Payable; Scott Jameson, Capital; Scott Jameson, Withdrawals; Translation Revenue; Rent Expense; Salaries Expense; Utilities Expense.

P2–4B Bobbie Singh provides writing services for small business. He blogs for companies that need professionally written content. His business records at November 15, 2020, are shown below:

(2) (3) (4) Journalizing transactions and posting to three-column ledger accounts

BLOG 4 U
Unadjusted Trial Balance
November 15, 2020

Account Number	Account Title	Debit	Credit
1100	Cash	$ 16,000	
1200	Accounts receivable	16,000	
1300	Computer supplies	1,200	
1900	Equipment	70,000	
2100	Accounts payable		$ 9,200
4000	B. Singh, capital		90,000
4100	B. Singh, withdrawals	4,600	
5000	Service revenue		14,200
6000	Rent expense	2,000	
6100	Salaries expense	3,600	
	Total	$113,400	$113,400

During the remainder of November, the business completed the following transactions:

Nov. 16 Collected $6,000 cash from a client on account.
17 Performed writing services for a client on account, $2,100.
21 Made a payment on account in the amount of $2,600.
22 Purchased computer supplies on account, $4,600.
23 Singh withdrew $2,100 cash for personal use.
24 Was advised that WeBlog4U was prepared to buy all of Blog 4 U for $67,800.
26 Received $11,900 cash for client's monthly blog that was just completed.
30 Paid employees' salaries, $2,700 cash.

Required

1. Record the transactions that occurred during November 16 through 30 on page 6 of the journal. Include an explanation for each entry.
2. Post the transactions to three-column accounts in the ledger, using dates, account numbers, journal references, and posting references. Open the ledger accounts listed in the trial balance together with their balances at November 15. Enter *Bal.* (for previous balance) in the Item column, and place a check mark (✓) in the journal reference column for the November 15 balance of each account.

P2–5B Haider Malik started a catering service called International Catering. During the first month of operations, October 2020, the business completed the following selected transactions:

(2) (3) (4) (5) Recording transactions, using three-column ledger accounts, preparing a trial balance

Oct. 2 Malik began the company with an investment of $50,000 cash and a food truck valued at $26,000. The business gave Malik owner's equity in the business.
6 Paid $8,000 cash for custom food service equipment.
78 Purchased supplies on account, $14,800.
17 Received $4,000 cash for catering at a street festival.
18 Catered to bands at a music festival and received payment on account, $8,600.

19 Paid employees salary for work on weekend, $2,600 cash.
24 Paid $12,000 cash as a partial payment for the supplies purchased on October 7.
26 Received a $1,600 bill for advertising expense that will be paid in the near future.
28 Received cash on account, $2,200.
29 Paid the following expenses with two separate cheques:
(1) BBQ rental, $3,000.
(2) Insurance, $1,600.
31 Malik withdrew $12,000 cash for personal use.

Required

1. Record the transactions in the journal.
2. Open the following three-column ledger accounts: Cash, #1100; Accounts Receivable, #1300; Supplies, #1500; Food Service Equipment, #1600; Food Truck, #1700; Accounts Payable, #2100; H. Malik, Capital, #3100; H. Malik, Withdrawals, #3200; Service Revenue, #4100; Advertising Expense, #5100; Insurance Expense, #5500; Rent Expense, #5700; Salaries Expense, #5800.
3. Post to the accounts and keep a running balance for each account.
4. Prepare the unadjusted trial balance of International Catering at October 31, 2020.

(2) (5) Correcting errors in a trial balance

P2–6B The trial balance for Mackle Fitness, shown below, does not balance.

MACKLE FITNESS Unadjusted Trial Balance July 31, 2020		
Cash	$ 47,000	
Accounts receivable	30,000	
Supplies	7,500	
Office furniture	34,500	
Fitness equipment	600,000	
Accounts payable		$ 30,000
Note payable		194,500
G. Mackle, capital		442,500
G. Mackle, withdrawals	55,500	
Service revenue		73,500
Salaries expense	42,500	
Rent expense	9,000	
Advertising expense	6,000	
Utilities expense	3,000	
Total	$835,000	$740,500

The following errors were detected:

a. The cash balance is overstated by $6,000.
b. Rent expense of $3,000 was posted as a credit rather than a debit.
c. The balance of Advertising Expense is $4,500, but it is listed as $6,000 on the trial balance.
d. A $9,000 debit to Accounts Receivable was posted as $900.
e. The balance of Utilities Expense is understated by $900.
f. A $19,500 debit to the G. Mackle, Withdrawals account was posted as a debit to G. Mackle, Capital.

g. A $1,500 purchase of supplies on account was neither journalized nor posted.

h. An $87,000 credit to Service Revenue was not posted.

i. Office furniture should be listed in the amount of $19,500.

Required Prepare the corrected trial balance at July 31, 2020. Journal entries are not required.

P2–7B Maquina Lodge, owned by Bob Palmiter, had the following account balances, in random order, on December 15, 2020 (all accounts have their "normal" balances):

(2) (3) (4) (5)
Journalizing entries, posting to ledger accounts, preparing a trial balance

Guest revenue	$309,000	Furniture	$57,800
Accounts receivable	8,800	Cash	3,800
Equipment rental expense	11,800	Notes receivable	26,000
B. Palmiter, capital	209,800	Utilities expense	21,000
Supplies expense	2,800	Supplies inventory	5,800
Mortgage payable	30,000	Accounts payable	12,000
Salaries expense	81,000	Office equipment	10,200
Insurance expense	6,800	Boating equipment	96,800
Building	200,000	Land	30,000

The following events also took place during the final weeks of the year:

Dec.	17	Signed an agreement to let a retired professor move in during the off season for a long stay, beginning today. The monthly rate is $3,200 payable at the beginning of each month. The professor paid $1,550 cash for the remainder of December.
	18	Collected an $18,000 note owed to Maquina and collected interest of $2,400 cash.
	21	Purchased boating equipment for $14,000 from Boats Unlimited. Maquina Lodge paid $5,000 cash, provided room rentals for $1,600 to Boats Unlimited, and promised to pay the balance in 60 days.
	23	Collected $2,800 cash for rooms for a conference held from December 16 to 23.
	24	Maquina Lodge paid $2,000 cash owing on the mortgage.
	27	Palmiter withdrew $14,000 cash for personal use.
	29	Provided meeting rooms to a lawyer for $2,000. The lawyer paid Maquina Lodge $1,100 cash and provided legal work for the balance.
	31	The accountant discovered that an error had been made in posting an entry to the Guest Revenue account on December 15. The entry was correctly journalized, but $4,200 was accidentally posted as $2,400 in the account.

Required

1. Where appropriate, record each transaction from December 17 to 29 in the journal. Include an explanation for each entry.
2. Enter the correct opening balances for each T-account dated as December 15.
3. Post entries in T-accounts and calculate the balance of each one.
4. Prepare the unadjusted trial balance of Maquina Lodge at December 31, 2020.

CHALLENGE PROBLEMS

P2–1C Some individuals, for whatever reason, do not pay income tax or pay less than they should. Often their business transactions are cash transactions, so there is no paper trail to prove how much or how little they actually earned. Canada Revenue Agency, however, has a way of dealing with these individuals; they use a model (based on the accounting equation) to calculate how much the individual must have earned.

(2)
Understanding the rules of debit and credit

Canada Revenue Agency is about to audit Donna Wynn for the period January 1, 2020, to December 31, 2020. Wynn buys and sells collectible coins for cash. Wynn had $8,000 cash and no other assets or liabilities at January 1, 2020.

Required

1. Use the accounting equation (specifically owner's equity) to explain how the Canada Revenue Agency model will be used to audit Donna.
2. What do you think are the accounting concepts underlying the model?

5 Analyzing a trial balance

P2–2C The owner of Archer Communications, Nancy Archer, is selling the business. She offers the trial balance shown below to prospective buyers.

ARCHER COMMUNICATIONS Unadjusted Trial Balance December 31, 2020		
Cash	$ 28,000	
Accounts receivable	30,500	
Prepaid expenses	6,000	
Land	64,000	
Accounts payable		$ 62,500
Note payable		38,000
N. Archer, capital		45,000
N. Archer, withdrawals	72,000	
Service revenue		151,000
Advertising expense	4,500	
Rent expense	39,000	
Supplies expense	10,500	
Salaries expense	42,000	
Total	$296,500	$296,500

Your best friend is considering buying Archer Communications. He seeks your advice in interpreting this information. Specifically, he asks whether this trial balance is the same as a balance sheet and an income statement. He also wonders whether Archer Communications is a sound company because all the accounts are in balance.

Required Write a short note to answer your friend's questions. To aid his decision, state how he can use the information on this unadjusted trial balance to compute Archer Communications's net income or net loss for the current period. State the amount of net income or net loss in your note.

Extending Your Knowledge

DECISION PROBLEMS

DP2–1

(2) (3) (4) (5)
Recording transactions directly in the ledger, preparing a trial balance, measuring net income or loss

3. Trial bal. total, $81,100

Your friend, Samina Hin, has asked your advice about the effects that certain business transactions will have on her business. Her business, Car Finders, finds the best deals on used cars for clients. Time is short, so you cannot journalize transactions. Instead, you must analyze the transactions and post them directly to T-accounts. Hin will continue in the business only if she can expect to earn monthly net income of $8,000. The business had the following transactions during March 2020:

a. Hin deposited $50,000 cash in a business bank account.
b. The business borrowed $8,000 cash from the bank, which is recorded as a note payable due within 1 year.
c. Purchased for cash a vehicle to drive clients to appointments, $27,000.
d. Paid $1,600 cash for supplies.
e. Paid cash for advertising in the local newspaper, $1,200.
f. Paid the following cash expenses for 1 month: commission, $12,400; office rent, $1,800; utilities, $600; gas, $1,000; interest, $200.
g. Earned revenue on account, $15,600.
h. Earned $7,500 revenue and received cash.
i. Collected cash from customers on account, $2,400.

Required

1. Open the following T-accounts: Cash; Accounts Receivable; Supplies; Vehicle; Note Payable; Samina Hin, Capital; Advising Revenue; Advertising Expense; Interest Expense; Rent Expense; Commission Expense; Gas Expense; Utilities Expense.
2. Record the transactions directly in the T-accounts without using a journal. Identify each transaction by its letter.
3. Prepare an unadjusted trial balance at March 31, 2020. List expenses alphabetically.
4. Compute the amount of net income or net loss for this first month of operations. Would you recommend Hin continue in business?

FINANCIAL STATEMENT CASES

FSC2–1

(1)
The process of creating financial statements

Refer to the Indigo Books & Music Inc.'s (Indigo) financial statements in Appendix A at the end of this book or on MyLab Accounting. Answer the following questions:

1. In what currency are Indigo's financial statements presented?
2. How are the dollar amounts on the Indigo financial statements presented?
3. What is the date of the most recent Indigo financial statements? Does the year-end at the same date as the previous year?
4. Does Indigo follow IFRS or ASPE? Where does it tell you this in the annual report? (Hint: The Notes to Consolidated Statements list this sort of information first.)
5. Management must approve the statements before they are published. When was this done for the current report?

②③ Journalizing transactions

FSC2–2

This problem helps to develop journalizing skills by using an actual company's account titles for a selected set of accounts. Refer to the TELUS Corporation's (TELUS) financial statements that appear on MyLab Accounting. Assume TELUS completed the following selected (fictitious) transactions during December 2016:

a. Made sales on account, $950.

b. Paid cash for goods, $1,100.

c. Paid annual financing costs of $520.

d. Collected accounts receivable of $2,100.

e. Paid cash for prepaid rent, $24.

f. Purchased equipment on account for $550.

g. Paid cash for services, $1,800.

Required

1. Set up T-accounts for this partial list of accounts: Cash (debit balance of $1,607); Accounts Receivable (debit balance of $2,621); Prepaid Expenses (debit balance of $209); Property, Plant, and Equipment (debit balance of $9,914); Accounts Payable and Accrued Liabilities (credit balance of $1,780); Service Revenue (credit balance of $11,049); Goods and Services Purchased (debit balance of $2,731); Financing Costs ($0 balance).
2. Journalize TELUS's Transactions a to g. Explanations are not required.
3. Post to T-accounts and compute the balance for each account. Identify each posting by its transaction letter.
4. For each of the accounts, compare your balances to TELUS's actual balances as shown on the December 31, 2016, balance sheet and income statement. All your amounts should agree with the actual figures rounded to the nearest dollar.

    Cash
    Accounts receivable
    Prepaid expenses
    Property, plant, and equipment
    Accounts payable and accrued liabilities
    Service revenue
    Goods and services purchased
    Financing costs

5. Balance sheet and income statement accounts listed are really categories representing summarized account balances. List three accounts that would be reflected in each of the following categories:

    a. Property, plant, and equipment

    b. Accounts payable and accrued liabilities

    c. General and administration expenses

Try It! Solutions for Chapter 2

1. a. E
   b. E
   c. A
   d. E
   e. A
   f. L
   g. A
   h. A
   i. E
   j. E

2. 10100 Cash
   10200 Accounts Receivable
   10400 Furniture and Fixtures
   20100 Accounts Payable
   20500 Income Taxes Payable
   30100 L. Starks, Capital
   30200 L. Starks, Withdrawals
   40100 Service Revenue
   50600 Rent Expense

3. a. DR
   b. DR
   c. CR
   d. CR
   e. CR
   f. CR
   g. DR
   h. CR
   i. DR
   j. CR

4. a. A company purchases supplies on account—invoice received from a vendor
   b. A company pays for the supplies it purchased in Transaction a.—bank cheque
   c. A company performs services on account for a college—invoice sent to a customer
   d. The college pays the company for the services performed in Transaction c.—bank deposit slip
   e. A customer pays the company immediately for services performed—bank deposit slip
   f. The company hires a student to provide office support during the summer—no source document since this is not a transaction.

5.

Date	Accounts and Explanation	Debit	Credit
Nov. 1	Cash	10,000	
	E. Martinez, Capital		10,000
	Owner contribution.		
15	Office Supplies	400	
	Accounts Payable		400
	Purchased office supplies on account.		
18	Advertising Expense	150	
	Cash		150
	Paid advertising expense.		
20	Cash	1,000	
	Service Revenue		1,000
	Performed services and received cash.		
28	E. Martinez, Withdrawals	500	
	Cash		500
	Owner withdrawal.		

6.

Supplies Expense

Debit	Credit
110	
290	
544	
944	

Accounts Payable

Debit	Credit
150	400
800	2,900
475	1,600
	750
	4,225

Cash

Debit	Credit
5,000	150
12,600	800
926	475
6,200	290
23,011	

Supplies Expense = \$110 + 290 + 544 = \$944
Accounts Payable = \$400 + 2,900 + 1,600 + 750 − 150 − 800 − 475 = \$4,225
Cash = \$5,000 + 12,600 + 926 + 6,200 − 150 − 800 − 475 − 290 = \$23,011

7. (1) The ending balance (X) for Cash is:

   X = \$10,000 + 20,000 − \$13,000
   X = \$17,000

   (2) We are given the beginning and ending balances. We can compute the debit entry as follows:

   \$12,800 + \$45,600 − X = \$23,500
   \$12,800 + \$45,600 − \$23,500 = X
   X = \$34,900

8.

COOPER FURNITURE REPAIR
Unadjusted Trial Balance
December 31, 2018

Account Title	Debit	Credit
Cash	\$ 7,000	
Equipment	10,000	
Accounts payable		\$ 2,300
Unearned revenue		4,500
M. Cooper, capital		12,200
M. Cooper, withdrawals	3,000	
Service revenue		8,000
Rent expense	5,000	
Advertising expense	1,200	
Utilities expense	800	
Total	\$27,000	\$27,000

3 Measuring Business Income: The Adjusting Process

CONNECTING CHAPTER 3

LEARNING OBJECTIVES

The **Summary** for Chapter 3 appears on page 141.
Key Terms with definitions for this chapter's material appear on page 142.

CPA competencies

This text covers material outlined in **Section 1: Financial Reporting of the CPA Competency Map**. The Learning Objectives for each chapter have been aligned with the CPA Competency Map to ensure the best coverage possible.

1.1.2 Evaluates the appropriateness of the basis of financial reporting

1.3.1 Prepares financial statements

Benjamin Rondel/Stockbyte/Getty Images

Liam Mills was surprised when he received his most recent quarterly bonus cheque from his employer, Custom Marketing, and the amount was smaller than he expected. Liam worked as a sales manager for western Canada. He was paid a monthly salary but also received a 3% bonus for revenue generated from advertising services provided to customers in his region. He was counting on his fourth-quarter (October–December) bonus cheque to be large enough to pay off the credit card debt he had accumulated over the holiday break. It had been a great year-end for Liam. He had successfully signed several annual advertising contracts. In addition, because of his negotiating skills, he was able to collect half of the payments for services up front instead of waiting for his customers to pay every month. Liam expected that his bonus cheque would be huge because of this new business, but it wasn't.

The next day, Liam stopped by the accounting office to discuss his bonus cheque. He was surprised to learn that his bonus was calculated by the revenue earned by his company through December 31. Although Liam had negotiated to receive half of the payments up front, the business had not yet earned the revenue from those payments by performing the advertising services. Eventually Liam will see the new business reflected in his bonus cheque, but he'll have to wait until the revenue has been earned.

In Chapter 2 we looked at recording transactions, posting to the ledger, and preparing the unadjusted trial balance. This is shown in Exhibit 3–1 steps ❶ to ❹ of the accounting cycle. The account balances in the trial balance include the effects of the transactions that occurred during the period—cash collections, purchases of assets, payments of bills, sales of assets, and so on. That certainly takes care of routine transactions. But not all transactions have source documents. It is a normal part of the accounting process to review account balances and bring the balances *up to date*. What does this mean? It will take a whole chapter to explain it.

EXHIBIT 3–1 | The Accounting Cycle

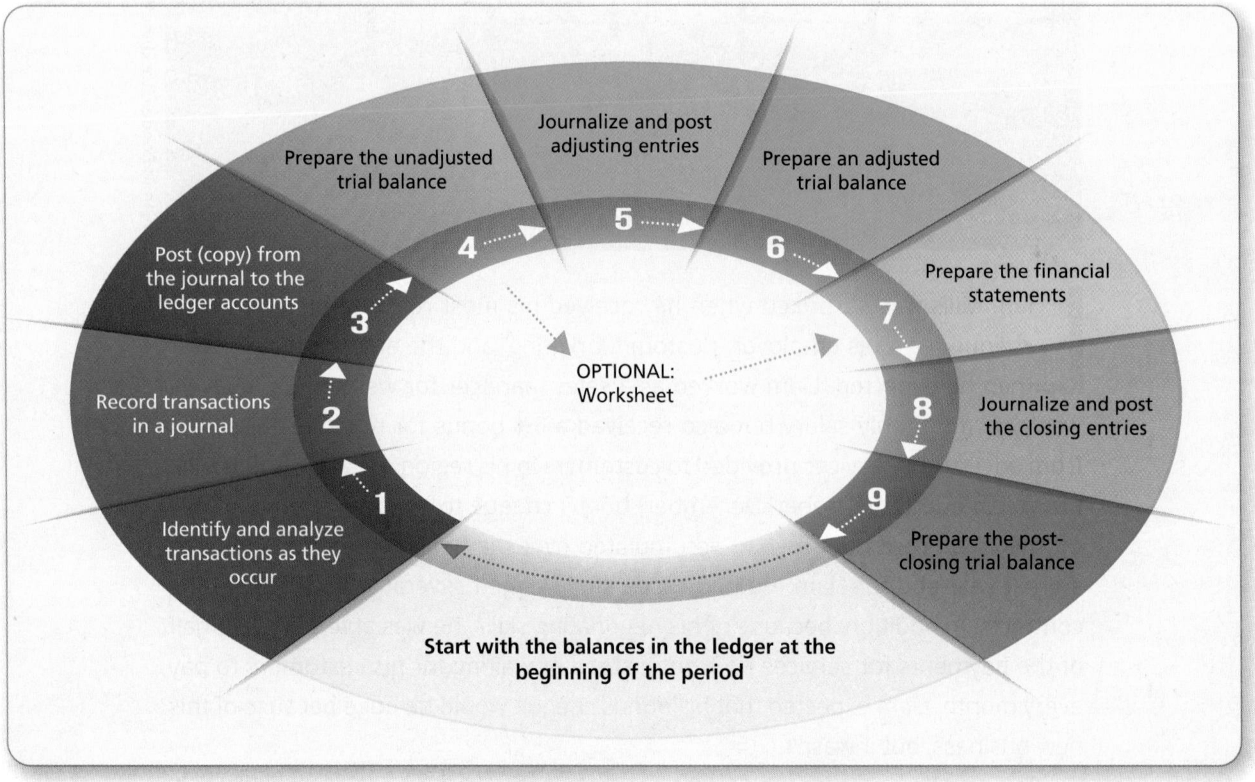

Journalize and post adjusting entries
Prepare the unadjusted trial balance
Prepare an adjusted trial balance
Post (copy) from the journal to the ledger accounts
Prepare the financial statements
Record transactions in a journal
OPTIONAL: Worksheet
Journalize and post the closing entries
Identify and analyze transactions as they occur
Prepare the post-closing trial balance
Start with the balances in the ledger at the beginning of the period
1
2
3
4
5
6
7
8
9

Whether the business is Custom Marketing or Hunter Environmental Consulting, a business must do some *adjusting entries* (step ❺) at the end of the period to bring the records up to date before preparing the financial statements (steps ❻ and ❼). In this chapter, we use the accounting concepts, assumptions, and principles found in the accounting framework (Exhibit 1–5) to measure income and prepare the financial statements of Hunter Environmental Consulting (HEC) for the month of May.

Time Period Assumption

LO ①
When does a sale really happen? And when do we record an expense?

Managers, investors, and creditors make decisions daily and need current information about the business's progress. They want to know how much profit the business has made during the period. The **time period assumption** ensures that accounting information is reported at regular intervals.

The most basic accounting period is one year, and virtually all businesses prepare annual financial statements. For many companies such as Custom Marketing, the annual accounting period is the calendar year from January 1 through December 31. Other companies use a **fiscal year** ending on some date other than December 31. Retailers traditionally make their fiscal year-end at the low point in their business activity following the after-Christmas sales in January. The fiscal year-end of Hudson's Bay Company is January 31 for that reason.

Managers and investors cannot wait until the end of the year to analyze a company's progress. Companies, therefore, prepare financial statements for **interim periods** that are less than a year. Statements can be prepared monthly, quarterly (three-month period), and semi-annually (six-month period). Given the fast pace of business, some companies such as car dealerships have accounting systems that produce daily financial reports and weekly summaries so managers can make decisions even more quickly. While many of the adjusting entries in this chapter are based on an annual accounting period, the procedures and statements can be applied to interim periods as well.

Recognition Criteria for Revenues and Expenses

Recognition (or "recognizing a transaction") is the process of including an item in the financial statements of a business.

Revenue Recognition

Revenue is the increase in owner's equity from delivering goods and/or services to customers in the course of operating a business. The **recognition criteria for revenues** tell accountants *when* to record revenue—that is, when to make a journal entry for a revenue transaction, and the *amount* of revenue to record.

When to Record Revenue Revenue recognition criteria state that revenue should be recorded when it has been *earned*—but not before. In most cases, revenue is earned when the business has delivered a good to the customer and/or completed a service. In other words, the business has satisfied its performance obligation.

Exhibit 3–2 shows two situations that provide guidance on when to record revenue. Situation 1 illustrates when *not* to record revenue, because the client merely states her plans. Situation 2 illustrates when revenue should be recorded—after the company has performed the service for the client.

The Amount of Revenue to Record The general principle is to record revenue equal to the cash value of the goods or the service transferred to the customer. Suppose that, in order to obtain a new client, Custom Marketing offers their advertising services for the discounted price of $5,000. Ordinarily the business would have charged $7,000 for this service. How much revenue should the business record? The answer is $5,000, because that was the cash value of the transaction.

Recognition Criteria for Expenses

Just as we have criteria that help us determine when to recognize revenue and how much revenue we should record, we also have criteria to help us determine when to recognize expenses. This is commonly referred to as the **matching objective**. Recall that expenses such as utilities and advertising are the costs of assets and

EXHIBIT 3–2 | Recording Revenue: The Recognition Criteria for Revenues

services that are consumed when earning revenue. The matching objective directs accountants to

1. Identify all expenses incurred during the accounting period.
2. Measure the expenses.
3. Match the expenses against the revenues earned during that period. This means subtracting related expenses from the revenues to compute net income or net loss.

Accountants follow the matching objective by identifying the revenues of a period and then the expenses that can be linked to particular revenues. For example, a business that pays sales commissions to its salespeople like Custom Marketing does will have commission expense for completed sales. Custom Marketing records the commission during the same period as the sale, even though the commission is paid later. If there are no sales in a period (so no revenue was earned), the business has no commission expense.

Other expenses are not so easy to link with particular sales. Custom Marketing's monthly rent expense occurs, for example, regardless of the revenues earned during the period. The matching objective directs accountants to identify these types of expenses with a particular time period, such as a month or a year. If Custom Marketing employs an office assistant at a monthly salary of $2,500, the business will record salary expense of $2,500 each month.

Try It!

1. Match the accounting terminology to the definitions.

A. Time period concept	i. Requires companies to record revenue when it satisfies each performance obligation (when it is earned).
B. Revenue recognition principle	ii. Assumes that a business's activities can be sliced into small time segments and that financial statements can be prepared for specific periods.
C. Matching objective	iii. Guides accounting for expenses, ensures that all expenses are recorded when they are incurred during the period, and matches those expenses against the revenues of the period.

Solutions appear at the end of this chapter and on **MyLab Accounting**

Accrual-Basis Accounting versus Cash-Basis Accounting

LO (2)

Why can't we wait to record transactions until the cash comes in or the cash goes out?

We can tie those three accounting principles together now as we look at two different ways to keep accounting records.

Accrual-Basis Accounting Recording the effect of every business transaction as it occurs, no matter when cash payments occur, is called **accrual-basis accounting**, or accrual accounting. Accrual accounting is based on the time period assumption and recognition criteria for revenues and expenses. Most businesses use the accrual basis because it is required as part of the generally accepted accounting principles (GAAP). Thus, accrual-basis accounting is the method covered in this text, and so far the accounts receivable and accounts payable accounts have helped us record information this way. We will look at a few more accounts to help us keep track of every transaction in the right period later in this chapter. The Canada Revenue Agency (CRA) requires accrual accounting for income tax purposes except in special cases.

Cash-Basis Accounting Recording transactions only when cash receipts and cash payments occur is called **cash-basis accounting**. Only very small businesses tend to use cash-basis accounting for their bookkeeping because they have less knowledge of accounting concepts and principles. Their accountant may later convert their financial records to the accrual basis when their tax returns are prepared.

Accrual-basis accounting provides more complete information than does cash-basis accounting. This difference is important, because the more complete the data, the better equipped decision makers are to reach accurate conclusions about the firm's financial health and future prospects.

Try It!

2. Total Pool Services earned $130,000 of service revenue during 2018. Of the $130,000 earned, the business received $105,000 in cash. The remaining amount, $25,000, was still owed by customers as of December 31. In addition, Total Pool Services incurred $85,000 of expenses during the year. As of December 31, $10,000 of the expenses still needed to be paid. In addition, Total Pool Services prepaid $5,000 cash in December 2018 for expenses incurred during the next year.
   a. Determine the amount of service revenue and expenses for 2018 using a cash-basis accounting system.
   b. Determine the amount of service revenue and expenses for 2018 using an accrual-basis accounting system.

Solutions appear at the end of this chapter and on **MyLab Accounting**

Adjusting the Accounts

LO (3)

What is the adjusting process, and why is it important?

At the end of the period, the accountant prepares the financial statements. This end-of-period process begins with the unadjusted trial balance that lists the accounts and their balances after the period's transactions have been recorded in the journal and posted to the accounts in the ledger. We prepared trial balances in Chapter 2, which is shown as step ❹ in Exhibit 3–1.

Let's return to follow the transactions of Hunter Environmental Consulting, the company we looked at in Chapters 1 and 2. For illustration purposes, assume Exhibit 3–3 is their unadjusted trial balance at May 31, 2019. (Account numbers are not shown. The balances and accounts are different from those described in earlier chapters because they reflect additional transactions that occurred during the month of May.)

EXHIBIT 3-3 | Unadjusted Trial Balance

HUNTER ENVIRONMENTAL CONSULTING Unadjusted Trial Balance May 31, 2019		
Account Title	**Debit**	**Credit**
Cash	$ 31,000	
Accounts receivable	14,000	
Office supplies	1,500	
Prepaid insurance	3,600	
Furniture	45,000	
Land	50,000	
Accounts payable		$ 12,000
Unearned service revenue		3,000
Lisa Hunter, capital		120,100
Lisa Hunter, withdrawals	6,000	
Service revenue		24,000
Rent expense	3,000	
Salaries expense	4,000	
Utilities expense	1,000	
Total	$159,100	$159,100

This monthly end-of-period process of updating the accounts is called "month end" and keeps many accounting department staff members very busy!

Accrual-basis accounting requires adjusting entries at the end of the period in order to produce correct balances for the financial statements. This is step 5 in Exhibit 3–1.

Adjusting entries assign revenues to the period in which they are earned and expenses to the period in which they are incurred. Adjusting entries also update the asset and liability accounts. They are needed to

- Properly measure the period's income on the income statement
- Bring related asset and liability accounts to correct balances for the balance sheet

Let's look at the end-of-period process of updating the accounts, which is called *adjusting the accounts, making the adjusting entries*, or *adjusting the books.*

Watch out! Accrual-basis accounting and accruals are not exactly the same thing! *Accrual-basis accounting* means recording transactions as they happen even if no cash is exchanged. There are two types of adjustments required to accomplish accrual-basis accounting: prepaids and *accruals*.

Prepaids and Accruals

Two basic types of adjustments are *prepaids* and *accruals.* In a *prepaid*-type adjustment, the cash is paid or received before the related expense or revenue is recorded. Prepaids are also called *deferrals* because the recording of the expense or the revenue is deferred (delayed) to periods after cash is paid or received. *Accrual*-type adjustments are the opposite of prepaids. For accruals, we record the expense or revenue before the related cash is paid or received. The timeline in Exhibit 3–4 helps to show how you can remember the difference between prepaids and accruals:

EXHIBIT 3–4 | Timeline for Adjusting Entries

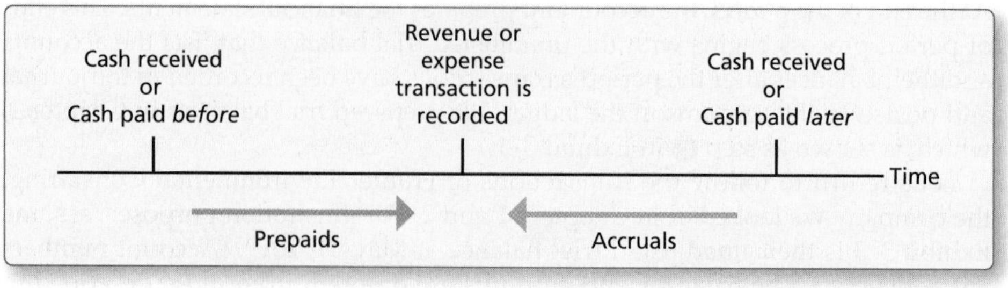

Adjusting entries can be further divided into five categories, as illustrated in Exhibit 3–5.

EXHIBIT 3–5 | Adjusting Entries

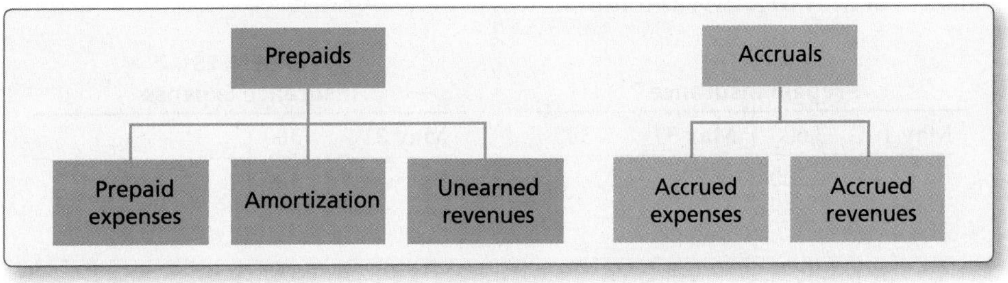

Study this material carefully because it is the most challenging topic in all of introductory accounting.

Prepaid Expenses

Prepaid expenses are assets that typically expire or are used up in the near future. They are assets since they represent a potential future economic benefit. Prepaid rent, prepaid insurance, and supplies are examples of prepaid expenses. They are called "prepaid" expenses because they are expenses that are paid in advance. Companies must later make adjustments regarding prepaid expenses to show what has been used up and to reflect an accurate asset balance on the balance sheet.

Prepaid expenses are assets, not expenses.

Prepaid Insurance Business insurance is usually paid in advance. This prepayment creates an asset for the policyholder because the policyholder has purchased the future benefit of insurance protection. Suppose HEC purchases a business liability insurance policy on May 1, 2019. The cost of the insurance is $3,600 for one year of coverage. The entry to record the payment is a debit to the asset account, Prepaid Insurance, as follows:

May 1	Prepaid Insurance	3,600	
	Cash		3,600
	Paid annual premium for business liability insurance.		

After posting, Prepaid Insurance appears as follows:

ASSETS
Prepaid Insurance

May 1	3,600	

The unadjusted trial balance at May 31, 2019, shown in Exhibit 3–3 lists Prepaid Insurance as an asset with a debit balance of $3,600. Throughout May, the Prepaid Insurance account maintains this balance. But $3,600 is *not* the amount of Prepaid Insurance for HEC's balance sheet at May 31, 2019. Why?

Adjusting a Prepaid Account At May 31, Prepaid Insurance should be adjusted to remove from its balance the amount of insurance that has been used up, which is one month's worth. By definition, the amount of an asset that has been used, or has expired, is an *expense*. This is an example of applying the matching objective. The adjusting entry transfers one-twelfth, or $300 ($3,600 × $\frac{1}{12}$), of the debit balance from Prepaid Insurance to Insurance Expense. The debit side of the entry records an increase in Insurance Expense, and the credit records a decrease in the asset Prepaid Insurance.

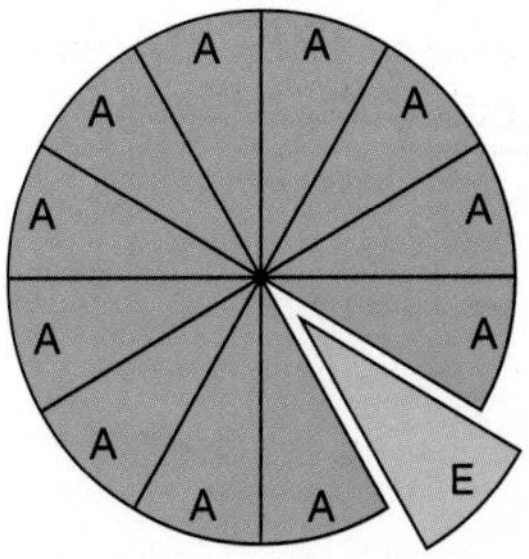

A = One month's Prepaid Insurance of $300, an asset (× 11 months = $3,300)

E = May's Insurance Expense of $300, an expense

The whole circle represents the full year of insurance coverage divided into 12 monthly pieces.

May 31	Insurance Expense	300	
	Prepaid Insurance		300
	To record insurance expense ($3, 600 × $\frac{1}{12}$) for May.		

Two rules to remember about adjusting entries:

1. Adjusting entries never involve the Cash account.
2. Adjusting entries either
   a. Increase a revenue account (credit revenue) or
   b. Increase an expense account (debit expense).

After posting, Prepaid Insurance and Insurance Expense show correct ending balances at May 31, 2019, as follows:

ASSETS

Prepaid Insurance

May 1	3,600	**May 31**	300
Bal.	3,300		

EXPENSES

Insurance Expense

May 31	300	
Bal.	300	

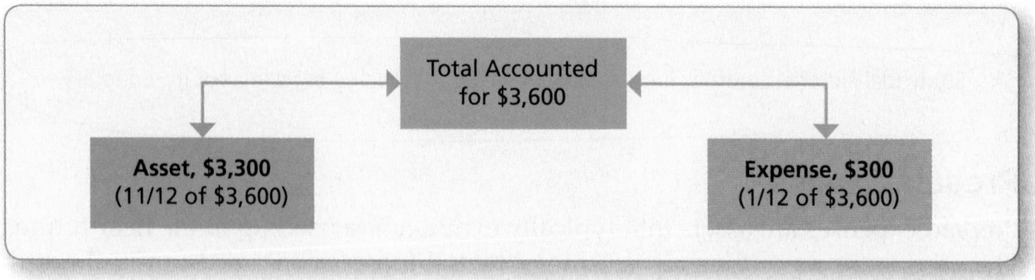

The full $3,600 has been accounted for. As shown in the diagram in the margin, eleven-twelfths measures the asset, and one-twelfth measures the expense.

A similar journal entry would be made at the end of the month for the next 11 months, eventually bringing the Prepaid Insurance balance to zero and the Insurance Expense balance to $3,600 over the life of the policy. In a computerized accounting system, the adjusting entry could be set up to occur automatically in each subsequent accounting period until the prepaid account has a zero balance.

The same analysis applies to a prepayment of rent. The only difference is in the account titles, which would be Prepaid Rent and Rent Expense instead of Prepaid Insurance and Insurance Expense.

The chapter appendix shows an alternative treatment of prepaid expenses where the expense is recorded first and the adjusting entry sets up the asset. The end result on the financial statements is the same as that for the method given here.

Supplies Supplies are accounted for in the same way as prepaid expenses. Suppose that, on May 2, HEC paid cash of $1,500 for office supplies:

May 2	Office Supplies	1,500	
	Cash		1,500
	Paid cash for office supplies.		

Assume that the business purchased no additional office supplies during April. The May 31 unadjusted trial balance, therefore, lists Office Supplies with a $1,500 debit balance as shown in Exhibit 3–3. But HEC's May 31 balance sheet should *not* report supplies of $1,500. Why?

During May, HEC used supplies in performing services for clients. The cost of the supplies used is the measure of *supplies expense* for the month. To measure HEC's supplies expense during May, Lisa Hunter counts the supplies on hand at the end of the month. This is the amount of the asset still available to the business. Assume the count indicates that supplies costing $1,000 remain. Subtracting the entity's $1,000 of supplies on hand at the end of May from the cost of supplies available during May ($1,500) measures supplies expense during the month ($500):

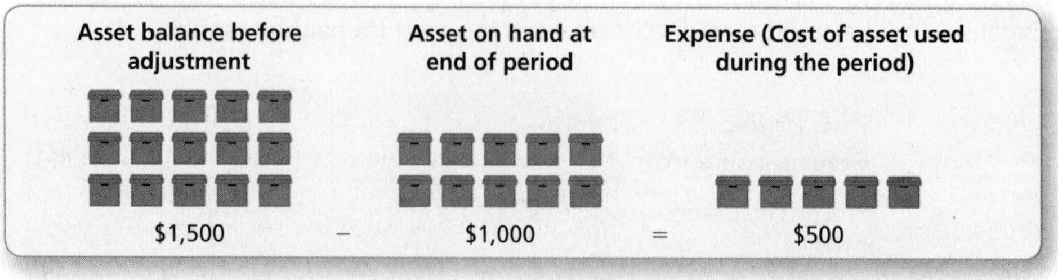

This same analysis could be done using a T-account:

ASSETS
Office Supplies

May 2	1,500		?
Bal.	1,000		

Asset balance before adjustment → May 2

Asset on hand at end of period → Bal.

Solve for the amount used during the period (in this case, expense is $1,500 – $1,000 = $500)

The May 31 adjusting entry updates the Office Supplies account and records the expense for supplies for May as follows:

May 31	Supplies Expense	500	
	Office Supplies		500
	To record supplies used during the month ($1,500 – $1,000).		

After posting, the Office Supplies and Supplies Expense accounts hold correct ending balances:

ASSETS
Office Supplies

May 2	1,500	**May 31**	**500**
Bal.	1,000		

→

EXPENSES
Supplies Expense

May 31	**500**		
Bal.	500		

The Office Supplies account enters the month of June with a $1,000 balance, and the adjustment process is repeated each month until the asset is used up.

Why It's Done This Way

Let's look at how the accounting framework explains why we need to adjust accounts prior to creating financial statements by looking more closely at prepaid accounts. Assume that a company has purchased its business insurance for the next year.

We can see that this transaction should be *recognized* as a financial transaction, and we should *measure* the transaction at its cost.

The company would categorize the insurance as an *asset* since there is future economic benefit to the company—the company has insurance coverage for the next year.

By recording and measuring the transaction in this manner, we have provided information that is *relevant* and *reliable* at the time the insurance is purchased.

The insurance coverage will expire a year from the date it was purchased, so the value of the prepaid asset declines with the passage of time. If we were to prepare the financial statements five months after the insurance was purchased, the balance sheet would not be *relevant* if it still showed the prepaid insurance at its original cost.

By completing the adjustment to expense the used portion, our financial statements remain both *reliable* and *relevant* to users, and the balance sheet and income statement will *communicate useful information to users*.

Amortization

The accrual basis of accounting also applies to how businesses account for capital assets. **Property, plant, and equipment (PPE)** are identifiable **tangible capital assets**, which are physical assets such as land, buildings, furniture, vehicles, machinery, and equipment. All these tangible capital assets except land decline in usefulness as they age. This decline is an *expense* to the business.

Accountants systematically spread the cost of each type of plant and equipment less any residual (or salvage) value over its *estimated* useful life. The *CPA Canada Handbook* calls this process of allocating the cost of plant and equipment to an expense account over its life **amortization**. (Another term for amortization in common usage is *depreciation*.)

Don't confuse current (and often increasing) real estate prices (market value) with the historic cost of the asset reported in the accounting records. Amortization expense is an accounting estimate that allocates the cost of the asset to an expense account as it is used over time. It is not intended to reflect current market values.

Many companies also own **intangible assets**, which are capital assets with no physical form, such as patents and trademarks. These assets will be discussed in more detail in Chapter 10.

Similarity to Prepaid Expenses The concept of accounting for amortization expense is the same as for prepaid expenses. In a sense, plant and equipment are large prepaid expenses that expire over a number of periods. For both prepaid expenses and plant and equipment, the business purchases an asset that wears out or is used up. As the asset is used, more and more of its cost is transferred from the asset account to the expense account. The major difference between prepaid expenses and capital assets is the length of time it takes for the asset to lose its usefulness (or expire). Prepaid expenses usually expire within a year, whereas plant and equipment assets remain useful for a number of years.

Consider HEC's operations. Suppose that, on May 3, the business purchased furniture for $45,000 and made this journal entry:

May 3	Furniture	45,000	
	Cash		45,000
	Purchased office furniture.		

Under IFRS, *depreciation* is the term used for amortizing tangible assets. *Amortization* is the term used for intangible assets. Many companies following ASPE also use this convention since the *CPA Canada Handbook* uses the term *amortization* but does not require it.

After posting, the Furniture account appears as follows:

ASSETS
Furniture

May 3 45,000	

In accrual-basis accounting, an asset is recorded when the furniture is acquired. Then, a portion of the asset's cost is transferred to Amortization Expense each period that the asset is used. This method matches the asset's expense to the revenue of the period, which is an application of the matching objective.

Straight-Line Method Lisa Hunter believes the furniture will remain useful for five years and be virtually worthless at the end of its life. One common way to calculate the amount of amortization to be recorded is the **straight-line method**. It divides the cost of the asset (less any **residual value** or *salvage value*) by its useful life so that the same amount of amortization is recorded for each period the asset provides value to its owner:

$$\text{Straight-line Amortization Expense} = \frac{\text{Cost} - \text{Residual value}}{\text{Useful life}}$$

$$= \frac{\$45{,}000 - \$0}{5 \text{ years}}$$

$$= \$9{,}000 \text{ per year}$$

In the case of HEC, the adjusting entries are prepared monthly, so the annual amortization expense must be divided by 12 to get the monthly cost. To find the monthly expense amount:

- Divide the annual amount by 12: $\$9,000 \div 12 = \$750$ per month.

Alternatively,

- The useful life could be shown as 60 months (5 years $\times$ 12 months $=$ 60 months).
- The calculation would be $(\$45,000 - \$0) \div 60 = \$750$ per month.

Amortization expense for May is recorded by the following adjusting entry:

May 31	Amortization Expense—Furniture	750	
	Accumulated Amortization—Furniture		750
	To record monthly amortization expense on furniture.		

The Accumulated Amortization Account Accumulated Amortization—Furniture is credited—not Furniture—because the original cost of any property, plant, and equipment acquisitions should remain in the asset account as long as the business uses the asset. This is an application of the cost principle you learned in Chapter 1. Accountants and managers may refer to the Furniture account to see how much the asset cost. This information is useful in a decision about whether to replace the furniture and the amount to pay. Accountants use the **Accumulated Amortization** account to show the cumulative sum of all amortization expense from the date of acquiring the tangible capital asset. Therefore, the balance in this account increases over the life of the asset—the account balance continues to "accumulate" over the life of the asset.

Use a separate Amortization Expense account and Accumulated Amortization account for each major type of tangible asset (Amortization Expense–Furniture, Amortization Expense–Buildings, and so on). Notice the format of the account names, which are expanded to describe the different assets.

Accumulated Amortization is a *contra asset* account. A **contra account** has two main characteristics:

- A contra account has a companion account.
- A contra account's normal balance (debit or credit) is the opposite of (or *contrary* to) the companion account's normal balance. (Recall from Chapter 2 that the normal balance of an account is the side of the account where increases are recorded.)

In this case, Accumulated Amortization—Furniture is the contra account that accompanies Furniture. It appears in the ledger directly after Furniture. Furniture has a debit balance, and therefore Accumulated Amortization—Furniture, a contra asset, has a credit balance. *All contra asset accounts have credit balances.*

After posting the amortization for one period, the related accounts of HEC are as follows:

ASSETS
Furniture

May 3	45,000	
Bal.	45,000	

CONTRA ASSET
Accumulated Amortization—Furniture

	May 31	750
	Bal.	750

EXPENSES
Amortization Expense—Furniture

May 31	750	
Bal.	750	

Book Value The balance sheet reports both Furniture and Accumulated Amortization—Furniture. Because it is a contra account, the balance of Accumulated Amortization—Furniture is subtracted from the balance of Furniture. This net amount (cost minus accumulated amortization) of a capital asset is called its **book value**, or *net book value*, or **carrying value**, which can be shown on a financial statement this way:

Furniture	$45,000
Less: Accumulated Amortization—Furniture	750
Furniture, net	$44,250

There is no rule or standard for how this financial information is presented. Some companies show brackets on the amount of a contra account. Other companies do not include the word *Less* in the statement. Everyone is correct.

The balance sheet at May 31 would report HEC's property, plant, and equipment as shown in Exhibit 3–6.

When a business shows a summary level of information such as "Furniture, net" in the balance sheet (perhaps they are a large corporation with many accounts), the details of the assets' cost and accumulated amortization are presented in the notes to the financial statement.

During May, HEC paid its employees' salaries of $4,000 on Thursday, May 15, and recorded the following entry:

May 15	Salaries Expense	4,000	
	Cash		4,000
	To pay salaries.		

After posting, the Salaries Expense account is as follows:

EXPENSES
Salaries Expense

May 15	4,000	

The unadjusted trial balance at May 31 (Exhibit 3–3) includes Salaries Expense with a debit balance of $4,000. Because May 31, the second payday of the month, falls on a Saturday, the second $4,000 payment will be made on Monday, June 2. Without an adjusting entry, this second $4,000 amount is not included in the May 31 trial balance amount for Salaries Expense, even though the expense has been incurred. Therefore, at May 31 the business adjusts for additional *salaries expense* and *salaries payable* of $4,000 by recording an increase in each of these accounts as follows:

All accrued expenses are recorded with similar entries—a debit to the appropriate expense account and a credit to the related liability account.

May 31	Salaries Expense	4,000	
	Salaries Payable		4,000
	To accrue salaries expense.		

After posting, the Salaries Expense and Salaries Payable accounts are updated to May 31:

EXPENSES
Salaries Expense

May 15	4,000	
May 31	4,000	
Bal.	8,000	

LIABILITIES
Salaries Payable

	May 31	4,000
	Bal.	4,000

The accounts at May 31 now contain the complete salaries information for the month of May. The expense account has a full month's salaries, and the liability account shows the portion that the business still owes at May 31.

Some companies, such as Custom Marketing, pay their employees on the last business day *before* the end of the period to allow employees to make rent and other payments due at the beginning of the month. In such a situation, no accrual for Salaries Expense would be made.

Future Payment of Accrued Salaries HEC will record the payment of this liability on Monday, June 2, as follows:

Jun. 2	Salaries Payable	4,000	
	Cash		4,000
	To record the payment of the salary payable.		

This payment entry does not affect May or June expenses because the May expense was recorded on May 15 and May 31. This entry only records the payment of the payable and is not considered to be an adjusting entry. June expense will be recorded in a like manner, starting on June 15.

Accrued Revenues

As we have just seen, expenses can occur before the cash payment, and that creates an accrued expense. Likewise, businesses often earn revenue before they collect the cash. Collection occurs later. Revenue that has been earned but not yet invoiced or collected is called an **accrued revenue**.

Assume HEC is hired on May 15 by Rock Creek Development to provide environmental consulting services on a monthly basis. Under this agreement, Rock Creek will pay HEC $3,000 monthly, with the first payment on June 15. During May, HEC will earn half a month's fee, $1,500, for work performed May 15 through May 31. On May 31, HEC makes the following adjusting entry to record an increase in Accounts Receivable and Service Revenue:

One way of thinking about an accrued revenue is that it is like an accounts receivable but without an invoice. In this case, it would be inappropriate to send an invoice for the part of the work completed as the agreement is for payment of a monthly amount on the 15th of the month. Some work was completed, so the revenue must be recognized with an adjusting entry.

May 31	Accounts Receivable	1,500	
	Service Revenue		1,500
	To accrue service revenue ($3, 000 × $\frac{1}{2}$).		

We see from the unadjusted trial balance in Exhibit 3–3 that Accounts Receivable has an unadjusted balance of $14,000. The Service Revenue unadjusted balance is $24,000. Posting the May 31 adjustment has the following effects on these two accounts:

ASSETS
Accounts Receivable

Bal.	14,000	
May 31	**1,500**	
Bal.	15,500	

REVENUES
Service Revenue

	Bal.	24,000
	May 31	1,000
	May 31	**1,500**
	Bal.	26,500

All accrued revenues are accounted for similarly: Debit a receivable account and credit a revenue account.

This adjusting entry illustrates the concept of revenue recognition. Without the adjustment, HEC's financial statements would be misleading—they would understate Accounts Receivable and Service Revenue by $1,500 each.

The chapter appendix shows an alternative treatment of unearned revenues and prepaid expenses.

Two rules to remember about adjusting entries:

1. Adjusting entries never involve the Cash account.
2. Adjusting entries either
   a. increase a revenue account (credit revenue) or
   b. increase an expense account (debit expense)

Try It!

3. Prepare the journal entries for Startech Surveillance Services' adjustments as of the end of the year. No explanations are required.
   a. Equipment amortization was $1,500.
   b. An advertising expense of $700 was incurred but not paid. (Use Advertising Payable.)
   c. Office Supplies on hand at the end of the year totalled $250. The beginning balance of Office Supplies was $600.
   d. Rent revenue of $1,200 was earned but not recorded or received.
   e. Unearned revenue of $3,000 had been earned.

Solutions appear at the end of this chapter and on **MyLab Accounting**

Summary of the Adjusting Process

Exhibit 3–7 summarizes the timing of adjusting entries (in blue) and shows the related journal entries made before or after them.

EXHIBIT 3–7 | Timing of Prepaid and Accrual Adjustments

PREPAIDS—Cash receipt or cash payment occurs first

Prepaid expenses

ORIGINAL ENTRY

Prepaid Insurance	XXX	
Cash		XXX
Pay for insurance in advance and record an asset first.		

ADJUSTING ENTRY

Insurance Expense	XXX	
Prepaid Insurance		XXX
Adjust for insurance used later and decrease the asset.		

Amortization

ORIGINAL ENTRY

Furniture	XXX	
Cash		XXX
Pay for furniture in advance and record an asset first.		

ADJUSTING ENTRY

Amortization Expense—Furniture	XXX	
Accum. Amort.—Furniture		XXX
Adjust for amortization (use) of asset later.		

Unearned revenues

ORIGINAL ENTRY

Cash	XXX	
Unearned Revenue		XXX
Receive cash in advance and record a liability first.		

ADJUSTING ENTRY

Unearned Revenue	XXX	
Revenue (e.g., Consulting)		XXX
Adjust for revenue earned later and decrease the liability.		

ACCRUALS—Cash receipt or cash payment occurs later.

Accrued expenses

ADJUSTING ENTRY

Salaries Expense	XXX	
Salaries Payable		XXX
Accrue for expense first and increase liability.		

LATER ENTRY

Salaries Payable	XXX	
Cash		XXX
Pay the liability later.		

Accrued revenues

ADJUSTING ENTRY

Accounts Receivable	XXX	
Revenue (e.g., Consulting)		XXX
Accrue the revenue earned first and increase the receivable.		

LATER ENTRY

Cash	XXX	
Accounts Receivable		XXX
Collect cash from the customer later.		

Exhibit 3–8 summarizes the adjusting entries of HEC at May 31 and shows the accounts after they have been posted. The adjustments are identified by their letter to save space.

EXHIBIT 3–8 | Journalizing and Posting the Adjusting Entries of Hunter Environmental Consulting

Panel A: Information for Adjustments at May 31, 2019

a. Prepaid insurance expired during May, $300
b. Supplies remaining on hand at May 31, $1,000
c. Amortization on furniture for the month of May, $750
d. Accrued salaries expense, $4,000
e. Accrued service revenue, $1,500
f. Amount of unearned service revenue that was earned during May, $1,000

Panel B: Adjusting Entries

a. Insurance Expense	300	
Prepaid Insurance		300
To record insurance expense.		
b. Supplies Expense	500	
Office Supplies		500
To record supplies used.		
c. Amortization Expense—Furniture	750	
Accumulated Amortization—Furniture		750
To record amortization on furniture.		

d. Unearned Service Revenue	1,000	
Service Revenue		1,000
To record unearned revenue that has been earned.		
e. Salaries Expense	4,000	
Salaries Payable		4,000
To accrue salaries expense.		
f. Accounts Receivable	1,500	
Service Revenue		1,500
To accrue service revenue.		

Panel C: Amounts Posted to T-Accounts

ASSETS

Cash

Bal. 31,000	

Accounts Receivable

Bal. 14,000	
(f) 1,500	
Bal. 15,500	

Office Supplies

Bal. 1,500	(b) 500
Bal. 1,000	

Prepaid Insurance

Bal. 3,600	(a) 300
Bal. 3,300	

Land

Bal. 50,000	

Furniture

Bal. 45,000	

Accumulated Amortization—Furniture

	(c) 750
	Bal. 750

LIABILITIES

Accounts Payable

	Bal. 12,000

Salary Payable

	(e) 4,000
	Bal. 4,000

Unearned Service Revenue

(d) 1,000	Bal. 3,000
	Bal. 2,000

OWNER'S EQUITY

Lisa Hunter, Capital

	Bal. 120,100

Lisa Hunter, Withdrawals

Bal. 6,000	

REVENUES

Service Revenue

	Bal. 24,000
	(e) 1,000
	(f) 1,500
	Bal. 26,500

EXPENSES

Amortization Expense—Furniture

(c) 750	
Bal. 750	

Insurance Expense

(a) 300	
Bal. 300	

Rent Expense

Bal. 3,000	

Salaries Expense

Bal. 4,000	
(e) 4,000	
Bal. 8,000	

Supplies Expense

(b) 500	
Bal. 500	

Utilities Expense

Bal. 1,000	

The Adjusted Trial Balance

This chapter began with the trial balance before any adjusting entries—the unadjusted trial balance (Exhibit 3–3). After the adjustments are journalized and posted, the accounts appear as shown in Exhibit 3–8, Panel C. A useful step in preparing the financial statements is to list the accounts, along with their adjusted balances, on an **adjusted trial balance**. This is step 6 in Exhibit 3–1. This document has the

LO 4
How do we get the accounting records ready to prepare the financial statements?

advantage of listing all the accounts and their adjusted balances in a single place. Exhibit 3–9 shows an adjusted trial balance.

EXHIBIT 3–9 | Adjusted Trial Balance

HUNTER ENVIRONMENTAL CONSULTING Adjusted Trial Balance May 31, 2019			
Account Title	Debit	Credit	
Cash	$ 31,000		Balance Sheet
Accounts receivable	15,500		
Office supplies	1,000		
Prepaid insurance	3,300		
Furniture	45,000		
Accumulated amortization—furniture		$ 750	
Land	50,000		
Accounts payable		12,000	
Salaries payable		4,000	
Unearned service revenue		2,000	
Lisa Hunter, capital		120,100	Statement of Owner's Equity
Lisa Hunter, withdrawals	6,000		
Service revenue		26,500	Income Statement
Amortization expense	750		
Insurance expense	300		
Rent expense	3,000		
Salaries expense	8,000		
Supplies expense	500		
Utilities expense	1,000		
Total	$165,350	$165,350	

> Some companies list expenses in descending order (largest first, smallest last). Other companies list expenses in account number or alphabetical order. What matters most is that the order is consistent between periods.

In Chapter 4 we will look at worksheets as an alternative tool for accountants to use when preparing an adjusted trial balance.

Try It!

4. Hooten Carpentry had the following accounts and account balances after adjusting entries. Assume all accounts have normal balances. Prepare the adjusted trial balance for Hooten Carpentry as of December 31, 2018.

Cash	$ 4,025	Hooten, Capital	$?
Land	5,000	Accounts Receivable	660
Utilities Expense	400	Office Supplies	120
Accounts Payable	225	Utilities Payable	210
Accumulated Amortization—Equipment	1,000	Service Revenue	12,000
Salaries Expense	550	Unearned Revenue	300
Supplies Expense	80	Amortization Expense—Equipment	800
Equipment	10,000	Hooten, Withdrawals	500

Preparing the Financial Statements from the Adjusted Trial Balance

LO 5

Remind me: How do we prepare the financial statements?

The May financial statements of Hunter Environmental Consulting (HEC) can be prepared from the adjusted trial balance in Exhibit 3–9. The right margin shows how the accounts are distributed to the financial statements. This is Step 7 in Exhibit 3-1.

- The income statement (Exhibit 3–10) is created using the revenue and expense accounts.
- The statement of owner's equity (Exhibit 3–11) shows the reasons for the change in the owner's capital account during the period.
- The balance sheet (Exhibit 3–12) reports the assets, liabilities, and owner's equity.

EXHIBIT 3–10 | Income Statement

HUNTER ENVIRONMENTAL CONSULTING Income Statement For the Month Ended May 31, 2019		
Revenue		
Service revenue		$26,500
Expenses		
Amortization expense	$ 750	
Insurance expense	300	
Rent expense	3,000	
Salaries expense	8,000	
Supplies expense	500	
Utilities expense	1,000	
Total expenses		13,550
Net income		$12,950

EXHIBIT 3–11 | Statement of Owner's Equity

❶

HUNTER ENVIRONMENTAL CONSULTING Statement of Owner's Equity For the Month Ended May 31, 2019	
Lisa Hunter, capital, May 1, 2019	$120,100
Add: Net income	12,950
	133,050
Less: Withdrawals	6,000
Lisa Hunter, capital, May 31, 2019	$127,050

EXHIBIT 3–12 | Balance Sheet

❷

HUNTER ENVIRONMENTAL CONSULTING Balance Sheet May 31, 2019				
Assets			**Liabilities**	
Cash		$ 31,000	Accounts payable	$ 12,000
Accounts receivable		15,500	Salaries payable	4,000
Office supplies		1,000	Unearned service revenue	2,000
Prepaid insurance		3,300	Total liabilities	18,000
Furniture	$45,000			
Less: Accumulated amortization—furniture	750	44,250	**Owner's Equity**	
Land		50,000	Lisa Hunter, capital	127,050
Total assets		$145,050	Total liabilities and owner's equity	$145,050

Relationships among the Three Financial Statements

The arrows in Exhibits 3–10, 3–11, and 3–12 illustrate the relationships among the income statement, the statement of owner's equity, and the balance sheet. Consider why the income statement is prepared first and the balance sheet last.

1. The income statement reports net income or net loss, calculated by subtracting expenses from revenues. Because revenues and expenses are owner's equity accounts, their net figure is then transferred to the statement of owner's equity.
2. Capital is a balance sheet account, so the ending balance in the statement of owner's equity is transferred to the balance sheet.

You may be wondering why the total assets on the balance sheet ($145,050 in Exhibit 3–12) do not equal the total debits on the adjusted trial balance ($165,350 in Exhibit 3–9). Likewise, the total liabilities and owner's equity do not equal the total credits on the adjusted trial balance ($165,350 in Exhibit 3–9). One reason for these differences is that Accumulated Amortization—Furniture and Lisa Hunter, Withdrawals are contra accounts. Recall that contra accounts are *subtracted* from their companion accounts on the balance sheet. However, on the adjusted trial balance, contra accounts are *added* as a debit or credit in their respective columns.

ETHICS When should accrued expenses be recorded?

Evan is in the process of recording the adjusting entries for Green Landscaping Services. Bob Green, owner and manager, has asked Evan to record all the adjusting entries except for accrued expenses. Bob has a meeting with the banker on Monday to apply for a business loan. Bob knows that the banker will review his balance sheet and income statement. Bob is concerned that by recording the accrued expenses, the business's liabilities will be significantly higher on the balance sheet and a net loss will be reported on the income statement (due to higher expenses). Bob has instructed Evan to delay recording the accrued expenses until after his meeting with the banker. What should Evan do?

Solution

Failing to record the adjusting entries for accrued expenses violates the matching principle. Recording the expenses now (before Monday) accurately matches the occurrence of the expenses with the revenues that were created during that period. If Evan does not record the adjusting entries, the financial statements will not accurately represent the financial position or operating performance of the business. The banker could be tricked into lending the company money. Then, if the business could not repay the loan, the bank would lose—all because the banker relied on incorrect accounting information supplied by the company.

Try It!

5. Prepare just the assets side of a balance sheet given the following accounts and balances, which are presented in random order. Exhibit 3–12 can be used as a model for the correct order of accounts.

Furniture	$21,000	Accounts Receivable	11,750
Accumulated Amortization—Furniture	7,500	Land	85,000
Prepaid Insurance	1,450	Office Supplies	1,100
Cash	63,200		

Solutions appear at the end of this chapter and on **MyLab Accounting**

EXHIBIT 3–13 | IFRS and Adjusting Entries

LO 6

How does IFRS apply to adjusting entries?

ASPE	IFRS
The concept of accrual accounting is accepted around the world. The accounting guidelines for all countries recommend the use of accrual accounting, so there are no process differences.	
Amortization is the term* used for the allocation of the cost of plant and equipment over its estimated useful life: • Amortization Expense • Accumulated Amortization Businesses may choose to use the term *depreciation* or *depletion* to be consistent with other companies in their industry.	*Depreciation* is the term used for amortization of tangible assets: • Depreciation Expense • Accumulated Depreciation *Amortization* is the term used for intangible assets.**
* This is the term used in Part II (ASPE), Section 3061, CPA Canada Handbook.	** IAS 16 and 38

Summary Problem for Your Review

The unadjusted trial balance of Smart Touch Learning Centre for November 30, 2019, which is the end of its fiscal accounting period, is shown below:

SMART TOUCH LEARNING CENTRE Unadjusted Trial Balance November 30, 2019		
Account Title	**Debit**	**Credit**
Cash	$ 13,800	
Accounts receivable	10,000	
Supplies	2,000	
Furniture	20,000	
Accumulated amortization—furniture		$ 8,000
Building	100,000	
Accumulated amortization—building		60,000
Land	44,000	
Accounts payable		4,000
Salaries payable		0
Unearned service revenue		16,000
Gina Ho, capital		64,000
Gina Ho, withdrawals	50,000	
Service revenue		120,000
Salaries expense	32,000	
Supplies expense	0	
Amortization expense—furniture	0	
Amortization expense—building	0	
Miscellaneous expense	200	
Total	$272,000	$272,000

Data needed for the adjusting entries include the following:

a. A count of supplies on November 30 shows $400 of supplies on hand.

b. Amortization for the year on furniture, $4,000.

c. Amortization for the year on building, $2,000.

d. Salaries owed at year-end but not yet paid, $1,000.

e. Service revenue that must be accrued, $2,600.

f. Of the $16,000 balance of unearned service revenue, $6,000 was earned during the year.

Required

1. Open the ledger accounts with their unadjusted balances using T-account format.
2. Journalize Smart Touch Learning Centre's adjusting entries at November 30, 2019. Identify entries by their letter as in Exhibit 3–8 and the date.
3. Post the adjusting entries into the T-accounts. Use a check mark as your posting reference since no account numbers have been provided.

4. Prepare an adjusted trial balance as at November 30, 2019.
5. Prepare the income statement, the statement of owner's equity for the year ended November 30, 2019, and the balance sheet as at November 30, 2019. Draw the arrows linking these three statements. List expenses in order from highest to lowest.

SOLUTION

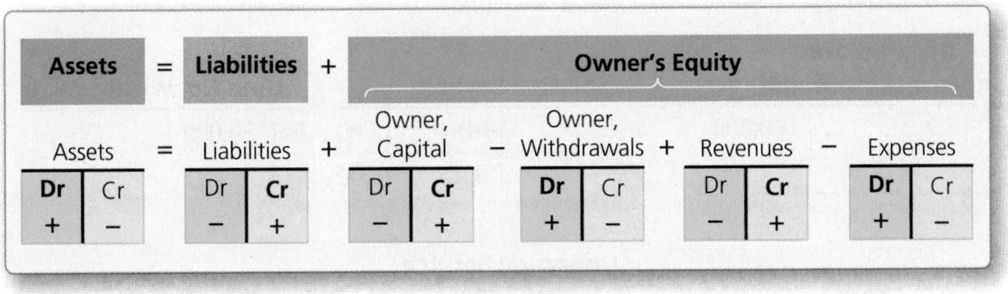

This might be a helpful tool to use when creating the journal entries.

Requirement 2

	Date	Account Titles and Explanations	Post. Ref.	Debit	Credit
	2019				
a.	Nov. 30	Supplies Expense	✓	1,600	
		Supplies	✓		1,600
		To record supplies used ($2,000 – $400).			
b.	Nov. 30	Amortization Expense—Furniture	✓	4,000	
		Accumulated Amortization—Furniture	✓		4,000
		To record amortization expense on furniture.			
c.	Nov. 30	Amortization Expense—Building	✓	2,000	
		Accumulated Amortization—Building	✓		2,000
		To record amortization expense on building.			
d.	Nov. 30	Salaries Expense	✓	1,000	
		Salaries Payable	✓		1,000
		To accrue salary expense.			
e.	Nov. 30	Accounts Receivable	✓	2,600	
		Service Revenue	✓		2,600
		To accrue service revenue.			
f.	Nov. 30	Unearned Service Revenue	✓	6,000	
		Service Revenue	✓		6,000
		To record unearned service revenue that has been earned.			

a. On the November 30, 2019, unadjusted trial balance, Supplies has a balance of $2,000. If the supplies on hand at year-end are $400, then make an adjusting entry for the $1,600 of supplies that were used ($2,000 – $400).

Requirements 1 and 3

For Requirement 1, create a T-account for each account name listed in the November 30, 2019, unadjusted trial balance on page 134. Insert the opening balances into the T-accounts from the trial balance, ensuring debit and credit balances on the trial balance are debit and credit balances in the T-accounts.

For Requirement 3, work slowly and check your work to make sure each transaction is posted to the proper T-account and no transactions were missed.

ASSETS

Cash

Bal.	13,800		

Building

Bal.	100,000		

Accounts Receivable

Bal.	10,000		
(e)	2,600		
Bal.	12,600		

Accumulated Amortization—Building

		Bal.	60,000
		(c)	2,000
		Bal.	62,000

Supplies

Bal.	2,000	(a)	1,600
Bal.	400		

Land

Bal.	44,000		

Furniture

Bal.	20,000		

Accumulated Amortization—Furniture

		Bal.	8,000
		(b)	4,000
		Bal.	12,000

LIABILITIES

Accounts Payable

		Bal.	4,000

Salaries Payable

		(d)	1,000
		Bal.	1,000

Unearned Service Revenue

(f)	6,000	Bal.	16,000
		Bal.	10,000

OWNER'S EQUITY

Gina Ho, Capital

		Bal.	64,000

Gina Ho, Withdrawals

Bal.	50,000		

REVENUE

Service Revenue

		Bal.	120,000
		(e)	2,600
		(f)	6,000
		Bal.	128,600

EXPENSES

Salaries Expense

Bal.	32,000		
(d)	1,000		
Bal.	33,000		

Supplies Expense

(a)	1,600		
Bal.	1,600		

Amortization Expense—Furniture

(b)	4,000		
Bal.	4,000		

Amortization Expense—Building

(c)	2,000		
Bal.	2,000		

Miscellaneous Expense

Bal.	200		

Requirement 4

SMART TOUCH LEARNING CENTRE Adjusted Trial Balance November 30, 2019		
Account Title	**Debit**	**Credit**
Cash	$ 13,800	
Accounts receivable	12,600	
Supplies	400	
Furniture	20,000	
Accumulated amortization—furniture		$ 12,000
Building	100,000	
Accumulated amortization—building		62,000
Land	44,000	
Accounts payable		4,000
Salaries payable		1,000
Unearned service revenue		10,000
Gina Ho, capital		64,000
Gina Ho, withdrawals	50,000	
Service revenue		128,600
Salaries expense	33,000	
Amortization expense—furniture	4,000	
Amortization expense—building	2,000	
Supplies expense	1,600	
Miscellaneous expense	200	
	$281,600	$281,600

The title of each statement must include the name of the company, the name of the statement, and either the specific period of time covered or the date of the statement.

Expenses are listed here from highest to lowest dollar amount. They could also be listed alphabetically.

Miscellaneous Expense is a catch-all account for expenses that do not fit in another category. It is usually reported last. Miscellaneous Expense should be a reasonably low dollar amount. If it is not, new accounts should be created for relevant expenses.

Ensure total debits equal total credits then double underline the totals to show they are final. Refer to Chapter 2 for help if the totals are not equal on your first try.

Requirement 5

Gather all the revenue and expense account names and amounts from the adjusted trial balance.

Expenses are listed in the same order they are found on the adjusted trial balance.

SMART TOUCH LEARNING CENTRE Income Statement For the Year Ended November 30, 2019		
Revenue		
Service revenue		$128,600
Expenses		
Salaries expense	$33,000	
Amortization expense—furniture	4,000	
Amortization expense—building	2,000	
Supplies expense	1,600	
Miscellaneous expense	200	
Total expenses		40,800
Net income		$ 87,800

Beginning owner's equity and withdrawals are from the adjusted trial balance. The net income amount is transferred from the income statement.

1

The owner's equity amount is transferred from the statement of owner's equity.

SMART TOUCH LEARNING CENTRE Statement of Owner's Equity For the Year Ended November 30, 2019	
G. Ho, capital, December 1, 2018	$ 64,000
Add: Net income	87,800
	151,800
Less: Withdrawals	50,000
G. Ho, capital, November 30, 2019	$101,800

Note that the date format is different for the balance sheet. This statement shows the financial position on one specific date.

Gather all the asset and liability accounts and amounts from the adjusted trial balance.

2

The owner's equity amount is transferred from the statement of owner's equity.

SMART TOUCH LEARNING CENTRE Balance Sheet November 30, 2019				
Assets			**Liabilities**	
Cash		$ 13,800	Accounts payable	$ 4,000
Accounts receivable		12,600	Salaries payable	1,000
Supplies		400	Unearned service revenue	10,000
Furniture	$ 20,000		Total liabilities	15,000
Less: Accumulated amortization	12,000	8,000	**Owner's Equity**	
Building	100,000		G. Ho, capital	101,800
Less: Accumulated amortization	62,000	38,000		
Land		44,000		
Total assets		$116,800	Total liabilities and owner's equity	$116,800

Check that total assets = total liabilities + owner's equity.

Chapter 3 Appendix

ALTERNATIVE TREATMENT OF ACCOUNTING FOR PREPAID EXPENSES AND UNEARNED REVENUES

Chapters 1 through 3 illustrate the most popular way to account for prepaid expenses and unearned revenues. This appendix illustrates an alternative—and equally appropriate—approach.

Prepaid Expense Recorded Initially as an Expense

LO A1

Is there another way to record prepaids?

Prepaid Insurance, Prepaid Rent, Prepaid Advertising, and Prepaid Legal Cost are all prepaid expenses. Supplies that will be used up in the current period or within one year are also accounted for as prepaid expenses.

In the body of the chapter, we showed that when a business prepays an expense it debits an *asset* account and later, as it is used up, debits an *expense* account.

Alternatively, the business can debit an expense account in the entry to record this cash payment. The thinking here is that the asset may be so short-lived that it will expire in the current accounting period—within one year or less. Let's see what happens when it does not expire before year-end. How do we then make an adjustment to ensure that the income statement for the period and the balance sheet at year-end are correct?

A $4,800 cash payment for an advertising contract (for one year, in advance) on August 1, 2019, may be debited to Advertising Expense:

Aug. 1	Advertising Expense	4,800	
	Cash		4,800
	Paid for a 12-month advertising contract.		

At December 31, 2019, only five months' prepayment has expired, leaving seven months' advertising still prepaid, which should be shown as an asset. In this case, the accountant must transfer $\frac{7}{12}$ of the original prepayment of $4,800, or $2,800, to Prepaid Advertising. At December 31, 2019, the business still has the benefit of the prepayment for January through July of 2019. The adjusting entry is as follows:

	Adjusting Entry		
Dec. 31	Prepaid Advertising	2,800	
	Advertising Expense		2,800
	To record prepaid advertising of $2,800 ($4,800 × 7/12).		

After posting, the two accounts appear as follows:

ASSETS
Prepaid Advertising

Dec. 31 Adj.	2,800	
Dec. 31 Bal.	2,800	

Seven months remaining

EXPENSES
Advertising Expense

Aug. 1 Payment	4,800	Dec. 31 Adj.	2,800
Dec. 31 Bal.	2,000		

Five months expired

The balance sheet for 2019 reports Prepaid Advertising of $2,800 ($400 per month for seven months), and the income statement for 2019 reports Advertising Expense of $2,000 ($400 per month for five months), regardless of whether the business initially debits the prepayment to an asset account or to an expense account.

Unearned Revenue Recorded Initially as a Revenue

LO A2

Is there another way to record unearned revenues?

Unearned (deferred) revenues arise when a business collects cash in advance of earning the revenue. The recognition of revenue is *deferred* until later when it is earned. Unearned revenues are liabilities because the business that receives cash owes the other party goods or services to be delivered later. In the chapter we saw that this liability was recognized when the cash was received.

Another way to account for the initial receipt of cash is to credit a *revenue* account when the business receives the cash. If the business then earns all the revenue within the period during which it received the cash, no adjusting entry is needed at the end of the period. However, if the business earns only a part of the revenue during the period, it must make adjusting entries at the end of the period.

Suppose on October 1, 2019, a consulting firm records as consulting revenue the receipt of $18,000 cash for revenue to be earned over nine months. The cash receipt entry is as follows:

Oct. 1	Cash	18,000	
	Consulting Revenue		18,000
	Received revenue to be earned over nine months.		

At December 31 the firm has earned only $\frac{3}{9}$ of the $18,000, or $6,000. Accordingly, the firm makes an adjusting entry to transfer the unearned portion ($\frac{6}{9}$ of $18,000, or $12,000) from the revenue account to a liability account as follows:

	Adjusting Entry		
Dec. 31	Consulting Revenue	12,000	
	Unearned Consulting Revenue		12,000
	Adjust for consulting revenue still to be earned.		

The adjusting entry moves the unearned portion ($\frac{6}{9}$ of $18,000, or $12,000) of the original amount into the liability account because the consulting firm still owes consulting service to the client during January through June of 2020. After posting, the total amount ($18,000), representing nine months of work, is properly divided between the liability account ($12,000, which is six months of work) and the revenue account ($6,000, which is three months of work) as follows:

LIABILITIES
Unearned Consulting Revenue

	Dec. 31 Adj. 12,000
	Dec. 31 Bal. 12,000

Six months of the receipt is still unearned

REVENUE
Consulting Revenue

Dec. 31 Adj. 12,000	Oct. 1 Receipt 18,000
	Dec. 31 Bal. 6,000

Three months of the receipt is earned

The firm's 2019 income statement reports consulting revenue of $6,000, and the balance sheet at December 31, 2019, reports as a liability the unearned consulting revenue of $12,000, regardless of whether the business initially credits a liability account or a revenue account.

Summary

Learning Objectives

① Apply the recognition criteria for revenues and expenses **Pg. 114**

When does a sale really happen? And when do we record an expense?

- The *time period assumption* ensures that accounting information is reported at regular intervals.
- The *recognition criteria for revenues* tell accountants when to record revenue and the amount of revenue to record.
- The *matching objective* guides accounting for expenses. It directs accountants to match expenses against the revenues earned during a particular period of time.

② Distinguish accrual-basis accounting from cash-basis accounting **Pg. 117**

Why can't we wait to record transactions until the cash comes in or the cash goes out?

- *Accrual-basis accounting*: Business events are recorded as they occur. This is part of GAAP and therefore is a basis for both ASPE and IFRS.
- *Cash-basis accounting*: Only those events that affect cash are recorded.

③ Prepare adjusting entries **Pg. 117**

What is the adjusting process, and why is it important?

- *Adjusting entries* are made at the end of the period to update the accounts for preparation of the financial statements. They can be divided into five categories: *prepaid expenses*, *amortization*, *unearned revenues, accrued expenses,* and *accrued revenues*.
- One method to calculate amortization is:

Straight-line amortization expense = (Cost − Residual value) ÷ Useful life

		Type of Account	
	Category of Adjusting Entry	**Debited**	**Credited**
Prepaid-type	Prepaid expense	Expense	Asset
	Amortization	Expense	Contra asset
	Unearned revenue	Liability	Revenue
Accrual-type	Accrued expense	Expense	Liability
	Accrued revenue	Asset	Revenue

④ Prepare an adjusted trial balance **Pg. 129**

How do we get the accounting records ready to prepare the financial statements?

- To prepare the *adjusted trial balance,* make a list of accounts and their balances from the ledger (T-account) totals.

⑤ Prepare the financial statements from the adjusted trial balance **Pg. 130**

Remind me: How do we prepare the financial statements?

- The three financial statements are related as follows: Income, shown on the *income statement*, increases owner's capital, which also appears on the *statement of owner's equity*. The ending balance of capital is the last amount reported on the *balance sheet.*

⑥ Describe the adjusting-process implications of International Financial Reporting Standards (IFRS) **Pg. 133**

How does IFRS apply to adjusting entries?

- There is no significant impact on the adjusting process since accrual accounting is necessary under both IFRS and ASPE.
- Companies reporting under IFRS generally use the term *depreciation* for PPE. ASPE uses the term *amortization*, but *depreciation* is also acceptable.

APPENDIX (A1) Account for a prepaid expense recorded initially as an expense

Pg. 139

Is there another way to record prepaids?

- Yes! First record the full amount of the payment made as an expense and then, at the end of the period, make an adjusting entry to record the portion of the payment that is still not used up.

APPENDIX (A2) Account for an unearned revenue recorded initially as a revenue Pg. 140

Is there another way to record unearned revenues?

- Yes! First record the full amount of the payment received as a revenue and then, at the end of the period, make an adjusting entry to record the portion of the revenue that is still not earned.

Key Terms for the chapter are shown next and are in the **Glossary** at the back of the book. **Similar Terms** are shown after **Key Terms**.

KEY TERMS

Accrual-basis accounting Accounting that recognizes (records) the impact of a business event as it occurs, regardless of whether the transaction affected cash *(p. 117)*.

Accrued expense An expense that has been incurred but not yet paid in cash. Also called an *accrued liability (p. 125)*.

Accrued revenue A revenue that has been earned but not yet received in cash *(p. 127)*.

Accumulated amortization The cumulative sum of all amortization expense from the date of acquiring a capital asset *(p. 123)*.

Adjusted trial balance A list of all the ledger accounts with their adjusted balances *(p. 129)*.

Adjusting entry An entry made at the end of the period to assign revenues to the period in which they are earned and expenses to the period in which they are incurred. Adjusting entries help measure the period's income and bring the related asset and liability accounts to correct balances for the financial statements *(p. 118)*.

Amortization The term the *CPA Canada Handbook* uses to describe the writing off that occurs to expense the cost of capital assets; also called *depreciation (p. 121)*.

Book value The asset's cost less accumulated amortization. Also called *carrying value (p. 123)*.

Carrying value (of property, plant, and equipment) The asset's cost less accumulated amortization. Also called *book value (p. 123)*.

Cash-basis accounting Accounting that records only transactions in which cash is received or paid *(p. 117)*.

Contra account An account that always has a companion account and whose normal balance is opposite that of the companion account *(p. 123)*.

Deferred revenue Another name for unearned revenue *(p. 124)*.

Fiscal year An accounting year of any 12 consecutive months that may or may not coincide with the calendar year *(p. 115)*.

Intangible asset An asset with no physical form giving a special right to current and expected future benefits *(p. 122)*.

Interim period In accounting, an interim period is less than a year *(p. 115)*.

Matching objective The basis for recording expenses. Directs accountants to identify all expenses incurred during the period, measure the expenses, and match them against the revenues earned during that same span of time *(p. 115)*.

Property, plant, and equipment (PPE) Long-lived tangible capital assets, such as land, buildings, and equipment, used to operate a business *(p. 121)*.

Recognition criteria for revenues The basis for recording revenues; tells accountants when to record revenue and the amount of revenue to record *(p. 115)*.

Residual value The expected cash value of an asset at the end of its useful life *(p. 122)*.

Straight-line method An amortization method in which an equal amount of amortization expense is assigned to each year (or period) of asset use *(p. 122)*.

Tangible capital asset Physical assets expected to be used beyond the current accounting period. Examples include land, building, and equipment *(p. 121)*.

Time period assumption Ensures that accounting information is reported at regular intervals *(p. 114)*.

SIMILAR TERMS

Accounting period	Reporting period
Accrual-basis accounting	Accrual accounting
Adjusting the accounts	Making the adjusting entries, adjusting the books
Amortization	Depreciation, depletion
Capital assets	Property, plant, and equipment
Carrying value	Book value, net carrying value, net book value
Deferred	Delayed
Property, plant, and equipment (PPE)	Capital asset, plant asset, fixed asset, tangible capital asset
Record	Journalize, recognize a transaction
Residual value	Scrap value, salvage value

SELF-STUDY QUESTIONS

Test your understanding of the chapter by marking the correct answer for each of the following questions:

1. Under the recognition criteria for revenues, revenue is recorded *(p. 115)*
   a. At the earliest acceptable time
   b. At the latest acceptable time
   c. As soon as it has been earned, but not before
   d. At the end of the accounting period
2. The matching objective provides guidance in accounting for *(p. 115)*
   a. Expenses
   b. Owner's equity
   c. Assets
   d. Liabilities
3. Accrual-basis accounting *(p. 117)*
   a. Results in higher income than cash-basis accounting
   b. Leads to the reporting of more complete information than does cash-basis accounting
   c. Is not acceptable under GAAP
   d. Omits adjusting entries at the end of the period
4. Adjusting entries *(p. 118)*
   a. Assign revenues to the period in which they are earned
   b. Help to properly measure the period's net income or net loss
   c. Bring asset and liability accounts to correct balances
   d. Do all of the above
5. A building-cleaning firm began November with supplies of $210. During the month, the firm purchased supplies of $250. At November 30, supplies on hand total $160. Supplies expense for the period is *(p. 120)*
   a. $160
   b. $340
   c. $300
   d. $500
6. A building that cost $150,000 has accumulated amortization of $70,000. The book value of the building is *(p. 123)*
   a. $70,000
   b. $80,000
   c. $150,000
   d. $190,000
7. Accumulated Amortization is reported on *(p. 124)*
   a. The balance sheet
   b. The income statement
   c. The statement of owner's equity
   d. Both a and b
8. A business received cash of $3,000 in advance for service that will be provided later. The cash receipt entry debited Cash and credited Unearned Revenue for $3,000. At the end of the period, $1,100 is still unearned. The adjusting entry for this situation will *(p. 124)*
   a. Debit Unearned Revenue and credit Revenue for $1,900
   b. Debit Unearned Revenue and credit Revenue for $1,100
   c. Debit Revenue and credit Unearned Revenue for $1,900
   d. Debit Revenue and credit Unearned Revenue for $1,100
9. The adjusting entry to accrue salaries expense *(p. 125)*
   a. Debits Salaries Expense and credits Cash
   b. Debits Salaries Payable and credits Salaries Expense
   c. Debits Salaries Payable and credits Cash
   d. Debits Salaries Expense and credits Salaries Payable
10. The links among the financial statements are *(p. 131)*
    a. Net income from the income statement to the statement of owner's equity
    b. Ending capital from the statement of owner's equity to the balance sheet
    c. Net income from the balance sheet to the income statement.
    d. Both a and b above

Answers to Self-Study Questions

1. c 2. a 3. b 4. d 5. c ($210 + $250 − $160 = $300) 6. b ($150,000 − $70,000 = $80,000) 7. a 8. a ($3,000 received − $1,100 unearned = $1,900 earned) 9. d 10. d

Assignment Material

MyLab Accounting Make the grade with MyLab Accounting: The Starters, Exercises, and Problems can be found on MyLab. You can practise them as often as you want, and most feature step-by-step guided instructions to help you find the right answer.

QUESTIONS

1. What is the difference between accrual-basis accounting and cash-basis accounting?
2. How often are financial statements prepared? What is a fiscal year? What is an interim period?
3. What two questions do the recognition criteria for revenues help answer?
4. Briefly explain the matching objective.
5. What is the purpose of making adjusting entries?
6. Why are adjusting entries usually made at the end of the accounting period, not during the period?
7. Name five categories of adjusting entries and give an example of each.
8. Why must the balance of Supplies be adjusted at the end of the period?
9. Kempenfelt Papers pays $4,800 for an insurance policy that covers four years. At the end of the first year, the balance of its Prepaid Insurance account contains two elements. What are the two elements, and what is the correct amount of each?
10. The title Prepaid Expense suggests that this type of account is an expense. If it is, explain why. If it is not, what type of account is it?
11. Snowbird Supports Company purchased a two-year insurance policy on October 1, 2018. On January 1, 2019, the balance in the Prepaid Insurance account was $3,150. What is the amount of expense to record in the year-end adjusting journal entry on December 31, 2019?
12. What is the process of allocating the cost of plant and equipment over its useful life called?
13. What is a contra account? Identify the contra account introduced in this chapter, along with the account's normal balance.
14. The manager of Qwik-Pick-Up, a convenience store, presents the company's balance sheet to a banker to obtain a loan. The balance sheet reports that the company's property, plant, and equipment have a book value of $155,000 and accumulated amortization of $75,000. What does *book value* of property, plant, and equipment mean? What was the cost of the property, plant, and equipment?
15. Give the entry to record accrued interest revenue of $7,200.
16. Why is unearned revenue a liability? Give an example.
17. What purposes does the adjusted trial balance serve?
18. Explain the relationships among the income statement, the statement of owner's equity, and the balance sheet.
19. Golf Simulator Experts Company failed to record the following adjusting entries at December 31, the end of its fiscal year: (a) accrued expenses, $1,500; (b) accrued revenues, $1,700; and (c) amortization, $3,000. Did these omissions cause net income for the year to be understated or overstated, and by what overall amount?
20. What are two possible differences between IFRS and ASPE in the terms used in amortization journal entries?
21. *A company pays $3,000 on February 1 to rent its office for February, March, and April. Make journal entries dated February 1 to illustrate the two ways this company can record its prepayment of rent.
22. **Diving Masters* magazine received $3,400 for magazine subscriptions in advance and recorded the cash receipt as Subscription Revenue. At the end of the year, only $1,400 of this revenue has been earned. What is the required year-end adjusting entry?

---

* These Questions cover Chapter 3 Appendix topics.

STARTERS

S3–1 In December, *Northern Kiteboarding* magazine collected $80,000 for subscriptions for the next calendar year. The company collects cash in advance and then downloads the magazines to subscribers each month.

① Applying the recognition criteria for revenues

Apply the recognition criteria for revenues to determine (a) when the company should record revenue for this situation and (b) the amount of revenue the company should record for the January-through-March downloads.

S3–2 Momentous Occasions is a photography business that rents photo booths for parties. A group paid $1,000 in advance on March 3 to guarantee services for its party to be held April 2. The total cost of the event was to be $2,500. On April 28, the balance of $1,500 was paid. Answer the following questions about the correct application of the revenue recognition criteria:

① Recognition criteria

a. Is the $1,000 reported as revenue on March 3?

b. On what date was the revenue earned?

c. Is the $1,500 reported as revenue on April 28?

S3–3 For each of the following, state whether you agree or disagree with the accounting treatment. What concept supports your view?

① Accounting theory

a. No utilities expense was recorded in December because the bill did not arrive until January.

b. A company records all revenue when earned, whether it has been collected or not.

c. Management of Custom Marketing requires the accountants to prepare weekly financial statements.

S3–4 Suppose you house-sit for people while they are away on vacation. Most of your customers pay you immediately after you finish a job. A few ask you to send them a bill. It is now June 30, and you have collected $600 from cash-paying customers. Your remaining customers owe you $1,400. How much service revenue would you have under the (a) cash basis and (b) accrual basis of accounting? Which method of accounting provides more information about your house-sitting business? Explain your answer.

② Comparing accrual-basis accounting and cash-basis accounting

Service revenue: Cash basis, $600

S3–5 Cryptocurrency Finder is buying the first computer for their new server farm. Suppose the company paid $5,000 for this computer, which it expects to last for three years. Describe how the company would account for the $5,000 expenditure under (a) the cash basis and (b) the accrual basis. State in your own words why the accrual basis is more realistic for this situation.

② Accrual-basis accounting versus cash-basis accounting for expenses

S3–6 Starrs Bakery started 12 months ago as a supplier of gluten-free desserts to restaurants all over the province. During its first year of operations, it earned $62,000 in revenues and incurred $51,000 in expenses. The business collected $58,000 from its customers and paid all but $2,500 to its suppliers. Starrs also prepaid $7,500 for prepaid rent and other expenses for the next year. Calculate the net income under the cash basis and then under the accrual basis.

② Accrual-basis accounting versus cash-basis accounting

S3–7 Check Yes or No in the following tables to indicate whether each of the accounts would usually require an adjusting entry to be made to the specific account listed.

② Adjusting entries introduction

Account	Yes	No	Account	Yes	No
Accounts Receivable			Supplies		
Building			Cash		
Interest Payable			Prepaid Insurance		

S3–8 On April 1, 2020, you prepaid three months of rent for a total of $18,000. Give your adjusting entry to record rent expense at April 30, 2020. Include the date of the entry and an explanation. Then, using T-accounts, post to the two accounts involved and show their balances at April 30, 2020.

③ Adjusting prepaid expenses

3
Adjusting Supplies
(c) $700

S3–9 At the beginning of the month, Supplies were $500. During the month, the company purchased $600 of supplies. At month's end, November 30, $400 of supplies were still on hand.

a. What was the cost of supplies used during the month? Where is this item reported?

b. Where is the ending balance of supplies reported?

c. Make the adjusting entry to update the Supplies account at the end of the month.

3
Recording amortization
(b) Amort. Expense, $750

S3–10 On May 1 your company paid cash of $27,000 for computers that are expected to remain useful for three years. At the end of three years, the value of the computers is expected to be zero. (Hint: Use the formula found on page 122.)

Make journal entries to record (a) the purchase of the computers on May 1 and (b) amortization on May 31. Include dates and explanations, and use the following accounts: Computer Equipment, Accumulated Amortization—Computer Equipment, and Amortization Expense—Computer Equipment.

3
Reporting amortization
2. Book value, $26,250

S3–11 Refer to the data in Starter 3–10.

1. Using T-accounts, post to the accounts listed in Starter 3–10 and show their balances at May 31.
2. What is the computer equipment's book value at May 31?
3. What amount is reported on the income statement on May 31?

3
Accruing and paying interest expense

S3–12 Suppose Resort Travel borrowed $60,000 on March 1 by signing a note payable to Royal Bank. Resort Travel's interest expense on the note payable for the remainder of its fiscal year (March through May) is $600.

1. Record Resort Travel's adjusting entry to accrue interest expense at May 31.
2. Post the adjusting entry to the T-accounts of the two accounts affected by the adjustment.

3
Accruing salaries

S3–13 Employees of Ralph's Llama Farm work Monday through Friday and are paid every Friday for work done that week. The daily payroll is $13,900 and the last payday was Friday, December 28. What is the required adjusting journal entry, if any, on Monday, December 31?

3
Accounting for unearned revenues

S3–14 *Shell Collector* magazine collects cash from subscribers in advance and then mails the magazines to subscribers over a one-year period. Give the adjusting entry that the company makes to record the earning of $10,000 of subscription revenue that was collected in advance on March 1, 2020.

3
Accounting for accrued revenues

S3–15 TentRentals Company sets up a large event tent for the local food festival. The tent will be rented to the Business Improvement Association for two weeks for a total cost of $3,500. The event takes place over the Canada Day weekend. So one week of the rental takes place in June, and the other week is in July. TentRentals will bill the Business Improvement Association on July 6 for the two-week rental. Record the June 30 adjusting entry to update TentRental's financial records for the one week they have earned rental revenue.

4
Preparing an adjusted trial balance
Trial Balance total, $84,850

S3–16 Blazing Software Consulting had the following accounts and account balances after adjusting entries. Assume all accounts have normal balances. Prepare the adjusted trial balance for Blazing Software Consulting's year-end of September 30, 2020.

Cash	$18,150	Computer Equipment	$15,000
Land	20,000	Accounts Receivable	2,250
Utilities Payable	350	Office Supplies	200
Accounts Payable	3,100	S. Scott, Capital	18,400
Accumulated Amortization—Computer Equipment	2,400	Utilities Expense	750
		Unearned Revenue	600
Service Revenue	60,000	Amortization Expense—Computer Equipment	1,200
Supplies Expense	800		
S. Scott, Withdrawals	22,000	Salaries Expense	4,500

S3–17 Compute Yessie Financial Advisors' net income for the year ended December 31, 2020, using the adjusted trial balance below.

(5) Computing net income
check figure of $11,500

YESSIE FINANCIAL ADVISORS Adjusted Trial Balance December 31, 2020		
Account Title	**Debit**	**Credit**
Cash	$ 300	
Office Supplies	300	
Equipment	20,600	
Accumulated amortization—equipment		$ 1,400
Accounts payable		500
Interest payable		800
Note payable		2,800
Y. Benoit, capital		4,200
Service revenue		17,500
Rent expense	3,200	
Interest expense	1,500	
Amortization expense—equipment	700	
Supplies expense	600	
Total	$ 27,200	$ 27,200

S3–18 Refer to the data in S3–17. Compute Yessie Financial Advisors' total assets at December 31, 2020. Remember that Accumulated Amortization is a contra asset.

(5) Computing total assets
Total assets, $19,800

S3–19 Do International Financial Reporting Standards (IFRS) for publicly accountable enterprises in Canada have an impact on the adjusting process for these companies?

(6) IFRS and adjusting entries

***S3–20** On July 31, 2020, Magnus's Muffins paid $18,000 for business insurance for the next year. Record the entries for the purchase of the insurance by recording it as an expense and then making a year-end entry on December 31, 2020, to adjust the accounts.

(A1) Alternative way to record prepaid expenses

***S3–21** On November 1, 2020, Freya Albatter's orthodontic office received a $2,500 prepayment from a client for dental work to be performed on November 22. The appointment got postponed until January 15, 2021. Prepare the journal entries for November 1, the December 31 year-end, and the January 15 appointment dates. Assume that the prepayment was recorded as a revenue because, at that time, it was assumed the work would be performed within the month.

(A2) Alternative way to record unearned revenues

---

* These Starters cover Chapter 3 Appendix topics.

EXERCISES

① Applying accounting assumptions, criteria, and objectives

E3–1 Identify the accounting assumption, criteria, or objective that gives the most direction on how to account for each of the following situations:

a. The owner of a business desires monthly financial statements to measure the financial progress of the business on an ongoing basis.

b. Expenses of $3,000 must be accrued at the end of the period to measure income properly.

c. A customer states her intention to switch travel agencies. Should the new travel agency record revenue based on this intention? Give the reason for your answer.

d. Expenses of the period total $6,000. This amount should be subtracted from revenue to compute the period's net income.

① Applying the recognition criteria for revenues and the matching objective

E3–2 Kobe Company receives two orders from Windsor Company for products costing $5,000. Answer the following questions about them.

1. The December 20, 2019, order will not be shipped until January 5, 2020. Kobe Company wants to record the revenue on December 20 so it can include it in the current year's financial statements. As Kobe's accountant, you object to this accounting treatment. Why?
2. On December 23, 2019, the order is shipped immediately. Kobe Company pays a commission of 5% of the selling price to its sales representative who received the order. This commission will not be paid until January 2020. Kobe's fiscal year-end is December 31. When should the journal entry needed to account for the sales commission be recorded? Explain.

② Cash vs accrual-basis accounting

E3–3 Chef's Catering completed the following selected transactions during May 2020:

May	1	Prepaid rent for three months, $2,400.
	5	Received and paid electricity bill, $700.
	9	Received cash for meals served to customers, $2,600.
	14	Paid cash for kitchen equipment, $3,000.
	23	Served a banquet on account, $2,800.
	31	Made the adjusting entry for rent (from May 1).
	31	Accrued salaries expense, $1,600.
	31	Recorded amortization for May on kitchen equipment, $50.

Required

1. Show whether each transaction would be handled as a revenue or an expense using both the cash basis and accrual basis accounting systems by completing the following table. (Expenses should be shown in parentheses.) Also, indicate the dollar amount of the revenue or expense. The May 1 transaction has been completed as an example.

Amount of Revenue (Expense) for May

Date	Cash Basis Amount of Revenue (Expense)	Accrual Basis Amount of Revenue (Expense)
May 1	*$(2,400)*	*$0*

2. After completing the table, calculate the amount of net income or net loss for Chef's Catering under the accrual basis and cash basis accounting systems for May.
3. Considering your results from Requirement 2, which method gives the best picture of the true earnings of Chef's Catering? Why?

E3–4 Write a memo to your supervisor explaining in your own words the concept of amortization as it is used in accounting. Use the following format:

3 Applying accounting concepts

Date:	(fill in)
To:	Supervisor
From:	(Student Name)
Subject:	The concept of amortization

E3–5 Compute the amounts indicated by question marks for each of the following Prepaid Rent situations. For situation A, make the needed journal entry. Consider each situation separately.

3 Allocating a prepaid expense to asset and expense accounts

C. Ending $6,800

	Situation				
	A	B	C	D	E
Beginning Prepaid Rent	$ 4,200	$ 5,000	$16,800	$ 5,900	$?
Payments for Prepaid Rent during the year	19,800	?	15,000	?	2,500
Total amount to account for	?	?	31,800	15,600	?
Ending Prepaid Rent	19,000	6,000	?	6,000	1,400
Rent Expense	?	$12,000	$25,000	$ 9,600	$2,600

E3–6 Check off the two effects of each of the following transactions:

3 Determining adjustments

Transaction	Revenue Earned	Expense Incurred	Liability Incurred	Liability Reduced	Asset Created	Asset Used Up
a. *Country Living* magazine sent magazines to customers who have paid their subscription.						
b. Young and Rubicam completed work on an advertising plan that will be billed and collected next month.						
c. Automotive Imports recorded the fact that it used up some of the cost of its building.						
d. Classic Ideas Consulting received a cellphone invoice that must be paid next month.						

E3–7 Journalize the entries for the following adjustments at January 31, the end of the accounting period:

3 Journalizing adjusting entries

a. Amortization, $5,000.

b. Prepaid insurance used, $500.

c. Interest expense accrued, $400.

d. Employee salaries owed for Monday through Thursday of a five-day workweek; the weekly payroll is $16,000.

e. Unearned service revenue that becomes earned, $2,000.

E3–8 Journalize the adjusting entry needed at December 31 for each of the following independent situations:

3 Journalizing adjusting entries

c. 22,500

a. On June 1, when we collected $48,000 rent in advance, we debited Cash and credited Unearned Rent Revenue. The tenant was paying for one year's rent in advance. At December 31, we must account for the amount of rent we have earned.

b. Interest revenue of $2,400 has been earned but not yet received on a $60,000 note receivable held by the business.

c. Salaries expense is $7,500 per day—Monday through Friday—and the business pays employees each Friday. This year December 31 falls on a Wednesday.

d. Equipment was purchased last year at a cost of $200,000. The equipment's useful life is five years. It will have no value after five years. Record the year's amortization.

e. On September 1, when we paid $6,000 for a one-year insurance policy, we debited Prepaid Insurance and credited Cash.

f. The business owes interest expense of $7,200 that it will pay early in the next period.

g. The unadjusted balance of the Supplies account is $13,500. The total cost of supplies remaining on hand on December 31 is $4,500.

(3)
Journalizing adjusting entries
a. $2,400

E3–9 Journalize the following December 31 transactions for Jieun Printing Services. No explanations are required.

a. Equipment cost is $24,000 and is expected to be useful for 10 years, at which time it will have no residual value. Calculate and record amortization for the current year.

b. Each Monday, Jieun pays employees for the previous week's work. The amount of weekly payroll is $5,600 for a seven-day workweek (Monday to Sunday). This year December 31 falls on a Thursday.

c. The beginning balance of Supplies was $2,500. During the year, Jieun purchased supplies for $3,000, and at December 31 the supplies on hand totalled $1,700.

d. Jieun prepaid one year of insurance coverage on August 1 of the current year, $5,280. Record insurance expense for the year ended December 31.

e. Jieun earned $3,200 of unearned revenue.

f. Jieun incurred $150 of interest expense on a note payable that will not be paid until February 28.

g. Jieun billed customers $6,000 for printing services performed.

(3)
Journalizing adjusting entries and related transactions
c. Dec 31, $1,800 adj.

E3–10 For each of these six independent situations, journalize the adjusting entry and the related transaction (either before or after it):

a. Dec. 1– business receives $2,000 for a 10-month service contract.

Dec. 31– year-end adjusting entry needed to update the balance in the account.

b. Mar. 31– work performed but not yet billed to customers for the month, $900.

Apr. 21 – received payment for the work that was completed.

c. Jun. 15 – purchased $3,500 of office supplies on account.

Dec. 31– a count of supplies shows that only $1,700 worth is left at year-end, so the balance in the account needs to be updated.

d. Feb. 2– business paid a $450 deposit for the last month's rental of a copier on a 10-month contract.

Nov. 30 – the rental period for the copier ended, so the balance in the prepaid account must be updated.

e. Jun. 1 – purchased truck for $39,900 (cash) with an expected useful life of seven years.

f. Dec. 31 – year-end adjusting entry needed to record amortization.

(3)
Journalizing adjusting entries and posting to T-accounts
3. Unearned Revenue bal. $800 CR

E3–11 The accounting records of Design a Tea Café include the following selected, unadjusted balances at March 31: Accounts Receivable, $1,500; Office Supplies, $700; Prepaid Rent, $2,240; Equipment, $8,000; Accumulated Amortization—Equipment, $0; Salaries Payable, $0; Unearned Revenue, $900; Service Revenue, $4,100; Salaries Expense, $800; Supplies Expense, $0; Rent Expense, $0; Amortization Expense—Equipment, $0.

The March 31 adjusting entries are as follows:

a. Service revenue accrued, $700

b. Unearned revenue that has been earned, $100

c. Office Supplies on hand, $300

d. Salaries owed to employees, $200

e. One month of prepaid rent has expired, $560

f. Amortization on equipment, $120

Required

1. Open a T-account for each account using the unadjusted balances given.
2. Journalize the adjusting entries using the letter and March 31 date in the date column.
3. Post the adjustments to the T-accounts, entering each adjustment by letter. Show each account's adjusted balance.

E3–12 The accounting records of Event Planners include the following unadjusted balances at March 31: Accounts Receivable, $5,400; Supplies, $2,700; Salaries Payable, $0; Unearned Service Revenue, $3,000; Service Revenue, $88,000; Salaries Expense, $22,000; Rent Expense, $18,000; Utilities Expense, $12,000; and Supplies Expense, $0.

(3) Recording adjustments in T-accounts

Service Revenue bal., $91,500

The company's accountant develops the following data for the March 31, 2020, adjusting entries:

a. Service revenue accrued, $2,500
b. Unearned service revenue that has been earned, $1,000
c. Supplies on hand, $800
d. Salaries owed to employees, $2,100

Open T-accounts as needed and record the adjustments directly in the accounts, identifying each adjustment amount by its letter instead of the date. Show each account's adjusted balance. Journal entries are not required.

E3–13 Refer to the data in E3–12. Prepare the adjusted trial balance for Event Planners for March 31, 2020. The remaining account balances you require (after adjustments) are as follows:

(4) Prepare an adjusted trial balance

Adjusted trial balance total, $117,900

Cash	$ 53,200
Accounts payable	9,500
Jin Singh, capital	12,800

E3–14 Prepare an adjusted trial balance for Toronto Mobile Pet Grooming as at June 30, 2020. Assume that all accounts have their normal balances. List expenses in alphabetical order.

(4) Prepare an adjusted trial balance

Accounts payable	$ 4,000
Accumulated amortization—truck	7,000
Amortization expense—truck	1,000
Cash	2,400
Truck	40,000
Insurance expense	200
Les Birman, capital	17,000
Les Birman, withdrawals	8,000
Prepaid insurance	1,800
Salaries expense	16,000
Salaries payable	2,000
Service revenue	44,000
Grooming supplies	4,000
Supplies expense	2,000
Unearned service revenue	1,400

E3–15 Refer to the data in E3–14. Prepare Toronto Mobile Pet Grooming's income statement and statement of owner's equity for the year ended June 30, 2020. Then prepare the balance sheet on that date.

(5) Preparing the financial statements

Total assets, $41,200

E3–16 On December 31, 2018, Grover Company made the following errors:

a. Did not accrue interest of $7,500 owed on loans due next year
b. Did not accrue service revenue in the amount of $9,200

(5) Effect of errors on financial statements

b. Net income understated

Assuming the financial statements are prepared before the errors are discovered, state the effects of each error on the financial statement elements by completing the chart below.

	Error a		Error b	
	Overstated	Understated	Overstated	Understated
Assets at Dec. 31, 2019, would be				
Liabilities at Dec. 31, 2019, would be				
Net income for 2019 would be				
Owner's equity at Dec. 31, 2019, would be				

3 A1

Recording prepaids in two ways

***E3-17** Let's look at recording the same supplies transactions two different ways. The business starts the year (January 1) with $1,800 of supplies on hand. On August 12, the business purchased $10,800 of supplies. On December 31, the count of supplies indicates $3,400 worth on hand.

Required

1. Assume that the business records supplies by initially debiting an asset account.
   a. Open T-accounts for Supplies and Supplies Expense, and place the beginning balance in the Supplies account.
   b. Record the August 12 purchase of the asset in the Supplies account.
   c. Record the December 31 adjusting entry into the T-accounts without using a journal.
2. Assume instead that the business records purchases of supplies by debiting an *expense* account.
   a. Open T-accounts for Supplies and Supplies Expense, and place the beginning balance in the Supplies account.
   b. Record the August 12 purchase (as an expense) directly in the Supplies Expense account.
   c. Record the December 31 adjusting entry into the T-accounts without using a journal.
3. Compare the ending account balances under both approaches. Are they the same? Explain.

3 A2

Recording unearned revenues in two ways

Unearned Service Revenue bal., $3,500

***E3-18** On January 1, a business had a liability to customers of $7,500 for unearned service revenue collected in advance. On May 31, the business received advance cash receipts of $20,000. At year-end, December 31, the company's liability to customers was $3,500 for unearned service revenue collected in advance.

Required

1. Assume that the company records unearned revenues by initially crediting a *liability* account.
   a. Open T-accounts for Unearned Service Revenue and Service Revenue, and place the beginning balance in Unearned Service Revenue.
   b. Journalize the May 31 and December 31 entries and post their dollar amounts into the T-accounts. No explanations are needed.
2. Assume that the company records unearned revenues by initially crediting a *revenue* account.
   a. Open T-accounts for Unearned Service Revenue and Service Revenue, and place the beginning balance on January 1 in the Unearned Service Revenue account.
   b. Journalize the May 31 cash collection (as a revenue). No explanation is needed. Post to the T-account.
   c. Journalize and post the December 31 adjusting entry to update the balance in the Unearned Service Revenue account to $3,500. No explanation is needed.
3. Compare the ending balances in the two accounts. Explain why they are the same or different.

---

* These Exercises cover Chapter 3 Appendix topics.

***E3–19** Fort Services initially records all prepaid expenses as expenses and all unearned revenues as revenues. Given the following information, prepare the necessary adjusting entries at December 31, 2020, the company's year-end.

A1 A2

Recording prepaids as expenses and unearned revenues as revenues, adjusting entries

Supplies Expense, Cr $700

a. On January 3, 2020, the company's first day of operations, $2,500 of supplies were purchased. A physical count revealed $700 of supplies still on hand at December 31, 2020.

b. On January 4, 2020, a $15,000 payment for insurance was made to an insurance agency for a 30-month policy.

c. On June 30, 2020, Fort Services received nine months' rent totalling $13,500 in advance from a tenant.

SERIAL EXERCISE

E3–20 *The Serial Exercise involves a company that will be revisited throughout relevant chapters in Volume 1 and Volume 2. You can complete the Serial Exercises using MyLab Accounting.*

3 4

Preparing adjusting entries and an adjusted trial balance

2. Adjusted trial balance total, $164,020

This exercise continues recordkeeping for the Canyon Canoe Company from previous chapters. You will need to use the unadjusted trial balance and posted T-accounts that you prepared in Chapter 2. If you did not complete the previous question, you can still work through this question using the following unadjusted trial balance:

CANYON CANOE COMPANY
Unadjusted Trial Balance
December 31, 2020

Account Title	Debit	Credit
Cash	$ 12,125	
Accounts receivable	5,750	
Office supplies	1,250	
Prepaid rent	3,000	
Land	85,000	
Building	35,000	
Canoes	12,000	
Accounts payable		$ 3,670
Unearned revenue		750
Note payable		7,200
Amber Wilson, capital		136,000
Amber Wilson, withdrawals	450	
Canoe rental revenue		12,400
Rent expense	1,200	
Salaries expense	3,300	
Utilities expense	445	
Telephone expense	500	
Total	$ 160,020	$ 160,020

At December 31, the business gathers the following information for the adjusting entries:

a. At December 31, the office supplies on hand totaled $165.

b. Prepaid rent of one month has been used. (Hint: Total is for three months.)

c. Determine the amortization on the building using straight-line amortization. Assume the useful life of the building is five years and the residual value is $5,000. (Hint: The building was purchased on December 1.)

d. $400 of unearned revenue has now been earned.

e. The employee who has been working the rental booth has earned $1,250 in salaries that will be paid January 15, 2021.

f. Canyon Canoe Company has earned $1,850 of canoe rental revenue that has not been recorded or received.

g. Determine the amortization on the canoes purchased on November 3 using the straight-line method. Assume the useful life of the canoes is four years and the residual value is $0.

h. Determine the amortization on the canoes purchased on December 2 using the straight-line amortization method. Assume the useful life of the canoes is four years and the residual value is $0.

i. Interest expense of $50 has accrued on the note payable.

Required

1. Journalize and post the adjusting entries using the T-accounts that you completed in Chapter 2. In the T-accounts, denote each adjusting amount as *Adj.* and an account balance as *Bal. You may require new T-accounts.* If you did not complete E2-22 then open and post to only the t-accounts which required adjusting entries.
2. Prepare an adjusted trial balance as of December 31, 2020. Add new accounts in the order they appear in the journal entries.

PRACTICE SET

(3) (4)
Preparing adjusting entries and preparing an adjusted trial balance

E3–21 *This problem continues the Crystal Clear Cleaning problem begun in Chapter 2 and continued through Chapter 9.*

Start from the unadjusted trial balance that Crystal Clear Cleaning prepared at November 30, 2019:

CRYSTAL CLEAR CLEANING
Unadjusted Trial Balance
November 30, 2019

Account Title	Debit	Credit
Cash	$ 51,650	
Accounts receivable	4,000	
Cleaning supplies	320	
Prepaid rent	4,000	
Prepaid insurance	4,800	
Equipment	5,400	
Truck	3,000	
Accounts payable		$ 1,245
Unearned revenue		15,000
Notes payable		36,000
A. Hideaway, capital		18,000
A. Hideaway, withdrawals	1,400	
Service revenue		5,100
Salaries expense	400	
Advertising expense	200	
Utilities expense	175	
Total	$ 75,345	$ 75,345

1. Using the data provided from the unadjusted trial balance and Chapter 2, prepare all required adjusting journal entries at November 30.
   a. Cleaning supplies on hand at the end of November were $50.
   b. One month's amortization was estimated to be $80 for the equipment and $70 for the truck. Record each as a separate journal entry, but use one expense account.

c. One month's rent was used up.
d. One month's insurance was used up.
e. Earned half a month's revenue that was collected in advance.
f. One month's interest expense is $59.

2. Prepare an adjusted trial balance as of November 30 for Crystal Clear Cleaning.

CHALLENGE EXERCISES

(5) Computing the financial statements

Supplies expense, $10,000

E3–22 The adjusted trial balances of Pacific Services at December 31, 2020, and December 31, 2019, include these amounts:

	2020	2019
Supplies	$ 4,000	$ 2,000
Salaries payable	5,000	8,000
Unearned service revenue	26,000	32,000

Analysis of the accounts at December 31, 2020, reveals these transactions for 2020:

Cash payment for supplies	$ 12,000
Cash payment for salaries	94,000
Cash receipts in advance for service revenue	160,000

Use T-accounts to compute the amount of supplies expense, salaries expense, and service revenue to report on the Pacific Services income statement for 2020.

BEYOND THE NUMBERS

BN3–1

Suppose a new management team is in charge of Wild Roses Inc., a microbrewery. Assume Wild Roses Inc.'s new top executives rose through the company ranks in the sales and marketing departments and have little appreciation for the details of accounting. The new president heard that adjusting entries take a lot of time and wants to receive the financial statements sooner. He says,

I want to avoid the hassle of adjusting the books every time we need financial statements. Sooner or later we receive cash for all our revenues, and we pay cash for all our expenses. I can understand cash transactions, but all these accruals confuse me. If I cannot understand our own accounting, I'm fairly certain the average person who invests in our company cannot understand it either. Let's start recording only our cash transactions. I bet it won't make any difference to anyone.

Write a business memo to the company president giving your response to the new policy. Identify at least five individual items (such as specific accounts) in the financial statements that will be reported incorrectly. Will outside investors care? Use the format of a business memo given with E3–4 on page 149.

ETHICAL ISSUE

EI3–1

The net income of EZ Furniture decreased sharply during 2020. Mariah Tessier, owner of the store, anticipates the need for a bank loan in 2021. Late in 2020, she instructs the accountant to record a $35,000 sale of furniture to the Tessier family, even though the goods will not be shipped from the manufacturer until January 2021. Tessier also tells the accountant not to make the following December 31, 2020, adjusting entries:

Salaries owed to employees	$27,000
Prepaid insurance that has expired	1,500

Required

1. Compute the overall effect of these transactions on the store's reported income for 2020.
2. Why did Tessier take this action? Is this action ethical? Give your reason, identifying the parties helped and the parties harmed by Tessier's action.
3. As a personal friend, what advice would you give to *the accountant*?

PROBLEMS (GROUP A)

① ② Cash-basis versus accrual-basis accounting

2. Net income, $5,700

P3–1A Kandi's Office Design had the following transactions during January:

Jan.	1	Paid for insurance for January through March, $2,400. It is company policy to record this sort of transaction in an asset account.
	4	Performed design service on account, $7,000.
	5	Purchased office furniture on account, $2,100.
	8	Paid advertising expense, $2,000 cash.
	15	Purchased office equipment for cash, $4,500.
	19	Performed design services and received cash, $9,000.
	24	Collected $3,500 on account for the January 4 service.
	26	Paid account payable from January 5.
	29	Paid salaries expense, $7,500 cash.
	31	Recorded adjusting entry for January insurance expense (see January 1).

Required

1. Show how each transaction would be accounted for using the accrual basis of accounting. Use the format below for your answer, and show your computations. Give the amount of revenue or expense for January. Journal entries are not required.

Amount of Revenue or Expense for January

Date	Revenue (Expense)	Amount

2. Compute January net income or net loss under the accrual basis of accounting.
3. State why the accrual basis of accounting is preferable to the cash basis.

① ② Applying accounting assumptions, criteria, and objectives

P3–2A Write a business memo to a new bookkeeper to explain the difference between the cash basis of accounting and the accrual basis. Mention the roles of the recognition criteria for revenues and the matching objective in accrual-basis accounting.

This is the format of the business memo:

Date:	(fill in)
To:	New Bookkeeper
From:	(Student Name)
Subject:	Difference between the *cash basis* of accounting and the *accrual basis* of accounting

③ Journalizing adjusting entries

a. Supplies Expense, $9,200

P3–3A Journalize the adjusting entry needed on December 31, the company's year-end, for each of the following independent cases affecting Envision Communications:

a. The beginning balance of Supplies was $4,800. During the year the company purchased supplies costing $7,600, and at December 31 the inventory of supplies remaining on hand is $3,200.

b. Each Friday the company pays its employees for the current week's work. The amount of the payroll is $15,000 for a five-day workweek. The current accounting period ends on Wednesday.

c. Envision has received notes receivable from some clients for professional services. During the current year, Envision has earned interest revenue of $800, which will be received next year.

d. The company is developing a wireless communication system for a large company, and the client paid Envision $120,000 at the start of the project. Envision recorded this amount as Unearned Consulting Revenue. The development will take several months to complete. Envision executives estimate that the company has earned three-fourths of the total fee during the current year.

e. Amortization for the current year includes the following: Office Furniture, $8,600, and Design Equipment, $16,000. Make a compound entry. (Hint: This means showing everything in one journal entry, not two.)

f. Details of Prepaid Insurance are shown in the account:

Prepaid Insurance		
Jan. 2 Bal.	6,000	

Envision Communications prepays a full year's insurance on January 2. Record insurance expense for the year ended December 31 as one annual adjustment for what was used for the year.

P3–4A FancyJohns, the luxury portable toilet rental company, has collected the following data for the December 31 adjusting entries:

③ Journalizing adjusting entries and subsequent journal entries

b. Insurance Expense, $9,500

a. Each Friday, FancyJohns pays employees for the current week's work. The amount of the weekly payroll is $7,000 for a five-day workweek. This year December 31 falls on a Wednesday. FancyJohns will pay its employees on January 2.

b. On January 1 of the current year, FancyJohns purchased an insurance policy that covers two years, $19,000.

c. The beginning balance of Cleaning Supplies was $4,000. During the year, FancyJohns purchased cleaning supplies for $5,200, and at December 31 the cleaning supplies on hand total $2,400.

d. During December, FancyJohns arranged for rentals at a Christmas and a New Year's Eve party at a resort. The client prepaid $7,000. FancyJohns recorded this amount as Unearned Revenue. FancyJohns estimates that the company has earned 45 percent of the total revenue in the current year and will earn the balance on January 3.

e. At December 31, FancyJohns had earned $3,500 of a two-month rental at the Outdoor Ice Place. The Outdoor Ice Palce has stated that they will pay FancyJohns the entire balance due for the two months on February 1.

f. Amortization for the current year includes Equipment, $3,700, and Trucks, $1,300. Make one compound entry to record the amortization, but use separate amortization accounts for each asset.

g. FancyJohns has incurred $300 of interest expense on a $450 interest payment due on January 15.

Required

1. Journalize the adjusting entry needed on December 31 for each of the previous items affecting FancyJohns. Assume FancyJohns records adjusting entries only at the end of the year.
2. Journalize the subsequent journal entries for adjusting entries a, d, and g.

③ ④ Journalizing and posting adjustments to T-accounts, preparing and using the adjusted trial balance

3. Adjusted trial bal. total, $74,035

P3–5A The unadjusted trial balance of Speedy Delivery at December 31, 2020, appears below. The data needed for the month-end adjustments follow the trial balance.

SPEEDY DRONE DELIVERY Unadjusted Trial Balance December 31, 2020		
Account Title	**Debit**	**Credit**
Cash	$ 5,400	
Accounts receivable	18,600	
Prepaid rent	4,500	
Supplies	1,200	
Drones	19,200	
Accumulated amortization—drones		$ 5,760
Accounts payable		3,400
Salaries payable		0
Unearned delivery revenue		2,400
F. Musk, capital		23,140
F. Musk, withdrawals	6,000	
Delivery revenue		36,500
Salaries expense	12,500	
Rent expense	0	
Amortization expense—drones	0	
Advertising expense	3,600	
Supplies expense	0	
Utilities expense	200	
Total	$71,200	$71,200

Adjustment data:

a. Unearned delivery revenue still remaining to be earned at December 31, $800.

b. Prepaid rent still available at December 31, $2,000.

c. Supplies used during the month, $450.

d. Amortization on drones for the month, $660.

e. Accrued utilities expense at December 31, $200 (credit Accounts Payable).

f. Accrued salaries expense at December 31, $1,975.

Required

1. Open T-accounts for the accounts listed in the unadjusted trial balance, inserting their December 31 balances.
2. Journalize the adjusting entries on December 31.
3. Post the adjusting entries to the T-accounts. Identify the posted amounts by their letter. Show the ending balance of each account.
4. Prepare the adjusted trial balance.

P3–6A Consider the unadjusted trial balance of Burrows Landscaping at December 31, 2020, and the related month-end adjustment data:

③ ④ ⑤ Preparing an adjusted trial balance and the financial statements

2. Total assets, $125,450

BURROWS LANDSCAPING
Unadjusted Trial Balance
December 31, 2020

Account Title	Debit	Credit
Cash	$ 34,500	
Accounts receivable	22,000	
Supplies	5,500	
Prepaid rent	9,000	
Equipment	66,000	
Accumulated amortization—equipment		$ 12,650
Accounts payable		7,200
Salaries payable		0
A. Burrows, capital		122,700
A. Burrows, withdrawals	25,000	
Landscaping design revenue		136,000
Salaries expense	82,000	
Rent expense	22,500	
Utilities expense	6,000	
Amortization expense—equipment	6,050	
Supplies expense	0	
Total	$278,550	$278,550

The following adjustments need to be made on December 31 before the financial statements for the year can be prepared:

a. Accrued landscaping design revenue, $8,500.

b. One month of the prepaid rent had been used. The unadjusted prepaid balance of $9,000 is for a period of four months.

c. Supplies remaining on hand, $900.

d. Amortization on equipment for the month of December. The equipment's expected useful life is 10 years; it will have no value at the end of its useful life, and the straight-line method of amortization is used.

e. An accrual for two days of salaries is needed. A five-day weekly payroll is $10,000.

Required

1. Sketch T-accounts in your notes to calculate the new balances. Prepare the adjusted trial balance of Burrows Landscaping at December 31, 2020.
2. Prepare the income statement (record expenses from largest to smallest on the income statement) and the statement of owner's equity for the year ended December 31, 2020, and the balance sheet at December 31, 2020. Draw the arrows linking the three financial statements, or write a short description of how they are linked.

③ ④ ⑤

Prepare adjusting entries, an adjusted trial balance, and financial statements

Net income, $158,075

P3–7A Online Security Buddies provides consulting services to small businesses that require computer security but are too small to have their own IT person on staff. The business had the following account balances:

ONLINE SECURITY BUDDIES Unadjusted Trial Balance December 1, 2020		
Account Title	**Debit**	**Credit**
Cash	$ 19,000	
Accounts receivable	23,200	
Supplies	5,000	
Prepaid advertising	1,500	
Computer equipment	69,000	
Accumulated amortization—computer equipment		$ 0
Server equipment	288,000	
Accumulated amortization—server equipment		0
Accounts payable		93,600
I. Steele, capital		186,000
I. Steele, withdrawals	79,000	
Consulting revenue		342,500
Salaries expense	120,000	
Supplies expense	0	
Utilities expense	17,400	
Total	$622,100	$622,100

The following transactions occurred during December:

a. On December 1, paid $11,500 cash to an advertising firm for four months of advertising work in advance.

b. On December 6, supplies in the amount of $3,700 were purchased on account.

c. On December 15, the company received a cash advance of $8,000 for work to be performed starting January 1, 2021.

d. On December 29, the company provided counselling services to a customer for $15,000, to be paid in 30 days.

The following information was available on December 31, 2020:

e. A physical count shows $7,600 of supplies remaining on hand on December 31.

f. The server equipment has an expected useful life of eight years with no expected value after eight years. The server equipment was purchased on January 2, and the straight-line method of amortization is used.

g. The computer equipment, purchased on January 2, is expected to be used for four years with no expected value after four years. The straight-line method of amortization is used.

h. The advertising firm has performed one-quarter of the work on the contract.

i. The company's senior consultant, who earns $800 per day, worked the last six days of the year and will be paid on January 4, 2018.

Required

1. Journalize the entries. Add new accounts if necessary.
2. Prepare an adjusted trial balance on December 31, 2020. List expenses in the order of dollar amount, from the greatest amount to the smallest.

3. Prepare an income statement for the year ended December 31, 2020. List expenses in the order of dollar amount, from the greatest amount to the smallest.
4. Prepare a statement of owner's equity for the year ended December 31, 2020. Assume there have been no changes to the capital account since January 1.
5. Prepare a balance sheet at December 31, 2020.

P3–8A Griffin Fishing Charters has collected the following data for the December 31 adjusting entries:

(3) (5) Journalizing adjusting entries and identifying the impact on financial statements

a. The company received its electric bill on December 31 for $375 but will not pay it until January 5. (Use the Utilities Payable account.)
b. Griffin purchased a three-month boat insurance policy on November 1 for $1,200.
c. As of December 31, Griffin had earned $3,000 of charter revenue that has not been recorded or received.
d. Griffin's fishing boat was purchased on January 1 at a cost of $33,500. Griffin expects to use the boat for 10 years and that it will have a residual value of $3,500.
e. On October 1, Griffin received $9,000 prepayment for a deep-sea fishing charter to take place in December. As of December 31, Griffin has completed the charter.

Required

1. Journalize the adjusting entries needed on December 31 for Griffin Fishing Charters. Assume Griffin records adjusting entries only at the end of the year.
2. If Griffin had not recorded the adjusting entries, indicate which specific category of accounts on the financial statements would be misstated and if the misstatement is overstated or understated. Use the following table as a guide.

Adjusting Entry	Specific Category of Accounts on the Balance Sheet	Over/ Understated	Specific Category of Accounts on the Income Statement	Over/ Understated

***P3–9A** Gonzales Sales and Service completed the following transactions during 2020:

(3) (A1) (A2) Recording prepaid rent and service revenue collected in advance in two ways

Rent Expense bal., $10,000

Aug. 31	Paid $15,000 store rent covering the six-month period ending February 28, 2021.
Dec. 1	Collected $6,400 cash in advance from customers. The service revenue earned will be $1,600 each month over the four-month period ending March 31, 2021.

Required

1. Journalize these entries by debiting an asset account for Prepaid Rent and by crediting a liability account for Unearned Service Revenue. Explanations are not required.
2. Journalize the related adjustments at December 31, 2020. Explanations are not required.
3. Post the entries to T-accounts and show their balances at December 31, 2020. Posting references are not required.
4. Repeat Requirements 1 through 3. This time debit Rent Expense for the rent payment and credit Service Revenue for the collection of revenue in advance.
5. Compare the account balances in Requirements 3 and 4. They should be equal.

* This Problem covers Chapter 3 Appendix topics.

PROBLEMS (GROUP B)

① ② Accrual-basis accounting

P3–1B DoItForYou Concierge Services experienced the following selected transactions during October:

Oct.	1	Paid for insurance for October through December, $9,000.
	4	Paid utility invoice with cash, $1,200.
	5	Performed services on account, $8,000.
	9	Purchased office equipment for cash, $7,000.
	12	Received cash for services performed, $4,400.
	14	Purchased office equipment on account, $2,400.
	28	Collected $3,000 on account from October 5.
	31	Paid salaries expense, $4,500 cash.
	31	Paid account payable from October 14.
	31	Recorded adjusting entry for October insurance expense (see October 1).

Required

1. Show how each transaction would be accounted for using the accrual basis of accounting. Use the format below for your answer, and show your computations. Give the amount of revenue or expense for October. Journal entries are not required.

Amount of Revenue or Expense for October		
Date	Revenue/Expense	Amount

2. Compute October net income or net loss under the accrual basis of accounting.
3. Why is the accrual basis of accounting preferable to the cash basis?

① ③ Applying accounting assumptions, criteria, and objectives

P3–2B As the controller of Best Security Systems, you have hired a new bookkeeper, whom you must train. She objects to making an adjusting entry for accrued salaries at the end of the period. She reasons, "We will pay the salaries soon. Why not wait until payment to record the expense? In the end, the result will be the same." Write a business memo to explain to the bookkeeper why the adjusting entry for accrued salaries expense is needed.

This is the format of the business memo:

Date:	(fill in)
To:	New Bookkeeper
From:	(Student Name)
Subject:	Why the adjusting entry for salaries expense is needed

③ Journalizing adjusting entries

P3–3B Journalize the adjusting entry needed on December 31, the company's year-end, for each of the following independent cases affecting Prairie Construction:

a. Details of Prepaid Rent are shown in the account:

Prepaid Rent		
Jan. 1 Bal.	4,500	
Mar. 31	9,000	
Sep. 30	9,000	

Prairie Construction pays office rent semi-annually on March 31 and September 30. At December 31, part of the last payment is still available to cover January to March of the next year. No rent expense was recorded during the year.

b. Prairie Construction has lent money to help employees find housing, receiving notes receivable in return. During the current year, the entity has earned interest revenue of $1,400 from employees' loans, which it will receive next year.

c. The beginning balance of Supplies was $5,100. During the year the company purchased supplies costing $16,500, and at December 31 the inventory of supplies remaining on hand is $5,500.

d. Prairie Construction is installing cable in a large building, and the owner of the building paid Prairie Construction $42,000 as the annual service fee. Prairie Construction recorded this amount as Unearned Service Revenue. Pete, the general manager, estimates that the company has earned one-fourth of the total fee during the current year.

e. Prairie Construction pays its employees each Friday. The amount of the weekly payroll is $5,000 for a five-day workweek, and the daily salary amounts are equal. The current accounting period ends on Wednesday.

f. Amortization expenses for the current year are Equipment, $14,000, and Trucks, $33,000. Record this as a compound entry.

P3–4B Lindsey Home Staging is almost done its accounting for the year. Lindsey just found the last December 31 adjusting entries that need to be recorded:

(3) Journalizing adjusting entries and subsequent journal entries

a. Each Friday Lindsey pays employees for the current week's work. The amount of the weekly payroll is $6,500 for a five-day workweek. This year December 31 falls on a Tuesday. Lindsey will pay the employees on January 3.

b. On January 1 of the current year, Lindsey purchases a business insurance policy that covers two years for $5,500.

c. The beginning balance of her decorating supplies account was $4,200. During the year she purchased more supplies for $5,100, and at December 31 the supplies on hand total $2,900.

d. During December Lindsey prepared a home remodelling plan, and the client prepaid $9,000. Lindsey recorded this amount as Unearned Revenue. The job will be completed by January 14. Lindsey estimates that the company earned 70 percent of the total revenue during the current year.

e. At December 31 Lindsey had earned $4,000 for staging services for Tomball Adamsey. Tomball has stated he will pay Lindsey on the closing date of his home, January 10.

f. Amortization for the current year includes Equipment, $3,600, and Vehicles, $1,400. Write this as one compound entry, but use separate amortization accounts for each asset.

g. Lindsey incurred $300 of interest expense on a $500 interest payment due on January 18.

Required

1. Journalize the adjusting entries needed on December 31 for each of the items affecting Lindsey's Home Staging. Assume Lindsey only records adjusting entries at the end of the year.
2. Journalize the subsequent journal entries for adjusting entries a, d, and g.

③ ④
Journalizing and posting adjustments to T-accounts, preparing the adjusted trial balance

P3–5B The unadjusted trial balance of Pigeon Delivery at December 31, 2020, appears below. The data needed for the month-end adjustments follow the trial balance.

PIGEON DELIVERY Unadjusted Trial Balance December 31, 2020		
Account Title	**Debit**	**Credit**
Cash	$ 24,180	
Accounts receivable	44,500	
Prepaid rent	8,800	
Supplies	2,100	
Trucks	69,000	
Accumulated amortization—trucks		$ 34,500
Accounts payable		5,800
Salaries payable		0
Unearned delivery revenue		6,400
M. Fowl, capital		75,180
M. Fowl, withdrawals	12,000	
Delivery revenue		48,000
Salaries expense	7,200	
Rent expense	0	
Amortization expense—trucks	0	
Advertising expense	2,100	
Supplies expense	0	
Total	$169,880	$169,880

Adjustment data at December 31:

a. Prepaid rent still available at December 31, $4,400.
b. Supplies used during the month, $1,800.
c. Amortization on trucks for the month, $670.
d. Accrued salaries expense at December 31, $950.
e. Unearned delivery revenue still remaining to be earned at December 31, $2,500.

Required

1. Open T-accounts for the accounts listed in the unadjusted trial balance, inserting their December 31 balances.
2. Journalize the adjusting entries
3. Post the adjusting entries to the T-accounts. Identify the posted amounts by their letter. Show the ending balance of each account.
4. Prepare the adjusted trial balance. Report expenses in alphabetical order.

P3–6B The unadjusted trial balance of Halifax Research at December 31, 2020, appears below:

(3) (4) (5)
Preparing an adjusted trial balance and the financial statements

HALIFAX RESEARCH Unadjusted Trial Balance December 31, 2020		
Account Title	**Debit**	**Credit**
Cash	$ 24,200	
Accounts receivable	38,500	
Supplies	2,400	
Prepaid rent	12,000	
Furniture	72,000	
Accumulated amortization—furniture		$ 13,800
Accounts payable		18,400
Salaries payable		0
J. Suzuki, capital		125,000
J. Suzuki, withdrawals	46,000	
Consulting revenue		121,500
Salaries expense	32,000	
Rent expense	33,000	
Utilities expense	12,000	
Amortization expense—furniture	6,600	
Supplies expense	0	
Total	$278,700	$278,700

Adjustment data:

a. Accrued consulting revenue at December 31, $3,800.

b. The prepaid balance of $12,000 represented one year of rent. Four months of prepaid rent have been used.

c. Supplies remaining on hand at December 31, $900.

d. The estimated useful life of the furniture is 10 years, it will have no value at the end of the 10 years, and the straight-line method of amortization is used. Amortization expense had only been taken for the first 11 months.

e. Accrue salaries expense at December 31 for three days. The five-day weekly payroll is $6,000.

Required

1. Prepare the adjusted trial balance of Halifax Research at December 31, 2020. List expense accounts showing highest to lowest amounts. Sketch T-accounts in your notes to calculate the new balances.

2. Prepare the income statement and the statement of owner's equity for the year ended December 31, 2020, and the balance sheet at December 31, 2020. Report income statement accounts showing highest to lowest amounts. Draw the arrows linking the three financial statements, or write a short description of how they are linked.

③ ④ ⑤
Prepare adjusting entries, an adjusted trial balance, and financial statements

P3–7B Millennial Communications provides management consulting services. The business had the following account balances:

MILLENNIAL COMMUNICATIONS Unadjusted Trial Balance December 1, 2020		
Account Title	**Debit**	**Credit**
Cash	$ 19,000	
Accounts receivable	17,100	
Supplies	3,900	
Prepaid advertising	13,000	
Computer equipment	54,000	
Accumulated amortization—computer equipment		$ 0
Furniture	120,000	
Accumulated amortization—furniture		0
Accounts payable		28,000
R. Watts, capital		98,000
R. Watts, withdrawals	45,000	
Consulting revenue		260,600
Salaries expense	82,500	
Supplies expense	0	
Travel expense	32,100	
Total	$386,600	$386,600

The following transactions occurred during December:

a. On December 1, paid cash for an Internet advertising consultant for four months of work in advance. The contract was for $3,200 per month. Work will begin on January 1, 2021.

b. On December 10, supplies in the amount of $2,975 were purchased on account.

c. On December 18, the company received a cash advance of $4,000 for work to be performed starting January 1.

d. On December 30, the company provided consulting services to a customer for $12,500; payment will be received in 30 days.

The following adjustments information was available on December 31, 2020:

e. A physical count shows $5,100 of supplies remaining on hand on December 31.

f. The computer equipment has an expected useful life of four years with no residual value after four years. The computers were purchased on January 2 of this year, and the straight-line method of amortization is used.

g. The furniture, purchased on January 2, is expected to be used for eight years with no expected value after eight years. The straight-line method of amortization is used.

h. On October 1, Millennial Consulting hired an advertising firm to prepare a marketing plan and agreed to pay the firm $2,200 per month. Millennial Consulting paid for five months' work in advance and has made no adjusting entries for this during 2020. Record the portion of the prepayment that has been used to date.

i. The company's office manager, who earns $400 per day, worked the last five days of the year and will be paid on January 5, 2021.

Required

1. Journalize the entries. Add new accounts if necessary.
2. Prepare an adjusted trial balance on December 31, 2020.
3. Prepare an income statement for the year ended December 31, 2020. List expenses in alphabetical order.
4. Prepare a statement of owner's equity for the year ended December 31, 2020. Assume there have been no changes to the capital account since January 1.
5. Prepare a balance sheet at December 31, 2020.

P3–8B Harrison Fly Fishing Charters has collected the following data for the December 31 adjusting entries:

(3) (5) Journalizing adjusting entries and identifying the impact on financial statements

a. The company received its electric bill on December 31 for $375 but will not pay it until January 5. (Use the Utilities Payable account.)

b. Harrison purchased a three-month boat insurance policy on November 1 for $3,600.

c. As of December 31, Harrison had earned $1,000 of charter revenue that has not been recorded or received.

d. Harrison's fishing boat was purchased on January 1 at a cost of $56,500. Harrison expects to use the boat for five years and that it will have a residual value of $6,500.

e. On October 1, Harrison received $5,000 prepayment for a deep-sea fishing charter to take place in December. As of December 31, Harrison has completed the charter.

Required

1. Journalize the adjusting entries needed on December 31 for Harrison Fly Fishing Charters. Assume Harrison records adjusting entries only at the end of the year.
2. If Harrison had not recorded the adjusting entries, indicate which specific category of accounts on the financial statements would be misstated and if the misstatement is overstated or understated. Use the following table as a guide:

Adjusting Entry	Specific Category of Accounts on the Balance Sheet	Over/ Understated	Specific Category of Accounts on the Income Statement	Over/ Understated

***P3–9B** Connect Air completed the following transactions during 2020:

(3) (A1) (A2) Recording prepaid advertising and flight travel revenue collected in advance in two ways

Oct. 15	Paid $10,000 for advertising and promotional material covering the four-month period ending February 15, 2021.
Nov. 1	Received $15,600 payment in advance for a series of charter flights. Revenue of $2,600 will be earned each month over the six-month period ending April 30, 2021.

Required

1. Open T-accounts for Advertising Expense, Prepaid Advertising, Unearned Flight Revenue, and Flight Revenue.
2. Journalize these entries by debiting an asset account for Prepaid Advertising and by crediting a liability account for Unearned Flight Revenue. Explanations are not required.
3. Journalize the related adjustments at December 31, 2020. Explanations are not required.

* This Problem covers Chapter 3 Appendix topics.

4. Post the entries to the T-accounts and show their balances at December 31, 2020. Posting references are not required.
5. Repeat Requirements 1 through 4. This time debit Advertising Expense instead of Prepaid Advertising, and credit Flight Revenue instead of Unearned Flight Revenue.
6. Compare the account balances in Requirements 4 and 5. They should be equal.

CHALLENGE PROBLEMS

(1) Application of the matching objective

P3–1C The matching objective is well established as a basis for recording expenses.

Required

1. New accountants sometimes state the objective as matching revenues against expenses. Explain to a new accountant why matching revenues against expenses is incorrect.
2. It has been suggested that not-for-profit organizations, such as churches and hospitals, should flip their income statements and show revenues as a deduction from expenses. Why do you think that the suggestion has been made?

(1) (2) Understanding the concepts underlying the accrual basis of accounting

P3–2C The following independent questions relate to the accrual basis of accounting:

1. It has been said that the only time a company's financial position is known for certain is when the company is wound up and its only asset is cash. Why is this statement true?
2. A friend suggests that the purpose of adjusting entries is to correct errors in the accounts. Is your friend's statement true? What is the purpose of adjusting entries if the statement is wrong?
3. The text suggested that furniture (and the other property, plant, and equipment assets that are amortized) is a form of prepaid expense. Do you agree? Why do you think some accountants view property, plant, and equipment this way?

Extending Your Knowledge

DECISION PROBLEMS

(3) (5) Making business decisions

DP3-1

One year ago, Tyler Stasney founded Swift Classified Ads. Stasney remembers that you took an accounting course while in college and comes to you for advice. He wishes to know how much net income his business earned during the past year in order to decide whether to keep the company going. His accounting records consist of the T-accounts from his ledger, which were prepared by an accountant who moved to another city. The ledger at December 31 follows. The accounts have *not* been adjusted.

Stasney indicates that at year-end, customers owe the business $1,600 for accrued service revenue. These revenues have not been recorded. During the year, Swift Classified Ads collected $4,000 service revenue in advance from customers, but the business earned only $900 of that amount. Rent expense for the year was $2,400, and the business used up $1,700 of the supplies. Swift determines that amortization on its equipment was $5,000 for the year. At December 31, the business owes an employee $1,200 accrued salary.

Help Swift Classified Ads compute its net income for the year. Advise Stasney whether to continue operating Swift Classified Ads.

Cash	
Dec. 31 5,800	

Accounts Payable	
	21,500 Dec. 31

T. Stasney, Capital	
	20,000 Dec. 31

Salaries Expense	
Dec. 31 17,000	

Accounts Receivable	
Dec. 31 12,000	

Unearned Revenue	
	4,000 Dec. 31

T. Stasney, Withdrawals	
Dec. 31 28,000	

Amortization Expense—Equipment	

Prepaid Rent	
Jan. 2 2,800	

Salaries Payable	

Service Revenue	
	59,500 Dec. 31

Rent Expense	

Office Supplies	
Jan. 2 2,600	

Utilities Expense	
Dec. 31 800	

Equipment	
Jan. 2 36,000	

Supplies Expense	

Accumulated Amortization—Equipment	

FINANCIAL STATEMENT CASES

FSC3–1

①②③④ Explaining the effects of accruals and deferrals on the financial statements

During the year ended April 1, 2017, Indigo Books & Music Inc. (Indigo) recorded numerous accruals and deferrals. As a long-term employee of Indigo's accounting and finance staff, it is your job to explain the effects of accruals and deferrals on Indigo's financial statements. (Indigo's financial statements appear in Appendix A at the end of this book and on MyLab Accounting.) Suppose the following questions were raised at the shareholders' meeting:

1. "Prepaid expenses" in the amount of $11,706,000 are listed on the April 1, 2017, balance sheet. What items could be included in this balance, and why is this account listed as a balance sheet account instead of an expense account?
2. "Accounts payable and accrued liabilities" is shown on the balance sheet in the amount of $170,611,000. Define an accrued liability, and give an example of items that could be included in this liability.
3. What is depreciation, and how much depreciation has been recorded for the computer equipment between April 2, 2016, and April 1, 2017? (Hint: Refer to Note 9 for this amount.)

FSC3–2

①②③④ Explaining the effects of accruals and deferrals on the financial statements

During the year ended December 31, 2016, TELUS Corporation (TELUS) recorded numerous accruals and deferrals. As a long-term employee of TELUS's accounting and finance staff, it is your job to explain the effects of accruals and deferrals on TELUS's 2016 financial statements. (TELUS's 2016 financial statements and notes appear on MyLab Accounting.) Suppose the following questions were raised at the shareholders' meeting:

1. Prepaid expenses are listed on the December 31, 2016, consolidated statements of financial position (balance sheet). What is the balance at this date? What items would be included in this balance, and why is this account listed as a balance sheet account instead of an expense account?
2. "Accounts payable and accrued liabilities" are shown on the December 31, 2016, consolidated statements of financial position in the amount of $2,330,000,000. Define an accrued liability. Use Note 23 to identify what accounts are specifically included in TELUS's statement.
3. What is depreciation, and how much would have been recorded for the year ended December 31, 2016, on the consolidated statements of income?

Try It! Solutions for Chapter 3

1. a. ii
   b. i
   c. iii

2. a. Service Revenue = cash received = $105,000
   Expenses = cash paid = $85,000 - $10,000 + $5,000 = $80,000
   b. Service Revenue = revenue earned = $130,000
   Expenses = expense incurred = $85,000

3.

Date	Accounts and Explanation	Debit	Credit
(a)	Amortization Expense—Equipment	1,500	
	Accumulated Amortization—Equipment		1,500
	To record amortization on equipment.		
(b)	Advertising Expense	700	
	Advertising Payable		700
	To accrue advertising expense.		
(c)	Supplies Expense	350	
	Office Supplies		350
	To record office supplies used. ($600–$250)		
(d)	Accounts Receivable (or Rent Receivable)	1,200	
	Rent Revenue		1,200
	To accrue rent revenue.		
(e)	Unearned Revenue	3,000	
	Service Revenue		3,000
	To record service revenue earned that was collected in advance.		

4.

HOOTEN CARPENTRY
Adjusted Trial Balance
December 31, 2018

Account Title	Debit	Credit
Cash	$ 4,025	
Accounts receivable	660	
Office supplies	120	
Land	5,000	
Equipment	10,000	
Accumulated amortization—equipment		$ 1,000
Accounts payable		225
Utilities payable		210
Unearned revenue		300
Hooten, capital		8,400
Hooten, withdrawals	500	
Service revenue		12,000
Amortization expense—equipment	800	
Salaries expense	550	
Supplies expense	80	
Utilities expense	400	
Total	$ 22,135	$ 22,135

5. The partial balance sheet is shown below:

Assets		
Cash		$ 63,200
Accounts receivable		11,750
Office supplies		1,100
Prepaid insurance		1,450
Furniture	$21,000	
Less: Accumulated amortization—furniture	7,500	13,500
Land		85,000
Total assets		$176,000

4 Completing the Accounting Cycle

CONNECTING CHAPTER 4

LEARNING OBJECTIVES

The **Summary** for Chapter 4 appears on pages 204–205.
Key Terms with definitions for this chapter's material appears on page 205.

CPA competencies

This text covers material outlined in **Section 1: Financial Reporting of the CPA Competency Map**. The Learning Objectives for each chapter have been aligned with the CPA Competency Map to ensure the best coverage possible.

1.1.2 Evaluates the appropriateness of the basis of financial reporting

1.3.1 Prepares financial statements

1.4.2 Evaluates financial statements including note disclosure

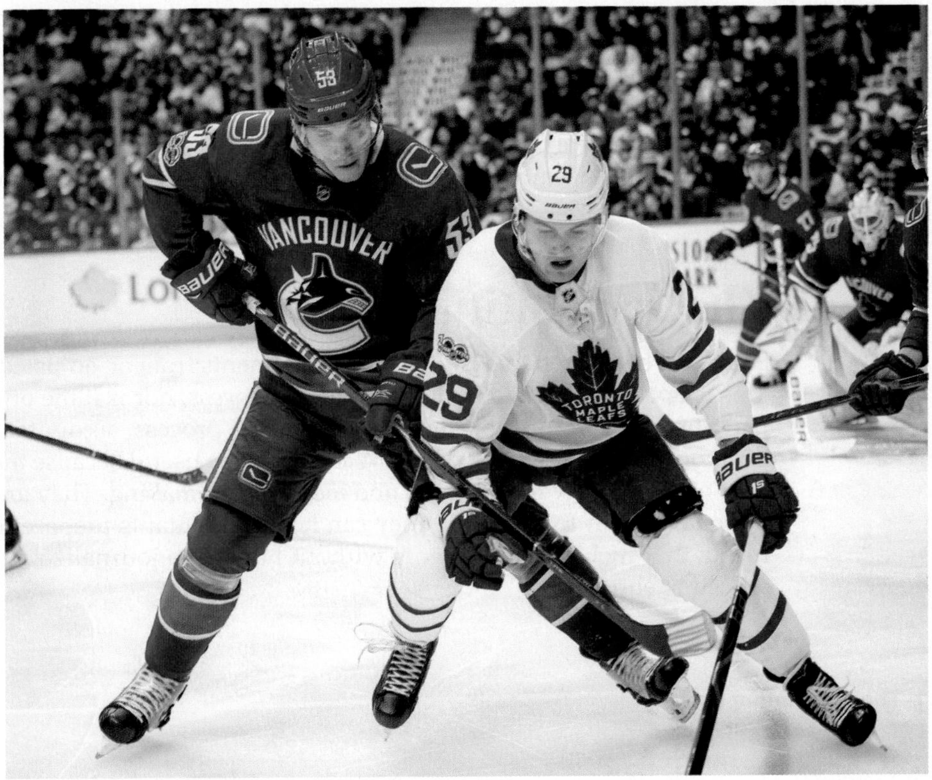

Dom Gagne/Cal Sport Media/Alamy Stock Photo

It's a beautiful day in late spring in Vancouver, but you are still immersed in hockey as you watch the Vancouver Canucks play the Toronto Maple Leafs in the sixth game of the Stanley Cup Final. The teams are playing a best-of-seven series, and the Leafs lead the series three games to two. The Canucks need to win this game or Toronto will win the Stanley Cup.

The game is tied 1–1 at the end of the second period. Toronto scores early in the third period to take a 2–1 lead. The Canucks fight back and score the tying goal with two minutes to go. There is no more scoring in regulation time, and the final result will be decided in overtime.

The game goes back and forth in overtime before the Canucks finally score to force a seventh game back in Toronto.

When the teams return to Toronto to play the seventh game, what will the scoreboard say at the start of the game? Will it be 3–2 to carry over the score from the previous game, or will the scoreboard be set back to zero? The answer should be obvious no matter what sport is being discussed: After a game is completed, the scoreboard is always set back to zero.

In the same way, the accounting process sets the company's financial scoreboard back to zero at the end of each fiscal year. The process is called *closing the books*, and that is the main topic in this chapter. The logic behind the closing process in accounting is the same as setting the scoreboard back to zero after a game. Companies need to see how well they are doing in each financial period.

In this chapter we take one final look at the accounting cycle and see how the accounting records are completed and made ready to start the next accounting period. We will also look at how to provide more useful information to readers of financial statements by introducing a detailed format for the balance sheet—a classified format. This more detailed format will make it easier to begin our first look at financial analysis at the end of the chapter.

The Accounting Cycle

So far, we have prepared the financial statements from an adjusted trial balance. This is not the final step in the accounting process, nor is it the only way to prepare information for reporting. As part of the process, accountants often use a document known as a worksheet. Worksheets are useful because they summarize a lot of data, allow for changes, and aid decision making. They are shown as an optional step in Exhibit 4–1. They can help accountants prepare financial statements that include adjustments without having to journalize and post all the adjusting entries.

EXHIBIT 4–1 | The Accounting Cycle

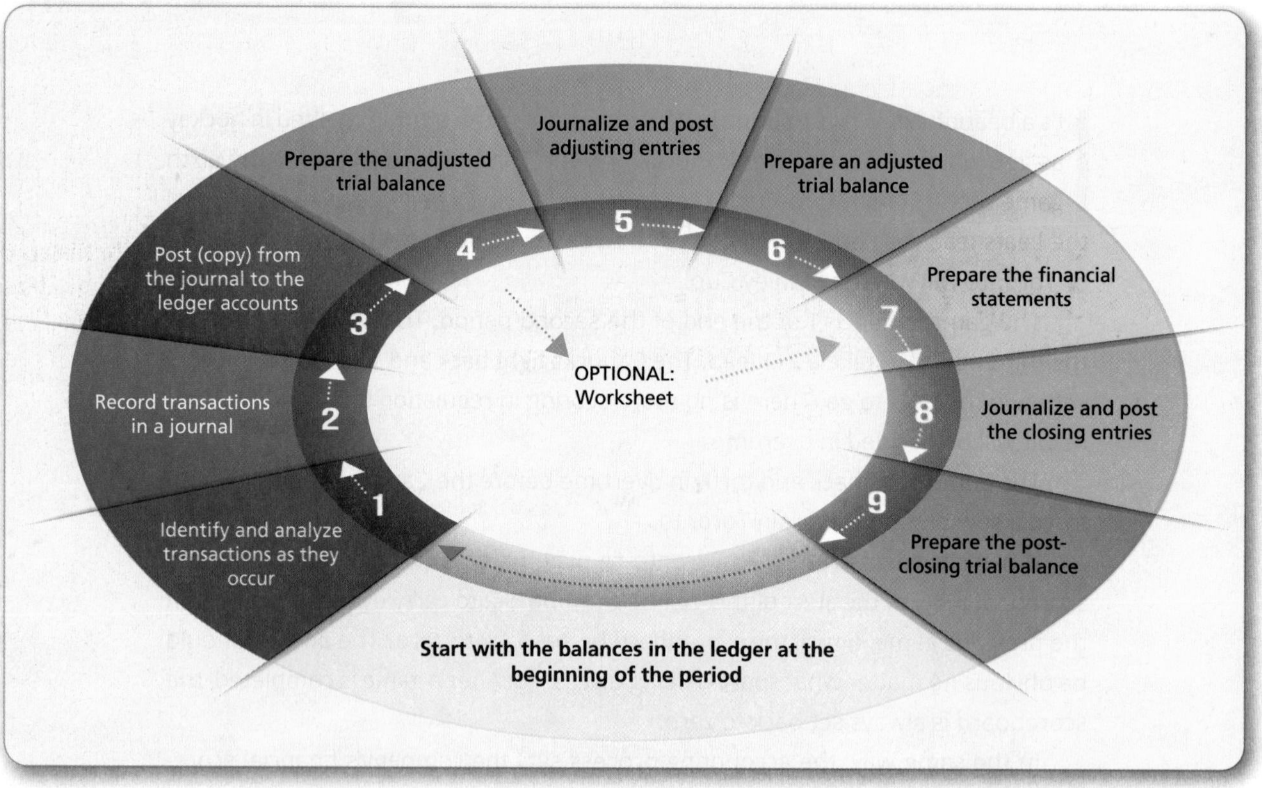

Journalize and post adjusting entries
Prepare the unadjusted trial balance
Prepare an adjusted trial balance
Post (copy) from the journal to the ledger accounts
Prepare the financial statements
Record transactions in a journal
OPTIONAL: Worksheet
Journalize and post the closing entries
Identify and analyze transactions as they occur
Prepare the post-closing trial balance
1
2
3
4
5
6
7
8
9
Start with the balances in the ledger at the beginning of the period

At the end of the accounting cycle, the scoreboard is reset for the next accounting period. These closing entries, shown as step 8 above, follow the same basic pattern for all service businesses. In Chapter 5 we will show how a company that earns revenue by selling products rather than services adjusts and closes its books.

The Worksheet

LO 1

How can we summarize data to prepare the financial statements?

Accountants often use a **worksheet**, a document with many columns, to help summarize data for the financial statements. Listing all the accounts and their unadjusted balances helps identify the accounts that need adjustment. After the adjusting entries are completed, the worksheet aids the closing process by listing the ending adjusted balances of all the accounts.

The worksheet is not part of the journal or the ledger, nor is it a financial statement. Therefore, it is not part of the formal accounting system. Instead, it is a summary device that exists for the accountant's convenience. An Excel spreadsheet works well for an accounting worksheet.

Exhibit 4–2 illustrates the worksheet for Hunter Environmental Consulting (HEC) at May 31, 2019. A step-by-step description of its preparation follows.

Even though this is not one of the formal financial statements, it uses a three-line heading for clarity and consistency. It shows the name of the business, the name of the document, and the period of time covered.

Set Up the Accounts and Unadjusted Trial Balance

Print the account titles in the first column and their unadjusted ending balances in the unadjusted trial balance columns of the worksheet, and total the amounts.

The account titles and balances come directly from the ledger accounts before any adjusting entries are prepared. This example uses the balances from Exhibit 3–4.

Accounts are usually listed in the order in which they appear in the ledger. Some accounts may have zero balances (for example, Amortization Expense). What do you do if one or more accounts are omitted from the unadjusted trial balance? Such accounts can always be written below the first column totals later when they are discovered. For example, if Supplies Expense was accidentally omitted, the accountant can write Supplies Expense beneath the Totals line later. Keep in mind that the worksheet is not the finished version of the financial statements, so the order of the accounts on the worksheet is not critical. Supplies Expense would be listed in its proper sequence on the income statement.

Before moving on to the next step, check that total debits equal total credits.

Record Adjusting Entries

Enter the adjusting entries in the Adjustments columns, and total the amounts.

Exhibit 4–2 includes these May adjusting entries that we made in Chapter 3 to prepare the adjusted trial balance:

a. Prepaid insurance expired during May, $300
b. Supplies remaining on hand at May 31, $1,000
c. Amortization on furniture for the month of May, $750
d. Accrued salaries expense, $4,000
e. Accrued service revenue, $1,500
f. Amount of unearned service revenue that was earned during May, $1,000

Cash needs no adjustment because all cash transactions are recorded as they occur during the period.

EXHIBIT 4–2 | Creating an Accounting Worksheet

	A	B	C	D	E	F	G	H	I	J	K	L	M
1	HUNTER ENVIRONMENTAL CONSULTING												
2	Accounting Worksheet												
3	For the Month Ended May 31, 2019												
4		Unadjusted Trial Balance		Adjustments				Adjusted Trial Balance		Income Statement		Balance Sheet	
5	**Account Title**	**Dr**	**Cr**		**Dr**		**Cr**	**Dr**	**Cr**	**Dr**	**Cr**	**Dr**	**Cr**
6	Cash	131,000						31,000				131,000	
7	Accounts receivable	14,000		(e)	1,500			15,500				15,500	
8	Office supplies	1,500				(b)	500	1,000				1,000	
9	Prepaid insurance	36,00				(a)	300	3,300				3,300	
10	Furniture	45,000						45,000				45,000	
11	Accum. amortization—furniture		0			(c)	750		750				750
12	Land	50,000						50,000				50,000	
13	Accounts payable		12,000						12,000				12,000
14	Salaries payable		0			(d)	4,000		4,000				4,000
15	Unearned service revenue		3,000	(f)	1,000				2,000				2,000
16	Lisa Hunter, capital		120,100						120,100				120,100
17	Lisa Hunter, withdrawals	6,000						6,000				6,000	
18	Service revenue		24,000			(e)	15,00		26,500		26,500		
19						(f)	1,000						
20	Amortization expense	0		(c)	750			750		750			
21	Insurance expense	0		(a)	300			300		300			
22	Rent expense	3,000						3,000		3,000			
23	Salaries expense	4,000		(d)	4,000			8,000		800			
24	Supplies expense	0		(b)	500			500		500			
25	Utilities expense	1,000						1,000		1,000			
26	Totals	159,100	159,100		8,050		8,050	165,350	165,350	13,550	26,500	151,800	138,850
27	Net income									12,950			12,950
28										26,500	26,500	151,800	151,800

Analyze each of these as you would have done in Chapter 3 to prepare the journal entry, but enter the amounts directly into the Adjustments column. A letter is used to link the debit and the credit of each adjusting entry.

After the adjustments are entered on the worksheet, the columns are totalled. Total debits must again equal total credits.

Note: The adjusting entries still need to be journalized. This interim step speeds up the preparation of the statements but does not replace the need to record journal entries.

Complete the Adjusted Trial Balance

Compute each account's adjusted balance by combining the unadjusted trial balance and the adjustment figures. Enter the adjusted amounts in the adjusted trial balance columns.

You may want to write out balances in T-accounts to help calculate balances, as shown in the margin.

Cash has no adjusting entry, so the total is reported in the debit column. Accounts Receivable's adjusted balance of $15,500 is computed by adding the $1,500 debit adjustment to the unadjusted trial balance debit amount of $14,000. Office Supplies' adjusted balance of $1,000 is determined by subtracting the $500 credit adjustment from the unadjusted debit balance of $1,500. An account may receive more than one adjustment, as in the case of Service Revenue.

Office Supplies

Bal.	1,500		
		Adj.	500
Bal.	1,000		

Generally, the rules are:

- Debit + Debit = Debit
- Credit + Credit = Credit
- Debit + Credit = Debit if total debits > total credits
- Debit + Credit = Credit if total credits > total debits

After all the amounts have been recorded in the Adjusted Trial Balance columns, calculate the total for each column and verify that total debits equal total credits.

Complete Income Statement and Balance Sheet Columns

Transfer the asset, liability, and owner's equity amounts from the adjusted trial balance to the balance sheet columns. Transfer the revenue and expense amounts to the income statement columns. Total the statement columns.

The asset, liability, and owner's equity accounts go to the balance sheet, and the revenues and expenses go to the income statement.

Every account is either a balance sheet account or an income statement account. Debits on the adjusted trial balance remain debits in the statement columns, and credits remain credits.

After all the amounts have been transferred to their appropriate column, calculate a subtotal for each income statement and balance sheet column.

Record the Net Income or Net Loss

On the income statement, compute net income or net loss and transfer that amount to the balance sheet.

The last step is to complete the accounting worksheet with the calculation of the net income or net loss. The amount is calculated as the difference between the debit and credit Income Statement columns.

Net Income Net income of $12,950 is entered as a "plug figure" in the Income Statement *debit* column. This brings total debits up to total credits on the income statement. Net income is also entered as a "plug figure" in the Balance Sheet *credit* column because an excess of revenues over expenses increases capital, and increases in capital are recorded by a credit. After completion, total debits equal total credits in the Income Statement columns and in the Balance Sheet columns.

Revenue (total *credits* on the income statement)	$26,500
Expenses (total *debits* on the income statement)	13,550
Net income	$12,950

Net Loss If expenses exceed revenues, the result is a net loss. In that event, *Net loss* is printed on the worksheet as shown below. The net loss amount should be entered in the *credit* column of the income statement (to balance out) and in the *debit* column of the balance sheet. This is because an excess of expenses over revenue decreases capital, and decreases in capital are recorded by a debit. After completion, total debits equal total credits in the Income Statement columns and in the Balance Sheet columns, as shown below (amounts are assumed).

	A	B	C	D	E	F	G	H	I	J	K	L	M
1	HUNTER ENVIRONMENTAL CONSULTING												
2	Accounting Worksheet (assumed amounts)												
3	For the Month Ended May 31, 2019												
4		Unadjusted Trial Balance		Adjustments				Adjusted Trial Balance		Income Statement		Balance Sheet	
5	Account Title	Dr	Cr		Dr		Cr	Dr	Cr	Dr	Cr	Dr	Cr
6	Cash	31,000						31,000				31,000	
7	Accounts receivable	14,000		(e)	1,500			15,500				15,500	
24	Supplies expense	0		(b)	500			500		500			
25	Utilities expense	1,000						1,000		1,000			
26		186,100	186,100		4,250		4,250	189,100	189,100	19,100	15,000	170,000	174,100
27	Net loss	You have a net loss when Income Statement debits > Income Statement credits. In other words, when expenses > revenues.									4,100	4,100	
28										19,100	19,100	174,100	174,100

Try It!

1. Indicate with a check mark where the final balance for each of the following accounts is extended in a worksheet. Assume each account has a normal balance.

	Income Statement		Balance Sheet	
	Debit	Credit	Debit	Credit
Cash				
Supplies				
Supplies Expense				
Unearned Revenue				
Service Revenue				
Owner's Equity				

2. The unadjusted trial balance of Sigrid's Off Road Adventures at December 31, 2020, the end of its fiscal year, is presented on the next page.

   Data needed for the adjusting entries are as follows:

   a. Supplies remaining on hand at year-end are worth $200.
   b. Amortization on furniture, $2,500.
   c. Amortization on building, $1,500.
   d. Salaries owed but not yet paid, $600.
   e. Service revenues to be accrued, $1,300.
   f. Of the $8,000 balance of Unearned Service Revenue, $2,000 was earned during 2020.

SIGRID'S OFF ROAD ADVENTURES Unadjusted Trial Balance December 31, 2020		
Account Title	**Debit**	**Credit**
Cash	$ 6,000	
Accounts receivable	5,000	
Supplies	1,000	
Furniture	10,000	
Accumulated amortization—furniture		$ 4,000
Building	60,000	
Accumulated amortization—building		30,000
Land	20,000	
Accounts payable		2,000
Salaries payable		0
Unearned service revenue		8,000
Sigrid Chu, capital		40,000
Sigrid Chu, withdrawals	25,000	
Service revenues		60,000
Salaries expense	16,000	
Supplies expense	0	
Amortization expense—furniture	0	
Amortization expense—building	0	
Miscellaneous expense	1,000	
Total	$144,000	$144,000

Prepare the worksheet of Sigrid's Off Road Adventures for the year ended December 31, 2020. Identify each adjusting entry by the letter corresponding to the data given.

To plan your worksheet, leave one blank line under the Service Revenues account.

Solutions appear at the end of this chapter and on **MyLab Accounting**

Working Through the Accounting Cycle

LO (2)

Remind me: How does this all fit together?

The worksheet helps to organize accounting data and to compute the net income or net loss for the period. It also helps accountants record the adjusting entries, prepare the financial statements, and close the accounts, but it is not required. Here is how the same work is done without a worksheet.

Recording the Adjusting Entries

Adjusting entries must be journalized and posted prior to closing the accounts.

The adjusting entries are a key element of accrual-basis accounting. The worksheet helps identify the accounts that need adjustments. But the actual adjustment of the accounts requires journal entries that are posted to the ledger accounts. In other words, steps 5 and 6 in the accounting cycle are not optional. They may be skipped temporarily to prepare interim statements more quickly, but eventually the adjusting entries must be recorded in the journals. Panel A of Exhibit 4–3 repeats the Hunter Environmental Consulting adjusting entries that we journalized in Chapter 3. Panel B shows the postings to the T-accounts, with "Adj." denoting an amount posted from an adjusting entry. Only the revenue and expense accounts are presented in the exhibit in order to focus on the closing process, which is discussed in the next section. T-accounts, instead of ledger accounts, are used for demonstration purposes.

EXHIBIT 4–3 | Journalizing and Posting the Adjusting Entries

Panel A: Journalizing

Adjusting Entries			Page 4
May 31	Insurance Expense	300	
	Prepaid Insurance		300
	To record insurance expense.		
31	Supplies Expense	500	
	Office Supplies		500
	To record supplies used.		
31	Amortization Expense—Furniture	750	
	Accumulated Amortization—Furniture		750
	To record amortization on furniture.		
31	Salaries Expense	4,000	
	Salaries Payable		4,000
	To accrue salaries expense.		
31	Accounts Receivable	1,500	
	Service Revenue		1,500
	To accrue service revenue.		
31	Unearned Service Revenue	1,000	
	Service Revenue		1,000
	To record unearned revenue that has been earned.		

Panel B: Posting the Adjustments to the Revenue and Expense T-Accounts

REVENUE

Service Revenue

Debit	Credit
	24,000
	Adj. 1,500
	Adj. 1,000
	Bal. 26,500

EXPENSES

Amortization Expense—Furniture

Debit	Credit
Adj. 750	
Bal. 750	

Insurance Expense

Debit	Credit
Adj 300	
Bal. 300	

Rent Expense

Debit	Credit
3,000	
Bal. 3,000	

Salaries Expense

Debit	Credit
4,000	
Adj. 4,000	
Bal. 8,000	

Supplies Expense

Debit	Credit
Adj. 500	
Bal. 500	

Utilities Expense

Debit	Credit
1,000	
Bal. 1,000	

Adj. = Amount posted from an adjusting entry
Bal. = Balance

The adjusting entries can be recorded in the journal as they are entered on the worksheet, but it is not necessary to journalize them at the same time. Most accountants prepare the financial statements immediately after completing the worksheet. They can wait to journalize and post the adjusting entries before they make the closing entries.

Preparing the Adjusted Trial Balance

The next step in the accounting cycle is to prepare the adjusted trial balance. For your convenience, it is presented in Exhibit 4–4. This is the same information as in the worksheet, but having it here lets us look at all the steps in the accounting cycle, and it will make it easier to see where the numbers come from for the closing entries, which are done next.

EXHIBIT 4–4 | Preparing the Adjusted Trial Balance

HUNTER ENVIRONMENTAL CONSULTING
Adjusted Trial Balance
May 31, 2019

Account Title	Debit	Credit
Cash	$ 31,000	
Accounts receivable	15,500	
Office supplies	1,000	
Prepaid insurance	3,300	
Furniture	45,000	
Accumulated amortization—furniture		$ 750
Land	50,000	
Accounts payable		12,000
Salaries payable		4,000
Unearned service revenue		2,000
Lisa Hunter, capital		120,100
Lisa Hunter, withdrawals	6,000	
Service revenue		26,500
Amortization expense	750	
Insurance expense	300	
Rent expense	3,000	
Salaries expense	8,000	
Supplies expense	500	
Utilities expense	1,000	
Total	$165,350	$165,350

Preparing the Financial Statements

The worksheet shows the amount of net income or net loss for the period, but it is still necessary to prepare the financial statements. (The financial statements can be prepared directly from the adjusted trial balance, as was shown in Chapter 3. This is why completion of the worksheet is optional and shown in Exhibit 4–1 as an alternative "route" to step 7.) Using the worksheet to sort the accounts to the balance sheet and the income statement eases the preparation of the statements. Exhibit 4–5 presents the May financial statements for Hunter Environmental Consulting, which are based on the data from the worksheet in Exhibit 4–2 or alternatively, they can be based on the adjusted trial balance found in Exhibit 4–4.

EXHIBIT 4–5 | May 2019 Financial Statements of Hunter Environmental Consulting

HUNTER ENVIRONMENTAL CONSULTING Income Statement For the Month Ended May 31, 2019		
Revenues		
Service revenue		$26,500
Expenses		
Amortization expense—furniture	$ 750	
Insurance expense	300	
Rent expense	3,000	
Salaries expense	8,000	
Supplies expense	500	
Utilities expense	1,000	
Total expenses		13,550
Net income		$12,950

HUNTER ENVIRONMENTAL CONSULTING Statement of Owner's Equity For the Month Ended May 31, 2019	
Lisa Hunter, capital, May 1, 2019	$120,100
Add: Net income	12,950
	133,050
Less: Withdrawals	6,000
Lisa Hunter, capital, May 31, 2019	$127,050

HUNTER ENVIRONMENTAL CONSULTING Balance Sheet May 31, 2019				
Assets			**Liabilities**	
Cash		$ 31,000	Accounts payable	$ 12,000
Accounts receivable		15,500	Salaries payable	4,000
Office supplies		1,000	Unearned service revenue	2,000
Prepaid insurance		3,300	Total liabilities	18,000
Furniture	$45,000			
Less: Accumulated amortization—furniture	750	44,250	**Owner's Equity**	
Land		50,000	Lisa Hunter, capital	127,050
Total assets		$145,050	Total liabilities and owner's equity	$145,050

Try It!

3. Using the worksheet created in Try It #2, prepare the financial statements of Sigrid's Off Road Adventures. Even if you did not complete the worksheet, you can use the solution shown at the end of the chapter as a starting point for this question.

Solutions appear at the end of this chapter and on **MyLab Accounting**.

Closing the Accounts

LO ③

What are closing entries, and how do we record them?

Closing the accounts occurs at the end of the period. Closing prepares the accounts for recording the transactions of the next period and consists of journalizing and posting the closing entries. Closing results in the balances of the revenue and expense accounts becoming zero in order to clearly measure the net income of each period separately from all other periods. We also close the owner's withdrawals account to reset its balance to zero. This is just like resetting the scoreboard after each game in the hockey playoff series discussed at the beginning of this chapter.

Recall that the income statement reports net income (or net loss) for a specific period. This is the "score" for the year. The revenue and expense accounts represent just what happened in the fiscal period, so they are closed (reset to zero) and are therefore called **temporary (or nominal) accounts**.

The Withdrawals account is also a temporary account because it measures withdrawals taken during a specific period. The Withdrawals account is also closed at the end of the period. *The closing process applies only to temporary accounts.*

To better understand the closing process, contrast the nature of the temporary accounts with the nature of the **permanent (or real) accounts**. They are *not* closed at the end of the period. The permanent accounts represent assets, liabilities, and owner's equity (the Capital account) that are on hand at a specific time. This is why their balances at the end of one accounting period carry over to become the beginning balances of the next period. For example, the Cash balance at December 31, 2019, is also the beginning Cash balance for January 1, 2020.

There is no account for net income, which is the net result of all revenue and expense accounts. Income Summary combines all revenue and expense amounts into one account, and its balance will equal the net income (or net loss). Income Summary does not appear on financial statements.

Closing entries transfer the revenue, expense, and withdrawal balances from their respective accounts to the Capital account. We show this in the statement of owner's equity, but we also need to update the journals and ledgers with the transfer. It is when we post the closing entries that the Capital account absorbs the impact of the balances in the temporary accounts.

As an intermediate step, however, the revenues and expenses are transferred first to a temporary account called **Income Summary**. The Income Summary account is like a temporary "holding tank" that is used only in the closing process. It represents the net income or net loss during the period.

Closing a Net Income The steps in closing the accounts of a service business like HEC that has a net income are as follows (the circled numbers are keyed to Exhibit 4–6 and Exhibit 4–7):

One way to remember the order of the closing entries is to use an acronym such as REISWC (pronounced rice-wick):

❶ **R**evenues

❷ **E**xpenses

❸ **I**ncome **S**ummary

❹ **W**ithdrawals to **C**apital

❶ Revenue account(s)
  Income Summary

Debit each revenue account for the amount of its credit balance. This closing entry transfers the sum of the revenues to the credit side of the Income Summary account.

❷ Income Summary
  Expense account(s)

Credit each expense account for the amount of its debit balance. This closing entry transfers the sum of the expenses to the debit side of the Income Summary account.

❸ Income Summary
  Capital account

The Income Summary account now holds the net income of the period, but only for a moment. To close net income, debit Income Summary for the amount of its credit. This closing entry transfers the net income from Income Summary to the Capital account and sets the Income Summary account to zero.

❹ Capital account
  Withdrawals account

This entry transfers the Withdrawals amount to the debit side of the Capital account. Withdrawals are not expenses and do not affect net income or net loss.

EXHIBIT 4–6 | Journalizing and Posting the Closing Entries

Panel A: Journalizing

It is not necessary to make separate closing entries for each revenue and expense account. Here there is one compound journal entry to close six accounts all at once.

		Closing Entries		Page 5
①	May 31	Service Revenue	26,500	
		Income Summary		26,500
		To close the revenue account and create the Income Summary account.		
②	31	Income Summary	13,550	
		Amortization Expense—Furniture		750
		Insurance Expense		300
		Rent Expense		3,000
		Salaries Expense		8,000
		Supplies Expense		500
		Utilities Expense		1,000
		To close the expense accounts.		
③	31	Income Summary	12,950	
		Lisa Hunter, Capital		12,950
		To close the Income Summary account and transfer net income to the Capital account (Income Summary balance = $26,500−$13,550).		
④	31	Lisa Hunter, Capital	6,000	
		Lisa Hunter, Withdrawals		6,000
		To close the Withdrawals account and transfer the Withdrawals amount to the Capital account.		

Panel B: Posting

Amortization Expense—Furniture

Adj.	750		
Bal.	750	Clo. ②	750

Insurance Expense

Adj.	300		
Bal.	300	Clo. ②	300

Rent Expense

Adj.	3,000		
Bal.	3,000	Clo. ②	3,000

Salaries Expense

	4,000		
Adj.	4,000		
Bal.	8,000	Clo. ②	8,000

Supplies Expense

Adj.	500		
Bal.	500	Clo. ②	500

Utilities Expense

	1,000		
Bal.	1,000	Clo. ②	1,000

Income Summary

Clo. ②	13,550	Clo. ①	26,500
Clo. ③	12,950	Bal.	12,950

Service Revenue

			24,000
		Adj.	1,500
		Adj.	1,000
Clo. ①	26,500	Bal.	26,500

Lisa Hunter, Withdrawals

Bal.	6,000	Clo. ④	6,000

Lisa Hunter, Capital

Clo. ④	6,000		120,100
		Clo. ③	12,950
		Bal.	127,050

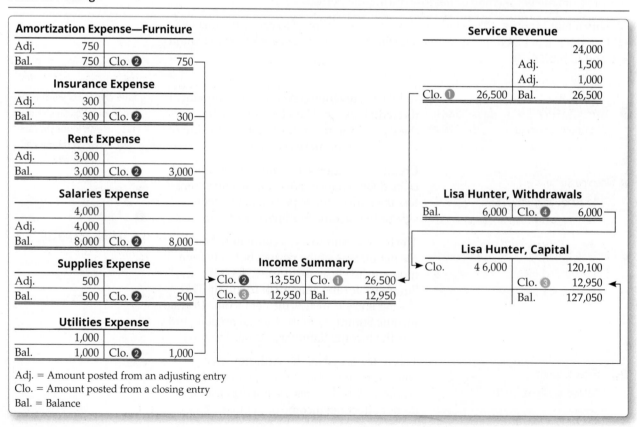

Adj. = Amount posted from an adjusting entry
Clo. = Amount posted from a closing entry
Bal. = Balance

These steps are best illustrated with an example. Suppose HEC closes the books at the end of May. Exhibit 4–6 presents the complete closing process for the business. The account balances to use are found in the adjusted trial balance (Exhibit 4–4). In Exhibit 4–6, Panel A gives the closing entries; Panel B shows the accounts after the closing entries have been posted.

The closing entries set the revenues, expenses, and the Withdrawals account back to zero. Now the Capital account includes the full effects of the May revenues, expenses, and withdrawals. These amounts, combined with the beginning Capital account's balance, give Lisa Hunter, Capital an ending balance of $127,050. Trace this ending Capital balance to the statement of owner's equity and also to the balance sheet in Exhibit 4–5.

Closing a Net Loss What would the closing entries be if HEC had suffered a net *loss* during May? Suppose that revenue was still $26,500 but for this example expenses totalled $27,500. The Income Summary account would appear as follows:

Income Summary

Clo. ❷	27,500	Clo. ❶	26,500
Bal.	1,000		

Closing entry ❸ would then credit Income Summary to close its debit balance and transfer the net loss to Lisa Hunter, Capital:

❸	May 31	Lisa Hunter, Capital	1,000	1,000
		Income Summary		
		To close the Income Summary account and transfer net loss to the Capital account.		

After posting, these two accounts would appear as follows:

Income Summary

Clo. ❷	27,500	Clo. ❶	26,500
Bal.	1,000	Clo. ❸	1,000

Lisa Hunter, Capital

Clo. ❸	1,000		120,100
		Bal.	119,100

Notice that the Capital balance is now $119,100. *The net loss decreases the Capital balance.*

❹ The Withdrawals balance would be closed to Capital, as before.

Exhibit 4–7 summarizes the four steps in the closing process.

The double underline at the bottom of an account indicates a zero balance is left in the account. It saves space since you do not need to write Bal. 0.

EXHIBIT 4–7 | The Closing Process for Net Income

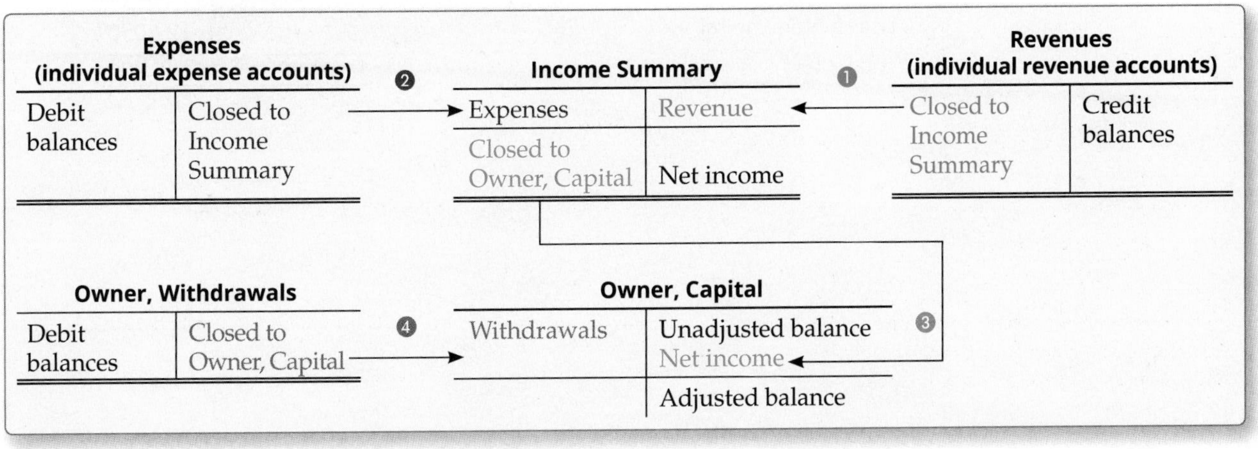

Accounting software does not use an Income Summary account. Entries are made to the Capital account (or for corporations the Retained Earnings account).

Closing Using Computers The closing process is fundamentally mechanical and is completely automated in a computerized system. Accounts are identified as either temporary or permanent when they are originally set up. The temporary accounts are closed automatically by selecting that option from the software's menu. Posting also occurs automatically. Many accounting programs allow for records to be open for two accounting periods at the same time. The beginning of a new period is open prior to closing the previous period. The reason for this is because time is needed to accumulate the information to properly adjust and close the accounts, but companies do not want to hold up processing the next period's transactions.

Post-Closing Trial Balance

The accounting cycle can end with step ⑨, the **post-closing trial balance**. See Exhibit 4–8 for HEC's post-closing trial balance. The post-closing trial balance is the final check on the accuracy of journalizing and posting the adjusting and closing entries. It lists the ledger's accounts and their adjusted balances after closing, and it is dated as of the end of the period for which the statements have been prepared.

The post-closing trial balance contains only the balance sheet information. It contains the ending balances of the permanent accounts—the assets, liabilities, and owner's equity (capital) accounts. No temporary accounts—revenues, expenses, or withdrawal accounts—are included because their balances have been closed. The ledger is up to date and ready for the next period's transactions.

EXHIBIT 4–8 | Post-Closing Trial Balance

HUNTER ENVIRONMENTAL CONSULTING
Post-Closing Trial Balance
May 31, 2019

Account Title	Debit	Credit
Cash	$ 31,000	
Accounts receivable	15,500	
Office supplies	1,000	
Prepaid insurance	3,300	
Furniture	45,000	
Accumulated amortization—furniture		$ 750
Land	50,000	
Accounts payable		12,000
Salaries payable		4,000
Unearned service revenue		2,000
Lisa Hunter, Capital		127,050
Total	$ 145,800	$145,800

Try It!

4. Benson Auto Repair had the following account balances after adjustments. Assume all accounts had normal balances.

Cash	$ 4,000	S. Benson, Capital	$35,700
Accounts Receivable	3,200	S. Benson, Withdrawals	2,100
Prepaid Rent	1,900	Service Revenue	1,600
Office Supplies	3,000	Amortization Expense—Equipment	300
Equipment	34,800	Salaries Expense	800
Accumulated Amortization—Equipment	1,600	Rent Expense	500
Accounts Payable	5,400	Utilities Expense	600
Note Payable (long-term)	7,000	Supplies Expense	100

Prepare the closing entries for Benson at December 31.

5. Prepare the post-closing trial balance for Benson Auto Repair at December 31, 2020, based on the balances in the accounts after completing Try It #4. If you did not complete question #4, you can start this question by using the solution on page 240.

Solutions appear at the end of this chapter and on **MyLab Accounting**.

Correcting Journal Entries

LO 4

How do we fix accounting errors?

In Chapter 2 we discussed errors that affect the trial balance: treating a debit as a credit and vice versa, transpositions, and slides. Here we show how to correct errors in journal entries. Knowing how to detect and correct errors is an important function in the preparation of accurate financial statements.

When the error is detected after posting, the accountant makes a *correcting entry* to correct an error. Correcting entries can appear on the worksheet with the adjusting entries at the end of a period, or they can be journalized and posted as soon as the error is detected.

Suppose HEC paid $10,000 cash for furniture and, in error, debited Office Supplies as follows:

Incorrect Entry			
May 13	Office Supplies	10,000	
	Cash		10,000
	Bought supplies.		

There are two ways to approach this sort of correction manually: either reverse the original entry and then create the correct journal entry, or create a journal entry that changes only the affected accounts. Exhibit 4–9 shows both approaches.

Notice that both approaches to correcting this error give the same results: Furniture reflects an increase of $10,000 and Office Supplies reflects an increase of $0, so both account balances are now correct.

Many software programs allow users to make a correction to the entry by changing the original transaction. The computer reverses the original entry and replaces it with the new, correct entry as we see on the left side of Exhibit 4–9.

Adjusting entries are not the same as correcting entries. Adjustments are made as part of the normal process of accounting. Corrections are made because of errors.

EXHIBIT 4-9 | Two Approaches for Correcting a Journal Entry Error

Correcting Entry: Reverse original and rewrite

May 15	Cash	10,000	
	Office Supplies		10,000
	To reverse the original transaction because it was entered incorrectly.		
May 15	Furniture	10,000	
	Cash		10,000
	To correct May 13 journal entry to reflect that furniture was purchased.		

This method is often preferred because it is easy to do and easy to follow through the journals to see what happened. It has a good *audit trail*—an easy-to-read transaction history to figure out what happened.

Correcting Entry: One step to change only affected accounts

May 15	Furniture	10,000	
	Office Supplies		10,000
	To correct May 13 entry. Furniture was purchased.		

The credit to Office Supplies in the correcting entry offsets the incorrect debit of the first entry. The debit to Furniture places the furniture's cost in the correct account. Now both Office Supplies and Furniture are correct.

Try It!

6. Suppose a company purchased $200 of supplies on account but in error credited Accounts Receivable for $200. Make the single journal entry on November 7 to correct this error, then correct the error using two journal entries using the same date. Provide an explanation for each journal entry.

Solutions appear at the end of this chapter and on **MyLab Accounting**

Classifying Assets and Liabilities

LO 5

How can assets and liabilities be classified for a more informative balance sheet?

Liquidity is a measure of how quickly an item can be converted to cash. All balance sheet accounts are listed in order of their liquidity or their *intended* disposition. Cash is the most liquid asset. Accounts receivable is a relatively liquid asset because the business expects to collect the amount in cash in the near future. Supplies are less liquid than accounts receivable, and furniture and buildings are even less so.

Users of financial statements are interested in liquidity because business difficulties often arise from a shortage of cash. How quickly can the business convert an asset to cash and pay a debt? How soon must a liability be paid?

These users need additional information to guide their decisions, so accounts are grouped into categories when they are presented in financial statements. Chapter 5 introduces a new subtotal on the income statement. In this chapter, we learn that a **classified balance sheet** lists assets and liabilities in the order of their relative liquidity by introducing subtotals to classify accounts as either *current* or *long-term*.

Assets

Current Assets **Current assets** are assets that are expected to be converted to cash, sold, or consumed during the next 12 months or within the business's normal operating cycle if longer than a year. The **operating cycle** is the time span during which cash is paid for goods and services that are sold to customers, who then pay the business cash:

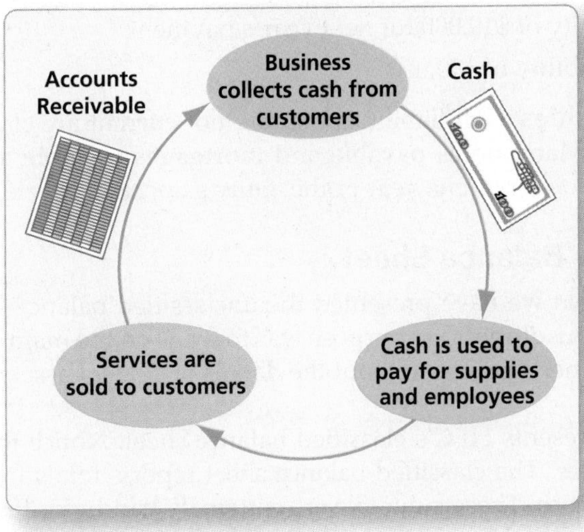

For most businesses, the operating cycle is a few months. Few types of business have operating cycles longer than a year.

Cash, Accounts Receivable, Notes Receivable due within a year or less, Supplies, and Prepaid Expenses are all current assets. **Merchandisers** such as Hudson's Bay Company and Canadian Tire Corporation and **manufacturing entities** such as Spin Master Corp. and Bombardier Inc. have an additional current asset, Inventory. This account shows the cost of goods that are held for sale to customers and will be examined in great detail in Chapter 5.

If a note receivable has some part that is due in the current period, the current portion is reported separately as a current asset and the rest of the receivable is reported as a long-term asset. In Exhibit 4–11 we can see that $51,600 is expected to be received in the current period while $48,400 will be received later.

Investment does not mean "owner's investment in the business," as that amount is included in equity. Instead, an investment shown as an asset is something (cash, shares, notes, bonds, or other assets) that is held with the expectation of it increasing in value through interest, dividends, or capital appreciation.

Long-Term Assets **Long-term assets** are all assets that are not classified as current assets. The term *long-term assets* is not a title on a financial statement—it is just a description of what is not current.

Property, plant, and equipment and intangible assets were introduced in Chapter 3. Two other categories of long-term assets are Long-Term Investments and Other Assets (a catch-all category for assets that are not classified more precisely). We discuss these categories in more detail in later chapters.

Liabilities

Financial statement users (such as creditors) are interested in the due dates of an entity's liabilities. Liabilities that must be paid the soonest create the greatest strain on cash. Therefore, the balance sheet lists liabilities in the order they are due to be paid. Balance sheets usually have at least two liability classifications: *current liabilities* and *long-term liabilities*. Knowing how many of a business's liabilities are current and how many are long-term helps creditors assess the likelihood of collecting from the entity.

Current Liabilities **Current liabilities** are debts that are due to be paid with cash or with goods and services within one year or the entity's operating cycle if the cycle is longer than a year. Accounts Payable, Salaries Payable, Interest Payable, and Unearned Revenue are all current liabilities.

If the long-term debt such as Notes Payable is paid in instalments, with the first instalment due within one year, the second instalment due the second year, and so on, then the first instalment would be a current liability and the remainder would be shown as a long-term liability. For example, a $100,000 notes payable to be paid $10,000 per year over 10 years would include the following:

- A current liability of $10,000 for next year's payment
- A long-term liability of $90,000

Long-Term Liabilities All liabilities that are not current are classified as **long-term liabilities**. Many notes payable and **mortgages payable** are long-term—payable after the longer of one year or the entity's operating cycle.

The Classified Balance Sheet

Thus far in this text we have presented the unclassified balance sheet of Hunter Environmental Consulting. Our purpose was to focus on the main points of assets, liabilities, and owner's equity without the details of current assets, current liabilities, and so on.

Exhibit 4–10 presents HEC's classified balance sheet. Notice that HEC has no long-term liabilities. The classified balance sheet reports totals for current assets and current liabilities. These subtotals are extremely handy for financial analysis, as you will see later in this chapter.

EXHIBIT 4–10 | Classified Balance Sheet of Hunter Environmental Consulting in Account Format

HUNTER ENVIRONMENTAL CONSULTING
Balance Sheet
May 31, 2019

Assets			**Liabilities**	
Current assets			Current liabilities	
Cash		$ 31,000	Accounts payable	$ 12,000
Accounts receivable		15,500	Salaries payable	4,000
Office supplies		1,000	Unearned service revenue	2,000
Prepaid insurance		3,300	Total current liabilities	18,000
Total current assets		50,800		
Property, plant, and equipment			**Owner's Equity**	
Furniture	$ 45,000		Lisa Hunter, capital	127,050
Less: Accumulated amortization	750	44,250		
Land		50,000		
Total property, plant, and equipment		94,250		
Total assets		$145,050	Total liabilities and owner's equity	$145,050

We saw this before on the income statement and in chapter 3 when these accounts were introduced. When there is information to be broken out into more detail, an extra column is added to the left.

The classified balance sheet of CAM Company is shown in Exhibit 4–11. It shows how a company with more accounts could present its data on a classified balance sheet. All the accounts have not been introduced to you yet. They are shown here so you have a model to use as they are added later.

Keep these pages handy! Bookmark them! They illustrate the formats to be followed when preparing a classified balance sheet.

Formats of Balance Sheets The balance sheet of CAM Company shown in Exhibit 4–11 lists the assets at the top with the liabilities and owner's equity below. This is the *report format*. HEC's balance sheet in Exhibit 4–10 lists the assets at the left with the liabilities and the owner's equity at the right. That is the *account* (or *equation*) *format*. Either format is acceptable.

EXHIBIT 4–11 | Classified Balance Sheet of CAM Company in Report Format

CAM COMPANY Balance Sheet June 30, 2019			
Assets			
Current assets			
Cash		$ 26,400	
Short-term investments		57,000	
Accounts receivable		235,000	
Interest receivable		26,800	
Current portion of note receivable		51,600	
Inventory		847,800	
Supplies		5,200	
Prepaid insurance		27,000	
Total current assets			$1,276,800
Long-term investments			
Note receivable		100,000	
Less: Current portion of note receivable		51,600	
Total long-term investments			48,400
Property, plant, and equipment			
Equipment	$ 60,000		
Less: accumulated amortization	18,000	42,000	
Furniture and fixtures	70,000		
Less: accumulated amortization	30,000	40,000	
Buildings	240,000		
Less: accumulated amortization	160,000	80,000	
Land		70,000	
Total property, plant, and equipment			232,000
Intangible assets			
Trademark			7,000
Total assets			$1,564,200
Liabilities			
Current liabilities			
Accounts payable	$357,000		
Salaries and wages payable	22,400		
Interest payable	24,600		
Goods and services tax payable	64,600		
Current portion of note payable	72,200		
Other current liabilities	23,600		
Total current liabilities		$ 564,400	
Long-term liabilities			
Note payable	220,000		
Less: current portion of note payable	72,200		
Total long-term liabilities		147,800	
Total liabilities			$ 712,200
Owner's Equity			
A. Lannister, capital			852,000
Total liabilities and owner's equity			$1,564,200

Did you notice that the Balance Sheet is called a Balance Sheet in the title and not a Classified Balance Sheet? The name of the document does not change, just the layout.

This example uses three columns for the dollar amounts. Other examples use two columns. This is done so you can see that there is not only one way to present information

Each time more detail is shown, the information is broken down into a column to the left of the total (e.g., $60,000 – $18,000 = $42,000).

Notice that even though it is the middle of the statement, there is a double underline representing the end of the assets section. This amount is a total of all the amounts directly above it.

This amount is a total of all the amounts directly above it. It also has a double underline to indicate that it is a final total.

Try It!

7. Create the classified balance sheet for Ticket Busters at December 31, 2020. Accounts listed in random order below have their normal balances. Use the report format of presentation. Optional: Try using three columns for the amounts as illustrated in Exhibit 4–11.

Yuri Sang, Capital	$ 14,160	Salaries Payable	$ 1,400
Cash	23,600	Accumulated Amortization—Furniture	240
Furniture	11,200	Mortgage Payable	20,000
Accounts Payable	11,200	Computers	7,000
Accumulated Amortization—Computers	200	Supplies	200
Accounts Receivable	7,600	Unearned Service Revenue	2,400

Why It's Done This Way

The top level of the accounting framework reminds us that financial statements are prepared to provide interested external users with information about the financial health of the company. These users have a variety of relationships with the company—some may be creditors who have lent money to the company, others may be shareholders or investors in the company. These groups want to understand how well the company has done in the past year. As well, they may want to predict how the company will do in the future.

The classified format of the balance sheet is an example of how liquidity information can be provided to help users get a better understanding about the financial condition of a business, which they can use as they calculate and interpret financial ratios.

Accounting Ratios

LO 6

How do decision makers evaluate a company using the current ratio and debt ratio?

The purpose of accounting is to provide information for decision making. Users of accounting information include managers, investors, and creditors. A creditor considering lending money must predict whether the borrower can repay the loan. If the borrower already has a large amount of debt, the probability of repayment is lower than if the borrower has a small amount of debt. To better understand complex information, decision makers use ratios they compute from a company's financial statements. A ratio is a useful way to show the relationship between numbers. Two of the most widely used decision aids in business are the current ratio and the debt ratio.

Current Ratio

The **current ratio** measures the ability of a business to pay its short-term debt obligations. In other words, it measures the company's ability to pay current liabilities with current assets.

$$\text{Current ratio} = \frac{\text{Total current assets}}{\text{Total current liabilities}}$$

A company prefers a high current ratio, which means the business has enough current assets to pay current liabilities when they come due, plus a cushion of additional current assets. An increasing current ratio from period to period generally indicates improvement in ability to pay current debts.

A general rule is that a strong current ratio would be in the range of 2.00, which indicates that the company has approximately $2.00 in current assets for every $1.00 in current liabilities. Such a company would probably have little trouble paying its current liabilities and could probably borrow money on better terms, such as at a lower rate of interest. Most successful businesses operate with current ratios between 1.30 and 2.00. A current ratio of 1.00 is considered quite low.

Let's examine HEC's current ratio, using the company's classified balance sheet in Exhibit 4–10:

	Current Ratio	Debt Ratio
Prefer ratio to be	high	low
Improvement when	increasing	decreasing

$$\text{Current ratio} = \frac{\text{Total current assets}}{\text{Total current liabilities}} = \frac{\$50{,}800}{\$18{,}000} = 2.82$$

HEC has $2.82 in current assets for every dollar the company owes in current liabilities. HEC's current ratio is very high, which makes the business look safe.

Debt Ratio

The **debt ratio** indicates the proportion of a company's assets that are financed with debt, as opposed to the proportion financed by the owner(s) of the company. This ratio measures a company's ability to pay both current and long-term debts—total liabilities.

$$\text{Debt ratio} = \frac{\text{Total liabilities}}{\text{Total assets}}$$

Think of the debt ratio in personal terms to help you remember the guideline that a lower debt ratio is preferred over a higher debt ratio. If you owned a car that is now worth $15,000 (your total assets) but had a loan on it for $17,000 (your total liabilities) this would be "bad." Your debt ratio would be 17,000/15,000 = 1.13. But if you owned the same $15,000 car and had a $10,000 loan on it, your debt ratio would be 10,000/15,000 = 0.67, which is certainly "better."

A low debt ratio is safer than a high debt ratio. Why? Because a company with low liabilities has low required payments. Such a company is less likely to get into financial difficulty. A rule of thumb is that a debt ratio below 0.60, or 60 percent, is considered safe for most businesses. Most companies have debt ratios in the range of 0.60 to 0.80. A decreasing ratio indicates improvement over time.

Let's examine HEC's debt ratio, using the company's balance sheet in Exhibit 4–10:

$$\text{Debt ratio} = \frac{\text{Total liabilities}}{\text{Total assets}} = \frac{\$18{,}000}{\$145{,}050} = 0.12, \text{ or } 12\%$$

The percentage of HEC's total assets that is financed with debt is 12 percent. A debt ratio of 12 percent is very safe.

Interpreting Ratios

Financial ratios are an important aid to decision makers. However, it is unwise to place too much confidence in a single ratio or group of ratios. For example, a company may have a high current ratio, which indicates financial strength, and it may also have a high debt ratio, which suggests weakness. Which ratio gives the more reliable signal about the company? Experienced managers, lenders, and investors evaluate a company by examining a large number of ratios over several years to spot trends and turning points. These people also consider other facts, such as the company's cash position and its trend in net income. No single ratio gives the whole picture about a company.

As you progress through the study of accounting, we will introduce key ratios used for decision making. Chapter 18 (in Volume 2) then summarizes all the ratios discussed in this text and provides an overview of ratios used in decision making.

Try It!

8. Refer to Try It #7, if you completed it, or the solution posted on page 241. Compute and evaluate the current ratio and the debt ratio for Ticket Busters.

Solutions appear at the end of this chapter and on **MyLab Accounting**

ETHICS Should revenue be recorded early?

Carnival Custom Painting's controller, Kristi Seay, is hoping to get a loan from a local bank. The business's van engine has just stopped working, and the business has no extra cash to replace the engine. It needs a short-term loan of $3,000. A teller at the bank has told Kristi that the bank will only approve the loan if the business has a current ratio that is above 1.2. Currently, Carnival's current ratio is 1.1. The business has just received a contract for painting a new commercial building. Kristi has told the teller that she expects revenue of $15,000 from the contract but won't receive payment until the job is completed. The business plans on starting the job next week but won't be finished for another two months, not soon enough to use the cash to replace the engine in the van. The teller has suggested to Kristi that she go ahead and record the revenue and cash receipt of the painting contract even though it hasn't been completed. This, he tells her, will increase the business's current assets and thereby increase the current ratio to 1.4, well above the bank minimum. What should Kristi do? What would you do?

Solution

Kristi should not record the revenue and cash receipt early. The revenue recognition principle requires that businesses record revenue only when it has been earned. Given that Carnival Custom Painting has not yet started the job, no revenue has been earned. Kristi should look for alternative sources of financing instead of trying to manipulate the current ratio to meet the minimum required by the bank. Another possibility would be for Kristi to renegotiate the contract with the new client to receive $3,000 in advance instead of after the completion of the job. This would allow Kristi to make the repairs on the van and not have to borrow the money from the bank.

LO 7

How does IFRS apply to the accounting cycle and financial reporting?

EXHIBIT 4–12 | Accounting Cycle and Financial Reporting Implications of IFRS

ASPE	IFRS
The accounting cycle for companies following IFRS is the same as that for companies following ASPE. While the approach to recording transactions is essentially the same under both reporting systems, the presentation of the information may be quite different. Canadian companies following IFRS will choose the financial statement names and formats that best meet their needs or are favoured by others in their industry.	
Balance sheet	Choice of name such as statement of financial position or balance sheet. A classified format is required.
Companies use a classified format, which lists the accounts in the order of liquidity in a **current then non-current** order.	Under IFRS, there is a choice between current then non-current *OR* **non-current then current** order (on the asset side of the balance sheet, they present the long-term assets first followed by the current assets; on the liability and equity side of the balance sheet, they present the equity section, then the long-term liabilities, followed by the current liabilities). The non-current then current order is sometimes called a *reverse order of liquidity*.
Income statement	Choice of name such as statement of comprehensive income or income statement And there is a choice of presentation: Prepare a separate income statement and statement of comprehensive income, or prepare one document that combines both.
Statement of owner's equity (statement of retained earnings for a corporation)	Choice of name such as statement of changes in equity or statement of retained earnings
Cash flow statement	Choice of name such as statement of cash flows or cash flow statement

Summary Problem for Your Review

The unadjusted trial balance of Cloud Break Consulting at the end of its fiscal year is presented below:

CLOUD BREAK CONSULTING Unadjusted Trial Balance November 30, 2020		
Account Title	**Debit**	**Credit**
Cash	$131,000	
Accounts receivable	104,000	
Supplies	4,000	
Prepaid rent	27,000	
Building	300,000	
Accumulated amortization—building		$155,000
Land	45,000	
Accounts payable		159,000
Salaries payable		0
Unearned service revenue		40,000
Michael Moe, capital		102,000
Michael Moe, withdrawals	7,000	
Service revenue		450,000
Salaries expense	255,000	
Supplies expense	0	
Rent expense	25,000	
Amortization expense—building	0	
Miscellaneous expense	8,000	
Total	$906,000	$906,000

Data needed for the adjusting entries include:

a. Supplies remaining on hand at year-end are worth $2,000.

b. Nine months of rent ($27,000) were paid in advance on September 1, 2020. No rent expense has been recorded since that date.

c. Amortization expense has not been recorded on the building for the 2020 fiscal year. Amortization is $14,000 per year on the building.

d. Employees work Monday through Friday. The weekly payroll is $5,000 and is paid every Friday. November 30, 2020, is a Monday.

e. Service revenue of $15,000 must be accrued.

f. Cloud Break Consulting received $40,000 in advance for consulting services to be provided evenly from June 1, 2020, through January 31, 2021. None of the revenue from this client has been recorded.

To plan your worksheet, check the adjusting entries data to see if the same account is affected more than once. If it is, leave one or two blank lines under the account name. Do this for Service Revenue on this worksheet.

Required

1. Prepare the worksheet of Cloud Break Consulting for the year ended November 30, 2020. Identify each adjusting entry by the letter corresponding to the data given.
2. Journalize the adjusting entries and post them to T-accounts. (Before posting to the T-accounts, enter into each T-account its balance as shown in the unadjusted trial balance. For example, enter the $104,000 balance in the Accounts Receivable account before posting its adjusting entry.) Identify adjusting entries by *letter.* Provide explanations. You can take the adjusting entries straight from the worksheet from Requirement 1. Find the ending balances of the permanent accounts.
3. Prepare the income statement for the year ended November 30, 2020. List expenses in order from largest to smallest but also list Miscellaneous Expense last among the expenses, which is a common practice.
4. Prepare the statement of owner's equity for the year ended November 30, 2020. Draw the arrow that links the income statement to the statement of owner's equity if both statements are on the same page. Otherwise, explain how they are linked.
5. Prepare the classified balance sheet at November 30, 2020. Use the report format. All liabilities are current. Draw the arrow that links the statement of owner's equity to the balance sheet if both statements are on the same page. Otherwise, explain how they are linked.
6. Journalize and post the closing entries. (Each T-account should carry its balance as shown in the adjusted trial balance.) Provide explanations. To distinguish closing entries from adjusting entries, identify the closing entries by *number.* Draw the arrows to illustrate the flow of data, as shown in Exhibit 4–6, Panel B, page 184. Indicate the balance of the Capital account after the closing entries are posted.

SOLUTION

Requirement 1

Using the trial balance given, write the account titles in the first column of the worksheet and the amounts in the Unadjusted Trial Balance columns, ensuring debit and credit balances on the trial balance are debit and credit balances on the worksheet.

When calculating the Adjusted Trial Balance amounts, remember to add and subtract the adjustments properly. For assets, withdrawals, and expenses, add debits and subtract credits. For contra assets, liabilities, owner's equity, and revenues, add credits and subtract debits.

	A	B	C	D	E	F	G	H	I	J	K	L	M
1	**CLOUD BREAK CONSULTING**												
2	Worksheet												
3	For the Year Ended November 30, 2020												
4		**Unadjusted Trial Balance**		**Adjustments**				**Adjusted Trial Balance**		**Income Statement**		**Balance Sheet**	
5	**Account Title**	**Debit**	**Credit**		**Debit**		**Credit**	**Debit**	**Credit**	**Debit**	**Credit**	**Debit**	**Credit**
6	Cash	131,000						131,000				131,000	
7	Accounts receivable	104,000		(e)	15,000			119,000				119,000	
8	Supplies	4,000				(a)	2,000	2,000				2,000	
9	Prepaid rent	27,000				(b)	9,000	18,000				18,000	
10	Building	300,000						300,000				300,000	
11	Accum. amort.—building		155,000			(c)	14,000		169,000				169,000
12	Land	45,000						45,000				45,000	
13	Accounts payable		159,000						159,000				159,000
14	Salaries payable		0			(d)	1,000		1,000				1,000
15	Unearned service revenue		40,000	(f)	30,000				10,000				10,000
16	Michael Moe, capital		102,000						102,000				102,000
17	Michael Moe, withdrawals	7,000						7,000				7,000	
18	Service revenue		450,000			(e)	15,000		495,000		495,000		
19						(f)	30,000						
20	Salaries expense	255,000		(d)	1,000			256,000		256,000			
21	Supplies expense	0		(a)	2,000			2,000		2,000			
22	Rent expense	25,000		(b)	9,000			34,000		34,000			
23	Amort. exp.—building	0		(c)	14,000			14,000		14,000			
24	Miscellaneous expense	8,000						8,000		8,000			
25		906,000	906,000		71,000		71,000	936,000	936,000	314,000	495,000	622,000	441,000
26	Net income									181,000			181,000
27										495,000	495,000	622,000	622,000

(a) Supplies on hand ($4,000) − supplies still on hand ($2,000) = $2,000 adjustment

(b) Of the $27,000 rent paid for nine months (or $3,000 per month), $9,000 should be recorded as rent expense for September, October, and November.

(f) Unearned Service Revenue started with a balance of $40,000, and $30,000 was earned for June to November, so that means there is still $10,000 to be earned, which is a liability.

The same "plug figure" ($181,000) must make the final Income Statement column totals equal and the final Balance Sheet column totals equal.

Requirement 2

Refer to the Adjustments columns of the worksheet. Prepare journal entries for all the transactions in the Adjustments columns.

a.	Nov. 30	Supplies Expense	2,000	
		Supplies		2,000
		To reflect supplies remaining on hand at year-end.		
b.	Nov. 30	Rent Expense	9,000	
		Prepaid Rent		9,000
		To record rent expense for September, October, and November (3 × $3,000 = $9,000).		
c.	Nov. 30	Amortization Expense—Building	14,000	
		Accumulated Amortization—Building		14,000
		To record annual amortization expense on building.		
d.	Nov. 30	Salaries Expense	1,000	
		Salaries Payable		1,000
		To record one day's salaries owed to employees ($5,000 ÷ 5 = $1,000).		
e.	Nov. 30	Accounts Receivable	15,000	
		Service Revenue		15,000
		To accrue service revenue at year-end.		
f.	Nov. 30	Unearned Service Revenue	30,000	
		Service Revenue		30,000
		To record service revenue earned from June to November ($40,000 ÷ 8 = $5,000 revenue per month; six months' revenue is 6 × $5,000 = $30,000).		

Create T-accounts only for the accounts affected by the adjusting entries.

Remember that the beginning balance in each of these T-accounts is the amount from the unadjusted trial balance columns of the worksheet.

When you post the adjusting entries, use the letters a to f to identify each adjustment to make it easier to follow your work later.

Find the balance of each T-account.

Accounts Receivable

104,000	
(e) 15,000	
Bal. 119,000	

Supplies

4,000	(a) 2,000
Bal. 2,000	

Prepaid Rent

27,000	
	(b) 9,000
Bal. 18,000	

Accumulated Amortization—Building

	155,000
	(c) 14,000
	Bal. 169,000

Salaries Payable

	(d) 1,000
	Bal. 1,000

Unearned Service Revenue

(f) 30,000	40,000
	Bal. 10,000

Service Revenue

	450,000
	(e) 15,000
	(f) 30,000
	Bal. 495,000

Salaries Expense

255,000	
(d) 1,000	
Bal. 256,000	

Supplies Expense

(a) 2,000	
Bal. 2,000	

Rent Expense

25,000	
(b) 9,000	
Bal. 34,000	

Amortization Expense—Building

(c) 14,000	
Bal. 14,000	

Requirement 3

CLOUD BREAK CONSULTING Income Statement For the Year Ended November 30, 2020		
Revenue		
Service revenue		$495,000
Expenses		
Salaries expense	$256,000	
Rent expense	34,000	
Amortization expense—building	14,000	
Supplies expense	2,000	
Miscellaneous expense	8,000	
Total expenses		314,000
Net income		$181,000

The title must include the name of the company, the name of the document, and the specific period of time covered.

Gather all the revenue and expense account names and amounts from the Income Statement columns of the worksheet.

Requirement 4

CLOUD BREAK CONSULTING Statement of Owner's Equity For the Year Ended November 30, 2020	
Michael Moe, capital, December 1, 2019	$102,000
Add: Net income	181,000
	283,000
Less: Withdrawals	7,000
Michael Moe, capital, November 30, 2020	$276,000

Watch that the line for the date indicates the specific period of time covered.

Beginning owner's equity and withdrawals are from the Balance Sheet columns of the worksheet. The net income amount is transferred from the income statement.

Requirement 5

CLOUD BREAK CONSULTING Balance Sheet November 30, 2020			
Assets			
Current assets			
Cash		$131,000	
Accounts receivable		119,000	
Supplies		2,000	
Prepaid rent		18,000	
Total current assets			$270,000
Property, plant, and equipment			
Building	$300,000		
Less: Accumulated amortization	169,000	131,000	
Land		45,000	
Total property, plant, and equipment			176,000
Total assets			$446,000
Liabilities			
Current liabilities			
Accounts payable		$159,000	
Salaries payable		1,000	
Unearned service revenue		10,000	
Total current liabilities			$170,000
Owner's Equity			
Michael Moe, capital			276,000
Total liabilities and owner's equity			$446,000

Notice that the balance sheet shows the financial position on one specific date.

The classified balance sheet uses the accounts and balances that appear in the Balance Sheet columns of the worksheet and includes additional headings and subtotals. Use Exhibit 4–11 as a model.

❶ To close revenue accounts, debit each revenue account for the amount reported in the Income Statement column of the worksheet. Credit Income Summary for the total of the debits.
❷ To close expense accounts, credit each expense account for the amount reported in the Income Statement column of the worksheet. Debit Income Summary for the total of the credits.
❸ To close the Income Summary account, calculate the difference between the total debits and total credits in the Income Summary account. This should match the net income or net loss amount on the worksheet. In this case, Income Summary has a credit balance. Therefore, debit Income Summary to close it and credit the Capital account. Using an Income Summary T-account may help you close Income Summary more easily.
❹ To close the Withdrawals account, credit the Withdrawals account for the amounts reported in the Balance Sheet columns of the worksheet, and debit the Capital account.

Requirement 6

❶	Nov. 30	Service Revenue	495,000	
		Income Summary		495,000
		To close the revenue account and create the Income Summary account.		
❷	Nov. 30	Income Summary	314,000	
		Salaries Expense		256,000
		Supplies Expense		2,000
		Rent Expense		34,000
		Amortization Expense—Building		14,000
		Miscellaneous Expense		8,000
		To close the expense accounts.		
❸	Nov. 30	Income Summary	181,000	
		Michael Moe, Capital		181,000
		To close the Income Summary account. (Income Summary balance = $495,000 − $314,000.)		
❹	Nov. 30	Michael Moe, Capital	7,000	
		Michael Moe, Withdrawals		7,000
		To close the Withdrawals account and transfer the Withdrawals amount to the Capital account.		

Identify the closing entries by their journal entry numbers 1, 2, 3, or 4.

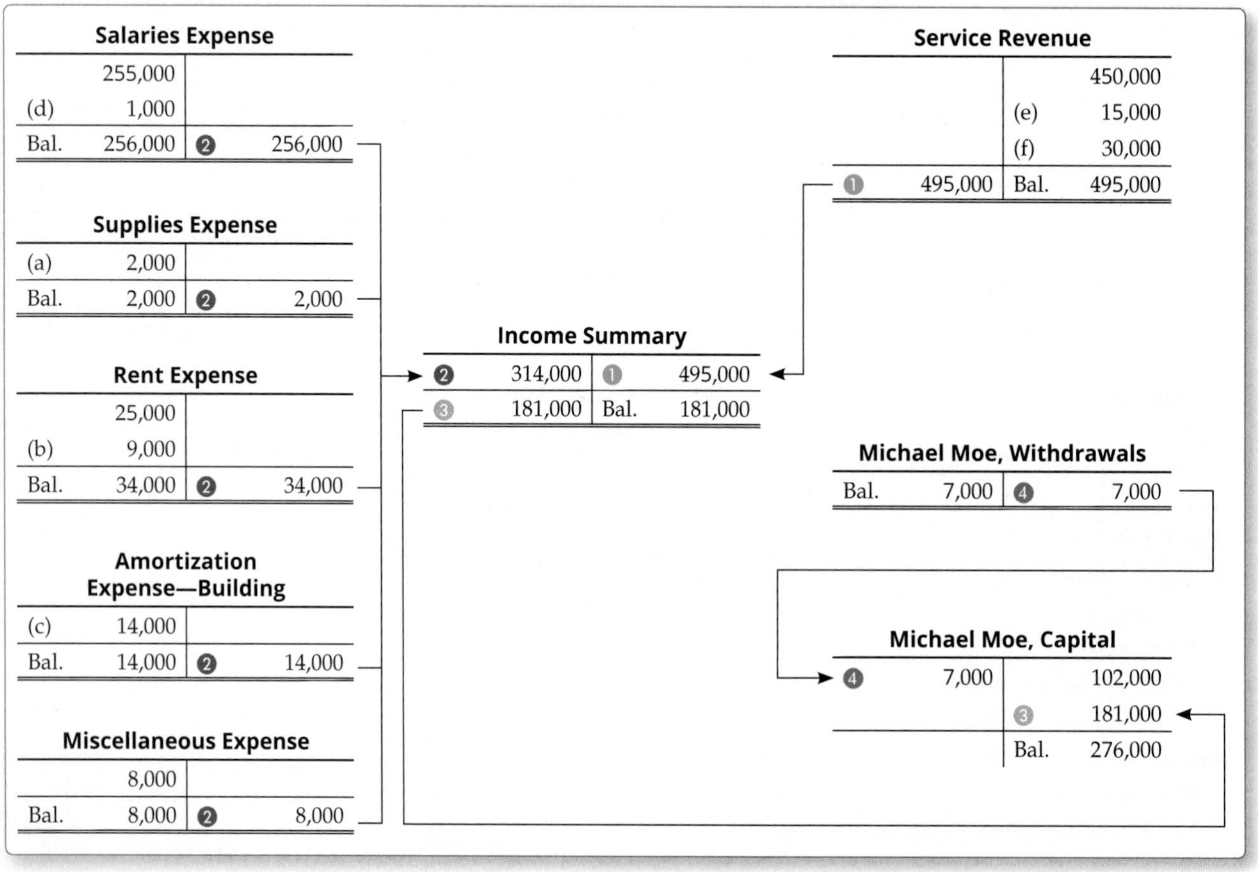

Chapter 4 Appendix

REVERSING ENTRIES: AN OPTIONAL STEP

Reversing entries are special types of entries that are used most often in conjunction with accrual-type adjustments such as accrued salaries expense and accrued service revenue. Reversing entries are *not* used for adjustments to record amortization and prepayments.

LO (A1)
What are reversing entries, and how do we record them?

Reversing Entries for Accrued Expenses

To see how reversing entries work, let's examine a business that pays its employees every Friday. Salaries expense is $5,000 per week, or $1,000 per day. In July 2019, month end is on a Wednesday.

Generally accepted accounting principles (GAAP) do not require reversing entries. They are used only for convenience and to save time.

July 2019						
S	M	T	W	T	F	S
	1	2	3	4	(5)	6
7	8	9	10	11	(12)	13
14	15	16	17	18	(19)	20
21	22	23	24	25	(26)	27
28	29	30	31	1	(2)	3

We need to record what was earned by the employees but not yet paid as at Wednesday, July 31, 2019. The adjusting entry for three days of a five-day work week would be:

Jul. 31	Salaries Expense	3,000	
	Salaries Payable		3,000

To record three days of salaries owed to employees in July. ($5,000 ÷ 5 = 1,000/day × 3 days)

The next payroll date is August 2. On that date, the business will pay $3,000 of accrued salaries plus $2,000 in salaries that the employees have earned in the first two days of August. There are two ways this next journal entry can be made: with or without the use of a reversing entry.

Accounting without a Reversing Entry

Aug. 2	Salaries Payable	3,000	
	Salaries Expense	2,000	
	Cash		5,000

To record payment of salaries payable from July and the salaries expense from the current month.

This method of recording the cash payment is correct. However, it wastes time because the company's accountant must refer to the adjusting entries of July 31 to recall how much was accrued. Searching the preceding period's adjusting entries takes time and, in business, time is money. To save time, accountants use reversing entries, which eliminates the need to search the preceding period's adjusting entries.

Making a Reversing Entry

A reversing entry is the exact opposite of a prior adjusting entry.

Ordinarily, the accountant who makes the adjusting entry prepares the reversing entry at the same time. The reversing entry is recorded on the first day of the next period so that it affects only the new period.

A reversing entry switches the debit and the credit of a previous adjusting entry. The business may choose to record this reversing entry:

To reverse the July 31 adjusting entry for salaries.

Aug. 1	Salaries Payable	3,000	
	Salaries Expense		3,000

Note how the accounts appear after the company posts the reversing entry:

Salaries Payable

	Jul. 31 3,000
Aug. 1 Rev. 3,000	Jul. 31 Bal. 3,000
Aug. 1 Bal. 0	

Salaries Expense

	Aug. 1 Rev. 3,000

This credit balance in Salaries Expense does not mean that the entity has negative salaries expense, as you might think. Instead, the odd credit balance is merely a temporary result of the reversing entry that will be eliminated on August 2.

The payment of the payroll does not include an entry to the Salaries Payable account because there is no balance in that account.

To record the weekly payroll payment.

Aug. 2	Salaries Expense	5,000	
	Cash		5,000

After posting the journal entry, the Salaries Expense account has its correct debit balance of $2,000, which is the amount of salaries expense incurred so far in August.

Salaries Expense

Aug. 2 5,000	Aug. 1 Rev. 3,000
Aug. 2 Bal. 2,000	

Exhibit 4A–1 shows these transactions side by side to highlight the differences and show that the results are the same whether or not reversing entries are used.

EXHIBIT 4A-1 | Comparison of Two Ways to Record Reversing Entries for Accrued Expenses

Start at month end. Accrue $3,000 Salaries Expense on July 31.

Jul. 31	Salaries Expense	3,000	
	Salaries Payable		3,000

Salaries Expense

Jul. 5 5,000	
Jul. 12 5,000	
Jul. 19 5,000	
Jul. 26 5,000	
Jul. 31 3,000	
Jul. 31 Bal. 23,000	Closing entries set this to zero at end of month

Salaries Payable

	Jul. 31 3,000
	Jul. 31 Bal. 3,000

No reversing entry on August 1.

Pay salaries on August 2. The cash payment of $5,000 includes $3,000 owed from July and $2,000 earned in August.

Aug. 2	Salaries Payable	3,000	
	Salaries Expense	2,000	
	Cash		5,000

Salaries Payable

Aug. 2 3,000	Jul. 31 Bal. 3,000
	Aug. 2 Bal. 0

Salaries Expense

Aug. 2 2,000	

Rev. = reversing entry; Clo. = closing entry; Bal. = balance

Reversing entry recorded August 1.

Aug. 1	Salaries Payable	3,000	
	Salaries Expense		3,000

Salaries Payable

	Jul. 31 3,000
Aug. 1 Rev. 3,000	Jul. 31 Bal. 3,000
Aug. 1 Bal. 0	

Salaries Expense

	Aug. 1 Rev. 3,000

Pay salaries on August 2. The cash payment of $5,000 updates the expense account to its correct balance.

Aug. 2	Salaries Expense	5,000	
	Cash		5,000

Salaries Payable

Salaries Expense

Aug. 2 5,000	Aug. 1 Rev. 3,000
Aug. 2 Bal. 2,000	

Reversing Entries for Accrued Revenues

While most reversing entries are made to accrued expenses, reversing entries may be made to accrued revenues. For example, if HEC had completed some consulting work for a client on May 31 and sent the invoice, an entry would be made to debit Accounts Receivable and credit Service Revenue at May 31, 2019. A reversing entry on June 1, 2019, would reduce Accounts Receivable and temporarily create a debit balance in Service Revenue. When the payment is received in June, the accountant would debit Cash and credit Service Revenue.

Summary

Learning Objectives

① Prepare an accounting worksheet **Pg. 175**

How can we summarize data to prepare the financial statements?

- The accountant's worksheet includes the following columns:

	Unadjusted Trial Balance		Adjustments		Adjusted Trial Balance		Income Statement		Balance Sheet	
Account Title	Dr	Cr	Dr	Cr	Dr	Cr	Dr	Cr	Dr	Cr

② Completing the accounting cycle **Pg. 179**

Remind me: How does this all fit together?

- A worksheet is an optional tool for preparing information used to create financial statements.

③ Close the revenue, expense, and withdrawal accounts **Pg. 183**

What are closing entries, and how do we record them?

- The temporary accounts are closed out to zero. Their balances are transferred to the Capital account.
- To remember what is closed, use the acronym REISWC (pronounced rice-wick):
  1. **R**evenues
  2. **E**xpenses
  3. **I**ncome **S**ummary
  4. **W**ithdrawals to **C**apital

④ Correct typical accounting errors **Pg. 187**

How do we fix accounting errors?

- Accountants use "correcting journal entries" to fix errors after journal entries have been posted. Either reverse the original journal entry and then write a new journal entry, or change only the affected accounts in a new journal entry.

⑤ Classify assets and liabilities as current or long-term, and prepare a classified balance sheet **Pg. 188**

How can assets and liabilities be classified for a more informative balance sheet?

- Classify assets and liabilities into one of the following groups:
  - Current (within one year or the company's operating cycle if longer than a year)
  - Long-term (non-current)

⑥ Use the current ratio and the debt ratio to evaluate a company **Pg. 192**

How do decision makers evaluate a company using the current ratio and debt ratio?

$$\text{Current ratio} = \frac{\text{Total current assets}}{\text{Total current liabilities}}$$

- The current ratio measures the company's ability to pay current liabilities with current assets.

$$\text{Debt ratio} = \frac{\text{Total liabilities}}{\text{Total assets}}$$

- The debt ratio measures the company's overall ability to pay liabilities. The debt ratio shows the proportion of the entity's assets that are financed with debt.

(7) Describe the accounting cycle and financial reporting implications of International Financial Reporting Standards (IFRS) Pg. 194

How does IFRS apply to the accounting cycle and financial reporting?

- There is no change to the accounting cycle if companies follow IFRS or ASPE.
- Canadian companies reporting under IFRS have several choices in the format of their balance sheet presentation.

(A1) Describe and prepare reversing entries Pg. 201

What are reversing entries, and how do we record them?

- A reversing entry is an optional step that switches the debit and credit of a previous adjusting entry to "undo" it.

Key Terms for the chapter are shown next and are in the **Glossary** at the back of the book. **Similar Terms** are shown after **Key Terms**.

KEY TERMS

Classified balance sheet A balance sheet that places each asset and liability into a specific category *(p. 188).*

Closing entries Entries that transfer the revenue, expense, and owner withdrawal balances from these respective accounts to the Capital account *(p. 183).*

Closing the accounts A step in the accounting cycle at the end of the period that prepares the accounts for recording the transactions of the next period. Closing the accounts consists of journalizing and posting the closing entries to set the balances of the revenue, expense, and owner withdrawal accounts to zero *(p. 183).*

Current asset An asset that is expected to be converted to cash, sold, or consumed during the next 12 months, or within the business's normal operating cycle if longer than a year *(p. 188).*

Current liability A debt due to be paid within one year or one of the entity's operating cycles if the cycle is longer than a year *(p. 189).*

Current ratio Current assets divided by current liabilities. Measures the company's ability to pay current liabilities from current assets *(p. 192).*

Current then non-current A balance sheet format that reports current assets before long-term assets, and current liabilities before long-term liabilities and equity. This format may be used for reporting under both ASPE and IFRS *(p. 194).*

Debt ratio Ratio of total liabilities to total assets. Gives the proportion of a company's assets that it has financed with debt *(p. 193).*

Income Summary A temporary "holding tank" account into which the revenues and expenses are transferred prior to their final transfer to the Capital account *(p. 183).*

Liquidity A measure of how quickly an item can be converted to cash *(p. 188).*

Long-term asset An asset not classified as a current asset *(p. 189).*

Long-term liability A liability not classified as a current liability *(p. 190).*

Manufacturing entity A company that earns its revenue by making products *(p. 189).*

Merchandiser A company that earns its revenue by selling products rather than services *(p. 189).*

Mortgage payable Long-term debts that include an agreement that if the debt is not paid, specific property is taken by the lender *(p. 190).*

Nominal account Another name for a *temporary account (p. 183).*

Non-current then current A balance sheet format that may be used for companies reporting under IFRS. Accounts are reported in the reverse order of liquidity, for example, long-term assets before current assets *(p. 194).*

Operating cycle The time span during which cash is paid for goods and services that are sold to customers who then pay the business in cash *(p. 188).*

Permanent account An asset, liability, or owner's equity account that is not closed at the end of the period. Also called a *real account (p. 183).*

Post-closing trial balance A list of the ledger accounts and their balances at the end of the period after the closing entries have been journalized and posted. The last step of the accounting cycle, it ensures that the ledger is in balance for the start of the next accounting period *(p. 186).*

Real account Another name for a *permanent account (p. 183).*

Reversing entry An entry that switches the debit and the credit of a previous adjusting entry. The reversing entry is dated the first day of the period following the adjusting entry *(p. 201).*

Temporary account The revenue and expense accounts that relate to a particular accounting period and are closed at the end of the period. For a proprietorship, the owner withdrawals account is also temporary. Also called a *nominal account (p. 183).*

Worksheet A columnar document designed to help move data from the trial balance to the financial statements *(p. 175).*

SIMILAR TERMS

Current ratio	Working capital ratio
Current then non-current	In order of liquidity
Non-current	Long-term
Non-current then current	In reverse order of liquidity
Permanent account	Real account
Temporary account	Nominal account

SELF-STUDY QUESTIONS

Test your understanding of the chapter by marking the correct answer to each of the following questions:

1. The worksheet is a (*p. 175*)
   a. Journal
   b. Ledger
   c. Financial statement
   d. Device for completing the accounting cycle
2. The usefulness of the worksheet is (*p. 175*)
   a. Identifying the accounts that need to be adjusted
   b. Summarizing the effects of all the transactions of the period
   c. Aiding the preparation of the financial statements
   d. All of the above
3. Which situation indicates a net loss within the Income Statement section of the worksheet? (*p. 178*)
   a. Total credits exceed total debits
   b. Total debits exceed total credits
   c. Total debits equal total credits
   d. Total debits plus credits is negative
4. Which of the following accounts is not closed? (*p. 183*)
   a. Supplies Expense
   b. Prepaid Insurance
   c. Interest Revenue
   d. Withdrawals
5. What do closing entries accomplish? (*p. 183*)
   a. Zero out the revenues, expenses, and Owner, Withdrawals
   b. Transfer revenues, expenses, and Owner, Withdrawals to the Owner, Capital account
   c. Bring the Owner, Capital account to its correct ending balance
   d. All of the above
6. The purpose of the post-closing trial balance is to (*p. 186*)
   a. Provide the account balances for preparation of the balance sheet
   b. Ensure that the ledger is in balance for the start of the next period
   c. Aid the journalizing and posting of the closing entries
   d. Ensure that the ledger is in balance for completion of the worksheet
7. A $500 payment on account to a supplier was recorded by debiting Supplies and crediting Cash. This entry was posted. The correcting entry is (p. *187*)

a. Accounts Payable	500	
Supplies		500
b. Supplies	500	
Accounts Payable		500
c. Cash	500	
Accounts Payable		500
d. Cash	500	
Supplies		500

8. The classification of assets and liabilities as current or long-term depends on (*p. 188*)
   a. Their order of listing in the ledger
   b. Whether they appear on the balance sheet or the income statement
   c. The relative liquidity of the item
   d. The format of the balance sheet—account format or report format
9. Clean Water Softener Systems has Cash of $600, Accounts Receivable of $900, and Office Supplies of $400. Clean owes $500 on Accounts Payable and has Salaries Payable of $200. Clean's current ratio is (*p. 192*)
   a. 2.71
   b. 2.50
   c. 0.63
   d. 0.37
10. A classified balance sheet format is required for companies that report under (*p. 194*)
    a. Cash basis of accounting
    b. ASPE
    c. IFRS
    d. Both ASPE and IFRS

Answers to Self-Study Questions

1. d 2. d 3. b 4. b 5. d 6. b 7. a 8. c 9. a 10. d

Assignment Material

MyLab Accounting Make the grade with MyLab Accounting: The Starters, Exercises, and Problems can be found on MyLab. You can practise them as often as you want, and most feature step-by-step guided instructions to help you find the right answer.

QUESTIONS

1. Identify the steps in the accounting cycle, distinguishing those that occur during the period from those that are performed at the end of the period.
2. Why is the worksheet a valuable accounting tool?
3. Name two advantages the worksheet has over the adjusted trial balance.
4. Why must the adjusting entries be journalized and posted if they have already been entered on the worksheet?
5. In what order are the financial statements prepared? Why?
6. Why should the adjusting entries be journalized and posted before the closing entries are made?
7. Which types of accounts are closed?
8. What purpose is served by closing the accounts?
9. Distinguish between permanent accounts and temporary accounts, indicating which type is closed at the end of the period. Give five examples of each type of account.
10. Is Income Summary a permanent account or a temporary account? When and how is it used?
11. Give the closing entries for the following accounts (balances in parentheses): Service Revenue ($5,000), Salaries Expense ($1,200), Income Summary (credit balance of $2,000), Withdrawals ($2,500).
12. What types of accounts are listed on the post-closing trial balance?
13. C'app Company purchased supplies of $120 on account. The accountant debited Inventory and credited Accounts Payable for $120. A week later, after this entry has been posted to the ledger, the accountant discovers the error. Describe two ways the accountant can correct the error.
14. Why are assets classified as current or long-term? On what basis are they classified?
15. Indicate which of the following accounts are current assets and which are long-term assets: Prepaid Rent, Building, Furniture, Accounts Receivable, Cash, Note Receivable (due within one year), Notes Receivable (due after one year).
16. In what order are assets and liabilities listed on the balance sheet?
17. A friend tells you that the difference between a current liability and a long-term liability is that they are payable to different types of creditors. Is your friend correct?
18. Why is the current ratio calculated? Should this ratio result in a high or low value?
19. Why is the debt ratio calculated? Should this ratio result in a high or low value?

*20. Why are reversing entries used?

*This question covers Chapter 4 Appendix topics.

STARTERS

① Start of a worksheet

S4–1 Scissors Hair Stylists has begun the preparation of its adjusted trial balance as follows:

	A	B	C	D	E	F	G
1	**SCISSORS HAIR STYLISTS**						
2	Preparation of Adjusted Trial Balance						
3	December 31, 2020						
4		**Unadjusted Trial Balance**		**Adjustments**		**Adjusted Trial Balance**	
5	**Account Title**	**Debit**	**Credit**	**Debit**	**Credit**	**Debit**	**Credit**
6	Cash	600					
7	Supplies	800					
8	Equipment	16,200					
9	Accumulated amortization—equipment		1,100				
10	Accounts payable		500				
11	Interest payable		0				
12	Note payable		2,900				
13	Suzanne Byrd, capital		5,300				
14	Service revenue		13,000				
15	Rent expense	4,800					
16	Supplies expense	0					
17	Amortization expense	0					
18	Interest expense	400					
19		22,800	22,800				

Year-end data:

a. Supplies remaining on hand, $300

b. Amortization, $1,100

c. Accrued interest expense, $700

Complete the company's adjusted trial balance. Identify each adjustment by its letter. To save time, you may write your answer in the spaces provided on the adjusted trial balance.

① Worksheet columns

S4–2 The following accounts appear in the adjusted trial balance columns of a worksheet:

a. ________ Service Revenue

b. ________ Unearned Service Revenue

c. ________ Land

d. ________ Salaries Expense

e. ________ Supplies Expense

f. ________ Supplies

g. ________ Accumulated Amortization

h. ________ Equipment

i. ________ Owner's Capital

j. ________ Owner's Withdrawals

State which of the following columns each account balance is extended to:

1. Income statement debit
2. Balance sheet debit
3. Income statement credit
4. Balance sheet credit

S4–3 A partial worksheet for Ramey Law Firm is presented below. Solve for the missing information.

① Determining net income or net loss using a worksheet

	A	J	K	L	M
5		Income Statement		Balance Sheet	
6		Debit	Credit	Debit	Credit
32	Sub-total	(a)	$24,850	$211,325	$202,950
33	Net (b)	8,375			(c)
34	Total	(d)	$24,850	(e)	(f)
35					

S4–4 A partial worksheet for Aaron Adjusters is presented below. Solve for the missing information.

① Determining net income or net loss using a worksheet

	A	J	K	L	M
5		Income Statement		Balance Sheet	
6		Debit	Credit	Debit	Credit
32	Sub-total	$22,400	(a)	(b)	$61,400
33	Net (c)		5,300	(d)	
34	Total	(e)	(f)	(g)	$61,400
35					

S4–5 Answer the following questions:

① ② Using the worksheet

1. What type of balance does the Owner, Capital account have—debit or credit?
2. Which income statement account has the same type of balance as the Capital account?
3. Which type of income statement account has the opposite type of balance as the Capital account?
4. What do we call the difference between total debits and total credits on the income statement? Into what account is the difference figure closed at the end of the period?

S4–6 Epic North Coffee started the year with a beginning capital balance of $20,000. During the year the business earned $40,000 of service revenue and incurred $21,000 of expenses. The owner withdrew $8,000 from the business. After the closing entries are recorded and posted, what will be the balance in the Capital account?

③ Capital account balance
$31,000

S4–7 Indicate whether each of these accounts is permanent (P) or temporary (T):

③ Permanent versus temporary accounts

_____	Furniture	_____	Service Revenue
_____	Interest Expense	_____	Salaries Payable
_____	Accounts Receivable	_____	Equipment
_____	Accumulated Amortization	_____	Notes Payable
_____	P. Norwood, Withdrawals	_____	P. Norwood, Capital

S4–8 It is December 31, 2020, and time to close the books. Journalize the following closing entries, with explanations, for Renee's Rice Treats:

③ Journalizing closing entries

a. Service revenue, $15,000
b. A compound closing entry for all the expenses: Salaries, $3,500; Rent, $2,000; Advertising, $2,500
c. Income Summary
d. Renee Van Etten, Withdrawals, $3,200

S4–9 This question should be completed by using the information in S4–8.

③ Analyzing the overall effect of the closing entries on the owner's Capital account
2. Renee Van Etten, Capital, $14,300

1. Set up all the T–accounts in S4–8 and insert their adjusted balances (denote as *Bal.*) at December 31, 2020. Also set up a T-account for Renee Van Etten, Capital, $10,500, and for Income Summary. Post the closing entries to the accounts, denoting posted amounts as *Clo.*
2. Compute the ending balance of Renee Van Etten, Capital.

③ Identifying and journalizing closing entries

S4–10 Currie Ice Road Trucking provided you with the following partial list of accounts:

Cash	$ 29,917
O. Currie	89,352
Revenues	28,596
Accounts Payable	6,866
Accounts Receivable	1,692
Amortization Expense—Equipment	2,090
Equipment	80,043
Interest Expense	726
Long-Term Liabilities	55,647

Prepare Currie Ice Road Trucking's closing entries for the above accounts. Include explanations.

③ Identifying accounts included on a post-closing trial balance

S4–11 For each account listed, identify whether the account would be included on a post-closing trial balance. Signify either Yes (Y) or No (N).

a. ______ Office Supplies
b. ______ Interest Expense
c. ______ J. Grey, Capital
d. ______ J. Grey, Withdrawals
e. ______ Service Revenue
f. ______ Accumulated Amortization—Furniture
g. ______ Rent Expense
h. ______ Unearned Revenue
i. ______ Accounts Payable

③ Preparing a post-closing trial balance

Post-closing trial bal. total, $15,200

S4–12 After closing its accounts at March 31, 2020, Watts Home Services had the following balances:

Cash	800	Service Revenue	0
Other Assets	1,600	Will Watts, Capital	8,900
Accounts Receivable	4,000	Supplies	300
Total Expenses	0	Long-Term Liabilities	1,600
Accounts Payable	1,800	Accumulated Amortization—Equipment	2,000
Equipment	8,500	Unearned Service Revenue	900

Prepare Watts Home Services' post-closing trial balance at March 31, 2020. List accounts in the order shown in Exhibit 4–8.

④ Correct an error with two entries

S4–13 Fred was having a bad day. He was checking his work and discovered that instead of recording the payment of Telephone Expense in the amount of $645 to the right account, he had instead debited Salaries Expense by $465. Fred is unsure how to fix it. Prepare the two journal entries to make the correction on October 22.

④ Correcting errors

S4–14 Suppose a company made the following journal entry to pay the account balance owing for supplies purchased earlier in the month:

Mar. 31	Accounts Receivable	175	
	Cash		175
	To pay for supplies purchased on account.		

Is this an error? If so, correct the error using both methods shown in this chapter. Provide an explanation for each journal entry.

④ Correcting errors

S4–15 Suppose a company made the following journal entry to close its revenue accounts:

Nov. 30	Income Summary	60,000	
	Service Revenue		55,000
	Other Revenue		5,000
	To close the revenue accounts.		

1. Make the single journal entry, with an explanation, to correct this error.
2. Show the alternative way to correct the error. Provide an explanation for each journal entry.

S4–16 Indicate where each of the following accounts would be reported in the financial statements for the year ended December 31, 2019:

(5) Classify accounts

1. ________ Prepaid Rent
2. ________ Unearned Revenue
3. ________ Note Payable (due June 30, 2022)
4. ________ Accounts Receivable
5. ________ Accounts Payable
6. ________ Accumulated Amortization
7. ________ Supplies
8. ________ Company Truck

a. Property, plant, and equipment
b. Current asset
c. Current liability
d. Long-term liability

S4–17 Stone Craft Brewing reported the following partial list of accounts:

(5) Classifying assets and liabilities as current or long-term

Current liabilities, $850

Service Revenue	$1,300	Building	$4,000
Cash	600	Accounts Payable	550
Accounts Receivable	500	Supplies	1,050
Interest Expense	90	Accumulated Amortization—	
Land	800	Building	2,400
Prepaid Expenses	250	Salaries Payable	300

1. Identify the assets (including contra assets) and liabilities.
2. Classify each asset and each liability as current or long-term.
3. Identify and compute the following amounts for Stone Craft Brewing:
   a. Total current assets
   b. Book value of the building
   c. Total current liabilities
   d. Total long-term liabilities

S4–18 Calculate the current ratio and the debt ratio for Tietz Consulting at December 31, 2020.

(6) Calculate ratios

Debt ratio = 0.30

Tietz Consulting Balance Sheet December 31, 2020		
Assets		
Current assets		
Cash		$27,200
Accounts receivable		5,400
Prepaid insurance		2,400
Total current assets		35,000
Property, plant, and equipment		
Furniture	$31,200	
Less: accumulated amortization	7,800	23,400
Total assets		$58,400
Liabilities		
Current liabilities		
Accounts payable	$15,800	
Unearned service revenue	1,600	
Total current liabilities		$17,400
Owner's Equity		
C. Tietz, capital		41,000
Total liabilities and owner's equity		$58,400

(6) Computing the current ratio and the debt ratio

Current ratio =2.02

S4–19 Garwood Racing has these account balances at December 31, 2020:

Accounts Payable	$ 8,700	Accum. Amortization—Equipment	$ 8,000
Accounts Receivable	12,500	Note Payable, Long-Term	18,000
Cash	6,500	Prepaid Rent	4,000
Supplies	3,000	Salaries Payable	4,200
Equipment	24,000	Service Revenue	62,000

Compute Garwood Racing's current ratio and debt ratio.

(6) Computing and using the current ratio and the debt ratio

1. $1.80

S4–20 You hear that Prime Developments has a current ratio of 1.8 and a debt ratio of 0.57.

1. How much in *current* assets does Prime Developments have for every dollar of *current* liabilities that it owes?
2. What does the current ratio measure?
3. What percentage of Prime Developments' total assets are financed with debt?

(7) Balance sheet presentation under IFRS

S4–21 Answer the following questions about IFRS:

1. What are the two main options (those illustrated in the chapter) for balance sheet presentation for companies following IFRS?
2. Explain what is meant by the term "reverse order of liquidity."
3. What is another name for a balance sheet that may be used by corporations reporting under IFRS?

(A1) Reversing entry for accrued revenues

***S4–22** Ocean Breeze Associates accrued $8,500 of Service Revenue at December 31. Ocean Breeze Associates received $14,500 on January 15, including the accrued revenue recorded on December 31.
Journalize the adjusting entry to accrue Service Revenue, the reversing entry, and the subsequent cash receipt.

EXERCISES

(1) Recording adjusting entries on a worksheet

2. Adjustments $3,700 total

E4–1 The worksheet of Best Jobs Employment Service follows but is incomplete.
The following data at April 30, 2020, are given for Best Jobs Employment Service:

a. Service revenue accrued, $700.
b. Office supplies used, $300.

	A	B	C	D	E	F	G
1	**BEST JOBS EMPLOYMENT SERVICE**						
2	Worksheet						
3	April 30, 2020						
4	**Account Names**	**Unadjusted Trial Balance**		**Adjustments**		**Adjusted Trial Balance**	
5		**Debit**	**Credit**	**Debit**	**Credit**	**Debit**	**Credit**
6	Cash	$ 1,100					
7	Accounts receivable	4,100					
8	Office supplies	1,200					
9	Equipment	32,700					
10	Accumulated amortization—equipment		$ 13,900				
11	Salaries payable						
12	K. Kubota, capital		25,200				
13	K. Kubota, withdrawals	5,300					
14	Service revenue		9,000				
15	Salaries expense	2,200					
16	Rent expense	1,500					
17	Amortization expense—equipment						
18	Supplies expense						
19	**Total**	**$48,100**	**$48,100**				
20							

* This Starter covers Chapter 4 Appendix topics.

c. Amortization on equipment, $1,300.

d. Salaries owed to employees, $1,400.

Required

1. Calculate and enter the adjustment amounts directly in the Adjustments columns. Use letters *a* through *d* to label the four adjustments.
2. Calculate and enter the adjusted account balances in the Adjusted Trial Balance columns.

E4–2 The unadjusted trial balance of Skydive Tours appears below:

1 Preparing a worksheet
Net income, $12,520

SKYDIVE TOURS Unadjusted Trial Balance September 30, 2020		
Cash	$ 14,240	
Accounts receivable	11,880	
Prepaid rent	2,400	
Supplies	6,780	
Equipment	65,200	
Accumulated amortization—equipment		$ 5,680
Accounts payable		10,320
Salaries payable		0
R. Puri, capital		72,060
R. Puri, withdrawals	6,000	
Service revenue		23,600
Amortization expense—equipment	0	
Salaries expense	3,600	
Rent expense	0	
Utilities expense	1,560	
Supplies expense	0	
Total	$111,660	$111,660

Additional information at September 30, 2020:

a. The business had corporate sales that were not recorded yet in the amount of $840. It must accrue this service revenue.

b. Equipment amortization in the amount of $260 needs to be recorded.

c. The business needs to accrue salaries expense of $2,100 for work done but not yet recorded.

d. Prepaid rent used in the amount of $1,200.

e. Supplies worth $3,200 were used up during the period.

Required

Complete the Skydive Tours worksheet for September 2020. What was net income for the month ended September 30, 2020?

E4–3 Review the steps in the accounting cycle, and answer the following questions:

2 Identifying steps in the accounting cycle

1. What is the first step?
2. Are any steps optional? If yes, which one(s)?

3. Which steps are completed throughout the period?
4. Which steps are completed only at the end of the period?
5. What is the last step in the accounting cycle?

(3) Journalizing adjusting and closing entries

E4–4 Journalize the adjusting and closing entries for Skydive Tours' information shown in E4–2. Include explanations.

(3) Posting adjusting and closing entries

R. Puri, Capital bal., $78,580

E4–5 Set up T-accounts for only those accounts affected by the adjusting and closing entries in E4–2. Post the adjusting and closing entries from E4–4 to the accounts, identifying adjustment amounts as *Adj.*, closing amounts as *Clo.*, and balances as *Bal.* Double underline the accounts with zero balances after you close them, and show the ending balance in each account.

(3) Identifying and journalizing closing entries

2. Capital balance, $135,600

E4–6 Michael's Esports Tutoring reported the following partial list of accounts in its June 30, 2020, financial records:

Michael Lucas, Capital	$118,400	Interest Expense	$ 8,800
Service Revenue	256,400	Accounts Receivable	56,000
Unearned Revenues	5,400	Salaries Payable	3,400
Salaries Expense	70,000	Amortization Expense	40,800
Accumulated Amortization	140,000	Rent Expense	23,600
Supplies Expense	11,800	Michael Lucas, Withdrawals	90,000
Interest Revenue	5,800	Supplies	5,600

Required

1. Prepare the company's closing entries. Include explanations.
2. Prepare a T-account for Michael Lucas, Capital. What is the ending Capital balance at June 30, 2020?

(3) Journalizing and posting closing entries

Income Summary credit bal., $1,400

E4–7 Lipsky Insurance Agency reported the following items at May 31:

Insurance Expense	$ 100	Cash	$1,000
Marketing Expense	1,600	Service Revenue	4,200
Other Assets	500	Accounts Payable	300
Amortization Expense	700	Rent Expense	400
C. Lipsky, Withdrawals	200	Accounts Receivable	1,200
Long-Term Liabilities	400	C. Lipsky, Capital	2,700

Required

1. Make Lipsky Insurance Agency's closing entries, as needed, for these accounts. Include explanations.
2. Set up T-accounts for those accounts that Lipsky Insurance Agency closed on May 31. Insert their account balances prior to closing, post the closing entries to these accounts, and show each account's ending balance after closing. Also show the Income Summary T-account. Label a balance as *Bal.* and a closing entry amount as *Clo.*

(3) Identifying and journalizing closing entries

2. V. Deep, Capital bal., $112,050

E4–8 The accountant for Perfect Paintball has posted adjusting entries (a) through (e) to the accounts at December 31, 2020. All the revenue, expense, and owner's equity accounts of the entity are listed in T-account form.

Required

1. Journalize Perfect Paintball's closing entries at December 31, 2020. Include explanations. Indicate if the business had a profit or loss for the year.
2. Determine Perfect Paintball's ending Capital balance at December 31, 2020.

Accounts Receivable	
41,000	
(a) 7,250	

Paintball Supplies	
6,000	(b) 5,500

Accumulated Amortization—Equipment	
	9,000
	(c) 1,650

Accumulated Amortization—Building	
	49,500
	(d) 6,000

Salaries Payable	
	(e) 1,050

V. Deep, Capital	
	110,600

V. Deep, Withdrawals	
122,100	

Service Revenue	
	166,500
	(a) 7,250

Salaries Expense	
36,000	
(e) 1,050	

Paintball Supplies Expense	
(b) 5,500	

Amortization Expense—Equipment	
(c) 1,650	

Amortization Expense—Building	
(d) 6,000	

E4–9 The adjusted trial balance for Pria's Music Lessons follows:

③ Recording closing entries

2. Net loss, $6,900

PRIA'S MUSIC LESSONS Adjusted Trial Balance December 31, 2020		
Cash	$ 27,600	
Supplies	7,500	
Prepaid rent	3,600	
Instruments	168,900	
Accumulated amortization—instruments		$ 26,050
Accounts payable		29,300
Salaries payable		3,250
Unearned service revenue		17,600
P. Chai, capital		153,300
P. Chai, withdrawals	15,000	
Service revenue		61,000
Salaries expense	45,200	
Rent expense	15,650	
Amortization expense—instruments	1,200	
Supplies expense	2,650	
Utilities expense	3,200	
	$290,500	$290,500

Required

1. Journalize the closing entries of Pria's Music Lessons at December 31, 2020. Include explanations.
2. How much net income or net loss did Pria's Music Lessons earn for the period ended December 31, 2020? How can you tell?

③ Preparing a post-closing trial balance

E4–10 Using the data provided in E4–9, prepare the post-closing trial balance for Pria's Music Lessons at December 31, 2020. You will need to calculate the new balance for the Capital account if you did not complete E4–9.

④ Recording correcting entries

E4–11 Unless your instructor states otherwise, you may use either one or two journal entries, with explanations, to make the following corrections:

1. Suppose HEC paid an account payable of $2,400 and erroneously debited Supplies. The error correction was recorded on June 5.
2. Suppose HEC made the following adjusting entry to record amortization:

May 31	Amortization Expense—Furniture	4,000	
	Furniture		4,000

3. Suppose, in closing the books to a profitable year, HEC made this closing entry:

Aug. 31	Income Summary	59,200	
	Service Revenue		59,200

④ Correcting accounting errors

E4–12 Prepare a correcting entry (or entries), with explanations, for each of the following accounting errors:

Nov. 3	Debited Supplies and credited Accounts Payable for a $9,000 purchase of office equipment on account.
Nov. 6	Accrued interest revenue of $3,000 by a debit to Accounts Receivable and a credit to Interest Revenue.
Nov. 8	Adjusted prepaid rent by debiting Prepaid Rent and crediting Rent Expense for $4,000. This adjusting entry should have debited Rent Expense and credited Prepaid Rent for $4,000.
Nov. 12	Debited Salaries Expense and credited Accounts Payable to accrue salaries expense of $12,000.
Nov. 19	Recorded the earning of $7,800 service revenue collected in advance by debiting Accounts Receivable and crediting Service Revenue.

⑤ Preparing a classified balance sheet

Total assets, $181,550

E4–13 Use the data from your solution to E4–10 to prepare Pria's Music Lesson's classified balance sheet at December 31, 2020. Use the report format. Alternatively, you may use the data from E4–9, but you will need to compute the ending balance of P. Chai, Capital first.

⑤ Preparing a classified balance sheet

E4–14 Based on the following adjusted trial balance, prepare a classified balance sheet for Warsaw Rentals on December 31, 2020. You will have to compute the owner's capital account balance on December 31, 2020, because the other financial statements are not being prepared.

WARSAW RENTALS Adjusted Trial Balance December 31, 2020		
Account Title	**Debit**	**Credit**
Cash	$ 29,200	
Accounts receivable	2,000	
Office supplies	1,400	
Prepaid insurance	2,400	
Building	30,100	
Accumulated amortization		$ 3,900
Accounts payable		16,800
Taxes payable		1,900
Unearned rental revenue		3,800

(Continued)

WARSAW RENTALS Adjusted Trial Balance December 31, 2020		
Account Title	**Debit**	**Credit**
W. Yachin, Capital		41,000
W. Yachin, Withdrawals	9,800	
Rental revenue		18,250
Advertising expense	2,800	
Amortization expense	1,300	
Supplies expense	1,100	
Insurance expense	2,650	
Utilities expense	2,900	
Total	$ 85,650	$85,650

E4–15 Refer to the Cloud Break Consulting classified balance sheet presented in the Summary Problem.

(6) Assessing the current ratio and debt ratio

Required

Compute Cloud Break Consulting's current ratio and debt ratio at November 30, 2020. Round your answers to two decimal places. One year ago the current ratio was 1.20 and the debt ratio was 0.45. Indicate whether Cloud Break Consulting's ability to pay its debts has improved or deteriorated during the current year.

E4–16 The fictional balance sheet of MAC Company using IFRS is shown below. Review it and describe at least three differences in their presentation from what is shown in Exhibit 4–11. Ignore the fact that MAC Company is a corporation.

(7) Balance sheet presentation choices under International Financial Reporting Standards (IFRS)*

	A	B	C	D	E	F
1			MAC COMPANY			
2			Balance Sheet			
3			June 30, 2019			
4			*(all amounts in Cad $)*			
5	**Assets**			**Shareholders' Equity**		
6	**Non-current assets**			Issued share capital		852,000
7	**Property, plant, and equipment**					
8	Equipment, net	42,000		**Liabilities**		
9	Furniture, net	40,000				
10	Buildings, net	80,000		**Non-current liabilities**		
11	Land	70,000		Note payable	220,000	
12	**Total property, plant, and equipment**		232,000	Less: current portion of note payable	72,200	
13	**Intangible assets**			**Total non-current liabilities**		147,800
14	Trademark		7,000			
15	**Long-term investments**		48,400			
16	**Total non-current assets**		287,400	**Current liabilities**		
17	**Current assets and receivables**			Other current liabilities	23,600	
18	Inventory	847,800		Goods and services tax payable	64,600	
19	Supplies	5,200		Current portion of note payable	72,200	
20	Prepaid insurance	27,000		Salaries and wages payable	22,400	
21	Interest receivable	26,800		Interest payable	24,600	
22	Current portion of note receivable	51,600		Accounts payable	357,000	
23	Accounts receivable	235,000		**Total current liabilities**		564,400
24	Short-term investments	57,000				
25	Cash	26,400		**Total liabilities**		712,200
26	**Total current assets and receivables**		1,276,800			
27	**Total assets**		1,564,200	**Total equity and liabilities**		1,564,200
28						

(A1) Journalizing reversing entries

***E4–17** On December 31, 2020, Rexall Industries recorded an adjusting entry for $10,000 of accrued interest revenue. On January 15, 2021, the company received interest payments in the amount of $22,000. Assuming Rexall Industries uses reversing entries, prepare the 2020 and 2021 journal entries for these interest transactions.

(A1) Journalizing reversing entries

***E4–18** On September 30, 2020, its fiscal year-end, NS Services recorded an adjusting entry for $2,000 of interest it owes at year-end and will include as part of its payment on October 31, 2020. On October 31, 2020, the company paid interest in the amount of $3,000. Assuming NS Services uses reversing entries, prepare the journal entries for these interest transactions.

---

*These Exercises cover Chapter 4 Appendix topics.

SERIAL EXERCISE PART 1

The Serial Exercise involves a company that will be revisited throughout relevant chapters in Volume 1 and Volume 2. You can complete the Serial Exercises using MyLab Accounting.

(1) Prepare accounting worksheet

Net income $4,970

E4–19 This exercise continues recordkeeping for the Canyon Canoe Company from previous chapters.

Required Complete the worksheet at December 31, 2020. Use the unadjusted trial balance from Chapter 2 and the adjusting entries from Chapter 3. If you have not completed them, you can still answer this question with the following information:

CANYON CANOE COMPANY
Unadjusted Trial Balance
December 31, 2020

Account Title	Debit	Credit
Cash	$ 12,125	
Accounts receivable	5,750	
Office supplies	1,250	
Prepaid rent	3,000	
Land	85,000	
Building	35,000	
Canoes	12,000	
Accounts payable		$ 3,670
Unearned revenue		750
Note payable		7,200
Amber Wilson, capital		136,000
Amber Wilson, withdrawals	450	
Canoe rental revenue		12,400
Rent expense	1,200	
Salaries expense	3,300	
Utilities expense	445	
Telephone expense	500	
Total	$ 160,020	$ 160,020

At December 31, the business gathers the following information for the adjusting entries:

a. At December 31, the office supplies on hand totaled $165.

b. Prepaid rent of one month has been used. (Hint: Total is for three months.)

c. Determine the amortization on the building using straight-line amortization. Assume the useful life of the building is five years and the residual value is $5,000. (Hint: The building was purchased on December 1.)

d. $400 of unearned revenue has now been earned.

e. The employee who has been working the rental booth has earned $1,250 in salaries that will be paid January 15, 2021.

f. Canyon Canoe Company has earned $1,850 of canoe rental revenue that has not been recorded or received.

g. Determine the amortization on the canoes purchased on November 3 using the straight-line method. Assume the useful life of the canoes is four years and the residual value is $0.

h. Determine the amortization on the canoes purchased on December 2 using the straight-line amortization method. Assume the useful life of the canoes is four years and the residual value is $0.

i. Interest expense of $50 has accrued on the note payable.

SERIAL EXERCISE PART 2

E4–20 This exercise continues recordkeeping for the Canyon Canoe Company. If you did not complete those exercises, or E4-19 then you can use the following information at this time:

(2) (3) (5)
Complete accounting cycle, closing, classified balance sheet

CANYON CANOE COMPANY
Adjusted Trial Balance
December 31, 2020

Account Title	Debit	Credit
Cash	$ 12,125	
Accounts receivable	7,600	
Office supplies	165	
Prepaid rent	2,000	
Land	85,000	
Building	35,000	
Accumulated amortization—building		$ 500
Canoes	12,000	
Accumulated amortization—canoes		350
Accounts payable		3,670
Unearned revenue		350
Salaries payable		1,250
Interest payable		50
Note payable		7,200
Amber Wilson, capital		136,000
Amber Wilson, withdrawals	450	
Canoe rental revenue		14,650
Rent expense	2,200	
Salaries expense	4,550	
Utilities expense	445	
Telephone expense	500	
Supplies expense	1,085	
Amortization expense—building	500	
Amortization expense—canoes	350	
Interest expense	50	
Total	$ 164,020	$ 164,020

Required

1. Prepare an income statement for the two months ended December 31, 2020.
2. Prepare a statement of owner's equity for the two months ended December 31, 2020.
3. Prepare a classified balance sheet (report form) at December 31, 2020. Assume the note payable is long-term.
4. Journalize the closing entries at December 31, 2020.
5. Open T-accounts for Income Summary and Amber Wilson, Capital. Post the entries from requirement 3 and determine the ending balance for both accounts. Denote each closing amount as *Clos.* and each account balance as *Bal.*
6. Prepare a post-closing trial balance at December 31, 2020.

PRACTICE SET

(1) (2) (3) (4) (5)
Completing the accounting cycle from adjusted trial balance to post-closing trial balance with an optional worksheet

E4–21 *This problem continues the Crystal Clear Cleaning problem begun in Chapter 2 and continued through Chapter 9. Refer to the Practice Set data provided in Chapter 3.*

Required

1. (Optional) Prepare a worksheet at November 30, 2019. Use the unadjusted trial balance from Chapter 2 and the adjusting entries from Chapter 3.
2. Prepare an income statement and statement of owner's equity for the month ended November 30, 2019. Also prepare a classified balance sheet at November 30, 2019, using the report format. Assume the Note Payable is long-term. Use the worksheet prepared in Requirement 1 or the adjusted trial balance from Chapter 3. Use the order of accounts in the trial balance to report the expenses on the income statement.
3. Prepare closing entries at November 30, 2019, and post to the accounts. Open T-accounts for Income Summary and A. Hideaway, Capital. Determine the ending balance in each account. Denote each closing amount as *Clos.* and each account balance as *Balance.*
4. Prepare a post-closing trial balance at November 30, 2019.

CHALLENGE EXERCISES

(2) (5)
Computing financial statement amounts
1. Net income, $50,000

E4–22 The unadjusted account balances of Stinson Consulting follow:

Cash	$ 1,900	Unearned Service Revenue	$ 5,300
Accounts Receivable	7,200	Scott Stinson, Capital	90,200
Supplies	2,100	Scott Stinson, Withdrawals	46,200
Prepaid Insurance	3,200	Service Revenue	80,600
Furniture	8,400	Salaries Expense	22,700
Accumulated Amortization—Furniture	1,300	Amortization Expense—Furniture	0
Building	53,800	Amortization Expense—Building	0
Accumulated Amortization—Building	14,900	Supplies Expense	0
		Insurance Expense	0
Land	51,200	Utilities Expense	2,700
Accounts Payable	7,100		

Adjusting data at the end of the year included the following:

a. Unearned service revenue that has been earned during the year, $4,600.
b. Work was completed but has not been invoiced. The company needs to accrue service revenue in the amount of $2,700.
c. Still need to record the supplies that were used up in operations, $1,900.
d. Employees have worked but have not been paid $2,400. The company needs to accrue salary expense.
e. Prepaid insurance was used up during the accounting period in the amount of $2,800.
f. Amortization expense that has not been recorded yet—furniture, $2,300; building, $3,100.

Scott Stinson, the proprietor of Stinson Consulting, has received an offer to sell his company. He needs to know the following information as soon as possible:

1. Net income for the year covered by these data
2. Total assets
3. Total liabilities
4. Total owner's equity
5. Proof that total assets equal total liabilities plus total owner's equity after all items are updated

Required

Without opening any accounts, making any journal entries, or using a worksheet, provide Scott Stinson with the requested information. Show all computations.

***E4–23** Refer to E4–21. Which adjusting entries (a, b, c, d, e, and/or f) can be reversed with reversing journal entries?

(A1) Reversing entries

* This Exercise covers Chapter 4 Appendix topics.

ETHICAL ISSUE

EI4–1

Grant Film Productions wishes to expand and has borrowed $100,000. As a condition for making this loan, the bank requires that the business maintain a current ratio of at least 1.50.

Business has been good but not great. Expansion costs have brought the current ratio down to 1.40 on December 15. Rita Grant, owner of the business, is considering what might happen if she reports a current ratio of 1.40 to the bank. One course of action for Grant is to record in December $10,000 of revenue that the business will earn in January of next year. The contract for this job has been signed.

Required

1. Journalize the revenue transaction, and indicate how recording this revenue in December would affect the current ratio.
2. Discuss whether it is ethical to record the revenue transaction in December. Identify the accounting principle relevant to this situation, and give the reasons underlying your conclusion.

FINANCIAL STATEMENT CASES

FSC4–1

(5) (6)
Reading a balance sheet of a publicly traded corporation
4. April 1, 2017, current ratio, 2.06

This case, based on Indigo Books & Music Inc.'s (Indigo's) balance sheet in Appendix A at the end of this text and on MyLab Accounting, will familiarize you with some of the assets and liabilities of this company. Answer these questions, using the company's balance sheet.

Required

1. Compare Indigo's balance sheet to the balance sheet in Exhibit 4–11. What differences in style do you notice between these two balance sheets? Describe these differences.
2. What was the value of Indigo's total current assets in 2017? In 2016?
3. What was the value of the total current liabilities in 2017? In 2016?
4. Compute Indigo's current ratio at April 1, 2017, and at April 2, 2016. Did the ratio improve or deteriorate during the year?
5. Compute Indigo's debt ratio for the fiscal years ended 2017 and 2016. Did the ratio improve or deteriorate during the year?

FSC4–2

(5) (6)
Working with a balance sheet for a corporation
7. Dec. 31, 2016, debt ratio, 0.71

This case, based on TELUS Corporation's balance sheet on MyLab Accounting, will familiarize you with some of the assets and liabilities of this company. Answer these questions, using the company's balance sheet.

Required

1. Compare TELUS's balance sheet (consolidated statement of financial position) to the balance sheet in Exhibit 4–11. What differences in style do you notice between these two balance sheets? Describe these differences.
2. What was TELUS's largest current asset in 2016? In 2015?
3. What was the company's largest current liability in 2016? In 2015?
4. What were total current assets in 2016? In 2015?
5. What were total current liabilities in 2016? In 2015?
6. Compute TELUS's current ratio at December 31, 2016, and at December 31, 2015. Did the ratio values improve or deteriorate during the year?
7. Compute TELUS's debt ratio at December 31, 2016, and at December 31, 2015. Did the ratio values improve or deteriorate during the year?

IFRS MINI-CASE

The IFRS Mini-Case is now available online, at **MyLab Accounting** in Chapter Resources.

Try It! Solutions for Chapter 4

1.

	Income Statement		Balance Sheet	
	Debit	Credit	Debit	Credit
a. Cash			✔	
b. Supplies			✔	
c. Supplies Expense	✔			
d. Unearned Revenue				✔
e. Service Revenue		✔		
f. Owner's Equity				✔

2. Using the trial balance given, write the account titles in the first column of the worksheet and the amounts in the unadjusted trial balance columns, ensuring debit and credit balances on the unadjusted trial balance are debit and credit balances on the worksheet. To make sure all the account balances have been entered correctly, trace each worksheet balance back to the December 31, 2020, trial balance.

When calculating the adjusted trial balance amounts, remember to add and subtract the adjustments properly. For assets, withdrawals, and expenses, add debits and subtract credits. For contra assets, liabilities, owner's equity, and revenues, add credits and subtract debits.

	A	B	C	D	E	F	G	H	I	J	K	L	M
1	SIGRID'S OFF ROAD ADVENTURES												
2	Worksheet												
3	December 31, 2020												
4		Unadjusted Trial Balance		Adjustments				Adjusted Trial Balance		Income Statement		Balance Sheet	
5		Dr	Cr		Dr		Cr	Dr	Cr	Dr	Cr	Dr	Cr
6	Cash	6,000						6,000				6,000	
7	Accounts receivable	5,000		(e)	1,300			6,300				6,300	
8	Supplies	1,000				(a)	800	200				200	
9	Furniture	10,000						10,000				10,000	
10	Accum. amort.—furniture		4,000			(b)	2,500		6,500				6,500
11	Building	60,000						60,000				60,000	
12	Accum. amort.—building		30,000			(c)	1,500		31,500				31,500
13	Land	20,000						20,000				20,000	
14	Accounts payable		2,000						2,000				2,000
15	Salaries payable		0			(d)	600		600				600
16	Unearned service revenue		8,000	(f)	2,000				6,000				6,000
17	Sigrid Chu, capital		40,000						40,000				40,000
18	Sigrid Chu, withdrawals	25,000						25,000				25,000	
19	Service revenues		60,000			(e)	1,300		63,300		63,300		
20						(f)	2,000						
21	Salaries expense	16,000		(d)	600			16,600		16,600			
22	Supplies expense			(a)	800			800		800			
23	Amort. exp.—furniture			(b)	2,500			2,500		2,500			
24	Amort. exp.—building			(c)	1,500			1,500		1,500			
25	Miscellaneous expense	1,000						1,000		1,000			
26	Total	144,000	144,000		8,700		8,700	149,900	149,900	22,400	63,300	127,500	86,600
27	Net income									40,900			40,900
28										63,300	63,300	127,500	127,500

3.

SIGRID'S OFF ROAD ADVENTURES Income Statement For the Month Ended December 31, 2020		
Revenue		
Service revenue		$63,300
Expenses		
Amortization expense—furniture	$2,500	
Amortization expense—building	1,500	
Miscellaneous expense	1,000	
Salaries expense	16,600	
Supplies expense	800	
Total expenses		22,400
Net income		$40,900

SIGRID'S OFF ROAD ADVENTURES Statement of Owner's Equity For the Year Ended December 31, 2020	
Sigrid Chu, capital, January 1, 2020	$40,000
Add: Net income	40,900
	80,900
Less: Withdrawals	25,000
Sigrid Chu, capital, December 31, 2020	$55,900

SIGRID'S OFF ROAD ADVENTURES Balance Sheet December 31, 2020		
Assets		
Cash		$ 6,000
Accounts receivable		6,300
Supplies		200
Furniture	$10,000	
Less: Accumulated amortization	6,500	3,500
Building	60,000	
Less: Accumulated amortization	31,500	28,500
Land		20,000
Total assets		$64,500
Liabilities		
Accounts payable		$ 2,000
Salaries payable		600
Unearned service revenue		6,000
Total liabilities		8,600
Owner's Equity		
Sigrid Chu, capital		55,900
Total liabilities and owner's equity		$64,500

4.

Date	Account Titles and Explanations	Debit	Credit
Dec. 31	Service Revenue	1,600	
	Income Summary		1,600
	To close the revenue account and create the Income Summary account.		
31	Income Summary	2,300	
	Amortization Expense—Equipment		300
	Salaries Expense		800
	Rent Expense		500
	Utilities Expense		600
	Supplies Expense		100
	To close the expense accounts.		
31	S. Benson, Capital	700	
	Income Summary		700
	To close the Income Summary account ($2,300 - $1,600).		
31	S. Benson, Capital	2,100	
	S. Benson, Withdrawals		2,100
	To close the Withdrawals account and transfer the Withdrawals amount to the Capital account.		

5.

BENSON AUTO REPAIR Post-Closing Trial Balance December 31, 2018		
Account Title	**Debit**	**Credit**
Cash	$ 4,000	
Accounts receivable	3,200	
Prepaid rent	1,900	
Office supplies	3,000	
Equipment	34,800	
Accumulated amortization—equipment		$ 1,600
Accounts payable		5,400
Note payable (long-term)		7,000
S. Benson, capital		32,900
Totals	$46,900	$46,900

6. With one entry:

Nov. 7	Accounts Receivable	200	
	Accounts Payable		200
	To correct a previous journal entry. Accounts Receivable had been debited in error for a purchase of supplies on account.		
	With two journal entries:		
Nov. 7	Accounts Receivable	200	
	Supplies		200
	To reverse incorrect entry.		
Nov. 7	Supplies	200	
	Accounts Payable		200
	To record purchase correctly as supplies.		

7.

TICKET BUSTERS Balance Sheet December 31, 2020			
Assets			
Current assets			
Cash		$23,600	
Accounts receivable		7,600	
Supplies		200	
Total current assets			$31,400
Property, plant, and equipment			
Computers	$ 7,000		
Less: Accumulated amortization—computers	200	6,800	
Furniture	11,200		
Less: Accumulated amortization—furniture	240	10,960	
Total property, plant, and equipment			17,760
Total assets			$49,160
Liabilities			
Current liabilities			
Accounts payable		$11,200	
Salaries payable		1,400	
Unearned service revenue		2,400	
Total current liabilities			$15,000
Long-term liabilities			
Mortgage payable		20,000	
Total long-term liabilities			20,000
Total liabilities			35,000
Owner's Equity			
Yuri Sang, capital			14,160
Total liabilities and owner's equity			$49,160

8.

Current ratio = Total current assets ÷ Total current liabilities

= $31,400 ÷ $15,000

= 20.9

Debt ratio = Total liabilities ÷ Total assets

= $35,000 ÷ $49,160

= 0.71

Ticket Busters' current ratio would be considered acceptable. It indicates that the business could adequately meet its current debt obligations. The debt ratio is acceptable but possibly a little high. This means that lenders are financing 71 percent of Ticket Busters' assets.

5 Merchandising Operations

CONNECTING CHAPTER 5

LEARNING OBJECTIVES

(A4) Prepare a merchandiser's financial statements under the periodic inventory system

How can we prepare financial statements for a company using the periodic inventory system?

Preparing the Financial Statements of a Merchandiser, page 275

(B1) Compare the perpetual and periodic inventory systems

How do the inventory systems compare?

Comparing the Perpetual and Periodic Inventory Systems, page 279

The **Summary** for Chapter 5 appears on pages 281–282.
Key Terms with definitions for this chapter's material appears on pages 283–284.

CPA competencies

This text covers material outlined in **Section 1: Financial Reporting of the CPA Competency Map**. The Learning Objectives for each chapter have been aligned with the CPA Competency Map to ensure the best coverage possible.

1.1.2 Evaluates the appropriateness of the basis of financial reporting

1.2.2 Evaluates treatment for routine transactions

1.3.1 Prepares financial statements

1.4.2 Evaluates financial statements including note disclosure

Tim Finlan/Toronto Star/Getty Images

SAIL* is Canada's "outdoor superstore" specializing in a wide range of outdoor products for camping, hunting, fishing, orienteering, and other outdoor pursuits. This Canadian company has been in business for over 40 years in the eastern provinces. It is currently owned by SAIL Plein Air Inc.

This is the first business we are looking at that sells goods and not services. This is a different business model with some new accounts. For this company, buying

*Fun fact: The name SAIL was originally an acronym for Surplus d'Armée Imrico Ltée.

and selling inventory plays a big part in their success. Their website tells us that in 2017 SAIL had over 500,000 items in each of their stores, including:

- Outdoor clothing, boots, and shoes
- Around 20 to 50 fully assembled tents
- 40 models of canoes and kayaks
- Up to 3,500 pairs of snowshoes (when in season)
- 1,550 models of fishing rods
- A variety of equipment for other outdoor activities

This chapter will illustrate how businesses record the purchase and sale of goods as well as how the new accounts needed for these sorts of transactions are reflected in their financial statements. In addition, we see how this information can help a business evaluate how well inventory is managed and how profitable it is. This is the first of two chapters about inventory. In the next chapter there is more information about tracking specific inventory items and their cost.

What comes to mind when you think of *merchandising*? You are familiar with Canadian retailers who sell you the clothing you purchase at a clothing store, the bread you buy at the grocery store, or the gas you purchase at your local service station. Merchandisers include Canadian Tire Corporation, SAIL Plein Air Inc., Shoppers Drug Mart Corporation, and Roots Canada Limited. Some businesses, such as department stores, gas stations, and grocery stores, buy their inventory ready for sale to customers. Others, such as Big Rock Brewery Inc. and BlackBerry Limited, manufacture their own products. A *merchandising entity* earns its revenue by selling products, called *merchandise inventory* or, simply, **inventory**.

How do the operations of merchandisers differ from those of the businesses we have studied so far? In the first four chapters, Hunter Environmental Consulting provided an illustration of a business that earns revenue by selling its services. Service enterprises include hotels, airlines, physicians, lawyers, public accountants, and the 12-year-old who cuts lawns in your neighbourhood.

This chapter illustrates transactions relating to the purchase and sale of inventory in a business and how this information is presented in the financial statements.

What Are Merchandising Operations?

LO (1)

How can we use sales information to evaluate a company?

Merchandisers have some new balance sheet and income statement items.

Let's compare service entities, with which you are familiar, with merchandising companies. Exhibit 5–1 shows how the financial statements of a service entity differ from those of a merchandiser. New accounts are bolded in the exhibit and explained further here.

Sales Revenue The selling price of merchandise sold by a business is called **sales revenue**, often abbreviated as **sales**. This results in an increase in capital from delivering inventory to customers.

The term *cost of goods* sold is often shortened to COGS or CGS.

Cost of Goods Sold The major expense of a merchandiser is **cost of goods sold** or **cost of sales**. It represents the entity's cost of the goods (the inventory) it sold to customers. While inventory is held by a business it is an asset, because the goods are an economic resource with future value to the company. When the inventory is sold, however, its cost becomes an expense to the seller to match against the revenue from the sale.

Gross Margin **Gross margin** (or **gross profit**) is calculated by deducting the cost of goods sold from the sales revenue. It is a measure of business success. A sufficiently high gross margin is important to a merchandiser, since all other expenses of the company are deducted from this gross margin.

Suppose SAIL's cost for a hiking jacket is $250 and SAIL sells the jacket to a customer for $600. SAIL's gross margin on the jacket is $350 ($600 − $250). The gross margin reported on SAIL's year-end income statement is the sum of the gross margins on all the products the company sold during its fiscal year.

Inventory The business's inventory includes all goods that the company owns and expects to sell to customers in the normal course of operations. Inventory is an asset reported in the current assets section of the balance sheet.

EXHIBIT 5–1 | Financial Statements of a Service Company and a Merchandiser

SERVICE CO. Income Statement For the Year Ended June 30, 2020		**MERCHANDISING CO.** Income Statement For the Year Ended June 30, 2020	
Service revenue	$XXX	**Sales revenue**	$XXX
Expenses		**Cost of goods sold**	X
Salaries expense	X	**Gross margin**	XX
Amortization expense	X	Operating expenses	
Net income	$ X	Salaries expense	X
		Amortization expense	X
		Net income	$ X

SERVICE CO. Balance Sheet June 30, 2020		**MERCHANDISING CO.** Balance Sheet June 30, 2020	
Assets		**Assets**	
Current assets		Current assets	
Cash	$ X	Cash	$ X
Accounts receivable, net	X	Accounts receivable, net	X
Prepaid expenses	X	**Inventory**	X
		Prepaid expenses	X

Service revenue
− Operating expenses
= Net Income

Sales revenue
− Cost of goods sold
= Gross margin

Expenses other than cost of goods sold, that are incurred in ongoing operations.

Gross margin
− Operating expenses
= Net Income

Inventory is included in current assets

What Goes into Inventory Cost?

The cost of inventory on a merchandiser's balance sheet represents all the costs incurred to bring the merchandise to the point of sale. Suppose SAIL purchases sleeping bags from a manufacturer in Asia. SAIL's cost of a sleeping bag would include the following:

Item	Explanation	Amount per sleeping bag
Cost of the sleeping bag		$50.00
Customs/duties	Paid to the Canadian government	5.00
Shipping costs (also called freight-in)	From manufacturer in Asia to SAIL store	2.50
Insurance	During transportation	1.50
Total Cost		**$59.00**

So SAIL's total cost for this sleeping bag is $59.00 ($50.00 + $5.00 + $2.50 + $1.50). We can now expand the definition of the cost principle of measurement as follows:

The cost of an asset = The sum of all the costs incurred to bring the asset to its intended use, net of all discounts

For merchandise inventory, the intended use is readiness for sale. After the goods are ready for sale, then other costs, such as advertising, display, and sales commissions, are expensed. These costs are *not* included as the cost of inventory.

The Operating Cycle for a Merchandising Business

Some merchandisers buy inventory, sell the inventory to their customers, and use the cash to purchase more inventory to repeat the cycle. Other merchandisers, like Canada Goose Inc. or Gilden Activewear Inc., manufacture their products and sell them to customers. The balance of this chapter considers the first group of merchandisers, which buys products and resells them. For a cash sale the operating cycle is from cash to inventory, which is purchased for resale, and back to cash. Exhibit 5–2 diagrams the operating cycle for *sales on account*. For a sale on account the cycle is from cash to inventory to accounts receivable and back to cash. Managers try to shorten the cycle, because the faster the sale of inventory and the collection of cash, the higher the profits because goods are sold at a profit more often within a period of time.

EXHIBIT 5–2 | Operating Cycle of a Merchandiser with Sales on Account

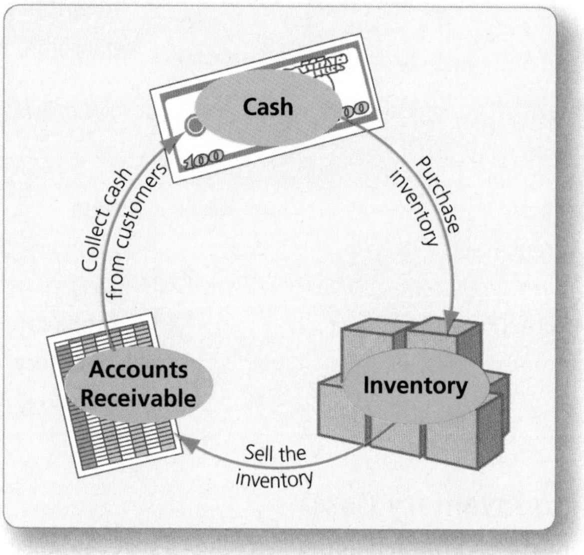

Inventory Systems: Perpetual and Periodic

There are two main types of inventory accounting systems:

- Periodic system
- Perpetual system

Periodic Inventory Systems

The **periodic inventory system** is used by businesses that sell relatively inexpensive goods. A very small grocery store without optical-scanning point-of-sale equipment to read UPC or bar codes does not keep a daily running record of every loaf of bread and litre of milk that it buys and sells. The cost of record keeping would be overwhelming. Instead, it counts its inventory periodically—at least once a year—to determine the quantities on hand. The inventory amounts are used to prepare the annual financial statements. Businesses such as restaurants and small retail stores also use the periodic inventory system.

Appendix A of this chapter covers the periodic inventory system.

Perpetual Inventory Systems

Under the **perpetual inventory system**, the business keeps a running record of inventory and cost of goods sold by updating these accounts every time a purchase, sale, or return occurs. The low cost of automated information systems has increased the use of perpetual systems. Using technology reduces the time required to manage inventory and thus increases a company's ability to control its merchandise. But even under a perpetual system, the business counts the inventory on hand at least once a year. The physical count establishes the correct amount of ending inventory for the financial statements (which may have been affected by theft or spoilage) and serves as a check on the perpetual records.

A perpetual inventory system records the following:

- Units purchased
- Units sold
- The quantity of inventory on hand

Inventory systems are often integrated with accounts receivable and sales. The computer can keep up-to-the-minute records, so managers can call up current inventory supplier or customer account information at any time. For example, in their perpetual system, the point-of-sale equipment at SAIL is a computer terminal that records sales and also updates the inventory records. Bar codes, such as the one shown in the margin, are scanned by a laser. The lines of the bar code represent inventory and cost data that keep track of each item.

Jameschipper/Fotolia

Perpetual Inventory System	Periodic Inventory System
• Keeps a running record of all inventory as it is bought and sold (units and price)	• Does *not* keep a running record of all goods bought and sold
• Inventory counted at least once a year	• Inventory counted at least once a year

Try It!

1. a. What is the gross margin if sales are $100,000 and cost of goods sold is $60,000?
b. If gross margin is $10,000 and cost of goods sold is $30,000, what was sales revenue?
c. If sales are $37,500 and gross margin is $7,500, what was cost of goods sold?

Solutions appear at the end of this chapter and on **MyLab Accounting**

Accounting for Inventory Purchases in the Perpetual Inventory System

LO 2 **How can we track the purchase and sale of inventory as transactions occur?**

The cycle of a merchandising entity begins with the purchase of inventory, as shown in Exhibit 5–2. The Inventory account is used only for purchases of merchandise for resale. Purchases of any other assets are recorded in a different asset account. For example, the purchase of supplies is debited to Supplies, not to Inventory.

The Purchase Invoice

In this section, we trace the steps that Slopes Ski Shop, a small ski clothing store located in Vancouver, British Columbia, takes to order, receive, and pay for inventory. Slopes Ski Shop (Slopes) sells ski jackets and other winter wear. Here we use documents to illustrate some of the transactions.

- Suppose Slopes wants to stock ski jackets from Neige Sportswear (Neige). Slopes prepares a **purchase order** for ski jackets and transmits it to Neige. A purchase order lists not only what Slopes wants to purchase from Neige but also all the details that are agreed upon, including price, quantity, and payment terms. These details will also appear on the invoice. Purchase orders are used to document what was agreed upon prior to the delivery of the goods.
- On receipt of the purchase order, Neige searches its warehouse for the inventory that Slopes has ordered. Neige ships the ski jackets and sends the invoice to Slopes on the same day. The **invoice** or **bill** is the seller's request for payment from the purchaser.
- Slopes waits until the inventory arrives to ensure that it is the correct type and quantity ordered and that it arrives in good condition. After the inventory is inspected and approved, Slopes pays Neige the invoice amount according to the terms of payment previously negotiated.

Exhibit 5–3 is a copy of an invoice from Neige Sportswear to Slopes Ski Shop.

EXHIBIT 5–3 | Purchase Invoice

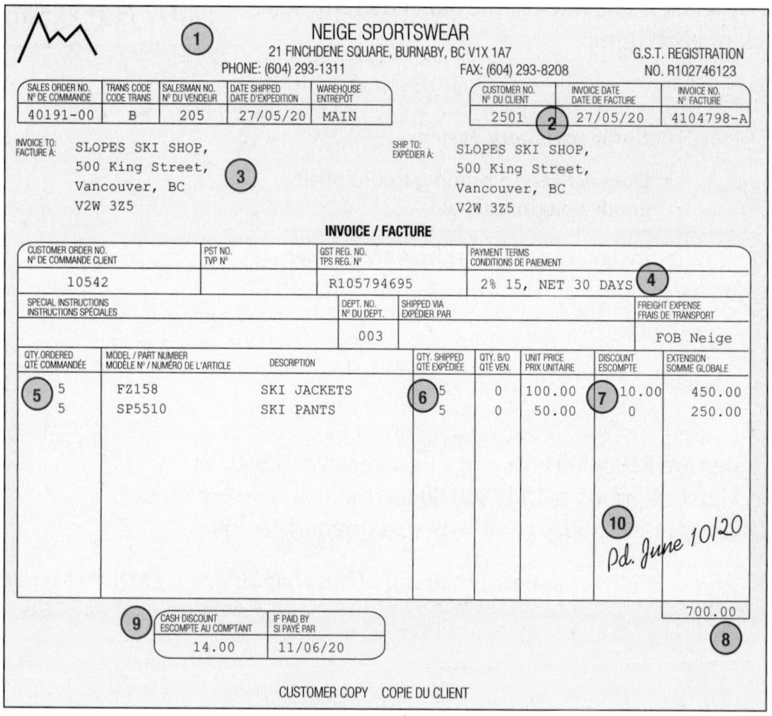
NEIGE SPORTSWEAR
21 FINCHDENE SQUARE, BURNABY, BC V1X 1A7
PHONE: (604) 293-1311 FAX: (604) 293-8208
G.S.T. REGISTRATION NO. R102746123

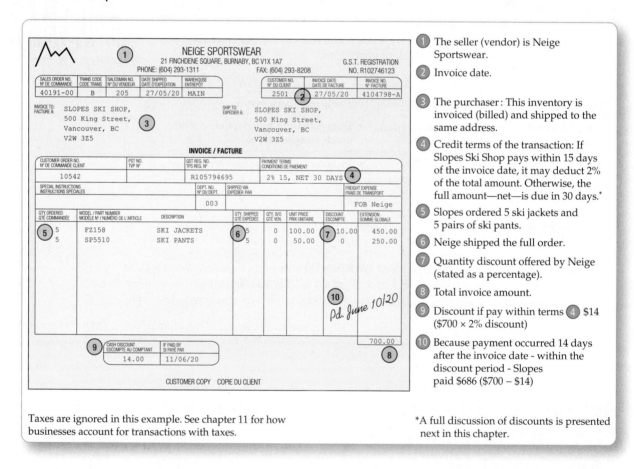

SALES ORDER NO. / Nº DE COMMANDE	TRANS CODE / CODE TRANS	SALESMAN NO. / Nº DU VENDEUR	DATE SHIPPED / DATE D'EXPÉDITION	WAREHOUSE / ENTREPÔT
40191-00	B	205	27/05/20	MAIN

CUSTOMER NO. / Nº DU CLIENT	INVOICE DATE / DATE DE FACTURE	INVOICE NO. / Nº FACTURE
2501	27/05/20	4104798-A

INVOICE TO: / FACTURE À: SLOPES SKI SHOP, 500 King Street, Vancouver, BC V2W 3Z5

SHIP TO: / EXPÉDIER À: SLOPES SKI SHOP, 500 King Street, Vancouver, BC V2W 3Z5

INVOICE / FACTURE

CUSTOMER ORDER NO. / Nº DE COMMANDE CLIENT	PST NO. / TVP Nº	GST REG. NO. / TPS REG. Nº	PAYMENT TERMS / CONDITIONS DE PAIEMENT
10542		R105794695	2% 15, NET 30 DAYS

SPECIAL INSTRUCTIONS / INSTRUCTIONS SPÉCIALES	DEPT. NO. / Nº DU DEPT.	SHIPPED VIA / EXPÉDIER PAR	FREIGHT EXPENSE / FRAIS DE TRANSPORT
	003		FOB Neige

QTY. ORDERED / QTÉ COMMANDÉE	MODEL / PART NUMBER / MODÈLE Nº / NUMÉRO DE L'ARTICLE	DESCRIPTION	QTY. SHIPPED / QTÉ EXPÉDIÉE	QTY. B/O / QTÉ VEN.	UNIT PRICE / PRIX UNITAIRE	DISCOUNT / ESCOMPTE	EXTENSION / SOMME GLOBALE
5	FZ158	SKI JACKETS	5	0	100.00	10.00	450.00
5	SP5510	SKI PANTS	5	0	50.00	0	250.00
							700.00

Pd. June 10/20

CASH DISCOUNT / ESCOMPTE AU COMPTANT	IF PAID BY / SI PAYÉ PAR
14.00	11/06/20

CUSTOMER COPY COPIE DU CLIENT

1. The seller (vendor) is Neige Sportswear.
2. Invoice date.
3. The purchaser: This inventory is invoiced (billed) and shipped to the same address.
4. Credit terms of the transaction: If Slopes Ski Shop pays within 15 days of the invoice date, it may deduct 2% of the total amount. Otherwise, the full amount—net—is due in 30 days.*
5. Slopes ordered 5 ski jackets and 5 pairs of ski pants.
6. Neige shipped the full order.
7. Quantity discount offered by Neige (stated as a percentage).
8. Total invoice amount.
9. Discount if pay within terms (4) $14 ($700 × 2% discount)
10. Because payment occurred 14 days after the invoice date - within the discount period - Slopes paid $686 ($700 – $14)

Taxes are ignored in this example. See chapter 11 for how businesses account for transactions with taxes.

*A full discussion of discounts is presented next in this chapter.

Discounts from Purchase Prices

There are two major types of discounts from purchase prices: quantity discounts and purchase discounts.

Quantity Discounts A **quantity** (or **volume**) **discount** works this way: The greater the quantity purchased, the lower the price per item. For example, Neige Sportswear may offer no quantity discount for the purchase of only one ski jacket and charge the *list* price—the full price—of $100 per unit. However, Neige may offer the following quantity discount terms in order to persuade customers to order more ski jackets:

Quantity	Quantity Discount	Net Price per Unit	
Minimum quantity, 2 ski jackets	5%	$95	← $100 − 0.05($100)
3–9 ski jackets	10%	$90	← $100 − 0.10($100)
More than 9 ski jackets	20%	$80	← $100 − 0.20($100)

There is no Quantity Discount account recorded at the time the order is placed. Instead, all accounting entries are based on the net price of a purchase after the quantity discount has been subtracted, as shown on the invoice.

Suppose Slopes purchases five ski jackets from Neige. The cost of each ski jacket is, therefore, $90. In Exhibit 5–3 we see that the total cost of the five jackets is $450, or five items purchased times a *net price* of $90 per unit. In addition to the jackets, Slopes purchases ski pants for a total invoice in the amount of $700, which Slopes will pay for later since it is "on account." Slopes records the May 27 purchase as follows:

May 27	Inventory	700	
	Accounts Payable		700
	Purchased inventory on account.		

Purchase Discounts Many businesses also offer purchase discounts to their customers. A purchase discount is totally different from a quantity discount. A **purchase discount** (also referred to as a **cash discount**) is a reward for prompt payment. The purchase discount is computed on the net purchase amount after the quantity discount has been subtracted, further reducing the cost of the inventory to the purchaser.

Neige Sportswear's credit terms of "2% 15, net 30 days," shown as item 4 in the exhibit, can also be expressed as **2/15, n/30**. This means that Slopes may deduct 2 percent of the total amount due if it pays within the **discount period**, which is within 15 days of the invoice date. Otherwise, the full amount—net—is due in 30 days.

Terms of "n/30" indicate that no discount is offered, and payment is due 30 days after the invoice date. Terms of **eom** mean that payment is due by the end of the current month. However, a purchase after the 25th of the current month on terms of *eom* can be paid at the end of the next month.

A computerized accounting system is typically programmed to make the owner aware of invoices as the date for taking the discount approaches so the business can take advantage of the purchase discount.

A business does not record a purchase discount until the payment is made and it knows for sure that the discount has been earned. Slopes paid within the discount period of 15 days, so its cash payment entry on June 10 is:

Jun. 10	Accounts Payable	700	
	Cash		686
	Inventory		14
	Paid on account within discount period. The discount is $14 ($700 × 0.02).		

Whether a company takes the purchase discount or not, the Accounts Payable account for the inventory purchase must always be $0 after final payment is made.

Accounts Payable			
Jun 10	700	May 27	700

The discount is credited to Inventory. This means the inventory cost Slopes $686 ($700 minus the purchase discount of $14), as shown in the following Inventory account:

	Inventory				
(Purchase)	May 27	700	**Jun. 10**	14	(Discount)
	Bal.	686			

However, if Slopes pays this invoice on June 25, after the discount period, it must pay the full invoice amount. In this case, the payment entry is:

Jun. 25	Accounts Payable	700	
	Cash		700
	Paid on account after discount period.		

Without the discount, Slopes' cost of the inventory is the full amount of $700.

Purchase Returns and Allowances

Most businesses allow their customers to *return* merchandise that is defective, damaged in shipment, or otherwise unsuitable. Or, if the buyer chooses to keep damaged goods, the seller may deduct an *allowance* from the amount the buyer owes. Both purchase returns and purchase allowances decrease the amount that the buyer must pay the seller.

Purchase Returns When a business returns merchandise to the seller, it may also send a business document known as a **debit memo**. This document states that the buyer no longer owes the seller for the amount of the returned purchases. Suppose the $90 ski jackets received by Slopes Ski Shop (in Exhibit 5–3) were not the model of jacket ordered. Slopes issues the debit memo shown in Exhibit 5–4.

EXHIBIT 5–4 | Debit Memo

Debit Memo **No. 122**

Date: June 3, 2020

Slopes Ski Shop
500 King Street
Vancouver, BC V2W 3Z5

Supplier Name Neige Sportswear
21 Finchdene Square
Vancouver, BC V1X 1A7

Reason for Debit Invoice 4107898-A, wrong model received

Description	Amount
5 model FZ158 (wrong model)	$450

Slopes returns the merchandise to the seller and records the purchase return as follows:

Jun. 3	Accounts Payable	450	
	Inventory		450
	Returned inventory to seller.		

Purchase Allowances Now assume that one pair of the Neige ski pants was damaged in shipment to Slopes. The damage is minor, and Slopes decides to keep the ski pants in exchange for a $25 allowance from Neige. To record this **purchase allowance**, Slopes makes this entry:

Jun. 4	Accounts Payable	25	
	Inventory		25
	Received a purchase allowance.		

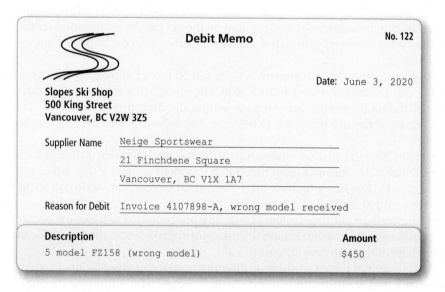

Assume that Slopes has not yet paid its liability to Neige. After these return ($450) and allowance ($25) transactions are posted, Slopes' accounts will show these balances:

Inventory

(Purchase)	May 27	700	Jun. 3	450	(Return)
			Jun. 4	25	(Allowance)
	Bal.	225			

Accounts Payable

Jun. 3	450	May 27	700
Jun. 4	25		
		Bal.	225

Slopes' cost of *inventory* is $225, and Slopes owes Neige $225 on *account payable*. If Slopes pays within the discount period, 2 percent will be deducted from these balances.

The return and the allowance had two effects:

- They decreased Slopes' liability, which is why we debit Accounts Payable.
- They decreased the net cost of the inventory, which is why we credit Inventory.

ETHICS How should you handle gifts from vendors?

Anthony Jackson works as a buyer for a department store that has decided to expand into selling seasonal home decor. Anthony has been charged with the responsibility of selecting the vendor for the new inventory that the store will sell. His purchasing manager has provided him with two possible vendors to choose from. One vendor, Abbey's Wholesalers, has a long-standing relationship with the store and can be counted on to provide high-quality goods on a timely basis. The other vendor, Zeta Wholesalers, is a new company that is just getting established as a home decor wholesaler. Anthony has contacted both vendors to set up meetings to discuss the new inventory and possible credit terms available. The day before the meeting with the potential vendors, Anthony receives a pair of hockey tickets to a major NHL game in the mail from Abbey's Wholesalers thanking him for his continued relationship with the wholesaler. What should Anthony do?

Solution

Anthony should contact his purchasing manager and explain the situation to him or her. By accepting the hockey tickets, Anthony might unknowingly be violating the code of ethics of the business. Most businesses have a code of ethics that relates to purchasing, specifically discussing conflicts of interest. Conflicts of interest occur when a vendor is selected above another vendor because of possible personal financial gain such as receiving gifts or entertainment from the selected vendor. Anthony should carefully discuss the situation with his manager before accepting the tickets.

Transportation Costs: Who Pays?

The transportation cost of moving inventory from seller to buyer can be significant. Someone must pay this cost. The purchase agreement specifies FOB (*free on board*) terms to indicate who pays the shipping charges. FOB governs:

Another term used for FOB shipping point is CIF destination, which stands for cost, insurance, and freight.

- When **legal title**, or ownership, passes from the seller to buyer.
- Who pays the freight:
  - Under **FOB shipping point** terms, legal title passes when the inventory leaves the seller's place of business—the shipping point. The buyer owns the goods while they are in transit, and therefore the buyer pays the transportation cost, or freight.
  - Under **FOB destination** terms, legal title passes when the goods reach the destination, so the seller pays the freight.

Exhibit 5-5 summarizes FOB terms.

EXHIBIT 5-5 | FOB Terms Determine Who Pays the Freight

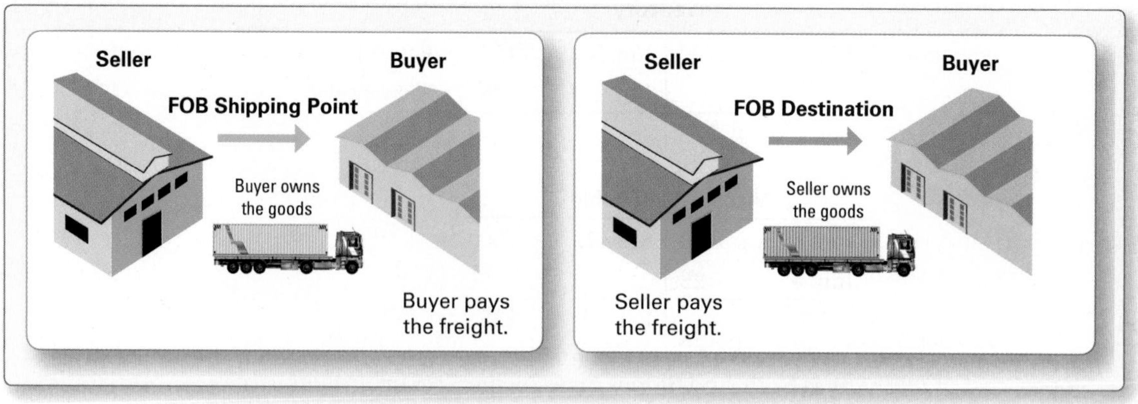

The perpetual method in this text records all discounts, returns, allowances, and freight-in the Inventory account to simplify recording, but most businesses have more detailed records.

Freight-in Freight-in is the transportation cost on *purchased* goods. FOB shipping point terms are the most common. The *buyer* owns the goods while they are in transit, so the buyer pays the freight. In accounting, the cost of an asset includes all costs incurred to bring the asset to its intended use. For inventory, cost therefore includes the following:

- *Net cost* after all discounts, returns, and allowances have been subtracted, plus
- *Freight-in*

Suppose Slopes receives a $100 shipping bill directly from the freight company. Slopes' entry to record payment of the freight charge is as follows:

Jun. 1	Inventory	100	
	Cash		100
	Paid a freight bill.		

Normally, no discount for early payment is offered on transportation costs.

The freight charge increases the cost of the inventory to $325 as follows:

	Inventory				
(Purchase)	May 27	700	Jun. 3	450	(Return)
(Freight)	Jun. 1	100	Jun. 4	25	(Allowance)
(Net cost)	Bal.	325			

Under FOB shipping point, the seller sometimes prepays the transportation cost as a convenience and adds this cost on the invoice. The buyer can debit Inventory for the combined cost of the inventory and the shipping cost because both costs apply to the merchandise. In this example, Neige could have charged Slopes $700 for the goods plus $100 shipping on the invoice, and the May 27 journal entry would have recorded an $800 debit to Inventory.

Freight-out The *seller* may pay freight charges to ship goods to customers. This is called *freight-out*. Freight-out is a selling expense that is debited to the Delivery Expense account.

Summary of Purchase Returns and Allowances, Discounts, and Transportation Costs Here are two ways of thinking about the Inventory purchase transactions and the **net purchases** of inventory when looking at the accounts for the entire month of June:

Purchases of Inventory	−	Purchase Returns and Allowances	−	Purchase Discounts	+	Freight-in	=	Inventory Cost (Net Purchases)
60,500	−	2,000	−	1,000	+	2,500	=	60,000

Inventory

Purchases	60,500	Purchase ret. & allow.	2,000
Freight-in	2,500	Purchase discounts	1,000
Bal.	60,000		

Selling Inventory and Recording Cost of Goods Sold

After a company buys inventory, the next step in the operating cycle is to sell the goods. We now shift to follow Slopes Ski Shop through some selling transactions. A sale earns income, or Sales Revenue. A sale also requires a cost in the form of an expense, Cost of Goods Sold, as the seller gives up the asset, Inventory.

The sale of inventory may be for cash or on account. Let's begin with a cash sale.

The recording of cost of goods sold along with sales revenue is an example of the matching objective—matching expense against revenue to measure net income.

Cash Sale Cash sales of merchandise in the amount $10,000 would be recorded by debiting Cash and crediting the new account, Sales Revenue, on July 9 as follows:

Jul. 9	Cash	10,000	
	Sales Revenue		10,000
	Cash sales.		

Suppose these goods cost the seller $6,000. An accompanying entry is needed to transfer the $6,000 cost of the goods from the Inventory account to the Cost of Goods Sold account as follows:

Jul. 9	Cost of Goods Sold	6,000	
	Inventory		6,000
	Recorded the cost of goods sold.		

Cost of goods sold is the cost of the inventory that the business has sold to customers. Assuming that Slopes started with $60,000 of inventory on July 2, we can see that the sale of goods that cost Slopes $6,000 will reduce the inventory balance as the goods are no longer in stock. After posting, the Cost of Goods Sold account holds the cost of the merchandise sold:

For many businesses, the cashier scans the bar code on the product and the computer automatically records the sale and cost of goods sold entry.

Inventory

Jul. 2 Bal. 60,000	Jul. 9 6,000

Cost of Goods Sold

Jul. 9 6,000	

Sale on Account Businesses generally sell to other businesses *on account* (on credit). On July 10, Slopes sells ski wear to High Hopes Ski Chalet for $24,000 on credit terms of 2/15, n/30. These goods cost Slopes $14,400. Slopes's entries to record this credit sale and the related cost of goods sold are as follows:

Jul. 10	Accounts Receivable	24,000	
	Sales Revenue		24,000
	Sale on account.		
10	Cost of Goods Sold	14,400	
	Inventory		14,400
	Recorded the cost of goods sold.		

In this chapter we provide you with the amount of cost of goods sold. You will learn how to calculate cost of goods sold in the next chapter.

Suppose Slopes collects the amount outstanding on July 31. To record this collection on account, Slopes debits Cash and credits Accounts Receivable for the same amount, as follows:

Jul. 31	Cash	5,000	
	Accounts Receivable		5,000
	Cash collection after the discount period.		

Why is there no July 31 entry to Sales Revenue, Cost of Goods Sold, or Inventory? The sales revenue, the related cost of goods sold, and the decrease in inventory for the goods sold were recorded on July 10.

Sales Discounts and Sales Returns and Allowances

Instead of the customer making an immediate payment, Slopes may experience any of the following:

- A sales return: The customer may return goods to Slopes Ski Shop.
- A sales allowance: Slopes may grant a sales allowance to reduce the amount of cash to be collected from the customer.
- A sales discount: If the customer pays within the discount period—under terms such as 2/10, n/30—Slopes collects the discounted (reduced) amount. No discount is recorded for a quantity, or volume, discount.
- Freight-out: Slopes may have to pay delivery expense to transport the goods to the buyer's location.

We saw that purchase discounts and purchase returns and allowances decrease the cost of inventory purchases. In the same way, **sales discounts** and **sales returns and allowances** decrease the revenue earned on sales. Sales Discounts and Sales Returns and Allowances are contra accounts to Sales Revenue. **Net Sales** or Net Sales Revenue is calculated as follows:

Sales Revenue	(Credit account balance)
Less: Sales Discounts	(Debit account balance)
Sales Returns and Allowances	(Debit account balance)
Net Sales Revenue (or Net Sales)	(Credit subtotal (*not* a separate account))

Companies keep a close watch on their customers' paying habits and on their own sales of defective and unsuitable merchandise. They maintain separate accounts for Sales Discounts and Sales Returns and Allowances to provide better information for decision making.

Sales Returns What if High Hopes Ski Chalet realized that some of the items they purchased were the wrong size and returned the outfits? These goods are not damaged and can be resold. Slopes then issues a **credit memo** to High Hopes like the one in Exhibit 5–6. The document issued by the seller for a credit to the customer's account receivable is called a credit memo, because the company gives the customer credit for the returned merchandise.

High Hopes returns goods that were sold by Slopes for $3,000. Slopes, the seller, records the sales return and the related decrease in Accounts Receivable as follows:

Jul. 12	Sales Returns and Allowances	3,000	
	Accounts Receivable		3,000
	Received returned goods.		

The sale of inventory and the return of goods by customers both require two separate journal entries.

Slopes receives the returned merchandise and updates the Inventory records. Slopes must also decrease Cost of Goods Sold as follows (the returned goods cost Slopes $1,800):

Jul. 12	Inventory	1,800	
	Cost of Goods Sold		1,800
	Returned goods to inventory.		

EXHIBIT 5–6 | Credit Memo

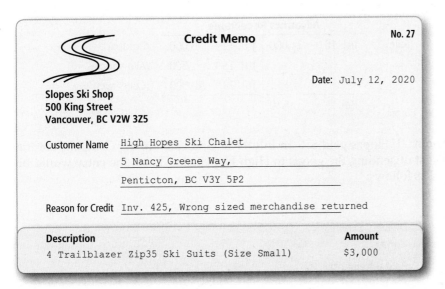

Credit Memo No. 27

Date: July 12, 2020

Slopes Ski Shop
500 King Street
Vancouver, BC V2W 3Z5

Customer Name High Hopes Ski Chalet
5 Nancy Greene Way,
Penticton, BC V3Y 5P2

Reason for Credit Inv. 425, Wrong sized merchandise returned

Description	Amount
4 Trailblazer Zip35 Ski Suits (Size Small)	$3,000

Sales Allowances Suppose Slopes grants High Hopes a $500 sales allowance for damaged goods on July 15. High Hopes has agreed to keep the goods and repair them in return for a reduced purchase price. Slopes then subtracts a further $500 from the customer's balance owing. Slopes journalizes this transaction as follows:

Jul. 15	Sales Returns and Allowances	500	
	Accounts Receivable		500
	Granted a sales allowance for damaged goods.		

No Inventory entry is needed for a sales allowance transaction because the seller, Slopes, receives no returned goods from the customer. Instead, Slopes will simply receive less cash from the customer.

Sales Discounts After the preceding entries are posted, all the accounts have up-to-date balances. The Accounts Receivable account for High Hopes has a $20,500 debit balance, as follows:

Accounts Receivable

(Sale)	Jul. 10	24,000	Jul. 12	3,000	(Return)
			Jul. 15	500	(Allowance)
	Bal.	20,500			

On July 24, which is within the discount period, Slopes collects this accounts receivable and records the discount that High Hopes took according to the agreed-upon terms. The collection entry and record of the Sales Discount is as follows:

Jul. 24	Cash	20,090		← $20,500 − $410 = $20,090
	Sales Discounts	410		← 0.02 × $20,500 = $410
	Accounts Receivable		20,500	
	Cash collection within the discount period.			

Now the Accounts Receivable balance is zero:

	Accounts Receivable				
(Sale)	Jul. 10	24,000	Jul. 12	3,000	(Return)
			Jul. 15	500	(Allowance)
			Jul. 24	20,500	(Collection)
	Bal.	0			

Freight-out If Slopes paid $50 on July 11 to Grant's Shipping Company for the freight cost of sending the goods to High Hopes Ski Chalet, the entry would be recorded as follows:

Jul. 11	Delivery Expense	50	
	Cash		50
	Paid a freight bill.		

Try It!

2. Journalize, without explanations, the following transactions of Royal Fashion Distributors, a wholesaler that uses the perpetual inventory system, during the month of June 2020:

Jun.	3	Purchased $14,500 of inventory from a manufacturer under terms of 1/10, n/eom and FOB shipping point.
	7	Returned $2,700 of defective merchandise purchased on June 3.
	9	Paid freight bill of $750 on June 3 purchase.
	10	Sold inventory for $11,500 to a retail store, collecting cash of $2,400. Payment terms on the remainder were 2/15, n/30. The goods cost Royal Fashion Distributors $6,900.
	12	Paid amount owed on credit purchase of June 3.
	16	Granted a sales allowance of $1,200 on the portion of the June 10 sale that was on account.
	23	Received cash from June 10 customer in full settlement of the debt.

Solutions appear at the end of this chapter and on **MyLab Accounting**

Adjusting and Closing the Accounts of a Merchandising Business

LO 3

How can we adjust for inventory shrinkage and begin the next cycle using the perpetual inventory system?

A merchandising business adjusts and closes the accounts the same way a service entity does. If a worksheet is used, the trial balance is entered and the worksheet is completed to determine net income or net loss. The worksheet provides the data for journalizing the adjusting and closing entries and for preparing the financial statements. Since there is very little difference between the worksheet of a service business and that of a merchandising business that uses the perpetual inventory system, we will not cover worksheets here. (However, worksheets are covered in Summary Problems for Your Review on **MyLab Accounting**, in Chapter Resources.)

Adjusting Inventory Based on a Physical Count

In theory, the Inventory account remains up to date at all times. However, the actual amount of inventory on hand may differ from what the books show. Losses due to theft and damage can be significant. Also, accounting errors can cause Inventory's balance to need adjustment either upward or, more often, downward. For this reason, virtually all merchandising businesses take a physical count of inventory at least once each year. The most common time for a business to count its inventory is at the end of the fiscal year, before the financial statements are prepared. The business then adjusts the Inventory account to the correct amount based on the physical count.

At year-end, Slopes Ski Shop's Inventory account shows an unadjusted balance of $174,000.

Inventory

}	}
Dec. 31 174,000	

With no **shrinkage**—a reduction in the amount of inventory due to theft, spoilage, or error—the business should have on hand inventory costing $174,000. But on December 31, Steve Austin, the owner of Slopes Ski Shop, counts the merchandise in the store, and the total cost of the goods on hand comes to only $168,000.

Inventory Balance Before Adjustment	−	Actual Inventory on Hand	=	Adjusting Entry to Inventory
$174,000	−	$168,000	=	Credit of $6,000

Slopes would record the inventory shrinkage of $6,000 with this adjusting entry:

Dec. 31	Cost of Goods Sold	6,000	
	Inventory		6,000
	Adjustment for inventory shrinkage.		

As a result of this inventory adjustment, cost of goods sold (an expense) is higher and gross margin is lower. The current asset Inventory has been reduced.

This entry brings Inventory to its correct balance.[1]

Inventory

	}		}
Dec. 31	174,000	Dec. 31 Adj.	6,000
Dec. 31 Bal.	168,000		

The physical count can also indicate that more inventory is present than the books show. A search of the records may reveal that Slopes Ski Shop received inventory but did not record the corresponding purchase entry. This would be entered

---

[1]Some companies record the inventory shrinkage of $6,000 with this adjusting entry:

Dec. 31	Loss on Inventory (or Inventory Shrinkage)	6,000	
	Inventory		6,000
	Adjustment for inventory shrinkage.		

This is done to highlight the shrinkage so that it can be monitored and to identify it as a loss.

as debit Inventory and credit Cash or Accounts Payable. If the reason for the excess inventory cannot be identified, the business adjusts the accounts by debiting Inventory and crediting Cost of Goods Sold.

Summary of Merchandising Cost Flows

The Inventory account balance at the end of the period is the amount of beginning inventory in the next period. To summarize the effects of transactions on the Inventory and Cost of Goods Sold accounts, Slopes Ski Shop's inventory activities are summarized in Exhibit 5–7. Note that key year-end amounts are shown; other transactions that would have occurred throughout the year are represented as "XXX." These transactions are typical of merchandisers using the perpetual inventory system.

EXHIBIT 5–7 | Summary of Activities Affecting the Inventory and Cost of Goods Sold Accounts

Inventory

Dec. 31, 2019, balance	XXX	XXX	Purchase discounts during 2020
Purchases of merchandise during 2020	XXX	XXX	Purchases returns and allowances during 2020
Freight-in costs incurred during 2020	XXX	421,000	Cost of sales transactions during 2020
Return of goods to inventory	XXX	6,000	Adjustment for shrinkage shrinkage after physical count
Dec. 31, 2020, balance	168,000		

Cost of Goods Sold

Cost of sales for 2020	421,000	XXX	Return of goods to inventory
Adjustment for shrinkage after physical count	6,000		
Dec. 31, 2020, balance	427,000		

Try It!

3. At December 31, 2020, a merchandising company's year-end, the accounting records show a balance of $125,000 in the Inventory account. Suppose a physical count of the goods in the warehouse shows inventory on hand costing $110,000. What journal entry would bring the Inventory account to its correct balance?
4. At December 31, 2020, a merchandising company's year-end, the accounting records show a balance of $75,000 in the Inventory account. Suppose a physical count of the goods in the warehouse shows inventory on hand costing $78,000. What journal entry would bring the Inventory account to its correct balance?

Solutions appear at the end of this chapter and on **MyLab Accounting**

Closing the Accounts of a Merchandising Business

Exhibit 5–8 presents Slopes Ski Shop's closing entries, which are similar to those you have seen in Chapter 4 except for the new accounts highlighted with bold text. All amounts, including an opening Capital balance of $90,000, assumed for demonstration purposes.

EXHIBIT 5–8 | Closing Entries for a Merchandiser

Debit Revenue accounts to close them

Debit Income Summary for total expenses plus contra revenue accounts

Operating expenses are wages, rent, insurance, supplies, and so on.

Closing Entries				
❶	Dec. 31	**Sales Revenue**	**777,000**	
		Interest Revenue	3,000	
		Income Summary		780,000
		To close the revenue accounts and create the Income Summary account.		
❷	Dec. 31	Income Summary	648,000	
		Cost of Goods Sold		**427,000**
		Sales Discounts		**7,500**
		Sales Returns and Allowances		**8,000**
		Operating Expenses		205,500
		To close the expense accounts.		
❸	Dec. 31	Income Summary*	132,000	
		Steve Austin, Capital		132,000
		To close the Income Summary account and transfer net income to the Capital account. *$780,000 − $648,000		
❹	Dec. 31	Steve Austin, Capital	65,000	
		Steve Austin, Withdrawals		65,000
		To close the Withdrawals account and transfer the Withdrawals amount to the Capital account.		

Income Summary

❷ Clo.	648,000	❶ Clo.	780,000
❸ Clo.	132,000	Bal.	0

Steve Austin, Withdrawals

Bal.	65,000	❹ Clo.	65,000
		Bal.	0

Steve Austin, Capital

❹ Clo.	65,000	Bal.	90,000
		❸ Clo.	132,000
		Bal.	157,000

Clo. = Amount posted from a closing entry
Bal. = Balance

Preparing a Merchandiser's Financial Statements

LO ④

How can we prepare financial statements for a company using the perpetual inventory system?

The following exhibits present Slopes Ski Shop's financial statements (prepared after all year-end adjusting entries have been entered).

Income Statement Special presentation is warranted for three items that appear on the merchandiser's income statement shown in Exhibit 5–9: operating expenses, income from operations, and other revenue and expense. **Operating expenses** are those expenses other than cost of goods sold incurred in the entity's major line of business—merchandising. Slopes Ski Shop's operating expenses include wages, rent, insurance, amortization of furniture and fixtures, and supplies.

EXHIBIT 5-9 | Merchandiser Multi-Step Income Statement

SLOPES SKI SHOP Income Statement For the Year Ended December 31, 2020		
Sales revenue		$777,000
Less: Sales discounts	$7,500	
Sales returns and allowances	8,000	15,500
Net sales revenue		761,500
Cost of goods sold		427,000
Gross margin		334,500
Operating expenses		201,000
Selling expenses	126,000	
General expenses	75,000	
Income from operations		133,500
Other revenue and expense		
Interest revenue	3,000	
Less: Interest expense	4,500	(1,500)
Net income		$132,000

These are activities outside the scope of selling merchandise.

Many companies report their operating expenses in two categories:

- *Selling expenses* are those expenses related to marketing the company's products— sales salaries; sales commissions; advertising; amortization, rent, utilities, and property taxes on store buildings; amortization on store furniture; delivery expense; and so on.
- *General and administrative expenses* include office expenses, such as the salaries of the executives and office employees; amortization, rent, utilities, and property taxes on the home office building; and office supplies.

In this chapter, we will report operating expenses in just one category—operating expenses or simply expenses—to keep the examples simple.

Gross margin minus operating expenses equals **income from operations**, or **operating income**. Many people view operating income as an important indicator of a business's performance because it measures the results of the entity's major ongoing activities.

The last section of Slopes Ski Shop's income statement is **other revenue and expense**. This category reports revenues and expenses that are outside the main operations of the business. Examples include gains and losses on the sale of long-term assets like property, plant, and equipment, and gains and losses on lawsuits. Accountants have traditionally viewed Interest Revenue and Interest Expense as "other" items because they arise from lending money and borrowing money.

Statement of Owner's Equity A merchandiser's statement of owner's equity as shown in Exhibit 5–10, looks exactly like that of a service business. In fact, you cannot determine whether the entity sells merchandise or services from looking at the statement of owner's equity.

EXHIBIT 5-10 | Merchandiser Statement of Owner's Equity

SLOPES SKI SHOP Statement of Owner's Equity For the Year Ended December 31, 2020	
Steve Austin, capital, January 1, 2020	$ 90,000
Add: Net income	132,000
	222,000
Less: Withdrawals	65,000
Steve Austin, capital, December 31, 2020	$157,000

Balance Sheet The balance sheet shows inventory as a current asset. As we saw in Chapter 4, the classified balance sheet can be prepared in one of two formats:

- The report format (assets on top, owner's equity at the bottom)
- The account format (assets at left, liabilities and owner's equity at right).

Exhibit 5–11 shows the balance sheet in the report format.

EXHIBIT 5–11 | Merchandiser Balance Sheet

SLOPES SKI SHOP Balance Sheet December 31, 2020		
Assets		
Current assets		
Cash	$ 6,000	
Accounts receivable	24,000	
Note receivable	32,000	
Interest receivable	1,000	
Inventory	168,000	
Prepaid insurance	600	
Supplies	500	
Total current assets		$232,100
Property, plant, and equipment		
Furniture and fixtures	120,000	
Less: Accumulated amortization	18,000	
Total property, plant, and equipment		102,000
Total assets		$334,100
Liabilities		
Current liabilities		
Accounts payable	$128,000	
Unearned sales revenue	1,500	
Wages payable	3,000	
Interest payable	500	
Total current liabilities		133,000
Long-term liabilities		
Notes payable		44,100
Total liabilities		177,100
Owner's Equity		
Steve Austin, capital		157,000
Total liabilities and owner's equity		$334,100

Income Statement Formats

There are also two basic formats for the income statement:

- The multi-step format (Exhibit 5–9)
- The single-step format (Exhibit 5–12)

Multi-Step Income Statement A **multi-step income statement** shows subtotals to highlight significant relationships and is the most popular format. In addition to net income, it also presents gross margin and operating income, or income from operations. Slopes Ski Shop's multi-step income statement appears in Exhibit 5–9.

Single-Step Income Statement The **single-step income statement** groups all revenues together and then lists and deducts all expenses together without drawing any subtotals. Thus, it clearly distinguishes revenues from expenses. The income statements in Chapters 1 through 4 were single-step. This format works well for service entities, because they have no gross margin to report, and for companies that have several types of revenues. Exhibit 5–12 shows a single-step income statement for Slopes Ski Shop.

EXHIBIT 5–12 | Single-Step Income Statement

SLOPES SKI SHOP Income Statement For the Year Ended December 31, 2020		
Revenues		
Sales revenue		$777,000
Less: Sales discounts	$ 7,500	
Sales returns and allowances	8,000	15,500
Net sales revenue		761,500
Interest revenue		3,000
Total revenues		764,500
Expenses		
Cost of goods sold	427,000	
Operating expenses	205,500	
Total expenses		632,500
Net income		$132,000

Interest expense of $4,500 is included in operating expenses.

Most published financial statements are highly condensed. Of course, condensed statements can be supplemented with desired details in the notes to the financial statements. For example, notes would disclose which system is being used—periodic or perpetual—as well as if inventory has been **pledged as collateral**, and so on.

Try It!

5. The adjusted trial balance of Patti's Party Supplies for the year ended December 31, 2020, appears below. Use this information to prepare the company's single-step income statement for the year ended December 31, 2020.

PATTI'S PARTY SUPPLIES Adjusted Trial Balance December 31, 2020		
Account Title	**Debit**	**Credit**
Cash	$ 5,600	
Accounts receivable	19,900	
Inventory	25,800	
Furniture	26,500	
Accumulated amortization—furniture		$ 23,800
Accounts payable		4,000
Interest payable		600
Unearned sales revenue		2,400
Note payable, long-term		35,000
Patti Grandy, capital		22,200
Patti Grandy, withdrawals	48,000	
Sales revenue		244,000
Interest revenue		2,000
Sales discounts	10,000	
Sales returns and allowances	8,000	
Cost of goods sold	81,000	
Operating expenses	106,300	
Interest expense	2,900	
Total	$334,000	$334,000

6. Refer to the Patti's Party Supplies adjusted trial balance in Try It #5. Use that information to prepare the company's multi-step income statement for the year ended December 31, 2020.

Solutions appear at the end of this chapter and on **MyLab Accounting**

Why It's Done This Way

Inventory is an asset and an element of the financial statements because it has future economic benefit to the company—the company hopes to sell the inventory for more than it cost to purchase it, creating a positive *gross margin*. When the inventory is sold, it becomes an expense referred to as the *cost of goods sold*. The future economic benefit of the inventory is realized when it is sold.

The *multi-step income statement* is an example of financial information being arranged in reports to provide more *useful* information to readers of financial statements. Recall that providing useful information is the primary objective of financial reporting.

Two Ratios for Decision Making

LO 5

How can we use ratios to evaluate a business?

Inventory is the most important asset to a merchandising business because it's the reason the business exists. Buying the inventory is risky because if it is not what customers want, it won't sell. If inventory doesn't sell, the merchandiser has invested a lot of its money in purchasing the inventory but has little income. To manage the business, owners and managers focus on the best way to sell the inventory. They use several ratios to evaluate operations, among them *gross margin percentage* and *inventory turnover.*

Gross margin (gross profit) is net sales minus cost of goods sold.

Gross Margin Percentage

Merchandisers strive to increase the **gross margin percentage**, which is computed for Slopes Ski Shop using amounts from Exhibit 5–9.

$$\textbf{Gross margin percentage} = \frac{\textbf{Gross margin}}{\textbf{Net sales revenue}} = \frac{\$334,500}{\$761,500} = 0.439, \text{ or } 43.9\%$$

EXHIBIT 5–13

Gross Margin on $1.00 of Sales for Two Merchandisers

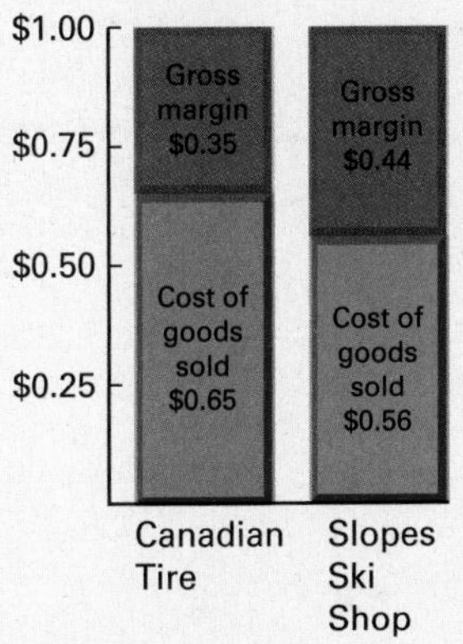

A 43.9 percent gross margin means that each dollar of sales generates almost 44 cents of gross profit. On average, the goods cost the seller 56 cents. The gross margin percentage (also called the *gross profit percentage*) is one of the most carefully watched measures of profitability.

Many businesses use the gross margin percentage as a means of determining how profitable a product line is. For example, if too much inventory is purchased and its selling price must be marked down, the gross margin percentage will decline. By monitoring the gross margin percentage, a business can correct problems quickly.

Exhibit 5–13 compares Slopes Ski Shop's gross margin percentage against Canadian Tire Corporation Ltd.'s gross margin percentage, which, at the time of writing, was 35.3 percent.

Inventory Turnover

Owners and managers strive to sell inventory as quickly as possible. This is because there is a cost to carrying inventory. If a company purchases inventory on credit (creating an account payable), there is a risk it may buy too much inventory and be unable to sell it before having to pay for the inventory. If this happens, the company either has to borrow funds to pay for the inventory and incur interest expense or use cash that could have been in a bank earning interest. For example, Dell Inc., the computer manufacturer and merchandiser, carries only *two hours* of parts inventory. Why? Prices of parts are continually declining, and Dell does not want to have any more inventory on hand than is absolutely necessary.

Dell is in a unique position in that it sells directly to customers and does not have to keep an inventory of computers on hand. Most retailers, such as Slopes Ski Shop, must keep inventory on hand for customers. Successful merchandisers purchase carefully to keep goods moving through the business at a rapid pace. **Inventory turnover**, the ratio of cost of goods sold to average inventory, indicates how rapidly inventory is sold. Slopes Ski Shop's inventory turnover using information from Exhibits 5–9 and 5–11 is as follows:*

$$\text{Inventory turnover} = \frac{\textbf{Cost of goods sold}}{\textbf{Average inventory}} = \frac{\textbf{Cost of goods sold}}{\frac{(\textbf{beginning inv}^* + \textbf{ending inv})}{2}} = \frac{\$427{,}000}{\frac{(\$158{,}400 + \$168{,}000)}{2}}$$

$$= 2.6 \text{ times per year}$$

*Taken from the balance sheet at the end of the preceding period

Inventory turnover can also be explained in terms of the number of days that inventory is held before being sold.

$$\text{Inventory turnover in days} = \frac{365 \text{ days}}{\text{inventory turnover}} = \frac{365 \text{ days}}{2.6} = 140 \text{ days}$$

Inventory turnover is usually computed for an annual period, and the relevant cost of goods sold figure is the amount from the entire year. The resulting inventory turnover statistic shows how many times the average level of inventory was sold during the year. A high rate of turnover is preferable to a low turnover rate. An increase in turnover rate usually means higher profits but may sometimes lead to a shortage of inventory to sell.

Inventory turnover varies from industry to industry. Grocery stores, for example, turn their goods over faster than automobile dealers do. Retailers of specialty sporting goods, such as Slopes Ski Shop, have an average turnover of 3.7 times per year. Exhibit 5–14 compares the inventory turnover rate of Slopes Ski Shop and Canadian Tire Corporation.

Exhibits 5–13 and 5–14 tell an interesting story. Canadian Tire sells lots of inventory at a relatively low gross profit margin. Compared to Slopes, Canadian Tire earns its profits by turning its inventory over rapidly—4.9 times during the year. Slopes Ski Shop, a small business, prices inventory to earn a higher gross margin on each dollar of sales and only turns over its inventory 2.6 times during the year.

EXHIBIT 5–14 | Rate of Inventory Turnover for Two Merchandisers

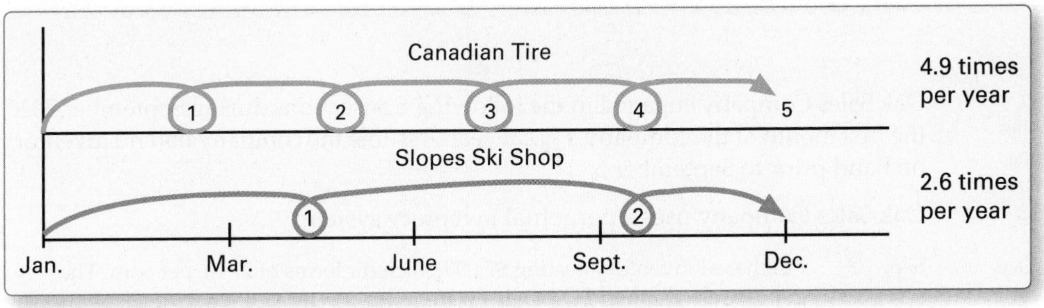

Gross margin percentage and rate of inventory turnover do not provide enough information to yield an overall conclusion about a merchandiser, but this example shows how owners and managers can use accounting information to evaluate a company.

Try It!

7. Refer to the Patti's Party Supplies multi-step income statement you created in Try It #6, or the solution on page 320. Calculate the gross margin percentage of this company.
8. Refer to the Patti's Party multi-step income statement you created in Try It #6, or the solution on page 320. Ending inventory at December 31, 2019, was $24,000. Calculate the inventory turnover of this company.

Solutions appear at the end of this chapter and on **MyLab Accounting.**

EXHIBIT 5–15 | The Effect of IFRS on Merchandising Operations

LO 6

How does IFRS affect companies that sell inventory?

ASPE	IFRS
"Revenue is recognized when the requirements as to performance are satisfied, provided that at the time of performance, ultimate collection is reasonably assured."[2]	There are five parts to recognition.[3] The business selling the goods must identify the customer contract; identify the separate performance obligations in the contract; determine the transaction price; allocate this price to the separate performance obligations in the contract; and recognize revenue when (or as) the business satisfies each performance obligation.
[2]CPA Canada Handbook Para. 3400.04	[3]IFRS 15

Summary Problem for Your Review

Two additional Summary Problems are available for this chapter in MyLab Accounting, in Chapter Resources. Summary Problem 1 (Perpetual) and 2 (Periodic) cover preparing worksheets, making adjusting and closing entries, preparing financial statements, and computing inventory turnover. Extra problem material is also available for Summary Problem 1 (Perpetual).

Oak Sales Company engaged in the following transactions during September 2020, the first month of the company's fiscal year. Assume the company had no inventory on hand prior to September 3.

Oak Sales Company uses a perpetual inventory system.

Sep. 3	Purchased inventory costing $7,000 on credit terms of 2/10, net eom. The goods were shipped FOB Oak's warehouse.
9	Returned 20 percent of the inventory purchased on September 3. It was defective.
12	Sold goods for cash, $6,000 (cost, $3,000).
15	Purchased inventory of $15,400, less a $400 quantity discount. Credit terms were 2/15, n/30. The goods were shipped FOB the supplier's warehouse.
16	Paid a $1,200 freight bill on the inventory purchased on September 15.
18	Sold inventory for $9,000 on credit terms of 2/10, n/30 (cost, $4,500).
22	Received merchandise returned from the customer from the September 18 sale, $2,000 (cost, $1,000). Merchandise was the wrong size.
24	Borrowed exactly enough money from the bank to pay for the September 15 purchase in time to take advantage of the discount offered. Signed a note payable to the bank for the net amount.
24	Paid supplier for goods purchased on September 15, less all returns and discounts.
28	Received cash in full settlement of the account from the customer who purchased inventory on September 18, less the return on September 22 and less the discount.
29	Paid the amount owed on account from the purchase of September 3, less the September 9 return.
30	Purchased inventory for cash, $4,640, less a quantity discount of $140.

Required

1. Journalize the transactions and include any calculations in the journal entry explanations.
2. Set up T-accounts and post the journal entries to show the ending balances in the Accounts Receivable, Inventory, Accounts Payable, and Cost of Goods Sold accounts.
3. Calculate Oak Sales' gross margin.

SOLUTION

Requirement 1

The perpetual method records purchases directly into the inventory account, which always has a running balance.

Notice that freight is not recorded in the Inventory entry because the shipping terms were FOB Oak Sales (i.e., paid by the seller).

2020			
Sep. 3	Inventory	7,000	
	Accounts Payable		7,000
	To record purchase on account, terms 2/10, net eom.		
9	Accounts Payable	1,400	
	Inventory		1,400
	Returned 20% of Sep. 3 purchase—goods were defective ($7,000 × 0.20).		

(Continued)

Sep. 12	Cash	6,000	
	Sales Revenue		6,000
	To record sale of goods for cash.		
12	Cost of Goods Sold	3,000	
	Inventory		3,000
	To record cost of the goods sold for cash on Sep. 12.		
15	Inventory	15,000	
	Accounts Payable		15,000
	To record purchase on account, terms 2/15, n/30. Received a quantity discount of $400 ($15,400 − $400 = $15,000).		
16	Inventory	1,200	
	Cash		1,200
	To record payment of the freight bill for the Sep. 15 purchase.		
18	Accounts Receivable	9,000	
	Sales Revenue		9,000
	To record sale of goods on account, terms 2/10, n/30.		
18	Cost of Goods Sold	4,500	
	Inventory		4,500
	To record cost of the goods sold on account on Sep. 18.		
22	Sales Returns and Allowances	2,000	
	Accounts Receivable		2,000
	To record return of goods sold on Sep. 18 —wrong size.		
22	Inventory	1,000	
	Cost of Goods Sold		1,000
	To record cost of the return of goods sold on Sep. 18—wrong size.		
24	Cash	14,700	
	Note Payable		14,700
	Borrowed money from the bank, signing a note payable, to pay for Sep. 15 purchase. Amount borrowed calculated as $14,700 [$15,000 − (0.02 × $15,000)].		
24	Accounts Payable	15,000	
	Inventory		300
	Cash		14,700
	To record payment of Sep. 15 purchase, taking the 2% discount. Cash payment is calculated as $14,700 [$15,000 − (0.02 × $15,000)]. The discount is $300 ($15,000 × 0.02).		

With every sale there is a Cost of Goods Sold/Inventory entry to update the Inventory balance and expense the cost.

The quantity discount is not recorded since it is deducted from the invoice at the time of sale.

Freight is recorded in the Inventory account under the perpetual system. The shipping terms were FOB supplier's warehouse, which means that once they left the supplier, title passed and the goods were Oak Sales' responsibility.

When goods are returned to the supplier, Inventory must also be updated to reflect this.

This transaction was eligible for a 2 percent discount, so the amount needed to finance this purchase has a $300 deduction.

A discount is recorded directly to the Inventory account using the perpetual method.

(Continued)

(Continued)

Sep. 28	Cash	6,860	
	Sales Discounts	140	
	Accounts Receivable		7,000
	To record receipt of payment from the Sep. 18 sale on account, less the Sep. 22 sales return and the sales discount. The sales discount was \$140 [(\$9,000 − \$2,000) × 0.02]. The cash received was \$6,860 [(\$9,000 − \$2,000) × 0.98].		
29	Accounts Payable	5,600	
	Cash		5,600
	To record payment of \$7,000 Sep. 3 purchase on account, less \$1,400 return on Sep. 9. Since the payment is not within the discount period, no discount is taken.		
30	Inventory	4,500	
	Cash		4,500
	To record cash purchase. Received a quantity discount of \$140, so final cost was \$4,500 (\$4,640 − \$140).		

Requirement 2

Accounts Receivable

Sep. 18	9,000	Sep. 22	2,000
		28	7,000
Bal.	0		

Accounts Payable

		Sep. 3	7,000
Sep. 9	1,400	15	15,000
24	15,000		
29	5,600		
		Bal.	0

Inventory

Sep. 3	7,000	Sep. 9	1,400
15	15,000	12	3,000
16	1,200	18	4,500
22	1,000	24	300
30	4,500		
Bal.	19,500		

Cost of Goods Sold

Sep. 12	3,000	Sep. 22	1,000
18	4,500		
Bal.	6,500		

Requirement 3

Sales	− Sales returns and discounts	− Cost of goods sold	= Gross margin
\$6,000 + \$9,000	− \$2,000 − \$140	− \$6,500	= \$6,360

Chapter 5 Appendix A

ACCOUNTING FOR MERCHANDISE IN A PERIODIC INVENTORY SYSTEM

Purchasing Merchandise in the Periodic Inventory System

LO A1

How can we track purchases and sales when we don't know how much inventory we have until the end of the period?

Some businesses find it too expensive to invest in a computerized (perpetual) inventory system that keeps up-to-the-minute records of merchandise on hand and cost of goods sold. Sometimes the nature of the inventory makes the perpetual inventory system impractical. These businesses use the periodic inventory system.

Recording Purchases of Inventory

All inventory systems use the Inventory account. But in a periodic inventory system, purchases, purchase discounts, purchase returns and allowances, and transportation costs are recorded in separate expense accounts bearing these titles. Let's account for the Slopes Ski Shop purchase of the Neige Sportswear goods shown in Exhibit 5–3. The following entries record the purchase and payment on account within the discount period:

May 27	Purchases	700	
	Accounts Payable		700
	Purchased inventory on account.		
Jun. 10	Accounts Payable	700	
	Cash		686
	Purchase Discounts		14
	Paid for inventory on account within the discount period. The discount is $14 ($700 × 0.02).		

The Inventory account is not updated until the end of the period.

Recording Purchase Returns and Allowances

Suppose instead that, prior to payment, Slopes returned to Neige goods costing $450 and also received from Neige a purchase allowance of $25. Slopes would record these transactions as follows:

Jun. 3	Accounts Payable	450	
	Purchase Returns and Allowances		450
	Returned inventory to seller.		
Jun. 4	Accounts Payable	25	
	Purchase Returns and Allowances		25
	Received a purchase allowance.		

During the period, the business records the cost of all inventory bought in the Purchases account. The balance of Purchases is the original or gross amount because it does not include subtractions for purchase discounts, returns, or allowances.

	Purchase (*debit* balance account)
(Contra account)	− **Purchase Discounts** (*credit* balance account)
(Contra account)	− **Purchase Returns and Allowances** (*credit* balance account)
	= **Net purchases** (a *debit* subtotal, not a separate account)

Recording Transportation Costs

Under the periodic system, costs to transport purchased inventory from seller to buyer are debited to a separate expense account, as shown for payment of a $100 freight bill:

Jun. 1	Freight-in	100	
	Cash		100
	Paid a freight bill.		

Recording Sales of Inventory

Recording sales is streamlined in the periodic system. ***With no running record of inventory to maintain***, we can record a $3,000 sale as follows:

Jul. 10	Accounts Receivable	3,000	
	Sales Revenue		3,000
	Sale on account.		

No accompanying entry to Inventory and Cost of Goods Sold is required in the periodic system.

Accounting for sales discounts and sales returns and allowances is the same as in the perpetual inventory system except that there are no entries to Inventory and Cost of Goods Sold.

Try It!

9. Refer to the Royal Fashion Distributors transactions in Try It #2 on page 256. Royal engaged in those transactions during June 2020, the first month of the company's fiscal year. Assume the company uses a periodic inventory system and had no inventory on hand prior to June 3. Journalize the transactions. No explanations are required.

Solutions appear at the end of this chapter and on **MyLab Accounting**

COST OF GOODS SOLD

LO (A2)

How do we compute the cost of goods sold amount under the periodic inventory system?

Under the periodic inventory method, the cost of goods sold is *calculated* at the end of the period instead of being tracked as a balance during the period in the perpetual inventory system. Once the cost of the goods remaining in inventory at the end of the period (ending inventory) is determined by the inventory count, then we can calculate the cost of the inventory sold during the period. To do this, follow these steps:

- Determine the cost of the goods that were in inventory at the beginning of the period, which is beginning inventory. This is the same amount as the prior period's ending inventory.
- Add the cost of goods purchased during the period. Adding beginning inventory and purchases will give the cost of the goods available for sale during the period.
- Subtract the cost of the goods on hand at the end of the period (ending inventory, based on the inventory count).

The formula for cost of goods sold is demonstrated in the graphic below:

Beginning Inventory + Cost of Goods Purchased = Goods Available for Sale − Ending Inventory = Cost of Goods Sold

Exhibit 5A–1, Panel A, is an expansion of the cost of goods sold formula showing how the Cost of Goods Purchased (or Net purchases fits into the calculation. Panel B is a different way to remember the same information.

EXHIBIT 5A–1 | Measuring Cost of Goods Sold in the Periodic Inventory System

Panel A

Beginning inventory
+ Net purchases ←
+ Freight-in
= Cost of goods available for sale
− Ending inventory
= Cost of goods sold ←

Purchases of inventory
− Purchase discounts
− Purchase returns and allowances
= Net Purchases

In a periodic system, cost of goods sold must be computed and is not a ledger account.

Panel B

Start + Buy − Count = Sold

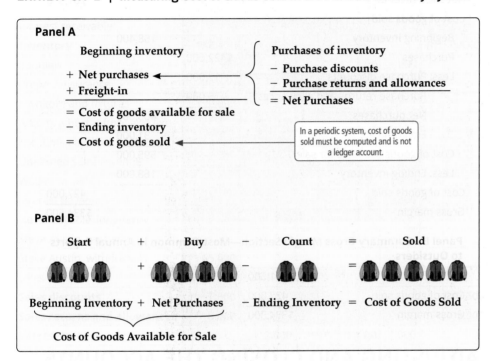

Beginning Inventory + Net Purchases − Ending Inventory = Cost of Goods Sold

Cost of Goods Available for Sale

Try It!

10. Refer to Royal Fashion Distributors journal entries created in Try It #9 on page 270. Calculate cost of goods sold and gross profit assuming ending inventory is $11,000 and beginning inventory was $0.

Solutions appear at the end of this chapter and on **MyLab Accounting**

Exhibit 5A–2 shows Slopes' net sales revenue, cost of goods sold (including net purchases and freight-in), and gross margin on the income statement for the periodic system. (All amounts are assumed.)

Journalizing the Closing Entries in the Periodic Inventory System

Exhibit 5A–4 gives Slopes' closing entries. Here is an explanation of each entry:

❶ Debits the revenue accounts and the contra expenses (Purchase Discounts and Purchase Returns and Allowances) and credits income summary.

❷ Debits Income Summary and credits the contra revenue accounts (Sales Discounts and Sales Returns and Allowances) and all the expenses, including Purchases and Freight-in.

Closing entries ❸ and ❹ are new.

❸ Debits Income Summary for the amount of the beginning balance of the Inventory account and credits Inventory.

❹ Debits Inventory for its ending balance, which was determined by the count of inventory at the end of the period and credits Income Summary.

Closing entries ❺ and ❻ finish the closing process by updating the profit or loss (Income Summary) to the owner's Capital account and closing the Withdrawals account to Capital.

EXHIBIT 5A–4 | Closing Entries for the Periodic Inventory System

	Closing Entries			
❶	Dec. 31	Sales Revenue	777,000	
		Interest Revenue	3,000	
		Purchase Discounts	12,000	
		Purchase Returns and Allowances	5,000	
		Income Summary		797,000
❷	Dec. 31	Income Summary	674,600	
		Sales Discounts		7,500
		Sales Returns and Allowances		8,000
		Purchases		422,600
		Freight-in		31,000
		Wages Expense		142,000
		Rent Expense		48,000
		Amortization Expense		6,000
		Insurance Expense		4,000
		Supplies Expense		1,000
		Interest Expense		4,500
❸	Dec. 31	Income Summary	158,400	
		Inventory (beginning balance)		158,400
❹	Dec. 31	Inventory (ending balance)	168,000	
		Income Summary		168,000
❺	Dec. 31	Income Summary	132,000	
		Steve Austin, Capital		132,000
		($797,000 – $674,600 – $158,400 + $168,000)		
❻	Dec. 31	Steve Austin, Capital	65,000	
		Steve Austin, Withdrawals		65,000

These entries update the Inventory ledger account

Now Inventory has its correct ending balance as shown below.

Inventory

Jan. 1 Bal.	158,400	Dec. 31 Clo. ❸	158,400
Dec. 31 Clo. ❹	168,000		
Dec. 31 Bal.	168,000		

Correct ending balance

The entries to the Inventory account deserve additional explanation. Recall that before the closing process Inventory still has the period's beginning balance. At the end of the period, this balance is one year old and must be replaced with the ending balance so that the financial statements can be prepared at December 31, 2020.

Try It!

11. Refer to Royal Fashion's journal entries created in Try It #10. on page 271. The inventory count at the end of June 2020 showed an amount of $11,000 on hand. Using this information, prepare the closing entries using the periodic inventory method.

PREPARING THE FINANCIAL STATEMENTS OF A MERCHANDISER

LO (A4)

How can we prepare financial statements for a company using the periodic inventory system?

Exhibit 5A–5 presents Slopes Ski Shop's financial statements. The *income statement* through gross margin repeats Exhibit 5A–2.

Net sales, cost of goods sold, operating income, and net income are unaffected by the choice of inventory system. You can prove this by comparing Slopes' financial statements given in Exhibit 5A–5 with the corresponding statements in Exhibit 5–9, 5–10, and 5–11. The only differences appear within the cost of goods sold section of the income statement.

EXHIBIT 5A–5 | Financial Statements of Slopes Ski Shop (Periodic Inventory System)

SLOPES SKI SHOP Income Statement For the Year Ended December 31, 2020			
Sales revenue			$777,000
Less: Sales discounts		$ 7,500	
Sales returns and allowances		8,000	15,500
Net sales revenue			761,500
Cost of goods sold			
Beginning inventory		158,400	
Purchases	$ 422,600		
Less: Purchase discounts	12,000		
Purchase returns and allowances	5,000		
Net purchases		405,600	
Freight-in		31,000	
Cost of goods available for sale		595,000	
Less: Ending inventory		168,000	
Cost of goods sold			427,000
Gross margin			334,500
Operating expenses			201,000
Income from operations			133,500
Other revenue and expense			
Interest revenue		3,000	
Less: Interest expense		4,500	1,500
Net income			$132,000

SLOPES SKI SHOP Statement of Owner's Equity For the Year Ended December 31, 2020	
Steve Austin, capital, January 1, 2020	$ 90,000
Add: Net income	132,000
	222,000
Less: Withdrawals	65,000
Steve Austin, capital, December 31, 2020	$157,000

SLOPES SKI SHOP Balance Sheet December 31, 2020					
Assets			**Liabilities**		
Current assets			Current liabilities		
Cash	$ 6,000		Accounts payable	$128,000	
Accounts receivable	24,000		Unearned sales revenue	1,500	
Note receivable	32,000		Wages payable	3,000	
Interest receivable	1,000		Interest payable	500	
Inventory	168,000		Total current liabilities		$133,000
Prepaid insurance	600		Long-term liabilities		
Supplies	500		Notes payable		44,100
Total current assets		$232,100	Total liabilities		177,100
Property, plant and equipment					
Furniture and fixtures	$120,000		**Owner's Equity**		
Less: Accumulated amortization	18,000		S. Austin, capital		157,000
Total property, plant, and equipment		102,000			
Total assets		$334,100	Total liabilities and owner's equity		$334,100

Summary Problem for Your Review

CHAPTER 5 APPENDIX A

Use the data for Oak Sales Company from page 266, except that this time assume that Oak Sales Company uses a periodic inventory system instead of the perpetual system in that example.

Another Summary Problem for Your Review for this appendix is available in MyLab Accounting, which covers preparing worksheets, making adjusting and closing entries, preparing financial statements, and computing inventory turnover.

Required

1. Journalize the transactions and include any calculations in the journal entry explanations.
2. The inventory count at the end of September 2020 showed $19,500 of inventory on hand. Using this information and the amounts from the journal entries created in Requirement 1, compute the cost of goods sold under the periodic inventory system for Oak Sales Company for the month ended September 30, 2020.
3. Prepare the closing entries under the periodic inventory system for Oak Sales Company for the month ended September 30, 2020. Assume no other transactions took place during September 2020.

SOLUTION

Requirement 1

2020			
Sep. 3	Purchases	7,000	
	Accounts Payable		7,000
	To record purchase on account, terms 1/10, net eom.		
9	Accounts Payable	1,400	
	Purchase Returns and Allowances		1,400
	Returned 20% of Sep. 3 purchase—goods were defective ($7,000 × 0.20).		
12	Cash	6,000	
	Sales Revenue		6,000
	To record sale of goods for cash.		
15	Purchases	15,000	
	Accounts Payable		15,000
	To record purchase on account, terms 2/15, n/30. Received a quantity discount of $400 ($15,400 − $400 = $15,000).		
16	Freight-in	1,200	
	Cash		1,200
	To record payment of the freight bill for the Sep. 15 purchase.		
18	Accounts Receivable	9,000	
	Sales Revenue		9,000
	To record sale of goods on account, terms 2/10, n/30.		

Using the periodic inventory system, acquisitions are recorded in a separate account and there is no running balance of inventory.

A separate account is used for purchase returns.

A separate account is used for freight-in, which is used in the calculation of cost of goods sold.

(*Continued*)

(Continued)

Sep. 22	Sales Returns and Allowances	2,000	
	Accounts Receivable		2,000
	To record return of goods sold on Sep. 18—wrong size.		
24	Cash	14,700	
	Note Payable		14,700
	Borrowed money from the bank, signing a note payable, to pay for Sep. 15 purchase. Amount borrowed calculated as $14,700 [$15,000 − (0.02 × $15,000)].		
24	Accounts Payable	15,000	
	Purchase Discounts		300
	Cash		14,700
	To record payment of Sep. 15 purchase, taking the 2% discount. Cash payment is calculated as $14,700 [$15,000 − (0.02 × $15,000)]. The discount is $300 ($15,000 × 0.02)].		
28	Cash	6,860	
	Sales Discounts	140	
	Accounts Receivable		7,000
	To record receipt of payment from the Sep. 18 sale on account, less the Sep. 22 sales return and less the sales discount. The sales discount was $140 [(9,000 − $2,000) × 0.02]. The cash received was $6,860 [(9,000 − $2,000) × 0.98].		
29	Accounts Payable	5,600	
	Cash		5,600
	To record payment of $7,000 Sep. 3 purchase on account, less $1,400 return on Sep. 9. Since the payment is not within the discount period, no discount is taken.		
30	Purchases	4,500	
	Cash		4,500
	To record cash purchase. Received a quantity discount of $140, so final cost was $4,500 ($4,640 − $140)].		

Using the periodic method, a separate account is used for purchase discounts and factors into the net purchases calculation.

Requirement 2

Cost of goods sold in the periodic inventory system is calculated as follows:

Beginning inventory (given)		$ 0
+ Net purchases, calculated as:		
Purchases of inventory ($7,000 + $15,000 + $4,500)	$ 26,500	
− Purchase discounts	300	
− Purchases returns and allowances	1,400	24,800
+ Freight-in		1,200
= Cost of goods available for sale		26,000
− Ending inventory (given)		19,500
= Cost of goods sold		$ 6,500

A company must complete a physical count to enter the ending inventory number.

Requirement 3

	2020			
❶	Sep. 30	Sales Revenue	15,000	
		Purchase Discounts	300	
		Purchase Returns and Allowances	1,400	
		Income Summary		16,700
		To close all revenue and contra expense accounts.		
❷	Sep. 30	Income Summary	29,840	
		Sales Discounts		140
		Sales Returns and Allowances		2,000
		Purchases		26,500
		Freight-in		1,200
		To close all expense and contra revenue accounts.		
❸	Sep. 30	Income Summary	0	
		Inventory		0
		To record the beginning inventory balance.		
❹	Sep. 30	Inventory	19,500	
		Income Summary		19,500
		To record the ending inventory balance.		
❺	Sep. 30	Income Summary	6,360	
		Capital		6,360
		To close net income from Income Summary ($16,700 − $29,840 + $19,500 = $6,360) to the Capital account		

[$6,000 + $9,000]

[$7,000 + $15,000 + $4,500]

Using the periodic method, this closing entry is the only way inventory is updated to carry forward a balance for the next period. This number is derived from a physical count

Chapter 5 Appendix B

COMPARING THE PERPETUAL AND PERIODIC INVENTORY SYSTEMS

Exhibit 5B–1 provides a side-by-side comparison of the two inventory accounting systems. It gives the journal entries, the T-accounts, and all financial statement effects of both inventory systems.

LO (B1)

How do the inventory systems compare?

EXHIBIT 5B–1 | Comparing the Perpetual and Periodic Inventory Systems (amounts assumed)

Panel A—Recording in the Journal and Posting to the Accounts

Perpetual System	Periodic System

1. Credit purchases of $600,000:

Inventory	600,000			Purchases	600,000		
Accounts Payable		600,000		Accounts Payable		600,000	

2. Credit sales of $1,000,000 (cost $550,000):

Accounts Receivable	1,000,000			Accounts Receivable	1,000,000		
Sales Revenue		1,000,000		Sales Revenue		1,000,000	

Cost of Goods Sold	550,000		Note that there is no Cost of Goods Sold entry.
Inventory		550,000	

3. End-of-period entries:

No entries required. Both Inventory and Cost of Goods Sold are up to date.

a. Transfer the cost of beginning inventory ($100,000) to Income Summary:

Income Summary	100,000	
Inventory		100,000

b. Record the cost of ending inventory ($150,000) based on a physical count:

Inventory	150,000	
Income Summary		150,000

c. Transfer the cost of purchases to Income Summary:

Income Summary	600,000	
Purchases		600,000

T-accounts after closing completed:

Inventory		Cost of Goods Sold		Inventory		Income Summary	
100,000*	550,000	550,000	550,000	100,000*	100,000	100,000	150,000
600,000				150,000		600,000	
150,000				150,000		550,000	550,000

* Beginning inventory was 100,000

Panel B—Reporting in the Financial Statements

Perpetual System	Periodic System

Income Statement (partial)

Perpetual		Periodic		
Sales revenue	$1,000,000	Sales revenue		$1,000,000
Cost of goods sold	550,000	Cost of goods sold		
Gross margin	$ 450,000	Beginning inventory	$100,000	
		Purchases	600,000	
		Cost of goods available for sale	700,000	
		Less: Ending inventory	150,000	
		Cost of goods sold		550,000
		Gross margin		$ 450,000

Balance Sheet (partial)

Perpetual			Periodic		
Current assets			Current assets		
Cash	$	XXX	Cash	$	XXX
Accounts receivable		XXX	Accounts receivable		XXX
Inventory		150,000	Inventory		150,000

Summary

Learning Objectives

① Use sales and gross margin to evaluate a company **Pg. 244**

How can we use sales information to evaluate a company?

- The major revenue of a merchandising business is sales revenue, or net sales. The major expense is cost of goods sold.

$$\text{Net sales} - \text{Cost of goods sold} = \text{Gross margin, or gross profit}$$

- Gross margin measures the business's success or failure in selling its products at a higher price than it paid for them.

② Account for the purchase and sale of inventory under the perpetual inventory system **Pg. 247**

How can we track the purchase and sale of inventory as transactions occur?

- The accounting cycle is from cash to inventory as the inventory is purchased for resale, and back to cash as the inventory is sold.
- An invoice is the document generated by a purchase or sale transaction.
- Most merchandisers offer purchase returns to their customers to allow them to return unsuitable merchandise and allowances for damaged goods that the buyer chooses to keep.
- Some suppliers offer their customers purchase discounts to encourage them to pay their invoice promptly within the discount period.
- A merchandiser keeps a continuous record for each inventory item to show the inventory on hand at all times.

$$\text{Sales revenue} - \text{Sales discounts} - \text{Sales returns and allowances} = \text{Net sales revenue}$$

③ Adjust and close the accounts of a merchandising business under the perpetual inventory system **Pg. 256**

How can we adjust for inventory shrinkage and begin the next cycle using the perpetual inventory system?

- The end-of-period adjusting and closing process of a merchandising business is similar to that of a service business.
- In addition, a merchandiser adjusts inventory for theft losses, damage, and accounting errors normally discovered from the physical count of the inventory.

④ Prepare a merchandiser's financial statements under the perpetual inventory system **Pg. 259**

How can we prepare financial statements for a company using the perpetual inventory system?

- The income statement may appear in the single-step format or the multi-step format.
  - The single-step format has only two sections—one for revenues and the other for expenses.
  - The multi-step format has subtotals for gross margin and income from operations. (It is the most widely used format.)

⑤ Use the gross margin percentage and the inventory turnover ratio to evaluate a business **Pg. 263**

How can we use ratios to evaluate a business?

$$\text{Gross margin percentage} = \frac{\text{Gross margin}}{\text{Net sales revenue}}$$

$$\text{Inventory turnover} = \frac{\text{Cost of goods sold}}{\text{Average inventory}} = \frac{\text{Cost of goods sold}}{\dfrac{\text{Beginning inventory} + \text{Ending inventory}}{2}}$$

$$\text{Inventory turnover in days} = \frac{365}{\text{inventory turnover}}$$

⑥ Describe the effect of IFRS on merchandising operations **Pg. 265**

How does IFRS affect companies that sell inventory?

- Revenue recognition standards differ in how specific they are about the process of 'recognizing' performance obligations. IFRS expectations are more detailed.

(A1) Account for the purchase and sale of inventory under the periodic inventory system **Pg. 269**

How can we track the purchases and sales when we don't know how much inventory we have until the end of the period?

- Under the periodic inventory system, merchandisers do not keep a continuous record of the inventory on hand. Instead, at the end of the period, the merchandiser makes a physical count of the inventory on hand and applies the cost per item to calculate the cost of the ending inventory.
  - Record purchases of inventory in the Purchases account.
  - Record freight-in, purchase discounts, and purchase returns and allowances in separate contra accounts.
  - When recording sales, there is no entry to record the cost of goods sold.

(A2) Compute the cost of goods sold under the periodic inventory system **Pg. 270**

How do we compute the cost of goods sold amount under the periodic inventory system?

- Cost of goods sold is computed at the end of the period using the cost of goods sold formula:

	Beginning inventory
+	Net purchases
+	Freight-in
=	Cost of goods available for sale
−	Ending inventory
=	Cost of goods sold

- The physical inventory count gives the amount of ending inventory that is required by the cost of goods sold formula.
- There is no Cost of Goods Sold account like there is under the perpetual inventory system.

(A3) Adjust and close the accounts of a merchandising business under the periodic inventory system **Pg. 272**

How do we update inventory using the year-end physical count and begin the next cycle using the periodic inventory system?

- Purchases, Purchase Returns and Allowances, and Freight-in accounts are all closed to the Income Summary account.
- The opening inventory amount is debited to Income Summary and credited to Inventory to remove opening inventory from the balance sheet.
- The closing inventory amount (based on the inventory count) is debited to Inventory and credited to Income Summary to place closing inventory on the balance sheet.
- The result of these inventory transactions in the Income Summary account is that the cost of goods sold amount appears on the income statement and Inventory on the balance sheet is the closing inventory at year-end.

(A4) Prepare a merchandiser's financial statements under the periodic inventory system **Pg. 275**

How can we prepare financial statements for a company using the periodic inventory system?

- The financial statements report the same results regardless of whether the merchandiser uses the periodic inventory system or the perpetual inventory system.

The only difference is on the income statement:

  - The cost of goods sold amount is an account balance under the perpetual inventory system.
  - The cost of goods sold amount is a calculation under the periodic inventory system.

(B1) Compare the perpetual and periodic inventory systems **Pg. 280**

How do the inventory systems compare?

- In the perpetual system:
  - Inventory purchases are recorded in the Inventory account.
  - Each sale has a transaction that records the cost of the sale and updates inventory, providing the current level.
- In the periodic system:
  - Inventory purchases are recorded in the Purchases account, which is an expense account.
  - Only the sale is recorded. There is no Inventory update. The cost of goods sold is calculated only at the end of the period.

- Both inventory systems:
  - Require a physical count of inventory at least once per year, usually at the end of the period.
  - Report the same financial results at the end of the period since both adjust Inventory to match the amount based on the physical count.

Key Terms for the chapter are shown next and are in the **Glossary** at the back of the book. **Similar Terms** are shown after **Key Terms**.

KEY TERMS

2/15, n/30 Credit terms offered by some merchandisers, meaning that if the invoice is paid within 15 days of the invoice date (the *discount period*), a 2 percent discount may be taken. If not, the full amount (net) is due in 30 days. Also shown as *2/15, net 30 (p. 249).*

Bill Another term for *invoice (p. 248).*

Cash discount Another name for a purchase discount *(p. 249).*

Cost of goods sold The cost of the inventory that the business has sold to customers; the largest single expense of most merchandising businesses. Also called *cost of sales (p. 244).*

Cost of sales Another name for *cost of goods sold (p. 244).*

Credit memo The document issued by a seller to reduce a customer's accounts receivable *(p. 254).*

Debit memo The document issued by a buyer to reduce the buyer's account payable to a seller *(p. 250).*

Discount period The time period during which a cash discount is available and a reduced payment can be made by the purchaser *(p. 249).*

Eom A credit term that means an invoice amount is due by the end of the month *(p. 249).*

FOB destination Legal title passes to the buyer only when the inventory reaches the destination (i.e., the seller pays the freight) *(p. 251).*

FOB shipping point Legal title passes to the buyer as soon as the inventory leaves the seller's place of business—the shipping point *(p. 251).*

Freight-in The transportation costs on purchased goods (i.e., from the wholesaler to the retailer) *(p. 252).*

Freight-out The transportation costs on goods sold (i.e., from the retailer to the customer) *(p. 252).*

Gross margin Excess of sales revenue over cost of goods sold. Also called *gross profit (p. 244).*

Gross margin percentage Gross margin divided by net sales revenue. A measure of profitability *(p. 263).*

Gross profit Another name for *gross margin (p. 250).*

Income from operations Another name for *operating income (p. 260).*

Inventory All goods that a company owns and expects to sell in the normal course of operation *(p. 244).*

Inventory turnover The ratio of cost of goods sold to average inventory. Measures the number of times a company sells its average level of inventory during a year *(p. 264).*

Invoice A seller's request for cash from the purchaser *(p. 248).*

Legal title The legal ownership of property *(p. 251).*

Multi-step income statement An income statement format that contains subtotals to highlight significant relationships. In addition to net income, it also presents gross margin and income from operations *(p. 261).*

Net purchases Purchases plus freight-in and less purchase discounts and purchase returns and allowances *(p. 252).*

Net sales Sales revenue less sales discounts and sales returns and allowances *(p. 254).*

Operating expense Expense, other than cost of goods sold, that is incurred in the entity's major line of business: rent, amortization, salaries, wages, utilities, property tax, and supplies expense *(p. 259).*

Operating income Gross margin minus operating expenses plus any other operating revenues. Also called *income from operations (p. 260).*

Other revenue and expense Revenues and/or expenses that are outside the main operations of a business, such as a gain or losson the sale of capital assets *(p. 260).*

Periodic inventory system A type of inventory accounting system in which the business does not keep a continuous record of the inventory on hand. Instead, at the end of the period the business makes a physical count of the on-hand inventory and applies the appropriate unit costs to determine the cost of the ending inventory *(p. 246).*

Perpetual inventory system A type of accounting inventory system in which the business keeps a continuous record for each inventory item to show the inventory on hand at all times *(p. 247).*

Pledged as collateral Ownership of asset is promised to a lender in case payment is not made, then the goods would be sold to pay balance owing *(p. 262).*

Purchase allowance A negotiated decrease in the amount the purchaser owes the seller. *(p. 250).*

Purchase discount A reduction in the purchase price granted to the purchaser for paying within the discount period. Also called a *cash discount (p. 249).*

Purchase order A legal document that represents a business's intention to buy goods *(p. 248).*

Quantity discount A reduction in the purchase price of an item based on the quantity of the item purchased; the greater the quantity purchased, the lower the price per item *(p. 248).*

Sales Another name for *sales revenue (p. 244).*

Sales discount A reduction in the amount receivable from a customer offered by the seller as an incentive for the customer to pay promptly. A contra account to sales revenue *(p. 254).*

Sales returns and allowances A decrease in the seller's receivable from a customer's return of merchandise or from granting the customer an allowance from the amount the customer owes the seller. A contra account to sales revenue *(p. 254)*.

Sales revenue The amount that a merchandiser earns from selling inventory before subtracting expenses. Also called *sales (p. 244)*.

Shrinkage A reduction in the amount of inventory due to theft, spoilage, or error *(p. 257)*.

Single-step income statement An income statement format that groups all revenues together and then lists and deducts all expenses together without drawing any subtotals *(p. 261)*.

SIMILAR TERMS

2/15, net 30	2/15, n/30
Cost of goods sold, COGS, CGS	Cost of sales
FOB destination	CIF destination (CIF stands for cost, insurance, and freight)
Freight-in or **Freight-out**	Freight; Transportation-in; Transportation costs
Gross margin	Gross profit
Gross margin percentage	Gross profit percentage
Operating income	Income from operations
Invoice	Bill
List price	Full price; Price with no discounts deducted
Purchase discount	Cash discount; Discount given to reward prompt payment
Quantity discount	Volume discount; Discount given to reward purchase of more than one of a particular item
Sales revenue	Sales

SELF-STUDY QUESTIONS

Test your understanding of the chapter by marking the correct answer for each of the following questions:

1. The major expense of a merchandising business is *(p. 244)*
   a. Cost of goods sold b. Amortization
   c. Rent d. Interest
2. Sales total $445,000, cost of goods sold is $220,000, and operating expenses are $175,000. How much is gross margin? *(p. 244)*
   a. $445,000 b. $50,000
   c. $270,000 d. $225,000
3. A purchase discount results from *(p. 249)*
   a. Returning goods to the seller
   b. Receiving a purchase allowance from the seller
   c. Buying a large enough quantity of merchandise to get the discount
   d. Paying within the discount period
4. Which of the following is *not* an account? *(p. 254)*
   a. Sales Revenue b. Net Sales
   c. Inventory d. Supplies Expense
5. If a merchandiser's beginning inventory was $60,000, it purchased $125,000 during the period, and a count shows $50,000 of inventory on hand at the end of the period, what was the cost of the goods sold? *(p. 258)*
   a. $110,000 b. $75,000
   c. $185,000 d. $135,000
6. Which account causes the main difference between a merchandiser's adjusting and closing process and that of a service business? *(p. 259)*
   a. Advertising Expense b. Interest Revenue
   c. Cost of Goods Sold d. Accounts Receivable
7. The closing entry for Sales Discounts includes *(p. 259)*
   a. Sales Discounts
      Income Summary
   b. Sales Discounts
      Sales Revenue
   c. Income Summary
      Sales Discounts
   d. Not used: Sales Discounts is a permanent account, which is not closed.
8. Which income statement format reports income from operations? *(p. 260)*
   a. Account format b. Single-step format
   c. Report format d. Multi-step format
9. A company has sales of $375,000, cost of goods sold of $225,000, average inventory during the year of $75,000, and ending inventory of $90,000. The company's inventory turnover for the year is *(p. 264)*
   a. 3.00 times b. 2.50 times
   c. 5.00 times d. 2.00 times
10. Refer to Self-Study Question 9. About how many days does it take the inventory to turn over? *(p. 264)*
    a. 122 b. 88
    c. 146 d. 73

Answers to Self-Study Questions

1. a 2. d ($445,000 − $220,000 = $225,000) 3. d 4. b 5. d 6. c 7. c
8. d 9. a 10. a (365 days ÷ 3.00 times = 122 days)

Assignment Material

MyLab Accounting Make the grade with MyLab Accounting: The Starters, Exercises, and Problems can be found on MyLab. You can practise them as often as you want, and most feature step-by-step guided instructions to help you find the right answer.

QUESTIONS

1. Gross margin is often mentioned in the business press as an important measure of success. What does gross margin measure, and why is it important?
2. Describe the operating cycle for (a) the purchase and cash sale of inventory, and (b) the purchase and sale of inventory on account.
3. What is cost of goods sold, and where is it reported?
4. What are two types of inventory accounting systems? Briefly describe each.
5. Indicate which accounts are debited and credited under the perpetual inventory system for (a) a credit purchase of inventory and the subsequent cash payment, and (b) a credit sale of inventory and the subsequent cash collection. Assume no discounts, returns, allowances, or freight.
6. Inventory costing $9,600 is purchased and invoiced on July 28 under terms of 2/10, n/30. Compute the payment amount on August 6. How much would the payment be on August 9? What explains the difference? What is the latest acceptable payment date under the terms of sale?
7. Inventory listed at $80,000 is sold subject to a quantity discount of $6,000 and under payment terms of 1/15, n/45. What is the net sales revenue on this sale if the customer pays within 15 days?
8. Name the new contra accounts introduced in this chapter.
9. Describe FOB shipping point. When does the buyer take ownership of the goods, and who pays the freight?
10. You are evaluating two companies as possible investments. One entity sells services; the other entity is a merchandiser. How can you identify the merchandiser by examining the two entities' balance sheets and income statements?
11. You are beginning the adjusting and closing process at the end of your company's fiscal year. Does the unadjusted trial balance carry the final ending amount of inventory if your company uses the perpetual inventory system? Why or why not?
12. Give the adjusting entry for inventory if shrinkage is $5,000 on December 31.
13. What is the identifying characteristic of the "other" category of revenues and expenses? Give an example of each.
14. Name and describe two formats for the income statement, and identify the type of business to which each format best applies.
15. Which financial statement reports sales discounts and sales returns and allowances? Show how they are reported, using any reasonable amounts in your illustration.
16. Does a merchandiser prefer a high or a low rate of inventory turnover? Explain.
17. In general, what does a low gross margin percentage suggest about a business's pricing strategy?

*18. In the periodic inventory system, what is meant by the term "cost of goods available for sale"?

*19. In a periodic inventory system, why must inventory be physically counted to determine cost of goods sold?

*20. Beginning inventory is $20,000, net purchases total $45,000, and freight-in is $4,000. If ending inventory is $29,000, what is cost of goods sold?

*21. Why do accountants use a Purchases account when inventory items are acquired in a periodic inventory system?

*22. How are purchase discounts accounted for in a periodic inventory system?

*23. Suppose you are starting a new retail business. What factors would you consider in determining whether to implement a periodic or a perpetual inventory system?

*These Questions cover Chapter 5 Appendix A or B topics.

STARTERS

(1) Practice using accounting terminology

S5-1 Match the accounting terminology to the definitions.

1. Cost of Goods Sold	a. An inventory system that requires businesses to obtain a physical count of inventory to determine quantities on hand.
2. Perpetual inventory system	b. Expenses, other than Cost of Goods Sold, that are incurred in the entity's major ongoing operations.
3. Periodic inventory system	c. Excess of Sales Revenue over Cost of Goods Sold.
4. Operating expenses	d. The cost of inventory that the business has sold to customers.
5. Gross margin	e. Goods the company owns and expects to sell to customers in the normal course of operations.
6. Inventory	f. An inventory system that keeps a running record of inventory.

(1) Compare the perpetual and periodic inventory systems

S5-2 For each statement below, identify whether the statement applies to the periodic inventory system or the perpetual inventory system:

a. Normally used for relatively inexpensive goods.
b. Keeps a running computerized record of inventory.
c. Achieves better control over inventory.
d. Requires a physical count of inventory to determine the quantities on hand.
e. Uses bar codes to keep up-to-the-minute records of inventory.

(2) Account for the total purchase cost of inventory

S5-3 Suppose Marks uses the perpetual inventory system to purchase T-shirts on account for $15,000 from an overseas supplier. It cost Marks $1,000 FOB supplier to ship the T-shirts as well as duty and excise fees of $200. Marks was also fined $300 for unloading the inventory in an unauthorized area.

1. Compute the cost of inventory to Marks.
2. Marks pays $500 cash to deliver the goods to three regional retail outlets. How would this cost be recorded?

(2) Compute inventory balance

S5-4 The following data pertain to Zari Scarf and Hat for the year ended December 31, 2020:

Beginning inventory	$190,300
Purchases of inventory on credit during the year	$450,000
Cost of goods sold during the year	65% of sales
Sales (75% on credit) during the year	$800,000

a. Prepare entries for the following transactions using a perpetual inventory system:
   i. Purchase of inventory during 2020
   ii. Sales during 2020
   iii. Cost of goods sold during 2020
b. Compute the balance in the Inventory account on December 31, 2020.

(2) Accounting for the purchase of inventory, purchase discount—perpetual

b. $85,750

S5-5 Suppose Toys Plus uses the perpetual inventory system and buys $100,000 of LEGO toys on credit terms of 2/15, n/45. Some of the goods are damaged in shipment, so Toys Plus returns $12,500 of the merchandise to LEGO. How much must Toys Plus pay LEGO:

a. After the discount period?
b. Within the discount period?

S5-6 Refer to the Toys Plus situation in S5-5 and journalize the following transactions on the books of Toys Plus. Explanations are not required.

a. Purchase of the goods on July 8, 2020.

b. Return of the damaged goods on July 12, 2020.

c. Payment on July 15, 2020.

d. In the end, how much did the inventory cost Toys Plus?

(2) Recording purchase, purchase return, and cash payment transactions—perpetual

c. Credit Cash, $85,750

S5-7 Details of purchase invoices, including shipping terms, credit terms, and returns, appear below. Compute the total amount to be paid in full settlement of each invoice, assuming that credit for returns is granted before the expiration of the discount period and payment is made within the discount period. (Hint: Assume FOB destination freight is included in the invoice price.)

(5) Purchases including shipping terms

a. $1,746

Invoice	Freight and Credit Terms	Transportation Charges	Returns and Allowances
a. $2,000	FOB destination, 3/10, n/45	$ 55	$200
b. $5,500	FOB shipping point, 2/10, n/30	$100	$ 50
c. $6,700	FOB shipping point, 2/10, n/45	$200	$350
d. $9,300	FOB destination, 2/10, n/60	$150	$550

S5-8 Consider the following transactions for Burlington Drug Store:

(2) Recording purchase transactions—perpetual

b. Net inventory cost, $18,278

Feb.	2	Burlington buys $23,800 worth of inventory on account with credit terms of 2/15, n/30, FOB shipping point.
	4	Burlington pays a $50 freight charge.
	9	Burlington returns $5,200 of the merchandise due to damage during shipment.
	14	Burlington pays the amount due, less return and discount.

Required

1. Journalize the purchase transactions. Explanations are not required.
2. In the final analysis, how much did the inventory cost Burlington Drug Store?

S5-9 Spanner Inc. sells $160,000 of women's sportswear to Lululime under credit terms of 2/10, net 30 on August 1, 2020. Spanner's cost of the goods is $76,000, and Spanner receives the appropriate amount of cash from Lululime on August 10, 2020. Assume Spanner Inc. uses the perpetual inventory system.

Journalize Spanner's transactions for August 1, 2020, and August 10, 2020.

(2) Recording sales transactions—perpetual

Cash receipt, $156,800

S5-10 Journalize the following sales transactions for Salem Sportswear. Explanations are not required.

(2) Recording sales, sales return, and collection entries—perpetual

Sales Discount, $1,860

Jul.	1	Salem sold $20,000 of men's sportswear for cash. Cost of goods sold is $10,000.
	3	Salem sold $62,000 of women's sportswear on account, credit terms are 3/10, n/30. Cost of goods is $31,000.
	5	Salem received a $4,500 sales return on damaged goods from the customer on July 1. Cost of goods damaged is $2,250. Money was refunded.
	10	Salem receives payment from the customer on the amount due, less discount.

S5-11 Beachcomber Paddle's Inventory account at January 31 showed a debit balance of $150,000. A physical count of inventory showed goods on hand of $147,000. Journalize the adjusting entry. Beachcomber Paddle uses the perpetual inventory system.

(3) Adjusting inventory for shrinkage—perpetual

③ Making closing entries—perpetual

Income Summary, $451,000

S5–12 Murphy RV Accessories' accounting records include the following accounts at December 31, 2020:

Cost of Goods Sold	$310,000	Accumulated Amortization	$300,000
Accounts Payable	24,000	Cash	20,000
Advertising Expense	40,000	Sales Revenue	620,000
Building	400,000	Amortization Expense	30,000
C. Murphy, Capital	355,000	C. Murphy, Withdrawals	30,000
Inventory	380,000	Sales Discounts	17,000
Land	100,000	Accounts Receivable	45,000
Selling Expenses	54,000		

Journalize the required closing entries for Murphy RV Accessories at December 31, 2020. The company uses the perpetual inventory system.

④ Preparing a merchandiser's income statement—perpetual

Net income, $23,000

S5–13 Suppose Dawson Communications uses the perpetual inventory system and reported these figures in its December 31, 2020, financial statements:

Accounts payable	$118,000
Accounts receivable	5,600
Accrued liabilities	3,200
Cash	7,600
Cost of goods sold	40,000
Equipment, net	17,400
Inventory	800
Long-term notes payable	1,800
Net sales revenue	100,000
Total operating expenses	37,000
V. Dawson, capital	18,400

Prepare Dawson Communications' multi-step income statement for the year ended December 31, 2020.

④ Preparing a merchandiser's balance sheet—perpetual

S5–14 Use the data in S5–13 to prepare Dawson Communications' classified balance sheet at December 31, 2020. Use the report format with all headings.

⑤ Computing inventory-related ratios

S5–15 Refer to the Dawson Communications situation in S5–13 and S5–14. Compute the gross margin percentage and rate of inventory turnover for 2020, rounding to one decimal place. One year earlier, at December 31, 2019, Dawson's Inventory balance was $600.

⑤ Computing gross margin percentage and inventory turnover

Gross margin percentage, 47.0%

S5–16 Networking Systems, which uses the perpetual inventory system, earned sales revenue of $66 million in 2020. Cost of goods sold was $35 million, and net income reached $16 million. Total current assets included inventory of $14.0 million at December 31, 2020. Last year's ending inventory was $13.2 million. The managers of Networking Systems need to know the company's gross margin percentage and rate of inventory turnover for 2020. Compute these amounts, rounding to one decimal place.

⑤ Shrinkage adjustment, computing and evaluating gross margin

S5–17 Georgian Book Shop's accounts at June 30, 2020, included the following unadjusted balances:

Inventory	$15,400
Cost of Goods Sold	40,300
Sales Revenue	85,300
Sales Discounts	1,400
Sales Returns and Allowances	2,000

Georgian Book Shop uses a perpetual inventory system. The cost calculated from the physical count of inventory on hand on June 30, 2020, was $5,000.

a. Journalize the adjustment for inventory shrinkage.

b. Compute the gross margin.

c. Compute the gross margin percentage. If the industry standard is 45%, how are they doing?

⑥ Accounting for a merchandiser using IFRS

S5–18 How do merchandisers who report under IFRS recognize revenue? Does this differ for companies that report under ASPE?

***S5–19** Suppose Toys Plus buys $200,000 of LEGO toys on January 15 on credit terms of 2/15, n/45. Some of the goods are damaged in shipment, so on January 20, Toys Plus returns $25,000 of the merchandise to LEGO. Assuming Toys Plus uses a periodic inventory system, how much must Toys Plus pay LEGO:

a. After the discount period?

b. Within the discount period?

c. Journalize the purchase of the goods. An explanation is not required.

d. Journalize the return of the damaged goods. An explanation is not required.

A1
Recording purchase and cash payment transactions—periodic system
b. $171,500

***S5–20** Spanner Inc. sells $160,000 of women's sportswear to Lululime under credit terms of 2/10, net 30 on August 1, 2020. Spanner's cost of goods sold is $76,000, and Spanner receives the appropriate amount of cash from Lululime on August 10, 2020. Assume Spanner Inc. uses a periodic inventory system.

Journalize Spanner's transactions for August 1, 2020, and August 10, 2020.

A1
Recording sales and cash collections—periodic system
Cash receipt, $156,800

***S5–21** Minit Company began the year with inventory of $16,000. During the year Minit purchased $180,000 of goods and returned $12,000 due to damage. Minit also paid freight charges of $1,500 on inventory purchases. At year-end, Minit's inventory based on the physical inventory count stood at $32,000. Minit uses the periodic inventory system.

Compute Minit Company's cost of goods sold for the year.

A2
Computing cost of goods sold—periodic system

***S5–22** The Wholesale Company began the year with inventory of $24,000. During the year, the company purchased $272,000 of goods and returned $18,000 due to damage. At year-end, the Inventory balance was $34,000. The Wholesale Company uses the periodic inventory system.

Compute the Wholesale Company's cost of goods sold for the year.

A2
Using the cost of goods sold formula in a periodic inventory system

***S5–23** Suppose MegaSports reported cost of goods sold totalling $150 million. Ending inventory was $65 million, and beginning inventory was $58 million. How much inventory did MegaSports purchase during the year?

A2
Computing inventory purchases
Purchase, $157 million

***S5–24** Suppose Helen's Clothing purchased T-shirts on account for $36,260. Credit terms are 1/15, n/45. Helen's Clothing paid within the discount period.

a. If Helen's Clothing uses a periodic inventory system, when will the purchase of inventory be recorded as an expense—when it is purchased or when it is sold?

b. If Helen's Clothing uses a perpetual inventory system, when will the purchase of inventory be recorded as an expense—when it is purchased or when it is sold?

B1
Comparing periodic and perpetual inventory systems

*These Starters cover Chapter 5 Appendix A or B topics.

EXERCISES

E5–1 City Computers reported the comparative information shown below. All amounts are shown in thousands of dollars.

1
Evaluating a company's revenues, gross margin, operating income, and net income
2. Gross margin 2020, $2,700 (in thousands)

CITY COMPUTERS Income Statement (in $000)		
	For the Year Ended	
	January 31, 2020	**January 31, 2019**
Sales revenue	$10,000	$9,550
Expenses		
Cost of goods sold	7,300	7,030
Selling, advertising, general, and administrative	1,830	1,710
Amortization	186	173
Other expenses	127	432
Total expenses	9,443	9,345
Net income	$ 557	$ 205

CITY COMPUTERS Balance Sheet (partial) (in $000)		
	January 31, 2020	**January 31, 2019**
Assets		
Current assets		
Cash	$ 690	$ 185
Accounts and other receivables	130	208
Inventory	1,990	1,800
Prepaid expenses and other current assets	40	80
Total current assets	$2,850	$2,273

Required

1. Is City Computers a merchandising entity, a service business, or both? How can you tell? List the items in City Computers' financial statements that influence your answer.
2. Compute City Computers' gross margin for fiscal years 2020 and 2019. Did the gross margin increase or decrease in 2020? Is this a good sign or a bad sign about the company?
3. Write a brief memo to the owner advising her of City Computers trend of sales revenue, gross margin, and net income. Indicate whether the outlook for City Computers is favourable or unfavourable based on these trends. Use the following memo format:

Date:	____________________
To:	The Owner
From:	Student Name
Subject:	Trend of sales revenue, gross margin, and net income for City Computers

(2) Journalizing transactions from a purchase invoice under the perpetual inventory system

3. Net cash paid, $2,197.80

E5–2 As the proprietor of Willow Auto Service, you receive the invoice below from a supplier (GST has been ignored):

LORDY AUTO PARTS WHOLESALE DISTRIBUTORS
2600 Victoria Avenue
Saskatoon, Saskatchewan S4P 1B3

Invoice date: May 14, 2020 **Payment terms:** 1/10, n/30
Sold to: Willow Auto Service
4219 Cumberland Avenue
Prince Albert, SK S7M 1X3

Quantity Ordered	Description	Quantity Shipped	Price	Amount
6	P135-X4 Radials	6	$ 90.00	$ 540.00
8	L912 Belted-bias	8	100.00	800.00
14	R39 Truck tires	14	120.00	1,680.00
	Total			$3,020.00

Due date:	**Amount:**
May 24, 2020	$2,989.80
May 25 through June 13, 2020	$3,020.00
Paid:	

Required

Journalize the following three transactions. No explanations are required. Willow Auto Services uses the perpetual inventory system.

1. On May 14, 2020, received the above invoice.
2. The L912 Belted-bias tires were ordered by mistake and therefore were returned to Lordy on May 19, 2020.
3. Payment was made May 22, 2020, to Lordy Auto Parts.

E5–3 Suppose The Bay uses the perpetual inventory system and purchases $300,000 of sporting goods on account from Nike on April 10, 2020. Credit terms are 1/10, net 30. The Bay pays electronically on April 20, 2002, and Nike receives the money the same day.

Journalize The Bay's (a) purchase and (b) cash payment transactions. What was The Bay's net cost of this inventory?

Note: E5–4 covers this same situation for the seller.

(2) Recording purchase transactions under the perpetual inventory system

Net inventory cost, $297,000

E5–4 Nike uses the perpetual inventory system and sells $300,000 of sporting goods to The Bay under credit terms of 1/10, net 30 on April 10, 2020. Nike's cost of the goods is $210,000, and it receives the appropriate amount of cash from The Bay on April 20, 2020.

Journalize Nike's transactions on April 10, 2020, and April 20, 2020. How much gross margin did Nike earn on this sale?

(2) Recording sales, cost of goods sold, and cash collections under the perpetual inventory system

Gross margin, $87,000

E5–5 Journalize the following transactions for Soul Art Gift Shop. Explanations are not required.

(2) Journalizing purchase and sales transactions

Feb.	3	Purchased $3,300 of inventory on account under terms 3/10, n/eom and FOB shipping point.
	7	Returned $900 of defective merchandise purchased on February 3.
	9	Paid freight bill of $400 on February 3 purchase.
	10	Sold inventory on account for $4,700. Payment terms were 2/15, n/30. These goods cost the company $2,350.
	12	Paid amount owed on credit purchase of February 3, less the return and the discount.
	28	Received cash from February 10 customer in full payment of their account.

E5–6 On April 30, 2020, Ladysmith Jewellers purchased inventory of $90,000 on account from Northern Gems Ltd., a jewellery importer. Terms were 2/15, n/45. On receiving the goods, Ladysmith checked the order and found $5,500 worth of items that were not ordered but included in the invoice. Therefore, Ladysmith returned this amount of merchandise to Northern on May 4. On May 14, Ladysmith paid Northern.

(2) Journalizing purchase and sales transactions under the perpetual inventory system

1. May 14 cash paid, $82,810

Required

1. Journalize all necessary transactions for Ladysmith Jewellers, which uses the perpetual inventory system. Explanations are not required.
2. Journalize the transactions of Northern Gems Ltd., which uses the perpetual inventory system. Northern's gross margin is 35 percent, so cost of goods sold is 65 percent of sales. Explanations are not required.

E5–7 The following documents describe two business transactions:

(2) Using business documents to record purchases, sales, and returns

Eddie's: Credit Cash for $1,835

INVOICE

Date: March 14, 2020
Sold to: **Eddie's Bicycle Shop**
Sold by: **Schwinn Company**
Terms: 2/10, n/30

Items Purchased: Bicycles

Quantity	Price	Total
8	$152	$1,216
2	112	224
10	96	960
Total		**$2,400**

Debit Memo

Date: March 20, 2020
Issued to: **Schwinn Company**
Issued by: **Eddie's Bicycle Shop**

Items Returned: Bicycles

Quantity	Price	Total
2	$152	$304
2	112	224
Total		**$528**

Reason: **Damaged in shipment**

Eddie's Bicycle Shop paid the balance due on March 21.

Both Eddie's Bicycle Shop and Schwinn Company use a perpetual inventory system.

Schwinn Company's cost of the bicycles sold to Eddie's Bicycle Shop was $1,280. Schwinn Company's cost of the returned merchandise was $256.

Round calculations to the nearest dollar. No explanations are required for the journal entries.

Required

1. Record these transactions and Eddie's cash payment on March 21 in the books of Eddie's Bicycle Shop.
2. Then beside each entry, record what the books of Schwinn Company, which makes and sells bicycles, would record.

Set up your answer in the following format:

Date	Eddie's Bicycle Shop Journal Entries	Schwinn Journal Entries

(2) Computing sales, cost of goods sold, and gross margin amounts

f. $74,600; g. $71,100

E5–8 Supply the missing income statement amounts in each of the following situations:

Sales	Sales Discounts	Net Sales	Cost of Goods Sold	Gross Margin
$94,500	$2,200	$92,300	$56,700	(a)
99,500	(b)	95,520	(c)	$36,000
68,700	2,100	(d)	37,700	(e)
(f)	3,500	(g)	52,500	18,600

(3) Computing inventory and cost of goods sold amounts

Inventory bal., $19,000

E5–9 The following amounts summarize Berloni Company's merchandising activities during 2020. Berloni uses the perpetual inventory system. Set up T-accounts for Inventory and Cost of Goods Sold. Post the amounts below directly into the accounts and calculate the balances. Briefly discuss the possible causes of the shrinkage amount.

Cost of inventory sold to customers	$93,000
Inventory balance, December 31, 2019	15,500
Invoice total for inventory purchases	98,000
Cost of freight-in	5,000
Cost of undamaged inventory returned by customers	10,000
Shrinkage calculated on December 31, 2020	12,000
Purchase discounts received	3,000
Purchase returns and allowances received	1,500

(3) Making closing entries under a perpetual inventory system

2. J. McClelland, Capital bal., $22,200

E5–10 McClelland Hardware Store's accounting records (partial) carried the following accounts at December 31, 2020:

Accounts Receivable	$ 39,500	Selling Expenses	$ 87,750
Interest Revenue	1,400	Sales Revenue	510,100
Accounts Payable	199,000	Interest Expense	12,000
Other Expense	64,500	Inventory	220,500
Cost of Goods Sold	210,050	General and Administrative	
J. McClelland, Withdrawals	168,000	Expenses	55,000

Note: For simplicity, all operating expenses have been summarized in the accounts Selling Expenses, and General and Administrative Expenses.

Required

1. Journalize all of this company's closing entries at December 31, 2020. The company uses the perpetual inventory system.
2. Set up T-accounts for the Income Summary account and the J. McClelland, Capital account. Post to these accounts, and calculate their ending balances. One year earlier, at December 31, 2019, the Capital balance was $108,000.

E5–11 Bubble Tea's accounts at December 31, 2020, included these unadjusted balances:

Inventory	$ 4,400
Cost of Goods Sold	31,200
Sales Revenue	46,800
Sales Discounts	1,250
Sales Returns and Allowances	700

(3) Adjusting and closing entries under the perpetual inventory system, computing gross margin

c. Gross margin, $12,950

The physical count of inventory showed $3,700 of inventory on hand. This is the only adjustment needed.

Required

1. Journalize the adjustment for inventory shrinkage. Include an explanation. Bubble Tea uses the perpetual inventory system.
2. Journalize the closing entries for the appropriate accounts.
3. Compute the gross margin.

E5–12

(3) Closing entries under the perpetual inventory system

Net income, $93,700

STAR CITY RESEARCH
Adjusted Trial Balance
December 31, 2020

Account Title	Debit	Credit
Cash	$ 17,000	
Accounts receivable	29,700	
Inventory	62,100	
Supplies	12,200	
Store fixtures	70,000	
Accumulated amortization		$ 42,000
Accounts payable		31,200
Salary payable		3,800
Note payable, long-term		12,500
B. Wells, capital		41,800
B. Wells, withdrawals	34,000	
Sales revenue		433,600
Sales discounts	4,300	
Cost of goods sold	245,800	
Selling expenses	51,800	
General expenses	36,900	
Interest expense	1,100	
Total	$564,900	$564,900

Required

Journalize Star City Research's closing entries at December 31, 2020. How much was the net income or net loss?

E5–13 Use the data in E5–12 to prepare the multi-step income statement of Star City Research for the year ended December 31, 2020.

(4) Preparing a multi-step income statement under the perpetual inventory system

Gross margin, $183,500

(4) Preparing a multi-step income statement under the perpetual inventory system

Net income, $5,735

E5-14 Bark Buddy reported the following figures from its adjusted trial balance for its first year of business, which ended on July 31, 2020:

Cash	$2,900	Cost of Goods Sold	$18,700
Selling Expenses	1,400	Equipment, Net	9,500
Accounts Payable	4,300	Accrued Liabilities	1,800
C. Camilia, Capital	4,365	Net Sales Revenue	29,200
Notes Payable, Long-Term	500	Accounts Receivable	3,200
Inventory	1,100	Interest Expense	65
Administrative Expenses	3,300		

Prepare Bark Buddy's multi-step income statement for the year ended July 31, 2020.

(5) Using the gross margin percentage and the rate of inventory turnover to evaluate profitability

Gross margin, 42.74%

E5-15 Refer to E5-13. After completing Star City Research's income statement for the year ended December 31, 2020, compute these ratios to evaluate Star City Research's performance:

1. Gross margin percentage
2. Inventory turnover (ending inventory one year earlier, at December 31, 2019, was $54,500)

Compare your figures with the 2019 gross margin percentage of 40.13 percent and the inventory turnover rate of 3.82 times. Does the two-year trend suggest that Star City Research's profits are increasing or decreasing?

(4) (5) Preparing a merchandiser's multi-step income statement under the perpetual inventory system to evaluate the business

3. worse

E5-16 Selected amounts from the accounting records of Waldron Video Sales for the year ended December 31, 2020, follow:

Journal Entries

Dec. 31	Sales Revenue	281,400	
	Interest Revenue	1,800	
	Income Summary		283,200
31	Income Summary	254,400	
	Cost of Goods Sold		161,200
	Sales Discounts		12,600
	Sales Returns and Allowances		6,900
	Selling Expenses		57,800
	General Expenses		15,900
31	Income Summary	28,800	
	B. Waldron, Capital		28,800
31	B. Waldron, Capital	28,000	
	B. Waldron, Withdrawals		28,000

Required

1. Waldron Video Sales uses the perpetual inventory system. Prepare the business's multi-step income statement for the year ended December 31, 2020.
2. Compute the rate of inventory turnover for the year. The inventory balance on December 31, 2019, was $25,400 and on December 31, 2020, was $28,600. Last year the turnover rate was 5.42 times. Does this two-year trend suggest improvement or deterioration in inventory turnover?
3. Compute the gross margin percentage and compare it with last year's value of 49.18 percent for Waldron Video Sales. Does this two-year trend suggest better or worse profitability during the current year?

***E5–17** Journalize, without explanations, the following transactions of Digbey Auto Parts, a distributor that uses the periodic inventory system, during the month of June 2020:

Jun.	3	Purchased $16,800 of inventory under terms of 2/10, n/eom and FOB shipping point.
	7	Returned $1,600 of defective merchandise purchased on June 3.
	9	Paid freight bill of $350 on June 3 purchase.
	10	Sold inventory for $22,400, collecting cash of $3,600. Payment terms on the remainder were 2/15, n/30.
	12	Paid amount owed on credit purchase of June 3.
	16	Granted a sales allowance of $1,200 on the June 10 sale.
	23	Received cash from the June 10 customer in full settlement of the debt.

(A1) Journalizing purchase and sale transactions under the periodic inventory system

June 23 cash receipt, $17,248

***E5–18** As the proprietor of OK Auto Repair, you receive this invoice from a supplier (GST has been ignored):

(A1) Journalizing transactions from a purchase invoice under the periodic inventory system

3. May 22 payment, $2,197.80

LORDY AUTO PARTS WHOLESALE DISTRIBUTORS
2600 Victoria Avenue
Saskatoon, Saskatchewan S4P 1B3

Invoice date: May 14, 2020 **Payment terms:** 1/10, n/30
Sold to: OK Auto Repair
4219 Cumberland Avenue
Prince Albert, SK S7M 1X3

Quantity Ordered	Description	Quantity Shipped	Price	Amount
6	P135-X4 Radials	6	$ 190.00	$ 540.00
8	L912 Belted-bias	8	100.00	800.00
14	R39 Truck tires	14	120.00	1,680.00
	Total			$3,020.00

Due date:	**Amount:**
May 24, 2020	$2,989.80
May 25 through June 13, 2020	$3,020.00
Paid:	

Required

Journalize the following three transaction. Willow Auto Services uses the periodic inventory system.

1. On May 14, 2020, received the above invoice.
2. The L912 Belted-bias tires were ordered by mistake and therefore were returned to Lordy on May 19, 2020.
3. Payment was made May 22, 2020, to Lordy Auto Parts.

***E5–19** On April 30, 2020, Ladysmith Jewellers purchased inventory of $45,000 on account from Northern Gems Ltd., a jewellery importer. Terms were 2/15, net 45. On receiving the goods, Ladysmith checked the order and found $5,500 of unsuitable merchandise. Therefore, Ladysmith returned the merchandise to Northern on May 4, 2020.

On May 14, 2020, Ladysmith Jewellers paid the net amount owed from April 30.

(A1) Journalizing purchase transactions under the periodic inventory system

May 14 cash received, $38,710

Required

1. Record the required transactions in the journal of Ladysmith Jewellers. Use the periodic inventory system. Explanations are not required.
2. Journalize the transactions of Northern Gems Ltd., which uses the periodic inventory system. Explanations are not required.

*These Exercises cover Chapter 5 Appendix A topics.

A2
Computing cost of goods sold in a periodic inventory system
Cost of goods sold, $80,600

***E5-20** The periodic inventory records of Presley Video Sales include these accounts at December 31, 2020:

Purchases	$86,250
Purchase Discounts	3,400
Purchase Returns and Allowances	4,300
Freight-in	3,650
Inventory, December 31, 2019	12,700
Inventory, December 31, 2020	14,300

Required

Compute Presley Video's cost of goods sold for 2020.

2
Computing inventory and cost of goods sold under the periodic inventory system
a. $700, f. $9,400, j. $20,100

***E5-21** Supply the missing income statement amounts in each of the following situations:

Case	Sales	Sales Discounts	Net Sales	Beginning Inventory	Net Purchases	Ending Inventory	Cost of Goods Sold	Gross Margin
1	$24,100	(a)	$23,400	$ 8,800	$16,700	$ 9,900	(b)	$7,800
2	20,600	$500	(c)	6,400	10,800	(d)	$11,100	(e)
3	23,400	400	23,000	(f)	11,200	5,700	14,900	(g)
4	(h)	800	(i)	10,100	(j)	12,100	18,100	9,700

A2
Computing cost of goods sold (periodic inventory system)
Net purchases, $219,500

***E5-22** For the year ended December 31, 2020, Home Distributors, a retailer of home-related products, reported net sales of $429,500 and cost of goods sold of $225,000. The company's balance sheets at December 31, 2019 and 2020, reported inventories of $173,000 and $167,500, respectively. What were Home Distributors' net purchases during 2020?

A2
Cost of goods sold in a periodic inventory system
c. Gross margin, $93,000

***E5-23** Rees Distributors uses the periodic inventory system. Rees reported these amounts at May 31, 2020:

Inventory, May 31, 2019	$ 29,000
Inventory, May 31, 2020	31,000
Purchases (of inventory)	82,000
Purchase Discounts	2,000
Purchase Returns	3,000
Freight-in	4,000
Sales Revenue	200,000
Sales Discounts	13,000
Sales Returns	15,000

Compute Rees Distributors':

a. Net sales revenue
b. Cost of goods sold
c. Gross margin

1 A1 B1
Describing periodic and perpetual inventory systems

***E5-24** The following characteristics are related to either periodic inventory or perpetual inventory systems.

A. Purchases of inventory are journalized to an asset account at the time of purchase.
B. Purchases of inventory are journalized to an expense account at the time of purchase.
C. Inventory records are constantly updated.
D. Sales made require a second entry to be journalized to record cost of goods sold.
E. Bar code scanners that record sales transactions are most often associated with this inventory system.
F. A physical count of goods on hand at year-end is performed.

Identify each characteristic as one of the following:

a. Periodic inventory system
b. Perpetual inventory system
c. Both periodic and perpetual inventory systems
d. Neither periodic nor perpetual inventory system

*These Exercises cover Chapter 5 Appendix A and B topics.

SERIAL EXERCISE PART 1

The Serial Exercise involves a company that will be revisited throughout relevant chapters in Volume 1 and Volume 2. You can complete the Serial Exercises using MyLab Accounting.

E5-25 This exercise continues recordkeeping for the Canyon Canoe Company. At the beginning of the new year, Canyon Canoe Company decided to carry and sell T-shirts with its logo printed on them. Canyon Canoe Company uses the perpetual inventory system to account for the inventory. During January 2021, Canyon Canoe Company completed the following merchandising transactions:

(2) Purchase and sale of inventory under the perpetual inventory system

Cash T-account balance $13,635

Jan.	1	Purchased 10 T-shirts at $4 each and paid cash.
	2	Sold 6 T-shirts for $10 each, total cost of $24. Received cash.
	3	Purchased 50 T-shirts on account at $5 each. Terms 2/10, n/30.
	7	Paid the supplier for the T-shirts purchased on January 3, less discount.
	8	Realized 4 T-shirts from the January 1 order were printed incorrectly and returned them for a cash refund.
	10	Sold 40 T-shirts on account for $10 each, total cost of $200. Terms 3/15, n/45.
	12	Received payment for the T-shirts sold on account on January 10, less discount.
	14	Purchased 100 T-shirts on account at $4 each. Terms 4/15, n/30.
	18	Canyon Canoe Company contacted the supplier from the January 14 purchase and told it that some of the T-shirts were the wrong color. The supplier offered a $50 purchase allowance.
	20	Paid the supplier for the T-shirts purchased on January 14, less the allowance and discount.
	21	Sold 60 T-shirts on account for $10 each, total cost of $220. Terms 2/20, n/30.
	23	Received a payment on account for the T-shirts sold on January 21, less discount.
	25	Purchased 320 T-shirts on account at $5 each. Terms 2/10, n/30, FOB shipping point.
	27	Paid freight associated with the January 25 purchase, $48.
	29	Paid for the January 25 purchase, less discount.
	30	Sold 275 T-shirts on account for $10 each, total cost of $1,300. Terms 2/10, n/30.
	31	Received payment for the T-shirts sold on January 30, less discount.

Required

1. Open T-accounts in the ledger, using the post-closing balances from Chapter 4. If you did not complete earlier questions, use this information:

CANYON CANOE COMPANY Post-Closing Trial Balance December 31, 2020		
Account Title	**Debit**	**Credit**
Cash	$ 12,125	
Accounts receivable	7,600	
Office supplies	165	
Prepaid rent	2,000	
Land	85,000	
Building	35,000	
Accumulated amortization—building		$ 500
Canoes	12,000	
Accumulated amortization—canoes		350
Accounts payable		3,670
Unearned revenue		350
Salaries payable		1,250
Interest payable		50
Note payable		7,200
Amber Wilson, capital		140,520
Total	$ 153,890	$ 153,890

Set up the following accounts with opening balances (Bal.) as 0: Inventory, Income Summary, Sales Revenue, Sales Discounts, Canoe Rental Revenue, Cost of Goods Sold, Rent Expense, Salaries Expense, Utilities Expense, Telephone Expense, Supplies Expense, Amortization Expense—Building, Amortization Expense—Canoes, Interest Expense.

2. Journalize and post the January transactions. Compute each account balance, and denote the balance as *Bal*. Explanations are not required.

SERIAL EXERCISE PART 2

(3) (4) (5)
Making adjusting and closing entries, preparing financial statements under the perpetual inventory system, and computing gross margin percentage

3. Net income $915

E5–26 *This exercise continues recordkeeping for the Canyon Canoe Company and focuses on non-merchandising transactions, adjusting and closing entries, and preparing financial statements.*

Canyon Canoe Company does not typically prepare adjusting and closing entries each month, but the company is surprised at how popular the shirts are and wishes to know the net income for January and would also like to understand how to prepare the closing entries for a merchandising company. During January 2021, Canyon Canoe Company completed the following non-merchandising transactions:

Jan.	2	Collected $4,500 on account.
	15	Paid the utilities and telephone bills from December ($295, $325).
	15	Paid the salaries accrued in December ($1,250).
	18	Rented canoes and received cash, $1,825
	20	Received bills for utilities ($360) and telephone ($275), which will be paid later.
	23	Paid various accounts payable, $1,800.
	30	Paid employee, $750.

Required

1. Journalize and post the January transactions. Omit explanations. Use the ledger from E5-25 for posting.
2. Journalize and post the adjusting entries for the month of January. Omit explanations. Denote each adjustment as *Adj*. Compute each account balance, and denote the balance as *Bal*. In addition to the adjusting entries from the data from previous chapters, Canyon Canoe Company provides this data:
   a. A physical count of the inventory at the end of the month revealed the cost was $470.
   b. Office supplies used, $55.
   c. The Unearned Revenue has now been earned.
   d. Interest expense accrued on the note payable, $50.
3. Prepare the month ended January 31, 2021, single-step income statement of Canyon Canoe Company.
4. Journalize and post the closing entries. Omit explanations. Denote each closing amount as *Clo.* and each balance as *Bal*. After posting all closing entries, prove the equality of debits and credits in the ledger by preparing a post-closing trial balance.
5. Compute the gross profit percentage for January for Canyon Canoe Company.

PRACTICE SET

E5-27 *This problem continues the Crystal Clear Cleaning practice set begun in Chapter 2 and continued through Chapter 9.*

(2) (4) (5)
Journalizing purchase and sale transactions, making closing entries, preparing financial statements, and computing the gross profit percentage

Crystal Clear Cleaning has decided that, in addition to providing cleaning services, it will sell cleaning products. Crystal Clear uses the perpetual inventory system. During December 2019, Crystal Clear completed the following transactions:

Dec.	2	Purchased 1,000 units of inventory for $4,000 on account from Sparkle Company on terms, 5/10, n/20.
	5	Purchased 1,200 units of inventory from Borax on account with terms 4/10, n/30. The total invoice was for $6,000, which included a $300 freight charge.
	7	Returned 300 units of inventory to Sparkle from the December 2 purchase (cost $1,200).
	9	Paid Borax. No discount is applied on the freight charge.
	11	Sold 500 units of goods to Happy Maids for $5,500 on account with terms n/30. Crystal Clear's cost of the goods was $2,000.
	12	Paid Sparkle.
	15	Received 100 units with a retail price of $1,100 back from customer Happy Maids. The goods cost Crystal Clear $400.
	21	Received payment from Happy Maids, settling the amount due in full.
	28	Sold 500 units of goods to Bridget, Inc. on account for $6,500 (cost $2,022). Terms 1/15, n/30.
	29	Paid cash for utilities of $550.
	30	Paid cash for Sales Commission Expense of $214.
	31	Received payment from Bridget, Inc., less discount.
	31	Recorded the following adjusting entries: a. Physical count of inventory on December 31 showed 800 units of goods on hand, with a cost of $3,848. b. Amortization expenses include $80 for the equipment and $70 for the truck. Continue to use one expense account but separate contra-asset accounts. c. Accrued salaries expense of $2,100. d. Prepaid insurance in the amount of $400 expired. e. Prepaid rent in the amount of $1,000 was used. f. Interest of $180 should be accrued. g. $1,250 of unearned service revenue has been earned.

Required

1. If you did not complete Chapter 4, open the following T-accounts in the ledger: Cash, $51,650; Accounts Receivable, $4,000; Inventory, $0; Cleaning Supplies, $50; Prepaid Rent, $3,000; Prepaid Insurance, $4,400; Equipment, $5,400; Accumulated Amortization—Equipment, $80; Truck, $3,000; Accumulated Amortization—Truck, $70; Accounts Payable, $1,245; Salaries Payable, $0; Interest Payable, $59; Unearned Revenue, $14,375; Notes Payable, $36,000; A. Hideaway, Capital, $19,671; A. Hideaway, Withdrawals, $0; Service Revenue, $0; Sales Revenue, $0; Sales Discounts, $0; Sales Returns and Allowances, $0; Cost of Goods Sold, $0; Salaries Expense, $0; Sales Commission Expense, $0; Utilities Expense, $0; Amortization Expense, $0; Rent Expense, $0; Insurance Expense, $0; Interest Expense, $0.

   If you did complete the work on this problem in Chapter 4, then open the following new T-accounts with zero balances: Inventory, Sales Revenue, Sales Discounts, Sales Returns and Allowances, Cost of Goods Sold, and Sales Commission Expense.
2. Journalize and post the December transactions. Omit explanations. Compute each account balance, and denote the balance as *Balance*. Identify each accounts payable and accounts receivable with the vendor or customer name in the journal entries. (For example, Accounts Payable—Sparkle Company)
3. Journalize and post the adjusting entries. Omit explanations. Denote each adjusting amount as *Adj*. Compute each account balance, and denote the balance as *Balance*. After posting all adjusting entries, prove the equality of debits and credits in the ledger by preparing an adjusted trial balance.
4. Prepare the multi-step income statement and statement of owner's equity for the month ended December 31, 2019. Also prepare a classified balance sheet at December 31, 2019. Assume the note payable is long-term. List expenses in the order they are shown in the adjusted trial balance.
5. Compute the gross profit percentage for December for the company.

BEYOND THE NUMBERS

1 5

Evaluating a company's profitability

Gross margin percentage in 2020, 26%

BN5–1

Wilson Distributors is a provider of motorcycle parts. The company recently reported the following:

WILSON DISTRIBUTORS
Consolidated Statements of Operations (Adapted)
For the Years Ended July 31, 2020 and 2019

	2020	2019
Sales	$1,320,000	$984,000
Cost of sales	980,000	752,000
Gross margin	340,000	232,000
Expenses		
Selling, general, and administrative	264,000	204,000
Amortization	34,000	21,000
Restructuring charges	84,000	—
Total expenses	382,000	225,000
Operating income (loss)	(42,000)	7,000
Other items (summarized)	(7,000)	(16,000)
Net income (loss)	$ (49,000)	$ (9,000)

Required Evaluate Wilson Distributors' operations during 2020 in comparison with 2019. Consider sales, gross margin, operating income, and net income. Compare the gross margin percentage and inventory turnover in both years. Wilson Distributors' inventories at December 31, 2020, 2019, and 2018, were $92,000, $145,000, and $122,000, respectively. In the annual report, management describes the restructuring charges in 2020—the costs of downsizing the company—as a one-time event. How does this additional information affect your evaluation?

ETHICAL ISSUE

EI5–1

Schafer Bearing Company makes all sales of industrial bearings under terms of FOB shipping point. The company usually receives orders for sales approximately one week before shipping inventory to customers. For orders received late in December, Bob Schafer, the owner, decides when to ship the goods. If profits are already at an acceptable level, the company delays shipment until January. If profits are lagging behind expectations, the company ships the goods during December.

Required

1. Under Schafer Bearing Company's FOB policy, when should the company record a sale?
2. Do you approve or disapprove of Schafer Bearing Company's means of deciding when to ship goods to customers? If you approve, give your reason. If you disapprove, identify a better way to decide when to ship goods. (There is no accounting rule against Schafer Bearing Company's practice.)

PROBLEMS (GROUP A)

P5–1A Kitchen Stuff is a mid-sized retailer in Canada. The appliances department of Kitchen Stuff purchases small appliances such as coffee makers and toasters from many well-known manufacturers. Kitchen Stuff uses a sophisticated perpetual inventory system.

(1) (2) Explaining the perpetual inventory system

Required You are the manager of a Kitchen Stuff store. Write a memo to a new employee in the appliances department that explains how the company accounts for the purchase and sale of inventory.

Use the following heading for your memo:

Date:	____________
To:	New employee
From:	Store manager
Subject:	Kitchen Stuff accounting system for inventories

P5–2A The following transactions occurred between Happy Pharmaceuticals and Zari Drug Store during February. Both companies use the perpetual inventory system.

(2) Accounting for the purchase and sale of inventory under the perpetual inventory system

Feb. 27 Cash amount, $31,000

Feb.	6	Zari purchased $60,000 of merchandise from Happy on credit terms of 1/10, n/30, FOB shipping point. Separately, Zari paid a $1,000 bill for freight-in. Happy invoiced Zari for $60,000 (these goods cost Happy $36,000).
	10	Zari returned $5,000 of the merchandise purchased on February 6. Happy issued a credit memo for this amount and returned the goods to inventory (cost, $3,000).
	15	Zari paid $24,000 of the invoice amount owed to Happy for the February 6 purchase. Happy allows its customers to take the cash discount on partial payments.
	27	Zari paid the remaining amount owed to Happy for the February 6 purchase.

Required Journalize these transactions, first on the books of Zari Drug Store and second on the books of Happy Pharmaceuticals.

(2)

Journalizing purchase and sale transactions under the perpetual inventory system

2. Inventory balance, $261,170

P5–3A Singh Distributing Company uses the perpetual inventory system and engaged in the following transactions during May of the current year:

May	3	Purchased office supplies for cash, $22,000.
	7	Purchased inventory on credit terms of 3/10, net eom, $76,000.
	8	Returned 25 percent of the inventory purchased on May 7. It was not the inventory ordered.
	10	Sold goods for cash, $34,000 (cost, $20,400).
	13	Sold inventory on credit terms of 2/15, n/45 for $148,200 less $13,500 quantity discount offered to customers who purchase in large quantities (cost, $90,480).
	16	Paid the amount owed on account from the purchase of May 7, less the discount and the return.
	17	Received wrong-sized inventory as a sales return from May 13 sale, $12,400, which is the net amount after the quantity discount. Singh's cost of the inventory received was $7,440.
	18	Purchased inventory of $164,000 on account. Payment terms were 2/10, net 30.
	26	Paid supplier for goods purchased on May 18.
	28	Received cash in full settlement of the account from the customer who purchased inventory on May 13.
	31	Purchased inventory for cash, $96,000, less a quantity discount of $9,600, plus freight charges of $2,200.

Required

1. Journalize the preceding transactions on the books of Singh Distributing Company.
2. Suppose the balance in Inventory was $60,000 on May 1. What is the balance in inventory on May 31?

(3)

Journalizing the closing entries of a merchandising business under the perpetual inventory system

2. Capital, $352,600

P5–4A The adjusted trial balance of Fifi's Fine Foods at December 31, 2020, is shown below:

FIFI'S FINE FOODS
Adjusted Trial Balance
December 31, 2020

Account Title	Debit	Credit
Cash	$ 6,200	
Accounts receivable	57,000	
Inventory	351,200	
Prepaid rent	24,000	
Equipment	108,000	
Accumulated amortization—equipment		$ 54,000
Accounts payable		43,200
Salary payable		7,000
Interest payable		2,600
Note payable, long-term		87,000
J. Marvin, capital		270,000
J. Marvin, withdrawals	153,000	
Sales revenue		835,400
Cost of goods sold	331,600	
Salary expense	125,600	
Rent expense	48,000	
Advertising expense	21,600	
Utilities expense	30,800	
Amortization expense—equipment	10,800	
Insurance expense	13,200	
Interest expense	5,200	
Miscellaneous expense	13,000	
Total	$1,299,200	$1,299,200

Required

1. Journalize the closing entries. assuming that Fifi's Fine Foods uses the perpetual inventory system. Explanations are not required.
2. Determine the December 31, 2020, Capital balance for Fifi's Fine Foods.

P5–5A Buono Adventures, which uses the perpetual inventory system, has the following account balances (in alphabetical order) on July 31, 2020:

③ ④
Adjusting and closing the accounts of a merchandising company, and preparing a merchandiser's financial statements under the perpetual inventory system

2. Net loss, $67,500

Accounts Payable	$ 21,600
Accounts Receivable	23,200
Accumulated Amortization—Equipment	64,600
Cash	8,400
Cost of Goods Sold	687,000
E. Buono, Capital	402,000
E. Buono, Withdrawals	92,000
Equipment	180,000
Interest Earned	4,000
Inventory	143,000
Operating Expenses	355,000
Sales Discounts	10,300
Sales Returns and Allowances	32,900
Sales Revenue	1,045,200
Supplies	14,600
Unearned Sales Revenue	9,000

Note: For simplicity, all operating expenses have been summarized in the account Operating Expenses.

Additional data at July 31, 2020:

a. A physical count of items showed $3,000 of supplies on hand. (Hint: Use the account Operating Expenses in the adjusting journal entry.)

b. An inventory count showed inventory on hand at July 31, 2020, of $140,000.

c. The equipment has an estimated useful life of eight years and is expected to have no scrap or residual value at the end of its life. (Hint: Use the account Operating Expenses in the adjusting journal entry.)

d. Unearned sales revenue of $5,600 was earned by July 31, 2020.

Required

1. Record all adjustments and closing entries that would be required on July 31, 2020.
2. Prepare the multi-step income statement and statement of owner's equity for the year ended July 31, 2020, and the classified balance sheet in report format as at July 31, 2020.

P5–6A Items from the accounts of Marchand Distributors at May 31, 2020, follow, listed in alphabetical order. Marchand Distributors uses the perpetual inventory system. The operating expenses are summarized in the General Expenses and the Selling Expenses accounts.

④
Preparing a single-step income statement for a merchandising business under the perpetual inventory system

1. Net income, $259,600

Accounts Payable	$ 51,000	Interest Payable	$ 2,800
Accounts Receivable	107,500	Interest Revenue	600
Accumulated Amortization—		Inventory, May 31, 2020	147,100
Equipment	96,900	Notes Payable, Long-Term	114,800
C. Marchand, Capital	167,800	Salaries Payable	7,200
C. Marchand, Withdrawals	66,900	Sales Discounts	26,500
Cash	19,900	Sales Returns and	
Cost of Goods Sold	1,086,900	Allowances	45,900
Equipment	340,800	Sales Revenue	1,991,500
General Expenses	206,800	Selling Expenses	357,200
Interest Expense	9,200	Supplies	33,100
		Unearned Sales Revenue	15,200

Required

1. Prepare the business's single-step income statement for the year ended May 31, 2020. Show Net Sales Revenue and not the individual accounts.
2. Prepare the statement of owner's equity for the year ended May 31, 2020.
3. Prepare Marchand Distributors' classified balance sheet in report format at May 31, 2020.

(4) (5)
Preparing a multi-step income statement and calculating gross margin percentage under the perpetual inventory system

1. Net income, $259,600

P5–7A 1. Use the data in P5–6A to prepare Marchand Distributors' multi-step income statement for the year ended May 31, 2020.
2. Corry Marchand, owner of the company, strives to earn a gross margin of at least 50 percent and a net income of 20 percent (Net income percentage = Net income ÷ Net sales revenue). Did Marchand Distributors achieve these goals? Show your calculations. Round these answers to one decimal place.

(3) (4) (5)
Making closing entries, computing gross margin percentage and inventory turnover under the perpetual inventory system

2. Gross margin percentage for 2020, 38.4%

P5–8A The adjusted trial balance of The Creative Space at November 30, 2020, is shown below.

THE CREATIVE SPACE Adjusted Trial Balance November 30, 2020		
Account Title	**Debit**	**Credit**
Cash	$ 4,000	
Accounts receivable	24,250	
Inventory	13,700	
Supplies	700	
Furniture	20,000	
Accumulated amortization—furniture		$ 12,000
Accounts payable		7,250
Salary payable		1,100
Unearned sales revenue		3,600
Note payable, long-term		22,500
A. Propp, capital		20,650
A. Propp, withdrawals	18,000	
Sales revenue		112,500
Sales returns	3,000	
Cost of goods sold	67,500	
Selling expenses	16,850	
General expenses	10,500	
Interest expense	1,100	
Total	$179,600	$179,600

Required

1. Journalize The Creative Space's closing entries. The Creative Space uses the perpetual inventory system.
2. Compute the gross margin percentage and the rate of inventory turnover for 2020, rounded to one decimal place. Inventory on hand one year ago was $10,700. For 2019, The Creative Space's gross margin was 32 percent and inventory turnover was 4.9 times during the year. Does the two-year trend in these ratios suggest improvement or deterioration in profitability?

***P5–9A** The following transactions occurred between Sweetums Candies and Corner Store Drug Store during February of the current year.

(A1) Accounting for the purchase and sale of inventory under the periodic system

Feb.	6	Corner purchased $50,000 of merchandise from Sweetums on credit terms 2/10, n/30, FOB shipping point. Separately, Corner paid a $2,000 bill for freight-in. Sweetums invoiced Corner for $50,000.
	15	Corner returned $7,000 of the merchandise purchased on February 6. Sweetums issued a credit memo for this amount.
	15	Corner paid $24,000 of the invoice amount owed to Sweetums for the February 6 purchase. This payment included none of the freight charge.
	27	Corner paid the remaining amount owed to Sweetums for the February 6 purchase.

Required Journalize these transactions, first on the books of Corner Store and second on the books of Sweetums Candies. Assume both companies use the periodic inventory system and discounts are allowed on partial payments.

***P5–10A** Kaur Distributing Company, which uses the periodic inventory system, engaged in the following transactions during May of the current year:

(A1) Journalizing purchase and sale transactions under the periodic inventory system

May	3	Purchased office supplies for cash, $22,000.
	7	Purchased inventory on credit terms of 3/10, net eom, $160,000.
	8	Returned 10 percent of the inventory purchased on May 7. It was not the inventory ordered.
	10	Sold goods for cash, $36,400.
	13	Sold inventory on credit terms of 2/15, n/45 for $60,300, less $8,800 quantity discount offered to customers who purchase in large quantities.
	16	Paid the amount owed on account from the purchase of May 7.
	17	Received wrong-sized inventory returned from May 13 sale, $3,200, which is the net amount after the quantity discount.
	18	Purchased inventory of $76,000 on account. Payment terms were 2/10, net 30.
	26	Paid supplier for goods purchased on May 18.
	28	Received cash in full settlement of the account from the customer who purchased inventory on May 13.
	29	Purchased inventory for cash, $26,000, less a quantity discount of $2,200, and paid freight charges of $600.

Required Journalize the preceding transactions on the books of Kaur Distributing Company.

***P5–11A** Selected accounts from the accounting records of Northern Windows had the balances shown below at December 31, 2020. Northern Windows uses the periodic inventory system.

(2) (5) (A2) Computing cost of goods sold and gross margin in a periodic inventory system, evaluating the business

1. Gross margin, $43,600

Purchases	$160,000
Selling Expenses	10,000
Furniture and Fixtures	40,000
Purchase Returns and Allowances	1,000
Salaries Payable	1,500
Sales Revenue	205,000
Sales Returns and Allowances	1,900
Inventory: December 31, 2019	36,000
Inventory: December 31, 2020	37,000
Accounts Payable	9,000
Accounts Receivable	15,000

*These Problems cover Chapter 5 Appendix A topics.

Cash	3,500
Freight-in	1,400
Accumulated Amortization—Furniture and Fixtures	16,000
Purchase Discounts	1,500
Sales Discounts	1,600
General Expenses	22,000
Amortization Expense—Furniture and Fixtures	4,000
S. Namrata, Capital	81,900
S. Namrata, Withdrawals	20,500

Required

1. Show the computation of Northern Windows' net sales, cost of goods sold, and gross margin for the year ended December 31, 2020.
2. Sal Namrata, the proprietor of Northern Windows, strives to earn a gross margin percentage of 25 percent. Did he achieve this goal?
3. Did the rate of inventory turnover reach the industry average of 3.8 times per year?

A3

Preparing a merchandiser's worksheet under the periodic inventory system

Net income, $235,600

***P5–12A** The unadjusted trial balance of Marvin's Fine Gems at December 31, 2020, is shown below:

MARVIN'S FINE GEMS
Unadjusted Trial Balance
December 31, 2020

Account Title	Debit	Credit
Cash	$ 6,200	
Accounts receivable	57,000	
Inventory	345,000	
Prepaid rent	28,000	
Equipment	108,000	
Accumulated amortization—equipment		$ 43,200
Accounts payable		43,200
Salary payable		0
Interest payable		0
Note payable, long-term		87,000
J. Marvin, capital		270,000
J. Marvin, withdrawals	153,000	
Sales revenue		835,400
Purchases	337,800	
Salary expense	118,600	
Rent expense	44,000	
Advertising expense	21,600	
Utilities expense	30,800	
Amortization expense—equipment	0	
Insurance expense	13,200	
Interest expense	2,600	
Miscellaneous expense	13,000	
Total	$1,278,800	$1,278,800

Additional data at December 31, 2020:

a. Rent expense for the year, $48,000.

b. The equipment has an estimated useful life of 10 years and is expected to have no value when it is retired from service.

c. Accrued salaries at December 31, $7,000.

d. Accrued interest expense at December 31, $2,600.

e. Inventory based on the inventory count on December 31, $351,200.

Required Complete Marvin's Fine Gems' worksheet for the year ended December 31, 2020. Key adjustments by letter. You do not need to complete the adjusted trial balance column as totals can be input directly into the financial statement columns. Marvin's Fine Gems uses the periodic inventory system.

***P5–13A** Refer to the data in P5–12A.

A3

Journalizing the adjusting and closing entries of a merchandising business under the periodic inventory system

2. Dec. 31, 2020, Capital bal., $352,600

Required

1. Journalize the adjusting and closing entries.
2. Determine the December 31, 2020, balance of Capital for Marvin's Fine Gems.

***P5–14A** Items from the accounts of Marchand Distributors at May 31, 2020, follow, listed in alphabetical order. Marchand Distributors uses the periodic inventory system. For simplicity, all operating expenses are summarized in the General Expenses and the Selling Expenses account.

5 A4

Preparing a multi-step income statement and a classified balance sheet under the periodic inventory system as well as calculating margin

1. Net income, $259,600

Accounts Payable	$ 71,000	Inventory May 31, 2019	$ 151,800
Accounts Receivable	107,500	Note Payable, Long-Term	114,800
Accumulated Amortization—		Purchases	1,102,200
Equipment	96,900	Salaries Payable	7,200
C. Marchand, Capital	167,800	Sales Discounts	26,500
C. Marchand, Withdrawals	66,900	Sales Returns and	
Cash	19,900	Allowances	45,900
Equipment	340,800	Sales Revenue	1,991,500
General Expenses	206,800	Selling Expenses	357,200
Interest Expense	9,200	Supplies	33,100
Interest Payable	2,800	Unearned Sales Revenue	15,200
Interest Revenue	600		

Required

1. Prepare the business's multi-step income statement for the year ended May 31, 2020. A physical count of inventory on May 31, 2020, valued it at $167,100.
2. Prepare Marchand Distributors' statement of owner's equity at May 31, 2020.
3. Prepare Marchand Distributors' classified balance sheet in report format at May 31, 2020.
4. Corry Marchand, owner of the company, strives to earn a gross margin of at least 50 percent and a net income of 20 percent (Net income percentage = Net income ÷ Net sales revenue). Did Marchand Distributors achieve these goals? Show your calculations. Round your answers to one decimal place.

A1 A2 A3 A4 B1

Journalizing, posting to T-accounts, year-end adjusting, preparing financial statements using the periodic inventory system, comparing to the perpetual system.

***P5–15A** Mumbai Sales Company engaged in the following transactions during September 2020, the first month of the company's operations. Assume the company had no inventory on hand prior to September 3 and a zero capital balance. Mumbai Sales Company has a periodic inventory system.

Sep.	3	Purchased inventory costing $7,000 on credit terms of 2/10, net eom. The goods were shipped FOB Mumbai's warehouse.
	9	Returned 20 percent of the inventory purchased on September 3. It was defective.
	12	Sold goods for cash, $6,000 (cost, $3,000).
	15	Purchased inventory of $15,400, less a $400 quantity discount. Credit terms were 2/15, n/30. The goods were shipped FOB the supplier's warehouse.
	16	Paid a $1,200 freight bill on the inventory purchased on September 15.
	18	Sold inventory for $9,000 on credit terms of 2/10, n/30 (cost, $4,500).
	22	Received merchandise returned from the customer from the September 18 sale, $2,000 (cost, $1,000). Merchandise was the wrong size.
	24	Borrowed exactly enough money from the bank to pay for the September 15 purchase in time to take advantage of the discount offered. Signed a short-term note payable to the bank for the net amount.
	24	Paid supplier for goods purchased on September 15, less all returns and discounts.
	28	Received cash in full settlement of the account from the customer who purchased inventory on September 18, less the return on September 22 and less the discount.
	29	Paid the amount owed on account from the purchase of September 3, less the September 9 return.
	30	Purchased inventory for cash, $4,640, less a quantity discount of $140.

Required

1. Journalize the transactions and include any calculations in the journal entry explanations.
2. Refer to the Mumbai Sales Company journal entries in Requirement 1 to set up T-accounts, and post the journal entries to calculate the ending balances for the cost of goods sold equation accounts. Set up a T-account for M. Mumbai, Capital at this time.
3. Calculate cost of goods sold using an ending inventory value of $16,000.
4. Assume Mumbai Sales has two year-end adjusting entries: (a) accrue accounting expenses of $1,000, and (b) accrue a sale of $2,000 that was completed on September 30 but unrecorded. Record and post the adjusting entries and closing entries for Mumbai Sales Company.
5. Prepare the financial statements under the periodic inventory system. (Note: Include a multi-step income statement, a statement of owners' equity, and a classified balance sheet.)
6. Refer to the Mumbai Sales Company journal entries in Requirement 1 above. Assume that the note payable signed on September 24 requires the payment of $250 interest expense. Was the decision to borrow funds to take advantage of the cash discount wise or unwise?
7. Compare the results of the Summary Problem on page 266 with this solution (periodic). What main differences do you notice?

PROBLEMS (GROUP B)

P5–1B Clearly Optical is a regional chain of optical shops. The company offers a large selection of eyeglass frames, and Clearly Optical stores provide while-you-wait service. Clearly Optical has launched a vigorous advertising campaign promoting its two-for-the-price-of-one frame sale.

① ② Explaining the perpetual inventory system

Required

Clearly Optical expects to grow rapidly and increase its level of inventory. As chief accountant of the company, you wish to install a perpetual inventory system. Write a memo to the company president to explain how the accounting system would work.

Use the following heading for your memo:

Date:	____________________
To:	Company President
From:	Chief Accountant
Subject:	How a perpetual inventory system works

P5–2B The following transactions occurred between Cloutier Pharmaceuticals and Arnold Drug Stores during June of the current year:

② Accounting for the purchase and sale of inventory under the perpetual inventory system

Jun.	8	Arnold purchased $29,400 of merchandise from Cloutier on credit terms 2/10, n/30, FOB shipping point. Separately, Arnold paid freight-in of $600. Cloutier invoiced Arnold for $29,400. These goods cost Cloutier $12,600.
	11	Arnold returned $3,600 of the merchandise purchased on June 8. Cloutier issued a credit memo for this amount and returned the goods, in excellent condition, to inventory (cost $1,500).
	17	Arnold paid $12,000 of the invoice amount owed to Cloutier for the June 8 purchase. This payment included none of the freight charge. Arnold took the purchase discount on the partial payment.
	26	Arnold paid the remaining amount owed to Cloutier for the June 8 purchase.

Required Journalize these transactions, first on the books of Arnold Drug Stores and second on the books of Cloutier Pharmaceuticals. Both companies use the perpetual inventory system.

P5–3B Coburn Furniture Company engaged in the following transactions during July of the current year:

② Journalizing purchase and sale transactions under the perpetual inventory system

Jul.	2	Purchased inventory for cash, $12,800, less a quantity discount of $1,800.
	5	Purchased store supplies on credit terms of net eom, $6,800.
	8	Purchased inventory of $54,000 less a quantity discount of 10 percent, plus freight charges of $2,200. Credit terms are 3/15, n/30.
	9	Sold goods for cash, $21,600. Coburn's cost of these goods was $13,000.
	11	Returned $2,000 (net amount after the quantity discount) of the inventory purchased on July 8. It was damaged in shipment.
	12	Purchased inventory on credit terms of 3/10, n/30, $60,000.
	14	Sold inventory on credit terms of 2/10, n/30 for $138,400, less a $13,840 quantity discount (cost, $83,000).
	16	Received and paid the electricity bill, $6,400.
	20	Received returned inventory from the July 14 sale, $5,000 (net amount after the quantity discount). Coburn shipped the wrong goods by mistake. Coburn's cost of the inventory received was $3,000.

21 Paid supplier for goods purchased on July 8 less the discount and the return.

23 Received $87,120 cash in partial settlement of the account from the customer who purchased inventory on July 14. Granted the customer a 1 percent discount and credited the customer's account receivable for $88,000.

31 Paid for the store supplies purchased on July 5.

Required

1. Journalize the preceding transactions on the books of Coburn Furniture Company. The company uses the perpetual inventory system.
2. Suppose the balance in inventory was $45,500 on July 1. What is the balance in inventory on July 31?

③ Journalizing closing entries of a merchandising business under the perpetual inventory system

P5–4B Gismondi Produce Company's adjusted trial balance at December 31, 2020, is as follows.

GISMONDI PRODUCE COMPANY
Adjusted Trial Balance
December 31, 2020

Account Title	Debit	Credit
Cash	$ 22,150	
Accounts receivable	109,600	
Inventory	116,500	
Store supplies	23,800	
Prepaid insurance	2,400	
Store fixtures	270,000	
Accumulated amortization—store fixtures		$ 189,000
Accounts payable		69,900
Salaries payable		5,500
Interest payable		1,600
Notes payable, long-term		47,000
F. Gismondi, capital		119,000
F. Gismondi, withdrawals	52,000	
Sales revenue		1,290,500
Cost of goods sold	729,700	
Salaries expense	244,100	
Rent expense	52,000	
Utilities expense	36,200	
Amortization expense—store fixtures	27,000	
Insurance expense	21,600	
Store supplies expense	5,000	
Interest expense	3,950	
Miscellaneous expense	6,500	
Total	$1,722,500	$1,722,500

Required

1. Journalize the closing entries of Gismondi Produce Company assuming that the perpetual inventory system is used. Explanations are not required.
2. Determine the December 31, 2020, balance in the Capital account.

P5–5B Singleton Sports Products, which uses the perpetual inventory system, has the following account balances (in alphabetical order) on August 31, 2020:

(3) (4) Adjusting and closing the accounts of a merchandising company, and preparing a merchandiser's financial statements under the perpetual inventory system

Accounts Payable	$ 61,500
Accounts Receivable	64,700
Accumulated Amortization—Equipment	124,000
Cash	14,400
C. Singleton, Capital	305,100
C. Singleton, Withdrawals	62,400
Cost of Goods Sold	789,900
Equipment	336,000
Interest Earned	2,600
Inventory	248,400
Operating Expenses	541,200
Sales Discounts	36,200
Sales Returns and Allowances	48,600
Sales Revenue	1,640,000
Supplies	27,600
Unearned Sales Revenue	36,200

Note: For simplicity, all operating expenses have been summarized in the account Operating Expenses.

Additional data at August 31, 2020:

a. A physical count of items showed $14,200 of supplies were on hand. (Hint: Use the account Operating Expenses in the adjusting journal entry.)

b. An inventory count showed inventory on hand at August 31, 2020, of $247,400.

c. The equipment is expected to last five years and to have no value at the end of this time. (Hint: Use the account Operating Expenses in the adjusting journal entry.)

d. Unearned sales of $9,600 were earned by August 31, 2020.

Required

1. Record all adjusting and closing entries required on August 31, 2020.
2. Prepare the multi-step income statement and statement of owner's equity for the year ended August 31, 2020, and the classified balance sheet in report format as at August 31, 2020.

P5–6B The accounts of Massood's Muffins at July 31, 2020, are listed in alphabetical order below. For simplicity, all operating expenses are summarized in the accounts Selling Expenses and General Expenses. Massood's Muffins uses the perpetual inventory system.

(4) Preparing a single-step income statement and a classified balance sheet under the perpetual inventory system

Accounts Payable	$ 31,000	Inventory	$262,500
Accounts Receivable	78,500	Notes Payable, Long-Term	250,000
Accumulated Amortization— Store Equipment	30,750	Salaries Payable	11,500
M. Sterling, Capital	451,700	Sales Discounts	12,500
M. Sterling, Withdrawals	41,150	Sales Returns and Allowances	26,400
Cash	3,100	Sales Revenue	945,600
Cost of Goods Sold	803,000	Selling Expenses	158,625
General Expenses	122,125	Store Equipment	242,000
Interest Expense	5,100	Supplies	8,100
Interest Payable	4,400	Unearned Sales Revenue	37,400
Interest Revenue	750		

Required

1. Prepare Massood's Muffins' single-step income statement for the year ended July 31, 2020. Show Net Sales Revenue and not the individual accounts.
2. Prepare Massood's Muffins' statement of owner's equity.
3. Prepare Massood's Muffins' classified balance sheet in report format at July 31, 2020.

(4) (5)
Preparing a multi-step income statement and calculating gross margin percentage under the perpetual inventory system

P5–7B 1. Use the data in P5–6B to prepare Massood's Muffins' multi-step income statement for the year ended July 31, 2020.
2. Massood Sterling, the owner of the company, strives to earn a gross margin of at least 50 percent and a net income of 20 percent (Net income percentage = Net income ÷ Net sales revenue). Did the business achieve these goals? Show your calculations. Round your answer to one decimal place.

(3) (5)
Making closing entries and computing gross margin percentage and inventory turnover under the perpetual inventory system

P5–8B The adjusted trial balance of Harrison Trading Company at September 30, 2020, appears below. Harrison Trading Company uses the perpetual inventory system.

HARRISON TRADING COMPANY
Adjusted Trial Balance
September 30, 2020

Account Title	Debit	Credit
Cash	$ 14,000	
Accounts receivable	9,000	
Inventory	42,000	
Supplies	3,000	
Building	280,000	
Accumulated amortization—building		$196,000
Land	70,000	
Accounts payable		11,000
Salary payable		2,400
Unearned sales revenue		1,600
Note payable, long-term		80,000
B. Harrison, capital		70,900
B. Harrison, withdrawals	55,000	
Sales revenue		355,000
Sales returns	14,000	
Cost of goods sold	167,000	
Selling expenses	36,500	
General expenses	22,400	
Interest expense	4,000	
Total	$716,900	$716,900

Required

1. Journalize Harrison Trading Company's closing entries.
2. Compute the gross margin percentage and the rate of inventory turnover for 2020, rounded to one decimal place. Inventory on hand at September 30, 2019, was $40,000. For 2019, Harrison Trading Company's gross margin percentage was 34.8 percent and the inventory turnover rate was 3.9 times. Does the two-year trend in these ratios suggest improvement or deterioration in profitability?

***P5–9B** The following transactions occurred between Wentworth Pharmaceuticals and Tweed Drug Stores during June of the current year:

(A1) Accounting for the purchase and sale of inventory under the periodic system

Jun.	6	Tweed purchased $29,400 of merchandise from Wentworth on credit terms 2/10, n/30, FOB shipping point. Separately, Tweed paid freight-in of $300. Wentworth invoiced Tweed for $29,400.
	10	Tweed returned $3,600 of the merchandise purchased on June 6. Wentworth issued a credit memo for this amount.
	15	Tweed paid $12,000 of the invoice amount owed to Wentworth for the June 6 purchase. This payment included none of the freight charge.
	27	Tweed paid the remaining amount owed to Wentworth for the June 6 purchase.

Required Journalize these transactions, first on the books of Tweed Drug Stores and second on the books of Wentworth Pharmaceuticals. Assume both companies use the periodic inventory system.

***P5–10B** Mid-Century Antiques, which uses a periodic inventory system, engaged in the following transactions during July of the current year:

(A1) Journalizing purchase and sale transactions under the periodic inventory system

Jul.	2	Purchased inventory for cash, $6,400, less a quantity discount of $900.
	5	Purchased store supplies on credit terms of net eom, $3,400.
	8	Purchased inventory of $27,000, less a quantity discount of 10 percent, plus freight charges of $1,100. Credit terms are 2/15, n/30.
	9	Sold goods for cash, $10,800.
	11	Returned $1,000 (net amount after the quantity discount) of the inventory purchased on July 8. It was damaged in shipment.
	12	Purchased inventory on credit terms of 2/10, n/30, for $30,000.
	14	Sold inventory on credit terms of 1/10, n/30, for $69,200, less a $6,920 quantity discount.
	16	Received and paid the electricity bill, $3,200.
	20	Received returned inventory from the July 14 sale, $2,500 (net amount after the quantity discount). Mid-Century shipped the wrong goods by mistake.
	21	Paid supplier for goods purchased on July 8.
	23	Received $43,120 cash in partial settlement of the account from the customer who purchased inventory on July 14. Granted the customer a 2 percent discount and credited the customer's account receivable for $44,000.
	30	Paid for the store supplies purchased on July 5.

Required Journalize the preceding transactions on the books of Mid-Century Antiques.

***P5–11B** Selected accounts from the accounting records of Burke Imports at September 30, 2020, are shown below. Burke Imports uses the periodic inventory system.

(2) (5) (A2) Computing cost of goods sold and gross margin in a periodic system, evaluating the business

Cash	$ 28,600
Purchases	206,200
Freight-in	6,200
Sales Revenue	376,400
Purchases Returns and Allowances	3,200
Salaries Payable	4,400
Glen Burke, Capital	66,800
Sales Returns and Allowances	10,600
Inventory: September 30, 2019	46,200
Inventory: September 30, 2020	51,400
Selling Expense	68,400
Equipment	96,000

*These Problems cover Chapter 5 Appendix A topics.

Purchase Discounts	2,730
Accumulated Amortization—Equipment	19,200
Sales Discounts	7,200
General Expenses	37,000
Accounts Payable	29,400
Accounts Receivable	34,400

Required

1. Using the financial statement format as a guide only, show the computation of Burke Imports' net sales, cost of goods sold, and gross margin for the year ended September 30, 2020.
2. Glen Burke, owner of Burke Imports, strives to earn a gross margin percentage of 41.5 percent. Did he achieve this goal?
3. Did the rate of inventory turnover reach the industry average of 3.4 times per year?

(A3) Preparing a merchandiser's worksheet under the periodic inventory system

***P5–12B** Tuttle Electronics' unadjusted trial balance below pertains to December 31, 2020.

TUTTLE ELECTRONICS
Unadjusted Trial Balance
December 31, 2020

Account Title	Debit	Credit
Cash	$ 22,150	
Accounts receivable	109,600	
Inventory	108,300	
Store supplies	28,800	
Prepaid insurance	18,000	
Store fixtures	270,000	
Accumulated amortization—store fixtures		$ 162,000
Accounts payable		69,900
Salaries payable		0
Interest payable		0
Note payable, long-term		47,000
F. Tuttle, capital		119,000
F. Tuttle, withdrawals	52,000	
Sales revenue		1,290,500
Purchases	737,900	
Salaries expense	238,600	
Rent expense	52,000	
Utilities expense	36,200	
Amortization expense—store fixtures	0	
Insurance expense	6,000	
Store supplies expense	0	
Interest expense	2,350	
Miscellaneous expense	6,500	
Total	$1,688,400	$1,688,400

*These Problems cover Chapter 5 Appendix A topics.

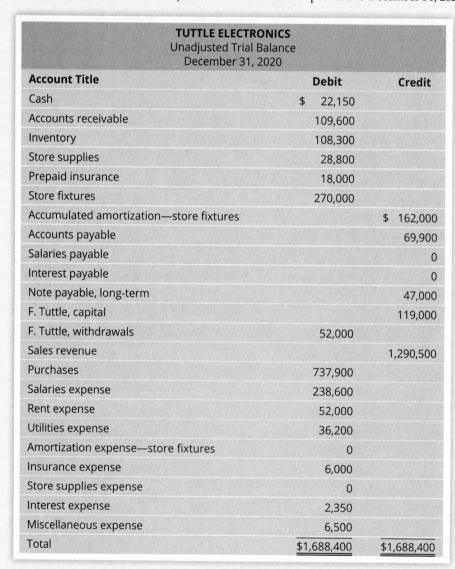

Additional data at December 31, 2020:

a. Insurance expense for the year should total $21,600.

b. Store fixtures have an estimated useful life of 10 years and are expected to have no value when they are retired from service.

c. Accrued salaries at December 31, $5,500.

d. Accrued interest expense at December 31, $1,600.

e. Store supplies on hand at December 31, $23,800.

f. Inventory based on the inventory count on December 31, $116,500.

Required Tuttle Electronics uses the periodic inventory system. Complete Tuttle Electronics' worksheet for the year ended December 31, 2020. Key adjustments by letter. You do not need to complete the adjusted trial balance column as totals can be input directly into the financial statement columns.

***P5–13B** Refer to the data in P5–12B.

A3 Journalizing the adjusting and closing entries of a merchandising business under the periodic inventory system

Required

1. Journalize the adjusting and closing entries of Tuttle Electronics.
2. Determine the December 31, 2020, balance in the Capital account.

***P5–14B** Selected accounts of Olsevik Janitorial Supplies, at July 31, 2020, are listed in alphabetical order below. For simplicity, all operating expenses are summarized in the Selling Expenses account and the General Expenses account. Olsevik Janitorial Supplies uses the periodic inventory system.

5 A4 Preparing a multi-step income statement and a classified balance sheet under the periodic inventory system and evaluate gross margin

Accounts Payable	$102,000	Inventory: July 31, 2019	$ 730,000
Accounts Receivable	117,000	Inventory: July 31, 2020	525,000
Accumulated Amortization— Equipment	61,500	Notes Payable, LongTerm	500,000
		Purchases	1,361,000
B. Olsevik, Capital	863,400	Salaries Payable	23,000
B. Olsevik, Withdrawals	42,300	Sales Discounts	25,000
Cash	46,200	Sales Returns and Allowances	52,800
Equipment	484,000		
General Expenses	284,250	Sales Revenue	1,891,200
Interest Expense	10,200	Selling Expenses	317,250
Interest Payable	8,800	Supplies	16,200
Interest Revenue	1,500	Unearned Sales Revenue	34,800

Required

1. Prepare the business's multi-step income statement for the year ended July 31, 2020.
2. Prepare Olsevik Janitorial Supplies' statement of owner's equity at July 31, 2020.
3. Prepare Olsevik Janitorial Supplies' classified balance sheet in report format at July 31, 2020.
4. Bev Olsevik, owner of the company, strives to earn a gross margin percentage of at least 28.5 percent and a net income percentage of 15.3 percent (Net income percentage = Net income ÷ Net sales revenue). Did Olsevik Janitorial Supplies achieve these goals? Show your calculations. Round answers to one decimal place.

---

*These Problems cover Chapter 5 Appendix A and B topics.

A1 A2 A3 A4 B1

Journalize, post to T-accounts, year-end adjustment and prepare financial statements with a comparison between periodic and perpetual methods

***P5–15B** Kellet International engaged in the following transactions during November 2020, the first month of the company's fiscal year. Assume the company had no inventory on hand prior to November 3. Kellet International has a periodic inventory system.

Nov.	3	Purchased inventory costing $7,000 on credit terms of 1/10, net eom. The goods were shipped FOB Kellet's warehouse.
	9	Returned 20 percent of the inventory purchased on November 3. It was defective.
	12	Sold goods for cash, $6,000 (cost, $3,000).
	15	Purchased inventory of $15,400, less a $400 quantity discount. Credit terms were 1/15, n/30. The goods were shipped FOB the supplier's warehouse.
	16	Paid a $1,200 freight bill on the inventory purchased on November 15.
	18	Sold inventory for $9,000 on credit terms of 1/10, n/30 (cost, $4,500).
	22	Received merchandise returned from the customer from the November 18 sale, $2,000 (cost, $1,000). Merchandise was the wrong size.
	24	Borrowed exactly enough money from the bank to pay for the November 15 purchase in time to take advantage of the discount offered. Signed a note payable to the bank for the net amount.
	24	Paid supplier for goods purchased on November 15, less all returns and discounts.
	28	Received cash in full settlement of the account from the customer who purchased inventory on November 18, less the return on November 22 and less the discount.
	29	Paid the amount owed on account from the purchase of November 3, less the November 9 return.
	30	Purchased inventory for cash, $4,640, less a quantity discount of $140.

Required

1. Journalize the transactions and include any calculations in the journal entry explanations.
2. Refer to the Kellet International journal entries in Requirement 1 to set up T-accounts, and post the journal entries to calculate the ending balances for the cost of goods sold equation accounts. Set up a t-account for H. Kellet, Capital at this time.
3. Calculate cost of goods sold using an ending inventory value of $16,000.
4. Assume Kellet International has two year-end adjusting entries: (a) accrue accounting expenses of $1,000, and (b) accrue a sale of $2,000 that was completed on November 30 but unrecorded. Record and post the adjusting entries and closing entries for Kellet International.
5. Prepare the financial statements under the periodic inventory system.
6. Refer to the Kellet International journal entries in Requirement 1 above. Assume that the note payable signed on November 24 requires the payment of $250 interest expense. Was the decision to borrow funds to take advantage of the cash discount wise or unwise?
7. Compare the results of the Summary Problem on page 266 with this solution (periodic). What main differences do you notice?

---

*These Problems cover Chapter 5 Appendix A topics.

CHALLENGE PROBLEMS

P5–1C You have been hired recently as an accountant by Apex, a small chain of stores that sells wireless products. One of your first activities is to review the accounting system for Apex.

(1) (2) (5)
Understanding purchasing and gross margin

In your review, you discover that the company determines selling prices by adding a standard markup on cost of 10 percent (i.e., cost plus 10 percent of cost) to the cost of all products. The company uses a perpetual inventory system. You also discover that your predecessor, a bookkeeper, had set up the accounting system so that all purchase discounts and purchase returns and allowances were accumulated in an account that was treated as "other income" for financial statement purposes because he believed that they were financing items and not related to operations.

Sarah Hussey, owner of Apex, uses modern decision-making techniques in running Apex. Two ratios she particularly favours are the gross margin percentage and inventory turnover ratio.

Required

1. What is a possible effect of the accounting system described on the pricing of products and thus operations of Apex stores?
2. What is the effect of the accounting system instituted by your predecessor on the two ratios Ms. Hussey favours?

***P5–2C** Rob Carson is concerned about theft by shoplifters in his chain of three discount stores and has come to your public accounting firm for advice. Specifically, he has several questions he would like you to answer:

(1) (B1)
Using an inventory system for control

a. He wonders if there is any inventory system he can use that will allow him to keep track of products that leave his stores as legitimate sales and will also allow him to determine if inventory has been lost or stolen.
b. He realizes that carrying inventory is expensive. He wants to know if you have any suggestions as to how he can keep close tabs on his inventory at the three stores so he can be sure that the stores don't run out of product or have too much on hand.
c. The space in the stores is limited. Rob wants to install an inventory system that will tell him when a product is slow-moving or obsolete so he can clear it out and replace it with a potentially faster-moving product.

Required Indicate whether a perpetual inventory system or a periodic inventory system will provide Rob with answers to the three questions he has asked. Explain how the inventory system indicated will provide the specific information he has requested.

---

*This Problem covers Chapter 5 Appendix B topic.

Extending Your Knowledge

DECISION PROBLEMS

(3) Evaluating an inventory error

DP5–1

The employees of Olford Furniture Company made an error when they performed the periodic inventory count at year-end, October 31, 2020. Part of one warehouse was not counted and therefore was not included in inventory. (Assume the error is not material, so the October 31, 2020, financial statements were not corrected.)

Required

1. Indicate the effect of the inventory error on cost of goods sold, gross margin, and net income for the year ended October 31, 2020.
2. Will the error affect cost of goods sold, gross margin, and net income in 2021? If so, what will be the effect?

(4) (5) Using financial statements to decide on a business expansion

Net income, $182,200

DP5–2

Meaghan Mirkle owns the Unicorn Day Spa, which has prospered during its second year of operation. To help Mirkle decide whether to open another spa in the area, her bookkeeper has prepared the current income statement of the business.

UNICORN DAY SPA Income Statement For the Year Ended December 31, 2020		
Sales revenue		$740,000
Interest revenue		30,000
Total revenue		770,000
Cost of goods sold		348,000
Gross margin		422,000
Operating expenses		
Salaries expense	$127,000	
Rent expense	32,000	
Amortization expense	24,500	
Interest expense	10,500	
Utilities expense	6,800	
Supplies expense	4,000	
Total operating expenses		204,800
Income from operations		217,200
Other revenues		
Sales discounts ($11,000) and returns ($24,000)		35,000
Net income		$252,200

Mirkle recently read in an industry trade journal that a successful two-year-old spa meets these criteria:

a. Gross margin is at least 48.7 percent.

b. Net income is at least $150,000.

Basing her opinion on the entity's income statement data, Mirkle believes the business meets both criteria. She plans to go ahead with the expansion plan and asks your advice.

When you point out that the income statement includes errors, Mirkle asks you to prepare a corrected statement prior to analyzing the results.

Required Prepare a correct multi-step income statement and make a recommendation about whether to undertake the expansion at this time.

FINANCIAL STATEMENT CASE

FSC5–1

(3) Closing entries for a corporation that sells merchandise

This problem uses both the statement of earnings (income statement) and the balance sheet of Indigo Books and Music Inc. (Indigo) that appear in Appendix A at the end of this book and on MyLabAccounting.

1. Journalize Indigo's closing entries for the year ended April 1, 2017, up to the line Operating profit. Instead of closing to a Capital account, close to the Retained Earnings account (since Indigo is a corporation, not a proprietorship). What was the amount closed to Retained Earnings?
2. What amounts go into the inventory value shown on the balance sheet? Why are online shipping costs excluded from the inventory total? See Note 7 in the annual report for this detail.
3. What amounts are shown on the balance sheet for the Inventory account for April 1, 2017, and April 2, 2016?

IFRS MINI-CASE

The IFRS Mini-Case is now available at **MyLab Accounting** in Chapter Resources.

Try It! Solutions for Chapter 5

1. a. Gross margin = $40,000
   b. Sales revenue = $40,000
   c. Cost of goods sold = $30,000
2.

2020				
Jun. 3	Inventory		14,500	
	Accounts Payable			14,500
7	Accounts Payable		2,700	
	Inventory			2,700
9	Inventory		750	
	Cash			750
10	Cash		2,400	
	Accounts Receivable		9,100	
	Sales Revenue			11,500
10	Cost of Goods Sold		6,900	
	Inventory			6,900
12	Accounts Payable*		11,800	
	Inventory**			118
	Cash***			11,682
16	Sales Return and Allowances		1,200	
	Accounts Receivable			1,200
23	Cash†		7,742	
	Sales Discounts††		158	
	Accounts Receivable†††			7,900

*($14,500 – $2,700)
**($11,800 × 0.01)
***($11,800 – $118)
†($7,900) – $158)
††($7,900 × 0.02)
†††($9,100 × $1,200)

3. The journal entry would be:

2020			
Dec. 31	Cost of Goods Sold	15,000	
	Inventory		15,000
	To record adjustment for inventory shrinkage, calculated as $125,000 – $110,000 = $15,000.		

4. The journal entry would be:

2020			
Dec. 31	Inventory	3,000	
	Cost of Goods Sold		3,000
	To record adjustment to inventory records based on physical count, calculated as $78,000 – $75,000 = $3,000.		

5.

PATTI'S PARTY SUPPLIES
Income Statement
For the Year Ended December 31, 2020

Revenues		
Sales revenue		$244,000
Less: Sales discounts	$ 10,000	
Sales returns and allowances	8,000	18,000
Net sales revenue		226,000
Interest revenue		2,000
Total revenue		228,000
Expenses		
Cost of goods sold	$ 81,000	
Operating expenses	106,300	
Interest expense	2,900	
Total expenses		190,200
Net income		$ 37,800

6.

PATTI'S PARTY SUPPLIES
Income Statement
For the Year Ended December 31, 2020

Sales revenue		$244,000
Less: Sales discounts	$10,000	
Sales returns and allowances	8,000	18,000
Net sales revenue		226,000
Cost of goods sold		81,000
Gross margin		145,000
Operating expenses		106,300
Operating income		38,700
Other revenue and expense		
Interest revenue	2,000	
Interest expense	2,900	(900)
Net income		$ 37,800

7. Gross margin percentage = Gross margin revenue / Net sales
= \$145,000 ÷ \$226,000 = 64.2%

8. Inventory turnover = Cost of goods sold / Average inventory
= \$81,000 + [(\$24,000 + \$25,800) ÷ 2]
= 3.25 times

9.

2020			
Jun. 3	Purchases	14,500	
	Accounts Payable		14,500
7	Accounts Payable	2,700	
	Purchases Returns and Allowances		2,700
9	Freight-in	750	
	Cash		750
10	Cash	2,400	
	Accounts Receivable	9,100	
	Sales Revenue		11,500
12	Accounts Payable	11,800	
	Purchases Discounts *		118
	Cash		11,682
16	Sales Return and Allowances	1,200	
	Accounts Receivable		1,200
23	Cash	7,742	
	Sales Discounts**	158	
	Accounts Receivable		7,900

*(\$14,500 − \$2,700) × 0.01 = \$118
**(\$9,100 − \$1,200) × 0.02 = \$158

10. Beginning Inventory + Net Purchases − Ending Inventory − Cost of Goods Sold
\$0 + (\$14,500 − \$2,700 − \$118 + \$750) − \$11,000 = \$1,432
Net Sales − Cost of Goods Sold = Gross Profit
(\$11,500 − \$1,200 − \$158) − \$1,432 = \$8,710

11. The closing entries are as follows:

2020			
Jun. 30	Sales Revenue	11,500	
	Purchases Returns and Allowances	2,700	
	Purchases Discounts	118	
	Income Summary		14,318
30	Income Summary	16,608	
	Purchases		14,500
	Freight-in		750
	Sales Returns and Allowances		1,200
	Sales Discounts		158
30	Income Summary	0	
	Inventory (Beginning)		0
30	Inventory (Ending)	11,000	
	Income Summary		11,000
30	Income Summary	8,710	
	Capital Account		8,710

6 Accounting for Merchandise Inventory

CONNECTING CHAPTER 6

LEARNING OBJECTIVES

The **Summary** for Chapter 6 appears on page 343.
Key Terms with definitions for this chapter's material appears on page 344.

CPA competencies

This textbook covers material outlined in **Section 1: Financial Reporting of the CPA Competency Map.** The Learning Objectives for each chapter have been aligned with the CPA Competency Map to ensure the best coverage possible.

1.2.2 Evaluates treatment for routine transactions

Courtesy of Plentea Inc.

The luxury tea market is growing in Canada. There is a wide variety of tea available: white, black, green, oolng, pu'erh, herbal, fruit, rooibos, chai and matcha are just a few of the popular ones.

Plentea Tea Bar is one of many hip tea emporiums which have popped up across the country serving hot tea, cold tea, tea lattes, and tea frappes.

Mohammed Binyahya and Tariq Al Barwani met as engineering students at the University of Calgary and later opened their shop in the trendy Toronto Parkdale neighbourhood. The partners thought of their unique version of a tea business by remembering the custom brewed teas which were popular where they grew up — in the United Arab Emirates. They felt that something similar could be successful in Toronto.

There isn't a tea bag to be found in this store. Plentea makes a custom blend for each customer as they walk in the door. Their wall of tea holds all the ingredients for them to either whip up one of their signature blends or to create something unique. Their slogan "make new patterns" reflects their passion for creating a customized tea experience with herbs and spices which are ground by pestle and mortar or pressed through a "teapresso" machine.

Sourcing, ordering, and managing inventory for this wide variety of teas, spices, and herbs is key to their successful business. Tea needs to be sold when fresh and it needs to be in stock when a customer comes into their shop. The accounting records that Plentea keeps will track what is purchased, when it is sold, and for how much.

The last chapter introduced accounting for merchandise inventory. It showed how Slopes Ski Shop, a sporting goods store, recorded the purchase and sale of its inventory. At that time, the cost of goods sold figure was either given to you (in the perpetual method) or calculated (in the periodic method). This chapter completes the accounting for merchandise inventory by showing how these costs are calculated under a couple of different costing methods.

Now we follow the fictitious transactions of a Canadian success story Plentea. What if Plentea decided to add their own custom blend of chai tea in a gift box for sale at Christmas? Then Plentea would need to select from several different accounting methods to track this new inventory purchased from their supplier. We will show how each method works so that by the end of this chapter, you will also be prepared to decide which accounting method is most appropriate if you ever start your own business.

First, let's review the balance sheet and the income statement. Exhibit 6–1 gives information found in The Second Cup Ltd.'s balance sheet and income statement. Inventories, cost of goods sold (sometimes called cost of sales), and gross margin are the focus of this chapter.

EXHIBIT 6–1 | The Second Cup Ltd.'s Financial Statements—Inventory-Related Sections

THE SECOND CUP LTD. Balance Sheet (partial, adapted) December 31, 2016	
Assets	(thousands)
Current assets	
Cash and cash equivalents	$3,004
Trade and other receivables	3,023
Inventories	200
Prepaid expenses and other assets	251

THE SECOND CUP LTD. Income Statement (partial, adapted) For the year ended December 31, 2016	
	(thousands)
Revenue	$14,663
Cost of goods sold	10,668
Gross margin	$ 3,395

Based on The Second Cup Ltd. in its 2016 annual report

As you can see in Exhibit 6–1, inventory is worth $200,000. Is this the "right" amount of inventory? Companies want to make sure that they carry enough inventory to meet customer demand. At the same time, if companies carry too much inventory, they risk "tying up" too much of the company's assets in inventory and the money invested in this asset could be better used elsewhere. In the case of Plentea or The Second Cup Ltd., managing the supply of inventory for freshness and cost may matter the most.

Inventory Costing Methods

Companies determine the number of units from perpetual inventory records that are verified by a physical count. Recall that the cost of inventory is

LO 1

Are there different methods used to account for perpetual inventory?

Inventory cost = Purchase price − Purchase discounts − Quantity discounts + Any costs necessary to put the unit in a saleable condition, such as freight-in, customs duties, and insurance

In this chapter we want to get more detailed about the unit cost of inventory. In other words, if there is \$60,000 of inventory, it would be more useful to know that there are 1,000 units at a cost of \$60 each.

We can use the inventory cost stated on a per-unit basis to determine the value of the ending inventory and cost of goods sold on the financial statements:

Ending Inventory = Number of units *on hand* × Unit cost

Cost of goods sold = Number of units *sold* × Unit cost

Let's imagine a three-month period where the boxes of tea were purchased first for \$55 each (including all discounts and transportation), then a month later for \$60 each, and then in the most recent month for \$65 each. Now what is the cost of each unit left in inventory after some of the tea is sold? Well, the answer to that question is "It depends!" It depends on what costing method is used. And that is what is discussed in the first part of this chapter.

The accounting profession has developed three costing methods that are compliant with accounting standards for private enterprises (ASPE) and acceptable to the Canada Revenue Agency:

- Specific-unit cost
- First-in, first-out (FIFO) cost
- Weighted-average cost

The method chosen will have a direct effect on the balance sheet, the income statement, and cash flows (since it affects the amount of income tax paid). Once it is chosen, however, the company should use the same method going forward for consistency and comparability.

Specific-Unit-Cost Method The **specific-unit-cost method**, also called the **specific identification method**, uses the specific cost of each unit of inventory for items that have a distinct identity. Some businesses deal in items that differ from unit to unit, such as automobiles, jewels, and real estate.

For example, a small used car dealership starts the month with no inventory. During the month it purchases two vehicles: a model with vehicle identification number (VIN) 010 that costs \$21,000 and a model with VIN 020 that costs \$27,000. This means that the cost of goods available for sale is \$48,000. If the dealer sells the model with VIN 020, cost of goods sold is \$27,000, the cost of the specific unit. Since the model with VIN 010 is the only unit left in inventory at the end of the period, ending inventory is \$21,000, the dealer's cost of that particular car.

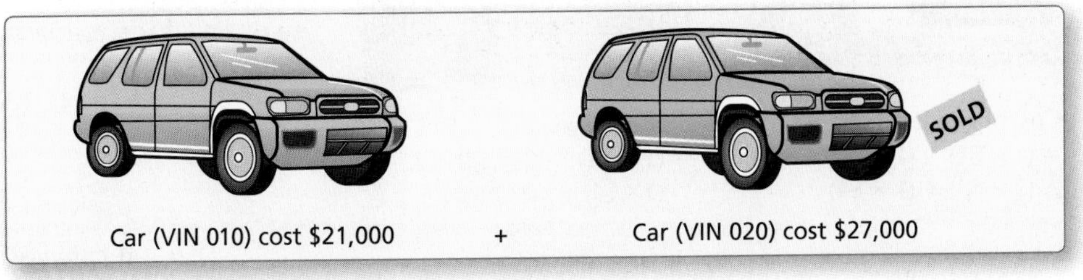

Beginning inventory	$ 0
Purchases	
VIN 010	$21,000
VIN 020	27,000
Cost of goods available for sale	48,000
Ending inventory (VIN 010)	$21,000
Cost of goods sold (VIN 020)	$27,000

Cost Flows for Identical Inventory . Many companies have units of inventory that are exactly the same—they cannot tell one unit of inventory from another. These companies use either the first-in, first-out method or the weighted-average-cost method to value inventory. These methods are *cost flow assumptions* that do not have to match the actual flow of inventory costs:

- Under the first-in, first-out (FIFO) method, the cost of goods sold is based on the oldest purchases. Perishables like milk or eggs are a good example: You have to sell the oldest inventory items first, before they go bad.

- Under the weighted-average-cost methods, the cost of goods sold is based on the weighted-average cost for the period. *Weighted* means that the quantity of goods purchased at each price influences the average. For example, if you buy three mugs at $10 each and one mug for $5, the weighted-average cost of the four mugs is $8.75 each (and not the average of the two *prices* paid, which is ($10 + $5)/2 = $7.50). The calculation of this weighted average is different depending on whether the periodic or perpetual method is used. When using the perpetual method, it is a moving weighted average (you calculate a new average after each transaction), and when using the periodic system, it is an average for the entire period. More details about these methods follow with examples of calculations and the related journal entries.

Exhibit 6–2 summarizes the inventory costing methods with a simple example that shows each method's effects on the income statement (sales, cost of goods sold, and gross margin) and the balance sheet (ending inventory).

EXHIBIT 6–2 | Inventory Costing Methods Illustrated

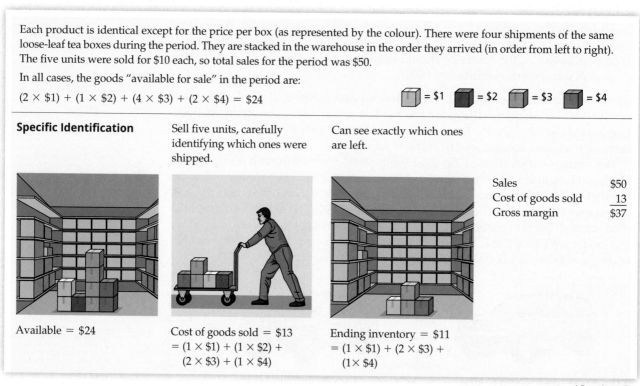

Each product is identical except for the price per box (as represented by the colour). There were four shipments of the same loose-leaf tea boxes during the period. They are stacked in the warehouse in the order they arrived (in order from left to right). The five units were sold for $10 each, so total sales for the period was $50.

In all cases, the goods "available for sale" in the period are:

$(2 \times \$1) + (1 \times \$2) + (4 \times \$3) + (2 \times \$4) = \$24$ □ = $1 ■ = $2 □ = $3 ■ = $4

Specific Identification Sell five units, carefully identifying which ones were shipped. Can see exactly which ones are left.

Sales	$50
Cost of goods sold	13
Gross margin	$37

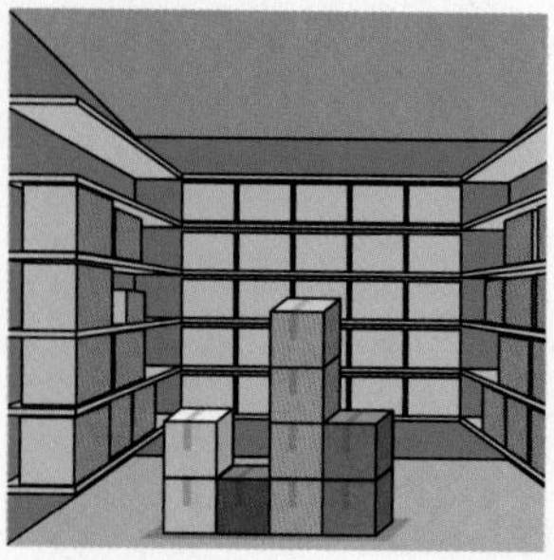

Available = $24

Cost of goods sold = $13
= (1 × $1) + (1 × $2) +
 (2 × $3) + (1 × $4)

Ending inventory = $11
= (1 × $1) + (2 × $3) +
 (1 × $4)

(Continued)

EXHIBIT 6–2 | Inventory Costing Methods Illustrated (*Continued*)

FIFO

The first boxes in are the first ones shipped out.

What's left are the most recent purchases.

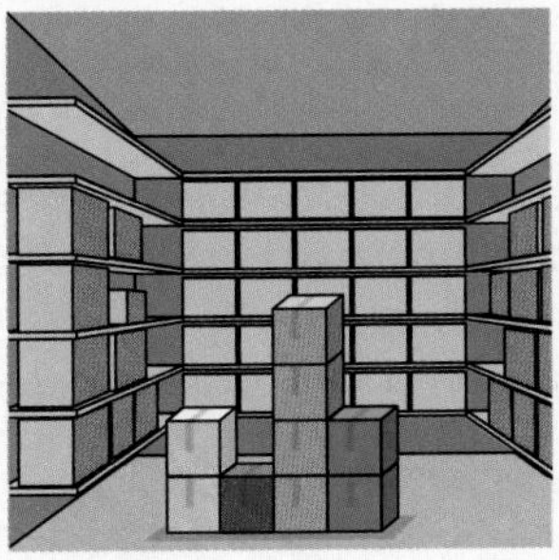

Available = $24

Cost of goods sold = $10
= (2 × $1) + (1× $2) +
(2 × $3)

Ending inventory = $14
= (2 × $3) + (2 × $4)

Sales	$50
Cost of goods sold	10
Gross margin	$40

Weighted Average*
Start with nine cases.

Sell five cases.

The four left are at an average price per unit.

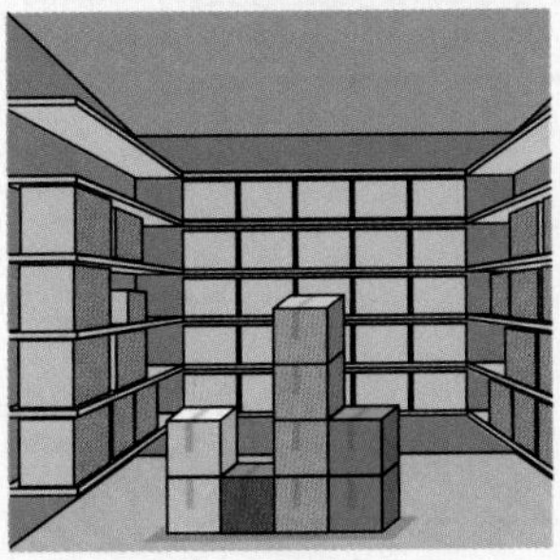

Available = $24
÷ 9 units = $2.67 each**

Cost of goods sold = $13.35
= 5 × $2.67

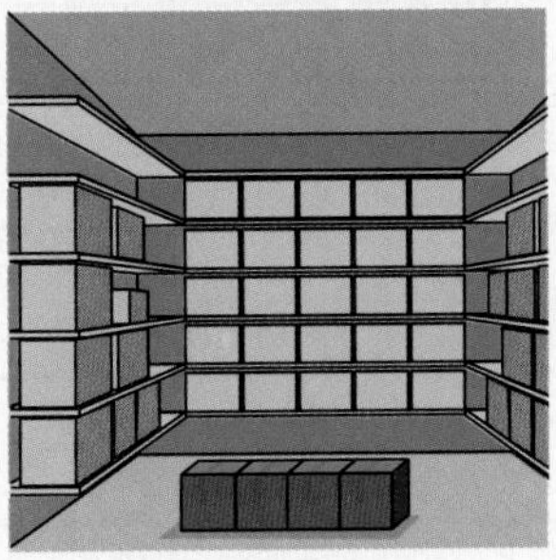

Ending inventory = $10.65**
= 4 × $2.67 = 10.68

Sales	$50.00
Cost of goods sold	13.35
Gross margin	$36.65

*After one shipment. This repeats to have a new average after each purchase or sale and is called a "moving weighted average" when the perpetual inventory method is used.

**Rounded to two decimal places. Notice the rounding difference.

Inventory Costing in a Perpetual System

We use the following transaction data for the next illustrations:

Chai Tea Box			Number of Units	Unit Cost
Nov.	1	Beginning inventory	10	$10
	5	Purchase	60	11
	15	Sale	30	
	26	Purchase	70	12
	30	Sale	90	

Plentea sells their most popular chai blend at $25 per gift box.
All purchase and sale transactions are on account.

Notice as we work through the examples that the inventory costing methods produce different amounts for:

- Ending inventory
- Cost of goods sold

First-in, First-out Method

FIFO assumes that goods in first are sold first; therefore, the last goods purchased are left in ending inventory.

Many companies use the **first-in, first-out (FIFO) method** to account for their inventory. FIFO costing is consistent with the physical movement of inventory for most companies. That is, they sell their oldest inventory first.

For Plentea, we can see how this works for their transactions as illustrated in the FIFO perpetual inventory record shown in Exhibit 6–3.

EXHIBIT 6–3 | Perpetual Inventory Record—FIFO Cost for Chai Tea Boxes

	A	B	C	D	E	F	G	H	I	J	
1	Chai Tea Boxes										
2		Purchases			Cost of Goods Sold			Inventory on Hand			
3	Date	Qty.	Unit Cost	Total Cost	Qty.	Unit Cost	Total Cost	Qty.	Unit Cost	Total Cost	
4	Nov. 1							10	× $10	= $100	Beginning inventory
5	5	60	× $11	= $ 660				10	× $10	= $100	$760
6								60	× $11	= $660	
7	15				30 { 10	× $10	= $ 100				
8					20	× $11	= $ 220	40	× $11	= $440	
9	26	70	× $12	= $ 840				40	× $11	= $440	$1,280
10								70	× $12	= $840	
11	30				90 { 40	× $11	= $ 440				
12					50	× $12	= $ 600	20	× $12	= $240	
13	Ending	130		$1,500	120		$1,360	20		$240	Ending inventory

Plentea began November with 10 chai tea boxes that cost $10 each. After the November 5 purchase of 60 boxes at $11 each, the inventory on hand consists of 70 boxes with a total cost of $760.

70 boxes on hand	10 at $10	=	$ 100
	60 at $11	=	660
	Inventory on hand	=	$760

On November 15, Plentea sold 30 boxes. Under FIFO costing, the first 10 boxes sold are costed at the oldest price ($10 per box). The next 20 boxes sold come from the shipment that cost $11 per box. That leaves 40 units in inventory on hand, and those units cost $11 each. The remainder of the inventory record follows that same pattern.

The FIFO monthly summary at November 30 is:

- Cost of goods sold: 120 boxes that cost a total of $1,360
- Ending inventory: 20 boxes that cost a total of $240

You can verify this by recalling that under this method, the most recent purchases are left in inventory (since the oldest goods are sold first), so the 20 remaining boxes would be from the November 26 purchase, which cost $12 per box (20 × $12 = $240).

You can also use the cost of goods sold model to check the accuracy of the inventory record, as follows:

Beginning inventory	$ 100	10 units at $10
Net purchases	1,500	60 units at $11 + 70 units at $12
Cost of goods available for sale	1,600	140 units
Less: Ending inventory	240	20 units at $12
Cost of goods sold	$1,360	120 units

Journal Entries under FIFO The journal entries under FIFO costing for the perpetual inventory system follow the data in Exhibit 6–3. For example, on November 5, Plentea purchased $660 of inventory on account and made the first journal entry. On November 15, Plentea sold 30 boxes of chai tea for $25 each, at which time it recorded the sale ($750) and the cost of goods sold ($320). The remaining journal entries (November 26 and 30) follow the inventory data in Exhibit 6–3.

Nov. 5	Inventory	660	
	Accounts Payable		660
	Purchased inventory on account (60 × $11 = $660).		
15	Accounts Receivable	750	
	Sales Revenue		750
	Sale on account (30 × $25 = $750).		
15	Cost of Goods Sold	320	
	Inventory		320
	Cost of goods sold (($10 × $10) + (20 × $11) = $320).		
26	Inventory	840	
	Accounts Payable		840
	Purchased inventory on account (70 × $12 = 840).		
30	Accounts Receivable	2,250	
	Sales Revenue		2,250
	Sale on account (90 × $25 = $2,250).		
30	Cost of Goods Sold	1,040	
	Inventory		1,040
	Cost of goods sold ((40 × $11) + ($12 × 50) = $1,040).		

Moving-Weighted-Average-Cost Method

Suppose Plentea uses the **moving-weighted-average-cost method** to account for its inventory. **With this method, the business computes a new weighted-average cost per unit after each purchase.** Ending inventory and cost of goods sold are then based on the same, most recent, weighted-average cost per unit. Exhibit 6–4 shows a perpetual inventory record for the moving-weighted-average-cost method. *We round average unit cost to the nearest cent and total cost to the nearest dollar for this example.*

EXHIBIT 6-4 | Perpetual Inventory Record—Moving-Weighted-Average Cost for Chai Tea Boxes

	A	B	C	D	E	F	G	H	I	J
1	Chai Tea Boxes									
2		Purchases			Cost of Goods Sold			Inventory on Hand		
3	Date	Qty.	Unit Cost	Total Cost	Qty.	Unit Cost	Total Cost	Qty.	Unit Cost	Total Cost
4	Nov. 1							10	× $10.00	= $ 100
5	5	60	× $11	= $ 660				70	× $10.86	= $ 760*
6	15				30	× $10.86	= $ 326	40	× $10.86	= $ 434
7	26	70	× $12	= $ 840				110	× $11.58	= $1,274
8	30				90	× $11.58	= $1,042	20	× $11.58	= $ 232
9	Ending	130		$1,500	120		$1,368	20		$ 232

*$10.86 × 70 = $760.20, rounded to $760. Rest of calculations are also rounded.

Beginning inventory

($100 + $660) ÷ 70 boxes = $10.857142 or $10.86

= $760 − $326

($434 + $840) ÷ 110 = $11.581818 or $11.58

Ending inventory

After each purchase, Plentea computes a new average cost per unit. For example, on November 5, the new weighted-average unit cost combines the cost and quantity of units on hand on November 1 with the November 5 purchase and is calculated as

Businesses typically don't round until the final calculation to be more accurate. In this chapter we round unit cost to the nearest cent and the rest of the calculations to the nearest dollar.

	Total cost of inventory on hand	÷	Number of units on hand	=	Average cost per unit
Nov. 5	$100 + $660 = $760	÷	70 boxes	=	$10.86*

*760 ÷ 70 = $10.857142, rounded to $10.86

The 30 boxes sold on November 15 cost $10.86 per box for a total cost rounded to $326. The total cost of inventory on hand on November 15 is $434 (calculated as $760 − $326 = $434).

Plentea computes a new average cost after the November 26 purchase, which is why it is called a "moving" weighted-average cost. In this case, the 70 boxes purchased at a higher price bring the average cost up to $11.58 per box.

The moving-weighted-average-cost summary at November 30 is:

- Cost of goods sold: 120 units that cost a total of $1,368
- Ending inventory: 20 units that cost a total of $232

Journal Entries under Moving-Weighted-Average-Cost Method The journal entries under moving-weighted-average costing follow the data in Exhibit 6-4.

Nov. 5	Inventory	660	
	Accounts Payable		660
	Purchased inventory on account (60 × $11 = $660).		
15	Accounts Receivable	750	
	Sales Revenue		750
	Sale on account (30 × $25 = $750).		
15	Cost of Goods Sold	326	
	Inventory		326
	Cost of goods sold (30 × $10.86 = $325.80, rounded to $326).		

(continued)

26	Inventory	840	
	Accounts Payable		840
	Purchased inventory on account (70 × \$12 = \$840).		
30	Accounts Receivable	2,250	
	Sales Revenue		2,250
	Sale on account (90 × \$25 = \$2,250).		
30	Cost of Goods Sold	1,042	
	Inventory		1,042
	Cost of goods sold, calculated as: Cost of inventory on hand: \$434 + \$840 = \$1,274 Moving-weighted-average cost per unit: \$1,274 ÷ 110 = \$11.58 Cost of goods sold = 90 × \$11.58 = \$1,042.20, rounded to \$1,042		

Try It!

1. Assume The Watch Shop began June with an inventory of 20 smart watches that cost \$60 each. The Watch Shop sells them for \$100 each. During June, The Watch Shop bought and sold inventory as follows:

Jun.	3	Sold 16 smart watches for \$100 each.
	16	Purchased 20 smart watches at \$65 each.
	23	Sold 16 smart watches for \$100 each.

Prepare a perpetual inventory record for The Watch Shop under each method:

- FIFO
- Moving-weighted-average cost (round all unit costs to two decimal places and total costs to the nearest whole dollar)

2. Refer to The Watch Shop data given in the previous question. Journalize all of The Watch Shop's inventory transactions for June for the FIFO and moving-weighted-average-cost methods. All transactions are on account.

Solutions appear at the end of this chapter and on **MyLab Accounting**

Comparing FIFO and Moving-Weighted-Average Cost

LO 2

What are the effects of two of the different methods?

What leads any company to select the moving-weighted-average-cost method or to use FIFO? The different methods have different benefits.

Exhibit 6–5 summarizes the assumed results for the two inventory methods for Plentea. It shows sales revenue based on \$25 per box for 120 boxes sold, cost of

EXHIBIT 6–5 | Comparative Results for FIFO and Moving-Weighted-Average Cost

		FIFO		Moving-Weighted-Average
Sales revenue		\$3,000		\$3,000
Cost of goods sold	(from Exhibit 6-3)	1,360	(from Exhibit 6-4)	1,368
Gross margin		\$1,640		\$1,632

goods sold, and gross margin for FIFO and moving-weighted-average costing. The cost of goods sold amounts come from Exhibits 6-3 and 6-4.

Exhibit 6–5 also shows that when inventory costs are increasing, FIFO costing produces the lower cost of goods sold and the higher gross margin compared to the moving-weighted-average costing. Net income is also higher under FIFO costing when inventory costs are rising. Many companies prefer high income to attract investors and borrow money on favourable terms. In an environment of increasing costs, FIFO costing offers this benefit.

The moving-weighted-average-cost method generates a gross margin that will be lower than the gross margin generated under FIFO costing when prices are rising. The opposite is true when inventory purchase prices are falling—the moving-weighted-average-cost method would generate a higher gross margin than FIFO costing.

Try It!

3. Refer to the information in Try It #1 and your journal entries created for Try It #2. Use that information to show the computation of gross margin for the FIFO and moving-weighted-average-cost methods for The Watch Shop.
4. Refer to Try It #3. Which method maximizes net income? Which method minimizes income taxes?
5. How would your answer to Try It #4 change if inventory purchase prices were falling during June?

Solutions appear at the end of this chapter and on **MyLab Accounting**

Inventory Costing in a Periodic System

LO (3)

Are there different methods used to account for periodic inventory?

Accounting is simpler in a periodic system because the company keeps no daily running record of inventory on hand. The only way to determine the ending inventory and cost of goods sold in a periodic system is to count the goods—usually at the end of the year. The periodic system works well for a small business where the owner can control inventory by visual inspection. Appendix A in Chapter 5 illustrates the periodic system in greater detail.

Exhibit 6–6 repeats most of Exhibit 5–2A. It shows the calculation of cost of goods sold in a periodic inventory system.

EXHIBIT 6–6 | Calculation of Cost of Goods Sold in a Periodic Inventory System

Cost of goods sold			
Beginning inventory		$158,400	
Purchases	$422,600		
Less: Purchase discounts	12,000		
Purchase returns and allowances	5,000		
Net purchases		405,600	
Freight-in		31,000	
Cost of goods available for sale		595,000	
Less: Ending inventory		168,000	
Cost of goods sold			$427,000

Inventory on hand at end of last period (→ Beginning inventory)

Inventory on hand at end of the current period (→ Less: Ending inventory)

To show how the periodic inventory system works for the FIFO and weighted-average-cost methods, we use the same Plentea data that we used for the perpetual system, as follows:

For more details, refer to Chapter 5, Appendix A to review the periodic inventory system.

Chai Tea Box			Number of Units	Unit Cost
Nov.	1	Beginning inventory	10	$10
	5	Purchase	60	11
	15	Sale	30	
	26	Purchase	70	12
	30	Sale	90	

Plentea sells their most popular chai blend at $25 per gift box.
All purchase and sale transactions are on account.

First-in, First-out (FIFO) Method

Plentea could use the FIFO costing method with a periodic inventory system. The FIFO computations are as follows:

Beginning inventory	$ 100	10 units at $10
Net purchases	1,500	60 units at $11 + 70 units at $12
Cost of goods available for sale	1,600	140 units
Less: Ending inventory	240	20 units at $12
Cost of goods sold	$1,360	120 units

The cost of goods available for sale is always the sum of beginning inventory plus purchases. Under FIFO costing, the ending inventory comes from the latest—the most recent—purchases, which cost $12 per unit. Ending inventory is therefore $240, and cost of goods sold is $1,360. **These amounts will always be the same as the amounts calculated under the perpetual system.**

There are fewer journal entries in the periodic system because Plentea would record a sale with only a single entry. For example, Plentea's sale on account of 30 boxes of chai tea for $25 each is recorded as follows:

Nov. 15	Accounts Receivable	750	
	Sales Revenue		750
	Sale on account (30 × $25).		

There is no cost of goods sold entry in the periodic inventory system.

Weighted-Average-Cost Method

In the **weighted-average-cost method**, we compute a single weighted-average cost per unit for the entire period as follows:

Cost of goods available for sale	÷	Number of units available for sale	=	Average cost per unit for the entire period
$1,600	÷	140 units	=	$11.43*

Using the weighted-average-cost method, ending inventory and cost of goods sold under the periodic system differ from the amounts in a perpetual system. Why? Because under the perpetual system, a new average cost is computed after each purchase (it is a "moving" weighted-average cost). *But the periodic system uses a single average cost that is determined at the end of the period.*

This average cost per unit (rounded to two decimal places) is then used to compute the ending inventory and cost of goods sold (rounded to the nearest whole dollar) as follows:

Beginning inventory	$ 100	10 units at $10
Net purchases	1,500	60 units at $11 + 70 units at $12
Cost of goods available for sale	1,600	140 units at weighted-average cost of $11.43*
Less: Ending inventory	229*	20 units at $11.43
Cost of goods sold	$1,371*	120 units at $11.43

*Numbers are rounded.

Try It!

6. Pemberton Company began March with 40 units of inventory that cost a total of $800. During March, Pemberton purchased and sold goods as follows:

March	8	Purchased 60 units at $12.50
	14	Sold 50 units at $25
	22	Purchased 40 units at $15
	27	Sold 60 units at $30

Calculate the gross margin amount using the FIFO method assuming Pemberton uses a periodic inventory system.

7. Refer to the Pemberton Company data in the previous question. Calculate the gross margin amount using the weighted-average method assuming Pemberton uses a periodic inventory system.

Solutions appear at the end of this chapter and on **MylLab Accounting**

Other Inventory Issues

LO 4

How do we address other inventory issues?

In addition to choosing between the FIFO and weighted-average costing methods for inventory, accountants face other inventory issues. This section covers:

- Accounting concepts related to inventory
- The lower-of-cost-and-net-realizable-value rule
- Effects of inventory errors
- Estimating ending inventory
- Ethical issues

Accounting Concepts and Inventories

Several accounting concepts, principles, or constraints have special relevance to inventories.

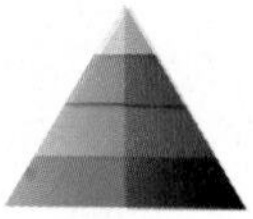

Consistency The **consistency principle** states that businesses should use the same accounting methods and procedures from period to period. Following the consistency principle ensures that the financial statements are *comparable* from one period to the next. **Comparability** is one of the qualitative characteristics that supports the objective of communicating useful information in financial reports (for others, refer to Exhibit 1–5).

Suppose you are analyzing a company's net income pattern over a two-year period. The company switched from moving-weighted-average to FIFO costing during that time. Its net income increased dramatically, but only as a result of the change in inventory method. If you did not know of the change, you might believe that the company's income increased because of improved operations. Therefore, companies must report any changes in the accounting methods they use.

Disclosure The **disclosure principle** holds that a company's financial statements should report enough information for outsiders to make knowledgeable decisions about the company. In short, the company should report *relevant*, *reliable*, *understandable*, and *comparable* information about itself. This means disclosing the method or methods used to value inventories. Suppose a banker is comparing two companies—one using weighted-average costing and the other using FIFO. The FIFO company reports higher net income, but only because it uses the FIFO inventory method. Without knowledge of these accounting methods, the banker could lend money to the wrong business. In addition, different categories of inventory should be disclosed, such as raw materials, work-in-process, and finished goods inventories.

Materiality The **materiality constraint** states that a company must perform strictly proper accounting *only* for items that are significant to the business's financial statements. Information is significant—or, in accounting terminology, *material*—when its presentation in the financial statements would influence a decision or cause someone to change a decision. The materiality constraint frees accountants from having to report every item in strict accordance with ASPE. For inventory, this means immaterial items can be expensed rather than included in inventory.

Accounting Conservatism **Conservatism** in accounting means reporting items in the financial statements at amounts that lead to the most cautious immediate results. Conservatism, which is not part of the conceptual framework, could be interpreted as:

- "Anticipate no gains, but provide for all probable losses."
- "If in doubt, record an asset at the lowest reasonable amount and a liability at the highest reasonable amount."
- "When there's a question, record as an expense rather than record as an asset."

The goal is for financial statements to report realistic figures. While we want to avoid overstating assets and understating liabilities, we also should not deliberately understate assets, revenues, and gains, nor deliberately overstate liabilities, expenses, and losses.

Why It's Done This Way

In this chapter, we have studied three methods used to account for inventory—specific-unit cost; first-in, first-out (FIFO); and weighted-average-cost. We use these methods to determine the cost of goods sold as well as the inventory value at year end. The specific-unit-cost method tells us the cost of the goods sold and the cost of ending inventory precisely. However, the other two methods are approximations of cost of goods sold and ending inventory. In these inventory situations, how do we ensure, based on the relevancy and reliability aspects of the accounting framework, that these flow methods will be useful to users? If FIFO and weighted-average-cost are approximations of inventory value and the cost of goods sold, shouldn't we use only the specific-unit-cost method to get a reliable value for the balance sheet and income statement?

The accounting framework addresses this concern under the constraints section with "materiality." Essentially, materiality allows the accountant to use estimates or approximations of the actual value of an element, like inventory, if the estimate closely reflects the real value. As long as a person reading the financial statements knows the inventory valuation method, this user will not be misled by the use of FIFO or weighted-average-cost. The cost of using the specific-unit-cost method would be more than the benefit of having slightly more accurate financial statements, thus violating the cost–benefit constraint. Thus, the financial statements are still considered relevant and reliable even though the inventory value on the balance sheet (and the cost of goods sold expense on the income statement) is estimated, since they lead to statements that communicate useful information to users at a reasonable cost.

Lower-of-Cost-and-Net-Realizable-Value Rule

The **lower-of-cost-and-net-realizable-value** rule (abbreviated as LCNRV) shows accounting conservatism in action. LCNRV requires that inventory be reported in the financial statements at the lower of its:

- Historic cost
- Net realizable value (market value)

Note that the matching objective of the cost principle of measurement is applied to ending inventory with LCNRV. The reduction in the value of the inventory is shown in the year the inventory declines in value, *not* in the year the inventory is sold.

For inventories, *net realizable value* generally means the expected selling price (i.e., the amount the business could get if it sold the inventory less the costs of selling it).

If the net realizable value of inventory falls below its historical cost, the business must write down the value of its goods. This write-down is known as an **impairment**. This situation may arise if inventory has become damaged or if it has become obsolete. On the balance sheet, the business reports ending inventory at its LCNRV.

At each year end, a new assessment of the net realizable value is made. If the circumstances that caused inventories to be written down below cost no longer exist, the amount of the write-down is reversed, up to the original cost of the inventory in question, which is called an **impairment reversal**. However, inventory is *never* written up to an amount greater than its original cost, since this would violate the LCNRV rule.

Suppose Plentea paid $6,000 for Christmas blend tea inventory on September 26. By December 31, the seasonal inventory can only be sold for $4,000, and the decline in value appears permanent. In order to sell the goods quickly, an online advertisement costing $500 will be required. Net realizable value is below FIFO cost, and the entry to write down the inventory to LCNRV is as follows:

Dec. 31	Costs of Goods Sold*	2,500	
	Inventory		2,500
	To write down inventory to net realizable value.		
	(cost, $6,000 − net realizable value, $4,000 − $500 advertisement)		

*Could also record this in an expense account, such as Holding Loss or Shrinkage.

In this case, Plentea's balance sheet would report this inventory as follows:

Balance Sheet (partial)	
Current assets	
Inventory, at market	$3,500
(which is lower than $6,000 cost)	

Companies often disclose LCNRV in notes to their financial statements, as shown here for The Second Cup Ltd. in its 2016 annual report:

> 3. Summary of Significant Accounting Policies
> g. Inventories
> Inventories are stated at the lower of cost and net realizable value, with cost being determined on an average cost basis. Net realizable value is the estimated recoverable amount less applicable selling expenses. If carrying value exceeds net realizable amount, a write-down in recognized. The write-downs are reversed if circumstances that caused the initial write-down no longer exist.

Effects of Inventory Errors

Businesses count their inventories at the end of the period. For the financial statements to be accurate, it is important to get a correct count of ending inventory. This can be difficult for a company with inventory in many locations.

An error in ending inventory creates a whole string of errors. To illustrate, suppose Plentea accidentally counted too much ending inventory. Therefore, ending inventory is overstated on the balance sheet. The following chart shows how an overstatement (or an understatement) of ending inventory affects cost of goods sold, gross margin, and net income:

	Ending Inventory Overstated	Ending Inventory Understated
Sales revenue	Correct	Correct
Cost of goods sold		
Beginning inventory	Correct	Correct
Net purchases	Correct	Correct
Cost of goods available for sale	Correct	Correct
Ending inventory	**ERROR: Overstated**	**ERROR: Understated**
Cost of goods sold	**Understated**	**Overstated**
Gross margin	**Overstated**	**Understated**
Operating expenses	Correct	Correct
Net income	**Overstated**	**Understated**

Recall that one period's ending inventory is the next period's beginning inventory. Thus, an error in ending inventory carries over into the next period. Exhibit 6–7 illustrates the effect of an inventory error. Period 1's ending inventory is overstated by $10,000. The error carries over to Period 2, but Period 3 is correct. In fact, both Period 1 and Period 2 should look like Period 3.

Use the jingle EI, NI, O to remember the effect on ending inventory. If ending inventory (EI) is overstated, net income (NI) is overstated (O).

EXHIBIT 6–7 | Inventory Errors: An Example

	A	B	C	D	E	F	G
1		**Period 1**		**Period 2**		**Period 3**	
2		**Ending Inventory Overstated by $10,000**		**Beginning Inventory Overstated by $10,000**		**Correct**	
3	Sales revenue		$100,000		$100,000		$100,000
4	Cost of goods sold						
5	Beginning inventory	$10,000		$20,000		$10,000	
6	Net purchases	50,000		50,000		50,000	
7	Cost of goods available for sale	60,000		70,000		60,000	
8	Less: Ending inventory	20,000		10,000		10,000	
9	Cost of goods sold		**40,000**		**60,000**		50,000
10	Gross margin		**$ 60,000**		**$ 40,000**		$ 50,000
11							
12				$100,000			
13	The correct gross margin is $50,000 for each period.						

Ending inventory is *subtracted* in computing cost of goods sold in one period, and the same amount is *added* as beginning inventory the next period. Therefore, an inventory error cancels out after two periods. The overstatement of cost of goods sold in Period 2 counterbalances the understatement for Period 1. Thus, the total gross margin for the two periods combined is correct. These effects are summarized in Exhibit 6–8.

EXHIBIT 6–8 | Effects of Inventory Errors

	Period 1		Period 2	
Inventory Error	**Cost of Goods Sold**	**Gross Margin and Net Income**	**Cost of Goods Sold**	**Gross Margin and Net Income**
Period 1 ending inventory *overstated*	Understated	Overstated	Overstated	Understated
Period 1 ending inventory *understated*	Overstated	Understated	Understated	Overstated

The effect of inventory errors also affects equity because the Income Summary account is closed to equity. However, by the end of Year 2, after closing entries are posted, the inventory errors have cancelled out in equity.

Ethical Issues

Companies whose profits do not meet expectations can be tempted to "cook the books" to increase reported income. The increase in reported income will make the business look more successful than it really is.

There are two main schemes for using inventory to increase reported income:

- The easier, and the more obvious, is to overstate ending inventory. As we have seen, a dollar change in ending inventory means a dollar change in net income. This is one reason auditors examine the ending inventory so carefully.
- The second way of using inventory to increase reported income involves sales. Fiat Chrysler Automobiles (FCA) is being investigated in the United States for fraud—for allegedly overstating sales in order to keep reporting consecutive sales increases for a longer "winning streak." As a result of the investigation, FCA Canada stated that their new sales reporting methodology starting July 2016 "involves reporting sales once a vehicle is shipped to the customer."[1]

ETHICS **Should the inventory be included?**

One of A'isha Sowell's main responsibilities at the end of the accounting period is to supervise the count of physical inventory for her employer. She knows that it is important that the business get an accurate count of inventory so that its financial statements are reported correctly. In reviewing the inventory count sheet, she realizes that a large crate of inventory that has already been sold but not yet delivered was included in the count of inventory. The crate has left her employer but is still in transit at fiscal year-end. A'isha does not believe that it should be included because the inventory was sold FOB shipping point. When A'isha went to her supervisor with this information, she was told that she shouldn't worry about it because the error would ultimately correct itself. What should A'isha do?

Solution

Companies whose profits are lagging can be tempted to increase reported income to make the business look more successful. One easy way to do this is to overstate ending inventory. A'isha is correct in her assumption that the inventory should not be included in the physical count of inventory. While this error will ultimately correct itself (in two years), in the current year, the business will be overstating gross profit and net income. This overstatement could cause investors to view the business more favourably than they should. A'isha should stand firm in her decision to not include the inventory in the count.

[1]http://business.financialpost.com/transportation/fiat-chryslers-canadian-sales-plunge-18-in-september-dragging-down-sales-data

Try It!

8. Suppose Luchenko Supplies paid $20,000 for inventory. By its year end, the company had sold 60 percent of the inventory but determined that the remaining inventory could be sold for only 60 percent of its original cost. The company anticipated that this decline was permanent.
   a. At what amount would inventory be reported on the year-end balance sheet?
   b. Suppose, one month later, a worldwide shortage of this inventory now gives it a net realizable value of $10,000. At what amount would this inventory be reported on the balance sheet one month later?
9. Roses Treasures, a craft store, uses a periodic inventory system. The inventory data for the year ended December 31, 2020, are as follows:

Sales revenue		$ 60,000
Cost of goods sold		
Beginning inventory	$11,000	
Net purchases	45,000	
Cost of goods available for sale	56,000	
Less: Ending inventory	12,000	
Cost of goods sold		44,000
Gross margin		$ 16,000

   a. Suppose it was discovered after the year end that $2,000 of craft supplies had dried up in their packages and should have been destroyed before year end. These supplies had been counted and recorded as ending inventory. What numerical effects did these obsolete craft supplies have on the accounting information above?
   b. What numerical effects will the obsolete craft supplies have on the accounting information for the following year?

Solutions appear at the end of this chapter and on **MyLab Accounting**

Estimating Ending Inventory

LO 5

How can we estimate inventory if there is a fire?

Sometimes a business needs to *estimate* the value of its ending inventory. Estimates are often calculated to provide inventory values for interim statements when it is not practical to do a full inventory count. They are also needed if there is a fire or other disaster that destroys inventory and records.

Gross Margin Method

The **gross margin method** (also known as the **gross profit method**) provides a way to estimate inventory using the cost of goods sold model (amounts are assumed for illustration):

	Beginning inventory (BI)	$ 20
+	Net purchases (NP)	100
=	Cost of goods available for sale	120
−	**Ending inventory (EI)**	**(40)**
=	**Cost of goods sold (COGS)**	**$ 80**

Once the cost of goods available for sale is calculated, you can calculate either the ending inventory (if you know the cost of goods sold) or the cost of goods sold (if you know the ending inventory):

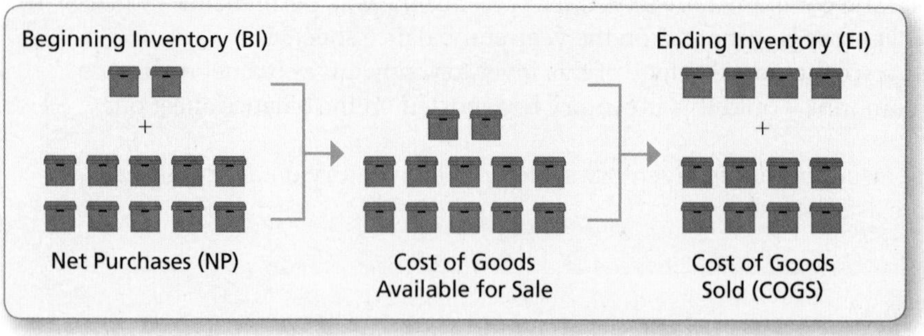

OR

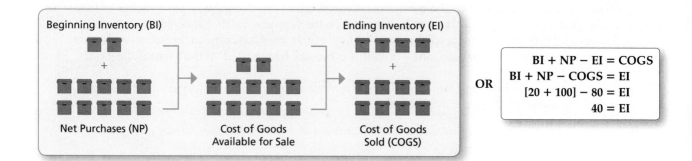

BI + NP − EI = COGS
BI + NP − COGS = EI
[20 + 100] − 80 = EI
40 = EI

The gross margin % + the cost of goods sold % = 100%. If gross margin is 35% of sales, then cost of goods sold is 65% of sales.

Suppose a fire destroys your inventory. To collect insurance, you must estimate the cost of the ending inventory. Using your normal *gross margin percent* (i.e., gross margin divided by net sales revenue), you can estimate cost of goods sold. Then subtract cost of goods sold from cost of goods available for sale to estimate ending inventory. Exhibit 6–9 illustrates the gross margin method using assumed amounts.

EXHIBIT 6–9 | Gross Margin Method of Estimating Inventory (amounts assumed)

Beginning inventory		$14,000
Net purchases		66,000
Cost of goods available for sale		80,000
Estimated cost of goods sold		
Sales revenue	$100,000	
Less: Estimated gross margin of 40%	40,000	
Estimated cost of goods sold (cost is 60% of sales revenue)		60,000
Estimated cost of ending inventory		$20,000

Equation solution: $14,000 + $66,000 − ($100,000 × 0.60) = $20,000

Retail Method

The **retail method** of estimating the cost of ending inventory is often used by retail establishments that use the periodic inventory system. This is because it is often easier for retail establishments to calculate the selling price, or retail price, of a wide range of items rather than to look at all the individual invoices to find the costs of each of those items.

Like the gross margin method, the retail method is based on the familiar cost of goods sold model, rearranged to calculate ending inventory:

	Beginning inventory (BI)
+	Net purchases (NP)
=	Cost of goods available for sale
−	Cost of goods sold (COGS)
=	Ending inventory (EI)

However, to use the retail method, a business must know both the total cost and the total selling price of its opening inventory, as well as both the total cost and the total selling price of its net purchases. Total selling price is determined by counting each item of inventory and multiplying it by the item's retail selling price (the price given on the price tag). By summing separately the costs and selling prices of beginning inventory and net purchases, the business knows the cost and retail selling price of the goods it has available for sale.

The business can calculate the total selling price of its sales because this is the sum of the amounts recorded on the cash register when sales are made.

Retail Ratio The retail ratio is the ratio of the cost of goods available for sale at *cost* to the cost of goods available for sale at *selling price*. To calculate the cost-to-retail percentage, first calculate the cost of the goods available for sale. Then divide the goods available for sale at cost by the goods available for sale at retail. It is usually expressed as a percentage, as shown in Exhibit 6–10.

EXHIBIT 6–10 | Retail Method of Estimating Inventory (amounts assumed)

	Cost	Selling Price
Beginning inventory (BI)	$151,200	$216,000
Net purchases (NP)	504,000	720,000
Cost of goods available for sale	$655,200	936,000
Net sales, at selling price (retail)		696,000
Ending inventory (EI), at selling price (retail)		$240,000
Estimated ending inventory (EI), at cost ($240,000 ×70%*)	$168,000	

*Retail ratio = ($655,200/$936,000) × 100 % = 70 %

BI at retail
+ NP at retail
= Selling price of goods for sale

Selling price of goods for sale
− Actual sales
= EI at selling price

EI at selling price × Retail or cost ratio = EI at cost

The retail method can be used to estimate inventory at any point in time, and it is acceptable to use the retail method to calculate year-end inventory cost for financial statement and income tax purposes, although an inventory count must be done at least once per year.

Try It!

10. Beginning inventory is $45,000, net purchases total $160,000, and net sales are $250,000. The normal gross margin is 40 percent of sales. Use the gross margin method to calculate ending inventory.
11. A beachwear shop needs to estimate the cost of its ending inventory for insurance purposes, and since it is summer it cannot close for a physical count of inventory. The insurance company will accept an estimate using the retail method. The shop's owner knows the cost of opening inventory was $25,000 from the previous year end's physical count and its selling price was $60,000. From invoices, the owner knows the cost of purchases was $100,000 and the retail selling prices totalled $240,000. Cash register receipts show that sales from the beginning of the year totalled $250,000. Calculate the cost of ending inventory for the insurance company.

Solutions appear at the end of this chapter and on **MyLab Accounting**

Summary Problem for Your Review

Suppose a division of GCA Computers that handles computer parts uses the periodic inventory system and has these inventory records for December 2020:

Date	Item	Quantity	Unit Cost	Sale Price
Dec. 1	Beginning inventory	100 units	$16	
10	Purchase	60 units	18	
15	Sale	70 units		$40
21	Purchase	100 units	20	
30	Sale	90 units		50

Company accounting records reveal that operating expenses for December were $4,000.

Required

Prepare the December 2020 income statement in multi-step format. Show amounts for FIFO cost and weighted-average cost. Label the bottom line "Operating income." (Round the average cost per unit to three decimal places and all other figures to whole-dollar amounts.) Show your computations, and use the periodic inventory model from pages 332–334 to compute cost of goods sold.

SOLUTION

The best approach to this solution is an organized one. One approach is to complete one income statement line before going to the next, until "Ending inventory." Notice that the amounts for sales revenue, beginning inventory, net purchases, and operating expenses are the same for the two inventory costing methods.

GCA COMPUTERS—Parts Division
Partial Income Statement
For the Month Ended December 31, 2020

	FIFO		Weighted-Average		Computations
Sales revenue		$7,300		$7,300	(70 × $40) + (90 × $50) = $7,300
Cost of goods sold					
Beginning inventory	$1,600		$1,600		100 × $16 = $1,600
Net purchases	3,080		3,080		(60 × $18) + (100 × $20) = $3,080
Cost of goods available for sale	4,680		4,680		
Less: Ending inventory	2,000		1,800		FIFO: 100 × $20 = $2,000; Weighted-Average: 100 × $18* = $1,800
Cost of goods sold		2,680		2,880	
Gross margin		4,620		4,420	
Operating expenses		4,000		4,000	
Operating income		$ 620		$ 420	

*$18 = $4,680 ÷ 260 units

Summary

Learning Objectives

① Account for perpetual inventory under the specific-unit-cost, FIFO, and moving-weighted-average-cost methods **Pg. 325**

Are there different methods used to account for perpetual inventory?

- In the perpetual inventory system:
  - Inventory is debited immediately at cost when an item is purchased (total number of items purchased × cost per item).
  - Inventory is credited immediately when an item is sold (cost of goods sold = total number of items sold × cost per item)
  - Ending inventory is calculated as the total number of items on hand × cost per item.
- If a company has inventory items that are unique or expensive, they typically use the *specific-unit-cost method* to determine the cost of goods sold and ending inventory.
- If a company has inventory items that are similar, they can assign costs using the *first-in, first-out (FIFO)* or *moving-weighted-average-cost methods* to determine the cost of goods sold and ending inventory.

② Compare the effects of the FIFO and moving-weighted-average-cost methods **Pg. 331**

What are the effects of two of the different methods?

- When prices are rising, moving-weighted-average costing produces the higher cost of goods sold and the lower income.

③ Account for periodic inventory under the FIFO and -weighted-average-cost methods **Pg. 332**

Are there different methods used to account for periodic inventory?

- The business does not keep an up-to-date balance for ending inventory. Instead, at the end of the period, the business counts the inventory on hand and updates its records.
- To compute ending inventory and cost of goods sold, a cost is assigned to each inventory item within that category.
- Two methods of assigning costs to similar items are *first-in, first-out (FIFO)* and *weighted-average*.
- FIFO costing produces identical balances for ending inventory and cost of goods sold under the periodic and perpetual inventory systems. However, the weighted-average method produces a different result under the periodic and perpetual systems.

④ Apply accounting concepts to inventory **Pg. 334**

How do we address other inventory issues?

- Key accounting concepts related to inventories include conservatism, the consistency principle, the disclosure principle, and the materiality constraint.
- The *lower-of-cost-and-net-realizable-value (LCNRV) rule*—an example of accounting conservatism—requires that businesses report inventory on the balance sheet at the lower of its cost and net realizable value or current replacement cost.
- Companies disclose their definition of "net realizable value" for purposes of applying the LCNRV rule in the notes to their financial statements.
- Although inventory overstatements in one period are counterbalanced by inventory understatements in the next period, effective decision making depends on accurate inventory information.

⑤ Estimate ending inventory by the gross margin method and the retail method? **Pg. 339**

How can we estimate inventory if there is a fire?

- The *gross margin method* and the *retail method* are techniques for estimating the cost of ending inventory.
- Both methods are useful for preparing interim financial statements and for estimating the cost of inventory destroyed by fire or other disasters.

Key Terms for the chapter are shown next and are in the **Glossary** at the back of the book. **Similar Terms** are shown after **Key Terms**.

KEY TERMS

Comparability A qualitative characteristic of accounting information that should enable users to compare one company's accounting information to another company's accounting information and to its own previous years' results *(p. 334)*.

Conservatism An accounting concept by which the least favourable figures are presented in the financial statements *(p. 335)*.

Consistency principle An accounting principle that states businesses must use the same accounting methods and procedures from period to period or disclose a change in method *(p. 334)*.

Disclosure principle An accounting concept that states a business's financial statements must report enough information for outsiders to make knowledgeable decisions about the business *(p. 335)*.

First-in, first-out (FIFO) method An inventory costing method by which the first costs into inventory are the first costs out to cost of goods sold. Ending inventory is based on the costs of the most recent purchases *(p. 328)*.

Gross margin method A way to estimate inventory based on a rearrangement of the cost of goods sold model: Beginning inventory + Net purchases = Cost of goods available for sale. Cost of goods available for sale − Cost of goods sold = Ending inventory. Also called the *gross profit method (p. 339)*.

Gross profit method Another name for the *gross margin method (p. 339)*.

Impairment A write-down in value that occurs when an asset, such as inventory, becomes worth less than its cost *(p. 336)*.

Impairment reversal A write-up in value that occurs when an asset that had been written down, such as inventory, increases in value up to the amount of the original write-down *(p. 336)*.

Lower-of-cost-and-net-realizable-value (LCNRV) Requires that an asset be reported in the financial statements at the lower of its historical cost or its market value (current replacement cost for inventory) *(p. 338)*.

Materiality constraint An accounting concept that states a company must perform strictly proper accounting only for items and transactions that are significant to the business's financial statements *(p. 335)*.

Moving-weighted-average-cost method A weighted-average-cost method where unit cost is changed to reflect each new purchase of inventory *(p. 329)*.

Retail method A method of estimating ending inventory based on the total cost and total selling price of opening inventory and net purchases *(p. 340)*.

Specific identification method Another name for the *specific-unit-cost method (p. 325)*.

Specific-unit-cost method An inventory costing method based on the specific cost of particular units of inventory. Also called the *specific identification method (p. 325)*.

Weighted-average-cost method An inventory costing method used for the periodic inventory system where the average cost is calculated at the end of the period. Weighted-average cost is determined by dividing the cost of goods available for sale by the number of units available for sale *(p. 333)*.

SIMILAR TERMS

Cost of goods sold	Cost of sales
Gross margin method	Gross profit method
LCNRV	Lower-of-cost-or-net-realizable-value

SELF-STUDY QUESTIONS

Test your understanding of the chapter by marking the correct answer to each of the following questions:

1. Which inventory costing method assigns to ending inventory the newest—the most recent—costs incurred during the period? *(p. 326)*
   a. Specific-unit cost
   b. First-in, first-out (FIFO)
   c. Moving-weighted-average cost
   d. None of the above

2. Assume Lids.ca began June with 20 units of inventory that cost a total of $760. During June, Lids.ca purchased and sold goods as follows:

Jun.	8	Purchased	60 units at $40
	14	Sold	50 units at $80
	22	Purchased	40 units at $44
	27	Sold	60 units at $80

   Under the FIFO inventory method and a perpetual inventory system, how much is Lids.ca's cost of goods sold for the transaction on June 14? *(p. 328)*
   a. $3,160
   b. $4,000
   c. $2,000
   d. $1,960

3. What is Lids.ca's journal entry on June 14 in Self-Study Question 2? *(p. 329)*

a. Accounts Receivable	1,960	
Inventory		1,960
b. Accounts Receivable	4,000	
Sales Revenue		4,000
c. Cost of Goods Sold	1,960	
Inventory		1,960

d. Both b and c

4. Given the following data, what is the weighted-average cost of ending inventory, rounded to the nearest whole dollar? *(p. 329)*

Sales revenue	100 units at $10 per unit
Beginning inventory	50 units at $8 per unit
Purchase	90 units at $9 per unit

a. $400
b. $360
c. $346
d. $864

5. Assume the following data for Burnette Sales for 2020:

Beginning inventory	10 units at $7 each
Mar. 18 Purchased	15 units at $9 each
Sold	20 units at $15 each
Jun. 10 Purchased	20 units at $10 each
Sold	12 units at $15 each
Oct. 30 Purchased	12 units at $11 each
Sold	10 units at $16 each

On December 31, a physical count reveals 15 units on hand.

Under the FIFO method (assuming a perpetual inventory system), what would ending inventory be valued at? *(p. 328)*

a. $105
b. $162
c. $115
d. $135

6. Which inventory costing method results in the lowest net income during a period of rising inventory costs? *(p. 331)*

a. Specific-unit cost
b. First-in, first out (FIFO)
c. Weighted-average cost
d. None of the above

7. Suppose Lids.ca used the weighted-average-cost method and a periodic inventory system. Use the Lids.ca data in Self-Study Question 3 to compute the cost of the company's inventory on hand at June 30. Round unit cost to the nearest cent. *(p. 329)*

a. $410
b. $420.80
c. $820
d. $841.60

8. Which principle or concept states that businesses should use the same accounting methods and procedures from period to period? *(p. 334)*

a. Disclosure
b. Conservatism
c. Consistency
d. Materiality

9. Review the following data:

Ending inventory at cost	$24,000
Ending inventory at net realizable value	23,600
Cost of goods sold (before consideration of the lower-of-cost-and-net-realizable-value rule)	37,000

Which of the following depicts the proper account balance after the application of the lower-of-cost-and-net-realizable-value rule? *(p. 336)*

a. Cost of goods sold will be $36,400.
b. Cost of goods sold will be $37,000.
c. Cost of goods sold will be $37,400.
d. Ending inventory will be $24,000.

10. At December 31, 2020, Malasky Company overstated ending inventory by $20,000. How does this error affect cost of goods sold and net income for 2020? *(p. 337)*

a. Overstates cost of goods sold and understates net income
b. Understates cost of goods sold and overstates net income
c. Overstates both cost of goods sold and net income
d. Leaves both cost of goods sold and net income correct because the errors cancel each other out

11. Suppose a Super Comics location suffered a fire loss and needs to estimate the cost of the goods destroyed. Beginning inventory was $50,000, net purchases totalled $300,000, and sales came to $500,000. Super Comics' normal gross margin is 45 percent. Use the gross margin method to estimate the cost of the inventory lost in the fire. *(p. 339)*

a. $150,000
b. $125,000
c. $75,000
d. $175,000

Answers to Self-Study Questions

1. b 2. d $(20 \times \$38) + (30 \times \$40) = \$1,960$ 3. d 4. c 5. b 6. c
7. a (Cost of goods available $= \$760 + \$2,400 + \$1,760 = \$4,920$; Number of units available $= 20 + 60 + 40 = 120$; $\$4,920/120$ units $= \$41$; $\$41 \times 10 = \$410$) 8. c 9. c
10. b 11. c

Assignment Material

MyLab Accounting Make the grade with MyLab Accounting: The Starters, Exercises, and Problems can be found on MyLab. You can practise them as often as you want, and most feature step-by-step guided instructions to help you find the right answer

QUESTIONS

1. Why is merchandise inventory so important to a retailer or wholesaler?
2. Suppose your business deals in made-to-order machinery. Which inventory system and method should you use to achieve good internal control over the inventory? If your business is a small store that sells inexpensive cell phone cases, which inventory system would you most likely use? Why?
3. Identify the accounts debited and credited in the standard purchase and sale entries under (a) the perpetual inventory system and (b) the periodic inventory system.
4. What is the role of the physical count of inventory in (a) the perpetual inventory system and (b) the periodic inventory system?
5. If beginning inventory is $60,000, purchases total $135,000, and ending inventory is $62,500, how much is cost of goods sold?
6. If beginning inventory is $44,000, purchases total $109,000, and cost of goods sold is $115,000, how much is ending inventory?
7. What two items determine the cost of ending inventory?
8. Briefly describe the three perpetual generally accepted inventory costing methods. During a period of rising prices, which method produces the higher reported income? Which produces the lower reported income?
9. Which inventory costing method produces the ending inventory valued at the most current cost?
10. Describe the impact on cost of goods sold of using the FIFO method as opposed to the weighted-average-cost method of valuing ending inventory when the price of inventory purchases is rising. Which method provides a more accurate value of the goods remaining in ending inventory at the end of an accounting period?
11. You read that companies should use the specific-unit-cost method to most accurately value items that have been sold and transferred to cost of goods sold, yet most companies do not use this method. Why not?
12. How does the consistency principle affect accounting for inventory?
13. What is the goal of conservatism when you apply it to inventory?
14. Discuss the materiality concept. Is the dollar amount that is material the same for a company that has annual sales of $10,000 compared with a company that has annual sales of $1,000,000?
15. Manley Company's inventory has a cost of $27,000 at the end of the year, and the net realizable value of the inventory is $32,500. At which amount should the company report the inventory on its balance sheet? Suppose the net realizable value of the inventory is $25,500 instead of $32,500. At which amount should Manley Company report the inventory? What rule governs your answers to these questions?
16. When does an inventory error cancel out, and why?
17. Gabriel Products accidentally overstated its ending inventory by $10,000 at the end of Period 1. Is the gross margin of Period 1 overstated or understated? Is the gross margin of Period 2 overstated, understated, or unaffected by the Period 1 error? Is the total gross margin for the two periods overstated, understated, or correct? Give the reason for your answers.
18. Identify two methods of estimating inventory amounts.
19. A fire destroyed the inventory of Bronk Supplies, but the accounting records were saved. The beginning inventory was $31,500, purchases for the period were $68,250, and sales were $120,000. Bronk's customary gross margin is 30 percent of sales. Use the gross margin method to estimate the cost of the inventory destroyed by the fire.
20. The retail method of estimating inventory seems simple but in reality can be difficult to apply. Why is this so?

STARTERS

S6–1 Garda's Equipment has the following items in its inventory on August 1:

Serial Number	Cost
6X6A1	$ 9,100
6Y6M5	9,300
6B6D8	8,700
6R7R5	10,950

The company uses the specific-unit-cost method for costing inventory. During August, it sold units 6X6A1 and 6B6B8 for $15,000 each and purchased unit 6A7M6 for $11,200. What is the value of the ending inventory at August 31?

① Computing ending inventory—specific-unit-cost method
Ending inventory, $31,450

S6–2 Refer to the information in S6–1. Calculate the gross margin for the month of August.

① Computing gross margin—specific-unit-cost method
Gross margin, $12,200

S6–3 Schwenn Cycles uses the FIFO inventory method. Schwenn started June with five bicycles that cost $190 each. On June 16, Schwenn bought 20 bicycles at $200 each. On June 30, Schwenn sold 15 bicycles. Prepare Schwenn's perpetual inventory record.

① Perpetual inventory record—FIFO
Ending inventory, $2,000

S6–4 Use the Schwenn Cycles data in S6–3 to journalize the following transactions:

a. The June 16 purchase of inventory on account

b. The June 30 sale of inventory on account; Schwenn sold each bicycle for $240

c. Cost of goods sold

① Recording inventory transactions—FIFO
c. COGS, $2,950

S6–5 Flynn Cycles uses the moving-weighted-average-cost method. Flynn started June with five bicycles that cost $190 each. On June 16, Flynn bought 20 bicycles at $200 each. On June 30, Flynn sold 15 bicycles. Prepare Flynn's perpetual inventory record.

Round average cost per unit to the nearest cent and all other amounts to the nearest dollar.

① Perpetual inventory record—moving-weighted-average cost
Ending inventory, $1,980

S6–6 Use the Flynn Cycles data in S6–5, except assume that Flynn uses the moving-weighted-average-cost method, and journalize the following transactions:

a. The June 16 purchase of inventory on account

b. The June 30 sale of inventory on account; Schwenn sold each bicycle for $240

c. Cost of goods sold

① Recording inventory transactions—moving-weighted-average-cost method
c. COGS, $2,970

S6–7 Examine S6–3 (FIFO costing) and S6–5 (moving-weighted-average costing). Focus on the sale of goods on June 30. Why is cost of goods sold different between FIFO costing and moving-weighted-average costing? Explain.

② Comparing cost of goods sold under FIFO and moving-weighted-average-cost methods

S6–8 Answer these questions in your own words:

a. Why does FIFO produce the lower cost of goods sold during a period of rising prices?

b. Why does moving-weighted-average costing produce the higher cost of goods sold during a period of rising prices?

c. Which inventory costing method—FIFO or moving-weighted-average—results in the higher and the lower cost of ending inventory? Prices are rising. Exhibits 6–3 and 6–4 on pages 328 and 330 provide the necessary information.

② Comparing cost of goods sold and ending inventory under FIFO and moving-weighted-average-cost methods during times of rising prices

S6–9 Kim's Shirt and Tie Shop uses a periodic inventory system. Kim's completed the following inventory transactions during April, its first month of operations:

Apr.	1	Purchased 10 shirts at $50 each
	7	Sold 6 shirts for $80 each
	13	Purchased 6 shirts for $55 each
	21	Sold 3 shirts for $85 each

a. Compute Kim's ending inventory and cost of goods sold under FIFO costing.

b. Then compute ending inventory and cost of goods sold under the weighted-average-cost method. Round average unit cost to three decimal places, but round all totals to the nearest cent.

c. Compute gross margin under both methods. Which method results in the higher gross margin?

③ Computing FIFO and weighted-average-cost amounts in a periodic system
Gross margin, FIFO, $335

4 Explaining inventory policy

S6–10 Why are standard setters interested in ensuring that companies use the same inventory costing method from one year to the next?

4 Apply the lower-of-cost-and-net-realizable-value rule to inventory

S6–11 Determine the value of the inventory to be reported on the balance sheet by applying lower-of-cost-and-net-realizable-value rule to the following data:

Item	Quantity	Cost Price/Unit	Market Price/Unit	Selling Costs
001	5	$29	$30	$100
002	8	$40	$35	$ 50

4 Measuring the effects of an inventory error

S6–12 Trump Luggage Sales uses a periodic inventory system. The inventory data for the year ended December 31, 2019, follow:

Sales revenue	$150,000
Cost of goods sold	
Beginning inventory	22,000
Net purchases	80,000
Cost of goods available for sale	102,000
Less: Ending inventory	24,000
Cost of goods sold	78,000
Gross margin	$ 72,000

Assume that the ending inventory was accidentally overstated by $4,000. What are the correct amounts of cost of goods sold and gross margin after correcting this error?

4 Next year's effect of an inventory error

S6–13 Refer back to the Trump Luggage Sales inventory data in S6–12. The ending inventory balance is stated correctly at the end of 2020. What effect would the overstatement of ending inventory made in 2019 have on cost of goods sold and gross margin for the year ended December 31, 2020?

5 Estimating ending inventory by the gross margin method

Estimated cost of ending inventory, $750,000

S6–14 Magic Carpets began the year with inventory of $1,400,000. Inventory purchases for the year totalled $3,200,000. Sales revenue for the year was $7,000,000, and the gross margin was 45 percent. How much is Magic Carpets' estimated cost of ending inventory? Use the gross margin method.

5 Estimating ending inventory by the retail method

Estimated cost of ending inventory, $35,228

S6–15 A fire wiped out Pichai Paper Company's inventory. The insurance company will accept an estimate using the retail method. Last year's balance sheet stated that the ending inventory was $15,000, and it would usually sell for $40,000. Mr. Pichai knows that the cost of purchases was $140,000, and the retail selling prices for the paper totalled $290,000. Credit card receipts indicate that there was $255,000 of sales since the beginning of the year. Calculate the cost of the lost ending inventory for the insurance company. Round the retail ratio to two decimal places and the final answer to the nearest dollar.

EXERCISES

1 Computing gross margin—specific-unit-cost method

2. Gross margin, $64,000

E6–1 Erickson Company buys transformers from manufacturers and sells them to utility companies. The units are costly, and the company keeps track of them using serial numbers. On April 1, the company had two transformers in stock:

Serial Number	Unit Cost
2010901	$55,000
2010905	59,200

During the month, the company purchased the following two transformers:

Serial Number	Unit Cost
20101001	$51,000
20101002	56,800

Erickson Company sold two transformers—serial numbers 2010905 and 20101002—during the month of April. The selling price of the transformers was $90,000 per unit.

Required

1. Erickson Company uses the specific-unit-cost method for costing inventory. Why would the company prefer to use this method?
2. Compute the gross margin for Erickson Company for the month of April.

E6–2 Elmo's Music carries a large inventory of guitars and other musical instruments. The store uses the FIFO method and a perpetual inventory system. Company records indicate the following for a particular line of guitars that sell for $1,600 each:

(1) Measuring ending inventory and cost of goods sold in a perpetual system—FIFO

Cost of goods sold, $6,180

Date	Item	Quantity	Unit Cost
May 1	Balance	5	$900
6	Sale	3	
8	Purchase	10	840
17	Sale	4	
30	Purchase	5	840

Required Prepare a perpetual inventory record for the guitars. Then determine the amounts Elmo's Music should report for ending inventory and cost of goods sold under the FIFO method.

E6–3 After preparing the FIFO perpetual inventory record in E6–2, journalize Elmo's Music's May 8 purchase of inventory on account and the cash sale on May 17.

(1) Recording perpetual inventory transactions

E6–4 Refer to the Elmo's Music inventory data in E6–2, except assume that the store uses the moving-weighted-average-cost method. Prepare Elmo's Music Store's perpetual inventory record for the guitars on the moving-weighted-average-cost basis. Round average cost per unit to the nearest cent and all other amounts to the nearest dollar.

(1) Applying the moving-weighted-average-cost method in a perpetual inventory system

Cost of goods sold, $6,100

E6–5 Lally Company accounting records yield the following data for the year ended December 31, 2020:

(2) Recording perpetual inventory transactions using FIFO

2. Inventory, $38,000

Inventory: January 1, 2020	$ 24,000
Purchases of inventory (on account)	147,000
Sales of inventory—70 percent on account,	
30 percent for cash (cost $133,000)	225,000
Inventory at FIFO cost December 31, 2020	?

Required

1. Journalize Lally Company's inventory transactions for the year in a perpetual system. Use December 31 as the transaction date. No explanations are necessary.
2. Report ending inventory, sales, cost of goods sold, and gross margin on the appropriate financial statement.

E6–6 In the space provided, write the name of the inventory method that best fits the description (specific-unit, FIFO, or weighted-average). Assume that the cost of inventory is rising.

(2) Identifying income and other effects of the three inventory methods

__________ a. Maximizes reported net income when inventory purchase prices are falling

__________ b. Results in a cost of ending inventory that is close to the current cost of replacing the inventory

__________ c. Maximizes reported net income when inventory purchase prices are rising

__________ d. Used to account for automobiles, jewellery, and art objects

__________ e. Provides a smoother measure of ending inventory and cost of goods sold over time

__________ f. Precisely matches cost of goods sold with net sales revenue

(2) Calculating gross margin under FIFO and the moving-weighted-average-cost method in a perpetual inventory system

Gross margin, moving-weighted-average-cost method, $5,100

E6–7 Use your results from E6-2, E6-3, and E6–4 to calculate the gross margin for Elmo's Music under both the FIFO and the moving-weighted-average-cost methods. Explain why the gross margin is higher under the moving-weighted-average-cost method.

(2) Comparing the moving-weighted-average and FIFO methods in a perpetual inventory system

Cost of goods sold, moving-weighted-average cost, $1,509,200

E6–8 Max Office Products markets the ink used in inkjet printers. Max started the year with 10,000 containers of ink (moving-weighted-average cost of $18 each; FIFO cost of $16 each). During the year, Max purchased 80,000 containers of ink at $22 on January 10 and sold 70,000 units for $46 each on January 22. Max paid a total of $500,000 in operating expenses on January 31. All transactions are on account.

Journalize Max's purchases, sales, and operating expense transactions using the following format. Max uses a perpetual inventory system to account for inkjet printer ink.

		Moving-Weighted-Average*		FIFO	
Date	**Accounts**	**Debit**	**Credit**	**Debit**	**Credit**

*Round moving-weighted-average unit cost to the nearest cent.

(3) Recording periodic inventory transactions using FIFO

2. Gross margin, $92,000

E6–9 Refer to the Lally Company data in E6–5, except assume that Lally is using FIFO in a periodic inventory system. Inventory on hand at December 31, 2020, was $38,000, based on a physical count.

Required

1. Journalize Lally Company's inventory transactions for the year in a periodic system. Use December 31 as the date. No explanations are required.
2. Report ending inventory, sales, cost of goods sold, and gross margin on the appropriate financial statement.
3. How do these amounts compare to the same amounts in the perpetual inventory system calculated in E6–5, Requirement 2?

(3) Computing FIFO and weighted-averages-cost amounts in a periodic system

Cost of goods sold, weighted-average, $1,540

E6–10 The periodic inventory records of Flexon Prosthetics indicate the following for the month of July:

Jul.	1	Beginning merchandise inventory	6 units at $ 60 each
	8	Purchase	5 units at $ 67 each
	15	Purchase	10 units at $ 70 each
	26	Purchase	5 units at $ 85 each

At July 31, Flexon counts four units of merchandise inventory on hand.

a. Compute ending merchandise inventory and cost of goods sold using the FIFO inventory costing method.

b. Compute ending merchandise inventory and cost of goods sold using the weighted-average-cost method.

(3) Computing ending inventory by applying three inventory costing methods in a periodic inventory system

3. FIFO cost of goods sold, $4,770

E6–11 Kelso Electrical's inventory records for industrial switches indicate the following at November 30, 2020:

Nov.	1	Beginning inventory	14 units at $160
	8	Purchase	4 units at $170
	15	Purchase	11 units at $180
	26	Purchase	5 units at $200

The physical count of inventory at November 30, 2020, indicates that six units remain in ending inventory and the company owns them.

Required Compute ending inventory and cost of goods sold using each of the following methods, assuming a periodic inventory system is used:

1. Specific-unit cost, assuming three $170 units and three $180 units are on hand on November 30, 2020
2. Weighted-average cost
3. First-in, first-out (FIFO)

E6–12 1. Supply the missing income statement amounts for each of the following companies for the year ended December 31, 2020:

③ Determining amounts for the income statement: periodic system

(c) $10,200

Company	Net Sales	Beginning Inventory	Net Purchases	Ending Inventory	Cost of Goods Sold	Gross Margin
Arc Co.	$46,500	$ 5,300	$31,400	$ 8,700	(a)	$18,500
Bell Co.	(b)	13,700	46,500	(c)	$50,000	26,300
Court Co.	50,000	(d)	27,900	11,300	38,700	(e)
Dolan Co.	51,200	6,400	(f)	4,100	(g)	23,700

2. Prepare the income statement for Bell Co., which uses the periodic inventory system. Bell's operating expenses for the year were $9,700.

E6–13 Williamson Landscape Supplies, which uses a perpetual inventory system and the FIFO costing method, has these account balances at December 31, 2020, prior to releasing the financial statements for the year:

① ④ Applying the lower-of-cost-and-net-realizable-value rule to inventories: perpetual system

Inventory

Beg. Bal. 50,000	
End. bal. 84,000	

Cost of Goods Sold

Bal. 500,000	

Sales Revenue

	Bal. 940,000

The company has determined that the net realizable value of the December 31, 2020, ending inventory is $79,500.

Required Prepare Williamson Landscape Supplies' partial balance sheet at December 31, 2020, to show how Williamson would apply the lower-of-cost-and-net-realizable-value rule to inventories. Include a complete heading for the statement.

E6–14 Before the following financial statement was released, it was discovered that the current net realizable value of ending inventory was $96,000.

③ ④ Applying the lower-of-cost-and-net-realizable-value rule to inventories: periodic system

2. Cost of goods sold, $229,700

1. Journalize the entry to apply the lower-of-cost-and-net-realizable-value rule to the inventory on August 31, 2020. No explanation is required.
2. Prepare a revised income statement to apply the lower-of-cost-and-net-realizable-value rule to Wire Solutions Company's inventory.
3. What is the inventory balance that would be reported on the Wire Solutions Company's balance sheet. How would it be reported?

WIRE SOLUTIONS COMPANY
Income Statement (partial)
For the Month Ended August 31, 2020

Sales revenue		$320,000
Cost of goods sold		
Beginning inventory	$ 82,000	
Net purchases	243,700	
Cost of goods available for sale	325,700	
Less: Ending inventory	105,700	
Cost of goods sold		220,000
Gross margin		$100,000

(4) Correcting an inventory error
Net income 2019, $34,100

E6–15 John's Septic Systems Company reported the comparative income statement for the years ended September 30, 2020, and 2019, shown below:

JOHN'S SEPTIC SYSTEMS COMPANY Income Statement For the Years Ended September 30, 2020 and 2019				
	2020		2019	
Sales revenue		$165,000		$146,000
Cost of goods sold				
Beginning inventory	$ 16,500		$15,400	
Net purchases	91,000		78,000	
Cost of goods available for sale	107,500		93,400	
Ending inventory	23,600		16,500	
Cost of goods sold		83,900		76,900
Gross margin		81,100		69,100
Operating expenses		40,000		30,000
Net income		$ 41,100		$ 39,100

During 2020, accountants for the company discovered that ending 2019 inventory was overstated by $5,000. Prepare the corrected comparative income statement for the two-year period, complete with a heading for the statement. What was the effect of the error on net income for the two years combined? Explain your answer.

(4) Assessing the effect of an inventory error on two years of statements

E6–16 Janet Chao, accountant of Seaward Electronics Ltd., learned that Seaward Electronics' $24 million cost of inventory at the end of last year was overstated by $3 million. She notified the company president, Eric Moffat, of the accounting error and the need to alert the company's lenders that last year's reported net income was incorrect. Moffat explained to Chao that there is no need to report the error to lenders because the error will counterbalance this year: This year's error will affect this year's net income in the opposite direction of last year's error. Even with no correction, Moffat reasons, net income for both years combined will be the same whether or not Seaward Electronics corrects its errors.

Required

1. Was last year's reported net income of $37 million overstated, understated, or correct? What was the correct amount of net income last year?
2. Is this year's net income of $41 million overstated, understated, or correct? What is the correct amount of net income for the current year?
3. Whose perspective is better, Chao's or Moffat's? Give your reason. Consider the trend of reported net income both without the correction and with the correction.

(3) (4) Ethical implications of inventory actions

E6–17 Determine whether each of the actions below in buying, selling, and accounting for inventories is ethical or unethical. Give your reason for each answer.

1. Frank's Tea Company knowingly overstated purchases to produce a high figure for cost of goods sold (and thus a low amount of net income). The real reason was to decrease the company's income tax payments to the government.
2. During a period of rising prices, Plentea delayed the purchase of inventory until after December 31, 2020, in order to keep 2020's moving-weighted-average cost of goods sold from growing too large. The delay in purchasing inventory helped net income of 2020 to reach the level of profit demanded by the company's investors.
3. In applying the lower-of-cost-and-net-realizable-value rule to inventories, Sam's Cookie Emporium recorded an excessively low realizable value for ending inventory. This allowed the company to pay no income tax for the year.
4. Hawk Distributors purchased a lot of inventory shortly before year end. The extra inventory that was purchased at a lower price decreased the moving-weighted-average cost of goods sold and increased reported income for the year to reach the level of profit demanded by the company's investors.
5. Lacombe Motorbike Sales deliberately overstated ending inventory in order to report higher profits (net income).

E6–18 Bathurst Company began April with inventory of $200,000. The business made net purchases of $600,000 and had net sales of $800,000 before a fire destroyed the company's inventory. For the past several years, Bathurst Company's gross margin on sales has been 34 percent.

(5)
Estimating inventory by the gross margin method
Estimated inventory cost, $272,000

Required

1. Estimate the cost of the inventory destroyed by the fire.
2. Identify another reason owners and managers use the gross margin method to estimate inventory on a regular basis.

E6–19 Assume Dollar Valu Store estimates its inventory by the gross margin method when preparing monthly financial statements (it uses the periodic method otherwise). For the past two years, the cost of goods purchased has averaged 60 percent of net sales. Assume further that the company's inventory records for its stores reveal the following data:

(5)
Estimating ending inventory by the gross margin method and preparing the income statement
Estimated cost of goods sold, $5,016,000

Inventory: June 1, 2020	$ 480,000
Transactions during June:	
Purchases	4,920,000
Sales	8,360,000

Required

1. Estimate the June 30, 2020, inventory using the gross margin method.
2. Prepare the June income statement through gross margin for Dollar Valu Store.

E6–20 Lids has three lines of hats: baseball, winter, and fashion. On May 18, 2020, Lids had a fire that destroyed the baseball hat inventory. Sales for the period January 1 to May 18 for the baseball hats were $800,000. Inventory at January 1, 2020, for the baseball hats was $95,000 (cost), $285,000 (retail). Purchases made from January 1 to May 18 for the baseball hats at cost were $240,000, and at retail were $720,000. Use the retail method to calculate the cost of the inventory lost in the fire. Hint: Use the format shown in Exhibit 6–9 to structure each calculation.

(5)
Estimating inventory by the retail method
Estimated ending inventory cost, baseball hats, $67,650

SERIAL EXERCISE

E6–21 *The Serial Exercise involves a company that will be revisited throughout relevant chapters in Volume 1 and Volume 2. You can complete the Serial Exercises using MyLab Accounting.*

(2)
Accounting for inventory using the perpetual inventory system—FIFO
Effects of FIFO, COGS $1,845

This exercise continues recordkeeping for the Canyon Canoe Company. You do not have to have completed any previous questions to complete this exercise.

At the beginning of January 2021, Canyon Canoe Company decided to carry and sell T-shirts with its logo printed on them. Canyon Canoe Company uses the perpetual inventory system to account for the inventory. During February 2021, Canyon Canoe Company completed the following merchandising transactions:

Feb.	2	Sold 60 T-shirts at $10 each.
	5	Purchased 50 T-shirts at $6 each.
	7	Sold 45 T-shirts for $10 each.
	8	Sold 20 T-shirts for $10 each.
	10	Canyon Canoe Company realized the inventory was running low, so it placed a rush order and purchased 20 T-shirts. The premium cost for these shirts was $7 each.
	12	Placed a second rush order and purchased 40 T-shirts at $7 each.
	13	Sold 20 T-shirts for $10 each.
	15	Purchased 50 T-shirts at $6 each.
	20	In order to avoid future rush orders, purchased 150 T-shirts. Due to the volume of the order, Canyon Canoe Company was able to negotiate a cost of $5 each.
	21	Sold 40 T-shirts for $10 each.
	22	Sold 35 T-shirts for $10 each.
	24	Sold 20 T-shirts for $10 each.
	25	Sold 45 T-shirts for $10 each.
	27	Sold 40 T-shirts for $10 each.

Required

1. Assume Canyon Canoe Company began February with 94 T-shirts in inventory that cost $5 each. Prepare the perpetual inventory records for February using the FIFO inventory costing method.
2. Provide a summary for the month, in both units and dollars, of the change in inventory in the following format:

	Number of T-shirts	Dollar Amount
Beginning Balance		
Add: Purchases		
Less: Cost of Goods Sold		
Ending Balance		

PRACTICE SET

① ④
Accounting for more detailed transactions—perpetual, FIFO

E6-22 *This problem continues the Crystal Clear Cleaning problem begun in Chapter 2 and continued through Chapter 9.*

Consider the December transactions for Crystal Clear Cleaning that were presented in Chapter 5. (Cost data have been removed from the sale transactions.) Crystal Clear uses the perpetual inventory system.

In this question, account for discounts and returns as a reduction of purchases, and adjust the unit costs in inventory accordingly.

Dec.	2	Purchased 1,000 units of inventory for $4,000 on account from Sparkle Company on terms 5/10, n/20.
	5	Purchased 1,200 units of inventory from Borax on account with terms 4/10, n/30. The total invoice was for $6,000, which included a $300 freight charge.
	7	Returned 300 units of inventory to Sparkle from the December 2 purchase.
	9	Paid Borax.
	11	Sold 500 units of goods to Happy Maids for $5,500 on account with terms n/30.
	12	Paid Sparkle.
	15	Received 100 units with a sales price of $1,100 of goods back from customer Happy Maids.
	21	Received payment from Happy Maids, settling the amount due in full.
	28	Sold 500 units of goods to Bridget, Inc. on account for $6,500. Terms 1/15, n/30.
	29	Paid cash for utilities of $550.
	30	Paid cash for Sales Commission Expense of $214.
	31	Received payment from Bridget, Inc., less discount.
	31	Recorded only the adjusting entry for inventory: a. Physical count of inventory on December 31 showed 800 units of goods on hand.

Required

1. Prepare a perpetual inventory record for December for Crystal Clear Cleaning using the FIFO inventory costing method. (Note: You must calculate the cost of goods sold on December 11, 28, and 31 [adjusting entry a].) Round per-unit costs to two decimal places.
2. Journalize the transactions for December 11, 28, and 31 using the perpetual inventory record created in Requirement 1.

CHALLENGE EXERCISES

E6–23 For each of the following situations, identify the inventory method that you are using or would prefer to use or, given the use of a particular method, state the strategy that you would follow to accomplish your goal.

(2) Inventory policy decisions

a. Inventory costs are increasing. Your business uses the FIFO method and is having an unexpectedly good year. It is near year end, and you need to keep net income from increasing too much.

b. Inventory costs have been stable for several years, and you expect costs to remain stable for the indefinite future. (Give your reason for your choice of method.)

c. Inventory costs are decreasing, and you want to maximize income.

d. Company management prefers an inventory policy that avoids extremes.

e. Your inventory turns over very rapidly, and the business uses a perpetual inventory system. Inventory costs are increasing, and the business prefers to report high income.

E6–24 CPA Auto Supplies made the following purchases and sales of windshield wipers during March:

(1) (2) (3) Comparing the effects of costing methods under perpetual and periodic inventory systems

			Units	Unit Cost	Unit Sale Price
Mar.	1	Beginning	10	$ 6	
	3	Purchase	70	8	
	10	Sale	50		$16
	14	Purchase	25	10	
	20	Purchase	100	11	
	26	Sale	125		16

Required

1. Assuming CPA Auto Supplies uses a perpetual inventory system, calculate the cost of goods sold during March using (a) the moving-weighted-average-cost method and (b) FIFO. Round all average amounts to the nearest cent.
2. Now assume CPA Auto Supplies uses a periodic inventory system. Calculate the cost of goods sold during March using (a) the weighted-average-cost method and (b) FIFO. Round all average amounts to the nearest cent. (c) Calculate gross margin for both methods. Which is higher?
3. What do you notice when you compare the FIFO results from Requirement 1 and Requirement 2?

BEYOND THE NUMBERS

BN6–1

The inventory costing method chosen by a company can affect the financial statements and thus the decisions of the users of those statements.

(2) (4) Assessing the impact of the inventory costing method on the financial statements

Required

1. A leading accounting researcher stated that one inventory costing method reports the more recent costs in the income statement, while another method reports the more recent costs in the balance sheet. In this person's opinion, this results in one or the other of the statements being "inaccurate" when prices are rising. What did the researcher mean?
2. Random Appliances follows conservative accounting and writes the value of its inventory of ovens down to net realizable value, which has declined below cost. The following year, an unexpected baking craze results in a demand for ovens that far exceeds supply, and the net realizable value increases well above the previous cost. What effect will conservatism have on the income of Random Appliances over the two years?
3. Why would you want management to be conservative in accounting for inventory if you were (a) a shareholder and (b) a prospective shareholder?

ETHICAL ISSUE

E16–1

During 2019, Bryant Electronics changed to the weighted-average-cost method of accounting for inventory. Suppose that during 2020 Bryant Electronics changes back to the FIFO method and in the following year switches back to the weighted-average-cost method again.

Required

1. What would you think of a company's ethics if it changed accounting methods every year?
2. What accounting principle would changing methods every year violate?
3. Who can be harmed when a company changes its accounting methods too often? How?

PROBLEMS (GROUP A)

1
Using the perpetual inventory system—FIFO
2. Cost of goods sold, $9,280

P6–1A Smart Lighting, an LED bulb superstore, uses the FIFO method for valuing inventories. It began August with 50 units of a smart light bulb that costs $80 each. During August, the store completed these inventory transactions:

			Units	Unit Cost	Unit Sale Price
Aug.	3	Sale	40		$140
	8	Purchase	80	$88	
	21	Sale	70		150
	30	Purchase	10	96	

Required

1. Prepare a perpetual inventory record for the smart light bulbs.
2. Determine the store's cost of goods sold for August.
3. Compute gross margin for August.

1
Accounting for inventory using the perpetual system—FIFO
1. Cost of goods sold, $37,850

P6–2A PEI Distributors purchases inventory in crates of merchandise. Assume the company began July with an inventory of 30 units that cost $300 each. During the month, the company engaged in the following business transactions:

Jul.	10	Purchased 30 units on account at $320.
	15	Sold 40 units on account at $700.
	22	Purchased 70 units on account at $350.
	29	Sold 75 units on account at $800.
	31	Reported monthly operating expenses of $30,000. The company paid one-third with cash and the rest was recorded on account.
	31	Paid $12,000 of the Accounts Payable balance

Assume PEI Distributors uses the FIFO cost method for valuing inventories. The company uses a perpetual inventory system.

Required

1. Prepare a perpetual inventory record, at FIFO cost, for this merchandise.
2. Make journal entries to record the company's transactions. No explanations are necessary.

1
Accounting for inventory using the perpetual system—moving-weighted-average cost
1. Cost of goods sold, $3,236

P6–3A Golf Unlimited carries an inventory of putters and other golf clubs. The sales price of each putter is $119. Company records indicate the following for a particular line of Golf Unlimited's putters:

Date		Item	Quantity	Unit Cost
Nov.	1	Balance	24	$53
	6	Sale	20	
	8	Purchase	30	70
	17	Sale	30	
	30	Sale	2	

Required

1. Prepare Golf Unlimited's perpetual inventory record for the putters assuming Golf Unlimited uses the moving-weighted-average inventory costing method. Round the average unit cost to the nearest cent and all other amounts to the nearest dollar. Then identify the cost of ending inventory and cost of goods sold for the month.
2. Journalize Golf Unlimited's inventory transactions using the moving-weighted-average inventory costing method. Include explanations. (Assume purchases and sales are made on account.)

P6–4A Refer to the PEI Distributors situation in P6–2A. Keep all the data unchanged, except assume that the company uses the moving-weighted-average-cost method.

(2) Accounting for inventory in a perpetual system—moving-weighted-average cost

Inventory balance, $5,117

Required

1. Prepare a perpetual inventory record using the moving-weighted-average cost. Round the average unit cost to the nearest cent and all other amounts to the nearest dollar.
2. Prepare a multi-step income statement for PEI Distributors for the month of July 2020 to calculate operating income.

P6–5A Refer to P6–2A and P6–4A to prepare a table comparing ending inventory, cost of goods sold, and gross margin under both the FIFO and the moving-weighted-average-cost methods. You will need to calculate gross margin for P6–2A. Explain why the gross margin is lower under the moving-weighted-average-cost method.

(2) Summarize perpetual inventory data and explain

FIFO gross margin, $50,150

P6–6A Gamsu's Office Depot sells office furniture. The company's fiscal year ends on March 31, 2020. On January 1, 2020, inventory consisted of 20 office dividers that cost $1,800 each. During the quarter, Gamsu's purchased inventory on account as follows:

(1) (2) Computing ending inventory by applying two inventory costing methods in a perpetual inventory system

Gross margin 1(a), $189,193

	Units	Unit Cost	Total
January	60	$1,850	$111,000
February	40	1,900	76,000
March	30	1,950	58,500

Sales for each month in the quarter were as follows:

	Units	Unit Selling Price	Total
January	50	$3,600	$180,000
February	20	3,700	74,000
March	34	3,800	129,200

Operating expenses in the quarter were $110,000.

Assume that the company uses a perpetual inventory system and that purchases of inventory occur on the first day of each month.

Required

1. Determine the cost of the divider ending inventory at March 31, 2020, under (a) moving-weighted-average costing and (b) FIFO costing. Round the average unit cost to the nearest cent and all other amounts to the nearest dollar.
2. Prepare a multi-step income statement for the quarter ended March 31, 2017, under each method described in Requirement 1.

P6–7A Refer to the information in P6–6A, Gamsu's Office Depot. Assume the company uses a periodic inventory system.

(3) Computing ending inventory by applying two inventory costing methods in a periodic inventory system

Gross margin 1(a), $188,026

Required

1. Determine the cost of the department's ending inventory at March 31, 2020, under (a) weighted-average-cost method and (b) the FIFO method. Round the average unit cost to the nearest cent and all other amounts to the nearest dollar. Assume the company determines cost of goods sold at the end of each quarter.
2. Prepare the department's multi-step income statement for the quarter ended March 31, 2020, under each method described in Requirement 1.

③
Computing inventory by two methods—periodic system
2. Gross margin, FIFO, $19,157

P6–8A Pongphop Noodles began April with 73 units of inventory that cost $50 each. During the month, Pongphop made the following purchases:

Apr.	4	113 units at $48
	12	81 units at $49
	19	167 units at $52
	25	34 units at $56

The company uses a periodic inventory system, and the physical count at April 30 shows 51 units of inventory on hand.

Required

1. Determine the ending inventory and cost of goods sold amounts for the April financial statements under (a) weighted-average cost and (b) FIFO cost. Round average cost per unit to the nearest cent and all other amounts to the nearest dollar.
2. Sales revenue for April totalled $40,000. Compute Pongphop's gross margin for April under each method.
3. Which method will result in higher net income for Pongphop? Why?

③
Using the periodic inventory system—weighted-average and FIFO costing
3. Gross margin, weighted-average, $399,040

P6–9A Winslow Products, which uses a periodic inventory system, began 2020 with 6,000 units of inventory that cost a total of $90,000. At year end, the physical count indicated 20,000 units of inventory on hand. During 2020, Winslow Products purchased merchandise on account as follows:

Purchase 1 (10,000 units at $14 per unit)	$140,000
Purchase 2 (20,000 units at $12 per unit)	240,000

Required

1. How many units did Winslow Products sell during the year? The sale price per unit was $38. Determine Winslow's sales revenue for the year.
2. Compute cost of goods sold by the weighted-average method. Round average cost per unit to the nearest cent and all other amounts to the nearest dollar. Then determine gross margin for the year.
3. Compute cost of goods sold by the FIFO method. Then determine gross margin for the year.
4. Compare the gross margins you calculated for each inventory method in Requirements 2 and 3. What conclusions can you draw about margins when the purchase prices for inventory are falling?

① ② ③
Using the perpetual and periodic inventory systems
2. Cost of goods sold, $22,380

P6–10A Northeast Tire began May with 50 units of inventory that cost $264 each. During May, Northeast Tire completed these inventory transactions:

			Units	Unit Cost	Unit Selling Price
May	2	Purchase	12	$270	
	8	Sale	27	264	$360
	13	Sale	23	264	360
		Sale	3	270	370
	17	Purchase	24	270	
	22	Sale	31	270	370
	29	Purchase	24	290	

Required

1. The above data are taken from Northeast Tire's perpetual inventory records. Which cost method does Northeast Tire use?
2. Compute Northeast Tire's cost of goods sold and gross margin for May under the
   a. Perpetual inventory system
   b. Periodic inventory system

P6–11A Hartley Home Furniture has had poor sales in the last year. The rate of inventory turnover has dropped, and some of the business's merchandise is gathering dust. At the same time, competition has forced the business to lower the selling prices of its inventory. It is now December 31, 2020. Assume the net realizable value of a Hartley Home Furniture store's ending inventory is $1,500 below what Hartley Home Furniture paid for the goods, which was $10,300. Before any adjustments at the end of the period, assume the store's Cost of Goods Sold account has a balance of $65,200.

(4)
Applying the lower-of-cost-and-net-realizable-value rule to inventories

Cost of goods sold, $66,700

Required

1. What action should Hartley Home Furniture take in this situation, if any?
2. What account is used to record the write-down? Is it debited or credited?
3. At what amount should Hartley Home Furniture report inventory on the balance sheet?
4. At what amount should the business report cost of goods sold on the income statement?
5. Discuss the accounting principle, concept, or constraint that is most relevant to this situation.

P6–12A The accounting records of Keller Music Stores show these data (in thousands):

(4)
Correcting inventory errors over a three-year period

1. Net income, 2018, $46,000

	2020		2019		2018	
Net sales revenue		$426		$366		$378
Cost of goods sold						
Beginning inventory	$ 56		$ 80		$ 96	
Net purchases	276		240		216	
Cost of goods available	332		320		312	
Less: Ending inventory	92		56		80	
Cost of goods sold		240		264		232
Gross margin		186		102		146
Operating expenses		148		92		110
Net income		$ 38		$ 10		$ 36

In early 2021, a team of auditors discovered that the ending inventory of 2018 had been understated by $10,000. Also, the ending inventory for 2020 had been overstated by $6,000. The ending inventory at December 31, 2019, was correct.

Required

1. Show corrected comparative income statements for the three years.
2. State whether each year's net income as reported here and the related owner's equity amounts are understated or overstated. For each incorrect figure, indicate the amount of the understatement or overstatement.

P6–13A Sang-beom Shoe Company has a periodic inventory system and uses the gross margin method of estimating inventories for interim financial statements. The company had the following account balances for the fiscal year ended August 31, 2020:

(3) (5)
Accounting for inventory by the periodic system, estimating inventory by the gross margin method

1. Estimated cost of goods sold, Aug. 31, 2020, $1,140,000

Inventory: Sep. 1, 2019	$ 195,000
Purchases	1,157,000
Purchases returns and allowances	23,000
Freight-in	11,000
Sales	1,922,000
Sales returns and allowances	22,000

Required

1. Use the gross margin method to estimate the cost of the business's ending inventory, assuming the business has an average cost of 60 percent. Hint: Review Exhibit 6–6 for calculation of cost of goods sold.

2. The business has done a physical count of the inventory on hand on August 31, 2020. For convenience, this inventory was calculated using the retail selling prices marked on the goods, which amounted to $252,000. Use the information from Requirement 1 and the gross margin method to calculate the cost of the inventory counted.

(1) (5)
Applying the moving-weighted-average and FIFO costing methods, estimating inventory by the gross margin method
3. Shortage, $45,360

P6–14A Danilov Computers uses a perpetual inventory system for the purchase and sale of their SSD inventory and had the following information available on November 30, 2020:

		Purchases and Sales	Number of Units
Nov.	1	Balance of inventory at $40 per unit	3,900
	7	Purchased at $56 per unit	6,000
	8	Sold for $76 each	4,500
	12	Purchased at $52 per unit	7,500
	16	Sold for $84 each	9,000
	21	Purchased at $52 per unit	4,500
	25	Purchased at $48 per unit	10,500
	29	Sold for $84 each	13,500

Required

1. Calculate the cost of goods sold and the cost of the ending inventory for November under each of the following inventory costing methods: (a) moving-weighted-average cost and (b) FIFO cost.
2. Prepare the journal entries required to record the transactions using the perpetual inventory system with FIFO costing.
3. An internal audit has discovered that a new employee—an accounting clerk—had been stealing merchandise and covering up the shortage by changing the inventory records. The external auditors examined the accounting records prior to the employment of the individual and noted that the company has an average gross margin rate of 37 percent. Use the gross margin method to estimate the cost of the inventory shortage (under the FIFO costing method). (Note: The physical count matched the estimate.) Explain the difference between the three inventory values—the accounting records, physical count, and estimates—and their importance in valuing inventory.

PROBLEMS (GROUP B)

(1)
Using the perpetual inventory system—FIFO

P6–1B Lengyel Lawn Supply, which uses the FIFO method, began March with 200 units of fertilizer inventory that cost $40 each. During March, Lengyel completed these inventory transactions:

			Units	Unit Cost	Unit Sale Price
Mar.	2	Purchase	48	$50	
	8	Sale	160		$144
	17	Purchase	96	60	
	22	Sale	124		148

Required

1. Prepare a perpetual inventory record for the fertilizer.
2. Determine Lengyel's cost of goods sold for March.
3. Compute gross margin for March.

P6–2B Kamlhani Imports is a furniture distributor that uses the FIFO cost method with its perpetual inventory system. The following information is for the first item that it is selling—bean bag chairs—for the month of November. The store engaged in the following business transactions:

① Accounting for inventory in a perpetual system—FIFO

Nov.	1	Opening inventory	50 chairs at $50
	3	Purchase on account	60 chairs at $55
	10	Sale on account	100 chairs at $120
	22	Purchase on account	90 chairs at $60
	24	Sale on account	70 chairs at $140
	28	Operating expenses were $14,400, with one-half paid in cash and the rest reported on account.	

Required

1. Prepare a perpetual inventory record, at FIFO cost, for the bean bag chair inventory.
2. Make journal entries to record the company's transactions. No explanations are required.

P6–3B Snowboard Solutions carries an inventory of snowboards, bindings, and accessories. The sales price of each binding is $125. Company records indicate the following for a popular slip-on binding:

① Accounting for inventory using the perpetual system—moving-weighted-average cost

Date		Item	Quantity	Unit Cost
Feb.	1	Balance	24	$ 61
	7	Sale	20	
	11	Purchase	35	68
	18	Sale	31	
	25	Sale	3	

Required

1. Prepare Snowboard Solutions' perpetual inventory record for the bindings assuming the business uses the moving-weighted-average inventory costing method. Round the average unit cost to the nearest cent and all other amounts to the nearest dollar. Then identify the cost of ending inventory and cost of goods sold for the month.
2. Journalize Snowboard Solutions' inventory transactions using the moving-weighted-average inventory costing method. Include explanations. (Assume purchases and sales are made on account.)

P6–4B Refer to the Kamlhani Imports transactions in P6–2B. Keep all the data unchanged, except that Kamlhani uses the moving-weighted-average-cost method.

① Accounting for inventory in a perpetual system—moving-weighted-average cost

Required

1. Prepare a perpetual inventory record at moving-weighted-average cost. Round the average unit cost to the nearest cent and all other amounts to the nearest dollar.
2. Prepare a multi-step income statement to calculate the net operating income (or loss) for Kamlhani Imports for the month ended of November 2019.

P6–5B Refer to P6–2B and P6–4B to prepare a table comparing ending inventory, cost of goods sold, and gross margin under both the FIFO and the moving-weighted-average-cost methods. You will need to calculate gross margin for P6–2B. Explain why the gross margin is lower under the moving-weighted-average-cost method.

② Summarize perpetual inventory data and explain

① ②
Computing ending inventory by applying two inventory costing methods in a perpetual inventory system

P6–6B Buntzell Industrial Supplies distributes industrial equipment. The company's fiscal year ends on March 31, 2020. One department in the company had 50 industrial sinks that cost $540 each on hand at January 1, 2020. During the quarter, the department purchased merchandise on account as follows:

	Units	Unit Cost	Total
January	120	$585	$70,200
February	24	360	8,640
March	48	450	21,600

Sales for each month in the quarter were as follows:

	Units	Unit Selling Price	Total
January	36	$1,260	$ 45,360
February	108	1,080	116,640
March	60	1,020	61,200

Operating expenses in the quarter were $95,000.

Assume that the company uses a perpetual inventory system. Also assume that monthly purchases of inventory occur on the first day of each month.

Required

1. Determine the cost of the department's ending inventory of sinks at March 31, 2020, under (a) moving-weighted-average cost and (b) FIFO cost. Round the average unit cost to the nearest cent and all other amounts to the nearest dollar.
2. Prepare the department's multi-step income statement for the quarter ended March 31, 2020, under each method described in Requirement 1.

③
Computing ending inventory by applying two inventory costing methods in a periodic inventory system

P6–7B Refer to the information in P6–6B. Assume that Buntzell Industrial Supplies uses a periodic inventory system.

Required

1. Determine the cost of the department's ending inventory of sinks at March 31, 2020, under (a) the weighted-average-cost method and (b) the FIFO method. Round the average unit cost to the nearest cent and all other amounts to the nearest dollar. Assume the company determines cost of goods sold at the end of the quarter.
2. Prepare the department's multi-step income statement for the quarter ended March 31, 2020, under each method described in Requirement 1.

③
Computing inventory by two methods—periodic system

P6–8B Comet Appliances and Supply began December with 280 units of inventory that cost $90 each. During December, the store made the following purchases:

Dec.	3	430 units at $91
	12	190 units at $92
	18	420 units at $93
	27	426 units at $92

The store uses the periodic inventory system, and the physical count at December 31 indicates that 358 units of inventory are on hand.

Required

1. Determine the ending inventory and cost of goods sold amounts for the December financial statements under the weighted-average-cost and FIFO methods. Round the average cost per unit to the nearest cent and all other amounts to the nearest dollar.
2. Sales revenue for December totalled $192,000. Compute Comet Appliances and Supply's gross margin for December under each method.
3. Which method will result in higher net income for Comet? Why?

P6–9B Cloutier Hardware, which uses a periodic inventory system, began 2020 with 9,000 units of inventory that cost a total of $90,000. At year end, the physical count indicated 10,000 units of inventory on hand. During 2020, Cloutier purchased merchandise on account as follows:

③ Using the periodic inventory system—FIFO and weighted-average

Purchase 1 (15,000 units)	$180,000
Purchase 2 (30,000 units)	420,000

Required

1. How many units did Cloutier sell during the year? The sale price per unit was $31. Determine Cloutier's sales revenue for the year.
2. Compute cost of goods sold by both the FIFO and the weighted-average-cost method. Then determine gross margin for the year under each method.

P6–10B The Cookie Company (TCC) began August 2020 with 100 units of inventory that cost $60 each. The sale price of each of those units was $100. During August, TCC completed these inventory transactions:

① ③ Using the perpetual and periodic inventory systems

			Units	Unit Cost	Unit Sale Price
Aug.	3	Sale	32	$60	$100
	8	Purchase	160	62	
	11	Sale	68	60	100
	22	Sale	88	62	104
	30	Purchase	36	64	
	31	Sale	12	62	104

Required

1. The above data are taken from TCC's perpetual inventory records. Which cost method does the company use?
2. Compute TCC's cost of goods sold and gross margin for August 2020 under the:
   a. Perpetual inventory system
   b. Periodic inventory system

P6–11B Senick Building Supplies has experienced declining sales in the last six months. The rate of inventory turnover has dropped, and some of the company's merchandise is gathering dust. At the same time, competition has forced Senick to lower the selling prices of its inventory. It is now December 31, 2020, and the net realizable value of Senick's ending inventory is $1,092 below what the business actually paid for the goods, which was $7,644. Before any adjustments at the end of the period, Senick's Cost of Goods Sold account has a balance of $44,928.

④ Applying the lower-of-cost-and-net-realizable-value rule to inventories

Required

1. What action should Senick Building Supplies take in this situation, if any?
2. Provide any journal entry required.
3. At what amount should Senick report inventory on the balance sheet? At what amount should the company report cost of goods sold on the income statement?
4. Discuss the accounting principle, concept, or constraint that is most relevant to this situation.

(4)
Correcting inventory errors over a three-year period

P6–12B The financial records of Sketch Drawing and Home Plans show these data (in thousands):

	2020		2019		2018	
Net sales revenue		$410		$345		$320
Cost of goods sold						
Beginning inventory	$ 49		$ 41		$ 52	
Net purchases	146		101		98	
Cost of goods available for sale	195		142		150	
Less: Ending inventory	52		49		41	
Cost of goods sold		143		93		109
Gross margin		267		252		211
Operating expenses		109		102		74
Net income		$158		$150		$137

In early 2021, a potential investor's auditors discovered that the ending inventory of 2018 had been overstated by $5,000. Also, the ending inventory for 2020 had been understated by $7,000. The ending inventory at December 31, 2019, was correct.

Required

1. Show corrected comparative income statements for the three years.
2. State whether each year's net income as reported here and the related owner's equity amounts are understated or overstated. For each incorrect figure, indicate the amount of the understatement or overstatement.

(3) (5)
Accounting for inventory by the periodic system and estimating inventory by the gross margin method

P6–13B Kenora Supplies has a periodic inventory system and uses the gross margin method of estimating inventories for interim financial statements. The business had the following account balances for the fiscal year ended August 31, 2020:

Inventory: Sep. 1, 2019	$ 136,000
Purchases	1,180,000
Purchases returns and allowances	36,000
Freight-in	24,000
Sales	2,100,000
Sales returns and allowances	50,000

Required

1. Use the gross margin method to estimate the cost of the business's ending inventory, assuming the business has an average gross margin rate of 45 percent.
2. The business has done a physical count of the inventory on hand on August 31, 2020. For convenience, this inventory was calculated using the retail selling prices marked on the goods, which amounted to $300,000. Use the information from Requirement 1 and the gross margin method to calculate the cost of the inventory counted.

(1) (5)
Applying moving-weighted-average and FIFO costing methods and estimating inventory by the gross margin method

P6–14B Stanislav IT Solutions uses the perpetual inventory system for the purchase and sale of jump drive inventory and had the following information available on August 31, 2020:

		Purchases and Sales	Number of Units
Aug.	1	Balance of inventory at $15 per unit	810
	7	Purchased at $14 per unit	2,250
	8	Sold for $25 each	1,800
	12	Purchased at $15 per unit	1,575
	16	Sold for $26 each	2,600
	21	Purchased at $17 per unit	1,800
	25	Purchased at $20 per unit	2,700
	29	Sold for $27 each	3,600

Required

1. Calculate the cost of goods sold and the cost of the ending inventory for August under (a) moving-weighted-average cost and (b) FIFO cost.
2. Prepare the journal entries required to record the August transactions using the perpetual inventory system with FIFO costing.
3. An internal audit has discovered that two new employees—an accounting clerk and an employee from the purchasing department—have been stealing merchandise and covering up the shortage by changing the inventory records. The external auditors examined the accounting records prior to the employment of the two individuals and noted that the company had an average gross margin rate of 50 percent. The physical count matched the estimate. Use the gross margin method to estimate the cost of the inventory difference (under the FIFO costing method). (Note: The physical count matched the estimate.) Explain the difference between the three inventory values—records, physical count, and estimates—and their importance in valuing inventory.

CHALLENGE PROBLEMS

P6–1C An anonymous source advised Canada Revenue Agency (CRA) that Jim Mayers, owner of Mayers Grocery Store, has been filing fraudulent tax returns for the past several years. You, a tax auditor with the CRA, are in the process of auditing Mayers Grocery Store for the year ended December 31, 2020. The tax returns for the past five years show a decreasing value for ending inventory. You have performed a quick survey of the large store and the attached warehouse and observed that both seemed very well stocked.

(4) (5) Measuring inventory and income

Required Does the information set forth above suggest anything to you that might confirm the anonymous tip? What would you do to confirm or deny your suspicions?

P6–2C It is Monday morning. You heard on the morning news that a client of your public accounting firm, Sundar Sweets, had a fire the previous Friday night that destroyed its office and warehouse. Since you had been at Sundar on the previous Friday preparing the monthly income statement for the previous month that ended on Thursday, you realize you probably have the only current financial information available for Sundar.

(5) Estimating inventory from incomplete records

Upon arrival at your firm's office, you meet your manager, who confirms your suspicions. Sundar Sweets lost its entire inventory and its records. She tells you that the company wants your firm to prepare information for a fire loss claim for Sundar's insurance company for the inventory.

You know the audit file for the fiscal year that ended three months earlier contains a complete section dealing with inventory and the four product lines Sundar carried, including the most recent gross margin rate for each line. The file will show total inventory and how much inventory there was by product line at year end. You also recall that the file contains an analysis of sales by product line for the past several years and that Sundar used a periodic inventory system.

Required Explain how you would use the information available to you to calculate the fire loss by product line.

Extending Your Knowledge

DECISION PROBLEM

DP6–1

③ Assessing the impact of a year-end purchase of inventory—periodic system

1. Without purchase: FIFO gross margin, $268,250
Weighted-average gross margin, $263,125

Kao Camping Supplies is nearing the end of its first year of operations on October 31, 2020. The company uses a periodic inventory system and made inventory purchases of $176,250 during the year as follows:

January	150 units at $165	=	$ 24,750
July	600 units at $195	=	117,000
November	150 units at $230	=	34,500
Totals	900		$176,250

Sales for the year will be 750 units for $410,000 revenue. Expenses other than cost of goods sold will be $105,000. The owner of the company is undecided about whether to adopt FIFO or weighted-average costing as the company's method. The company rounds all unit prices to two decimal places in interim calculations.

The company has storage capacity for 600 additional units of inventory. Inventory prices are expected to stay at $230 per unit for the next few months. The president is considering purchasing 150 additional units of inventory at $230 each before the end of the year. He wishes to know how the purchase would affect net income before taxes under both the FIFO and weighted-average costing methods.

Required

1. To help the owner make the decision, prepare income statements under FIFO costing and weighted-average costing, both without and with the year-end purchase of 150 units of inventory at $230 per unit.
2. Compare net income before taxes under FIFO costing without and with the year-end purchase. Make the same comparison under weighted-average costing. Under which method does the year-end purchase have the greater effect on net income before taxes?
3. If the company wanted to manipulate net income for the year, is one method more manipulative than the other?

FINANCIAL STATEMENT CASE

FSC6–1

① ④ Inventories

The notes are an important part of a company's financial statements, giving valuable details that would clutter the tabular data presented in the statements. This problem will help you learn how to use a company's inventory notes. Refer to page 43 of the Indigo Books and Music Inc. April 1, 2017, annual report (and Note 7, Inventories) in Appendix A and on MyLab Accounting.

Required Refer to Note 7, Inventories on page 43 to answer the following questions:

1. What was the amount of the write-down of inventory as a result of the application of the lower-of-cost-and-net-realizable-value policy in 2017 and 2016?
2. Was there a reversal of any previous write-down?

Try It! Solutions for Chapter 6

1. Perpetual inventory records:

FIFO

	A	B	C	D	E	F	G	H	I	J
1	Smart watches									
2			Purchases			Cost of Goods Sold			Inventory on Hand	
3	Date	Qty.	Unit Cost	Total Cost	Qty.	Unit Cost	Total Cost	Qty.	Unit Cost	Total Cost
4	Jun. 1							20	$60	$1,200
5	3				16	$60	$ 960	4	60	240
6	16	20	$65	$1,300				4	60	240
7								20	65	1,300
8	23				4	60	240			
9					12	65	780	8	65	520
10	Ending	20		1,300	32		1,980	8		520

Notice that the June 3 items are sold from the opening batch of inventory, which all cost the same amount. However, the June 23 items are sold from two batches of inventory that have different costs. Remember, under FIFO, items from the oldest batch are assumed to be sold first.

Moving-Weighted-Average Costing

	A	B	C	D	E	F	G	H	I	J
1	Smart watches									
2			Purchases			Cost of Goods Sold			Inventory on Hand	
3	Date	Qty.	Unit Cost	Total Cost	Qty.	Unit Cost	Total Cost	Qty.	Unit Cost	Total Cost
4	Jun. 1							20	$60.00	$1,200
5	3				16	$60.00	$ 960	4	60.00	240
6	16	20	$65.00	$1,300				24	64.17	1,540
7	23				16	64.17	1,027	8	64.17	513
8	Ending	20		1,300	32		1,987	8		513

Notice that the June 3 items are sold from the opening batch of inventory, which all cost the same amount. However, the June 23 items are sold from two batches of inventory that have different costs. The moving-weighted-average-cost calculation is given in the solutions for the next question. Under the moving-weighted-average-cost method, both cost of goods sold and ending inventory amounts are calculated using the same moving-weighted-average unit cost.

2. Journal entries:

		FIFO		Moving-Weighted-Average	
Jun. 3	Accounts Receivable	1,600		1,600	
	Sales Revenue		1,600		1,600
3	Cost of Goods Sold	960		960	
	Inventory		960		960
16	Inventory	1,300		1,300	
	Accounts Payable		1,300		1,300
23	Accounts Receivable	1,600		1,600	
	Sales Revenue		1,600		1,600
23	Cost of Goods Sold	1,020*		1,027**	
	Inventory		1,020		1,027

Notice the following:
- Only the June 23 COGS entries differ. Refer to the calculations provided.

*(4units × $60) + (12 units × $65) = $1,020
**(4 units × $60) + (20 units × $65) = $1,540; $1,540/24units + $64.17 per unit;
16units × $64.17 + $1,027 (rounded)

3.

	FIFO	Moving-Weighted-Average	
Sales revenue	$3,200	$3,200	($1,600 + $1,600)
Cost of goods sold	1,980		($960 + $1,020)
		1,987	($960 + $1,027)
Gross margin	$1,220	$1,213	

The sales and COGS amounts are gathered from the journal entries in the previous question.

Gross margin = Sales revenue − COGS

4. The method with:
   - The greatest gross margin will maximize net income
   - The lowest gross margin will minimize income taxes

   When inventory purchase prices are rising, as they are in this question, FIFO maximizes net income. Of the methods allowed in Canada, moving-weighted-average minimizes income taxes.
5. When inventory purchase prices are falling, moving-weighted-average maximizes net income and FIFO minimizes income taxes.
6. Under FIFO:

Sales revenue*	$3,050
Cost of goods sold**	1,700
Gross margin	$1,350

*Sales are calculated as (50 × $25) + (60 × $30) = $1,250 + $1,800 = $3,050

**Cost of goods sold are calculated as:

Beginning inventory (40 units, total cost given)	$ 800
Net purchases (60 units × $12.50) + (40 × $15)	1,350
Cost of goods available for sale (140 units)	2,150
Less: Ending inventory (30 units × $15)	(450)
Cost of goods sold (110 units)	$1,700

7. Under weighted-average:

Sales revenue*	$3,050
Cost of goods sold**	1,689
Gross margin	$1,361

*Sales are calculated as (50 × $25) + (60 × $30) = $1,250 + $1,800 = $3,050

**Cost of goods sold are calculated as:

Beginning inventory (40 units, total cost given)	$ 800
Net purchases (60 units × $12.50) + (40 × $15)	1,350
Cost of goods available for sale (140 units)	2,150
Less: Ending inventory (30 units × ($2,150/140 units))	461
Cost of goods sold (110 units × ($2,150/140 units))	$1,689

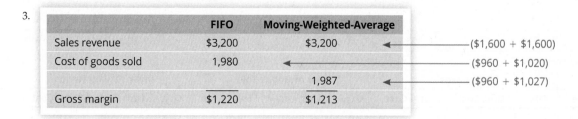

8. a. Amount of inventory remaining at cost: $20,000 − ($20,000 × 60%) = $8,000
Net realizable value of remaining inventory: $8,000 × 60% = $4,800
Since the net realizable value ($4,800) is lower than the original cost of the remaining inventory ($8,000), the balance sheet should reflect the net realizable amount of $4,800.
b. Amount of inventory at original cost: $20,000 − ($20,000 × 60%) = $8,000
Net realizable value of remaining inventory one month later: $10,000
Current carrying value of this inventory: $4,800
Since the net realizable value ($10,000) is greater than the original cost of the remaining inventory ($8,000) and its current carrying value ($4,800), the balance sheet one month later should reflect the original cost amount of $8,000. The lower-of-cost-and-net-realizable-value rule prevents this inventory from being written up to $10,000 since its original cost is lower than its net realizable value.

9. a. The ending inventory is overstated by $2,000, which has the following effects:

	Current balance	Effect	Balance should be:
Sales revenue	$ 60,000	correct	$ 60,000
Cost of goods sold			
Beginning inventory	11,000	correct	11,000
Net purchases	45,000	correct	45,000
Cost of goods available for sale	56,000	correct	56,000
Less: Ending inventory	12,000	overstated	10,000
Cost of goods sold	44,000	understated	46,000
Gross margin	$ 16,000	overstated	$ 14,000

b. The previous year's ending inventory (the next year's beginning inventory) is overstated by $2,000.

At the end of the second year, the first year's overstatement and the second year's understatement of gross margin cancel each other out, for a net effect of nil. However, both years' balances are still incorrect.

10.

Beginning inventory		$ 45,000
Net purchases		160,000
Cost of goods available for sale		205,000
Estimate of cost of goods sold		
Sales revenue	$ 250,000	
Less: Estimated gross margin of 40%	100,000	
Estimated cost of goods sold		150,000
Estimated cost of *ending inventory*		$ 55,000

11. Using the retail method to estimate ending inventory:

	Cost	Selling Price
Beginning inventory	$ 25,000	$ 60,000
Net purchases	100,000	240,000
Goods available for sale	$125,000	300,000
Net sales, at selling price (retail)		250,000
Ending inventory, at selling price (retail)		$ 50,000
Ending inventory, at cost ($50,000 × 42%*)	$ 21,000	

*Retail ratio = ($125,000 ÷ $300,000) × 100 = 42%

7 Accounting Information Systems

CONNECTING CHAPTER 7

LEARNING OBJECTIVES

(1) Describe an effective accounting information system

What is an effective accounting system?

(2) Explain the elements of computerized and manual accounting systems

How do accounting systems work?

(3) Journalize and post transactions using the sales journal, the cash receipts journal, and the accounts receivable subsidiary ledger

How are transactions involving customers recorded in an efficient way?

(4) Journalize and post transactions using the purchases journal, the cash payments journal, and the accounts payable subsidiary ledger

How are transactions involving suppliers of goods and services recorded in an efficient way?

(5) Journalize and post entries not recorded in a special journal

Is the general journal still required when special journals are used?

(A1) Use special journals to record and post transactions with sales taxes

How do we deal with taxes in an accounting system?

Special Journals and Sales Taxes (this Appendix can be found in MyLab Accounting, Chapter Resources)

The **Summary** for Chapter 7 appears on page 398.
Key Terms with definitions for this chapter's material appears on page 399.

CPA competencies

This text covers material outlined in **Section 1: Financial Reporting of the CPA Competency Map**. The Learning Objectives for each chapter have been aligned with the CPA Competency Map to ensure the best coverage possible.

1.1.3 Evaluates reporting processes to support reliable financial reporting

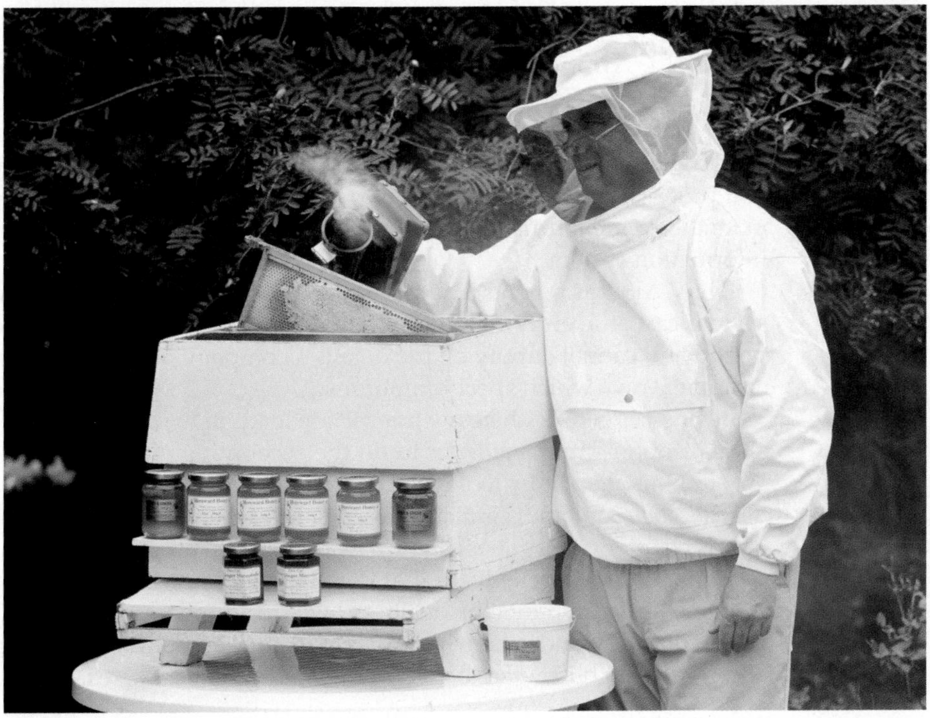
Parkerphotography/Alamy Stock Photo

Sven Lanzinger started beekeeping with his father when he was very young. After completing his apprenticeship as a mechanic and starting a family, he did some research to figure out what sort of small business he and his spouse could set up to bring in extra income. He settled on the idea of using his beekeeping skills to sell honey and related products at the local farmers' markets and to stores in the region.

Sven is not an accountant, but, like many small business owners, he needs an accounting system to track all of his product sales and his expenses. He also needs the financial results for his annual income tax return for the Canada Revenue Agency.

Sven's accounting system began as the classic "shoebox" operation: All the slips for cash received and receipts for payments made were kept in a box, which was then sent to an accountant at year end to prepare the financial statements and tax returns.

His accounting system had to change when the number of business transactions and types of products grew. Sales to stores expanded when his bees produced bigger crops than he had expected, and he started remitting the Harmonized Sales Tax. Sven heard that both QuickBooks and Sage 50 are great accounting software packages that allow him to track all his revenues and expenses on his computer. He chose QuickBooks because that is what his accountant preferred.

To ensure he enters all transactions into his accounting system, Sven checks his bank account balances online daily. The software tracks what each of his customers owe him, so he can review the reports and collect his money on time. At the end of the year, he passes all the files over to his accountant so she can record any year-end adjusting entries and complete the income tax returns.

Sven is delighted that his accounting system is effective and easy to use. It frees him from bookkeeping and allows him to focus his energies on what he does best: beekeeping.

Every organization needs an **accounting information system (AIS)**. An AIS is a set of interrelated components (people, procedures, documents, hardware, software, etc.) that collect, process, store, and disseminate financial information to internal and external users. The system collects information, processes it, and produces reports that meet users' needs. So far in this text, we have used a manual general journal and general ledger to create the records in an accounting information system.

Every AIS has a general journal and a general ledger. However, this manual system can efficiently handle a limited number of transactions per accounting period and cannot supply all the details a company needs, such as which specific customers owe which specific amounts.

Businesses cope with heavy transaction loads in two ways: computerization and specialization. We *computerize* to do the accounting efficiently and more reliably. We start this chapter by looking at computers and accounting information systems. *Specialization* combines similar transactions to speed up the process. The second half of this chapter covers special journals that can be used for repetitive transactions as well as subsidiary ledgers that detail amounts owed to a business by specific customers and amounts the business owes to suppliers.

You may be wondering why we cover manual accounting information systems at all, since many businesses use computerized systems. There are four main reasons:

- Learning a manual system will equip you to work with both manual and electronic systems. The accounting is the same regardless of the system.
- Few small businesses have computerized all their accounting. Even companies that use QuickBooks or Sage 50 keep some manual accounting records. For businesses that use manual systems, these systems follow the principles and procedures that we illustrate in this chapter.
- Learning a manual system will help you master accounting. A number of small business owners only know which keys to use in QuickBooks, but if they had accounting knowledge they could better manage their businesses. You will also see how special journals, subsidiary ledgers, and computer modules link to each other to create the final set of financial statements.
- Learning a manual system will help you recognize a computer system that is not set up properly or is not working as intended.

Effective Accounting Information Systems

LO 1

What is an effective accounting system?

Exhibit 7–1 shows examples of business transactions and activities that are completed when using an accounting information system. A lot of data needs to be captured and organized in order to produce information that is useful for decision makers.

An effective system—whether computerized or manual—provides the following:

- Control
- Compatibility
- Flexibility
- Reports that meet users' needs
- A favourable cost–benefit relationship

Features

Chapter 8 presents more information about internal controls.

Control Owners and managers must *control* the business and manage risk. *Internal controls* safeguard assets and eliminate waste. They are the methods and procedures used to authorize transactions, to ensure adherence to management policy, to safeguard assets and records, to prevent and detect error and fraud, to provide

EXHIBIT 7-1 | Business Transactions and AIS Activities

Business Transactions	AIS Activities
Sell merchandise inventory	Receipt of customer order Approval of credit sale Check availability of merchandise inventory Shipment of inventory to customer Processing of sales invoice Receipt of customer payment
Purchase of goods or services	Request for purchase of goods or services Approval of vendor Receipt of goods or services Processing of vendor invoice Payment for goods or services
Payroll	Approval of new employees Collection of time records Preparation and payment of payroll Preparation and payment of payroll taxes

security by limiting access to assets and records, and to ensure that information produced is relevant, accurate, and timely. You will see examples of these controls throughout this chapter, such as the use of cheques for all cash payments and the comparison of the general ledger account total to the detailed listing of individual customer, inventory, or payable balances at the end of the month to reconcile any discrepancies.

For example, in companies such as Indigo Books and Music Inc., managers control cash payments to avoid theft through unauthorized payments. VISA, MasterCard, and other credit card companies keep accurate records of their accounts receivable to ensure that customers are billed and collections are received on time.

Compatibility A *compatible* system is one that works smoothly with the business's operations, personnel, and organizational structure. For example, branches of Scotiabank report how much revenue is generated and how many bank loans are issued from each branch so that the head office can track these numbers in each region. If revenue and loan numbers in Alberta or Nova Scotia are down, the managers can concentrate their collection efforts in those regions. They may relocate some branch offices, open new branches, or hire new personnel to increase their revenues and net income. A compatible accounting information system conforms to the particular needs of the business.

Flexibility Organizations evolve. They develop new products, sell off unprofitable operations and acquire new ones, adjust employee pay scales, and decide to "go green." Changes in the business often call for changes in the accounting system. A well-designed system is *flexible* if it accommodates changes without needing a complete overhaul. Consider Sven's honey business. If he adds products he purchases for resale, such as bee-themed T-shirts, then his accounting system must adapt to handle purchase transactions and multiple inventory balances. Sven would not want to get new software every time he evolved his business.

Reports that Meet Users' Needs If the accounting system processes the information collected but does not produce reports that are relevant or useful, then the accounting system is lacking. To address this, most accounting packages allow users to program their preferences for financial statement presentation and allow users to create special reports.

Favourable Cost–Benefit Relationship Achieving control, compatibility, and flexibility can be expensive. Managers strive for a system that offers maximum benefits at a minimum cost—that is, a system that has a favourable *cost–benefit* *relationship*. Most small companies use off-the-shelf computerized accounting packages, such as Sage 50 or QuickBooks. Less-expensive accounting software may have limited flexibility and limited capabilities. Large companies, such as the yoga-wear company lululemon athletica, have specialized needs for information. For them, customized programming is a must because the benefits—in terms of information tailored to the company's needs—far outweigh the cost of the system. The result? Better decisions.

All these features are needed whether the accounting information system is computerized or manual. Let's begin with a computerized system.

Components of a Computerized Accounting Information System

A computerized accounting information system has two basic components (hardware and software) in addition to the personnel and procedures to operate it.

Hardware is the electronic equipment and the network that connects them. Most systems require a **network** to link computers. In a networked system, a **server** stores the program and the data.

Access to computer information must be strictly controlled. At a TELUS store, it would be improper for all employees to gain access to customer accounts. An unauthorized employee could change a customer's account balance or learn confidential information about the customer. Hence, access codes limit access to certain information. Source documents should support all sensitive changes to computer files.

Software is the set of programs that drives the computer. Accounting software reads, edits, and stores transaction data. It also generates the reports you can use to run the business.

Many companies are now moving their data "into the cloud" to save money. A business using **cloud computing** pays a third party to store the business's information on a third-party server instead of at the business. Employees access the software and data via the Internet.

For large enterprises, such as the Molson Coors Brewing Company or the Royal Bank of Canada, the accounting software is integrated into the company **database**, or computerized storehouse of information. Many business databases, or *management information systems*, include both accounting and non-accounting data. For example, VIA Rail Canada, in negotiating a union contract, often needs to examine the relationship between the employment history and salary levels of company employees. VIA's database provides the data that managers need to negotiate effectively with their labour unions. During negotiations, both parties carry laptops so that they can access the database and analyze data on the spot.

Personnel who operate the system must be properly trained. In addition, management of a computerized accounting information system requires careful consideration of data security and screening of the people in the organization who will have access to the data. Security is usually achieved with *passwords*, codes that restrict access to computerized records.

Try It!

1. Every business needs an accounting information system (AIS). Which of the following is the reason why?
   a. It is mandatory to set up a company bank account.
   b. The Canada Revenue Agency requires every business to have an AIS.
   c. Owners and managers of businesses must make decisions, and they need information to run the organization.
   d. The provincial corporation of finance may audit your business.
2. Suppose you are the controller for a small industrial ventilation company that wants to change its accounting information system. The new system you are considering will not accept the current alpha characters in the job-order numbers. Each job is assigned a number and then, as extras are added to the job, an alpha character is added to the job-order number, for example, job 1645a. Which feature of a good accounting information system is being compromised, and what could you do to solve this dilemma?

Solutions appear at the end of this chapter and on **MyLab Accounting**

How Accounting Systems Work

LO 2 How do accounting systems work?

As we discuss the stages of data processing, observe the differences between a computerized system and a manual system. The relationship among the three stages of data processing—inputs, processing, and outputs—is shown in Exhibit 7–2.

EXHIBIT 7–2 | The Three Stages of Data Processing

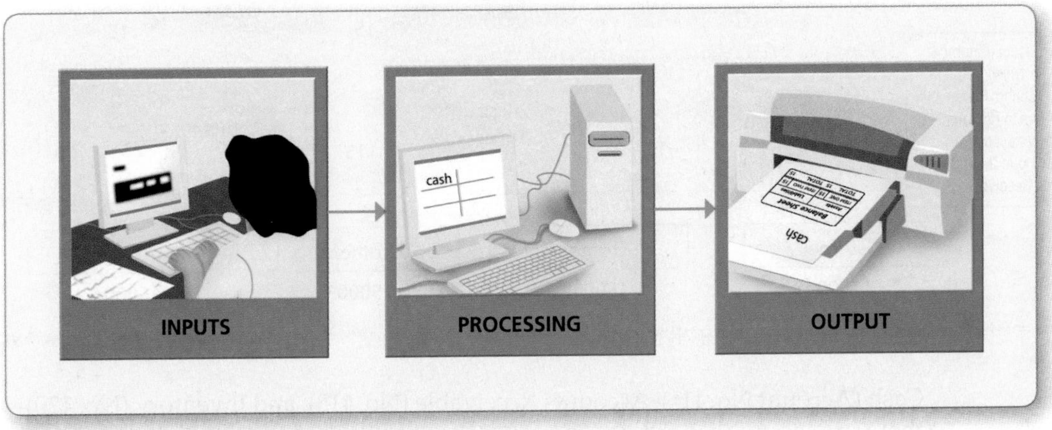

Inputs Inputs come from source documents, such as orders received from customers, sales receipts, and bank deposit slips. Inputs are usually grouped by type. For example, a firm would enter cash sales separately from credit sales and purchases.

Processing In a manual system, *processing* includes journalizing transactions, posting to the accounts, and preparing the financial statements. In a computerized system, the initial data entered will be posted automatically to the ledger and then processed into reports (including the journal and account details) and financial statements. Often account numbers or the first letters of a name are used to quickly enter the data into the correct accounts.

Outputs *Outputs* are the reports used for decision making, including the financial statements. Business owners can make better decisions with the reports produced by a good accounting system. In a computerized accounting system, a trial balance is a report (an output). But a manual system would treat the trial balance as a *processing* step leading to the preparation of financial statements.

Often a cash register doubles as a computer terminal, called a point-of-sale terminal. The cashier passes the Universal Product Code (UPC) of merchandise over the scanner, which identifies the merchandise to the computer. The use of a scanner eliminates errors in recording sales and automatically updates inventory records (costs and units) in a perpetual inventory system.

Designing an Accounting System: The Chart of Accounts

An accounting system begins with the chart of accounts. Recall from Chapter 2, Exhibit 2–3 that the chart of accounts lists all accounts in the general ledger and their account numbers. In the accounting system of most companies, the account *numbers* take on added importance. It is efficient for data entry to represent a complex account title, such as Accumulated Amortization—Photographic Equipment, with a number (e.g., 15570).

Recall that asset accounts often begin with the digit 1, liabilities with the digit 2, owner's equity accounts with the digit 3, revenues with 4, and expenses with 5. This is because the reporting component of any accounting system relies on *account number ranges* to translate accounts and their balances into properly organized financial statements and other reports. For example, the accounts numbered 101–399 (assets, liabilities, and owner's equity) are sorted to the balance sheet, and the accounts numbered 401–599 (revenues and expenses) go to the income statement.

Exhibit 7–3 illustrates one structure for computerized accounts. Assets in this case are divided into current assets; property, plant, and equipment; and other assets. Among the current assets we illustrate only three general ledger accounts:

EXHIBIT 7–3 | Sample Account Number Structure

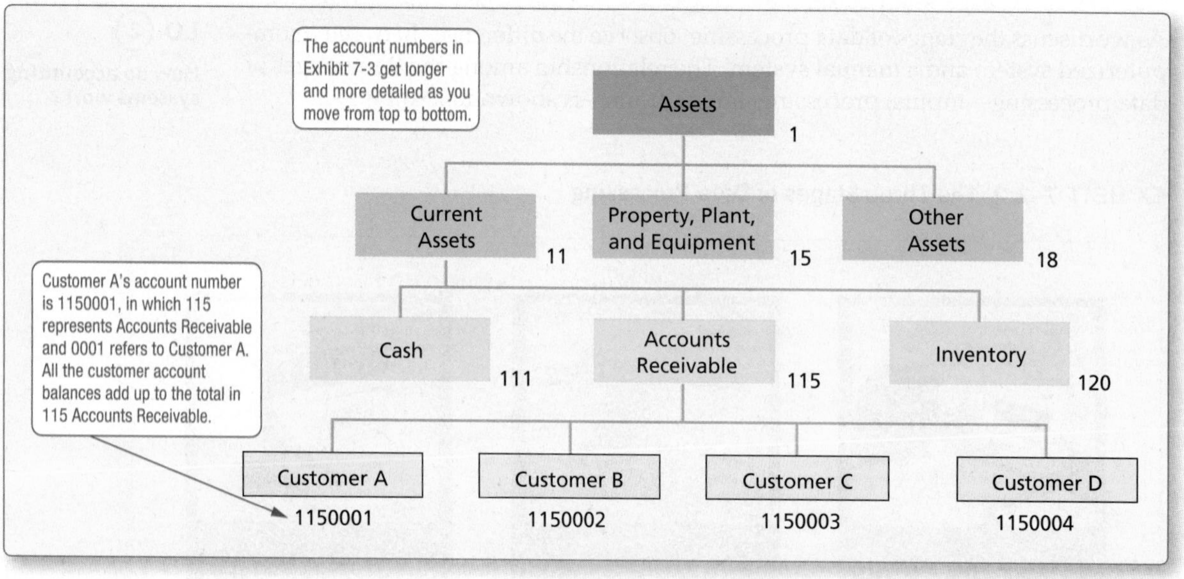

Cash (Account No. 111), Accounts Receivable (No. 115), and Inventory (No. 120)—there are others that are not shown. Accounts Receivable holds the *total* dollar amount receivable from customers A, B, C, and D.

Many computer systems have long account numbers, such as 100000 for Assets, 110000 for Current Assets, 111000 for Cash, and so on to allow for the addition of new accounts in the future.

Processing Transactions

Recording transactions in a full accounting system requires an additional step that we have skipped thus far. A business of any size *classifies transactions by type* for efficient handling. In an expanded manual system, credit sales, purchases on account, cash receipts, and cash payments are treated as separate categories. Each category of transactions has its own special journal. (We discuss these journals in detail later in this chapter.) For example:

Payroll payments are another category of transactions and are recorded in the *payroll journal or payroll register*, which we discuss in detail in Chapter 11. Companies can create other special journals for categories of transactions that are important to their own operations or are specific to their industry. The special journals shown here tend to be used most often.

Transactions that do not fit any of the special journals, such as the adjusting and closing entries at the end of the period, are recorded in the *general journal*, which serves as the "journal of last resort."

Computerized systems are organized by function, or task, which mirror the special journals just mentioned. You can select a function, such as recording sales on account, from a menu. A **menu** is a list of options for choosing computer functions. In such a *menu-driven* system, you first access the main menu. You then choose from a submenu until you reach the function you want. Some accounting packages call these submenu items **modules**.

Posting in a computerized system can be performed continuously (**online processing** or **real-time processing**) or later for a group of similar transactions (**batch processing**). The posting then updates the account balances automatically. Outputs—accounting reports—are the final stage of data processing. In a computerized system, the financial statements can be printed automatically. Spreadsheets can be linked to accounting packages to help prepare more complex reports.

Exhibit 7-4 summarizes the accounting cycle in a computerized system and in a manual system. As you study the exhibit, compare and contrast the two types of systems.

You may think a computer skips steps when data are entered because the computer performs some of the steps such as posting internally. However, a computerized accounting system performs all the steps a manual system does, except for the worksheet.

EXHIBIT 7-4 | Comparison of the Accounting Cycle in a Computerized and a Manual System

Computerized systems post and process data very quickly and ***accurately***, assuming data are entered correctly. Programs can block journal entries that are out of balance until the error is corrected or display a reminder if an entry seems unusual. Financial statements and special reports can be generated quickly whenever they are needed.

Start with the account balances in the ledger at the beginning of the period.

Manual systems may be easier to understand. The trail from journal to ledger to financial statements is easy to see and follow compared to computerized systems, where much of the processing is done "behind the scenes."

COMPUTERIZED SYSTEM	ACCOUNTING CYCLE STEPS	MANUAL SYSTEM
Analyze and classify business transactions by type. Access appropriate menus for data entry.	1 & 2	Analyze and classify business transactions by type. Journalize transactions in special journals or the general journal.
Computer automatically posts transactions as a batch or when entered online.	3	Post journal entries to the ledger accounts.
The unadjusted balances are generated immediately after each posting. The trial balance, if needed, can be accessed as a report.	4	Compute the unadjusted balance in each account at the end of the period. Enter the trial balance on the worksheet and complete. (optional)
Enter and post adjusting entries. Print the financial statements.	5, 6, & 7	Journalize and post the adjusting entries. Prepare the financial statements.
Run automatic closing procedures after backing up the period's accounting records. The next period's opening balances are created automatically as a result of closing.	8 & 9	Journalize and post the closing entries. Prepare the post-closing trial balance. This trial balance becomes Step 1 for the next period.

Enterprise Resource Planning

Many small and medium-sized businesses use accounting software such as QuickBooks or Sage 50. However, larger companies often use **enterprise resource planning (ERP)** systems that feed accounting and other data into software for all company activities—from purchasing to production and customer service. These systems can be expensive to implement but can save money in the long run by integrating all of a company's data and systems.

The larger ERP systems, such as SAP, Oracle Cloud ERP, and JD Edwards, are popular for a number of reasons, including the wide range of functionality they offer. Some of the largest providers of ERP software also have financial packages developed specifically for certain industries; they spend a great deal of time learning what specific industries require and then target those needs. For example, SAP provides the following and more with their ERP software:

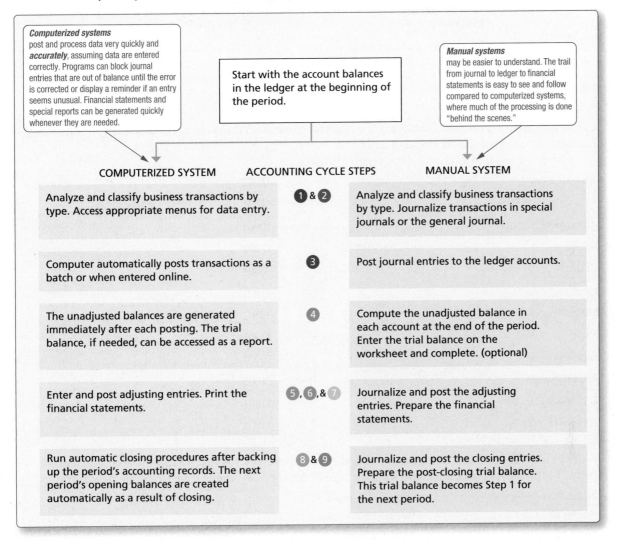

- Accounting
- Financial management
- Treasury and financial risk management
- Travel management
- Talent management
- Service delivery
- Receivables management
- Streamlined essential business processes
- Workforce analytics
- Payroll
- Strategic workforce management
- E-recruiting
- Operations analytics
- Procurement and logistics execution
- Product development and manufacturing
- Sales and service
- Integrated modules

Try It!

3. Create a chart of accounts by matching the account name with the most appropriate account number. Assume expenses are listed alphabetically.

Accounts Payable	18001
Accounts Receivable	54001
Advertising Expense	12001
Building	17001
Cash	30001
Land	41001
Miscellaneous Expenses	25001
Notes Payable	51001
Salaries Expense	59001
Sales Revenue	21001
T. Pioneer, Capital	11001
T. Pioneer, Withdrawals	31001

4. Refer to the information in the previous question. Suppose you needed to add the accounts listed below to the chart of accounts. Specify the range of numbers available for each of the new accounts.

Notes Receivable	Supplies Expense
Automobile	Unearned Revenue
Supplies	Service Revenue

Solutions appear at the end of this chapter and on **MyLab Accounting**

Special Journals

LO 3

How are transactions involving customers recorded in an efficient way?

The journal entries illustrated so far have been made in the **general journal**. However, it is not efficient to record all transactions in the general journal, so we use special journals. A **special journal** is an accounting journal designed to record one specific type of transaction.

Exhibit 7–5 shows a typical accounting system for a merchandising business. The remainder of this chapter describes how this system works.

EXHIBIT 7–5 | An Accounting System with Special Journals for a Merchandising Business

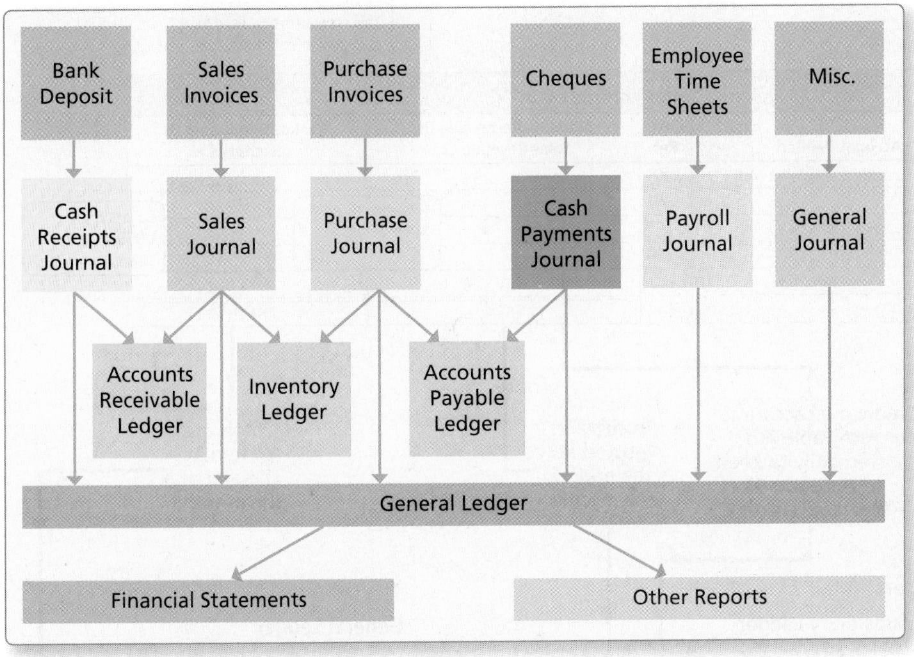

The exhibit shows that source documents are entered into the appropriate journal for that type of transaction. All totals are posted to the **general ledger** (as shown in earlier chapters). Some information is updated into **subsidiary ledgers** (or subledgers) which are individual records within a general ledger account. For example, Exhibit 7–3 showed that the general ledger account for accounts receivable is broken down further into a series of individual customer accounts. So when the general ledger account is updated, we also need to update the individual account balance.

While companies can create as many special journals as they like, most transactions fall into one of five categories, so accountants use at least five different journals. This system saves time and money, as we will see. The payroll journal will be discussed in Chapter 11. The five types of transactions, the special journals used, and the posting abbreviations are as follows:

Transaction	Special Journal	Posting Abbreviation
Sale on account	Sales journal	S
Cash receipt	Cash receipts journal	CR
Purchase on account	Purchases journal	P
Cash payment	Cash payments journal	CP
All others	General journal	G

The Sales Journal

Transactions are recorded in either the general journal or a special journal, but not in both.

Most merchandisers sell inventory on account. These *credit sales* are recorded in the **sales journal**. Credit sales of assets other than inventory—for example, buildings—occur infrequently and may be recorded in the general journal.

Exhibit 7–6 illustrates a sales journal (Panel A) and the related posting to the ledgers (Panel B) of Slopes Ski Shop, a small ski shop we introduced in Chapter 5. Each entry in the Accounts Receivable Dr/Sales Revenue Cr column of the sales journal in Exhibit 7–6 is a debit (Dr) to Accounts Receivable and a credit (Cr) to Sales Revenue, as the heading above this column indicates. For each transaction, the accountant enters the following:

- Date
- Invoice number

EXHIBIT 7–6 | Sales Journal and Posting to Ledgers under the Perpetual Inventory System

Panel A: Sales Journal

This account is only used for perpetual inventory systems.

Sales Journal					Page 3
Date 2020	Invoice No.	Account Debited	Post. Ref	Accounts Receivable Dr Sales Revenue Cr	Cost of Goods Sold Dr Inventory Cr
Nov. 2	422	Claudette Cabot 115009	✓	935	505
13	423	Brent Harmon 115115	✓	694	361
18	424	Susan Levy 115249	✓	907	517
27	425	Clay Schmidt 115391	✓	1,783	431
30		Total		4,319	1,814
				(115/410)	(511/131)

GJ entry:
A/R 935
Sales 935

GJ entry:
COGS 505
Inven. 505

As you post to the ledgers, print the journal page number in the account to identify the source of the data. All transaction data in Exhibit 7–6 originated on Page 3 of the Sales journal, so all posting references in the ledger accounts are S.3.

Individual accounts receivable are posted daily to keep Accounts Receivable current.

Totals are posted at the end of the month.

Totals are posted at the end of the month.

Panel B: Posting to Ledgers

Accounts Receivable Subsidiary Ledger

Claudette Cabot					115009
Date		Jrnl. Ref.	Debit	Credit	Balance
Nov. 2		S.3	935		935

Brent Harmon					115115
Date		Jrnl. Ref.	Debit	Credit	Balance
Nov.13		S.3	694		694

Susan Levy					115249
Date		Jrnl. Ref.	Debit	Credit	Balance
Nov.18		S.3	907		907

Clay Schmidt					115391
Date		Jrnl. Ref.	Debit	Credit	Balance
Nov.27		S.3	1,783		1,783

Note that some Accounts Receivable subsidiary ledger accounts may have opening balances. For simplicity, they are not shown here.

General Ledger

Accounts Receivable					No. 115
Date	Item	Jrnl. Ref.	Debit	Credit	Debit Balance
Nov.30		S.3	4,319		4,319

Inventory					No. 131
Date	Item	Jrnl. Ref.	Debit	Credit	Debit Balance
Nov. 1		Bal			3,885
30		S.3		1,814	2,071

Sales Revenue					No. 410
Date	Item	Jrnl. Ref.	Debit	Credit	Credit Balance
Nov.30		S.3		4,319	4,319

Cost of Goods Sold					No. 511
Date	Item	Jrnl. Ref.	Debit	Credit	Debit Balance
Nov.30		S.3	1,814		1,814

- Customer name and number
- Transaction amounts

This streamlined way of recording sales on account saves time that, in a manual system, would be spent entering account names and dollar amounts in the general journal for every transaction.

In recording credit sales in the previous chapters, we did not record the names of credit-sale customers. In practise, the business must know the amount receivable from each customer. How else can the company identify who owes it money, when payment is due, and how much?

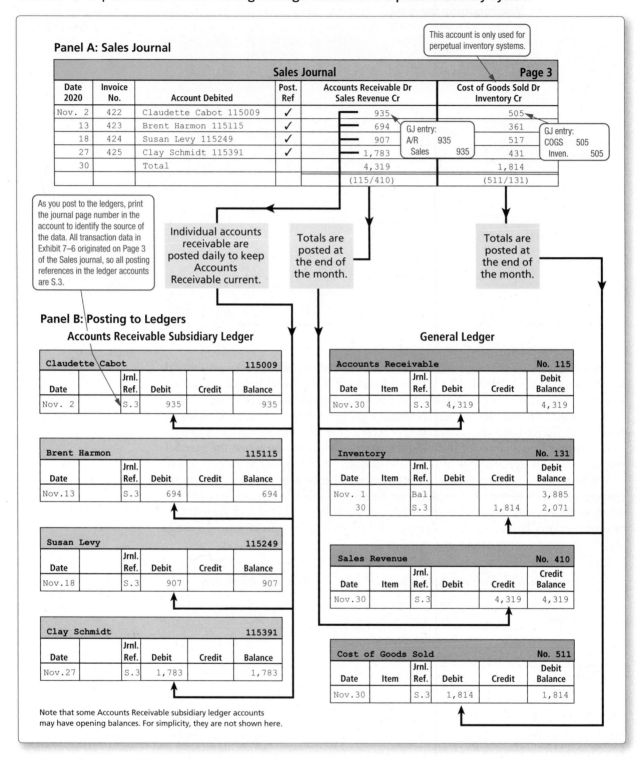

Consider the first transaction in Panel A. On November 2, 2020, Slopes Ski Shop sold ski equipment on account to Claudette Cabot for $935. The invoice number is 422. All this information appears on a single line in the sales journal. No explanation is necessary. The transaction's presence in the sales journal means that it is a credit sale, debited to Accounts Receivable—Claudette Cabot and credited to Sales Revenue. To gain any additional information about the transaction, we would look at the original invoice.

Only credit sales of merchandise are recorded in the sales journal.

Recall from Chapter 5 that Slopes uses a *perpetual* inventory system. When recording the sale, Slopes also records the cost of goods sold and the decrease in inventory. The far-right column of the sales journal records the cost of goods sold and inventory amount—$505 for the goods sold to Claudette Cabot. If Slopes used a *periodic* inventory system, it would not record cost of goods sold or the decrease in inventory at the time of sale. The sales journal would need only one column to debit Accounts Receivable and to credit Sales Revenue for the amount of the sale.

Additional data can be recorded in the sales journal. For example, a company may add a column to record sale terms, such as 2/10, n/30. The design of the journal depends on the managers' needs for information. Special journals are flexible—they can be tailored to meet any special needs of a business.

Posting to the General Ledger The only ledger we have used so far is the general ledger, which holds the accounts reported in the financial statements. Exhibit 7–7 uses Panel A from Exhibit 7–6 to explain how the accounts are posted to the general ledger at the end of each month.

EXHIBIT 7–7 | Posting References to the General Ledger

The checkmark indicates that this transaction has been posted to the subledger.

Panel A: Sales Journal

Sales Journal					Page 3
Date 2020	Invoice No.	Account Debited	Post. Ref	Accounts Receivable Dr Sales Revenue Cr	Cost of Goods Sold Dr Inventory Cr
Nov. 2	422	Claudette Cabot 115009	✓	935	505
13	423	Brent Harmon 115115	✓	694	361
18	424	Susan Levy 115249	✓	907	517
27	425	Clay Schmidt 115391	✓	1,783	431
30		Total		4,319	1,814
				(115/410)	(511/131)

Showing these account numbers here indicates that $4,319 has been posted to these two accounts (Accounts Receivable and Sales Revenue) at the end of the month.

These account numbers indicate that $1,814 has been posted to the Cost of Good Sold and Inventory accounts at the end of the month.

Posting to the Accounts Receivable Subsidiary Ledger The $4,319 debit to Accounts Receivable does not identify the amount receivable from any specific customer. A business may have many customers. For example, TELUS has a customer account for each of its subscribers.

Businesses must create an account for each customer in a subsidiary ledger called the accounts receivable subsidiary ledger. A subsidiary ledger is a file of the individual accounts that make up a total for a general ledger account. The customer accounts in the subsidiary ledger are usually arranged in alphabetical order, but they often have a customer number as well so that reports can be created by name or by customer number.

The purpose of an Accounts Receivable subsidiary ledger account is to provide detail of a *customer's* account or history to facilitate billing and collection.

Amounts in the sales journal are posted to the subsidiary ledger continuously, or at least daily, to keep a current record of the amount receivable from each customer. The amounts are debits. Daily posting allows the business to answer customer inquiries promptly. Suppose Claudette Cabot telephones Slopes on November 11

Posting to the subsidiary ledger and to the general ledger is *not* double posting since the subsidiary ledger is *not* part of the general ledger and will *not* appear on the trial balance. Posting to both is necessary to keep the two in balance.

to ask how much money she owes. The subsidiary ledger readily provides that information: $935 in Exhibit 7–6, Panel B:

Accounts Receivable Subsidiary Ledger

Claudette Cabot					115009
Date		Jrnl. Ref.	Debit	Credit	Balance
Nov. 2		S.3	935		935

To simplify the process, when each transaction amount is posted to the subsidiary ledger in a manual system, a check mark or some other notation is printed in the posting reference column of the sales journal to indicate that the subsidiary ledger has been updated (see Exhibit 7–7). A general ledger account number would not be used here because it refers to the Accounts Receivable **control account** in the general ledger, which is the total of all the subsidiary ledger account balances.

Balancing the Ledgers The arrows in Exhibit 7–6 indicate the direction of the information. The arrows show the links between the individual customer accounts in the subsidiary ledger and the Accounts Receivable account. After posting, the Accounts Receivable debit balance in the general ledger should equal the sum of the individual customer balances in the subsidiary ledger. The subsidiary ledger's information is often summarized in a list. This list of the customers and their balances is called a **schedule**. So the process of checking that the schedule of accounts receivable is equal to the general ledger (control account) balance is called balancing or **proving** the ledgers as shown below:

Accounts Receivable debit balance in the General Ledger:

Accounts Receivable	$4,319

Control account

After *all* postings, the balance in the control account should equal the sum of all the subsidiary accounts.

Data from the Accounts Receivable Subsidiary Ledger:
Schedule of Accounts Receivable
November 30, 2020

Lists the individual customer accounts and balances from the subsidiary ledger.

115009	Claudette Cabot	$ 935
115115	Brent Harmon	694
115249	Susan Levy	907
115391	Clay Schmidt	1,783
Total accounts receivable		$4,319

For those of you more comfortable with T-accounts, we can prove the same balances this way:

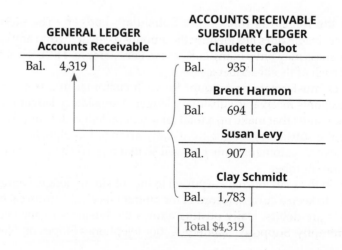

GENERAL LEDGER
Accounts Receivable

Bal. 4,319	

ACCOUNTS RECEIVABLE SUBSIDIARY LEDGER

Claudette Cabot

Bal. 935	

Brent Harmon

Bal. 694	

Susan Levy

Bal. 907	

Clay Schmidt

Bal. 1,783	

Total $4,319

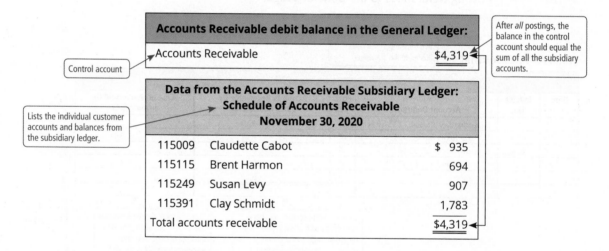

The Cash Receipts Journal

Cash transactions are common in most businesses because cash receipts from customers keep a business going. To record a large number of cash receipt transactions, accountants use the **cash receipts journal**.

Exhibit 7–8, Panel A, illustrates the cash receipts journal for Slopes Ski Shop transactions in November 2020. The related posting to the ledgers is shown in Panel B.

Every transaction recorded in this journal is a cash receipt, so the first column is for debits to the Cash account. In a typical merchandising business, the main sources of cash are collections on account and cash sales. The next column is for debits to Sales Discounts on collections from customers.

The cash receipts journal has credit columns for Accounts Receivable, Sales Revenue, and Other Accounts. The Other Accounts columns list sources of cash other than cash sales and collections on account and are also used to record the names and account numbers of customers from whom cash is received on account.

Every entry in the cash receipts journal includes a debit to Cash. *Cash* sales are recorded here; *Credit* sales are recorded in the sales journal.

In Exhibit 7–8, cash sales occurred on November 6, 19, and 28. Observe the debits to Cash and the credits to Sales Revenue ($517, $853, and $1,802).

Different businesses have different types of transactions, and they design their special journals to meet their particular needs for information. In this case, Slopes uses the Other Accounts Credit column as a catch-all to record all non-routine cash receipt transactions. For example, on November 25, Slopes collected $762 of interest revenue.

Total debits must equal total credits in the cash receipts journal. This equality holds for each transaction and for the monthly totals. For the month in Exhibit 7–8, total debits equal total credits, as shown:

Debit Columns		Credit Columns	
Cash	$6,134	Accounts Receivable	$1,235
Sales Discounts	35	Sales Revenue	3,172
Cost of Goods Sold	1,707	Other Accounts	1,762
		Inventory	1,707
Total	$7,876	Total	$7,876

Total debits must equal total credits for each special journal.

Posting to the General Ledger The column totals are usually posted monthly. Trace the posting to Cash and the other accounts from the cash receipts journal to the general ledger in Exhibit 7–8.

Monthly posting is typical in a manual system. Computers post transactions either as they happen or in a batch at the end of the day.

The column total for Other Accounts is *not* posted. Instead, these credits are posted individually. In Exhibit 7–8, the November 12 transaction reads "Note Payable to Scotiabank." This account's number (222) in the Post. Ref. column indicates that the transaction amount was posted individually. The November 25 collection of interest revenue is also posted individually. These amounts can be posted to the general ledger at the end of the month, but their date in the ledger accounts should be their actual date in the journal to make it easy to trace each amount back to the cash receipts journal. The check mark (✓), instead of an account number, below the column total means that the column total was not posted because individual items above were posted.

Posting to the Subsidiary Ledger Amounts from the cash receipts journal are posted to the accounts receivable subsidiary ledger *daily* to keep the individual balances up to date. The postings to the accounts receivable ledger are credits. For example, trace the $935 credit to Claudette Cabot's account. It reduces the balance in her account to zero. The $300 receipt from Brent Harmon reduces his accounts receivable balance to $394.

EXHIBIT 7–8 | Cash Receipts Journal and Posting to the Ledgers under the Perpetual Inventory System

The customer's name and account number appear in the Other Accounts/Account Title column to make sure the payment received is posted to the subsidiary ledger.

For this transaction, we enter the account title, Note Payable, in the Other Accounts/Account Title Column.

Each sale entry is accompanied by an entry that debits Cost of Goods Sold and credits Inventory for the cost of the merchandise sold, since the perpetual inventory system is being used.

Slopes borrowed $1,000 from Scotiabank. Cash is debited, and Note Payable to Scotiabank is credited in the Other Accounts column because it is an unusual transaction.

Slopes collected $900 from Claudette Cabot. Referring back to Exhibit 7–6, we see that on November 2 Slopes sold merchandise for $935 to Claudette Cabot.

The terms of sale allowed a $35 discount for prompt payment within the discount period.

Panel A: Cash Receipts Journal

Cash Receipts Journal — Page 5

Date 2020	Debits: Cash	Debits: Sales Discounts	Credits: Accounts Receivable	Credits: Sales Revenue	Other Accounts: Account Title	Post. Ref.	Amount	Cost of Goods Sold Dr Inventory Cr
Nov. 6	517			517				290
12	1,000				Note Payable to Scotiabank	222	1,000	
14	900	35	935		Claudette Cabot 115009*	✓		
19	853			853				426
22	300		300		Brent Harmon 115115	✓		
25	762				Interest Revenue	460	762	
28	1,802			1,802				991
30	6,134	35	1,235	3,172	Totals		1,762	1,707
	(101)	(420)	(115)	(410)			(✓)**	(511/131)

Totals are posted at the end of the month.

Individual accounts receivable are posted daily.

Individual amounts are posted at the end of the month.

Total is not posted.

Total is posted at the end of the month.

Panel B: Posting to Ledgers

Accounts Receivable Subsidiary Ledger

Claudette Cabot — 115009

Date		Jrnl. Ref.	Debit	Credit	Balance
Nov. 2		S.3	935		935
14		CR.5		935	0

Brent Harmon — 115115

Date		Jrnl. Ref.	Debit	Credit	Balance
Nov.13		S.3	694		694
22		CR.5		300	394

Susan Levy — 115249

Date		Jrnl. Ref.	Debit	Credit	Balance
Nov.18		S.3	907		907

Clay Schmidt — 115391

Date		Jrnl. Ref.	Debit	Credit	Balance
Nov.27		S.3	1,783		1,783

General Ledger

Cash — No. 101

Date	Item	Jrnl. Ref.	Debit	Credit	Debit Balance
Nov.30		CR.5	6,134		6,134

Accounts Receivable — No. 115

Date	Item	Jrnl. Ref.	Debit	Credit	Debit Balance
Nov.30		S.3	4,319		4,319
30		CR.5		1,235	3,084

Inventory — No. 131

Date	Item	Jrnl. Ref.	Debit	Credit	Debit Balance
Nov. 1		Bal.	3,885		3,885
30		S.3		1,814	2,071
30		CR.5		1,707	364

Note Payable to Scotiabank — No. 222

Date	Item	Jrnl. Ref.	Debit	Credit	Credit Balance
Nov.12		CR.5		1,000	1,000

Sales Revenue — No. 410

Date	Item	Jrnl. Ref.	Debit	Credit	Credit Balance
Nov. 1		S.3		4,319	4,319
30		CR.5		3,172	7,491

Sales Discounts — No. 420

Date	Item	Jrnl. Ref.	Debit	Credit	Debit Balance
Nov. 30		CR.5	35		35

Interest Revenue — No. 460

Date	Item	Jrnl. Ref.	Debit	Credit	Credit Balance
Nov.25		CR.5		762	762

Cost of Goods Sold — No. 511

Date	Item	Jrnl. Ref.	Debit	Credit	Debit Balance
Nov.30		S.3	1,814		1,814
30		CR.5	1,707		3,521

Note: The posting reference CR.5 should not be confused with the abbreviation for credit, CR. The posting reference for cash receipts always includes a page number.

* A customer name can appear in the Account Title column because we are recording a cash receipt to a subsidiary-ledger account as well as to the Accounts Receivable control account.
** The total is not posted but the ✓ indicates that each item in the column was posted individually.

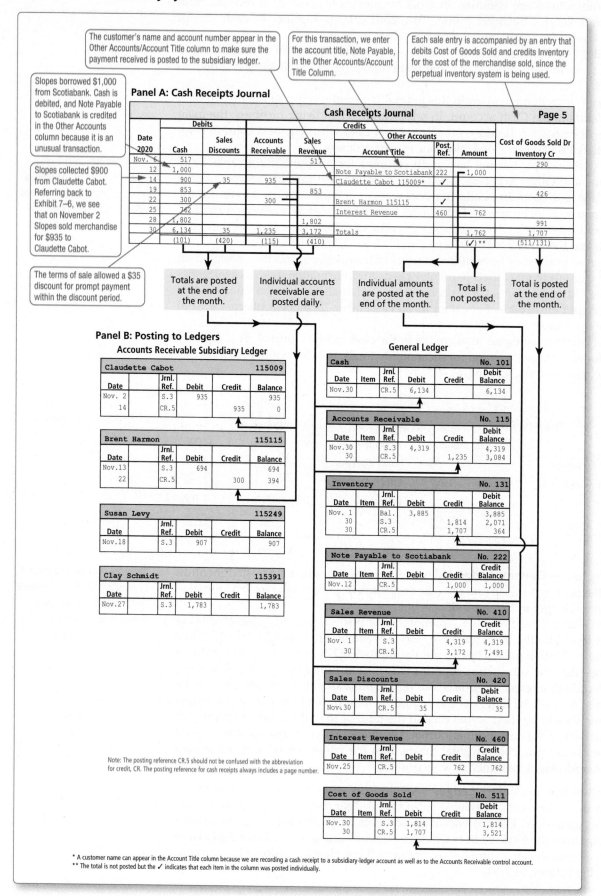

Balancing the Ledgers After posting, the sum of the individual balances that remain in the accounts receivable subsidiary ledger equals the general ledger balance in Accounts Receivable.

Accounts Receivable debit balance in the General Ledger:	
Accounts Receivable	$3,084

Data from the Accounts Receivable Subsidiary Ledger: Schedule of Accounts Receivable November 30, 2020		
115115	Brent Harmon	$ 394
115249	Susan Levy	907
115391	Clay Schmidt	1,783
Total accounts receivable		$3,084

Slopes' list of account balances from the subsidiary ledger helps it follow up on slow-paying customers if it determines how long each customer's accounts receivable balance has been unpaid. (This is covered in Chapter 9.) Good accounts receivable records help a business manage its cash.

Try It!

5. Refer to the Slopes Ski Shop information given in this chapter. Suppose you worked in the accounting department of the company. If Slopes did not use an accounts receivable subsidiary ledger and Claudette Cabot asked you for her account balance in the middle of the month, could you answer her?

6. Sidney Company experienced the following transactions during February 2020:

Feb.	2	Issued invoice no. 291 for a sale on account to Limpert Design Ltd., $400. Sidney's cost of this inventory was $240.
	3	Purchased inventory on credit terms of 1/10, n/30 from Dunning Co., $2,600. The invoice was dated February 3.
	4	Sold inventory for cash, $300 (cost, $204).
	5	Issued cheque no. 45 to Office Depot to purchase office furniture for cash, $1,400.
	8	Received payment on account, $200. The discount period had expired.
	10	Purchased inventory from Mega Corp. for cash, $1,300, issuing cheque no. 46.
	13	Received $400 cash from Limpert Design Ltd. in full settlement of its account receivable.
	13	Issued cheque no. 47 to pay Dunning Co. the net amount owed from February 3.
	14	Purchased supplies on account from Office Corp., $500. Payment is due in 30 days. The invoice was dated February 14.
	15	Sold inventory on account to Frankie's Diner, issuing invoice no. 292 for $800 (cost, $550).
	20	Purchased inventory on credit terms of net 30 from Super Sales Ltd., $1,600. The invoice was dated February 19.
	22	Issued cheque no. 48 to pay for insurance coverage, debiting Prepaid Insurance for $2,000.
	25	Issued cheque no. 49 to pay utilities, $450.
	28	Sold goods for $550 cash (cost, $325).

(Continued)

a. Which of these transactions would be recorded in the sales journal? Record those transactions in a sales journal using the format shown in Exhibit 7–6.
b. Which of these transactions would be recorded in the cash receipts journal? Record those transactions in a cash receipts journal using the format shown in Exhibit 7–8.

7. Identify the effect of each of the following transactions on the accounts receivable subsidiary ledger:

	Debit, Credit, or No Effect
a. Sale of merchandise on account	__________
b. Payment to supplier for goods	__________
c. Accrued rent owing at the end of the month	__________
d. Purchase of inventory on account	__________

Solutions appear at the end of this chapter and on **MyLab Accounting**

The Purchases Journal

LO 4

How are transactions involving suppliers of goods and services recorded in an efficient way?

A merchandising business like Slopes Ski Shop purchases inventory and supplies frequently. Such purchases are usually made on account. The **purchases journal** is designed to account for all purchases of inventory, supplies, and other assets *on account*. It can also be used to record expenses incurred *on account*. Cash purchases are normally paid by cheque and are recorded in the cash payments journal.

Exhibit 7–9 illustrates Slopes' purchases journal (Panel A) and posting to the ledgers (Panel B).[1] The purchases journal in Exhibit 7–9 has amount columns for:

The source document for entries in the purchases journal is the supplier's (creditor's) invoice or bill.

- Credits to Accounts Payable
- Debits to Inventory, Supplies, and Other Accounts

The Other Accounts columns record purchases of assets other than inventory and supplies. Each business designs its purchases journal to meet its own needs for information and efficiency. Accounts Payable is credited for all transactions recorded in the purchases journal.

Companies design journals to meet their special needs. A repair service might not use a Supplies column but might need a Small Tools column for frequent purchases of tools.

On November 2, Slopes purchased ski poles inventory costing $700 from JVG Canada Inc. The supplier's name (JVG Canada Inc.) and account number are entered in the Supplier Account Credited column. The purchase terms of 3/15, n/30 are also entered in the Terms column to help identify the due date and the discount available. Accounts Payable is credited and Inventory is debited for the transaction amount. On November 19, a purchase of supplies on account is entered as a debit to Supplies and a credit to Accounts Payable.

Note the November 9 purchase of equipment from City Office Supply Co. The purchases journal contains no column for Equipment, so the Other Accounts debit column is used. Because this was a credit purchase, the accountant enters the supplier name (City Office Supply Co.) and account number in the Supplier Account Credited column and writes "Equipment" in the Other Accounts/Account Title column.

The total credits in the purchases journal ($2,876) must equal the total debits ($1,706 + $103 + $1,067 = $2,876).

[1]This is the only special journal that we illustrate with the credit column placed to the left and the debit columns to the right. This arrangement of columns focuses on Accounts Payable, which is credited for each entry to this journal, and on the individual supplier to be paid.

EXHIBIT 7–9 | Purchases Journal and Posting to the Ledgers under the Perpetual Inventory System

A periodic inventory system would replace the Inventory column with a column entitled "Purchases."

The check mark below the column total indicated that the column total was *not* posted because individual items in the column were posted.

Panel A: Purchases Journal

Purchases Journal — Page 8

					Credits	Debits				
								Other Accounts		
Date 2020	Supplier Account Credited	Invoice Date	Terms	Post. Ref.	Accounts Payable	Inventory	Supplies	Account Title	Post. Ref.	Amount
Nov. 2	JVG Canada Inc. 210240	01/11/20	3/15, n/30	✓	700	700				
5	Gr. Rossignol Cda Inc. 210152	05/11/20	n/30	✓	319	319				
9	City Office Supply Co. 210079	09/11/20	2/10, n/30	✓	440			Equipment	191	440
12	Audio Electronics Inc. 210015	11/11/20	n/30	✓	236	236				
13	JVG Canada Inc. 210240	12/11/20	3/15, n/30	✓	451	451				
19	City Office Supply Co. 210079	19/11/20	2/10, n/30	✓	103		103			
23	O'Leary Furniture Corp. 210322	22/11/20	n/60	✓	627			Furniture	181	627
30	Totals				2,876	1,706	103			1,067
					(210)	(131)	(161)			(✓)

Individual accounts payable are posted daily.

Totals are posted at the end of the month.

Total is not posted.

Individual amounts are posted at the end of the month.

P. 8 indicates the source of the posted amounts—that is, Page 8 of the purchases journal.

Panel B: Posting to Ledgers

Accounts Payable Subsidiary Ledger

Audio Electronics Inc. — 210015

Date		Jrnl. Ref.	Debit	Credit	Balance
Nov. 12		P.8		236	236

City Office Supply Co. — 210079

Date		Jrnl. Ref.	Debit	Credit	Balance
Nov. 9		P.8		440	440
19		P.8		103	543

Groupe Rossignol Canada Inc. — 210152

Date		Jrnl. Ref.	Debit	Credit	Balance
Nov. 5		P.8		319	319

JVG Canada Inc. — 210240

Date		Jrnl. Ref.	Debit	Credit	Balance
Nov. 2		P.8		700	700
13		P.8		451	1,151

O'Leary Furniture Corp. — 210322

Date		Jrnl. Ref.	Debit	Credit	Balance
Nov. 23		P.8		627	627

General Ledger

Inventory — No. 131

Date	Item	Jrnl. Ref.	Debit	Credit	Debit Balance
Nov. 1		Bal.			3,885
30		S.3		1,814	2,071
30		CR.5		1,707	364
30		P.8	1,706		2,070

Supplies — No. 161

Date	Item	Jrnl. Ref.	Debit	Credit	Debit Balance
Nov. 30		P.8	103		103

Furniture — No. 181

Date	Item	Jrnl. Ref.	Debit	Credit	Debit Balance
Nov. 23		P.8	627		627

Equipment — No. 191

Date	Item	Jrnl. Ref.	Debit	Credit	Debit Balance
Nov. 9		P.8	440		440

Accounts Payable — No. 210

Date	Item	Jrnl. Ref.	Debit	Credit	Credit Balance
Nov. 30		P.8		2,876	2,876

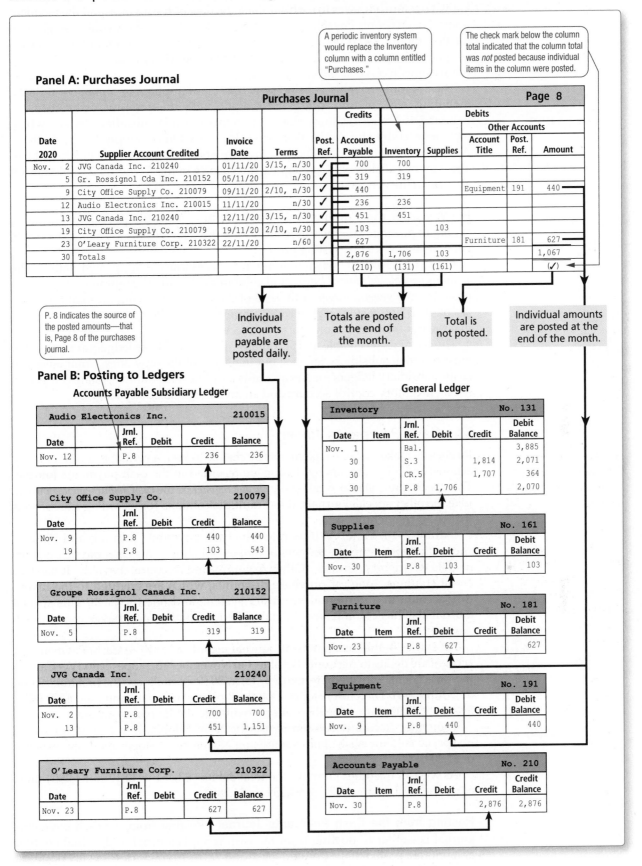

Accounts Payable Subsidiary Ledger To pay debts on time, a company must know how much it owes to each supplier, the date of the invoice, and the payment terms. The Accounts Payable account in the general ledger shows only a single total for the amount owed on account. It does not indicate the amount owed to each supplier. Companies keep an accounts payable subsidiary ledger that is similar to the accounts receivable subsidiary ledger.

The accounts payable subsidiary ledger lists suppliers in alphabetical order, including account numbers if used, along with the amounts owed to them. Exhibit 7–9, Panel B, shows Slopes' accounts payable subsidiary ledger, which includes accounts for Audio Electronics Inc., City Office Supply Co., and others. After the daily and period-end postings are done, the total of the individual balances in the subsidiary ledger equals the balance in the Accounts Payable control account in the general ledger.

Posting from the Purchases Journal Posting from the purchases journal is similar to posting from the sales journal and the cash receipts journal. Exhibit 7–9, Panel B, illustrates the posting process.

Individual accounts payable in the purchases journal are posted daily to the *accounts payable subsidiary ledger*, and column totals and other amounts are usually posted to the *general ledger* at the end of the month. The column total for Other Accounts is not posted; each account's number in the Post. Ref. column indicates that the transaction amount was posted individually.

The accounts receivable and accounts payable subsidiary ledgers are two of the most common subsidiary ledgers, but they are not the only ones. Companies can create subsidiary ledgers for any accounts they like. For example, many companies use an inventory control account and an inventory subsidiary ledger.

The Cash Payments Journal

Businesses make most cash payments by cheque to keep a verifiable record of transactions, and all payments by cheque are recorded in the **cash payments journal**. This special journal is also called the *cheque register* or the *cash disbursements journal*. Like the other special journals, it has multiple columns for recording transactions that occur frequently.

Exhibit 7–10, Panel A, illustrates the cash payments journal, and Panel B shows the posting to the ledgers of Slopes Ski Shop. This cash payments journal has two debit columns—Other Accounts and Accounts Payable. It has two credit columns—one for purchase discounts, which are credited to the Inventory account in a perpetual inventory system, and one for Cash. This special journal also has columns for the date, cheque number, and payee of each cash payment.

All entries in the cash payments journal include a credit to Cash. Payments on account are debits to Accounts Payable. On November 15, Slopes paid JVG Canada Inc. on account, with credit terms of 3/15, n/30 (for details, see the first transaction in Exhibit 7–9). Therefore, Slopes took the 3 percent discount and paid $679 ($700 less the $21 discount). The discount is credited to the Inventory account.

The Other Accounts column is used to record debits to accounts for which no special column exists. For example, on November 3 Slopes paid rent expense of $1,200.

As with all the other journals, the total debits ($3,461 + $819 = $4,280) must equal the total credits ($21 + $4,259 = $4,280).

Posting from the Cash Payments Journal Posting from the cash payments journal is similar to posting from the cash receipts journal. Individual creditor amounts are posted daily. Column totals and Other Accounts are usually posted at the end of the month. Exhibit 7–10, Panel B, illustrates the posting process.

EXHIBIT 7–10 | Cash Payments Journal and Posting to the Ledgers under the Perpetual Inventory System

If using a periodic inventory system the only difference in the cash payments journal would be a heading for Purchase Discounts instead of Inventory.

Panel A: Cash Payments Journal

Cash Payments Journal — Page 6

Date 2020	Ch. No.	Payee	Account Debited	Post. Ref.	Debits: Other Accounts	Debits: Accounts Payable	Credits: Inventory	Credits: Cash
Nov. 3	101	R. Landis Ltd.	Rent Expense	541	1,200			1,200
8	102	Grand and Toy	Supplies	161	61			61
15	103	JVG Canada Inc.	JVG Canada Inc. 210240	✓		700	21	679
20	104	Gr. Rossignol Cda Inc.	Gr. Rossignol Cda Inc. 210152	✓		119		119
26	105	Yu Supplies Ltd.	Inventory	131	2,200			2,200
30			Totals		3,461	819	21	4,259
					(✓)	(210)	(131)	(101)

Rent Expense, Supplies, and Inventory are posted individually, which required the posting reference to be noted as as you see here.

Total is not posted.

Totals are posted at the end of the month.

Individual accounts payable are posted daily.

Individual amounts are posted at the end of the month.

Panel B: Posting to Ledgers

Accounts Payable Subsidiary Ledger

Audio Electronics Inc. 210015

Date		Jrnl. Ref.	Debit	Credit	Balance
Nov.12		P.8		236	236

City Office Supply Co. 210079

Date		Jrnl. Ref.	Debit	Credit	Balance
Nov. 9		P.8		440	440
19		P.8		103	543

Groupe Rossignol Canada Inc. 210152

Date		Jrnl. Ref.	Debit	Credit	Balance
Nov. 5		P.8		319	319
20		CP.6	119		200

JVG Canada Inc. 210240

Date		Jrnl. Ref.	Debit	Credit	Balance
Nov. 2		P.8		700	700
13		P.8		451	1,151
15		CP.6	700		451

O'Leary Furniture Co. 210322

Date		Jrnl. Ref.	Debit	Credit	Balance
Nov.23		P.8		627	627

General Ledger

Cash No. 101

Date	Item	Jrnl. Ref.	Debit	Credit	Debit Balance
Nov.30		CR.5	6,134		6,134
30		CP.6		4,259	1,875

Inventory No. 131

Date	Item	Jrnl. Ref.	Debit	Credit	Debit Balance
Nov. 1		Bal.			3,885
30		S.3		1,814	2,071
30		CR.5		1,707	364
30		P.8	1,706		2,070
26		CP.6	2,200		4,270
30		CP.6		21	4,249

Supplies No. 161

Date	Item	Jrnl. Ref.	Debit	Credit	Debit Balance
Nov.30		P.8	103		103
8		CP.6	61		164

This reference indicates that this amount originated in the purchases journal (P) on Page 8.

Accounts Payable No. 210

Date	Item	Jrnl. Ref.	Debit	Credit	Credit Balance
Nov.30		P.8		2,876	2,876
30		CP.6	819		2,057

Likewise, this reference indicates that this amount originated in the cash payments journal (CP) on Page 6.

Rent Expense No. 541

Date	Item	Jrnl. Ref.	Debit	Credit	Debit Balance
Nov. 3		CP.6	1,200		1,200

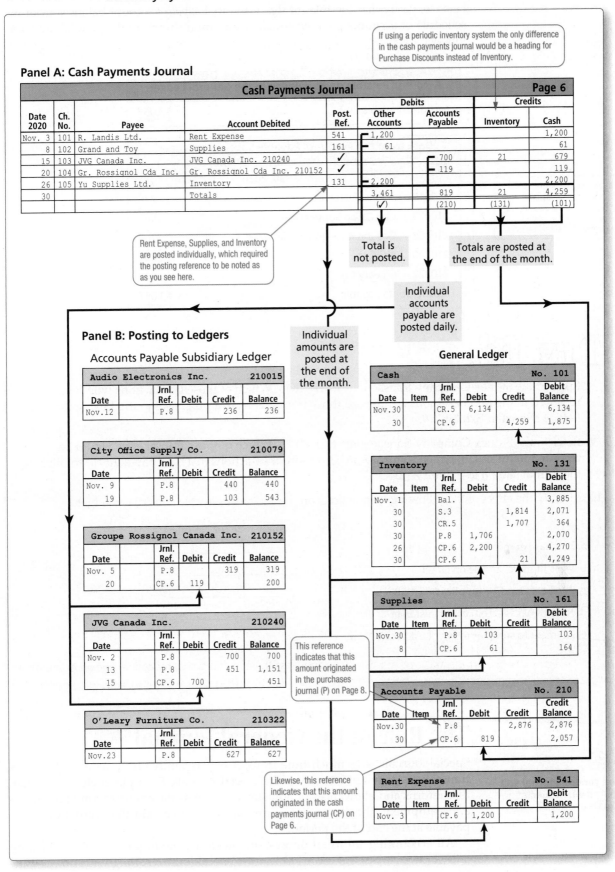

Balancing the Ledgers To review their accounts payable, companies list the individual supplier balances in the accounts payable subsidiary ledger. To prove the balance, verify that the total of the individual *supplier* account balances from the schedule of accounts payable equals the amount shown in the general ledger as follows:

Accounts Payable debit balance in the General Ledger:	
Accounts Payable	$2,057

Balance of the Accounts Payable control account = Sum of all the creditor balances in the accounts payable subsidiary ledger

Data from the Accounts Payable Subsidiary Ledger: Schedule of Accounts Payable November 30, 2020		
210015	Audio Electronics Inc.	$ 236
210079	City Office Supply Co.	543
210152	Groupe Rossignol Canada Inc.	200
210240	JVG Canada Inc.	451
210322	O'Leary Co.	627
Total accounts payable		$2,057

Try It!

8. Refer to the Sidney Company transactions in Try It #6. Which of those transactions would be recorded in the purchases journal? Record those transactions in a purchases journal using the format shown in Exhibit 7–9.

9. Refer to the Sidney Company transactions in Try It #6. Which of those transactions would be recorded in the cash payments journal? Record those transactions in a cash payments journal using the format shown in Exhibit 7–10.

10. Identify the effect of the following transactions on the accounts payable subsidiary ledger.

	Debit, Credit, or No Effect
a. Purchase of merchandise on credit	________
b. Sales of merchandise on credit	________
c. Purchase of office supplies on credit	________
d. Receipt of cash from credit customer	________
e. Payment to supplier to pay the account balance	________

Solutions appear at the end of this chapter and on **MyLab Accounting**

The Role of the General Journal

LO 5

Is the general journal still required when special journals are used?

Special journals save much time in recording repetitive transactions. But some transactions do not fit into any of the special journals. Examples include merchandise returns and allowances or adjustments such as the amortization of buildings and equipment, the expiration of prepaid insurance, and the accrual of salary payable at the end of the period.

All accounting information systems need a general journal. The adjusting and closing entries are recorded in the general journal, along with non-routine transactions.

Exhibit 7–11 summarizes a process you can follow to choose the special journal to use for a transaction.

Remember these four important points when recording transactions using special journals and subsidiary ledgers:

- Transactions are entered into one of the special journals (or modules in a computerized system) or the general journal, but *not both*.
- Entries involving accounts receivable or accounts payable and inventory that are recorded in a special journal or the general journal must be posted to both the subsidiary ledger account and the related general ledger control account.
- At the end of the month or more often, a schedule of subsidiary ledger accounts must be reconciled or proved to the related control account in the general ledger to ensure the sum of all the amounts in the subsidiary ledger equals the balance in the control account.
- The trial balance and financial statements are created using the general ledger account balances at the end of the month or period. Using special journals does not affect this process.

EXHIBIT 7–11 | A Method of Choosing the Special Journal to Use for a Transaction

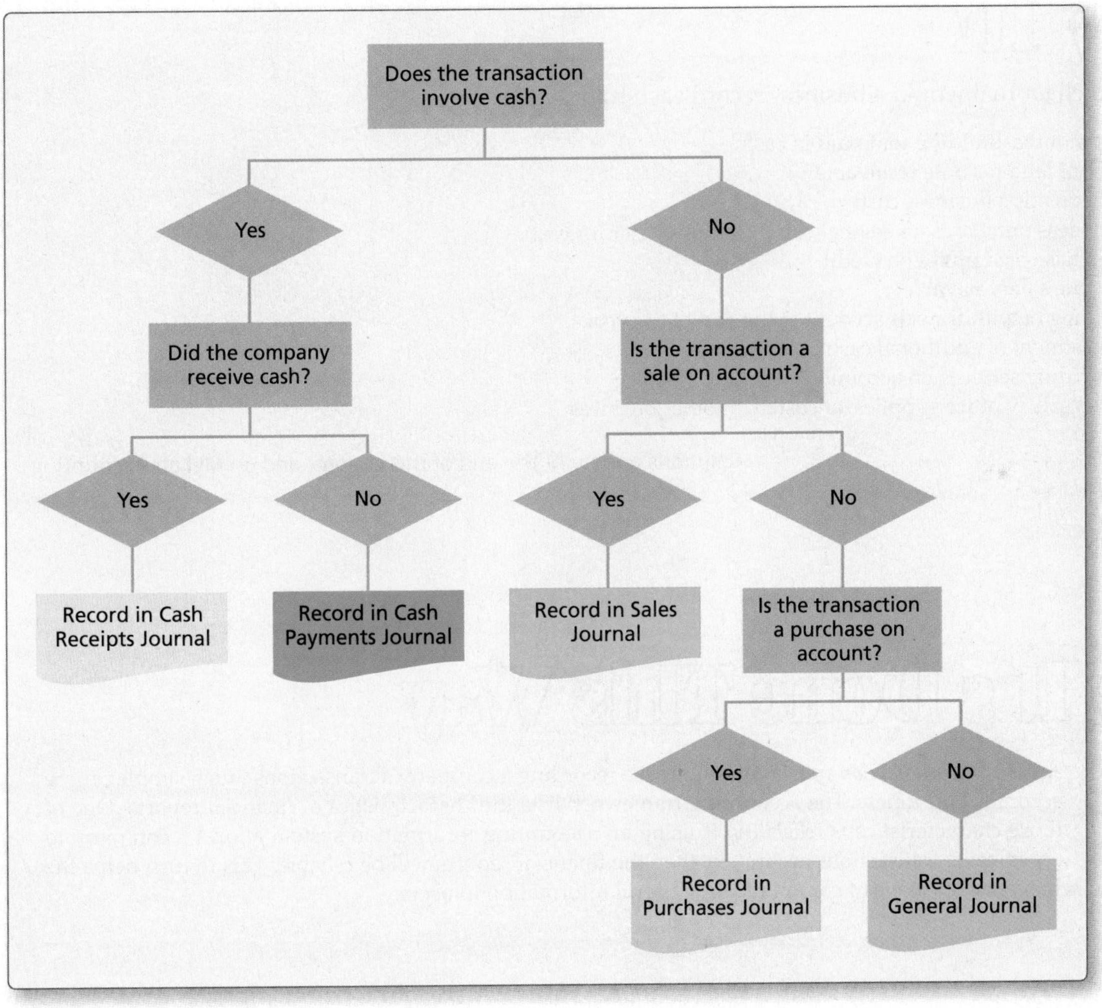

ETHICS Should I change the transaction?

Girmanesh Landin is responsible for recording all the transactions for Marshall's Home Care. This is Girmanesh's first job as a staff accountant, and she wants to do a good job. Last week, she recorded several cash payments for bills in the computerized accounting information system. She now realizes that she selected the incorrect cash account. She selected the savings account instead of the chequing account. Girmanesh knows that she could go back into each transaction and make the correction without anyone knowing that she made the mistake, but she is unsure of what to do. Should Girmanesh make the correction?

Solution

Because Girmanesh is new to the job, she should find out the procedure for making corrections in the accounting information system before she changes each transaction. Attempting to hide her mistakes could cause her integrity to be questioned because it would appear that she was trying to cover up things rather than ask for clarification and help. Most businesses will prefer that Girmanesh make a separate correcting entry instead of going back in and changing the incorrect transaction. This procedure allows for businesses to have a record of the original transaction and then the correcting entry. It is generally never a good idea to change transactions that have already been recorded, and many software systems will not allow such actions as a method to prevent fraud.

Try It!

11. In which journal would a business record each transaction?

a. Six months' building rent paid in cash
b. Sale of land for note receivable
c. Bank lends a business cash
d. Business purchases a personal computer for owner for cash
e. Purchase of supplies on credit
f. Accrue salary payable
g. Closing of withdrawals account at the end of the year
h. Investment of additional cash in the business
i. Providing services on account
j. Cash sale of office supplies, at cost, to another business

Solutions appear at the end of this chapter and on **MyLab Accounting**

Why It's Done This Way

Accounting information systems exist to make recording a company's transactions much simpler, more accurate, and timely. The accounting framework lists the characteristics of financial reports. One of those characteristics is *reliability*. If using an accounting information system allows a company to organize its transactions accurately, then the financial reports will be reliable. This in turn helps the company to achieve the objective of communicating useful information to users.

Summary Problem for Your Review

Taylor Company, a furniture supplier that uses the perpetual inventory system, completed the following selected transactions during March 2020:

Mar.	1	Sold $1,300 of lighting to Jen Zrilladich, terms n/30, invoice 310 (cost, $850).
	3	Purchased inventory on credit terms of 1/10, n/60 from Lane Corp., $4,000.
	4	Received $1,000 from a cash sale to a customer (cost $638).
	6	Received $120 on account from Jim Bryant. The full invoice amount was $130, but Bryant paid within the discount period to earn the $10 discount.
	9	Received $2,160 on a note receivable from Lesley Cliff. This amount includes the $2,000 note receivable plus $160 of interest revenue.
	10	Purchased lighting from an artisan, $300, issuing cheque no. 401.
	15	Sold $2,500 of outdoor seating to Pajo's Restaurant, terms n/30, invoice 311 (cost, $1,700).
	15	Received $1,600 from a cash sale to a customer (cost, $1,044).
	24	Borrowed $4,400 by signing a note payable to Scotiabank.
	27	Received $2,400 on account from Lance Au. Payment was received after the discount period lapsed.
	29	Paid Lane Corp. for the purchase made on May 3, cheque no. 402.

The general ledger showed the following balances at February 29, 2020: Cash, $2,234; Accounts Receivable, $5,580; Note Receivable—Lesley Cliff, $2,000; Inventory, $3,638; Jim Taylor, Capital, $13,452. The accounts receivable subsidiary ledger at February 29 contained debit balances as follows: Lance Au, $3,680; Melinda Fultz, $1,770; Jim Bryant, $130.

Required

1. Record the transactions in the cash receipts journal (Page 7), cash payments journal (Page 5), sales journal (Page 8), and purchases journal (Page 4). Taylor Company uses a perpetual inventory system.
2. Compute column totals at March 31, 2020, in all the special journals. Show that total debits equal total credits in each of the special journals.
3. Post to the general ledger, the accounts receivable subsidiary ledger, and the accounts payable subsidiary ledger. Use complete posting references, including the following account numbers: Cash, 11; Accounts Receivable, 12; Note Receivable—Lesley Cliff, 13; Inventory, 14; Accounts Payable, 20; Note Payable—Scotiabank, 22; Jim Taylor, Capital, 30; Sales Revenue, 41; Sales Discounts, 42; Interest Revenue, 46; and Cost of Goods Sold, 51. Insert Bal. in the Posting Reference column (Jrnl. Ref.) for each February 29 account balance.
4. Create a schedule of accounts receivable to balance the accounts receivable subsidiary ledger with Accounts Receivable in the general ledger. Create a schedule of accounts payable to balance the accounts payable subsidiary ledger with Accounts Payable in the general ledger.

SOLUTION

Requirements 1 and 2

Items recorded in the Other Accounts columns must be listed and posted individually.

These accounts are used because the company is using a perpetual system.

Cash Receipts Journal								Page 7
	Debits		Credits					
					Other Accounts			
Date 2020	Cash	Sales Discounts	Accounts Receivable	Sales Revenue	Account Title	Post. Ref.	Amount	Cost of Goods Sold Dr Inventory Cr
Mar. 4				1,000				638
6	120	10	130		Jim Bryant	✓		
9	2,160				Note Receivable—			
					Lesley Cliff	13	2,000	
					Interest Revenue	46	160	
15	1,600			1,600				1,044
24	4,400				Note Payable—			
					Scotiabank	22	4,400	
27	2,400		2,400		Lance Au	✓		
31	11,680	10	2,530	2,600	Total		6,560	1,682
	(11)	(42)	(12)	(41)			(✓)	(51/14)

Total Dr = 11,690

Total Cr = 11,690

Make sure all amounts in the Debits columns equal all amounts in the Credits columns.

Indicates posting to the subledger; account numbers are not used.

Indicates that posting has been completed for all items individually.

Selected transactions are explained more fully:

Mar. 4 and 15: For each of these sales transactions, the cost of goods sold and inventory reduction are also recorded.

Mar. 6: The debit columns include the $120 cash received (invoice amount less the discount) and the $10 discount. Accounts Receivable is credited for $130, and Jim Bryant is entered in the Other Accounts/Account Title column so that his accounts receivable subsidiary ledger account balance is reduced by $130.

Mar. 9: This is an example of a compound entry with infrequently used accounts. Therefore, the Note Receivable—Lesley Cliff and Interest Revenue accounts are listed in the Other Accounts columns.

Note that the Inventory column under the Credits heading is used to record the reduction in inventory when cash discounts are taken. This is different from the March 10 purchase of inventory for cash, which is recorded in the Other Accounts column and posted separately.

Cash Payments Journal — Page 5

				Debits		Credits	
Date 2020	Chq. No.	Accounts Debited	Post. Ref.	Other Accounts	Accounts Payable	Inventory	Cash
Mar. 10	401	Inventory	14	300			300
29	402	Lane Corp.	✓		4,000		4,000
31				300	4,000		4,300
				✓	(20)		(11)

Total Dr = $4,300 Total Cr = $4,300

Recall that Taylor Company uses the perpetual inventory system. As a result, record the cost of the goods sold and the inventory reduction for each sale transaction. Taylor's sales journal has a column at the far right for this purpose.

Sales Journal — Page 8

Date 2020	Invoice No.	Accounts Debited	Post. Ref.	Account Receivable Dr	Sales Revenue Cr	Cost of Goods Sold Dr Inventory Cr
Mar. 1	310	J. Zrilladich	✓	1,300	1,300	850
15	311	Pajo's Restaurant	✓	2,500	2,500	1,700
31				3,800	3,800	2,550
				(12)	(41)	(51/14)

Total Dr = $3,800 Total Cr = $3,800

For each transaction, make sure all amounts in the Debits columns equal all amounts in the Credits columns.

Purchases Journal — Page 4

					Credits	Debits			
							Other Accounts		
Date 2020	Account Credited	Invoice Date	Terms	Post. Ref.	Accounts Payable	Inventory	Account Title	Post. Ref.	Amount
Mar. 3	Lane Corp.	03/03/14	1/10, n/60	✓	4,000	4,000			
31					4,000	4,000			
					(20)	(14)			

Total Cr = $4,000 Total Dr = $4,000

Requirement 3

Accounts Receivable Subsidiary Ledger

Lance Au

Date	Item	Jrnl. Ref.	Debit	Credit	Balance
Feb. 29		Bal.			3,680
Mar. 27		CR.7		2,400	1,280

Jim Bryant

Date	Item	Jrnl. Ref.	Debit	Credit	Balance
Feb. 29		Bal.			130
Mar. 6		CR.7		130	0

Melinda Fultz

Date	Item	Jrnl. Ref.	Debit	Credit	Balance
Feb. 29		Bal.			1,770

Pajo's Restaurant

Date	Item	Jrnl. Ref.	Debit	Credit	Balance
Mar. 15		S.8	2,500		2,500

Jen Zrilladich

Date	Item	Jrnl. Ref.	Debit	Credit	Balance
Mar. 1		S.8	1,300		1,300

Accounts Payable Subsidiary Ledger

Lane Corp.

Date	Item	Jrnl. Ref.	Debit	Credit	Credit Balance
Mar. 3		P.4		4,000	4,000
Mar. 29		CP.5	4,000		0

The year (2020) has been omitted from all ledgers.

General Ledger

Cash **No. 11**

Date	Item	Jrnl. Ref.	Debit	Credit	Debit Balance
Feb. 29		Bal.			2,234
Mar. 31		CR.7	11,680		13,914
31		CP.5		4,300	9,614

Accounts Receivable **No. 12**

Date	Item	Jrnl. Ref.	Debit	Credit	Debit Balance
Feb. 29		Bal.			5,580
Mar. 31		CR.7		2,530	3,050
31		S.8	3,800		6,850

Note Receivable—Lesley Cliff **No. 13**

Date	Item	Jrnl. Ref.	Debit	Credit	Debit Balance
Feb. 29		Bal.			2,000
Mar. 9		CR.7		2,000	0

Inventory **No. 14**

Date	Item	Jrnl. Ref.	Debit	Credit	Debit Balance
Feb. 29		Bal.			3,638
Mar. 10		CP.5	300		3,938
31		CR.7		1,682	2,256
31		S.8		2,550	(294)
31		P.4	4,000		3,706

Accounts Payable **No. 20**

Date	Item	Jrnl. Ref.	Debit	Credit	Credit Balance
Mar. 31		P.4		4,000	4,000
31		CP.5	4,000		0

Note Payable — Scotiabank **No. 22**

Date	Item	Jrnl. Ref.	Debit	Credit	Credit Balance
Mar. 24		CR.7		4,400	4,400

Jim Taylor, Capital **No. 30**

Date	Item	Jrnl. Ref.	Debit	Credit	Credit Balance
Feb. 29		Bal.			13,452

Sales Revenue **No. 41**

Date	Item	Jrnl. Ref.	Debit	Credit	Credit Balance
Mar. 31		CR.7		2,600	2,600
31		S.8		3,800	6,400

Sales Discounts **No. 42**

Date	Item	Jrnl. Ref.	Debit	Credit	Debit Balance
Mar. 31		CR.7	10		10

Interest Revenue **No. 46**

Date	Item	Jrnl. Ref.	Debit	Credit	Credit Balance
Mar. 9		CR.7		160	160

Cost of Goods Sold **No. 51**

Date	Item	Jrnl. Ref.	Debit	Credit	Debit Balance
Mar. 31		CR.7	1,682		1,682
31		S.8	2,550		4,232

Requirement 4

From the general ledger:	
Accounts Receivable	$6,850

At month end, customer account balances from the accounts receivable subsidiary ledger are listed and compared to the general ledger control account.

From the accounts receivable subsidiary ledger: Schedule of Accounts Receivable March 31, 2020	
Lance Au	$1,280
Melinda Fultz	1,770
Pajo's Restaurant	2,500
Jen Zrilladich	1,300
Total accounts receivable	$6,850

Note: If Taylor Company had used the periodic inventory system, account No. 51, Cost of Goods Sold, would not exist, so there would be no Cost of Goods Sold column in the cash receipts journal. As well, there would be no $1,682 credit posting to Inventory originating from the cash receipts journal. The same is true for the Cost of Goods Sold and Inventory columns in the sales journal.

At March 31, 2020, the Accounts Payable balance in the general ledger is nil. All accounts in the accounts payable subsidiary ledger are nil, so both the control account and subsidiary ledger are in balance.

Summary

Learning Objectives

(1) Describe an effective accounting information system Pg. 372

What is an effective accounting system?

An effective accounting information system captures and summarizes transactions to provide timely, accurate information to users and decision makers. The five major features are as follows:

- Control over operations
- Compatibility with the particular features of the business
- Flexibility in response to changes in the business
- Reports that meet users' needs
- A favourable cost–benefit relationship, with benefits outweighing costs

(2) Explain the elements of computerized and manual accounting systems Pg. 375

How do accounting systems work?

- Computerized systems process inputs faster than manual systems do and can generate more types of reports.
- Account numbers play a bigger role in the operation of computerized systems than they do in manual systems because computers classify accounts by account numbers. Both computerized and manual accounting systems require transactions to be classified by type.
- The computerized accounting system can be designed so that data are entered and the computer does the rest: posting, trial balances, financial statements, and closing procedures.
- Computerized accounting systems are integrated so that the different modules of the system are updated automatically.

(3) Journalize and post transactions using the sales journal, the cash receipts journal, and the accounts receivable subsidiary ledger Pg. 378

How are transactions involving customers recorded in an efficient way?

- Many accounting systems use special journals to record transactions by category.
- Credit sales are recorded in a sales journal, and cash receipts in a cash receipts journal.
- Posting from these journals is to both the general ledger and to the accounts receivable subsidiary ledger, which lists each customer and the amount receivable from that customer.
- Accounts receivable subsidiary ledger customer account balances are totalled and compared or proved to the Accounts Receivable control account in the general ledger.

(4) Journalize and post transactions using the purchases journal, the cash payments journal, and the accounts payable subsidiary ledger Pg. 386

How are transactions involving suppliers of goods and services recorded in an efficient way?

- Credit purchases are recorded in a purchases journal, and cash payments in a cash payments journal.
- Posting from these journals is to both the general ledger and the accounts payable subsidiary ledger.
- Accounts payable subsidiary ledger supplier account balances are totalled and compared or proved to the Accounts Payable control account in the general ledger.

(5) Journalize and post entries not recorded in a special journal Pg. 390

Is the general journal still required when special journals are used?

- Transactions that do not fit into any of the special journals are recorded in the general journal. Examples include sales returns and allowances, year-end adjusting entries for amortization, accruals, deferrals, and prepaids, as well as the period-end closing entries.

Key Terms for the chapter are shown next and are in the **Glossary** at the back of the book. **Similar Terms** are shown after **Key Terms**.

KEY TERMS

Accounting information system (AIS) The combination of personnel, records, and procedures that a business uses to meet its need for financial data *(p. 372)*.

Batch processing Computerized accounting for similar transactions in a group or batch *(p. 377)*.

Cash payments journal A special journal used to record cash payments made by cheque *(p. 388)*.

Cash receipts journal A special journal used to record all types of cash receipts *(p. 383)*.

Cloud computing A subscription-based service where an external company provides software, processing capability, and data storage that the customer accesses using the Internet. Customers gain the software capabilities without investing in the hardware and software themselves *(p. 374)*.

Control account An account whose balance equals the sum of the balances in a group of related accounts in a subsidiary ledger *(p. 382)*.

Database A computerized storehouse of information that can be systematically assessed in a variety of report forms *(p. 374)*.

Enterprise resource planning (ERP) A computer system that integrates all company data into a single data warehouse *(p. 377)*.

General journal The journal used to record all transactions that do not fit into one of the special journals *(p. 378)*.

General ledger Ledger of accounts that are reported in the financial statements *(p. 379)*.

Hardware Electronic equipment that includes computers, disk drives, monitors, printers, and the network that connects them *(p. 374)*.

Menu A list of options for choosing computer functions *(p. 376)*.

Module Separate compatible units of an accounting package that are integrated to function together *(p. 376)*.

Network The system of electronic linkages that allow different computers to share the same information *(p. 374)*.

Online processing Computerized processing of related functions, such as the recording and posting of transactions, on a continuous basis *(p. 377)*.

Proving The process of ensuring the balance in the general ledger equals the sum of the individual balances in the subsidiary ledgers *(p. 382)*.

Purchases journal A special journal used to record all purchases of inventory, supplies, and other assets on account *(p. 386)*.

Real-time processing Computerized processing of related functions, such as the recording and posting of transactions, on a continuous basis. Also called *online processing (p. 377)*.

Sales journal A special journal used to record credit sales *(p. 379)*.

Schedule A report that breaks down details in an account balance *(p. 382)*.

Server The main computer in a network where the program and data are stored *(p. 374)*.

Software A set of programs or instructions that cause the computer to perform the desired work *(p. 374)*.

Special journal An accounting journal designed to record one specific type of transaction *(p. 378)*.

Subsidiary ledger The book of accounts that provides supporting details on individual balances, the total of which appears in a general ledger account *(p. 379)*.

SIMILAR TERMS

Accounts payable ledger, accounts payable subledger	Accounts payable subsidiary ledger
Accounts receivable ledger, accounts receivable subledger	Accounts receivable subsidiary ledger
AIS	Accounting information system
Balancing the ledgers	Proving the ledgers, reconciling the ledgers, reconciling receivables and payables
Cash payments journal	Cash disbursements journal, cheque register
CP	Cash payments journal
CR	Cash receipts journal
ERP	Enterprise resource planning
Online processing	Real-time processing
P	Purchases journal
Prove	Proving
S	Sales journal
Subledger	Subsidiary ledger

SELF-STUDY QUESTIONS

Test your understanding of the chapter by marking the correct answer for each of the following questions:

1. Which feature of an effective information system is most concerned with safeguarding assets? *(p. 372)*
   a. Control
   b. Flexibility
   c. Compatibility
   d. Reports that meet users' needs
   e. Favourable cost–benefit relationship
2. The account number 211031 most likely refers to *(p. 375)*
   a. Liabilities
   b. Current liabilities
   c. Accounts payable
   d. An individual supplier
3. Special journals help most by *(p. 378)*
   a. Limiting the number of transactions that have to be recorded
   b. Improving the efficiency of operating the accounting system
   c. Improving accuracy in posting to subsidiary ledgers
   d. Easing the preparation of the financial statements
4. Centex Sound Systems purchased inventory costing $8,000 from Sony on account. Where should Centex record this transaction, and what account is credited? *(p. 386)*
   a. Cash payments journal; credit Cash
   b. Sales journal; credit Sales Revenue
   c. Purchases journal; credit Accounts Payable
   d. General journal; credit Inventory
5. Every transaction recorded in the cash receipts journal includes a *(p. 383)*
   a. Credit to Cash
   b. Debit to Accounts Receivable
   c. Debit to Sales Discounts
   d. Debit to Cash
6. Entries in the purchases journal are posted to the *(p. 386)*
   a. General ledger only
   b. General ledger and the accounts payable subsidiary ledger
   c. General ledger and the accounts receivable subsidiary ledger
   d. Accounts receivable subsidiary ledger and the accounts payable subsidiary ledger
7. Every transaction recorded in the cash payments journal includes a *(p. 383)*
   a. Debit to Accounts Payable
   b. Debit to an Other Account
   c. Credit to Inventory
   d. Credit to Cash
8. The individual accounts in the accounts receivable subsidiary ledger identify *(p. 383)*
   a. Payees
   b. Debtors
   c. Amounts to be paid
   d. Suppliers
9. A company uses a sales journal, a purchases journal, a cash receipts journal, a cash payments journal, and a general journal. A sales return for credit would be recorded in the *(p. 389)*
   a. Sales journal
   b. General journal
   c. Sales return and allowances journal
   d. Cash payments journal
   e. Accounts payable subsidiary ledger
10. Which of the following transactions would be recorded in the general journal? *(p. 390)*
    a. Cash payment of rent
    b. Amortization of office furniture
    c. Sales of inventory on account
    d. Purchases of inventory on account

Answers to Self-Study Questions

1. a 2. d 3. b 4. c 5. d 6. b 7. d 8. b 9. b 10. b

Assignment Material

MyLab Accounting Make the grade with MyLab Accounting: The Starters, Exercises, and Problems can be found on MyLab. You can practise them as often as you want, and most feature step-by-step guided instructions to help you find the right answer.

QUESTIONS

1. What is an accounting information system (AIS)?
2. What are two common entry-level accounting software systems used by small businesses?
3. Describe the five criteria of an effective accounting system and give an example of each.
4. What accounting categories correspond to the account numbers 1, 2, 3, 4, and 5 in the chart of accounts in a typical computerized accounting system?
5. Why might the number 112 be assigned to Accounts Receivable and the number 1120708 to Carl Erickson, a customer?
6. Name four special journals used in accounting systems. For what type of transaction is each designed?
7. Describe the two advantages that special journals have over recording all transactions in the general journal.
8. What is a control account, and how is it related to a subsidiary ledger? Name two common control accounts.
9. Graff Company's sales journal has amount columns headed Accounts Receivable Dr and Sales Revenue Cr. In this journal, 86 transactions are recorded. How many posting references or (✓) appear in the journal? State what each posting reference represents.
10. Provide some examples of transactions that would be recorded in the Other Accounts CR column of the cash receipts journal.
11. At what two times is posting done from a special journal? What items are posted at each time?
12. What is the purpose of balancing, proving, or reconciling the ledgers?
13. Posting from the journals of Barnstormer Brewery is complete. But the total of the individual balances in the accounts payable subsidiary ledger does not equal the balance in the Accounts Payable control account in the general ledger. Does this mean that the trial balance is out of balance? Explain.

STARTERS

S7–1 Suppose you started a company that prints rubberized logos on T-shirts. The business is growing fast, and you need a better accounting information system. Consider the features of an effective system, as discussed on pages 372–374. Which do you regard as most important? Why? Which feature must you consider if your financial resources are limited?

(1) Features of an effective information system

S7–2 Match each component of a computerized accounting information system with an example. Components may be used more than once.

(1)(2) Defining components of an accounting information system

Example	Component
1. Server	A. Inputs
2. Bank cheques	B. Processing and storage
3. Reports	C. Outputs
4. Keyboard	
5. Software	
6. Financial statements	
7. Bar code scanner	

①②
Assigning account numbers

S7–3 Complete the crossword puzzle.

Across:

2. Electronic linkage that allows different computers to share the same information
3. Main computer in a networked system
7. Cost–______ relationship must be favourable

Down:

1. Managers need ______ over operations to authorize transactions and safeguard assets
3. Programs that drive a computer
4. Electronic computer equipment
5. A ______ ible information system accommodates changes as the organization evolves
6. The opposite of debits

②
Identifying the elements of computerized and manual accounting systems

S7–4 Identify each of the following items as an element of a computerized accounting system (c), a manual accounting system (m), or both (b).

1. The trial balance transferred to or entered on the worksheet
2. Automatic posting to the general ledger
3. The use of UPC codes for inventory
4. Printing financial statements
5. Closing the accounts by debiting Income Summary and crediting expenses
6. Starting the cycle with account balances in the general ledger

②
Identifying data processing stages of an accounting system

S7–5 Indicate whether the items described below are inputs (I), outputs (O), or neither input nor output (N) of a computerized or manual accounting system.

1. Bank statement	______	7. Balance sheet	______
2. Sales invoice	______	8 Debit memo from supplier	______
3. Cheque from customer	______	9. Post-closing trial balance	______
4. Cheque payable to supplier	______	10. Unadjusted trial balance	______
5. Bank deposit slip	______	11. Auditor's report	______
6. Inventory printout	______		

②
Accounting system vocabulary

S7–6 From the list below, identify the headings and the account names of LP Gas Co. Assign an account number to each account. Use the following numbers: 151, 191, 201, 281, 301, 311, 411, and 531.

Assets	LP, Capital
Current Assets	LP, Withdrawals
Inventory	Revenues
Accounts Payable	Salaries Expense

S7–7 Given the following unidentified journal, write an explanation for each transaction.

③ Identifying transactions in a special journal

	Debits		Credits				
Date	**Cash**	**Sales Dis.**	**Acc. Rec.**	**Sales Rev.**	**Other Acct.**	**Amount**	**COGS Dr Inv. Cr**
Aug. 8	3,000			3,000			1,250
10	2,500				Ruff, Capital	2,500	
15	340		340		Lucille Adams		
27	490	10	500		Marshall Field		

S7–8 Use the sales journal and the related ledger accounts in Exhibit 7–6, page 380, to answer these questions about Slopes Ski Shop.

③ Using the sales journal and the related ledgers

1. How much inventory did Slopes have on hand at the end of November? Where can you get this information?
2. What amount did Slopes post to the Sales Revenue account? When did Slopes post to the Sales Revenue account? Assume a manual accounting system.
3. After these transactions, how much does Susan Levy owe Slopes? Where did you obtain this information? Be specific.
4. If there were no discounts, how much would Slopes hope to collect from all its customers? Where is this amount stored in a single figure?

S7–9 1. A business that sells on account must have good accounts receivable records to ensure collection from customers. What is the name of the detailed record of amounts collectible from individual customers?

③ Using accounts receivable records and balancing the ledgers

2. Where does the total amount receivable from all the customers appear? Be specific.
3. A key control feature of Slopes Ski Shop's accounting system lies in the agreement between the detailed customer receivable records and the summary total in the general ledger. Use the data in Exhibit 7–6, page 380, to reconcile Slopes' accounts receivable records at November 30, 2020.

S7–10 The cash receipts journal of Slopes Ski Shop appears in Exhibit 7–8, page 384, along with the company's various ledger accounts. Use the data in Exhibit 7–8 to answer the following questions raised by Steve Austin, owner of the business.

③ Using cash receipts data

1. How much were total cash receipts during November?
2. How much cash did Slopes collect on account from customers? How much in total discounts did customers earn by paying quickly? How much did Slopes' accounts receivable decrease because of collections from customers during November?
3. How much were cash sales during November?
4. How much did Slopes borrow during November? Where else could you look to determine whether Slopes has paid off part of the loan?

S7–11 Use Slopes Ski Shop's purchases journal (Exhibit 7–9, page 387) to address these questions that Steve Austin, the owner of the business, is faced with.

④ Using the purchases journal

1. How much were Slopes' total purchases of inventory during November?
2. Suppose it is December 1 and Slopes wishes to pay the full amount that Slopes owes on account. Examine only the purchases journal. Then make a general journal entry to record payment of the correct amount on December 1. Include an explanation. What other entry would have to be made to keep the ledgers in balance?

S7–12 Refer to Slopes Ski Shop's purchases journal (Exhibit 7–9, page 387) and cash payments journal (Exhibit 7–10, page 389). Steve Austin, the owner, has raised the following questions about the business.

④ Using the purchases journal and the cash payments journal

1. Increase in accounts payable, $2,876

1. By how much did total credit purchases of inventory, supplies, equipment, and furniture increase Slopes' accounts payable during November?
2. How much of the accounts payable balance did Slopes pay off during November?
3. At November 30, after all purchases and all cash payments, how much does Slopes owe JVG Canada Inc.? How much in total does Slopes owe on account?

(3)(4) Using all the journals

2. Net sales revenue, $7,456

S7–13 Answer the following questions about the November transactions of Slopes Ski Shop. You will need to refer to Exhibits 7–6 through 7–10, which begin on page 378.

1. How much cash does Slopes have on hand at November 30?
2. Determine Slopes' gross sales revenue and net sales revenue for November.
3. How did Slopes purchase furniture—for cash or on account? Indicate the basis for your answer.
4. From whom did Slopes purchase supplies on account? How much in total does Slopes owe this company on November 30?

(3)(4) Using all the journals

S7–14 Indicate the special journal in which you would find the following column headings (the heading could appear in more than one special journal):

a. Interest Revenue Cr
b. Sales Discounts Dr
c. Accounts Receivable Cr
d. Supplies Dr
e. Cash Dr
f. Cost of Goods Sold Dr
g. Accounts Payable Dr
h. Accounts Payable Cr
i. Purchases Dr
j. Cash Cr

(3)(4)(5) Using the journals

S7–15 Use the following abbreviations to indicate the journal in which you would record transactions a through o:

G = General journal	P = Purchases journal
S = Sales journal	CP = Cash payments journal
CR = Cash receipts journal	

Transactions:

a. ________ Cash sale of inventory
b. ________ Payment of rent
c. ________ Amortization of computer equipment
d. ________ Purchases of inventory on account
e. ________ Collection of accounts receivable
f. ________ Expiration of prepaid insurance
g. ________ Sale on account
h. ________ Payment on account
i. ________ Cash purchase of inventory
j. ________ Collection of dividend revenue earned on an investment
k. ________ Prepayment of insurance
l. ________ Borrowing money on a long-term note payable
m. ________ Purchase of equipment on account
n. ________ Cost of goods sold along with a credit sale
o. ________ Return of merchandise

S7–16 Identify all the journals in which the following accounts would be debited or credited. Use P for purchases journal, S for sales journal, CP for cash payments journal, CR for cash receipts journal, and G for general journal. Some accounts may be used in more than one journal. Assume a perpetual inventory system.

(3)(4)(5) Identifying journals

1. Cost of goods sold ____________
2. Accounts payable ____________
3. Amortization expense ____________
4. Cash ____________
5. Accounts payable ____________
6. Sales revenue ____________
7. Sales returns and allowances ____________
8. Inventory ____________

EXERCISES

E7–1 The head office of East Coast Choppers wants to "go green" and reduce paper use and unnecessary reports. Which features of an effective accounting information system will allow for this initiative? Discuss.

(1) Features of an effective accounting information system

E7–2 It is important to set up a properly numbered chart of accounts, especially in a computerized accounting system. Use account numbers 101 through 106, 201, 221, 301, 321, 401, 501, and 521 to correspond to the following selected accounts from the general ledger of Kelowna Music Festival. List the accounts and their account numbers in proper order, starting with the most liquid current asset.

(2) Setting up a chart of accounts

M. Wyant, Capital	Amortization Expense—Music Equipment
Accounts Receivable	Cost of Goods Sold
Cash	Note Payable, Long-Term
Accounts Payable	M. Wyant, Withdrawals
Music Equipment	Inventory
Supplies	Sales Revenue
Accumulated Amortization—Music Equipment	

E7–3 Refer to Exhibit 7–4 on page 375. Which steps are automatic in a computerized accounting system as compared to a manual accounting system?

(2) Elements of computerized and manual accounting systems

E7–4 The sales and cash receipts journals of Manitoba Maple Products include the following entries:

(3) Using the sales and cash receipts journals (perpetual inventory system)

Total debits to Cash, $1,060

Sales Journal					
Date	Invoice No.	Account Debited	Post. Ref.	Accounts Receivable Dr Sales Revenue Cr	Cost of Goods Sold Dr Inventory Cr
May 7	671	I. Pax	✓	220	72
10	672	W. Singh	✓	120	58
10	673	F. Zehr	✓	120	50
12	674	J. Legg	✓	240	120
31		Total		700	300

Cash Receipts Journal								
	Debits		Credits					
					Other Accounts			
Date	Cash	Sales Discounts	Accounts Receivable	Sales Revenue	Account Title	Post. Ref.	Amount	Cost of Goods Sold Dr Inventory Cr
May 16					I. Pax	✓		
19					F. Zehr	✓		
24	600			600				380
30					W. Singh	✓		

Required Complete the cash receipts journal for those transactions indicated. There are no sales discounts. Also, total the journal and show that total debits equal total credits.

③ Using the sales and cash receipts journals (perpetual inventory system)

E7–5 The cash receipts journal of Crab Harvest follows:

Cash Receipts Journal							Page 7
	Debits		Credits				
					Other Accounts		
Date	Cash	Sales Discounts	Accounts Receivable	Sales Revenue	Account Title	Post. Ref.	Amount
Jan. 2	790	40	830		Mandarin Corp.	(a)	
9	490		490		Big Fish Inc.	(b)	
19	4,480				Note Receivable	(c)	4,000
					Interest Revenue	(d)	480
30	310	20	330		S. Breakwell	(e)	
31	4,230			4,230			
31	10,300	60	1,650	4,230	Totals		4,480
	(f)	(g)	(h)	(i)		(j)	

Crab Harvest's chart of accounts (general ledger) includes the following selected accounts, along with their account numbers:

Number	Account	Number	Account
110	Cash	510	Sales Revenue
120	Accounts Receivable	512	Sales Discounts
125	Note Receivable	515	Sales Returns
140	Land	520	Interest Revenue

Required

Indicate whether each posting reference (a) through (j) should be

- A check mark (✓) for a posting to a customer account in the accounts receivable subsidiary ledger
- An account number for a posting to an account in the general ledger. If so, give the account number
- A letter (X) for an amount not posted

E7–6 During February, Sanier Animation had the following transactions:

③ Recording transactions in the sales journal

2. Accounts Receivable Dr, Sales Revenue Cr column total, $1,465

Feb.	1	Sold merchandise inventory on account to Theatre Co., $1,025. Cost of goods, $780. Invoice no. 401.
	6	Sold merchandise inventory for cash, $860 (cost, $640).
	12	Collected interest revenue of $80.
	15	Received cash from Theatre Co. in full settlement of its account receivable. There was no discount.
	20	Sold merchandise inventory on account to Delgado Co., issuing invoice no. 402 for $440 (cost, $330).
	22	Sold merchandise inventory for cash, $560 (cost, $420).
	26	Sold office supplies to an employee for cash of $80.
	28	Received $431 from Delgado Co. in full settlement of its account receivable. Delgado earned a discount by paying early. Terms are 2/10, n/15.

Required

1. Prepare headings for the company's sales journal. Journalize the transactions that should be recorded in Page 9 of the sales journal. (Round the sales discount to a whole dollar.)

   Assume the company uses a perpetual inventory system.
2. Total each column of the sales journal.

E7–7 Refer to the information in E7–6.

③ Recording transactions in the cash receipts journal

2. Accounts Receivable Cr column total, $1,465

Required

1. Prepare headings for a cash receipts journal. Journalize the transactions that should be recorded in Page 4 of the cash receipts journal.
2. Total each column of the cash receipts journal.

E7–8 Using the information in the following unidentified journals, state how the numbers identified as a) through h) would be posted using the selections below:

③ Posting from the cash receipts journal and the sales journal

1. Posted to a general ledger account as a debit
2. Posted to a general ledger account as a credit
3. Posted to a subsidiary ledger account as a debit
4. Posted to a subsidiary ledger account as a credit
5. Posted to the general ledger as a debit and a credit
6. Not posted

Date	Account Debited	Acc. Rec. Dr Sales Rev. Cr	Cost of Goods Sold Dr Inventory Cr
Feb. 9	Jones Company	3,540	2,300
10	Sails and Boats	10,900	b) 5,550
26	Davis Enterprises	c) 7,000	g) 3,250
28	Totals	a) 21,440	11,100

Date	Debits Cash	Sales Dis.	Acc. Rec.	Sales Rev.	Credits Other Acct.	Amount	COGS Dr Inv. Cr
Sep. 8	3,000			3,000			1,750
10	2,500				Ross, Capital	2,500	
13	50				Int. Revenue	50	
15	582	18	600		Jane Gibson		
30	e) 6,132	d) 18	600	3,000	Totals	f) 2,550	h) 1,750

a. 21,440 ______
b. 5,550 ______
c. 7,000 ______
d. 18 ______
e. 6,132 ______
f. 2,550 ______
g. 3,250 ______
h. 1,750 ______

3 Identifying transactions from postings to the accounts receivable subsidiary ledger

E7–9 A customer account in the accounts receivable subsidiary ledger of Peterborough Coffee Company follows:

Canal Lumber Inc.				112590
Date	**Jrnl. Ref.**	**Dr**	**Cr**	**Debit Balance**
Dec. 1				1,600
9	S.5	4,720		6,320
18	J.8		760	5,560
30	CR.9		2,800	2,760

Required Describe the three posted transactions.

3 Posting from the purchases journal, balancing the ledgers

3. Total Accounts Payable, $2,990

E7–10 The purchases journal of Lightning Snowboards follows:

Purchases Journal										Page 7
								Other Accounts Dr		
Date	**Account Credited**	**Invoice Date**	**Terms**	**Post. Ref.**	**Accounts Payable Cr**	**Inventory Dr**	**Supplies Dr**	**Acct. Title**	**Post. Ref.**	**Amt. Dr**
Sep. 2	Brotherton Inc.	02/09	n/30		800	800				
5	Rolf Office Supply	05/09	n/30		340		340			
13	Brotherton Inc.	13/09	2/10, n/30		1,400	1,400				
26	Marks Equipment Company	25/09	n/30		450			Equipment		450
30	Totals				2,990	2,200	340			450

Required

1. Open three-column general ledger accounts for Inventory (account #131), Supplies (account #141), Equipment (account #171), and Accounts Payable (account #210). Post to these accounts from the purchases journal. Use dates and posting references in the ledger accounts.

2. Open accounts in the accounts payable subsidiary ledger for Brotherton Inc., Rolf Office Supply, and Marks Equipment Company. Post from the purchases journal. Use dates and journal references in the ledger accounts.
3. Balance the Accounts Payable control account in the general ledger with the total of the balances in the accounts payable subsidiary ledger.
4. Does Lightning Snowboards use a perpetual or a periodic inventory system?

E7–11 During February, Johnston Cranberries wrote the following cheques:

(4) Using the cash payments journal

3. Total credit to Cash, $37,790

Feb.	3	Used cheque number 87655 to pay $490 on account to Musk Co. net of a $10 discount for an earlier purchase of inventory.
	6	Purchased inventory for $3,800. Paid using cheque number 87656.
	11	Paid $300 for supplies on cheque number 87657.
	15	Purchased inventory on account from Monroe Corporation, $1,548.
	16	Paid $24,100 on account to LaGrange Ltd.; there was no discount. Used cheque number 87658.
	21	Purchased furniture for $2,800. Paid using cheque number 87659.
	26	Paid $3,900 on account to Graff Software Ltd. for an earlier $4,000 purchase of inventory. The purchase discount was $100. Issued cheque number 87660 for this payment.
	28	Made a semi-annual interest payment of $2,400 on a long-term note payable. Paid using cheque number 87661. The entire payment was for interest. (Assume none of the interest had been accrued previously.)

Required

1. Prepare a cash payments journal similar to the one illustrated in this chapter. Omit the payee column.
2. Record the transactions in the cash payments journal. Which transaction should not be recorded in the cash payments journal? In what journal does it belong?
3. Total the amount columns of the cash payments journal. Determine that the total debits equal the total credits.

E7–12 Morali Consulting makes most of its sales and purchases on account. It uses the five journals described in this chapter (sales, cash receipts, purchases, cash payments, and general journal). Identify the journal most likely used to record the postings for the transactions indicated by numbers in the following T-accounts.

(3) (4) Identifying transactions from postings to the T-accounts

Cash

	Debit	Credit	
1.	5,000	400	2.

Prepaid Supplies

Debit	Credit	
1,000	600	3.

Accounts Receivable

	Debit	Credit	
4.	10,000	5,000	5.

Accounts Payable

	Debit	Credit	
6.	400	2,000	7.
		200	12.

Inventory

	Debit	Credit
8.	2,000	

Service Revenue

Debit	Credit	
	10,000	9.

Supplies Expense

	Debit	Credit
10.	600	

Delivery Expense

	Debit	Credit
11.	200	

(3) (4)
Special journals perpetual inventory system

Total debit to Cash from cash receipts journal, $8,000

E7–13 Bright's Patio Shop sells garden and patio furniture. Record the following transactions in the appropriate special journals. Total each journal at May 31.

May	1	Sold $2,600 of patio furniture to Jen Williams, terms n/30, invoice 310 (cost, $1,700).
	2	Purchased inventory on credit terms of 1/10, n/60 from Sisco Corp., $8,000. Invoice date is May 2.
	5	Sold inventory for cash, $400 (cost, $220).
	10	Purchased $600 of patio lanterns from an artisan. Issued cheque no. 401.
	15	Sold $5,000 of outdoor seating to Pat's Restaurant, terms n/30, invoice 311 (cost, $3,400).
	22	Received payment from Jen Williams (May 1).
	26	Received payment from Pat's Restaurant (May 15).
	29	Paid Sisco Corp. for the purchase made on May 2, cheque no. 402.

(4) (5)
Recording purchase transactions in the general journal and purchases journal

Purchases journal: Total credit to Accounts Payable, $8,110

E7–14 During April, Xitang Company completed the following credit purchase transactions:

Apr.	5	Purchased supplies, $400, from Central Co.
	11	Purchased inventory, $1,200, from McDonald Ltd. Xitang Company uses a perpetual inventory system.
	14	Issued cheque to pay Central Co.
	19	Purchased equipment, $4,300, from Baker Corp.
	20	Issued cheque to pay Baker Corp.
	22	Purchased inventory, $2,210, from Khalil Inc.

Required Record these transactions first in the general journal—with explanations—and then in the purchases journal. Omit credit terms, posting references, and invoice dates. In the general journal use a separate Accounts Payable account name for each customer (i.e. Accounts Payable—Central Co.) Assuming you have the purchases journal form, which procedure for recording transactions is quicker? Why?

(3) (5)
Recording transactions in the cash receipts journal, sales journal, and general journal

E7–15 M and N Sporting Goods reported these selected transactions for the month of July:

Jul.	9	Issued invoice no. 159 for a sale on account to Evans Company, $4,600, terms 1/10, n/30. The cost of the merchandise was $2,700.
	10	Issued invoice no. 160 for a sale on account to Sails and Boats, $5,700, terms 2/15, n/45. The cost of the merchandise was $2,450.
	12	Sold $3,000 of merchandise to Bruce Services for cash. The cost of the merchandise was $1,250.
	16	Owner invested $3,400 into the business.
	18	Collected $580 from Lucille Adams on account.
	20	Issued a credit memo to Sails and Boats for $2,800 for merchandise returned. The cost of the returned merchandise was $1,200.

Required Record the above transactions in either the sales journal, the cash receipts journal, or the general journal, using Exhibits 7–6 and 7–8 as templates. M and N Sporting Goods uses a perpetual inventory system.

SERIAL EXERCISE

E7–16 *The Serial Exercise involves a company that will be revisited throughout relevant chapters in Volume 1 and Volume 2. You can complete the Serial Exercises using MyLab Accounting.*

③④⑤
Accounting for both merchandising and service transactions under the perpetual inventory system using special journals

Total Sales Revenue $3,750

This exercise continues recordkeeping for the Canyon Canoe Company. You do not have to have completed any previous questions to complete this exercise.

At the beginning of the new year, Canyon Canoe Company decided to carry and sell T-shirts with its logo printed on them. Canyon Canoe Company uses the perpetual inventory system to account for the inventory. During January 2021, Canyon Canoe Company completed the following merchandising transactions:

Jan.	1	Purchased 10 T-shirts at $4 each and paid cash.
	2	Sold 6 T-shirts for $10 each, total cost of $24. Received cash.
	3	Purchased 50 T-shirts on account at $5 each. Terms 2/10, n/30.
	7	Paid the supplier for the T-shirts purchased on January 3, less discount.
	8	Realized 4 T-shirts from the January 1 order were printed wrong and returned them for a cash refund.
	10	Sold 40 T-shirts on account for $10 each, total cost of $200. Terms 3/15, n/45.
	12	Received payment for the T-shirts sold on account on January 10, less discount.
	14	Purchased 100 T-shirts on account at $4 each. Terms 4/15, n/30.
	18	Canyon Company called the supplier from the January 14 purchase and told them that some of the T-shirts were the wrong colour. The supplier offered a $50 purchase allowance.
	20	Paid the supplier for the T-shirts purchased on January 14, less the allowance and discount.
	21	Sold 60 T-shirts on account for $10 each, total cost of $220. Terms 2/20, n/30.
	23	Received a payment on account for the T-shirts sold on January 21, less discount.
	25	Purchased 320 T-shirts on account at $5 each. Terms 2/10, n/30, FOB shipping point.
	27	Paid freight associated with the January 25 purchase, $48.
	29	Paid for the January 25 purchase, less discount.
	30	Sold 275 T-shirts on account for $10 each, total cost of $1,300. Terms 2/10, n/30.
	31	Received payment for the T-shirts sold on January 30

Required

1. Enter the transactions in a sales journal (Page 2, omit the invoice number column), a cash receipts journal (Page 5), a purchases journal (Page 7, omit the supplier name and invoice date column), a cash payments journal (Page 6, omit the cheque number and payee), and a general journal (Page 4), as appropriate.
2. Total each column of the special journals. Show that total debits equal total credits in each special journal.

PRACTICE SET

③④⑤ Using all journals

E7–17 *This problem continues the Crystal Clear Cleaning problem begun in Chapter 2 and continued through Chapter 9.*

Crystal Clear Cleaning has decided that, in addition to providing cleaning services, it will sell cleaning products. Crystal Clear uses the perpetual inventory system. During December 2019, Crystal Clear completed the following transactions:

Dec.	2	Purchased 1,000 units of inventory for $4,000 on account from Sparkle Company with terms 5/10, n/20.
	5	Purchased 1,200 units of inventory from Borax on account with terms 4/10, n/30. The total invoice was for $6,000, which included a $300 freight charge.
	7	Returned 300 units of inventory to Sparkle from the December 2 purchase (cost, $1,200).
	9	Paid Borax. Issued cheque no. 566.
	11	Sold 500 units of goods to Happy Maids for $5,500 on account with terms n/30. Crystal Clear's cost of the goods was $2,000.
	12	Paid Sparkle. Issued cheque no. 567.
	15	Received 100 units with a retail price of $1,100 back from customer Happy Maids. The goods cost Crystal Clear $400.
	21	Received payment from Happy Maids, settling the amount due in full.
	28	Sold 500 units of goods to Bridget, Inc. on account for $6,500 (cost, $2,022). Terms 1/15, n/30.
	29	Paid cash for utilities of $550.
	30	Paid cash for sales commission expense of $214.
	31	Received payment from Bridget, Inc., less discount.

Required

1. Record the preceding transactions in the appropriate journal (sales journal (omit the Invoice No. column), cash receipts journal, purchases journal, cash payments journal, or general journal.)
2. Total each column of the special journals. Show that total debits equal total credits in each special journal.

CHALLENGE EXERCISES

③④ Using the special journals

1. Gross margin $3,935

E7–18 1. Slopes Ski Shop's special journals in Exhibits 7–6 through 7–10 (p. 378) provide the manager with much of the data needed for preparing the financial statements. Slopes uses the *perpetual* inventory system, so the amount of cost of goods sold is simply the ending balance in that account. The manager needs to know the business's gross margin for November. Compute the gross margin.

2. Suppose Slopes used the *periodic* inventory system. In that case, the business must compute cost of goods sold by the following formula:

Cost of goods sold:	
Beginning inventory	$ 3,885
+ Net purchases	XXX
= Cost of goods available for sale	XXXX
− Less: Ending inventory	4,249
= Cost of goods sold	$ XXX

Perform this calculation of cost of goods sold for Slopes. Does this computation of cost of goods sold agree with your answer to Requirement 1?

BEYOND THE NUMBERS

BN7–1

③ ④ Designing a special journal

Queen Technology Associates creates and sells cutting-edge network software. Queen's quality control officer estimates that 20 percent of the company's sales and purchases of inventory are returned for additional debugging. Queen needs special journals for:

- Sales returns and allowances
- Purchase returns and allowances

Required

1. Design on paper or on a computer the two special journals. For each journal, include a column for the appropriate business document.
2. Enter one transaction in each journal, using the Slopes Ski Shop transaction data llustrated on pages 380. Show all posting references, including those for column totals. In the purchase returns and allowances journal, assume debit memo number 14.

ETHICAL ISSUE

EI7–1

On a recent trip to Brazil, Lou Delgado, sales manager of Cyber Systems, took his wife along for a vacation and included her airfare and meals on his expense report, which he submitted for reimbursement. Donna Alliksar, vice-president of sales and Delgado's boss, thought his total travel and entertainment expenses seemed excessive. However, Alliksar approved the reimbursement because she owed Delgado a favour. Alliksar, well aware that the company president routinely reviews all expenses recorded in the cash payments journal, had the accountant record the expenses of Delgado's wife in the general journal as follows:

	Sales Promotion Expense	9,000	
	Cash		9,000

Required

1. Does recording the transaction in the general journal rather than in the cash payments journal affect the amounts of cash and total expenses reported in the financial statements?
2. Why did Alliksar want this transaction recorded in the general journal?
3. What is the ethical issue in this situation? What role does accounting play in the ethical issue?

PROBLEMS (GROUP A)

① Safeguarding customer data

P7–1A Sally Green has recently been hired as the CEO for a startup Internet-based retail store, ShopCan.ca. Her main job duties include responsibility for the information technology and computer systems of the business. Sally was reviewing the security of customer data and realized that customer service representatives had access to all customer data, including credit card information and billing addresses.

Required

1. What should Sally do?
2. What data breach happened to Canadian Tire in 2017? What customer data was stolen or released?

(2) Computerized accounting system

P7–2A Winnie Lu is in the process of setting up the chart of accounts for a company that is converting its manual system to a computerized accounting system. Below is a proposed chart of accounts:

T. Pioneer, Capital	30001
Advertising Expense	51001
Building	17001
Accounts Payable	21001
Sales Revenue	41001
Miscellaneous Expenses	59001
Cash	11001
T. Pioneer, Withdrawals	21002
Land	18001
Notes Payable	25001
Accounts Receivable	12001
Salaries Expense	54001

Required

1. Can you see a problem with the numbering system that has been decided upon by Winnie? How would this affect the financial reports?
2. What could happen during the closing process?

(3) Correcting errors in the cash receipts journal (perpetual inventory system)

Corrected cash receipts journal: Total debit to Cash, $83,000

P7–3A The cash receipts journal shown below contains five entries. All five entries are for legitimate cash receipt transactions, but the journal contains some errors in recording the transactions. In fact, only one entry is correct, and each of the other four entries contains one error.

Cash Receipts Journal — **Page 22**

	Debits		Credits					
					Other Accounts			
Date	Cash	Sales Discounts	Accounts Receivable	Sales Revenue	Account Title	Post. Ref.	Amount	Cost of Goods Sold Dr Inventory Cr
Jan. 4		4,200		4,200				2,030
7	6,000	220			Debbie Hughes	✓	6,220	
13	57,400				Note Receivable	13	53,900	
					Interest Revenue	45	3,500	
20				4,620				2,100
30	15,400		10,780					
31	78,800	4,420	10,780	8,820	Totals		63,620	4,130
	(11)	(42)	(12)	(41)			(✓)	(51/13)

Total Dr = $83,220 Total Cr = $83,220

Required

1. Identify the correct entry in the cash receipts journal above.
2. Identify the error in each of the other four entries.
3. Using the following format, prepare a corrected cash receipts journal. All column totals are correct in the cash receipts journal that follows.

								Page 22
Cash Receipts Journal								
	Debits		Credits					
					Other Accounts			
Date	Cash	Sales Discounts	Accounts Receivable	Sales Revenue	Account Title	Post. Ref.	Amount	Cost of Goods Sold Dr Inventory Cr
Jan. 4								
7					Debbie Hughes	✓		
13					Note Receivable	13		
					Interest Revenue	45		
20								
30								
31	83,000	220	17,000	8,820	Totals		57,400	4,130
	(11)	(42)	(12)	(41)			(✓)	(51/13)

Total Dr = $83,220 Total Cr = $83,220

P7–4A The Nova Scotia Beekeepers Supply Company, which uses the perpetual inventory system and makes all credit sales on terms of 2/10, n/30, completed the following transactions during July. The business records all sales returns and all purchase returns in the general journal.

③④⑤ Using all the journals, the accounts receivable subsidiary ledger, and the accounts payable subsidiary ledger

Jul. 2 Issued invoice no. 913 for sale on account to White Harbour Restaurant, $12,300. The cost of this inventory was $5,400.

3 Purchased inventory on credit terms of 3/10, n/60 from The Country Store, $7,401. The invoice was dated July 3.

5 Sold inventory for cash, $3,231 (cost, $1,440).

5 Issued cheque no. 532 to purchase beekeeping equipment for cash, $6,555.

8 Collected interest revenue of $3,325.

9 Issued invoice no. 914 for sale on account to Bell Ltd., $16,650 (cost, $6,930).

10 Purchased inventory for cash, $3,429, issuing cheque no. 533.

12 Received cash from White Harbour Restaurant in full settlement of its account receivable from the sale on July 2.

13 Issued cheque no. 534 to pay The Country Store the net amount owed from July 3.

13 Purchased supplies on account from Manley Inc., $4,323. Terms were net end of month. The invoice was dated July 12.

15 Sold inventory on account to O. Brown, issuing invoice no. 915 for $1,995 (cost, $720).

17 Issued credit memo to O. Brown for $1,995 for merchandise sent in error and returned by Brown. Also accounted for receipt of the inventory.

18 Issued invoice no. 916 for credit sale to White Harbour Restaurant, $1,071 (cost, $381).

19 Received $16,317 from Bell Ltd. in full settlement of its account receivable from July 9.

20 Purchased inventory on credit terms of net 30 from Burgess Distributing Ltd., $6,141. The invoice was dated July 20.

22 Purchased furniture on credit terms of 3/10, n/60 from The Country Store, $1,935. The invoice was dated July 22.

22 Issued cheque no. 535 to pay for insurance coverage, debiting Prepaid Insurance for $3,000.

24 Sold supplies to an employee for cash of $162, which was the cost of the supplies.

25 Issued cheque no. 536 to pay utilities, $3,359

28	Purchased inventory on credit terms of 2/10, n/30 from Manley Inc., $4,025. The invoice was dated July 28.
29	Returned damaged inventory to Manley Inc., issuing a debit memo for $2,025.
29	Sold goods on account to Bell Ltd., issuing invoice no. 917 for $1,488 (cost, $660).
30	Issued cheque no. 537 to pay Manley Inc. $1,323.
31	Received cash in full on account from White Harbour Restaurant.
31	Issued cheque no. 538 to pay monthly salaries of $7,041.

Required Use the following abbreviations to indicate the journal in which you would record each of the July transactions. Key each transaction by date. Also indicate whether the transaction would be recorded in the accounts receivable subsidiary ledger or the accounts payable subsidiary ledger.

G = General journal
S = Sales journal
CR = Cash receipts journal
P = Purchases journal
CP = Cash payments journal

③ ⑤

Using the sales, cash receipts, and general journals (with the perpetual inventory system)

1. Cash receipts journal: Total debit to Cash, $142,872

P7–5A The general ledger of Yilin Groceries includes the following selected accounts, along with their account numbers:

Cash	11	Land	18
Accounts Receivable	12	Sales Revenue	41
Inventory	13	Sales Discounts	42
Notes Receivable	15	Sales Returns and Allowances	43
Supplies	16	Cost of Goods Sold	51

All credit sales are on the company's standard terms of 2/10, n/30. Transactions in July that affected sales and cash receipts were as follows:

Jul.	2	Sold inventory on credit to Fortin Inc., $2,800. Cannin's cost of these goods was $1,600.
	4	As a favour to a competitor, sold supplies at cost, $3,400, receiving cash.
	7	Cash sales of merchandise for the week totalled $7,560 (cost, $6,560).
	9	Sold merchandise on account to A. L. Price, $29,280 (cost, $20,440).
	10	Sold land that cost $50,000 for cash of $50,000.
	11	Sold goods on account to Sloan Forge Ltd., $20,416 (cost, $14,080).
	12	Received cash from Fortin Inc. in full settlement of its account receivable from July 2.
	14	Cash sales of merchandise for the week were $8,424 (cost, $6,120).
	15	Sold inventory on credit to the partnership of Wilkie & Blinn, $14,600 (cost, $9,040).
	18	Received inventory sold on July 9 to A. L. Price for $2,400. The goods shipped were the wrong size. These goods cost Cannin $1,760.
	20	Sold merchandise on account to Sloan Forge Ltd., $2,516 (cost, $1,800).
	21	Cash sales of merchandise for the week were $3,960 (cost, $2,760).
	22	Received $8,000 cash from A. L. Price in partial settlement of his account receivable.
	25	Received cash from Wilkie & Blinn for its account receivable from July 15.
	25	Sold goods on account to Olsen Inc., $6,080 (cost, $4,200).
	27	Collected $10,500 on a note receivable.
	28	Cash sales of merchandise for the week were $15,096 (cost, $9,840).
	29	Sold inventory on account to R. O. Bankston Inc., $968 (cost, $680).
	30	Received goods sold on July 25 to Olsen Inc. for $160. The wrong items were shipped. The cost of the goods was $100.
	31	Received $18,880 cash on account from A. L. Price.

Required

1. Use the appropriate journal to record the above transactions: a sales journal (omit the Invoice No. column), a cash receipts journal, or a general journal. Yilin Groceries records sales returns and allowances in the general journal.
2. Total each column of the sales journal and the cash receipts journal. Show that total debits equal total credits.
3. Show how postings would be made from the journals by writing the account numbers and check marks in the appropriate places in the journals.

P7–6A The general ledger of Katie's Supplies includes the following accounts:

(4) (5) Using the purchases, cash payments, and general journals

1. Cash payments journal: Total credit to Cash, $19,981

Cash	111	Furniture	187
Inventory	131	Accounts Payable	211
Prepaid Insurance	161	Rent Expense	564
Supplies	171	Utilities Expense	583

Transactions in August that affected purchases and cash payments were as follows:

Aug.	1	Purchased inventory on credit from Stiples Corp., $6,900. Terms were 2/10, n/30. The invoice was dated August 1.
	1	Paid monthly rent, debiting Rent Expense for $2,000.
	5	Purchased supplies on credit terms of 2/10, n/30 from Bella Supply Ltd., $450. The invoice date was August 5.
	8	Paid electricity bill, $600.
	9	Purchased furniture on account from Rite Office Supply, $9,100. Payment terms were net 30. The invoice date was August 8.
	10	Returned the furniture to Rite Office Supply. It was the wrong colour.
	11	Paid Stiples Corp. the amount owed on the purchase of August 1.
	12	Purchased inventory on account from Wynne Inc., $4,400. Terms were 3/10, n/30. The invoice was dated August 12.
	13	Purchased inventory for cash, $650.
	14	Paid a semi-annual insurance premium, debiting Prepaid Insurance, $1,200.
	15	Paid the account payable to Bella Supply Ltd. from August 5.
	18	Paid gas and water bills with cash, $100.
	21	Purchased inventory on credit terms of 1/10, n/45 from Cyber Software Ltd., $5,200. The invoice was dated August 21.
	21	Paid account payable to Wynne Inc. from August 12.
	22	Purchased supplies on account from Favron Sales, $2,740. Terms were net 30. The invoice was dated August 21.
	25	Returned $1,200 of the inventory purchased on August 21 to Cyber Software Ltd.
	31	Paid Cyber Software Ltd. the net amount owed from August 21.

Required

1. Katie's Supplies records purchase returns in the general journal. Use the appropriate journal to record the above transactions: a purchases journal, a cash payments journal (omit the Cheque No. column), or a general journal.
2. Total each column of the special journals. Show that total debits equal total credits in each journal.
3. Show how postings would be made from the journals by writing the account numbers and check marks in the appropriate places in the journals.

③ ④ ⑤
Using all the journals, posting, balancing the ledgers

6. Total Accounts Receivable, $2,976; total Accounts Payable, $26,152

P7–7A Callahan Distributors, which uses the perpetual inventory system and makes all credit sales on terms of 1/10, n/30, completed the following transactions during July:

Jul.	2	Issued invoice no. 913 for sale on account to Ishikawa Inc., $24,600. Callahan's cost of this inventory was $10,800. Credit sales terms are 1/10, n/30.
	3	Purchased inventory on credit terms of 3/10, n/60 from Nakkach Corp., $14,802. The invoice was dated July 3.
	5	Sold inventory for cash, $6,462 (cost, $2,880).
	5	Issued cheque no. 532 to purchase furniture for cash, $13,110.
	8	Collected interest revenue of $6,650.
	9	Issued invoice no. 914 for sale on account to Bell Ltd., $33,300 (cost, $13,860). Credit sales terms are 1/10, n/30.
	10	Purchased inventory for cash, $6,858, issuing cheque no. 533.
	12	Received cash from Ishikawa Inc. in full settlement of its account receivable from the sale on July 2.
	13	Issued cheque no. 534 to pay Nakkach Corp. the net amount owed from July 3. (Round to the nearest dollar.)
	13	Purchased supplies on account from Manley Inc., $8,646. Terms were net end of month. The invoice was dated July 13.
	15	Sold inventory on account to M. O. Brown, issuing invoice no. 915 for $3,990 (cost, $1,440). Credit sales terms are 1/10, n/30.
	17	Issued credit memo to M. O. Brown for $3,990 for merchandise sent in error and returned by Brown. Also accounted for receipt of the inventory.
	18	Issued invoice no. 916 for credit sale to Ishikawa Inc., $2,142 (cost, $762). Credit sales terms are 1/10, n/30.
	19	Received $32,967 from Bell Ltd. in full settlement of its account receivable from July 9.
	20	Purchased inventory on credit terms of net 30 from Burgess Distributing Ltd., $12,282. The invoice was dated July 20.
	22	Purchased furniture on credit terms of 3/10, n/60 from Nakkach Corp., $3,870. The invoice was dated July 22.
	22	Issued cheque no. 535 to pay for insurance coverage, debiting Prepaid Insurance for $6,000.
	24	Sold supplies to an employee for cash of $324, which was the cost of the supplies.
	25	Issued cheque no. 536 to pay utilities, $6,718.
	28	Purchased inventory on credit terms of 2/10, n/30 from Manley Inc., $8,050. The invoice date was July 28.
	29	Returned damaged inventory to Manley Inc., issuing a debit memo for $4,050.
	29	Sold goods on account to Bell Ltd., issuing invoice no. 917 for $2,976 (cost, $1,320). Credit sales terms are 1/10, n/30.
	30	Issued cheque no. 537 to pay Manley Inc. $2,646.
	31	Received cash in full on account from Ishikawa Inc.
	31	Issued cheque no. 538 to pay monthly salaries of $14,082.

Required

1. Open the following three-column general ledger accounts using the account numbers given:

Cash	111	Sales Revenue	411
Accounts Receivable	112	Sales Discounts	412
Supplies	116	Sales Returns and Allowances	413
Prepaid Insurance	117	Interest Revenue	419
Inventory	118	Cost of Goods Sold	511
Furniture	151	Salaries Expense	531
Accounts Payable	211	Utilities Expense	541

2. Open these accounts in the subsidiary ledgers: accounts receivable subsidiary ledger—Bell Ltd., M. O. Brown, and Ishikawa Inc.; accounts payable subsidiary ledger—Nakkach Corp., Manley Inc., and Burgess Distributing Ltd.
3. Enter the transactions in a sales journal (Page 7), a cash receipts journal (Page 5), a purchases journal (Page 10), a cash payments journal (Page 8), and a general journal (Page 6), as appropriate.
4. Post daily to the accounts receivable subsidiary ledger and to the accounts payable subsidiary ledger. Post the individual amounts to the general ledger on the date recorded in the journal; post column totals to the general ledger on July 31.
5. Total each column of the special journals. Show that total debits equal total credits in each journal.
6. Balance or reconcile the accounts receivable subsidiary ledger and Accounts Receivable in the general ledger. Do the same for the accounts payable subsidiary ledger and Accounts Payable in the general ledger.

PROBLEMS (GROUP B)

P7–1B Josh Gruen has recently been hired as the CEO for an online vitamin startup, VitaCan.ca. His main job duties include responsibility for the information technology and computer systems of the business. Josh was reviewing the security of customer data and realized that customer service representatives had access to all customer data and health records, including credit card information and billing addresses.

(1) Safeguarding customer data

Required

1. What should Josh do?
2. What happened to Bell Canada in 2017? What customer data was stolen or released?

P7–2B Hanna Na is in the process of setting up the chart of accounts for a company that is converting their manual system to a computerized accounting system. Below is a proposed chart of accounts:

(2) Computerized accounting system

T. Forgere, Capital	30001
Advertising Expense	51001
Building	17001
Accounts Payable	21001
Sales Revenue	41001
Miscellaneous Expenses	59001
Cash	11001
T. Forgere, Withdrawals	31002
Land	18001
Notes Payable	25001
Accounts Receivable	12001
Salaries Expense	54001
Net Income	60000

Required

1. Can you see a problem with the numbering system that Hanna has decided on?
2. How would this affect the financial reports?

③ Correcting errors in the cash receipts journal (perpetual inventory system)

P7-3B The cash receipts journal below contains five entries. All five entries are for legitimate cash receipt transactions, but the journal contains some errors in recording the transactions. In fact, only one entry is correct, and each of the other four entries contains one error.

Cash Receipts Journal								**Page 16**
	Debits		**Credits**					
					Other Accounts			
Date	**Cash**	**Sales Discounts**	**Accounts Receivable**	**Sales Revenue**	**Account Title**	**Post. Ref.**	**Amount**	**Cost of Goods Sold Dr Inventory Cr**
May. 3	7,110	340	7,450		Alcon Labs Ltd.	✓		
9			3,460	3,460	Carl Ryther	✓		
10	110,000			110,000	Land	19		
19	730							440
30	10,600			11,330				6,310
31	128,440	340	10,910	124,790	Totals			6,750
	(11)	(42)	(12)	(41)			✓	(51/13)

Total Dr = $128,780   Total Cr = $135,700

Required

1. Identify the correct entry in the cash receipts journal above.
2. Identify the error in each of the other four entries.
3. Using the following format, prepare a corrected cash receipts journal. All column totals are correct in the cash receipts journal that follows.

Cash Receipts Journal								**Page 16**
	Debits		**Credits**					
					Other Accounts			
Date	**Cash**	**Sales Discounts**	**Accounts Receivable**	**Sales Revenue**	**Account Title**	**Post. Ref.**	**Amount**	**Cost of Goods Sold Dr Inventory Cr**
May. 3					Alcon Labs Ltd.	✓		
9					Carl Ryther	✓		
10					Land	19		
19								
30								
31	131,900	340	10,910	11,330	Totals		110,000	6,750
	(11)	(42)	(12)	(41)			✓	(51/13)

Total Dr = $132,240   Total Cr = $132,240

P7–4B Butala Sales Company, which uses the perpetual inventory system and makes all credit sales with terms 1/10, n/30, had the following transactions during January. Butala records all sales returns and all purchase returns in the general journal.

(3)(4)(5) Using all the journals and the accounts receivable and accounts payable subsidiary ledgers

Jan.	2	Issued invoice no. 191 for sale on account to Wooten Design Ltd., $9,400. Butala's cost of this inventory was $5,560.
	3	Purchased inventory on credit terms of 1/10, n/60 from Delwood Co., $23,600. The invoice was dated January 3.
	4	Sold inventory for cash, $3,232 (cost, $2,040).
	5	Issued cheque no. 473 to purchase furniture for cash, $14,348.
	8	Collected interest revenue of $10,760.
	9	Issued invoice no. 192 for sale on account to Vachon Inc., $25,000 (cost, $13,200).
	10	Purchased inventory for cash, $3,104, issuing cheque no. 474.
	12	Received $9,212 cash from Wooten Design Ltd. in full settlement of its account receivable.
	13	Issued cheque no. 475 to pay Delwood Co. net amount owed from January 3.
	13	Purchased supplies on account from Lehigh Corp., $5,756. Terms were net end of month. The invoice date was January 13.
	15	Sold inventory on account to Franklin Ltd., issuing invoice no. 193 for $2,972 (cost, $1,640).
	17	Issued credit memo to Franklin Ltd. for $2,972 for merchandise sent in error and returned to Butala by Franklin. Also accounted for receipt of the inventory.
	18	Issued invoice no. 194 for credit sale to Wooten Design Ltd., $7,300 (cost, $3,880).
	19	Received $24,500 from Vachon Inc. in full settlement of its account receivable from January 9.
	20	Purchased inventory on credit terms of net 30 from Jasper Sales Ltd., $5,600. The invoice was dated January 19.
	22	Purchased furniture on credit terms of 1/10, n/60 from Delwood Co., $13,100. The invoice was dated January 22.
	22	Issued cheque no. 476 to pay for insurance coverage, debiting Prepaid Insurance for $5,380.
	24	Sold an old computer to an employee for cash of $1,344, which was the value of the computer.
	25	Issued cheque no. 477 to pay utilities, $4,552.
	28	Purchased inventory on credit terms of 1/10, n/30 from Lehigh Corp., $1,684. The invoice was dated January 28.
	29	Returned damaged inventory to Lehigh Corp., issuing a debit memo for $1,684.
	29	Sold goods on account to Vachon Inc., issuing invoice no. 195 for $5,268 (cost, $3,256).
	30	Issued cheque no. 478 to pay Lehigh Corp. on account from January 13.
	31	Received cash in full on account from Wooten Design Ltd. for credit sale of January 18. There was no discount.
	31	Issued cheque no. 479 to pay monthly salaries of $17,400.

Required Use the following abbreviations to indicate the journal in which you would record each of the January transactions. Key each transaction by date. Also indicate whether the transaction would be recorded in the accounts receivable subsidiary ledger or the accounts payable subsidiary ledger.

G = General journal
S = Sales journal
CR = Cash receipts journal
P = Purchases journal
CP = Cash payments journal

(3) (5)

Using the sales, cash receipts, and general journals (with the perpetual inventory system)

P7–5B The general ledger of Beauchamp Supply includes the following accounts:

Cash	111	Land	142
Accounts Receivable	112	Sales Revenue	411
Notes Receivable	115	Sales Discounts	412
Inventory	131	Sales Returns and Allowances	413
Equipment	141	Cost of Goods Sold	511

All credit sales are on the company's standard terms of 1/10, n/30. Transactions in November that affected sales and cash receipts were as follows:

Nov.	1	Sold inventory on credit to Ijri Ltd., $4,000. Beauchamp Supply's cost of these goods was $2,228.
	5	As a favour to another company, sold new equipment for its cost of $23,080, receiving cash in this amount.
	6	Cash sales of merchandise for the week totalled $8,400 (cost, $5,400).
	8	Sold merchandise on account to Izzo Ltd., $14,320 (cost, $11,854).
	9	Sold land that cost $64,000 for cash of $64,000.
	11	Sold goods on account to Dryer Builders Inc., $12,198 (cost, $7,706).
	11	Received cash from Ijri Ltd. in full settlement of its account receivable from November 1.
	13	Cash sales of merchandise for the week were $7,980 (cost, $5,144).
	15	Sold inventory on credit to Rapp and Howe, a partnership, $3,200 (cost, $2,068).
	18	Received inventory sold on November 8 to Izzo Ltd. for $480. The goods shipped were the wrong colour. These goods cost Beauchamp Supply $292.
	19	Sold merchandise on account to Dryer Builders, $14,400 (cost, $11,854).
	20	Cash sales of merchandise for the week were $9,320 (cost, $6,296).
	21	Received $6,400 cash from Izzo Ltd. in partial settlement of its account receivable. There was no discount.
	22	Received payment in full from Rapp and Howe for its account receivable from November 15.
	22	Sold goods on account to Diamond Inc., $8,088 (cost, $5,300).
	25	Collected $6,400 on a note receivable.
	27	Cash sales of merchandise for the week totalled $8,910 (cost, $5,808).
	27	Sold inventory on account to Littleton Corporation, $7,580 (cost, $5,868).
	28	Received goods sold on November 22 to Diamond Inc. for $2,720. The goods were shipped in error so were returned to inventory. The cost of these goods was $1,920.
	28	Received $7,440 cash on account from Izzo Ltd.

Required

1. Use the appropriate journal to record the above transactions: a sales journal (omit the Invoice No. column), a cash receipts journal, and a general journal. Beauchamp Supply records sales returns and allowances in the general journal.
2. Total each column of the sales journal and the cash receipts journal. Show that total debits equal total credits.
3. Show how postings would be made from the journals by writing the account numbers and check marks in the appropriate places in the journals.

P7–6B The general ledger of Argyle Supply Company includes the following accounts:

(4) (5) Using the purchases, cash payments, and general journals

Cash	111	Equipment	189
Inventory	131	Accounts Payable	211
Prepaid Insurance	161	Rent Expense	562
Supplies	171	Utilities Expense	565

Transactions in November that affected purchases and cash payments were as follows:

Nov.	1	Paid monthly rent, debiting Rent Expense for $17,000.
	3	Purchased inventory on credit from Sylvania Ltd., $4,000. Terms were 2/15, n/45. The invoice was dated November 3.
	4	Purchased supplies on credit terms of 2/10, n/30 from Harmon Sales Ltd., $1,600. The invoice was dated November 4.
	7	Paid utility bills, $1,812.
	10	Purchased equipment on account from Epee Corp., $12,200. Payment terms were 2/10, n/30. The invoice was dated November 10.
	11	Returned the equipment to Epee Corp. It was defective.
	12	Paid Sylvania Ltd. the amount owed on the purchase of November 3.
	12	Purchased inventory on account from Epee Corp., $42,000. Terms were 2/10, n/30. The invoice was dated November 12.
	14	Purchased inventory for cash, $3,200.
	15	Paid an insurance premium, debiting Prepaid Insurance, $4,832.
	16	Paid the account payable to Harmon Sales Ltd. from November 4.
	17	Paid electricity bill with cash, $1,400.
	20	Paid the November 12 account payable to Epee Corp., less the purchase discount.
	21	Purchased supplies on account from Master Supply Ltd., $15,080, terms net 30. The invoice was dated November 20.
	22	Purchased inventory on credit terms of 1/10, n/30 from Linz Brothers Inc., $6,800. The invoice was dated November 22.
	26	Returned $1,000 of inventory purchased on November 22 to Linz Brothers Inc.
	30	Paid Linz Brothers Inc. the net amount owed.

Required

1. Use the appropriate journal to record the above transactions: a purchases journal, a cash payments journal (do not use the Cheque No. column), or a general journal. Argyle Supply Company records purchase returns in the general journal.
2. Total each column of the special journals. Show that total debits equal total credits in each journal.
3. Show how postings would be made from the journals by writing the account numbers and check marks in the appropriate places in the journals.

(3)(4)(5)
Using all the journals, posting, balancing the ledgers (perpetual inventory system)

P7–7B Zwicky Sales Company, which uses the perpetual inventory system and makes all credit sales with terms 1/10, n/30, had these transactions during January:

Jan.	2	Issued invoice no. 191 for sale on account to Wooten Design Ltd., $9,400. Zwicky's cost of this inventory was $5,560. Credit sales terms are 1/10, n/30.
	3	Purchased inventory on credit terms of 3/10, n/60 from Delwood Co., $23,600. The invoice was dated January 3.
	4	Sold inventory for cash, $3,232 (cost, $2,040).
	5	Issued cheque no. 473 to purchase furniture for cash, $4,348.
	8	Collected interest revenue of $10,760.
	9	Issued invoice no. 192 for sale on account to Piver Inc., $25,000 (cost, $13,200). Credit sales terms are 1/10, n/30.
	10	Purchased inventory for cash, $3,104, issuing cheque no. 474.
	12	Received $9,306 cash from Wooten Design Ltd. in full settlement of its account receivable.
	13	Issued cheque no. 475 to pay Delwood Co. net amount owed from January 3.
	13	Purchased supplies on account from Lehigh Corp., $5,756. Terms were net end of month. The invoice was dated January 13.
	15	Sold inventory on account to Cradick Ltd., issuing invoice no. 193 for $2,972 (cost, $1,640). Credit sales terms are 1/10, n/30.
	17	Issued credit memo to Cradick Ltd. for $2,972 for merchandise sent in error and returned to Zwicky by Cradick. Also accounted for receipt of the inventory.
	18	Issued invoice no. 194 for credit sale to Wooten Design Ltd., $7,300 (cost, $3,880). Credit sales terms are 1/10, n/30.
	19	Received $24,750 from Piver Inc. in full settlement of its account receivable from January 9.
	20	Purchased inventory on credit terms of net 30 from Jasper Sales Ltd., $5,600. The invoice was dated January 19.
	22	Purchased furniture on credit terms of 3/10, n/60 from Delwood Co., $13,100. The invoice was dated January 22.
	22	Issued cheque no. 476 to pay for insurance coverage, debiting Prepaid Insurance for $5,380.
	24	Sold supplies to an employee for cash of $1,344, which was the value of the supplies.
	25	Issued cheque no. 477 to pay utilities, $4,552.
	28	Purchased inventory on credit terms of 2/10, n/30 from Lehigh Corp., $1,684. The invoice was dated January 28.
	29	Returned damaged inventory to Lehigh Corp., issuing a debit memo for $1,684.
	29	Sold goods on account to Piver Inc., issuing invoice no. 195 for $5,268 (cost, $3,256). Credit sales terms are 1/10, n/30.
	30	Issued cheque no. 478 to pay Lehigh Corp. on account from January 13.
	31	Received cash in full on account from Wooten Design Ltd. for credit sale of January 18. There was no discount.
	31	Issued cheque no. 479 to pay monthly salaries of $7,400.

Required

1. For Zwicky Sales Company, open the following three-column general ledger accounts using the account numbers given:

Cash	111	Sales Revenue	411
Accounts Receivable	112	Sales Discounts	412
Supplies	116	Sales Returns and Allowances	413
Prepaid Insurance	117	Interest Revenue	419
Inventory	118	Cost of Goods Sold	511
Furniture	151	Salaries Expense	531
Accounts Payable	211	Utilities Expense	541

2. Open these accounts in the subsidiary ledgers: accounts receivable subsidiary ledger—Piver Inc., Cradick Ltd., and Wooten Design Ltd.; accounts payable subsidiary ledger—Delwood Co., Lehigh Corp., and Jasper Sales Ltd.
3. Enter the transactions in a sales journal (Page 8), a cash receipts journal (Page 3), a purchases journal (Page 6), a cash payments journal (Page 9), and a general journal (Page 4), as appropriate.
4. Post daily to the accounts receivable subsidiary ledger and to the accounts payable subsidiary ledger. Post the individual amounts to the general ledger on the date recorded in the journal; post column totals to the general ledger on January 31.
5. Total each column of the special journals. Show that total debits equal total credits in each journal.
6. Balance or reconcile the accounts receivable subsidiary ledger and Accounts Receivable in the general ledger. Do the same for the accounts payable subsidiary ledger and Accounts Payable in the general ledger.

CHALLENGE PROBLEMS

P7–1C An accounting information system that provides timely, accurate information to management is an important asset of any organization. This is especially true as organizations become larger and move into different parts of the world. The integration of computers into many organizations' information systems has enhanced their usefulness to the organization.

① Advantage of an effective accounting information system

Required Assume your older sister is a pharmacist. She regards an information system as simply an accounting system that keeps track of her company's revenues and expenses. Explain to her how an effective accounting information system can make her a more effective pharmacist.

P7–2C Information technology is increasingly sophisticated, and everyone wants the latest technology. Your brother has asked you about installing this "wonderful" computer system in his car dealership and auto repair business. The salesperson has promised your brother that the system "will do everything he wants and then some." Your brother has come to you for advice about acquiring this new computerized accounting information system. At present he uses Sage 50 with only the general ledger module.

② Providing advice about a computerized accounting system

Required Provide the advice your brother wants, focusing on the costs of the new computerized accounting information system; your brother has been told all the positive aspects of purchasing the system.

Extending Your Knowledge

DECISION PROBLEMS

DP7–1

3

Reconstructing transactions from amounts posted to the accounts receivable subsidiary ledger

Cash receipts journal: Total debit to Cash, $31,632

A fire destroyed some accounting records of Critter Hollow Company. The owner, Jennifer Chu, asks for your help in reconstructing the records. *She needs to know the beginning and ending balances of Accounts Receivable and the credit sales and cash receipts on account from customers during March.* All Critter Hollow Company sales are on credit, with payment terms of 2/10, n/30. All cash receipts on account reached Critter Hollow Company within the 10-day discount period, except as noted. The only accounting record preserved from the fire is the accounts receivable subsidiary ledger, which follows:

Adam Chi

Date		Jrnl. Ref.	Debit	Credit	Balance
Mar. 1	Balance				0
8		S.6	15,000		15,000
16		S.6	3,000		18,000
18		CR.8		15,000	3,000
19		J.5		600	2,400
27		CR.8		2,400	0

Anna Fowler

Date		Jrnl. Ref.	Debit	Credit	Balance
Mar. 1	Balance				3,300
5		CR.8		3,300	0
11		S.6	1,200		1,200
21		CR.8		1,200	0
24		S.6	12,000		12,000

Norris Associates Ltd.

Date		Jrnl. Ref.	Debit	Credit	Balance
Mar. 1	Balance				9,000
15		S.6	9,000		18,000
29		CR.8		8,700*	9,300

*Cash receipt did not occur within the discount period.

Robertson Inc.

Date		Jrnl. Ref.	Debit	Credit	Balance
Mar. 1	Balance				1,500
3		CR.8		1,500	0
25		S.6	12,000		12,000
29		S.6	3,600		15,600

DP7–2

(3) (4) Understanding an accounting system

The external auditor must ensure that the amounts shown on the balance sheet for Accounts Receivable represent actual amounts that customers owe the company. Each customer account in the accounts receivable subsidiary ledger must represent an actual credit sale to the person or company indicated, and the customer's balance must not have been collected. This auditing concept is called *validity*, or *validating* the existence of the accounts receivable.

The auditor must also ensure that all amounts that the company owes are included in Accounts Payable and other liability accounts. For example, all credit purchases of inventory made by the company (and not yet paid) should be included in the balance of the Accounts Payable account. This auditing concept is called *completeness*.

Required Suggest how an auditor might test a customer's Account Receivable balance for validity. Indicate how the auditor might test the balance of the Accounts Payable account for completeness.

COMPREHENSIVE PROBLEMS FOR PART 1

Two Comprehensive Problems are available in MyLab, Chapter Resources

1. Completing A Merchandiser's Accounting Cycle.
2. Completing The Accounting Cycle for a Merchandising Entity.

Try It! Solutions for Chapter 7

1. C
2. The feature of an effective accounting information system most compromised in this example would be compatibility. The new system is not compatible with the old system, and the new system would have to have other valuable features or qualities to consider changing to it. To solve this dilemma, it might be possible to change the job-order numbers to "-1" instead of the alpha character, assuming the new system would accept this. For example, instead of job number 1645a, you could use job number 1645-1. Students might also make a case for "flexibility".
3.

Cash	11001
Accounts Receivable	12001
Building	17001
Land	18001
Accounts Payable	21001
Notes Payable	25001
T. Pioneer, Capital	30001
T. Pioneer, Withdrawals	31001
Sales Revenue	41001
Advertising Expense	51001
Salaries Expense	54001
Miscellaneous Expenses	59001

Note that the expenses are assumed to be listed in the chart of accounts in alphabetical order. They could also be listed in another order, with Salaries Expense having account number 51001 and Advertising Expense having account number 54001. However, Miscellaneous Expense is always listed last on an income statement and would typically have the final account number of the expenses, although this may not always be the case.

4. Possible ranges of account numbers in the chart of accounts are:

Notes Receivable	12002 to 17000, although likely in the middle part of the range since Supplies are more liquid and an Automobile is less liquid than Notes Receivable
Automobile	12002 to 17000, although likely in the end part of the range since Supplies and Notes Receivable are more liquid than an Automobile
Supplies	12002 to 17000, although likely in the earlier part of the range since Supplies are more liquid than Notes Receivable and an Automobile
Supplies Expense	54002 to 59000, since alphabetically this account would follow Salaries Expense
Unearned Revenue	21002 to 25000 or 25002 to 29999, depending on how soon Unearned Revenue would be earned compared to Note Payable being paid
Service Revenue	41002 to 49999

5. If Slopes Ski Shop did not use an accounts receivable subsidiary ledger and Claudette Cabot asked you for her account balance, it would be difficult to answer her. A subsidiary ledger is needed for ready access to the data for each customer. The inefficient alternative is to look through all transactions in the general journal for the ones involving Claudette Cabot—definitely an error-prone and time-consuming alternative.
6. a. The sales journal records sales on account. The transactions on February 2 and 15, 2020, were sales on account and are shown in the sales journal below.
   b. The cash receipts journal records cash received from all sources. The transactions on February 4, 8, 13, and 28, 2020, were cash receipts from all sources and are shown in the cash receipts journal below.

Sales Journal — **Page 2**

Date 2020	Invoice No.	Account Debited	Post. Ref.	Accounts Receivable Dr Sales Revenue Cr	Cost of Goods Sold Dr Inventory Cr
Feb. 2	291	Limpert Design Ltd.		400	240
15	292	Frankie's Diner		800	550
29				1,200	790

Cash Receipts Journal — **Page 5**

	Debits		Credits					
					Other Accounts			
Date 2020	Cash	Sales. Disc	Accounts Receivable	Sales Revenue	Account Title	Post. Ref.	Amount	Cost of Goods Sold Dr Inventory Cr
Feb. 4	300			300				204
8	200	0	200					
13	400	0	400		Limpert Design Ltd.			
28	550			550				325
29	1,450	0	600	850				529

7. a. Debit
   b. No Effect
   c. No Effect
   d. No Effect

8. The purchases journal records all purchases made on account. The transactions on February 3, 14, and 20, 2020, were purchases on account and are shown in the purchases journal below.

Purchases Journal									Page 9
					Credits	Debits			
							Other Accounts		
Date 2020	Supplier Account Credited	Invoice Date	Terms	Post Ref.	Accounts Payable	Inventory	Account Title	Post. Ref.	Amount
Feb. 3	Dunning Co.	03/02/20	1/10, n/30		2,600	2,600			
14	Office Corp.	14/02/20	n/30		500		Supplies		500
20	Super Sales Ltd.	19/02/20	n/30		1,600	1,600			
28					4,700	4,200			500

9. The cash payments journal records all cash payments paid by cheque. The transactions on February 5, 10, 13, 22, and 25, 2020, were cash payments paid by cheque and are shown in the cash payments journal below.

Cash Payments Journal							Page 6
				Debits		Credits	
Date 2020	Chq. No.	Payee/Accounts Debited	Post Ref.	Other Accounts	Accounts Payable	Inventory	Cash
Feb. 5	45	Office Depot/Office Furniture		1,400			1,400
10	46	Mega Corp./Inventory		1,300			1,300
13	47	Dunning Co.			2,600	26	2,574
22	48	Insurance/Prepaid Insurance		2,000			2,000
25	49	Utilities/Utilities Expense		450			450
28				5,150	2,600	26	7,724

10. a. Credit
    b. No Effect
    c. Credit
    d. No effect
    e. Debit

11. a. Cash payments journal
    b. General journal
    c. Cash receipts journal
    d. Cash payments journal
    e. Purchases journal
    f. General journal
    g. General journal
    h. Cash receipts journal
    i. Sales journal
    j. Cash receipts journal

8 Internal Control and Cash

CONNECTING CHAPTER 8

LEARNING OBJECTIVES

1 Define internal control

What is internal control?

2 List and describe the components of internal control and control procedures

What should we think about when designing an internal control system?

3 Prepare a bank reconciliation and the related journal entries

What do we do when the bank statement balance and the cash account balance are not the same?

4 Apply internal controls to cash receipts and cash payments

How do we implement internal controls for cash receipts and cash payments?

5 Apply internal controls to petty cash

How do we implement internal controls for petty cash?

6 Make ethical business judgments

Are there steps we can follow when making ethical business judgments?

The **Summary** for Chapter 8 appears on pages 457–458.

Key Terms with definitions for this chapter's material appears on pages 458–459.

CPA competencies

This text covers material outlined in **Section 1: Financial Reporting of the CPA Competency Map** and the Professional and Ethical Behavior section of the Enabling Competencies. The Learning Objectives for each chapter have been aligned with the CPA Competency Map to ensure the best coverage possible.

1.1.3 Evaluates reporting processes to support reliable financial reporting

EC 1.1.1 Identifies situations involving existing or potential ethical issues

Joseph Belanger/123RF

Rachel Adawe scoured through the stacks of printouts. She had been hired to work on an embezzlement (stealing cash or assets of an entity) investigation for a local school board. The superintendent had called her because he suspected one of the volunteers was stealing money from the school council's hot dog funds. He had heard of the case in Ottawa where a volunteer parent council treasurer took almost $15,000 and then went on to volunteer at a different school.[1] He wanted to make sure that this wasn't happening in his district.

Rachel enjoyed searching through the financial statements, identifying a problem, and then finding the transactions that documented the embezzlement. She always treated these cases as a puzzle that needed to be solved.

Where will Rachel start looking when she begins searching for the stolen money? She'll start at the source, by reviewing documents such as invoices, sales receipts, and bank deposit slips. She will then review the transactions that were recorded (or not recorded) from those documents. These two pieces will help Rachel determine whether money was stolen and how it happened. It's important to Rachel that she not only catch the thief but also help prevent losses in the future. She will use her knowledge and experience in accounting to help her.

Sometimes businesses or charities are unfortunate enough to have employees steal from them, and they need help in providing enough evidence to the police. They often turn to an accountant, such as Rachel, who specializes in fraud, often called a certified fraud examiner (CFE). In addition, businesses hire accountants to help protect their assets by identifying potential problems in their record keeping and control of cash and assets.

The use of strong internal controls and procedures likely would have prevented this theft. This chapter discusses the importance of internal controls, especially over cash, and how companies can create good internal control policies.

[1]"How $15,000 Vanished from an Ottawa School Council's Bank Account—and Stayed Secret," *National Post*, February 10, 2017.

This chapter discusses **internal control**—the organizational plan that companies use to protect their assets and records. Internal controls are important to *all* managers, not just the accounting manager, because assets in every department throughout the company need to be protected.

The chapter applies internal control techniques mainly to cash, because cash is an attractive asset for unethical employees (and in the case we saw in the vignette, volunteers) to steal. The chapter also provides a framework for making ethical judgments in business.

Internal Control

LO 1
What is internal control?

One of a business manager's key responsibilities is to control operations. Owners and managers set goals, hire people to lead the way, and expect employees to carry out the plan.

Internal control consists of the processes put in place by management to provide reasonable assurance that the organization will achieve its key internal control objectives of:

- **Encouraging operational efficiency.** A company must optimize the use of resources, minimize expenses, and ensure management's business policies are implemented and followed while operating in agreement with regulations and reporting requirements.
- **Preventing and detecting error and fraud.** Companies must prevent and detect error and fraud, which lead to a waste of company resources.
- **Safeguarding assets and records.** A company must protect its assets so that company resources are not wasted needlessly. Safeguarding records ensures they are accurate and complete when needed for decision making.
- **Providing accurate, reliable information.** A company must provide accurate, reliable information, including accounting records. This is essential for decision making.

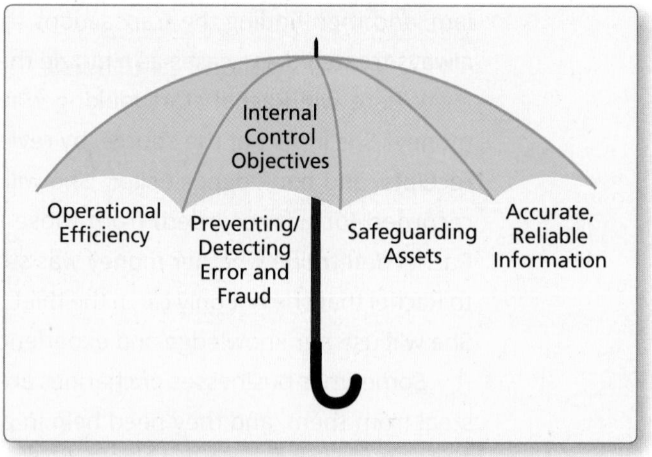

Without reliable records, a manager cannot tell what investments to make or how much to charge for products, and banks cannot determine whether to make a loan.

How critical are internal controls? They are so important that US and Canadian legislators have passed laws that require public companies (those that sell their shares of stock to the public) to maintain a system of internal controls.

The Sarbanes-Oxley Act and Its Canadian Implications

The Enron Corporation and WorldCom accounting scandals in 2001–2002 continue to affect business today. WorldCom reported expenses as assets and overstated both profits and assets. Enron overstated profits and went out of business almost overnight. Its former chief executive officer, Edmonton-born Bernie Ebbers, was convicted of securities fraud and sentenced to 25 years in prison. The same accounting firm, Arthur Andersen LLP, had audited both companies' financial statements. Arthur Andersen voluntarily closed its doors in 2002 after nearly 90 years in public accounting.

As the scandals unfolded, many people asked, "How could this happen? Where were the auditors?" To address investor confidence, the US Congress passed the **Sarbanes-Oxley Act**, abbreviated as **SOX**. This act requires companies to review internal control and take responsibility for the accuracy and completeness of their financial reports. The Dodd-Frank Act amended SOX, granting authority to the Public Company Accounting Oversight Board to inspect foreign auditing firms that practise in the United States. In addition, the act requires that foreign firms comply with SOX when they are employed by US public companies that list on a US stock exchange. In 2002–2003, Canadian securities regulators enacted similar legislation (included in Bill 198), which is also known as "Canadian-SOX" or *C-SOX*.

Why Does Fraud Happen?

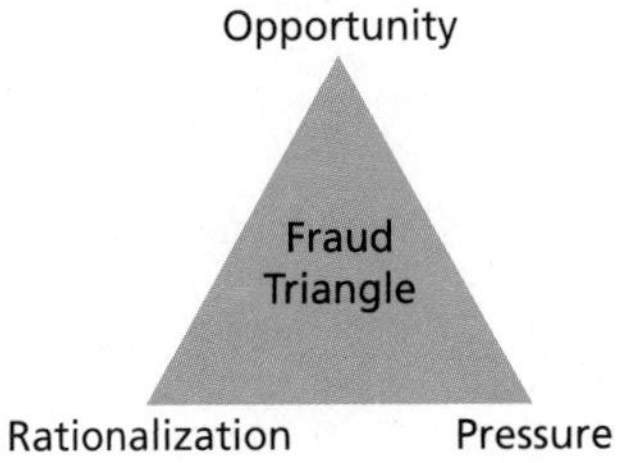

When businesses set up internal controls, it is important not to start with the mindset that people are inherently bad and out to steal from their employers. There are a number of theories about why fraud happens.

The fraud triangle is a common framework for thinking about this issue.

- **Opportunity** Some people may perceive that there is an opportunity to steal when a business has weak or ineffective internal controls. In other words, the business makes it easy for something to go missing or unaccounted for. This is the easiest part of the triangle to control.
- **Pressure** Some employees may be faced with situations in which they are pressured to commit fraud. The pressure might be external (e.g., excessive personal debt) or related to work (e.g., they didn't get a pay raise and feel they deserve extra compensation).
- **Rationalization** It is human nature to find good reasons for doing something wrong. For example, in a large corporation, a person might justify theft by saying that no one is really hurt by it.

Managers need to be aware of these risks and set up internal controls to anticipate and prevent at least the *opportunity* side of the triangle.

The Components of Internal Control

LO 2
What should we think about when designing an internal control system?

The **Committee of Sponsoring Organizations (COSO)** provides leadership related to internal control, risk management, and fraud deterrence. Their framework helps companies achieve internal controls. Their five components can be remembered by using the acronym CRIME:

- Control procedures
- Risk assessment
- Information system
- Monitoring of controls
- Environment

} CRIME

Control Procedures Control procedures are designed to ensure that the business's goals are achieved. The next section discusses procedures such as assigning responsibilities, separating duties, and using security devices to protect assets in detail.

Risk Assessment A company must identify its risks. For example, food manufacturers face the risk that their food products may harm people; music companies face copyright infringement risks; and all companies face the risk of bankruptcy.

Companies facing difficulties might be tempted to falsify their financial statements to make themselves look better than they really are. As part of the internal control system, the company's business risk, as well as the risk concerning individual accounts, must be assessed. The higher the risk, the more controls a company must put in place to safeguard its assets and accounting records.

Information System Controls must be in place within the information system to ensure that only authorized users have access to various parts of the accounting information system. In addition, controls must be put in place to ensure adequate approvals for recorded transactions are required. The decision makers need accurate information to keep track of assets and measure profits and losses.

Monitoring of Controls In large companies, internal auditors monitor company controls to safeguard assets, whereas in small businesses the owner or manager ensures controls are operating as they should.

Environment Organizations need to operate honestly and efficiently. They often use codes of ethics or rules of professional conduct to provide this guidance/structure to employees about ethics and integrity. It starts with the owner and top managers. This is the "tone at the top" of the business. Managers must have goal-oriented rules and processes, and they must behave in a way that sets a good example for company employees. For example, managers who cheat on expense claims and brag about it will likely have employees who do the same.

Internal control is a management priority, not merely a part of the accounting system. Therefore, it is a responsibility not only of accountants but also of managers in all functional areas throughout the organization.

In annual reports, top managers take responsibility for the financial statements and the related system of internal control. A typical report states, "Management is responsible for establishing and maintaining adequate internal control over financial reporting to provide reasonable assurance regarding the reliability of financial reporting and the preparation of financial statements for external purposes in accordance with GAAP."

Exhibit 8–1 diagrams the components of internal control, using car ownership as an example.

EXHIBIT 8–1 | The Components of Internal Control (Applied to Car Ownership)

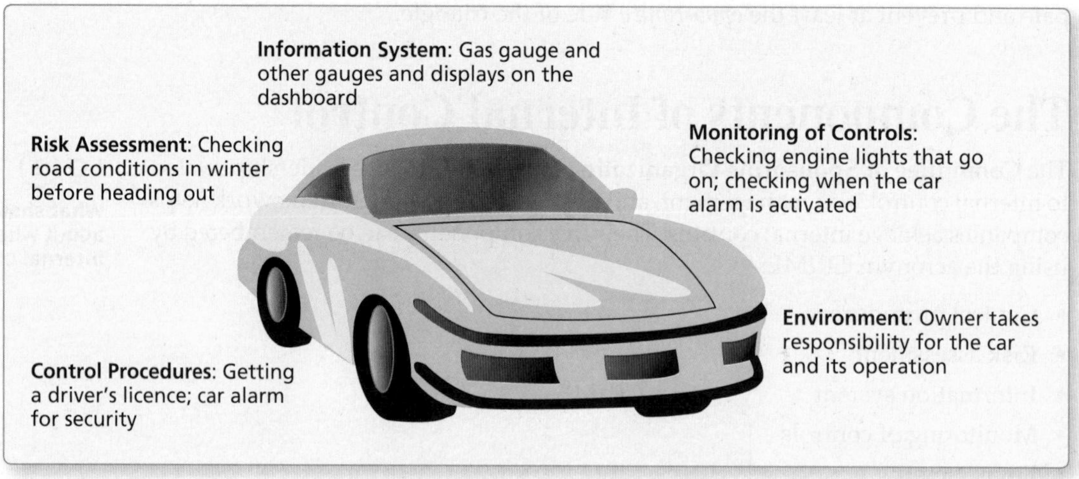

Let's examine in detail how businesses create an effective system of internal control.

Internal Control Procedures

Whether we are talking about a large multinational company, a local department store, or a school board, they all need to implement internal control procedures such as those discussed below.

Competent, Reliable, and Ethical Personnel Companies must hire qualified, well-educated, and skilled employees and pay them fairly. Companies must also train employees to do their job and must supervise their work. This will help build a competent staff. Internal controls are most effective when employees at all levels and in all areas adopt the organization's goals and ethical standards.

Assignment of Responsibilities In a business with good internal controls, each employee has carefully defined responsibilities and access to only certain information. For example, two important duties are writing cheques and doing the accounting. In a large company, the **treasurer** is responsible for cash management whereas the **controller** is the chief accounting officer. The controller approves invoices (bills) for payment and the treasurer signs the cheques.

Most banks and retail businesses assign each cashier a money tray and hold the cashier responsible if that fund is short at the end of the shift. This internal control device clearly assigns responsibility to each employee. Discrepancies can be traced to the person responsible.

In small companies, a clerk prepares invoices for payment and adjusts the accounting records, but the controller or owner signs the cheques. With clearly assigned responsibilities, all duties are carried out.

Separation of Duties Smart management divides the responsibilities for transactions between two or more people or departments. *Separation of duties* (also called *segregation of duties*) limits the chances for fraud and promotes the accuracy of accounting records by dividing up the three tasks of custody, authorization, and recording. Separation of duties can be divided into three parts:

The three parts can be remembered as CAR:
- Custody of assets
- Authorization of transactions
- Record keeping

- *Separate the custody of assets from accounting.* Accountants must not handle cash, and cashiers must not have access to the accounting records. If one employee has both cash-handling and accounting duties, as in the chapter-opening vignette about the school council's stolen funds, theft is made easier.

  Likewise, only warehouse employees with no accounting duties should have custody of inventory. If they were allowed to account for the inventory, they could steal it and make fake journal entries so that inventory disappears from the accounting records without actually being sold.
- *Separation of the authorization of transactions from the custody of related assets.* Persons who authorize transactions should not handle the related asset. For example, the same individual should not authorize the payment of a supplier's invoice and also sign the cheque to pay the invoice.
- *Separate operations from record keeping.* Accounting should be completely separate from operating departments, such as production and sales. Sales figures could be inflated, and top managers wouldn't know how much the company actually sold unless an impartial department records the information.

Even the smallest businesses should have internal controls and some separation of duties. For example, if the bookkeeper writes all cheques and keeps the general ledger records, the owner should sign all cheques and reconcile the monthly bank statement.

Proper Authorization An organization generally has written rules that outline approved procedures. Any deviation from policy requires *proper authorization.* For example, managers or assistant managers of retail stores often ask for ID when verifying payment by a customer or approving returns.

Audits An **audit** is an examination of the organization's financial statements and the accounting systems, controls, and records that produced them.

One of the auditor's first steps in auditing a business is to understand and evaluate its internal controls. If a company has good controls, then misstatements are minimized and are usually corrected before the financial statements are prepared. If the control system is weak, then misstatements can go undetected, as mentioned in the chapter-opening vignette.

Audits can be internal or external. *Internal auditors* are employees of the organization. They strive to ensure that other employees are following company policies and that operations are running efficiently. Internal auditors also determine whether the company is following legal requirements, such as privacy protection.

External auditors are completely independent of the organization. External audits provide users of financial information and management with reasonable assurance that the financial statements *fairly present* the financial position of an organization and the results of its operations and that the organization's financial statements have been prepared in accordance with generally accepted accounting principles. Auditors can also be from other agencies, such as tax auditors from the Canada

In some audits, procedures and even the audit itself may occur as a surprise to the employees so that they cannot cover up fraud or weaknesses in the system.

If a clerk in a retail store makes a mistake on the sales receipt, the receipt is not destroyed but is marked **VOID**. Most businesses use prenumbered sales receipts, so a missing receipt would be noticed.

The Personal Information Protection and Electronic Documents Act is legislation requiring companies to safeguard private information about individuals. There are 10 principles of fair information practices. As an example, principle #7 states: **Safeguards**: Protect personal information against loss or theft; safeguard the information from unauthorized access, disclosure, copying, use or modifications; protect personal information regardless of the format in which it is held.

Revenue Agency. Both internal and external auditors should be independent of the operations they examine, and both should suggest improvements that can help the business run efficiently. Although proprietorships do not require external audits, proprietorships may have external audits completed to satisfy bankers or other financial statement users.

Use of Documents and Records Business *documents and records* provide the details of business transactions. Such documents include sales invoices and purchase orders, and records include journals and ledgers. Documents should be prenumbered because a gap in the numbered sequence draws attention to a possible missing document.

A concert event promoter, for example, may use a paper wristband as a key document. The promoter can check on cashiers by comparing the number of wristbands issued against the amount of cash received. By multiplying the number of wristbands by the price per ticket to estimate the revenue and comparing this amount with each day's cash receipts, the manager can see whether all of the revenues are being collected.

Use of Electronic Devices and Computer Controls Businesses use electronic devices to protect assets. For example, retailers like The Bay control their inventories by attaching an *electronic sensor* to merchandise. The cashier removes the sensor at checkout. If a customer tries to remove an item from the store with the sensor attached, an alarm sounds. According to Checkpoint Systems, which manufactures electronic sensors, these devices reduce loss due to theft by as much as 50 percent.

Other Controls Businesses of all types keep cash and important documents in *fireproof vaults. Burglar alarms* protect buildings, and *security cameras* protect other property. *Loss-prevention specialists* train employees to spot suspicious activity.

Retailers receive most of their cash from customers on the spot. To safeguard cash, they use *point-of-sale terminals* that serve as a cash register and also record each transaction. Several times each day a supervisor removes the cash for deposit in the bank. Regular data backups help businesses reduce the risk of losing important information from theft or accidents.

Employees who handle cash might have an opportunity to steal it. Some businesses purchase **fidelity bonds** on cashiers; we say cashiers are "bonded." The bond is an insurance policy that reimburses the company for any losses from the employee's theft. Before issuing a fidelity bond, the insurance company investigates the employee's record.

Mandatory vacations and *job rotation* are also important internal controls. Vancity Credit Union, for example, moves employees from job to job. This improves morale by giving employees a broad view of the business. Also, knowing that someone else will be doing that job next month keeps an employee honest. Fraud is often discovered when someone takes vacation or is hospitalized unexpectedly because the person is not there to cover up the fraudulent activities, and the person filling in questions those activities.

Internal Controls for Ecommerce

Ecommerce creates its own unique types of risks. Hackers may gain access to confidential information, such as account numbers and passwords, that would normally be unavailable in face-to-face transactions. Confidentiality is a significant challenge for companies doing business online. To convince people to buy online, companies must ensure security of customer data.

Pitfalls

Some of the most common security pitfalls of ecommerce include:

- *Computer viruses and Trojans.* A **computer virus** is a malicious program that (1) enters program code without consent and (2) performs destructive actions. A **Trojan** hides inside a legitimate program and works like a virus. Viruses can destroy or alter data, make bogus calculations, and infect files.

- *Phishing expeditions.* **Phishing** is when thieves create legitimate-sounding bogus websites to attract lots of visitors that the thieves use to obtain account numbers and passwords from the unsuspecting visitors.
- *Identity theft.* Identity theft occurs when thieves obtain and control your personal data to steal your assets, make purchases, or obtain loans in your name without your knowledge or permission. This can often have devastating effects on a person's finances by leaving them with no assets or large debts or by ruining their credit record.
- *Stolen credit card numbers.* Malware installed in the security and payments systems can lead to the misappropriation of private customer information. This results in not only a financial loss but also a loss of trust and reputation for the business.

Equifax (a consumer credit score company) incurred a data breach of Canadian, American, and British files in the summer of 2017. Information affecting up to 143 million people was taken due to "a vulnerability in its website."

Security Measures To address the risks posed by ecommerce, companies have devised a number of security measures, including encryption and firewalls.

- *Encryption.* The server holding confidential information should always be secure, but sometimes hackers try to enter a server to get access to customer data. One technique for protecting customer data is encryption. **Encryption** rearranges messages by a mathematical process. The encrypted message cannot be read by anyone who does not know the process. An accounting example uses check-sum digits for account numbers. Each account number has its last digit equal to the sum of the previous digits, for example, Customer Number 2237, where $2 + 2 + 3 = 7$. Any account number that fails this test triggers an error message.
- *Firewalls.* **Firewalls** limit access to a local network. Network members can access the network, but non-members cannot. Usually several firewalls are built into the system. At the point of entry, passwords, PINs, and signatures are used to restrict entry. More sophisticated firewalls are used deeper in the network.

Blockchain technology will facilitate increased online security.

The Limitations of Internal Control

Unfortunately, most internal controls can be circumvented or overcome by two limitations: collusion and the cost–benefit constraint.

Collusion When two or more people work as a team to beat internal controls, this is called **collusion**. Consider the Classic Theatre. Geoff and Lana can design a scheme in which Geoff accepts the admission money from 10 customers but does not give them tickets. Lana, the ticket taker, admits 10 customers without tickets. Geoff and Lana then split the cash. To prevent this situation, the manager must take additional steps, such as counting the people in the theatre and matching that figure against the number of ticket stubs retained. But that takes time away from other duties.

Cost–benefit The stricter the internal control system, the more it costs. A complex system of internal control may strangle the business with red tape. How tight should the controls be? Internal controls must be judged in light of the costs and benefits. An example of a good cost–benefit constraint is a security guard at a store, who costs about $28,000 a year. On average, each guard prevents about $50,000 of theft. The net benefit to the store is $22,000.

Indigo Books and Music's management acknowledges the limitations of internal controls of their 2017 Annual Report:

> All internal control systems, no matter how well designed, have inherent limitations. Therefore, even those systems determined to be effective can provide only reasonable assurance with respect to consolidated financial statements preparation and presentation. Additionally, management is necessarily required to use judgment in evaluation controls and procedures.[2]

A control system, no matter how well conceived or operated, can provide only reasonable, not absolute, assurance that the objectives of the system are met.

---

[2]From Indigo Books and Music Inc., 2017 Annual Report (page 25), https://static.indigoimages.ca/2017/corporate/Indigo-FY17-Q4-Report.pdf.

Try It!

1. Match the terms to the definitions.

Sarbanes-Oxley Act	________	a. Organizational plan and all the related measures adopted by an entity to safeguard assets, encourage employees to follow company policies, promote operational efficiency, and ensure accurate and reliable accounting records
Phishing	________	b. Employees of the business who ensure that the company's employees are following company policies and meeting legal requirements and that operations are running efficiently
Internal control	________	c. Rearranging plain-text messages by a mathematical process—the primary method of achieving security in ecommerce
Encryption	________	d. Requires companies to review internal control and take responsibility for the accuracy and completeness of their financial reports
Separation of duties	________	e. Dividing responsibilities between two or more people
Internal auditors	________	f. Collecting passwords and personal data using bogus websites
Computer virus	________	g. Using passwords and PINs to limit access to a local network
Trojan	________	h. A malicious and destructive program that enters program code without consent
Firewall	________	i. A malicious program that hides inside a legitimate program to corrupt data

2. What problems can result when a sales clerk can also grant credit approval and record the sales in addition to handling the cash?

Solutions appear at the end of this chapter and on **MyLab Accounting**

The Bank Account as a Control Device

LO 3

What do we do when the bank statement balance and the cash account balance are not the same?

Cash—which includes cash on hand in funds such as *petty cash*, cash on deposit in banks and trust companies (both Canadian cash and cash in other currencies), and cash equivalents, such as term deposits or **Treasury bills** (very safe, short-term financial instruments issued by the federal government)—is the most liquid asset an organization has. Accordingly, it is usually the first item under the heading "Current Assets" on the balance sheet and can also be called "Cash and Cash Equivalents." Cash does *not* include **postdated cheques** (which are cheques that can only be cashed on a future date) or **stale-dated cheques** (cheques that are more than six months old) since banks will not include them as part of a company's cash balance. Cash's liquidity is an advantage because it is easily exchangeable for other assets. However, cash's liquidity is also a disadvantage because it is the most attractive asset to steal, and therefore it must be protected with good internal controls and risk management policies. The next learning objective will explain how organizations protect their cash by using internal controls.

Keeping cash in a *bank account* helps because banks have established practices for safeguarding customers' money. Banks also provide customers with detailed records of their transactions. To take full advantage of these control features, a business should deposit all cash receipts in the bank and make all cash payments through the bank rather than paying for things out of the cash register. An exception is petty cash, which we look at later.

The documents related to the use of a bank account include the following:

Signature Card Banks require each person authorized to transact business through an account to sign a *signature card*. The signature card shows each authorized person's signature. This helps protect against forgery. The teller sees an electronic copy of this card when processing a transaction on the account.

Deposit Slip Banks supply standard forms such as *deposit slips* or *deposit books*. The customer fills in the dollar amount of each deposit. As proof of the transaction, the customer keeps a deposit receipt. A bank machine also gives a receipt, but even the smallest business should use deposit books or deposit slips to ensure proper documentation. There is an example of this source document on page 67 in Chapter 2.

Cheque To pay from a bank account, the company writes a **cheque**, which is the document that tells the bank to pay the designated person or company a specified amount of money. There are three people or organizations involved with every cheque:

- The *maker*, who signs the cheque
- The *payee*, to whom the cheque is paid
- The *bank* on which the cheque is drawn

Exhibit 8–2 shows a cheque drawn on the bank account of Business Research Inc., the maker. The cheque has two parts: the cheque itself and the **remittance advice**, an optional attachment that tells the payee the reason for payment.

EXHIBIT 8–2 | Cheque with Remittance Advice

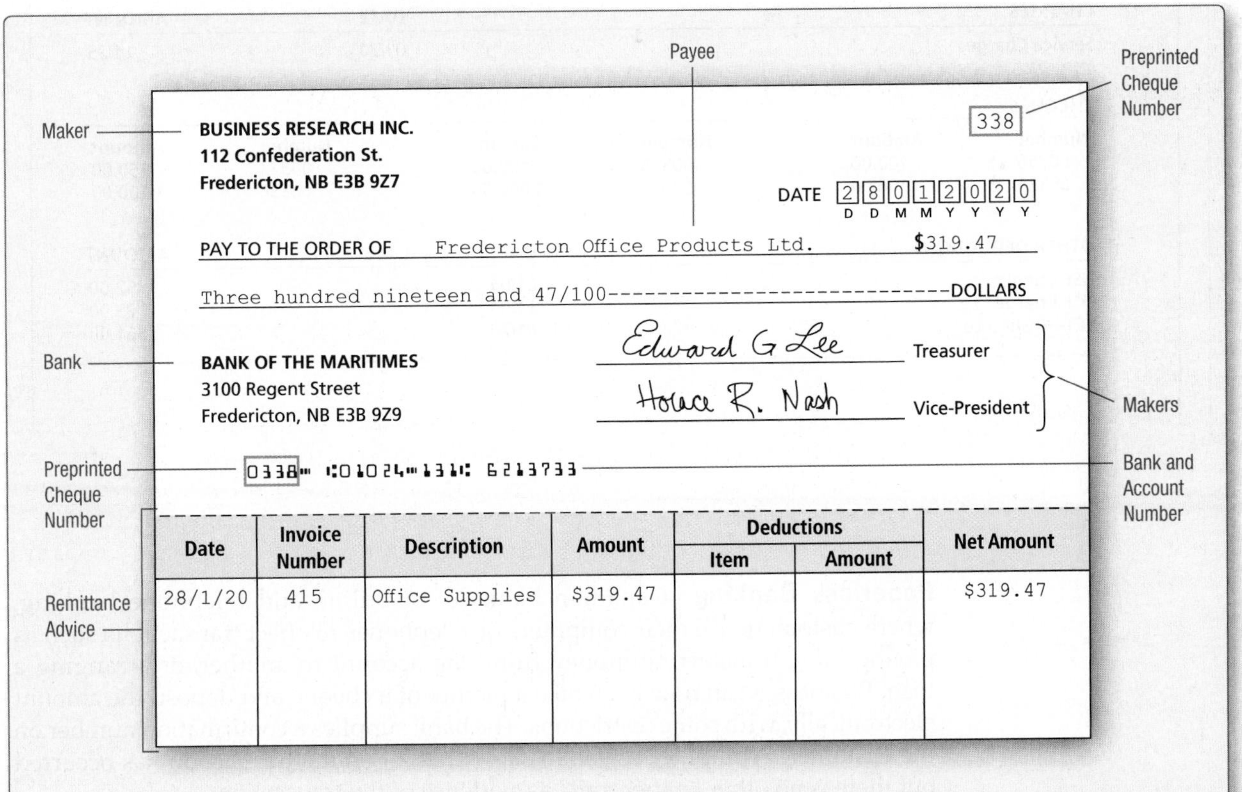

BUSINESS RESEARCH INC.
112 Confederation St.
Fredericton, NB E3B 9Z7

338

DATE 2 8 0 1 2 0 2 0
D D M M Y Y Y Y

PAY TO THE ORDER OF Fredericton Office Products Ltd. $319.47

Three hundred nineteen and 47/100---------------------------DOLLARS

BANK OF THE MARITIMES
3100 Regent Street
Fredericton, NB E3B 9Z9

Edward G Lee Treasurer
Horace R. Nash Vice-President

0338 ⑈ ⑆01024⑈131⑆ 6213733

Date	Invoice Number	Description	Amount	Deductions		Net Amount
				Item	Amount	
28/1/20	415	Office Supplies	$319.47			$319.47

Bank Statement Banks send monthly statements to their customers, or they can be downloaded online as needed. A **bank statement** reports what the bank did with the customer's cash. The statement shows the account's beginning and ending balances for the period and lists cash receipts and payments transacted through the bank. Included with the statement are either the maker's *cancelled cheques* that have been cashed by the payee or copies of these cheques. The statement also lists deposits and other changes in the account. Exhibit 8–3 is the bank statement of Business Research Inc. for the month ended January 31, 2020.

EXHIBIT 8–3 | Bank Statement

BANK OF THE MARITIMES
3100 REGENT STREET, FREDERICTON, NEW BRUNSWICK E3B 9Z9

BANK STATEMENT
CALL OUR INFOLINE
1-800-386-2093
QUEBEC 1-800-386-1600
TORONTO 416-987-7735

Business Research Inc.
112 Confederation St.
Fredericton, NB E3B 9Z7

BRANCH NO. 1024
ACCOUNT NO. 1316213733
JANUARY 01, 2020 to JANUARY 31, 2020

BEGINNING BALANCE	TOTAL DEPOSITS	TOTAL WITHDRAWALS	SERVICE CHARGES	ENDING BALANCE
$6,556.12	4,348.61	4,988.00	14.25	$5,902.48

TRANSACTIONS

DEPOSITS	DATE	AMOUNT
Deposit	01/04	1,112.00
Deposit	01/08	194.60
EFT—Rent Collection	01/17	900.00
Bank Collection	01/26	2,114.00
Interest	01/31	28.01

CHARGES	DATE	AMOUNT
Service Charges	01/31	14.25

CHEQUES

Number	Amount	Number	Amount	Number	Amount
00256	100.00	00335	100.00	00333	150.00
00334	100.00	00332	3,000.00	00336	1,100.00

OTHER DEDUCTIONS	DATE	AMOUNT
NSF Cheque	01/04	52.00
NSF Charge	01/04	25.00
EFT—Insurance	01/20	361.00

Paperless Banking Canadian banks offer online and telephone banking, where customers use their computers or telephones to effect transactions such as paying bills, transferring money from one account to another, or arranging a loan. Businesses can now even take a picture of a cheque and deposit the amount electronically, with some restrictions. The bank supplies a confirmation number on the customer's computer screen to show that an online transaction has occurred but there is no other "paper trail" as evidence of the transaction.

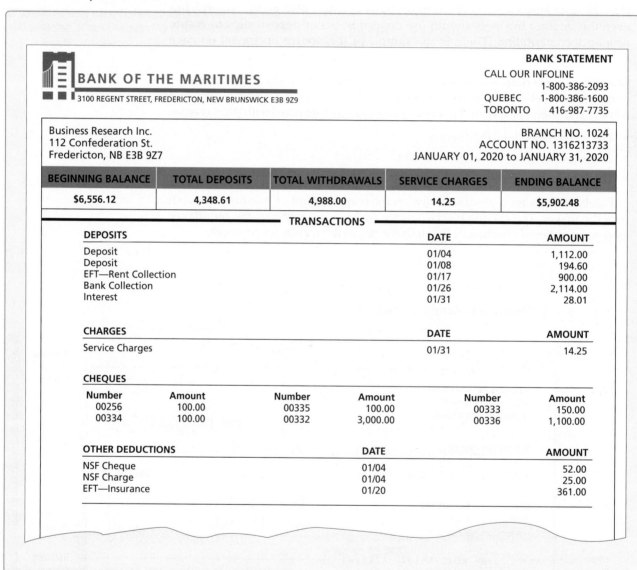

Electronic funds transfer (EFT) moves cash by electronic communications rather than by paper documents. It is much cheaper for a company to pay employees by this sort of **direct deposit** than by issuing hundreds of payroll cheques. Also, like many people, companies make mortgage, insurance, credit card, and other payments through automatic withdrawals, which are EFTs. Other than the original contract, there may be no separate document provided as evidence of each subsequent transaction.

Debit cards are another form of electronic payment. Purchases made using a debit card result in an immediate withdrawal for money from the customer's bank account and deposit into the store's bank account. Receipts are issued but they are often difficult to track.

Each of these transactions is confirmed by its appearance on a subsequent bank statement or printout from the online banking website. Businesses must implement additional procedures to carefully track and record these transactions. Often the bank statement is the only way the company knows about them.

Cheque truncation, or taking a picture of the cheque to be deposited is becoming more common.

The Bank Reconciliation

A business might assume that the amount of cash in its bank account is the same as the amount of cash in its accounting records. However, this is rarely the case, so the two amounts must be compared and reconciled.

- The bank statement shows the cash receipts and payments transacted through the bank during the month of January. In Exhibit 8–3, the bank shows an ending balance of $5,902.48 for Business Research Inc.
- The general ledger for the Cash account. Exhibit 8–4 shows that Business Research Inc.'s January 31 ending cash balance is $3,294.21.

EXHIBIT 8–4 | Cash Records of Business Research Inc.

General Ledger

Account: Cash					Account No. 1100
Date	**Item**	**Jrn. Ref.**	**Debit**	**Credit**	**Balance**
Jan. 1	Balance	✓			6,556.12 Dr
2	Cash receipt	CR. 9	1,112.00		7,668.12 Dr
3	Cheque 332	CP. 16		3,000.00	4,668.12 Dr
5	Cheque 333	CP. 16		510.00	4,415.12 Dr
5	Cheque 334	CP. 16		100.00	4,058.12 Dr
6	Cheque 335	CP. 16		100.00	3,958.12 Dr
7	Cash receipt	CR. 9	194.60		4,152.72 Dr
10	Cheque 336	CP. 17		1,100.00	3,052.72 Dr
11	Cheque 337	CP. 17		286.00	2,766.72 Dr
15	Cheque 338	CP. 17		319.47	2,447.25 Dr
20	Cheque 339	CP. 17		83.00	2,364.25 Dr
25	Cheque 340	CP. 17		203.14	2,161.11 Dr
28	Cheque 341	CP. 17		458.53	1,702.58 Dr
31	Cash receipt	CR. 10	1,591.63		3,294.21 Dr

CR - Cash Receipts Journal
CP - Cash Payments Journal
See chapter 7 for more detailed information about special journals.

The books and the bank statement usually show different cash balances. Differences arise because of a time lag in recording transactions, called a **timing difference**. Three examples of timing differences follow:

- When companies write a cheque, they immediately deduct the amount of the cheque from their Cash account balance. But the bank does not subtract this amount from the company's account until the bank pays it. That may take days, even weeks, if the payee waits to cash the cheque.
- Likewise, companies immediately add the amount of the cash receipt for each deposit that they make to their account. But it may take a day or more for the bank to add deposits to the company's balance.
- Any EFT payments and cash receipts are recorded by the bank before companies learn of them.

To ensure accurate cash records, companies need to update their records—either online or after they receive their bank statement. As part of this updating process a document called the **bank reconciliation** is prepared by the company (not the bank), usually monthly. The bank reconciliation accomplishes the following:

- It explains the differences between the company's cash records and the bank balance.
- It ensures that all cash transactions have been accounted for.
- It establishes that the bank and book records of cash are correct.

The person who prepares the bank reconciliation should have no other cash duties. Otherwise, he or she could steal cash and manipulate the bank reconciliation to hide the theft.

Since bank statements are usually received monthly, a bank reconciliation is often performed only once a month. However, with online access to bank account information, you are able to print your bank account history at any time. Thus, companies and individuals often prepare bank reconciliations more frequently than once a month.

Items on the Bank Reconciliation Exhibit 8–5 lists the items that appear on a bank reconciliation. They all cause differences between the bank balance and the book balance. (We refer to the company's cash records as the "Book" records.) The items are defined and explained in the annotations.

EXHIBIT 8–5 | Items that Appear on the Bank Reconciliation

Bank (Not yet recorded by the bank)	Books (Not yet recorded in the books)
End-of-month bank balance	End-of-month book balance
+ Deposits in transit	+ Bank collections
− Outstanding cheques	+/ − EFT receipts or payments
+/ − Bank errors	− Bank service charges
	+ Interest revenue
	− NSF cheques
	− Cheque printing costs
	+/ − Book errors

Outstanding deposits. The company has recorded (posted) these deposits, but the bank has not.

Cheques issued by the company and recorded on its books, but the bank has not yet paid or processed them.

Bank collections are cash receipts. Many businesses have their customers pay directly to the company bank account.

The bank may receive or pay cash on behalf of the company. An EFT may be a cash receipt or a cash payment.

Bank charges or fees for processing the company's transactions.

Depositors may earn interest on cash in their accounts.

These are cash receipts or cheques that turn out to be worthless. NSF cheques (sometimes called *bounced cheques*, *rubber cheques*, or *hot cheques*) are cash removed from the bank account because there was no money collected after all.

Preparing the Bank Reconciliation

You may want to start by reviewing the bank reconciliation shown in Exhibit 8–6. Panel A, lists the reconciling items for easy reference, and Panel B shows the completed reconciliation. The bank reconciliation can be prepared using a side-by-side format as shown in Exhibit 8–6 or in a vertical format as shown in the solution to

EXHIBIT 8–6 | Bank Reconciliation

Panel A: Reconciling Items

① Deposit in transit, $1,591.63	⑥ Interest earned on bank balance, $28.01
② Bank error: The bank deducted $100 for a cheque written by another company. Add $100 to bank balance.	⑦ Book error: cheque no. 333 for $150.00 paid to Brown Corp. on account was recorded as $510.00
③ Outstanding cheques: no. 337, $286.00; no. 338, $319.47; no. 339, $83.00; no. 340, $203.14; no. 341, $458.53	⑧ Bank service charges, $39.25 ($25.00 + $14.25)
④ EFT receipt of rent revenue, $900.00	⑨ NSF cheque from L. Ross, $52.00
⑤ Bank collection of note receivable, $2,114.00, including interest revenue of $114.00	⑩ EFT payment of insurance expense, $361.00

Panel B: Bank Reconciliation

BUSINESS RESEARCH INC.
Bank Reconciliation
January 31, 2020

BANK			BOOKS		
Bank Balance, January 31, 2020		**$5,902.48**	**Book Balance, January 31, 2020**		**$3,294.21**
Add:			Add:		
① Deposit of January 31 in transit	1,591.63		④ EFT receipt of rent revenue	900.00	
② Correction of bank error—Business Research Associates cheque erroneously charged against company account	100.00		⑤ Bank collection of note receivable, including interest revenue of $114.00	2,114.00	
		$7,594.11	⑥ Interest revenue earned on bank balance	28.01	
			⑦ Correction of book error—overstated amount of cheque no. 333	360.00	
③ Subtract: outstanding cheques					6,696.22
No. 337	$ 286.00		Subtract:		
338	319.47		⑧ Service charges	$ 39.25	
339	83.00		⑨ NSF cheque	52.00	
340	203.14				
341	458.53	(1,350.14)	⑩ EFT payment of insurance expense	361.00	(452.25)
Adjusted bank balance		**$6,243.97**	**Adjusted book balance**		**$6,243.97**

Amounts should agree

Each reconciling item is treated in the same way in every situation. Here is a summary of how to treat the various reconciling items:

BANK BALANCE—ALWAYS

- *Add* deposits in transit.
- *Subtract* outstanding cheques.
- *Add* or *subtract* corrections of bank errors.

BOOK BALANCE—ALWAYS

- *Add* bank collections, interest revenue, and EFT receipts.
- *Subtract* service charges, NSF cheques, and EFT payments.
- *Add* or *subtract* corrections of book errors.

the Summary Problem for Your Review on page 455. The format is important and should look neat and organized, but there is no standard presentation since this is an internal company document.

The steps in preparing a bank reconciliation are as follows:

1. After setting up your bank reconciliation form, start with two figures, the balance in the business's Cash account in the general ledger (*balance per books*) and the balance shown on the bank statement (*balance per bank*) on the same date – January 31, 2020. Using Exhibit 8–3, the balance per bank would be $5,902.48, and using Exhibit 8–4 the balance per books would be $3,294.21. These two amounts are different because of the timing differences discussed earlier.

Who doesn't know about this item yet? is a question to ask to help determine whether to add or subtract from the bank balance or the book balance. For example, for deposits in transit, the bank does not know about the transactions, so the bank's side of the reconciliation is updated.

2. Add to or subtract from the *bank* balance those items that appear correctly on the books but not on the bank statement (refer to Exhibit 8–5):
   a. Add **deposits in transit** to the bank balance. Deposits in transit are identified by comparing the deposits listed on the bank statement for that month to the business's list of cash receipts (based on the deposit book). They appear as cash receipts on the books but not as deposits on the bank statement. Normally they will be deposits on the bank statement within days, so they are added to the bank balance.
   b. Subtract **outstanding cheques** from the bank balance. Outstanding cheques are identified by comparing the cancelled cheques returned with the bank statement to the business's list of cheques written. Outstanding cheques appear as cash payments on the books but not as paid cheques on the bank statement. Since they will normally be paid by the bank very soon, they are subtracted from the bank balance. If cheques were outstanding on the bank reconciliation for the preceding month and have still not been cashed, add them to the list of outstanding cheques on this month's bank reconciliation. Outstanding cheques, are usually the most numerous item on a bank reconciliation.

Errors can be made by the bank or on the books. The balance that is adjusted for the error depends on where the error occurred. If the bank makes the error, the bank statement balance is adjusted then the bank must be notified so it can correct the error. If the error is on the books, the book balance is adjusted on the reconciliation and corrected with a journal entry.

3. Add to or subtract from the *book* balance those items that appear on the bank statement but not on the company books (refer to Exhibit 8–5):
   a. Add to the book balance: **bank collections**, EFT cash receipts, and interest revenue earned on the money in the bank. These items are identified by comparing the deposits listed on the bank statement with the business's list of cash receipts. They show up as cash receipts on the bank statement but not on the books.
   b. Subtract from the book balance: EFT cash payments, service charges, the cost of printed cheques, and other bank charges (e.g., fees for handling **nonsufficient funds (NSF) cheques** or stale-dated cheques). These items are identified by comparing the other charges listed on the bank statement to the cash payments recorded on the business's books. They appear as subtractions on the bank statement but not as cash payments on the books.
4. Compute the *adjusted bank balance* and *adjusted book balance*. The two adjusted balances should be equal.

Journalizing Transactions from the Reconciliation

The bank reconciliation is an accountant's tool that is separate from the company's journals and ledgers. It explains the effects of all cash receipts and all cash payments through the bank. But the bank reconciliation does *not* enter any transactions into the journals. To ensure that the transactions are entered into the accounts, we must make journal entries for the reconciling items on the books side of the bank reconciliation and post to the ledger to update the Cash account. These journal entries are made on January 31, 2020, and are shown in Exhibit 8–7. The numbers in circles correspond to the reconciling items listed in Exhibit 8–6, Panel A and shown in Panel B.

The journal entries in Exhibit 8–7 update the company's books once they are posted.

Journal entries are only made for items on the book side of the reconciliation to update the company's cash balance. These items must be recorded on the business's books because they are cash amounts that have increased or decreased the cash in the bank account, but they have not been recorded in the accounting records. This will make the Cash balance equal to the reconciled bank balance.

EXHIBIT 8–7 | Business Research Inc. Journal Entries Resulting from the Bank Reconciliation

General Journal — **Page 11**

	Date 2020	Account Titles and Explanations	Post. Ref.	Debit	Credit
❹	Jan. 31	Cash		900.00	
		Rent Revenue			900.00
		Receipt of monthly rent.			
❺	Jan. 31	Cash		2,114.00	
		Note Receivable			2,000.00
		Interest Revenue			114.00
		Note receivable collected by bank.			
❻	Jan. 31	Cash		28.01	
		Interest Revenue			28.01
		Interest earned on bank balance.			
❼	Jan. 31	Cash		360.00	
		Accounts Payable—Brown Corp.			360.00
		Correction of cheque no. 333.			
❽	Jan.31	Bank Charges Expense		39.25	
		Cash			39.25
		Bank service charges ($25.00 NSF + $14.25).			
❾	Jan. 31	Accounts Receivable—L. Ross		52.00	
		Cash			52.00
		NSF cheque returned by bank.			
❿	Jan. 31	Insurance Expense		361.00	
		Cash			361.00
		Payment of monthly insurance.			

L. Ross did not have enough cash in his chequing account to cover the cheque, so the bank removed the cash from Business Research's account as a withdrawal.

Business Research has set up the receivable again and must now try to collect it. At this point an additional charge could also be administered by the company for the default.

How Owners and Managers Use the Bank Reconciliation

The bank reconciliation is part of a system of internal controls, as the following example illustrates.

Randy Vaughn is a CPA in Regina, Saskatchewan. Vaughn owns several apartment complexes that are managed by his cousin, Alexis Vaughn. His accounting practice keeps him busy, so he has little time to devote to the properties. Vaughn's cousin approves tenants, collects the monthly rent cheques, arranges custodial and maintenance work, hires and fires employees, writes the cheques, and performs the bank reconciliation. This concentration of duties in one person is terrible from an internal control standpoint—Vaughn's cousin could be stealing from him. Vaughan is aware of this possibility, so he exercises some internal controls over his cousin's activities:

- Periodically, he drops by his properties to see whether the apartments are in good condition.
- To control cash, Vaughn uses a bank reconciliation. On an irregular basis, he examines the bank reconciliations as prepared by his cousin. He matches every cheque that cleared the bank to the journal entry on the books. Vaughn would know

immediately if his cousin were writing cheques to herself. Vaughn sometimes prepares his own bank reconciliation to see whether it agrees with his cousin's work.

- To keep his cousin on her toes, Vaughn lets her know that he periodically checks her work.
- Vaughn has a simple method for controlling cash receipts. He knows the occupancy level of his apartments. He also knows the monthly rent he charges, and he requires all tenants to pay by cheque. He multiplies the number of apartments—say 100—by the monthly rent (which averages $500 per unit) to arrive at an expected monthly rent revenue of $50,000. By tracing the $50,000 revenue to the bank statement, Vaughn can tell that his rent money went into his bank account.

Control activities such as these (often referred to as **executive controls**) are critical in small businesses. With only a few employees, a separation of duties may not be feasible. The owner must oversee and, if possible, become involved in the operations of the business, or the assets may disappear.

Try It!

3. List the three items that can appear on the bank side of a bank reconciliation. Why does the company *not* need to record the reconciling items that appear on the bank side of the bank reconciliation?
4. Jonas Company's July 31, 2020, bank statement balance is $9,000 and shows a service charge of $30, interest earned of $10, and an NSF cheque for $600. Deposits in transit total $2,400, and outstanding cheques are $1,150. The bookkeeper incorrectly recorded as $152 a cheque of $125 in payment of an account payable. The company's book balance at July 31, 2020, was $10,843.
   a. Prepare the bank reconciliation for Jonas Company at July 31, 2020. Calculate the adjusted bank balance first, then calculate the adjusted book balance below it. Draw an arrow to show that both adjusted balances agree.
   b. Prepare the journal entries needed to update the company's books.

Solutions appear at the end of this chapter and on **MyLab Accounting**

Why It's Done This Way

Cash, the subject of this chapter, is always reported at its fair value, simply by virtue of what cash is. The accounting framework presented in Exhibit 1–5 in Chapter 1 describes the elements of the financial statements, one of which is assets. Cash is an asset, since it is controlled by a company and has an expected future benefit.

This chapter mentioned that postdated cheques received are not included in the cash balance. This is because the cash is not available to the company, and it would be misleading to include postdated cheques in the cash balance since it would overstate the amount of cash the company has that is expected to produce a future benefit.

Internal Control Over Cash Receipts

LO 4
How do we implement internal controls for cash receipts and cash payments?

Internal control over cash receipts (also includes credit card receipts and debit card payments) ensures that all cash receipts are deposited daily. Companies receive cash over the counter, electronically, and through the mail. Each source of cash has its own security measures.

Controls over Cash Receipts

Cash Receipts over the Counter Consider a Canadian Tire store. The cash register, which is often a computer terminal, is positioned so that customers can see the amounts the cashier scans into the terminal. No person willingly pays more than the marked price for an item, so the customer helps prevent the sales clerk from overcharging. For each transaction, Canadian Tire issues a receipt to ensure that each sale is recorded.

The cash drawer opens only when the clerk enters a transaction and the machine records it. At the end of the day, a manager ensures the amount of cash is correct by comparing the cash in the drawer against the machine's record of sales. This step helps prevent theft by the clerk.

At the end of the day—or several times a day if business is brisk—the cashier or another employee with cash-handling duties records all the cash on a deposit slip and deposits the cash in the bank. The machine tape or digital information then goes to the accounting department as the basis for the journal entry to record sales revenue. These security measures, coupled with oversight by a manager, discourage theft.

It is important to deposit *all* the cash received at least daily to know the amount of total cash sales. Neither managers nor employees should use cash received to make purchases or other cash payments. In some rare circumstances where records are destroyed or missing, the bank statement can be used to reconstruct transactions.

Electronic Cash Receipts Many companies receive payments via the Internet. For example, the online payment service PayPal enables small businesses to send electronic payments without a credit card and receive electronic payments without a merchant account. PayPal can connect to the company bank account for both sending and receiving payments, but businesses still need to be aware of the safety and security of this system.

Cash Receipts by Mail Many companies receive payments (cheques and credit card authorizations) by mail. Exhibit 8–8 shows how large companies with many staff members segregate duties and control payments received by mail.

1. All incoming mail is opened by a mailroom employee who sends all customer payments to the treasurer.
2. The treasurer has the cashier deposit the money in the bank.
3. The remittance advices, or records of payment, go to the accounting department so that journal entries can be recorded in the Cash and customers' accounts.
4. As a final step, the controller compares the records of the day's cash receipts (step 2 to step 3) to ensure that they match. The debit to Cash should equal the amount deposited in the bank. All cash receipts are safe in the bank, and the company books are up to date.

EXHIBIT 8–8 | Cash Receipts by Mail

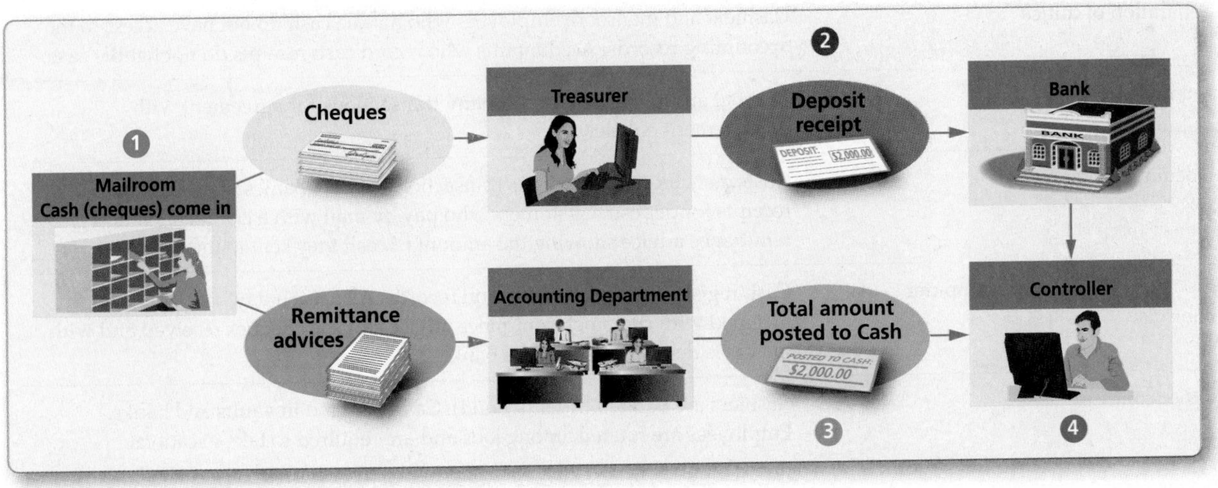

In small companies with few staff members, the manager or owner should check the mail clerk's work or make the cash deposit to ensure the procedures are working properly when it's not possible to segregate duties.

Some companies use a lock-box system. Customers send their cheques to a post office box belonging to the bank; the bank deposits the cheques directly to the company's bank account. Internal control is tight because company personnel never touch incoming cash.

The Cash Short and Over account can have a debit or credit balance. A credit balance would be classified as Other Revenue. Since customers tend to notify the cashier when they don't receive enough change, Cash Short and Over is more likely to have a debit balance and be an expense for the business.

Cash Short and Over

When the recorded cash balance exceeds cash on hand, we have a *cash short* situation. When the actual cash exceeds the recorded Cash balance, we have a *cash over* situation. Suppose the tapes from a cash register at Little Short Stop convenience store indicated sales revenue of $15,000, but the cash received was $14,980. To record the day's sales for that register, the store would make this entry:

Dec. 18	Cash	14,980	
	Cash Short and Over	20	
	Sales Revenue		15,000
	Daily cash sales.		

In this entry, **Cash Short and Over** is an expense account because sales revenue exceeds cash receipts. This account is credited when cash receipts exceed sales. The Cash Short and Over account's balance should be small. The debits and credits for cash shorts and overs collected over an accounting period tend to cancel each other out. A large balance signals the accountant to investigate. For example, too large a debit balance may mean an employee is stealing. Cash Short and Over, then, acts as an internal control device.

Exhibit 8–9 summarizes the internal controls over cash receipts.

EXHIBIT 8–9 | Internal Controls over Cash Receipts

Internal Control Procedures	Internal Controls over Cash Receipts
Competent, reliable, ethical personnel	Screen employees for undesirable personality traits. Create effective training programs.
Assignment of responsibilities	Specific employees are designated as cashiers, supervisors, and accountants.
Proper authorization	Only designated employees can approve cheque cashing above a certain amount, approve purchases on credit, etc.
Separation of duties	Cashiers and mailroom employees who handle cash do not have access to the accounting records. Accountants who record cash receipts do not handle cash.
Internal audits	Internal auditors examine company transactions for agreement with management policies.
Documents and records	Customers receive receipts as transaction records. Bank statements list cash receipts for deposit. Customers who pay by mail with a cheque include a remittance advice showing the amount of cash they sent to the company.
Electronic devices and computer controls	Cash registers serve as transaction records. Also, each day's receipts are matched with customer remittance advices for the cheques received and with the day's deposit slip with the bank.
Other controls	Cashiers are bonded (fidelity bond). Cash is stored in vaults and banks. Employees are rotated among jobs and are required to take vacations.

Internal Control Over Cash Payments

Cash payments are as important as cash receipts. It is therefore critical to control cash payments for goods and services by cheque. Prior to issuing the cheque, authorization for payment would be required. Companies often pay small amounts from a petty cash fund.

Controls over Payments by Cheque

Payment by cheque is an important internal control:

- The cheque provides a record of the payment.
- The cheque must be signed by an authorized official. An even better control is to require two signatures.
- Before signing the cheque, the official should verify the evidence supporting the payment.

As noted in our discussion on internal controls, companies need a good separation of duties among ordering goods, possession of goods, updating the accounting records, and writing cheques for cash payments.

Controls over Purchase and Payment To illustrate the internal control over cash payments, let's suppose the business is paying for merchandise inventory. The purchasing and payment process follows these steps, as outlined in Exhibit 8–10:

EXHIBIT 8–10 | Cash Payments by Cheque

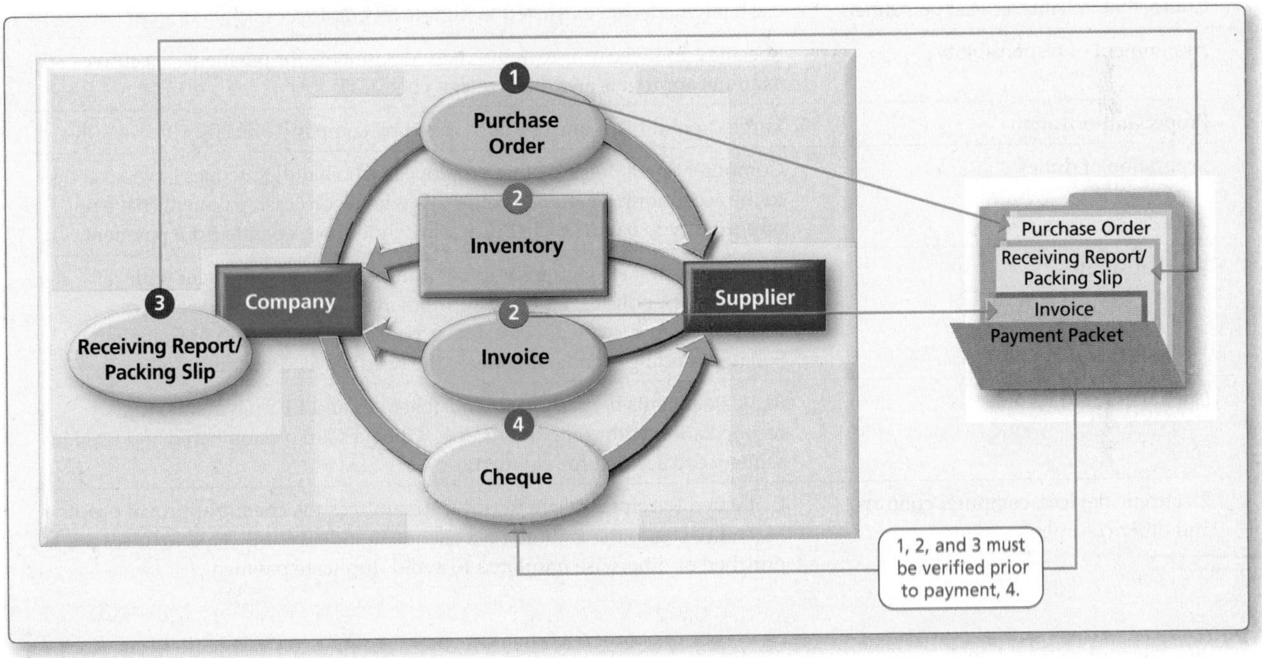

❶ The company sends an authorized *purchase order* to the supplier.

❷ The supplier ships the merchandise and mails the *invoice*, or bill.

❸ The company receives the goods. The receiving department checks the goods for damage and either checks off the items received on the packing slip that accompanies the goods or prepares a list of the goods received on a *receiving report*.

❹ After the accounting department checks and confirms all the forgoing documents using a *payment packet* or voucher, the company sends a *cheque* to the supplier only for the goods received.

For good internal control, the purchasing agent should neither receive the goods nor approve the payment. If these duties are not separated, a purchasing agent could buy goods and have them shipped to his or her home. Or the purchasing agent could increase the price of purchases, approve the payment, and then split the price increase with the supplier.

After payment, the cheque signer should punch a hole through the payment packet or otherwise mark the packet and its contents as paid. These actions alert the company that it has paid the bill. Dishonest employees and suppliers have been known to present a bill for cash payment two or more times.

Streamlined Procedures Technology is streamlining payment procedures, especially for large companies. **Evaluated Receipt Settlement (ERS)** compresses the approval process into a single step: comparing the receiving report with the purchase order. If the two documents match, that proves that the company received the merchandise it ordered. Then the company pays the supplier.

An even more streamlined process bypasses people and documents altogether. In **Electronic Data Interchange (EDI)**, Canadian Tire's computers can communicate directly with the computers of suppliers like General Tire, Rubbermaid, and Procter & Gamble. When Canadian Tire's inventory of automobile tires reaches a certain (low) level, the computer sends a purchase order to General Tire. General Tire ships the tires and invoices Canadian Tire electronically. General Tire receives funds directly from Canadian Tire's bank via an EFT.

Exhibit 8–11 summarizes the internal controls over cash payments.

EXHIBIT 8–11 | Internal Controls over Cash Payments

Element of Internal Control	Internal Controls over Cash Payments
Competent, reliable, ethical personnel	Cash payments are entrusted to high-level employees.
Assignment of responsibility	Specific employees approve purchase documents for payment. Executives examine approvals and then co-sign cheques.
Proper authorization	Large expenditures must be authorized by company officials.
Separation of duties	Computer operators and other employees who handle cheques have no access to the accounting records. Accountants who record cash payments have no opportunity to handle cash. Purchasing should be separate from payment.
Internal audits	Internal auditors examine company transactions for agreement with management policies. External auditors may also be hired to review compliance to specific policies, like expense claims (the recent Canadian Senate spending scandal illustrates the need for external auditors).
Documents and records	Bank statements list cash payments (cheques and EFT payments) for reconciliation with company records. Cheques are prenumbered and used in sequence to account for payments.
Electronic devices, computer controls, and other controls	Evaluated Receipt Settlement (ERS) streamlines the cheque approval process. Machines stamp the amount on a cheque in indelible ink. Paid invoices are punched or otherwise mutilated to avoid duplicate payment.

Try It!

5. When cash is received by mail, what keeps the mailroom employee from pocketing a customer cheque and destroying the remittance advice?
6. Suppose the tapes from the cash registers at a Burger King restaurant indicated sales revenue of $7,252, but the cash received was $7,262. Journalize the day's sales.
7. Two officers' signatures are required for cheques over $1,000. One officer is going on vacation and presigns several cheques. The cheques are locked in the vault. What is the internal control feature in this scenario, and is it effective?

Solutions appear at the end of this chapter and on **MyLab Accounting**

Internal Control Over Petty Cash

LO 5

How do we implement internal controls for petty cash?

It is wasteful to write a cheque for an employee's taxi fare (while on company business) or the delivery of a package across town. To meet these needs, companies keep cash on hand to pay small amounts. This fund is called **petty cash**.

Even though petty cash payments are small, employee theft is often seen with this fund. Therefore, internal controls such as the following are important:

- Designate a **custodian** of the petty cash fund.
- Keep a specific amount of cash on hand in a secure location.
- Support all fund payments for expenses with a **petty cash ticket or voucher**.
- Do surprise audits of the fund to ensure receipts and cash total the assigned amount.

Creating the Petty Cash Fund

The petty cash fund is opened when a cheque is written for the designated amount. The cheque is made payable to the employee responsible for petty cash. Banks do not like to cash cheques made out to "Cash" or "Petty Cash" unless they know the customer. Assume that on January 31 the business creates a petty cash fund of $400.

The petty cash custodian cashes a $400 cheque and places the money in the fund (a locked metal box or other secure location). Starting the fund is recorded as follows:

Jan. 31	Petty Cash	400	
	Cash		400
	To open the petty cash fund.		

For each petty cash payment, the custodian prepares a *petty cash ticket* or *petty cash voucher* like the one illustrated in Exhibit 8–12. Prior to replenishment of the fund, each petty cash voucher should have a receipt, invoice, or other documentation to support the payment.

EXHIBIT 8–12 | Petty Cash Ticket

PETTY CASH TICKET

Date Mar. 25, 2020 **No.** 45

Amount $34.00

For Payment for delivery of contract.

Debit Delivery Expense, Acct. No. 545

Received by Lewis Wright **Fund Custodian** MAR

Signatures (or initials) identify the recipient of the cash (Lewis Wright) and the fund custodian (MAR). Requiring both signatures reduces fraudulent payments. The custodian keeps all the prenumbered petty cash tickets in the petty cash fund box or location. The sum of the cash plus the total of the ticket amounts should equal the opening balance ($400) at all times. Also, the Petty Cash account in the financial records keeps its $400 balance at all times.

No journal entries are made for petty cash payments until the fund is replenished. At that time, all petty cash payments will be recorded in a summary entry. This procedure avoids the need to journalize many payments for small amounts.

As the use of company credit cards increases, the use of Petty Cash accounts is decreasing.

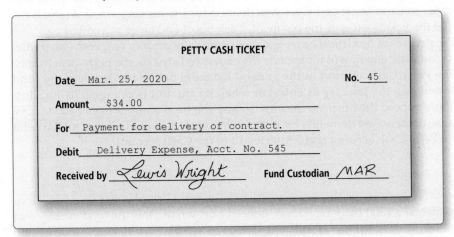

Replenishing the Petty Cash Fund

Maintaining the Petty Cash account at its designated balance is the nature of an **imprest system**. This system clearly identifies the amount of cash for which the fund custodian is responsible and is the system's main internal control feature. Imprest systems are also used for branch offices that keep cash for the office in a fund. Payments reduce the cash in the fund, so the fund must be replenished periodically.

On March 31, the petty cash fund holds $230 in petty cash and $164 in petty cash tickets.

We can see that $6 is missing:

Fund balance		$400
Cash on hand	$230	
Petty cash tickets	164	
Total accounted for		$394
Amount of cash missing		$ 6

To replenish the petty cash fund, we need to bring the cash on hand up to $400. The company writes a cheque, payable to the fund custodian, for $170 ($400 − $230). The fund custodian cashes this cheque and puts $170 back into the fund. Now the fund holds $400 cash, as it should.

Notice that replenishing the fund does not affect the Petty Cash account balance.

The petty cash tickets identify the accounts to debit, as shown in the entry to replenish the fund (items are assumed for this illustration):

Mar. 31	Office Supplies	46	
	Delivery Expense	34	
	Cash Short and Over	6	
	Selling Expense	84	
	Cash		170
	To replenish the petty cash fund.		

The cash payments have exceeded the sum of the tickets, since the fund was short $6, so Cash Short and Over was debited for the missing amount ($6). If the sum of the tickets exceeds the payment, Cash Short and Over is credited.

The petty cash fund *must* be replenished, especially prior to year end. Otherwise, the income statement will understate the expenses listed on the petty cash tickets.

The Petty Cash account in the general ledger is debited only when the fund is started (see the January 31 entry) or when its amount is changed. In our illustration, suppose the business decides to raise the fund amount from $400 to $500 because of increased demands for petty cash. This step would require a $100 debit to the Petty Cash account and a $100 credit to the Cash account.

Try It!

8. Leitch Design Studios established a $300 petty cash fund. James C. Brown (JCB) is the fund custodian. At the end of the first week, the petty cash fund contains the following:
   - Cash: $163
   - Petty cash tickets:

No.	Amount	Issued to	Signed by	Account Debited
1	$14	B. Jarvis	B. Jarvis and JCB	Office Supplies
2	39	S. Bell	S. Bell	Delivery Expense
4	43	R. Tate	R. Tate and JCB	—
5	33	G. Blair	G. Blair and JCB	Travel Expense

a. Identify three internal control weaknesses revealed in the given data.
b. Prepare the general journal entries to record the following:
   i. January 1: Establishment of the petty cash fund
   ii. June 30: Replenishment of the fund. Assume petty cash ticket no. 4 was issued for the purchase of office supplies

Solutions appear at the end of this chapter and on **MyLab Accounting**

Ethics and Accounting

LO 6

Are there steps we can follow when making ethical business judgments?

Robert Schad, former president and CEO of Husky Injection Molding Systems Ltd. in Bolton, Ontario, said, "Ethical practice is, quite simply, good business." The late Anita Roddick, founder of The Body Shop, said, "Being good is good business." Both Roddick and Schad were in business long enough to recognize the danger in unethical behaviour. Sooner or later unethical conduct comes to light, as was true in our chapter-opening vignette about the school board. Moreover, ethical behaviour wins out in the end because it is the right thing to do.

Corporate and Professional Codes of Ethics

Most companies have a code of ethics to encourage employees to behave ethically. But codes of ethics are not enough by themselves. Owners and managers must set a high ethical tone. They must make it clear that the company will not tolerate unethical conduct.

Accountants have additional incentives to behave ethically. As professionals, they are expected to maintain higher standards than society in general. Their ability to attract business depends entirely on their reputation.

Chartered Professional Accountants (CPAs) must adhere to the code of ethics and the rules of professional conduct set out by CPA Canada. These documents set minimum standards of conduct for members. Unacceptable actions can result in expulsion from the organization, which makes it impossible for the person to remain a professional accountant.

Ethical Issues in Accounting

In many situations the ethical choice is easy. For example, stealing money, as in the chapter-opening vignette, is illegal and unethical. In other cases, the choices are more difficult. But in every instance ethical judgments are a personal decision. What should I do in a given situation? Let's consider an ethical issue in accounting.

Sonja Kleberg is preparing the income tax return of a client who earned more income than expected. On January 2, the client pays for advertising to run in late January and asks Sonja to backdate the expense to the preceding year. Backdating would decrease the client's taxable income of the earlier year and postpone a few dollars in tax payments. No big deal, right? After all, there is a difference of only two days between January 2 and December 31. This client is important to Kleberg. *What should she do?* She should refuse the request because the transaction took place in January of the new year.

What internal control device could prove that Kleberg behaved unethically if she backdated the transaction in the accounting records? A Canada Revenue Agency audit could prove that the expense occurred in January rather than in December by reviewing the documentation. Falsifying tax returns is both illegal and unethical.

Weighing tough ethical judgments requires a decision framework. A framework is shown in the box on the top of the next page. Consider the six questions shown there as general guidelines; they will guide you through answering tough ethical questions.

Decision Guidelines: Making Ethical Judgments

Decision	Guideline
1. What are the facts?	*Determine the facts.*
2. What is the ethical issue, if any?	*Identify the ethical issues.* CPA Canada says that an "ethical issue is a situation or problem in which your actions, the actions of people you advise, or the actions of an organization you help to shape, might harm one or more people or stakeholder groups, or might violate what is considered to be right or good."[3]
3. What are the alternatives?	*Specify the alternatives.* "Do nothing" is always an alternative.
4. Who is involved in the situation?	*Identify the stakeholders*, the people involved.
5. What are the possible consequences of each alternative in question 3?	*Assess the possible outcomes of each alternative.*
6. What should be done?	*Make a decision.*

[3]From CPA Canada's "The CPA Way 7—Ethical Behaviour," https://www.cpacanada.ca/-/media/site/become-a-cpa/docs/national-education-resources/en-the-cpa-way-7-ethical-behaviour.pdf.

Try It!

9. Suppose David Duncan, the lead external auditor for Axiom Corporation, thinks Axiom may be understating its liabilities on the balance sheet. Axiom's transactions are very complex, and outsiders may never figure this out. Duncan asks his firm's standards committee how he should handle the situation. They reply, "Require Axiom to report all its liabilities." Axiom is Duncan's most important client, and Axiom is pressuring Duncan to certify the liabilities. Duncan tries to rationalize that Axiom's reported amounts are okay. What should Duncan do? To make his decision, Duncan could follow the decision guidelines outlined in this chapter. Apply those guidelines to David Duncan's situation.

Solutions appear at the end of this chapter and on **MyLab Accounting**

Summary Problem for Your Review

The Cash account of Atlantic Dental Associates at February 29, 2020, follows:

Cash

Feb. 1	Bal.	7,990	Feb. 3	800
6		1,600	12	6,200
15		3,600	19	2,200
23		2,200	25	1,000
28		4,800	27	1,800
29	Bal.	8,190		

Atlantic Dental Associates receives the February 2020 bank statement data in the first week of March 2020 (negative amounts appear in parentheses):

BANK STATEMENT FOR FEBRUARY 2020

DESCRIPTION	WITHDRAWALS	DEPOSITS	DATE	BALANCE
Balance Forward			Feb01	$ 7,990
Deposits		1,600	Feb07	9,590
Cheques total for day	800		Feb08	8,790
Deposits		3,600	Feb15	12,390
Cheques total for day	6,200		Feb16	6,190
Cheques total for day		2,200	Feb23	3,990
Deposits	2,200		Feb24	6,190
NSF cheque, M. E. Crown	1,400		Feb24	4,790
Bank collection of note receivable		2,000*	Feb26	6,790
EFT rent expense	660		Feb28	6,130
Service charge	20		Feb29	6,110
Interest		5	Feb29	6,115
	11,280	9,405		

*Includes principal of $1,762 plus interest of $238.

Required

1. Prepare the bank reconciliation of Atlantic Dental Associates at February 29, 2020.
2. Journalize the entries based on the bank reconciliation.

Before creating the bank reconciliation, compare the Cash account and the bank statement. Cross out all items that appear in both places. The items that remain are the reconciling items.

Begin with the ending balance on the bank statement.

Add deposits (debits) from the Cash account not on the bank statement.

Deduct cheques (credits) from the Cash account not on the bank statement.

Begin with the ending balance in the Cash general ledger account.

Add money received by the bank on behalf of the company (increases to the bank statement balance).

Deduct bank charges, NSF cheques, or preauthorized payments (decreases to the bank statement balance).

SOLUTION

Requirement 1

Atlantic Dental Associates Bank Reconciliation February 29, 2020		
Bank		
Bank Balance, February 29, 2020		$ 6,115
Add: Deposit of February 28 in transit		4,800
		10,915
Subtract: Outstanding cheques		
Feb. 25	$1,000	
Feb. 27	$1,800	(2,800)
Adjusted bank balance, February 29, 2020		$ 8,115
Books		
Book Balance, February 29, 2020		$ 8,190
Add: Bank collection of note receivable, including interest of $238		2,000
Add: Interest earned on bank balance		5
		10,195
Subtract: Service charge	$ 20	
NSF cheque	1,400	
EFT—Rent expense	660	(2,080)
Adjusted book balance, February 29, 2020		$ 8,115

Requirement 2

Prepare journal entries for all reconciling items from the "books" section of the bank reconciliation.

Feb. 29	Cash	2,000	
	Note Receivable		1,762
	Interest Revenue		238
	Note receivable collected by bank ($2,000 − $238).		
29	Cash	5	
	Interest Revenue		5
	Interest earned on bank balance.		
29	Bank Charges Expense	20	
	Cash		20
	Bank service charge.		
29	Accounts Receivable—M. E. Crown	1,400	
	Cash		1,400
	NSF cheque returned by bank.		
29	Rent Expense	660	
	Cash		660
	Monthly rent expense.		

Summary

Learning Objectives

① Define internal control Pg. 432

What is internal control?

- Internal control is the organizational plan and all related measures adopted by an entity to meet the following management objectives:
  - Encouraging operational efficiency
  - Prevention and detection of fraud and error
  - Safeguarding assets and records
  - Providing accurate, reliable information
- The Sarbanes-Oxley Act and the Dodd-Frank Act are legislation implemented in the United States that affect Canadian companies listed on US stock exchanges. Canada has implemented similar legislation requiring companies to have internal controls and management to take responsibility for them.

② List and describe the components of internal control and control procedures Pg. 433

What should we think about when designing an internal control system?

- Internal control objectives can be achieved by applying these components (**CRIME**):
  - **C**ontrol procedures
  - **R**isk assessment
  - **I**nformation system
  - **M**onitoring of controls
  - **E**nvironment
- An effective system of internal control has these procedures:
  - Competent, reliable, and ethical personnel
  - Clear assignment of responsibilities
  - Separation of duties
  - Proper authorization
  - Internal and external audits
  - Documents and records
  - Electronic devices and computer controls
- Other controls companies also make use of include fireproof vaults, point-of-sale terminals, fidelity bonds, mandatory vacations, surveillance cameras, and job rotation.
- Two limitations of internal controls are collusion and the cost–benefit constraint.

③ Prepare a bank reconciliation and the related journal entries Pg. 438

What do we do when the bank statement balance and the cash account balance are not the same?

- The bank reconciliation explains the reasons for the difference between the company's cash balance in its accounting records and the cash balance in its bank account.

④ Apply internal controls to cash receipts and cash payments Pg. 446

How do we implement internal controls for cash receipts and cash payments?

- To control cash receipts over the counter, companies use point-of-sale terminals that customers can see and require cashiers to provide customers with receipts.
- A duplicate tape inside the machine or a link to a central computer records each sale and cash transaction.
- To control cash receipts by mail:
  - A mailroom employee should be assigned the responsibility for opening the mail as an essential separation of duties—the accounting department should not open the mail.
  - At the end of the day, the controller compares the two records of the day's cash receipts: the bank deposit amount from the cashier and the debit to Cash from the accounting department.
- To control cash payments, cheques should be issued and signed only when supporting documents, including the purchase order, invoice (bill), and receiving report (all with appropriate signatures), have been reviewed.

⑤ Apply internal controls to petty cash **Pg. 451**

How do we implement internal controls for petty cash?

- Designate an employee or custodian of the petty cash fund.
- Keep a specific amount of cash on hand in a secure location.
- Support all fund payments for expenses with a petty cash ticket or voucher.
- Perform unannounced checks or audits on the petty cash fund to count the balance.

⑥ Make ethical business judgments **Pg. 453**

Are there steps we can follow when making ethical business judgments?

- To make ethical decisions, businesspeople should follow six guidelines:
  1. Determine the facts
  2. Identify the ethical issues
  3. Specify the alternatives
  4. Identify the stakeholders
  5. Assess the possible outcomes of each alternative
  6. Make the decision

Key Terms for the chapter are shown next and are in the **Glossary** at the back of the book. **Similar Terms** are shown after **Key Terms.**

KEY TERMS

Audit The examination of financial statements by outside accountants. The conclusion of an audit is the accountant's professional opinion about the financial statements *(p. 435).*

Bank collection Collection of money by the bank on behalf of a depositor *(p. 444).*

Bank reconciliation The process of explaining the reasons for the difference between a depositor's records and the bank's records about the depositor's bank account *(p. 442).*

Bank statement A document for a particular bank account showing its beginning and ending balances and listing the month's transactions that affected the account *(p. 440).*

Cash The most liquid asset an organization has; includes cash on hand, cash on deposit in banks and trust companies, and cash equivalents *(p. 438).*

Cash short and over When the recorded cash balance does not match the actual amount counted *(p. 448).*

Cheque A document that instructs the bank to pay the designated person or business a specified amount of money *(p. 439).*

Cheque truncation The conversion of a physical cheque into an electronic format (i.e., taking a picture) for processing through the banking system to save time and resources *(p. 441).*

Collusion When two or more people work as a team to beat internal controls and steal from a company *(p. 437).*

Committee of Sponsoring Organizations (COSO) A committee that provides thought leadership related to enterprise risk management, internal control, and fraud deterrence *(p. 433).*

Computer virus A malicious computer program that reproduces itself, gets included in program code without consent, and destroys program code *(p. 436).*

Controller The chief accounting officer of a company *(p. 435).*

Custodian A person designated to be responsible for something of value, like the petty cash fund *(p. 451).*

Deposit in transit A deposit recorded by the company but not yet by its bank *(p. 444).*

Direct deposit Funds that are deposited and transferred directly to a bank account, such as employee payroll *(p. 441).*

Electronic Data Interchange (EDI) The transfer of structured data by electronic means and standards between organizations from one computer system to another without human intervention *(p. 450).*

Electronic funds transfer (EFT) A system that transfers cash by digital communication rather than paper documents *(p. 451).*

Encryption The process of rearranging plain-text messages by some mathematical formula to achieve confidentiality *(p. 437).*

Evaluated Receipt Settlement (ERS) A streamlined payment procedure that compresses the approval process into a single step: comparing the receiving report with the purchase order *(p. 450).*

Executive controls Management involvement in internal controls *(p. 446).*

Fidelity bond An insurance policy that reimburses the company for any losses due to the employee's theft. Before hiring, the bonding company checks the employee's background *(p. 436).*

Firewall Barriers used to prevent entry into a computer network or a part of a network. Examples include passwords, personal identification numbers (PINs), and fingerprints *(p. 437).*

Imprest system A way to account for petty cash by maintaining a constant balance in the Petty Cash account, supported by the fund (cash plus disbursement tickets) totalling the same amount *(p. 452).*

Internal control The organizational plan and all the related measures adopted by an entity to meet management's objectives of discharging statutory responsibilities, profitability, prevention and detection of fraud and error, safeguarding assets, reliability of accounting records, and timely preparation of reliable financial information *(p. 432).*

Nonsufficient funds (NSF) cheque A "bounced" cheque, one for which the maker's bank account has insufficient money to pay the cheque *(p. 444).*

Outstanding cheque A cheque issued by the company and recorded on its books but not yet paid by its bank *(p. 444).*

Petty cash A fund containing a small amount of cash that is used to pay minor expenditures *(p. 451).*

Petty cash ticket (voucher) A document indicating that money has been removed from the petty cash fund and a receipt is required to verify the expense *(p. 451).*

Phishing A method of gathering account numbers and passwords from people who visit legitimate-sounding bogus websites. The data gathered are then used for illicit purposes *(p. 437).*

Postdated cheques Cheques that are written for a future date *(p. 438).*

Remittance advice An optional attachment to a cheque that tells the payee the reason for payment *(p. 439).*

Sarbanes-Oxley Act American legislation that requires publicly-traded companies to review internal controls and take responsibility for the accuracy and completeness of their financial reports *(p. 433).*

Stale-dated cheques Cheques that are older than six months and need to be reissued *(p. 438).*

Timing difference A time lag in recording transactions *(p. 442).*

Treasurer The person in a company responsible for cash management *(p. 435).*

Treasury bill A financial instrument issued by the federal government that has a term of one year or less. It is sold at a discount and matures at par. The difference between the cost and maturity value is the purchaser's income *(p. 438).*

Trojan A computer virus that does not reproduce but gets included into program code without consent and performs actions that can be destructive *(p. 436).*

Void A business document marked void means that it is cancelled. Numbered documents should not be discarded but rather marked as void and kept in the files *(p. 436).*

SIMILAR TERMS

Cash receipts	Cash, cheques, and other negotiable instruments received
COSO	Committee of Sponsoring Organizations
CRIME	**C**ontrol procedures, **r**isk assessment, **i**nformation systems, **m**onitoring of controls, and **e**nvironment
C-SOX	Canadian-SOX Canadian internal control legislation (Bill 198)
EDI	Electronic Data Interchange
EFT	Electronic funds transfer
ERS	Evaluated Receipt Settlement
Invoice	Bill
NSF	Non-sufficient funds cheques, bounced cheques, rubber cheques, hot cheques
Separation of duties	Segregation of duties, division of duties
SOX	Sarbanes-Oxley Act

SELF-STUDY QUESTIONS

Test your understanding of the chapter by marking the correct answer for each of the following questions:

1. Janice Gould receives cash from customers. Her other assigned job is to post the collections to customer accounts receivable. Her company has weak *(p. 435)*
   a. Ethics
   b. Assignment of responsibilities
   c. Computer controls
   d. Separation of duties
2. What internal control function is performed by auditors? *(p. 435)*
   a. Objective opinion on the fair presentation of the financial statements
   b. Assurance that all transactions are accounted for correctly
   c. Communication of the results of the audit to regulatory agencies
   d. Guarantee that company employees have behaved ethically
3. Encryption *(p. 437)*
   a. Creates firewalls to protect data
   b. Cannot be broken by hackers
   c. Avoids the need for separation of duties
   d. Rearranges messages by a special process
4. The bank account serves as a control device over *(p. 438)*
   a. Cash receipts
   b. Cash payments
   c. Both of the above
   d. None of the above
5. Which of the following items appears on the bank side of a bank reconciliation? *(p. 442)*
   a. Book error
   b. Outstanding cheque
   c. NSF cheque
   d. Interest revenue earned on bank balance
6. Which of the following items appears on the book side of a bank reconciliation? *(p. 442)*
   a. Outstanding cheques
   b. Deposits in transit
   c. Both of the above
   d. None of the above
7. Which of the following reconciling items requires a journal entry on the books of the company? *(p. 444)*
   a. Book error
   b. Outstanding cheque
   c. NSF cheque
   d. Interest revenue earned on bank balance
   e. All of the above except (b)
   f. None of the above
8. The internal control feature that is specific to petty cash is *(p. 451)*
   a. Separation of duties
   b. Assignment of responsibility
   c. Proper authorization
   d. The imprest system
9. The petty cash fund had an initial balance of $100. It currently has $20 and petty cash tickets totalling $75 for office supplies. The entry to replenish the fund would contain a *(p. 452)*
   a. Credit to Cash Short and Over for $5.
   b. Credit to Petty Cash for $80.
   c. Debit to Cash Short and Over for $5.
   d. Debit to Petty Cash for $80.
10. Ethical judgments in accounting and business *(p. 453)*
    a. Require employees to break laws to get ahead
    b. Force decision makers to think about what is good and bad
    c. Always hurt someone
    d. Are affected by internal controls but not by external controls

Answers to Self-Study Questions

1. d 2. a 3. d 4. c 5. b 6. d 7. e 8. d 9. c 10. b

Assignment Material

MyLab Accounting Make the grade with MyLab Accounting: Most of the Starters, Exercises, and Problems can be found on MyLab. You can practise them as often as you want, and most feature step-by-step guided instructions to help you find the right answer.

QUESTIONS

1. Which of the features of effective internal control is the most fundamental? Why?
2. Which company employees bear primary responsibility for a company's financial statements and for maintaining the company's system of internal control? How do these individuals carry out this responsibility?
3. Identify at least seven procedures found in effective systems of internal control. What is one inherent limit/weakness of any internal control system?
4. Separation of duties may be divided into three parts. What are they?
5. What is an audit? Identify the two types of audit and the differences between them.
6. Why are documents and records a feature of internal control systems?
7. Suppose a company has six bank accounts, two petty cash funds, and three certificates of deposit that can be withdrawn on demand. How many cash amounts would this company likely report separately on its balance sheet?
8. Briefly state how each of the following serves as an internal control measure over cash: bank account, signature card, deposit slip, and bank statement.
9. What purpose does a bank reconciliation serve?
10. Why is it necessary to record journal entries after the bank reconciliation has been prepared? Which side of the bank reconciliation requires journal entries?
11. What role does a cash register play in an internal control system?
12. Describe internal control procedures for cash received by mail.
13. Discuss the specific characteristics of an effective internal control system for cash receipts over the counter.
14. What documents make up the payment packet? Describe three procedures that use the payment packet to ensure that each payment is appropriate.
15. What is Evaluated Receipt Settlement (ERS), and how does it streamline payment procedures?
16. Why should the same employee not account for cash payments, sign cheques, and mail the cheques to payees?
17. When are the only times the Petty Cash account is used in a journal entry?
18. What balance does the Petty Cash account have at all times? Does this balance always equal the amount of cash in the fund? When are the two amounts equal? When are they unequal?
19. Why should accountants adhere to a higher standard of ethical conduct than many other members of society do?
20. "Our managers know that they are expected to meet budgeted profit figures. We don't want excuses. We want results." Discuss the ethical implications of this policy.

STARTERS

S8–1 Internal controls are designed to safeguard assets; encourage employees to follow company policies; promote operational efficiency; provide accurate, reliable information; and ensure accurate records. Which objective mentioned must the internal controls accomplish for the business to survive? Give your reason.

(1) Definition of internal control

S8–2 How does the Dodd-Frank amendment of the Sarbanes-Oxley Act affect Canadian companies with regard to internal controls?

(1) Applying the definition of internal controls

S8–3 Explain in your own words why separation of duties is often described as the cornerstone of internal control for safeguarding assets. Describe what can happen if the same person has custody of an asset and also accounts for the asset.

(1) Applying the definition of internal controls

S8–4 How do external auditors differ from internal auditors? How does an external audit differ from an internal audit? How are the two types of audits similar?

(2) Characteristics of an effective system of internal control

② Analyzing internal controls

S8-5 Geoff works the late shift at Classic Movie Theatre. Occasionally Geoff must sell tickets *and* take the tickets as customers enter the theatre. Standard procedure requires that Geoff tear the tickets, give half to the customer, and keep the other half. To control cash receipts, the manager compares each night's cash receipts with the number of ticket stubs on hand.

a. How could Geoff take money from the theatre's cash receipts and hide the theft? What additional steps should the manager take to strengthen the internal control over cash receipts?

b. What is the internal control weakness in this situation? Explain the weakness.

c. What electronic device is often used at concerts and events to ensure legitimate tickets are presented by the patrons?

③ Aspects of a bank reconciliation

S8-6 Answer the following questions about the bank reconciliation:

1. Is the bank reconciliation a journal, a ledger, an account, or a financial statement? If it is none of these, what is it?
2. What is the difference between a bank statement and a bank reconciliation?

③ Aspects of a bank reconciliation

S8-7 Each of the items in the following list must be accounted for in the bank reconciliation. Next to each item, enter the appropriate letter from the following possible treatments: (a) bank side of reconciliation—add the item; (b) bank side of reconciliation—subtract the item; (c) book side of reconciliation—add the item; and (d) book side of reconciliation—subtract the item.

______ Outstanding cheque
______ NSF cheque
______ Bank service charge
______ Cost of printed cheques
______ EFT receipt
______ Bank error that decreased the bank balance
______ Deposit in transit
______ Bank collection
______ EFT payment
______ Customer cheque returned because of unauthorized signature
______ Book error that increased balance of Cash account

③ Calculating aspects of a bank reconciliation

S8-8 In the month of July, The Red Apple Co. wrote and recorded cheques in the amount of \$4,520. In August, the company wrote and recorded cheques in the amount of \$6,340. Of these cheques, \$3,760 were paid by the bank in July and \$2,580 were paid in August. What is the amount of the outstanding cheques at the end of July and at the end of August?

③ Preparing a bank reconciliation

Adjusted balance, \$6,200

S8-9 The Cash account of Hunter Security Systems reported a balance of \$4,960 at May 31, 2020. There were outstanding cheques totalling \$1,800 and a May 31 deposit in transit of \$400. The bank statement, which came from Royal Bank, listed a May 31 balance of \$7,600. Included in the bank balance was a collection of \$1,260 on account from Latha Vithanages, a Hunter customer who pays the bank directly. The bank statement also shows a \$40 service charge and \$20 of interest revenue that Hunter earned on its bank balance. Prepare Hunter's bank reconciliation at May 31, 2020.

③ Recording transactions from a bank reconciliation

S8-10 After preparing Hunter Security Systems' bank reconciliation in S8-9, journalize the company's transactions that arise from the bank reconciliation. Date each transaction May 31, 2020, and include an explanation with each entry.

④ Apply internal controls to cash receipts

S8-11 Caturday Afternoon sells cat and kitten supplies and food and handles all sales with a cash register. The cash register displays the amount of the sale. It also shows the cash received and any change returned to the customer. The register also produces a customer receipt but keeps no internal record of the transactions. At the end of the day, the clerk counts the cash in the register and gives it to the cashier for deposit in the company bank account.

1. Identify the internal control weakness over cash receipts.
2. What could the store do to correct the weakness?

S8–12 Francois sells furniture for Monet Furniture Company. He is having financial problems and takes $300 that he received from a customer. He recorded the sale through the cash register. What will alert Giles DuBois, the owner, that something is wrong?

(4) Control over cash receipts

S8–13 Shawn works in the purchasing department of Partha Distribution. He receives the goods that he purchased and also approves payment for the goods. How could he cheat his employer? How could Partha Distribution avoid this internal control weakness?

(4) Internal control over payments by cheque

S8–14 C9 Gaming Supplies started a petty cash fund on November 15, with a balance of $100. By November 27, it had $5 in cash and $95 in petty cash tickets. This included $55 of courier receipts, which they report as delivery expenses, and $40 of RONA receipts, which will be recorded as maintenance expenses. They recognized that the petty cash account was too small, so on December 1, it was increased to have a $300 balance.

Record the petty cash transactions. Explanations are not required.

(5) Petty cash transactions

S8–15 Record the following petty cash transactions of Lexite Laminated Surfaces in general journal form (explanations are not required):

Apr.	1	Established a petty cash fund with a $200 balance.
	30	The petty cash fund has $19 in cash and $187 in petty cash tickets that were issued to pay for office supplies ($117) and entertainment expenses ($70). Replenished the fund with $181 of cash and recorded the expenses.

(5) Petty cash not balancing

April 30, Credit Cash Short and Over for $6

S8–16 Angela Brennan, an accountant for Dublin Co., discovers that her supervisor, Barney Stone, made several errors last year. Overall, the errors overstated the company's net income by 15 percent. It is not clear whether the errors were deliberate or accidental. What should Brennan do?

(6) Making an ethical judgment

EXERCISES

E8–1 The 2017 annual report of Bank of Montreal, contained the following excerpt in the "Independent Auditors' Report of Registered Public Accounting Firm":

> We also have audited, in accordance with the standards of the Public Company Accounting Oversight Board (United States), the Bank's internal control over financial reporting as of October 31, 2017, based on the criteria established in Internal Control – Integrated Framework (2013) issued by the Committee of Sponsoring Organizations of the Treadway Commission (COSO), and our report dated December 5, 2017 expressed an unmodified (unqualified) opinion on the effectiveness of the Bank's internal control over financial reporting.

Why is this a requirement of a Canadian company?

(1) Internal control and COSO

E8–2 Yorkshire Bike Shop has a liberal return policy. A customer can return any product for a full refund within 14 days of purchase. When a customer returns merchandise, Yorkshire policy specifies the following:

- Store clerk issues a prenumbered return slip, refunds cash from the cash register, and keeps a copy of the return slip for review by the manager.
- Store clerk places the returned goods back on the shelf or on the floor as soon as possible.

Yorkshire uses a periodic inventory system.

(2) Identifying and correcting an internal control weakness

Required

1. How can a dishonest store clerk steal from Yorkshire? What part of company policy enables the store clerk to steal without getting caught?
2. How can Yorkshire improve its internal controls to prevent this theft?

(2) Correcting an internal control weakness

E8–3 Jonathan Todd Schwartz was a CPA who worked for GSO Business Management LLC. He was sent to prison for six years for embezzling millions of dollars from celebrities, including the Canadian singer-songwriter Alanis Morissette. Schwartz withdrew funds by reporting them as cash expenses and personally handled the cash. Client bank statements were sent to GSO, where he modified the information and then sent out financial statements to his clients.

What internal control weaknesses at GSO Business Management LLC allowed this to happen? How could the losses have been avoided?

(2) Identifying internal control strengths and weaknesses

E8–4 The following situations suggest either a strength or a weakness in internal control. Identify each as a *strength* or a *weakness* and give your reason for each answer.

a. Top managers delegate all internal control procedures to the accounting department.

b. The accounting department orders merchandise and approves invoices for payment.

c. Cash received over the counter is controlled by the clerk, who enters the sale and places the cash in the register. The clerk matches the total recorded by the register to each day's cash sales.

d. The vice-president, who signs cheques, assumes the accounting department has matched the invoice with other supporting documents and therefore does not examine the payment packet.

(2) Identifying internal controls

E8–5 Identify the missing internal control procedure in the following situations:

a. In the course of auditing the records of a company, you find that the same employee orders merchandise and approves invoices for payment.

b. Business is slow at the Vogue Theatre on Tuesday, Wednesday, and Thursday nights. To reduce expenses, the owner decides not to use a ticket taker on those nights. The ticket seller (cashier) is told to keep the tickets as a record of the number sold.

c. The same trusted employee has served as cashier for 10 years.

d. When business is brisk, Hasties Convenience Store deposits cash in the bank several times during the day. The manager at the convenience store wants to reduce the time employees spend delivering cash to the bank, so he starts a new policy. Cash will build up over weekends, and the total will be deposited on Monday.

e. Grocery stores such as No Frills purchase large quantities of their merchandise from a few suppliers. At one grocery store, the manager decides to reduce paperwork. He eliminates the requirement that a receiving department employee prepare a receiving report, which lists the quantities of items received from the supplier.

f. The treasurer of the Beta Soccer Association was elected for a third term to manage all the financial affairs of the club. The president and secretary have signing authority, so sound internal controls are in place.

g. A pancake breakfast is held every year to raise funds (over $10,000) for charity. The organizer's 15-year-old daughter is hired to sell tickets and handle the funds collected.

(2) Explaining the role of internal control

E8–6 The following questions pertain to internal control. Consider each situation separately.

1. Cali Company requires that all documents supporting a cheque be cancelled (stamped Paid) by the person who signs the cheque. Why do you think this practice is required? What might happen if it were not?
2. Separation of duties is an important consideration if a system of internal control is to be effective. Why is this so?
3. Cash may be a relatively small item on the financial statements. Nevertheless, internal control over cash is very important. Why is this true?
4. Many managers think that safeguarding assets is the most important objective of internal control systems, while auditors emphasize internal control's role in ensuring reliable accounting data. Explain why managers are more concerned about safeguarding assets and auditors are more concerned about the quality of the accounting records.

E8–7 Portal & Sons owns the following assets at the balance sheet date:

③ Cash and equivalents

Cash in bank—chequing account	$3,250
Treasury bills	3,000
Postdated cheques from customers	500
Cash in bank—savings account	5,000
Cash on hand in cash register	250
Cash refund due from Canada Revenue Agency	2,000

What amount of cash should be reported on the balance sheet?

E8–8 The following items could appear on a bank reconciliation:

③ Classifying bank reconciliation items

a. Outstanding cheques
b. Deposits in transit for current month
c. NSF cheque
d. Bank collection of a note receivable on the company's behalf
e. Bank credit memo for interest earned on bank balance
f. Bank debit memo for service charge
g. Book error: We credited Cash for $200. The correct credit was $2,000
h. Bank error: The bank decreased our account for a cheque written by another customer
i. Outstanding cheques from the previous month that are still outstanding
j. EFT payment by a customer
k. Bank error in recording a deposit for $464 should have been $446

Required

1. Classify each item as (1) an addition to the book balance, (2) a subtraction from the book balance, (3) an addition to the bank balance, or (4) a subtraction from the bank balance.
2. Indicate (a) the items that will result in an adjustment to the company's records, and (b) why the other items do not require an adjustment.

E8–9 Adams Enterprises began operations on January 2, 2020, depositing $40,000 in the bank. During this first month of business, the following transactions occurred that affected the Cash account in the general ledger:

③ Preparing a bank reconciliation

Adjusted balance, $14,560

Date	Description	Dr	Cr
Jan. 2	Deposit	$40,000	
5	Payment, cheque 001		$12,000
8	Payment, cheque 002		16,000
9	Cash sales	16,000	
15	Payment, cheque 003		10,000
18	Cash sales	12,000	
20	Bank loan	50,000	
26	Equipment purchase, cheque 004		74,000
30	Payment on account, cheque 005		17,000
31	Cash sales	25,600	

Shortly after the end of January the company received its first bank statement:

BANK STATEMENT FOR JANUARY 2020

Description	Withdrawals	Deposits	Date	Balance
Balance Forward			Jan01	0
Deposit		40,000	Jan02	40,000
Chq#001	12,000		Jan07	28,000
Deposit		16,000	Jan09	44,000
Chq#002	16,000		Jan13	28,000
Deposit		12,000	Jan18	40,000
Bank Loan		50,000	Jan20	90,000
Chq#004	74,000		Jan28	16,000
Deposit		2,000	Jan29	18,000
Service Charge	48		Jan31	17,952
Interest		8	Jan31	17,960
	102,048	120,008		

In preparing to do the bank reconciliation, Adams Enterprises noticed that the $2,000 deposit on January 29 was a bank error and informed the bank. The bank will correct the error on the next bank statement.

Required Prepare Adams Enterprises' bank reconciliation at January 31, 2020.

(3) Preparing a bank reconciliation

Adjusted balance $19,334

E8–10 Padilha Rental Company's general ledger Cash account showed the following transactions during October 2020:

Date	Description	Dr	Cr	Balance
Oct. 1	Opening balance			$ 2,800
2	Deposit	$20,000		22,800
5	Payment, cheque 233		$ 6,000	16,800
8	Payment, cheque 234		18,000	(1,200)
9	Deposit	18,000		16,800
15	Payment, cheque 235		5,000	11,800
18	Deposit	5,200		17,000
26	Payment, cheque 236		3,300	13,700
30	Payment, cheque 237		4,750	8,950
31	Deposit	10,500		19,450

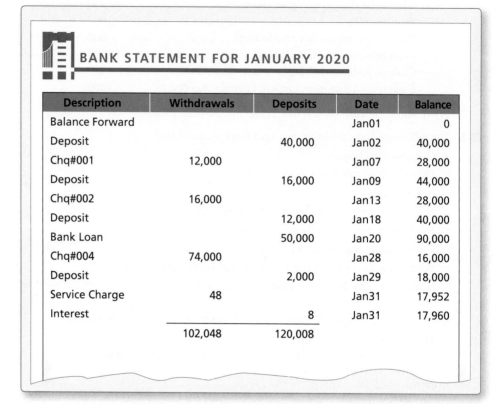

The bank statement for the month ending October 31, 2020, is shown below:

BANK STATEMENT FOR OCTOBER 2020

Description	Withdrawals	Deposits	Date	Balance
Balance Forward			Oct01	2,800
Deposit		20,000	Oct02	22,800
Chq#00233	6,000		Oct07	16,800
Deposit		18,000	Oct09	34,800
Chq#00234	18,000		Oct10	16,800
Deposit		5,200	Oct18	22,000
Chq#00235	5,000		Oct18	17,000
Service Charge	120		Oct31	16,880
Service Charge	120		Oct31	16,760
Interest		4	Oct31	16,764
	29,240	43,204		

Padilha Rental Company informed its bank that the bank charged a service charge twice. The bank has agreed to reverse one of the bank charges on the next month's bank statement.

Required Prepare Padilha Rental Company's bank reconciliation at October 31, 2020.

E8–11 Nate Nanzer's chequebook lists the entries shown here:

(3) Preparing a bank reconciliation

Adjusted balance, $17,356

Date	Cheque No.	Item	Cheque	Deposit	Balance
Jul. 1					$ 3,868
4	622	West Coast ESports	$ 208		3,660
9		Dividends received		$ 400	4,060
13	623	TELUS	304		3,756
14	624	Esso	276		3,480
18	625	Cash	268		3,212
26	626	Mastercard	132		3,080
28	627	Belfour Apartments	2,932		148
31		Paycheque		17,332	17,480

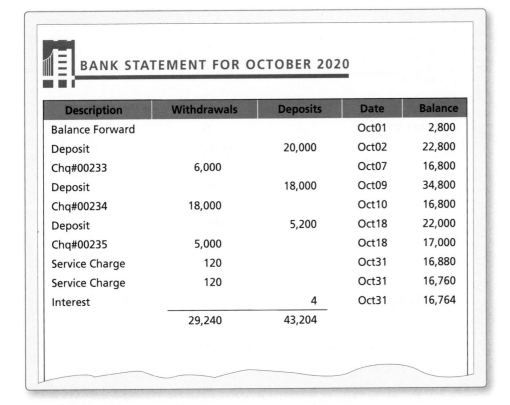

Nanzer's July bank statement is shown below:

BANK STATEMENT FOR JULY 2020

	No.	Amount	
Balance			$3,868
Add: Deposits			400
Subtract cheques:	No.	Amount	
	622	$ 208	
	623	304	
	624	316*	
	625	268	(1,096)
Other charges			
Printed cheques		$ 52	
Service charge		32	(84)
Balance			$3,088

*This is the correct amount of cheque number 624.

Required Prepare Nate Nanzer's bank reconciliation at July 31, 2020. How much cash does Nanzer actually have on July 31?

(3) Using a different bank statement format when preparing a reconciliation and preparing related journal entries

Adjusted balance, $4,070

E8–12 The Cash account of Baylor Associates at February 28, 2019, follows:

Cash

Beg. Bal.	3,995	400	Feb. 3
Feb. 6	800	3,100	Feb. 12
Feb. 15	1,800	1,100	Feb. 19
Feb. 23	1,100	500	Feb. 25
Feb. 28	2,400	900	Feb. 27
End. Bal.	4,095		

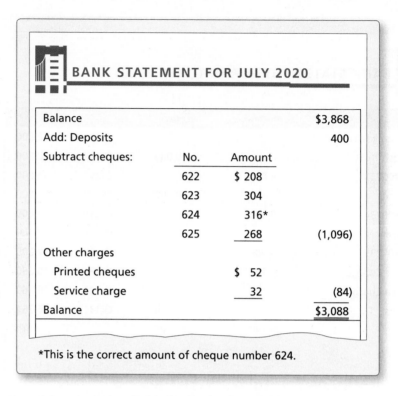

Baylor Associates received the following bank statement on February 28, 2019:

BANK STATEMENT

BANK OF TOMORROW
123 PETER PAN RD, WHISTLER, BC V0N 7X7

Baylor Associates
14 W Gadsden St
Garibaldi, BC V0N 9R9

CHEQUING ACCOUNT 136–213734
FEBRUARY 28, 2019

BEGINNING BALANCE	TOTAL DEPOSITS	TOTAL WITHDRAWALS	SERVICE CHARGES	ENDING BALANCE
$3,995	4,715	5,630	10	$3,070

TRANSACTIONS

DEPOSITS	DATE	AMOUNT
Deposit	02/07	800
Deposit	02/15	1,800
EFT—Collection of note	02/17	1,000
Deposit	02/24	1,100
Interest	02/28	15

CHARGES	DATE	AMOUNT
Service Charge	02/28	10

CHEQUES

Number	Amount	Number	Amount	Number	Amount
102	400	103	1,100		
101	3,100				

OTHER DEDUCTIONS	DATE	AMOUNT
EFT—EZ Rent	02/01	330
NSF Cheque	02/13	700

Additional data:

Baylor deposits all cash receipts in the bank and makes all payments by cheque.

Required

1. Prepare the bank reconciliation of Baylor Associates at February 28, 2019. Use the cheque date instead of a cheque number in your reconciliation.
2. Journalize the entries based on the bank reconciliation.

E8–13 In the months of February and March, Apex Ski Shop wrote and journalized cheques in the amount of $6,532 and $9,764, respectively. Of these cheques, $5,220 cleared the bank in February and $8,223 cleared the bank in March. What is the amount of outstanding cheques at the end of February and at the end of March?

(3) Following outstanding cheques over multiple months

E8–14 A jury convicted the treasurer of GTX Company of stealing cash from the company. Over a three-year period, the treasurer allegedly took almost $100,000 and attempted to cover the theft by manipulating the bank reconciliation.

(2) (3) Applying internal controls to the bank reconciliation

Required What is a likely way that a person would manipulate a bank reconciliation to cover a theft? What internal control arrangement could have avoided this theft?

E8–15 When you pay for goods at La Tienda Foods, the cash register displays the amount of the sale, the cash received, and any change returned to you. Suppose the register also produces a customer receipt but keeps no record of the sales transactions. At the end of the day, the clerk counts the cash in the register and gives it to the cashier for deposit in the company bank account.

(4) Evaluating internal control over cash receipts

Required Write a memo to Mia Francesca, the owner. Identify the internal control weakness over cash receipts, and explain how the weakness gives an employee the opportunity to steal cash. State how to prevent such a theft.

(4) Evaluating internal control over cash payments

E8–16 Gary's Motors purchases high-performance auto parts from a Winnipeg vendor. Joel Sieben, the accountant for Gary's, verifies receipt of merchandise and then prepares, signs, and mails the cheque to the vendor.

Required

1. Identify the internal control weakness over cash payments in this scenario.
2. What could the business do to correct the weakness?

(4) (5) Applying internal controls to cash payments, including petty cash transactions

E8–17 A-1 Machines is located in Saskatoon, Saskatchewan, with a sales territory covering the entire province.

The company has established a large petty cash fund to handle small cash payments and cash advances to the salespeople to cover frequent sales trips.

The controller, Margaret Hamm, has decided that two people (Anne Bloom and Tom Hurry) should be in charge of the fund since money is often needed when one person may be out for coffee or lunch. Hamm also feels this will increase internal control, as the work of one person will serve as a check on that of the other.

Regular small cash payments are handled by either Bloom or Hurry, who make the payment and have the person receiving the money sign a sheet of paper listing the date and reason for the payment. Whenever a salesperson requires an advance for a trip, he or she simply signs a receipt for the money received. The salespeople later submit receipts for the cost of the trip to either Bloom or Hurry to offset the cash advance.

Hamm is puzzled that the fund is almost always out of balance and either over or short.

Required Comment on the internal control procedures of A-1 Machines. Suggest changes that you think would improve the system.

(5) Apply internal controls to cash payments

E8–18 The petty cash fund had the following petty cash tickets:

Toner for a printer	$ 42
Freight to deliver goods sold	39
Freight on inventory purchased	112
Miscellaneous expense	10
Postage expense	25
	$228

Assume that the business has established a petty cash fund in the amount of $250 and that the amount of cash in the fund at the time of replenishment is $20. The business uses a perpetual inventory system.

Prepare the entry to replenish the fund on February 28.

(5) Petty cash, cash short and over

E8–19 Record the following selected transactions of Kelly's Organics in general journal format (explanations are not required):

Jun.	1	Established a petty cash fund with a $200 balance.
	2	Journalized the day's cash sales. Cash register tapes show a $4,875 total, but the cash in the register is $4,885.
	10	The petty cash fund had $56.50 in cash and $134.00 in petty cash tickets issued to pay for office supplies ($21.00), delivery expenses ($69.50), and entertainment expenses ($43.50). Replenished the fund.

(5) Control over petty cash
3. Petty Cash balance, $300

E8–20 1. Explain how an *imprest* petty cash system works.

2. Atlantic Press maintains an imprest petty cash fund of $300, which is under the control of Gladys Yu. At November 30, the fund holds $80 cash and petty cash tickets for $140 of office supplies and $100 of delivery expenses.

   Journalize (a) the establishment of the petty cash fund on November 1 and (b) the replenishment of the fund on November 30.

3. Prepare a T-account for Petty Cash and post to the account. What is Petty Cash's balance at all times?

E8–21 Maritime Distributors created a $500 imprest petty cash fund on September 7 with the expectation that when the balance reached below $100, it would be replenished. During the first few weeks of use, the fund custodian authorized and signed petty cash tickets as shown below.

(5) Accounting for petty cash

Date	Ticket No.	Item	Account Debited	Amount
Sep. 8	1	Delivery of flyers to customers	Delivery Expense	$228.80
Sep. 22	2	Stamp purchase	Postage Expense	85.98
Sep. 29	3	Newsletter	Supplies Expense	60.40
Oct. 3	4	Key to closet	Miscellaneous Expense	9.52
Oct. 13	5	Staples	Supplies Expense	14.72

Required Make general journal entries to (a) create the petty cash fund and (b) record its replenishment at October 15. Cash in the fund totals $97.58. Include explanations.

E8–22 Refer to the Maritime Distributors petty cash fund data in E8–21. Suppose, one month later, on November 15, the company decided to decrease the petty cash fund by $100 due to theft and break-ins in the area. Journalize the decrease in the petty cash fund.

(5) Accounting for petty cash

E8–23 You have a part-time job in a local coffee shop, which is part of a chain of cafés. You received the job through your parents' friendship with Tina Presley, the coffee shop manager. The job is going well, but you are puzzled by the actions of Tina and her husband, Sean. Each day, one or both of them fills takeout orders and takes them to Tina's office. Later you notice Sean and Tina enjoying the takeout orders, sometimes with friends. You know the orders were not rung through the checkout counter. When you ask a co-worker about the practice, you are told that Tina is the boss and can do as she wishes, and besides, many employees help themselves to meals.

(6) Evaluating the ethics of conduct by a manager

Required Apply the decision guidelines for ethical judgments outlined in the box on page 454 to decide whether a manager of a coffee shop should help herself or himself to meals on a regular basis and not pay for what she or he takes.

USING EXCEL

E8–24 Download an Excel template for this problem online in MyLab Accounting. Lori Anders of Wilderness Associates is getting ready to prepare the October bank reconciliation.

(3) Using Excel for a Bank Reconciliation

The cash balance on the books of Wilderness Associates on October 31 is $3,546. Lori reviews the bank statement and notes the cash balance at October 31 of $2,445. The bank statement also reveals that the bank collected a note receivable on behalf of Wilderness Associates—the principal was $1,500 and the interest was $15. One customer's cheque for $29 was returned by the bank for insufficient funds. Two additional items on the bank statement were the monthly EFT for the utilities, $250, and the bank service fee of $12. Lori notes that the cash deposit made on October 31 of $3,300 does not appear on the statement and that three cheques totalling $975 had not cleared the bank account when the bank statement was prepared.

Required

1. Prepare the bank reconciliation for Wilderness Associates at October 31, 2018 using Excel. Format appropriate cells with dollar signs, underlines, and double underlines. Use formulas to calculate subtotals and totals.
2. Journalize the entries based on the bank reconciliation. For dollar amounts, use cell references on the bank reconciliation.

Excel Skills

1. Use Excel's data validation to enter descriptions into the bank reconciliation and accounts into the journal entries.
2. Format cells using borders and number formatting.
3. Use formulas to calculate subtotals and totals.

SERIAL EXERCISE

(3) Prepare bank reconciliation and journal entries
Adjusted Bank Balance $14, 315

E8-25 *The Serial Exercise involves a company that will be revisited throughout relevant chapters in Volume 1 and Volume 2. You can complete the Serial Exercises using MyLab Accounting.*

This exercise continues recordkeeping for the Canyon Canoe Company. You can do this question even if you have not completed prior questions from this series.

Canyon Canoe Company has decided to open a new chequing account at River Nations Bank during March 2021. Canyon Canoe Company's March Cash T-account for the new cash account from its general ledger is as follows:

Cash—River Nations Bank Chequing Account

Mar.	1	Bal.	0	200	Mar.	2	Chq#101
	2	Deposit	10,000	4,300		4	Chq#102
	13	Deposit	2,325	750		9	Chq#103
	20	Deposit	2,750	1,675		14	Chq#104
	27	Deposit	4,500	1,500		21	Chq#105
	31	Deposit	3,490	175		28	Chq#106
				300		30	Chq#107
		Bal.	14,165				

(3) Prepare bank reconciliation and journal entries

Canyon Canoe Company's bank statement dated March 31, 2021, follows:

BANK STATEMENT FOR MARCH 2021

Beginning balance, March 1, 2021		$ 0
Deposits and other credits		
Mar. 2	$10,000	
14	2,325	
21	2,750	
28	4,500	
29 EFT Sport Shirts(1)	500	
31 Interest Revenue	45	20,120
Cheques and other debits		
Mar. 2 EFT to Bank Cheques(2)	55	
3 Chq#101	200	
6 Chq#102	4,300	
15 Chq#104	1,675	
16 Chq#103	750	
28 EFT to Rivers Energy(3)	270	
29 Chq#106	175	
31 Bank service charge	70	(7,495)
Ending balance, March 31, 2021		$ 12,625

(1) Sport Shirts is a customer making a payment on account.
(2) Bank Cheques is a company that prints business cheques (Use the Bank Charges Expense account.)
(3) Rivers Energy is a utility provider.

Required

1. Prepare the bank reconciliation at March 31, 2021.
2. Journalize any transactions required from the bank reconciliation.
3. Compute the adjusted account balance for the Cash T-account, and denote the balance as *Bal*. Does the adjusted balance of the Cash T-account match the adjusted book balance on the bank reconciliation?

PRACTICE SET

E8–26 *This problem continues the Crystal Clear Cleaning practise set begun in Chapter 2 and continued through Chapter 9.*

(3) Preparing a bank reconciliation and journal entries

In March 2020, Crystal Clear Cleaning opened a new chequing account at First Provincial Bank. The bank statement dated March 31, 2020, for Crystal Clear Cleaning follows:

BANK STATEMENT

MARCH 1, 2020

BEGINNING BALANCE	TOTAL DEPOSITS	TOTAL WITHDRAWALS	SERVICE CHARGES	ENDING BALANCE
$0	103,300	9,240	25	$94,035

TRANSACTIONS

DEPOSITS	DATE	AMOUNT
Deposit	03/02	33,000
Deposit	03/10	900
Deposit	03/18	19,000
Deposit	03/20	50,000
EFT Peg's Restaurant(1)	03/23	350
Interest Revenue	03/31	50

CHARGES	DATE	AMOUNT
Service Charge	03/31	25

CHEQUES

Number	Amount	Number	Amount	Number	Amount
235	2,400	236	2,900	240	300
237	1,500	239	2,000		

OTHER DEDUCTIONS	DATE	AMOUNT
EFT to Cheque Art(2)	03/02	10
EFT to Canadian Energy(3)	03/28	130

(1) Peg's Restaurant is a customer making a payment on account.

(2) Cheque Art is a company that prints business cheques (considered a bank charges expense) for Crystal Clear Cleaning.

(3) Canadian Energy is a utility provider.

Crystal Clear Cleaning's Cash account in the general ledger shows the following transactions for March:

Cash—First Provincial Bank Chequing Account

Balance		0				
Mar. 2	Deposit	33,000	2,400	Mar. 2	Chq#235
10	Deposit	900	2,900	4	Chq#236
18	Deposit	19,000	1,500	5	Chq#237
20	Deposit	50,000	400	10	Chq#238
31	Deposit	1,770	2,000	21	Chq#239
			300	23	Chq#240
			300	29	Chq#241
Balance		94,870			

Required

1. Prepare the bank reconciliation at March 31, 2020.
2. Journalize any required entries from the bank reconciliation. Post to the Cash T-account to verify the balance of the account matches the adjusted book balance from the bank reconciliation.

CHALLENGE EXERCISES

(2) (3)
Bank reconciliation, detecting theft, and internal controls

E8–27 Winfray Co. records all cash receipts on the basis of its cash register tapes. Winfray Co. discovered during January 2020 that one of its sales clerks had stolen an undetermined amount of cash receipts when she took the daily deposits to the bank. The following data have been gathered for January:

Note collection	$ 2,500
Bank service charges	80
Interest earned	500
Outstanding cheques as of January 31, 2020	6,450
Cash in the bank per the general ledger account	31,000
Cash according to the January 31, 2020, bank statement	36,938

There were no outstanding deposits on January 31, 2020.

Required

1. Determine the amount of cash receipts stolen by the sales clerk.
2. What accounting controls would have prevented or detected this theft?

(3)
Assessing outstanding cheques
1. Sep. 30, $2,338

E8–28 The accounting records of Abacus Supplies showed the following:

Outstanding cheques:

- The July 31 bank reconciliation reported outstanding cheques of $489. In the month of August, the Abacus accounting records showed that cheques in the Amount of $14,089 were written. Total cheques that cleared the bank according to the bank statement were $13,089 in August.
- In September, cash payments from the accounting records were $19,349 and the total cheques that cleared the bank were $18,500.

Outstanding deposits:

- The July 31 bank reconciliation reported that deposits outstanding totalled $889. In August, the cash account (according to the ledger) showed deposits of $18,322, but the bank statement listed the total deposits of $17,322.
- In September, the bank statement listed deposits of $16,766 and the deposits recorded in the cash receipts journal totalled $15,667.

Required

1. What was the amount of outstanding cheques at August 31 and at September 30?
2. What was the amount of outstanding deposits at August 31 and at September 30?

BEYOND THE NUMBERS

BN8–1

(1) (4) Correcting an internal control weakness

Theta Construction Company, headquartered in Calgary, built a Roadway Inn in High River, 64 kilometres south of Calgary. The construction foreman, whose name was Slim, moved into High River in March to hire the 40 workers needed to complete the project. Slim hired the construction workers, had them fill out the necessary tax forms, and sent the employment documents to the home office, which opened a payroll file for each employee.

Work on the motel began on April 1 and ended September 1. Each Thursday evening Slim filled out an electronic time card that listed the hours worked by each employee during the five-day workweek that ended at 5:00 p.m. on Thursday. Slim emailed the time sheets to the home office, which prepared the payroll cheques on Friday morning. A courier delivered the payroll cheques to Slim, and at 5:00 p.m. on Friday he distributed the payroll cheques to the workers.

Required

1. Describe in detail the internal control weakness in this situation. Specify what negative result(s) could occur because of the internal control weakness.
2. Describe what you would do to correct the internal control weakness.

ETHICAL ISSUE

EI8–1

Arjun Samji owns apartment buildings in Ontario. Each property has a manager who collects rent, arranges for repairs, and runs advertisements in the local newspaper. The property managers transfer cash to Samji monthly and prepare their own bank reconciliations.

The manager in Hamilton has been stealing large sums of money. To cover the theft, she understates the amount of outstanding cheques on the monthly bank reconciliation. As a result, each monthly bank reconciliation appears to balance. However, the balance sheet reports more cash than Samji actually has in the bank. In negotiating the sale of the Hamilton property, Samji is showing the balance sheet to prospective investors.

Required

1. Identify two parties other than Samji who can be harmed by this theft. In what ways can they be harmed?
2. Discuss the role accounting plays in this situation.

PROBLEMS (GROUP A)

(1) Define internal control

P8–1A An employee of Ellerback Event Planning recently stole thousands of dollars of the company's cash. The company has decided to install a new system of internal controls.

Required As controller of Ellerback Event Planning, write a memo to the owner, Nick Flewelling, explaining what internal controls are and how they can benefit the company.

(1) (2) Identifying the procedures found in an effective internal control system

P8–2A Use the information in P8–1A to explain how separation of duties helps to safeguard assets.

2
Identifying internal control weaknesses

P8–3A Each of the following situations has an internal control weakness:

a. Syspro Software Associates sells accounting software. Recently, the development of a new software program stopped while the programmers redesigned Syspro Software Associates' accounting system. Syspro Software Associates' own accountants could have performed this task.

b. Judy Sloan has been your trusted employee for 30 years. She performs all cash-handling and accounting duties. She has just purchased a new Lexus and a new home in an expensive suburb. As the owner of the company, you wonder how she can afford these luxuries because you pay her $35,000 per year and she has no sources of outside income.

c. Sanchez Hardwoods Ltd., a private corporation, falsified sales and inventory figures to get a large loan. The company prepared its own financial statements. The company received the loan but later went bankrupt and couldn't repay the loan.

d. The office supply company from which The Family Shoe Store purchases sales receipts recently notified Family that the last shipped receipts were not prenumbered. Louise Bourseault, the owner of Family, replied that she never uses the receipt numbers, so the omission is not important.

e. Discount stores such as Dollar Mart make most of their sales for cash, with the remainder in debit card and credit card sales. To reduce expenses, one store manager ceases purchasing fidelity bonds on the cashiers.

Required

1. Identify the missing internal control procedure in each situation.
2. Identify the potential problem that could be caused by each control weakness.
3. Propose a solution to each internal control problem.

3
Using the bank reconciliation as a control device
1. Adjusted balance, $28,060

P8–4A The cash receipts and the cash payments of Spinners Bowling for November 2020 are as follows:

Cash Receipts

Date	Cash Debit
Nov. 5	$ 3,436
7	470
13	1,723
15	1,065
19	441
24	10,875
30	2,598
Total	$20,608

Cash Payments

Cheque No.	Cash Credit
1221	$ 1,819
1222	1,144
1223	429
1224	111
1225	816
1226	109
1227	4,468
1228	998
1229	330
1230	2,724
Total	$12,948

The Cash account of Spinners Bowling shows a balance of $26,983 on November 30, 2020. Outstanding amounts from the previous month's bank reconciliation were cheque number 1219 for $500, cheque number 1218 for $400, and an October 31 deposit in the amount of $2,000. On December 3, 2020, Spinners Bowling received this bank statement:

BANK STATEMENT FOR NOVEMBER 2020

Description	Withdrawals	Deposits	Date	Balance
Balance Forward			Nov01	18,223
Deposit		2,000	Nov01	20,223
EFT Rent Collection		880	Nov01	21,103
Deposit		3,436	Nov06	24,539
NSF Cheque	433		Nov08	24,106
Chq#001221	1,819		Nov09	22,287
Deposit		470	Nov10	22,757
Chq#001222	1,144		Nov13	21,613
Chq#001223	429		Nov14	21,184
Deposit		1,723	Nov14	22,907
Chq#001224	111		Nov15	22,796
Deposit		1,065	Nov15	23,861
EFT Insurance	275		Nov19	23,586
Deposit		441	Nov20	24,027
Chq#001225	816		Nov22	23,211
Deposit		10,875	Nov25	34,086
Chq#001226	109		Nov29	33,977
Chq#001227	4,968		Nov30	29,009
Bank Collection		1,430	Nov30	30,439
Chq#001219	500		Nov30	29,939
Service Charge	25		Nov30	29,914
	10,629	22,320		

Explanations: EFT—electronic funds transfer, NSF—nonsufficient funds

Additional data for the bank reconciliation is as follows:

a. The EFT deposit was a receipt of monthly rent. The EFT debit was payment for monthly insurance.

b. The NSF cheque was received late in October from a customer.

c. The $1,430 bank collection of a note receivable on November 30 included $100 interest revenue.

d. The correct amount of cheque number 1227, a payment on account, is $4,968. (Spinners Bowling's accountant mistakenly recorded the cheque for $4,468.)

Required

1. Prepare the bank reconciliation of Spinners Bowling at November 30, 2020.
2. Describe how a bank account and the bank reconciliation help Spinners Bowling's managers control the business's cash.
3. How are outstanding items from the previous month's bank reconciliation that clear on the November bank statement dealt with?

P8–5A Spottify Electronics had a computer failure on October 1, 2020, that resulted in the loss of data, including the balance of its Cash account and its bank reconciliation from September 30, 2020. The accountant, Crisanto Danila, has been able to obtain the following information from the records of the company and its bank:

a. An examination showed that two cheques (#244 for $305.00 and #266 for $632.50) had not been cashed as of October 1. Danila recalled that there was only one

(3)

Preparing a bank reconciliation and related journal entries

1. Adjusted balance, $7,714.00

deposit in transit on the September 30 bank reconciliation but was unable to recall the amount.

b. The cash receipts and cash payments journals contained the following entries for October 2020:

Cash Receipts
Amounts
$ 908.50
1,748.00
3,726.00
1,975.00
736.00
$ 9,093.50

Cash Payments	
Cheque No.	**Amount**
275	$ 310.50
276	448.50
277	466.90
278	811.90
279	577.30
280	3,886.90
281	void
282	488.50
283	1,058.00
	$8,048.50

c. The company's bank provided the following statement as of October 31, 2020:

BANK STATEMENT FOR OCTOBER 2020

Date	Cheques and Other Debits		Deposits and Other Credits		Balance
Oct. 1	#276	448.50		2,346.00	6,520.50
2	#266	632.50			5,888.00
5	#277	466.90			5,421.10
8				908.50	6,329.60
14	#275	310.50		1,196.00	7,215.10
17	EFT	529.00			6,686.10
19			EFT	414.00	7,100.10
22	#279	577.30		1,748.00	8,270.80
22	#280	3,976.90	EFT	1,196.00	5,489.90
24			EFT	471.50	5,961.40
27	NSF	805.00		3,726.00	8,882.40
28	SC	20.00			8,862.40
31	#283	1,058.00		1,975.00	9,779.40

d. The deposit made on October 14 was for the collection of a note receivable ($1,100.00) plus interest.

e. The electronic funds transfers (EFTs) had not yet been recorded by Spottify Electronics because the bank statement was the first notification of them.

- The October 17 EFT was for the monthly payment on an insurance policy for Spottify Electronics.
- The October 19 and 24 EFTs were collections on accounts receivable.
- The October 22 EFT was in error—the transfer should have been to the Spottify Horse Farm.

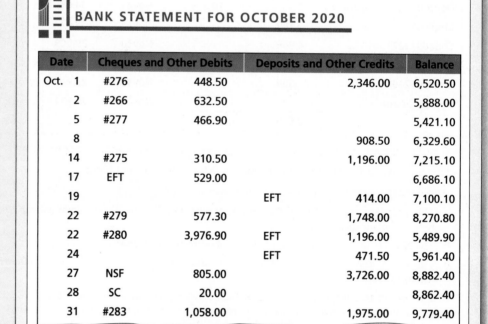

f. The NSF cheque on October 27 was received from a customer as payment for electronics purchased for $805.00.

g. Cheque #280 was correctly written for $3,976.90 for the purchase of inventory (assume a periodic system) but incorrectly recorded by the cash payments clerk.

Required

1. Prepare a bank reconciliation as of October 31, 2020, including the calculation of the book balance of October 31, 2020.
2. Prepare all journal entries that would be required by the bank reconciliation. No explanations are needed.

P8–6A The December cash records of Davidson Insurance follow:

(5) Preparing a bank reconciliation and journal entries

1. Adjusted Balance $18,025

Cash Receipts	
Date	**Cash Debit**
Dec. 4	$4,240
9	550
14	600
17	1,900
31	1,860

Cash Payments	
Cheque No.	**Cash Credit**
1416	$ 810
1417	180
1418	630
1419	1,390
1420	1,490
1421	700
1422	600

Davidson's Cash account shows a balance of $17,450 at December 31.

On December 31, Davidson Insurance received the following bank statement:

BANK STATEMENT FOR DECEMBER

BEGINNING BALANCE	TOTAL DEPOSITS	TOTAL WITHDRAWALS	SERVICE CHARGES	ENDING BALANCE
$14,100	9,040	4,175	10	$18,955

TRANSACTIONS

DEPOSITS	DATE	AMOUNT
EFT	12/01	350
Deposit	12/05	4,240
Deposit	12/10	550
Deposit	12/15	600
Deposit	12/18	1,900
BC	12/22	1,400

CHARGES	DATE	AMOUNT
Service Charge	12/31	10

CHEQUES

Number	Amount	Number	Amount	Number	Amount
1416	810	1418	630		
1417	180	1419	1,930		

OTHER DEDUCTIONS	DATE	AMOUNT
NSF	12/08	400
EFT	12/19	225

Explanations: BC–bank collection; EFT–electronic funds transfer; NSF–nonsufficient funds cheques; SC–service charge

Additional data for the bank reconciliation follow:

a. The EFT credit was a receipt of rent. The EFT debit was an insurance payment.

b. The NSF cheque was received from a customer.

c. The $1,400 bank collection (BC) was for a note receivable.

d. The correct amount of cheque #1419, for rent expense, is $1,930. Davidson's controller mistakenly recorded the cheque for $1,390.

Required

1. Prepare the bank reconciliation of Davidson Insurance at December 31, 2020.
2. Journalize any required entries from the bank reconciliation.

(3) Preparing a bank reconciliation and related journal entries
1. Adjusted balance, $36,242

P8–7A The October 31, 2020, bank statement of Jazzera Distributors has just arrived. To prepare Jazzera Distributors' bank reconciliation, you gather the following data:

a. The October 31 bank balance is $38,212.

b. The bank statement includes two deductions for NSF cheques from customers. One was for $168 and the other was for $370.

c. The following Jazzera Distributors' cheques are outstanding at October 31:

Cheque No.	Amount
312	$1,098
522	1,086
534	114
539	112
540	416
541	894

d. A few customers pay their accounts by EFT. The October bank statement lists a $12,732 deposit against customer accounts.

e. The bank statement includes two special deposits: $1,766, which is the amount of GST refund (GST Receivable), the bank received on behalf of Jazzera Distributorsand $160, the interest revenue Jazzera earned on its bank balance during October.

f. Jazzera's owner wrote a cheque for $818 for the purchase of auction equipment items. The cheque was processed by the bank, but the owner did not notify his accounting staff until they discovered the blank cheque stub, so the cheque was not recorded until after October 31.

g. On October 31, the company deposited $932, but this deposit does not appear on the bank statement.

h. The bank statement includes an $818 deduction for a cheque drawn by Jazz Communications. Jazzera promptly notified the bank of its error.

i. The bank statement lists a $132 subtraction for the bank service charge.

j. Jazzera's Cash account shows a balance of $23,072 on October 31.

Required

1. Prepare the bank reconciliation for Jazzera Distributors at October 31, 2020.
2. Record in general journal form the entries necessary to bring the book balance of Cash into agreement with the adjusted book balance on the reconciliation. Include an explanation for each entry.

(4) Identifying internal control weakness in cash receipts

P8–8A Calibre Interiors makes all sales on credit. Cash receipts arrive by mail, usually within 30 days of sale. Sarah Romano opens envelopes and separates the cheques from the accompanying remittance advices. Romano forwards the cheques to another employee, who makes the daily bank deposit but has no access to the accounting records. Romano sends the remittance advices, which show the amount of cash received, to the accounting department for entry in the accounts. Her only other duty is to grant sales allowances to customers. (Recall that a *sales allowance* decreases the amount that the customer must pay.) When she receives a customer cheque for less than the full amount of the invoice, she records the sales allowance and forwards the document to the accounting department.

Required You are a new management employee of Calibre Interiors. Write a memo to the company president, Mary Briscoll, identifying the internal control weakness in this situation. State how to correct the weakness.

P8–9A Suppose that, on June 4, Devine Design creates a petty cash fund with an imprest balance of $400. During June, Lucie Chao, the fund custodian, signs the following petty cash tickets:

(5) Accounting for petty cash transactions

2. Fund should hold $23.50

Date	Ticket No.	Item	Amount
Jun. 6	101	Office supplies	$ 26.64
9	102	Cab fare for executive	60.00
12	103	Delivery of package across town	29.32
19	104	Dinner money for sales manager entertaining a customer	133.34
26	105	Office supplies	127.20

On June 30, prior to replenishment, the fund contains these tickets plus $34.40. The accounts affected by petty cash payments are Office Supplies Expense, Travel Expense, Delivery Expense, and Entertainment Expense.

Required

1. Explain the characteristics and internal control features of an imprest fund.
2. On June 30, how much cash should the petty cash fund hold before it is replenished?
3. Make general journal entries to (a) create the fund and (b) replenish it. Include explanations.
4. Make the July 1 entry to increase the fund balance to $500. Include an explanation, and briefly describe what the custodian does in this case.

P8–10A Jennifer Black, CPA, is the controller of Arc Industries, a large manufacturing company. Company president, Allen Arc, informed Jennifer that if the company failed to report a "healthy bottom line" this year the bank would turn down its application for a $1,000,000 loan. The company has suffered losses for the past two years, and current economic conditions have caused a downturn in demand for the company's product. Arc suggested that Jennifer use "creative accounting" if necessary to ensure the company reported a profit. As a reward Jennifer would receive a substantial year-end bonus. If you were Jennifer, how would you respond to the president?

(6) Making ethical business judgments

PROBLEMS (GROUP B)

P8–1B Kyanoga Real Estate prospered during the past 10 years. Business was so good that the company bothered with few internal controls. The recent decline in the local real estate market, however, has caused Kyanoga to experience a shortage of cash. John Flannigan, the company owner, is looking for ways to save money.

(1) Define internal control

Required As controller of the company, write a memorandum to convince John Flannigan of the company's need for a good system of internal control. Include the definition of internal control, and briefly discuss key internal control objectives.

(2) Identifying the procedures found in an effective internal control system

P8–2B Using the information from P8–1B, briefly discuss the internal control procedures, beginning with hiring competent, reliable, and ethical personnel.

2 Identifying internal control weaknesses

P8–3B Each of the following situations has an internal control weakness:

a. Upside-Down Applications develops custom programs to customers' specifications. Recently, development of a new program stopped while the programmers redesigned Upside-Down's accounting system. Upside-Down's accountants could have performed this task.

b. Norma Rottler has been your trusted employee for 24 years. She performs all cash-handling and accounting duties. Ms. Rottler just purchased a new Lexus and a new home in an expensive suburb. As owner of the company, you wonder how she can afford these luxuries because you pay her only $30,000 a year and she has no source of outside income.

c. Izzie Hardwoods, a private company, falsified sales and inventory figures in order to get an important loan. The loan went through, but Izzie later went bankrupt and could not repay the bank.

d. The office supply company where Pet Grooming Goods purchases sales receipts recently notified Pet Grooming Goods that its documents were not prenumbered. Howard Mustro, the owner, replied that he never uses receipt numbers.

e. Discount stores such as Cusco make most of their sales in cash, with the remainder in credit card sales. To reduce expenses, one store manager ceases purchasing fidelity bonds on the cashiers.

f. Cornelius's Corndogs keeps all cash receipts in a shoebox for a week because Cornelius likes to go to the bank on Tuesdays when another employee can watch the store for him.

Required

1. Identify the missing internal control procedure in each situation.
2. Identify the problem that could be caused by each control weakness.
3. Propose a solution to each internal control problem.

3 Using the bank reconciliation as a control device

P8–4B The cash receipts and the cash payments of Ace Hardware for January 2020 are as follows:

Cash Receipts	
Date	**Cash Debit**
Jan. 3	$20,988
8	1,480
10	1,980
16	7,788
22	20,736
29	2,404
31	1,428
Total	$56,804

Cash Payments	
Cheque No.	**Cash Credit**
311	$ 3,672
312	1,668
313	12,562
314	2,584
315	8,588
316	3,900
317	1,304
318	6,268
319	800
320	12,664
Total	$54,010

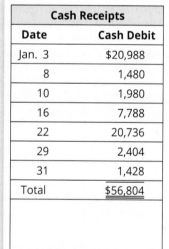

The Cash account of Ace Hardware shows a balance of $39,478 at January 31, 2020.

Ace Hardware received the following bank statement on January 31, 2020:

BANK STATEMENT FOR JANUARY 2020

Description	Withdrawals	Deposits	Date	Balance
Balance Forward			Jan01	36,684
EFT Dividend Collection		1,052	Jan01	37,736
Deposit		20,988	Jan04	58,724
Chq#00311	3,672		Jan07	55,052
Deposit		1,480	Jan09	56,532
Deposit		1,980	Jan12	58,512
Chq#00313	12,436		Jan13	46,076
NSF Cheque	3,456		Jan14	42,620
Chq#00312	1,668		Jan15	40,952
Deposit		7,788	Jan17	48,740
Chq#00314	2,584		Jan18	46,156
EFT Insurance	1,316		Jan21	44,840
Bank Collection		12,744	Jan22	57,584
Deposit		20,736	Jan23	78,320
Chq#00315	8,588		Jan26	69,732
Chq#00316	3,900		Jan30	65,832
Service Charge	40		Jan31	65,792
	37,660	66,768		

Additional data for the bank reconciliation:

a. The EFT deposit was a receipt of monthly rent. The EFT debit was payment of monthly insurance.

b. The NSF cheque was received from A. Levine.

c. The $12,744 bank collection of a note receivable on January 22 included $200 interest revenue.

d. The correct amount of cheque number 313, a payment on account, is $12,436. (Ace Hardware's accountant mistakenly recorded the cheque for $12,562.)

Required

1. Prepare the Ace Hardware bank reconciliation at January 31, 2020.
2. Describe how a bank account and the bank reconciliation help Ace Hardware's owner control the business's cash.
3. How would you handle items that were outstanding (bank side) from the previous month's bank reconciliation?

P8–5B Excel Communications had a computer failure on August 1, 2020, which resulted in the loss of data, including the balance of its Cash account and its bank reconciliation from July 31, 2020. The accountant, Brad Eyers, has been able to obtain the following information from the records of the company and its bank:

(3) Preparing a bank reconciliation and related journal entries

a. An examination showed that two cheques (#461 for $645.00 and #492 for $225.00) had not been cashed as of August 1. Eyers recalled that there was only one deposit in transit on the July 31 bank reconciliation but was unable to recall the amount.

b. The cash receipts and cash payments journal contained the following entries for August 2020:

Cash Receipts	Cash Payments	
Amounts	Cheque #	Amount
$ 876.00	499	$ 678.00
1,230.00	500	651.00
1,545.00	501	2,578.50
612.00	502	846.00
2,460.00	503	327.00
$6,723.00	504	820.00
	505	void
	506	314.00
	507	543.00
		$6,757.50

c. The bank provided the following statement as of August 31, 2020:

BANK STATEMENT FOR AUGUST 2020

Date	Cheques and Other Debits		Deposits and Other Credits		Balance
Aug. 1	#500	651.00		660.00	3,579.00
3	#492	225.00			3,354.00
5	#501	2,578.50			775.50
8				876.00	1,651.50
16	#499	678.00		585.00	1,558.50
17	EFT	442.50			1,116.00
19			EFT	720.00	1,836.00
21	#503	327.00		1,230.00	2,739.00
22	#504	860.00	EFT	336.50	2,215.50
24			EFT	471.00	2,686.50
26	NSF	1,792.50		1,545.00	2,439.00
27	SC	37.50			2,401.50
31	#507	543.00		612.00	2,470.50

d. The deposit made on August 16 was for the collection of a note receivable ($540.00) plus interest.

e. The EFTs had not yet been recorded by Excel Communications since the bank statement was the first notification of them.
   - The August 17 EFT was for the monthly payment on an insurance policy for Excel Communications.
   - The August 19 and 24 EFTs were collections on accounts receivable.
   - The August 22 EFT was in error—the transfer should have been to Accel Communications.

f. The NSF cheque on August 26 was received from a customer as payment of $1,792.50 for installation of a satellite purchased from Excel.

g. Cheque #504 was correctly written for $860.00 for the purchase of inventory (assume a perpetual system) but incorrectly recorded by the cash payments clerk.

Required

1. Prepare a bank reconciliation as of August 31, 2020, including the calculation of the book balance of August 31, 2020.
2. Prepare all journal entries that would be required by the bank reconciliation. Explanations are not required.

(5) Preparing a bank reconciliation and journal entries

P8–6B The May cash records of Donald Insurance follow:

Cash Receipts	
Date	**Cash Debit**
May 4	$ 4,230
9	520
14	530
17	1,950
31	1,840

Cash Payments	
Cheque No.	**Cash Credit**
1416	$ 890
1417	120
1418	630
1419	1,090
1420	1,420
1421	900
1422	670

Donald's Cash account shows a balance of $17,750 at May 31.

On May 31, Donald Insurance received the following bank statement:

BANK STATEMENT FOR MAY

BEGINNING BALANCE	TOTAL DEPOSITS	TOTAL WITHDRAWALS	SERVICE CHARGES	ENDING BALANCE
$14,400	9,380	5,015	35	$18,730

TRANSACTIONS

DEPOSITS	DATE	AMOUNT
EFT	05/01	450
Deposit	05/05	4,230
Deposit	05/10	520
Deposit	05/15	530
Deposit	05/18	1,950
BC	05/22	1,700

CHARGES	DATE	AMOUNT
Service Charge	05/31	35

CHEQUES

Number	Amount	Number	Amount	Number	Amount
1416	890	1418	630		
1417	120	1419	1,900		

OTHER DEDUCTIONS	DATE	AMOUNT
NSF	05/08	1,100
EFT	05/19	375

Explanations: BC–bank collection; EFT–electronic funds transfer; NSF–nonsufficient funds cheques; SC–service charge

Additional data for the bank reconciliation follow:

a. The EFT credit was a receipt of rent. The EFT debit was an insurance payment.

b. The NSF cheque was received from a customer.

c. The $1,700 bank collection (BC) was for a note receivable.

d. The correct amount of cheque no. 1419, for rent expense, is $1,900. Donald's controller mistakenly recorded the cheque for $1,090.

Required

1. Prepare the bank reconciliation of Donald Insurance at May 31, 2020.
2. Journalize any required entries from the bank reconciliation.

③ Preparing a bank reconciliation and the related journal entries

P8–7B The June 30, 2020, bank statement of Copps Shoes has just arrived from the bank. To prepare the Copps Shoes bank reconciliation, you gather the following data:

a. The Copps Shoes Cash account shows a balance of $39,518 on June 30.

b. The bank statement includes two charges for returned cheques from customers. One is a $3,558 cheque received from Trinity Western and deposited on June 20, returned by Trinity Western's bank with the imprint "Unauthorized Signature." The other is an NSF cheque in the amount of $988 received from Mavis Jones. This cheque had been deposited on June 17.

c. Copps Shoes pays rent ($5,650), utilities ($2,000), and cellphone charges ($120) each month by EFT.

d. The following Copps Shoes' cheques are outstanding at June 30:

Cheque No.	Amount
291	$ 306
322	1,074
327	4,312
329	82
330	3,096
331	432
332	1,860

e. The bank statement includes a deposit of $11,466, collected by the bank on behalf of Copps Shoes. Of the total, $11,208 is collection of a note receivable and the remainder is interest revenue.

f. The bank statement shows that Copps Shoes earned $26 in interest on its bank balance during June. This amount was added to Copps Shoes' account by the bank.

g. The bank statement lists a $144 subtraction for the bank service charge.

h. On June 30, the Copps Shoes accountant deposited $3,378, but this deposit does not appear on the bank statement.

i. The bank statement includes a $4,200 deposit that Copps Shoes did not make. The bank had erroneously credited the Copps Shoes' account for another bank customer's deposit.

j. The June 30 bank balance is $50,534.

Required

1. Prepare the bank reconciliation for Copps Shoes at June 30, 2020.
2. Record in general journal form the entries that bring the book balance of Cash into agreement with the adjusted book balance on the reconciliation. Include an explanation for each entry.

④ Identifying internal control weaknesses in cash receipts

P8–8B Inno Bakery makes all sales of its bread to retailers on account. Cash receipts arrive by mail, usually within 30 days of the sale. Gary Cho opens envelopes and separates the cheques from the accompanying remittance advices. Cho forwards the cheques to another employee, who makes the daily bank deposit but has no access to the accounting records. Cho sends the remittance advices, which show the amount of cash received, to the accounting department for entry in the accounts. Cho's only other duty is to grant sales allowances to customers. (Recall that a *sales allowance* decreases the amount that the customer must pay.) When he receives a customer cheque for less than the full amount of the invoice, he records the sales allowance and forwards the document to the accounting department.

Required You are the new controller of Inno Bakery. Write a memo to the company president, John Senick, identifying the internal control weakness in this situation. State how to correct the weakness.

P8–9B Suppose that on September 1, Stellar Sundials opens a new showroom in Napanee, Ontario, and creates a petty cash fund with an imprest balance of $400. During September, Lisa Manfield, the fund custodian, signs the petty cash tickets shown below:

5 Accounting for petty cash transactions

Date	Ticket No.	Item	Amount
Sep. 4	1	Courier for package received	$ 49.67
18	2	Refreshments for showroom opening	101.00
21	3	Computer disks	88.07
22	4	Office supplies	7.50
28	5	Dinner for sales manager entertaining a customer	87.50

On September 30, prior to replenishment, the fund contains these tickets plus $61.34. The accounts affected by petty cash payments are Office Supplies Expense, Entertainment Expense, and Delivery Expense.

Required

1. Explain the characteristics and the internal control features of an imprest fund.
2. On September 30, how much cash should this petty cash fund hold before it is replenished?
3. Make the general journal entries to (a) create the fund and (b) replenish it. Include explanations.
4. Due to the risk of robbery, make the entry on October 1 to decrease the fund balance to $300. Include an explanation.

P8–10B Hans Bozzell is a vice-president of the Western Bank in Markham, Ontario. Active in community affairs, Bozzell serves on the board of directors of Orson Tool & Dye. Orson is expanding rapidly and is considering relocating its factory. At a recent meeting, board members decided to try to buy 20 hectares of land on the edge of town. The owner of the property is Sherri Fallon, a customer of Western Bank. Fallon is a recent widow. Bozzell knows that Fallon is eager to sell her local property. In view of Fallon's anguished condition, Bozzell believes she would accept almost any offer for the land. Realtors have appraised the property at $4 million.

6 Making an ethical judgment

Required Apply the ethical judgment framework outlined in the box on page 454 to help Bozzell decide what his role should be in Orson's attempt to buy the land from Fallon.

CHALLENGE PROBLEMS

P8–1C
- "Effective internal control must begin with top management."
- "The 'tone at the top' is a necessary condition if an organization is to have an effective system of internal control."

1 Management's role in internal control

Statements such as these are becoming a more important part of internal control literature and thought.

The chapter lists a number of characteristics that are important for an effective system of internal control. Many of these characteristics have been part of the internal control literature for years.

Required Explain why you think a commitment to good internal control by top management is fundamental to an effective system of internal control.

(4) (5)

Applying internal controls to cash payments, including petty cash transactions

P8–2C MEI Distributors is located in Moncton, New Brunswick, with a sales territory covering the Maritime provinces and Newfoundland. Employees live in New Brunswick and all report to work at the company's offices in Moncton.

The company has established a large petty cash fund to handle cash payments and cash advances to its salespeople to cover trips to and from New Brunswick on sales calls.

The controller, Jelisa Valji, has decided that two people (Sarah Wong and Martha Dekinder) should be in charge of the petty cash fund, since money is often needed when one person is out of the office. Valji also feels this will increase internal control, because the work of one person will serve as a check on that of the other.

Regular small cash payments are handled by either Wong or Dekinder, who make the payment and have the person receiving the money sign a sheet of paper giving the date and reason for the payment. Whenever a salesperson requires an advance for a sales trip, that person simply signs a receipt for the money received. The salesperson later submits receipts covering the costs incurred to either Wong or Dekinder to offset the cash advance.

Valji, a family friend as well as the controller, doesn't think the system is working and, knowing you are studying accounting, has asked for your advice.

Required Write a memo to Valji commenting on the internal control procedures of MEI. Suggest changes that you think would improve the system.

Extending Your Knowledge

DECISION PROBLEM

(3)

Using the bank reconciliation to detect a theft

Adjusted bank balance, $12,200

IT Solutions has poor internal control over cash. Recently Sanjay Gupda, the owner, has suspected the cashier of stealing. Details of the business's cash position at April 30, 2020, follow:

a. The Cash account in the ledger shows a balance of $12,900.

b. The April 30 bank statement shows a balance of $8,600. The bank statement lists a $400 credit for a bank collection, a $20 debit for the service charge, and an $80 debit for an NSF cheque. C. J. Ellis, the IT Solutions accountant, has not recorded any of these items on the books.

c. At April 30 the following cheques are outstanding:

Cheque No.	Amount
402	$ 200
527	600
531	1,200
561	400

d. There is a $6,000 deposit in transit at April 30, 2020.

e. Cindy Bing, the cashier, handles all incoming cash and makes bank deposits. She also writes cheques and reconciles the monthly bank statement.

Gupda asks you to determine whether Bing has stolen cash from the business and, if so, how much. Perform a bank reconciliation. There are no bank or book errors. Gupda also asks you to evaluate the internal controls and recommend any changes needed to improve them.

FINANCIAL STATEMENT CASES

FSC8–1

① ④
Audit opinion, management responsibility, internal controls, and cash

6. Decreased by $86,050,000

Review Indigo Books and Music Inc.'s (Indigo's) 2017 annual report, given in Appendix A at the end of this book and on MyLab Accounting. Answer the following questions about Indigo's internal controls and cash position:

1. What is the name of Indigo's outside auditing firm? What is the date of the annual report? Who is the chief executive officer (CEO) of Indigo Books and Music Inc.?
2. Who bears primary responsibility for the financial statements? How can you tell?
3. Who bears primary responsibility for internal controls?
4. Examine the independent auditor's report. What standard of auditing did the outside auditors use in examining Indigo's financial statements? By what accounting standards were the statements evaluated?
5. What are cash equivalents? Where do you find detailed information about cash and cash equivalents in the 2017 annual report?
6. By how much did Indigo's cash and cash equivalents change during fiscal 2017?

FSC8–2

① ④
Audit opinion, management responsibility, internal controls, and cash

Study the "Report of independent registered public accounting firm" in the TELUS annual report given on MyLab Accounting and answer the following questions about TELUS's internal controls and cash position:

1. What is the name of TELUS's outside auditing firm? What office of this firm signed the auditor's report? How long after TELUS's year end did the auditors issue their opinion?
2. Who bears responsibility for the financial statements? How can you tell?
3. Does the auditor guarantee that internal controls are effective? Explain.
4. What standard of auditing did the outside auditors use in examining TELUS's financial statements? By what accounting standards were the statements evaluated?
5. By how much did TELUS's cash and temporary investments balance change during 2016?

Try It! Solutions for Chapter 8

1. Sarbanes-Oxley Act – d
   Phishing – f
   Internal control – a
   Encryption – c
   Separation of duties – e
   Internal auditors – b
   computer virus – h
   Trojan – i
   Firewall – g
2. A number of problems can result when a sales clerk can also grant credit approval and record the sales in addition to handling the cash. The clerk could grant credit approval to friends and others who do not meet the credit standards; the clerk could also steal merchandise and hide the theft in the accounting records. In addition, the clerk could fail to do all three jobs well and make mistakes or forget to perform a task when the sales floor is busy.
3. The three items that can appear on the bank side of a bank reconciliation are deposits in transit, outstanding cheques, and corrections of bank errors. The company does *not* need to record the reconciling items that appear on the bank side of the bank reconciliation because those items have already been recorded on the company books or are errors of the bank that should not be entered on the company books.
4. a.

JONAS COMPANY Bank Reconciliation July 31, 2020	
Bank	
Bank balance, July 31, 2020	$ 9,000
Add: Deposits in transit	2,400
	$11,400
Less: Outstanding cheques	1,150
Adjusted bank balance	**$10,250**
Books	
Book balance, July 31, 2020	$10,843
Add: Interest revenue earned	10
Correction of book error—overstated a cheque	27
	$10,880
Less: Bank charges	30
NSF cheque	600
Adjusted book balance	**$10,250**

b. Journal entries to update the company's books:

Cash	10	
Interest Revenue		10
To record interest earned during July 2020.		

Cash	27	
Accounts Payable		27
To correct a cheque recorded as $152 that should have been recorded as $125($152 − $125 = $27).		

Bank Charges Expense	30	
Cash		30
To record bank service charge for July 2020.		

Accounts Receivable	600	
Cash		600
To reinstate the account receivable for an NSF cheque.		

5. When cash is received by mail, a mailroom employee cannot pocket a customer cheque and destroy the remittance advice because the customer will notify the company. If a customer gets a statement from the company listing the invoice and amount a second time, the customer can show the paid cheque to prove that he or she has already paid. That would indicate that the company has a dishonest employee.
6. The journal entry for the day's sales would be:

Cash	7,262	
Sales Revenue		7,252
Cash Short and Over		10
To record the day's sales, along with the cash overage.		

7. The internal control feature in this scenario is proper authorization. Two signatures are required to ensure that no unauthorized expenditures are made. Presigning the cheques defeats the control and should be discouraged.
8. a. The three internal control weaknesses are
   - Petty cash ticket no. 3 is missing. There is no indication of what happened to this ticket. The company should investigate.
   - The petty cash custodian (JCB) did not sign petty cash ticket no. 2. This omission may have been an oversight on his part. However, it raises the question of whether he authorized the payment. Both the fund custodian and the recipient of the cash should sign the ticket.
   - Petty cash ticket no. 4 does not indicate which account to debit and presumably has no receipt attached. What did Tate do with the money, and what account should be debited? At worst, the funds have been stolen. At best, asking the custodian to reconstruct the transaction from memory is haphazard. Since we are instructed in requirement (b) to assume petty cash ticket no. 4 was issued for the purchase of office supplies, debit Office Supplies.

   A fourth control weakness is that, after only one week, the fund is already short $8. This implies a lack of control over petty cash disbursements.

   While it is not specifically asked for in this question, always check for the following when reviewing a petty cash fund:

   - Ensure the cash in the fund plus the total of all petty cash ticket amounts equal the opening balance of the petty cash fund ($300 in this case).

- Sequence all petty cash tickets by their ticket number and ensure all ticket numbers in the sequence are accounted for.
- Ensure all transaction details are filled in on each petty cash ticket and that receipts are attached.
- Ensure the fund custodian signs each petty cash ticket.
- Investigate any significant cash short and over amounts.

b. Petty cash journal entries

i. Entry to establish the petty cash fund:

Jan. 1	Petty Cash	300	
	Cash		300
	To open the petty cash fund.		

This journal entry is only made once, when the petty cash fund is created. Funds are transferred from one Cash account to another Cash account.

ii. Entry to replenish the fund:

Jun. 30	Office Supplies	57	
	Delivery Expense	39	
	Travel Expense	33	
	Cash Short and Over	8	
	Cash		137
	To replenish the petty cash fund.		

Ensure the cash in the fund ($163) plus the total of all petty cash ticket amounts ($129) equal the opening balance of the petty cash fund ($300). If the total is less than $300, the fund is short. If the total is greater than $300, the fund is over.

9. Each step of the framework for making ethical judgments is answered below for David Duncan's situation:
   1. *Determine the facts.* The facts are given in the situation description.
   2. *Identify the ethical issues.* Duncan's ethical dilemma is to decide what he should do with the information he has uncovered.
   3. *Specify the alternatives.* For Duncan, the alternatives include (a) go along with Axiom's liabilities as reported (i.e., do nothing), or (b) force Axiom's management to report liabilities at more correct amounts.
   4. *Identify the stakeholders.* Individuals who could be affected include Duncan, the partners and staff of his auditing firm, the management and employees at Axiom, Axiom's investors, Axiom's creditors, the federal and various provincial governments.
   5. *Assess the possible outcomes of each alternative.*
      a. If Duncan certifies Axiom's present level of liabilities—and if no one ever objects—Duncan will keep this valuable client. But if Axiom's actual liabilities turn out to be higher than reported, Axiom's investors and creditors may lose money and take Duncan to court. That would damage his reputation as an auditor and hurt his firm.
      b. If Duncan follows the policy suggestion of his company, he must force Axiom to increase its reported liabilities. That will anger Axiom, and Duncan and his firm may get fired as Axiom's auditor. In this case Duncan will save his reputation, but it will cost him and his firm business in the short run.
   6. *Make a decision.* In the end, Duncan went along with Axiom and certified Axiom's liabilities. He went directly against his firm's policies. Axiom later admitted understating its liabilities, Duncan had to retract his audit opinion, and Duncan's firm collapsed soon after. Duncan should have followed company policy. Rarely is one person smarter than a team of experts. Not following company policy cost him and many others dearly.

9 Receivables

CONNECTING CHAPTER 9

LEARNING OBJECTIVES

The **Summary** for Chapter 9 appears on pages 516–517.

Key terms with definitions for this chapter's material appears on page 518.

CPA competencies

This text covers material outlined in **Section 1: Financial Reporting of the CPA Competency Map.** The Learning Objectives for each chapter have been aligned with the CPA Competency Map to ensure the best coverage possible.

1.1.2 Evaluates the appropriateness of the basis of financial reporting

1.2.2 Evaluates treatment for routine transactions

1.4.2 Evaluates financial statements including note disclosure

Pierre Rochon photography/Alamy Stock Photo

Rogers Communications Inc. is one of Canada's largest communications companies. It owns radio and television stations, magazines, cable and wireless businesses, the Rogers Centre in Toronto, a portion of the Toronto Blue Jays baseball team, and other Canadian businesses.

You may recognize this company because you might receive monthly cellphone bills from Rogers or one of its subsidiaries, such as Fido or Chatr. When a person signs up for a cellphone contract, their credit history is evaluated to see if they are likely to pay their bills. The credit department at Fido decides which customers are allowed to have an account.

While a company like Rogers does its best to carefully choose customers, it recognizes that not all customers pay their bills. Why doesn't Rogers ask all customers to prepay their accounts? Sales increase when people are allowed to pay later. But if they eventually don't pay, this creates a loss for the business.

To keep the accounting records accurate, Rogers has to make an estimate of how much they might not get paid. According to the Rogers's 2017 annual report, which includes all of their businesses and not just the wireless division, they estimated that they might not get paid $61 million of accounts receivable. This chapter will look at how all businesses estimate potential bad debts and report different types of receivables.

As Rogers Communications' business grows, so do its revenues and receivables. This chapter builds on what you have already learned about receivables and introduces more specific transactions related to this type of account to answer such questions as "What if customers don't pay?" and "How do we account for longer-term receivables?"

Receivables: An Introduction

LO 1

What are receivables, and how are they reported on the balance sheet?

A **receivable** arises when a business (or person) sells goods or services to another party on credit. The receivable is the seller's claim for the amount of the transaction. A receivable also arises when one person or business lends money to another. Each credit transaction involves at least two parties:

- The **creditor**, who sells something and obtains a receivable, which is an asset
- The **debtor**, who makes the purchase and has a payable, which is a liability

This chapter focuses on accounting for receivables by the seller (the creditor).

Types of Receivables

The three major types of receivables are:

- Accounts receivable
- Notes receivable
- Other receivables

Accounts Receivable Accounts receivable, also called *trade receivables*, are amounts to be collected from customers. Accounts receivable are *current assets* because they are typically collected within 30 to 60 days.

Selling on credit (on account) creates an account receivable. The related journal entries (amounts and the perpetual method are assumed) are as follows:

Service Company			
Feb. 4	Accounts Receivable—Sullivan Company	10,000	
	Service Revenue		10,000
	Performed service on account.		

Merchandiser			
Feb. 4	Accounts Receivable—Sullivan Company	10,000	
	Sales Revenue		10,000
	Sold goods on account.		
Feb. 4	Cost of Goods Sold	4,000	
	Inventory		4,000
	Cost of goods sold on account.		

The business collects cash for most receivables and makes this entry:

Feb. 27	Cash	10,000	
	Accounts Receivable—Sullivan Company		10,000
	Collected cash on account.		

Note that we now include the name of the company next to the Accounts Receivable account title. This is so we can better track who owes the money. In addition, the general ledger balance is now supported by a *subsidiary ledger* that lists the amount receivable from each customer.

The Accounts Receivable account in the general ledger serves as a *control account* because it summarizes the total of the receivables from all customers. At March 1, the balances would be shown as follows:

GENERAL LEDGER

Accounts Receivable

Bal.	13,000	

ACCOUNTS RECEIVABLE SUBSIDIARY LEDGER

Aston

Bal.	5,000	

Harris

Bal.	8,000	

Sullivan Company

Bal.	0	

Total $13,000

Notes Receivable *Notes receivable* are more formal than accounts receivable. The debtor promises in writing to pay the creditor a definite sum at a definite future date. A written document known as a *promissory note* serves as the evidence of the receivable. Notes receivable due within one year, or one operating cycle if longer than one year, are current assets. Notes due beyond one year are classified as long-term assets. These accounts usually have interest charged on their balances. This is explained in greater detail later in this chapter.

Other Receivables *Other receivables* is a miscellaneous category that includes any other type of receivable where there is a right to receive cash in the future. It may include loans to employees or owners (called *shareholder loans* if the business is a corporation), taxes receivable, or interest receivable. When they are long-term receivables, the portion that is due within one year or less is classified as a current asset. Receivables can be reported as shown in Exhibit 9–1, where they are bolded for emphasis (amounts assumed).

EXHIBIT 9–1 | Receivables on the Balance Sheet

EXAMPLE COMPANY Balance Sheet (partial)—Assets Section Date		
Assets		
Current assets		
Cash		$ 1,000
Accounts receivable	**$20,000**	
Less: Allowance for doubtful accounts	**1,500**	**18,500**
Notes receivable, short-term		**5,000**
Inventories		7,000
Prepaid expenses		1,500
Total current assets		33,000
Investments and long-term receivables		
Investments	6,000	
Notes receivable, long-term	**16,000**	
Other receivables	**4,000**	
Total non-current assets		26,000
Property, plant, and equipment, net		15,000
Total assets		$74,000

Note: If there is a credit balance for any customers, it is reported as a liability.

This new account reflects "what might not get paid."

This balance could also include the short-term portion of long-term receivables.

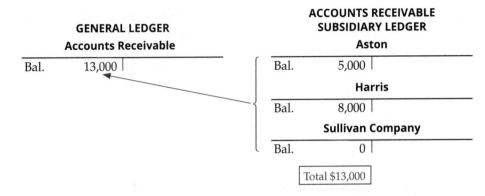

Accounting for Uncollectible Accounts

LO 2

Why would companies estimate their uncollectible accounts receivable, and how could they do that?

Selling on credit provides both a benefit and a cost to the selling company.

- *The benefit:* The business increases sales revenues and profits by making sales to a wide range of customers. Customers can buy now but pay later.
- *The cost:* The company will be unable to collect from some customers, and that creates an expense. The expense is called **bad debt expense**, **uncollectible account expense**, or **doubtful account expense**. Bad-debt expense is an operating expense, the same as salaries expense and amortization expense.

There is no single indicator that an account has become delinquent and will not be paid. Some clues would be:

- Receivable is past due
- Customer does not respond to company calls or attempts to collect
- Customer files for bankruptcy
- Company finds out that the business has closed
- The customer has left town or cannot be located

Accounts receivable are essentially interest-free loans to the buyer because the seller does not receive the cash to use in the business. Some sellers charge late fees to offset the costs of these interest-free loans.

Bad debt expense varies from company to company. The older the receivable, the less valuable it is because of the decreasing likelihood of collection. If a customer doesn't pay and there is a chance of recovering some or all of the balance, then the receivable can be turned over to a collection agency. If the customer doesn't pay and there is no chance any amount will be received, then the balance would be worthless.

How do companies account for these uncollectible accounts? They use the allowance method or, in certain limited cases, the direct write-off method. We begin the next section with the allowance method because it is required when reporting under ASPE.

The Allowance Method

The amount of the allowance depends on the volume of credit sales, industry norms, the effectiveness of the credit department, and the diligence of the collection department.

Most companies use the **allowance method** to measure bad debts. The key concept is to record bad debt expense in the same period as the sales revenue, which is an application of the *matching objective*. The business doesn't wait to see which customers will not pay. Instead, it records bad debt expense on the basis of estimates developed from past experience or professional judgment.

The business records bad debt expense for the estimated amount and sets up **Allowance for Doubtful Accounts** (or **Allowance for Uncollectible Accounts**), a contra account to Accounts Receivable. The allowance is the amount of receivables that the business expects *not* to collect. Subtracting the allowance from Accounts Receivable yields the net amount that the company does expect to collect, as shown in the following partial balance sheet (using assumed numbers):

Accounts receivable	$10,000	◄ Customers owe this amount.
Less: Allowance for doubtful accounts	900	◄ The company estimates it will not collect this amount.
Accounts receivable, net	$ 9,100	◄ This is what the company thinks it will actually get paid.

In this example, $9,100 is the **net realizable value (NRV)** of the accounts receivable.

Companies may also choose to present their information this way:

Accounts receivable	$10,000	
Allowance for doubtful accounts	(900)	$9,100

Many Canadian companies do not provide information on their gross receivables and allowance for doubtful accounts; rather, they simply report the net receivable. They sometimes report the details in the notes to the financial statements.

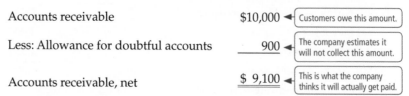

Rogers Communication Inc. presented the following information about their accounts receivable on the balance sheet of their 2016 annual report:

As at December 31 (in millions of dollars)	Note	2016	2015
Accounts receivable	14	1,949	1,792

In the notes to the financial statement, it provides this additional information:

As at December 31 (In millions of dollars)	2016	2015
Customer accounts receivable	1,455	1,329
Other accounts receivable	553	549
Allowance for doubtful accounts	(59)	(86)
Total accounts receivable	1,949	1,792

Estimating Uncollectibles

How are bad debts estimated? Companies base estimates on their past experience. There are three ways to estimate uncollectibles:

- Percent-of-sales method
- Aging-of-accounts-receivable method
- Percent-of-accounts-receivable method

The three approaches all normally require an adjusting entry at the end of the period.

Percent-of-Sales Method The **percent-of-sales method** computes bad debt expense as a percentage of net credit sales. This method is called an **income statement approach** because the estimate is based on credit sales for the period (an income-statement figure). Assume it is December 31, 2020, and the accounts have these balances *before the year-end adjustments*:

Accounts Receivable		Allowance for Doubtful Accounts	
100,000			1,000

Based on prior experience, the company's bad debt expense is 2 percent of net credit sales, which were $500,000 in 2020.

Percent-of-Sales Method:
Bad Debt Expense = Net credit sales × estimated%

The adjusting entry to record bad debt expense for 2020 and to update the allowance is:

2020			
Dec. 31	Bad Debt Expense	10,000	
	Allowance for Doubtful Accounts		10,000
	To record bad debt expense for the year ($500,000 × 0.02).		

After posting, the accounts are ready for reporting on the 2020 balance sheet.

Accounts Receivable		Allowance for Doubtful Accounts	
100,000			1,000
		Adj.	10,000
		Bal.	11,000

Net accounts receivable, $89,000

Now the allowance for doubtful accounts is realistic. The balance sheet will report accounts receivable at the net amount of $89,000 ($100,000 − $11,000). The income statement will report the estimated bad debt expense of $10,000, along with revenue and other operating expenses for the period.

Aging-of-Accounts-Receivable Method Another method for estimating uncollectible accounts is the **aging-of-accounts-receivable method**. This method is called a **balance sheet approach** because it focuses on accounts receivable, a balance sheet account.

In the aging-of-accounts-receivable method, the company groups each customer account (Baring Tools Co., etc.) according to how long amounts due have been outstanding. All accounting software offers reports that can sort customer accounts by age. Exhibit 9–2 shows an aging schedule with the calculation of the expected amount of doubtful accounts. Notice that the percentage uncollectible increases as a customer account gets older.

EXHIBIT 9–2 | Accounts Receivable Aging Schedule, December 31, 2020

	A	B	C	D	E	F
1		Age of Accounts Receivable				
2	**Customer Name**	**1–30 Days**	**31–60 Days**	**61–90 Days**	**Over 90 Days**	**Total**
3	Baring Tools Co.	$20,000				$ 20,000
4	Calgary Drills Ltd.	10,000				10,000
5	Red Deer Pipe Corp.		$3,000	$ 5,000		8,000
6	Seal Coatings Inc.			9,000	$ 900	9,900
7	Other accounts*	30,000	2,000	12,000	8,100	52,100
8	Totals	$60,000	$5,000	$26,000	$ 9,000	$100,000
9						
10	Estimated percent uncollectible	× 1%	× 2%	× 5%	× 90%	
11	Allowance for Doubtful Accounts	$ 600	$ 100	$ 1,300	$ 8,100	$ 10,100

*Each of the "Other accounts" would appear individually.

1. Target balance

Customers owe the company $100,000, but the company expects *not* to collect $10,100 of this amount.

How the Aging-of-Accounts-Receivable Method Works The aging-of-accounts-receivable method starts with a calculation of what the credit balance of the allowance account needs to be—$10,100 in this case. Because we started with a balance of $1,000 in this account from a previous period, we need to *update* it to the new balance that we calculated in Exhibit 9–2.

The longer an account is outstanding, the less chance there is of collection. Even if a past-due account is collected in full, there is a cost associated with collecting an account late.

Allowance for Doubtful Accounts

		1,000
	Adj.	9,100
	Bal.	10,100

Step 2: The bad debt expense adjusting entry amount must be calculated: $10,100 − $1,000 = $9,100

Step 1: Calculate the target balance (what you calculated from the aging schedule), which is "what the balance should be."

To adjust the allowance, the company makes this adjusting entry at the end of the period:

2020			
Dec. 31	Bad Debt Expense	9,100	
	Allowance for Doubtful Accounts		9,100
	To update the Allowance account to its target balance ($10,100 − $1,000) and record bad debt expense for the period.		

2. Journalize the adjustment

After posting, the accounts are ready for reporting on the balance sheet at net realizable value ($89,900) because that is the amount the company expects to realize, or collect in cash.

Accounts Receivable		Allowance for Doubtful Accounts	
100,000			1,000
			Adj. 9,100
			Bal. 10,100

Net accounts receivable, $89,900

The income statement reports the bad debt expense—in this case, $9,100.

Percent-of-Accounts-Receivable Method Another balance sheet–based method of determining the allowance for doubtful accounts is the **percent-of-accounts-receivable method**. This method is similar to the aging-of-accounts-receivable method; companies can determine what the credit balance of the Allowance account needs to be by calculating it as a percent of the Accounts Receivable balance.

Percent-of-Accounts-Receivable Method:

Target Allowance Balance = Accounts Receivable Balance × estimated %

Bad Debts Expense = Target Allowance Balance − Actual Allowance Balance

For example, assume Accounts Receivable are $100,000 and Allowance for Doubtful Accounts has a credit balance of $1,000 at December 31, 2020, *before the year-end adjustment*. Based on experience, the company determines that the allowance should be 5 percent of Accounts Receivable, or $5,000. This is the target balance. The adjusting entry is calculated as follows:

Allowance for Doubtful Accounts	
	1,000
	Adj. 4,000
	Bal. 5,000

Step 2: The bad debt expense adjusting entry amount must be calculated: $5,000 − $1,000 = $4,000

Step 1: Calculate the target balance as a percentage of the total receivable balance outstanding. In this case it is $100,000 × .05 = $5,000

To adjust the allowance, the company makes this adjusting entry at the end of the period:

2020			
Dec. 31	Bad Debt Expense	4,000	
	Allowance for Doubtful Accounts		4,000
	To update the Allowance account to its target balance ($10,100 − $1,000) and record bad debt expense for the period.		

What if There Is a Debit Balance in the Allowance Account before Adjustments? This would happen when a company has written off more accounts receivable than expected during the year. In this case, let's assume there is a $500 debit balance in the Allowance for Doubtful Accounts prior to adjustment, and the balance in this account should be $5,000, like in the previous example:

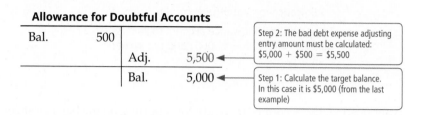

Allowance for Doubtful Accounts

Bal.	500		
		Adj.	5,500
		Bal.	5,000

Step 2: The bad debt expense adjusting entry amount must be calculated: $5,000 + $500 = $5,500

Step 1: Calculate the target balance. In this case it is $5,000 (from the last example)

The expense for the period and the increase to the Allowance account would be recorded as $5,500 in a journal entry.

Using the Allowance Methods Together In practice, many companies use the percent-of-sales and the aging-of-accounts-receivable or the percent-of-accounts-receivable methods together.

- For *interim statements* (monthly or quarterly), companies use the percent-of-sales method because it is easier to apply. The percent-of-sales method focuses on the amount of bad debt *expense*, calculated by multiplying sales by a chosen percent.
- At the end of the year, these companies use the aging-of-accounts-receivable method or the percent-of-accounts-receivable method to ensure that Accounts Receivable is reported at *expected net realizable value*. These two methods focus on the amount of the receivables—the *asset*—that is uncollectible.

Exhibit 9–3 summarizes and compares the three methods.

EXHIBIT 9–3 | Comparing the Allowance Methods for Estimating Uncollectibles

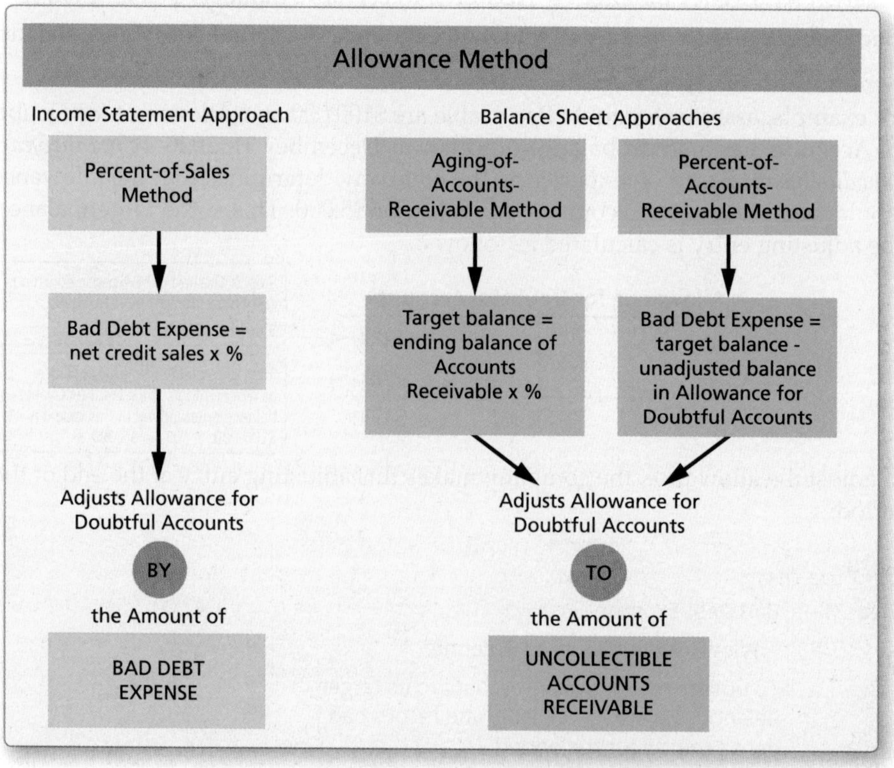

Writing Off Uncollectible Accounts

Let's assume that during early 2021 the company collects on most of its $100,000 of accounts receivable and records the cash receipts as follows:

2021			
Jan.–Mar.	Cash	80,000	
	Accounts Receivable		80,000
	To record collections on account.		

Suppose that, after repeated attempts to collect, the company's credit department determines that it cannot collect a total of $1,200 from customers Seal Coatings Inc. ($900) and one of the "other" customers, Kirsh ($300). The company then **writes off** or removes the balances of these customers from the Accounts Receivable control account and subsidiary ledger:

2021			
Mar. 31	Allowance for Doubtful Accounts	1,200	
	Accounts Receivable—Seal Coatings Inc.		900
	Accounts Receivable—Kirsh		300
	To write off uncollectible accounts.		

Since Allowance for Doubtful Accounts is a contra-asset account, the write-off of uncollectible accounts has no effect on total assets, liabilities, or equity:

	Assets	=	Liabilities	+	Owner's Equity
Allowance for Doubtful Accounts	+1,200	=	0	+	0
Accounts Receivable	−1,200				

A write-off of uncollectible accounts affects neither an expense account nor the net amount of receivables.

This is because the expense was recognized when the allowance was set up. Now both the accounts receivable and the allowance balance are updated to reflect the amount deemed impossible to collect.

	Before Write-off	**After Write-off**
Accounts receivable	$ 20,000	$ 18,800
Less: Allowance for doubtful accounts	5,000	3,800
Accounts receivable, net	$ 15,000	$ 15,000

These written-off customers must be eliminated from the accounts receivable records because the company does not want to waste time and money pursuing collections from them. In other words, they need to be removed from the list of customers we expect to pay their invoices (Accounts Receivable), and they need to be removed from the list of people we estimate may not pay their invoices (Allowance for Doubtful Accounts)—because we now know for sure that nothing will be paid. However, a record of these customers will still be retained in the system or by the credit department for future reference and possible future credit applications.

Recovery of Accounts Previously Written Off

When an account receivable is written off as uncollectible, the customer still owes the money. However, the company may stop pursuing collection.

Some companies turn delinquent receivables over to a lawyer or a collection agency to help recover some of the cash. If the lawyer or collection agency is able to get cash from the customer and pay it to the company, it is called a **recovery**.

Let's see how to record the recovery of an account that we wrote off earlier. Recall that on March 31, 2021, the company wrote off the $900 receivable from customer Seal Coatings Inc. Suppose it is now October 4, 2021, and the company unexpectedly receives $900 from Seal Coatings Inc. To account for this recovery, the company makes two journal entries to ❶ reverse the earlier write-off and ❷ record the cash collection, as follows:

	2021			
❶	Oct. 4	Accounts Receivable—Seal Coatings Inc.	900	
		Allowance for Doubtful Accounts		900
		Reinstated Seal Coatings Inc. account receivable.		
❷	Oct. 4	Cash	900	
		Accounts Receivable— Seal Coatings Inc.		900
		To record collection on account.		

Follow through the entries to Seal Coating's subsidiary ledger account, shown in the T-account below: first the credit sale, then the write-off, then the reversal of the write-off, and finally the credit to the account when the company pays in full. The customer's subsidiary account shows the complete credit history—an important feature of the subsidiary ledger system and one of the reasons why both steps are shown separately in the journals—so there is a detailed record of what happened with this customer.

Accounts Receivable—Seal Coatings Inc.

Sale – 2020	900	900	Write-off – Mar. 31, 2021
❶ Reinstate – Oct. 4, 2021	900	900	❷ Collection – Oct. 4, 2021

Try It!

1. Acadia Building Supplies is a chain of hardware and building supply stores concentrated in the Maritimes. The company's year-end balance sheet on December 31, 2019, reported:

Accounts receivable	$4,000,000
Less: Allowance for doubtful accounts	175,000

a. Journalize, without explanations, December 31, 2020, adjusting entries for Acadia Building Supplies:
   i. Estimated bad debt expense was $140,000 for the first three-quarters of the year, based on the percent-of-sales method.
   ii. Write-offs of Accounts Receivable totalled $160,000.
   iii. December 31, 2020, aging of receivables indicates, using estimated amounts, that $192,000 of total receivables are uncollectible.

b. Post all three transactions to the T-account for Allowance for Doubtful Accounts, as follows:

Allowance for Doubtful Accounts

2020 Write-offs	?	Dec. 31, 2019, Bal.	175,000
		2020 Expense	?
		Bal. before Adj.	?
		Dec. 31, 2020, Adj	?
		Dec. 31, 2020, Bal.	192,000

c. Report Acadia Building Supplies' receivables and related allowance on the December 31, 2020, balance sheet. Accounts Receivable at that date totals $4,155,000.
d. What is the expected net realizable value of receivables at December 31, 2020? How much is bad debt expense for 2020?

2. Poco Supplies wrote off the following accounts receivable as uncollectible for the year ended December 31, 2020:

Carl Rogers $3,250, Vince Tran $4,100, Dan Saerose $2,200, Total = $9,550

The company prepared the following aging schedule for its accounts receivable on December 31, 2020:

Aging	Receivables Balance on December 31, 2020	Estimated Percent Uncollectible
0 – 30 days	$115,000	1%
31 – 60 days	55,000	2%
61 – 90 days	35,000	20%
91 – 120 days	15,000	30%
Over 120 days	10,000	50%

a. Journalize the write-offs and the year-end adjusting entry for 2020 using the allowance method. Assume that Allowance for Doubtful Accounts had a beginning credit balance of $15,000 on January 1, 2020, and the company uses the aging method.
b. Determine the net realizable value of accounts receivable on December 31, 2020.

Solutions appear at the end of this chapter and on **MyLab Accounting**

Why It's Done This Way

Accountants and users have agreed that a company should *estimate* its bad debts, and this chapter presented various methods that companies can use to do that.

In terms of the accounting framework, is this a good idea? We need to focus on the characteristics of financial information that make it beneficial to users. Think about relevance and reliability. Reporting an allowance for doubtful accounts is less *reliable* than either waiting to record the revenue until cash payment is received or waiting for a bad debt to be confirmed. It does, however, add *relevance* to the financial statements: It allows revenue to be recorded in the period it occurred and allows accounts receivable to not be overstated by setting up an Allowance for Doubtful Accounts to reflect the possibility that some accounts will not be collected.

While neither situation is perfect, the trade-off between using an estimate to make information more relevant and losing some reliability seems appropriate in this situation, leading to financial statements that communicate useful information to users.

The Direct Write-off Method

LO 3 What is the direct write-off method?

There is another way to account for uncollectible receivables—the **direct write-off method**. It is not appropriate for most companies because it does not follow generally accepted accounting principles (GAAP).

Under the direct write-off method, the company waits until it decides that a customer's account receivable is uncollectible to record the expense. The company writes off the customer's account receivable by debiting Bad Debt Expense and crediting the customer's Account Receivable, as follows (using assumed data):

2020			
Mar. 6	Bad Debt Expense	2,000	
	Accounts Receivable—Sterling		2,000
	Wrote off an uncollectible account from Dec. 10, 2019, sale.		

The direct write-off method is inferior to the allowance method for two reasons:

- It does not set up an Allowance for Doubtful Accounts. As a result, the direct write-off method always reports the receivables at their full amount. Assets are then overstated on the balance sheet, since the business likely does not expect to collect the full amount of accounts receivable.
- It does not match the bad debt expense against revenue very well. In this example, the company made the sale to Sterling in 2019 and should have estimated and recorded the bad debt expense during 2019, matching the bad debt expense to its related sales revenue. That is the only way to measure net income properly. By recording the bad debt expense in 2020, the company overstates net income in 2019 and understates net income in 2020. Both years' net income amounts are incorrect.

The direct write-off method is acceptable only if uncollectibles are not considered *material* in amount or if the difference between using an allowance method and the direct write-off method is very small. It works for retailers such as neighbourhood stores or bakeries, because those companies report almost no receivables and cannot reasonably make an estimate in advance.

Try It!

3. Cersei Crowley is a home decorator. She uses the direct write-off method to account for uncollectible receivables. At January 31, 2020, Cersei's accounts receivable totalled $15,000. During February, she reported $18,000 of sales on account and collected $19,000 on account. She wrote off one account with Jane Eyre in the amount of $1,800 on February 26, 2020.

a. Journalize the write-off. No explanation is required.

b. What is Cersei's accounts receivable balance at the end of February?

Solutions appear at the end of this chapter and on **MyLab Accounting**

Exercising Internal Control over Accounts Receivable

Businesses that sell goods or services on account receive cash by mail, usually in the form of a cheque or online payments via electronic funds transfer (EFT), so internal control over collections is important. As we discussed in the previous chapter, a critical element of internal control is the separation of cash-handling and cash-accounting duties.

Most large companies also have a credit department to evaluate customers' credit applications to determine if they meet the company's credit approval standards. The extension of credit is a balancing act. The company does not want to lose sales to good customers, but it also wants to avoid receivables that will never be collected. For good internal control over cash collections from receivables, separation of duties must be maintained. The credit department should have no access to cash, and those who handle cash should not be in a position to grant credit to customers. If a credit department employee also handles cash, he or she could pocket money received from a customer. The employee could then label the customer's account as uncollectible, and the company would stop billing that customer. In this scenario, the employee may have covered his or her theft.

ETHICS Should the uncollectible accounts be underestimated?

Norah Wang is in the process of recording adjusting entries for her employer, Happy Kennels. She is evaluating the uncollectible accounts and determining the amount of bad debts expense to record for the year. Her manager, Gillian Tedesco, has asked that Norah underestimate the amount of uncollectible accounts for the year. Gillian is hoping to get a bank loan for an expansion of the kennel facility, and she is concerned that the net income of the company will be too low for a loan to be approved. What should Norah do?

Solution

It is important that accounts receivable be reported at the appropriate amount on the balance sheet. This involves determining an accurate estimate of uncollectible accounts and recognizing the associated bad debts expense. In understating the amount of uncollectible accounts, Norah would be misleading the bank on the amount of cash that Happy Kennels expects to collect in the future. Norah would also understate the Bad Debts Expense account and overstate net income on the income statement.

Other Payment Methods

Credit Card Sales

LO 4 **How do we record credit card, debit card, and online transactions?**

Credit card sales are common in both traditional and online retailing. American Express, VISA, and MasterCard are popular. The customer uses the credit card to pay for purchases. The credit card company pays the seller and then bills the customer, who pays the credit card company.

Credit cards offer the convenience of buying without having to pay the cash immediately. A VISA customer receives a monthly statement detailing each of their credit card transactions. The customer can write a cheque or make an online payment to cover the total of these credit card purchases.

Retailers accept credit cards from customers to increase revenue. Not only are credit cards more convenient for the customer but also research shows that customers purchase more with credit cards than with cash only. This transaction is essentially a sale of the receivable to the credit card company. The credit card company previously performed the credit check and now assumes the risk of uncollectible accounts. Hence, retailers do not have to keep accounts receivable records, and they do not have to collect cash from customers.

These benefits to the seller do not come free. The seller pays a fee to the credit card company and, therefore, receives less than the full amount of the sale. The credit card company takes a fee of 1 to 5 percent[1] on the sale. Accounting for credit card sales differs for bank credit cards and for non-bank credit cards.

Bank Credit Cards VISA, MasterCard, and American Express are popular *bank credit cards*. With bank credit cards, the seller uses chip technology to immediately process credit transactions that are electronically deposited into the merchant's bank account. Smaller retailers may still need to bundle and deposit the VISA or MasterCard receipts at the bank for processing. Suppose you and your family have lunch at The Keg restaurant. You pay the bill—$100—with a VISA card. The Keg's entry to record the $100 VISA card sale, subject to the credit card company's (assumed) 2 percent discount, which is an *expense* to The Keg for a credit card transaction, is as follows:

Mar. 2	Cash	98	
	Credit Card Discount Expense	2	
	Sales Revenue		100
	Recorded VISA credit card sale less a 2 percent credit card discount expense.		

[1]The rate varies among companies and over time.

Non-bank Credit Cards Credit cards other than VISA, MasterCard, and American Express are known as *non-bank credit cards* and are rarely seen in the marketplace. With non-bank credit cards, the seller mails the credit card receipts to the credit card company and awaits payment, less the credit card company's fee. Suppose instead that you pay the bill at The Keg—$100—with a Diners Club card, a non-bank credit card. The Keg's entry to record the $100 non-bank credit card sale is subject to the credit card company's (assumed) 2 percent discount:

Mar. 2	Accounts Receivable	98	
	Credit Card Discount Expense	2	
	Sales Revenue		100
	Recorded Diners Club credit card sale less a 2 percent credit card discount expense.		

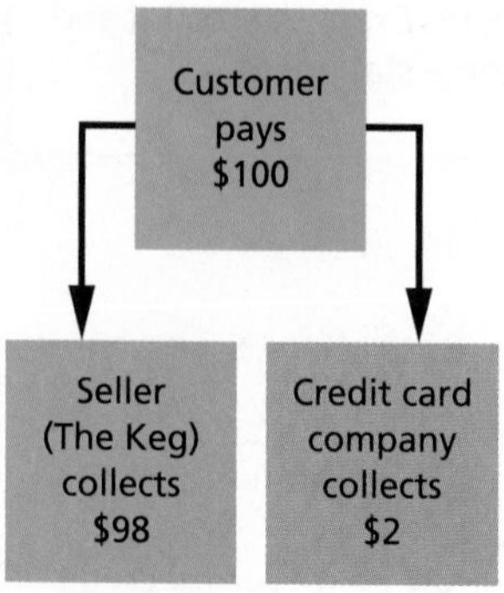
Customer pays $100
Seller (The Keg) collects $98
Credit card company collects $2

In both the bank credit card and the non-bank credit card examples, the customer pays either VISA or Diners Club the $100 after later receiving the monthly statement from the credit card company. The Keg receives $98 from the credit card company, and the credit card company keeps $2 for this transaction.

Debit Card Sales

Debit cards are fundamentally different from credit cards. Using a *debit card* is like paying with cash, except that you don't have to carry cash or write a cheque. All banks issue debit cards. When a business makes a sale, the customer "swipes" her debit card through an Interac or similar card reader and enters her personal identification number (PIN). The bank deducts the cost of the purchase from the customer's account immediately and transfers the purchase amount, less a debit card service fee for processing the transaction, into the business's account. The journal entry for the business is almost the same as the journal entry for a bank credit card sale except the expense account may be named Debit Card Service Fee so that the transaction costs can be tracked.

Online Payments

PayPal, Apple Pay, and other providers of online payment solutions are usually accounted for in the same way as bank debit and credit card transactions. Payments are deposited directly into a company's bank account at the time of the transaction, less a percentage discount and sometimes an additional transaction fee.

Companies that accept **cryptocurrencies** such as Bitcoin incur no transaction fees when the sale is made. There is a cost associated with turning those funds into Canadian dollars at a later date.

Try It!

4. Restaurants do a large volume of business by customer credit cards and debit cards. Suppose MasterCard charges merchants 2 percent, the non-bank credit card companies charge 3 percent, and the debit card transactions incur a charge of 2.5 percent.

   Record these sale transactions for a Swiss Chalet restaurant on June 12:

MasterCard credit card sales	$15,000
Non-bank credit card sales	3,000
Debit card sales	5,000

Solutions appear at the end of this chapter and on **MyLab Accounting**

Accounting for Notes Receivable

LO 5

What are notes receivable, and how do we account for these assets?

Notes receivable are more formal than accounts receivable. The debtor signs a promissory note accepting the conditions of borrowing. The note also serves as evidence of the transaction.

Exhibit 9–4 illustrates a promissory note and explains the special terms used for notes receivable.

Identifying the Maturity Date of a Note

Some notes specify the maturity date, as shown in Exhibit 9–4. Other notes state the period of the note in days or months. When the period is given in months, the note matures on the same day of the month as the date the note was issued. A six-month note dated February 16 matures on August 16.

EXHIBIT 9–4 | A Promissory Note

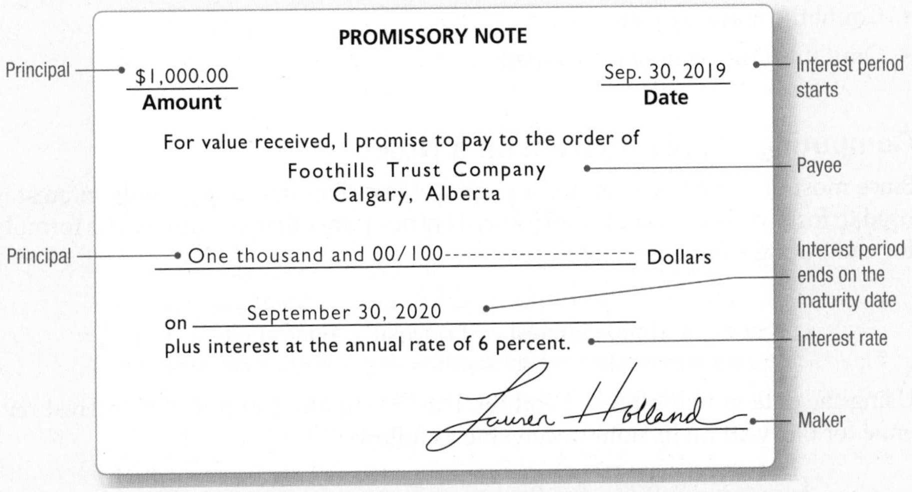

Promissory note: A written promise to pay a specified sum of money at a particular future date.
Maker of the note (*debtor*): The entity that signs the note and promises to pay the required amount; the maker of the note is the *debtor*.
Payee of the note (*creditor*): The entity to whom the maker promises future payment; the payee of the note is the *creditor*.
Principal: The amount lent by the payee and borrowed by the maker of the note.
Interest: The revenue to the payee for lending the money; interest is an expense to the debtor.
Interest period: The period of time during which interest is to be computed, extending from the original date of the note to the maturity date; also called the **note term** or simply the **time period**.
Interest rate: The percentage rate of interest specified by the note, always stated for a period of one year; therefore, a 6 percent note means that the amount of interest for *one year* is 6 percent of the note's principal amount.
Maturity date (also called **due date**): The date on which final payment of the note is due.
Maturity value: The sum of the principal plus interest due at maturity.

September, April, June, and November have 30 days. All the rest have 31, except February, which has 28 and one day more every four years.

A 120-day note dated September 14, 2019, matures on January 12, 2020, as shown below:

Month	Number of Days	Cumulative Total
Sep. 2019	16*	16
Oct. 2019	31	47
Nov. 2019	30	77
Dec. 2019	31	108
Jan. 2020	12	120

*30 − 14 = 16

When the period is given in days, the maturity date is determined by counting the days from date of issue. The 120-day note dated September 14, 2019, would have to be *repaid* by January 12, 2020. In counting the days remaining for a note, remember to:

- Count the maturity date
- Omit the date the note was issued

Computing Simple Interest on a Note

Since most of these notes are for a period of less than one year, simple interest is used to focus on the concepts and journal entries rather than formulae. The formula for computing simple interest is:

Time means interest period.

Amount of simple interest = Principal × Interest rate × Time

Using the data in Exhibit 9–4, Foothills Trust Company computes its interest revenue for one year on its notes receivable as follows:

The time element is one (1) because the note's term is one year.

Amount of simple interest = Principle × Interest rate × Time
= \$1,000 × 0.06 × 1 (year)
= \$60

The maturity value of the note is \$1,060 (\$1,000 principal +\$60 interest).

Interest on a \$2,000 note at 10 percent per year for three months is computed as follows:

When the term of a note is stated in months, we compute the interest based on the 12-month year.

Amount of simple interest = Principle × Interest rate × Time
= \$2,000 × 0.10 × $^3/_{12}$
= \$50

The interest on a \$5,000 note at 12 percent for 60 days is computed as follows:

When the interest period of a note is stated in days, we usually compute interest based on a 365-day year.

Amount of simple interest = Principle × Interest rate × Time
= \$5,000 × 0.12 × $^{60}/_{365}$
= \$98.63

Keep in mind that interest rates are stated as an annual rate. Therefore, the time in the interest formula should also be expressed in terms of a year.

Recording Notes Receivable

Notes Receivable is not a common account. There are a limited number of situations where the account might be used. Each is discussed below.

Note Received in Return for Cash Consider the loan agreement shown in Exhibit 9–4. After Lauren Holland signs the note and presents it to Foothills Trust Company, the trust company gives her $1,000 cash. At the maturity date, Holland pays the trust company $1,060 ($1,000 principal + $60 interest). The trust company's entries (assuming it has a September 30 year end) are as follows:

2019			
Sep. 30	Notes Receivable—L. Holland	1,000	
	Cash		1,000
	Lent money at 6% for 1 year.		
2020			
Sep. 30	Cash	1,060	
	Notes Receivable—L. Holland		1,000
	Interest Revenue		60
	Collected note at maturity with interest (Interest revenue = $1,000 × 0.06 × 1)		

Note was Received as Payment for Sale Some companies sell merchandise in exchange for notes receivable. This arrangement often occurs when the payment term extends beyond the customary accounts receivable period, which ranges from 30 to 60 days, as indicated by the company's credit terms of 2/10, net 30 or net 60.

Suppose that, on October 20, 2020, Midland Plumbing services a boiler for $15,000 at Western Builders' head office. Western signs a 90-day promissory note at 10 percent interest. Midland's entries to record the service and collection from Western (Midland's year end is June 30) are as follows:

2020			
Oct. 20	Notes Receivable—Western Builders	15,000.00	
	Service Revenue		15,000.00
	To record service provided. Note at 10% for 90 days.		
2021			
Jan. 18	Cash	15,369.86	
	Notes Receivable—Western Builders		15,000.00
	Interest Revenue		369.86
	To record collection at maturity with interest. (Interest revenue = $15,000 × 0.10 × $^{90}/_{365}$)		

Note was Received in Exchange for an Account Receivable A company may accept a notes receivable from a trade customer who fails to pay an account receivable on time. The customer signs a promissory note and gives it to the creditor.

Suppose Clifford Sales sees that it will not be able to pay off its account payable with Fridoris Supply, which is due in 15 days. Fridoris Supply may accept a 12-month, $6,000 notes receivable with 9 percent interest from Clifford Sales on October 1, 2020. Fridoris Supply's entry is as follows:

2020			
Oct. 1	Notes Receivable—Clifford Sales	6,000	
	Accounts Receivable—Clifford Sales		6,000
	Received a note at 9% for 12 months.		

Accruing Interest Revenue

A notes receivable may be outstanding at the end of the accounting period. The interest revenue earned on the note up to the year end is part of that year's earnings. Recall that interest revenue is earned over time, not just when cash is received. We saw in Chapter 3, on page 127, that accrued revenue creates an asset for the amount that has been earned but not received.

Let's continue with the Fridoris Supply notes receivable from Clifford Sales. Fridoris Supply's accounting period ends December 31.

How much of the total interest revenue does Fridoris Supply earn in 2020 (for October, November, and December)?

$$\$6{,}000 \times 0.09 \times {}^3/_{12} = \$135$$

Fridoris Supply makes this adjusting entry to accrue interest revenue at December 31, 2020:

2020			
Dec. 31	Interest Receivable	135	
	Interest Revenue		135
	To accrue interest revenue earned in 2020 but not yet received ($6,000 × 0.09 × 3/12).		

How much interest revenue does Fridoris Supply earn in 2021 (for January through September)?

$$\$6{,}000 \times 0.09 \times {}^9/_{12} = \$405$$

On the note's maturity date, Fridoris Supply makes this entry:

2021			
Sep. 30	Cash	6,540	
	Notes Receivable—Clifford Sales		6,000
$6,000 × 0.09 × 3/12 = $135	Interest Receivable		135
$6,000 × 0.09 × 9/12 = $405	Interest Revenue		405
	To collect a notes receivable on which interest has been previously accrued.		

The entries for accrued interest at December 31, 2020, and for collection in 2021 assign the correct amount of interest revenue to each year.

$540 total interest revenue ($6,000 × 0.09 × 1 year)

$135 interest (3 months in 2020) $405 interest (9 months in 2021)

Oct. 1, 2020	Dec. 31, 2020	Sep. 30, 2021
Set up note	Accrued Interest	Received cash for note
	(Receivable/Revenue)	plus interest

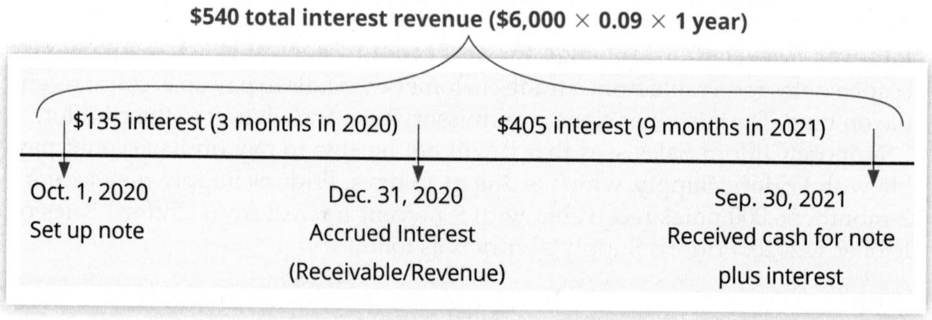

A company holding a note may need cash before the note matures. A procedure for selling the note, called *discounting a notes receivable*, appears in the Chapter 9 Appendix.

Dishonoured Notes Receivable

If the maker of a note does not pay it at maturity, the maker **dishonours a note** or **defaults on the note**. Because the note has expired, it is no longer in force. However, the debtor still owes the payee. The payee must transfer the amount of the note to Accounts Receivable since Notes Receivable contains only notes that have not yet matured.

Suppose Whitehorse Hardware has a six-month, 10 percent notes receivable for $5,000 from Northern Cabinets. On the February 3 maturity date, Northern Cabinets defaults. Whitehorse Hardware would record the default as follows:

Feb. 3	Accounts Receivable—Northern Cabinets	5,250		← $5,000 + ($5,000 × 0.10 × 6/12) = $5,250
	Notes Receivable—Northern Cabinets		5,000	
	Interest Revenue		250	← $5,000 × 0.10 × 6/12 = $250
	To record the default on a note.			

Whitehorse Hardware would pursue collection from Northern Cabinets for this account receivable and would account for the receivable in the normal way. According to the recognition for revenues, further accrual of interest from this point until payment is received could only be recorded if collection is likely.

Try It!

5. On April 1, 2019, Mediterranean Importers loaned $20,000 cash to Bud Shriver on a one-year, 7 percent note. Record the loan transaction and any year-end transactions for Mediterranean.
6. Refer to the previous question. The loan was repaid on April 1, 2020, with its related interest. Record the repayment for Mediterranean, assuming no reversing entries were used.
7. Refer to Try It #5. Suppose Shriver defaulted on the note at maturity instead of repaying it. How would Mediterranean Importers record the default?

Solutions appear at the end of this chapter and on **MyLab Accounting**

Using Accounting Information for Decision Making

LO 6

How can we evaluate how effectively a company manages its current assets?

The relationships between assets, liabilities, and revenues provide new information about how well a business and its managers are doing. Let's examine two important ratios using the accounts presented in Exhibit 9–5.

EXHIBIT 9–5 | ABC Ltd.'s Financial Statement Information (partial)

Balance Sheet (partial)	2020	2019
Current Assets		
Cash	$ 19,796	$ 10,000
Accounts receivable, net	63,175	57,308
Inventories	68,117	74,742
Prepaid expenses	2,060	1,945
Supplies	3,363	2,702
Total current assets	$156,511	$146,697
Current Liabilities		
Accounts payable and accrued expenses	$ 33,298	$ 38,061
Income taxes payable	2,017	5,037
Total current liabilities	$ 35,315	$ 45,098
Sales revenue from the income statement	$512,037	

Acid-Test (or Quick) Ratio

Corporate stakeholders, investors, managers, government, and other readers of financial reports use ratios for decision making. In Chapter 4, for example, we discussed the current ratio, which indicates the ability to pay current liabilities with current assets. A more stringent measure of the ability to pay current liabilities is the **acid-test ratio** (or **quick ratio**). The acid-test ratio tells whether the entity could pay all its current liabilities if they came due immediately.

$$\textbf{Acid-test ratio} = \frac{\textbf{Cash + Short-term investments + Net current receivables}}{\textbf{Total current liabilities}}$$

$$2020: \frac{\$19{,}796 + \$0 + \$63{,}175}{\$35{,}315} = 2.35$$

$$2019: \frac{\$10{,}000 + \$0 + \$57{,}308}{\$43{,}098} = 1.56$$

The higher the acid-test ratio, the better able the business is to pay its current liabilities. ABC's ratio in 2020 is 2.35, showing excellent liquidity. There is more than twice as much in assets coming in to the company as opposed to leaving the company. A comparison of 2020 to 2019 indicates that the ratio has improved from 1.56 to 2.35.

What is an acceptable acid-test ratio value? In general, an acid-test ratio of 1.00 is considered safe. However, the answer depends on the industry. Automobile dealers can operate smoothly with an acid-test ratio of 0.20. The acid-test ratio for most department stores clusters about 0.80, while travel agencies average 1.10.

Days' Sales in Receivables

After a business makes a credit sale, the next critical event in the business cycle is collection of the receivable. Several financial ratios centre on receivables. **Days' sales in receivables**, also called *days sales uncollected*, days sales in average accounts receivable, or the **collection period**, indicates how many days it takes to collect the average level of receivables. The shorter the collection period, the more quickly the organization has cash to use for operations. The longer the collection period, the less cash is available to pay bills and expand. Days' sales in receivables can be computed in two steps, as follows:

$$❶\ \textbf{One day's sales} = \frac{\textbf{Net sales}}{\textbf{365 days}}$$

$$❷\ \textbf{Days' sales in receivables} = \frac{\textbf{Average net accounts receivable}}{\textbf{One days'sales}} = \frac{\left(\begin{array}{l}\textbf{Beginning net receivables}\\ \textbf{+ Ending net receivables}\end{array}\right) \div 2}{\textbf{One day's sales}}$$

For ABC Ltd., the days' sales in receivables for 2020 is:

$$❶\ \textbf{One day's sales} = \frac{\$512{,}037}{365} = \$1{,}403 \textbf{ per day}$$

$$❷\ \textbf{Day's sales in receivables} = \frac{(\$57{,}308 + \$63{,}175) \div 2}{\$1{,}403} = 42.94 \textbf{ days}$$

On average, it takes ABC Ltd. about 43 days to collect its accounts receivable. The length of the collection period depends on the credit terms of the sale and the terms that are common in a particular industry. For example, sales on net 30 terms should be collected within approximately 30 days. When there is a discount, such as 2/10, net 30, the collection period may be shorter. Terms of net 45 result in a longer collection period. If the terms are net 45, then 43 days is good; however, if the terms are net 30, 43 days to collect is not an efficient collection result and should be improved.

Refer to Chapter 5, page 251, if you need help recalling how to read "terms."

Accounts Receivable Turnover

Another common way to express a company's ability to collect cash from its customers is to use the accounts receivable turnover formula, which is:

$$\textbf{Accounts receivable turnover} = \frac{\textbf{Net credit sales}}{\textbf{Average net accounts receivable}}$$

For this chapter's ratio calculations, assume that all sales are on account unless otherwise stated. ABC Ltd.'s result is:

$$\textbf{Accounts receivable turnover} = \frac{\$512{,}037}{(\$57{,}308 + \$63{,}175) \div 2} = 8.5 \text{ turns}$$

The results for days sales in receivables and the accounts receivable turnover are related—they say the same thing in a different way. Notice that if you divide 365 days by 8.5 turns you get a result of 42.9 days. So why is the same result calculated in different ways? People interpret information in different ways, so both ratios are used in businesses.

A company should watch its collection period closely. Whenever the collection period lengthens, the business must find other sources of financing, such as borrowing. During recessions customers pay more slowly, and a longer collection period may be unavoidable. Cash flow or lack thereof is a serious issue since companies need cash to operate. This is covered in more detail in Chapters 17 and 18.

Days sales in receivables = 365 ÷ accounts receivable turnover

When the days' sales in receivables result is lower than the industry standard, this may mean that credit is too tight and potential sales might be lost.

Try It!

8. Use the data in Exhibit 9–5 to compute ABC Ltd.'s current ratio at December 31, 2020. Then compare ABC Ltd.'s current ratio and acid-test ratio. Why is the current ratio higher?
9. Can days' sales in receivables be computed in one step instead of two? If so, what would be the formula?

Solutions appear at the end of this chapter and on **MyLab Accounting**

EXHIBIT 9–6 | The Impact of IFRS on Accounts Receivable

ASPE	IFRS
Assets categorized as current, including accounts receivable, are essentially reported at their fair values. How do we know this? We subtract the allowance for doubtful accounts from the gross receivables and show the anticipated amount that a company will be able to collect. Because of this deduction, we are really presenting the account at its estimated collectible amount, or its fair value.	
Accounts Receivable is the usual term used.	Trade Receivables is the usual term used.

LO 7

How does IFRS affect accounts receivable?

Summary Problem for Your Review

Akerlof Investigations has an Accounts Receivable balance of $34,000 and an Allowance for Doubtful Accounts credit balance of $3,000 at the December 31, 2018, fiscal year end.

Required

Record the journal entries for the following Akerlof Investigations transactions. No explanations are needed. In calculations, round final amounts to the nearest whole dollar.

2019	
Apr. 1	Lent $20,000 to Blatchford Agencies. Received a six-month, 10 percent note.
Jun. 21	J. Schiller called to say there was no way he could pay his $1,000 balance and Akerlof should stop calling.
Oct. 1	Collected the Blatchford Agencies' note at maturity.
Nov. 30	Lent $15,000 to Fane Industries on a three-month, 12 percent note.
Dec. 31	Accrued interest revenue on the Fane Industries' note.
Dec. 31	Recorded estimated uncollectible as 1 percent of the $550,000 of credit sales.
2020	
Feb. 28	Collected the Fane Industries' note at maturity.
Mar. 3	J. Shiller wanted to do further business with Akerlof Investigations and paid the $1,000 balance from 2019.

SOLUTION

2019				
Apr. 1	Notes Receivable—Blatchford Agencies	20,000		
	Cash		20,000	All notes receivable in this company are stated in terms of months, so interest is calculated based on 12 months in a year (not 365 days in a year).
June 21	Allowance for Doubtful Accounts	1,000		
	Accounts Receivable—J. Schiller		1,000	
Oct. 1	Cash	21,000		
	Notes Receivable—Blatchford Agencies		20,000	
	Interest Revenue		1,000	← ($20,000 × 0.10 × $^6/_{12}$)
Nov. 30	Notes Receivable—Fane Industries	15,000		Accrue interest for only one month. This is how much time has passed.
	Cash		15,000	
Dec. 31	Interest Receivable	150		
	Interest Revenue		150	← ($15,000 × 0.12 × $^1/_{12}$)
Dec. 31	Bad Debt Expense	5,500		
	Allowance for Doubtful Accounts		5,500	← ($550,000 × .01)
2020				
Feb. 28	Cash	15,450		← $15,000 + ($15,000 × 0.12 × $^3/_{12}$)
	Notes Receivable—Fane Industries		15,000	
	Interest Receivable		150	
	Interest Revenue		300	← ($15,000 × 0.12 × $^2/_{12}$) The revenue is reported for the two months that the loan was outstanding in 2020.
Mar. 3	Accounts Receivable—J. Schiller	1,000		
	Allowance for Doubtful Accounts		1,000	
Mar. 3	Cash	1,000		
	Accounts Receivable—J. Schiller		1,000	

Chapter 9 Appendix

DISCOUNTING (SELLING) A NOTES RECEIVABLE

LO (A1) **Is it possible to receive cash from a notes receivable prior to the note's maturity date?**

A payee of a notes receivable may need cash before the maturity date of the note. When this occurs, the payee may sell the note, a practice called **discounting a notes receivable**. The price to be received for the note is determined by a present-value calculation. We discuss these concepts in detail in Chapter 15. The transaction between the seller and the buyer of the note can take any form agreeable to the two parties. Here we illustrate one procedure used for discounting short-term notes receivable. To receive cash immediately, the seller is willing to accept a lower price than the note's maturity value.

Proceeds Are More than the Note To illustrate, suppose EMCO Ltd. lent $15,000 to Dartmouth Builders on October 20, 2019. The maturity date of the 90-day, 10 percent Dartmouth note is January 18, 2020. Suppose EMCO discounts the Dartmouth Builders note at the National Bank on December 9, 2019, when the note is 50 days old. The bank applies a 12 percent annual interest rate in computing the discounted value of the note.

The bank will use a discount rate that is higher than the interest rate on the note in order to earn some interest on the transaction. EMCO may be willing to accept this higher rate in order to get cash quickly. The discounted value, called the *proceeds*, is the amount EMCO receives from the bank. The proceeds can be computed in five steps, as shown in Exhibit 9–1A. At maturity the bank collects $15,370 from the maker of the note and earns $202 interest revenue from holding the note.

EXHIBIT 9–1A | Discounting (Selling) a Notes Receivable: EMCO Ltd. Discounts the Dartmouth Builders Note

Steps	Computations		
1. Compute the original amount of interest on the notes receivable.	$15,000 × 0.10 × 90/365	=	$370
2. Maturity value of note = Principal + Interest	$15,000 + $370	=	$15,370
3. Determine the period (number of days, months, or years) the bank will hold the note (the discount period).	Dec. 9, 2019 to Jan. 18, 2020	=	40 days
4. Compute the bank's discount on the note. This is the bank's interest revenue from holding the note.	$15,370 × 0.12 × 40/365	=	$202
5. Seller's proceeds from discounting the notes receivable* = Maturity value of note − Bank's discount on the note	$15,370 − $202	=	$15,168

*(Buyer's cost of purchasing)

EMCO Ltd.'s entry to record discounting (selling) the note on December 9, 2019, is:

2019			
Dec. 9	Cash	15,168	
	Notes Receivable—Dartmouth Builders		15,000
	Interest Revenue		168
	To record discounting a note.		

$370 total interest on note (1)
−$202 bank's interest revenue (4)
$168 left for EMCO as revenue

Proceeds Are Less than the Note When the proceeds from discounting a notes receivable are less than the principal amount of the note, the payee records a debit to Interest Expense for the amount of the difference. For example, EMCO could discount the note for cash proceeds of $14,980. The entry to record this transaction would be:

2019			
Dec. 9	Cash	14,980	
	Interest Expense	20	
	Notes Receivable—Dartmouth Builders		15,000

In the discounting of the notes receivable just described, interest revenue accrued from the original date of the note (October 20, 2019) to the date of discounting (December 9, 2019) was not recognized because the discount fee was greater than the amount of interest earned between October 20 and December 9. The company incurred an additional $20 plus the forgone interest revenue of $370 that it could have earned if held to maturity. The bank will collect $15,370 from Dartmouth, and the bank paid EMCO $14,980, thereby earning a profit of $390 on discounting this note.

Pledging Accounts Receivable

Just as a company can sell a notes receivable, a company can also sell accounts receivable for less than full value to receive cash right away. Another option for a business to increase their cash would be to *pledge* their accounts receivable, or legally promise the receivables to a lender, as security for a loan. Rogers Communications Inc. states in the notes to their 2016 annual report that they have pledged $250 million of receivables.

Try It!

10. If a 60-day note dated April 16 is discounted on May 2, what is the discount period?

Solutions appear at the end of this chapter and on **MyLab Accounting**

Summary

Learning Objectives

① Define common types of receivables, and report receivables on the balance sheet Pg. 494

What are receivables, and how are they reported on the balance sheet?

- A *receivable* arises when a business (or person) sells goods or services to another party on credit.
- The receivable is the seller's claim for the amount of the transaction.
- A receivable also arises when one person lends money to another.
- Each credit transaction involves two parties: the *creditor*, who sells something and obtains a receivable, which is an asset, and the *debtor*, who makes the purchase and has a payable, which is a liability.
- All accounts receivable, notes receivable, and allowance accounts appear in the balance sheet in the current asset section when they are due within one year.

② Use the allowance method to account for uncollectibles, and estimate uncollectibles by the percent-of-sales, aging-of-accounts-receivable, and the percent-of-accounts-receivable methods Pg. 496

Why would companies estimate their uncollectible accounts receivable, and how could they do that?

- The *allowance method* matches expenses to sales revenue and also results in a more realistic measure of net accounts receivable.
- The *percent-of-sales method*, the *aging-of-accounts-receivable method*, and the *percent-of-accounts-receivable method* are the main approaches to estimating bad debts under the allowance method.
- Here is where each of the journal entries is recorded in the T-accounts and the order in which they usually occur:

Accounts Receivable (Debit)	Accounts Receivable (Credit)	Allowance for Doubtful Accounts (Debit)	Allowance for Doubtful Accounts (Credit)
1. Sales on credit	2. Customer payments on account		3. Estimate of uncollectible
	4. Write off uncollectible	4. Write off uncollectible	
5. Recovery of account reinstated			5. Recovery of account reinstated

(3) Use the direct write-off method to account for uncollectibles **Pg. 503**

What is the direct write-off method?

- Businesses using the *direct write-off method* only recognize bad debts when they are writing them off. This is easy to apply, but it fails to match the bad debt expense to the corresponding sales revenue.
- Accounts Receivable are reported at their full amount, which is misleading because it suggests that the company expects to collect all its accounts receivable.

(4) Account for credit card, debit card, and online sales **Pg. 505**

How do we record credit card, debit card, and online payment transactions?

- When customers pay for their purchases using a *credit card*, the credit card company pays the vendor and collects from the customer.
- Non-bank credit cards, such as Diners Club, reimburse vendors at a later date, creating a receivable for the vendor until payment is received from the credit card company.
- When a customer pays with a *debit card*, the issuer removes the amount of the purchase from the customer's bank account and puts it into the vendor's account.
- The vendor pays a fee for each credit card and debit card transaction.
- Online payments through PayPal or other providers are accounted for like credit and debit card transactions.

(5) Account for notes receivable **Pg. 507**

What are notes receivable, and how do we account for these assets?

- *Notes receivable* are formal credit agreements.
- The formula used for computing interest on most notes receivable is as follows:

$$\textbf{Amount of simple interest} = \textbf{Principal} \times \textbf{Interest rate} \times \textbf{Time}$$

(6) Use the acid-test ratio and days' sales in receivables to evaluate a company **Pg. 511**

How can we evaluate how effectively a company collects its accounts receivable?

- The *acid-test ratio* measure s a company's ability to pay current liabilities from the most liquid current assets:

$$\text{Acid-test ratio} = \frac{\text{Cash} + \text{Short-term investments} + \text{Net current receivables}}{\text{Total current liabilities}}$$

- *Days' sales in receivables* indicates how long it takes to collect the average level of receivables:

$$\text{Days' sales in receivables} = \frac{\text{Average net accounts receivable}}{\text{One days'sales}} = \frac{\left(\begin{array}{l}\text{Beginning net receivables} \\ + \text{Ending net receivables}\end{array}\right) \div 2}{\text{One day's sales}}$$

- Another way to measure how well receivables are being collected is by calculating the *accounts receivable turnover*:

$$\text{Account receivable turnover} = \frac{\text{Net credit sales}}{\text{Average net accounts receivable}}$$

(7) Understand the impact on accounts receivable of International Financial Reporting Standards (IFRS) **Pg. 513**

How does IFRS affect accounts receivable?

- Receivables are reported at fair value. Both sets of standards are essentially *converged*.
- There is one presentation difference—IFRS report Accounts Receivable as "Trade Receivables."

(A1) Discount a notes receivable **Pg. 515**

Is it possible to receive cash from a notes receivable prior to the note's maturity date?

- The payee of a notes receivable will sometimes discount, or sell, the note to a bank or other third party before the maturity date of the note.

Key Terms for the chapter are shown next and are in the **Glossary** at the back of the book. **Similar Terms** are shown after **Key Terms**.

KEY TERMS

Acid-test ratio Ratio of the sum of cash plus short-term investments plus net current receivables to current liabilities. Tells whether the entity could pay all its current liabilities if they came due immediately. Also called the *quick ratio (p. 512)*.

Aging-of-accounts-receivable method A way to estimate bad debts by analyzing individual accounts receivable according to the length of time they have been due *(p. 498)*.

Allowance for Doubtful Accounts A contra account, related to accounts receivable, that holds the estimated amount of collection losses. Also called *allowance for uncollectible accounts (p. 496)*.

Allowance for Uncollectible Accounts Another name for *allowance for doubtful accounts (p. 496)*.

Allowance method A method of recording collection losses based on estimates made prior to determining that the business will not collect from specific customers *(p. 496)*.

Bad debt expense The cost to the seller of extending credit. Arises from the failure to collect from credit customers. Also called *doubtful accounts expense* or *uncollectible accounts expense (p. 496)*.

Balance sheet approach Another name for the *aging-of-accounts-receivable method* of estimating uncollectibles *(p. 498)*.

Collection period Another name for *days' sales in receivables (p. 512)*.

Creditor The party to a credit transaction who sells a service or merchandise and obtains a receivable *(p. 494)*.

Cryptocurrencies Digital currencies that operate independently of a central bank *(p. 506)*.

Days' sales in receivables Ratio of average net accounts receivable to one day's sales. Indicates how many days' sales remain in Accounts Receivable awaiting collection. Also called the *collection period (p. 512)*.

Debtor The party to a credit transaction who makes a purchase and creates a payable *(p. 494)*.

Default on a note Failure of the maker of a note to pay at maturity. Also called *dishonour of a note (p. 511)*.

Direct write-off method A method of accounting for bad debts by which the company waits until the credit department decides that a customer's account receivable is uncollectible and then debits Bad Debt Expense and credits the customer's Account Receivable *(p. 503)*.

Discounting a notes receivable Selling a notes receivable before its maturity date *(p. 515)*.

Dishonour a note Failure of the maker of a note to pay a notes receivable at maturity. Also called *default on a note (p. 511)*.

Doubtful account expense Another name for *bad debt expense (p. 496)*.

Due date The date on which the final payment of a note is due. Also called the *maturity date (p. 507)*.

Income statement approach Another name for the *percent-of-sales method* of estimating uncollectibles *(p. 497)*.

Interest The revenue to the payee for loaning out the principal, and the expense to the maker for borrowing the principal *(p. 507)*.

Interest period The period of time during which interest is to be computed, extending from the original date of the note to the maturity date. Also called the *note term* or the *time period (p. 507)*.

Interest rate The percentage rate that is multiplied by the principal amount to compute the amount of interest on a note *(p. 507)*.

Maker of a note The person or business that signs the note and promises to pay the amount required by the note agreement. The maker is the *debtor (p. 507)*.

Maturity date The date on which the final payment of a note is due. Also called the *due date (p. 507)*.

Maturity value The sum of the principal and interest due at the maturity date of a note *(p. 507)*.

Net realizable value (NRV) Accounts receivable minus allowance for doubtful accounts equals the amount of accounts receivable the company hopes to realize, or collect *(p. 496)*.

Note term Another name for the *interest period* of a note *(p. 507)*.

Payee of a note The person or business to whom the maker of a note promises future payment. The payee is the *creditor (p. 507)*.

Percent-of-accounts-receivable method A method of estimating uncollectible receivables by determining the balance of Allowance for Doubtful Accounts based on a percentage of accounts receivable *(p. 499)*.

Percent-of-sales method A method of estimating uncollectible receivables as a percent of the net credit sales (or net sales). Also called the *income statement approach (p. 497)*.

Principal The amount loaned out by the payee and borrowed by the maker of a note *(p. 507)*.

Promissory note A written promise to pay a specified amount of money at a particular future date *(p. 507)*.

Quick ratio Another name for the *acid-test ratio (p. 512)*.

Receivable A monetary claim against a business or an individual, acquired mainly by selling goods and services and by lending money *(p. 494)*.

Recovery When a previously written off receivables amount is collected *(p. 502)*.

Time period Another name for the *interest period (p. 507)*.

Uncollectible accounts expense Another name for *bad debt expense (p. 496)*.

Write-off Remove the balance of the customer's account from the Accounts Receivable control account and subsidiary ledger in the accounting records since the customer will not pay what it owes *(p. 501)*.

SIMILAR TERMS

Acid-test ratio	Quick ratio
Aging-of-accounts-receivable method (of estimating uncollectibles)	Balance sheet approach (of estimating uncollectibles)
Allowance for Doubtful Accounts	Allowance for Uncollectible Accounts; Allowance for Bad Debts
Bad debt expense	Uncollectible accounts expense; Doubtful accounts expense
Days' sales in receivables	Collection period, days' sales uncollected
Dishonour a note	Default on a note
Interest period	Note period; Note term; Time
Maturity date	Due date
Percent-of-Accounts-Receivable Method (of estimating uncollectibles)	Balance sheet approach (of estimating uncollectibles)
Percent-of-Sales Method (of estimating uncollectibles)	Income statement approach (of estimating uncollectibles)
Pledge	Promise
Trade receivables	Accounts receivable

SELF-STUDY QUESTIONS

Test your understanding of the chapter by marking the correct answer for each of the following questions:

1. The party that holds a receivable is called the (*p. 494*)
   a. Creditor
   b. Debtor
   c. Maker
   d. Security holder
2. Keady Marina made the following general journal entry related to uncollectibles:

Bad Debt Expense	700	
Allowance for Doubtful Accounts		700

   The purpose of this entry is to (*p. 497*)
   a. Write off uncollectibles
   b. Close the expense account
   c. Age the accounts receivable
   d. Estimate and record bad debt expense
3. The credit balance in Allowance for Doubtful Accounts is $12,600 prior to the adjusting entries at the end of the period. The aging of the accounts indicates that an allowance of $81,200 is needed. The amount of expense to record is (*p. 498*)
   a. $12,600
   b. $68,600
   c. $81,200
   d. $93,800
4. Keady Marina also made this general journal entry:

Allowance for Doubtful Accounts	1,800	
Accounts Receivable (detailed)		1,800

   The purpose of this entry is to (*p. 501*)
   a. Write off uncollectibles
   b. Close the expense account
   c. Age the accounts receivable
   d. Record bad debt expense
5. Keady Marina also made this general journal entry:

Accounts Receivable (detailed)	640	
Allowance for Doubtful Accounts		640

   The purpose of this entry is to (*p. 502*)
   a. Write off uncollectibles
   b. Close the expense account
   c. Reverse the write-off of receivables
   d. Record bad debt expense
6. Which of the following is a limitation of the direct write-off method of accounting for uncollectibles? (*p. 503*)
   a. The direct write-off method overstates assets on the balance sheet.
   b. The direct write-off method does not match expenses against revenue very well.
   c. The direct write-off method does not set up an allowance for uncollectibles.
   d. All of the above
7. The function of the credit department is to (*p. 504*)
   a. Collect accounts receivable from customers
   b. Report bad credit risks to other companies
   c. Evaluate customers who apply for credit
   d. Write off uncollectible accounts receivable
8. A six-month, $40,000 note specifies interest of 8 percent. The full amount of interest on this note will be (*p. 508*)
   a. $400
   b. $800
   c. $1,600
   d. $3,200
9. The maturity value of a note is equal to the (*p. 508*)
   a. Principal plus total interest due
   b. Face value of the note
   c. Principal minus total interest due
   d. Principal times the interest rate

10. The note in Self-Study Question 8 was issued on August 31, and the company's accounting year ends on December 31. The year-end balance sheet will report interest receivable of (*p. 510*)
    a. $533
    b. $1,067
    c. $1,600
    d. $3,200

11. At year end, Schultz Company has cash of $11,600, current accounts receivable of $48,900, merchandise inventory of $37,900, and prepaid expenses totalling $5,100. Liabilities of $55,900 must be paid next year. What is Schultz's acid-test ratio? (*p. 512*)
    a. 1.08
    b. 0.21
    c. 1.76
    d. Cannot be determined from the data given

12. *Cottage Canoes holds a $40,000, 10 percent, 120-day notes receivable from Painter's Hall. Prior to maturity, Cottage Canoe discounts the note and sells it for proceeds of $41,000. The journal entry to record the discounting of the note would include (*p. 515*)
    a. A debit to notes receivable of $40,000
    b. A credit to notes receivable of $41,000
    c. A debit to interest expense of $1,000
    d. A credit to interest revenue of $1,000

*This question covers Chapter 9 Appendix topics.

Answers to Self-Study Questions

1. a 2. d 3. b ($81,200 − $12,600 = $68,600) 4. a 5. c 6. d 7. c
8. c ($40,000 × 0.08 × $^6/_{12}$ = $1,600) 9. a 10. b ($40,000 × 0.08 × $^4/_{12}$ = $1,067)
11. a 12. d

Assignment Material

MyLab Accounting Make the grade with MyLab Accounting: The Starters, Exercises, and Problems can be found on MyLab. You can practise them as often as you want, and most feature step-by-step guided instructions to help you find the right answer.

QUESTIONS

1. Name the two parties to a receivable/payable transaction. Which party has the receivable? Which has the payable? The asset? The liability?
2. What is the difference between accounts receivable and notes receivable?
3. What type of account must the sum of all the subsidiary accounts be equal to?
4. What is the name of the contra account for receivables that may not be collected?
5. Which of the two methods of accounting for uncollectible accounts—the allowance method or the direct write-off method—is preferable? Why?
6. Identify the accounts debited and credited to account for uncollectibles under (a) the allowance method, and (b) the direct write-off method.
7. Which entry decreases net income under the allowance method of accounting for uncollectibles: the entry to record bad debt expense or the entry to write off an uncollectible account receivable?
8. Show three ways to report Accounts Receivable of $50,000 and Allowance for Doubtful Accounts of $1,400 Cr on the balance sheet or in the related notes.

9. Suppose a company records a credit sale to a new customer in 2019. In 2020, the company discovers the customer is bankrupt; the company will be unable to collect its receivable from the customer. The bad debt expense for this customer is recorded in 2020. What are the accounting problems with this situation? Is recording the bad debt expense in 2020 incorrect?

10. Briefly describe how a company may use both the percent-of-sales method and aging-of-accounts-receivable method (or the percent-of-accounts-receivable method) to account for uncollectibles.

11. a. How accurately does the direct write-off method measure income?

    b. How accurately does the direct write-off method value accounts receivable?

12. How does a credit balance arise in a customer's account receivable? How does the company report this credit balance on its balance sheet?

13. What are the benefits of credit card sales to a retailer? What is the cost to the retailer? How is the cost of a credit card sale recorded?

14. Use the terms *maker*, *payee*, *principal*, *maturity date*, *promissory note*, and *interest* in an appropriate sentence or two describing a notes receivable.

15. Name three situations in which a company might receive a notes receivable. For each situation, show the account debited and the account credited to record receipt of the note.

16. For each of the following notes receivable, compute the amount of interest revenue earned during 2020:

	Principal	*Interest Rate*	*Interest Period*	*Maturity date*
a. Note #1	$ 10,000	4%	60 days	Nov. 30, 2020
b. Note #2	$ 50,000	6	3 months	Sep. 30, 2020
c. Note #3	$100,000	4	1/2 year	Dec. 31, 2020

17. When the maker of a note dishonours the note at maturity, what accounts does the payee debit and credit?

18. Yellowknife Hardware has a policy of charging 2 percent interest on overdue (past 60 days) accounts receivable. Northern Cabinets has declared bankruptcy, and it is unlikely that full payment on this account will be collected. Should Yellowknife charge additional interest on the Northern Cabinets account receivable?

19. Why is the acid-test ratio a more stringent measure of the ability to pay current liabilities than is the current ratio?

20. Which measure of days' sales in receivables is preferable, 30 or 40? Give your reason.

21. *Why would a payee sell a notes receivable before its maturity date?

*This question covers Chapter 9 Appendix topics.

STARTERS

S9–1 From the following alphabetical list of adjusted account balances, prepare the current assets section of Versi-Vista Berries' September 30, 2020, balance sheet. Use a multi-column format, as shown in Exhibit 9–1.

(1) Reporting receivables on the balance sheet

Current assets, $186,050

Account Title	**Debit**	**Credit**
Accounts receivable	75,000	
Allowance for doubtful accounts		2,800
Bad debt expense	500	
Cash	112,000	
Farm equipment	122,000	
Office supplies	1,200	
Prepaid rent	650	

S9–2 During its first year of operations, Spring Break Travel earned revenue of $700,000 on account. Industry experience suggests that Spring Break's bad debts will amount to 1 percent of revenues. At December 31, 2019, accounts receivable total $80,000. The company uses the allowance method to account for uncollectibles.

(2) Applying the allowance method (percent of sales) to account for uncollectibles

1. Journalize Spring Break Travel's bad debt expense using the percent-of-sales method.

2. Show how Spring Break should report accounts receivable on its balance sheet at December 31, 2019.

2. Accounts Receivable, net, $73,000

S9–3 This exercise continues the situation of S9–2, in which Spring Break Travel ended 2019 with Accounts Receivable at $80,000 and Allowance for Doubtful Accounts at $7,000.

(2) Applying the allowance method (percent of sales) to account for uncollectibles

4. Bad Debt Expense, $8,000

During 2020, Spring Break Travel completed these transactions:

- Service revenue on account, $800,000 (assume no cost of goods sold).
- Collections on account, $840,000.
- Write-offs of uncollectibles, $6,000.
- Bad debt expense, 1 percent of service revenue.

Journalize Spring Break Travel's 2020 transactions at the end of the first quarter (March 31, 2020), and show the updated balance sheet totals.

2
Applying the allowance method (percent-of-receivables) to account for uncollectibles

S9–4 The Accounts Receivable balance for Lake Company at December 31, 2019, was $20,000. During 2020, Lake earned revenue of $454,000 on account and collected $325,000 on account. Lake wrote off $5,600 receivables as uncollectible. Industry experience suggests that uncollectible accounts will amount to 5 percent of accounts receivable.

1. Assume Lake had an unadjusted $2,700 credit balance in Allowance for Bad Debts at December 31, 2020. Journalize Lake's December 31, 2020, adjustment to record bad debts expense using the percent-of-receivables method.
2. Assume Lake had an unadjusted $2,400 debit balance in Allowance for Bad Debts at December 31, 2020. Journalize Lake's December 31, 2020, adjustment to record bad debts expense using the percent-of-receivables method.

2
Applying the allowance method (aging-of-receivables) to account for uncollectibles

S9–5 Surf and Sun had the following balances at December 31, 2020, before the year-end adjustments:

Accounts Receivable		Allowance for Doubtful Accounts	
81,000			2,063

The aging of accounts receivable yields the following data:

	Age of Accounts Receivable		
	0–60 Days	Over 60 Days	Total Receivables
Accounts Receivable	$ 78,000	$ 3,000	$ 81,000
Estimated percent uncollectible	× 2%	× 23%	

1. Journalize Surf and Sun's entry to record bad debt expense for 2020 using the aging-of-receivables method.
2. Prepare a T-account to compute the ending balance of Allowance for Doubtful Accounts.

2
Account balances

2. $122,550

S9–6 Harrison Real Estate reported the following information for 2020:

Accounts receivable, Jan. 1, 2020	$118,000
Allowance for doubtful accounts, Dec. 31, 2020, prior to adjustment	600
Net credit sales during 2020	195,000
Collections on account during 2020	87,000
Cash sales during 2020	27,000

1. If uncollectible accounts are determined by the percent-of-sales method to be 3 percent of net credit sales, what is the bad debt expense for 2020?
2. If uncollectible accounts are determined by the aging of receivables to be $3,450, what is the amount of net accounts receivable after adjusting entries for 2020?

2
Collecting a receivable previously written off

S9–7 University Cycle Shop had trouble collecting its account receivable from Matt Reid. On January 19, University finally wrote off Reid's $2,400 account receivable. University turned the account over to a lawyer, who pursued Reid for payment for the rest of the year. On December 31, Reid sent a $2,400 cheque to University Cycle Shop with a note that said, "Here's your money. Please call off your bloodhound!"

Journalize the following transactions for University Cycle Shop:

Jan.	19	Write-off of Reid's account against Allowance for Doubtful Accounts
Dec.	31	Reinstatement of Reid's account
	31	Collection of cash from Reid

S9–8 Tolco Importers Inc. had the following balances at the end of the year, before the year-end adjustments:

2

Applying the allowance method (aging-of-accounts-receivables and percent-of-accounts-receivable) to account for uncollectibles

1. Bad Debt Expense, $1,800

Accounts Receivable		Allowance for Doubtful Accounts	
148,000			4,000

The aging of accounts receivable yields these data:

	A	B	C	D
1		Age of Accounts Receivable		
2		0–60 Days	Over 60 Days	Total Receivables
3	Accounts receivable	$140,000	$8,000	$148,000
4	*Percent uncollectible*	*3%*	*20%*	

1. Journalize Tolco Importers Inc.'s entry to adjust the Allowance account to its correct balance at year end.
2. Prepare the T-account for Allowance for Doubtful Accounts.
3. Repeat question 1 assuming that, instead of aging the accounts, the allowance is calculated as 3.5 percent of the Accounts Receivable balance.

S9–9 Branson Shipping uses the direct write-off method in dealing with uncollectible accounts because it is highly unusual that the business ever has bad debts, and when they do they are not material in relation to total sales.

3

Use the direct write-off method

2019	
Oct. 15	Shipped goods for Marine Specialties on account, $2,200.
2020	
May 15	Received notice of bankruptcy from Marine Specialties and wrote off the amount they owed from the October 15 sale.

1. Journalize the transactions.
2. What is the major flaw in using the direct write-off method as opposed to the allowance method?

S9–10 Larry Libbey is a lawyer in Calgary. He uses the direct write-off method to account for uncollectible receivables because he rarely has delinquent accounts.

3

Applying the direct write-off method to account for uncollectibles

1. Bad Debt Expense, $6,000

At May 31, Libbey's accounts receivable totalled $32,000. During June, he earned revenue of $40,000 on account and collected $36,000 on account. He also wrote off uncollectible receivables of $6,000 on June 12.

1. Use the direct write-off method to journalize Libbey's write-off of the uncollectible receivables.
2. What is Libbey's balance of Accounts Receivable at June 30? Does he expect to collect the full amount? Explain.

S9–11 What job must be withheld from a company's credit department in order to safeguard its cash? If the credit department does perform this job, what can a credit department employee do to hurt the company?

3

Ensuring internal control over the collection of receivables

S9–12 Northern Consultants accepts American Express credit cards from its customers. Assume Northern makes a sale of $2,000 and the credit card company charges a 3 percent fee. Provide the journal entry on June 22 to record the sales revenue.

4

Recording credit card sales

S9–13 Gas stations do a large volume of business by customer credit cards and debit cards. An Esso station had these transactions on July 17:

4

Recording credit card and debit card sales

Debit cards, Cash, $15,680

MasterCard credit card sales	$20,000
Non-bank credit card sales	5,000
Debit card sales	16,000

Suppose MasterCard charges merchants 3 percent, non-bank credit card companies charge 4 percent, and the bank charges 2 percent for debit card transactions. Record these sale transactions for the Esso station.

(5) Defining common terms

S9–14 Match the terms with their correct definition.

Terms	Definitions
1. Accounts receivable	a. The party to a credit transaction who takes on an obligation/payable.
2. Other receivables	b. The party who receives a receivable and will collect cash in the future.
3. Debtor	c. A written promise to pay a specified amount of money at a particular future date.
4. Notes receivable	d. The date when the notes receivable is due.
5. Maturity date	e. A miscellaneous category that includes any other type of receivable where there is a right to receive cash in the future.
6. Creditor	f. The right to receive cash in the future from customers for goods sold or for services performed.

(5) Computing interest amounts on notes receivable

Note #1, $8,000

S9–15 For each of the following notes receivable, compute the amount of interest revenue earned during 2020. Use a 365-day year or base your calculations on the number of months, depending on how the interest period is stated, and round only your answer to the nearest dollar.

	Principal	Interest Rate	Interest Period During 2020
Note 1	$200,000	8%	6 months
Note 2	30,000	4%	75 days
Note 3	20,000	9%	60 days
Note 4	100,000	5%	3 months

(5) Accounting for notes receivable

2. Debit Cash, $201,973

S9–16 HSBC Bank lent $200,000 to Johann Schroeder on a 90-day, 4 percent note. Record the following transactions for HSBC, rounding to the nearest dollar (explanations are not required):

1. Lending the money on May 6.
2. Collecting the principal and interest at maturity. Specify the date. For the computation of interest, use a 365-day year.

(5) Accounting for notes receivable

3. $43

S9–17 Portage Planners accepted a $12,900 note from M. Bonicalzi in settlement of an old account receivable. The 4 percent note was dated October 2, 2019, and was due in four months.

1. What is the journal entry on Portage Planners' books on October 2, 2019?
2. Assume that Portage Planners' year end is December 31. How much interest revenue is accrued on December 31, 2019?
3. What is the amount of interest revenue in 2020?

(6) Collection period for receivables

1. 25 days

S9–18 Swift Media Sign Company sells on account. Recently, Swift reported these figures:

	2020	2019
Net sales	$600,060	$570,000
Receivables at year end	42,800	38,200

Required

1. Compute Swift Media Sign Company's days' sales in average receivables for 2020.
2. Suppose Swift's normal credit terms for a sale on account are 2/10, net 30. How well does Swift's collection period compare to the company's credit terms? Is this good or bad for Swift? Explain.

S9–19 Surfwood Co. and Berry's Bait Inc. are similar companies that operate within the same industry. The following information is available:

6 Computing key ratios for a company and assessing their meaning

		Surfwood Co.			Berry's Bait		
	Industry Average	2020	2019	2018	2020	2019	2018
Days' sales in receivables	32	28.3	31.8	33.9	36.7	30.5	29.9

Which company has the greater number of days in uncollected accounts in 2020? Is the days' sales in receivables generally favourable or unfavourable? Which company is showing an unfavourable trend in terms of managing accounts receivable?

S9–20 In determining how accounts should be presented, accountants are concerned about the values being both relevant and reliable. Is the accounts receivable value presented on the balance sheet both relevant and reliable under IFRS?

7 Receivables under IFRS

***S9–21** Bonavista Outdoors Store sells on account. When a customer account becomes three months old, Bonavista Outdoors Store converts the account to a notes receivable and immediately discounts the note to a bank. During the year, Bonavista Outdoors Store completed these transactions:

A1 Accounting for notes receivable, including a discounted note

Sep. 1 debit to Cash, $7,440

May	29	Sold goods on account to Raj Diwali, $9,600.
Sep.	1	Received an $8,000, 60-day, 8 percent note and cash of $1,600 from Raj Diwali in satisfaction of his past-due account receivable.
	1	Sold the Diwali note by discounting it to a bank for proceeds of $7,440.

Required

Record the transactions in Bonavista Outdoors Store's journal.

*This Exercise covers Chapter 9 Appendix topics.

EXERCISES

E9–1 From the following list of adjusted account balances, prepare the current asset section of Delainey's Hardscaping for December 31, 2020. Assume all accounts have normal balances.

1 Reporting receivables on the balance sheet

Accounts receivable	$51,000	Inventory	$22,000
Bad debt expense	1,200	Cash	15,000
Notes receivable, due August 31, 2021	12,000	Accumulated Amortization—Equipment	5,000
Supplies	1,440	Allowance for doubtful accounts	3,500
Notes receivable, due August 31, 2023	5,300	Equipment	25,000

E9–2 BooBoo's Home Health Care has the following adjusted account balances at April 30, 2020. All accounts have normal balances. Prepare the current asset section of BooBoo's balance sheet.

1 Reporting receivables on the balance sheet

Current assets, $313,050

Account Title	Balance
Accounts receivable	$ 51,000
Accumulated amortization—furniture	8,500
Allowance for doubtful accounts	2,500
Bad debt expense	4,100
Cash	98,700
Furniture	22,000
Inventory	122,750
Notes receivable, due July 1, 2020	41,000
Notes receivable, due November 1, 2023	68,000
Prepaid expenses	2,100

(2)
Using the allowance (percent-of sales) method for bad debts

2. Accounts Receivable, net $29,400

E9–3 On February 28, Big White Ski Equipment had a $25,500 debit balance in Accounts Receivable. During March, the company had sales of $65,500, which included $60,000 in credit sales. March collections were $53,000, and write-offs of uncollectible receivables totalled $1,250. Other data include:

a. February 28 credit balance in Allowance for Doubtful Accounts is $1,300.
b. Bad debt expense is estimated as 3 percent of credit sales.

Required

1. Prepare journal entries to record sales, collections, write-offs of uncollectibles during March, and bad debt expense by the allowance method (using the percent-of-sales method). Use March 31 as the journal entry date. Explanations are not required.
2. Prepare T-accounts to show the ending balances in Accounts Receivable and Allowance for Doubtful Accounts. Compute *net* Accounts Receivable at March 31. How much does Big White expect to collect?

(2)
Using the allowance (aging-of-accounts-receivable) method for bad debts

E9–4 Lui Dental began operations in January 2020 selling dental appliances to dentists. The following transactions occurred during the first six months of operations:

Jan. 15	Sold appliances to Dr. Hall on account for $15,750; cost $6,400.
Feb. 22	Received payment in full from Dr. Hall.
Mar. 4	Sold merchandise to Dr. Evans on account for $4,400; cost $1,250.
Apr. 20	Sold merchandise to Dr. Murray on account for $6,700; cost $2,990.
May 31	Sold merchandise to Dr. Kim on account for $3,200; cost $1,100.
Jun. 28	Received $3,000 on account from Dr. Evans.

Required

1. Complete the following aged listing of customer accounts as of June 30, 2020:

	A	B	C	D	E	F
1		Age of Accounts Receivable				
2	Customer	1–30 Days	31–60 Days	61–90 Days	Over 90 Days	Total
3	Dr. Evans					
4	Dr. Hall					
5	Dr. Kim	3,200				3,200
6	Dr. Murray					
7	Totals:					

2. Estimate the Allowance for Doubtful Accounts required at June 30, 2020, assuming the following uncollectible rates: 30 days, 2%; 60 days, 5%; 90 days, 15%; > 90 days, 50%.
3. Show how Lui Dental would report its accounts receivable on its June 30, 2020, balance sheet. What amounts would be reported on an income statement prepared for the six-month period ended June 30, 2020?
4. If Dr. Evans's account needed to be written off in September 2020, how accurate is Lui Dental at estimating its bad debts?

(1) (2)
Using the aging approach to estimate bad debts and reporting receivables on the balance sheet

2. Accounts Receivable, net, $288,500

E9–5 At December 31, 2020, the Accounts Receivable balance of Stenner's Electronics is $300,000. The Allowance for Doubtful Accounts has an $8,900 credit balance. Accountants for Stenner's Electronics prepare the following aging schedule for its accounts receivable:

	A	B	C	D	E	F
1		Age of Accounts Receivable				
2		1–30 Days	31–60 Days	61–90 Days	Over 90 Days	Total
3	Accounts Receivable	$140,000	$80,000	$70,000	$10,000	$300,000
4	Estimated percent uncollectible	0.5%	2.0%	6.0%	50.0%	
5	Allowance Needed					

Required

1. Journalize the adjusting entry for doubtful accounts based on the aging schedule. Show the T-account for the allowance at December 31, 2020.
2. Show how Stenner's Electronics will report Accounts Receivable on its December 31, 2020, balance sheet.
3. Suppose all the facts of this situation are the same except that Allowance for Doubtful Accounts has a $900 debit balance. Calculate the amount of the adjusting entry.

E9–6 Angel Landscaping Services started the year 2020 with an Accounts Receivable balance of $40,500 and an Allowance for Doubtful Accounts balance of $4,310. During the year, $4,290 of accounts receivable were identified as uncollectible. Sales revenue for 2020 was $429,000, including credit sales of $422,400. Cash collections on account were $415,600 during the year.

(2)
Using the allowance method to account for uncollectibles

5. Accounts receivable, net, $40,711

The aging of accounts receivable yields these data:

	A	B	C	D	E	F
1		**Age of Accounts Receivable**				
2		**0–30 Days**	**31–60 Days**	**61–90 Days**	**Over 90 Days**	**Total**
3	Amount of receivable	$26,400	$6,600	$5,500	$4,510	$43,010
4	*Percent uncollectible*	1%	1%	3%	40%	

You are the accountant preparing the December 31, 2020, year-end entries.

Required

1. Journalize Angel's (a) credit sales, (b) cash collections on account, (c) write-off of the accounts receivable identified as uncollectible, and (d) bad debt expense based on 0.5 percent of credit sales.
2. Prepare a T-account for the Accounts Receivable and Allowance for Doubtful Accounts accounts.
3. Calculate the balance in Allowance for Doubtful Accounts based on the aging-of-accounts-receivable method.
4. Make any adjustment required to the Allowance for Doubtful Accounts based on your calculation in Requirement 3.
5. Show how Angel Landscaping Services should report Accounts Receivable on the balance sheet.

E9–7 Acme Cell Phones had a debit balance in Accounts Receivable of $100,000 on January 1, 2020. On that date, Acme sold $80,000 of merchandise to Brodie Trucking Company on account. Ignore the cost of goods sold.

(2) (3)
Sales, write-offs, and bad debt recovery using the allowance method and the direct write-off method

3. Accounts Receivable, ending bal., $100,000

On January 28, Brodie paid only $56,000 of the account receivable.

After repeated attempts to collect, Acme finally wrote off its accounts receivable from Brodie on May 31.

On December 1, Acme received Brodie's cheque for $24,000 with a note apologizing for the late payment.

Required

1. Journalize the Acme Cell Phones transactions.
2. Record the May 31 and December 1 journal entries as if Acme Cell Phones were using the direct write-off method.
3. What amount of net Accounts Receivable would Acme Cell Phones report on its December 31, 2020, balance sheet under the direct write-off method? Does Acme expect to collect this much of the receivable? Give your reasons.

(2) (3) Interpreting amounts from T-accounts resulting from the allowance method

E9–8 Wellington Corp. summarized its accounts receivable activity in the following two T-accounts:

Accounts Receivable		
Dec. 31, 2019 Bal.	80,000	
	320,000	350,000
		5,800
	500	500
Dec. 31, 2020 Bal.	44,200	

Allowance for Doubtful Accounts		
	6,000	Dec. 31, 2019 Bal.
	500	
5,800	4,900	
	5,600	Dec. 31, 2020 Bal.

Required

Analyze the information presented in the T-accounts and identify the amount related to each of the following:

a. Credit sales during the period.
b. Collection of credit sales during the period.
c. Write-off of a delinquent account.
d. Recovery of an account previously written off.
e. Adjusting entry to estimate bad debts.

(4) Accounting for debit card sales and credit card sales

E9–9 Record the following transactions in the general journal of Jesse's Quick Clean Service. Assume Scotiabank charges merchants $0.50 per debit card transaction and MasterCard charges 4 percent of sales as service fees.

Mar.	31	Scotiabank debit card sales of $22,000, consisting of 1,500 transactions.
	31	MasterCard credit card sales of $33,000.
Mar.	31	FleetPlan card accepted for $2,800 of payments. This card requires that receipts are submitted for payment manually. A 2 percent fee applies.
Apr.	10	Payment was received from FleetPlan.

(5) Recording notes receivable and accruing interest revenue

Nov. 30 Interest Revenue, $310.02

E9–10 Record the following transactions in the journal of Seaview Supplies, which ends its accounting year on November 30:

Oct.	1	Lent $88,000 cash to Joe Lazarus on a one-year, 2 percent note.
Nov.	3	Sold goods to Highwater Inc., receiving a 100-day, 4 percent note for $3,162.50. Cost of the goods was $2,000.00. Seaview uses a perpetual inventory system.
	16	Received a $2,200, six-month, 8 percent note on account from STM Inc. when the receivable for that amount could not be paid on time.
	30	Accrued interest revenue on all notes receivable.

Hint: Recall that you divide by days or months depending on the terms of the note.

(5) Notes receivable transactions

$36.99 accrual

E9–11 Tropical North Company, which has a December 31 year end and uses a periodic inventory system, completed the following transactions during 2019 and 2020:

2019		
Oct.	14	Sold merchandise to OFTR Racing, receiving a 60-day, 6 percent note for $5,000.
Nov.	16	Sold merchandise to Sunshine Racing, receiving a 72-day, 4 percent note for $7,500.
Dec.	13	Received amount due from OFTR Racing.
Dec.	31	Accrued interest on the Sunshine Racing note.
2020		
Jan.	27	Collected in full from Sunshine Company.

Required

Prepare the necessary journal entries to record the above transactions. Assume that a 365-day year is used for calculations. Round all answers to the nearest cent.

E9–12 On September 30, 2019, Team Bank loaned $94,000 to Kendall Warner on a one-year, 6 percent note. Team's fiscal year ends on December 31.

(5) Journalizing notes receivable transactions including a dishonoured note

Required

1. Journalize all entries for Team Bank related to the note for 2019 and 2020.
2. Which party has a
   a. Notes receivable?
   b. Note payable?
   c. Interest revenue?
   d. Interest expense?
3. Suppose that Kendall Warner defaulted on the note. What entry would Team record for the dishonoured note?

E9–13 Unique Media Sign Incorporated sells on account. Recently, Unique reported the following figures:

(6) Analyzing receivables

	2019	2018
Net Credit Sales	$594,920	$602,000
Net Receivables at end of year	38,500	47,100

Required

1. Compute Unique's days' sales in receivables and accounts receivable turnover for 2019. (Round to the nearest day.)
2. Suppose Unique's normal credit terms for a sale on account are 2/10, net 30. How well does Unique's collection period compare to the company's credit terms? Is this good or bad for Unique?

E9–14 Vision Electronics, which makes DVD players, reported the following items at February 28, 2020 (amounts in thousands, with last year's—2019—amounts also given as needed):

(6) Using ratios to evaluate a company

a. 0.78

Accounts Payable	$1,796	Accounts Receivable, net	
Cash	860	February 29, 2020	$ 440
Inventories		February 28, 2019	300
February 29, 2020	380	Cost of Goods Sold	4,800
February 28, 2019	320	Short-term Investments	330
Net Sales Revenue	7,720	Other Current Assets	180
Long-term Assets	820	Other Current Liabilities	290
Long-term Liabilities	20		

Compute for 2020 Vision Electronics' (a) acid-test ratio, (b) days' sales in average receivables, (c) current ratio, (d) debt ratio, (e) gross margin percent, (f) inventory turnover. Evaluate each ratio value as strong or weak. Assume Vision Electronics sells on terms of net 30.

E9–15 Franklin Ltd., a gift store, reported the following amounts in its 2020 financial statements. The 2019 figures are given for comparison.

(6) Evaluating ratio data

1. 2020, 0.72

	2020		2019	
Current assets				
Cash		$ 12,000		$ 26,000
Short-term investments		46,000		22,000
Accounts receivable	$120,000		$148,000	
Less: Allow. for doubtful accts	20,000	100,000	18,000	130,000
Inventory		384,000		378,000
Prepaid insurance		4,000		4,000
Total current assets		$ 546,000		$ 560,000
Total current liabilities		$ 218,000		$ 224,000
Net sales		$1,460,000		$1,464,000

Required

1. Determine whether Franklin Ltd.'s acid-test ratio improved or deteriorated from 2019 to 2020. How does Franklin Ltd.'s acid-test ratio compare with the industry average of 0.90?
2. Compare the days' sales in receivables measure for 2020 with the company's credit terms of net 30. What action, if any, should Franklin Ltd. take?
3. Indicate the most likely effect of the following changes in credit policy on the days' sales in receivables (+ for increase, − for decrease, and NE for no effect):
   a. Granted credit to people with poor credit history.
   b. Increased collection techniques or methods.
   c. Granted credit with discounts for early payment.

(6) Using the acid-test ratio, accounts receivable turnover ratio, and days' sales in receivables to evaluate a company

E9–16 Silver Clothiers reported the following selected items at April 30, 2020 (previous year's—2019—amounts also given as needed):

Accounts Payable	$ 328,000	Accounts Receivable, net	
Cash	573,720	April 30, 2020	$ 11,000
Inventory		April 30, 2019	165,000
April 30, 2020	250,000	Cost of Goods Sold	1,200,000
April 30, 2019	210,000	Short-term Investments	148,000
Net Credit Sales Revenue	3,212,000	Other Current Assets	100,000
Long-term Assets	350,000	Other Current Liabilities	188,000
Long-term Liabilities	130,000		

Compute Silver's (a) acid-test ratio, (b) accounts receivable turnover ratio, and (c) days' sales in receivables (using the turnover ratio) for the year ending April 30, 2020. Evaluate each ratio value as strong or weak. Silver sells on terms of net 30. (Round days' sales in receivables to a whole number.)

(A1) Discounting a notes receivable
Cash proceeds, $199,233

***E9–17** Suncare Company installs switching systems and receives its pay in the form of notes receivable. It installed a system for the City of Edson, Alberta, receiving a nine-month, 10 percent, $200,000 notes receivable on May 31, 2020. To obtain cash quickly, Suncare discounted the note with HSBC Bank on June 30, 2020. The bank charged a discount rate of 11 percent.

Compute Suncare's cash proceeds from discounting the note. Follow the five-step procedure outlined in Exhibit 9–1A on page 515. Round to the nearest dollar.

(5) (A1) Accounting for notes receivable, including a discounted note
Jun. 30 debit to Cash, $199,233

***E9–18** Use your answers to E9–17 to journalize Suncare Company's transactions as follows (round to the nearest dollar):

May	31	Sold a telecommunications system, receiving a nine-month, 10 percent, $200,000 note from the city of Edson, Alberta. Suncare Company's cost of the system was $131,250.
Jun.	30	Received cash for interest revenue for one month.
	30	Discounted the note to HSBC Bank at a discount rate of 11 percent.

*These Exercises cover Chapter 9 Appendix topics.

USING EXCEL

Using Excel for Aging Accounts Receivable

E9–19 *Download an Excel template for this problem online in MyLab Accounting.* The Lake Lucerne Company uses the allowance method of estimating bad debts expense. An aging schedule is prepared in order to calculate the balance in the allowance account.

The percentage uncollectible is calculated as follows:

1–30 Days	1%
31–60 Days	2%
61–90 Days	5%
91–365 Days	50%

After 365 days, the account is written off.

Required

Use the Excel file provided online to:

1. Calculate the number of days each receivable is outstanding
2. Complete the Schedule of Accounts Receivable.
3. Journalize the adjusting entry for bad debt expense.

Excel Skills

1. Use the DAYS function to calculate the number of days between the invoice date and the date of the aging schedule.
2. Use the VLOOKUP function to provide the uncollectible accounts percentage based on the days outstanding.
3. Use IF and AND functions to determine in which column of the Accounts Receivable Schedule to place the amount for each customer.
4. Format cells using number and percentage formats.
5. Use formulas to calculate totals.
6. Use the Increase Indent button to indent the credit account for the journal entry.
7. Use absolute references to refer to a table in the vlookup formula.

SERIAL EXERCISE

E9-20 *The Serial Exercise involves a company that will be revisited throughout relevant chapters in Volume 1 and Volume 2. You can complete the Serial Exercises using MyLab Accounting.*

① ② Receivables using the allowance method

1 c. June 30, 2021, Allowance balance, $689

This exercise continues recordkeeping for the Canyon Canoe Company. Students do not have to complete prior exercises in order to answer this exercise.

Canyon Canoe Company has experienced rapid growth in its first few months of operations and has had a significant increase in customers renting canoes and purchasing T-shirts. Many of these customers are asking for credit terms. Amber Wilson, owner and company manager, has decided it is time to review the business transactions and update some of the business practices. Her first step is to make decisions about handling accounts receivable. So far, year-to-date credit sales have been $15,500. A review of outstanding receivables resulted in the following aging schedule:

	A	B	C	D	E	F
1	**Age of Accounts as of June 30, 2021**					
2	**Customer Name**	**1–30 Days**	**31–60 Days**	**61–90 Days**	**Over 90 Days**	**Total**
3	Canyon Youth Club	$ 250				$ 250
4	Crazy Tees	200	$150			350
5	Early Start Daycare				$500	500
6	Lakefront Pavilion	575				575
7	Outdoor Center			$300		300
8	Rivers Canoe Club	350				350
9	Sport Shirts	450	120			570
10	Zack's Marina	75	75	75		225
11	Totals	$1,900	$345	$375	$500	$3,120

Required

1. The company wants to use the allowance method to estimate bad debts. Determine the estimated bad debts expense under the following methods at June 30, 2021. Assume a zero beginning balance for Allowance for Doubtful Accounts. Round to the nearest dollar.
   a. Percent-of-sales method, assuming 4.5% of credit sales will not be collected.
   b. Percent-of-receivables method, assuming 22.5% of receivables will not be collected.

c. Aging-of-receivables method, assuming 5% of invoices 1–30 days will not be collected, 20% of invoices 31–60 days, 40% of invoices 61–90 days, and 75% of invoices over 90 days.

2. Journalize the entry at June 30, 2021, to adjust for bad debts expense using the percent-of-sales method.
3. Journalize the entry at June 30, 2021, to record the write-off of the Early Start Daycare invoice.
4. At June 30, 2021, open T-accounts for Accounts Receivable and Allowance for Doubtful Accounts before requirements 2 and 3. Post entries from requirements 2 and 3 to those accounts. Assume a zero beginning balance for Allowance for Doubtful Accounts.
5. Show how Canyon Canoe Company will report net accounts receivable on the balance sheet on June 30, 2021.

PRACTICE SET

(1) (2) (3)
Accounting for uncollectible accounts using the allowance method and reporting net accounts receivable on the balance sheet

E9-21 *This problem continues the Crystal Clear Cleaning problem begun in Chapter 2 and continued through Chapter 8.*

Crystal Clear Cleaning uses the allowance method to estimate bad debts. Consider the following April 2020 transactions for Crystal Clear Cleaning:

Apr.	1	Performed cleaning service for Shiree's Home Staging for $13,000 on account with terms n/20.
	10	Borrowed money from First Provincial Bank, $30,000, making a 180-day, 12% note.
	12	After discussions with customer More Shine, Crystal Clear has determined that $230 of the receivable owed will not be collected. Wrote off this portion of the receivable.
	15	Sold goods to Warner for $9,000 on account with terms n/30. Cost of Goods Sold was $4,500.
	28	Sold goods to Lelaine, Inc. for cash of $2,800 (cost $840).
	28	Collected from More Shine $230 of receivable previously written off.
	29	Paid cash for utilities of $150.
	30	Create an aging schedule for Crystal Clear Cleaning for accounts receivable. Crystal Clear determined that $7,000 of receivables outstanding for 1–30 days were 3% uncollectible, $10,000 of receivables outstanding for 31–60 days were 20% uncollectible, and $5,870 of receivables outstanding for more than 60 days were 30% uncollectible. Then determine the total amount of estimated uncollectible receivables and adjust the Allowance for Doubtful Accounts. Assume the account had an unadjusted credit balance of $260. (Round to nearest whole dollar.) Write the adjusting entry.

Required

1. Prepare all required journal entries for Crystal Clear. Omit explanations.
2. Show how net accounts receivable would be reported on the balance sheet as of April 30, 2020.

CHALLENGE EXERCISES

(4)
Evaluating credit card sales for profitability

Net income with bank credit cards, $489,200

E9-22 Trendy Fashions provides store credit and manages its own receivables. Average experience for the past three years has been as follows:

	Cash	Credit	Total
Sales	$1,040,000	$700,000	$1,740,000
Cost of Goods Sold	624,000	420,000	1,044,000
Bad Debt Expense	—	38,000	38,000
Other Expenses	115,600	106,000	221,600

Helen Tran, the owner, is considering whether to accept bank credit cards and discontinue providing store credit. Typically, the availability of bank credit cards increases credit sales by 15 percent. But the bank credit card companies charge approximately

4 percent of credit card sales. If Tran switches to bank credit cards, she can save $5,000 on accounting and other expenses and will eliminate bad debt expense. She figures that cash customers will continue buying in the same volume regardless of the type of credit the store offers.

Required

Should Trendy Fashions start offering bank credit card service and discontinue providing store credit? Show the computations of net income under the present plan and under the bank credit card plan.

BEYOND THE NUMBERS

BN9–1

1 Reporting receivables on the balance sheet

Aug. 31, 2020, Accounts Receivable, $126,250

Bhatti Communications' cash flow statement reported the following *cash* receipts and *cash* payments (the amount in brackets) for the year ended August 31, 2020:

BHATTI COMMUNICATIONS Cash Flow Statement For the Year Ended August 31, 2020	
Cash flows from operating activities	
Cash receipts from customers	$827,500
Interest received	2,300
Cash flows from investing activities	
Loans made on notes receivable	(13,750)
Collection of loans on notes receivable	27,500

Bhatti's balance sheet one year earlier—at August 31, 2019—reported Accounts Receivable of $93,750 and Notes Receivable of $20,750. Credit sales for the year ended August 31, 2020, totalled $860,000, and the company collects all of its accounts receivable because uncollectibles rarely occur.

Bhatti Communications needs a loan, and the manager is preparing the company's balance sheet at August 31, 2020. To complete the balance sheet, the owner needs to know the balances of Accounts Receivable and Notes Receivable at August 31, 2020. Supply the needed information; T-accounts are helpful.

ETHICAL ISSUE

EI9–1

Dylan worked for a propane gas distributor as an accounting clerk in a small town. Last winter, his brother Mike lost his job at the machine plant. By January, temperatures were sub-zero, and Mike had run out of money. Dylan saw that Mike's account was overdue, and he knew Mike needed another delivery to heat his home. He decided to credit Mike's account and debit the balance to the parts inventory because he knew the parts manager, the owner's son, was incompetent and would never notice the extra entry. Months went by, and Dylan repeated the process until an auditor ran across the charges by chance. When the owner fired Dylan, he said, "If you had only come to me and told me about Mike's situation, we could have worked something out."

Required

1. What can a business like this do to prevent employee behaviour of this kind?
2. What effect would Dylan's actions have on the balance sheet? The income statement?
3. How much discretion does a business have with regard to accommodating hardship situations?

PROBLEMS (GROUP A)

(2) Using the percent-of-sales and aging-of-accounts-receivable approaches for uncollectibles

3. Accounts Receivable, net in 2020, $319,361

P9–1A The September 30, 2020, balance sheet of Kroenke Products reported the following:

Accounts Receivable	$310,000
Allowance for Doubtful Accounts (credit balance)	10,000

During the last quarter of 2020, Kroenke Products completed the following selected transactions:

Dec.	30	Wrote off the following accounts receivable as uncollectible: Barry White, $2,500; Carlos Media, $2,200; and Doug Zabellos, $1,100.
	31	Recorded bad debt expense (rounded up to the nearest dollar) based on the aging of accounts receivable, as follows:

	A	B	C	D	E	F
1	**Age of Accounts Receivable**					
2		**1–30 Days**	**31–60 Days**	**61–90 Days**	**Over 90 Days**	**Total**
3	Accounts Receivable	$179,000	$95,000	$37,500	$17,000	$328,500
4	Estimated percent uncollectible	0.1%	0.3%	5.0%	40.0%	
5						

Required

1. Record the transactions in the general journal.
2. Open the Allowance for Doubtful Accounts three-column ledger account and post entries affecting that account. Keep a running balance.
3. Most companies report two-year comparative financial statements. If Kroenke Products' Accounts Receivable balance was $320,000 and the Allowance for Doubtful Accounts stood at $12,000 at December 31, 2019, show how the company will report its Accounts Receivable in a comparative balance sheet for 2020 and 2019.
4. Suppose, on December 31, the bad debt expense was based on an estimate of 4 percent of the accounts receivable balance rather than on the aging of accounts receivable. Record the December 31, 2020, entry for bad debt expense in the general journal.

(2) Use the percent-of-sales, aging-of-accounts-receivable, and percent-of-accounts-receivable methods for uncollectibles

3. Net Accounts Receivable, $129,282.50

P9–2A Matiere Co. completed the following transactions during 2019 and 2020:

2019		
Dec.	31	Estimated that bad debt expense for the year was 3 percent of credit sales of $385,000 and recorded that amount as expense.
	31	Made the closing entry for bad debt expense.
2020		
Mar.	26	Sold inventory to Mabel Sanders, $10,037.50, on credit terms of 2/10, n/30. Ignore cost of goods sold.
Sep.	15	Wrote off Mabel Sanders's account as uncollectible after repeated efforts to collect from her.
Nov.	10	Received $5,500 from Sanders, along with a letter stating her intention to pay her debt in full within 30 days. Reinstated her account in full.
Dec.	5	Received the balance due from Sanders.
	31	Made a compound entry to write off the following accounts as uncollectible: Curt Major, $2,200; Bernadette Lalonde, $962.50; Ellen Smart, $1,470.
	31	Estimated that bad debt expense for the year was 2 percent of credit sales of $490,000 and recorded the expense.
	31	Made the closing entry for bad debt expense.

Matiere records all amounts to the nearest cent. Present all amounts to two decimal places.

Required

1. Open three-column general ledger accounts for Allowance for Doubtful Accounts and Bad Debt Expense. Keep running balances.
   2. Record the transactions in the general journal and post to the ledger accounts.
   3. The December 31, 2020, balance of Accounts Receivable is $146,000. Show how Accounts Receivable would be reported at that date.
4. Assume that Matiere Co. begins aging accounts receivable on December 31, 2020. The balance in Accounts Receivable is $146,000, the credit balance in Allowance for Doubtful Accounts is $16,717.50 (use your calculations from Requirement 3), and the company estimates that $19,900 of its accounts receivable will prove uncollectible.
   a. Make the adjusting entry for uncollectibles.
   b. Show how Accounts Receivable will be reported on the December 31, 2020, balance sheet after this adjusting entry.

P9–3A The Generation Employment Agency started business on January 1, 2020. The company produced monthly financial statements and had total sales of $525,000 (of which $400,000 was on account) during the first four months.

On April 30, Accounts Receivable had a balance of $236,400 (no accounts have been written off to date), which was made up of the following accounts aged according to the date of the sale:

① ②

Estimating uncollectibles using the aging-of-accounts method and reporting receivables on the balance sheet

2. a. Accounts Receivable, net May 31, $258,624

	A	B	C	D	E
1			Month of Sale		
2	**Customer**	**January**	**February**	**March**	**April**
3	Golden Distributors	$ 3,600	$ 1,000	$ 2,000	$ 1,800
4	PG Courier	1,000	1,200	3,400	2,400
5	Personnel Solutions	5,000	14,000	8,000	4,000
6	Natures Design	2,000	7,400	8,120	28,400
7	Other Accounts Receivable	23,760	16,360	53,480	49,480
8		$35,360	$39,960	$75,000	$86,080

The following accounts receivable transactions took place in May 2020:

May 12 Decided the PG Courier account was uncollectible and wrote it off.

15 Collected $6,600 from Golden Distributors for sales made in the first three months.

21 Decided the Personnel Solutions account was uncollectible and wrote it off.

24 Collected $2,000 from Natures Design for sales made in the month of January.

26 Received a cheque from Personnel Solutions for $18,200 plus four cheques of $3,200 each, postdated to June 26, July 26, August 26, and September 26.

31 Total sales in the month were $380,000; 90 percent of these were on account, and 75 percent of the sales on account were collected in the month.

Required

1. The Generation Employment Agency has heard that other companies in the industry use the allowance method of accounting for uncollectibles, with many of these estimating the uncollectibles through an aging of accounts receivable.
   a. Journalize the adjustments that would have to be made on April 30 (for the months of January through April), assuming the following estimates of uncollectibles:

Age of Accounts Receivable	Percent Estimated Uncollectible
From current month	3%
From prior month	4
From two months prior	10
From three months prior	20
From four months prior	45

(Round your total estimate to the nearest whole dollar.)

b. Journalize the transactions of May 2020.

c. Journalize the month-end adjustment, using the information from the table that appears in Requirement 1a.

2. For the method of accounting for the uncollectibles used above, show:

a. The balance sheet presentation of the accounts receivable.

b. The overall effect of the uncollectibles on the income statement for the months of April and May 2020.

(2) (3)

Accounting for uncollectibles by the direct write-off and allowance methods

4. Net Accounts Receivable, allowance method, $361,300

P9-4A On March 31, 2020, Summitt Manufacturing had a $290,000 debit balance in Accounts Receivable. During April, the business had sales revenue of $1,150,000, which included $990,000 in credit sales. Other data for April include the following:

a. Collections on accounts receivable, $910,000.

b. Write-offs of uncollectible receivables, $4,500.

Required

1. Record bad debt expense for April by the direct write-off method. Use T-accounts to show all April activity in Accounts Receivable and Bad Debt Expense.
2. Record bad debt expense and write-offs of customer accounts for April by the allowance method. Use T-accounts to show all April activity in Accounts Receivable, Allowance for Doubtful Accounts, and Bad Debt Expense. The March 31 unadjusted balance in Allowance for Doubtful Accounts was $1,200 (debit). Bad debt expense was estimated at 1 percent of credit sales.
3. What amount of bad debt expense would Summitt report on its April income statement under the two methods? Which amount better matches expense with revenue? Give your reason.
4. What amount of *net* accounts receivable would Summitt report on its April 30 balance sheet under the two methods? Which amount is more realistic? Give your reason.

(5)

Accounting for notes receivable, including accruing interest revenue

1. Note (a), $9,090.00

P9-5A The Door Company received the following notes during 2020:

	A	B	C	D	E	F	G	H
1	Note	Date	Principal Amount	Interest Rate	Term	Due Date	Interest	Maturity Value
2	(a)	Aug. 30	$ 9,000	4%	3 months			
3	(b)	Nov. 19	12,000	3	60 days			
4	(c)	Dec. 1	15,000	5	1 year			
5	(d)	Dec. 1	20,000	6	2 years			

Required

1. Determine the due date, interest cost, and maturity value of each note. Round all interest amounts to the nearest cent.
2. Journalize a single adjusting entry at December 31, 2020, to record accrued interest revenue on the notes. An explanation is not required.
3. Journalize the collection of principal and interest on note (b). Explanations are not required.
4. Show how these notes will be reported on the balance sheet at December 31, 2020.

P9–6A Record the following selected transactions in the general journal of WM Gaming Supplies and show all your answers to two decimal places. Explanations are not required.

(4) (5) Accounting for credit card sales, notes receivable, dishonoured notes, and accrued interest revenue

Jan. 20, 2020, Interest Revenue. $39.46

2019		
Nov.	21	Received an $18,000, 60-day, 4 percent note from Barb Nuefield on account.
	30	Recorded VISA credit card sales of $26,000. VISA charges 3 percent of sales.
Dec.	31	Made an adjusting entry to accrue interest on the Nuefield note.
	31	Made an adjusting entry to record bad debt expense based on 3 percent of credit sales of $1,950,000.
	31	Made a compound closing entry for Interest Revenue and Bad Debt Expense (ignore credit card sales and charges).
2020		
Jan.	20	Collected the maturity value of the Nuefield note.
Mar.	14	Lent $20,000 cash to Morgan Supplies, receiving a six-month, 5 percent note.
	30	Received a $5,600, 30-day, 10 percent note from Quin Carson on his past-due account receivable.
May	29	Carson dishonoured (failed to pay) his note at maturity; after attempting to collect his note for one month, wrote off the account as uncollectible.
Sep.	14	Collected the maturity value of the Morgan Supplies note.
	30	Wrote off as uncollectible the accounts receivable of Sue Parsons, $3,250, and Mac Gally, $5,200.

P9–7A Assume that Brechin Farm Equipment completed the following selected transactions:

(4) (5) Journalizing uncollectible notes receivable and accrued interest revenue

Dec. 2, 2020, cash received, $11,241.42

2019		
Dec.	1	Sold equipment to Fifty Acres Farms, receiving a $40,000, six-month, 5 percent note. Ignore cost of goods sold.
	31	Made an adjusting entry to accrue interest on the Fifty Acres Farms note.
	31	Made an adjusting entry to record bad debt expense based on an aging of accounts receivable. The aging analysis indicates that $56,200 of accounts receivable will not be collected. Prior to this adjustment, the credit balance in Allowance for Doubtful Accounts is $47,500.
2020		
Jun.	1	Collected the maturity value of the Fifty Acres Farms note.
	30	Sold repair services for $16,000 on MasterCard. MasterCard charges 1.75 percent.
Jul.	21	Sold merchandise to Marco Donolo, receiving a 45-day, 3 percent note for $11,200. Ignore cost of goods sold.
Sep.	4	Donolo dishonoured (failed to pay) his note at maturity; converted the maturity value of the note to an account receivable.
Nov.	11	Sold merchandise to Solomon Tractor for $9,600, receiving a 120-day, 5 percent note. Ignore cost of goods sold.
Dec.	2	Collected in full from Donolo.
	31	Accrued the interest on the Solomon Tractor note.

Required Record the transactions in the general journal. Explanations are not required. Round all answers to two decimal places.

P9–8A Eastern Supply uses the allowance method in accounting for uncollectible accounts with the estimate based on the aging-of-accounts-receivable method. The company had the following account balances on August 31, 2020:

(2) (5) Using the allowance method of accounting for uncollectibles, estimating uncollectibles by the percent-of-sales and the aging-of-accounts-receivable methods, accounting for notes receivable

2. Bad Debt Expense, debit, $48,960

Accounts Receivable	$687,000
Allowance for Doubtful Accounts (credit balance)	72,600

The following transactions took place during September 2020:

Sep. 2 Elbow Inc., which owes $48,000, is unable to pay on time and has given a 25-day, 8 percent note in settlement of the account.

6 Received from Irma Good the amount owed on an August 7 dishonoured note, plus extra interest for 30 days at 4 percent computed on the maturity value of the note ($12,600). This dishonoured note had been converted to an account receivable on August 7.

9 Received notice that a customer (Tony Goad) has filed for bankruptcy. Goad owes $19,200. The courts will confirm the amount recoverable at a later date.

11 Determined the account receivable from Kay Walsh ($9,120) was uncollectible and wrote it off.

18 Received a cheque from the courts in the amount of $15,000 as final settlement of Goad's account.

27 Elbow Inc. paid the note received on September 2.

27 Determined the account receivable for Dave Campbell ($5,040) was uncollectible and wrote it off.

30 Sales for the month totalled $720,000 (of which 85 percent were on account), and collections on account totalled $601,200.

30 Eastern Supply did an aging of accounts receivable that indicated that $75,000 is expected to be uncollectible. The company recorded the appropriate adjustment.

Required

1. Record the above transactions in the general journal. Show all amounts to two decimal places.
2. What would be the adjusting entry required on September 30 if the company used the percent-of-sales method with an estimate of uncollectibles equal to 8 percent of credit sales?
3. Which of the two methods of estimating uncollectible accounts would normally be more accurate? Why?

6

Using ratio data to evaluate a company's financial position

For 2019: a. 1.66

P9–9A The comparative financial statements of Bita Company for 2020, 2019, and 2018 included the following selected data:

	2020	2019	2018
		(in thousands)	
Balance Sheet			
Current assets			
Cash	$ 80	$ 80	$ 40
Short-term investments	280	400	240
Receivables, net	760	600	480
Inventories	1,680	1,520	1,360
Prepaid expenses	120	120	80
Total current assets	$ 2,920	$ 2,720	$2,200
Total current liabilities	$ 1,920	$ 1,640	$1,520
Income Statement			
Sales revenue	$10,400	$10,000	$7,600

Required

1. Compute these ratios for 2020 and 2019, assuming that all sales are on account:
   a. Current ratio (round to two decimal places)
   b. Acid-test ratio (round to two decimal places)
   c. Days' sales in receivables (round to nearest full day)
   d. Accounts receivable turnover (round to nearest full turn)

2. Write a brief memo explaining to Adrian Crane, owner of Bita Company, which ratio values showed improvement from 2019 to 2020 and which ratio values deteriorated. Discuss whether this trend is favourable or unfavourable for the company.

***P9–10A** A company received the following notes during 2020. The notes were discounted on the dates and at the rates indicated.

A1
Discounting notes receivable
2. Proceeds from discounting: Note (a), $20,063.16

	A	B	C	D	E	F	G
1	Note	Date	Principal Amount	Interest Rate	Term	Date Discounted	Discount Rate
2	(a)	Jun. 15	$20,000	8%	60 days	Jul. 15	12%
3	(b)	Aug. 1	9,000	10	90 days	Aug. 27	12
4	(c)	Nov. 21	12,000	15	90 days	Dec. 4	15

Required Identify each note by letter, compute interest using a 365-day year for all notes, and round all interest amounts to the nearest cent. Explanations are not required.

1. Determine the due date and maturity value of each note.
2. Determine the discount and proceeds from the sale (discounting) of each note.
3. Write the general journal entry to record the discounting of note (b).

PROBLEMS (GROUP B)

P9–1B The November 30, 2020, balance sheet of Thyme Company reported the following:

2
Using the percent-of-sales, aging-of-accounts-receivable, and percent-of-accounts-receivable methods for uncollectibles

Accounts Receivable	$358,000
Allowance for Doubtful Accounts (credit balance)	7,700

At the end of each quarter, Thyme estimates bad debt expense to be 2 percent of credit sales. At the end of the year, the company ages its accounts receivable and adjusts the balance in Allowance for Doubtful Accounts to correspond to the aging schedule. During the last month of 2020, Thyme completes the following selected transactions:

Dec. 9 Made a compound entry to write off the following uncollectible accounts: M. Yang, $710; Tory Ltd., $315; and S. Roberts, $1,050.

18 Wrote off as uncollectible the $1,360 account receivable from Acme Ltd. and the $790 account receivable from Data Services.

31 Receivables clerk posts quarterly update of bad debt expense based on credit sales of $420,000.

31 Accountant makes year-end adjustment to update the balance in the Allowance for Doubtful Accounts balance based on the following summary of the aging of accounts receivable:

	A	B	C	D	E	F
1		Age of Accounts Receivable				
2		1–30 Days	31–60 Days	61–90 Days	Over 90 Days	Total
3	Accounts Receivable	$188,400	$78,500	$40,500	$34,500	$341,900
4	Estimated percent uncollectible	0.15%	0.5%	7.0%	35.0%	

Required

1. Record the transactions in the general journal.
2. Open the Allowance for Doubtful Accounts three-column ledger account and post entries affecting that account. Keep a running balance.

*This Problem covers Chapter 9 Appendix topics.

3. Most companies report two-year comparative financial statements. If Thyme Company's Accounts Receivable balance was $299,500 and the Allowance for Doubtful Accounts stood at $9,975 on December 31, 2019, show how the company will report its accounts receivable on a comparative balance sheet for 2020 and 2019.
4. Suppose, on December 31, 2020, the bad debt expense was based on an estimate of 3 percent of the accounts receivable balance rather than on the aging of accounts receivable. Record the December 31, 2020, entry for bad debt expense in the general journal.

(2) Using the percent-of-sales and aging-of-accounts methods for uncollectibles

P9–2B Choices Clothing completed the following selected transactions during 2019 and 2020:

2019

Dec. 31	Estimated that bad debt expense for the year was 3 percent of credit sales of $748,000 and recorded that amount as expense.
31	Made the closing entry for the bad debt expense account.

2020

Feb. 17	Sold inventory to Bruce Jones, $1,412, on credit terms of 2/10, n/30. Ignore the cost of goods sold.
Jul. 29	Wrote off Jones's account as uncollectible after repeated efforts to collect from the customer.
Sep. 6	Received $1,150 from Bruce Jones, along with a letter stating his intention to pay his debt in full within 45 days. Reinstated the account in full.
Oct. 21	Received the balance due from Jones.
Dec. 31	Made a compound entry to write off the following accounts as uncollectible: Sean Rooney, $1,610; Sargent Ltd., $3,075; and Linda Lod, $11,580.
31	Estimated that bad debt expense for the year was 3 percent of credit sales of $860,000 and recorded the expense.
31	Made the closing entry for the bad debt expense.

Choices records all amounts to the nearest cent. Present all amounts to two decimal places.

Required

1. Open three-column general ledger accounts for Allowance for Doubtful Accounts and Bad Debt Expense. Keep running balances.
2. Record the transactions in the general journal and post to the two ledger accounts.
3. The December 31, 2020, balance of Accounts Receivable is $501,000. Show how Accounts Receivable would be reported at that date.
4. Assume that Choices Clothing begins aging its accounts on December 31, 2020. The balance in Accounts Receivable is $501,000, the credit balance in Allowance for Doubtful Accounts is $31,975, and the company estimates that $32,000 of its accounts receivable will prove uncollectible.
   a. Make the adjusting entry for uncollectibles.
   b. Show how Accounts Receivable will be reported on the December 31, 2020, balance sheet.

(1) (2) Estimating uncollectibles using the aging-of-accounts-receivable method and reporting receivables on the balance sheet

P9–3B Canmore Services Inc. started business on March 1, 2020. The company produces monthly financial statements and had total sales of $600,000 (of which $570,000 were on account) during the first four months.

On June 30, the Accounts Receivable account had a balance of $210,000 (no accounts have been written off to date), which was made up of the following accounts aged according to the date the services were provided:

	A	B	C	D	E
1		Month of Service			
2	**Customer**	**March**	**April**	**May**	**June**
3	Torrance Trucks	$ 2,520	$ 1,200	$ 1,800	$ 1,440
4	Vesuvus Ltd.	1,500	1,140	1,632	4,344
5	Lou Del Rio	6,876	4,464	9,168	7,908
6	Mort Black	6,408	3,468	12,624	15,912
7	Other Accounts Receivable	14,760	23,916	31,380	57,540
8		$32,064	$34,188	$56,604	$87,144

The following accounts receivable transactions took place in July 2020:

Jul. 12 Determined the account of Vesuvus Ltd. was uncollectible and wrote it off.

15 Collected $4,200 from Torrance Trucks for services in the first three months.

21 Decided the account of Lou Del Rio was uncollectible and wrote it off.

24 Collected $6,408 from Mort Black for services in the month of March.

26 Received a cheque from Lou Del Rio for $9,600 plus two cheques, of $9,408 each, postdated to September 10 and November 10.

31 Total sales of service in the month were $162,000; 90 percent of these were on on account and 60 percent of the sales on account were collected in the month.

Required

1. Canmore Services Inc. has heard that other companies in the industry use the allowance method of accounting for uncollectibles, with many of these estimating the uncollectibles through an aging of accounts receivable.
   a. Journalize the adjustments that would have to be made on June 30 (for the months of March through June), assuming the following estimates of uncollectibles:

Age of Accounts Receivable	**Estimated Percent Uncollectible**
From current month	1%
From prior month	3
From two months prior	6
From three months prior	20
From four months prior	40

   (Round your total estimate to the nearest whole dollar.)

   b. Journalize the transactions of July 2020.
   c. Journalize the month-end adjustment, using the information from the table that appears in Requirement 1a.
2. For the method of accounting for the uncollectibles used above, show:
   a. The balance sheet presentation of the accounts receivable.
   b. The overall effect of the uncollectibles on the income statement for the months of June and July 2020.

P9–4B On June 30, 2020, Alberta Wireless had a $100,000 debit balance in Accounts Receivable. During July, the company had sales revenue of $150,000, which included $140,000 in credit sales. Other data for July include:

a. Collections of accounts receivable, $120,000.
b. Write-offs of uncollectible receivables, $4,000.

(1) (2) (3)
Accounting for uncollectibles by the direct write-off and allowance methods

Required

1. Record bad debt expense for July by the direct write-off method. Use T-accounts to show all July activity in Accounts Receivable and Bad Debt Expense.
2. Record bad debt expense and write-offs of customer accounts for July by the allowance method. Use T-accounts to show all July activity in Accounts Receivable, Allowance for Doubtful Accounts, and Bad Debt Expense. The June 30 unadjusted balance in Allowance for Doubtful Accounts was $3,000 (credit). Bad debt expense was estimated at 2 percent of credit sales.
3. What amount of bad debt expense would Alberta Wireless report on its July income statement under the two methods? Which amount better matches expense with revenue? Give your reason.
4. What amount of *net* accounts receivable would Alberta Wireless report on its July 31 balance sheet under the two methods? Which amount is more realistic? Give your reason.

(5) Accounting for notes receivable, including accruing interest revenue

P9–5B Unaday Loans issued the following notes during 2020:

	A	B	C	D	E	F	G	H
1	Note	Date	Principal Amount	Interest Rate	Term	Due Date	Interest	Maturity Value
2	(a)	Oct. 31	$33,000	6%	6 months			
3	(b)	Nov. 10	12,000	5	60 days			
4	(c)	Dec. 1	21,000	7	1 year			

Required

1. Determine the due date, interest cost, and maturity value of each note. Round all interest amounts to two decimal places.
2. Journalize a single adjusting entry at December 31, 2020, to record accrued interest revenue on all three notes. An explanation is not required.
3. Journalize the collection of principal and interest on note (b). Explanations are not required.
4. Show how these notes will be reported on the balance sheet at December 31, 2020.

(4) (5) Accounting for debit card sales, notes receivable, dishonoured notes, and accrued interest revenue

P9–6B Record the following selected transactions in the general journal of J&S Event Planners. Explanations are not required.

2019

Dec.	12	Received a $5,775, 120-day, 8 percent note from Jacques Alard to settle his $5,775 account receivable balance.
	31	Made an adjusting entry to accrue interest on the Alard note.
	31	Made an adjusting entry to record bad debt expense in the amount of 4 percent of credit sales of $288,200.
	31	Recorded $88,000 of debit card sales. Royal Bank's debit card service fee is 2 percent.
	31	Made a compound closing entry for sales revenue, interest revenue, bad debt expense, and debit card service fees.

2020

Apr.	11	Collected the maturity value of the Alard note.
Jun.	1	Lent $16,500 cash to Mercury Inc., receiving a six-month, 7 percent note.
Oct.	31	Received a $3,025, 60-day, 8 percent note from Jay Nakashi on his past-due account receivable.
Dec.	1	Collected the maturity value of the Mercury Inc. note.
	30	Jay Nakashi dishonoured (failed to pay) his note at maturity as it was confirmed that he had moved; wrote off the receivable as uncollectible, debiting Allowance for Doubtful Accounts.
	31	Wrote off as uncollectible the account receivable of Art Pierce, $853, and of John Grey, $623.

P9–7B HyLooi Food Products completed the following selected transactions:

④ ⑤ Journalizing credit card sales, uncollectibles, notes receivable, and accrued interest revenue

2019

Nov.	1	Sold goods to NoExtras Foods, receiving a $300,000, six-month, 5 percent note. Ignore cost of goods sold.
Dec.	5	Recorded VISA credit card sale of $30,000. VISA charges a 4 percent fee.
	31	Made an adjusting entry to accrue interest on the NoExtras note.
	31	Made an adjusting entry to record bad debt expense based on an aging of accounts receivable. The aging analysis indicates that $154,000 of accounts receivable will not be collected. Prior to this adjustment, the credit balance in Allowance for Doubtful Accounts is $140,000.

2020

May	1	Collected the maturity value of the NoExtras note.
	15	Received a 60-day, 8 percent, $7,200 note from Sherwood Market on account.
Jun.	23	Sold merchandise to Meadows Foods, receiving a 30-day, 6 percent note for $18,000. Ignore cost of goods sold.
Jul.	14	Collected the maturity value of the Sherwood Market note.
	23	Meadows Foods dishonoured (failed to pay) its note at maturity; onverted the maturity value of the note to an account receivable.
Nov.	16	Lent $25,000 cash to Urban Provisions, receiving a 120-day, 8 percent note.
Dec.	5	Collected in full from Meadows Foods.
	31	Accrued the interest on the Urban Provisions note.

Required Record the transactions in the general journal. Explanations are not required. Round all answers to two decimal places.

P9–8B Halifax Supplies uses the allowance method to account for uncollectible accounts with the estimate based on an aging of accounts receivable. The company had the following account balances on September 30, 2020:

② ⑤ Using the allowance method of accounting for uncollectibles, estimating uncollectibles by the percent-of-sales and the aging-of-accounts-receivable methods, accounting for notes receivable

Accounts Receivable	$1,947,000
Allowance for Doubtful Accounts (credit balance)	56,000

The following transactions took place during the month of October 2020:

Oct.	2	Albert Morrison, who owes $40,000, is unable to pay on time and has given a 20-day, 8 percent note in settlement of the account.
	6	Received from Al Klassen the amount owed on a September 6 dishonoured note, plus extra interest for 30 days at 4 percent computed on the maturity value of the note ($15,300). This dishonoured note had been converted to an account receivable on September 6.
	9	Received notice that a customer (Will Wong) has filed for bankruptcy. Wong owes $35,000. The courts will confirm the amount recoverable at a later date.
	11	Determined the account receivable for Susan Knight ($7,200) was uncollectible and wrote it off.
	18	Received a cheque from the courts in the amount of $23,000 as final settlement of Wong's account.
	22	Morrison paid the note received on October 2.
	25	Determined the account receivable for Donald Purcell ($8,200) was uncollectible and wrote it off.
	31	Sales for the month totalled $743,000 (of which 95 percent were on account) and collections on account totalled $520,000.
	31	Halifax Supplies did an aging of accounts receivable that indicated that $60,000 is expected to be uncollectible. The company recorded the appropriate adjustment.

Required

1. Record the above transactions in the general journal. Show all amounts to two decimal places.
2. What would be the adjusting entry required on October 31 if the company used the percent-of-sales method with an estimate of uncollectibles equal to 4 percent of sales on account?
3. Which of the two methods of estimating uncollectible accounts would normally be more accurate? Why?

(6) Using ratio data to evaluate a company's financial position

P9–9B The comparative financial statements of Kaur Investments for 2020, 2019, and 2018 included the selected data shown below:

	2020	2019	2018
		(in millions)	
Balance Sheet			
Current assets			
Cash	$ 580	$ 560	$ 520
Short-term investments	280	340	252
Receivables, net	560	520	488
Inventories	720	680	600
Prepaid expenses	100	40	80
Total current assets	$ 2,240	$ 2,140	$1,940
Total current liabilities	$ 1,160	$ 1,200	$1,320
Income Statement			
Sales revenue	$11,680	$10,220	$8,400

Required

1. Compute these ratios for 2020 and 2019, assuming that all sales are on account:
   a. Current ratio (round to two decimal places)
   b. Acid-test ratio (round to two decimal places)
   c. Days' sales in receivables (round to nearest full day)
   d. Accounts receivable turnover (round to nearest full turn)
2. Write a memo explaining to Amarpreet Kaur, owner of Kaur Investments, which ratio values showed improvement from 2019 to 2020 and which ratio values showed deterioration. Discuss whether these factors convey a favourable or an unfavourable impression about the company.

(A1) Discounting notes receivable

***P9–10B** A company received the following notes during 2020. The notes were discounted on the dates and at the rates indicated.

	A	B	C	D	E	F	G
1	Note	Date	Principal Amount	Interest Rate	Term	Date Discounted	Discount Rate
2	(a)	Aug. 18	$10,000	11%	6 months	Nov. 18	13%
3	(b)	Jul. 15	9,000	9	90 days	Jul. 26	12
4	(c)	Sep. 1	16,000	10	180 days	Nov. 2	13

Required Identify each note by letter, compute interest using a 365-day year for all notes, and round all interest amounts to the nearest cent. Explanations are not required.

1. Determine the due date and maturity value of each note.
2. Determine the discount and proceeds from the sale (discounting) of each note.
3. Write the general journal entry to record the discounting of note (a).

*This Problem covers Chapter 9 Appendix topics.

CHALLENGE PROBLEMS

P9–1C New Market Builders Supply is a six-store chain of retail stores selling home renovation materials and supplies mainly on credit; the company has its own credit card and does not accept other cards. New Market Builders Supply had a tendency to institute policies that conflicted with each other. Management rarely became aware of these conflicts until they became serious.

①② Understanding accounts receivable management

Recently, the owner, Angela Kim, who has been reading all the latest management texts, has instituted a new bonus plan. All managers are to be paid bonuses based on the success of their department. For example, the bonus for George Tatulis, the sales manager, is based on how much he can increase sales. The bonus for Sonia Petrov, the credit manager, is based on reducing the bad debt expense.

Required Describe the conflict that the bonus plan has created for the sales manager and the credit manager. How might the conflict be resolved?

P9–2C Days' sales in receivables is a good measure of a company's ability to collect the amounts owed to it. You have owned shares in Stapler Office Ltd. for some years and follow the company's progress by reading the annual report. You noticed the most recent report indicated that the days' sales in receivables had increased over the previous year, and you are concerned.

⑥ Explaining days' sales in accounts receivable

Required Suggest reasons that may have resulted in the increase in the number of days' sales in receivables.

Extending Your Knowledge

DECISION PROBLEMS

DP9–1

②③ Comparing the allowance and direct write-off methods for uncollectibles

2. $40,260

Hamed Hazara Advertising has always used the direct write-off method to account for uncollectibles. The company's revenues, bad debt write-offs, and year-end receivables for the most recent year follow.

Year	Revenues	Write-Offs	Receivables at Year End
2020	$187,000	$3,300	$44,000

Hamed Hazara is applying for a bank loan, and the loan officer requires figures based on the allowance method of accounting for bad debts. Hazara estimates that bad debts run about 2 percent of revenues each year.

Required Hamed Hazara must give the banker the following information:

1. How much more or less would net income be for 2020 if Hazara were to use the allowance method for bad debts?
2. How much of the receivables balance at the end of 2020 does Hazara expect to collect?

Compute these amounts, and then explain for Hazara why net income is more or less for 2020 using the allowance method versus the direct write-off method for uncollectibles.

FINANCIAL STATEMENT CASES

FSC9–1

(2) (6)
Trade receivables and related uncollectibles

Indigo Books & Music Inc. (Indigo)—like all other businesses—makes adjusting entries prior to year end to measure assets, liabilities, revenues, and expenses properly.

Examine Indigo's balance sheet in Appendix A at the back of this book and on MyLab Accounting to answer the questions below.

Required

1. Indigo has accounts receivable of $7,448,000. What types of customers account for these receivables? (Hint: Most of this information can be found in Note 21, specifically in the section Credit Risk.)
2. How many days' sales are in Accounts Receivable at April 1, 2017? Show all calculations. What does this ratio mean to the company?

FSC9–2

(2) (6)
Accounts receivable and related uncollectibles

Answer the following questions using the financial statements for TELUS Corporation that appear on MyLab Accounting.

1. What is the total Accounts Receivable at December 31, 2016? What was the total Accounts Receivable at December 31, 2015?
2. What is TELUS's Allowance for Doubtful Accounts balance, and how is the estimate calculated? (See Note 4(b).)
3. Does TELUS age its accounts receivable? (Hint: See Note 4(b).)
4. How much did TELUS write off as doubtful accounts expense during 2016? (Again, see Note 4(b).)
5. How many days' sales are in Accounts Receivable at December 31, 2016? Discuss these results.

IFRS MINI-CASE

The IFRS Mini-Case is now available online, at **MyLab Accounting** in Chapter Resources.

Try It! Solutions for Chapter 9

1. a. i.

Dec. 31	Bad Debt Expense	140,000	
	Allowance for Doubtful Accounts		140,000

ii.

Dec. 31	Allowance for Doubtful Accounts	160,000	
	Accounts Receivable		160,000

iii.

Dec. 31	Bad Debt Expense	37,000	
	Allowance for Doubtful Accounts		37,000

Recall that write-offs reduce the Allowance for Doubtful Accounts and Accounts Receivable. They do *not* affect the bad debt expense.

b.

Allowance for Doubtful Accounts

		Dec. 31, 2019, Bal.	175,000
2020 Write-offs (ii)	160,000	2020 Expense Estimate (i)	140,000
		Bal. before Adj.	155,000
		Dec. 31, 2020, Adj. (iii)	37,000
		Dec. 31, 2020, Bal.	192,000

First, determine the balance in Allowance for Doubtful Accounts by filling in this T-account. Add the expense amount from (a) i. and deduct the write-offs from (a) ii.

The final balance in Allowance for Doubtful Accounts must be $192,000 (given in (a) iii.). The balance in the T-account before the adjustment is already $155,000 (calculated above). Therefore, Bad Debt Expense and Allowance for Doubtful Accounts must be increased by the difference of $37,000.

c.

Accounts receivable	$4,155,000
Less: Allowance for doubtful accounts	192,000
Accounts receivable, net	$3,963,000

d.

Expected realizable value of receivables at December 31, 2020 ($4,155,000 − $192,000)	$3,963,000
Bad debt expense for 2020 ($140,000 + $37,000)	$ 177,000

2 a.

Dec. 31	Allowance for doubtful accounts	9,550	
	Accounts Receivable—Carl Rogers		3,250
	Accounts Receivable—Vince Tran		4,100
	Accounts Receivable—Dan Saerose		2,200
Dec. 31	Bad Debt Expense	13,300*	
	Allowance for Doubtful Accounts		13,300

Balance in account should be $115,000 \times 0.01 + 55,000 \times 0.02 + 35,000 \times 0.20 + 15,000 \times 0.30 + 10,000 \times 0.50 = \$18,750$

Allowance for Doubtful Accounts

		15,000 Opening Balance
Write-off	9,550	X*
		18,750 Calculated Balance

$*X = 18,750 - 15,000 + 9,550 = 13,300$
This is the journal entry amount.

b.

Accounts receivable	$ 230,000
Less: Allowance for doubtful accounts	18,750
Accounts receivable, net	$ 211,250

3 a.

Feb. 26	Bad Debt Expense	1,800	
	Accounts Receivable—Jane Eyre		1,800

b. Balance in Accounts Receivable = $15,000 + $18,000 − $19,000 − $1,800 = $12,200

4.

Jun. 12	Cash	14,700	
	Credit Card Discount Expense	300	
	Sales Revenue		15,000
	To record MasterCard credit card sales for the day less a 2 percent credit card discount expense.		
Jun. 12	Accounts Receivable—credit card company	2,910	
	Credit Card Discount Expense	90	
	Sales Revenue		3,000
	To record non-bank credit card sales for the day less a 3 percent credit card discount expense.		
Jun. 12	Cash	4,875	
	Debit Card Service Fee	125	
	Sales Revenue		5,000
	To record debit card sales for the day less a 2.5 percent service fee.		

5.

2019			
Apr. 1	Notes Receivable—Bud Shriver	20,000	
	Cash		20,000
	Loaned money at 7% for 1 year.		
Dec. 31	Interest Receivable	1,050	
	Interest Revenue		1,050
	To accrue interest revenue earned in 2019 but not yet received ($\$20{,}000 \times 7\% \times 9/12 = \$1{,}050$).		

6.

2020			
Apr. 1	Cash	21,400	
	Notes Receivable—Bud Shriver		20,000
	Interest Receivable		1,050
	Interest Revenue		350
	To record collection of notes receivable from Bud Shriver on which interest has been accrued previously. Interest Receivable is $350 ($\$20{,}000 \times 7\% \times 3/12 = \$350$).		

7.

2020			
Apr. 1	Accounts Receivable—Bud Shriver	21,400	
	Notes Receivable—Bud Shriver		20,000
	Interest Receivable		1,050
	Interest Revenue		350
	To record default on the notes receivable from Bud Shriver on which interest has been accrued previously. Interest Receivable is $350 ($\$20{,}000 \times 7\% \times 3/12 = \$350$).		

8. $$\text{Current ratio} = \frac{\text{Total current assets}}{\text{Total current liabilities}}$$

$$= \$156{,}511 \div \$35{,}315$$

$$= 4.43$$

$$\text{Acid-test ratio} = \frac{\text{Cash and cash equivalents} + \text{Accounts receivable}}{\text{Total current liabilities}}$$

$$= (\$19{,}796 + \$63{,}175) \div \$35{,}315$$

$$= 2.35$$

The current ratio is higher because it includes all the current assets and not just cash, short-term investments, and receivables.

9. Yes. By inserting the "one day's sales" formula into the "days' sales in average accounts receivable" formula, the single formula becomes:

Days' sales in average accounts receivable

$$= \frac{\text{Average net accounts receivable}}{\text{Net sales}} \times 365$$

10. The discount period is 44 days. Method: Compute the number of days the note was held prior to discounting (April 16 to May 2 is 16 days). Subtract the days held from the length of the note ($60 - 16 = 44$). This method eliminates the necessity of determining the maturity date and then having to count from the discount date to the maturity date.

10 Property, Plant, and Equipment; and Goodwill and Intangible Assets

CONNECTING CHAPTER 10

LEARNING OBJECTIVES

The **Summary** for Chapter 10 appears on pages 576–577.
Key terms with definitions for this chapter's material appears on pages 578–579.

CPA competencies

This text covers material outlined in **Section 1: Financial Reporting of the CPA Competency Map**. The Learning Objectives for each chapter have been aligned with the CPA Competency Map to ensure the best coverage possible.

1.1.2 Evaluates the appropriateness of the basis of financial reporting

1.2.2 Evaluates treatment for routine transactions

Kawartha Dairy Ltd.

Kawartha Dairy Limited is a 100 percent Canadian-owned ice cream and dairy processor located in Bobcaygeon, Ontario, and is still operated by the same family that started it back in 1937. It not only operates its own production facility but also runs a chain of eight of its own retail stores. Kawartha Dairy brand products are also wholesaled to other businesses, who in turn offer the products in their own stores. In addition to ice cream and milk, Kawartha Dairy produces specialized products like buttermilk for the baking industry and private-label items for other companies.

A firm like this has a huge investment in assets. Kawartha Dairy owns buildings, land, production equipment, and office furniture that it uses to run the business. It also has a fleet of trucks to deliver its goods to its own retail outlets, independent specialty shops, grocery stores, and institutional customers.

How does the company record the purchase of these trucks in their accounting records? Do they expense them or set them up as assets? Because they help the company earn revenue over several periods, they are reported as assets.

How should Kawartha Dairy account for the use of the trucks? They record amortization over each truck's useful life. Managers estimate how long they can use the truck and how much they can sell it for when it is taken out of service. They don't amortize this last amount because they get it back when they sell the truck or trade it in for a new one.

Because most companies keep assets for as long as they can, they also need to make repairs and maintain the trucks. *How do you decide when work done on the truck is part of the cost or considered a repair?* Professional judgment is just as important in these decisions as are the generally accepted accounting principles. Managers at Kawartha and other companies need to know how to account for these assets.

This chapter covers these and other matters about property, plant, and equipment, the long-term tangible assets that a business uses to operate, such as airplanes for Air Canada and automobiles for Discount Car and Truck Rentals. It also looks at *intangibles*—those assets with no physical form, such as trademarks and copyrights, and finally, this chapter shows how to account for natural resources such as oil and timber.

Property, plant, and equipment are **identifiable tangible assets**. They are often referred to by their initials, PPE. On many financial statements, these are a major component of the total assets owned by a company. These assets have some special characteristics:

Property, plant, and equipment are sometimes referred to as long-lived assets, capital assets, fixed assets, or long-term assets.

- You hold them for use in the business—not to sell as inventory—and they are *tangible*, which means you can touch them. Other assets are *intangible*, and we will explore those later in the chapter.
- They are used in the operation of the business to help create revenue. (On the other hand, a vacant plot of land would be shown as an *investment* because it is not being used in the operation of the business.)
- They are relatively expensive, and their cost can be a challenge to determine.
- They last a long time—usually for several years. If these assets wear out or become obsolete, you need to amortize them.
- They may be sold or traded in.

Measuring the Cost of PPE

LO 1

What are property, plant, and equipment (PPE), and how do we measure their cost?

The *cost principle of measurement* directs a business to carry an asset on the balance sheet at its cost—the amount paid for the asset, or the market value if the asset is transferred into the business.

The cost of an asset = The sum of all the costs incurred to bring the asset to its intended purpose, net of all discounts

The cost of *property, plant, and equipment* is the purchase price plus taxes plus other acquisition costs, including commissions, and all other necessary costs incurred to ready the asset for its intended use. In Chapter 5 we applied this principle to determine the cost of inventory. The goods and services tax (GST) and the harmonized sales tax (HST), which are paid on the purchase, are never included as part of the cost since these amounts are recoverable by the purchaser. Provincial sales tax (PST) *is* included in the cost of a tangible capital asset. We discuss this in more detail in Chapter 11.

Property

Generally speaking, the *property* portion of long-lived tangible assets refers to land and land improvements. We will review each category separately.

Land The cost of land includes the following costs paid (or to be paid) by the purchaser:

- The purchase price
- The brokerage commission
- The closing costs (which may include the survey, legal, registration, title, and transfer fees)
- Any property taxes in **arrears**
- The cost for grading and clearing the land
- The costs for demolishing or removing any unwanted buildings

Suppose Kawartha Dairy pays $500,000 to purchase 100 hectares of land. The company also pays $30,000 in brokerage commission, $10,000 in transfer taxes, $5,000 for removal of an old building, $2,000 for a new advertising sign saying "Coming Soon!" and a $1,000 survey fee. What is the cost of this land? Exhibit 10–1 shows all the *necessary* costs incurred to bring the land to its intended use.

EXHIBIT 10–1 | Measuring the Cost of Land

Purchase price of land		$500,000
Add related costs		
Brokerage commission	$30,000	
Transfer taxes	10,000	
Removal of building	5,000	
Survey fee	1,000	
Total land costs		46,000
Total cost of land		$546,000

Kawartha's entry to record the purchase of the land is as follows:

Feb. 1	Land	546,000	
	Cash		546,000

We would say that Kawartha Dairy **capitalized** the cost of the land at $546,000. This means that the company debited an asset account (Land) for $546,000. The advertising sign cost would be expensed since it was not a necessary cost to ready the land for use.

Capitalize has nothing to do with the Capital (or equity) account. In this case, it means the amount paid is added to the cost of the asset.

Land Improvements Land and Land Improvements are two separate asset accounts because one is amortized and the other is not. Land improvements are amortized over their useful lives and include the following:

- Lighting
- Signs
- Fences
- Paving
- Sprinkler systems
- Landscaping

Suppose Kawartha Dairy spent $35,000 for the construction of fences around the land it had purchased above. The entry to record the expenditure is as follows:

Mar. 7	Land Improvements	35,000	
	Cash		35,000

The cost of land is not amortized because it does not wear out. Since there is an *infinite useful life*, no adjustment is made to its reported value.

It could be argued that decorative items such as trees and shrubs should be classified as land, since they may have an infinite useful life. The accountant would need to use professional judgment to determine the proper classification. (This is a situation where there are not always rules for all decisions.)

Plant (Buildings)

Plant refers to buildings a company owns, such as manufacturing facilities, stores, and offices.

The cost of constructing a building includes the following:

- Architectural fees
- Building permits
- Contractors' charges
- Payments for materials, labour, and overhead

The time to complete a new building can be many months, even years, and the separate expenditures can be numerous. If the company constructs its own assets, the cost of the building may also include the cost of interest on money borrowed to finance the construction.

When an existing building is purchased, its cost includes all the costs to repair and renovate the building for its intended use.

Equipment

There are several different types of assets that fall under this category.

Equipment is not necessarily a subheading on a financial statement. It is merely a broad term that refers to assets that a company owns, which may include:

- Company vehicles
- Furniture
- Computers
- Manufacturing equipment
- Display shelves
- Storage racks

They are all *recorded separately* but may be *reported* in categories such as "Machinery and Equipment" and "Furniture and Fixtures."

Machinery and Equipment The equipment category includes the productive assets a company builds or acquires to produce, store, manage, or distribute the products it sells. There are many different types of equipment. WestJet has baggage-handling equipment and planes, your campus copy company has copy equipment, and Kawartha Dairy has delivery trucks.

The cost of machinery and equipment includes the following:

- Purchase price (less any discounts)
- Transportation charges
- Insurance while in transit
- Provincial sales tax (PST)
- Purchase commission
- Installation costs
- Cost of testing the asset before it is used

After the asset is set up, tested, and ready to be used, we stop capitalizing these costs to the Machinery and Equipment account. Thereafter, insurance, taxes, and maintenance costs are recorded as expenses.

Furniture and Fixtures This category includes desks, chairs, filing cabinets, and display racks.

Computers Depending on the type of business, computers might be reported as equipment (when they control machinery), furniture and fixtures (as part of the office), or their own separate account (if there are a lot of them).

Leasehold Improvements

The Leasehold Improvements account includes alterations to assets the company is leasing. For example, suppose TELUS Corporation, known for its Fido wireless business, leases some of its store locations. The company might renovate the stores to include a lockable storage room. This improvement of the leased space is an asset for TELUS even though the company does not own the store itself. The cost of leasehold improvements should be amortized over the term of the lease (including the renewal option) or the useful life of the leased asset, whichever is shorter.

Lump-Sum Purchase of Assets

A company may pay a single price for several assets purchased as a group—a "basket purchase." For example, suppose a company pays one price for land and an office building. For accounting purposes, the company must identify the cost of each asset in its own account.

It does not matter what the seller claims each asset is worth or what the book value is on the seller's books. The market (fair) value is determined by appraisal or some other objective method.

Suppose Kawartha Dairy purchases land and a building in Barrie to be used as a warehouse. The combined purchase price of the land and building is $540,000. An **appraisal**, which is an expert assessment of the value of an asset, indicates that the land's market value is $200,000 and the building's market value is $400,000. Notice that the appraisal is more than what was paid for the land and building—a good deal. It is also possible for an appraisal to come in at a lower value. The issue is that the appraisal amounts and the purchase price are not the same, so we need to determine what value to assign to each asset.

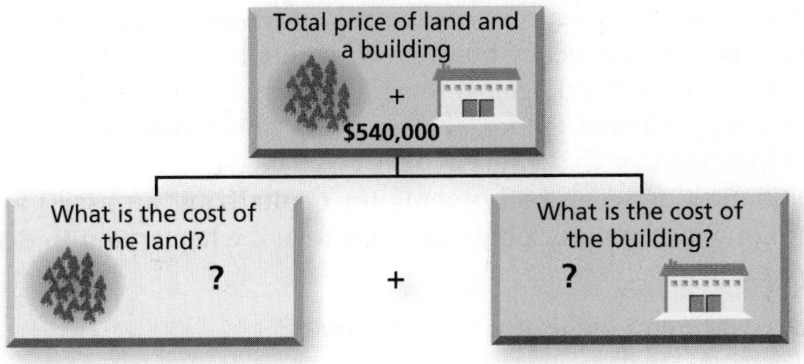

Relative-Fair-Value Method The **relative-fair-value method** is a cost allocation technique where the total cost is divided among the assets according to their relative fair market values.

1. Calculate the ratio of each asset's market value to the total market value of both assets combined. Total appraised value is $200,000 + $400,000 = $600,000. Thus, the land, valued at $200,000, is one-third, or 33.33 percent, of the total market value. The building's appraised value is two-thirds, or 66.67 percent, of the total.
2. Apply that ratio to the total purchase price.

The cost of each asset is determined as follows:

	A	B	C	D	E	F	G	H	I	J
1	Asset	Market Value		❶ Fraction of Total Value				❷ Total Purchase Price		Cost of Each Asset
2	Land	$200,000	÷	$600,000	=	.33	×	$540,000	=	$180,000
3	Building	$400,000	÷	$600,000	=	.67	×	$540,000	=	$360,000
4	Total	$600,000								$540,000

Suppose Kawartha Dairy pays $90,000 cash and takes out a **mortgage** for the balance. The entry to record the purchase of the land and building is as follows:

Apr. 6	Land	180,000	
	Building	360,000	
	Cash		90,000
	Mortgage Payable		450,000

Betterments versus Repairs

When a company spends money on a capital asset it already owns, it must decide whether to debit an asset account for betterments or an expense account for repairs.

A capital expenditure causes the asset's cost to increase, which means future amortization needs to be revised.

Betterments are debited to an asset account because they increase the capacity or efficiency of the asset or extend its useful life. For example, the cost of a major engine overhaul that extends a Kawartha Dairy truck's useful life is a betterment. The amount of the expenditure, said to be *capitalized*, is a debit to the asset account Truck.

Repairs, such as maintenance expenses and truck repair expenses, do not extend the asset's capacity or efficiency but merely maintain the asset in working order. These expenses are matched against revenue. Examples could include repainting a truck, repairing a dented fender, and replacing tires. These costs are debited to Repair and Maintenance Expense.

The distinction between betterments (or capitalizing an asset) and repairs requires judgment. Here are some questions to ask when trying to decide if the cost is a betterment:

- Does the cost extend the useful life of the asset?
- Does the cost increase output or decrease operating costs?
- Does it increase the quality of the output?
- What about the materiality constraint? Most companies have a minimum dollar limit for betterments. For example, a $400 betterment to a truck would be expensed if the company had a $500 minimum dollar limit for betterments.

Exhibit 10–2 illustrates the distinction between betterments (capital expenditures) and repairs (expenses) for several delivery truck expenditures.

EXHIBIT 10–2 | Delivery Truck Expenditures—Betterment or Repair?

Betterment: Debit an Asset Account	**Repair:** Debit Repair and Maintenance Expense
Capitalized:	*Expensed:*
Major engine overhaul	Repair of headlights or other mechanism
Modification of truck for new use	Oil change, lubrication, and so on
Addition to storage capacity of truck	Replacement tires or windshield
Painting logo on truck	Repainting (to fix rust or damage)

Ethical Issues

When there are choices to be made in accounting, such as whether a cost should be expensed or capitalized or how to allocate costs using the relative-fair-value method, accountants may face an ethical dilemma. On the one hand, companies want to save on taxes. This motivates companies to expense as many costs as possible or include more costs to assets other than land (which is not amortized) to decrease taxable income. But they also want their financial statements to look as good as possible, with high net income and high reported amounts for assets, which means they want to capitalize as many costs as possible.

In most cases, whether a cost is capitalized or expensed for tax purposes, it must be treated the same way for accounting purposes in the financial statements. What, then, is the ethical path? Accountants should follow this general guideline for capitalizing a cost:

Capitalize all costs that provide a future benefit for the business and expense all other costs.

Many companies have gotten into trouble by capitalizing costs that really should have been expensed. They made their financial statements look better than the facts warranted. WorldCom committed this type of accounting fraud (among others), and its former top executives are now in prison as a result.

Try It!

1. Which of the following would you include in the cost of machinery? (Note: There can be more than one correct answer.)
   a. Installation charges
   b. Testing of the machine
   c. Repair to machinery necessitated by operator's error on first day of use
   d. First-year maintenance cost
2. Budget Banners pays $200,000 cash for the purchase of land, building, and equipment. At the time of acquisition, the land has a market value of $22,000, the building $187,000, and the equipment $11,000. Journalize the lump-sum purchase on May 31.
3. Classify each of the following as a betterment or a repair (assume all costs are material in amount):
   a. Installing new tires on a cement truck
   b. Repainting a delivery truck that was damaged in an accident
   c. Replacing the motor in a delivery truck
   d. Installing an elevating device in a delivery truck
   e. Safety test on a delivery truck when the licence is renewed
   f. Installing carrying racks on the roof of the delivery truck

Solutions appear at the end of this chapter and on **MyLab Accounting**

Amortization

LO 2 **How do we calculate and account for amortization?**

As we have seen in Chapter 3, **amortization**[1] is defined as the allocation of the cost of property, plant, and equipment (except for land) less salvage value or residual value to expense over its useful life. Amortization matches the asset's cost (expense) against the revenue earned by the asset. Thus, the primary purpose of amortization accounting is to measure income correctly in each period.

Suppose Kawartha Dairy buys a reefer truck (one with a refrigerated trailer). Kawartha believes it will get 20 years' service from the truck. Using the straight-line amortization method, Kawartha Dairy expenses 1/20th of the asset's cost in each of its 20 years' use.

Let's contrast what amortization *is* with what it *is not*.

- *Amortization is not a process of valuation.* Businesses do not record amortization based on the market (fair) value of their property, plant, and equipment; they use their actual cost.
- *Amortization does not mean that the business sets aside cash to replace assets* as they become fully amortized.
- *Amortization is sometimes related to physical wear and tear.* All assets except land wear out. For some tangible assets, physical wear and tear creates the need to amortize their value. For example, physical factors wear out the trucks that Kawartha Dairy drives. The same is true of The Bay's store fixtures.
- *Amortization is sometimes related to obsolescence.* Assets such as computers or jet aircraft may become obsolete before they wear out. An asset is obsolete when another asset can do the job more efficiently. Thus an asset's useful life may be shorter than its physical life. Accountants usually amortize computers over a short period of time—perhaps two to four years—even though they know the computers could be used much longer. This is because computers are typically replaced with newer models before they wear out. In all cases, the asset's cost is amortized over its *expected useful life*.

[1]This is the term used in Part II (ASPE), Section 3061, *CPA Canada Handbook*.

EXHIBIT 10–3 | Property, Plant, and Equipment, Goodwill, and Intangible Assets and Their Related Expenses

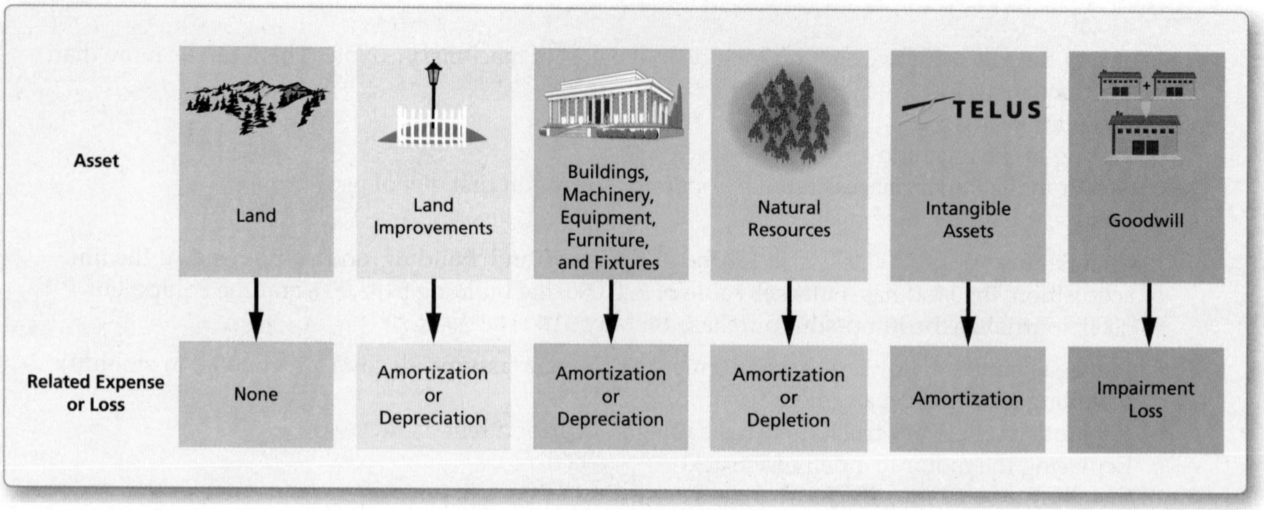

Property, plant, and equipment, goodwill, and intangible assets have their own terminology. Exhibit 10–3 shows which expense or loss applies to each category and when to use the terms *amortization*, *depreciation*, *depletion*, and *impairment*. We will look at each of these in turn.

Amortization Methods

Amortization for a capital asset is based on three factors:

- Cost
- Estimated useful life
- Estimated residual value

The asset's cost is known because we have an invoice and know what was paid for it. The other two factors must be estimated, so amortization itself is an estimated amount. It is impossible to quantify the *exact* amount of the useful life of an asset that has been used up during the period, but there is no doubt that a portion of the asset has been consumed. It is important that these estimates be as accurate as possible because they have an impact on the amount of net income reported in each period that the asset is used.

Note that the residual value is the portion of the asset's cost that will *not* be consumed or used; therefore, it should *not* be amortized.

Estimated useful life is the length of the service period expected from the asset. Useful life may be expressed in years, units of output, kilometres, or other measures. For example, a building's useful life is stated in years, a bookbinding machine's in the number of books the machine can bind, and a delivery truck's in kilometres.

Estimated residual value—also called salvage value—is the asset's expected cash value at the end of its useful life. Scrap value is the asset's value at the end of its physical life. For example, a business may believe that a machine's useful life will be seven years. After that time, the company expects to sell the machine as scrap metal. The expected cash receipt is the machine's residual value. The estimated residual value is *not* amortized because the business expects to receive this amount when the machine is sold.

A company stops recording amortization once the asset's book value is equal to the **amortizable cost**.

Cost − Residual value = Amortizable cost

Three methods are widely used in Canada for computing amortization:

- Straight-line
- Units-of-production
- Double-declining-balance

Exhibit 10–4 presents the data we will use to illustrate amortization for a Kawartha Dairy delivery truck.

EXHIBIT 10–4 | Data for Recording Amortization for a Kawartha Dairy Truck

Cost of truck	$65,000	Estimated useful life:	
Estimated residual value	5,000	Years	5 years
Amortizable cost	$60,000	Units of production	400,000 units (kilometres)

Straight-Line Method

The **straight-line method** allocates an equal amount of amortization to each year of asset use. This method was introduced in Chapter 3. The equation for straight-line amortization expense applied to the Kawartha Dairy delivery truck data from Exhibit 10–4 is:

$$\text{Straight-line amortization} = \frac{\text{Cost} - \text{Residual value}}{\text{Useful life}}$$

$$= \frac{\$65{,}000 - \$5{,}000}{5 \text{ years}}$$

$$= \$12{,}000 \text{ per year}$$

The entry to record each year's amortization is:

Dec. 31	Amortization Expense—Delivery Truck	12,000	
	Accumulated Amortization—Delivery Truck		12,000

Notice that when there is more than one asset being amortized in a business, we update the account names to include the specific asset information.

Assume that this truck was purchased on January 1, 2020, and the business's fiscal year-ends on December 31. A *straight-line* **amortization schedule** is presented in Exhibit 10–5.

EXHIBIT 10–5 | Straight-Line Amortization for a Truck

	A	B	C	D	E	F	G	H	I
1			Amortization for the Year						
2		Asset	Amortization		Amortizable		Amortization	Accumulated	Asset
3	Date	Cost	Rate		Cost		Expense	Amortization	Book Value
4	Jan. 1, 2020	$65,000							**$65,000**
5	Dec. 31, 2020		$\frac{1}{5}$	×	$60,000	=	$12,000	$12,000	53,000
6	Dec. 31, 2021		$\frac{1}{5}$	×	60,000	=	12,000	**24,000**	**41,000**
7	Dec. 31, 2022		$\frac{1}{5}$	×	60,000	=	12,000	36,000	29,000
8	Dec. 31, 2023		$\frac{1}{5}$	×	60,000	=	12,000	48,000	17,000
9	Dec. 31, 2024		$\frac{1}{5}$	×	60,000	=	12,000	60,000	5,000

Residual value

The final column of Exhibit 10–5 shows the asset's *book value* (also referred to as the *carrying value*), which is cost less accumulated amortization. The bolded amounts show that at the end of the second year, the asset's book value is $41,000, calculated as cost less accumulated amortization, or $65,000 − $24,000.

As an asset is used, accumulated amortization increases and the asset's book value decreases.

The partial balance sheet presentation of the Property, Plant, and Equipment section at December 31, 2021, would be:

Delivery truck	$65,000
Less: Accumulated amortization—delivery truck	24,000
Delivery truck, net	$41,000

Book value

Sometimes the formula for straight-line amortization is restated to show the useful life as a rate or percentage, known as the **amortization rate**. For example, if an asset has a five-year useful life, then or 20 percent is amortized each year. The formula for the expense can then be restated as follows:

$$\textbf{Straight-line amortization} = (\textbf{Cost} - \textbf{Residual value}) \times \frac{\textbf{1}}{\textbf{Useful life in years}}$$

$$= \textbf{Amortizable cost} \times \textbf{Amortization rate}$$

Units-of-Production Method

A unit of output can be a kilometre driven/flown, hours, or a part manufactured.

The **units-of-production (UOP) method** allocates a fixed amount of amortization to each unit of output produced by the asset. Think of this as a two-step process:

❶ Calculate amortization cost per unit.

❷ Multiply the cost per unit by the number of units produced or used in the period.

The equation to calculate the UOP method amortization expense, applied to the Exhibit 10–4 data, is:

❶ **Units-of-production amortization per unit of output**

$$= \frac{\textbf{Cost} - \textbf{Residual value}}{\textbf{Useful life in units of production}}$$

$$= \frac{\$65{,}000 - \$5{,}000}{400{,}000 \textbf{ kilometres}}$$

$$= \$0.15 \textbf{ per kilometre}$$

This truck was driven 90,000 kilometres in the first year, 120,000 in the second, 100,000 in the third, 60,000 in the fourth, and 30,000 in the fifth. The amount of UOP amortization per period varies with the number of units the asset produces. Exhibit 10–6 shows the UOP amortization schedule for this asset.

EXHIBIT 10–6 | Units-of-Production Amortization for a Truck

	A	B	C	D	E	F	G	H	I
1			Amortization for the Year						
2–3	Date	Asset Cost	Amortization Per Kilometre		Number of Kilometres		Amortization Expense	Accumulated Amortization	Asset Book Value
4	Jan. 1, 2020	$65,000	❶		❷				$65,000
5	Dec. 31, 2020		$0.15	×	90,000	=	$13,500	$13,500	51,500
6	Dec. 31, 2021		0.15	×	120,000	=	18,000	31,500	33,500
7	Dec. 31, 2022		0.15	×	100,000	=	15,000	46,500	18,500
8	Dec. 31, 2023		0.15	×	60,000	=	9,000	55,500	9,500
9	Dec. 31, 2024		0.15	×	30,000	=	4,500	60,000	5,000

Residual value

Double-Declining-Balance Method

The **double-declining-balance (DDB) method** computes annual amortization expense by multiplying the asset's book value by a constant percentage, which is two times (double) the straight-line amortization rate. This is an *accelerated* amortization model, which means it expenses more of the cost of the asset at the start of its life and less at the end of its useful life.

There are two steps to calculate the amortization expense:

To do the calculation in one step, compute 2 ÷ Useful life in years. Express the result as a fraction or a percent, then multiply by the book value at the beginning of the period.

❶ Compute the straight-line amortization rate per year, for example, for the truck: (1 ÷ 5 years = 20% per year).

Multiply the straight-line rate by 2 to get the **DDB rate**. For the truck example, the DDB rate is 20% × 2 = 40%; or you can think of it as the annual rate of one-fifth, which is then doubled to $^2/_5$, which is 40%.

❷ Multiply the asset's book value (cost less accumulated amortization) at the beginning of the year by the DDB rate. Ignore residual value except for the last year. The formula for the amortization expense can be stated as follows:

$$\textbf{DDB amortization} = (\textbf{Cost} - \textbf{Accumulated amortization}) \times 2 \times \frac{1}{\textbf{Useful life}}$$

The first year's amortization for the truck in Exhibit 10–4 can also be calculated in one step like this:

$$\begin{aligned}\textbf{DDB amortization} &= \textbf{Asset book value of the period} \times \textbf{DDB rate}\\ &= \$65{,}000 \times 0.40\\ &= \$26{,}000\end{aligned}$$

The DDB formula is unique. Rather than use amortizable cost (as the other methods do), the formula for DDB is *book value* × DDB rate. Residual value is not used in the DDB formula until the final year's amortization calculation.

The same approach is used to compute DDB amortization for all later years, except for the final year.

The final year's amortization is the amount needed to reduce the asset's book value to its residual value. In the DDB amortization schedule in Exhibit 10–7, the fifth and final year's amortization is $3,424—the $8,424 book value less the $5,000 residual value.

Since amortization is an estimate, accountants usually round the final answer for calculations to the nearest whole dollar.

EXHIBIT 10–7 | Double-Declining-Balance Amortization for a Truck

	A	B	C	D	E	F	G	H	I
1			Amortization for the Year						
2		Asset	DDB		Asset		Amortization	Accumulated	Asset
3	Date	Cost	Rate		Book Value		Expense	Amortization	Book Value
4	Jan. 1, 2020	$65,000	❶		❷				$65,000
5	Dec. 31, 2020		0.40	×	$65,000	=	$26,000	$26,000	39,000
6	Dec. 31, 2021		0.40	×	39,000	=	15,600	41,600	23,400
7	Dec. 31, 2022		0.40	×	23,400	=	9,360	50,960	14,040
8	Dec. 31, 2023		0.40	×	14,040	=	5,616	56,576	8,424
9	Dec. 31, 2024					=	3,424*	60,000	5,000

*Amortization in 2024 is the amount needed to reduce the asset's book value to the residual value of $5,000 ($8,424 – $5,000 = $3,424).

Residual value

The DDB method differs from the other methods in two ways:

- Residual value is ignored until the last period. In the first year, amortization is calculated on the asset's full cost.
- Final-year amortization is the amount needed to bring the asset's book value to the residual value. It is a "plug" figure.

With declining-balance amortization, the asset's book value will rarely equal its residual value in the final year. Amortization expense in the final year is the amount that will reduce the asset's book value to the residual value.

Comparing Amortization Methods

Let's compare the three methods we have just discussed. Each method allocates different amounts of amortization expense to each period, but they all result in the same amortization over the life of the asset.

	Amount of Amortization per Year		
Year	**Straight-Line**	**Units-of-Production**	**Double-Declining-Balance**
2020	$12,000	$13,500	$26,000
2021	12,000	18,000	15,600
2022	12,000	15,000	9,360
2023	12,000	9,000	5,616
2024	12,000	4,500	3,424
Total	**$60,000**	**$60,000**	**$60,000**

Which method is best? That depends on the asset. For managers, it is the one that best represents the situation. A business should match an asset's expense against the revenue that the asset produces. A company can use different methods for different assets.

Method	Asset Characteristics	Effect on Amortization	Example
Straight-line	Generates revenue evenly over time	Equal amount each period	Building
Units-of-Production	Wears out because of physical use rather than obsolescence	More usage causes larger amortization	Vehicles (miles) Machinery (hours)
Double-Declining-Balance	Produces more revenue or is more productive in early years	Higher expense in early years, less later	Computers

Exhibit 10–8 graphs the relationship between annual amortization amounts for the three methods.

EXHIBIT 10–8 | Amortization Expense Patterns for the Various Methods

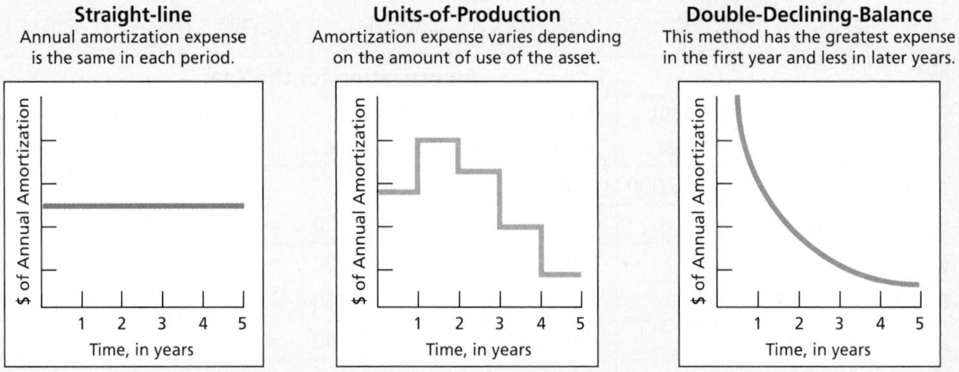

Try It!

4. Sonoma Industrial Products purchased equipment on January 2, 2020, for $176,000. The expected life of the equipment is 10 years or 100,000 units of production, and its residual value is $16,000. Using three amortization methods, the annual amortization expense and total accumulated amortization at the end of 2020 and 2021 are as follows:

	Method A		Method B		Method C	
	Annual Amortization Expense	Accumulated Amortization	Annual Amortization Expense	Accumulated Amortization	Annual Amortization Expense	Accumulated Amortization
2020	$16,000	$16,000	$35,200	$35,200	$ 4,800	$ 4,800
2021	16,000	32,000	28,160	63,360	22,400	27,200

a. Identify the amortization method used in each instance, and show the equation and computation for each. (Round off to the nearest dollar.)

b. Assume continued use of the same method through the year 2022. Determine the annual amortization expense, accumulated amortization, and book value of the equipment for 2020 through 2022 under each method, assuming 12,000 units of production in 2022.

Solutions appear at the end of this chapter and on **MyLab Accounting**

Why It's Done This Way

The accounting framework provides guidance on how to record transactions. We can focus on two principles: *recognition* and *measurement*. When an asset such as equipment is acquired by a business, a financial transaction has occurred, and we should record it (*recognition*). We can determine the cost of the equipment easily, so we have satisfied the *cost principle of measurement*.

Next, into which account should the equipment be placed? Is it an asset or is it an expense? The framework also discusses elements. *Assets* are economic resources controlled by an entity that are expected to benefit the entity in the future. Does equipment fit that description? Yes, because the company expects to receive benefits from having the equipment for many years.

Part of its economic benefit is used up each year and needs to be *expensed*. We calculate amortization expense and, through that account, we recognize part of the cost of the equipment each year. In this way, we *match* the expense of the asset to the period of economic benefit. This supports *the matching objective*, which we learned is an expense recognition criteria.

Other Issues in Accounting for PPE

LO 3 How do we account for other amortization issues?

Amortization usually differs depending on whether it is being calculated for accounting or income tax purposes. At certain times amortization must be calculated for partial years; it also happens that amortization assumptions have to be revised. This section covers these topics.

Amortization and Income Taxes

Most companies use the straight-line method for reporting capital asset values and amortization expense to their owners and creditors on their financial statements. Businesses often keep a separate set of records for calculating the amortization expense they claim on their tax returns because the Canada Revenue Agency (CRA) specifies the maximum amortization taxpayers can deduct for income tax purposes. This amount is usually different from amortization expense reported on the income statement.

Capital Cost Allowance The CRA allows corporations as well as individuals with business or professional income to compute deductions from income to recognize the consumption or use of capital assets. The deductions are called **capital cost allowance (CCA)**, the term the CRA uses to describe amortization for tax purposes. The CRA specifies the *maximum* rates allowed for each asset class (type of asset), called *CCA rates*. A taxpayer may claim anything from zero to the maximum CCA allowed in a year. Most taxpayers claim the maximum CCA since this provides the largest deduction from taxable income as quickly as possible. Claiming the maximum CCA reduces taxable income and thus tax payable, leaving more cash available for investment or other business uses.

The CCA rate is applied to the balance in the asset class at the end of the year (cost minus accumulated CCA claimed to date) in the same manner as the DDB method.

Some CRA rates and classes in effect at the time of publication are as follows:

	Rate	Class
Automobiles costing over $30,000	30%	10.1
Most buildings bought after 1987	4%	1
Computer software	100%	12
Office furniture and fixtures	20%	8
Computers	55%	50

Half-Year Rule The CRA allows the taxpayer to claim only 50 percent of the normal CCA rate in the year of acquisition. This is referred to as the **half-year rule**. The half-year rule is currently suspended for eligible property as part of a temporary federal government strategy to increase investment in Canada.

Accelerated Investment Incentive Eligible property put into use before 2028 will qualify for an *enhanced* CCA in the year of purchase. The allowance is calculated on 1.5 times the net qualifying addition to the class for the year. (Manufacturing and processing machinery have a 100 percent deduction in the first year.) This incentive is phased out with declining rates from 2024–2027.

CCA is studied more fully in advanced accounting and tax courses.

Amortization for Partial Years

Companies purchase property, plant, and equipment whenever they need them—for example, on February 8 or August 17. They do not wait until the beginning of a year or a month. Therefore, companies develop policies to compute amortization for partial years. One possibility is to set a company rule that a full month's amortization be recorded if the asset is bought on or before the 15th of the month, and no amortization for the month if purchased after the 15th. Another possibility is to pro-rate the cost based on the exact days.

For the purpose of most homework questions, companies will follow the guideline of recording a full month of amortization if the asset is purchased before the 15th of the month.

Suppose a company purchases a building as a maintenance shop on April 4, 2020, for $600,000. The building's estimated life is 18 years, and its estimated residual value is $60,000. The company's fiscal year-ends on December 31. How does the company compute amortization for the year-ended December 31, 2020?

Many companies compute partial-year amortization by first calculating a full year's amortization. They then multiply full-year amortization by the fraction of the year during which they used the asset. In this case, the company needs to record nine months' amortization, for April to December. Assuming the straight-line method, the 2020 amortization for the maintenance shop is $22,500, computed as follows:

$$\textbf{Full-year amortization: } \frac{\$600{,}000 - \$60{,}000}{18 \text{ years}} = \$30{,}000$$

$$\textbf{Partial-year amortization: } \$30{,}000 \times 9/12 = \$22{,}500$$

Each company must make its own policies to ensure consistent treatment of partial years. Professional judgment is used rather than there being specific guidance available.

If the company purchased the building above on August 17, then it would record no amortization for August. In this case, the year's amortization for four months (September to December) would be ($10,000 ($30,000 × $^4/_{12}$).

Partial-year amortization is computed under the DDB amortization method in the same way—by applying the appropriate percentage of the year during which the asset is used.

For the UOP amortization method, partial-year and full-year amortization are calculated the same way because amortization is based on the number of units produced. Amortization for the UOP method is *not* a function of time, so partial-year amortization is not an issue as it is for the other amortization methods.

For the purpose of simplicity, we are rounding calculations to the nearest dollar. Spreadsheets or custom software can calculate amortization to the level of detail required by a company.

Change in the Useful Life of an Amortizable Asset

Estimating the useful life of property, plant, and equipment subject to amortization poses an accounting challenge. As previously discussed, a business must estimate the useful life of these assets to compute amortization. This prediction is the most difficult part of accounting for amortization. As the asset is used, the business may change the asset's estimated useful life based on experience and new information. Such a change is called a *change in accounting estimate*.

To *record* a change in an accounting estimate, the asset's remaining amortizable book value is spread over its adjusted, or new, remaining useful life. The change is accounted for **prospectively**, meaning from this point on into the future.

The equation for revised straight-line amortization is:

$$\text{Revised straight-line amortization} = \frac{\text{Cost} + \text{Betterments} - \text{Accumulated amortization} - \text{New residual value}}{\text{Estimated remaining useful life}}$$

Assume that an ice cream–making machine owned by Kawartha Dairy cost \$400,000, and the company originally believed the asset had a 16-year useful life with no residual value. The company uses the straight-line method and has used the machine for four years. There were no betterments during this time. First, let's calculate the accumulated amortization up to this point in time:

$$400{,}000 \div 16 \text{ years} = \$25{,}000 \text{ amortization per year}$$
$$\$25{,}000 \times 4 \text{ years} = \$100{,}000 \text{ accumulated amortization}$$

From its experience with the asset during the first four years, management believes the asset will remain useful for the next 20 years and at that time have no residual value. In Year 5, the company would compute the revised annual amortization amount as follows:

$$\text{Revised Annual Amortization} = \frac{\$400{,}000 + \$0 - \$100{,}000 - \$0}{20 \text{ years}} = \$15{,}000 \text{ per year}$$

Use the remaining useful life here.

The yearly amortization journal entry based on the new estimated useful life is:

Dec. 31	Amortization Expense—Ice Cream Machine	15,000	
	Accumulated Amortization—Ice Cream Machine		15,000

Using Fully Amortized Assets

A *fully amortized asset* is one that has reached the end of its *estimated* useful life. No more amortization is recorded for the asset. If the asset is no longer useful, it is disposed of. But the asset may still be useful, and the company may continue using it. The asset account and its accumulated amortization remain on the books, but no additional amortization is recorded.

Try It!

5. On April 17, 2020, Logan Services purchased a used crane for \$65,000. The company expects the crane to remain useful for four years (600 hours of use) and to have a residual value of \$5,000. The company expects the crane to be used for 130 hours until December 31, 2020, the company's year-end. Compute the amortization expense for 2020 using the following amortization methods: (a) straight-line, (b) UOP, and (c) DDB.
6. On January 10, 2000, ABC Co. purchased for \$800,000 a building that had an estimated residual value of \$50,000 and a useful life of 40 years. On January 13, 2020, a \$200,000 addition to the building increased its residual value by \$50,000. Calculate straight-line amortization expense for 2020.

Solutions appear at the end of this chapter and on **MyLab Accounting**

Disposing of PPE

LO 4 **How do we account for the disposal of PPE?**

Eventually, an amortizable asset no longer serves its purpose. The asset may be worn out, obsolete, or no longer useful to the business for some other reason. The owner may sell the asset or exchange it. If the asset cannot be sold or exchanged, then it is discarded, or **junked**. While each situation is accounted for differently, there are some common steps that occur. In all cases, the business should:

1. Bring amortization up to date. If the disposal occurs partway through the year, a partial year's amortization must be recorded to update accumulated amortization.
2. Calculate whether there is a loss/gain on the disposal.
3. Remove the asset and contra-asset accounts from the books, and record the gain/loss and payment with a journal entry:
    - Debit the asset's accumulated amortization account
    - Credit the asset account
    - Record any gain or loss
    - Record payment and/or trade-in (if applicable)

Discarding PPE

When an asset is discarded, there is no cash received. Let's look at the journal entries, which vary depending on whether the asset is fully amortized or not.

Discarding Assets at Book Value Suppose Kawartha Dairy is disposing of an ice cream cone machine, and the final year's amortization expense has just been recorded on December 31. The cost was $60,000, and there is no residual value. The machine's accumulated amortization totals $60,000. Assume this asset cannot be sold or exchanged, so it is discarded or junked.

1. Amortization is up to date because this is recorded at year-end. No further adjustment is needed.
2. There is no gain or loss because the net book value is zero.
3. The entry to record its disposal is:

Dec. 31	Accumulated Amortization—Cone Machinery	60,000	
	Cone Machinery		60,000
	To dispose of a fully amortized machine.		

Now both accounts have zero balances, as shown in the T-accounts below:

Cone Machinery			
Dec. 31	60,000	**Dec. 31**	60,000

Accumulated Amortization—Cone Machinery			
Dec. 31	60,000	Dec. 31	60,000

When an asset is disposed of, a gain or loss on the sale is determined by comparing the proceeds from the disposition to the asset's book value:

- Proceeds > Book value → Gain
- Proceeds < Book value → Loss

Discarding Assets at a Loss If assets are discarded before being fully amortized, the company records a loss equal to the asset's book value. Let's now suppose Kawartha Dairy's store fixtures that cost $40,000 are junked. If the accumulated amortization is $30,000, the book value is therefore $10,000.

1. Amortization is up to date because this is recorded at year-end.
2. There is a loss because there is a book value of $10,000 but no payment received for it.

Cash received from selling the asset		$ 0
Book value of asset sold:		
Cost	$40,000	
Less: Accumulated amortization up to date of sale	30,000	
Net book value		10,000
Gain (loss) on sale of the asset		($10,000)

③ Disposal of these store fixtures generates a loss, that is recorded as follows:

Dec. 31	Accumulated Amortization—Store Fixtures	30,000	
	Loss on Disposal of Store Fixtures	10,000	
	Store Fixtures		40,000
	To dispose of store fixtures.		

A Gain or Loss on Disposal of Property, Plant, and Equipment is reported on the income statement in the "other gains and losses" section.

Selling PPE

Let's use the following information from Kawartha Dairy for the next example about selling surplus office furniture:

Sales date:	September 30, 2020
Selling price:	$50,000 cash
Original cost:	$100,000
Purchased:	January 1, 2017

The furniture has been amortized on a straight-line basis with a 10-year useful life and no residual value.

❶ Bring the amortization up to date. If Kawartha Dairy uses the calendar year as its accounting period, partial amortization must be recorded for nine months from January 1, 2020, to the sale date of September 30. The straight-line amortization entry for nine months at September 30, 2020, is:

Sep. 30	Amortization Expense—Furniture	7,500	
	Accumulated Amortization—Furniture		7,500
	To update amortization ($100,000 ÷ 10 years × 9/12).		

After this entry is posted, the Furniture and the Accumulated Amortization—Furniture accounts appear as follows:

Furniture

Jan. 1, 2017	100,000		

Accumulated Amortization—Furniture

		Dec. 31, 2017	10,000
		Dec. 31, 2018	10,000
		Dec. 31, 2019	10,000
		Sep. 30, 2020	**7,500**
		Balance	37,500

Book value = $62,500

Annual amortization = ($100,000 cost − $0 residual value) ÷ 10 years = $10,000

❷ Calculate if there is a gain or loss on the sale. The loss is computed as follows:

Cash received from selling the asset		$50,000
Book value of asset sold		
Cost	$100,000	
Less: Accumulated amortization up to date of sale	37,500	
Net book value		62,500
Gain (loss) on sale of the asset		($12,500)

❸ Record the journal entry to remove the balances in the asset and its contra account. Kawartha Dairy's entry to record the sale of the furniture for $50,000 cash is:

When disposing an asset, make sure to adjust both the asset and its accumulated amortization account balances to zero.

Sep. 30	Cash	50,000	
	Loss on Disposal of Furniture	12,500	
	Accumulated Amortization—Furniture	37,500	
	Furniture		100,000
	To dispose of furniture.		

If the sale price had been $70,000, Kawartha Dairy would have had a gain of $7,500 (Cash, $70,000 – Asset book value, $62,500). The entry to record this gain would be as follows:

Sep. 30	Cash	70,000	
	Accumulated Amortization—Furniture	37,500	
	Furniture		100,000
	Gain on Disposal of Furniture		7,500
	To dispose of furniture.		

Exchanging PPE

Businesses often exchange old tangible assets (property, plant, and equipment) for newer, more efficient assets. The most common exchange transaction is a *trade-in*.

The first thing to determine in any exchange transaction is whether the transaction has commercial substance.[2] **Commercial substance** exists when the entity's future cash flows from the new asset received will differ in risk, timing, or amount from the cash flows from the old asset given up in the exchange. This is almost always the case. Exhibit 10–9 summarizes the accounting treatment for exchanges.

EXHIBIT 10–9 | Accounting for Exchanges of Non-Monetary Assets

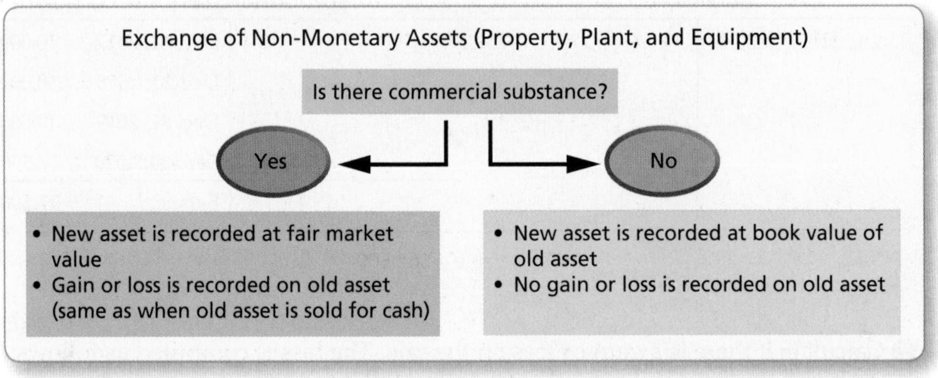

Suppose Kawartha Dairy owns a milk truck that it purchased for $42,000 on January 2, 2016. The old truck was expected to last seven years and was amortized on a straight-line basis. Accumulated amortization was up to date in the records at $30,000. On January 2, 2021, Kawartha Dairy exchanged this truck for a newer truck

[2]Part II, Section 3831, of the *CPA Canada Handbook*, "Non-monetary Transactions," guides the accounting treatment of tangible asset exchanges because property, plant, and equipment are defined as non-monetary assets.

that had a fair market value of $53,000. Kawartha Dairy received a trade-in allowance of $8,000 for the old truck and paid the seller $45,000 cash. Kawartha Dairy will receive better gas mileage with the new truck and will be able to save delivery expenses by delivering more with the new truck. Therefore, *this exchange of assets has commercial substance*. The entry to record this exchange would be as follows:

Why is the trade-in allowance usually different from the book value? The book value depends on the asset's *historical cost* and on the amortization method used. The trade-in allowance is based on the *market value* of the asset being traded in.

Jan. 2	New Truck	53,000	
	Loss on Exchange of Assets	4,000	
	Accumulated Amortization—Old Truck	30,000	
	Cash		45,000
	Old Truck		42,000
	To record exchange of the old milk truck and cash for a new milk truck.		

Payment for asset (trade-in allowance)		$8,000
Cost of asset	$42,000	
Less: Accum. Amort.	30,000	
Book value of old asset		12,000
Loss on the exchange		($4,000)

Try It!

7. ABC Catering Service purchased equipment on January 8, 2018, for $58,500. The equipment is expected to last six years and to have a residual value of $4,500.
   a. Suppose ABC sold the equipment for $43,000 on December 29, 2020. Journalize the sale of the equipment, assuming straight-line amortization is used.
   b. Suppose ABC sold the equipment for $23,000 on December 29, 2020. Journalize the sale of the equipment, assuming straight-line amortization is used.
8. In January 2018, Luk's Catering purchased a portable food heater for $3,100 cash. The journal entry to record the purchase included a debit to Catering Equipment. During 2018 and 2019, Luk's Catering recorded total amortization of $2,200 on the heater. On January 2, 2020, Luk's Catering traded in the old food heater for a new one that is more efficient, paying $2,900 and accepting $500 for the trade-in. This exchange transaction has commercial substance. Journalize Luk's Catering's exchange of equipment.

Solutions appear at the end of this chapter and on **MyLab Accounting**

Accounting for Natural Resources

LO 5

How do we account for natural resources?

Natural resources are tangible capital assets that are often called *wasting assets* because they are used up in the process of production. Examples include iron ore, coal, oil, gas, and timber. Natural resources are like inventories in the ground (coal) or on top of the ground (timber). Natural resources are expensed through amortization. Some companies use the word **depletion** to describe amortization of natural resources. Amortization expense, or *depletion expense*, is that portion of the cost of natural resources that is used up in a particular period. It is computed the same way as the units-of-production (UOP) method:

$$\text{① Amortization per unit of resource} = \frac{\text{Cost} - \text{Residual value}}{\text{Estimated total units of natural resource}}$$

$$\text{② Amortization expense} = \text{Amortization per unit of resource} \times \text{Number of units of resource}$$

An oil well may cost $300,000 and contain an estimated 10,000 barrels of oil. (Natural resources usually have no residual value.) If 3,000 barrels are extracted during the first year, amortization expense is calculated as follows:

❶ **Amortization per unit of resource** $= \dfrac{(\$300{,}000 - \$0)}{10{,}000 \text{ barrels}} = \$30$ **per barrel**

❷ **Amortization expense** $=$ **$30/barrel × 3,000 barrels extracted**

$=$ **$90,000**

The journal entry to record the amortization for the year would be shown as follows:

Dec. 31	Amortization Expense—Oil	90,000	
	Accumulated Amortization—Oil		90,000

Accumulated Amortization for natural resources is a contra account similar to Accumulated Amortization for property, plant, and equipment. Natural resource assets can be reported on the balance sheet, as is shown for oil in the following example. See Exhibit 4–11 on to see how this fits into the rest of the balance sheet.

Property, plant, and equipment			
Land			$120,000
Buildings	$800,000		
Less: Accumulated amortization	305,000	$495,000	
Equipment	160,000		
Less: Accumulated amortization	105,000	55,000	
Net property, plant, and equipment			550,000
Oil and gas properties			
Oil		**300,000**	
Less: Accumulated amortization		**90,000**	
Net oil and gas properties			210,000

Future Removal and Site Restoration Costs

There is increasing concern on the part of individuals and governments about the environment. In the past, a company exploiting natural resources, such as a mining company, would simply abandon the site once the ore body was mined completely. Now there is legislation in most jurisdictions requiring a natural resource company to remove buildings, equipment, and waste and to restore the site once a location is to be dismantled and abandoned.

The *CPA Canada Handbook* refers to future removal and site restoration costs as an **asset retirement obligation**, which is estimated at the time the asset is acquired or the obligation becomes known. The liability (a credit) for the asset retirement obligation is measured at the end of each period at the best estimate of the future expenditures. This estimate is determined by the judgment of management, supplemented by experience of similar transactions and perhaps reports from independent experts. The same amount is recorded as an asset retirement cost (a debit) and added to the carrying amount of its related asset (such as a mine). The asset retirement cost must then be expensed using an amortization method and time frame that matches that of the related asset.

Asset retirement obligations are reviewed at each balance sheet date and adjusted to reflect the current best estimate.

Try It!

9. Suppose West Fraser Timber Co. Ltd. purchases, for $600,000, land that contains an estimated 400,000 fbm (foot-board measures) of timber. West Fraser harvests 200,000 fbm in the year of purchase. How much amortization should be recorded?

Solutions appear at the end of this chapter and on **MyLab Accounting**

Intangible Assets and Goodwill

LO 6

How do we account for intangible assets and goodwill?

As we discussed earlier in this chapter, **intangible assets** have no physical form. Instead, these assets convey special rights from ownership of patents, copyrights, trademarks, franchises, leaseholds, and goodwill.

In our technology-driven economy, intangibles are very important. Consider the online auctioneer eBay Inc. The company has no physical products—only the software it uses to provide the service that helps people buy and sell everything from toys to bathroom tiles millions of times each month.

The **intellectual capital** of eBay or a company like BlackBerry Ltd. is difficult to measure, but when one company buys another we get a glimpse of the value of the acquired intellectual capital. Intangibles can account for most of a company's market value, so companies must value their purchased intangibles just as they do their physical and financial assets.

Intangibles are expensed as they expire through amortization. Amortization is computed over the lesser of the asset's legal life or estimated useful life. Obsolescence often shortens an intangible asset's useful life. Amortization expense for intangibles can be written off directly against the intangible asset account with *no accumulated amortization account*. The residual value of most intangibles is zero.

Specific Intangibles

Patents **Patents** are federal government grants conveying an exclusive right for 20 years to produce and sell an invention. The invention may be a product or a process. Patented products include Bombardier Ski-Doos and the BlackBerry Ltd.'s BlackBerry cellphone. Suppose BlackBerry Ltd. pays $2,000,000 to acquire a patent, and it believes the expected useful life of the patent is five years before competitors enter the market. Amortization expense is $400,000 per year ($2,000,000 ÷ 5 years). The company's entries for this patent are as follows:

Jan. 1	Patent	2,000,000	
	Cash		2,000,000
	To record purchase of a patent.		
Dec. 31	Amortization Expense—Patent	400,000	
	Patent		400,000
	To amortize the cost of a patent ($2,000,000 ÷ 5).		

At the end of the first year, BlackBerry would report the patent on the balance sheet at $1,600,000 ($2,000,000 minus the first year's amortization of $400,000).

Intangibles do not have a related accumulated amortization account. The amortization expense is written off directly against the intangible asset.

Copyrights **Copyrights** are exclusive rights to reproduce and sell software, a book, a musical composition, a film, or some other creative work. Issued by the federal government, copyrights extend 50 years beyond the end of the creator's life. A company may pay a large sum to purchase an existing copyright from the owner. For example, the publisher Penguin Random House (Canada) may pay the author

The symbol ® means that the name has been registered as a trademark.

of a popular novel tens of thousands of dollars or more for the book's copyright. The useful life of a copyright for a popular book may be two or three years; on the other hand, some copyrights, especially of musical compositions, such as works by the Beatles, seem to remain valuable over several decades.

Trademarks and Brand Names **Trademarks** and **brand names** (or **trade names**) are distinctive identifiers of products or services. For example, the Edmonton Oilers and Toronto Blue Jays have insignia that identify their respective teams. Molson Canadian, Swiss Chalet, WestJet, and Roots are everyday trade names. Advertising slogans such as Speedy Muffler's "At Speedy You're a Somebody" are also legally protected for a period of 15 years (which can be renewed). **Soundmarks** (distinctive sounds used to perform the same function as a trademark, such as the THX sound system sound at the movies and the Intel sound in its commercials) are also protected. The cost of a trademark, soundmark, or trade name is amortized over its useful life.

Franchises and Licences **Franchises** and **licences** are privileges granted by a private business or a government to sell a product or service in accordance with specified conditions. The Winnipeg Jets hockey organization is a franchise granted to its owners by the National Hockey League. Tim Hortons and Re/Max Ltd. are other well-known franchises. The acquisition cost of a franchise or licence is amortized over its useful life.

Leaseholds A **leasehold** is a right arising from a prepayment that a lessee (tenant) makes to secure the use of an asset from a lessor (landlord). For example, most malls lease the space to the mall stores and shops that you visit. Often, leases require the lessee to make this prepayment in addition to monthly rental payments. The prepayment is a debit to an intangible asset account entitled Leaseholds. This amount is amortized over the life of the lease by debiting Rent Expense and crediting Leaseholds.

Sometimes lessees modify or improve the leased asset. For example, a lessee may construct a fence on leased land. The lessee debits the cost of the fence to a separate intangible asset account, **Leasehold Improvements**, and amortizes its cost over the lesser of the term of the lease and its useful life.

Goodwill

Goodwill is a truly unique asset. *Goodwill* in accounting is a more limited term than in everyday use, as in "friendly or cooperative feelings." In accounting, **goodwill** is the excess of the cost to purchase a company over the market value of its net assets (assets minus liabilities). Why might an acquiring company pay an amount greater than the market value of net assets acquired when purchasing a business? The business being acquired might have good customer relations, a unique software code, a good location, efficient operations, a monopoly in the marketplace, strong sources of financing, and other factors that make it more valuable than just the net assets being acquired.

Another way to think about this calculation is that there is goodwill of $2 million because the payment of $10 million is more than the market value of $8 million.

Suppose Kawartha Dairy wants to expand outside of Ontario and acquires Truro Dairy at a cost of $10 million. The market value of Truro Dairy's assets is $9 million, and its liabilities total $1 million. In this case, Kawartha Dairy paid $2 million for goodwill, computed as follows:

Purchase price paid for Truro Dairy		$10 million
Sum of the market value of Truro Dairy's assets	$9 million	
Less: Truro Dairy's liabilities	1 million	
Market value of Truro Dairy's net assets		8 million
Excess is called *goodwill*		$ 2 million

Kawartha Dairy's entry to record the acquisition of Truro Dairy, including its goodwill, would be:

June 30	Assets (Cash; Receivables; Inventories; Property, Plant, and Equipment; all at market value)	9,000,000	
	Goodwill	2,000,000	
	Liabilities		1,000,000
	Cash		10,000,000
	Purchased Truro Dairy.		

Goodwill has the following special features:

- Goodwill is recorded at its cost only by the company that purchases another company. A purchase transaction provides objective evidence of the value of the goodwill.
- Goodwill has an indefinite life, so it is not amortized like other intangibles. According to ASPE, the purchaser must assess the goodwill every year and, if its value is **impaired** (if the fair value falls below the carrying value in the accounting records), the goodwill must be written down to reflect the *impairment*. The write-down amount is accounted for as a loss in the year of the write-down. For example, suppose the goodwill—purchased above—is worth only $1,500,000 at the end of the first year due to a strike or some bad publicity at Truro Dairy. In that case, Kawartha Dairy would make this entry:

Dec. 31	Loss on Goodwill (or Impairment Loss)	500,000	
	Goodwill		500,000
	Recorded loss on goodwill ($2,000,000 − $1,500,000).		

Goodwill can be written down, but it cannot be written up if there is a reversal of circumstances.

Kawartha Dairy would then report this goodwill on the balance sheet at its current value of $1,500,000.

Try It!

10. Suppose a company paid $650,000 on January 5, 2020, to acquire a patent that it believes will have a five-year useful life. The company's year-end is December 31.
    a. Journalize the purchase of the patent and the amortization entry at year-end.
    b. Suppose this same patent was acquired on May 13, 2020. Journalize the purchase of the patent and the amortization entry at year-end assuming that the company chose to amortize by rounding to the closest whole month.
11. Suppose TELUS Corporation acquires Novel Networks, a small company that produces specialized computer programs, for $2,000,000 on October 12. Novel Networks' assets have a book value of $500,000 on October 12 and a market value of $400,000. Its liabilities have a market value of $300,000. Record the acquisition of Novel Networks by TELUS Corporation.

Solutions appear at the end of this chapter and on **MyLab Accounting**

LO 7

How does IFRS apply to PPE, intangible assets, and goodwill?

EXHIBIT 10–10 | The Impact of IFRS on PPE, Intangibles, and Goodwill

ASPE	IFRS
Property, Plant, and Equipment (PPE)	
Amortization is the term often used for tangible and intangible assets.	*Depreciation* is the term often used for tangible assets, whereas amortization is often used for intangible assets.
There is no guidance on the level of detail required in reporting PPE.	After an asset has been capitalized, companies must capitalize replacement parts and **derecognize** the parts that are replaced. In other words, each part of an item of PPE that is significant relative to the total cost of the asset must be depreciated separately. This is called **componentization**. If a company purchases a building, it has to depreciate the significant components (roof, heating) of the building separately.
Cost is measured at acquisition. Follow historic cost principle, and show this cost in later years unless there is an impairment.	In the years following acquisition, companies have the *option* to follow a **revaluation method**. Under the revaluation approach, the carrying amount of the PPE is its fair value at the date of revaluation. PPE must be tested for impairment annually and depreciation revised for future periods.
PPE must be tested for impairment when it is apparent.	To assess impairment under IFRS, assets may be looked at individually or they can be divided into **cash generating units (CGUs)**, the smallest identifiable group of assets that generates cash flows that are largely independent of the cash flows from other assets. The recoverable amount of the asset is compared annually with the carrying value to assess whether or not there is any write-down needed.
Assets that were written down *cannot* have their impairment reversed.	Assets that were written down can have their impairment reversed in a future period.
Intangible Assets and Goodwill	
Only purchased intangible assets can be reported and amortized.	*Internally generated* intangible assets must be analyzed to determine whether they will provide a future benefit to the company. If they will, they can be capitalized and amortized.
Companies may only use the historic cost principle to value assets.	Companies have the option of using a cost model or the revaluation model to determine the carrying amount of the intangible asset.

Summary Problems for Your Review

Problem 1

Uhuru Industrial Products purchased equipment on January 2, 2020, for $176,000. The expected life of the equipment is 10 years, or 100,000 units of production, and its residual value is $16,000. Management has amortized the equipment using the DDB method. On July 2, 2022, Uhuru sold the equipment for $100,000 cash.

Required

Record Uhuru Industrial Products' amortization for 2022 using the DDB method and the sale of the equipment on July 2, 2022.

Problem 2

Meben Logistics purchased a building at a cost of $500,000 on January 2, 2016. Meben has amortized the building by using the straight-line method, a 35-year useful life, and a residual value of $150,000. On January 2, 2020, the business changed the useful life of the building from 35 years to 25 years from the date of purchase. The fiscal year of Meben Logistics ends on December 31.

Required

Record amortization for 2020 assuming no change in the building's residual value.

SOLUTIONS

Problem 1

	A	B	C	D
1		Double-Declining-Balance		
2	Year	Annual Amortization Expense	Accumulated Amortization	Book Value
3	Start			$176,000
4	2020	$35,200	$ 35,200	140,800
5	2021	28,160	63,360	112,640
6	2022	22,528	85,888	90,112

2020			
Jul. 2	Amortization Expense—Equipment	11,264	
	Accumulated Amortization—Equipment		11,264
	To record amortization expense for the period Jan. 1, 2022, to Jun. 30, 2022. ($112,640 × 0.20* × ½)		
Jul. 2	Cash	100,000	
	Accumulated Amortization—Equipment**	74,624	
	Loss on Sale of Equipment	1,376	
	Equipment		176,000
	To record sale of equipment.		

*10-year amortization using DDB = 1/10 × 2, or 0.20
**$35,200 + $28,160 + $11,264 = $74,624.

Amortization expense must first be recorded for the portion of the year that the asset was used before it was sold.

If Cash > Book value, then record a gain on disposal.

If Cash < Book value, then record a loss on disposal.

Problem 2

The equation for revised straight-line amortization is:

$$\text{Revised straight-line amortization} = \frac{\text{Cost} + \text{Betterments} - \text{Accumulated amortization} - \text{New residual value}}{\text{Estimated remaining useful life}}$$

Notice that these solutions are rounded to the nearest dollar. Please check with your instructor to see if rounding to two decimal places is more appropriate for your course.

Cost	= \$500,000 (given)
Betterments	= \$0 (given)
Accumulated amortization	= [(\$500,000 − \$150,000) ÷ 35 years] × 4 years = \$40,000
New residual value	= \$150,000 (the same as old residual value)
Estimated remaining useful life in years	= 25 − 4 = 21 years

The expected useful life changed from 35 years to 25 years. Since amortization has already been expensed for 4 years, 21 years remain in the building's new 25-year useful life.

Therefore,

$$\text{Revised straight-line amortization} = \frac{\$500{,}000 + \$0 - \$40{,}000 - \$150{,}000}{21 \text{ years}} = \$14{,}762 \text{ per year, rounded}$$

2020			
Dec. 31	Amortization Expense—Building	14,762	
	Accumulated Amortization—Building		14,762
	To record annual amortization for 2020.		

Summary

Learning Objectives

① Measure the cost of property, plant, and equipment Pg. 552

What are property, plant, and equipment (PPE), and how do we measure their cost?

- Property, plant, and equipment (PPE) are tangible, long-lived assets that the business uses in its operations.
  - The cost is the purchase price plus applicable provincial taxes (but not GST or HST), purchase commissions, and all other necessary amounts incurred to acquire the asset and to prepare it for its intended use.
  - Capitalize only those costs that add to the asset's usefulness or its useful life.
  - Expense all other costs as maintenance or repairs.

② Calculate and account for amortization Pg. 557

How do we calculate and account for amortization?

- Straight-line method:

$$\text{Straight-line amortization} = \frac{\text{Cost} - \text{Residual value}}{\text{Useful life}}$$

- Units-of-production (UOP) method:

$$\text{Units-of-production amortization per unit of output} = \frac{\text{Cost} - \text{Residual value}}{\text{Useful life in units of production}}$$

- Double-declining-balance (DDB) method:

DDB amortization = Asset book value × DDB rate

- Use the method that best matches amortization expense against the revenues produced by the asset.

③ Account for other issues: Amortization for income tax purposes, partial years, and revised assumptions **Pg. 563**

How do we account for other amortization issues?

- Amortization for financial statement purposes and income tax purposes often differs. This is both legal and ethical.
- CRA allows companies and individuals to claim capital cost allowance (CCA) against taxable income.
- When assets are purchased or sold during the year, calculate partial-year amortization.
- When significant changes occur to an asset's cost, residual value, or useful life, annual amortization expense must be revised for all future years to reflect the changes.

$$\text{Revised straight-line amortization} = \frac{\text{Cost} + \text{Betterments} - \text{Accumulated amortization} - \text{New residual value}}{\text{Estimated remaining useful life}}$$

④ Account for the disposal of property, plant, and equipment **Pg. 565**

How do we account for the disposal of PPE?

- When disposing of PPE, always follow these three steps:
  1. Update amortization to date of sale, disposal, or trade.
  2. Calculate the gain or loss on disposal and report the gain or loss on the income statement.
  3. Remove the book balances from the asset account and its related accumulated amortization account.

⑤ Account for natural resources **Pg. 569**

How do we account for natural resources?

- Natural resources are expensed through amortization (depletion) on a UOP basis.

⑥ Account for intangible assets and goodwill **Pg. 571**

How do we account for intangible assets and goodwill?

- Intangible assets are assets that have no physical form.
  - They give their owners a special right to current and expected future benefits.
  - The major types of intangible assets are patents, copyrights, trademarks, franchises, leaseholds, and licences.
  - Amortization is computed on a straight-line basis over the lesser of the legal life or the useful life.
  - Goodwill is not amortized, but its carrying value is assessed annually and written down if its market value is less than its carrying value.

⑦ Describe the impact of IFRS on property, plant, and equipment, intangible assets, and goodwill **Pg. 574**

How does IFRS apply to PPE, intangible assets, and goodwill?

- ASPE and IFRS are converged in many aspects, but there are a few differences:
  - Under IFRS, each part of an item of PPE that is significant relative to the total cost of the asset must be amortized separately. This is known as componentization.
  - IFRS allows fair market valuation of PPE assets at each balance sheet date subsequent to acquisition if the company so chooses. Depreciation is then revised.
  - ASPE and IFRS allow impairment assessment each year, but under IFRS assets may be looked at individually or they can be divided into cash generating units (CGUs).
  - IFRS allows assets that were written down to have the impairment reversed in a future period, while this is not possible under ASPE.
  - Under IFRS, internally generated intangible assets can be capitalized and amortized if they will provide a future benefit to the company.

Key Terms for the chapter are shown next and are in the **Glossary** at the back of the book. **Similar Terms** are shown after **Key Terms**.

KEY TERMS

Amortizable cost The asset's cost minus its estimated residual value *(p. 558)*.

Amortization The systematic charging of the cost of a capital asset. It is often called depletion when applied to natural resources. The term is also used to describe the writing off to expense of capital assets *(p. 557)*.

Amortization rate The amount of amortization written off to expense stated as a percentage *(p. 560)*.

Amortization schedule A table or chart that shows the amortization expense and asset values by period *(p. 559)*.

Appraisal An expert assessment of the value of an asset *(p. 554)*.

Arrears A legal term for debt that is overdue because of at least one missed payment *(p. 552)*.

Asset retirement obligation A liability that records the future cost to settle a present obligation, such as future removal and site restoration costs *(p. 570)*.

Betterment An expenditure that increases the capacity or efficiency of an asset or extends its useful life. Capital expenditures are debited to an asset account *(p. 555)*.

Brand name A distinctive identification of a product or service *(p. 572)*.

Capital cost allowance (CCA) Amortization allowed for income tax purposes by the Canada Revenue Agency; the rates allowed are called capital cost allowance rates *(p. 563)*.

Capitalize To record as an asset *(p. 553)*.

Cash generating unit (CGU) Under IFRS, the smallest identifiable group of assets that generates cash flows that are largely independent of the cash flows from other assets *(p. 574)*.

Commercial substance In an exchange of tangible capital assets, commercial substance exists when an entity's future cash flows from the new asset received will differ in risk, timing, or amount from the cash flows from the old asset given up *(p. 568)*.

Componentization Under IFRS, recording each identifiable component of an asset separately to calculate depreciation on each part *(p. 574)*.

Copyright The exclusive right to reproduce and sell software, a book, a musical composition, a film, or other creative work. Issued by the federal government, copyrights extend 50 years beyond the creator's life *(p. 571)*.

DDB rate Double-declining-balance percentage applied to an asset to calculate its amortization or depreciation. It is twice the straight-line amortization rate *(p. 560)*.

Depletion Another word to describe the amortization of natural resources or wasting assets *(p. 569)*.

Derecognize Under IFRS, to remove an asset from the accounting records because it has been replaced *(p. 574)*.

Double-declining-balance (DDB) method A type of amortization method that expenses a relatively larger amount of an asset's cost nearer the start of its useful life than does the straight-line method *(p. 560)*.

Estimated residual value The expected cash value of an asset at the end of its useful life. Also called *residual value*, *scrap value*, or *salvage value (p. 558)*.

Estimated useful life Length of the service that a business expects to get from an asset; may be expressed in years, units of output, kilometres, or other measures *(p. 558)*.

Franchise Privileges granted by a private business or a government to sell a product or service in accordance with specified conditions *(p. 572)*.

Goodwill Excess of the cost of an acquired company over the sum of the market values of its net assets (assets minus liabilities) *(p. 572)*.

Half-year rule The Canada Revenue Agency allows businesses to claim only 50 percent of the normal CCA rate in the year an asset is acquired *(p. 564)*.

Identifiable tangible asset An asset that is physical—it can be seen and touched—and can be separated from other assets; used to describe property, plant, and equipment *(p. 552)*.

Impaired When the fair value falls below the carrying value in the accounting records *(p. 573)*.

Intangible asset An asset with no physical form that conveys a special right to current and expected future benefits *(p. 571)*.

Intellectual capital The knowledge of the people who work in a business *(p. 571)*.

Junked Discarded *(p. 566)*.

Leasehold A right arising from a prepayment that a lessee (tenant) makes to secure the use of an asset from a lessor (landlord) *(p. 572)*.

Leasehold improvements Changes to a leased asset that are amortized over the term of the lease or the useful life of the asset, whichever is shorter *(p. 572)*.

Licence Privileges granted by a private business or a government to sell a product or service in accordance with special conditions *(p. 572)*.

Mortgage A long-term notes payable that includes a borrower's promise to transfer legal title to specific assets if the debt is not paid *(p. 555)*.

Patent A federal government grant giving the holder the exclusive right for 20 years to produce and sell an invention *(p. 571)*.

Prospectively In the future (*p. 564*).

Relative-fair-value method The allocation of the cost of assets according to their fair market value (*p. 555*).

Repair An expenditure that merely maintains an asset in its existing condition or restores the asset to good working order. Repairs are expensed (matched against revenue) (*p. 556*).

Revaluation method Under IFRS, when an asset's value is restated in the accounting records to reflect the asset's current market value (*p. 574*).

Soundmark A distinctive sound meant to function the same as a trademark (*p. 572*).

Straight-line method An amortization method in which an equal amount of amortization expense is assigned to each year (or period) of asset use (*p. 559*).

Trademark Distinctive identifications of a product or service. Also called *trade name* (*p. 572*).

Trade name Another term for trademark (*p. 572*).

Units-of-production (UOP) method An amortization method by which a fixed amount of amortization is assigned to each unit of output produced by the capital asset (*p. 560*).

SIMILAR TERMS

Amortization	Depreciation (for assets such as property, plant, and equipment); Depletion (for natural resources)
Book value	Carrying value
Brand name	Trade mark; Trade name
CCA	Capital cost allowance
CGU	Cash generating unit
CRA	Canada Revenue Agency
DDB	Double-declining-balance method of amortization
Fair value	Market value
Junked	Scrapped, discarded
Natural resources	Wasting assets
PPE	Property, plant, and equipment
Property, plant, and equipment	Long-lived assets; Long-term assets; Capital assets
Residual value	Salvage value; Scrap value
Trade name	Brand name, trademark
UOP	Units-of-production method of amortization

SELF-STUDY QUESTIONS

Test your understanding of the chapter by marking the correct answer for each of the following questions:

1. Which of the following payments is *not* included in the cost of land? (*p. 552*)
   a. Removal of old building
   b. Legal fees
   c. Property taxes in arrears paid at acquisition
   d. Cost of fencing and lighting

2. Niall Home Builders plans to build a custom home. In the first quarter, they spent the following amounts:

Land purchase	$70,000
Surveys and legal fees	2,800
Land clearing	3,000
Install fences around the property	3,100
Install lighting and signage	400

   What amount should be recorded as the land cost? (*p. 553*)
   a. $78,900 b. $76,200
   c. $75,800 d. $79,300

3. Willard Windows paid $150,000 for two machines valued at $120,000 and $60,000. Willard will record these machines at costs of (*p. 554*)
   a. $120,000 and $60,000 b. $75,000 each
   c. $100,000 and $50,000 d. $90,000 and $60,000

4. Which of the following items is a repair? (*p. 555*)
   a. New brakes for delivery truck
   b. Paving of a company parking lot
   c. Cost of a new engine for a truck
   d. Building permit paid to construct an addition to an existing building
5. Which of the following definitions fits amortization? (*p. 557*)
   a. Allocation of the asset's market value to expense over its useful life
   b. Allocation of the asset's cost to expense over its useful life
   c. Decreases in the asset's market value over its useful life
   d. Increases in the fund set aside to replace the asset when it is worn out
6. Which amortization method's amounts are not computed based on time? (*p. 558*)
   a. Straight-line
   b. Units-of-production (UOP)
   c. Double-declining-balance (DDB)
   d. All are based on time
7. A copy machine costs $45,000 when new and has accumulated amortization of $44,000. Suppose Print and Photo Centre discards this machine and receives nothing. What is the result of the disposal transaction? (*p. 566*)
   a. No gain or loss
   b. Gain of $1,000
   c. Loss of $1,000
   d. Loss of $45,000
8. A company paid $900,000 for a building and was amortizing it by the straight-line method over a 40-year life, with estimated residual value of $60,000. After 10 years it became evident that the building's *remaining* useful life would be 40 years with a residual value of $50,000. Amortization for the 12th year is (*p. 564*)
   a. $16,000
   b. $17,250
   c. $21,000
   d. $28,000
9. A truck costs $50,000 when new and has accumulated amortization of $35,000. Suppose Wilson Towing exchanges the truck for a new truck. The new truck has a market value of $60,000, and Wilson pays cash of $40,000. Assume the exchange has commercial substance. What is the result of this exchange? (*p. 568*)
   a. No gain or loss
   b. Gain of $5,000
   c. Loss of $5,000
   d. Gain of $45,000
10. Amortization of a natural resource is computed in the same manner as which amortization method? (*p. 569*)
    a. Straight-line
    b. UOP
    c. Double-declining-balance
    d. CCA
11. On March 1, 2019, Gregor Goldfields purchased a mineral deposit for $400,000 that is expected to be in operation for 10 years. A geological report estimated the mineral deposit contained 125,000 tonnes of gold. Management expects the asset to have a zero residual value when fully amortized. During 2019, 34,000 tonnes of gold were mined. What is the amount of amortization expense at the company's year-end, December 31, 2019? (*p. 569*)
    a. $33,333
    b. $40,000
    c. $75,000
    d. $108,800
12. Vasdev Company paid $1,100,000 to acquire Gentech Systems. Gentech's assets had a market value of $1,800,000, and its liabilities were $800,000. In recording the acquisition, Vasdev will record goodwill of (*p. 572*)
    a. $100,000
    b. $1,000,000
    c. $1,100,000
    d. $0

Answers to Self-Study Questions

1. d 2. c 3. c [$120,000 ÷ ($120,000 + $60,000)] × $150,000 = $100,000; [$60,000 ÷ ($120,000 + $60,000)] × $150,000 = $50,000 4. a 5. b 6. b 7. c
8. a Amortizable cost = $900,000 − $60,000 = $840,000
$840,000 ÷ 40 years = $21,000 per year
$900,000 − ($21,000 × 10 years) = $690,000
($690,000 − 50,000) ÷ 40 years = $16,000 per year
9. b 10. b 11. d 12. a $1, 100,000 − ($1,800,000 − $800,000) = $100,000

Assignment Material

MyLab Accounting Make the grade with MyLab Accounting: The Starters, Exercises, and Problems can be found on MyLab. You can practise them as often as you want, and most feature step-by-step guided instructions to help you find the right answer.

QUESTIONS

1. Describe how to measure the cost of property, plant, and equipment. Would an ordinary cost of repairing the asset after it is placed in service be included in the asset's cost?
2. Suppose land with a building on it is purchased for $1,050,000. How do you account for the $65,000 cost of removing this unwanted building?
3. When assets are purchased as a group for a single price and no individual asset cost is given, how is each asset's cost determined?
4. What does the word *capitalize* mean?
5. Define amortization and explain the concept of useful life of an asset.
6. To what types of assets does amortization expense apply under ASPE?
7. Which amortization method does each of the graphs at the bottom of the page characterize: straight-line, UOP, or DDB?
8. Explain the concept of accelerated amortization. Which of the three amortization methods results in the most amortization in the first year of the asset's life?
9. The level of business activity fluctuates widely for Orillia Schoolbus Co., reaching its slowest time in July and August each year. At other times, business is brisk. What amortization method is most appropriate for the company's fleet of school buses? Why?
10. Shania Data Centre uses the most advanced computers available to keep a competitive edge over other data service centres. To maintain this advantage, the company usually replaces its computers before they are worn out. Describe the major factors affecting the useful life of a property, plant, and equipment asset, and indicate which seems more relevant to this company's computers.
11. Which amortization method does not consider estimated residual value in computing amortization during the early years of the asset's life?
12. What is capital cost allowance (CCA)?
13. Describe how to compute amortization for less than a full year.
14. Hudson Company paid $25,000 for office furniture. The company expected it to remain in service for six years and to have a $1,000 residual value. After two years' use, company accountants believe the furniture will last for the next seven years. How much amortization will Hudson record for each of these last seven years, assuming straight-line amortization and no change in the estimated residual value? (Round your answer to the nearest dollar.)
15. When a company sells property, plant, and equipment before the year's end, what must it record before accounting for the sale?
16. Describe how to determine whether a company experiences a gain or a loss when an existing piece of equipment is exchanged for a new piece of equipment.
17. What expense applies to natural resources? By which amortization method is this expense computed?
18. How do intangible assets differ from most other assets? Why are they assets at all? What expense applies to intangible assets?
19. Why is the cost of patents and other intangible assets often expensed over a shorter period than the legal life of the asset?
20. Woodstock Industrial Products Inc. is recognized as a world leader in the manufacture of industrial products. The company's success has created vast amounts of business goodwill. Would you expect to see this goodwill reported on Woodstock's financial statements? Why, or why not?
21. To which types of assets does amortization expense apply under IFRS?
22. Under IFRS, companies need to calculate amortization separately for the major components of an amortizable asset. Does this provide better information for the users of financial information?

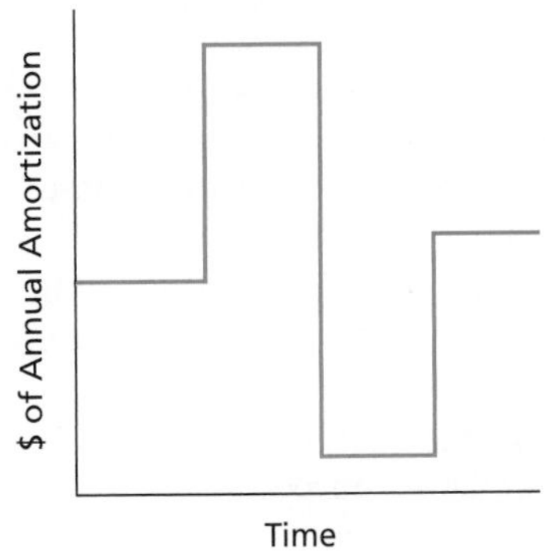

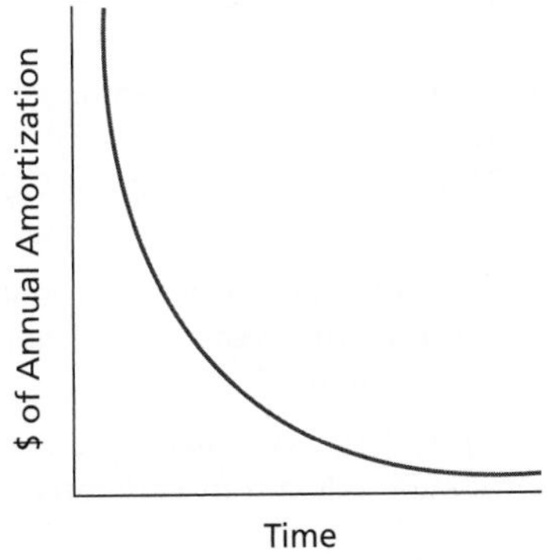

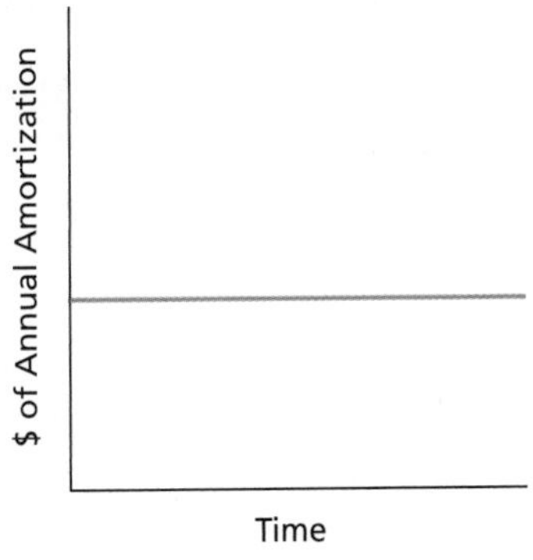

STARTERS

① Measuring the cost of property, plant, and equipment

S10–1 Highland Clothing purchased land, paying $96,000 cash and signing a $300,000 note payable. In addition, Highland paid delinquent property tax of $1,100, title insurance costing $600, and $4,600 to level the land and remove an unwanted building. Calculate to total cost of the land to be reported on the balance sheet.

① Calculate asset values
Land, $82,500

S10–2 Wishbone Landscapers bought land, a building, and equipment for a lump sum of $550,000. Following are the appraised fair market values of the newly acquired assets: Land, $97,500; Building, $390,000; and Equipment, $162,500. Calculate the cost of each asset to be reported on the balance sheet.

① Lump-sum purchase of assets
Land, $213,316

S10–3 Suppose you make a lump-sum purchase of land, building, and equipment on April 30. At the time of your purchase, the land has a current market value of $240,000, the building's market value is $350,000, and the equipment's market value is $175,000. Journalize the lump-sum purchase of the three assets for a total cost of $680,000. You sign a note payable for this amount. Round percent to two decimal places and your final answer to the nearest dollar.

① Capitalizing versus expensing amortizable asset costs

S10–4 FlyFast Airways repaired one of its Boeing 767 aircraft at a cost of $600,000, which FlyFast paid in cash. FlyFast erroneously capitalized this cost as part of the cost of the plane on June 16. How will this accounting error affect FlyFast's net income that month? Ignore amortization.

② Understanding amortization methods

S10–5 Give the amortization method(s) described by the following statements:

a. Amortization expense declines over the life of the asset
b. Book value declines over the life of the asset
c. Amortization expense fluctuates with use
d. Amortization expense is the same each period
e. This method best fits an asset that amortizes because of physical use
f. This method best fits an asset that generates revenue evenly each period
g. This method is the most common
h. This method records the most amortization over the life of the asset

② Computing amortization by three methods—first year only
2. Book value, $40,800,000

S10–6 On January 1, 2020, FlyFast Airways purchased a used Bombardier jet at a cost of $50,000,000. FlyFast expects the plane to remain useful for five years (6,000,000 miles) and to have a residual value of $4,000,000. FlyFast expects the plane to be flown 750,000 miles the first year. (Note: "Miles" is the unit of measure used in the airline industry.)

1. Compute FlyFast's first-year amortization on the jet using the following methods:
   a. Straight-line b. UOP c. DDB
2. Show the jet's book value at the end of the first year under the straight-line method.

② Computing amortization by three methods—second year
DDB, $12,000,000

S10–7 On January 1, 2020, FlyFast Airways purchased a used Bombardier aircraft at a cost of $50,000,000. FlyFast expects the plane to remain useful for five years (6,000,000 miles) and to have a residual value of $4,000,000. FlyFast expects the plane to be flown 750,000 miles the first year and 500,000 miles the second year. Compute second-year amortization on the plane using the following methods:

a. Straight-line b. UOP c. DDB

② Calculating capital cost allowance
1. CCA in first year, $15,000,000

S10–8 UpSky Airways purchased a small jet on January 1 at a cost of $40,000,000. UpSky expects the plane to remain useful for six years and to have a residual value of $4,000,000. UpSky is comparing the CCA method used for income tax purposes with the straight-line amortization method.

1. Calculate the amount of CCA, at a rate of 25 percent, that UpSky will be able to claim in its first year. Is this more or less than what it would show using the straight-line method?
2. Why does the Government of Canada, through the CCA, regulate the amount of amortization that a company can claim for income tax purposes?

S10–9 On March 31, 2020, Northern Mining purchased a dump truck at a cost of $4,000,000. Northern expects to use the truck for nine years and expects it to have a residual value of $400,000. Compute Northern's amortization on the truck for the year ended December 31, 2020, using the straight-line method.

(3) Partial-year amortization

S10–10 Assume the Goldeyes Baseball Club paid $60,000 for a hot dog stand with a 10-year useful life and no residual value. After using the hot dog stand for four years, the club determines that the asset will remain useful for only two more years. Record amortization on the hot dog stand for Year 5 on December 31. The company uses the straight-line method for amortizing assets.

(3) Computing and recording amortization after a change in useful life

S10–11 Red Pine Printers purchased equipment on January 1, 2016, for $250,000. The estimated residual value is $25,000, and the estimated useful life is 15 years. Red Pine Printers uses the straight-line method for amortization of its equipment. On January 1, 2019, Red Pine Printers revised the useful life to be 9 more years rather than 12. How much amortization would be recorded on December 31, 2019?

(3) Revised amortization

2019, $20,000

S10–12 A fully amortized asset has a cost of $100,000 and zero residual value.

1. What is the asset's accumulated amortization? What is its carrying value?
2. The asset cost $100,000. Now suppose its residual value is $10,000. How much is its accumulated amortization if it is fully amortized?

(3) Using fully amortized assets

S10–13 Alpha Communication purchased equipment on January 1, 2020, for $27,500. Suppose Alpha Communication sold the equipment for $20,000 on December 31, 2022. Accumulated amortization as of December 31, 2022, was $10,000. Journalize the cash sale of the equipment, assuming straight-line amortization was used.

(4) Recording a gain or loss on disposal

Gain on sale, $2,500

S10–14 Peter Company purchased equipment on January 1, 2019, for $28,000. Suppose Peter Company sold the equipment for $4,000 on December 31, 2020. Accumulated amortization as of December 31, 2020, was $11,000. Journalize the sale of the equipment, assuming straight-line amortization was used.

(4) Recording a gain or loss on disposal

Loss on sale, $13,000

S10–15 In 2018, Global Millwrights purchased a milling machine for $4,000, debiting Milling Equipment. During 2018 and 2019, Global recorded total amortization of $2,000 on the machine. In January 2020, Global traded in the machine for a new one with a fair market value of $4,200, paying $2,700 cash. This exchange transaction has commercial substance. Journalize Global Millwrights' exchange of machines on January 15.

(4) Exchanging property, plant, and equipment assets

Loss on exchange, $500

S10–16 Suppose Quik Trip Stores' comparative income statement for two years included these items (dollars in thousands):

(4) Understanding a gain/loss on the sale of PPE

	2020	2019
Net sales	$7,200	$6,800
Income from operations	49	65
Gain on sale of store facilities	28	—
Income before income taxes	$ 77	$ 65

Which was the better year for Quik Trip: 2020 or 2019? Explain.

S10–17 EnCana, the giant oil company, holds huge reserves of oil and gas assets. Assume that at the end of 2020 EnCana's cost of oil and gas assets totalled approximately $18 billion, representing 2.4 billion barrels of oil and gas reserves in the ground.

1. Which amortization method does EnCana use to compute its annual amortization expense for the oil and gas removed from the ground?
2. Suppose EnCana removed 0.8 billion barrels of oil during 2020. Record EnCana's amortization expense for 2020.

(5) Accounting for the amortization of natural resources

2. Amortization Expense, $6.0 billion

(6) Accounting for goodwill

1. Goodwill, $200,000

S10–18 Media-related companies have little in the way of property, plant, and equipment. Instead, their main asset is goodwill. When one media company buys another, goodwill is often the most costly asset acquired. Assume that Media Watch paid $800,000 on March 22 to acquire *The Thrifty Dime*, a weekly advertising paper. At the time of the acquisition, *The Thrifty Dime*'s balance sheet reported total assets of $1,300,000 and liabilities of $600,000. The fair market value of *The Thrifty Dime*'s assets was $1,200,000.

1. How much goodwill did Media Watch purchase as part of the acquisition of *The Thrifty Dime*?
2. Journalize Media Watch's acquisition of *The Thrifty Dime*.

(6) Accounting for a patent

$4,500

S10–19 Blue Consultants purchased a patent at a cost of $45,000 on June 30, 2019. It is estimated that the patent has a remaining useful life of five years in spite of the fact that it will expire in seven years from the date of purchase. Record the amortization for the December 31, 2019, year-end.

(6) Accounting for patents and for research and development cost

Net income, $700,000

S10–20 InnoTech Applications paid $1,300,000 in research costs for a new software program. InnoTech also paid $1,000,000 to acquire a patent on other software. After readying the software for production, InnoTech's sales revenue for the first year totalled $3,400,000. Cost of goods sold was $400,000, and selling expenses were $800,000. All of these transactions occurred during 2020. InnoTech expects the patent to have a useful life of five years. Prepare InnoTech Applications' single-step income statement for the year ended December 31, 2020, complete with a heading. Report expenses in order of highest to lowest amounts.

(7) Componentization

S10–21 Under IFRS, companies need to calculate amortization separately for the major components of an amortizable asset. Does this provide better information for the users of financial information? Why or why not?

(7) Internally generated assets under IFRS

S10–22 Suppose your publicly traded company has developed a process that will make the manufacture of a product more efficient and will streamline costs. The only costs associated with this internally generated patent are the legal costs of registering the patent. Your company immediately sells the patent to another publicly traded company for about 100 times the cost of the patent. How would your company value the patent before it is sold? How will the acquiring company record the acquisition of the patent?

EXERCISES

(1) Determining the cost of property, plant, and equipment

Land, $375,000

E10–1 The accounting firm of Chutter Danislav, CPAs, purchased land, paying $350,000 cash. In addition, the company paid property tax in arrears of $3,000, a legal fee of $1,500, and a $20,500 charge for levelling the land and removing an unwanted building. The company constructed an office building on the land at a cost of $1,200,000. It also paid $30,000 for a fence around the boundary of the property, $8,500 for the company sign near the entrance to the property, and $11,500 for special lighting of the grounds. During installation of the fence, $2,000 of damage to the fence was incurred. Determine the cost of the company's land, land improvements, and building.

(1) Allocating cost to assets acquired in a lump-sum purchase

Truck 1, $21,600

E10–2 Phillipines Trucking bought three used trucks for $60,000. An independent appraisal of the trucks produced the following figures:

Truck	Appraised Value
1	$24,000
2	23,000
3	20,000

Phillipines Trucking paid $21,000 in cash and signed a note for the remainder. Record the purchase in the general journal on February 1, identifying each truck's individual cost in a separate Truck account. Phillipines Trucking rounds percentage calculations to two decimal places and all costs to the nearest whole dollar as it feels greater precision is not material.

E10–3 Classify each of the following expenditures related to the cost of a machine:

① Measuring the cost of an asset, distinguishing betterments from repairs

	Cost or Betterment	Repair or Expense	Other
a. Purchase price			
b. Provincial sales tax paid on the purchase price			
c. Transportation and insurance while the machine is in transport from seller to buyer			
d. Installation			
e. Training of personnel for initial operation of the machine			
f. Special reinforcement to the machine platform			
g. Income tax paid on income earned from the sale of products manufactured by the machine			
h. Major overhaul to extend the machine's useful life by three years			
i. Ordinary recurring repairs to keep the machine in good working order			
j. Lubrication before the machine is placed in service			
k. Periodic lubrication after the machine is placed in service			
l. GST on the purchase price			

E10–4 Firestone Shoes is a family-owned retail shoe operation with two stores. Assume that early in Year 1 Firestone Shoes purchased computerized point-of-sale and operating systems costing $150,000. Bob Firestone expects this equipment will support the inventory and accounting requirements for four years. Because of technology obsolescence, no residual value is anticipated. Through error, Firestone Shoes accidentally expensed the entire cost of the equipment at the time of the purchase. Firestone Shoes' accounting policy for equipment amortization is the straight-line amortization method. The company is operated as a sole proprietorship, so it pays no corporate income tax.

① Capitalizing versus expensing, measuring the effect of an error

Required

Compute the overstatement or understatement in these accounts immediately after purchasing the equipment:

1. Equipment
2. Net income

E10–5 Crispy Fried Chicken bought equipment on January 2, 2018, for $33,000. The equipment was expected to remain in service for four years. At the end of the equipment's useful life, Crispy estimates that its residual value will be $6,000.

② Straight-line method

Year 3 expense, $6,750

Prepare a schedule of *amortization expense*, *accumulated amortization*, and *book value* per year for the equipment under the straight-line method. Show your computations.

E10–6 My Porto Chicken bought equipment on January 2, 2018, for $33,000. The equipment was expected to remain in service for four years and to operate for 6,750 hours. At the end of the equipment's useful life, My Porto estimates that its residual value will be $6,000. The equipment operated for 675 hours the first year, 2,025 hours the second year, 2,700 hours the third year, and 1,350 hours the fourth year.

② UOP method

Year 3 expense, $10,800

Prepare a schedule of *amortization expense*, *accumulated amortization*, and *book value* per year for the equipment under the units-of-production method. Show your computations.

E10–7 Gigi's Baked Chicken bought equipment on January 2, 2018, for $33,000. The equipment was expected to remain in service for four years. At the end of the equipment's useful life, Gigi's estimates that its residual value will be $6,000.

② DDB method

Year 3 expense, $2,250

Prepare a schedule of *amortization expense*, *accumulated amortization*, and *book value* per year for the equipment under the double-declining-balance method. Show your computations.

(2) Calculate amortization three ways

UOP Year 1 expense, $24,000

E10–8 On January 1, 2020, Murray Demolition, a Hamilton, Ontario, company specializing in blasting and removing buildings, purchased and took delivery of a new dump truck to add to its growing fleet. Murray Demolition has a high-class reputation and uses only the best and newest equipment on their worksites. The business spent $140,000 plus HST on the truck, which is expected to be useful to the business for four years, at which time it should be able to be sold for $60,000. Murray Demolition has always used the straight-line basis of calculating amortization. The new owners want to see the amortization schedules for the straight-line, UOP, and DDB methods just to be sure this makes sense. The business expects the truck to be useful for 200,000 kilometres—60,000 kilometres in Year 1, 50,000 kilometres in each of Years 2 and 3, and 40,000 kilometres in Year 4. Is there a problem with continuing to use the straight-line method?

(2) Determining amortization amounts by three methods

1. Amortization expense in 2020: Straight-line, $150,000; UOP, $157,500; DDB, $306,667

E10–9 Zhang Machine and Dye bought a machine on January 2, 2020, for $460,000. The machine was expected to remain in service for three years and produce 2,000,000 parts. At the end of its useful life, company officials estimated that, due to technological changes, the machine's residual value would only be $10,000. The machine produced 700,000 parts in the first year, 660,000 in the second year, and 650,000 in the third year.

Required

1. Prepare a schedule of *amortization expense* per year for the machine using the straight-line, UOP, and DDB amortization methods. Assume that in all cases the machine is valued at $10,000 at the end of the third year, and the third-year amortization is adjusted (set as a plug) to ensure this happens.
2. Which amortization method results in the highest net income in the second year? Does this higher net income mean the machine was used more efficiently under this method?
3. Which method tracks the wear and tear on the machine most closely? Why?
4. After one year under the DDB method, the company switched to the straight-line method. Prepare a schedule of amortization expense for this situation, showing all calculations.

(3) CCA versus straight-line amortization

E10–10 In 2019, Maxwell Inc. paid $625,000 for equipment that is expected to have a five-year life. In this industry, the residual value is estimated to be 5 percent of the asset's cost. Maxwell Inc. plans to use straight-line amortization for accounting purposes. For income tax purposes, Maxwell chooses to use the maximum CCA rate of 20 percent. The office equipment is in class 8 and considered eligible for the accelerated investment incentive.

Required

1. Calculate the amortization expense in 2019 and 2020 for accounting and tax purposes.
2. Why does the federal government regulate the amount of amortization a company can deduct when calculating income for income tax purposes?

(3) Changing the useful life of property, plant, and equipment

Amortization for Year 21, $25,000

E10–11 Jacoby Legal Services purchased land and a building for $1,100,000. The land had a fair value of $300,000 and the building $800,000. The building was amortized on a straight-line basis over a 50-year period. The estimated residual value was $50,000. After using the building for 20 years, the company realized that wear and tear on the building would force the company to replace it before 50 years. Starting with the 21st year, the company began amortizing the building over a revised *total* life of 40 years with zero residual value. Record amortization expense on the building for Years 20 and 21.

(2) (4) Analyzing the effect of a sale of property, plant, and equipment; DDB amortization

Loss on sale, $25,050

E10–12 On January 13, 2019, Bill's Birdfeeders purchased store fixtures for $65,000 cash, expecting the fixtures to remain in service for 10 years. Bill's Birdfeeders has amortized the fixtures on a DDB basis with an estimated residual value of $5,000. On September 30, 2020, Bill's Birdfeeders sold the fixtures for $19,150 cash because they were not environmentally friendly. Record the amortization expense on the fixtures for the years ended December 31, 2019, and 2020, and the sale of the fixtures on September 30, 2020. Round all final amounts to the nearest dollar.

E10–13 Prepare journal entries for the following transactions. Explanations are not required.

(2) (4) Purchase and sale of assets

Loss on sale, $2,600

2019

Jan. 1	Purchased a bulldozer for $64,000 cash, $4,000 residual value, 20-year expected life, double-declining-balance amortization.
May 1	Purchased office furniture for $15,000 cash, $3,000 residual value, 10-year expected life, straight-line amortization.
Dec. 31	Recorded amortization on the bulldozer and furniture.

2020

June 30	Sold the furniture for $11,000 cash. (Record amortization to date for 2020 before selling the furniture.)
Dec. 31	Recorded amortization on the bulldozer.

E10–14 Triad Freight is a large warehousing and distribution company that operates throughout Eastern Canada. Triad Freight uses the UOP method to amortize its trucks because its managers believe UOP amortization best measures the wear and tear on the trucks. Triad Freight trades in used trucks often to keep driver morale high and to maximize fuel efficiency. Consider these facts about one Mack truck in the company's fleet:

(1) (2) (4) Measuring the cost of property, plant, and equipment using UOP amortization; trading in a used asset

Gain on exchange of trucks, $123,000

When acquired in 2016, the tractor/trailer rig cost $585,000 and was expected to remain in service for eight years, or 1,500,000 kilometres. Estimated residual value was $60,000. The truck was driven 150,000 kilometres in 2014, 195,000 kilometres in 2018, and 235,000 kilometres in 2019. After 100,000 kilometres in 2020, the company traded in the Mack truck for a Freightliner rig with a fair market value of $510,000 on August 15. Triad Freight paid cash of $40,000. This trade-in will bring in significantly more income to Triad Freight by reducing operating costs. Determine Triad Freight's cost of the new truck. Prepare the journal entry to record the trade-in.

E10–15 Beau Lac Mining Ltd. paid $900,000 for the right to extract ore from a 300,000-tonne mineral deposit. In addition to the purchase price, the company also paid a $1,000 filing fee, a $5,000 licence fee to the province of Quebec, and $75,000 for a geological survey. Because Beau Lac Mining Ltd. purchased the rights to the minerals only, the company expected the asset to have zero residual value when fully depleted. During the first year of production, the company removed 65,000 tonnes of ore. Make general journal entries to record (a) purchase of the mineral rights (debit Mineral Asset) on January 1, 2020, (b) payment of fees and other costs on January 1, 2020, and (c) amortization for first-year production as at December 31, 2020.

(5) Recording natural resources and amortization

c. Amortization Expense, $212,550

E10–16 Biikman Company manufactures flat-screen monitors for the graphics industry. It purchased a patent for the design of a new monitor for $525,000. Although it gives legal protection for 20 years, the patent is expected to provide Biikman Company with a competitive advantage for only 10 years.

(3) (6) Recording intangibles, amortization, and a change in the asset's useful life

3. Amortization for final year, $420,000

After using the patent for two years, Biikman Company learns at an industry trade show that another company is designing an even higher quality monitor. Based on this new information, Biikman Company decides to amortize the remaining cost of the patent over the year, giving the patent a total useful life of three years.

Required

1. Prepare the journal entry to record the purchase of the patent on January 1, 2020.
2. Assume straight-line amortization is used. Record the journal entry for amortization at December 31, 2020.
3. Record amortization for the year ended December 31, 2022.

E10–17 Genji Toys acquired companies with assets with a market value of $55 million and liabilities of $30 million. Genji paid $27 million for these acquisitions during the year ended December 31, 2020.

(6) Measuring goodwill

2. Goodwill, $2 million

Required

1. How would a value be assigned to the net assets acquired?
2. What value would be assigned to goodwill?
3. Will the goodwill be amortized? If so, by how much?

(6)
Accounting for goodwill
1. Goodwill, $22,900

E10-18 The financial statements of Mei's Foods for the year ended December 31, 2019, reported the following details of acquisitions (adapted):

	In Thousands
Assets	
Cash	$3,400
Accounts receivable	8,400
Equipment	72,000
Intangibles	700
	$84,500
Liabilities	
Long-term debt	$16,400

Mei's Foods paid $91,000 cash for the acquisitions. Assume that the book value of the assets is equal to their fair value.

Required

1. How much goodwill did Mei's Foods purchase as part of the 2019 acquisitions?
2. Prepare the summary journal entry to record the acquisition at December 31, 2019.
3. Assume that, in 2020, the annual review of goodwill at December 31 identified a 15 percent impairment of the goodwill acquired in 2019. Prepare the journal entry required to record this impairment.

(6)
Computing and recording goodwill
1. Goodwill, $1,100,000

E10-19 In 2020, Camden Electronics purchased Winston Electronics, paying $2.4 million in a note payable. The market value of Winston Electronics' assets was $3.1 million, and Winston Electronics had liabilities of $1.8 million.

Required

1. Compute the cost of the goodwill purchased by Camden Electronics.
2. Record the purchase by Camden Electronics.
3. At 2020 year-end, the annual review of goodwill value indicated no impairment of goodwill. Record the entry Camden will make for goodwill at December 31, 2020.
4. At 2021 year-end, the annual review of goodwill value indicated a 40 percent impairment of the Winston Electronics goodwill. Record the entry for the goodwill impairment at December 31, 2021.

(7)
IFRS depreciation calculation

E10-20 Under IFRS, components of an asset may have different depreciation methods. Prime Printers Ltd. shows the following information about its special printing unit for banners on a spreadsheet that tracks its assets:

	A	B	C	D	E	F
1		**Banner Printer**				
2	**Component**	**Purchase Date**	**Cost**	**Estimated Residual**	**Depreciation Method**	**Estimated Life**
3	Monitor	Jan. 1, 2020	$ 1,800	$ 0	Straight-line	4 years
4	Base Unit	Jan. 1, 2020	75,000	5,000	UOP	200,000 copies
5	CPU	Jan. 1, 2020	4,700	200	Straight-line	3 years
6	Printer trays	Jan. 1, 2020	15,000	2,000	Straight-line	10 years
7			96,500			

Required

Compute depreciation for the banner printer for the year ended December 31, 2020. Assume that 17,000 copies were made during the year.

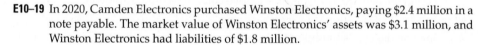

E10–21 Note 1 of the notes to the financial statements (page 75) of the Loblaw 2016 Annual Report reads as follows:

7 IFRS terms and concepts

> For the purpose of impairment testing, assets are grouped together into the smallest group of assets that generate cash inflows from continuing use that are largely independent of cash inflows of other assets or groups of assets. This grouping is referred to as a cash generating unit ("CGU"). The Company has determined that each location is a separate CGU for purposes of impairment testing.

Required

1. What is the "cash generating unit" for Loblaw?
2. What is *impairment testing*?

SERIAL EXERCISE

E10–22 *The Serial Exercise involves a company that will be revisited throughout relevant chapters in Volume 1 and Volume 2. You can complete the Serial Exercises using MyLab Accounting.*

2 3 Calculating and journalizing partial-year amortization

Total book value of PPE on
2. December 31, 2020, $131,150

This problem continues the Canyon Canoe Company situation from Chapter 9. This exercise continues recordkeeping for the Canyon Canoe Company. Students do not have to complete prior exercises in order to answer this exercise.

Amber Wilson is continuing to review business practices. Currently, she is reviewing the company's property, plant, and equipment and has gathered the following information:

	A	B	C	D	E	F	G
1	Asset	Acquisition Date	Cost	Estimated Life	Estimated Residual Value	Amortization Method*	Monthly Amortization Expense
2	Canoes	Nov. 3, 2020	$ 4,800	4 years	$ 0	SL	$ 100
3	Land	Dec. 1, 2020	85,000			n/a	
4	Building	Dec. 1, 2020	35,000	5 years	5,000	SL	500
5	Canoes	Dec. 2, 2020	7,200	4 years	0	SL	150
6	Computer	Mar. 2, 2020	3,600	3 years	300	DDB	
7	Office Furniture	Mar. 3, 2020	3,000	5 years	600	SL	

*SL = Straight-line; DDB = Double-declining-balance

Required

1. Calculate the amount of monthly amortization expense for the computer and office furniture for 2021.
2. For each asset, determine the book value as of December 31, 2020. Then, calculate the amortization expense for the first six months of 2021 and the book value as of June 30, 2021.
3. Prepare a partial balance sheet showing Property, Plant, and Equipment as of June 30, 2021.

CHALLENGE EXERCISES

E10–23 Great Lake Furniture Limited's 2020 financial statements reported these amounts (in thousands of dollars):

2 4 Reconstructing transactions from the financial statements

1. $118,000

	December 31			
	2020		2019	
	Cost	Accumulated Amortization	Cost	Accumulated Amortization
Land	$ 41,378	—	$ 35,073	—
Buildings	116,832	$ 51,566	105,325	$ 46,981
Equipment	17,940	11,712	16,575	10,678
Vehicles	13,994	11,533	13,513	10,680
Computer hardware and software	6,869	4,335	5,885	3,614
Leasehold improvements	26,178	7,461	21,081	6,220
	$223,191	$ 86,607	$197,452	$ 78,173
Net book value		$136,584		$119,279

In the 2020 annual report, Great Lake Furniture Limited reported amortization expense of $8,552,000. In addition, the company reported it had disposed of certain property, plant, and equipment assets and acquired others. The gain on disposal of property, plant, and equipment was $56,000.

Required

1. What was the accumulated amortization of the assets disposed of during 2020?
2. Assume that Great Lake Furniture Limited acquired assets costing $27,681,000 during 2020. What was the cost price of the assets sold during the year?
3. Write the journal entry to record the disposal of the property, plant, and equipment at the end of the year.

BEYOND THE NUMBERS

BN10–1

The following questions are unrelated except that they apply to property, plant, and equipment:

1. Julian Lyon, the owner of Lyon's Actuarial Services, regularly debits the cost of repairs and maintenance of amortizable assets to Property, Plant, and Equipment. Why would he do that, since he knows he is violating ASPE?
2. It has been suggested that, since many intangible assets have no value except to the company that owns them, they should be valued at $1 or zero on the balance sheet. Many accountants disagree with this view. Which view do you support? Why?
3. Jasmine Singh, the owner of Lakeshore Motors, regularly buys property, plant, and equipment and debits the cost to Repairs and Maintenance Expense. Why would she do that, since she knows this action violates ASPE?

ETHICAL ISSUE

EI10–1

Canam Group Developers purchased land and a building for a lump sum of $8 million. To get the maximum tax deduction, Canam's owner allocated 85 percent of the purchase price to the building and only 15 percent to the land. A more realistic allocation would have been 75 percent to the building and 25 percent to the land.

Required

1. Explain the tax advantage of allocating too much to the building and too little to the land.
2. Was Canam Group Developers' allocation ethical? If so, state why. If not, why not? Identify who was harmed.

PROBLEMS (GROUP A)

(2) Explaining the concept of amortization

P10–1A The board of directors of Downtown Shared Offices is having its regular quarterly meeting. Accounting policies are on the agenda, and amortization is being discussed. Anita Ma, a new board member, has some strong opinions about two aspects of amortization policy. She argues that amortization must be coupled with a fund to replace company assets. Otherwise, she argues, there is no substance to amortization. Ma also challenges the five-year estimated life over which Downtown Shared Offices is amortizing the company's computers. She notes that the computers will last much longer and should be amortized over at least 10 years.

Required Write a paragraph or two to explain the concept of amortization to Ma and to answer her arguments.

(2) Computing amortization by three methods

1. Book value, Dec. 31, 2022: Straight-line $88,675; UOP $85,696; DDB $42,000

P10–2A On January 5, 2020, Paige Construction purchased a used crane at a total cost of $200,000. Before placing the crane in service, Paige spent $12,500 transporting it, $4,800 replacing parts, and $11,400 overhauling the engine. Karen Paige, the owner, estimates that the crane will remain in service for four years and have a residual value of $42,000. The crane's annual usage is expected to be 2,400 hours in each of the first three years and 2,200 hours in the fourth year. In trying to decide which amortization method to use, Mary Blundon, the accountant, requests an amortization schedule for each of the following generally accepted amortization methods: straight-line, UOP, and DDB.

Required

1. Assuming Paige Construction amortizes this crane individually, prepare an amortization schedule for each of the three amortization methods listed, showing asset cost, amortization expense, accumulated amortization, and asset book value. Assume a December 31 year-end. Round amortization per hour to four decimal places and the final answer to the nearest dollar.
2. Paige Construction prepares financial statements for its bankers using the amortization method that maximizes reported income in the early years of asset use. Identify the amortization method that meets the company's objective.

P10–3A Digital Warehousing incurred the following costs in acquiring land and a building, making land improvements, and constructing and furnishing an office building for its own use:

(1) (2) (3)
Identifying the elements of property, plant, and equipment's cost; partial-year amortization

2. Amortization Expense:
Land Improvements, $5,333
Office Building, $28,771

a.	Purchase price of two hectares of land, including an old building that will be used for storage of maintenance equipment (land appraised market value is $1,300,000; building appraised market value is $300,000)	$1,150,000
b.	Real estate taxes in arrears on the land to be paid by Digital Warehousing	6,000
c.	Additional dirt and earth moving	6,000
d.	Legal fees on the land acquisition	4,500
e.	Fence around the boundary of the land	70,000
f.	Building permit for the office building	1,000
g.	Architect fee for the design of the office building	40,000
h.	Company signs near front and rear approaches to the company property	14,000
i.	Renovation of the storage building	150,000
j.	Concrete, wood, steel girders, and other materials used in the construction of the office building	700,000
k.	Masonry, carpentry, roofing, and other labour to construct the office building	550,000
l.	Parking lots and concrete walks on the property	31,500
m.	Lights for the parking lot, walkways, and company signs	12,500
n.	Salary of construction supervisor (90 percent to office building and 10 percent to storage building)	100,000
o.	Office furniture for the office building	125,000
p.	Transportation of furniture from seller to the office building	2,000

Digital Warehousing amortizes buildings over 40 years, land improvements over 20 years, and furniture over 6 years, all on a straight-line basis with zero residual value.

Required

1. Set up columns (or T-accounts) for Land, Land Improvements, Office Building, Storage Building, and Furniture. Show how to account for each of Digital's costs by listing the cost under the correct account. Determine the total cost of each asset.
2. Assuming that all construction was complete and the assets were placed in service on February 25, record amortization for the year ended December 31. Round figures to the nearest dollar.

①②③④ Recording property, plant, and equipment transactions; exchanges; changes in useful life

Dec. 31, 2020, Amortization Expense—Buildings, $700,000

P10–4A Accurate Research surveys Canadian opinions about environmental issues. The company's balance sheet reports the following assets under Property, Plant, and Equipment: Land, Buildings, Office Furniture, Communication Equipment, and Computers. The company has a separate Accumulated Amortization account for each of these assets except land. Assume that the company completed the following transactions during 2020:

Feb.	2	Traded in communication equipment with a book value of $26,000 (cost of $202,000) for similar new equipment with a fair market value of $196,000. The seller gave Accurate a trade-in allowance of $36,000 on the old equipment, and the company paid the remainder in cash. This transaction meets the criteria for commercial substance.
Jul.	19	Sold a building that had cost $1,050,000 and had accumulated amortization of $740,000 through December 31, 2019. Amortization is computed on a straight-line basis. The building has a 30-year useful life and a residual value of $90,000. Accurate received $150,000 cash and a $1,300,000 note receivable.
Oct.	21	Purchased used communication equipment and some computers from the A. C. Neilsen Company of Canada Ltd. Total cost was $200,000 paid in cash. An independent appraisal valued the communication equipment at $170,000 and the computers at $80,000.
Dec.	31	Equipment is amortized by the DDB method over a six-year life. Amortization on the equipment purchased on February 2 and on October 21 is recorded separately. Amortization on buildings is computed by the straight-line method. The company had assigned buildings an estimated useful life of 30 years and a residual value that is 30 percent of cost. After using the buildings for 10 years, the company has come to believe that their total useful life will be 20 years. Residual value remains unchanged. The buildings cost $15,000,000. Amortization for the year must be recorded.

Required Record the transactions in the journal of Accurate Research. Round all transactions to the nearest dollar.

①②③④ Journalizing property, plant, and equipment transactions; asset exchanges; betterments versus repairs

Dec. 31, 2020, Amortization Expense, $3,600

P10–5A Assume that Rees Warehousing completed the following transactions:

2019		
Mar.	3	Paid $8,000 cash for a used forklift.
	5	Paid $1,500 to have the forklift engine overhauled.
	7	Paid $1,000 to have the forklift modified for specialized moving of large flat-screen televisions.
Nov.	3	Paid $550 for an oil change and regular maintenance.
Dec.	31	Used the DDB method to record amortization on the forklift. (Assume a three-year life and no residual value.)
2020		
Feb.	13	Replaced the forklift's broken fork for $400 cash, the deductible on Rees Warehousing's insurance. The new fork will not increase the useful life of the forklift.
Jul.	10	Traded in the forklift for a new forklift costing $18,000. The dealer granted a $3,000 allowance on the old forklift, and Rees Warehousing paid the balance in cash. Recorded 2020 amortization for the year to date and then recorded the exchange of forklifts. This transaction has commercial substance.
Dec.	31	Used the DDB method to record amortization on the new forklift. (Assume a five-year life and no residual value.)

Rees Warehousing's amortization policy indicates that the company will take a full month's amortization on purchases occurring up to and on the 15th day of the month and will not take any amortization for the month if the transaction occurs after the 15th day of the month.

Required Record the transactions in the general journal, indicating whether each transaction amount should be capitalized as an asset or expensed. Round all calculations to the nearest dollar.

P10–6A Pride Parts Co. has a fiscal year ending December 31. The company completed the following selected transactions:

(1) (1) (3) (4)
Identifying the elements of property, plant, and equipment's cost; accounting for amortization by two methods; accounting for disposal of property, plant, and equipment; distinguishing betterments from repairs

2. Total Property, Plant, and Equipment, $590,727

2019

July 2 Paid $640,000 plus $20,000 in legal fees (pertaining to all assets purchased) to purchase the following assets from a competitor that was going out of business:

	A	B	C	D
1	Asset	Appraised Value	Estimated Useful Life	Estimated Residual Value
2	Land	$360,000	—	—
3	Buildings	240,000	8 years	$20,000
4	Equipment	120,000	3 years	2,000

Pride Parts Co. plans to use the straight-line amortization method for the building and for the equipment.

Sep. 2 Purchased a delivery truck with a list price of $39,000 for $36,000 cash. The truck is expected to be used for three years and driven a total of 280,000 kilometres; it is then expected to be sold for $4,000. It will be amortized using the UOP method.

3 Paid $3,000 to paint the truck with the company's colours and logo.

Dec. 31 Recorded amortization on the assets. The truck had been driven 20,000 kilometres since it was purchased.

2020

May 4 Pride Parts Co. paid $11,000 to Drag Services Ltd. for work done on the equipment. The job consisted of annual maintenance ($1,200) and the addition of automatic controls ($9,800) that allow the equipment to remain useful for the next five years and increase its expected residual value by $1,000.

Nov. 25 Sold the truck for $23,600. The truck had an odometer reading of 140,000 kilometres.

Dec. 31 Recorded amortization on the assets.

Required

1. Record the above transactions of Pride Parts Co. Round all amounts to the nearest dollar.
2. Show the balance sheet presentation of the assets at December 31, 2020.

P10–7A Oilco Canada Limited sells refined petroleum products. The company's balance sheet includes reserves of oil assets.

(5)
Accounting for natural resources

Amortization Expense, $994,975

Suppose that Oilco paid $15 million cash for an oil lease that contained an estimated reserve of 1,990,000 barrels of oil on January 1. Assume that on the same date the company also paid $550,000 for additional geological tests of the property and $170,000 to prepare the surface for drilling. The company signed a $120,000 note payable to have a portable building moved onto the property. Because the building provides onsite headquarters for the drilling effort and will be abandoned when the oil is depleted, its cost is debited to the Oil Properties account and included in amortization charges. During the first year of production, which ended on December 31, Oilco removed 125,000 barrels of oil, which it sold on credit for $75 per barrel.

Required

1. Make general journal entries to record all transactions related to the oil and gas property, including amortization and sale of the first-year production.
2. Show the accounts and amounts that would be presented on the balance sheet.

(6) Accounting for intangibles and goodwill

P10–8A *Part 1* WhiteWater West Industries is a waterpark construction company located in British Columbia. Assume that WhiteWater purchased another company that had the following totals on its financial statements:

Book value of assets	$1,536,000
Market value of assets	1,800,000
Liabilities	540,000

Required

1. Make the general journal entry to record WhiteWater's purchase of the other company for $1,620,000 cash on April 3.
2. How should WhiteWater account for goodwill at year-end and in the future? Explain in detail.

Part 2 Suppose BlackBerry Ltd. purchased a patent for $1,400,000 on January 1. Before using the patent, BlackBerry incurred an additional cost of $250,000 for a lawsuit to defend the company's right to purchase it. Even though the patent gives BlackBerry legal protection for 20 years, company management has decided to amortize its cost over an 8-year period because of the industry's fast-changing technologies.

Required

1. Make general journal entries to record the patent transactions, including straight-line amortization for one year at December 31.
2. Show the accounts and amounts that would be presented on the balance sheet.

PROBLEMS (GROUP B)

(2) Explaining the concept of amortization

P10–1B The board of directors of Chipman Developments is reviewing the 2020 annual report. A new board member, a dermatologist with little business experience, questions the company accountant about the amortization amounts. The dermatologist wonders why amortization expense has decreased from $250,000 in 2018, to $230,000 in 2019, to $215,000 in 2020. He states that he could understand the decreasing annual amounts if the company had been disposing of properties each year, but that has not occurred. Further, he notes that growth in the city is increasing the values of company properties. Why is the company recording amortization when the property values are increasing?

Required Write a short response to explain the concept of amortization to the dermatologist and to answer his questions.

(2) Computing amortization by three methods

P10–2B On January 5, 2020, Overwatch Corp. paid $438,000 for equipment used in manufacturing computer equipment. In addition to the basic purchase price, the business paid $2,200 transportation charges, $600 insurance for the goods in transit, $35,200 provincial sales tax, and $20,000 for a special platform on which to place the equipment in the plant and move the payload. Overwatch Corp.'s owner estimates that the equipment will remain in service for four years and have a residual value of $10,000. The equipment will produce 85,000 units in the first year, with annual production decreasing by 10,000 units during each of the next three years (that is, 75,000 units in Year 2, 65,000 units in Year 3, and so on). In trying to decide which amortization method to use, owner Sven Overwatch has requested an amortization schedule for each of three generally accepted amortization methods: straight-line, UOP, and DDB.

Required

1. For each of the amortization methods listed above, prepare an amortization schedule showing asset cost, amortization expense, accumulated amortization, and asset book value. Assume a December 31 year-end.
2. Overwatch Corp. prepares financial statements for its creditors using the amortization method that maximizes reported income in the early years of asset use. Identify the amortization method that meets the business's objective.

P10–3B The owner of Cheetle Moving and Storage incurred the following costs in acquiring land, making land improvements, and constructing and furnishing the company's office building in the year ended December 31, 2020:

① ② ③
Identifying the elements of property, plant, and equipment's cost

a.	Purchase price of four hectares of land, including an old building that will be used for a garage (land appraised market value is $450,000; building appraised market value is $50,000)	$400,000
b.	Additional dirt and earth moving	8,000
c.	Fence around the boundary of the land	25,000
d.	Legal fee for title search on the land	2,000
e.	Real estate taxes in arrears on the land to be paid by Cheetle Moving and Storage	4,800
f.	Company signs at front of the company property	4,000
g.	Building permit for the office building	2,000
h.	Architect fee for the design of the office building	75,000
i.	Masonry, carpentry, roofing, and other labour to construct office building	850,000
j.	Concrete, wood, steel girders, and other materials used in the construction of the office building	650,000
k.	Renovation of the garage	30,000
l.	Flowers and plants	15,000
m.	Parking lot and concrete walks on the property	48,500
n.	Lights for the parking lot, walkways, and company signs	14,500
o.	Salary of construction supervisor (95 percent to office building and 5 percent to garage renovation)	100,000
p.	Office furniture for the office building	160,000
q.	Transportation and installation of office furniture	2,500

Cheetle Moving and Storage amortizes buildings over 35 years, land improvements over 15 years, and furniture over 5 years, all on a straight-line basis with zero residual value.

Required

1. Set up columns for Land, Land Improvements, Office Building, Garage Building, and Furniture. Show how to account for each of Cheetle Moving and Storage's costs by listing the cost under the correct account. Determine the total cost of each asset.
2. Assuming that all construction was complete and the assets were placed in service on June 30, record amortization for the year ending December 31, 2020. Round final amounts to the nearest dollar.

P10–4B Belkin Freight provides general freight service in Canada. The business's balance sheet includes the following assets under Property, Plant, and Equipment: Land, Buildings, and Trucks. Belkin Freight has a separate accumulated amortization account for each of these assets except land.

① ② ③ ④
Recording property, plant, and equipment transactions; exchanges; changes in useful life

Assume that Belkin Freight completed the following transactions during 2020:

Feb. 6	Traded in the old moving truck with a book value of $86,000 (cost of $280,000) for a similar new truck with a fair market value of $330,000. Belkin Freight received a trade-in allowance of $120,000 on the old truck and paid the remainder in cash. This transaction met the criteria for commercial substance.
Jun. 3	Sold a building that had cost $1,250,000 and had accumulated amortization of $577,500 through December 31, 2019. Amortization is computed on a straight-line basis. The building has a 40-year useful life and a residual value of $150,000. Belkin Freight received $300,000 cash and a $1,000,000 note receivable.
Sep. 25	Purchased land and a building for cash for a single price of $790,000. An independent appraisal valued the land at $250,000 and the building at $375,000.

Dec. 31 The truck has an expected useful life of four years and an estimated residual value of 6 percent of its cost. Amortization is computed using the DDB method.

Amortization on buildings is computed by the straight-line method. The company had assigned to its older buildings, which cost $3,900,000, an estimated useful life of 30 years with a residual value equal to 30 percent of the asset cost. However, the owner of Belkin Freight has come to believe that the buildings will remain useful for a total of 35 years. Residual value remains unchanged. The company has used all its buildings, except for the one purchased on September 25, for 10 years. The new building carries a 35-year useful life and a residual value equal to 30 percent of its cost.

Make separate entries for amortization on the building acquired on September 25 and the other buildings purchased in earlier years.

Required Record the transactions in Belkin Freight's general journal.

① ② ③ ④
Journalizing property, plant, and equipment transactions; betterments versus repairs

P10–5B Assume that On Call Limousines completed the following transactions:

2019

Jan.	5	Paid $40,000 cash for a used limousine. Set up an asset account called Limousines.
	6	Paid $4,000 to have the engine overhauled.
	9	Paid $1,500 to repair damage to the limousine as it sat in the parking lot.
Jun.	15	Paid $600 for a minor tune-up after the limousine was put into use.
Dec.	31	Recorded amortization on the limousine by the DDB method. (Assume a five-year life.)

2020

Mar.	9	Traded in the used limousine for a new limousine costing $75,000. The dealer granted a $25,000 allowance on the old limousine, and the company paid the balance in cash. First record the amortization for the current year to date and then record the exchange of the limousines. This transaction has commercial substance.
Aug.	9	Repaired the new limousine's damaged fender for $2,500 cash.
Dec.	31	Recorded amortization on the new limousine by the DDB method. (Assume an eight-year life and a residual value of $20,000.)

On Call Limousines' amortization policy states that the company will take a full month's amortization on purchases occurring up to and on the 15th day of the month and will not take any amortization for the month if the purchase occurs after the 15th day of the month.

Required Record the transactions in the general journal, indicating whether each transaction amount should be capitalized as an asset or expensed. Round all calculations to the nearest dollar.

① ② ③ ④
Identifying the elements of property, plant, and equipment's cost; accounting for amortization by two methods; accounting for disposal of property, plant, and equipment; distinguishing betterments from repairs

P10–6B Megatron Inc. owns a small television station in the interior of British Columbia. Its year-end is June 30. The company completed the following transactions:

2020

Apr. 1 Paid $2,175,000 plus $75,000 in legal fees (pertaining to all assets purchased) to purchase the following assets from a competitor that was going out of business:

	A	B	C	D
1	**Asset**	**Appraised Value**	**Estimated Useful Life**	**Estimated Residual Value**
2	Land	$600,000	—	—
3	Buildings	960,000	30 years	$120,000
4	Equipment	840,000	5 years	80,000

		Megatron Inc. plans to use the straight-line amortization method for both the building and equipment.
May	1	Purchased a mobile broadcast unit truck with a list price of $295,000 for $245,000 cash. It is expected that the mobile truck will be used for seven years and driven a total of 200,000 kilometres; it is then expected to be sold for $55,000. It will be amortized using the UOP method.
	3	Paid $10,000 to paint the truck with the station's colours and logo.
Jun.	30	Recorded amortization on the assets. The truck had been driven 12,500 kilometres since it was purchased.
Dec.	30	Megatron Inc. paid $25,500 to Maxwell Maintenance for work done on the equipment. The job consisted of annual maintenance ($1,500) and the addition of automatic controls ($24,000) that allow the equipment to remain useful for the next six years and increase its expected residual value by $10,000.
2021		
Jun.	1	Sold the mobile unit truck for $200,000. The truck had an odometer reading of 82,000 kilometres.
	30	Recorded amortization on the assets.

Required

1. Record the above transactions of Megatron Inc. Round all amounts to the nearest dollar.
2. Show the balance sheet presentation of the assets at June 30, 2021.

P10–7B Kitkan Inc. is a global producer and marketer of rolled aluminum products.

(5) Accounting for natural resources

Suppose Kitkan Inc. paid $4.4 million cash on July 1, 2019, for a lease giving the firm the right to work a mine that contained an estimated 400,000 tonnes of bauxite. Assume that the company also paid $30,000 to remove unwanted buildings from the land and $130,000 to prepare the surface for mining. Further assume that Kitkan Inc. signed a $140,000 note payable to a landscaping company to return the land surface to its original condition after the lease ends. During the first year, Kitkan Inc. removed 37,000 tonnes of bauxite, which it sold on account for $40 per tonne.

Required

1. Make general journal entries to record all transactions related to the bauxite, including amortization and sale of the first year's production on June 30, 2020.
2. Show the accounts and amounts that would be presented on the balance sheet.

P10–8B *Part 1* Diesel Roasters operates franchised coffee shops. Assume that Diesel Roasters purchased another company that carried these figures:

(6) Accounting for goodwill and intangibles

Book value of assets	$3.6 million
Market value of assets	4.4 million
Liabilities	2.2 million

Required

1. Make the general journal entry to record Diesel Roasters' purchase of the other company for $2.5 million cash on March 31.
2. How should Diesel Roasters account for goodwill at year-end and in the future? Explain in detail.

Part 2 Suppose Susan McMillan purchased a Diesel Roasters franchise licence for $150,000 on January 1. In addition to the basic purchase price, McMillan also paid a lawyer $6,000 for assistance with the negotiations. McMillan believes the appropriate amortization period for the cost of the franchise licence is 10 years.

Required

1. Make general journal entries to record the franchise transactions, including straight-line amortization for one year at December 31.
2. Show the accounts and amounts that would be presented on the balance sheet.

CHALLENGE PROBLEMS

① ②
Understanding amortization and betterments and repairs

P10–1C The owner of newly formed Lake of the Woods Air Taxi, a friend of your family, knows you are taking an accounting course and asks for some advice. Mr. Linden tells you that he is pretty good at running the company but doesn't understand accounting. Specifically, he has two concerns:

1. The company has just paid $400,000 for two used float planes. His accountants tell him that he should use accelerated amortization for his financial statements, but he understands that straight-line amortization will result in lower charges to expense in the early years. He wants to use straight-line amortization.
2. A friend told him that Lake of the Woods Air Taxi should capitalize all repairs to the planes and "spread the cost out over the life of the planes." He wonders if there is anything wrong with this advice.

Required Respond to Mr. Linden's questions using your understanding of amortization and betterments and repairs.

③
Solve for missing information

P10–2C Due to a computer crash, some accounting data were corrupted at Ace Industries. For the Furniture account, only some of the data were still accessible. The balance in the Accumulated Amortization—Furniture account was $75,000. The furniture had been amortized a total of 60 percent of its original cost. Prior notes indicate that the double-declining-balance method was used for all furniture. The estimated useful life was eight years, and its residual value is expected to be 20 percent of its original cost.

Required Determine the age of the furniture to the nearest month.

Extending Your Knowledge

DECISION PROBLEMS

②
Measuring profitability based on different inventory and amortization methods

1. Net income: Zastre Associates, $116,000

DP10–1

Suppose you are considering investing in two businesses, Zastre Associates and Chen Co. The two companies are virtually identical, and both began operations at the beginning of 2020. During the year, each company purchased inventory as follows:

Jan. 10	12,000	units at $7	=	$ 84,000
Mar. 11	5,000	units at $9	=	45,000
Jul. 9	10,000	units at $10	=	100,000
Oct. 12	12,000	units at $11	=	132,000
Totals	39,000			$361,000

During 2020, both companies sold 30,000 units of inventory.

In early January 2020, both companies purchased equipment costing $400,000 that had a five-year estimated useful life and a $40,000 residual value. Zastre Associates uses the first-in, first-out (FIFO) method for its inventory and straight-line amortization for its equipment. Chen Co. uses the weighted-average method for inventory and DDB amortization. Both companies' trial balances at December 31, 2020, included the following:

Sales revenue	$560,000
Operating expenses (excluding amortization expense)	110,000

Required

1. Prepare both companies' income statements.
2. Write a memo to address the following long-term investment questions for your clients: Which company appears to be more profitable? Which company will have more cash to invest in promising projects? Which company would you prefer to invest in? Why?

FINANCIAL STATEMENT CASES

FSC10–1

(2) (4) (6)
Property, plant, and equipment and intangible assets

Refer to Indigo Books & Music Inc.'s financial statements in Appendix A at the end of this book and on MyLab Accounting to answer the following questions:

1. With respect to PPE, which amortization/depreciation method does Indigo use for the purpose of reporting to shareholders and creditors in the financial statements? What rates are used, and where did you find your answer?
2. What was the total amount of depreciation expense for 2017 as shown in Note 9?
3. Indigo lists intangible assets on the balance sheet. Where do you find more information about them? What types of intangible assets does Indigo have?

FSC10–2

(2) (4) (6)
Property, plant, and equipment and intangible assets

2. Amortization expense 2013, $423,000,000

Refer to the financial statements of TELUS Corporation on MyLab Accounting to answer the following questions:

1. Which amortization method does TELUS use for property, plant, and equipment for the purpose of reporting to shareholders and creditors in the financial statements? What rates are used? Where did you find your answer?
2. According to Note 17, what was the total depreciation for 2016?
3. According to Note 17, how much was spent on network assets (additions) during 2016?
4. What types of intangible assets does TELUS have listed on the 2016 financial statements?

IFRS MINI-CASE

The IFRS Mini-Case is now available online, at **MyLab Accounting** in Chapter Resources.

Try It! Solutions for Chapter 10

1. Include (a) installation charges and (b) testing of the machine in the cost of machinery because these costs are incurred to bring the machine to its intended purpose. However, do not include (c) repair to machinery and (d) first-year maintenance cost because they maintain the asset once it is put in to use.

2.

Asset	Market Value	Percentage of Total Value	× Total Purchase Price		= Cost of Each Asset
Land	$ 22,000	$22,000 / $220,000 = 10%	× $200,000	=	$ 20,000
Building	187,000	$187,000 / $220,000 = 85%	× $200,000	=	170,000
Equipment	11,000	$11,000 / $220,000 = 5%	× $200,000	=	10,000
Total	$220,000	100%			$200,000

Date	Accounts and Explanation	Debit	Credit
May 31	Land	20,000	
	Building	170,000	
	Equipment	10,000	
	Cash		200,000
	To record purchase of land, building, and equipment with cash.		

3. a. Installing new tires on a cement truck—repair
   b. Repainting a delivery truck that was damaged in an accident—repair
   c. Replacing the motor in a delivery truck—betterment
   d. Installing an elevating device in a delivery truck—betterment
   e. Safety test on a delivery truck when the licence is renewed—repair
   f. Installing carrying racks on the roof of the delivery truck—betterment

4. a. One approach is to look for patterns in the annual amortization expenses for each method, then check your guesses by calculating the expenses using the data given. Equal annual expenses indicate the straight-line method. A random pattern indicates the units-of-production method. Declining annual expenses indicate the double-declining-balance method.

Method A: Straight-line method
Amortizable cost = $160,000($176,000 − $16,000)
Each year: $160,000 ÷ 10 years = $16,000

Method B: Double-declining-balance method
Rate = 100% ÷ 10 years = 10%; 10% × 2 = 20%
2020: 0.20 × $176,000 = $35,200
2018: 0.20 × ($176,000 − $35,200) = $28,160

Method C: Units-of-production method
Calculating the number of units for 2020 and 2021 is not necessary, but it helps you prepare for the calculation you'll make in Requirement b.

Amortization per unit = ($176,000 − $16,000) ÷ 100,000 units = $1.60
2020: $1.60 × 3,000 units = $4,800 (since $4,800 ÷ $1.60 = 3,000 units)
2018: $1.60 × 14,000 units = $22,400 (since $22,400 ÷ $1.60 = 14,000 units)

4. b. Use the amortization rates calculated in Requirement a for the 2022 computations.

Method A Straight-Line Method			
Year	Annual Amortization Expense	Accumulated Amortization	Book Value
Start			$176,000
2020	$16,000	$16,000	160,000
2021	16,000	32,000	144,000
2022	16,000	48,000	128,000

Method B Double-Declining-Balance Method			
Year	Annual Amortization Expense	Accumulated Amortization	Book Value
Start			$176,000
2020	$35,200	$35,200	140,800
2021	28,160	63,360	112,640
2022	22,528	85,888	90,112

Method C Units-of-Production Method			
Year	Annual Amortization Expense	Accumulated Amortization	Book Value
Start			$176,000
2020	$ 4,800	$ 4,800	171,200
2021	22,400	27,200	148,800
2022	19,200	46,400	129,600

Computations for 2022:

Straight-line: $160,000 ÷ 10 years = $16,000
Double-declining-balance: 0.20 × $112,640 = $22,528
Units-of-production: $1.60 × 12,000 units = $19,200

5. a. Straight-line: ($65,000 − $5,000) ÷ 4 years = $15,000 per year
For 8 months (May–December 2020), $15,000 × 8/12 = $10,000

b. Units-of-production: ($65,000 − $5,000) ÷ 600 hours = $100 per hour
For the period April 17–December 31, 2020, 130 hours × $100/hour = $13,000

c. Double-declining-balance: Amortization rate = 2 × 25% = 50%
50% × $65,000 = $32,500 for full first year
For 8 months (May–December 2020), $32,500 × 8/12 = $21,667

6. Calculate the new book value:

Cost ($800,000 old + $200,000 new addition)	$1,000,000
Less: Accumulated amortization (20 years × $18,750/year*)	375,000
Revised book value	$ 625,000

Revised straight-line amortization:
= ($625,000 − $100,000**) ÷ 20
= $26,250 per year

*($800,000 − $50,000) ÷ 40 years = $18,750 per year amortization

**$50,000 old residual value + $50,000 additional residual value = $100,000

7. a. First take amortization for 2020. Annual amortization is ($58,500 − 4,500) ÷ 6 = $9,000 per year.

Cash received from selling the equipment		$43,000
Book value of the equipment		
Cost	$58,500	
Less: Accumulated amortization at sale date (3 years × $9,000/year)	27,000	
Net book value of equipment		31,500
Gain on sale of equipment		$11,500

Dec. 29	Cash	43,000	
	Accumulated Amortization—Equipment	27,000	
	Equipment		58,500
	Gain on Sale of Equipment		11,500
	To record the sale of equipment.		

b. First take amortization for 2020. Annual amortization is ($58,500 − 4,500) ÷ 6 = $9,000 per year.

Cash received from selling the equipment		$23,000
Book value of the equipment		
Cost	$58,500	
Less: Accumulated amortization at sale date (3 years * $9,000/year)	27,000	
Net book value of equipment		31,500
Gain (loss) on sale of equipment		($8,500)

Dec. 29	Cash	23,000	
	Accumulated Amortization—Equipment	27,000	
	Loss on Sale of Equipment	8,500	
	Equipment		58,500
	To record the sale of equipment.		

8.

Jan. 2	Catering Equipment (new)	3,400	
	Accumulated Amortization—Catering Equipment (old)	2,200	
	Loss on Sale of Catering Equipment	400	
	Catering Equipment (old)		3,100
	Cash		2,900
	To record the exchange of catering equipment.		

9. The amount of amortization expense to be recorded is:

$$\frac{\text{Cost} - \text{Residual value}}{\text{Estimated total units}} \times \text{Number of units produced}$$
$= (\$600{,}000 \div 400{,}000 \text{ fbm}) \times 200{,}000 \text{ fbm}$
$= \$1.50/\text{fbm} \times 200{,}000 \text{ fbm}$
$= \$300{,}000$

10. a.

Jan. 5	Patent	650,000	
	Cash		650,000
	To record the purchase of a patent with an expected useful life of five years.		

Dec. 31	Amortization Expense—Patent	130,000	
	Patent		130,000
	To record one year's amortization of patent ($650,000 ÷ 5 = $130,000).		

b.

May 13	Patent	650,000	
	Cash		650,000
	To record the purchase of a patent with an expected useful life of five years.		

Dec. 31	Amortization Expense—Patent	86,667	
	Patent		86,667
	To record 2020 partial-year amortization of patent ($650,000 ÷ 5 = $130,000; $130,000 × 8/12 = $86,667).		

11.

Oct. 12	Assets (all assets acquired, at market value)	400,000	
	Goodwill	1,900,000	
	Liabilities (all accts listed)		300,000
	Cash		2,000,000
	To record purchase of Novel Networks.		

11 Current Liabilities and Payroll

CONNECTING CHAPTER 11

LEARNING OBJECTIVES

The **Summary** for Chapter 11 appears on page 634.
Key Terms with definitions for this chapter's material appears on pages 634–635.

CPA competencies

This text covers material outlined in **Section 1: Financial Reporting of the CPA Competency Map.** The Learning Objectives for each chapter have been aligned with the CPA Competency Map to ensure the best coverage possible.

1.1.2 Evaluates the appropriateness of the basis of financial reporting

1.2.2 Evaluates treatment for routine transactions

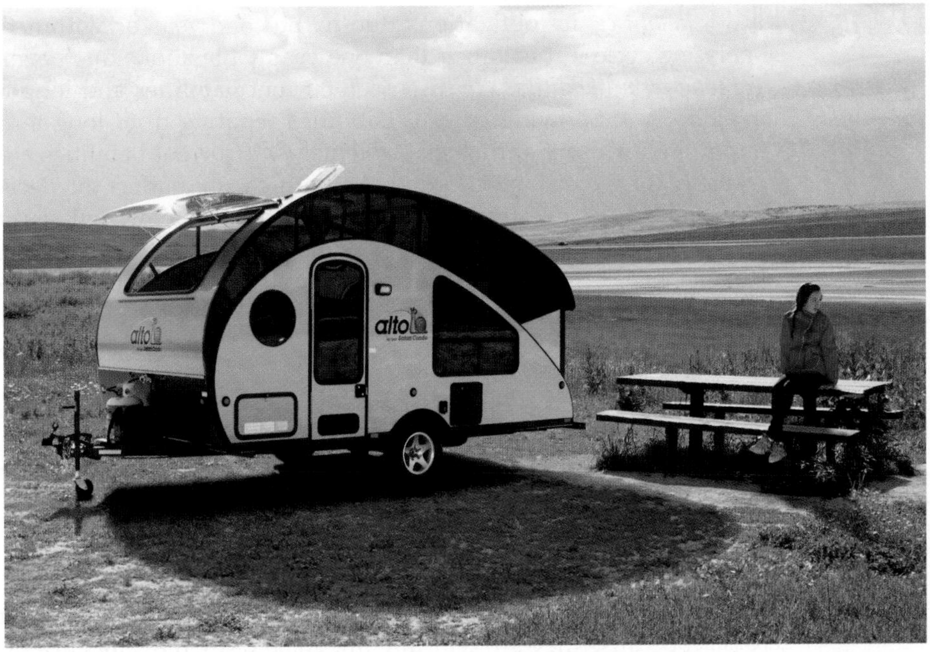

Safari Condo

Safari Condo is a Canadian innovator in the recreational vehicle (RV) market. They build both motorhomes and travel trailers. The picture here shows their Alto R series model with a retractable roof. It is a small, all-aluminum travel trailer made from recyclable materials that is aerodynamic and lightweight. It is designed so that it can be towed by vehicles that are smaller in size than what is typically required to pull a travel trailer.

Even though their product is unique, their accounting isn't. RV manufacturers have many of the same current liabilities as other businesses. They owe money to suppliers for goods and services provided and to the government for payroll and sales taxes, and they likely have loans outstanding.

In addition, manufacturers may have some liabilities they must estimate. RV manufacturers offer warranties on their products—a guarantee for a period of time that specific problems with their product will be fixed. But because Safari Condo does not know for certain if there will even be any warranty claims, how do they record a liability for an unknown amount? They make an *estimate* based on their own experience and the experience of others in their industry. Safari Condo might use the information found supplied by Warranty Week to estimate an amount for warranty expense. How much is reasonable? According to a study of American RV companies,[1] 2.2 percent of revenues is a reasonable estimate. Is this the right amount for Safari Condo to use in their accounting records? Given that they have high construction standards and use aluminum, they may record a different amount.

This chapter will look at how companies like Safari Condo record known liabilities and those that must be estimated.

[1]"Recreational Vehicle Warranties," October 19, 2017, http://www.warrantyweek.com/archive/ww20171019.html

Current *liabilities* are obligations due within one year or within the company's operating cycle if it is longer than one year. Obligations due beyond that period are *long-term liabilities*. We discussed current liabilities and long-term liabilities in Chapter 4. Showing current liabilities separate from long-term liabilities is important for users of financial statements. If current liabilities are not recorded correctly (or worse, not recorded at all), this would affect the decisions made by users thinking of investing in a company. In this chapter we will see how companies account for their current liabilities, which include product warranties, accounts payable, sales taxes, and payroll, among others. Exhibit 11–12 shows how they are presented in a balance sheet.

Current Liabilities of a Known Amount

LO 1
What are current liabilities, and how do we account for them?

The amounts of most current liabilities are known. A few current liabilities must be estimated. Let's begin with current liabilities of known amount.

Accounts Payable

Amounts owed for products or services that are purchased on account are *accounts payable*. Because they are typically due in 30 days, they are current liabilities. We have seen many accounts payable examples in previous chapters. Accounts payable occur because the business receives the goods or services before the payment has been made.

If Safari Condo purchased $600 of inventory, the transaction would be recorded as follows:

Nov. 22	Inventory	600	
	Accounts Payable		600
	To record purchase of inventory on account.		

The payment of the amount owing to the supplier would be shown as:

Dec. 5	Accounts Payable	600	
	Cash		600
	To record payment of account.		

Short-Term Notes Payable

This is similar to the notes receivable from Chapter 9—just from the opposite perspective of the borrower.

Short-term notes payable are a common form of financing. Short-term notes payable are promissory notes that must be paid with interest within one year. The following entries are typical for a short-term note payable that Safari Condo might have issued in 2019 to purchase inventory:

2019			
Oct. 31	Inventory	16,000	
	Note Payable, Short-Term		16,000
	Purchase of inventory by issuing a one-year, 10 percent note payable.		

At year end, it is necessary to accrue interest expense for two months. You may recall from Chapter 3 that the term *accrued expense* refers to an expense that the business has incurred but has not yet recorded, so it creates a liability. The interest on a note is separate from the principal. The accrued interest should be credited to Interest Payable—not to Note Payable.

2019			
Dec. 31	Interest Expense	267	
	Interest Payable		267
	Accrued interest expense at year end ($16,000 × 0.10 × 2/12).		

Remember that the calculation for interest is Principal × Interest rate × Time.

At maturity (the end of the loan), the note is paid back with interest:

2020			
Oct. 31	Note Payable, Short-Term	16,000	
	Interest Payable	267	
	Interest Expense	1,333	
	Cash		17,600
	Paid a note payable and interest at maturity. Interest expense is $1,333 ($16,000 × 0.10 × 10/12). Cash paid is $17,600 [$16,000 + ($16,000 × 0.10)].		

No longer a liability, the amount previously accrued must be eliminated with a debit to Interest Payable.

Interest expense of $267 was allocated to the year ended December 31, 2019. Safari Condo's interest expense for 2020 will be $1,333. At maturity, Safari Condo will pay a full year's interest, $1,600, allocated as shown in Exhibit 11–1.

EXHIBIT 11–1 | Matching Objective: Putting Interest in the Correct Fiscal Year

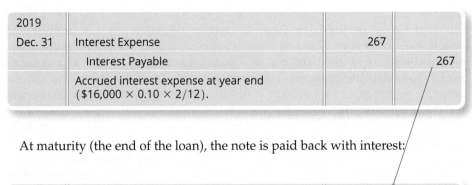

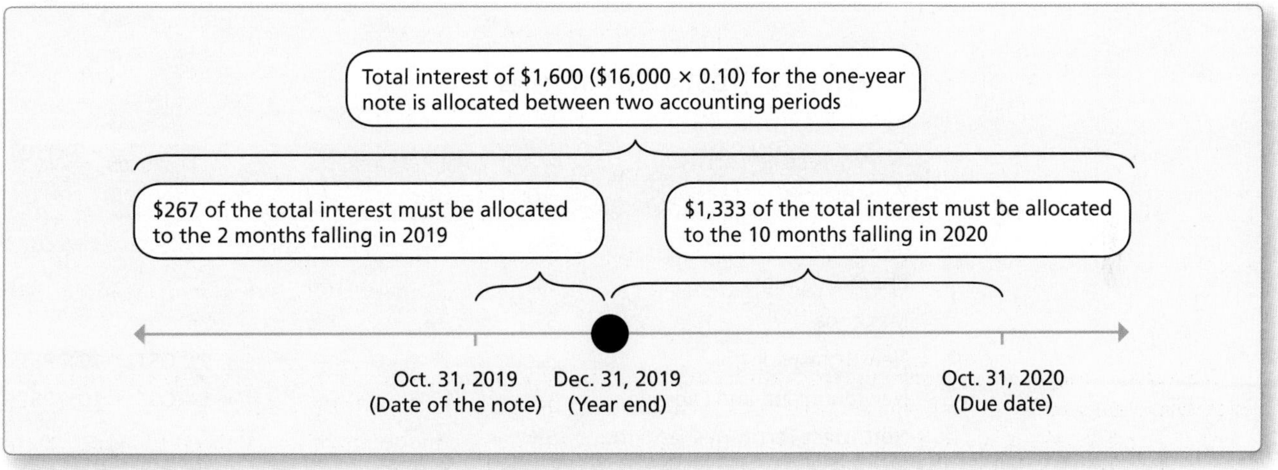

Short-Term Bank Loans and Operating Lines of Credit

Short-term bank loans are similar to short-term notes payable. They are arranged with a bank or other financial institution and are for a fixed time period at an interest rate negotiated between the bank and the borrower. If the bank loan is due in less than one year, or less than the company's operating cycle, it is considered short term. Interest expense is recorded separately from the loan, and interest expense on a bank loan is accrued at the end of the year in the same way as for a note payable.

Many companies, and many people as well, arrange an operating **line of credit** with a financial institution to have cash available in case of a temporary cash shortfall. A line of credit is like a bank loan that is negotiated once and then used

Crowdfunding is a way of raising money online for a new idea or product. Businesses like Kickstarter and Indiegogo connect contributors who donate funds in order to be among the first to receive the new product or service. The transaction results in a liability—the business owes a product or service—which must be reported on the financial statements.

when needed. Interest is payable monthly only on the amount of the line of credit actually used—if the line of credit is not used, no interest is payable. Interest paid on a line of credit is recorded as interest expense. While most lines of credit are payable on demand (the bank can demand immediate repayment at any time), banks rarely demand repayment without warning. Typically, the amount of the principal to be repaid each month is flexible, often with a minimum repayment required every month.

Many lines of credit are *secured*, meaning that assets are **pledged as security** in case the borrower cannot repay the loan. Unsecured lines of credit do not have assets pledged as security. However, they often charge a higher rate of interest than secured lines of credit because there is a greater risk the financial institution will not receive the money it lent when there are no assets to be sold to recover the funds.

Goods and Services Tax, Harmonized Sales Tax, and Sales Tax Payable

There are two basic consumption taxes levied on purchases in Canada that are *visible* to consumers: the goods and services tax (GST) levied by the federal government and the provincial sales taxes (PST) levied by some provinces. In some provinces these two taxes are combined into a harmonized sales tax (HST). There are also excise or luxury taxes, which are a form of sales tax levied by the federal and provincial governments on products such as cigarettes, gasoline, jewellery, and alcoholic beverages; these taxes are *hidden* in that they are collected by the manufacturer and consumers do not see it as a separate tax on their invoice. The focus of discussion in this section will be on the visible consumption taxes; GST, HST, and PST will be discussed in turn below.

A summary of basic rates in effect on July 1, 2018, is presented in Exhibit 11–2. Rates vary with the item sold. These rates change occasionally but were correct at the time of writing.

EXHIBIT 11–2 | GST/HST/PST Rates

Province or Territory	2018 Rates			Notes
	GST	HST	PST	
Alberta	5%	—	—	
British Columbia	5%	—	7%	
Manitoba	5%	—	8%	
New Brunswick	—	15%	—	= 5% GST + 10% PST
Newfoundland and Labrador	—	15%	—	= 5% GST + 10% PST
Northwest Territories	5%	—	—	
Nova Scotia	—	15%	—	= 5% GST + 10% PST
Nunavut	5%	—	—	
Ontario	—	13%	—	= 5% GST + 8% PST
Quebec	5%	—	9.975%	Called QST, not PST
Prince Edward Island	—	15%	—	= 5% GST + 10% PST
Saskatchewan	5%	—	6%	
Yukon	5%	—	—	

Goods and Services Tax (GST) The federal government, through the Canada Revenue Agency (CRA), collects the GST on *most* goods and services consumed in Canada.

There are three categories of goods and services with respect to the GST:

- **Zero-rated supplies**, such as basic groceries, prescription drugs, goods and services exported from Canada to nonresidents, and medical devices
- **Exempt supplies**, such as educational services, health care services, and financial services
- **Taxable supplies**, which basically includes everything that is not zero-rated or exempt

GST Charged on Sales The tax is collected by the individual or business (called the **registrant**) selling the taxable good or service (called *taxable supplies*). The account for these transactions is often called GST Payable.

GST Paid on Purchases Businesses who supply taxable goods and services have to pay tax on their purchases. Businesses are able to deduct the amount of GST paid (called an **input tax credit**, or **ITC**) from the GST they have collected from their sales in calculating the amount due. Some businesses use an account called GST Recoverable for these transactions.

GST Remittance The GST return and the net tax must be remitted quarterly for most registrants and monthly for larger registrants. GST **recoverable** means there is a tax refund paid from the government to the business. A payment of tax is called a *remittance*.

For example, Mary Janicek, who lives in Whitehorse, Yukon, where there is no provincial tax, purchased a new sound system on July 2, with the intention of earning money by working as a disc jockey at weddings and local nightclubs.[2] The equipment cost $2,400 plus GST in the amount of $120. Because Janicek is planning to use the equipment exclusively to perform at special events, she could recover the $120. Assuming she were a registrant, she would have to charge all her customers the 5 percent GST for her services and remit it to the government. During the first three months of business, Janicek earned revenue of $4,000 and collected $200 of GST. She spent $105: $100 plus GST of $5 on advertising supplies. The entries to record these transactions would be as follows:

Jul. 2	Equipment	2,400	
	GST Recoverable	120	
	Cash		2,520
	To record purchase of a new sound system.		
Jul.-Sep.	Advertising Expense	100	
	GST Recoverable	5	
	Cash		105
	To record advertising costs for the period.		
Jul.-Sep.	Cash	4,200	
	Disc Jockey Revenue		4,000
	GST Payable		200
	To record revenue from various events.		

This is how you calculate the GST recoverable when both GST and PST are included in the total cost of a product purchased: Divide the total cost of the product by the sum of 1 + the PST rate + the GST rate; then multiply the result by the GST rate.

For example, suppose a company purchases an item in Saskatchewan (where PST is 6 percent) with a total cost of $226, which includes PST and GST. What is the possible GST recoverable?

A: $226 ÷ (1 + 0.06 + 0.05) = $203.60

$203.60 × 0.05 = $10.18

The GST recoverable on this purchase is $10.18.

[2]If a business earns less than $30,000 per year it does not have to be registered for GST or HST purposes. If this were the case, the owner would neither charge GST or HST to his or her clients nor be able to claim an input tax credit. This scenario assumes that Janicek plans to make over $30,000 per year. A business is only *required* to become a GST or HST registrant if taxable revenues exceed $30,000 for the last four consecutive quarters.

Janicek receives an input tax credit of $125 for the GST paid on the purchase of the sound system and advertising ($120 + $5), so she would credit the GST Recoverable account to bring its balance to zero. She will also debit the GST Payable account to bring its balance to zero. In this case she will remit the difference.

When Janicek remits her first quarterly GST payment, she sends $75 to the Receiver General. The entry would be as follows:

Oct. 31	GST Payable	200	
	GST Recoverable		125
	Cash		75
	To record payment of GST payable net of input tax credits to the Receiver General.		

Alternative Presentations In the Mary Janicek example, we used two accounts—GST Recoverable and GST Payable—to illustrate input tax credits and GST collections to be remitted to the Receiver General. Some registrants use only one account—GST Payable—to record input tax credits *and* GST collections. When the GST return is sent to the Receiver General, the final account balance in the GST Payable account is remitted if the balance is a credit, or a refund is requested if the balance is a debit. However, since the CRA wants a report of both amounts, we will continue to use the two-account approach to illustrate input tax credits and GST collections.

Most companies include GST Payable as a current liability and report GST Recoverable as a current asset on their balance sheets. One can be subtracted from the other on the balance sheet if a company prefers to show it as one amount.

Harmonized Sales Tax (HST) Several provinces have combined their respective provincial sales taxes with the GST to create a harmonized sales tax (HST). While GST is consistent at 5 percent, the amount of provincial sales tax varies. See Exhibit 11–2 for rates in each province.

The entries to record HST collection and remittance to the CRA would be almost identical to the GST entries shown above. Let's assume that Mary Janicek lives in Ontario, which has HST of 13 percent, and look at the same transactions again:

Jul. 2	Equipment	2,400	
	HST Recoverable	312	
	Cash		2,712
	To record purchase of a new sound system.		
Jul.–Sep.	Advertising Expense	100	
	HST Recoverable	13	
	Cash		113
	To record advertising costs for the period.		
Jul.–Sep.	Cash	4,520	
	Disc Jockey Revenue		4,000
	HST Payable		520
	To record revenue from various events.		

In Ontario, Janicek would be required to remit $195 ($520 – $312 – $13) as her first quarterly payment. The entry would be as follows:

Oct. 31	HST Payable	520	
	HST Recoverable		325
	Cash		195
	To record payment of HST payable net of input tax credits to Receiver General.		

Provincial Sales Tax (PST) Some provinces levy a tax on sales to the final consumers of products; sales tax is not levied on sales to wholesalers or retailers (unless they are the final consumers of the product, such as for office supplies). The final sellers charge their customers the PST in addition to the price of the item sold. PST is often referred to as an **end-user tax** for this reason.

Consider Super Stereo Products, an electronics superstore located in Winnipeg. Super Stereo does not pay PST on its purchase of a TV set from Panasonic because it is inventory for resale, but you, as a consumer, would have to pay the 8 percent PST and the 5 percent GST to Super Stereo when you buy a Panasonic TV from the store. Super Stereo pays the PST it collected from you to the province of Manitoba and the GST to the federal government.

Suppose on September 16, sales at the Super Stereo store totalled $20,000. The business would record that day's sales as follows:

Sep. 16	Cash	22,600	
	Sales Revenue		20,000
	GST Payable		1,000
	Sales Tax Payable		1,600
	To record cash sales of $20,000 and the related taxes. GST = $20,000 × .05 = $1,000 PST = $20,000 × .08 = $1,600		

Sometimes called PST Payable

Taxes are charged on the base price of the item before other taxes.

Companies forward the sales tax they collect on behalf of the provincial government to the taxing authority at regular intervals (typically monthly for large companies and quarterly for small companies), at which time they debit Sales Tax Payable and credit Cash. There is no refundable tax, so there is only one payable account for a provincial tax.

Current Portion of Long-Term Debt

Some long-term notes payable and bonds payable are paid in instalments, which means that portions of the principal are repaid at specific time intervals. The **current portion of long-term debt** is the amount of the principal that is payable within one year—a current liability. The remaining portion of the long-term debt is a long-term liability.

Suppose Safari Condo borrowed $100,000 on January 1, 2020. This loan is to be repaid in instalments of $10,000 per year for 10 years on December 31 each year. On December 31, 2020, the first principal repayment of $10,000 is made (ignore interest), leaving a loan balance of $90,000. Exhibit 11–3 illustrates this example.

A current liability is due within one year, or within the company's operating cycle if it is longer than one year. The portion of a long-term debt payable within the year is classified as a current liability.

EXHIBIT 11–3 | Current Portion of Long-term Debt

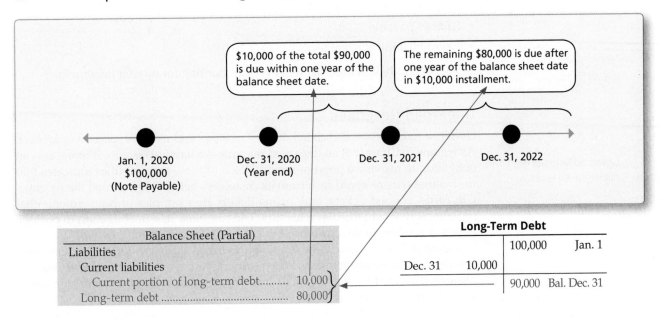

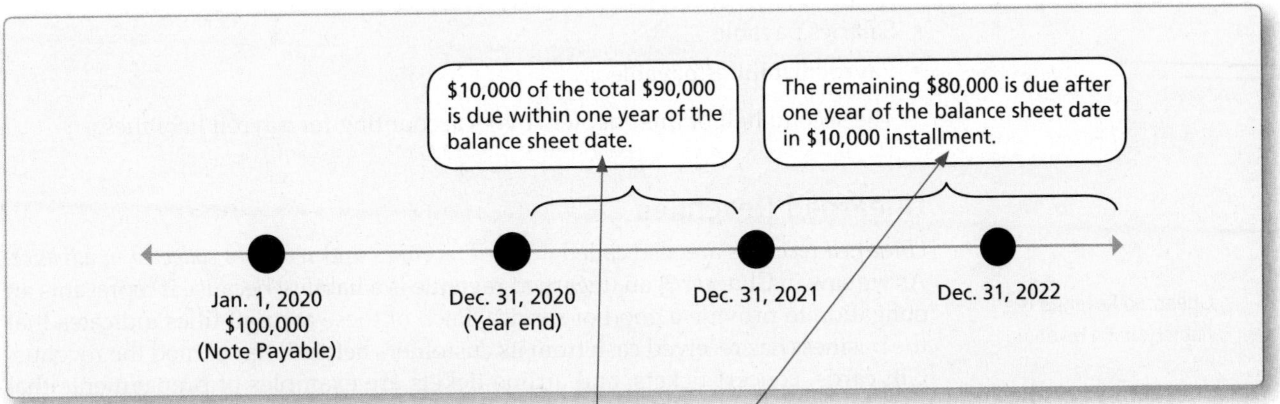

Balance Sheet (Partial)

Liabilities	
Current liabilities	
Current portion of long-term debt..........	10,000
Long-term debt	80,000

Long-Term Debt

		100,000	Jan. 1
Dec. 31	10,000		
		90,000	Bal. Dec. 31

Exhibit 11–3 shows that the December 31, 2020, balance sheet reports the $10,000 portion due to be repaid on December 31, 2021, as a current liability and reports the remaining $80,000 portion as long-term debt. On December 31, 2020, the company *may* make an adjusting entry to shift the current instalment of the long-term debt to a current liability account as follows:

The interest payable is classified separately from the principal.

2020			
Dec. 31	Long-Term Debt	10,000	
	Current Portion of Long-Term Debt		10,000
	To transfer the portion of long-term debt due in 2021 to the current liability account.		

The reason we say *may* make the adjusting entry is that this is a reporting requirement on the balance sheet. A company could just show this on the balance sheet without making the actual journal entry. This example shows that accounting includes both *recording* transactions properly and *reporting* the information on the financial statements, which highlights that reporting is every bit as important as recording.

The liabilities for the current portion of long-term debt do not include any accrued interest payable. The account, Current Portion of Long-Term Debt, represents only the appropriate portion of the *principal amount owed*. Interest Payable is a separate account for a different liability—the interest that must be paid.

What would be the effect if a company reported its full liability as all long term? Two ratios that would have been distorted by this accounting error are the current ratio and the acid-test ratio. Reporting a liability as long term could mislead external users because it understates current liabilities, overstating these two ratios and reporting an overly positive view of the company.

Accrued Expenses (Accrued Liabilities)

An **accrued expense** is an expense that has not yet been paid. An accrued expense creates a liability, which explains why accrued expenses are also called **accrued liabilities**. We introduced accrued expenses in Chapter 3.

Every journal entry to set up an accrued expense involves a debit to an *expense* and a credit to a *liability*.

Typical accrued expenses include the following:

- Interest payable
- Property taxes payable
- Salaries payable
- Payroll liabilities payable

The second half of this chapter covers accounting for payroll liabilities.

Unearned Revenues

Unearned Revenue is a liability, *not* a revenue.

Unearned revenues are also called *deferred revenues* and *revenues collected in advance*. As we saw in Chapter 3, an unearned revenue is a liability because it represents an obligation to provide a good or service. Each of these account titles indicates that the business has received cash from its customers before it has earned the revenue. Gift cards, concert tickets, and airline tickets are examples of prepayments that the company must record as a liability. The company has an obligation to provide goods or services to the customer. Let's consider an example.

Canadian Business magazine may be purchased individually or by means of a subscription (16 issues per year). When subscribers pay in advance to have *Canadian Business* delivered to their home or business, Rogers Media Inc. incurs a liability to provide future service. The liability account is called Unearned Subscription Revenue (which could also be titled Unearned Subscription Income or Deferred Subscription Income).

Assume that Rogers Media charges $20 (ignore taxes) for Bob Baylor's one-year subscription to *Canadian Business*. Rogers Media's entries would be:

2020			
Sep. 3	Cash	20	
	Unearned Subscription Revenue		20
	To record receipt of cash at the start of a one-year subscription.		

After receiving the cash on September 3, Rogers Media owes its customer magazines that it will provide over the next 12 months. Rogers Media's liability is:

Unearned Subscription Revenue

Debit		Credit	
		Sep. 3	20

Cash

Debit		Credit	
Sep. 3	20		

During 2020, Rogers Media delivers four of the magazines and earns $5 ($\$20 \times 4/16$) of the subscription revenue. At December 31, 2020, it makes the following adjusting entry to decrease (debit) the liability Unearned Subscription Revenue and increase (credit) Subscription Revenue:

2020			
Dec. 31	Unearned Subscription Revenue	5	
	Subscription Revenue		5
	Earned revenue that was collected in advance ($\$20 \times 4/16$).		

After posting, Rogers Media still owes the subscriber $15 for magazines to be delivered during 2021 (this is unearned revenue for Rogers). Rogers Media has earned $5 of the revenue, as follows:

Unearned Subscription Revenue

Debit		Credit	
Dec. 31	5	Sep. 3	20
		Bal.	15

Subscription Revenue

Debit		Credit	
		Dec. 31	5

Customer Deposits Payable

Some companies require cash deposits from customers as security on borrowed assets. These amounts are called Customer Deposits Payable because the company must refund the cash to the customer under certain conditions. Utility companies and businesses that lend tools and appliances commonly demand a deposit as protection against damage and theft. Certain manufacturers of products sold through individual dealers, such as Avon or Mary Kay, require deposits from the dealers who sell their products; the deposit is usually equal to the cost of the sample kit provided to the dealer. Companies whose products are sold in returnable containers collect deposits on those containers. Because the deposit is returned to the customer, the amount collected represents a liability.

Try It!

1. Suppose Magnus' Private Tutoring in Victoria, British Columbia, made cash sales of $3,000 in April subject to 5 percent GST and 7 percent PST. Record sales and the related consumption taxes. Also record payment of the PST to the provincial government and the GST to the Receiver General on May 10. Assume input tax credits amount to $69.
2. On September 1, 2019, Snippy Hair Salons borrowed $20,000. A portion of the loan is to be paid back each year on September 1 as follows: in 2020, $6,000; in 2021, $5,000; in 2022, $4,000; in 2023, $3,000; and in 2024, $2,000. Interest of 5 percent on the outstanding amount is paid on August 31 each year. At December 31, 2019, Snippy Hair Salons reported the long-term debt payable as follows:

Current Liabilities (in part)	
Portion of long-term debt due within one year	$ 6,000
Interest payable*	333
Long-Term Liabilities (in part)	
Long-term debt	$14,000

Assuming the company makes the loan repayments as scheduled, show how Snippy Hair Salons would report its loan liability on the year-end balance sheet one year later—December 31, 2020.

*Calculated as $\$20{,}000 \times 0.05 \times {}^{4}/_{12}$

Solutions appear at the end of this chapter and on **MyLab Accounting**

Current Liabilities that must be Estimated

LO 2

Why would we estimate liabilities, and how do we account for them?

A business may know that a liability exists but not know the exact amount. It cannot simply ignore the liability. This liability must be reported on the balance sheet.

Estimated Warranty Payable

Many companies guarantee their products against defects under **warranty** agreements. At the time of the sale, the company does not know the exact amount of warranty expense, but the business must estimate its warranty expense and the related liability.

A warrantied product may be sold in one year but repaired in another year. When should the repair be expensed—in the year the product is sold or in the year the product is repaired? The matching objective requires matching the warranty expense with the revenue from the sale in the year of the sale.

The matching objective leads us to record the *warranty expense* in the same period we record the revenue. The expense occurs when you make a sale, not when you pay the warranty claim.

BlackBerry Ltd. explains its treatment of product warranties:

> The Company's estimates of costs are based upon historical experience and expectations of future return rates and unit warranty repair costs. If the Company experiences increased or decreased warranty activity, or increased or decreased costs associated with servicing those obligations, revisions to the estimated warranty liability would be recognized in the reporting period when such revisions are made.[3]

To illustrate the journal entries, let's assume that Collico Fabricating made sales in 2019 of $80 million. Collico offers its customers a one-year warranty on its products. In the past, the warranty provision and actual warranty cost was 1 percent of fabricating sales. Assume the company believes that 1 percent of the value of products sold in 2019 is the appropriate estimate of the cost of warranty work to be

[3]BlackBerry Ltd.'s Notes to the Consolidated Financial Statements, 2017.

performed in the future. The company would record the sales of $80 million and the warranty expense of $800,000 ($80,000,000 × 0.01) in the same period as follows:

2019			
Various	Accounts Receivable	80,000,000	
Dates	Sales Revenue		80,000,000
	Sales on account.		
Dec. 31	Warranty Expense	800,000	
	Estimated Warranty Payable		800,000
	To accrue warranty expense on $80 million of sales.		

Assume that the costs paid to repair defective merchandise during 2020 total $700,000. If Collico repairs the defective products, Collico makes this journal entry:

2020			
Various	Estimated Warranty Payable	700,000	
Dates	Cash		700,000
	To pay repair costs for defective products sold under warranty.		

If Collico replaces the defective products rather than repairs them, Collico makes this journal entry:

2020			
Various	Estimated Warranty Payable	700,000	
Dates	Inventory		700,000
	To replace defective products sold under warranty.		

After paying these warranty claims, Collico's liability account would have a credit balance of $100,000 at the December 31, 2020, year end:

Estimated Warranty Payable

2020 Adj.	700,000	800,000	Dec. 31, 2019
		100,000	Dec. 31, 2020, Bal.

Notice there is a balance left in the account. There is no adjustment made at this time. The accountants for Collico Fabricating will decrease their next estimate based on the fact that there was a lower amount of warranty claims than their previous estimate. If there were a debit balance in this account, then the next year's estimate would be increased.

While warranty expense is often calculated as a percentage of sales dollars, it can also be calculated as a percentage of units of product sold. For example, suppose a tire company sells 50,000 tires in one year. It estimates, based on experience, that 0.5 percent of them, or 250 tires, will need to be replaced in the future. If the tires cost $50 each, the warranty expense is estimated to be $12,500 (250 × $50). The accounts used in the journal entry to record the warranty expense are the same as those shown above.

Estimated Vacation Pay Liability

All Canadian companies are required by law to grant paid vacations to their employees. The employees receive this benefit when they take their vacation, but they earn the compensation by working the other days of the year. The law requires most employers to provide a minimum number of weeks' holiday per year (usually two, but sometimes more based on the number of years worked). To match expense with revenue properly, the company accrues the vacation pay expense and liability for each of the 50 workweeks of the year. Then, the company records payment during the two-week vacation period. Employee turnover, terminations, and ineligibility (e.g., no vacation allowed until one full year has been worked) force companies to estimate the vacation pay liability and accrue vacation expense incurred.

Two weeks of annual vacation divided by 50 workweeks in a year results in a rate of 4 percent.

Suppose a company's January payroll is $100,000 and vacation pay adds 4 percent, or $4,000. In January, the company records the vacation pay accrual as follows:

Employees may earn more than two weeks of vacation depending on their employer.

Jan. 31	Vacation Pay Expense	4,000	
	Estimated Vacation Pay Liability		4,000
	To record vacation accrual for January.		

Each month thereafter, the company makes a similar entry.

If an employee takes a two-week vacation in August, his or her $2,000 monthly salary, made up of vacation and regular pay, is recorded as follows:

Aug. 31	Estimated Vacation Pay Liability	1,000	
	Salaries Expense	1,000	
	Various Withholding Accounts and Cash*		2,000
	To record payment of salary and vacation pay.		

*The various payroll accounts are discussed later in the chapter.

Employees are often encouraged to take vacation to eliminate large balances accumulating in these liability accounts.

Income Tax Payable (for a Corporation)

Corporations pay income tax in the same way as individual taxpayers do. Corporations file their income tax returns with the Canada Revenue Agency (CRA) and their provincial governments after the end of the fiscal year, so they must estimate their income tax payable for reporting on the balance sheet.

During the year, corporations make monthly tax instalments (payments) to the government(s) based on their estimated tax for the year. A corporation with an estimated tax liability of $1,200,000 for the year would record each month's payment of the instalment as shown here for September:

Calculating and reporting corporate income taxes is introduced in Chapter 13.

Sep. 30	Income Tax Expense	100,000	
	Cash		100,000
	To pay monthly income tax instalment.		

If the corporation has a December 31 year end, then the last monthly payment would be made as usual, and then a reconciliation would be performed. If at that point the *actual* tax expense for the year was calculated to be $1,240,000, then the corporation would accrue an additional $40,000. On December 30, the corporation pays the last monthly instalment of $100,000. It will have reported $1,200,000 of income tax expense for the year.

Then, at December 31, the corporation calculates *actual* tax expense for the year to be $1,240,000. It must accrue the additional $40,000:

Dec. 31	Income Tax Expense	40,000	
	Income Tax Payable		40,000
	To accrue income tax at year end.		

The corporation will pay off the balance of this tax liability during the next year when it files its federal and provincial tax returns, so Income Tax Payable is a current liability.

Contingent Liabilities

A **contingent liability** is a potential liability that depends on a *future* event arising out of past events. For example, Packenham town council may sue North Ontario Electric Supply Ltd., the company that installed new street lights in Packenham, claiming that the electrical wiring is faulty. The past transaction is the street-light installation. The future event is the court case that will decide the suit. North Ontario Electric Supply Ltd. thus faces a contingent liability, which may or may not become an actual obligation.

The *CPA Canada Handbook* generally requires *contingent losses* to be accrued or disclosed in the financial statements but does not allow *contingent gains* to be recognized *until* they are realized. The accounting treatment for contingencies requires the application of judgment, which follows the concept of *conservatism*. The accounting profession divides contingent liabilities into three categories. Each category indicates a likelihood that a contingency will cause a loss and become an actual liability. The three categories of contingent liabilities, along with how to report them, are shown in Exhibit 11–4.

EXHIBIT 11–4 | Contingent Liabilities: Three Categories

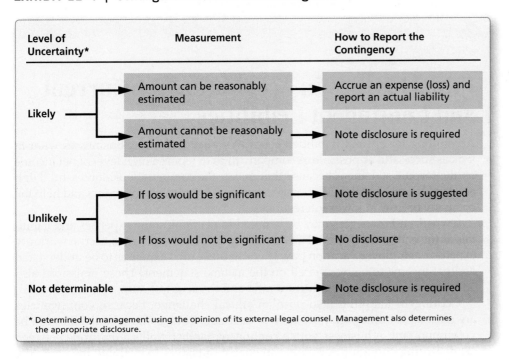

Level of Uncertainty*	Measurement	How to Report the Contingency
Likely	Amount can be reasonably estimated	Accrue an expense (loss) and report an actual liability
	Amount cannot be reasonably estimated	Note disclosure is required
Unlikely	If loss would be significant	Note disclosure is suggested
	If loss would not be significant	No disclosure
Not determinable		Note disclosure is required

* Determined by management using the opinion of its external legal counsel. Management also determines the appropriate disclosure.

Accrual As shown earlier in this chapter, an accrual is a journal entry. Increase (debit) an expense account and increase (credit) a liability account so that the future payment is reported on the balance sheet.

Disclosure The *disclosure principle* of accounting (see Chapter 6) requires a company to report any information deemed relevant to outsiders of the business for decision making. The notes to the financial statements provide some of this information. BlackBerry Ltd. discusses how it deals with contingencies in Note 14. Commitments and Contingencies, (c) Litigation, of its 2017 annual report:

> As of February 28, 2017, there are claims outstanding for which the Company has assessed the potential loss as both probable to result and reasonably estimable; therefore, no accrual has been made. Further, there are claims outstanding for which the Company has assessed the potential loss as reasonably possible to result, however an estimate of the amount of loss cannot reasonably be made.

Why It's Done This Way

This chapter is a great example of how the framework for financial reporting influences decisions about recording and reporting transactions.

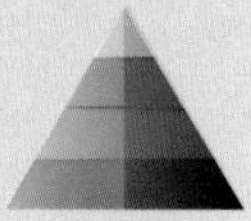

- A company may purchase inventory that is received on the first day of the month, but the invoice does not have to be paid until the end of the month. In this case, the company has a liability because it has received the inventory (*recognition*) at an agreed-upon amount (*measurement*) that will be paid in the near future.
- Suppose you purchase an airline ticket from WestJet for a flight from Toronto to Winnipeg that you will take at the end of the semester. You have paid for the flight, so why shouldn't WestJet simply recognize your payment as revenue? Because WestJet still owes you the flight. If, for some reason, WestJet cannot fulfill the contract with you, it must refund your fare. Thus, WestJet's unearned revenue for your flight is a liability until it provides the flight.
- Warranties and vacation pay are expenses that are estimated in order to be able to record an expense at the time the revenue is recognized (*matching objective*).
- Contingent liabilities are accrued or included in the notes to the financial statements when they are relevant to the business in order to satisfy the *disclosure principle*.

Of course, by recording all of these transactions, the business complies with the characteristics of *relevance* and *reliability*, leading to financial statements that *communicate useful information to users*.

Ethical Issues in Accounting for Current and Contingent Liabilities

Accounting for current liabilities poses an ethical challenge. Businesses want to look as successful as possible. A company likes to report a high level of net income on the income statement because that makes the company look successful. High asset values and low liabilities make the company look safe to lenders and help the company borrow at lower interest rates.

Owners and managers may be tempted to overlook some expenses and liabilities at the end of the period. For example, a company can fail to accrue warranty expense or employee vacation pay. This will cause total expenses to be understated and net income to be overstated on the income statement. These omissions also affect the ratios, such as the current ratio and the acid-test ratio.

Contingent liabilities also pose an ethical challenge. Because contingencies are *potential* liabilities, they are easy to overlook. But a contingent liability can be very important. A business with a contingent liability walks a tightrope between (1) disclosing enough information to enable outsiders to evaluate the company realistically, and (2) not giving away too much information, which could harm the company.

Ethical business owners ensure their accounting records are complete and accurate. Falsifying financial statements can ruin one's reputation in the business community and lead to criminal convictions. In addition to legal repercussions, missing liabilities such as warranty liabilities, accrued liabilities, and contingent liabilities can be detrimental to proper financial disclosure and can have serious consequences for all the stakeholders involved.

Try It!

3. Chez Nous Limited, a new company, made sales (all on account) of $400,000. The company estimated warranty repairs at 3 percent of sales. Chez Nous' actual warranty payments were $9,000. Record sales, warranty expense, and warranty payments on December 31. How much is Chez Nous' estimated warranty payable at the end of the period?

Solutions appear at the end of this chapter and on **MyLab Accounting**

Accounting for Payroll

LO 3 **How are payroll amounts calculated?**

Payroll is a major expense of many businesses. For service organizations—such as public accounting firms and real estate brokers—payroll is *the* major expense. Salaries, wages, and related employment expenses usually cause an accrued liability at year end.

Labour costs require special calculations that are repeated, so most businesses develop or purchase a special payroll system or use the payroll module of their accounting software. This software is updated regularly by the software manufacturer to ensure that the tax rates and any changes in laws are kept current in the system.

Employee compensation can be provided in a number of different forms:

Salary	Pay stated at an annual, monthly, or weekly rate, such as $48,000 per year, $4,000 per month, or $1,000 per week.
Wages	Pay amounts stated at an hourly rate, such as $20 per hour.
Straight time	Base rate for a set period of time.
Overtime	Higher rate of pay for additional hours worked.
Commission	Pay stated as a percentage of a sale amount, such as a 5 percent commission on a sale. A realtor thus earns $5,000 on a $100,000 sale of real estate.
Piecework	Pay based on the number of pieces produced by the employee, such as number of trees planted or shirts sewn.
Bonus	Pay over and above base salary (wage or commission). A bonus is usually paid for exceptional performance—often a single amount after year end.
Benefits	Extra compensation items that aren't paid directly to the employee. Benefits could include health, life, and disability insurance. The employer pays the insurance company, which then provides coverage for the employee. Another type of benefit, a pension, sets aside money for the employee for his or her retirement.

Let's take a moment to see how overtime pay is calculated. Lucy Guild is an administrator and bookkeeper for MicroAge Electronics Inc. Lucy earns $20 per hour for **straight time** (40 hours). The company pays *time and a half* for **overtime**. That rate is 150 percent (1.5 times) the straight-time rate. Thus Lucy earns $30 for each hour of overtime ($\$20 \times 1.5 = \$30$). For working 42 hours during a week, she earns $860, computed as follows:

Straight-time pay for 40 hours	$800
Overtime pay for 2 overtime hours (2 × $30.00)	60
Gross or total pay	$860

Gross Pay and Net Pay

Two pay amounts are important for accounting purposes:

- **Gross pay** is the total amount of salary, wages, commission, piecework, and bonus earned by the employee during a pay period. Gross pay is the amount before income taxes or any other deductions. Gross pay is the employer's expense. In the preceding example, Lucy Guild's gross pay was $860.
- **Net pay**, also called *take-home pay*, is the amount the employee keeps. Net pay equals gross pay minus all *deductions*. The employer writes a paycheque to each employee or makes an electronic funds transfer to each employee's bank account for his or her net pay.

Exhibit 11–5 illustrates gross and net pay.

EXHIBIT 11–5 | Gross Pay and Net Pay

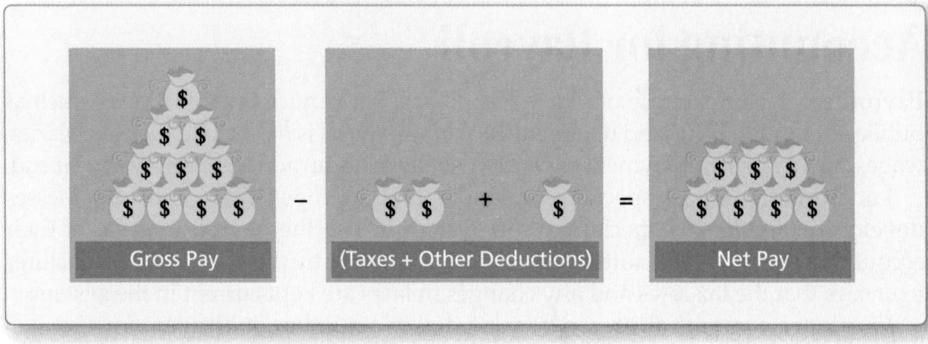

Payroll Deductions

Payroll deductions create the difference between gross pay and net pay. They are **withheld** from employees' pay and fall into two categories:

- *Required* (or *statutory*) *deductions*. The federal government and most provincial governments require by law that employers act as collection agents for employees' income taxes, Canada Pension Plan (CPP) or Quebec Pension Plan (QPP) contributions, and Employment Insurance (EI) premiums, which are deducted from employee paycheques.
- *Optional deductions*. These deductions include union dues (which may be automatic deductions for all unionized employees), insurance premiums, charitable contributions to organizations such as the United Way and other amounts that are withheld at the employee's request.

After being withheld, payroll deductions become current liabilities of the employer, which assumes responsibility for paying the outside party. For example, the employer pays the government the employee income tax withheld and pays the union the employee union dues withheld.

Required Payroll Deductions

Employees' Income Tax Payable For most employees, this deduction is the largest. The amount withheld depends on the employee's gross pay and on the amount of nonrefundable tax credits the employee claims. Each employee files both a provincial and a federal Personal Tax Credits Return (Form TD1), which is used by employers to determine how much income tax to withhold from an employee's gross pay. Factors on the TD1 that affect the amount of income tax to withhold include dependents, age, and student fees.

The employer accumulates both federal and provincial taxes withheld in the Employee Income Tax Payable account. The payable is eliminated when the employer pays (remits) these taxes to the government.

The CRA provides tables that the employer uses to calculate the amount to deduct from each employee's pay. The CRA also provides a free **Payroll Deductions Online Calculator (PDOC)** that provides more accurate calculations in a user-friendly format.

Employees' Canada (or Quebec) Pension Plan Contributions Payable The **Canada Pension Plan (CPP)** or **Quebec Pension Plan (QPP)** provides retirement, disability, and death benefits to employees who are covered by it. Employers are required to deduct premiums from each employee required to make a contribution (basically all employees between 18 and 70 years of age).

The federal government, through the CRA, determines annually the maximum pensionable earnings level (which is the maximum for deducting CPP), the basic annual exemption, and the contribution rate. In 2018, the following information was applicable:

Maximum pensionable earnings	$ 55,900
Basic annual exemption	3,500
Maximum contributory earnings ($55,900 – $3,500)	52,400
Contribution rate	× 4.95%
Maximum employee contribution for the year	$ 2,593.80

Divide the annual exemption of $3,500 by the number of pay periods in a year and deduct this from earnings before multiplying the contribution rate. This will ensure the correct amount of CPP exemption is calculated. For weekly pay periods, divide by 52; for two-week pay periods, divide by 26.

Once the employee reaches the maximum contribution of $2,593.80, the employer stops deducting CPP from the employee for that year. Some employees may have had more than one employer in a year; for example, you may have had a job for the summer and now have a part-time job while you are back at school. You recover any overpayment when you file your income tax return for the year.

The Canada Pension Plan system is changing starting in 2019. The contribution rate will gradually increase (to 5.95% in 2023) to allow for greater benefits to be paid out.

Employees' Employment Insurance Premiums Payable The Employment Insurance Act requires employers to deduct **Employment Insurance (EI)** premiums from each employee each time that employee is paid until the employee reaches the maximum. The purpose of EI is to provide assistance to contributors to the fund who cannot work for a variety of reasons. The most common reason is that the employee has been laid off; another reason is maternity leave or parental leave. As with the CPP, the CRA requires every employer to deduct EI premiums from every eligible employee. Those who are self-employed or related to the employer are not eligible.

2019 employee rates
CPP: 5.1% to max of $2,748.90 on $57,400 of earnings
EI: 1.62% to max of $860.22 on $53,100 of earnings

The federal government, through the CRA, establishes annually the maximum annual insurable earnings level and the EI premium rate. In early 2018, the following information was applicable:

Maximum insurable earnings	$51,700
Premium rate	× 1.66%
Maximum employee contribution	$858.22

The CRA provides tables and a Payroll Deductions Online Calculator that the employer uses to calculate the amount to deduct from each employee's gross pay each pay period, although this is easy to calculate manually. For example, if you earned $2,000 per month, $33.20 ($2,000 × 1.66%) would be deducted for EI each month.

If an employee exceeds the maximum contribution, for example, by having multiple employers, the overpayment can be recovered when he or she files an income tax return.

Remittance The employer must remit the income tax, CPP (or QPP) contributions, and EI premiums withheld and the employer's share, discussed below, to the CRA. The amount of withholdings determines how often the employer submits payroll payments. Most employers remit to the government at least monthly. Larger employers must remit two or four times a month depending on the total amounts withheld.

Other Payroll Deductions

As a convenience to their employees, many companies make optional payroll deductions and disburse cash according to employee instructions. Insurance payments, registered pension plan or retirement savings plan payments such as a **registered retirement savings plan (RRSP)** contribution, payroll savings plans, and donations to charities such as the United Way are examples.

Some employees have union dues as a required deduction. They would be recorded in an account such as Employee Union Dues Payable.

Employer Payroll Costs

Employers also incur expenses for at least three payroll costs:

- CPP (or QPP) contributions
- EI premiums
- Workers' compensation plan premiums

Employer Canada (or Quebec) Pension Plan Contributions In addition to being responsible for deducting and remitting the employee contribution to the CPP (or QPP), the employer must also pay into the program at the same time. The employer must match exactly the employee's contribution. Every employer must do so whether or not the employee also contributes elsewhere. Unlike the employee, the employer may not obtain a refund for overpayment.

Employer Employment Insurance Premiums The employer calculates the employee's EI premium and remits it together with the employer's share, which is generally 1.4 times the employee's premium, to the CRA. The maximum dollar amount of the employer's contribution would be 1.4 times the maximum employee's contribution of $858.22, which amounts to $1,201.51 (in 2018).

Workers' Compensation Premiums Unlike the previous two programs, which are administered by the federal government (the Quebec government for the QPP), **workers' compensation** plans are administered provincially. The purpose of the program is to provide financial support for workers injured on the job. The cost of the coverage is borne by the employer; the employee does not pay a premium to the fund. Workers' compensation payments are remitted quarterly.

In Manitoba, for example, almost all employees are covered by the program. There are over 70 different categories that the Workers Compensation Board uses to determine the cost of coverage. The category a group of workers is assigned to is based on the risk of injury to workers in that group, which is based on that group's and similar groups' experience. The employer pays a premium equal to the rate assessed times the employer's gross payroll, up to a maximum assessable.

Additional Provincial Payroll Taxes Certain provinces levy taxes on employers to pay for provincial health care, while others levy a combined health care and post-secondary education tax to pay for provincial health care and post-secondary education.

Payroll Withholding Tables

We have discussed the rates that employers use in calculating the withholdings that must be made from employees' wages for income taxes, CPP (or QPP) contributions, and EI premiums. The CRA's website provides tables that show the amounts to deduct for weekly, bi-weekly (every two weeks), semi-monthly, and monthly pay periods.

Payroll Deductions Online Calculator (PDOC)

As mentioned earlier, the CRA provides an online tool employers can use to calculate the required deductions. Exhibit 11–6 shows a screenshot of the PDOC for an employee named Hanna West, who is paid a salary of $1,500 per week.

EXHIBIT 11–6 | The CRA's Payroll Deductions Online Calculator (PDOC)

Français

Government of Canada Gouvernement du Canada

Home → Canada Revenue Agency → Payroll Deductions Online Calculator

Payroll Deductions Online Calculator

- How to use PDOC to
  - Result screen information
  - FAQ
- Need help?
  - Contact Us

Salary calculation: Result

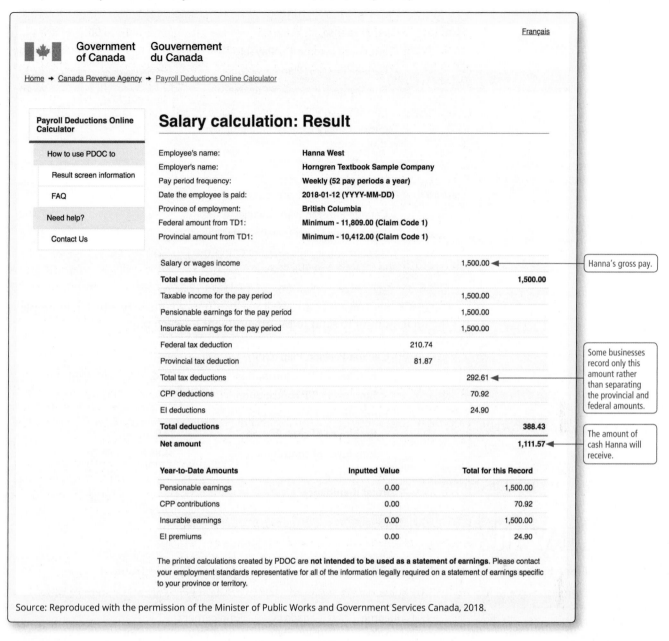

Employee's name:	**Hanna West**
Employer's name:	**Horngren Textbook Sample Company**
Pay period frequency:	**Weekly (52 pay periods a year)**
Date the employee is paid:	**2018-01-12 (YYYY-MM-DD)**
Province of employment:	**British Columbia**
Federal amount from TD1:	**Minimum - 11,809.00 (Claim Code 1)**
Provincial amount from TD1:	**Minimum - 10,412.00 (Claim Code 1)**

Salary or wages income		1,500.00 ← Hanna's gross pay.	
Total cash income			**1,500.00**
Taxable income for the pay period		1,500.00	
Pensionable earnings for the pay period		1,500.00	
Insurable earnings for the pay period		1,500.00	
Federal tax deduction	210.74		
Provincial tax deduction	81.87		
Total tax deductions		292.61 ← Some businesses record only this amount rather than separating the provincial and federal amounts.	
CPP deductions		70.92	
EI deductions		24.90	
Total deductions			**388.43**
Net amount			**1,111.57** ← The amount of cash Hanna will receive.

Year-to-Date Amounts	**Inputted Value**	**Total for this Record**
Pensionable earnings	0.00	1,500.00
CPP contributions	0.00	70.92
Insurable earnings	0.00	1,500.00
EI premiums	0.00	24.90

The printed calculations created by PDOC are **not intended to be used as a statement of earnings.** Please contact your employment standards representative for all of the information legally required on a statement of earnings specific to your province or territory.

Exhibit 11–7 shows the disbursement of Hanna's payroll costs by her employer.

EXHIBIT 11–7 | Disbursement of Hanna West's Payroll Costs by an Employer Using the PDOC (B.C.)

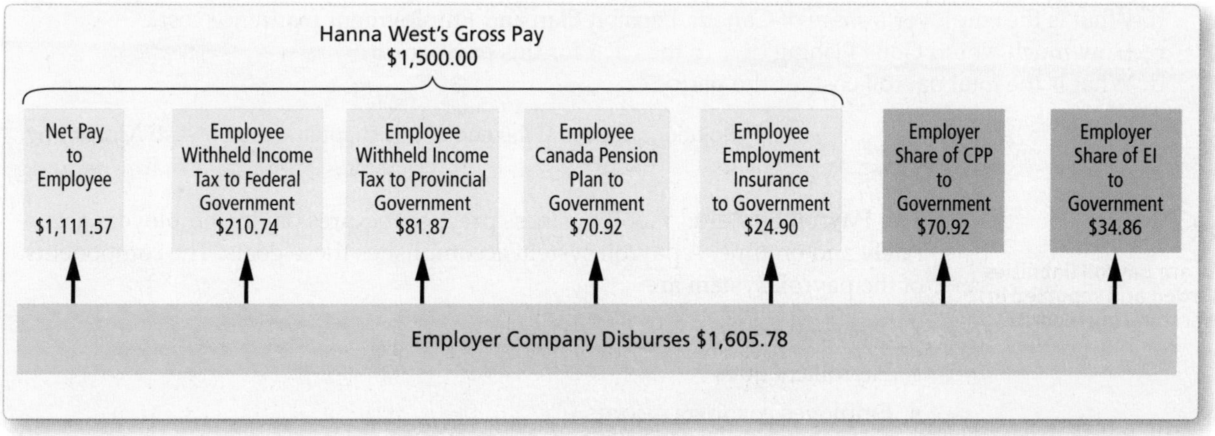

The journal entries to record this information would include:

Jan. 15	Salary Expense	1,500.00	
	Employee Income Tax Payable		292.61
	Canada Pension Plan Payable		70.92
	Employment Insurance Payable		24.90
	Salaries Payable		1,111.57
	To record salary expense and employee withholdings		

Jan. 15	Employee Benefits Expense	105.78	
	Canada Pension Plan Payable		70.92
	Employment Insurance Payable		34.86
	To record employer's share of CPP (1.0 × \$70.92) and EI (1.4 × \$24.90).		

The PDOC also provides an employer remittance summary which tells employers the total amount to send to the government for each pay:

Canada Pension Plan (CPP)		
Employee CPP contribution	\$70.92	
Employer CPP contribution	70.92	\$141.84
Employment Insurance (EI)		
Employee EI contribution	24.90	
Employer EI contribution	34.86	59.76
Tax Deductions		292.61
Total Remittance		\$494.21

Try It!

4. Gone Fishing records the following information for its sole employee, Charlie Trout:

	A	B	C	D	E	F	G	H
1	Hours	Pay Rate	Gross Pay	Income Tax Payable	Canada Pension Plan Payable	Employment Insurance Payable	Total Deductions	Net Pay
2	35	\$17.25		89.05	29.89	10.02		

a. What is the net pay for this employee?
b. What is the employer's share of Canada Pension Plan and Employment Insurance cost?
c. How much would Gone Fishing owe to the CRA for this pay period?
d. What is the total payroll cost for the period?

Solutions appear at the end of this chapter and on **MyLab Accounting**

LO 4

How are payroll liabilities recorded and reported in the accounting records?

The Payroll System Good business practice requires paying employees accurately and on time. A payroll system accomplishes these goals. The components of the payroll system are:

- A payroll register
- Payroll cheques
- Employee earnings records

Many accounting software packages have a payroll module that records the entries, creates the register, and prints the cheques and other payroll documents. There are also companies that specialize in providing payroll and human resource information services. Ceridian Canada Ltd. and ADP Canada Co. are examples of companies that provide payroll registers, cheques, earnings records, and other payroll documents.

Payroll Register

Each pay period the company organizes payroll data in a special journal called the *payroll register*. The payroll register is like a cash payments journal (see Chapter 7) and serves as a cheque register for recording payroll cheques.

Exhibit 11–8 (on the next page) is a payroll register for Leduc Petroleum. The payroll register has columns for each employee's gross pay, deductions, and net pay. To keep the journal entries more familiar looking to you, the general journal entries to record salary expense for the pay period are as follows:

Payroll liabilities are accrued liabilities. These liabilities are separate liability accounts because each liability is paid to a different entity.

2018			
Dec. 31	Office Salaries Expense	4,464.00	
	Sales Salaries Expense	9,190.00	
	Employee Income Tax Payable		2,858.90
	Canada Pension Plan Payable		402.70
	Employment Insurance Payable		235.12
	United Way Payable		155.00
	Salaries Payable		10,002.28
	To record payroll expenses for the pay period ended December 31, 2018.		

Owed to the government (Employee Income Tax Payable, Canada Pension Plan Payable, Employment Insurance Payable)

Owed to outside organizations (United Way Payable)

To the employees (Salaries Payable)

This next journal entry represents the liability for the employer's share of CPP and EI. Remember, the employer's share is 1.0 times the employee's share of CPP and 1.4 times the employee's share of EI.

2018			
Dec. 31	Employee Benefits Expense	731.87	
	Canada Pension Plan Payable		402.70
	Employment Insurance Payable		329.17
	To record the cost of employer's portion of payroll expenses for the pay period ended December 31, 2018.		

Employer CPP is same as employee amount.

Employer EI is 1.4 times the employee amount ($235.12 × 1.4).

Recording Cash Payments for Payroll

Companies record at least three cash disbursements: for payments of net pay to employees, for payments of payroll withholdings to the government, and for payments to third parties for employee benefits. Let's review them briefly for use with the payroll register in Exhibit 11–8.

Net Pay to Employees Reconciling the bank account can be time-consuming because of the large number of paycheques that may be outstanding. Some companies use one bank account strictly for payroll purposes. This helps to keep the payroll charges and outstanding cheques separate from the company's day-to-day business charges and cheques, making each account's reconciliation easier and reducing the chance for errors. The company would make the following entry in

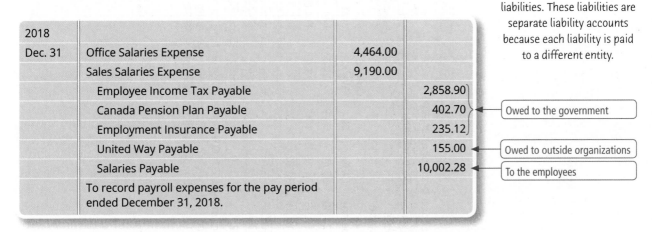

EXHIBIT 11–8 | Payroll Register for Leduc Petroleum

	A	B	C	D	E	F	G	H	I	J	K	L	M	N	O
1	Pay period ended December 31, 2018														
2			Gross Pay					Deductions				Net Pay		Account Debited	
3	Employee Name	Hours	Straight Time	Overtime	Total	Federal Income Tax	Prov. Income Tax (Alberta)	CPP	EI	United Way	Total	(*c* − *i*) Amount	Cheque No.	Office Salaries Expense	Sales Salaries Expense
4	Chen, W. L.*	40	620.00		620.00	56.40	24.80	30.69	10.29	2.00	124.18	495.82	1621	620.00	
5	Drumm, C. L.	44	600.00	90.00	690.00	51.50	15.55	34.16	11.45	2.00	114.66	575.34	1622		690.00
6	Elias, M.	41	640.00	24.00	664.00	53.11	18.91	32.87	11.02		115.91	548.09	1623	664.00	
15	Vokovich, E. A.**	40	1,360.00		1,360.00	196.40	93.90			15.00	305.30	1,054.70	1641		1,360.00
16	Total		12,940.00	714.00	13,654.00	1,966.18	892.72	402.70	235.12	155.00	3,651.72	10,002.28		4,464.00	9,190.00

*W. L. Chen earned gross pay of $620. His net pay was $495.82, paid with cheque number 1621. Chen is an office worker, so his salary is debited to Office Salaries Expense.

**E.A. Vokovich has exceeded maximum pensionable earnings of $55,900, so he has had the Canada Pension Plan maximum, $2,593.80, already deducted. Vokovich has also exceeded the maximum insurable Employment Insurance earnings of $51,700, so he has already had the maximum, $858.22, deducted.

January to record the cash payment (column L in Exhibit 11–8) for the December 31, 2018, weekly payroll if they were paying a payroll company or if they were transferring the funds into a separate bank account for payroll:

2019			
Jan. 4	Salaries Payable	10,002.28	
	Cash		10,002.28
	Cash payment for December 31, 2018, weekly payroll.		

Payroll Cheques Employees are paid by cheque or by electronic funds transfer (EFT). A *payroll cheque* has an attachment, or stub, that details the employee's gross pay, payroll deductions, and net pay. Employees paid by EFT must receive a statement of earnings with the same information on it. These amounts come from the payroll register. Exhibit 11–9 shows payroll cheque number 1622, issued to C. L. Drumm for net pay of $575.34 earned during the pay period ended December 31, 2018. To practise using payroll data, trace all amounts on the cheque attachment to the payroll register in Exhibit 11–8.

EXHIBIT 11–9 | Payroll Cheque

Leduc Petroleum
Payroll Account
Red Deer, Alberta

1622

January 4, 2019

Pay to the Order of C.L. Drumm $ 575.34

Five hundred and seventy five ------------------- 36/100 Dollars

The Bank of Nova Scotia
Red Deer
Alberta

Anna Figaro
Treasurer

⑆11190003⑆ 0787⑈ 50000454⑈

Pay			Deductions								
Straight Time	Over-time	Gross	Federal Income Tax	Prov. Income Tax	CPP	Employ-ment Ins.	United Way	Total	Net Pay	Cheque No.
600.00	90.00	690.00	51.50	15.55	34.16	11.45	2.00	114.66	575.34	1622

Payroll Withholdings to the Government and Other Organizations The employer must send income taxes withheld from employees' pay and the employee deductions and employer's share of CPP (or QPP) contributions and EI premiums to the Canada Revenue Agency (or the Quebec government in the case of QPP). The payment for a given month is due on or before the 15th day of the following month. In addition, the employer has to remit any withholdings for union dues, charitable donations, and the like; the payment would probably be made in the following month.

Assume that the summary of the payroll register at the end of the month included the following information for the entire month:

Federal income tax	$8,938.98
Province of Alberta income tax	$3,460.12
Employee CPP contributions	$2,047.72
Employee EI contributions	$1,232.14
United Way contributions	$ 620.00

Based on those amounts, the business would record payments to the CRA and the United Way for the month of December 2018 as follows:

Each payment that requires a separate cheque also requires a separate journal entry

2019			
Jan. 10	Employee Income Tax Payable	12,399.10	
	Canada Pension Plan Payable	4,095.44	
	Employment Insurance Payable	2,957.14	
	Cash		19,451.68
	To record payment to the CRA for December 2018 withholdings. CPP Payable = $2,047.72 + $2,047.72 EI Payable = $1,232.14 + (1.4 × $1,232.14)		
Jan. 10	United Way Payable	620.00	
	Cash		620.00
	To record payment to United Way for December 2018 withholdings.		

If the employer had deducted union dues or benefits payments from the employees, then they would be reported in the same manner as the United Way example. The deduction is accrued in a payable account (Employee Union Dues Payable, Employee Dental Benefits Payable, etc.) and then paid in the following month.

Other Liabilities and Remittances Sometimes the employer has additional payments that it makes for employees, such as benefits paid by the employer. If the company has a dental benefits plan for its employees for which it pays the premiums, it would record the cost each month and pay the premium when it is due.

2018			
Dec. 31	Employee Dental Benefits Expense	1,092	
	Employee Benefits Payable		1,092
	To record employee benefits payable by employer.		

If there were a quarterly remittance to the benefits provider, it would look like this:

2019			
Feb. 1	Employee Benefits Payable	3,276	
	Cash		3,276
	To record payment to Mega Dental for employee benefits for October to December.		

There would also be workers' compensation, which is paid completely by the employer. It also needs to be accrued and reconciled and paid at a later date.

2018			
Dec. 31	Workers' Compensation Expense	332	
	Workers' Compensation Payable		332
	To record workers' compensation premiums payable by employer.		

Small businesses may pay this annually, so the remittance for one year of premiums could look like this:

2019			
Apr. 15	Workers' Compensation Payable	3,712	
	Cash		3,712
	To record payment for workers' compensation premium accrued in last calendar year.		

Larger businesses would remit payments quarterly or monthly.

Earnings Record

The employer must file Summary of Remuneration Paid returns with the CRA on a calendar-year basis and must provide the employee with a Statement of Remuneration Paid, Form T4, by February 28 of the following year. Therefore, employers maintain an earnings record for each employee. (These earnings records are also used for EI claims.) Exhibit 11–10 (on the next page) is a six-week excerpt from the earnings record of employee Jason C. Jenkins.

The employee earnings record is not a journal or a ledger. It is an accounting tool—like the worksheet—that the employer uses to prepare payroll withholdings reports. The information provided on the employee earnings record with respect to year-to-date earnings also indicates when an employee has earned $55,900, the point at which the employer should stop withholding CPP contributions. (Unlike the employee, the employer may not obtain a refund for overpayment of CPP.) The same is true for EI deductions: the employer stops withholding EI contributions after the employee has earned $51,700. There is no maximum income tax deduction.

Exhibit 11–11 (found on page 629) is the Statement of Remuneration Paid, Form T4, for employee Jason C. Jenkins. The employer prepares this form for each employee, as well as a form called a T4 Summary—Summary of Remuneration Paid, which summarizes the information on all the T4s issued by the employer for that year. The employer sends the T4 Summary and one copy of each T4 to the CRA by February 28 each year. The CRA uses the documents to ensure that the employer has correctly paid to the government all amounts withheld on its behalf from employees, together with the employer's share.

The employee gets two copies of the T4; one copy must be filed with the employee's income tax return, while the second copy is for the employee's records.

The CRA matches the income on the T4 filed by the employer against the income reported on the employee's income tax return, filed by the employee, to ensure that the employee properly reported his or her income from employment.

Employers and employees can use the internet to file T4 information for reporting as well as to file tax information.

EXHIBIT 11–10 | Employee Earnings Record for 2018

Employee Name and Address:
Jenkins, Jason C.
XX Camousen Crescent
Victoria, BC

Social Insurance No.: 111 111 111
Marital Status: Married
Net Claims Code: 4
Pay Rate: $700 per week; overtime $26.25 per hour
Job Title: Web Development Support

	A	B	C	D	E	F	G	H	I	J	K	L	M	N
1			Gross Pay						Deductions				Net Pay	
2	Week Ended	Hours	Straight Time	Overtime	Total	To Date	Federal Income Tax	Province of BC Income Tax	CPP	EI	United Way	Total	Amount	Cheque No.
3	Jan. 4	40	700.00		700.00	700.00	47.60	18.16	31.32	11.62	2.00	110.70	589.30	403
50	Dec. 3	40	700.00		700.00	35,437.50	47.60	18.16	31.32	11.62	2.00	110.70	589.30	1525
51	Dec. 10	40	700.00		700.00	36,137.50	47.60	18.16	31.32	11.62	2.00	110.70	589.30	1548
52	Dec. 17	44	700.00	105.00	805.00	36,942.50	62.28	25.27	36.52	13.36	2.00	139.43	665.57	1574
53	Dec. 24	48	700.00	210.00	910.00	37,852.50	81.48	32.99	41.71	15.11	2.00	173.29	736.71	1598
54	Dec. 31	46	700.00	157.50	857.50	38,710.00	70.47	29.13	39.11	14.24	2.00	154.95	702.55	1632
55	Total		36,400.00	2,310.00	38,710.00	38,710.00	2,798.16	1,082.28	1,742.90	642.59	104.00	6,369.93	32,340.07	

EXHIBIT 11–11 | Employee Statement of Remuneration Paid (Form T4)

Employer's name – Nom de l'employeur

Example Company

Canada Revenue Agency | Agence du revenu du Canada

Year / Année: 2018

T4
Statement of Remuneration Paid
État de la rémunération payée

Box	Description	Amount
54	Employer's account number / Numéro de compte de l'employeur	12345-6789
12	Social insurance number / Numéro d'assurance sociale	111-111-111
28	Exempt – Exemption: CPP/QPP, EI, PPIP / RPC/RRQ, AE, RPAP	
10	Province of employment / Province d'emploi	BC
29	Employment code / Code d'emploi	
14	Employment income – line 101 / Revenus d'emploi – ligne 101	38710 00
22	Income tax deducted – line 437 / Impôt sur le revenu retenu – ligne 437	3880 44
16	Employee's CPP contributions – line 308 / Cotisations de l'employé au RPC – ligne 308	1742 90
24	EI insurable earnings / Gains assurables d'AE	38710 00
17	Employee's QPP contributions – line 308 / Cotisations de l'employé au RRQ – ligne 308	
26	CPP/QPP pensionable earnings / Gains ouvrant droit à pension – RPC/RRQ	38710 00
18	Employee's EI premiums – line 312 / Cotisations de l'employé à l'AE – ligne 312	642 59
44	Union dues – line 212 / Cotisations syndicales – ligne 212	
20	RPP contributions – line 207 / Cotisations à un RPA – ligne 207	
46	Charitable donations – line 349 / Dons de bienfaisance – ligne 349	104 00
52	Pension adjustment – line 206 / Facteur d'équivalence – ligne 206	
50	RPP or DPSP registration number / N° d'agrément d'un RPA ou d'un RPDB	
55	Employee's PPIP premiums – see over / Cotisations de l'employé au RPAP – voir au verso	
56	PPIP insurable earnings / Gains assurables du RPAP	

Employee's name and address – Nom et adresse de l'employé

Last name (in capital letters) – Nom de famille (en lettres moulées)	First name – Prénom	Initial – Initiale
JENKINS	Jason	C

XX Camousen Crescent
Victoria, BC

Other information (see over) / Autres renseignements (voir au verso)

Box – Case	Amount – Montant	Box – Case	Amount – Montant	Box – Case	Amount – Montant

Protected B when completed / Protégé B une fois rempli

T4 (14)

Source: Reproduced with the permission of the Minister of Public Works and Government Services Canada, 2018.

Independent Contractors

A company's payments to people who are not employees—outsiders called **independent contractors**—are *not* company payroll expenses. Consider two technical writers, Elena and Scott. Elena is the company's technical writer; Scott is a contractor hired to help Elena during the busy season. Elena is an employee of the company, and her compensation is a debit to Salaries Expense. The company must deduct income taxes, CPP, and EI from her paycheque and remit the employer port of CPP and EI for her. Scott, however, performs writing services for many clients, and the company debits Contract Labour Expense when it pays the invoice he presents for the work completed. Any payment for services performed by a person outside the company is recorded with a debit to an expense account other than payroll.

The CRA provides guidance for employers to determine if there is a *contract of service* (employer-employee relationship) or a *contract for service* (business relationship).

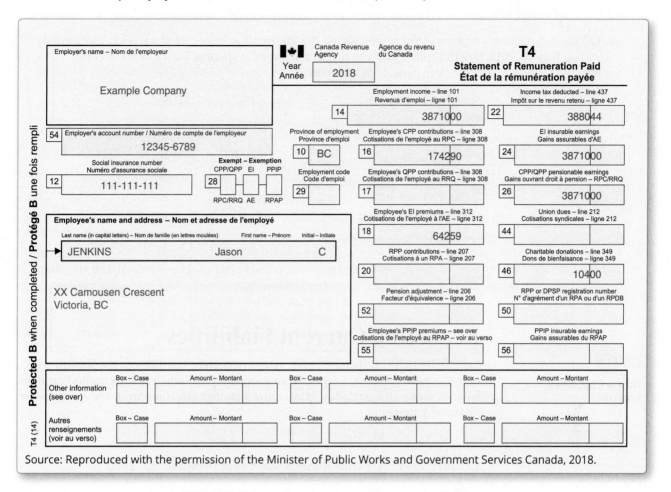

Try It!

5. The payroll register for Quesnel Quarries showed the information below for the weekly pay period ending July 10, 2018. Use this information to record the payroll expenses for the week and the employer's portion of payroll expenses for the week.

Straight-time wages	$21,840
Overtime wages	2,500
Deductions	
Federal income tax	1,850
Provincial income tax	980
Canada Pension Plan	1,200
Employment Insurance	445
Union Dues	420

Solutions appear at the end of this chapter and on **MyLab Accounting**

Reporting Current Liabilities

LO 5

How are liabilities reported?

Exhibit 11–12 illustrates the presentation of current liabilities in the liabilities section of a balance sheet. Large corporations may include less information on their balance sheet and put additional, more detailed information in the notes to the financial statements.

EXHIBIT 11–12 | Partial Balance Sheet as at December 31, 2020

SASHY'S FLOWERS Balance Sheet (partial) December 31, 2020		
Liabilities		
Current liabilities		
Accounts payable	$97,000	
Salaries payable	61,000	
Estimated warranty payable	21,250	
Current portion of long-term debt	10,000	
GST payable	19,447	
Interest payable	661	
Employee income tax payable	8,100	
Canada Pension Plan payable	2,970	
Employment Insurance payable	1,120	
Contingent liability (Note 17)	25,000	
Other current liabilities	1,500	
Total current liabilities		$248,048
Long-term liabilities		
Note payable	90,000	
Less: Current portion of long-term debt	10,000	
Total long-term liabilities		80,000
Total liabilities		$328,048

Try It!

6. From the following information, determine whether the accounts are current or long-term liabilities. Show how each of the current liabilities would be presented on the balance sheet at December 31, 2019, assuming a separate line on the balance sheet for each item. Perform any calculations that may be required. Calculate interest based on the days in a 365-day year and round all numbers to the nearest whole dollar for balance sheet presentation.
   a. A one-year, 3 percent note payable for $3,000 was issued on November 3, 2019.
   b. A $10,000, 180-day, 5 percent bank loan was arranged and effective on September 17, 2019.
   c. A $10,000, two-year, 3 percent bank loan was arranged and effective on September 17, 2019. The loan must be repaid in full on September 17, 2021.
   d. A $10,000, two-year, 5 percent bank loan was arranged and effective on January 2, 2019. Half of the loan must be repaid on January 2, 2020, and the remainder repaid on January 2, 2021.
   e. Of the $5,000 unearned subscription revenue that was recorded during the year, $4,200 was earned by December 31.
   f. The company expects to pay future warranty costs of 3 percent of sales for the $350,000 of goods sold during 2019.

Solutions appear at the end of this chapter and on **MyLab Accounting**

EXHIBIT 11–13 | The Impact of IFRS on Current Liabilities

LO 6
How does IFRS affect current liabilities?

ASPE	IFRS
Where the Canadian standard is substantially the same as the international standard, we say that the standards are *converged*. This is the case with current liabilities. For example, both IFRS and ASPE require that liabilities are carried at their fair value.	
Accounts payable and *accrued liabilities* are the usual terms used.	*Trade payables* and *provisions* are the more common terms.
A contingent liability must be *likely* to occur in order to be recognized.	A contingent liability has a slightly lower standard for when it should be recognized; it must be *probable* that it will occur.

The following illustration highlights the differences in interpretation:

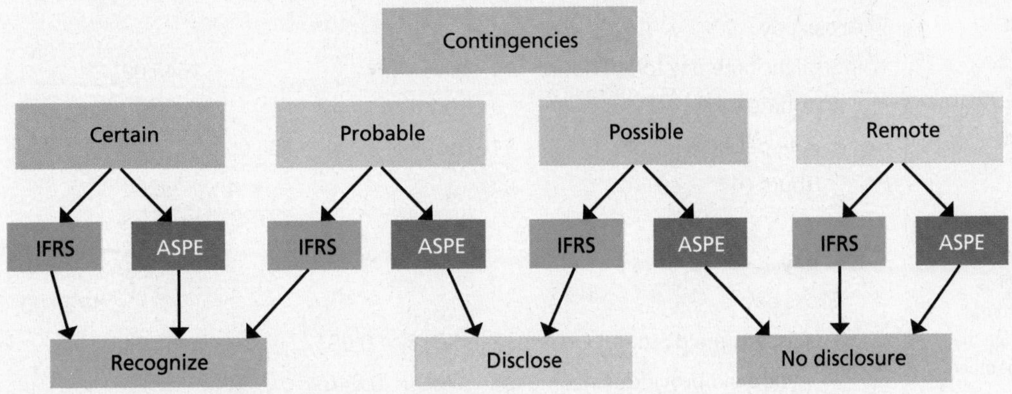

Summary Problem for Your Review

Best Threads, a clothing store in New Brunswick, employs one salesperson, Sheila Kingsley. Her straight-time pay is $640 per week. She earns time and a half for hours worked in excess of 40 per week. For Kingsley's wage rate and net claim code on her Personal Tax Credits Return (TD1), the federal income tax withholding rate is approximately 9 percent, and the provincial rate is 4.6 percent. CPP is 4.95 percent on income, and EI premiums are 1.66 percent. In addition, Best Threads pays Kingsley's Blue Cross supplemental health insurance premiums of $31.42 a month and dental insurance premiums of $18.50 a month.

During the week ended March 31, 2018, Kingsley worked 44 hours.

Required

1. Compute Kingsley's gross pay and net pay for the week.
2. Record the following payroll entries that Best Threads would make:

Mar. 31	Sales salary expense for Kingsley's wages including overtime pay (ignore the basic CPP exemption). Wages Payable is the account used for the accrued gross pay.
31	Cost of employer's share of Kingsley's withholdings (ignore the basic CPP exemption)
31	Expense for medical and dental benefits
Apr. 6	Payment of cash to Kingsley
10	Payment Best Threads must make to the CRA for the March 31 payroll
25	Payment of medical and dental benefits from the March 31 payroll

2. How much total payroll expense did Best Threads incur for the week?
3. What payroll-related accounts and amounts would appear on the balance sheet at March 31, 2018?

SOLUTION

Requirement 1

To compute gross pay, first separate hours worked into straight-time and overtime hours. Then multiply each by the appropriate hourly pay rate.

For this example, use the rates provided. Normally a business would compute the amount of each withholding by entering the information in the PDOC or other payroll software.

Gross pay			
Straight-time pay for 40 hours		$640.00	
Overtime pay			
Rate per hour ($640 ÷ 40 = $16/hour × 1.5)	$24.00		
Hours (44 − 40)	× 4	96.00	
		$736.00	
Net pay			
Gross pay			$736.00
Less: Withheld federal income tax ($736 × 0.09)		$ 66.24	
Withheld provincial income tax ($736 × 0.046)		33.86	
Withheld CPP ($736 × 0.0495)		36.43	
Withheld EI ($736 × 0.0166)		12.22	148.75
Net pay			$587.25

Gross pay − Total withholdings = Net pay

Requirement 2

This journal entry uses the gross pay, withholdings, and net pay amounts calculated in Requirement 1.

Mar. 31	Sales Salary Expense	736.00	
	Employee Income Tax Payable		100.10
	Canada Pension Plan Payable		36.43
	Employment Insurance Payable		12.22
	Wages Payable		587.25
	To record expense for S. Kingsley's wages.		
Mar. 31	Employee Benefits Expense	53.54	
	Canada Pension Plan Payable		36.43
	Employment Insurance Payable		17.11
	To record cost of employer's portion of S. Kingsley's wages. CPP is \$36.43 (\$36.43 × 1). EI is \$17.11 (\$12.22 × 1.4).		
Mar. 31	Medical and Dental Expense	49.92	
	Employee Benefits Payable		49.92
	To record expense of benefits (\$31.42 + \$18.50).		
Apr. 6	Wages Payable	587.25	
	Cash		587.25
	To record payment of wages to S. Kingsley.		
Apr. 10	Employee Income Tax Payable	100.10	
	Canada Pension Plan Payable	72.86	
	Employment Insurance Payable	29.33	
	Cash		202.29
	To record payment to the CRA. CPP = \$36.43 + \$36.43; EI = \$12.22 + \$17.11		
Apr. 25	Employee Benefits Payable	49.92	
	Cash		49.92
	To record payment of monthly benefits.		

Add federal and provincial taxes (\$66.24+\$33.86) to show one amount for Employee Income Tax Payable.

"Wages Payable" is the amount of net pay.

Remember that the employer's EI expense is 1.4 times the employee's EI withholding.

This journal entry issues the paycheque or sends the funds by EFT to the employee's bank account. Notice that the name of the payable account matches the account used in the first journal entry.

Employers pay to the CRA:

- Federal and provincial taxes withheld from the employee
- EI premiums withheld from employee + paid by employer
- CPP (or QPP) withholdings from employee + paid by employer

Requirement 3

Best Threads incurred *total payroll expense* of \$836.46 (gross salary of \$736.00 + employer's cost of CPP of \$36.43 + employer's cost of EI of \$17.11 + benefits of \$49.92).

Total payroll expense = Gross salary + EI expense + CPP expense + benefits

Requirement 4

The accounts and amounts that would appear on the March 31, 2018, balance sheet are as follows:

Employee Income Tax Payable	\$100.10
Canada Pension Plan Payable	72.86
Employment Insurance Payable	29.33
Employee Benefits Payable	49.92
Wages Payable	587.25

Summary

Learning Objectives

(1) Account for current liabilities of a known amount **Pg. 604**

What are current liabilities, and how do we account for them?

- Current liabilities may be divided into those of *known amount* and those that must be *estimated*. Trade accounts payable, short-term notes payable, interest payable, GST payable, HST payable, PST payable, employee benefits payable, and unearned revenues are current liabilities of known amount.

(2) Account for current liabilities that must be estimated **Pg. 612**

Why would we estimate liabilities, and how do we account for them?

- Current liabilities that must be estimated include warranties payable, vacation pay, and the corporation's income tax payable.
- *Contingent liabilities* are not actual liabilities but potential liabilities that may arise in the future.
- Contingent liabilities, like current liabilities, may be of known amounts or indefinite amounts. The likelihood of the contingency and the ability to estimate the amount determine whether the contingency is recorded as a liability, recorded in the notes to the financial statements, or not recorded at all.

(3) Compute payroll amounts **Pg. 617**

How are payroll amounts calculated?

- *Payroll* accounting handles the expenses and liabilities arising from compensating employees.
- Employers must withhold federal and provincial income taxes, CPP (or QPP) contributions, and EI premiums from employees' pay and send these *withholdings* together with the employer's share of the latter two to the appropriate government agency.
- Many employers allow their employees to pay for insurance and union dues and to make gifts to charities through payroll deductions.
- An employee's net pay is the gross pay less all withholdings and optional deductions.

(4) Record basic payroll transactions **Pg. 622**

How are payroll liabilities recorded and reported in the accounting records?

- An *employer's* payroll expenses include the employer's share of CPP (or QPP) contributions and EI premiums; employers also pay provincial health care taxes in those provinces that levy them as well as workers' compensation.
- A basic *payroll system* consists of a payroll register, a payroll bank account, payroll cheques or EFTs, and an earnings record for each employee.

(5) Report current liabilities on the balance sheet **Pg. 630**

How are liabilities reported?

- The company reports on the balance sheet all current liabilities that it owes: current liabilities of known amount, including payroll liabilities, and current liabilities that must be estimated.

(6) Describe the impact of IFRS on current liabilities **Pg. 631**

How does IFRS affect current liabilities?

- Under IFRS, the usual terms are *trade payables* and *provisions* for *accounts payable* and *accrued liabilities*, but these terms are optional for Canadian companies reporting under ASPE.

Key Terms for the chapter are shown next and are in the **Glossary** at the back of the book. **Similar Terms** are shown after **Key Terms**.

KEY TERMS

Accrued expense An expense that has been incurred but not yet paid in cash; also called an *accrued liability (p. 610).*

Accrued liability Another name for an *accrued expense (p. 610).*

Canada (or Quebec) Pension Plan (CPP or QPP) All employees and self-employed persons in Canada (except in Quebec, where the pension plan is the Quebec Pension Plan) between 18 and 70 years of age are required to contribute to the Canada Pension Plan administered by the Government of Canada *(p. 619).*

Contingent liability A potential liability from a past event that depends on an uncertain future event not within the business's control *(p. 615)*.

Current portion of long-term debt The amount of the principal that is payable within one year *(p. 609)*.

Employee compensation Payroll, a major expense of many businesses *(p. 617)*.

Employment Insurance (EI) Most employees and employers in Canada must contribute to the Employment Insurance fund, which provides assistance to unemployed workers *(p. 619)*.

End-user tax A consumption tax that is only paid by the final consumer *(p. 609)*.

Exempt supplies Goods and services that are not required to have GST or HST charged on them *(p. 607)*.

Gross pay Total amount of salary, wages, commissions, or any other employee compensation before taxes and other deductions are taken out *(p. 618)*.

Independent contractors Individuals who do work for a business but are not employees. They invoice the business for their contracted work *(p. 629)*.

Input tax credit (ITC) The sales tax that will be refunded by the government *(p. 607)*.

Line of credit Similar to a bank loan, it is negotiated once then drawn upon when needed. Interest is paid monthly only on the amount of the line of credit actually used *(p. 605)*.

Net pay Gross pay minus all deductions; the amount of employee compensation that the employee actually takes home *(p. 618)*.

Overtime For additional hours above the standard, employees are paid at a higher rate *(p. 617)*.

Payroll Employee compensation, a major expense of many businesses *(p. 617)*.

Payroll Deductions Online Calculator (PDOC) An online tool provided by the Canada Revenue Agency for calculating federal and provincial payroll deductions for all provinces (except Quebec) and territories *(p. 619)*.

Pledged as security A phrase that indicates an asset is held as collateral for a loan. In other words, if the loan is not paid, the asset will be taken as payment for the outstanding debt *(p. 606)*.

Recoverable In terms of accounting for taxes, this term means that the tax is refunded by the government *(p. 607)*.

Registered retirement savings plan (RRSP) A federal government plan where contributions towards retirement savings have special tax advantages. *(p. 620)*.

Registrant A business or individual that is registered with the government to collect and remit sales taxes *(p. 607)*.

Short-term note payable A note payable that is due within one year, a common form of financing *(p. 604)*.

Straight time A set period during which the base rate is paid to an employee *(p. 617)*.

Taxable supplies Goods and services that, when sold, have GST or HST charged on them *(p. 607)*.

Warranty When a business guarantees its products or services against defects *(p. 612)*.

Withheld Deducted from pay and kept by the employer to be remitted to another party *(p. 618)*.

Workers' compensation A provincially administered plan that is funded by contributions by employers and that provides financial support for workers injured on the job *(p. 620)*.

Zero-rated supplies Goods and services that have a GST or HST rate of zero percent *(p. 607)*.

SIMILAR TERMS

Accounts payable	Trade payables
Accrued expense	Accrued liability; Provisions
Accrued liabilities	Provisions; Accrued expenses
CPP	Canada Pension Plan
CRA	Canada Revenue Agency
Deduction	Withholding
EI	Employment Insurance
GST	Goods and services tax
HST	Harmonized sales tax
ITC	Input tax credit
Net pay	Take-home pay
Payroll register	Payroll journal; Payroll record
PDOC	Payroll Deductions Online Calculator
PST	Provincial sales tax
QPP	Quebec Pension Plan
QST	Quebec (provincial) sales tax
RRSP	Registered retirement savings plan
T4	Statement of Remuneration Paid
TD1	Personal Tax Credit Return
Unearned revenues	Deferred revenues; Revenues collected in advance; Customer prepayments

SELF-STUDY QUESTIONS

Test your understanding of the chapter by marking the correct answer for each of the following questions:

1. A $10,000, 9 percent, one-year note payable was issued on July 31. The balance sheet at December 31 will report interest payable of (*p. 604*)
   a. $0 because the interest is not due yet
   b. $522.74
   c. $375
   d. $900
2. Your company sells $180,000 (sales price) of goods and collects 5 percent GST. What current liability does the sale create? (*p. 606*)
   a. GST payable of $9,000
   b. Sales revenue of $189,000
   c. Unearned revenue of $9,000
   d. GST payable of $171,000
3. Jade Larson Antiques owes $20,000 on a truck purchased for use in the business. Assume the company makes timely principal payments of $5,000 each year at December 31 plus interest at 8 percent. Which of the following is true? (*p. 609*)
   a. After the first payment is made, the company owes $15,000 plus three years' interest.
   b. After the first payment, $15,000 would be shown as a long-term liability.
   c. After the first payment is made, $5,000 would be shown as the current portion due on the long-term note.
   d. Just before the last payment is made, $5,000 will appear as a long-term liability on the balance sheet.
4. Which of the following liabilities creates no expense accrual for the company? (*p. 610*)
   a. Interest
   b. Sales tax
   c. Employment Insurance
   d. Warranty
5. Suppose Super Tires estimates that warranty costs will equal 1 percent of tire sales. Assume that November tire sales totalled $900,000, and the company's outlay in replacement tires and cash to satisfy warranty claims was $7,400. How much warranty expense should the November income statement report? (*p. 612*)
   a. $1,600
   b. $7,400
   c. $9,000
   d. $16,400
6. A contingent liability that is likely and can be reasonably estimated should be (*p. 615*)
   a. Accrued as an expense and reported as a liability
   b. Only disclosed in a note to the financial statements
   c. Either disclosed in a note or accrued with a journal entry depending on the amount
   d. Ignored until the liability materializes
7. Nouvou Diet Systems Company is a defendant in a lawsuit that claims damages of $55,000. On the balance sheet date, it appears unlikely that the court will render a judgment against the company. How should Nouvou Diet Systems Company report this event in its financial statements? (*p. 615*)
   a. Omit mention because no judgment has been rendered
   b. Disclose the contingent liability in a note
   c. Report the loss on the income statement and the liability on the balance sheet
   d. Do both b and c
8. Darcy Renick's weekly pay for 40 hours is $600 plus time and a half for overtime. The federal tax rate, based on her income level and deductions, is 10.5 percent, the provincial rate is 8.8 percent, the CPP rate is 4.95 percent on her weekly earnings, and the EI rate is 1.88 percent on her weekly earnings. What is Darcy's take-home pay for a week in which she works 50 hours? (*p. 617*)
   a. $554.05
   b. $581.74
   c. $609.42
   d. $660.65
9. Which of the following represents a cost to the employer? (*p. 620*)
   a. Withheld income tax
   b. Canada Pension Plan
   c. Employment Insurance
   d. Both b and c
10. Which of the following items is reported as a current liability on the balance sheet? (*p. 630*)
    a. Short-term notes payable
    b. Estimated warranties
    c. Payroll withholdings
    d. All of the above

Answers to Self-Study Questions

1. c $10,000 × 0.09 × 5/12 = $375 2. a 3. c 4. b 5. c $900,000 × 0.01 = $9,000 6. a 7. b 8. c Overtime pay: $600 ÷ 40 = $15; $15 × 1.5 = $22.50 per hour; $22.50 per hour × 10 hours = $225; Gross pay: $600 + $225 = $825; Deductions = ($825 × 0.105) + ($825 × 0.088) + ($825 × 0.0495) + ($825 × 0.0188) = $86.63 + $72.60 + $40.84 + $15.51 = $215.58; Take-home pay: $825.00 − $215.58 = $609.42 9. d 10. d

Assignment Material

MyLab Accounting Make the grade with MyLab Accounting: The Starters, Exercises, and Problems can be found on MyLab. You can practise them as often as you want, and most feature step-by-step guided instructions to help you find the right answer.

QUESTIONS

1. What distinguishes a current liability from a long-term liability?
2. Explain how GST that is paid by consumers is a liability of the store that sold the merchandise. To whom is GST paid?
3. What is another name for "GST paid on purchases"?
4. A company purchases a machine by signing a $50,000, 4 percent, one-year note payable on June 30. Interest is to be paid at maturity. What two current liabilities related to this purchase does the company report on its December 31 balance sheet? What is the amount of each current liability?
5. Kalyaniwalla Planners has a $5,000 note payable that is paid in $1,000 installments over five years. How would the portion that must be paid within the next year be reported on the balance sheet? And the balance?
6. Why is it important for a business to separate the current portion of long-term debt from the long-term debt?
7. Why is an accrued expense a liability?
8. Describe the similarities and differences between an account payable and a short-term note payable.
9. At the beginning of the school term, what type of account is the tuition that your college or university collects from students? What type of account is the tuition at the end of the school term?
10. Why is a customer deposit a liability? Give an example.
11. Murray Company warrants its products against defects for two years from date of sale. During the current year, the company made sales of $1,000,000. Management estimated warranty costs on those sales would total $50,000 over the two-year warranty period. Ultimately, the company paid $35,000 cash on warranties. What is the company's warranty expense for the year? What accounting principle or objective governs this answer?
12. What distinguishes a contingent liability from other liabilities?
13. What accounting concept supports accruing contingent losses but not recording contingent gains until they are realized?
14. Why is payroll expense relatively more important to a service business such as a public accounting firm than it is to a merchandisers company such as Canadian Tire?
15. What determines the amount of income tax that is withheld from employee paycheques?
16. Identify three required deductions from employee paycheques.
17. Identify the employee benefit expenses an employer pays.
18. How much EI has been withheld from the pay of an employee who has earned $56,288 during 2018? What is the employer's EI expense for this employee?
19. Why do some companies use a special payroll bank account?
20. Under IFRS, what is the standard that must be met to report a contingent liability? Is it a higher or lower standard than under ASPE?

STARTERS

S11–1 On July 31, 2019, Mission Co. purchased $32,000 of inventory on a one-year, 6 percent note payable. Journalize the company's (a) accrual of interest expense on December 31, 2019, and (b) payment of the note plus interest on July 31, 2020.

(1) Accounting for a note payable
b. Credit Cash for $33,920

S11–2 Refer to the data in S11–1. Show what Mission Co. reports for the note payable and related interest payable on its balance sheet at December 31, 2019, and on its income statement for the year ended on that date.

(1) Reporting a short-term note payable and the related interest
Interest Expense, $800

S11–3 On July 10, Keller Company, a business located in Alberta, purchased $15,000 of inventory for resale on account. On July 25, Keller recorded the sale of that merchandise on account for $20,000 plus tax. On August 10, Keller remitted GST to the Receiver General. They had no other sales or input tax credits. Journalize all three transactions.

(1) Recording GST

(1) Current portion of long-term debt

S11–4 On January 1, The Kraft-Kwon Group purchased $280,000 of equipment with a long-term note payable. The debt is payable in annual instalments of $56,000 due on December 31 of each year. At the date of purchase, how will The Kraft-Kwon Group report the note payable?

(1) Recording unearned revenue

S11–5 On July 1, *Owl* magazine collected cash of $5,000 for annual subscriptions (12 issues per year) starting on August 1. Journalize the transaction to record the collection of cash on July 1 and the transaction required at December 31, the magazine's year end, assuming no revenue has been recorded so far. (Round the adjustment to the nearest whole dollar.)

(1) Accounting for a note payable

May 31 interest, $600

S11–6 On December 31, 2019, Jabot purchased $16,000 of equipment on a one-year, 9 percent note payable. Journalize the company's purchase of equipment, the accrual of interest expense on May 31, 2020 (its fiscal year end), and the payment of the note plus interest on December 31, 2020.

(2) Warranty journal entries

Balance, $1,570

S11–7 Central Yard Equipment offers warranties on all its lawn mowers. It estimates warranty expense at 1.4 percent of sales. At the beginning of 2019, the Estimated Warranty Payable account had a credit balance of $2,200. During the year, Central Yard Equipment had $580,000 of sales and had to pay out $8,750 in warranty payments for repairs.

1. Prepare the required journal entries to record warranty expense and payments. Use December 31 for the journal entry date.
2. What is the balance of the warranty liability at the end of 2019? Indicate whether the balance is a debit or a credit.

(2) Accounting for warranty expense and warranty payable

2. Estimated Warranty Payable bal., $2,000

S11–8 Snow Wayfarers guarantees its snowmobiles for three years. Company experience indicates that warranty costs will be 2 percent of sales.

Assume that a Snow Wayfarers dealer made sales totalling $600,000 during 2020, its first year of operations. The company received cash for 30 percent of the sales and notes receivable for the remainder. Warranty payments totalled $10,000 during 2020.

1. Record the sales, warranty expense, and warranty payments for Snow Wayfarers.
2. Post to the Estimated Warranty Payable T-account. At the end of 2020, what is the Estimated Warranty Payable balance for Snow Wayfarers?

(2) Reporting warranties in the financial statements

S11–9 Refer to the data given in S11–8.

What amount of warranty expense will Snow Wayfarers report during 2020? Does the warranty expense for the year equal the year's cash payments for warranties? Which accounting principle or objective addresses this situation?

(2) Recording vacation accrual

$660

S11–10 Asjid and Associates has nine employees. Six employees earn vacation at a rate of 4 percent per pay. Asjid pays each of these employees a weekly salary of $1,250 for a five-day workweek. The remaining three employees are managers who earn $2,000 per week and accrue vacation at a rate of 6 percent. Journalize the entry for the vacation accrual for the business for one pay period—the week ended January 10, 2020.

(2) Interpreting an actual company's contingent liabilities

S11–11 Bombardier Inc., the Canadian aircraft manufacturer, included the following note (adapted) in its 2017 annual report:

> **Notes to the Consolidated Financial Statements**
>
> *39 b) (in Part): Commitments and Contingencies*
>
> In connection with the signing of firm orders for the sale of new aircraft, the Corporation enters into specified-price trade-in commitments with certain customers. These commitments give customers the right to trade-in their pre-owned aircraft as partial payment for the new aircraft purchased.

1. Why are these *contingent* (versus real) liabilities?
2. How can a contingent liability become a real liability for Bombardier?

S11–12 Suppose you work for an accounting firm all year and earn a monthly salary of $4,000. There is no overtime pay. Your withheld deductions are 20 percent of gross pay. In addition to payroll deductions, you choose to contribute 4 percent monthly to your pension plan. Your employer also deducts $60 monthly for your payment of the health insurance premium.

Compute your net pay for November.

(3) Computing payroll amounts

Net pay, $2,980

S11–13 Mike Klyn is paid $840 for a 40-hour workweek and time and a half for hours worked above 40.

1. Compute Klyn's gross pay for working 50 hours during the first week of February.
2. Klyn is single, and his income tax withholding is 20 percent of total pay. His only payroll deductions are taxes withheld, CPP of 4.95 percent, and EI of 1.66 percent. Compute Klyn's net pay for the week.

(3) Computing an employee's total pay

2. Net pay, $847.66

S11–14 Return to the Mike Klyn payroll situation in S11–13. Klyn's employer, Jones Ski Corp., pays all the standard payroll expenses plus benefits for employee pensions (5 percent of gross pay), BC health insurance ($15 per employee per week), and disability insurance ($2 per employee per week). Assume February has four pay periods.

Compute Jones Ski Corp.'s total expense of employing Mike Klyn for the 50 hours that he worked during the first week of February. Show amounts to the nearest cent.

(3) Computing the payroll expense of an employer

Total expense, $1,313.76

S11–15 The PDOC for Ishant Sharma shows the following information:

Salary income			$2,000.00
Federal tax deduction	212.26		
Provincial tax deduction	137.38		
Total tax deductions		349.64	
CPP deductions		91.78	
EI deductions		37.60	
Total deductions			479.02
Net amount			$1,520.98

Prepare the journal entries to record the accrual of this payroll and the related employer's liability on June 30. No explanations are required.

(3) Payroll accruals

Employer EI expense, $52.64

S11–16 After solving S11–13 and S11–14, journalize for Jones Ski Corp. the following expenses related to the employment of Mike Klyn on February 7:

a. Salary expense with payment to the employee

b. Benefits

c. Employer payroll expenses

Round all amounts to the nearest cent.

(4) Making payroll entries

a. Salary Expense, $1,155

S11–17 After solving S11–13, S11–14, and S11–16, journalize for Jones Ski Corp. the remittance of this payroll to the CRA on March 15 (assuming that there was no additional payroll paid in February).

(4) Making payroll entries

S11–18 Refer to the payroll information in S11–13, S11–14, and S11–16.

1. How much was the company's total payroll expense for the week for Mike Klyn?
2. How much cash did Mike Klyn take home for his work?
3. How much did the *employee* pay this week for
   a. Income tax?
   b. CPP and EI?
4. How much expense did the *employer* have this week for
   a. CPP and EI?
   b. Benefits?

(4) Making payroll entries

1. Total expense $1,313.76

(4) Payroll journal entries

Employee benefits expense, $11,290.40

S11–19 GC Company has employees who are paid their salaries on a monthly basis. Information from the company preparing the payroll for August of the current year is given below in a spreadsheet.

	A	B	C	D	E	F	G	H
1		Gross Pay	Income Taxes	CPP	EI	Donations	Union Dues	
2	Aug. 30	155,000.00	31,250.00	7,320.00	2,836.00	375.00	1,050.00	
3								

Prepare the journal entries to record the August 30 payroll payment and the payroll benefits expense for GC Company. Also prepare the entries to record the payment of payroll withholdings to the government and other agencies on September 15. Explanations are not required.

(5) Reporting liabilities on the balance sheet

S11–20 Identify the proper classification of each item below. In the space beside each item, write C for a current liability, L for long-term liability, or N if it is not a liability.

________ a. Bank loan payments due in the next 12 months
________ b. Income taxes payable
________ c. Estimated property taxes
________ d. Warranty liability
________ e. Unearned revenue
________ f. Note payable in 120 days
________ g. Mortgage payable, payments do not start for 13 months
________ h. Bank overdraft

EXERCISES

(1) Recording note payable transactions

June 1, 2020, Credit Cash, $91,160

E11–1 Record the following note payable transactions of Lambda Company in the company's general journal. Explanations are not required.

2019		
Jun.	1	Purchased delivery truck costing $86,000 by issuing a one-year, 6 percent note payable.
Dec.	31	Accrued interest on the note payable.
2020		
Jun.	1	Paid the note payable at maturity.

(1) Recording HST on a series of transactions

E11–2 Prepare the journal entries for Passport merchandisers, assuming that Passport merchandisers uses a perpetual inventory system. Passport merchandisers charges GST on all its sales at the rate of 5 percent and pays GST on all its purchases at the rate of 5 percent. Explanations are not required.

May	8	Purchased inventory, on account, FOB destination, from Seguin Wholesale, $2,000 plus applicable GST.
	10	Returned defective merchandise to Seguin, $300 plus applicable GST.
	12	Sold merchandise to Dainty Store on account for $3,000 plus applicable GST. Cost of the merchandise sold was $1,300.
	28	Collected balance on account from Dainty Store.
	30	Paid balance on account to Seguin.
Jun.	15	Prepare the remittance payment of GST based on only the above transactions in May.

E11–3 Prepare the journal entries for Kingston Dance Supplies, assuming that Kingston Dance Supplies uses a perpetual inventory system. The HST rate is 13 percent in Ontario. Explanations are not required.

1
Recording GST on a series of transactions

Aug.	3	Purchased inventory, on account, from Shoe-tastic, $3,000 plus applicable HST.
	11	Returned defective merchandise to Shoe-tastic, $400 plus applicable HST.
	19	Sold merchandise to Jazz Masters on account for $1,000 plus applicable HST. Cost of the merchandise sold was $500.
	30	Paid balance on account to Shoe-tastic.
Sep.	23	Record the refund of HST based on only the above transactions.

E11–4 Make general journal entries to record the following transactions of Mehta Products for a two-month period:

1
Recording sales tax and GST
June 30, Debit Cash, $129,950

Jun.	30	Recorded cash sales of $115,000 for the month plus PST of 8 percent collected on behalf of the province of Manitoba and GST of 5 percent. Record the two taxes in separate accounts.
Jul.	6	Sent June PST and GST to the appropriate authorities (Minister of Finance for PST and Receiver General for GST). Assume no GST input tax credits in this period.

E11–5 Suppose Detweiler Technologies borrowed $2,000,000 on December 31, 2016, by issuing 4 percent long-term debt that must be paid in four equal annual instalments plus interest on the outstanding balance commencing January 2, 2018.

1
Current portion of long-term debt
2017: Current portion of long-term debt, $500,000; Interest payable, $80,000

Required Insert the appropriate amounts in the following excerpts from the company's partial balance sheet to show how Detweiler Technologies should report its current and long-term liabilities for this debt.

	December 31,			
	2017	**2018**	**2019**	**2020**
Current liabilities				
Current portion of long-term debt	$ ____	$ ____	$ ____	$ ____
Interest payable	$ ____	$ ____	$ ____	$ ____
Long-term liabilities				
Long-term debt	$ ____	$ ____	$ ____	$ ____

E11–6 The management of Epsot Marketing Services examines the following company accounting records at August 29, immediately before the end of the year, August 31:

1
Recording current liabilities

Total current assets	$ 325,000
Property, plant, and equipment	1,079,500
	$1,404,500
Total current liabilities	$ 192,500
Long-term liabilities	247,500
Owner's equity	964,500
	$1,404,500

Epsot's banking agreement with Royal Bank requires the company to keep a current ratio (current assets ÷ current liabilities) of 2.0 or better. How much in current liabilities should Epsot pay off within the next two days in order to comply with its borrowing agreements?

E11–7 The law firm Garner & Brown received from a large corporate client an annual retainer fee of $60,000 on January 2, 2020. The fee is based on anticipated monthly services of $5,000.

1
Accounting for unearned revenue
2. Services to be provided, $55,000

Required

1. Using the account title Retainer Fees for unearned revenue, journalize (a) Garner & Brown's receipt of retainer fees, and (b) the provision of services in the month of January 2020.
2. Post the journal entries in Requirement 1 to the unearned revenue account (Retainer Fees) T-account. What is the value of services to be provided to the client in the remaining 11 months?

(1) Accounting for unearned revenue

2. Unearned subscription revenue, $50

E11–8 Assume the *National Post* completed the following transactions for one subscriber during 2020:

Oct. 1	Sold a six-month subscription, collecting cash of $100 plus PST of 8 percent and GST of 5 percent.
Nov. 15	Remitted (paid) the PST to the province of Manitoba and the GST to the Receiver General. Remember: Write two cheques.
Dec. 31	Made the necessary adjustment at year end to record the amount of subscription revenue earned during the year.

Required

1. Using the account title Unearned Subscription Revenue, journalize the transactions above.
2. Post the entries to the Unearned Subscription Revenue T-account. How much does the *National Post* owe the subscriber at December 31, 2020?
3. How would the entries in Requirement 1 be different if the *National Post* were in a different province that uses a 12 percent HST rate? Record the entries.

(2) Accounting for warranty expense and the related liability

2. Estimated Warranty Payable bal., $28,040

E11–9 The accounting records of RM Cycle included the following at January 1, 2020:

Estimated Warranty Payable	
	Jan 1 24,800

In the past, RM Cycle's warranty expense has been 3 percent of sales. During 2020, RM Cycle made sales of $1,038,000 and paid $27,900 to satisfy warranty claims.

Required

1. Record RM Cycle's warranty expense and warranty payments during 2020. Explanations are not required.
2. What balance of Estimated Warranty Payable will RM Cycle report on its balance sheet at December 31, 2020?

(2) Accounting for warranty expense using units in calculations

2. Est. Warranty Payable bal., $5,000

E11–10 Chez Nous Limited, a new company, made sales of 20,000 units at a cost of $40 per unit. The company offers a one-year warranty that replaces any defective units with a new one. The company estimated warranty replacements at 3 percent of units sold. Chez Nous' actual warranty replacements were 475 units. Record the warranty expense, and warranty payments on December 31. How much is Chez Nous' estimated warranty payable at the end of the period?

(2) Reporting a contingent liability

E11–11 Ludeman Security Systems is a defendant in lawsuits brought against the monitoring service of its installed systems. Damages of $1 million are claimed against Ludeman Security Systems, but the company denies the charges and is vigorously defending itself. In a recent newspaper interview, the president of the company stated that he could not predict the outcome of the lawsuits. Nevertheless, he said management does not believe that any actual liabilities resulting from the lawsuits will significantly affect the company's financial position.

Required Describe what, if any, disclosure Ludeman Security Systems should provide of this contingent liability. Total liabilities are $4 million. If you believe note disclosure is required, write the note to describe the contingency.

(2) Accruing a contingency

E11–12 Refer to the Ludeman Security Systems situation in E11–11. Suppose that Ludeman Security Systems' lawyers advise that a preliminary judgment of $300,000 has been rendered against the company on April 16. The company will appeal the decision.

Required Describe how to report this situation in the Ludeman Security Systems' financial statements. Journalize any entry required under ASPE. Explanations are not required.

E11–13 Blue Water Dredging recorded $10,000 in estimated income taxes on the last day of each month and made the payment on the 15th of the following month. On December 31, 2019, Blue Water's year end, it was determined that total income tax expense for the year was $126,000. Record the final instalment on December 31 and its payment on January 15, 2020.

(2) Accounting for income taxes

E11–14 Sylvia Chan is a clerk in the shoe department of the Hudson's Bay store in Winnipeg. She earns a base monthly salary of $1,875 plus a 7 percent commission on her sales. Through payroll deductions, Chan donates $40 per month to a charitable organization and pays benefit premiums of $49.15. Compute Chan's gross pay and net pay for December, assuming her sales for the month are $50,000. The income tax rate on her earnings is 20 percent, the CPP contribution rate is 4.95 percent (account for the $3,500 basic annual exemption), and the EI premium rate is 1.66 percent. Chan has not yet reached the CPP or EI maximum earning levels.

(3) Computing net pay

Net pay, $3,870

To account for the CPP basic exemption, deduct 3,500 ÷ 12 from the pay just for the CPP calculation.

E11–15 Record the payroll, payroll deductions, and employer payroll costs given the following information about an Ontario company at March 31:

(3) Recording payroll journal entries

	A	B	C	D	E	F	G	H
1		Gross Pay	Income Taxes	CPP	EI	RRSP Contribution	Union Dues	
2	Mar. 31	190,000	22,800	9,300	3,500	10,000	2,945	
3								

In addition to the Registered Retirement Savings Plans (RRSPs) deducted from employees, the employer made a contribution of 1 percent of gross pay to the company pension plan on behalf of employees.

E11–16 Brad Jackson works for a Bob's Burgers takeout for straight-time earnings of $15.25 per hour with time and a half for hours in excess of 35 per week. Jackson's payroll deductions include income tax of 21 percent, CPP of 4.95 percent on earnings (account for the $3,500 basic annual exemption), and EI of 1.66 percent on earnings. In addition, he contributes $10 per week to his Registered Retirement Savings Plan (RRSP). Assume Jackson worked 40 hours during the week. He has not yet reached the CPP or EI maximum earning levels.

(3)(4) Computing and recording gross pay and net pay

1. Net pay, $462.51

Required

1. Compute Jackson's gross pay and net pay for the week.
2. Make a compound general journal entry for June 14 to record the restaurant's wage expense for Jackson's work, including his payroll deductions and the employer payroll costs. Round all amounts to the nearest cent. An explanation is not required. Remember, in a compound entry, all debits are entered first, then all credits. Check that total debits equals total credits.

E11–17 Twisted Indian Restaurant incurred salaries expense of $95,000 for September. The company's payroll expense includes CPP of 4.95 percent and EI of 1.4 times the employee payment, which is 1.66 percent of earnings. Also, the company provides the following benefits for employees: dental insurance (cost to the company of $5,723.09), life insurance (cost to the company of $441.09), and pension benefits through a private plan (cost to the company of $1,745.60). Record Twisted Indian Restaurant's payroll expenses for CPP, EI, and employee benefits on September 30. Ignore the CPP basic exemption.

(3)(4) Recording a payroll

Total of CPP and EI Expense, $6,910.30

E11–18 Study the Employee Earnings Record for Jason C. Jenkins in Exhibit 11–10, page 628. In addition to the amounts shown in the exhibit, the employer also paid all employee benefits plus (a) an amount equal to 5 percent of gross pay into Jenkins's pension retirement account, and (b) dental insurance for Jenkins at a cost of $35 per month and parking of $10 per month. Compute the employer's total payroll expense for employee Jason C. Jenkins during 2018. Carry all amounts to the nearest cent.

(4) Using a payroll system to compute total payroll expense

Total payroll expense, $43,828.03

① ⑤ Reporting current and long-term liabilities

Total current liabilities, $594,503

E11–19 Assume Salem Electronics completed these selected transactions during December 2019:

1. Music For You Inc., a chain of music stores, ordered $105,000 worth of CD players. With its order, Music For You Inc. sent a cheque for $105,000. Salem Electronics will ship the goods on January 3, 2020.
2. The December payroll of $600,000 is subject to employee withheld income tax of 16 percent, CPP expenses of 4.95 percent for the employee and 4.95 percent for the employer, EI deductions of 1.66 percent for the employee and 1.4 times the employee rate of 1.66 percent for the employer. On December 31, Salem Electronics pays employees but accrues all tax amounts. Employees have not reached CPP or EI maximums.
3. Sales of $30,000,000 are subject to estimated warranty cost of 1 percent. This was the first year the company provided a warranty, and no warranty claims have been recorded or paid.
4. On December 2, Salem Electronics signed a $50,000 note payable that requires annual payments of $10,000 plus 5 percent interest on the unpaid balance each December 2. Salem calculates interest on this note based on days, not months.

Required Report these liabilities on Salem Electronics' balance sheet at December 31, 2019. Round all amounts to the nearest dollar.

SERIAL EXERCISE

③ ④ Recording a payroll

1. Net pay, $1,639.59

E11–20 *The Serial Exercise involves a company that will be revisited throughout relevant chapters in Volume 1 and Volume 2. You can complete the Serial Exercises using MyLab Accounting.*

This exercise continues recordkeeping for the Canyon Canoe Company. Students do not have to complete prior exercises in order to answer this question.

On January 1, Amber Wilson hired a part-time employee to work in the rental booth. The employee is paid $2,000 monthly. The following additional payroll information is available for the January 31, 2021, pay date:

Federal income tax to be withheld	$138.55
Provincial income tax to be withheld	99.70
CPP	84.56
EI	33.20

Required

1. Compute the rental-booth employee's gross pay and net pay for the month.
2. Make one general journal entry to record Canyon Canoe Company's salary expense for the rental-booth employee, including the payroll deductions and the employer payroll costs. Round all amounts to the nearest cent.

CHALLENGE EXERCISES

① ⑤ Accounting for and reporting current liabilities

1. Current ratio 2020, 2.10

E11–21 Suppose the balance sheets of a corporation for two years reported these figures:

	Millions	
	2020	**2019**
Total current assets	$24.50	$22.92
Property, plant, and equipment, net	44.74	40.96
Total assets	$69.24	$63.88
Total current liabilities	$11.66	$15.12
Long-term liabilities	29.92	23.32
Shareholders' equity	27.66	25.44
Total liabilities and shareholders' equity	$69.24	$63.88

The notes to the 2020 financial statements report that because of some refinancing arrangements, the corporation was able to reclassify $7 million from current liabilities to long-term liabilities during 2020.

Required

1. Compute the corporation's current ratio (current assets ÷ current liabilities) at the end of each year. Describe the change between the years that you observe.
2. Suppose that the corporation had not refinanced and not been able to reclassify the $7 million of current liabilities as long term during 2020. Recalculate the current ratio for 2020 to include the $7 million. Why do you think the corporation decided to reclassify the liabilities as long term?

E11–22 Vallarta Company recently reported notes payable and accrued payrolls and benefits as follows:

(1)(5) Analyzing current liability accounts

1. Payment of notes payable, $55 million

	December 31, 2020	December 31, 2019
	(in millions of dollars)	
Current liabilities (partial)		
Notes payable	$ 26	$ 78
Accrued payrolls and benefits	270	298

Assume that, during 2020, Vallarta Company borrowed $3 million on notes payable. Also assume that Vallarta paid $250 million for employee compensation and benefits during 2020.

Required

1. Compute Vallarta Company's payment of notes payable during 2020.
2. Compute Vallarta Company's employee compensation expense for 2020.

BEYOND THE NUMBERS

BN11–1

Suppose a large manufacturing company is the defendant in numerous lawsuits claiming unfair trade practices. The company has strong incentives not to disclose these contingent liabilities. However, ASPE requires companies to report their contingent liabilities.

Required

1. Why would a company prefer not to disclose its contingent liabilities?
2. Describe how a bank could be harmed if a company seeking a loan did not disclose its contingent liabilities.
3. What is the ethical tightrope that companies must walk when they report their contingent liabilities?

BN11–2

The following questions are independent of each other.

a. A warranty is like a contingent liability in that the amount to be paid is not known at year end. Why are warranties payable shown as a current liability, whereas contingent liabilities are often reported in the notes to the financial statements?

b. Auditors have procedures for determining whether they have discovered all of a company's contingent liabilities, often called "a search for unrecorded liabilities." These procedures differ from the procedures used for determining that accounts payable are stated correctly. How would an auditor identify a client's contingent liabilities?

ETHICAL ISSUE

EI11–1

Many small businesses have to squeeze costs any way they can just to survive. One way some businesses do this is by hiring "independent contractors" rather than regular employees. Unlike

Try It! Solutions for Chapter 11

1.

April	Cash	3,360	
	Sales Revenue		3,000
	GST Payable		150
	Sales Tax Payable		210
	To record cash sales and related GST and PST. GST Payable is $150 (3,000 × 0.05). Sales Tax Payable is $210 ($3,000 × 0.07).		

May 10	GST Payable	150	
	Cash		81
	GST Recoverable		69
	To pay GST to the Receiver General, less the input tax credit.		

Separate journal entries are required for GST and PST payments because cheques are sent to two different governments.

May 10	Sales Tax Payable	210	
	Cash		210
	To pay sales tax to the provincial government.		

2. Snippy Hair Salons' balance sheet at December 31, 2020, would be as follows:

Current Liabilities (in part)	
Portion of long-term debt due within one year	$5,000
Interest payable*	233
Long-Term Debt (in part)	
Long-term debt	$9,000

*Calculated as $14,000 × 0.05 × 4/12, rounded to the nearest dollar

Total long-term debt amount at Dec. 31, 2020, is $14,000 ($5,000 current portion payable in 2021 + $9,000 long-term portion)

3.

Dec. 31	Accounts Receivable	400,000	
	Sales Revenue		400,000
	To record sales made on account during the year.		
Dec. 31	Warranty Expense	12,000	
	Estimated Warranty Payable		12,000
	To record warranty expense, calculated as $400,000 × 0.03.		
Dec. 31	Estimated Warranty Payable	9,000	
	Cash		9,000
	To record payments for repairs under warranty.		

Estimated Warranty Payable

Payments 9,000	Estimate 12,000
	Bal. 3,000

4. a. Gross pay: 35 hours × $17.25 = $603.75
Net pay: $603.75 − 89.05 − 29.89 − 10.02 = $474.79

b. Employer CPP = $29.89
Employer EI = $10.02 × 1.4 = 14.03
Total employer cost = 43.92

c. Total remittance to CRA
= $89.05 + 29.89 + 29.89 + 10.02 + 14.03 = $172.88
(income tax + employee CPP and EI + employer CPP and EI)

d. Total employer cost = $603.75 + 43.92 = $647.67

5.

July 10	Wages Expense*	24,340	
	Employee Federal Income Tax Payable		1,850
	Employee Provincial Income Tax Payable		980
	Canada Pension Plan Payable		1,200
	Employment Insurance Payable		445
	Union Dues Payable		420
	Wages Payable		19,445
	To record payroll for the week.		
	*$21,840 + $2,500 = $24,340		
July 10	Employee Benefits Expense	1,823	
	Canada Pension Plan Payable		1,200
	Employment Insurance Payable**		623
	To record employer payroll costs for the week.		
	**$445 × 1.4 = $623		

6. The *current liabilities* section would appear as follows:
   a. Interest Payable = $\$3,000 \times 0.03 \times 58/365 = \$14.30$

Note Payable, Short-Term	$3,000
Interest Payable	14

   b. Interest Payable = $\$10,000 \times 0.05 \times 105/365 = \$143.84$

Bank Loan Payable	$10,000
Interest Payable	144

   c. The loan would be listed as a long-term liability.
   Interest Payable = $\$10,000 \times 0.03 \times 105/365 = \$86.30$

Interest Payable	$86

   d. The remainder of the loan, $5,000, would be listed as a long-term liability.

   Interest Payable = $\$10,000 \times 0.05 \times 363/365 = \$497.26$

Bank Loan Payable	$5,000
Interest Payable	497

   e. $\$5,000 - \$4,200 = \$800$

Unearned Subscription Revenue	$800

   f. $\$350,000 \times .03 = \$10,500$

Estimated Warranty Payable	$10,500

Appendix A

Portions of Indigo's 2017 Annual Report are reproduced here. The information here is needed to complete each chapter's Financial Statement Case 1. To download your own copy of the full annual report, please go to the Chapter Resources section of MyAccountingLab. In addition, the TELUS 2016 Annual Report is available there, which is needed to complete the Financial Statement Case 2 in each chapter.

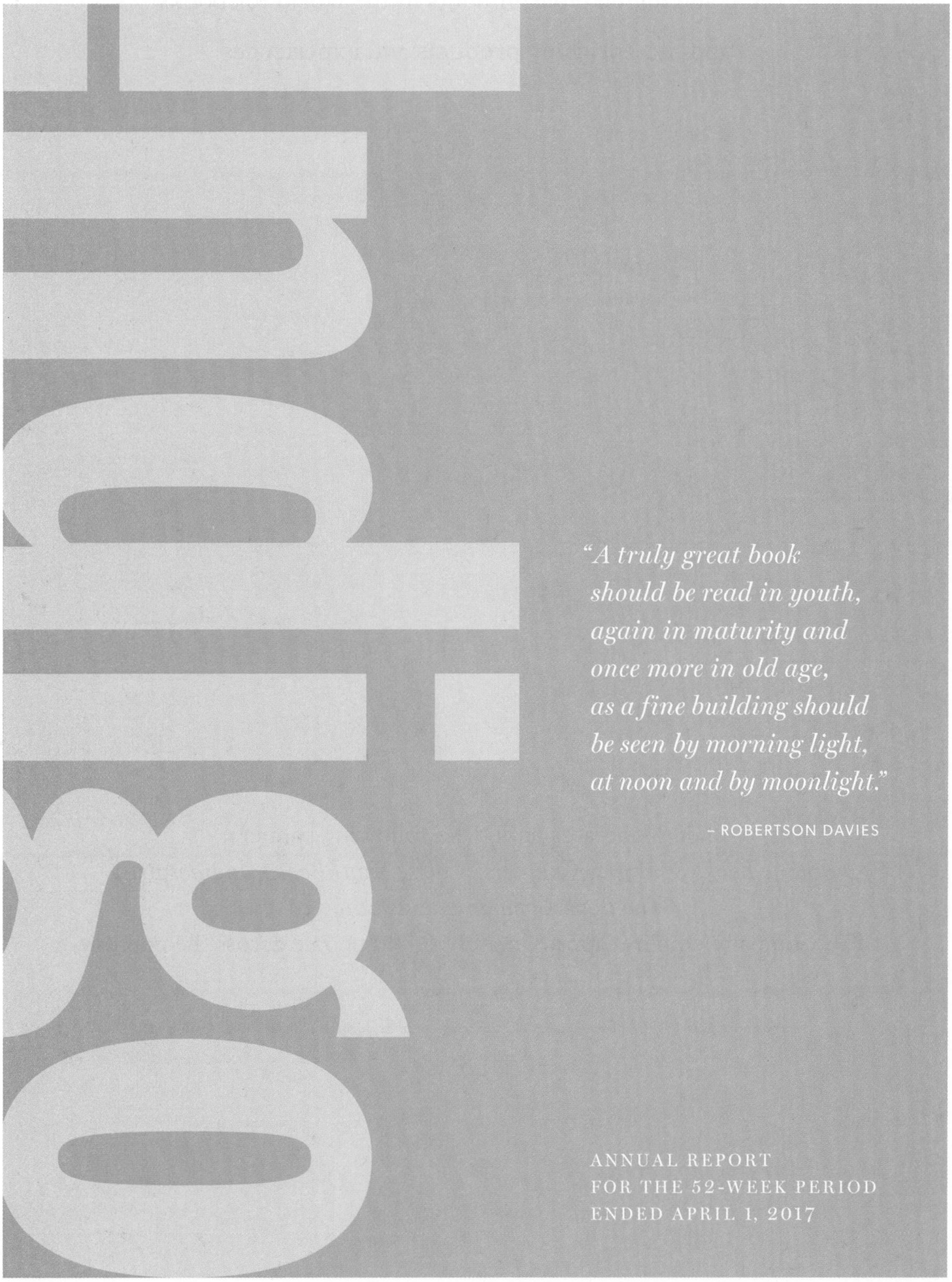

indigo
"A truly great book should be read in youth, again in maturity and once more in old age, as a fine building should be seen by morning light, at noon and by moonlight."
– ROBERTSON DAVIES
ANNUAL REPORT
FOR THE 52-WEEK PERIOD
ENDED APRIL 1, 2017

The Indigo Mission

To provide our customers with the most inspiring retail and digital environments in the world for books and life-enriching products and experiences.

Indigo operates under the following banners:
Indigo Books & Music, *Chapters*, *Coles*, *SmithBooks*, *Indigospirit*, *The Book Company*, and *indigo.ca*.
The Company employs approximately 6,500 people across the country.

Table of Contents

Report of the CEO

Dear Shareholder,

It is my pleasure to once again write to you in this, our year-end Annual Report.

2016/17 was a solid year for Indigo. We broke through the billion-dollar mark in total net revenue for the first time, increased our EBITDA by 21%, achieved best-in-class levels of employee engagement, won some prestigious awards, and perhaps best of all, earned very high ratings from our customers on our overall brand experience.

In May 2016, we launched the first of our true cultural department store formats at the wonderfully re-imagined CF Sherway Gardens, Toronto, Ontario. Everyone of our stakeholders has responded wonderfully to the new concept. Our publisher partners, the real estate community, our customers, and our employees have all shared their enthusiasm. Most exciting – this new store which replaced a store of almost the same size across the street, is producing 25% higher sales!

As a result of the warm reception to the new concept, we set the groundwork this year to begin a major three-year initiative to renovate our entire store network. This will be a big and exciting effort, designed to spur our growth and further strengthen our relationship with our customers.

At the same time, we also began work on what will be major advances in our digital experience, our supply chain, and our overall move to become a highly customer responsive omni-channel retailer.

We learned a great deal this year. From this learning will come the opportunity for valuable advances in all of the above areas.

In a snap shot – here are the key performance metrics for this past year:

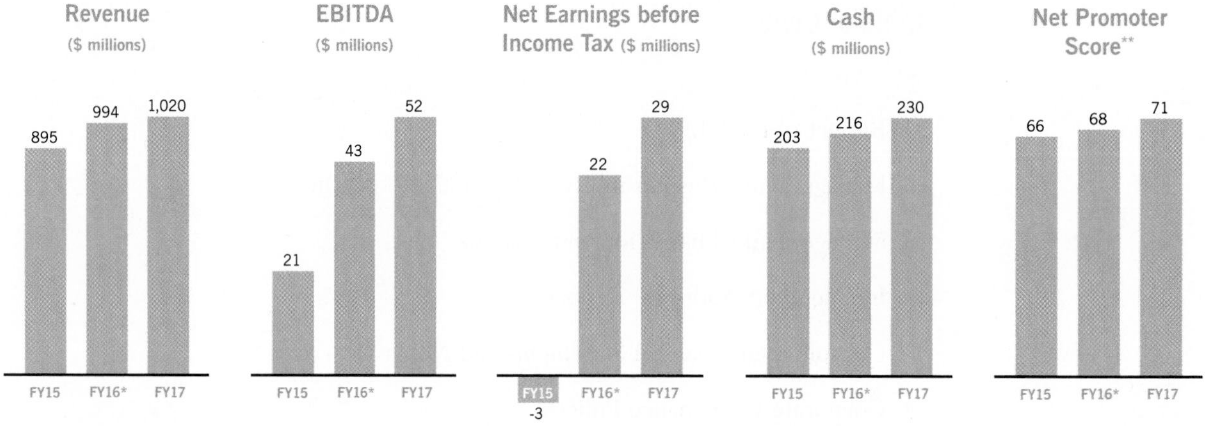

* 2016 includes a 53rd week

** Net Promoter Score as defined by Opinion Lab

We are pleased that once again this year Randstad Corporation has announced that Indigo is the top retail employer brand and the fourth most favoured brand overall to work for in Canada.

In September 2016, Forrester Research announced that Indigo was ranked #1 in providing Best-In-Class Retail Customer Experience for Traditional Retailers (Stores and Digital) in Canada, out of 27 retailers. Indigo's customer experience was also ranked #3 out of 194 brands within 27 different industries in Canada. Indigo's Forrester CX Index score increased from 2015 and, in 2016, 51% of Indigo customers gave the Company an "Excellent" ranking. Each year, Forrester Research benchmarks the customer experience for more than 800 brands in eight global markets with their CX index.

Every year for the last 12 years I have used this report to share what we are doing on the "giving back" side. I am proud to share that the Indigo Love of Reading Foundation has once again made a big difference in the lives of literally thousands of children. This past year, together with Indigo's customers, the Foundation put another 235,000 books into the hands of Canadian children. In total, the Foundation contributed $2.4 million to high-needs schools throughout Canada. We also produced a documentary titled "Read Between the Lines" about the deep literacy challenges faced by teachers and children in high-needs schools. We hope this documentary will educate and inspire policy makers to take action to ensure that all children in this country have the opportunity to be highly literate.

As always, by the time this report comes out, we are well engaged in our new fiscal year.

There is a lot underway in every aspect of the organization as we look to continue to grow sales, improve profitability, and build a long term sustainable organization.

I want to thank all our shareholders for their continued support. Know we are working hard on your behalf.

I also want to thank our Directors who have provided such steady and valuable support both in formal meetings and informally between our meetings. Your engagement is truly valued.

Finally, and for me, most important, I want to say a big thank you to everyone who brings such passion to work every day. You are the best! You so embrace our mission to enrich the lives of our customers and of your colleagues. I feel fortunate to be working with all of you.

Until next year...

Heather Reisman

Heather Reisman
Chair and Chief Executive Officer

Management's Responsibility for Financial Reporting

Management of Indigo Books & Music Inc. (the "Company") is responsible for the preparation and integrity of the consolidated financial statements as well as the information contained in this report. The following consolidated financial statements of the Company have been prepared in accordance with International Financial Reporting Standards, which involve management's best judgments and estimates based on available information.

The Company's accounting procedures and related systems of internal control are designed to provide reasonable assurance that its assets are safeguarded and its financial records are reliable. In recognizing that the Company is responsible for both the integrity and objectivity of the consolidated financial statements, management is satisfied that the consolidated financial statements have been prepared according to and within reasonable limits of materiality and that the financial information throughout this report is consistent. The Board of Directors, along with the Company's management team, have reviewed and approved the consolidated financial statements and information contained within this report.

The Board of Directors monitors management's internal control and financial reporting responsibilities through an Audit Committee composed entirely of independent directors. This Committee meets regularly with senior management and the Company's internal and independent external auditors to discuss internal control, financial reporting, and audit matters. The Audit Committee also meets with the external auditors without the presence of management to discuss audit results.

Ernst & Young LLP, whose report follows, were appointed as independent auditors by a vote of the Company's shareholders to audit the consolidated financial statements.

Heather Reisman
Chair and Chief Executive Officer

R. Craig Loudon
Interim Chief Financial Officer

Management's Discussion and Analysis

The following Management's Discussion and Analysis ("MD&A") is prepared as at May 30, 2017 and is based primarily on the consolidated financial statements of Indigo Books & Music Inc. (the "Company" or "Indigo") for the 52-week period ended April 1, 2017 and the 53-week period ended April 2, 2016. The Company's consolidated financial statements and accompanying notes are reported in Canadian dollars and have been prepared in accordance with International Financial Reporting Standards ("IFRS") as issued by the International Accounting Standards Board ("IASB") using the accounting policies described therein.

This MD&A should be read in conjunction with the consolidated financial statements and accompanying notes contained in the attached Annual Report. The Annual Report and additional information about the Company, including the Annual Information Form, can be found on SEDAR at *www.sedar.com*.

Overview

Indigo is Canada's largest book, gift, and specialty toy retailer, operating stores in all ten provinces and one territory in Canada and offering online sales through the *indigo.ca* website and the Company's mobile applications. As at April 1, 2017, the Company operated 89 superstores under the banners *Chapters* and *Indigo* and 123 small format stores under the banners *Coles*, *Indigospirit*, *SmithBooks*, and *The Book Company*.

As at April 1, 2017, the Company also employed approximately 6,500 people (on a full-time and part-time basis) and generated annual revenue of $1,019.8 million. The Company also has a 50% interest in Calendar Club of Canada Limited Partnership ("Calendar Club"), which operates seasonal kiosks and year-round stores in shopping malls across Canada.

The Company operates a separate registered charity under the name Indigo Love of Reading Foundation (the "Foundation"). The Foundation provides new books and learning material to high-needs elementary schools across the country through donations from Indigo, its customers, its suppliers, and its employees.

General Development of the Business

It has been 20 years since the Company launched its first superstore with a commitment to enriching Canadians' lives through books and complementary products. Much has changed since then, and continues to change, in both the book industry and the larger retail landscape. Indigo has been proactive in transforming its business in both its retail stores and digital offerings. The *indigo.ca* website has expanded dramatically, offering customers an increased number of titles at a lower cost than a traditional physical bookstore along with a broad range of general merchandise, much of which is unique to Indigo. In addition, digital channels have provided customers with instant accessibility, wide selection, and lower prices.

The Company opened a new store concept at CF Sherway Gardens in Toronto, Ontario, at the beginning of fiscal 2017. The new store concept reflects Indigo's transformation from a bookstore to a cultural department store for booklovers; it is a digital and physical place inspired by and filled with books, ideas, and beautifully designed products. The Company is committed to investing in Indigo's brand and the customer experience, with plans to renovate further superstores to this new store concept. The Company's priorities remain focused on continuing to transform its physical and digital platforms, building a high performance organization, and optimizing its cost structure.

The Company's key strategies going forward are outlined below.

Be the Preeminent Destination for Books

Print books remain the core focus of the business, across both physical and digital channels. The Company has invested, and will continue to invest, in book growth, enhancing the overall customer experience and improving productivity. In fiscal 2017, the Company optimized the book assortment in superstores, continued to refine its bestseller program, and expanded the staff picks and local authors programs. The Company will continue to adapt and improve all aspects of its book offering in both physical and digital channels through fiscal 2018 and beyond.

Grow as a Gifting Destination

Concurrently, Indigo remains committed to becoming the premier year-round gifting destination in Canada. The Company continues to expand its lifestyle and paper offerings, as well as its assortment of toys and games, with either dedicated toy sections or expanded toy offerings in all of its superstores and online. In fiscal 2017, the Company began selling Indigo's entire assortment of American Girl®[1] products on *indigo.ca*.

The Company's design and global sourcing team in New York leads the design and development of Indigo's proprietary merchandise. These private-label products are created by the Company's in-house creative team and are manufactured by third parties exclusively for Indigo. The Company is committed to adapting and improving its proprietary product development capability, expanding its line of gift and lifestyle merchandise which includes home, paper merchandise, and fashion accessories. This aspect of the business is part of the Company's focus on providing customers with meaningful and life-enriching merchandise only available at Indigo.

Transform Physical and Digital Platforms

The distinction between physical retail and digital retail is increasingly blurred as customers expect to have a seamless experience with the Indigo brand regardless of channel. Recognizing this, the Company is continuing to focus on improving the omni-channel customer experience with initiatives that better integrate physical and digital retail. The Company's "buy online, ship to store" initiative allows customers to buy products online and have them shipped to one of Indigo's stores at no charge. This service drives valuable traffic to stores and provides customers with additional flexibility to decide where and when purchases are picked up.

The Company's physical stores are being renovated and refreshed as part of rolling out Indigo's new store concept and the Company's focus on being the preeminent destination for books and becoming a top-of-mind gifting destination for Canadians. The Company rebranded and renovated one superstore and three small format stores in fiscal 2017. The Company will continue to renovate and transform its physical stores in fiscal 2018. The Company also continues to explore opportunities both within Canada and globally.

In addition to reshaping Indigo's physical store offerings, the Company continues to invest heavily into its digital platforms. The Company has launched a dedicated team solely focused on the agile delivery of digital products and services to further enhance the customer experience. The Company continues its strong social media presence across Facebook, Instagram, Pinterest, and Twitter, with half a million followers on Facebook and over 150,000 on Instagram. The Company launched a dedicated Indigobaby® Instagram in fiscal 2017. In fiscal 2018 and beyond, Indigo will continue to enhance all aspects of its digital platforms and presence, including an improved mobile experience. Furthermore, the Company continues to sell the eReaders and eReading services customers have come to love.

Optimizing the Company's plum rewards loyalty program was also a key area of focus in fiscal 2017. The Company's two loyalty programs, irewards and plum rewards, offer member discounts, and plum rewards also offers redeemable points on almost all product purchases in-store and online. The success of these programs creates a rich understanding of the Company's customers, as well as direct marketing and communication opportunities with Indigo's best customers. Going forward, the Company will increase its capabilities to utilize this data to personalize each touchpoint with customers across all channels and provide a rich omni-channel shopping experience.

[1] American Girl is a registered trademark of American Girl, LLC.

Drive Productivity Improvement

While a key focus of the Company's business is evolving to meet the emerging needs of customers, Indigo is also focused on driving productivity improvements to support the Company's continued evolution and new business strategies. The challenge for the Company is to continually look for innovative ways to drive costs down while improving the services Indigo delivers to its customers.

In fiscal 2017, the Company focused on implementing supply chain productivity initiatives designed to deliver improved operating margins and improve service to customers. The initiatives implemented to date have not yet brought the Company's supply chain and information management capabilities to a level that can efficiently support all of Indigo's planned strategies. Going forward, Indigo will continue to focus on driving end-to-end productivity and process efficiency in the supply chain and across the Company. The Company is also continuing the process of implementing a new product information management system.

Employee Engagement

In fiscal 2017, Indigo reached record-high employee engagement with an overall engagement index score of 89%. The Company's strategic efforts continue to focus on building and maintaining high levels of employee engagement through enhanced transparency, where all employees have a voice, as well as operating a more networked organization where employees are encouraged to connect regardless of hierarchy. Other initiatives driving our long-term engagement include the use of values-based leadership and the development of high-performing teams where individuals are encouraged to chart their own career paths and apply their strengths to meaningful work that allows them to bring their best selves to work at Indigo.

In April 2017, Indigo's employee engagement focus was again recognized outside of the Company, being named the top Canadian retail employer brand, and number four overall employer brand nationally, according to the annual award given by Randstad Canada, a staffing, recruitment, and HR company. The Randstad award rewards and encourages best practices in building the best employer brands and is the only employer award where winners are chosen entirely by workers and by job seekers in search of employment opportunities within Canada's leading organizations. The Company has ranked in the Top 20 Most Attractive Employer Brands in Canada since Randstad launched the program in 2011.

Results of Operations

The following three tables summarize selected financial and operational information for the Company. The classification of financial information presented below is specific to the Company and may not be comparable to that of other retailers. The selected financial information is derived from the audited consolidated financial statements for the 52-week period ended April 1, 2017 and the 53-week period ended April 2, 2016.

Key elements of the consolidated statements of earnings and comprehensive earnings for the periods indicated are shown in the following table:

(millions of Canadian dollars)	52-week period ended April 1, 2017	% Revenue	53-week period ended April 2, 2016	% Revenue
Revenue	1,019.8	100.0	994.2	100.0
Cost of sales	(565.6)	55.5	(551.2)	55.4
Cost of operations	(299.0)	29.3	(294.1)	29.6
Selling, administrative, and other expenses	(103.0)	10.1	(105.8)	10.7
Adjusted EBITDA[1]	52.2	5.1	43.1	4.3

1 Earnings before interest, taxes, depreciation, amortization, impairment, asset disposals, and equity investment. Also see "Non-IFRS Financial Measures".

Adjusted EBITDA is a key indicator used by the Company to measure performance against internal targets and prior period results and is commonly used by financial analysts and investors to assess performance. This measure is specific to Indigo and has no standardized meaning prescribed by IFRS. Therefore, adjusted EBITDA may not be comparable to similar measures presented by other companies.

Selected financial information of the Company for the last three fiscal years is shown in the following table:

(millions of Canadian dollars, except per share data)	52-week period ended April 1, 2017	53-week period ended April 2, 2016	52-week period ended March 28, 2015
Revenue			
Superstores	702.1	695.3	625.2
Small format stores	140.7	140.2	127.8
Online (including store kiosks)	148.2	133.3	114.0
Other	28.8	25.4	28.4
	1,019.8	994.2	895.4
Earnings (loss) before income taxes	29.0	22.1	(3.2)
Income tax recovery (expense)	(8.1)	6.5	(0.3)
Net earnings (loss)	20.9	28.6	(3.5)
Total assets	608.6	584.0	538.4
Long-term debt (including current portion)	–	0.1	0.2
Working capital	248.1	217.9	198.7
Basic earnings (loss) per share	$0.79	$1.10	$(0.14)
Diluted earnings (loss) per share	$0.78	$1.09	$(0.14)

Selected operating information of the Company for the last three fiscal years is shown in the following table:

	52-week period ended April 1, 2017	53-week period ended April 2, 2016	52-week period ended March 28, 2015
Comparable Sales Growth[1]			
Total retail and online	4.1%	12.9%	6.5%
Superstores	2.9%	12.8%	6.8%
Small format stores	0.9%	10.9%	0.8%
Stores Opened			
Superstores	1	–	–
Small format stores	1	1	–
	2	1	–
Stores Closed			
Superstores	–	3	4
Small format stores	1	5	4
	1	8	8
Number of Stores Open at Year-End			
Superstores	89	88	91
Small format stores	123	123	127
	212	211	218
Selling Square Footage at Year-End (in thousands)			
Superstores	1,953	1,925	2,019
Small format stores	304	305	311
	2,257	2,230	2,330

1 See "Non-IFRS Financial Measures".

Revenue

Total consolidated revenue for the 52-week period ended April 1, 2017 increased $25.6 million or 2.6% to $1,019.8 million from $994.2 million for the 53-week period ended April 2, 2016. Higher revenue was driven by continued double-digit growth in general merchandise, particularly in the lifestyle and toy categories. Print sales remained solid, as sales of *Harry Potter and the Cursed Child* partially offset the declining trend for adult colouring books. On a normalized 52-week basis, total revenue was 4.0% higher compared to the same period last year.

Online revenue increased by $14.9 million or 11.2% to $148.2 million for the 52-week period ended April 1, 2017 compared to $133.3 million last year. Online sales continued to grow in both print and general merchandise, with exceptional growth in lifestyle and toys. On a normalized 52-week basis, total online revenue was 12.8% higher compared to the same period last year.

Total comparable sales, which includes online sales, increased by 4.1% from last year. Comparable retail store sales for the year increased 2.9% in superstores and 0.9% in small format stores. Increases in comparable sales were primarily driven by the same reasons discussed above. Total comparable sales is based on comparable retail store sales and includes online sales for the same period. Comparable retail store sales are defined as sales generated by stores that have been open for more than 12 months on a 52-week basis. These measures exclude sales fluctuations due to store openings and closings, permanent relocation, material changes in square footage, and the impact of a 53-week fiscal year. Both measures are key performance indicators for the Company but have no standardized meaning prescribed by IFRS and may not be comparable to similar measures presented by other companies. During the 52-week period ended April 1, 2017, the Company opened one new superstore and decided to operate a previously-opened pop-up store on a permanent basis. In the same period, the Company closed one small format store.

Revenue from other sources includes revenue generated through cafés, irewards card sales, revenue from unredeemed gift cards ("gift card breakage"), revenue from unredeemed plum points ("plum breakage"), corporate sales, and revenue-sharing with Rauten Kobo Inc. ("Kobo"). Revenue from other sources increased $3.4 million or 13.4% to $28.8 million for the 52-week period year ended April 1, 2017 compared to $25.4 million last year as higher gift card breakage and corporate sales were partially offset by lower Kobo revenue and irewards membership income. Subtle changes in consumer behaviour have impacted historic gift card redemption patterns and drove a $3.3 million increase in gift card breakage revenue compared to last year. The $2.2 million increase in corporate sales was driven by sales of slow-moving inventory. These increases were partially offset by a $1.1 million decrease in combined Kobo revenue share and irewards card sales. Kobo revenue share decreased due to the slowing pace of eBook sales while irewards card sales continued to decrease as members move to the free plum rewards program. On a normalized 52-week basis, total revenue from other sources was up 16.1% compared to the same period last year.

Revenue by channel is highlighted below:

(millions of Canadian dollars)	52-week period ended April 1, 2017	53-week period ended April 2, 2016	% increase (decrease)	Comparable store sales % increase (decrease)
Superstores	702.1	695.3	1.0	2.9
Small format stores	140.7	140.2	0.4	0.9
Online (including store kiosks)	148.2	133.3	11.2	12.8
Other	28.8	25.4	13.4	N/A
Total	1,019.8	994.2	2.6	4.1

Revenue by product line is as follows:

	52-week period ended April 1, 2017	53-week period ended April 2, 2016
Print [1]	58.6%	61.9%
General merchandise [2]	37.7%	34.5%
eReading [3]	1.2%	1.5%
Other [4]	2.5%	2.1%
Total	100.0%	100.0%

1 Includes books, magazines, newspapers, and shipping revenue.
2 Includes lifestyle, paper, toys, calendars, music, DVDs, electronics, and shipping revenue.
3 Includes eReaders, eReader accessories, Kobo revenue share, and shipping revenue.
4 Includes cafés, irewards, gift card breakage, Plum breakage, and corporate sales.

Reconciliations between total revenue and comparable sales are provided below:

(millions of Canadian dollars)	52-week period ended April 1, 2017	53-week period ended April 2, 2016
Total retail store revenue	842.8	835.5
Total online revenue	148.2	133.3
Adjustments for stores not in both fiscal periods	(39.6)	(41.6)
Adjustments for week 53 revenues	–	(13.0)
Total comparable sales	951.4	914.2

	Superstores		Small format stores	
(millions of Canadian dollars)	52-week period ended April 1, 2017	53-week period ended April 2, 2016	52-week period ended April 1, 2017	53-week period ended April 2, 2016
Total revenue by format	702.1	695.3	140.7	140.2
Adjustments for stores not in both fiscal periods	(33.2)	(36.4)	(6.4)	(5.2)
Adjustments for week 53 revenue	–	(9.2)	–	(1.9)
Comparable retail store sales	668.9	649.7	134.3	133.1

Cost of Sales

Cost of sales includes the landed cost of goods sold, online shipping costs, inventory shrink and damage reserve, less all vendor support programs. Cost of sales increased $14.4 million to $565.6 million for the 52-week period ended April 1, 2017, compared to $551.2 million last year. The increase was driven by higher sales volumes, as discussed above. As a percent of total revenue, cost of sales increased 0.1% to 55.5% compared to 55.4% last year. Higher discounts driven by promotional discounting of *Harry Potter and the Cursed Child* and increased summer markdowns on slow-moving general merchandise were partially offset by greater sell-through of full-priced goods during the November/December holiday season.

Cost of Operations

Cost of operations includes all store, store support, online, and distribution centre costs. Cost of operations increased $4.9 million to $299.0 million for the 52-week period ended April 1, 2017, compared to $294.1 million last year. As a percent of total revenue, cost of operations decreased by 0.3% to 29.3% this year, compared to 29.6% last year.

Store-level operating costs decreased by $3.0 million primarily due to lower occupancy costs from having one fewer week in fiscal 2017 compared to last year and improved selling and administration efficiencies within retail store operations. Total distribution centre costs, which includes both retail and online, increased by $7.9 million due to both higher sales volume and increased labour costs. Higher distribution centre labour costs were partly driven by increased wage rates, which were required to attract seasonal labour in an increasingly competitive market.

During the year, the Company also went live with new systems and processes intended to improve the productivity of its online distribution centre. These initiatives did not achieve the productivity improvements envisioned. The launch resulted in some stabilization challenges which impacted the Company's online fulfilment capabilities during peak holiday season days and resulted in additional project costs to achieve delivery commitments. However, the Company has developed a plan to address these challenges and achieve improved performance.

Selling, Administrative, and Other Expenses

Selling, administrative, and other expenses include marketing, head office costs, and operating expenses associated with the Company's strategic initiatives. These expenses decreased $2.8 million to $103.0 million for the 52-week period ended April 1, 2017, compared to $105.8 million last year. As a percent of total revenue, selling, administrative, and other expenses decreased by 0.6 % to 10.1%, compared to 10.7% last year. Last year, the Company received one-time net proceeds of $4.5 million related to exiting a lease, without which current year expenses would have decreased by $7.3 million.

Lower expenses in the current year were driven primarily by a decrease in bonus accruals this year compared to the exceptional performance of the prior year and by non-recurring proceeds resulting from a reconciliation of café charges. These reductions were partly offset by increased marketing costs and a lower foreign exchange gain. Increased marketing costs are consistent with the Company's revenue growth and have remained flat year-over-year as a percentage of revenue. In the current year, there was a foreign exchange gain of $0.2 million, compared to a $0.6 million gain last year.

Adjusted EBITDA

Adjusted EBITDA, defined as earnings before interest, taxes, depreciation, amortization, impairment, asset disposals, and equity investment increased $9.1 million to $52.2 million for the 52-week period ended April 1, 2017, compared to $43.1 million for the 53-week period ended April 2, 2016. Adjusted EBITDA as a percent of revenue increased to 5.1% this year from 4.3% last year. As indicated above, the Company had a one-time impact of receiving $4.5 million from exiting a lease last year. Excluding this impact, adjusted EBITDA increased $13.6 million compared to last year. Higher adjusted EBITDA was driven by continued growth in revenue and margin and by lower head office costs, partially offset by higher operating costs at the retail and online distribution centres. A reconciliation of adjusted EBITDA to net earnings before taxes has been included in the "Non-IFRS Financial Measures" section of Management's Discussion and Analysis.

Capital Assets

Depreciation and amortization for the 52-week period ended April 1, 2017 increased by $1.4 million to $25.2 million compared to $23.8 million last year. The increase in amortization was driven by higher capital asset additions in fiscal 2016 compared to fiscal 2015.

Capital expenditures in fiscal 2017 totalled $30.6 million compared to $29.2 million last year. Capital expenditures in the current year were driven by the opening of a new superstore, continued implementation of changes across Indigo's retail outlets, and investments in the Company's digital business through back-end productivity initiatives, including increased distribution centre automation and a new product information management system. Fiscal 2017 capital expenditures included

$17.4 million for retail store renovations and equipment, $3.1 million for technology equipment, and $10.1 million primarily for application software and internal development costs. None of the capital expenditures were financed through leases.

Certain distribution centre automation initiatives and certain work completed towards a new product information management system did not meet the Company's expectations during the year. Management reviewed these projects and identified capitalized costs related to processes which are no longer expected to be used by the Company and therefore must be derecognized. As at April 1, 2017, $2.8 million of capital assets were written down for these projects.

The Company also assessed whether indicators of capital asset impairment or impairment reversals existed at each reporting date. For capital assets that could be reasonably and consistently allocated to individual stores, the store level was used as the cash-generating unit ("CGU"). During the year, impairment and reversal indicators were identified for certain CGUs. As a result of identifying impairment and reversal indicators, the Company performed testing that resulted in a reversal of previously recorded impairment losses. Recoverable amounts for CGUs being tested were based on value in use, which was calculated from discounted cash flow projections over the remaining lease terms, plus any renewal options where renewal was likely.

The Company had $1.0 million of capital asset impairment reversals during fiscal 2017 compared to net capital asset impairment reversals of $1.6 million last year. Impairment reversals in both years were driven by improved store performance and the likelihood of lease term renewals. Last year, impairment losses of $0.6 million arose due to a store closure. All impairment reversals and losses were spread across a number of CGUs at the store level.

Net Interest Income

The Company recognized net interest income of $2.2 million for the 52-week period ended April 1, 2017, compared to $0.8 million last year. The Company nets interest income against interest expense. Compared to last year, the Company generated more interest income by maintaining a higher average cash balance in short-term investments at higher interest rates.

The Company also had lower expenses in the current year. Last year, the Company paid interest and penalties of $0.7 million to the government as the result of Canada Revenue Agency ("CRA") tax audits on prior year returns of the Company and Calendar Club. The CRA has not yet responded to the Company's Notice of Objection filed last year, which disputed the interest and penalties resulting from the audit findings.

Earnings from Equity Investment

The Company uses the equity method to account for its investment in Calendar Club and recognizes its share of Calendar Club's earnings as part of consolidated net earnings. Calendar Club is primarily a seasonal operation that is dependent on the November/December holiday sales season to generate revenue. The Company recognized net earnings from Calendar Club of $1.6 million for the 52-week period ended April 1, 2017, compared to net earnings of $1.4 million last year.

Earnings Before Income Taxes

The Company recorded earnings before income taxes of $29.0 million for the 52-week period ended April 1, 2017, compared to earnings before income taxes of $22.1 million in the 53-week period last year. Excluding the Company's one-time proceeds from disposal of a lease in the prior year period, the Company recognized adjusted pre-tax earnings of $17.6 million last year. Higher pre-tax earnings in the current year were driven by improved revenue and margin and lower head office costs, partially offset by higher distribution centre operating costs and increased capital asset disposals.

Income Taxes

The Company recognized a primarily non-cash income tax expense of $8.1 million for the 52-week period ended April 1, 2017, compared to recognizing a net non-cash income tax recovery of $6.5 million in the 53-week period last year. Income tax expense in the current year primarily relates to a decrease in deferred tax assets. Last year, the Company fully reversed a previously-recorded valuation allowance against deferred tax assets based on management's best estimate of future taxable income the Company expected to achieve, which resulted in an income tax recovery. Excluding the impact of the valuation allowance, income tax expense in the comparative prior year period was $5.9 million. The Company's current year effective tax rate was 28.0% compared to (29.3%) last year due to the one-time impact of the valuation allowance reversal.

Net Earnings

The Company recognized net earnings of $20.9 million for the 52-week period ended April 1, 2017 ($0.79 net earnings per common share), compared to net earnings of $28.6 million ($1.10 net earnings per common share) in the 53-week period last year. As discussed above, the decrease in net earnings was primarily driven by the recognition of income tax expense in the current year compared to a net income tax recovery last year.

Other Comprehensive Income

During the first quarter of fiscal 2017, the Company implemented a formal hedging policy to mitigate foreign exchange risk, entering into contracts to manage the currency fluctuation risk associated with forecasted U.S. dollar expenses, primarily for general merchandise inventory purchases. All contracts entered into during the year have been designated as cash flow hedges for accounting purposes.

During 52-week period ended April 1, 2017, the Company entered into forward contracts with total notional amounts of C$173.4 million, respectively, to buy U.S. dollars and sell Canadian dollars. As at April 1, 2017, the Company had remaining forward contracts in place representing a total notional amount of C$70.3 million. These contracts extend over a period not exceeding 12 months. The total fair value of the outstanding contracts as at April 1, 2017 resulted in an unrealized net gain of $0.3 million. During the 52-week period ended April 1, 2017, net gains of $1.2 million from settled contracts were reclassified from other comprehensive income to inventory and expenses. Reclassified amounts resulting from hedge ineffectiveness were immaterial for the 52-week period ended April 1, 2017.

Seasonality and Fourth Quarter Results

Indigo's business is highly seasonal and follows quarterly sales and profit (loss) fluctuation patterns, which are similar to those of other retailers that are highly dependent on the November/December holiday sales season. A disproportionate amount of revenues and profits are earned in the third quarter. As a result, quarterly performance is not necessarily indicative of the Company's performance for the rest of the year. The following table sets out revenue, net earnings (loss), basic and diluted earnings (loss) per share for the preceding eight fiscal quarters. Under an accounting convention common in the retail industry, the Company follows a 52-week reporting cycle which periodically necessitates a fiscal year of 53 weeks. Fiscal year 2017 was 52 weeks, while fiscal year 2016 was 53 weeks.

	Fiscal quarters							
(millions of Canadian dollars, except per share data)	Q4[1] Fiscal 2017	Q3[1] Fiscal 2017	Q2[1] Fiscal 2017	Q1[1] Fiscal 2017	Q4[2] Fiscal 2016	Q3[1] Fiscal 2016	Q2[1] Fiscal 2016	Q1[1] Fiscal 2016
Revenue	209.5	400.3	216.9	193.1	220.4	383.2	205.7	184.9
Total net earnings (loss)	(8.9)	40.0	(1.2)	(9.0)	(13.4)	52.8	(1.8)	(9.0)
Basic earnings (loss) per share	($0.33)	$1.51	($0.04)	($0.34)	($0.51)	$2.03	$(0.07)	$(0.35)
Diluted earnings (loss) per share	($0.33)	$1.48	($0.04)	($0.34)	($0.51)	$2.02	$(0.07)	$(0.35)

[1] 13 week period
[2] 14 week period

On a 13-week basis, total comparable sales, which includes online sales, increased by 0.8% in the fourth quarter. Comparable retail store sales for the same period decreased 2.5% in superstores and 5.2% in small format stores. The increase in total comparable sales was primarily driven by continued general merchandise growth and strong online sales growth, offset by the shift in Boxing Week, which was included in the third quarter this year. The decline in the trend for adult colouring books also had a greater impact on small format stores, where the product mix is more focused towards print categories.

For the 13-week period ended April 1, 2017, total consolidated revenue decreased by $10.9 million to $209.5 million compared to $220.4 million for the 14-week period ended April 2, 2016. Retail revenue decreased by $17.0 million, or 9.3%, to $165.5 million compared to $182.5 million in the same quarter last year. The decrease was driven by a shorter quarter in the current year and the shift in the timing of Boxing Week sales discussed above. Online revenue showed continued growth, increasing by $4.5 million, or 14.5%, to $35.6 million compared to $31.1 million in the same quarter last year. The growth in online revenue was driven by the success of an increased number of March Break promotions in the current period.

Net loss for the 13-week period ended April 1, 2017 was $8.9 million compared to a loss of $13.4 million for the 14-week period ended April 2, 2016. As previously discussed, the Company had lower bonus accruals this period compared to the exceptional performance of the prior period and non-recurring proceeds resulting from a reconciliation of café charges. Additionally, the impact of foreign exchange in the current quarter was a gain of $0.1 million compared to a loss of $1.9 million in the same quarter last year due to implementation of a hedging program in fiscal 2017. These expense reductions were partially offset by higher capital asset disposals driven by the previously discussed capital asset derecognitions. The Company also recognized a $3.1 million net income tax recovery in the fourth quarter of fiscal 2017 compared to a $4.3 million net income tax recovery in the same quarter last year.

Overview of Consolidated Balance Sheets

Assets

As at April 1, 2017, total assets increased $24.6 million to $608.6 million, compared to $584.0 million as at April 2, 2016. The increase was driven by higher inventory, cash, and short-term investments, partly offset by lower deferred tax assets. The inventories increase of $13.8 million was primarily driven by higher trade book inventory as sales of key titles were lower than anticipated. The $14.0 million increase in combined cash, cash equivalents, and short-term investments was driven by higher cash balances from continued improvements in revenue and margin. Deferred tax assets were applied to offset the Company's estimated tax expense, resulting in a $7.9 million decrease in assets.

On February 17, 2017, the Company formalized a Letter of Intent with Starbucks Coffee Canada Inc. ("Starbucks") whereby, among other things, the Company and Starbucks mutually agreed to terminate the Company's license to operate Starbucks-branded cafes within 11 retail locations. Based on the terms of the Letter of Intent, the Company agreed to transfer to Starbucks the café inventories and capital assets from the terminated licensed locations, and the Company classified these inventories and capital assets as assets held for sale. Subsequent to the transfer, the Company will sublease space in each of the previously licensed locations for Starbucks to operate corporate-run cafes, similar to the 72 other Starbucks-branded cafes Starbucks operates in the Company's retail locations. The transfer and subsequent subleasing were completed on May 1, 2017.

Liabilities

As at April 1, 2017, total liabilities decreased $3.2 million to $236.8 million, compared to $240.0 million as at April 2, 2016. The decrease was primarily the result of a $2.6 million decrease in current and long-term accounts payable and accrued liabilities. As previously discussed, bonus accruals included as part of total accounts payable and accrued liabilities were lower than last year and the Company also recorded a one-time $3.6 million payable last year related to CRA audits, resulting in lower payables for the current year.

Equity

Total equity at April 1, 2017 increased $27.8 million to $371.8 million, compared to $344.0 million as at April 2, 2016. The increase in total equity was driven by net earnings of $20.9 million for the current year. Share capital increased by $6.7 million due to the exercise of stock options and Directors' deferred share units ("DSUs"). Correspondingly, contributed surplus decreased due to exercise of stock options, but the decrease was substantially offset by the issuance of new stock options.

The weighted average number of common shares outstanding for fiscal 2017 was 26,384,775 compared to 25,949,068 last year. As at May 30, 2017, the number of outstanding common shares was 26,352,484 with a book value of $216.0 million.

Working Capital and Leverage

The Company reported working capital of $248.1 million as at April 1, 2017, compared to $217.9 million as at April 2, 2016. Increased working capital compared to last year was driven by higher current assets. As previously discussed, inventories increased by $13.8 million and combined cash, cash equivalents, and short-term investments increased by $14.0 million.

The Company's leverage position (defined as Total Liabilities to Total Equity) decreased slightly at 0.6:1 as April 1, 2017 compared to 0.7:1 as at April 2, 2016 as total liabilities increased at a slower rate than total equity.

Overview of Consolidated Statements of Cash Flows

Cash and cash equivalents decreased $86.1 million during fiscal 2017 compared to an increase of $13.3 million last year. The current year decrease was driven by non-redeemable short-term investments which do not meet the criteria for recognition as cash equivalents. Excluding the impact of short-term investments, cash and cash equivalents increased by $14.0 million in fiscal 2017. Cash used for investing activities was $127.4 million, driven by short-term investments. This use of cash was partially offset by cash flows generated from operating activities of $35.6 million, financing activities of $4.9 million, and the effect of foreign currency exchange rate changes on cash and cash equivalents of $0.9 million.

Cash Flows from Operating Activities

The Company generated cash flows of $35.6 million from operating activities in fiscal 2017 compared to generating $38.6 million last year, a decrease of $3.0 million. The decrease was driven by a reduction in cash generated from working capital, partly offset by the usage of deferred tax assets in the current year. The Company used $17.2 million of cash for working capital this year compared to using $5.1 million of cash for working capital last year, primarily driven by the timing of prepaid expenses and higher print inventories in the current year. Last year, the Company did not use deferred tax assets due to the offset from the previously discussed valuation allowance.

Cash Flows Used for Investing Activities

The Company used cash flows of $127.4 million for investing activities in fiscal 2017 compared to $27.0 million used for investing activities last year, an increase of $100.4 million. The Company reported $100.0 million of non-redeemable short-term investments in the current year. In the previous year, the Company's short-term investments all met the criteria for classification as cash equivalents. The Company spent $30.6 million on capital projects this year compared to spending $29.2 million last year. As discussed above, the Company is investing in a number of initiatives to improve productivity and enhance the customer experience. Cash was also used for the construction of a new superstore which opened during the first quarter of fiscal 2017.

Cash was used for capital projects as follows:

(millions of Canadian dollars)	52-week period ended April 1, 2017	53-week period ended April 2, 2016
Construction, renovations, and equipment	17.4	17.0
Intangible assets (primarily application software and internal development costs)	10.1	9.0
Technology equipment	3.1	3.2
Total	30.6	29.2

Cash Flows from Financing Activities

The Company generated cash flows of $4.9 million from financing activities in fiscal 2017 compared to generating $1.5 million last year, an increase of $3.4 million. The increase was driven by a greater number of option exercises in the current year. Proceeds from share issuances due to option exercises increased by $2.3 million this year compared to last year. Last year, cash generated was partially offset by interest and penalties paid to the CRA of $0.7 million, as previously discussed.

Liquidity and Capital Resources

The Company has a highly seasonal business that generates a significant portion of its revenue and cash flows during the November/December holiday season. The Company has minimal accounts receivable and a majority of book products are purchased on trade terms with the right to return. The Company's main sources of capital are cash flows generated from operations, cash and cash equivalents, and short-term investments.

The Company's contractual obligations due over the next five years are summarized below:

(millions of Canadian dollars)	Less than 1 year	1-3 years	4-5 years	After 5 years	Total
Total obligations	57.7	73.8	34.9	60.2	226.6

Based on the Company's liquidity position and cash flow forecast, management expects its current cash position and future cash flows generated from operations to be sufficient to meet its working capital needs for fiscal 2018. In addition, the Company has the ability to reduce capital spending if necessary; however, a long-term decline in capital expenditures may negatively impact revenue and profit growth.

Accounting Policies

Critical Accounting Judgments and Estimates

The discussion and analysis of the Company's operations and financial condition are based upon the consolidated financial statements, which have been prepared in accordance with IFRS. The preparation of the consolidated financial statements in conformity with IFRS requires the Company to use judgment and estimation to assess the effects of several variables that are inherently uncertain. These judgments and estimates can affect the reported amounts of assets, liabilities, revenues, and expenses. The Company bases its judgments and estimates on historical experience and other assumptions that management believes to be reasonable under the circumstances. The Company also evaluates its judgments and estimates on an ongoing basis. Methods for determining all material judgments and estimates are consistent with those used in prior periods. The critical accounting judgments and estimates and significant accounting policies of the Company are described in notes 3 and 4 of the consolidated financial statements.

The following items in the consolidated financial statements involve significant judgment or estimation.

Use of judgments

The preparation of the consolidated financial statements in conformity with IFRS requires the Company to make judgments, apart from those involving estimation, in applying accounting policies that affect the recognition and measurement of assets, liabilities, revenues, and expenses. Actual results may differ from the judgments made by the Company. Information about judgments that have the most significant effect on recognition and measurement of assets, liabilities, revenues, and expenses is discussed below. Information about significant estimates is discussed in the following section.

Impairment

An impairment loss is recognized for the amount by which the carrying amount of an asset or a cash-generating unit ("CGU") exceeds its recoverable amount. Impairment losses are reversed if the recoverable amount of the capital asset, CGU, or group of CGUs exceeds its carrying amount, but only to the extent that the carrying amount of the asset does not exceed the carrying amount that would have been determined, net of depreciation or amortization, if no impairment loss had been recognized. The Company uses judgment when identifying CGUs and when assessing for indicators of impairment or reversal.

Intangible assets

Initial capitalization of intangible asset costs is based on the Company's judgment that technological and economic feasibility are confirmed and the project will generate future economic benefits by way of estimated future discounted cash flows that are being generated.

Leases

The Company uses judgment in determining whether a lease qualifies as a finance lease arrangement that transfers substantially all the risks and rewards incidental to ownership.

Deferred tax assets

The recognition of deferred tax assets is based on the Company's judgment. The assessment of the probability of future taxable income in which deferred tax assets can be utilized is based on management's best estimate of future taxable income that the Company expects to achieve from reviewing its latest forecast. This estimate is adjusted for significant non-taxable income and expenses and for specific limits to the use of any unused tax loss or credit. Deferred tax assets are recognized to the extent that it is probable that taxable profit will be available against which the deductible temporary differences and the carryforward of unused tax credits and unused tax losses can be utilized. Any difference between the gross deferred tax asset and the amount recognized is recorded on the balance sheet as a valuation allowance. If the valuation allowance decreases as a result of subsequent events, the previously recognized valuation allowance will be reversed. The recognition of deferred tax assets that are subject to certain legal or economic limits or uncertainties are assessed individually by the Company based on the specific facts and circumstances.

Use of estimates

The preparation of the consolidated financial statements in conformity with IFRS requires the Company to make estimates and assumptions in applying accounting policies that affect the recognition and measurement of assets, liabilities, revenues, and expenses. Actual results may differ from the estimates made by the Company, and actual results will seldom equal estimates. Information about estimates that have the most significant effect on the recognition and measurement of assets, liabilities, revenues, and expenses are discussed below.

Revenue

The Company recognizes revenue from unredeemed gift cards ("gift card breakage") if the likelihood of gift card redemption by the customer is considered to be remote. The Company estimates its average gift card breakage rate based on historical redemption rates. The resulting gift card breakage revenue is recognized over the estimated period of redemption based on historical redemption patterns commencing when the gift cards are sold.

The Indigo plum rewards program ("Plum") allows customers to earn points on their purchases. The fair value of Plum points is calculated by multiplying the number of points issued by the estimated cost per point. The estimated cost per point is based on many factors, including expected future redemption patterns and associated costs. On an ongoing basis, the Company monitors trends in redemption patterns (redemption at each reward level), historical redemption rates (points redeemed as a percentage of points issued) and net cost per point redeemed, adjusting the estimated cost per point based upon expected future activity.

Inventories
The future realization of the carrying amount of inventory is affected by future sales demand, inventory levels, and product quality. At each balance sheet date, the Company reviews its on-hand inventory and uses historical trends and current inventory mix to determine a reserve for the impact of future markdowns that will take the net realizable value of inventory on-hand below cost. Inventory valuation also incorporates a write-down to reflect future losses on the disposition of obsolete merchandise. The Company reduces inventory for estimated shrinkage that has occurred between physical inventory counts and each reporting date based on historical experience as a percentage of sales. In addition, the Company records a vendor settlement accrual to cover any disputes between the Company and its vendors. The Company estimates this reserve based on historical experience of settlements with its vendors.

Share-based payments
The cost of equity-settled transactions with counterparties is based on the Company's estimate of the fair value of share-based instruments and the number of equity instruments that will eventually vest. The Company's estimated fair value of the share-based instruments is calculated using the following variables: risk-free interest rate; expected volatility; expected time until exercise; and expected dividend yield. Risk-free interest rate is based on Government of Canada bond yields, while all other variables are estimated based on the Company's historical experience with its share-based payments.

Impairment
To determine the recoverable amount of an impaired asset, the Company estimates expected future cash flows and determines a suitable discount rate in order to calculate the present value of those cash flows. In the process of measuring expected future cash flows, the Company makes assumptions about certain variables, such as future sales, gross margin rates, expenses, capital expenditures, working capital investments, and lease terms, which are based upon historical experience and expected future performance. Determining the applicable discount rate involves estimating appropriate adjustments to market risk and to Company-specific risk factors.

Property, plant, equipment, and intangible assets (collectively, "capital assets")
Capital assets are depreciated over their useful lives, taking into account residual values where appropriate. Assessments of useful lives and residual values are performed on an ongoing basis and take into consideration factors such as technological innovation, maintenance programs, and relevant market information. In assessing residual values, the Company considers the remaining life of the asset, its projected disposal value, and future market conditions.

Accounting Standards Implemented in Fiscal 2017

Presentation of Financial Statements ("IAS 1")
In December 2014, the IASB issued amendments to IAS 1 as part of the IASB's Disclosure Initiative. These amendments encourage entities to apply professional judgment regarding disclosure and presentation in their financial statements and are effective for annual periods beginning on or after January 1, 2016. Implementation of these amendments in fiscal 2017 did not have a significant impact on the Company's financial statements and disclosures.

New Accounting Pronouncements

Statement of Cash Flows ("IAS 7")
In January 2016, the IASB issued amendments to IAS 7 as part of the IASB's Disclosure Initiative. These amendments require entities to provide additional disclosures that will enable financial statement users to evaluate changes in liabilities arising from financing activities, including changes arising from cash flows and non-cash changes. These amendments are effective for annual periods beginning on or after January 1, 2017 with early application permitted. Adopting these amendments will not have a significant impact on the Company's results of operations, financial position, or disclosures. The Company applied this standard beginning April 2, 2017.

Revenue from Contracts with Customers ("IFRS 15")

In May 2014, the IASB issued IFRS 15, a new standard that specifies how and when to recognize revenue as well as requiring entities to provide users of financial statements with more informative, relevant disclosures. IFRS 15 supersedes IAS 18, "Revenue," IAS 11, "Construction Contracts," and a number of revenue-related interpretations. Application of IFRS 15 is mandatory for all IFRS reporters and it applies to nearly all contracts with customers: the main exceptions are leases, financial instruments, and insurance contracts.

IFRS 15 must be applied retrospectively using either the retrospective or cumulative effect method for annual reporting periods beginning on or after January 1, 2018. The Company plans to apply this standard beginning April 1, 2018 but has not yet determined which transition method it will apply.

Implementation of IFRS 15 is expected to impact the allocation of deferred plum program revenue. Revenue is currently allocated to plum points using the residual fair value method. Under IFRS 15, revenue will be allocated based on relative stand-alone selling prices between plum points and the goods on which points were earned. The Company is currently assessing the impact of this change and other impacts of adopting this standard on its results of operations, financial position, and disclosures.

Financial Instruments ("IFRS 9")

In July 2014, the IASB issued the final version of IFRS 9, which reflects all phases of the financial instruments project and replaces IAS 39, "Financial Instruments: Recognition and Measurement," and all previous versions of IFRS 9. The standard introduces new requirements for classification and measurement, impairment, and hedge accounting. IFRS 9 is effective for annual periods beginning on or after January 1, 2018. The Company plans to apply this standard beginning on April 1, 2018.

IFRS 9 more closely aligns hedge accounting with risk management activities and applies a more qualitative and forward-looking approach to assessing hedge effectiveness. The Company is currently assessing the impact of this change and other impacts of adopting this standard on its results of operations, financial position, and disclosures.

Leases ("IFRS 16")

In January 2016, the IASB issued IFRS 16, which supersedes existing standards and interpretations under IAS 17, "Leases." IFRS 16 introduces a single lessee accounting model, eliminating the distinction between operating and finance leases. The new lessee accounting model requires substantially all leases to be reported on a company's balance sheet and will provide greater transparency on companies' leased assets and liabilities. IFRS 16 substantially carries forward the lessor accounting in IAS 17 with the distinction between operating leases and finance leases being retained. The Company is assessing the impact of adopting this standard on its results of operations, financial position, and disclosures.

The new standard will apply for annual periods beginning on or after January 1, 2019. The Company plans to apply this standard beginning March 31, 2019. For leases where the Company is the lessee, it has the option of adopting a full retrospective approach or a modified retrospective approach on transition to IFRS 16. The Company has not yet determined which transition method it will apply or whether it will use the optional exemptions or practical expedients available under the standard.

Risks and Uncertainties

The Company is exposed to a variety of risk factors and has identified the principal risks inherent in its business. The relative severity of these principal risks is impacted by the external environment and the Company's business strategies and, therefore, will vary from time to time.

The Company cautions that the following discussion of risk factors that may affect future results is not exhaustive. The Company's performance may also be affected by other specific risks that may be highlighted from time to time in other public filings of the Company available on the Canadian securities regulatory authorities' website at *sedar.com*. When relying upon forward-looking information to make decisions with respect to the Company, investors and others should carefully consider these factors, as well as other uncertainties, assumptions, potential events, industry, and Company-specific factors that may adversely affect future results. The Company assumes no obligation to update or revise previously filed public documents to reflect new events or circumstances, except as required by law.

Economic Environment

Traditionally, retail businesses are highly susceptible to market conditions in the economy. Economic conditions, both on a global scale and in particular markets, may have significant effects on consumer confidence and spending. A decline in consumer spending, especially over the November/December holiday season, could have an adverse effect on the Company's financial condition. Other variables, such as unanticipated increases in merchandise costs, higher labour costs, increases in shipping rates or interruptions in shipping service, foreign exchange fluctuations, or higher interest rates or unemployment rates, could also unfavourably impact the Company's financial performance.

Competition

The retail industry is highly competitive and continues to experience fundamental changes in a rapidly changing environment.

Specialty bookstores, independents, other book superstores, regional multi-store operators, supermarkets, drug stores, warehouse clubs, mail order clubs, Internet booksellers, mass merchandisers, and other retailers continue to sell and even expand physical book offerings, often at substantially discounted prices. The number of retailers selling eBooks and eReaders has also increased. Furthermore, technology continues to evolve and eReader technology is now widely available on tablets and mobile devices. This increased competition could negatively impact the Company's revenues and margins.

The general merchandise retail landscape also contains a significant amount of competition from established retailers and there can be no assurances that the Company will be able to gain market share. The Company competes with local, regional, national, and international retailers that sell gift and specialty toy products through both physical and digital platforms. New competitors frequently enter the market and existing competitors may increase market presence, expand merchandise offerings, add new sales channels, or change their pricing methods, all of which increase competition for customers. If the Company is unable to gain market share, Indigo's revenue could be adversely affected.

Aggressive merchandising or discounting by competitors could also reduce the Company's revenue, market share, and operating margins.

Real Estate

The Company leases all of its retail locations and attempts to renew these leases as they come due on favourable terms and conditions, but is susceptible to volatility in the market for supercentre and shopping mall space. Unforeseen increases in occupancy costs, or costs incurred as a result of unanticipated store closings or relocations, could also unfavourably impact the Company's performance.

Strategic Initiatives

The retail industry is constantly changing and management is committed to the Company's continued growth and success. Expansion into new markets or the launch of new initiatives could place a significant strain on the Company's management, operations, technical performance, financial resources, and internal financial control and reporting functions. The Company will continue to change and modify its strategy based on its economic environment and there can be no assurances that Indigo's strategy will be successful.

Relationships with Suppliers

The Company relies heavily on suppliers to provide book and general merchandise at appropriate margins and in accordance with agreed-upon terms and timelines. Failure to maintain favorable terms and relationships with suppliers, or the absence of key suppliers, may affect the Company's ability to compete in the marketplace. As Indigo continues to source a greater portion of its products from overseas, events causing disruptions of imports, changes in restrictions, or currency fluctuations could negatively impact the Company's revenues and margins.

The Company is also reliant on third parties to provide services essential to daily operations. Any disruption to these third-party services could have an unfavourable impact on the Company's performance and reputation, including significant negative impact in areas such as supply chain logistics, software development and support, transaction processing, and other key processes. The Company cannot make any assurances that it would be able to arrange for alternate or replacement contracts, transactions, or business relationships to mitigate the impact of disruptive events.

Inventory Management

The Company must manage its inventory levels to successfully operate the business. Inventory purchases are based on a number of variables, such as market trends and sales forecasts. Inability to respond to changing customer preferences or sales forecasts which do not match customer demand may result in excess inventory that must be sold at lower prices or an inventory shortage. While the majority of the Company's book purchases are eligible for return to suppliers at full credit, the growth of the general merchandise business means the Company has an increasing amount of non-returnable inventory. The Company monitors the impact of customer trends on inventory turnover and obsolescence, but inappropriate inventory levels could negatively impact the Company's revenue and financial performance.

Product Quality and Product Safety

The Company sells products produced by third-party manufacturers and relies on vendors to provide quality merchandise compliant with all applicable laws. Some of these products may expose the Company to potential liabilities and costs associated with defective products, product handling, and product safety. As part of its growth in general merchandise, the Company also sells food products and is subject to risks associated with food safety.

These risks could result in harm to the Company's customers and expose Indigo to product liability claims, damage the Company's reputation, and lead to product recalls. Liabilities and costs related to product quality and product safety may also have a negative impact on the Company's revenue and financial performance.

The Company has policies and controls in place to manage these risks, including maintaining liability insurance and providing third-party manufacturers with product safety guidance.

Technology and Digital Platforms

Information management and technology are key components to the ongoing competitiveness and daily operation of the business. If the Company's investment in technology fails to support growth initiatives or keep pace with technological changes, Indigo's competitiveness may be compromised. The Company also continues to invest in the digital customer experience, but there can be no assurance that Indigo will be able to recoup its investment costs. Furthermore, if systems are damaged or cease to function properly, capital investment may be required and the Company may suffer business interruptions in the interim. Such systems are pervasive throughout the Company and failures in their maintenance or development could have a significant adverse effect on the business.

Cybersecurity

A failure in, or breach of, the Company's IT operational or security systems or physical infrastructure, or those of Indigo's third-party vendors, cloud-based services, and other service providers, including as a result of cyberattacks, could disrupt the business, result in the disclosure or misuse of confidential or proprietary information, damage Indigo's brand and reputation, lead to temporary or permanent loss of data, increase the Company's remediation costs and legal liabilities, and impact its financial position and/or ability to achieve its strategic objectives. Although Indigo has business continuity plans and other safeguards in place, along with robust information security procedures, employee security awareness training and controls, the Company's business operations may be adversely affected by significant and widespread disruption to Indigo's physical IT infrastructure or operating systems that support the Company's business and customers. As cyber threats continue to evolve and become more difficult to detect, the Company may be required to expend significant additional resources to continue to modify or enhance Indigo's protective measures to protect against, among other things, security breaches, computer viruses and malware, phishing, hacktivism, cyberterrorism, denial-of-service attacks, credentials compromise, or to investigate and remediate any information security vulnerabilities.

Disaster Recovery and Business Continuity

Weather conditions, as well as events such as political or social unrest, natural disasters, disease outbreaks, or acts of terrorism, could have a material adverse effect on the Company's operations and financial performance. Moreover, if such events were to occur at peak times in the Company's business cycle, the impact of these events on operating performance could be significantly greater than they would otherwise have been. The Company has procedures in place to reduce the impact of business interruptions, crises, and potential disasters, but there can be no assurance that these procedures can fully eliminate the negative impact of such events.

Key Personnel

The Company's continued success will depend to a significant extent upon securing and retaining sufficient talent in management and other key areas. Employees have developed specialized skills and an in-depth knowledge of the business. Failure to effectively attract and retain talented and experienced employees or failure to establish adequate succession planning could result in a lack of requisite knowledge, skill and experience. If the Company does not continue to attract qualified individuals, train them in Indigo's business model, support their development, and retain them, the Company's performance could be adversely affected and growth could be limited. The loss of the services of key personnel, particularly Ms. Reisman, could have a material adverse effect on the Company. To mitigate the risk of personnel loss, the Company has implemented a number of employee engagement and retention strategies.

Corporate Reputation

The Company's corporate reputation and those of its retail banners are very important to Indigo's success and competitive position. The Company's reputation and, consequently, its brand, may be negatively affected by various factors, some of which may be outside of Indigo's control. Adverse events may damage the Company's reputation and brand at the corporate or retail level. Should negative factors materialize and diminish Indigo's brand equity, there could be a material adverse effect on the Company's operations and financial performance.

Credit, Foreign Exchange, and Interest Rate Risks

The Company is exposed to credit risk resulting from the possibility that counterparties may default on their financial obligations to the Company. Credit risk primarily arises from accounts receivable, cash and cash equivalents, short-term investments, and derivative financial instruments.

Accounts receivable primarily consists of receivables from retail customers who pay by credit card, recoveries of credits from suppliers for returned or damaged products, and receivables from other companies for sales of products, gift cards, and other services. Credit card payments have minimal credit risk and the limited number of corporate receivables is closely monitored.

The Company limits its exposure to counterparty credit risk related to cash and cash equivalents, short-term investments, and derivative financial instruments by transacting only with highly-rated financial institutions and other counterparties and by managing within specific limits for credit exposure and term to maturity.

The Company's foreign exchange risk is largely limited to currency fluctuations between the Canadian and U.S. dollars. Decreases in the value of the Canadian dollar relative to the U.S. dollar could negatively impact net earnings since the purchase price of some of the Company's products are negotiated with vendors in U.S. dollars, while the retail price to Indigo's customers is set in Canadian dollars. The Company also has a New York office that incurs U.S. dollar expenses. The Company maintains a hedging program to mitigate foreign exchange risk.

The Company's interest income is sensitive to fluctuations in Canadian interest rates, which affect the interest earned on Indigo's cash and cash equivalents and short-term investments. The Company has minimal interest rate risk and does not use any interest rate swaps to manage its risk. The Company does not currently have any debt.

Legal Proceedings

In the normal course of business, Indigo becomes involved in various claims and litigation. While the final outcome of such claims and litigation pending as at April 1, 2017 cannot be predicted with certainty, management believes that any such amount would not have a material impact on the Company's financial position.

Regulatory Environment

The Company's operations and activities are subject to a number of laws and regulations in Canada and in other countries. Changes to statutes, laws, regulations or regulatory policies, including tax laws, accounting principles, and environmental regulations, or changes in their interpretation, implementation or enforcement, could adversely affect the Company's operations and performance. The Company may incur significant costs in the course of complying with any such changes.

The Company is also subject to continuous examination of its regulatory filings by various securities regulators, tax authorities, and environmental stewards. As a result, authorities may disagree with the positions and conclusions taken by the Company in its filings, resulting in a reassessment. Reassessments could also arise from amended legislation or new interpretations of current legislation. Any reassessment could adversely affect the Company's financial performance.

Failure to comply with applicable regulations could also result in judgment, sanctions, or financial penalties that could adversely impact the Company's reputation and financial performance. The Company believes that it has taken reasonable measures designed to ensure compliance with applicable regulations, but there is no assurance that the Company will always be deemed to be in compliance.

Additionally, the distribution and sale of books is a regulated industry in which foreign ownership is generally not permitted under the Investment Canada Act. As well, the sourcing and importation of books is governed by the Book Importation Regulations to the Copyright Act (Canada). There is no assurance that the existing regulatory framework will not change in the future or that it will be effective in preventing foreign-owned retailers from competing in Canada. An increased number of competitors could have an adverse effect on the Company's financial performance.

Compliance with Privacy Laws

A number of federal and provincial statutes govern the privacy rights of the Company's employees and customers. These Canadian privacy laws create certain obligations regarding the Company's handling of personal information, including obligations relating to obtaining appropriate consent, limitations on use, retention, and disclosure of personal information, and ensuring appropriate security safeguards are in place. In the course of its business, the Company maintains records containing sensitive information identifying or relating to individual customers and employees. Although the Company has implemented systems and processes to comply with applicable privacy laws in connection with the collection, use, retention, and disclosure of such personal information, if a significant failure of such systems was to occur, the Company's business and reputation could be adversely affected.

Workplace Health and Safety

The failure of the Company to adhere to appropriate health and safety procedures and to ensure compliance with applicable laws and regulations could result in employee injuries, productivity loss, and liabilities to the Company. To reduce the risk of workplace incidents, the Company has health and safety programs in place and has established policies and procedures aimed at ensuring compliance with applicable legislative requirements.

Disclosure Controls and Procedures

Management is responsible for establishing and maintaining a system of disclosure controls and procedures to provide reasonable assurance that all material information relating to the Company is gathered and reported on a timely basis to senior management, including the Chief Executive Officer ("CEO") and interim Chief Financial Officer ("interim CFO"), so that appropriate decisions can be made by them regarding public disclosure.

As required by National Instrument 52-109, "Certification of Disclosure in Issuers' Annual and Interim Filings," the CEO and interim CFO have evaluated, or caused to be evaluated under their supervision, the effectiveness of such disclosure controls and procedures. Based on that evaluation, they have concluded that the design and operation of the system of disclosure controls and procedures were effective as at April 1, 2017.

Internal Controls over Financial Reporting

Management is also responsible for establishing and maintaining adequate internal controls over financial reporting to provide reasonable assurance regarding the reliability of financial reporting and the preparation of consolidated financial statements for external purposes in accordance with International Financial Reporting Standards.

All internal control systems, no matter how well designed, have inherent limitations. Therefore, even those systems determined to be effective can provide only reasonable assurance with respect to consolidated financial statement preparation and presentation. Additionally, management is necessarily required to use judgment in evaluating controls and procedures.

As required by National Instrument 52-109, "Certification of Disclosure in Issuers' Annual and Interim Filings," the CEO and interim CFO have evaluated, or caused to be evaluated under their supervision, the effectiveness of such internal controls over financial reporting using the framework established in the Internal Control – Integrated Framework ("COSO Framework") published in 2013 by the Committee of Sponsoring Organizations of the Treadway Commission. Based on that evaluation, they have concluded that the design and operation of the Company's internal controls over financial reporting were effective as at April 1, 2017.

Changes in Internal Controls over Financial Reporting

Management has also evaluated whether there were changes in the Company's internal controls over financial reporting that occurred during the period beginning on January 1, 2017 and ended on April 1, 2017 that have materially affected, or are reasonably likely to materially affect, the Company's internal controls over financial reporting. The Company has determined that no material changes in internal controls over financial reporting have occurred in this period.

Cautionary Statement Regarding Forward-Looking Statements

The above discussion includes forward-looking statements. All statements other than statements of historical facts included in this discussion that address activities, events, or developments that the Company expects or anticipates will or may occur in the future are forward-looking statements. These statements are based on certain assumptions and analysis made by the Company in light of its experience, analysis, and its perception of historical trends, current conditions, and expected future developments as well as other factors it believes are appropriate in the circumstances. However, whether actual results and developments will conform to the expectations and predictions of the Company is subject to a number of risks and uncertainties, including the general economic, market, or business conditions; competitive actions by other companies; changes in laws or regulations; and other factors, many of which are beyond the control of the Company. Consequently, all of the forward-looking statements made in this discussion are qualified by these cautionary statements and there can be no assurance that results or developments anticipated by the Company will be realized or, even if substantially realized, that they will have the expected consequences to, or effects on, the Company.

Non-IFRS Financial Measures

The Company prepares its consolidated financial statements in accordance with International Financial Reporting Standards ("IFRS"). In order to provide additional insight into the business, the Company has also provided non-IFRS data, including comparable sales and adjusted EBITDA, in the discussion and analysis section above. These measures are specific to Indigo and have no standardized meaning prescribed by IFRS. Therefore, these measures may not be comparable to similar measures presented by other companies.

Total comparable sales (including online), comparable retail store sales, and adjusted EBITDA are key indicators used by the Company to measure performance against internal targets and prior period results. These measures are commonly used by financial analysts and investors to compare the Company to other retailers.

Total comparable sales is based on comparable retail store sales and includes online sales for the same period. Comparable retail store sales are defined as sales generated by stores that have been open for more than 12 fiscal periods on a 52-week basis. These measures exclude sales fluctuations due to store openings and closings, permanent relocation, material changes in square footage, and the impact of a 53-week fiscal year. Both measures are key performance indicators for the Company. Adjusted EBITDA is defined as earnings before interest, taxes, depreciation, amortization, impairment, asset disposals, and equity investment. The method of calculating adjusted EBITDA is consistent with that used in prior periods.

Reconciliations between total comparable sales, comparable retail store sales, and revenue (the most comparable IFRS measure) were included earlier in this report. A reconciliation between adjusted EBITDA and earnings (loss) before income taxes (the most comparable IFRS measure) is provided below:

(millions of Canadian dollars)	52-week period ended April 1, 2017	53-week period ended April 2, 2016
Adjusted EBITDA	52.2	43.1
Depreciation of property, plant, and equipment	(16.6)	(14.7)
Amortization of intangible assets	(8.6)	(9.1)
Net reversal of capital asset impairments	1.0	1.6
Loss on disposal of capital assets	(2.8)	(1.0)
Net interest income	2.2	0.8
Share of earnings from joint venture	1.6	1.4
Earnings before income taxes	29.0	22.1

The Company has also provided non-GAAP normalized revenue data to remove the effect of having a 52-week fiscal year in 2017 compared to the 53-week fiscal year ended April 2, 2016. Normalized revenue was calculated by excluding fiscal 2016 week 53 revenue.

A reconciliation between full year fiscal 2016 revenue (the most comparable IFRS measure) and normalized fiscal 2016 revenue is provided below:

(millions of Canadian dollars)	Fiscal 2017 revenue	Fiscal 2016 revenue (full year)	Fiscal 2016 revenue (week 53)	Fiscal 2016 revenue (normalized)
Superstores	702.1	695.3	9.2	686.1
Small format stores	140.7	140.2	1.9	138.3
Online (including store kiosks)	148.2	133.3	1.9	131.4
Other	28.8	25.4	0.6	24.8
Total	1,019.8	994.2	13.6	980.6

Independent Auditors' Report

To the Shareholders of Indigo Books & Music Inc.

We have audited the accompanying consolidated financial statements of Indigo Books & Music Inc., which comprise the consolidated balance sheets as at April 1, 2017 and April 2, 2016, and the consolidated statements of earnings and comprehensive earnings, changes in equity, and cash flows for the 52 week period ended April 1, 2017 and the 53 week period ended April 2, 2016, and a summary of significant accounting policies and other explanatory information.

Management's responsibility for the consolidated financial statements

Management is responsible for the preparation and fair presentation of these consolidated financial statements in accordance with International Financial Reporting Standards, and for such internal control as management determines is necessary to enable the preparation of consolidated financial statements that are free from material misstatement, whether due to fraud or error.

Auditors' responsibility

Our responsibility is to express an opinion on these consolidated financial statements based on our audits. We conducted our audits in accordance with Canadian generally accepted auditing standards. Those standards require that we comply with ethical requirements and plan and perform the audit to obtain reasonable assurance about whether the consolidated financial statements are free from material misstatement.

An audit involves performing procedures to obtain audit evidence about the amounts and disclosures in the consolidated financial statements. The procedures selected depend on the auditors' judgment, including the assessment of the risks of material misstatement of the consolidated financial statements, whether due to fraud or error. In making those risk assessments, the auditors consider internal control relevant to the entity's preparation and fair presentation of the consolidated financial statements in order to design audit procedures that are appropriate in the circumstances, but not for the purpose of expressing an opinion on the effectiveness of the entity's internal control. An audit also includes evaluating the appropriateness of accounting policies used and the reasonableness of accounting estimates made by management, as well as evaluating the overall presentation of the consolidated financial statements.

We believe that the audit evidence we have obtained in our audits is sufficient and appropriate to provide a basis for our audit opinion.

Opinion

In our opinion, the consolidated financial statements present fairly, in all material respects, the financial position of Indigo Books & Music Inc. as at April 1, 2017 and April 2, 2016, and its financial performance and its cash flows for the 52-week period ended April 1, 2017 and for the 53-week period ended April 2, 2016 in accordance with International Financial Reporting Standards

Ernst & Young LLP

Toronto, Canada
May 30, 2017

Chartered Professional Accountants
Licensed Public Accountants

Consolidated Balance Sheets

(thousands of Canadian dollars)	As at April 1, 2017	As at April 2, 2016
ASSETS		
Current		
Cash and cash equivalents (note 6)	130,438	216,488
Short-term investments (note 6)	100,000	–
Accounts receivable	7,448	7,663
Inventories (note 7)	231,576	217,788
Income taxes recoverable	–	25
Prepaid expenses	11,706	11,290
Derivative financial instruments (note 8)	266	–
Assets held for sale (note 11)	1,037	–
Total current assets	482,471	453,254
Property, plant, and equipment (note 9)	65,078	60,973
Intangible assets (note 10)	15,272	16,506
Equity investment (note 22)	1,800	1,421
Deferred tax assets (note 12)	43,981	51,836
Total assets	608,602	583,990
LIABILITIES AND EQUITY		
Current		
Accounts payable and accrued liabilities (note 21)	170,611	171,112
Unredeemed gift card liability	50,396	50,969
Provisions (note 13)	110	34
Deferred revenue	12,852	13,232
Income taxes payable	360	–
Current portion of long-term debt	–	53
Total current liabilities	234,329	235,400
Long-term accrued liabilities (note 21)	2,378	4,483
Long-term provisions (note 13)	51	109
Total liabilities	236,758	239,992
Equity		
Share capital (note 15)	215,971	209,318
Contributed surplus (note 16)	10,671	10,591
Retained earnings	145,007	124,089
Accumulated other comprehensive income (note 8)	195	–
Total equity	371,844	343,998
Total liabilities and equity	608,602	583,990

See accompanying notes

On behalf of the Board:

Heather Reisman

Heather Reisman
Director

Michael Kirby
Director

Consolidated Statements of Earnings and Comprehensive Earnings

(thousands of Canadian dollars, except per share data)	52-week period ended April 1, 2017	53-week period ended April 2, 2016
Revenue (note 17)	1,019,845	994,181
Cost of sales	(565,640)	(551,194)
Gross profit	454,205	442,987
Operating, selling, and administrative expenses (notes 9, 10 and 17)	(428,981)	(423,037)
Operating profit	25,224	19,950
Net interest income	2,196	753
Share of earnings from equity investment (note 22)	1,617	1,397
Earnings before income taxes	29,037	22,100
Income tax recovery (expense) (note 12)		
Current	(335)	50
Deferred	(7,784)	6,431
Net earnings	20,918	28,581
Other comprehensive income (note 8)		
Items that are or may be reclassified subsequently to net earnings:		
Net change in fair value of cash flow hedges		
(net of taxes of (496); 2016 – 0)	1,357	–
Reclassification of net realized gain		
(net of taxes of 425; 2016 – 0)	(1,162)	–
Other comprehensive income	195	–
Total comprehensive earnings	21,113	28,581
Net earnings per common share (note 18)		
Basic	$0.79	$1.10
Diluted	$0.78	$1.09

See accompanying notes

Consolidated Statements of Changes in Equity

(thousands of Canadian dollars)	Share Capital	Contributed Surplus	Retained Earnings	Accumulated Other Comprehensive Income	Total Equity
Balance, March 28, 2015	205,871	9,770	95,508	–	311,149
Net earnings	–	–	28,581	–	28,581
Exercise of options (notes 15 and 16)	3,156	(484)	–	–	2,672
Directors' deferred share units converted (note 15)	291	(291)	–	–	–
Share-based compensation (notes 16 and 17)	–	1,212	–	–	1,212
Directors' compensation (note 16)	–	384	–	–	384
Other comprehensive income (note 8)	–	–	–	–	–
Balance, April 2, 2016	209,318	10,591	124,089	–	343,998
Balance, April 2, 2016	209,318	10,591	124,089	–	343,998
Net earnings	–	–	20,918	–	20,918
Exercise of options (notes 15 and 16)	5,983	(1,017)	–	–	4,966
Directors' deferred share units converted (note 15)	670	(670)	–	–	–
Share-based compensation (notes 16 and 17)	–	1,400	–	–	1,400
Directors' compensation (note 16)	–	367	–	–	367
Other comprehensive income (note 8)	–	–	–	195	195
Balance, April 1, 2017	215,971	10,671	145,007	195	371,844

See accompanying notes

Consolidated Statements of Cash Flows

(thousands of Canadian dollars)	52-week period ended April 1, 2017	53-week period ended April 2, 2016
CASH FLOWS FROM OPERATING ACTIVITIES		
Net earnings	20,918	28,581
Add (deduct) items not affecting cash		
Depreciation of property, plant and equipment (note 9)	16,612	14,739
Amortization of intangible assets (note 10)	8,573	9,073
Net reversal of capital asset impairments (notes 9 and 10)	(963)	(1,620)
Loss on disposal of capital assets (notes 9 and 10)	2,770	1,039
Share-based compensation (note 16)	1,400	1,212
Directors' compensation (note 16)	367	384
Deferred tax assets (note 12)	7,784	(7,595)
Assets held for sale (note 11)	(1,037)	–
Other	147	(58)
Net change in non-cash working capital balances (note 19)	(17,196)	(5,102)
Interest expense	36	1,000
Interest income	(2,232)	(1,753)
Income taxes received	51	50
Share of earnings from equity investment (note 22)	(1,617)	(1,397)
Cash flows from operating activities	35,613	38,553
CASH FLOWS FROM INVESTING ACTIVITIES		
Purchase of property, plant, and equipment (note 9)	(19,774)	(20,243)
Addition of intangible assets (note 10)	(10,089)	(9,000)
Short-term investments (note 6)	(100,000)	–
Proceeds from disposal of capital assets	–	6
Distributions from equity investment (note 22)	1,238	702
Interest received	1,190	1,522
Cash flows used for investing activities	(127,435)	(27,013)
CASH FLOWS FROM FINANCING ACTIVITIES		
Repayment of long-term debt	(53)	(175)
Interest paid	(28)	(995)
Proceeds from share issuances (note 15)	4,966	2,672
Cash flows from financing activities	4,885	1,502
Effect of foreign currency exchange rate changes on cash and cash equivalents	887	284
Net increase (decrease) in cash and cash equivalents during the period	(86,050)	13,326
Cash and cash equivalents, beginning of period	216,488	203,162
Cash and cash equivalents, end of period	130,438	216,488

See accompanying notes

Notes to Consolidated Financial Statements

April 1, 2017

1. CORPORATE INFORMATION

Indigo Books & Music Inc. (the "Company" or "Indigo") is a corporation domiciled and incorporated under the laws of the Province of Ontario in Canada. The Company's registered office is located at 468 King Street West, Toronto, Ontario, M5V 1L8, Canada. The consolidated financial statements of the Company comprise the Company, its equity investment in Calendar Club of Canada Limited Partnership ("Calendar Club"), and its wholly-owned subsidiary, Indigo Design Studios Inc. (formerly Soho Studios Inc.) The Company is the ultimate parent of the consolidated organization.

2. NATURE OF OPERATIONS

Indigo is Canada's largest book, gift and specialty toy retailer and was formed as a result of an amalgamation of Chapters Inc. and Indigo Books & Music Inc. under the laws of the Province of Ontario, pursuant to a Certificate of Amalgamation dated August 16, 2001. The Company operates a chain of retail bookstores across all ten provinces and one territory in Canada, including 89 superstores (2016 – 88) under the *Indigo* and *Chapters* names, as well as 123 small format stores (2016 – 123) under the banners *Coles*, *Indigospirit*, *SmithBooks*, and *The Book Company*. In addition, online sales are generated through the *indigo.ca* website and the Company's mobile applications. These digital platforms sell an expanded selection of books, gifts, toys, and paper products. The Company also operates seasonal kiosks and year-round stores in shopping malls across Canada through Calendar Club.

The Company's operations are focused on the merchandising of products and services in Canada. As such, the Company presents one operating segment in its consolidated financial statements.

The Company also has a separate registered charity, the Indigo Love of Reading Foundation (the "Foundation"). The Foundation provides new books and learning material to high-needs elementary schools across the country through donations from Indigo, its customers, its suppliers, and its employees.

3. BASIS OF PREPARATION

Statement of Compliance

These consolidated financial statements have been prepared in accordance with International Financial Reporting Standards ("IFRS") as issued by the International Accounting Standards Board ("IASB") and using the accounting policies described herein.

These consolidated financial statements were approved by the Company's Board of Directors on May 30, 2017.

Fiscal Year

The fiscal year of the Company ends on the Saturday closest to March 31. Under an accounting convention common in the retail industry, the Company follows a 52-week reporting cycle, which periodically necessitates a fiscal year of 53 weeks. The year ended April 1, 2017 contained 52 weeks, while the year ended April 2, 2016 contained 53 weeks. The next 53-week period will be for the fiscal year ending April 3, 2021.

Use of Judgments

The preparation of the consolidated financial statements in conformity with IFRS requires the Company to make judgments, apart from those involving estimation, in applying accounting policies that affect the recognition and measurement of assets, liabilities, revenues, and expenses. Actual results may differ from the judgments made by the Company. Information about judgments that have the most significant effect on recognition and measurement of assets, liabilities, revenues, and expenses is discussed below. Information about significant estimates is discussed in the following section.

Impairment

An impairment loss is recognized for the amount by which the carrying amount of an asset or a cash-generating unit ("CGU") exceeds its recoverable amount. Impairment losses are reversed if the recoverable amount of the capital asset, CGU, or group of CGUs exceeds its carrying amount, but only to the extent that the carrying amount of the asset does not exceed the carrying amount that would have been determined, net of depreciation or amortization, if no impairment loss had been recognized. The Company uses judgment when identifying CGUs and when assessing for indicators of impairment or reversal.

Intangible assets

Initial capitalization of intangible asset costs is based on the Company's judgment that technological and economic feasibility are confirmed and the project will generate future economic benefits by way of estimated future discounted cash flows that are being generated.

Leases

The Company uses judgment in determining whether a lease qualifies as a finance lease arrangement that transfers substantially all the risks and rewards incidental to ownership.

Deferred tax assets

The recognition of deferred tax assets is based on the Company's judgment. The assessment of the probability of future taxable income in which deferred tax assets can be utilized is based on management's best estimate of future taxable income that the Company expects to achieve from reviewing its latest forecast. This estimate is adjusted for significant non-taxable income and expenses and for specific limits to the use of any unused tax loss or credit. Deferred tax assets are recognized to the extent that it is probable that taxable profit will be available against which the deductible temporary differences and the carryforward of unused tax credits and unused tax losses can be utilized. Any difference between the gross deferred tax asset and the amount recognized is recorded on the balance sheet as a valuation allowance. If the valuation allowance decreases as a result of subsequent events, the previously recognized valuation allowance will be reversed. The recognition of deferred tax assets that are subject to certain legal or economic limits or uncertainties are assessed individually by the Company based on the specific facts and circumstances.

Use of Estimates

The preparation of the consolidated financial statements in conformity with IFRS requires the Company to make estimates and assumptions in applying accounting policies that affect the recognition and measurement of assets, liabilities, revenues, and expenses. Actual results may differ from the estimates made by the Company, and actual results will seldom equal estimates. Information about estimates that have the most significant effect on the recognition and measurement of assets, liabilities, revenues, and expenses are discussed below.

Revenue

The Company recognizes revenue from unredeemed gift cards ("gift card breakage") if the likelihood of gift card redemption by the customer is considered to be remote. The Company estimates its average gift card breakage rate based on historical redemption rates. The resulting gift card breakage revenue is recognized over the estimated period of redemption based on historical redemption patterns commencing when the gift cards are sold.

The Indigo plum rewards program ("Plum") allows customers to earn points on their purchases. The fair value of Plum points is calculated by multiplying the number of points issued by the estimated cost per point. The estimated cost per point is based on many factors, including expected future redemption patterns and associated costs. On an ongoing basis, the Company monitors trends in redemption patterns (redemption at each reward level), historical redemption rates (points redeemed as a percentage of points issued) and net cost per point redeemed, adjusting the estimated cost per point based upon expected future activity.

Inventories

The future realization of the carrying amount of inventory is affected by future sales demand, inventory levels, and product quality. At each balance sheet date, the Company reviews its on-hand inventory and uses historical trends and current inventory mix to determine a reserve for the impact of future markdowns that will take the net realizable value of inventory on-hand below cost. Inventory valuation also incorporates a write-down to reflect future losses on the disposition of obsolete merchandise. The Company reduces inventory for estimated shrinkage that has occurred between physical inventory counts and each reporting date based on historical experience as a percentage of sales. In addition, the Company records a vendor settlement accrual to cover any disputes between the Company and its vendors. The Company estimates this reserve based on historical experience of settlements with its vendors.

Share-based payments

The cost of equity-settled transactions with counterparties is based on the Company's estimate of the fair value of share-based instruments and the number of equity instruments that will eventually vest. The Company's estimated fair value of the share-based instruments is calculated using the following variables: risk-free interest rate; expected volatility; expected time until exercise; and expected dividend yield. Risk-free interest rate is based on Government of Canada bond yields, while all other variables are estimated based on the Company's historical experience with its share-based payments.

Impairment

To determine the recoverable amount of an impaired asset, the Company estimates expected future cash flows and determines a suitable discount rate in order to calculate the present value of those cash flows. In the process of measuring expected future cash flows, the Company makes assumptions about certain variables, such as future sales, gross margin rates, expenses, capital expenditures, working capital investments, and lease terms, which are based upon historical experience and expected future performance. Determining the applicable discount rate involves estimating appropriate adjustments to market risk and to Company-specific risk factors.

Property, plant, equipment, and intangible assets (collectively, "capital assets")

Capital assets are depreciated over their useful lives, taking into account residual values where appropriate. Assessments of useful lives and residual values are performed on an ongoing basis and take into consideration factors such as technological innovation, maintenance programs, and relevant market information. In assessing residual values, the Company considers the remaining life of the asset, its projected disposal value, and future market conditions.

4. SIGNIFICANT ACCOUNTING POLICIES

The accounting policies set out below have been applied consistently to all periods presented in these consolidated financial statements.

Basis of Measurement

The Company's consolidated financial statements are prepared on the historical cost basis of accounting, except as disclosed in the accounting policies set out below.

Basis of Consolidation

The consolidated financial statements comprise the financial statements of the Company and entities controlled by the Company. Control exists when the Company is exposed to, or has the right to, variable returns from its involvement with the controlled entity and when the Company has the current ability to affect those returns through its power over the controlled entity. When the Company does not own all of the equity in a subsidiary, the non-controlling interest is disclosed as a separate line item in the consolidated balance sheets and the earnings accruing to non-controlling interest holders are disclosed as a separate line item in the consolidated statements of earnings (loss) and comprehensive earnings (loss).

The financial statements of the subsidiary are prepared for the same reporting period as the parent company, using consistent accounting policies. Subsidiaries are fully consolidated from the date of acquisition, being the date on which the Company obtains control, and continue to be consolidated until the date that such control ceases. Once control ceases, the Company will reassess the relationship with the former subsidiary and revise Indigo's accounting policy based on the Company's remaining percentage of ownership. All intercompany balances and transactions and any unrealized gains and losses arising from intercompany transactions are eliminated in preparing these consolidated financial statements.

Equity Investment

The equity method of accounting is applied to investments in companies where Indigo has the ability to exert significant influence over the financial and operating policy decisions of the company but lacks control or joint control over those policies. Under the equity method, the Company's investment is initially recognized at cost and subsequently increased or decreased to recognize the Company's share of earnings and losses of the investment, and for impairment losses after the initial recognition date. The Company's share of losses that are in excess of its investment is recognized only to the extent that Indigo has incurred legal or constructive obligations or made payments on behalf of the company. The Company's share of earnings and losses of its equity investment are recognized through profit or loss during the period. Cash distributions received from the investment are accounted for as a reduction in the carrying amount of the Company's equity investment.

Cash and Cash Equivalents

Cash and cash equivalents consist of cash on hand, balances with banks, and highly liquid investments that are readily convertible to known amounts of cash with maturities of three months or less at the date of acquisition. Cash equivalents of fixed deposits or similar instruments with an original term of longer than three months are also included in this category if they are readily convertible to a known amount of cash throughout their term and are subject to an insignificant risk of change in value assessed against the amount at inception. Cash is considered to be restricted when it is subject to contingent rights of a third-party customer, vendor, or government agency.

Short-term Investments

Short-term investments consist of guaranteed investment securities with an original maturity date greater than 90 days and remaining term to maturity of less than 365 days from the date of acquisition. These investments are non-redeemable until the maturity date.

Inventories

Inventories are valued at the lower of cost, determined on a moving average cost basis, and market, being net realizable value. Costs include all direct and reasonable expenditures that are incurred in bringing inventories to their present location and condition. Net realizable value is the estimated selling price in the ordinary course of business. When the Company permanently reduces the retail price of an item and the markdown incurred brings the retail price below the cost of the item, there is a corresponding reduction in inventory recognized in the period. Vendor rebates are recorded as a reduction in the price of the products and corresponding inventories are recorded net of vendor rebates.

Prepaid Expenses

Prepaid expenses include store supplies, rent, license fees, maintenance contracts, and insurance. Store supplies are expensed as they are used while other costs are amortized over the term of the contract.

Income Taxes

Current income taxes are the expected taxes payable or receivable on the taxable earnings or loss for the period. Current income taxes are payable on taxable earnings for the period as calculated under Canadian taxation guidelines, which differ from taxable earnings under IFRS. Calculation of current income taxes is based on tax rates and tax laws that have been enacted, or substantively enacted, by the end of the reporting period. Current income taxes relating to items recognized directly in equity are recognized in equity and not in the consolidated statements of earnings (loss) and comprehensive earnings (loss).

Deferred income taxes are calculated at the reporting date using the liability method based on temporary differences between the carrying amounts of assets and liabilities and their tax bases. However, deferred tax assets and liabilities on temporary differences arising from the initial recognition of goodwill, or of an asset or liability in a transaction that is not a business combination, will not be recognized when neither accounting nor taxable profit or loss are affected at the time of the transaction.

Deferred tax assets arising from temporary differences associated with investments in subsidiaries are provided for if it is probable that the differences will reverse in the foreseeable future and taxable profit will be available against which the tax assets may be utilized. Deferred tax assets on temporary differences associated with investments in subsidiaries are not provided for if the timing of the reversal of these temporary differences can be controlled by the Company and it is probable that reversal will not occur in the foreseeable future.

Deferred tax assets and liabilities are calculated, without discounting, at tax rates that are expected to apply to their respective periods of realization, provided they are enacted or substantively enacted by the end of the reporting period. Deferred tax assets and liabilities are offset only when the Company has the right and intention to set off current tax assets and liabilities from the same taxable entity and the same taxation authority.

Deferred tax assets are recognized to the extent that it is probable that taxable profit will be available against which the deductible temporary differences and the carryforward of unused tax credits and unused tax losses can be utilized. Any difference between the gross deferred tax asset and the amount recognized is recorded on the consolidated balance sheets as a valuation allowance. If the valuation allowance decreases as the result of subsequent events, the previously recognized valuation allowance will be reversed.

Property, Plant, and Equipment

All items of property, plant, and equipment are initially recognized at cost, which includes any costs directly attributable to bringing the asset to the location and condition necessary for it to be capable of operating in the manner intended by the Company. Subsequent to initial recognition, property, plant, and equipment assets are shown at cost less accumulated depreciation and any accumulated impairment losses.

Depreciation of an asset begins once it becomes available for use. The depreciable amount of an asset, being the cost of an asset less the residual value, is allocated on a straight-line basis over the estimated useful life of the asset. Residual value is estimated to be nil unless the Company expects to dispose of the asset at a value that exceeds the estimated disposal costs. The residual values, useful lives, and depreciation methods applied to assets are reviewed based on relevant market information and management considerations.

The following useful lives are applied:

Furniture, fixtures, and equipment	5 – 10 years
Computer equipment	3 – 5 years
Equipment under finance leases	3 – 5 years
Leasehold improvements	over the shorter of useful life and lease term plus expected renewals, to a maximum of 10 years

Items of property, plant, and equipment are assessed for impairment as detailed in the accounting policy note on impairment and are derecognized either upon disposal or when no future economic benefits are expected from their use. Any gain or loss arising on derecognition is included in earnings when the asset is derecognized.

Leased assets

Leases are classified as finance leases when the terms of the lease transfer substantially all the risks and rewards related to ownership of the leased asset to the Company. At lease inception, the related asset and corresponding long-term liability are recognized at the lower of the fair value of the leased asset or the present value of the minimum lease payments.

Depreciation methods and useful lives for assets held under finance lease agreements correspond to those applied to comparable assets that are legally owned by the Company. If there is no reasonable certainty that the Company will obtain ownership of the financed asset at the end of the lease term, the asset is depreciated over the shorter of its estimated useful life or the lease term. The corresponding long-term liability is reduced by lease payments less interest paid. Interest payments are expensed as part of net interest on the consolidated statements of earnings (loss) and comprehensive earnings (loss) over the period of the lease.

All other leases are treated as operating leases. Payments on operating lease agreements are recognized as an expense on a straight-line basis over the lease term. Associated costs, such as maintenance and insurance, are expensed as incurred.

The Company performs quarterly assessments of contracts that do not take the legal form of a lease to determine whether they convey the right to use an asset in return for a payment or series of payments and therefore need to be accounted for as leases. As at April 1, 2017, the Company had no such contracts.

Leased premises

The Company conducts all of its business from leased premises. Leasehold improvements are depreciated over the lesser of their economic life or the initial lease term plus renewal periods where renewal has been determined to be reasonably certain ("lease term"). Leasehold improvements are assessed for impairment as detailed in the accounting policy note on impairment. Leasehold improvement allowances are depreciated over the lease term. Other inducements, such as rent-free periods, are amortized into earnings over the lease term, with the unamortized portion recorded in current and long-term accounts payable and accrued liabilities. As at April 1, 2017, all of the Company's leases on premises were accounted for as operating leases. Expenses incurred for leased premises include base rent, taxes, common area maintenance, and contingent rent based upon a percentage of sales.

Intangible Assets

Intangible assets are initially recognized at cost, if acquired separately, or at fair value, if acquired as part of a business combination. After initial recognition, intangible assets are carried at cost less accumulated amortization and any accumulated impairment losses.

Amortization commences when the intangible assets are available for their intended use. The useful lives of intangible assets are assessed as either finite or indefinite. Intangible assets with finite lives are amortized over their useful economic life. Intangible assets with indefinite lives are not amortized but are reviewed at each reporting date to determine whether the indefinite life continues to be supportable. If not, the change in useful life from indefinite to finite is made on a prospective basis. Residual value is estimated to be zero unless the Company expects to dispose of the asset at a value that exceeds the estimated disposal costs. The residual values, useful lives, and amortization methods applied to assets are reviewed annually based on relevant market information and management considerations.

The following useful lives are applied:

Computer application software	3 – 5 years
Internal development costs	3 years
Domain name	Indefinite useful life – not amortized

There are no legal, regulatory, contractual, competitive, economic or other factors that limit the useful life of the domain name to the Company. Therefore, useful life of the domain name is deemed to be indefinite.

Intangible assets are assessed for impairment as detailed in the accounting policy note on impairment. An intangible asset is derecognized either upon disposal or when no future economic benefit is expected from its use. Any gain or loss arising on derecognition is included in earnings when the asset is derecognized.

Computer application software

When computer application software is not an integral part of a related item of computer hardware, the software is treated as an intangible asset. Computer application software that is integral to the use of related computer hardware is recorded as property, plant, and equipment.

Internal development costs

Costs that are directly attributable to internal development are recognized as intangible assets provided they meet the definition of an intangible asset. Development costs not meeting these criteria are expensed as incurred. Capitalized development costs include external direct costs of materials and services and the payroll and payroll-related costs for employees who are directly associated with the projects.

Impairment Testing

Capital assets

For the purposes of assessing impairment, capital assets are grouped at the lowest levels for which there are largely independent cash inflows and for which a reasonable and consistent allocation basis can be identified. For capital assets that can be reasonably and consistently allocated to individual stores, the store level is used as the CGU for impairment testing. For all other capital assets, the corporate level is used as the group of CGUs. Capital assets and related CGUs or groups of CGUs are tested for impairment quarterly and whenever events or changes in circumstances indicate that the carrying amount may not be recoverable. Events or changes in circumstances that may indicate impairment include a significant change to the Company's operations, a significant decline in performance, or a change in market conditions that adversely affects the Company.

An impairment loss is recognized for the amount by which the carrying amount of a CGU or group of CGUs exceeds its recoverable amount. To determine the recoverable amount, management uses a value-in-use calculation to determine the present value of the expected future cash flows from each CGU or group of CGUs based on the CGU's estimated growth rate. The Company's growth rate and future cash flows are based on historical data and management's expectations. Impairment losses are charged pro rata to the capital assets in the CGU or group of CGUs. Capital assets and CGUs or groups of CGUs are subsequently reassessed for indicators that a previously recognized impairment loss may no longer exist. An impairment loss is reversed if the recoverable amount of the capital asset, CGU, or group of CGUs exceeds its carrying amount, but only to the extent that the carrying amount of the asset does not exceed the carrying amount that would have been determined, net of depreciation or amortization, if no impairment loss had been recognized.

Financial assets

Individually significant financial assets are tested for impairment on an individual basis. The remaining financial assets are assessed collectively in groups that share similar credit risk characteristics. Financial assets are tested for impairment whenever events or changes in circumstances indicate that the carrying amount may not be recoverable. Evidence of impairment may include indications that a debtor or a group of debtors are experiencing significant financial difficulty, default, or delinquency in interest or principal payments, and observable data indicating that there is a measurable decrease in the estimated future cash flows.

A financial asset is deemed to be impaired if there is objective evidence that one or more loss events having a negative effect on future cash flows of the financial asset occur after initial recognition and the loss can be reliably measured. The impairment loss is measured as the difference between the carrying amount of the financial asset and the present value of the estimated future cash flows, discounted at the original effective interest rate. The impairment loss is recorded as an allowance and recognized in net earnings. If the impairment loss decreases as a result of subsequent events, the previously recognized impairment loss is reversed.

Assets Held for Sale

Non-current assets are classified as assets held for sale if their carrying amounts will be recovered principally through a sale transaction rather than through continuing use. To qualify as assets held for sale, the sale must be highly probable, assets must be available for immediate sale in their present condition, and management must be committed to a plan to sell assets that should be expected to close within one year from the date of classification. Assets held for sale are recognized at the lower of their carrying amount and fair value less costs to sell and are not depreciated.

Provisions

A provision is a liability of uncertain timing or amount. Provisions are recognized when the Company has a present legal or constructive obligation as a result of past events for which it is probable that the Company will be required to settle the obligation and a reliable estimate of the settlement can be made. The amount recognized as a provision is the best estimate of the consideration required to settle the present obligation at the end of the reporting period, taking into account risks and uncertainties of cash flows. Where the effect of discounting to present value is material, provisions are adjusted to reflect the time value of money. Examples of provisions include decommissioning liabilities, onerous leases, and legal claims.

Borrowing Costs

Borrowing costs are primarily composed of interest on the Company's long-term debt, if any. Borrowing costs are capitalized using the effective interest rate method to the extent that they are directly attributable to the acquisition, production, or construction of qualifying assets that require a substantial period of time to get ready for their intended use or sale. All other borrowing costs are expensed as incurred and reported in the consolidated statements of earnings (loss) and comprehensive earnings (loss) as part of net interest.

Total Equity

Share capital represents the nominal value of shares that have been issued. Retained earnings include all current and prior period retained profits. Dividend distributions payable to equity shareholders are recorded as dividends payable when the dividends have been approved by the Board of Directors prior to the reporting date.

Share-based Awards

The Company has established an employee stock option plan for key employees. The fair value of each tranche of options granted is estimated on the grant date using the Black-Scholes option pricing model. The Black-Scholes option pricing model is based on variables such as: risk-free interest rate; expected volatility; expected time until exercise; and expected dividend yield. Expected stock price volatility is based on the historical volatility of the Company's stock for a period approximating the expected life. The grant date fair value, net of estimated forfeitures, is recognized as an expense with a corresponding increase to contributed surplus over the vesting period. Estimates are subsequently revised if there is an indication that the number of stock options expected to vest differs from previous estimates. Any consideration paid by employees on exercise of stock options is credited to share capital with a corresponding reduction to contributed surplus.

Revenue Recognition

The Company recognizes revenue when the substantial risks and rewards of ownership pass to the customer. Revenue is measured at the fair value of the consideration received or receivable by the Company for goods supplied, inclusive of amounts invoiced for shipping and net of sales discounts, returns, and amounts deferred related to the issuance of Plum points. Return allowances are estimated using historical experience.

Revenue is recognized when the amount can be measured reliably, it is probable that economic benefits associated with the transaction will flow to the Company, the costs incurred or to be incurred can be measured reliably, and the criteria for each of the Company's activities (as described below) have been met.

Retail sales

Revenue for retail customers is recognized at the time of purchase.

Online and kiosk sales

Revenue for online and kiosk customers is recognized when the product is shipped.

Commission revenue

The Company earns commission revenue through partnerships with other companies and recognizes revenue once services have been rendered and the amount of revenue can be measured reliably.

Gift cards

The Company sells gift cards to its customers and recognizes the revenue as gift cards are redeemed. The Company also recognizes gift card breakage if the likelihood of gift card redemption by the customer is considered to be remote. The Company determines its average gift card breakage rate based on historical redemption rates. Once the breakage rate is determined, the resulting revenue is recognized over the estimated period of redemption based on historical redemption patterns, commencing when the gift cards are sold. Gift card breakage is included in revenue in the Company's consolidated statements of earnings (loss) and comprehensive earnings (loss).

Indigo irewards loyalty program

For an annual fee, the Company offers loyalty cards to customers that entitle the cardholder to receive discounts on purchases. Each card is issued with a 12-month expiry period. The fee revenue related to the issuance of a card is deferred and amortized into revenue over the expiry period based upon historical sales volumes.

Indigo plum rewards program

Plum is a free program that allows members to earn points on their purchases in the Company's stores and on *indigo.ca*. Members can then redeem points for discounts on future purchases of merchandise in stores and online.

When a plum member purchases merchandise, the Company allocates the payment received between the merchandise and the points. The payment is allocated based on the residual method, where the amount allocated to the merchandise is the total payment less the fair value of the points. The portion of revenue attributed to the merchandise is recognized at the time of purchase. Revenue attributed to the points is recorded as deferred revenue and recognized when points are redeemed.

The fair value of points is calculated by multiplying the number of points issued by the estimated cost per point. The estimated cost per point is determined based on a number of factors, including the expected future redemption patterns and associated costs. On an ongoing basis, the Company monitors trends in redemption patterns (redemption at each reward level), historical redemption rates (points redeemed as a percentage of points issued) and net cost per point redeemed, adjusting the estimated cost per point based upon expected future activity. Points revenue is included as part of total revenue in the Company's consolidated statements of earnings (loss) and comprehensive earnings (loss).

Interest income

Interest income is reported on an accrual basis using the effective interest method and included as part of net interest in the Company's consolidated statements of earnings (loss) and comprehensive earnings (loss).

Vendor Rebates

The Company records cash consideration received from vendors as a reduction to the price of vendors' products. This is reflected as a reduction in cost of goods sold and related inventories when recognized in the consolidated financial statements. Certain exceptions apply where the cash consideration received is a reimbursement of incremental selling costs incurred by the Company, in which case the cash received is reflected as a reduction in operating, selling, and administrative expenses.

Earnings per Share

Basic earnings per share is determined by dividing the net earnings attributable to common shareholders by the weighted average number of common shares outstanding during the period. Diluted earnings per share is calculated in accordance with the treasury stock method and is based on the weighted average number of common shares and dilutive common share equivalents outstanding during the period. The weighted average number of shares used in the computation of both basic and fully diluted earnings per share may be the same due to the anti-dilutive effect of securities.

Financial Instruments

Financial assets and financial liabilities are recognized when the Company becomes a party to the contractual provisions of the financial instrument. Financial assets are derecognized when the contractual rights to the cash flows from the financial asset expire, or when the financial asset and all substantial risks and rewards are transferred. A financial liability is derecognized when it is extinguished, discharged, cancelled, or expires. Where a legally enforceable right to offset exists for recognized financial assets and financial liabilities and there is an intention to settle the liability and realize the asset simultaneously, or to settle on a net basis, such related financial assets and financial liabilities are offset.

For the purposes of ongoing measurement, financial assets and liabilities are classified according to their characteristics and management's intent. All financial instruments are initially recognized at fair value.

After initial recognition, financial instruments are subsequently measured as follows:

Financial assets

(i) Loans and receivables – These are non-derivative financial assets with fixed or determinable payments that are not quoted in an active market. These assets are measured at amortized cost, less impairment charges, using the effective interest method. Gains and losses are recognized in earnings through the amortization process or when the assets are derecognized.

(ii) Financial assets at fair value through profit or loss – These assets are held for trading if acquired for the purpose of selling in the near term or are designated to this category upon initial recognition. These assets are measured at fair value, with gains or losses recognized in earnings. Derivatives are classified as fair value through profit or loss unless they are designated as effective hedging instruments.

(iii) Held-to-maturity investments – These are non-derivative financial assets with fixed or determinable payments and fixed maturities that the Company intends, and is able, to hold until maturity. These assets are measured at amortized cost, less impairment charges, using the effective interest method. Gains and losses are recognized in earnings through the amortization process or when the assets are derecognized.

(iv) Available-for-sale financial assets – These are non-derivative financial assets that are either designated to this category upon initial recognition or do not qualify for inclusion in any of the other categories. These assets are measured at fair value, with unrealized gains and losses recognized in other comprehensive income until the asset is derecognized or determined to be impaired. If the asset is derecognized or determined to be impaired, the cumulative gain or loss previously reported in accumulated other comprehensive income is included in earnings.

Financial liabilities

(i) Other liabilities – These liabilities are measured at amortized cost using the effective interest rate method. Gains and losses are recognized in earnings through the amortization process or when the liabilities are derecognized.

(ii) Financial liabilities at fair value through profit or loss – These liabilities are held for trading if acquired for the purpose of selling in the near term or are designated to this category upon initial recognition. These liabilities are measured at fair value, with gains or losses recognized in earnings.

The Company's financial assets and financial liabilities are generally classified and measured as follows:

Financial Asset/Liability	Category	Measurement
Cash and cash equivalents	Loans and receivables	Amortized cost
Short-term investments	Held-to-maturity	Amortized cost
Accounts receivable	Loans and receivables	Amortized cost
Accounts payable and accrued liabilities	Other liabilities	Amortized cost
Derivative instruments	Fair value through profit or loss	Fair value

All other consolidated balance sheet accounts are not considered financial instruments.

All financial instruments measured at fair value after initial recognition are categorized into one of three hierarchy levels for measurement and disclosure purposes. Each level reflects the significance of the inputs used in making the fair value measurements.

Level 1: Fair value is determined by reference to unadjusted quoted prices in active markets.
Level 2: Valuations use inputs based on observable market data, either directly or indirectly, other than the quoted prices.
Level 3: Valuations are based on inputs that are not based on observable market data.

The following methods and assumptions were used to estimate the fair value of each type of financial instrument by reference to market data and other valuation techniques, as appropriate:

(i) The initial fair values of cash and cash equivalents, short-term investments, accounts receivable, and accounts payable and accrued liabilities approximate their carrying values given their short maturities;

(ii) The initial fair value of long-term debt, if any, is estimated based on the discounted cash payments of the debt at the Company's estimated incremental borrowing rates for debt of the same remaining maturities. The fair value of long-term debt approximates its carrying value. These instruments are subsequently measured at amortized cost; and

(iii) The fair value of derivative financial instruments are estimated using quoted market rates at the measurement date adjusted for the maturity term of each instrument. Derivative financial instruments are classified as level 2 in the fair value hierarchy.

Derivative financial instruments and hedge accounting

The Company enters into various derivative financial instruments as part of its strategy to manage foreign currency exposure. All contracts entered into during the year have been designated as cash flow hedges for accounting purposes. The Company does not hold or issue derivative financial instruments for trading purposes. All derivative financial instruments, including derivatives embedded in financial or non-financial contracts not closely related to the host contracts, are measured at fair value. The gain or loss that results from remeasurement at each reporting period is recognized in net income immediately unless the derivative is designated and effective as a hedging instrument, in which case the timing of the recognition in net income depends on the nature of the hedge relationship.

At the inception of a hedge relationship, the Company documents the relationship between the hedging instrument and the hedged item along with the Company's risk management objectives and strategy for undertaking various hedge transactions. Furthermore, at inception and on an ongoing basis, the Company documents whether the hedging instrument is highly effective in offsetting changes in cash flows of the hedged item attributable to the hedged risk. Such hedges are expected to be highly effective in achieving offsetting changes in cash flows and are assessed on an ongoing basis to determine that they actually have been highly effective throughout the financial reporting periods for which they were designated.

Accordingly, the effective portion of the change in the fair value of the foreign exchange forward contracts that are designated and qualify as cash flow hedges is recognized in other comprehensive income (loss) until related payments have been made in future accounting periods. Associated gains and losses recognized in other comprehensive income (loss) are reclassified to earnings in the periods when the hedged item is recognized in earnings. These earnings are included within the same line of the consolidated statement of earnings (loss) as the recognized item. However, when the hedged forecast transaction results in the recognition of a non-financial asset, the gains and losses previously recognized in other comprehensive income (loss) are transferred from equity and included in the initial measurement of the cost of the non-financial asset. The gain or loss relating to the ineffective portion is recognized immediately in the consolidated statements of earnings (loss).

Retirement Benefits

The Company provides retirement benefits through a defined contribution retirement plan. Under the defined contribution retirement plan, the Company pays fixed contributions to an independent entity. The Company has no legal or constructive obligations to pay further contributions after its payment of the fixed contribution. The costs of benefits under the defined contribution retirement plan are expensed as contributions are due and are reversed if employees leave before the vesting period.

Foreign Currency Translation

The consolidated financial statements are presented in Canadian dollars, which is the functional currency of the Company. Sales transacted in foreign currencies are aggregated monthly and translated using the average exchange rate. Transactions in foreign currencies are translated at rates of exchange at the time of the transaction. Monetary assets and liabilities denominated in foreign currencies that are held at the reporting date are translated at the closing consolidated balance sheet rate. Non-monetary items are measured at historical cost and are translated using the exchange rates at the date of the transaction. Non-monetary items measured at fair value are translated using exchange rates at the date when fair value was determined. The resulting exchange gains or losses are included in earnings.

Accounting Standards Implemented in Fiscal 2017

Presentation of Financial Statements ("IAS 1")

In December 2014, the IASB issued amendments to IAS 1 as part of the IASB's Disclosure Initiative. These amendments encourage entities to apply professional judgment regarding disclosure and presentation in their financial statements and are effective for annual periods beginning on or after January 1, 2016. Implementation of these amendments in 2017 did not have a significant impact on the Company's financial statements and annual disclosures.

5. NEW ACCOUNTING PRONOUNCEMENTS

Statement of Cash Flows ("IAS 7")

In January 2016, the IASB issued amendments to IAS 7 as part of the IASB's Disclosure Initiative. These amendments require entities to provide additional disclosures that will enable financial statement users to evaluate changes in liabilities arising from financing activities, including changes arising from cash flows and non-cash changes. These amendments are effective for annual periods beginning on or after January 1, 2017 with early application permitted. Adopting these amendments will not have a significant impact on the Company's results of operations, financial position, or disclosures. The Company applied this standard beginning April 2, 2017.

Revenue from Contracts with Customers ("IFRS 15")

In May 2014, the IASB issued IFRS 15, a new standard that specifies how and when to recognize revenue as well as requiring entities to provide users of financial statements with more informative, relevant disclosures. IFRS 15 supersedes IAS 18, "Revenue," IAS 11, "Construction Contracts," and a number of revenue-related interpretations. Application of IFRS 15 is mandatory for all IFRS reporters and it applies to nearly all contracts with customers: the main exceptions are leases, financial instruments, and insurance contracts.

IFRS 15 must be applied retrospectively using either the retrospective or cumulative effect method for annual reporting periods beginning on or after January 1, 2018. The Company plans to apply this standard beginning April 1, 2018 but has not yet determined which transition method it will apply.

Implementation of IFRS 15 is expected to impact the allocation of deferred plum program revenue. Revenue is currently allocated to plum points using the residual fair value method. Under IFRS 15, revenue will be allocated based on relative stand-alone selling prices between plum points and the goods on which points were earned. The Company is currently assessing the impact of this change and other impacts of adopting this standard on its results of operations, financial position, and disclosures.

Financial Instruments ("IFRS 9")

In July 2014, the IASB issued the final version of IFRS 9, which reflects all phases of the financial instruments project and replaces IAS 39, "Financial Instruments: Recognition and Measurement," and all previous versions of IFRS 9. The standard introduces new requirements for classification and measurement, impairment, and hedge accounting. IFRS 9 is effective for annual periods beginning on or after January 1, 2018. The Company plans to apply this standard beginning on April 1, 2018.

IFRS 9 more closely aligns hedge accounting with risk management activities and applies a more qualitative and forward-looking approach to assessing hedge effectiveness. The Company is currently assessing the impact of this change and other impacts of adopting this standard on its results of operations, financial position, and disclosures.

Leases ("IFRS 16")

In January 2016, the IASB issued IFRS 16, which supersedes existing standards and interpretations under IAS 17, "Leases." IFRS 16 introduces a single lessee accounting model, eliminating the distinction between operating and finance leases. The new lessee accounting model requires substantially all leases to be reported on a company's balance sheet and will provide greater transparency on companies' leased assets and liabilities. IFRS 16 substantially carries forward the lessor accounting in IAS 17 with the distinction between operating leases and finance leases being retained. The Company is assessing the impact of adopting this standard on its results of operations, financial position, and disclosures.

The new standard will apply for annual periods beginning on or after January 1, 2019. The Company plans to apply this standard beginning March 31, 2019. For leases where the Company is the lessee, it has the option of adopting a full retrospective approach or a modified retrospective approach on transition to IFRS 16. The Company has not yet determined which transition method it will apply or whether it will use the optional exemptions or practical expedients available under the standard.

6. CASH, CASH EQUIVALENTS, AND SHORT-TERM INVESTMENTS

Cash and cash equivalents consist of the following:

(thousands of Canadian dollars)	April 1, 2017	April 2, 2016
Cash	63,872	102,862
Restricted cash	1,343	3,460
Cash equivalents	65,223	110,166
Cash and cash equivalents	130,438	216,488

Restricted cash represents cash pledged as collateral for letter of credit obligations issued to support the Company's purchases of offshore merchandise.

As at April 1, 2017, the Company held $100.0 million of short-term investments (April 2, 2016 – no such investments). Short-term investments consist of guaranteed investment securities with an original maturity date greater than 90 days and remaining term to maturity of less than 365 days from the date of acquisition. These investments are non-redeemable until the maturity date, and therefore they are classified separately from cash and cash equivalents.

7. INVENTORIES

The cost of inventories recognized as an expense was $571.9 million in fiscal 2017 (2016 – $561.5 million). Inventories consist of the landed cost of goods sold and exclude online shipping costs, inventory shrink and damage reserve, and all vendor support programs. The amount of inventory write-downs as a result of net realizable value lower than cost was $9.0 million in fiscal 2017 (2016 – $10.1 million), and there were no reversals of inventory write-downs that were recognized in fiscal 2017 (2016 – nil). The amount of inventory with net realizable value equal to cost was $2.8 million as at April 1, 2017 (April 2, 2016 – $1.5 million).

8. DERIVATIVE FINANCIAL INSTRUMENTS

The Company's derivative financial instruments consist of foreign exchange forward contracts. These contracts were entered into in order to manage the currency fluctuation risk associated with forecasted U.S. dollar payments, primarily for general merchandise inventory purchases, and have been designated as cash flow hedges for accounting purposes. The fair value of a foreign exchange forward contract is estimated by discounting the difference between the contractual forward price and the current forward price for the residual maturity of the contract using a risk-free interest rate.

During the fiscal year ended April 1, 2017, the Company entered into forward contracts with total notional amounts of C$173.4 million to buy U.S. dollars and sell Canadian dollars. As at April 1, 2017, the Company had remaining forward contracts in place representing a total notional amount of C$70.3 million (April 2, 2016 – no forward contracts). These contracts extend over a period not exceeding 12 months.

The total fair value of the forward contracts as at April 1, 2017 resulted in an unrealized net gain of $0.3 million (April 2, 2016 – no forward contracts) recognized as other comprehensive income. The carrying value of the derivative financial instruments is equivalent to the pre-tax unrealized gain at period end.

During the fiscal year ended April 1, 2017, net gains of $1.2 million from settled contracts (April 2, 2016 – nil) were reclassified from other comprehensive income to inventory and expenses. Reclassified amounts resulting from hedge ineffectiveness were immaterial for the period ended April 1, 2017 (April 2, 2016 – nil).

9. PROPERTY, PLANT, AND EQUIPMENT

(thousands of Canadian dollars)	Furniture, fixtures, and equipment	Computer equipment	Leasehold improvements	Equipment under finance leases	Total
Gross carrying amount					
Balance, March 28, 2015	64,607	11,742	51,270	767	128,386
Additions	8,611	3,207	8,390	–	20,208
Transfers/reclassifications	1	(467)	501	–	35
Disposals	(2,127)	(102)	(372)	(166)	(2,767)
Assets with zero net book value	(2,952)	(2,253)	(5,818)	–	(11,023)
Balance, April 2, 2016	68,140	12,127	53,971	601	134,839
Additions	9,596	3,123	7,859	–	20,578
Transfers/reclassifications	–	(1,032)	997	–	(35)
Disposals	(28)	(17)	(1)	(465)	(511)
Assets with zero net book value	(4,950)	(2,038)	(6,931)	–	(13,919)
Transferred to assets held for sale	(914)	(2)	(501)	–	(1,417)
Balance, April 1, 2017	71,844	12,161	55,394	136	139,535
Accumulated depreciation and impairment					
Balance, March 28, 2015	33,335	5,638	33,990	537	73,500
Depreciation	6,134	2,347	6,092	166	14,739
Transfers/reclassifications	–	(5)	5	–	–
Disposals	(1,265)	(29)	(270)	(166)	(1,730)
Net impairment losses (reversals)	(459)	(5)	(1,156)	–	(1,620)
Assets with zero net book value	(2,952)	(2,253)	(5,818)	–	(11,023)
Balance, April 2, 2016	34,793	5,693	32,843	537	73,866
Depreciation	6,867	2,182	7,502	61	16,612
Transfers/reclassifications	–	–	–	–	–
Disposals	(22)	(3)	(1)	(465)	(491)
Net impairment losses (reversals)	(384)	(4)	(575)	–	(963)
Assets with zero net book value	(4,950)	(2,038)	(6,931)	–	(13,919)
Transferred to assets held for sale	(430)	(1)	(217)	–	(648)
Balance, April 1, 2017	35,874	5,829	32,621	133	74,457
Net carrying amount					
April 2, 2016	33,347	6,434	21,128	64	60,973
April 1, 2017	35,970	6,332	22,773	3	65,078

Property, plant and equipment are assessed for impairment at the CGU level, except for those assets which are considered to be corporate assets. As certain corporate assets cannot be allocated on a reasonable and consistent basis to individual CGUs, they are tested for impairment at the corporate level.

A CGU has been defined as an individual retail store as each store generates cash inflows that are largely independent from the cash inflows of other stores. CGUs and groups of CGUs are tested for impairment if impairment indicators exist at the reporting date. Recoverable amounts for CGUs being tested are based on value in use, which is calculated from discounted cash flow projections. For stores that are at risk of closure, cash flows are projected over the remaining lease terms, including any renewal options if renewal is likely. Cash flows for stores expected to operate beyond the current lease term and renewal options are projected using a terminal value calculation. Corporate asset testing calculates discounted cash flow projections over a five-year period plus a terminal value.

The key assumptions from the value-in-use calculations are those regarding growth rates and discount rates. Cash flow projections for the next three fiscal years are calculated separately for each CGU being tested and are based on management's best estimate of future income. Following these three fiscal years, projections are extrapolated using average long-term growth rates ranging from 0.0% to 3.0% (2016 – 0.0% to 3.0%). Management's estimate of the discount rate reflects the current market assessment of the time value of money and the risks specific to the Company. The pre-tax discount rate used to calculate value in use for store assets was 16.9% (2016 – 19.7%).

Impairment and reversal indicators were identified during fiscal 2017 for certain retail stores. Accordingly, the Company performed testing, which resulted in the reversal of impairment losses for certain Indigo retail stores. There were $1.0 million of property, plant, and equipment impairment reversals recognized in fiscal 2017 (2016 – $2.3 million). The Company did not recognize any impairments in fiscal 2017 (2016 – $0.6 million resulting from a store closure). Impairment reversals in both years arose due to improved store performance and were spread across a number of CGUs. The recoverable amount of the CGUs impacted by impairments or reversals was $7.4 million (2016 – $16.3 million) and was determined using each CGU's value in use. All impairments and reversals are recorded as part of operating, selling, and administrative expenses in the consolidated statements of earnings and comprehensive earnings.

10. INTANGIBLE ASSETS

(thousands of Canadian dollars)	Computer application software	Internal development costs	Domain name	Total
Gross carrying amount				
Balance, March 28, 2015	25,751	14,681	–	40,432
Additions	4,678	4,282	75	9,035
Transfers/reclassifications	(35)	–	–	(35)
Disposals	(16)	–	–	(16)
Assets with zero net book value	(12,561)	(5,543)	–	(18,104)
Balance, April 2, 2016	17,817	13,420	75	31,312
Additions	6,791	3,263	–	10,054
Transfers/reclassifications	35	–	–	35
Disposals	(2,023)	(814)	–	(2,837)
Assets with zero net book value	(5,733)	(4,023)	–	(9,756)
Balance, April 1, 2017	16,887	11,846	75	28,808
Accumulated amortization and impairment				
Balance, March 28, 2015	15,940	7,905	–	23,845
Amortization	5,149	3,924	–	9,073
Disposals	(8)	–	–	(8)
Assets with zero net book value	(12,561)	(5,543)	–	(18,104)
Balance, April 2, 2016	8,520	6,286	–	14,806
Amortization	4,568	4,005	–	8,573
Disposals	(1)	(86)	–	(87)
Assets with zero net book value	(5,733)	(4,023)	–	(9,756)
Balance, April 1, 2017	7,354	6,182	–	13,536
Net carrying amount				
April 2, 2016	9,297	7,134	75	16,506
April 1, 2017	9,533	5,664	75	15,272

The useful life of the domain name has been deemed to be indefinite because there are no legal, regulatory, contractual, competitive, economic, or other factors that limit the useful life of this asset to the Company.

Impairment testing for intangible assets is performed using the same methodology, CGUs, and groups of CGUs as those used for property, plant and equipment. The key assumptions from the value-in-use calculations for intangible asset impairment testing are also identical to the key assumptions used for property, plant and equipment testing. Impairment and reversal indicators were identified during fiscal 2017 for Indigo's retail stores. Accordingly, the Company performed impairment and reversal testing but there were no intangible asset impairment losses or reversals for retail stores in fiscal 2017 (2016 – no impairment losses or reversals). All impairments and reversals are recorded as part of operating, selling, and administrative expenses in the consolidated statements of earnings and comprehensive earnings.

The Company also identified specific projects that did not achieve expected results during the year and reviewed assets capitalized as part of these projects to determine whether they continued to meet the criteria for capitalization. As a result, the Company recorded $2.8 million of intangible asset disposals for derecognized project assets in fiscal 2017.

11. ASSETS HELD FOR SALE

On February 17, 2017, the Company formalized a Letter of Intent with Starbucks Coffee Canada Inc. ("Starbucks") whereby, among other things, the Company and Starbucks mutually agreed to terminate the Company's license to operate Starbucks-branded cafes within 11 retail locations.

Based on the terms of the Letter of Intent, the Company agreed to transfer to Starbucks the café inventories and capital assets from the terminated licensed locations, and the Company classified these inventories and capital assets as assets held for sale. Subsequent to the transfer, the Company will sublease space in each of the previously licensed locations for Starbucks to operate corporate-run cafes, similar to the 72 other Starbucks-branded cafes Starbucks operates in the Company's retail locations. The transfer and subsequent subleasing were completed on May 1, 2017.

12. INCOME TAXES

Deferred tax assets are recognized to the extent that it is probable that taxable profit will be available against which the deductible temporary differences and the carryforward of unused tax credits and unused tax losses can be utilized. As at April 1, 2017, the Company has recorded $44.0 million in gross value of deferred tax assets based on management's best estimate of future taxable income that the Company expected to achieve (April 2, 2016 – $51.8 million gross value of deferred tax assets).

Deferred income taxes reflect the net tax effects of temporary differences between the carrying amounts of assets and liabilities for financial reporting purposes and the amounts used for income tax purposes. Significant components of the Company's deferred tax assets are as follows:

(thousands of Canadian dollars)	April 1, 2017	April 2, 2016
Reserves and allowances	1,300	1,938
Tax loss carryforwards	22,243	23,597
Corporate minimum tax	2,871	2,511
Book amortization in excess of cumulative eligible capital deduction	214	217
Book amortization in excess of capital cost allowance	17,353	23,573
Total deferred tax assets	43,981	51,836

Significant components of income tax expense (recovery) are as follows:

(thousands of Canadian dollars)	52-week period ended April 1, 2017	53-week period ended April 2, 2016
Current income tax expense	360	–
Adjustment for prior periods	(25)	(50)
	335	(50)
Deferred income tax expense (recovery)		
Origination and reversal of temporary differences	6,119	6,586
Change in valuation allowance	–	(12,432)
Deferred income tax expense relating to utilization of loss carryforwards	1,649	–
Adjustment to deferred tax assets resulting from increase in substantively enacted tax rate	–	(451)
Change in tax rates due to change in expected pattern of reversal	38	(134)
Other, net	(22)	–
	7,784	(6,431)
Total income tax expense (recovery)	8,119	(6,481)

The reconciliation of income taxes computed at statutory income tax rates to the effective income tax rates is as follows:

(thousands of Canadian dollars)	52-week period ended April 1, 2017	%	53-week period ended April 2, 2016	%
Earnings before income taxes	29,037		22,100	
Tax at combined federal and provincial tax rates	7,771	26.8%	5,885	26.6%
Tax effect of expenses not deductible for income tax purposes	587	2.0%	793	3.6%
Decrease in valuation allowance	–	0.0%	(12,432)	(56.3%)
Adjustment to deferred tax assets resulting from increase in substantively enacted tax rate	–	0.0%	(451)	(2.0%)
Change in tax rates due to change in expected pattern of reversal	38	0.1%	(134)	(0.6%)
Other, net	(277)	(1.0%)	(142)	(0.6%)
	8,119	27.9%	(6,481)	(29.3%)

As at April 1, 2017, the Company has combined non-capital loss carryforwards of approximately $83.2 million for income tax purposes that expire in 2031 if not utilized.

13. PROVISIONS

Provisions consist primarily of amounts recorded in respect of decommissioning liabilities, onerous lease arrangements, and legal claims. Activity related to the Company's provisions is as follows:

(thousands of Canadian dollars)	52-week period ended April 1, 2017	53-week period ended April 2, 2016
Balance, beginning of period	143	1,023
Charged	85	33
Utilized / released	(67)	(913)
Balance, end of period	161	143

The Company is subject to payment of decommissioning liabilities upon exiting certain leases. The amount of these payments may fluctuate based on negotiations with the landlord. Onerous lease provisions unwind over the term of the related lease and were discounted using a pre-tax discount rate of 19.0%. Legal claim provisions fluctuate depending on the outcomes when claims are settled.

14. COMMITMENTS AND CONTINGENCIES

(a) Commitments

As at April 1, 2017, the Company had operating lease commitments in respect of its stores, support office premises, and certain equipment. The Company also had operating lease commitments related to the future relocation of its corporate home office. The leases expire at various dates between calendar 2017 and 2033, and may be subject to renewal options. Annual store rent consists of a base amount plus, in some cases, additional payments based on store sales. The Company also generates sublease income in respect of some of its premises leases. Over the next five fiscal years and thereafter, the Company expects to generate $5.5 million from these subleases.

The Company's minimum contractual obligations due over the next five fiscal years and thereafter are summarized below. Operating lease expenditures are presented net of their related subleases:

(millions of Canadian dollars)	Total
2018	57.7
2019	45.0
2020	28.8
2021	20.2
2022	14.7
Thereafter	60.2
Total obligations	226.6

(b) Legal Claims

In the normal course of business, the Company becomes involved in various claims and litigation. While the final outcome of such claims and litigation pending as at April 1, 2017 cannot be predicted with certainty, management believes that any such amount would not have a material impact on the Company's financial position or financial performance, except for those amounts that have been recorded as provisions on the Company's consolidated balance sheets.

15. SHARE CAPITAL

Share capital consists of the following:

Authorized

Unlimited Class A preference shares with no par value, voting, convertible into common shares on a one-for-one basis at the option of the shareholder

Unlimited common shares, voting

	52-week period ended April 1, 2017		53-week period ended April 2, 2016	
	Number of shares	Amount C$ (thousands)	Number of shares	Amount C$ (thousands)
Balance, beginning of period	25,797,351	209,318	25,495,289	205,871
Issued during the period				
Directors' deferred share units converted	67,108	670	29,142	291
Options exercised	487,025	5,983	272,920	3,156
Balance, end of period	26,351,484	215,971	25,797,351	209,318

16. SHARE-BASED COMPENSATION

The Company has established an employee stock option plan (the "Plan") for key employees. The number of common shares reserved for issuance under the Plan as at April 1, 2017 is 3,452,723. Most options granted between May 21, 2002 and March 31, 2012 have a ten-year term and have one fifth of the options granted exercisable one year after the date of issue with the remainder exercisable in equal instalments on the anniversary date over the next four years. Subsequently, most options granted after April 1, 2012 have a five-year term and have one third of the options granted exercisable one year after the date of issue with the remainder exercisable in equal instalments on the anniversary date over the next two years. A small number of options have special vesting schedules that were approved by the Board. Each option is exercisable into one common share of the Company at the price specified in the terms of the option agreement.

The Company uses the fair value method of accounting for stock options, which estimates the fair value of the stock options granted on the date of grant, net of estimated forfeitures, and expenses this value over the vesting period. During fiscal 2017, the pre-forfeiture fair value of options granted was $2.8 million (2016 – $1.4 million). The weighted average fair value of options issued in fiscal 2017 was $4.19 per option (2016 – $2.35 per option).

The fair value of the employee stock options is estimated at the date of grant using the Black-Scholes option pricing model with the following weighted average assumptions during the periods presented:

	52-week period ended April 1, 2017	53-week period ended April 2, 2016
Black-Scholes option pricing assumptions		
Risk-free interest rate	0.6%	0.5%
Expected volatility	33.8%	32.7%
Expected time until exercise	3.0 years	3.0 years
Expected dividend yield	–	–
Other assumptions		
Forfeiture rate	27.3%	28.4%

A summary of the status of the Plan and changes during both periods is presented below:

	52-week period ended April 1, 2017		53-week period ended April 2, 2016	
	Number #	Weighted average exercise price C$	Number #	Weighted average exercise price C$
Outstanding options, beginning of period	1,751,800	10.07	1,561,150	9.94
Granted	657,000	17.94	597,500	10.34
Forfeited	(257,850)	13.50	(133,930)	10.36
Exercised	(487,025)	10.20	(272,920)	9.79
Outstanding options, end of period	1,663,925	12.60	1,751,800	10.07
Options exercisable, end of period	734,900	9.68	651,550	9.59

A summary of options outstanding and exercisable is presented below:

	April 1, 2017				
	Outstanding			Exercisable	
Range of exercise prices C$	Number #	Weighted average exercise price C$	Weighted average remaining contractual life (in years)	Number #	Weighted average exercise price C$
8.00 – 9.41	322,500	8.30	1.3	322,500	8.30
9.42 – 10.28	306,050	10.09	3.4	75,050	10.09
10.29 – 10.77	343,375	10.56	1.9	258,400	10.59
10.78 – 17.38	172,000	12.92	3.2	78,950	11.91
17.39 – 18.00	520,000	18.00	4.4	–	–
8.00 – 18.00	1,663,925	12.60	3.0	734,900	9.68

Directors' Compensation

The Company has established a Directors' Deferred Share Unit Plan ("DSU Plan"). Under the DSU Plan, Directors annually elect whether to receive their annual retainer fees and other Board-related compensation in the form of deferred share units ("DSUs") or receive up to 50% of this compensation in cash. All fiscal 2017 Directors' compensation was in the form of DSUs (2016 – all DSUs).

The number of shares reserved for issuance under this plan is 500,000. The Company issued 21,788 DSUs with a value of $0.4 million during fiscal 2017 (2016 – 32,175 DSUs with a value of $0.4 million). The number of DSUs to be issued to each Director is based on a set fee schedule. The grant date fair value of the outstanding DSUs as at April 1, 2017 was $3.5 million (April 2, 2016 – $3.8 million) and was recorded in contributed surplus. The fair value of DSUs is equal to the traded price of the Company's common shares on the grant date.

17. SUPPLEMENTARY OPERATING INFORMATION

Supplemental product line revenue information:

(thousands of Canadian dollars)	52-week period ended April 1, 2017	53-week period ended April 2, 2016
Print[1]	598,107	615,410
General merchandise[2]	384,097	343,488
eReading[3]	12,510	14,452
Other[4]	25,131	20,831
Total	1,019,845	994,181

1 Includes books, magazines, newspapers, and shipping revenue.
2 Includes lifestyle, paper, toys, calendars, music, DVDs, electronics, and shipping revenue.
3 Includes eReaders, eReader accessories, Kobo revenue share, and shipping revenue.
4 Includes cafés, irewards, gift card breakage, plum breakage, and corporate sales.

Supplemental operating and administrative expenses information:

(thousands of Canadian dollars)	52-week period ended April 1, 2017	53-week period ended April 2, 2016
Wages, salaries, and bonuses	180,893	178,147
Short-term benefits expense	19,444	19,897
Termination benefits expense	2,922	6,559
Retirement benefits expense	1,575	1,418
Share-based compensation	1,400	1,212
Total employee benefits expense	206,234	207,233

Termination benefits arise when the Company terminates certain employment agreements.

Minimum lease payments recognized as an expense during fiscal 2017 were $60.4 million (2016 – $55.9 million). Contingent rents recognized as an expense during fiscal 2017 were $1.6 million (2016 – $1.6 million).

18. EARNINGS PER SHARE

Earnings per share is calculated based on the weighted average number of common shares outstanding during the period. In calculating diluted earnings per share amounts under the treasury stock method, the numerator remains unchanged from the basic earnings per share calculations as the assumed exercise of the Company's stock options and DSUs do not result in adjustment to net earnings. The reconciliation of the denominator in calculating diluted earnings per share amounts for the periods presented is as follows:

(thousands of shares)	52-week period ended April 1, 2017	53-week period ended April 2, 2016
Weighted average number of common shares outstanding, basic	26,385	25,949
Effect of dilutive securities – stock options	566	212
Weighted average number of common shares outstanding, diluted	26,951	26,161

As at April 1, 2017, 552,000 (April 2, 2016 – 672,500) anti-dilutive stock options were excluded from the computation of diluted net earnings per common share.

19. STATEMENTS OF CASH FLOWS

Supplemental cash flow information:

(thousands of Canadian dollars)	52-week period ended April 1, 2017	53-week period ended April 2, 2016
Accounts receivable	215	(2,767)
Inventories	(13,788)	(9,393)
Income taxes recoverable	(26)	(50)
Prepaid expenses	(416)	(5,813)
Accounts payable and accrued liabilities (current and long-term)	(2,606)	11,109
Unredeemed gift card liability	(573)	2,758
Provisions (current and long-term)	18	(880)
Income taxes payable	360	–
Deferred revenue	(380)	(66)
Net change in non-cash working capital balances	(17,196)	(5,102)

20. CAPITAL MANAGEMENT

The Company's main objectives when managing capital are:

- Ensuring sufficient liquidity to support financial obligations and to execute operating and strategic objectives;
- Maintaining financial capacity and flexibility through access to capital to support future development of the business;
- Minimizing the cost of capital while taking into consideration current and future industry, market, and economic risks and conditions.

There were no changes to these objectives during the year. The primary activities engaged by the Company to generate attractive returns for shareholders include transforming physical and digital platforms and driving productivity improvement through investments in information technology and distribution to support the Company's sales networks. The Company's main sources of capital are its current cash position, short-term investments, and cash flows generated from operations. Cash flow is primarily used to fund working capital needs and capital expenditures. The Company manages its capital structure in accordance with changes in economic conditions.

21. FINANCIAL RISK MANAGEMENT

The Company's activities expose it to a variety of financial risks, including risks related to foreign exchange, interest rate, credit, and liquidity.

Foreign Exchange Risk

The Company's foreign exchange risk is largely limited to currency fluctuations between the Canadian and U.S. dollars. Decreases in the value of the Canadian dollar relative to the U.S. dollar could negatively impact net earnings since the purchase price of some of the Company's products are negotiated with vendors in U.S. dollars, while the retail price to customers is set in Canadian dollars. In particular, a significant amount of the Company's general merchandise inventory purchases is denominated in U.S. dollars. The Company also has a New York office that incurs U.S. dollar expenses.

The Company uses derivative instruments in the form of forward contracts to manage its exposure to fluctuations in U.S. dollar exchange rates. As the Company has hedged a significant portion of the cost of its near-term forecasted U.S. dollar purchases, a change in foreign currency rates will not impact that portion of the cost of those purchases.

In fiscal 2017, the effect of foreign currency translation on net earnings was a gain of $0.2 million (2016 – gain of $0.6 million).

Interest Rate Risk

The Company's interest income is sensitive to fluctuations in Canadian interest rates, which affect the interest earned on the Company's cash, cash equivalents, and short-term investments. The Company has minimal interest rate risk and does not use any interest rate swaps to manage its risk. The Company does not currently have any debt.

Credit Risk

The Company is exposed to credit risk resulting from the possibility that counterparties may default on their financial obligations to the Company. Credit risk primarily arises from accounts receivable, cash and cash equivalents, short-term investments, and derivative financial instruments. Fair values of financial instruments reflect the credit risk of the Company and counterparties when appropriate.

Accounts receivable primarily consist of receivables from retail customers who pay by credit card, recoveries of credits from suppliers for returned or damaged products, and receivables from other companies for sales of products, gift cards, and other services. Credit card payments have minimal credit risk and the limited number of corporate receivables are closely monitored.

The Company limits its exposure to counterparty credit risk related to cash and cash equivalents, short-term investments, and derivative financial instruments by transacting only with highly-rated financial institutions and other counterparties, and by managing within specific limits for credit exposure and term to maturity. The Company's maximum credit risk exposure if all counterparties default concurrently is equivalent to the carrying amounts of accounts receivable, cash and cash equivalents, short-term investments, and derivative financial instruments.

Liquidity Risk

Liquidity risk is the risk that the Company will be unable to meet its obligations relating to its financial liabilities. The Company manages liquidity risk by preparing and monitoring cash flow budgets and forecasts to ensure that the Company has sufficient funds to meet its financial obligations and fund new business opportunities or other unanticipated requirements as they arise.

The contractual maturities of the Company's current and long-term liabilities as at April 1, 2017 are as follows:

(thousands of Canadian dollars)	Payments due in the next 90 days	Payments due between 90 days and less than a year	Payments due after 1 year	Total
Accounts payable and accrued liabilities	141,622	28,989	–	170,611
Unredeemed gift card liability	50,396	–	–	50,396
Provisions	7	103	–	110
Long-term accrued liabilities	–	–	2,378	2,378
Long-term provisions	–	–	51	51
Total	192,025	29,092	2,429	223,546

22. EQUITY INVESTMENT

The Company holds a 50% equity ownership in its associate, Calendar Club, to sell calendars, games, and gifts through seasonal kiosks and year-round stores in Canada. The Company uses the equity method of accounting to record Calendar Club results. In fiscal 2017, the Company received $1.2 million (2016 – $0.7 million) of distributions from Calendar Club.

The following tables represent financial information for Calendar Club along with the Company's share therein:

	Total		Company's share	
(thousands of Canadian dollars)	April 1, 2017	April 2, 2016	April 1, 2017	April 2, 2016
Cash and cash equivalents	2,576	3,969	1,288	1,985
Total current assets	5,833	9,713	2,917	4,857
Total long-term assets	363	483	181	242
Total current liabilities	2,596	7,353	1,298	3,677

	Total		Company's share	
(thousands of Canadian dollars)	52-week period ended April 1, 2017	53-week period ended April 2, 2016	52-week period ended April 1, 2017	53-week period ended April 2, 2016
Revenue	38,858	36,200	19,429	18,100
Expenses	(35,438)	(33,166)	(17,719)	(16,583)
Depreciation	(187)	(239)	(93)	(120)
Net earnings	3,233	2,795	1,617	1,397

Changes in the carrying amount of the investment were as follows:

(thousands of Canadian dollars)	Carrying value
Balance, March 28, 2015	726
Equity income from Calendar Club	1,397
Distributions from Calendar Club	(702)
Balance, April 2, 2016	1,421
Equity income from Calendar Club	1,617
Distributions from Calendar Club	(1,238)
Balance, April 1, 2017	1,800

23. RELATED PARTY TRANSACTIONS

The Company's related parties include its key management personnel, shareholders, defined contribution retirement plan, equity investment in Calendar Club, and subsidiary. Unless otherwise stated, none of the transactions incorporate special terms and conditions and no guarantees were given or received. Outstanding balances are usually settled in cash.

Transactions with Key Management Personnel

Key management of the Company includes members of the Board of Directors as well as members of the Executive Committee. Key management personnel remuneration includes the following expenses:

(thousands of Canadian dollars)	52-week period ended April 1, 2017	53-week period ended April 2, 2016
Wages, salaries, and bonus	7,733	7,529
Short-term benefits expense	233	230
Termination benefits expense	424	454
Retirement benefits expense	61	69
Share-based compensation	833	675
Directors' compensation	367	384
Total remuneration	9,651	9,341

Transactions with Shareholders

During fiscal 2017, the Company purchased goods and services from companies in which Mr. Gerald W. Schwartz, who is the controlling shareholder of Indigo, holds a controlling or significant interest. In fiscal 2017, the Company paid $6.0 million for these transactions (2016 – $4.5 million). As at April 1, 2017, Indigo had less than $0.1 million payable to these companies under standard payment terms and $1.0 million of restricted cash pledged as collateral for letter of credit obligations issued to support the Company's purchases of merchandise from these companies (April 2, 2016 – $0.1 million payable and $2.8 million restricted cash). All transactions were measured at fair market value and were in the normal course of business, under normal commercial terms, for both Indigo and the related companies.

Transactions with Defined Contribution Retirement Plan

The Company's transactions with the defined contribution retirement plan include contributions paid to the retirement plan as disclosed in note 17. The Company has not entered into other transactions with the retirement plan.

Transactions with Associate

The Company's associate, Calendar Club, is a seasonal operation that is dependent on the December holiday sales season to generate revenue. During the year, the Company loans cash to Calendar Club for working capital requirements and Calendar Club repays the loans once profits are generated in the third quarter. In fiscal 2017, Indigo loaned $11.6 million to Calendar Club (2016 – $11.1 million). All loans were repaid in full as at April 1, 2017.

Corporate Governance Policies

A presentation of the Company's corporate governance policies is included in the Management Information Circular, which is mailed to all shareholders. If you would like to receive a copy of this information, please contact Investor Relations at Indigo.

Executive Management and Board of Directors

EXECUTIVE MANAGEMENT

Heather Reisman
Chair and Chief Executive Officer

Kirsten Chapman
Executive Vice President, E-Commerce and Chief Marketing Officer

Gildave (Gil) Dennis
Executive Vice President, Retail and Human Resources

Kathleen Flynn
Executive Vice President, Real Estate, General Counsel and Corporate Secretary

Scott Formby
Chief Creative Officer

R. Craig Loudon
Interim Chief Financial Officer

Tod Morehead
Executive Vice President and Group General Merchandise Manager

Krishna Nikhil
Executive Vice President, Print and Chief Strategy Officer

Bahman (Bo) Parizadeh
Executive Vice President and Chief Technology Officer

Hugues Simard
Executive Vice President and Chief Financial Officer (effective June 1, 2017)

BOARD OF DIRECTORS

Frank Clegg
Volunteer Chairman and Chief Executive Officer
C4ST (Canadians for Safe Technology)

Jonathan Deitcher
Investment Advisor
RBC Dominion Securities Inc.

Mitchell Goldhar
Chairman of the Board
SmartREIT and
President and Chief Executive Officer
Penguin Investments Inc.

Howard Grosfield
Executive Vice President, US Consumer Marketing Services
American Express

Robert Haft
Managing Partner
Morgan Noble Healthcare

Andrea Johnson
Principal
Envelo Properties Corp.

Michael Kirby
Corporate Director
Chair of Partners for Mental Health

Anne Marie O'Donovan
President
O'Donovan Advisory Services Ltd.

Heather Reisman
Chair and Chief Executive Officer
Indigo Books & Music Inc.

Gerald Schwartz
Chairman and Chief Executive Officer
Onex Corporation

Joel Silver
President and Chief Executive Officer
David's Tea Inc.

Five-Year Summary of Financial Information

For the years ended (millions of Canadian dollars, except share and per share data)	April 1, 2017	April 2, 2016	March 28, 2015	March 29, 2014	March 30, 2013
SELECTED STATEMENTS OF EARNINGS (LOSS) AND COMPREHENSIVE EARNINGS (LOSS) INFORMATION					
Revenue					
Superstores	702.1	695.3	625.2	607.2	615.2
Small format stores	140.7	140.2	127.8	127.4	137.6
Online	148.2	133.3	114.0	102.0	91.9
Other	28.8	25.4	28.4	31.1	34.1
Total revenue	1,019.8	994.2	895.4	867.7	878.8
Adjusted EBITDA[1,2]	52.2	43.1	20.5	0.1	28.5
Earnings (loss) before income taxes	29.0	22.1	(3.2)	(26.9)	4.2
Net earnings (loss)	20.9	28.6	(3.5)	(31.0)	4.3
Dividends per share	–	–	–	$ 0.33	$ 0.44
Net earnings (loss) per common share	$ 0.79	$ 1.10	$(0.14)	$(1.21)	$ 0.17
SELECTED CONSOLIDATED BALANCE SHEET INFORMATION					
Working capital	248.1	217.9	198.7	189.7	224.3
Total assets	608.6	584.0	538.4	512.6	569.1
Long-term debt (including current portion)	–	0.1	0.2	0.8	1.5
Total equity	371.8	344.0	311.1	311.7	350.3
Weighted average number of shares outstanding	26,384,775	25,949,068	25,722,640	25,601,260	25,529,035
Common shares outstanding at end of period	26,351,484	25,797,351	25,495,289	25,298,239	25,297,389
STORE OPERATING STATISTICS					
Number of stores at end of period					
Superstores	89	88	91	95	97
Small format stores	123	123	127	131	134
Selling square footage at end of period (in thousands)					
Superstores	1,953	1,925	2,019	2,163	2,199
Small format stores	304	305	311	321	329
Comparable sales growth[2]					
Total retail and online	4.1%	12.9%	6.5%	(0.3%)	(3.7%)
Superstores	2.9%	12.8%	6.8%	(0.9%)	(4.6%)
Small format stores	0.9%	10.9%	0.8%	(5.0%)	(2.4%)
Sales per selling square foot					
Superstores	360	361	310	281	280
Small format stores	463	460	411	397	418

1 Earnings before interest, taxes, depreciation, amortization, impairment, asset disposals, and equity investment.
2 See "Non-IFRS Financial Measures" in the Company's Management Discussion and Analysis section of the Annual Report.

Investor Information

CORPORATE HOME OFFICE

468 King Street West
Suite 500
Toronto, Ontario
Canada M5V 1L8
Telephone (416) 364-4499
Fax (416) 364-0355

INVESTOR CONTACT

InvestorRelations@indigo.ca
www.chapters.indigo.ca/investor-relations/

MEDIA CONTACT

Janet Eger
Vice President, Public Affairs
Telephone (416) 342-8561

STOCK LISTING

Toronto Stock Exchange

TRADING SYMBOL

IDG

TRANSFER AGENT AND REGISTRAR

CST Trust Company
P.O. Box 700, Station B
Montreal, Quebec
Canada H3B 3K3
Telephone (Toll Free) 1-800-387-0825
(Toronto) (416) 682-3860
Fax: 1-888-249-6189
Email: inquiries@canstockta.com
Website: www.canstockta.com

AUDITORS

Ernst & Young LLP
Ernst & Young Tower
Toronto-Dominion Centre
Toronto, Ontario
Canada M5K 1J7

ANNUAL MEETING

The Annual Meeting represents an opportunity for shareholders to review and participate in the management of the Company as well as meet with its directors and officers.

Indigo's Annual Meeting will be held on
July 17, 2017 at 10:00 a.m. at
Torys LLP
79 Wellington Street West, 33rd Floor
Toronto, Ontario
Canada M5K 1N2

Shareholders are encouraged to attend and guests are welcome.

Une traduction française de ce document est disponible sur demande.

Indigo's Commitment to Communities Across Canada

The Indigo Love of Reading Foundation (the "Foundation") exists to enrich the lives of Canadian children by providing funds through the donations of Indigo, its leadership, its customers, its employees, and suppliers to support the purchase of new and engaging books and educational resources for the libraries of high-needs elementary schools. Since 2004, the Foundation has committed over $25 million in more than 3,000 high-needs schools, impacting over 900,000 children. The Foundation runs two signature programs each year. In May 2017, the Indigo Love of Reading Literacy Fund grant provided transformational support of $1.5 million to 30 high-needs elementary schools that lack the resources to build and maintain healthy school libraries. Additionally, each fall, the Indigo Adopt a School program unites Indigo staff, local schools, and their communities to raise money for new library books for their local schools. In October 2016, Indigo Adopt a School contributed over $800,000 to more than 500 schools.

On May 17, 2017, the Foundation released *Read Between the Lines*, a documentary commissioned by the Foundation to raise awareness for the literacy challenges facing Canada due, in part, to the underfunding of high-needs elementary school libraries.

Our Beliefs

- We exist to add joy to customers' lives – when they interact with us and, when they interact with our products.
- Each and every person in the company should understand how his or her work contributes to the creation of joyful customer moments.
- We owe to each other, irrespective of role or position, the same level of respect and caring as we would show to a valued friend.
- We have a responsibility to create an environment where each individual is inspired to perform to the best of his or her ability.
- Passion, creativity and innovation are the keys to sustainable growth and profitability. Each individual working at Indigo should reflect this in his or her work. Our role, as a company, is to encourage and reward the demonstration of these attributes.
- We have a responsibility to give back to the communities in which we operate.

Printed in Canada

FSC
Recycled
Supporting responsible use of forest resources
www.fsc.org Cert no. SW-COC-1700

Appendix B

TYPICAL CHART OF ACCOUNTS FOR SERVICE PROPRIETORSHIPS (ASPE)

Students: Add to this list as you see more account names so you have a record of what is commonly used. Add a list of merchandising terms too.

ASSETS

Cash
Petty Cash
Accounts Receivable
Allowance for Doubtful Accounts
Notes Receivable, Short-Term
GST Recoverable
HST Recoverable
Interest Receivable
Supplies
Prepaid Rent
Prepaid Insurance

Furniture
Accumulated Amortization—Furniture
Equipment
Accumulated Amortization—Equipment
Building
Accumulated Amortization—Building
Computer Equipment
Accumulated Amortization—Computer Equipment
Land Improvements
Accumulated Amortization—Land Improvements
Leasehold Improvements
Land
Notes Receivable, Long-Term
Patents
Goodwill

LIABILITIES

Accounts Payable
Note Payable
Notes Payable, Short-Term
Salaries Payable
Wages Payable
GST Payable
HST Payable
Sales Tax Payable
Employee Income Tax Payable
Employment Insurance Payable
Canada Pension Plan Payable
Quebec Pension Plan Payable
Employee Benefits Payable
RRSP Contribution Payable
Interest Payable
Unearned Revenue
Estimated Warranty Payable
Estimated Vacation Pay Liability
Current Portion of Long-Term Debt

Notes Payable, Long-Term

OWNER'S EQUITY

Owner, Capital
Owner, Withdrawals

REVENUES AND GAINS

Service Revenue
Interest Revenue
Gain on Sale of Land (or Furniture, Equipment, or Building)

EXPENSES AND LOSSES

Amortization Expense—Furniture
Amortization Expense—Equipment
Amortization Expense—Building
Amortization Expense—Computer Equipment
Amortization Expense—Land Improvements
Bad Debt Expense
Bank Charge Expense
Cash Short and Over
Credit Card Discount Expense
Debit Card Service Fee
Delivery Expense
Employee Benefits Expense
General Expense
Interest Expense
Insurance Expense
Miscellaneous Expense
Property Tax Expense
Rent Expense
Repairs Expense
Selling Expense
Supplies Expense
Utilities Expense
Vacation Pay Expense
Warranty Expense

Loss on Sale (or Exchange) of Land (or Furniture, Equipment, or Buildings)

Glossary

2/15, n/30 Credit terms offered by some merchandisers, meaning that if the invoice is paid within 15 days of the invoice date (the discount period), a 2 percent discount may be taken. If not, the full amount (net) is due in 30 days. Also shown as *2/15, net 30* (p. 249).

Account The detailed record of the changes that have occurred in a particular asset, liability, or item of owner's equity during a period (p. 13).

Accounting The system that measures business activities, processes that information into reports and financial statements, and communicates the findings to decision makers (p. 4).

Accounting equation The most basic tool of accounting: Assets = Liabilities + Owner's Equity (proprietorship) or Assets = Liabilities + Shareholders' Equity (corporation) (p. 12).

Accounting Standards Board The Canadian Accounting Standards Board establishes accounting standards for non-publicly accountable enterprises and contributes to the development of International Financial Reporting Standards (p. 24).

Accounting Standards for Private Enterprises (ASPE) Canadian accounting standards that specify the generally accepted accounting principles applicable to private enterprises and those corporations that chose not to apply IFRS (p. 10).

Account payable The oral or implied promise to pay off debts arising from credit purchases. A liability that is backed by the general reputation and credit standing of the debtor (p. 14).

Account receivable An asset; a promise to receive cash in the future from customers to whom the business has sold goods or services (p. 13).

Accounting cycle The process by which accountants produce an entity's financial statements and update the financial reports for a period of time (p. 58).

Accounting information system (AIS) The combination of personnel, records, and procedures that a business uses to meet its need for financial data (p. 372).

Accounting period The time frame, or period of time, covered by financial statements and other reports (p. 58).

Accrual-basis accounting Accounting that recognizes (records) the impact of a business event as it occurs, regardless of whether the transaction affected cash (p. 117).

Accrued expense An expense that has been incurred but not yet paid in cash. Also called an *accrued liability* (p. 125).

Accrued liability Another name for an *accrued expense* (p. 610).

Accrued revenue A revenue that has been earned but not yet received in cash (p. 127).

Accumulated amortization The cumulative sum of all amortization expense from the date of acquiring a capital asset (p. 123).

Acid-test ratio Ratio of the sum of cash plus short-term investments plus net current receivables to current liabilities. Tells whether the entity could pay all its current liabilities if they came due immediately. Also called the *quick ratio* (p. 512).

Adjusted trial balance A list of all the ledger accounts with their adjusted balances (p. 129).

Adjusting entry An entry made at the end of the period to assign revenues to the period in which they are earned and expenses to the period in which they are incurred. Adjusting entries help measure the period's income and bring the related asset and liability accounts to correct balances for the financial statements (p. 118).

Aging-of-accounts-receivable method A way to estimate bad debts by analyzing individual accounts receivable according to the length of time they have been due (p. 495).

Allowance for Doubtful Accounts A contra account, related to accounts receivable, that holds the estimated amount of collection losses. Also called *allowance for uncollectible accounts* (p. 496).

Allowance for Uncollectible Accounts Another name for allowance for doubtful accounts (p. 496).

Allowance method A method of recording collection losses based on estimates made prior to determining that the business will not collect from specific customers (p. 496).

Amortizable cost The asset's cost minus its estimated residual value (p. 558).

Amortization The term the CPA Canada Handbook uses to describe the writing off that occurs to expense the cost of capital assets; also called *depreciation* (p. 121).

Amortization rate The amount of amortization written off to expense stated as a percentage (p. 560).

Amortization schedule A table or chart that shows the amortization expense and asset values by period (p. 559).

Appraisal An expert assessment of the value of an asset (p. 554).

Arrears A legal term for debt that is overdue because of at least one missed payment (p. 552).

Asset An economic resource a business owns that is expected to be of benefit in the future (p. 13).

Asset retirement obligation A liability that records the future cost to settle a present obligation, such as future removal and site restoration costs (p. 570).

Audit The examination of financial statements by outside accountants. The conclusion of an audit is the accountant's professional opinion about the financial statements (p. 6).

Bad debt expense The cost to the seller of extending credit. Arises from the failure to collect from credit customers. Also called *doubtful accounts expense* or *uncollectible accounts expense* (p. 496).

Balance sheet A list of an entity's assets, liabilities, and owner's equity (proprietorship) or shareholders' equity (corporation) as of a specific date. Also called the *statement of financial position* (p. 21).

Balance sheet approach Another name for the aging-of-accounts-receivable method of estimating uncollectibles (p. 498).

Bank cheque A document that instructs the bank to pay the designated person or business the specified amount of money (p. 64).

Bank collection Collection of money by the bank on behalf of a depositor (p. 444).

Bank deposit slip A document that shows the amount of cash deposited into a person's or business's bank account (p. 64).

Bank reconciliation The process of explaining the reasons for the difference between a depositor's records and the bank's records about the depositor's bank account (p. 442).

Bank statement A document for a particular bank account showing its beginning and ending balances and listing the month's transactions that affected the account (p. 440).

Batch processing Computerized accounting for similar transactions in a group or batch (p. 377).

Betterment An expenditure that increases the capacity or efficiency of an asset or extends its useful life. Capital expenditures are debited to an asset account (p. 555).

Bill Another term for invoice (p. 248).

Book value The asset's cost less accumulated amortization. Also called *carrying value* (p. 123).

Bookkeeping A procedural element of accounting; the keeping of the financial records and the recording of financial information (p. 4).

Brand name A distinctive identification of a product or service (p. 572).

Business One or more individuals selling goods or services with the intent of making a profit (p. 4).

Canada (or Quebec) Pension Plan (CPP or QPP) All employees and self-employed persons in Canada (except in Quebec, where the pension plan is the Quebec Pension Plan) between 18 and 70 years of age are required to contribute to the Canada Pension Plan administered by the Government of Canada (p. 619).

Capital Another name for the owner's equity of a business (p. 14).

Capital cost allowance (CCA) Amortization allowed for income tax purposes by the Canada Revenue Agency; the rates allowed are called capital cost allowance rates (p. 563).

Capitalize To record as an asset (p. 553).

Carrying value (of property, plant, and equipment) The asset's cost less accumulated amortization. Also called *book value* (p. 123).

Cash The most liquid asset an organization has; includes cash on hand, cash on deposit in banks and trust companies, and cash equivalents (p. 438).

Cash-basis accounting Accounting that records only transactions in which cash is received or paid (p. 117).

Cash discount Another name for a purchase discount (p. 249).

Cash flow statement Reports cash receipts and cash payments classified according to the entity's major activities: operating, investing, and financing (p. 22).

Cash generating unit (CGU) Under IFRS, the smallest identifiable group of assets that generates cash flows that are largely independent of the cash flows from other assets (p. 574).

Cash payments journal A special journal used to record cash payments made by cheque (p. 388).

Cash receipts journal A special journal used to record all types of cash receipts (p. 383).

Cash short and over When the recorded cash balance does not match the actual amount counted (p. 448).

Chart of accounts A list of all the accounts and their account numbers in the ledger (p. 59).

Chartered Professional Accountant (CPA) An accountant who has met the examination and experience requirements of CPA Canada (p. 6).

Cheque A document that instructs the bank to pay the designated person or business a specified amount of money (p. 439).

Cheque truncation The conversion of a physical cheque into an electronic format (i.e., taking a picture) for processing through the banking system to save time and resources (p. 441).

Classified balance sheet A balance sheet that places each asset and liability into a specific category (p. 188).

Closing entries Entries that transfer the revenue, expense, and owner withdrawal balances from these respective accounts to the Capital account (p. 183).

Closing the accounts A step in the accounting cycle at the end of the period that prepares the accounts for recording the transactions of the next period. Closing the accounts consists of journalizing and posting the closing entries to set the balances of the revenue, expense, and owner withdrawal accounts to zero (p. 183).

Cloud computing A subscription-based service where an external company provides software, processing capability, and data storage that the customer accesses using the Internet. Customers gain the software capabilities without investing in the hardware and software themselves (p. 374).

Collection period Another name for days' sales in receivables (p. 512).

Collusion When two or more people work as a team to beat internal controls and steal from a company (p. 437).

Commercial substance In an exchange of tangible capital assets, commercial substance exists when an entity's future cash flows from the new asset received will differ in risk, timing, or amount from the cash flows from the old asset given up (p. 568).

Committee of Sponsoring Organizations (COSO) A committee that provides thought leadership related to enterprise risk management, internal control, and fraud deterrence (p. 433).

Comparable A qualitative characteristic of accounting information that says financial statements should be able to be measured against results in previous years or other businesses in the same industry (p. 11).

Comparability A qualitative characteristic of accounting information that should enable users to compare one company's accounting information to another company's accounting information and to its own previous years' results (p. 334).

Componentization Under IFRS, recording each identifiable component of an asset separately to calculate depreciation on each part (p. 574).

Compound journal entry A journal entry with more than one debit and credit (p. 72).

Computer virus A malicious computer program that reproduces itself, gets included in program code without consent, and destroys program code (p. 438).

Conservatism An accounting concept by which the least favourable figures are presented in the financial statements (p. 335).

Consistency principle An accounting principle that states businesses must use the same accounting methods and procedures from period to period or disclose a change in method (p. 334).

Contingent liability A potential liability from a past event that depends on an uncertain future event not within the business's control (p. 615).

Contra account An account that always has a companion account and whose normal balance is opposite that of the companion account (p. 123).

Control account An account whose balance equals the sum of the balances in a group of related accounts in a subsidiary ledger (p. 382).

Controller The chief accounting officer of a company (p. 435).

Copyright The exclusive right to reproduce and sell software, a book, a musical composition, a film, or other creative work. Issued by the federal government, copyrights extend 50 years beyond the creator's life (p. 571).

Corporation A business owned by shareholders that begins when the federal or provincial government approves its articles of incorporation. A corporation is a legal entity, an "artificial person," in the eyes of the law (p. 8).

Cost–benefit constraint An accounting constraint that says the benefits of the information produced should exceed the costs of producing the information (p. 12).

Cost of goods sold The cost of the inventory that the business has sold to customers; the largest single expense of most merchandising businesses. Also called *cost of sales* (p. 244).

Cost of sales Another name for cost of goods sold (p. 244).

Cost principle of measurement States that assets and services are recorded at their purchase cost and that the accounting record of the asset continues to be based on cost rather than current market value (p. 12).

Credit The right side of an account (p. 61).

Credit memo The document issued by a seller to reduce a customer's accounts receivable (p. 254).

Creditor The party to a credit transaction who sells a service or merchandise and obtains a receivable (p. 494).

Creditors Businesses or individuals to which payment is owed (p. 5).

Cryptocurrencies Digital currencies that operate independently of a central bank (p. 506).

Current asset An asset that is expected to be converted to cash, sold, or consumed during the next 12 months, or within the business's normal operating cycle if longer than a year (p. 188).

Current liability A debt due to be paid within one year or one of the entity's operating cycles if the cycle is longer than a year (p. 189).

Current portion of long-term debt The amount of the principal that is payable within one year (p. 609).

Current ratio Current assets divided by current liabilities. Measures the company's ability to pay current liabilities from current assets (p. 192).

Current then non-current A balance sheet format that reports current assets before long-term assets, and current liabilities before long-term liabilities and equity. This format may be used for reporting under both ASPE and IFRS (p. 194).

Custodian A person designated to be responsible for something of value, like the petty cash fund (p. 451).

Database A computerized storehouse of information that can be systematically assessed in a variety of report forms (p. 374).

Days' sales in receivables Ratio of average net accounts receivable to one day's sales. Indicates how many days' sales remain in Accounts Receivable awaiting collection. Also called the *collection period* (p. 512).

DDB rate Double-declining-balance percentage applied to an asset to calculate its amortization or depreciation. It is twice the straight-line amortization rate (p. 560).

Debit The left side of an account (p. 61).

Debit memo The document issued by a buyer to reduce the buyer's account payable to a seller (p. 250).

Debtor The party to a credit transaction who makes a purchase and creates a payable (p. 494).

Debt ratio Ratio of total liabilities to total assets. Gives the proportion of a company's assets that it has financed with debt (p. 193).

Default on a note Failure of the maker of a note to pay at maturity. Also called *dishonour of a note* (p. 511).

Deferred revenue Another name for unearned revenue (p. 124).

Depletion Another word to describe the amortization of natural resources or wasting assets (p. 569).

Deposit in transit A deposit recorded by the company but not yet by its bank (p. 444).

Derecognize Under IFRS, to remove an asset from the accounting records because it has been replaced (p. 574).

Designated accountants Accountants who have met the education, examination, and experience requirements of an accounting body (p. 6)

Direct deposit Funds that are deposited and transferred directly to a bank account, such as employee payroll (p. 441).

Direct write-off method A method of accounting for bad debts by which the company waits until the credit department decides that a customer's account receivable is uncollectible and then debits Bad Debt Expense and credits the customer's Account Receivable (p. 503).

Disclosure principle An accounting concept that states a business's financial statements must report enough information for outsiders to make knowledgeable decisions about the business (p. 335).

Discount period The time period during which a cash discount is available and a reduced payment can be made by the purchaser (p. 249).

Discounting a notes receivable Selling a notes receivable before its maturity date (p. 515).

Dishonour a note Failure of the maker of a note to pay a notes receivable at maturity. Also called *default on a note* (p. 511).

Dividends Distributions by a corporation to its shareholders (p. 14).

Double-declining-balance (DDB) method A type of amortization method that expenses a relatively larger amount of an asset's cost nearer the start of its useful life than does the straight-line method (p. 560).

Doubtful account expense Another name for bad debt expense (p. 496).

Due date The date on which the final payment of a note is due. Also called the *maturity date* (p. 507).

Economic entity assumption The accounting assumption that an organization or a section of an organization stands apart from other organizations and individuals as a separate economic unit for accounting purposes (p. 12).

Electronic Data Interchange (EDI) The transfer of structured data by electronic means and standards between organizations from one computer system to another without human intervention (p. 450).

Electronic funds transfer (EFT) A system that transfers cash by digital communication rather than paper documents (p. 451).

Employee compensation Payroll, a major expense of many businesses (p. 617).

Employment Insurance (EI) Most employees and employers in Canada must contribute to the Employment Insurance fund, which provides assistance to unemployed workers (p. 619).

Encryption The process of rearranging plain-text messages by some mathematical formula to achieve confidentiality (p. 437).

End-user tax A consumption tax that is only paid by the final consumer (p. 609).

Enterprise resource planning (ERP) A computer system that integrates all company data into a single data warehouse (p. 377).

Eom A credit term that means an invoice amount is due by the end of the month (p. 249).

Estimated residual value The expected cash value of an asset at the end of its useful life. Also called *residual value, scrap value,* or *salvage value* (p. 558).

Estimated useful life Length of the service that a business expects to get from an asset; may be expressed in years, units of output, kilometres, or other measures (p. 558).

Ethics Rules of behaviour based on what is good or bad (p. 7).

Evaluated Receipt Settlement (ERS) A streamlined payment procedure that compresses the approval process into a single step: comparing the receiving report with the purchase order (p. 450).

Executive controls Management involvement in internal controls (p. 446).

Exempt supplies Goods and services that are not required to have GST or HST charged on them (p. 607).

Expenses Costs incurred when running a business (or the using up of assets). Decrease in owner's equity that occurs in the course of delivering goods or services to customers or clients (p. 14).

External users Readers of financial information who do not work for the business (p. 5).

Fidelity bond An insurance policy that reimburses the company for any losses due to the employee's theft. Before hiring, the bonding company checks the employee's background (p. 436).

Financial accounting The branch of accounting that provides information to people outside the business (p. 5).

Financial statements Business documents that report financial information about an entity to persons and organizations outside the business (p. 4).

Firewall Barriers used to prevent entry into a computer network or a part of a network. Examples include passwords, personal identification numbers (PINs), and fingerprints (p. 437).

First-in, first-out (FIFO) method An inventory costing method by which the first costs into inventory are the first costs out to cost of goods sold. Ending inventory is based on the costs of the most recent purchases (p. 328).

Fiscal year An accounting year of any 12 consecutive months that may or may not coincide with the calendar year (p. 115).

FOB destination Legal title passes to the buyer only when the inventory reaches the destination (i.e., the seller pays the freight) (p. 251).

FOB shipping point Legal title passes to the buyer as soon as the inventory leaves the seller's place of business— the shipping point (p. 251).

Franchise Privileges granted by a private business or a government to sell a product or service in accordance with specified conditions (p. 572).

Freight-in The transportation costs on purchased goods (i.e., from the wholesaler to the retailer) (p. 252).

Freight-out The transportation costs on goods sold (i.e., from the retailer to the customer) (p. 252).

General journal The journal used to record all transactions that do not fit into one of the special journals (p. 378).

General ledger Ledger of accounts that are reported in the financial statements (p. 379).

Generally accepted accounting principles (GAAP) Accounting guidelines, formulated by the Accounting Standards Board, that specify the standards for how accountants must record, measure, and report financial information (p. 9).

Going concern assumption An accounting assumption that the business will continue operating in the foreseeable future (p. 12).

Goodwill Excess of the cost of an acquired company over the sum of the market values of its net assets (assets minus liabilities) (p. 572).

Gross margin Excess of sales revenue over cost of goods sold. Also called *gross profit* (p. 244).

Gross margin method A way to estimate inventory based on a rearrangement of the cost of goods sold model: Beginning inventory + Net purchases = Cost of goods available for sale. Cost of goods available for sale − Cost of goods sold = Ending inventory. Also called the *gross profit method* (p. 339).

Gross margin percentage Gross margin divided by net sales revenue. A measure of profitability (p. 263).

Gross pay Total amount of salary, wages, commissions, or any other employee compensation before taxes and other deductions are taken out (p. 618).

Gross profit Another name for gross margin (p. 250).

Gross profit method Another name for the *gross margin method* (p. 339).

Half-year rule The Canada Revenue Agency allows businesses to claim only 50 percent of the normal CCA rate in the year an asset is acquired (p. 564).

Hardware Electronic equipment that includes computers, disk drives, monitors, printers, and the network that connects them (p. 374).

Identifiable tangible asset An asset that is physical—it can be seen and touched—and can be separated from other assets; used to describe property, plant, and equipment (p. 552).

Impaired When the fair value falls below the carrying value in the accounting records (p. 573).

Impairment A write-down in value that occurs when an asset, such as inventory, becomes worth less than its cost (p. 336).

Impairment reversal A write-up in value that occurs when an asset that had been written down, such as inventory, increases in value up to the amount of the original write-down (p. 336).

Imprest system A way to account for petty cash by maintaining a constant balance in the Petty Cash account, supported by the fund (cash plus disbursement tickets) totaling the same amount (p. 452).

Income from operations Another name for operating income (p. 260).

Income statement A list of an entity's revenues, expenses, and net income or net loss for a specific period. Also called the *statement of earnings* or *statement of operations* (p. 20).

Income statement approach Another name for the percent-of-sales method of estimating uncollectibles (p. 497).

Income Summary A temporary "holding tank" account into which the revenues and expenses are transferred prior to their final transfer to the Capital account (p. 183).

Independence In accounting, this refers to there being no financial interest outside of the current business relationship. Auditors and other accountants must not be influenced by personal or professional gain from their auditing or accounting decisions (p. 6).

Independent contractors Individuals who do work for a business but are not employees. They invoice the business for their contracted work (p. 629).

Inflation A rise in the general level of prices (p. 12).

Input tax credit (ITC) The sales tax that will be refunded by the government (p. 607).

Intangible asset An asset with no physical form giving a special right to current and expected future benefits (p. 122).

Intellectual capital The knowledge of the people who work in a business (p. 571).

Interest The revenue to the payee for loaning out the principal, and the expense to the maker for borrowing the principal (p. 507).

Interest period The period of time during which interest is to be computed, extending from the original date of the note to the maturity date. Also called the *note term* or the *time period* (p. 507).

Interest rate The percentage rate that is multiplied by the principal amount to compute the amount of interest on a note (p. 507).

Interim period In accounting, an interim period is less than a year (p. 115).

Internal control The organizational plan and all the related measures adopted by an entity to meet management's objectives of discharging statutory responsibilities, profitability, prevention and detection of fraud and error, safeguarding assets, reliability of accounting records, and timely preparation of reliable financial information (p. 432).

Internal users Readers of financial information who either own the business or are employed by it and who are making decisions on behalf of the business (p. 5).

International Accounting Standards Board (IASB) The body that sets International Financial Reporting Standards (p. 10).

International Financial Reporting Standards (IFRS) The accounting standards that specify the generally accepted accounting principles that must be applied by publicly accountable enterprises in Canada and many other countries (p. 10).

Inventory All goods that a company owns and expects to sell in the normal course of operation (p. 244).

Inventory turnover The ratio of cost of goods sold to average inventory. Measures the number of times a company sells its average level of inventory during a year (p. 264).

Investors A person or business that provides capital (usually money) to a business with the expectation of receiving financial gain (p. 5).

Invoice A seller's request for cash from the purchaser (p. 248).

Journal The chronological accounting record of an entity's transactions (p. 59).

Junked Discarded (p. 566).

Leasehold A right arising from a prepayment that a lessee (tenant) makes to secure the use of an asset from a lessor (landlord) (p. 572).

Leasehold improvements Changes to a leased asset that are amortized over the term of the lease or the useful life of the asset, whichever is shorter (p. 572).

Ledger The book (or printout) of accounts (p. 59).

Legacy designation The accounting designation of CPAs who joined as part of the initial merger of accounting bodies. It is the name of their prior accounting designation that must be used in conjunction with the CPA designation until November 1, 2022 (p. 6).

Legal title The legal ownership of property (p. 251).

Liability An economic obligation (a debt) payable to an individual or an organization outside the business (p. 14).

Licence Privileges granted by a private business or a government to sell a product or service in accordance with special conditions (p. 572).

Limited liability partnership (LLP) A form of partnership in which each partner's personal liability for the business's debts is limited to a certain amount (p. 8).

Limited personal liability The owner's legal and financial liability is limited to the amount he or she invested into the business (p. 9).

Line of credit Similar to a bank loan, it is negotiated once then drawn upon when needed. Interest is paid monthly only on the amount of the line of credit actually used (p. 605).

Liquidity A measure of how quickly an item can be converted to cash (p. 188).

Listed companies Corporations that have shares traded on a stock exchange (p. 10).

Long-term asset An asset not classified as a current asset (p. 189).

Long-term liability A liability not classified as a current liability (p. 190).

Lower-of-cost-and-net-realizable-value (LCNRV) Requires that an asset be reported in the financial statements at the lower of its historical cost or its market value (current replacement cost for inventory) (p. 338).

Maker of a note The person or business that signs the note and promises to pay the amount required by the note agreement. The maker is the debtor (p. 507).

Management accounting The branch of accounting that generates information for internal decision makers of a business (p. 5).

Manufacturing entity A company that earns its revenue by making products (p. 189).

Matching objective The basis for recording expenses. Directs accountants to identify all expenses incurred during the period, measure the expenses, and match them against the revenues earned during that same span of time (p. 115).

Materiality The accounting constraint that says information should be reported if it is material to the user—that is, if knowing it might affect a decision maker's decision (p. 12).

Materiality constraint An accounting concept that states a company must perform strictly proper accounting only for items and transactions that are significant to the business's financial statements (p. 335).

Maturity date The date on which the final payment of a note is due. Also called the due date (p. 507).

Maturity value The sum of the principal and interest due at the maturity date of a note (p. 507).

Measurement The process of determining the amount at which an item is included in the financial statements (p. 12).

Menu A list of options for choosing computer functions (p. 376).

Merchandiser A company that earns its revenue by selling products rather than services (p. 189).

Merchandising business A business that resells products previously bought from suppliers (p. 17).

Module Separate compatible units of an accounting package that are integrated to function together (p. 376).

Mortgage A long-term notes payable that includes a borrower's promise to transfer legal title to specific assets if the debt is not paid (p. 555).

Mortgage payable Long-term debts that include an agreement that if the debt is not paid, specific property is taken by the lender (p. 190).

Moving-weighted-average-cost method A weighted-average cost method where unit cost is changed to reflect each new purchase of inventory (p. 329).

Multi-step income statement An income statement format that contains subtotals to highlight significant relationships. In addition to net income, it also presents gross margin and income from operations (p. 261).

Net earnings Excess of total revenues over total expenses. Also called *net income* or *net profit* (p. 20).

Net income Excess of total revenues over total expenses. Also called *net earnings* or *net profit* (p. 20).

Net loss Excess of total expenses over total revenues (p. 20).

Net pay Gross pay minus all deductions; the amount of employee compensation that the employee actually takes home (p. 618).

Net profit Excess of total revenues over total expenses. Also called *net earnings* or *net income* (p. 20).

Net purchases Purchases plus freight-in and less purchase discounts and purchase returns and allowances (p. 252).

Net realizable value (NRV) Accounts receivable minus allowance for doubtful accounts equals the amount of accounts receivable the company hopes to realize, or collect (p. 496).

Net sales Sales revenue less sales discounts and sales returns and allowances (p. 254).

Network The system of electronic linkages that allow different computers to share the same information (p. 374).

Nominal account Another name for a temporary account (p. 183).

Non-current then current A balance sheet format that may be used for companies reporting under IFRS. Accounts are reported in the reverse order of liquidity, for example, long-term assets before current assets (p. 194).

Nonsufficient funds (NSF) cheque A "bounced" cheque, one for which the maker's bank account has insufficient money to pay the cheque (p. 444).

Normal balance The balance that appears on the side of an account—debit or credit—where we record increases (p. 63).

Note payable A liability evidenced by a written promise to make a future payment (p. 14).

Note receivable An asset evidenced by another party's written promise that entitles you to receive cash in the future (p. 13).

Note term Another name for the interest period of a note (p. 507).

Online processing Computerized processing of related functions, such as the recording and posting of transactions, on a continuous basis (p. 377).

Operating cycle The time span during which cash is paid for goods and services that are sold to customers who then pay the business in cash (p. 188).

Operating expense Expense, other than cost of goods sold, that is incurred in the entity's major line of business: rent, amortization, salaries, wages, utilities, property tax, and supplies expense (p. 259).

Operating income Gross margin minus operating expenses plus any other operating revenues. Also called *income from operations* (p. 260).

Other revenue and expense Revenues and/or expenses that are outside the main operations of a business, such as a gain or loss on the sale of capital assets (p. 260).

Outstanding cheque A cheque issued by the company and recorded on its books but not yet paid by its bank (p. 444).

Overdraw To remove more money from a bank account than exists in the bank account. This puts the bank account into a negative balance. This becomes a loan from the bank (p. 63).

Overtime For additional hours above the standard, employees are paid at a higher rate (p. 617).

Owner's equity In a proprietorship, the claim of an owner of a business to the assets of the business. Also called *capital* (p. 14).

Owner withdrawals Amounts removed from the business by an owner (p. 14).

Partners' equity The name for owner's equity when there is more than one owner. In this case, the owners are called partners (p. 14).

Partnership An unincorporated business with two or more owners (p. 8).

Patent A federal government grant giving the holder the exclusive right for 20 years to produce and sell an invention (p. 571).

Payee of a note The person or business to whom the maker of a note promises future payment. The payee is the creditor (p. 507).

Payroll Employee compensation, a major expense of many businesses (p. 617).

Payroll Deductions Online Calculator (PDOC) An online tool provided by the Canada Revenue Agency for calculating federal and provincial payroll deductions for all provinces (except Quebec) and territories (p. 619).

Percent-of-accounts-receivable method A method of estimating uncollectible receivables by determining the balance of Allowance for Doubtful Accounts based on a percentage of accounts receivable (p. 499).

Percent-of-sales method A method of estimating uncollectible receivables as a percent of the net credit sales (or net sales). Also called the *income statement approach* (p. 497).

Periodic inventory system A type of inventory accounting system in which the business does not keep a continuous record of the inventory on hand. Instead, at the end of the period the business makes a physical count of the on-hand inventory and applies the appropriate unit costs to determine the cost of the ending inventory (p. 246).

Permanent account An asset, liability, or owner's equity account that is not closed at the end of the period. Also called a *real account* (p. 183).

Perpetual inventory system A type of accounting inventory system in which the business keeps a continuous record for each inventory item to show the inventory on hand at all times (p. 247).

Petty cash A fund containing a small amount of cash that is used to pay minor expenditures (p. 451).

Petty cash ticket (voucher) A document indicating that money has been removed from the petty cash fund and a receipt is required to verify the expense (p. 451).

Phishing A method of gathering account numbers and passwords from people who visit legitimate-sounding bogus websites. The data gathered are then used for illicit purposes (p. 437).

Pledged as collateral Ownership of asset is promised to a lender in case payment is not made, then the goods would be sold to pay balance owing (p. 262).

Pledged as security A phrase that indicates an asset is held as collateral for a loan. In other words, if the loan is not paid, the asset will be taken as payment for the outstanding debt (p. 606).

Post-closing trial balance A list of the ledger accounts and their balances at the end of the period after the closing entries have been journalized and posted. The last step of the accounting cycle, it ensures that the ledger is in balance for the start of the next accounting period (p. 186).

Postdated cheques Cheques that are written for a future date (p. 438).

Posting Transferring of amounts from the journal to the ledger (p. 66).

Posting reference A column in the journal that indicates to the reader to which account the journal entry has been posted (p. 77).

Prepaid expense A category of assets that are paid for first, then expire or get used up in the near future (p. 13).

Principal The amount loaned out by the payee and borrowed by the maker of a note (p. 507).

Private accountants Accountants that only work for one employer that is not a public accounting firm (p. 6).

Private enterprise A corporation that does not offer its shares for sale to the public (p. 10).

Professional designations Acknowledgement of educational achievement from an agency to assure qualification to perform a job (p. 6).

Profit Excess of total revenues over total expenses. Also called *net earnings, net income,* or *net profit* (p. 4).

Promissory note A written promise to pay a specified amount of money at a particular future date (p. 13).

Property, plant, and equipment (PPE) Long-lived tangible capital assets, such as land, buildings, and equipment, used to operate a business (p. 121).

Proprietorship An unincorporated business with a single owner (p. 7).

Prospectively In the future (p. 564).

Proving The process of ensuring the balance in the general ledger equals the sum of the individual balances in the subsidiary ledgers (p. 382).

Public accountants Designated accountants that provide services to clients in the practice of public accounting (p. 6).

Publicly accountable enterprise A corporation that has its shares traded on a stock exchange or for which a strong public interest exists (p. 10).

Publicly traded companies Businesses that are incorporated and list/sell their shares on a public stock exchange. (p. 6).

Purchase allowance A negotiated decrease in the amount the purchaser owes the seller. (p. 250).

Purchase discount A reduction in the purchase price granted to the purchaser for paying within the discount period. Also called a *cash discount* (p. 249).

Purchase invoice A document from a vendor that shows a customer what was purchased, when it was purchased, and how much it cost (p. 64).

Purchase order A legal document that represents a business's intention to buy goods (p. 248).

Purchases journal A special journal used to record all purchases of inventory, supplies, and other assets on account (p. 386).

Quantity discount A reduction in the purchase price of an item based on the quantity of the item purchased; the greater the quantity purchased, the lower the price per item (p. 248).

Quick ratio Another name for the acid-test ratio (p. 512).

Real account Another name for a permanent account (p. 183).

Real-time processing Computerized processing of related functions, such as the recording and posting of transactions, on a continuous basis. Also called *online processing* (p. 377).

Receivable A monetary claim against a business or an individual, acquired mainly by selling goods and services and by lending money (p. 494).

Recognition criteria for revenues The basis for recording revenues; tells accountants when to record revenue and the amount of revenue to record (p. 115).

Recoverable In terms of accounting for taxes, this term means that the tax is refunded by the government (p. 607).

Recovery When a previously written off receivables amount is collected (p. 502).

Registered retirement savings plan (RRSP) A federal government plan where contributions towards retirement savings have special tax advantages. (p. 620).

Registrant A business or individual that is registered with the government to collect and remit sales taxes (p. 607).

Relative-fair-value method The allocation of the cost of assets according to their fair market value (p. 555).

Relevant Information that might influence a decision is considered relevant (p. 10).

Reliable A qualitative characteristic of accounting information that says financial information is only useful if it accurately represents the impact of transactions—that is, it is free of error and bias (p. 11).

Remittance advice An optional attachment to a cheque that tells the payee the reason for payment (p. 439).

Repair An expenditure that merely maintains an asset in its existing condition or restores the asset to good working order. Repairs are expensed (matched against revenue) (p. 556).

Residual value The expected cash value of an asset at the end of its useful life (p. 122).

Retail method A method of estimating ending inventory based on the total cost and total selling price of opening inventory and net purchases (p. 340).

Revaluation method Under IFRS, when an asset's value is restated in the accounting records to reflect the asset's current market value (p. 574).

Revenue Amounts earned from delivering goods or services to customers. The increase in owner's equity that is earned by delivering goods or services to customers or clients (p. 14).

Reversing entry An entry that switches the debit and the credit of a previous adjusting entry. The reversing entry is dated the first day of the period following the adjusting entry (p. 201).

Sales Another name for sales revenue (p. 244).

Sales discount A reduction in the amount receivable from a customer offered by the seller as an incentive for the customer to pay promptly. A contra account to sales revenue (p. 254).

Sales invoice A seller's request for cash from the purchaser. This document gives the seller the amount of revenue to record (p. 64).

Sales journal A special journal used to record credit sales (p. 379).

Sales returns and allowances A decrease in the seller's receivable from a customer's return of merchandise or from granting the customer an allowance from the amount the customer owes the seller. A contra account to sales revenue (p. 254).

Sales revenue The amount that a merchandiser earns from selling its inventory before subtracting expenses. Also called *sales* (p. 17).

Sarbanes-Oxley Act American legislation that requires publicly-traded companies to review internal controls and take responsibility for the accuracy and completeness of their financial reports (p. 433).

Schedule A report that breaks down details in an account balance (p. 382).

Security An asset that will become the property of the lender if the debt that is owed to the lender is not paid (p. 13).

Server The main computer in a network where the program and data are stored (p. 374).

Service proprietorship An unincorporated business with one owner that earns income from selling services (p. 14).

Service revenue The amount of revenue that a business earns from selling services (p. 17).

Shareholder A person or company who owns one or more shares of stock in a corporation (p. 8).

Shareholders' equity The name for owner's equity when the business is a corporation. In this case, the owners are called shareholders (p. 14).

Short-term note payable A note payable that is due within one year, a common form of financing (p. 604).

Shrinkage A reduction in the amount of inventory due to theft, spoilage, or error (p. 257).

Single-step income statement An income statement format that groups all revenues together and then lists and deducts all expenses together without drawing any subtotals (p. 261).

Slide A type of error in which one or several zeros are added or deleted in a figure; for example, writing $30 as $300 (p. 78).

Software A set of programs or instructions that cause the computer to perform the desired work (p. 374).

Soundmark A distinctive sound meant to function the same as a trademark (p. 572).

Source document A document that is evidence of a transaction, such as an invoice (p. 64).

Special journal An accounting journal designed to record one specific type of transaction (p. 378).

Specific identification method Another name for the specific-unit-cost method (p. 325).

Specific-unit-cost method An inventory costing method based on the specific cost of particular units of inventory. Also called the *specific identification method* (p. 325).

Stable monetary unit assumption Accountants' basis for ignoring the effect of inflation and making no adjustments for the changing value of the dollar (p. 12).

Stale-dated cheques Cheques that are older than six months and need to be reissued (p. 438).

Statement of earnings Another name for the income statement (p. 20).

Statement of financial position Another name for the balance sheet (p. 21).

Statement of operations Another name for the income statement. Also called the *statement of earnings* (p. 20).

Statement of owner's equity A summary of the changes in an entity's owner's equity during a specific period (p. 21).

Straight-line method An amortization method in which an equal amount of amortization expense is assigned to each year (or period) of asset use (p. 122).

Straight time A set period during which the base rate is paid to an employee (p. 617).

Subsidiary ledger The book of accounts that provides supporting details on individual balances, the total of which appears in a general ledger account (p. 379).

Tangible capital asset Physical assets expected to be used beyond the current accounting period. Examples include land, building, and equipment (p. 121).

Taxable supplies Goods and services that, when sold, have GST or HST charged on them (p. 607).

Temporary account The revenue and expense accounts that relate to a particular accounting period and are closed at the end of the period. For a proprietorship, the owner withdrawals account is also temporary. Also called a *nominal account* (p. 183).

Three-column format One common type of ledger format that includes three columns for dollar amounts—one for debit amounts, one for credit amounts, and the other for a running balance (p. 76).

Time period Another name for the interest period (p. 507).

Time period assumption Ensures that accounting information is reported at regular intervals (p. 114).

Timing difference A time lag in recording transactions (p. 442).

Trademark Distinctive identifications of a product or service. Also called *trade name* (p. 572).

Trade name Another term for trademark (p. 572).

Transaction An event that has a financial impact on a business and that can be reliably measured (p. 15).

Transposition A type of error in which two digits in a number are shown in reverse order (p. 78).

Treasurer The person in a company responsible for cash management (p. 435).

Treasury bill A financial instrument issued by the federal government that has a term of one year or less. It is sold at a discount and matures at par. The difference between the cost and maturity value is the purchaser's income (p. 438).

Trial balance A list of all the ledger accounts with their balances (p. 59).

Trojan A computer virus that does not reproduce but gets included into program code without consent and performs actions that can be destructive (p. 436).

Uncollectible accounts expense Another name for bad debt expense (p. 496).

Understandable A qualitative characteristic of accounting information that says users should be able to understand the information in financial statements (p. 11).

Unearned revenue An unearned revenue is a liability created when a business collects cash from customers in advance of doing work for the customer. The obligation to provide a product or service in the future (p. 14).

Units-of-production (UOP) method An amortization method by which a fixed amount of amortization is assigned to each unit of output produced by the capital asset (p. 560).

Unlimited personal liability When the debts of a business are greater than its resources, the owner is (owners are) responsible for their payment (p. 9).

Void A business document marked void means that it is cancelled. Numbered documents should not be discarded but rather marked as void and kept in the files (p. 436).

Warranty When a business guarantees its products or services against defects (p. 612).

Weighted-average-cost method An inventory costing method used for the periodic inventory system where the average cost is calculated at the end of the period. Weighted-average cost is determined by dividing the cost of goods available for sale by the number of units available for sale (p. 333).

Withheld Deducted from pay and kept by the employer to be remitted to another party (p. 618).

Workers' compensation A provincially administered plan that is funded by contributions by employers and that provides financial support for workers injured on the job (p. 620).

Worksheet A columnar document designed to help move data from the trial balance to the financial statements (p. 175).

Write-off Remove the balance of the customer's account from the Accounts Receivable control account and subsidiary ledger in the accounting records since the customer will not pay what it owes (p. 501).

Zero-rated supplies Goods and services that have a GST or HST rate of zero percent (p. 607).

Index

Note: Page numbers followed by *n* represents footnotes.

B